Treatments of
Psychiatric Disorders

Volume 2

American Psychiatric Association Task Force on Treatments of Psychiatric Disorders

TREATMENTS OF PSYCHIATRIC DISORDERS

A Task Force Report of the American Psychiatric Association

VOLUME 2

Published by the
American Psychiatric Association
1400 K Street, N.W.
Washington, DC 20005
1989

The findings, opinions, and conclusions of this report do not necessarily represent the views of the officers, trustees, or all members of the Association. Each report, however, does represent the thoughtful judgment and findings of the task force of experts who composed it. These reports are considered a substantive contribution to the ongoing analysis and evaluation of problems, programs, issues, and practices in a given area of concern.

The paper used in this publication meets the minimum requirements of the American National Standard for Information Sciences—Permanence of Paper for Printed Library Materials ANSI Z39.48-1984.   ∞

Correspondence regarding copyright permissions should be directed to the Division of Publications and Marketing, American Psychiatric Association, 1400 K Street, N.W., Washington, DC 20005.

The correct citation for this book is:

American Psychiatric Association: Treatments of Psychiatric Disorders: A Task Force Report of the American Psychiatric Association. Washington, DC, American Psychiatric Association, 1989.

Library of Congress Cataloging-in-Publication Data
Treatments of psychiatric disorders.

   "American Psychiatric Association Task Force on Treatments of Psychiatric Disorders" —P. facing t.p.
   Includes bibliographies and indexes.
   1. Psychiatry. 1. American Psychiatric Association. Task Force on Treatments of Psychiatric Disorders. [DNLM: 1. Mental Disorders—therapy. WM 400 T7866]
RC454.T69   1989   616.89′1   89-248
ISBN 0-89042-201-X (set : alk. paper)

ISBN 0-89042-202-8   VOLUME 1
ISBN 0-89042-203-6   VOLUME 2
ISBN 0-89042-204-4   VOLUME 3
ISBN 0-89042-205-2   INDEXES

Contents

VOLUME 1

SECTION 1
Mental Retardation

C. Thomas Gualtieri, M.D., *Chairperson*

Pharmacotherapy

Psychological, Educational, Vocational, and Residential Services

SECTION 2
Pervasive Developmental Disorders

Magda Campbell, M.D., *Co-Chairperson*
Eric Schopler, Ph.D., *Co-Chairperson*

Treatment of Bulimia Nervosa

SECTION 7
Paraphilias and Gender Identity Disorders
James L. Mathis, M.D., *Chairperson*

SECTION 8
Tic Disorders

Donald J. Cohen, M.D., *Co-Chairperson*
James F. Leckman, M.D., *Co-Chairperson*
Kenneth E. Towbin, M.D., *Co-Chairperson*

SECTION 9
Elimination Disorders

Mark A. Riddle, M.D., *Chairperson*

SECTION 10
Other Disorders of Infancy, Childhood, or Adolescence

Joseph M. Green, M.D., *Chairperson*

VOLUME 2

SECTION 11
Organic Mental Syndromes
Lissy F. Jarvik, M.D., Ph.D., *Chairperson*

SECTION 12

Psychoactive Substance Use Disorders (Alcohol)

Marc Galanter, M.D., *Chairperson*

Treatment of Alcoholism

Special Treatment Contexts

SECTION 14

Schizophrenia

Robert Cancro, M.D., *Chairperson*

SECTION 15
Delusional (Paranoid) Disorders

Sir Martin Roth, M.D., F.R.C.P., F.R.C.Psych., *Chairperson*

VOLUME 3

SECTION 18
Anxiety Disorders

Martin T. Orne, M.D., Ph.D., *Co-Chairperson*
Fred H. Frankel, M.B.Ch.B., D.P.M., *Co-Chairperson*

SECTION 23
Sleep Disorders

David J. Kupfer, M.D., *Co-Chairperson*
Charles F. Reynolds III, M.D., *Co-Chairperson*

SECTION 24
Impulse Control Disorders Not Elsewhere Classified

Richard C. Marohn, M.D., *Chairperson*

SECTION 25
Adjustment Disorder

Joseph D. Noshpitz, M.D., *Co-Chairperson*
R. Dean Coddington, M.D., *Co-Chairperson*

SECTION 26
Personality Disorders
John G. Gunderson, M.D., *Chairperson*

Treatment Modalities

Treatment of Specific Disorders

INDEXES

List of Consultants

C. Alex Adsett, M.D.
W. Stewart Agras, M.D.
C. Knight Aldrich, M.D.
Arnold Allen, M.D.
Kenneth Z. Altshuler, M.D.
Wayne R. Anable, D.O.
Nancy C. Andreasen, M.D., Ph.D.
Paul A. Andrulonis, M.D.
Laurie Appelbaum, M.D.
Gary K. Arthur, M.D.
Stuart S. Asch, M.D.
Boris M. Astrachan, M.D.

Hrair M. Babikian, M.D.
Thomas H. Babor, Ph.D.
William E. Bakewell, Jr., M.D.
Cornelis B. Bakker, M.D.
Ross J. Baldessarini, M.D.
Gail M. Barton, M.D.
B. Lynn Beattie, M.D., F.R.C.P. (C)
Aaron T. Beck, M.D.
Alan S. Bellack, Ph.D.
Jules Bemporad, M.D.
Elissa P. Benedek, M.D.
R. Scott Benson, M.D.
Norman B. Bernstein, M.D.
Norman R. Bernstein, M.D.
Shashi K. Bhatia, M.D.
Subash C. Bhatia, M.D.
Raman Bhavsar, M.D.
Kay H. Blacker, M.D.
Barry Blackwell, M.D.
Barton J. Blinder, M.D., Ph.D.
Irvin Blose, M.D.
Daniel B. Borenstein, M.D.
Jonathan F. Borus, M.D.
Peter G. Bourne, M.D.
Malcolm B. Bowers, Jr., M.D.
David L. Braff, M.D.
Reed Brockbank, M.D.

Kirk Brower, M.D.
William E. Bunney, Jr., M.D.
Ann W. Burgess, R.N., D.N.Sc.
Ewald W. Busse, M.D.

Dennis P. Cantwell, M.D.
Bernard J. Carroll, M.D., Ph.D.
Stanley Cath, M.D.
Richard D. Chessick, M.D., Ph.D., P.C.
Eve S. Chevron, M.S.
James Claghorn, M.D.
Norman A. Clemens, M.D.
C. Robert Cloninger, M.D.
Raquel E. Cohen, M.D.
Calvin A. Colarusso, M.D.
Bernice E. Coleman, M.D.
Gregory B. Collins, M.D.
Liane Colsky, M.D.
Shirley M. Colthart, M.D.
Arnold M. Cooper, M.D.
Rex W. Cowdry, M.D.
Thomas J. Craig, M.D., M.P.H.
Miles K. Crowder, M.D.
Thomas J. Crowley, M.D.
Homer Curtis, M.D.
Thomas E. Curtis, M.D.

Amin N. Daghestani, M.D.
I. Deborah Dauphinais, M.D.
John M. Davis, M.D.
Jorge G. De La Torre, M.D.
Marian K. DeMyer, Ph.D.
Martha B. Denckla, M.D.
Bharati Desai, M.D.
Daniel A. Deutschman, M.D.
Robert De Vito, M.D.
William G. Dewhurst, M.D.
Leon Diamond, M.D.
Alberto Di Mascio, Ph.D.
David F. Dinges, Ph.D.

C. Wesley Dingman II, M.D.
Susan R. Donaldson, M.D.
John Donnelly, M.D.
Mina K. Dulcan, M.D.
David L. Dunner, M.D.
Jack Durell, M.D.
Maurice Dysken, M.D.

Felton Earls, M.D.
Marshall Edelson, M.D., Ph.D.
Irene Elkin, Ph.D.
Donald E. Engstrom, M.D.
Nathan B. Epstein, M.D.
Jack R. Ewalt, M.D.

Louis F. Fabre, Jr., M.D.
Peter J. Fagan, Ph.D.
Howard Farkas, B.A.
Beverly J. Fauman, M.D.
Ronald R. Fieve, M.D.
Stuart M. Finch, M.D.
Max Fink, M.D.
Paul J. Fink, M.D.
Joseph A. Flaherty, M.D.
Stephen Fleck, M.D.
Don E. Flinn, Jr., M.D.
Marc A. Forman, M.D.
Richard J. Frances, M.D.
Robert O. Friedel, M.D.

Warren J. Gadpaille, M.D.
Pierre N. Gagne, M.D.
Robert S. Garber, M.D.
Max Gardner, M.D.
Russell Gardner, Jr., M.D.
Joseph Gaspari, M.D.
Francine L. Gelfand, M.D.
Robert W. Gibson, M.D.
Stanley Gitlow, M.D.
Rachel Gittelman, Ph.D.
Alexander H. Glassman, M.D.
Ira D. Glick, M.D.
Richard L. Goldberg, M.D.
Charles Goldfarb, M.D.
Stuart J. Goldman, M.D.

Gerald Goldstein, M.D.
Michael J. Goldstein, Ph.D.
Donald Goodwin, M.D.
Tracy Gordy, M.D.
Fred Gottlieb, M.D.
Marvin E. Gottlieb, M.D.
Louis A. Gottschalk, M.D., Ph.D.
Paul Graffagnino, M.D.
Harry Grantham, M.D.
Wayne H. Green, M.D.
Harvey R. Greenberg, M.D.
Lester Grinspoon, M.D.
William N. Grosch, M.D.
Mortimer D. Gross, M.D., S.C.

Seymour Halleck, M.D.
Abraham L. Halpern, M.D.
James A. Hamilton, M.D.
Edward Hanin, M.D.
Richard K. Harding, M.D.
Saul I. Harrison, M.D.
Lawrence Hartmann, M.D.
Irwin N. Hassenfeld, M.D.
Leston Havens, M.D.
David R. Hawkins, M.D.
Robert G. Heath, M.D.
John E. Helzer, M.D.
Hugh C. Hendrie, M.B.Ch.B.
Marvin I. Herz, M.D.
David B. Herzog, M.D.
A. Lewis Hill, M.D.
Douglas P. Hobson, M.D.
James Hodge, M.D.
Charles J. Hodulik, M.D.
Charles C. Hogan, M.D., P.C.
Jimmie C.B. Holland, M.D.
Steven D. Hollon, Ph.D.
Harry C. Holloway, M.D.
Daniel W. Hommer, M.D.
Jeffrey L. Houpt, M.D.

David Israelstam, M.D., Ph.D.

Marc Jacobs, M.D.
Kay R. Jamison, Ph.D.

Michael S. Jellinek, M.D.
Keith H. Johansen, M.D.
Mary Ann Johnson, M.D.
Merlin H. Johnson, M.D.
Charles R. Joy, M.D.
Lewis L. Judd, M.D.
Nalini V. Juthani, M.D.

Nicholas Kanas, M.D.
Sylvia R. Karasu, M.D.
Jack L. Katz, M.D.
Edward Kaufman, M.D.
Jerald Kay, M.D.
David Kaye, M.D.
Alan E. Kazdin, Ph.D.
John F. Kelley, M.D.
Philippe J. Khouri, M.D.
Elizabeth Khuri, M.D.
Chase P. Kimball, M.D.
Donald F. Klein, M.D.
Arthur H. Kleinman, M.D.
Lawrence Y. Kline, M.D.
William Klykylo, M.D.
Peter T. Knoepfler, M.D.
Michael F. Koch, M.D.
Jonathan E. Kolb, M.D.
Lawrence C. Kolb, M.D.
Donald S. Kornfeld, M.D.
Douglas A. Kramer, M.D.
Peter D. Kramer, M.D.
Robert F. Kraus, M.D.
Daniel Kripke, M.D.
Markus Kruesi, M.D.
John W. Kuldau, M.D.

Yves Lamontagne, M.D., F.R.C.P.(C)
Ronald Langevin, Ph.D.
Donald G. Langsley, M.D.
Camille Laurin, M.D.
Ruth L. La Vietes, M.D.
Robert L. Leon, M.D.
Denis Lepage, M.D.
Joseph B. Leroy, M.D.
Stanley Lesse, M.D.
H.J. Leuchter, M.D.

Stephen B. Levine, M.D.
Peritz H. Levinson, M.D.
David J. Lewis, M.D., F.R.C.P.(C)
Robert Paul Liberman, M.D.
Paul Lieberman, M.D.
Rudolf W. Link, M.D.
Margaret W. Linn, Ph.D.
John R. Lion, M.D.
Marvin H. Lipkowitz, M.D.
Zbigniew J. Lipowski, M.D.
Melvin M. Lipsett, M.D.
James W. Lomax, M.D.
Catherine E. Lord, Ph.D.
Maria Lorenz, M.D.
Earl L. Loschen, M.D.
Reginald S. Lourie, M.D.
Eugene L. Lowenkopf, M.D.
Joseph F. Lupo, M.D.

K. Roy MacKenzie, M.D.
John A. MacLeod, M.D.
Leslie F. Major, M.D.
Michael J. Maloney, M.D.
David B. Marcotte, M.D.
John Markowitz, M.D.
Judd Marmor, M.D.
Ronald L. Martin, M.D.
Jules H. Masserman, M.D.
Thomas A. Mathews, M.D.
Kenneth L. Matthews, M.D.
Teresita McCarty, M.D.
Layton McCurdy, M.D.
John J. McGrath, M.D.
F. Patrick McKegney, Jr., M.D.
George N. McNeil, M.D.
Beverly T. Mead, M.D.
Herbert Y. Meltzer, M.D.
James R. Merikangas, M.D.
Harold Merskey, D.M.
Heino F. L. Meyer-Bahlburg, Dr.rer.nat.
Robert Michels, M.D.
Larry Michelson, Ph.D.
Ira Mintz, M.D.
Steven M. Mirin, M.D.
Arnold H. Modell, M.D.

Gordon L. Moore II, M.D.
Robert A. Moore, M.D.
Loren R. Mosher, M.D.
David A. Mrazek, M.D., M.R.C.Psych.
Frances J. Mulvihill, M.D.
Cecil Mushatt, M.D.

Carol C. Nadelson, M.D.
Theodore Nadelson, M.D.
Donald F. Naftulin, M.D.
Carlos Neu, M.D.
Theodore W. Neumann, Jr., M.D.
Robert G. Niven, M.D.
Grayson Norquist, M.D.
John I. Nurenberger, Jr., M.D.

Charles P. O'Brien, M.D., Ph.D.
William C. Offenkrantz, M.D.
Donald Oken, M.D.
Harold S. Orchow, M.D.
Emily Carota Orne, B.A.
Morris G. Oscherwitz, M.D.
Helen J. Ossofsky, M.D.

Lee C. Park, M.D.
Dean X. Parmalee, M.D., F.A.A.C.P.
Robert J. Pary, M.D.
Robert O. Pasnau, M.D.
William Patterson, M.D.
Chester A. Pearlman, Jr., M.D.
William S. Pearson, M.D.
Roger Peele, M.D.
William E. Pelham, Jr., Ph.D.
Irwin N. Perr, M.D.
Helen M. Pettinati, Ph.D.
Betty Pfefferbaum, M.D.
Irving Philips, M.D.
Edward Pinney, M.D.
William Pollin, M.D.
Harrison C. Pope, Jr., M.D.
Robert M. Post, M.D.
Harry Prosen, M.D.
Brigette Prusoff, Ph.D.
Joaquim Puig-Antich, M.D.
H. Paul Putman II, M.D.

Robert Racusin, M.D.
Judith L. Rapoport, M.D.
Allen Raskin, Ph.D.
Robert J. Reichler, M.D.
William H. Reid, M.D., M.P.H.
Karl Rickels, M.D.
Arthur Rifkin, M.D.
Louis Rittelmeyer, M.D.
Lee N. Robins, M.D.
Nicholas L. Rock, M.D.
Paul Rodenhauser, M.D.
Rita R. Rogers, M.D.
John Romano, M.D.
Howard P. Rome, M.D.
Patricia Rosebush, M.D.
Maj-Britt Rosenbaum, M.D.
Milton Rosenbaum, M.D.
Loren H. Roth, M.D.
Bruce Rounsaville, M.D.
Donald K. Routh, Ph.D.
Lester Rudy, M.D.

Benjamin Sadock, M.D.
Virginia Sadock, M.D.
Clifford J. Sager, M.D.
Watt T. Salmon, M.D.
Carl Salzman, M.D.
Alberto Santos, M.D.
Burhan Say, M.D.
Nina R. Schooler, Ph.D.
John Schowalter, M.D.
John J. Schwab, M.D.
Harvey J. Schwartz, M.D.
James H. Scully, M.D.
Peter M. Semkiw, M.D.
Mohammad Shaffii, M.D.
Charles Shagass, M.D.
Brian Shaw, M.D.
Kailie R. Shaw, M.D.
Michael H. Sheard, M.D.
David V. Sheehan, Ph.D.
Edwin Shneidman, Ph.D.
Miles Shore, M.D.
Michael Shostak, M.D.
Lorraine D. Siggins, M.D.

Peter M. Silberfarb, M.D.
Donald J. Silberman, M.D.
Archie A. Silver, M.D.
Joel J. Silverman, M.D.
Everett C. Simmons, M.D.
Bennett Simon, M.D.
George M. Simpson, M.D.
Margaret Singer, M.D.
Phillip R. Slavney, M.D.
William Sledge, M.D.
Gary W. Small, M.D.
Joyce G. Small, M.D.
Erwin R. Smarr, M.D.
Gail Solomon, M.D.
David Spiegel, M.D.
Robert L. Spitzer, M.D.
Daniel J. Sprehe, M.D.
Robert St. John, M.D.
Stephen M. Stahl, M.D., Ph.D.
Monica N. Starkman, M.D.
Dorothy A. Starr, M.D.
Roy Steinhouse, M.D.
Peter E. Stokes, M.D.
John S. Strauss, M.D.
Max Sugar, M.D.
David W. Swanson, M.D.

Zebulin C. Taintor, M.D.
John A. Talbott, M.D.
Allan Tasman, M.D.
Sam D. Taylor, M.D.
Lenore C. Terr, M.D.
Alexander Thomas, M.D.
Gary Tischler, M.D.
Arnold Tobin, M.D.
Garfield Tourney, M.D.
Darold A. Treffert, M.D.
Margaret Owen Tsaltas, M.D.
Gary J. Tucker, M.D.
William M. Tucker, M.D.
Ann R. Turkel, M.D.

Kathleen Bell Unger, M.D.
Yogendra Upadhyay, M.D.

George E. Vaillant, M.D.
Bessel Van der Kolk, M.D.
Christian D. Van der Velde, M.D.
Hugo Van Dooren, M.D.
Herman M. van Praag, M.D., Ph.D.
Ilza Veith, Ph.D., M.D.
Milton Viederman, M.D.

Thomas Wadden, Ph.D.
Raymond Waggoner, M.D.
Richard L. Weddige, M.D.
Walter Weintraub, M.D.
James M.A. Weiss, M.D.
Kenneth J. Weiss, M.D.
Sidney H. Weissman, M.D.
William D. Weitzel, M.D.
Elizabeth B. Weller, M.D.
Charles E. Wells, M.D.
Paul H. Wender, M.D.
Jack C. Westman, M.D.
Kerrin L. White, M.D.
Wayne Whitehouse, Ph.D.
Roy M. Whitman, M.D.
Jan N. Williams, M.D.
C. Philip Wilson, M.D.
G. Terence Wilson, Ph.D.
Ronald Wintrob, M.D.
Michael G. Wise, M.D.
Joseph Wolpe, M.D.
Edward A. Wolpert, M.D., Ph.D.
David R. Wood, M.D.
William M. Wood, M.D.
Sherwin M. Woods, M.D.
Henry H. Work, M.D.
Richard W. Worst, M.D.
Lyman C. Wynne, M.D., Ph.D.

Irvin D. Yalom, M.D.
Alayne Yates, M.D.

Robert G. Zadylak, M.D.
Leonard S. Zegans, M.D.
Norman Zinberg, M.D.
Charlotte M. Zitrin, M.D.
Joel P. Zrull, M.D.

Foreword

T. Byram Karasu and the hundreds of our colleagues who have contributed to this massive effort deserve our highest respect and admiration.

The sheer magnitude of the undertaking would have discouraged most, but the enormous complexity provided the challenge that Dr. Karasu and the APA Task Force on Treatments of Psychiatric Disorders needed to endure this seven-year process. The APA is particularly grateful to Dr. Karasu for his patience, thoughtfulness, and comprehensive intelligence about psychiatric therapies. The result is a work of unprecedented significance. Even though, in its present four volumes, it is by no means a definitive work, this report is a major contribution to the literature and a basis on which much more will be accomplished in the years to come.

Coming to fruition just at the end of my presidency of the American Psychiatric Association, the report advances two of my major interests and concerns. It is the first major attempt to clarify and specify the tools available to psychiatry. As such it will serve as the basis for our continuing effort to describe and define our profession within the world of medicine.

The eradication of stigma has been the theme of my presidency, and it is my hope that *Treatments of Psychiatric Disorders* can help us to demonstrate to the public the positive effective treatments in the psychiatric armamentarium. In its present form it serves to educate the profession, but I hope it will be refined and condensed into material for the general public so that there can be broader understanding of the effectiveness of psychiatric treatment.

Paul J. Fink, M.D.
President, American Psychiatric Association (1988–1989)

Introduction

Science provides only interim knowledge.

Psychiatric treatment, like the rest of medicine, is inherently a flexible and open system which will continuously be influenced by new knowledge. This report represents a description of clinically useful current approaches for the treatment of mental disorders with a balanced perspective. It is important to emphasize that a treatment plan inherently must be an open system. Thus, this report is a working document reflecting a combination of cumulative scientific knowledge and clinical judgment about the treatment of psychiatric patients.

Historical Background

This undertaking began with the establishment of a previous Commission on Psychiatric Therapies in 1977 by Jules Masserman, M.D., then the president of the American Psychiatric Association. The charge was to examine critically the somatic, dyadic, group/family, and social therapies in current use—and to recommend criteria for evaluating therapeutic approaches.

In its attempt to meet this difficult task, the Commission produced two publications, both published by the American Psychiatric Association. The first was a critical review of a large body of evaluation research, entitled *Psychotherapy Research: Methodological and Efficacy Issues* (American Psychiatric Association Commission on Psychiatric Therapies 1982). This work pointed to the complexity of the variables involved in defining both the nature of a psychotherapeutic treatment and its outcome. The second publication, *The Psychiatric Therapies* (American Psychiatric Association Commission on Psychiatric Therapies 1984), was a comprehensive compendium of the many psychosocial and somatic treatment modalities currently in use.

In continuation of the previous Commission, Daniel X. Freedman, M.D., then the president of the APA, established a Task Force on Treatment of Psychiatric Disorders in 1982 to produce a comprehensive document that would describe the state of the art for treatment of psychiatric disorders.

The Process of Development

Because of the multiplicity of psychiatric disorders and their related approaches, the Task Force designated Chairpersons for 26 Panels, each of whom would draw together a working group to review the treatment of a different disorder or group of disorders. Chairpersons and Panel members were chosen from among many well-qualified individuals on the basis of certain criteria: the publication of research or clinical reports concerned with the treatment of a specific category of mental illness; and nomination by peers based on acknowledged eminence in clinical practice, national reputation, past accomplishments, and broad perspective. In order to assist them in their task, each Panel was empowered to retain the specialized services of a wide variety of consultants and representatives of consultant organizations.

The consultants were selected so as to represent a breadth of disciplines and orientations, in appreciation of the diverse patient and treatment variables important in these fields. They encompass expertise in general psychiatry, child psychiatry, psychoanalysis, psychotherapy, pharmacotherapy, and biological and social psychiatry, as well as exposure to treatments in diverse settings. This method of selecting contributors and consultants, and the desire for integration and synthesis of divergent views, led to multiple responses and challenges. We believe this approach has had a salutary effect on the outcome of the report.

Panels were assigned psychiatric diagnostic groups for which they were to provide treatment considerations. They identified distinct categories within the given diagnostic groupings which deserved full narration and discussed the variation of treatment as applied to other categories. The Panels operated on the basis of the clinical model that assumes that, for an individual with specific characteristics who is suffering from a given disorder or combination of disorders, there are one or more preferred treatments and/or combinations as well as acceptable alternative and possibly adjunct treatments.

Once a draft was prepared by the contributors, that document marked the beginning of an elaborate review process, as follows: 1) it was sent to a number of consultants, chosen by the contributor(s) for comments; 2) Draft II was prepared by the contributor(s) on the basis of the consultants' suggestions; 3) the Task Force sent Draft II to five to ten consultants; 4) the comments and critiques of these individuals were sent to the original contributors(s) for preparation of Draft III; and 5) Draft III was then reviewed and finalized by the Task Force. This complex process of consultation and review produced sections that reflect the input and ideas of many experts. Although in some sections a single author, in others a group of authors, and in still others individual chapters are given credits depending upon the level of contribution, the completed product represents the original work of the primary author(s), views of the Chairperson and Consultants of each Panel, and the Members of the Task Force.

Format

As there was no precedent for us to use as a model, and also recognizing that the consideration of treatment for various disorders may require different approaches to their subjects, the Panels were given a relatively free rein as to the format, style, and length of their presentations.

The sections do not deal with the issues of diagnosis, but assume the reader's prior knowledge. Where there was a need for further elaboration of the *Diagnostic and Statistical Manual of Mental Disorders* in its utilization for treatment planning, these issues were discussed. The work progressed during the transitional stage from DSM-III to DSM-III-R. Whenever we were able, we tried to keep the pace.

Naturally, some topics were repeated to varying degrees in different chapters. This also helped to state some of the finer points between them. At times a clinical example was presented to clarify differential diagnostic issues.

In discussion of treatment of a condition from more than one perspective, an attempt was made to integrate multiple points of view within a single section. Wherever this was not feasible, multiple chapters are included from diverse perspectives. A clinician must be able to consider each clinical problem at several conceptual levels in designing the most appropriate treatment program. Often combined applications are included to describe complementary models that are in use. Wherever empirical data were available, they were cited. In newer fields there are detailed discussions of studies instead of conclusions, to allow a proper perspective on the data. Special references were added in the text for readers who may want to study the subject in greater depth.

Use of This Report

This report is a professional document designed to suggest useful treatments for psychiatric disorders as an aid for treatment planning. It is not intended to impose rigid methods. It aims to demonstrate the complexity of the treatment planning process and its application, the true nature of comprehensive diagnosis, and the depth and breadth of knowledge that is required to assess a patient's need for the provision of treatment.

Proper use of this document requires specialized training that provides both a body of knowledge and clinical skills. Furthermore, many specific factors will influence the treatment needs for a particular individual. The chapters in this report do not dictate an exclusive course of treatment or procedures to be followed and should not be construed as excluding other acceptable methods of practice. Therefore, it would be incorrect to assert that any single treatment in this book automatically fits any single patient. Sound use of this book requires a clinician's judgment based on knowledge of a patient and a valid background of training and practice in psychiatry. Ultimately, it is individual practitioners—based upon their clinical judgment, experience, and assessment of the scientific literature—who will determine the usefulness of various therapeutic approaches. Futhermore, the mental disorders discussed in this report do not encompass all of the conditions that a psychiatrist may legitimately treat.

Future Directions

It is also important to note that this report reflects current assessment from an evolving knowledge base. Psychiatry participates in the continual expansion of knowledge that is taking place in all areas of science and medicine. New psychotropic drugs and other somatic approaches are constantly being tested and evaluated. Similarly, new psychotherapeutic and psychosocial techniques are being developed and assessed. In addition, combinations of treatment which hold promise are being evaluated. The continual accrual of new information will need to be integrated into these formulations in an ongoing way.

An important implication of the attempt to systemize our knowledge is that as the Task Force proceeded with its work, both what is known as well as what needs to be known became more evident. In particular, there is a need for increasing refinement of significant variables toward a greater understanding of individual differences in response to different therapeutic approaches. Such refinement will depend upon ongoing research which must take into account specific interventions, specific disorders or patient subgroups of responders and nonresponders, specific dosages, specific durations, and specific combinations and sequences of the treatments—in short, the ultimate establishment of carefully delineated criteria for titrating the nature and timing of various therapies and their combinations to be utilized in a biopsycho-social approach to the treatment of psychiatric disorders (Karasu 1982).

Toksoz Byram Karasu, M.D.

References

American Psychiatric Association Commission on Psychiatric Therapies: Psychother-apy Research: Methodological and Efficacy Issues. Washington, DC, American Psychiatric Association, 1982
American Psychiatric Association Commission on Psychiatric Therapies: The Psychi-atric Therapies. Volume 1 (Somatic Therapies) and Volume 2 (Psychosocial Ther-apies). Washington, DC, American Psychiatric Association, 1984
Karasu TB: Psychotherapy and pharmacotherapy: toward an integrative model. Am J Psychiatry 139:7, 1982

Acknowledgments

This work was accomplished with the generous help of many people. Both the size of this project as well as the spirit of cooperation by which it was undertaken are demonstrated by the large number of clinicians involved and cited as contributors and consultants. I am deeply indebted to all.

I would like to thank the Chairpersons of the Panels and all contributors who not only prepared scholarly documents, but also gracefully allowed their original works to be modified through the consultation process. I would also like to express my gratitude to the consultants for their productive criticism.

I am most thankful for the support of Daniel X. Freedman, M.D., founder President of the Task Force, and Paul J. Fink, M.D., who presided during the crucial stage of the project, as well as to Keith H. Brodie, M.D., George Tarjan, M.D., John A. Talbott, M.D., Carol C. Nadelson, M.D., Robert O. Pasnau, M.D., George H. Pollock, M.D., Herbert Pardes, M.D., who served as Presidents, and also Lawrence Hartmann, M.D., William R. Sorum, M.D., Harvey Bluestone, M.D., Fred Gottlieb, M.D., Roger Peele, M.D., Irvin M. Cohen, M.D., and John S. McIntyre, M.D., who served as Speakers of the Assembly during the lifetime of the Task Force.

My special thanks to Melvin Sabshin, M.D., Medical Director of the American Psychiatric Association, for his unfailing leadership and the wisdom which he provided with great generosity, and to Harold Alan Pincus, M.D., Director, Office of Research, who gave administrative direction to the project and who, jointly with Paul J. Fink, M.D., the chairman of the Joint Ad Hoc Review Committee, weathered the most complicated organizational issues and skillfully brought this project to a successful conclusion.

I want to express my gratitude to Sandy Ferris for her organizational ability; to Philomena Lee, who maintained the highly complicated correspondence with a large number of people and corrected final drafts with exemplary patience, good humor, and dedication; to Betty Meltzer for her elegant editorial assistance; and to Louise Notarangelo, Rita Segarra, and Shirley Kreitman, who assisted them with equal competence and generosity.

My sincere appreciation and gratitude to Ronald E. McMillen, General Manager of the American Psychiatric Press, Inc., Timothy R. Clancy, Editorial Director, and Richard E. Farkas, Production Manager, for their leadership, and to their dedicated staff, Christine Kalbacher, Project Coordinator, Karen E. Sardinas-Wyssling and Lindsay E. Edmunds, Principal Manuscript Editors; to Editorial Experts, Inc., specifically Mary Stoughton and the staff editors, Pat Caudill and the staff proofreaders, and June Morse and the staff indexers, and to Robert Elwood and Nancy Borza at Harper Graphics, Typesetter, and Tom Reed at R. R. Donnelley & Sons Company, Printer, whose expert labors have facilitated the transformation of the raw material into four carefully wrought and handsome volumes.

Toksoz Byram Karasu, M.D.

Cautionary Statement

This report does not represent the official policy of the American Psychiatric Association. It is an APA task force report, signifying that members of the APA have contributed to its development, but it has not been passed through those official channels required to make it an APA policy document.

THIS REPORT IS NOT INTENDED TO BE CONSTRUED AS OR TO SERVE AS A STANDARD FOR PSYCHIATRIC CARE.

SECTION 11

Organic Mental Syndromes

Chapter 91

The Importance of Diagnosis

Medical training introduces clinicians to the concept of a manual as a quick guide to diagnosis and treatment, best exemplified by the Merck manual (1982). Here we find that a patient presenting with symptoms of somnolence, confusion, psychosis, constipation, and muscle weakness may have an elevated calcium level and need symptomatic treatment with hydration, low-calcium intake, and physical activity, pending diagnosis of the etiology of the hypercalcemia. Another patient may present with altered consciousness, fever, and a stiff neck; unless we consider the diagnosis of meningitis and get a lumbar puncture, we may fail to initiate appropriate life-saving antibiotic therapy. As we become more and more immersed in psychiatric practice, we encounter fewer and fewer examples of the kind described above (e.g., diseases that fit a clear-cut standard diagnostic and treatment format).

Nonetheless, our panel has tried to bring, whenever possible, the Merck manual orientation to DSM-III-R (American Psychiatric Association 1987). We have tried to make clear that accurate diagnosis still remains the cornerstone of successful treatment, even though at our current state of knowledge there are organic mental syndromes for which symptomatic treatment is our only option. Indeed, in preparing this section, we have come to realize how limited is our knowledge and how vast our ignorance. Nevertheless, for all of the organic mental syndromes, as for all diseases in medicine, the search for underlying causes and accurate diagnosis remains of paramount importance. It is only when the psychiatrist's diagnostic acumen, augmented by modern medicine's technological resources, has been exhausted that it becomes appropriate to resort to symptomatic treatment.

It is our hope that this section will aid in sharpening the psychiatrist's diagnostic skill in focusing on specific treatments where available, and in understanding symptomatic treatments for the organic mental syndromes. We want to point out that we have not been all-inclusive in our approach. To cite just three examples, we confined ourselves to adult patients only (see Section 5); we omitted special sections for the alcohol- and drug-abusing patient (see Sections 12 and 13); and we limited our discussion of experimental treatments primarily to those for multi-infarct and Alzheimer type dementias. We did include discussions of economic, ethical, and legal considerations in treatment, topics that are assuming ever-increasing importance to our patients and their families as well as to society-at-large.

Finally, we want to make clear that all of our contributors labored hard and revised their chapters on more than one occasion in an effort to provide the most accurate, up-to-date information. Nonetheless, we are well aware of the fact that perfection can be pursued but not attained. Hence, your comments will assist us in improving the next edition. Indeed, it is our fervent hope that as the 20th century draws to a close, research in psychiatry will provide reliable markers to guide us through that vast and largely uncharted field that we subsume today under the designation of organic mental syndromes so that much of what we have to say in the present section will have become obsolete by the time of the next edition.

Chapter 92

The Geriatric Patient

Aging and Organic Mental Syndromes

Substantial advances in the treatment of organic mental syndromes in older adults occurred only after the changes associated with normal aging were differentiated from the changes caused by disease in later life. The blurring of normal aging with illness had stalled progress in the clinical approach to the older patient, particularly in the area of cognitive functioning. When it is considered normal to display marked cognitive decrement ("senility") with aging, clinical resignation, if not nihilism, is the response.

Cognitive Changes with Aging

What does the literature reveal about normal cognitive function with aging? Owens (1966) reported on a longitudinal study of intellectual performance in 96 men, with an average age of 61 years, who had originally been tested in 1919 as freshmen at Iowa State University. The key finding of this study was that, on the average, there was little change in intellectual test scores as these men aged from 50 to 60 years. A previous report by Owens (1953) had shown increments in verbal ability and total score of intellectual performance as these men moved from age 20 to age 50 years, although numerical ability showed a slight decline. These studies were among the first to raise serious doubts about the presumed normal decline in mental abilities with advancing age that had been inferred from earlier cross-sectional studies.

In 1955, a 12-year longitudinal study of men, median age 71, was initiated at the National Institute of Mental Health (Granick and Patterson 1971). The goal of the study was to examine a broad range of variables in individuals of advanced age in whom disease was absent or minimal, in an effort to differentiate the impact of aging versus that of illness. Of note in these healthy aging subjects, as they moved on the average from their 70s to their 80s, was that while various intellectual functions declined, others improved. Speed in carrying out different operations, quality of

Draw-a-Person, and quality of sentence completions declined. On the other hand, vocabulary and picture arrangement improved. In terms of everyday life, these findings suggest that certain activities requiring quick reactions or a high degree of precision might not be carried out as well by older adults in general, although the ability to understand one's situation and learn from new experiences is maintained in later life. Moreover, it was found that decrements in intellectual performance with advancing age were significantly greater in subjects who also developed arteriosclerotic cardiovascular disease than in subjects who remained healthy. The study illustrated the impact of illness on intellectual functioning with aging, while showing how intellectual functioning is maintained in aging individuals who remain healthy.

Similar results were obtained in the only study of intellectual functioning in aging twins. This New York State Psychiatric Institute study also showed that a critical rate of decline on some subtests (vocabulary, similarities, and digit symbol substitution) of the Wechsler Adult Intelligence Scale (Wechsler 1944) could be used as a predictor of mortality (Jarvik and Bank 1983). Since then, the "terminal drop" hypothesis has been controversial; on balance, however, the hypothesis that certain intellectual declines relate to a foreshortened lifespan has held up.

Orientation Toward Treatment

Even when clinical changes in the elderly are viewed as potential signals of underlying illness, too often there is a delay in seeking treatment. This phenomenon is an example of the general obstacle of differentiating disease in older adults from changes associated with aging per se. Prompt treatment is all the more important in the elderly, given the greater potential in the frail geriatric patient for physical damage or deterioration with acute episodes of illness.

Acute changes, in fact, are often not even recognized as being acute in the older person. Consider the development of disorientation to time and place in a given individual. If the individual is 32 years old, such symptoms will likely elicit alarm and immediate action; if the individual is 82 years old, such symptoms may elicit dismay and reflection about the person's age. How often, however, do family members or physicians ask themselves whether this 82-year-old ever showed disorientation before? Might this be the first episode, and could it be signaling a hypertensive crisis that could lead to stroke and permanent organic mental syndrome unless treated immediately?

The Course of Illness with Aging

A fundamental clinical aspect that distinguishes the older from the younger patient is the greater likelihood of the former having more than one illness and receiving more than one treatment concurrently. Thus one must pay greater attention to illness-illness interactions along with treatment-treatment interactions (e.g., polypharmacy issues) in geriatric patients with organic mental syndromes (Cohen 1985). Often, aggravation of the course of an organic mental syndrome in the older patient is due to the interplay of these factors.

Inadequate recognition of how disorders can be brought into remission throughout the life cycle also has an impact on treatment of the geriatric patient. If an illness flares up in a younger patient, the hope, if not the expectation, is that remission can be achieved. In the older patient, however, the predictable expectation is that the course will be downhill as a phenomenon of aging instead of as a phenomenon of the illness. Hence, even though a disease process is recognized, negative stereotypes about the elderly can prevent the use of standard clinical approaches that should be employed independent of the patient's age.

Related to an inadequate understanding of the course of illness in later life is poor recognition of the potential role of rehabilitation for the geriatric patient. Certainly if an organic mental syndrome is of a nonprogressive nature or exhibits extended periods of clinical plateaus, the opportunity exists for some level of rehabilitation.

Service Utilization, Service Delivery, and Financing Issues

For many years the scientific literature has been pointing to the problems of low mental health service utilization and delivery for older patients (Redick and Taube 1980). While those age 65 and older represent 11 percent of the population, less than 5 percent of patients seen at public and private outpatient mental health facilities are in this older age group. Again, many explanations have been offered to explain this pattern (Cohen 1976). On the utilization end, difficulties in physical mobility, poor transportation, fear of crime, low income, and stigma issues have been described as among the factors affecting the behavior of older adults in seeking out mental health services. On the delivery end, negative stereotypes of the elderly, inadequate training in geriatric mental health, and poor reimbursement provisions on the part of private and public insurance programs have been portrayed as factors affecting the behavior of the mental health care delivery system in providing services for older patients. Meanwhile, progress is occurring along all these fronts (Cohen 1980).

Reimbursement Change for Alzheimer's Disease and Related Disorders

It was in the fall of 1984 that a specific group of organic mental syndromes in the aged led to what had been regarded as the most important change in Medicare coverage for mental disorders since the inception of Medicare over 20 years ago (Goldman et al. 1985). In September of that year, a major Task Force Report on Alzheimer's disease was released by the US Department of Health and Human Services (1984). Within the report there was a special financing recommendation that was announced as being implemented in conjunction with the release of the report. The purpose of the recommendation was to remove limitations on services (for Alzheimer's disease and related disorders) provided outside the hospital setting. Specifically, the recommendation read as follows:

> Current Medicare statute limits medically appropriate physician services provided outside of the hospital setting for patients with Alzheimer's disease when coded as a mental disorder. The Department should clarify that, except for psychotherapy, physician treatment services for patients with Alzheimer's disease and related disorders are not subject to the $250 limitations. In other words, in determining whether services for these patients are subject to the limit, the nature of the physician's service is the deciding factor, not the diagnostic code. Therefore, physician treatment services provided outside the hospital setting for patients with Alzheimer's disease and related disorders coded 290.X (in DSM-III and ICD-9) should be reimbursed in the same manner as services for Alzheimer's disease coded 331 (ICD-9). (p. xv)

The intent of this administrative change was to correct an inconsistency by which reimbursement for the same service differed depending on which diagnostic code for the treatment of Alzheimer's disease was used (290.X versus 331), although both codes referred to Alzheimer's disease and related disorders. The intent, too, was to reimburse for office visits for the medical management of Alzheimer's disease (including pharmacotherapy and other nonpsychotherapy treatment interventions) on an 80:20 reimbursement/copayment formula, as opposed to the dollar limit and 50:50 reimbursement/copayment formula that still holds for psychotherapy. This change should substantially improve the ability of those patients suffering from the organic mental syndrome of Alzheimer's disease or a related disorder to seek state-of-the-art clinical interventions.

The Social Situation of the Older Adult

The interplay of social factors with biomedical and psychological variables is particularly prominent with geriatric patients (Palmore 1980) and is most apparent with persons of an advanced age (over 85), referred to as the "old-old," in whom the risk of an organic mental syndrome is greatest. Management of clinical problems among the frail in this age group is considerably complicated by the social phenomenon that the children of these patients are themselves likely to be senior citizens. In addition, older women have an even more difficult situation because they are much more likely to be without a spouse to help them manage their health problems. By age 65, 50 percent of women who had been married are widowed, by age 75, 70 percent. This social situation of lacking a helping spouse, coupled with females living longer than males, largely explains why most of the residents in nursing homes are women (US Department of Health, Education, and Welfare 1978).

Within the community, availability of informal support systems to assist in the management of illness in those of an advanced age, and in those with organic mental syndromes in particular, is a growing dilemma as the age group 85 years and older moves toward increasing sevenfold in numbers between the years 1980 and 2050—from 2.2 to 16 million (US Senate 1984). The need for help with basic activities becomes a major consideration for many people at this stage of the life cycle. In managing illness in this age group, one must constantly pay close attention to changes in the older person's social situation, especially those that result in a thinning of the support system. For example, one in seven men age 65 years and older live alone, whereas one in three women in this age group live by themselves.

The social support network thus becomes a key factor in determining how well and how long the geriatric patient with an organic mental syndrome can remain in the community. Still, too often, dispositions for the older patient are decided in narrow dichotomous terms (i.e., home versus nursing home). The fact is that there are many options in between, such as the utilization of homemaker, respite, and/or day-care programs that can help keep these ill elderly individuals in the community and closer to their families. Part of the challenge to skill and creativity in geriatric management is dealing with these complex biopsychosocial variables. The geriatric patient with an organic mental syndrome represents no exception to this challenge and opportunity.

Chapter 93

Delirium

Definition and Diagnostic Criteria

Delirium may be defined in general terms as an organic mental syndrome characterized by acute onset, transient duration, and global cognitive dysfunction secondary
to diffuse impairment of cerebral metabolism (Beresin 1983; Lipowski 1980). It is more
specifically defined phenomenologically by the set of DSM-III-R (American Psychiatric
Association 1987) diagnostic criteria, shown in Table 1.

The principal clinical characteristics of delirium have been summarized by Lipowski (1980) as follows: Manifest impairments are present in thinking, registration,
recent memory, and orientation, and there is notable disturbance in attentional mechanisms. Arousal is either reduced or heightened, and there is a disturbance of the
sleep-wakefulness cycle, at times with diurnal rhythm reversal. There tends to be
fluctuation in the deficits in cognition and attention, which are unpredictable but
which tend to become more prominent in the presence of sleep disturbance. Psychomotor activity may be increased or decreased, often alternating with wide swings

---

Table 1.   DSM-III-R Diagnostic Criteria for Delirium

A. Reduced ability to maintain attention to external stimuli (e.g., questions must be repeated
because attention wanders) and to appropriately shift attention to new external stimuli
(e.g., perseverates answer to a previous question).

B. Disorganized thinking, as indicated by rambling, irrelevant, or incoherent speech.

C. At least two of the following:

    (1) reduced level of consciousness, e.g., difficulty keeping awake during examination
    (2) perceptual disturbances: misinterpretations, illusions, or hallucinations
    (3) disturbance of sleep-wake cycle with insomnia or daytime sleepiness
    (4) increased or decreased psychomotor activity
    (5) disorientation to time, place, or person
    (6) memory impairment, e.g., inability to learn new material, such as the names of
        several unrelated objects after five minutes, or to remember past events, such as
        history of current episode of illness

D. Clinical features develop over a short period of time (usually hours to days) and tend
to fluctuate over the course of a day.

E. Either (1) or (2):

    (1) evidence from the history, physical examination, or laboratory tests of a specific
        organic factor (or factors) judged to be etiologically related to the disturbance
    (2) in the absence of such evidence, an etiologic organic factor can be presumed if the
        disturbance cannot be accounted for by any nonorganic mental disorder, e.g., Manic
        Episode accounting for agitation and sleep disturbance

from one to another. Disturbances in perception are common, with vivid visual hallucinations or illusions and disturbance of other perceptual modalities as well. Restlessness, fear, and persecutory delusions and paranoia, which may be poorly systematized and short lived, are often intermixed with hallucinations. Patients often experience lucid intervals with transitory improvement in clinical signs and symptoms and relatively good insight into the nature of their difficulty. The duration of delirium is quite variable, but most patients recover within one week.

Associated Features

Clinical features associated with delirium include affective disturbances, such as apprehension, fear, depression, euphoria, apathy, irritability, and rage. Abnormal signs on physical and neurologic examinations are common. These include abnormal involuntary movements such as tremor and asterixis, impaired coordination, dysphasia, urinary incontinence, focal neurologic signs, autonomic nervous system dysfunction, and seizures. These associated features tend to be seen more commonly in elderly patients with delirium than in younger adults (Liston 1982).

Clinical Subtypes

Three clinical subtypes of delirium can be seen: the hyperactive type, characterized by psychomotor overactivity; the hypoactive type, with a reduced level of psychomotor activity and alertness; and the mixed type, with features of both the hyperactive and hypoactive variants (Lipowski 1980; Steinhart 1978/1979). The hyperactive variant and the less common mixed type are usually recognized easily because of the manifest agitation, psychotic behavior, and so forth. However, even the astute physician may misdiagnose or overlook the delirious patient with a hypoactive stuporous subtype who is quiet and appears to be calm and in no distress (Morse and Litin 1971; Wells 1985a).

Epidemiology

Delirium is a common disorder; estimates of its incidence among medical-surgical patients range between 10 and 15 percent (Beresin 1983). It is more frequently seen in the very young and the elderly, with estimated incidence rates of 50 percent or higher among older patients on psychiatric wards. Furthermore, there is some suggestion that patients older than age 75 years have incidence rates approximately twice as high as those for patients between the ages of 65 and 75 years (Liston 1982).

Most patients recover fully with appropriate treatment but recovery is related inversely to age and to duration of illness. Thus early diagnosis and treatment are important. Mortality rates may be substantial, especially for elderly individuals, in whom death associated with delirium ranges between 15 and 30 percent (Liston 1984; Rabins and Folstein 1982).

Etiology

Virtually any illness or disease process may be causally associated with the development of delirium, although in many instances the specific etiology is never elucidated (Wells 1985a). A listing of some of the more common conditions known to contribute to or cause delirium is presented in Table 2. A number of factors predisposing to the development of delirium are known, including chronic illness, advanced age, structural brain disease, multiple medications, abuse of drugs or alcohol, loss of sensory modalities, sleep deprivation, weakened psychological defense mechanisms, social isolation, and unfamiliar environment (Liston 1982, 1984). Moreover, premorbid personality structure, cultural background, and the setting in which the delirium develops may also contribute to its manifestations and variability (Romano and Engel 1944).

The role of medications and of drug and alcohol abuse is especially important. Many of these substances, either in combination or when used in excess, not only may induce delirium directly through toxicity but, particularly in the case of sedative-hypnotics, may cause a withdrawal delirium on abrupt discontinuation. In addition, age-related changes in pharmacokinetics may result in toxic levels of medications even at the usual therapeutic dosages (Liston 1982).

Differential Diagnosis

The differential diagnosis of delirium includes dementia, amnestic syndrome, organic hallucinosis, organic mood syndrome, organic anxiety syndrome, schizophrenia, schizophreniform disorder, and factitious disorder with psychological symptoms. However, the distinguishing, essential clinical features of delirium are reduced ability to maintain attention to external stimuli and to shift attention appropriately to new external stimuli, and disorganized thinking, as manifested by rambling, irrelevant, or incoherent speech (American Psychiatric Association 1987).

Dementia is perhaps the most important condition to be differentiated from delirium; the distinction can usually be accomplished by careful assessment of history and clinical manifestations (Liston 1984). Delirium may also be simulated by dissociative disorder, including an apparent clouding of consciousness; but in the latter cases serial electroencephalograms (EEGs) are within normal limits, and these patients frequently evince a positive response to amobarbital (Beresin 1983). If there is doubt concerning the differential diagnosis, delirium should be the presumptive diagnosis until reasonably ruled out.

Table 2. Underlying Conditions Commonly Associated with Delirium

Central Nervous System Disorders	Metabolic Disorders	Cardiopulmonary Disorders	Miscellaneous Conditions
Head trauma	Uremia	Myocardial infarction	Medications
Seizures	Hepatic failure	Congestive heart failure	"Street" drugs
Postictal states	Anemia	Cardiac arrhythmias	Toxins, heavy metals
Infection	Hypoglycemia	Shock	Severe trauma
Neoplasm	Thiamine	Respiratory failure	Sepsis
Vascular disease	deficiency		Sensory deprivation
Degenerative	Endocrinopathies		Temperature dysregulation
disease	Fluid, electrolyte		Postoperative states
	imbalance		
	Acid-base		
	imbalance		

Patient Evaluation

The diagnosis of delirium is made essentially on clinical grounds by history and examination. In almost all patients lacking evidence of organic brain dysfunction on examination, a functional (i.e., nonorganic) cause of the disorder will be found (Liston 1982). As Wells (1985a) emphasized, the psychiatrist should have a high index of suspicion of delirium whenever recent alteration in behavior, thinking, or arousal is noted, especially among patients with a negative history for prior psychiatric disorder. Standard psychiatric, medical, and neurologic histories and examinations will usually make the diagnosis. However, they can be complemented by simple bedside assessment tools such as the Mental Status Questionnaire (Kahn et al. 1960) and the Face-Hand Test (Fink et al. 1952). Appropriate laboratory investigations, such as those listed in Table 3, may be necessary to determine the underlying cause of the delirium. The choice of specific tests to be used will depend on the results of the clinical evaluation.

General Treatment Considerations

Correction of Underlying Disorders

The first principle in the treatment of delirium is the identification and correction of the organic causes that underlie the delirium, with proper attention to its phenomenologic, physiologic, anatomic, and pathologic components. However, the presentation of life-threatening delirium may demand therapeutic intervention before a definitive etiology can be established (Wells 1985a; Wells and McEvoy 1982). Brain damage must be prevented by counteracting hypoglycemia, hypoxia or anoxia, hyperthermia, and thiamine deficiency. In delirium of unknown etiology, iv treatment with 50 ml of a 50 percent glucose solution should be given after obtaining blood and

---

Table 3. Laboratory Evaluation of Delirium

Screening studies
  Complete blood count
  Urinalysis, including glucose and acetone
  Blood chemistries: Electrolytes, creatinine, glucose, liver function tests, thyroid function
    studies
  Chest X ray
  Electrocardiogram
  Electroencephalogram

Additional studies
  Computed tomography scan of the head
  Lumbar puncture
  Serum vitamin B_{12} and folate
  Toxic screens: Blood or urine for drugs, alcohol, toxins, heavy metals
  Serum drug levels (e.g., digoxin, lithium)
  Arterial blood gases
  Cultures: Blood, urine
  Serial electroencephalograms
  Magnetic Resonance Imaging of the brain

---

urine for diagnostic studies. Hypoxia and anoxia may result from myocardial infarction, hypotension, cardiac arrhythmias, obstructive or restrictive pulmonary disease, severe anemia, and carbon monoxide poisoning; appropriate steps to treat these conditions must be taken without delay. Hyperthermia, above 40.5 C (105 F), must be corrected by rapid cooling techniques such as alcohol sponges and baths, ice packs, and fanning. Wernicke's encephalopathy is indicated by the presence of delirium in conjunction with ataxia, peripheral neuropathy, horizontal or vertical nystagmus, paresis or paralysis of the lateral rectus muscles, and disconjugate gaze. It should be treated by immediate administration of thiamine HCl 100 mg iv, followed by 50 mg im each day for one week or until oral vitamin supplements can be taken (Wells 1985a; Wells and McEvoy 1982).

General Management

Hospitalization.   Patients with delirium should usually be managed in an acute hospital setting, although after the underlying causes have been identified and etiologic treatment has begun, some patients with milder symptoms may be managed adequately in skilled nursing facilities.

Consultations.   The psychiatrist is commonly asked to consult when a patient with delirium is on a medical or surgical unit. However, patients with delirium may present as emergencies either in psychiatric outpatient settings or while hospitalized on an inpatient psychiatric unit. In the latter cases, it is important for the attending psychiatrist to obtain consultation from other medical colleagues. Joint management of the delirious patient by the psychiatrist, internist, neurologist, pediatrician, or other primary care or specialty physician will help to ensure appropriate comprehensive evaluation and care.

Physiologic support.   The severity of delirium is often related to the general physical status of the patient; accordingly, optimal physiologic health should be maintained. Adequate hydration and nutrition are important, as is correction of electrolyte imbalances and life-threatening conditions such as those noted above.

Environmental support.   It is often necessary to adjust the environment of the patient with delirium to make it more familiar and to avoid ambiguous and confusing sensory stimulation. Recommended manipulations of the patient's environment include allowing the patient to keep a favorite object or picture nearby, having a relative stay with the patient, leaving a light on at night to decrease nocturnal exacerbation, frequent reorientation with calendars and clocks, and the use of a radio or television to help with orientation and to decrease sensory monotony or understimulation.

Nursing care.   Prevention or modification of disorganized behavior through repeated orientations and assistance in communication may be accomplished by skilled nursing care. Psychological support can be maintained by a gentle and uncritical approach and attitude toward the patient. Consultation with a clinical nurse specialist may be useful to the nursing staff in helping them carry out these activities and their responsibilities to observe, record, and manage the fluctuations in the patient's clinical state, as well as to watch for developing complications.

Protection.   Agitated and restless patients with delirium are often fearful and paranoid and may be belligerent, combative, or assaultive, leading to injury to themselves or others. Precautionary measures to avert such situations include medication (as described below), special duty nurses or attendants, and, for patients who may injure themselves in attempting to climb over side rails, placing the patient on a mattress on the floor. Physical restraints, while needed in severe cases, should be avoided if possible; they may worsen disorganized behavior and may cause patients to sustain soft tissue damage from struggling against them.

Medication. Except for the treatment of underlying, causative conditions, the indications for medication in delirium are principally for sedation, control of psychotic manifestations, and normalization of sleep. The choice of medication to accomplish these aims tends to be based on personal preference and experience rather than determined by systematic clinical investigation. As guiding principles, one should use lower dosages in the brain-impaired patient than in the patient with so-called functional psychosis; long-acting sedatives and medications that may potentiate the delirium, such as those with anticholinergic properties, should be avoided; dosages for the elderly should be less than those for younger adults.

For sleep induction, triazolam, a short-acting benzodiazepine with a half-life of 1.7 to 3.0 hours, may be selected, 0.25 to 0.5 mg administered orally; the dosage may be increased in 0.125- to 0.25-mg increments as required to induce sleep. Triazolam should be used with caution in the elderly because of the possibility of paradoxical agitation and impairment of mentation (Byerley and Gillin 1984). For a more sustained hypnotic effect in patients who have middle or terminal insomnia, an intermediate duration benzodiazepine such as temazepam (half-life 10 to 20 hours) 15 to 30 mg po; lorazepam (half-life 10 to 20 hours) 2 to 4 mg po, im, or iv; or oxazepam (half-life 8 to 12 hours) 15 to 45 mg po may be chosen and given at bedtime. Note that severely agitated patients, as well as those with physiologic dependence on hypnotic-sedative drugs, may fail to show the expected soporific response at usual dosages and may require larger amounts. Except in the case of withdrawal delirium, barbiturates should be avoided because of their tendency to cause cardiorespiratory depression and rapid eye movement (REM) suppression; these effects are not generally seen with benzodiazepines. Chloral hydrate, 1 to 2 g po, also produces REM depression but is an effective hypnotic with a short duration of action (half-life 4 to 12 hours). Antihistamines should not be used because of their anticholinergic effect, nor should phenothiazines because they not only have significant anticholinergic properties but also lower seizure threshold and produce temperature dysregulation (Byerley and Gillin 1984; Greenblatt and Shader 1975).

Sedation may be effected by daytime use of the same intermediate duration benzodiazepines as are used for sleep, given in similar or lower dosages every 4 to 6 hours during the day as needed to keep the restless and agitated patient calm, while avoiding an obtunding effect. However, agitation is often accompanied by psychotic behavior, which requires intervention to prevent harm to the patient or to others and to prevent the patient from pulling out iv tubing, electrocardiograph (ECG) leads, and so on. For these purposes, many clinicians select haloperidol, a butyrophenone, as the drug of choice. The butyrophenones possess potent antipsychotic, anxiolytic, and antiemetic properties; unlike many other neuroleptics, they do not tend to potentiate delirium. Haloperidol may be administered 2 to 10 mg po or 1 to 5 mg im, every four to six hours, individually titrated to the desired effect. More rapid response may be obtained by giving 5 mg im each hour until target symptoms subside, followed by oral maintenance (Moore 1977). The need for continuing medication should be reevaluated frequently once symptoms are controlled.

In the agitated, psychotic patient with delirium, the butyrophenone, droperidol, would appear to be a superior agent, although there are only sporadic reports of its use in delirium per se. Droperidol is used widely in Europe to treat psychotic disorders, but in the United States its use for a number of years has been as an adjunct to anesthesia, owing to its sedative and antiemetic properties. Indeed, its only common major side effect is sedation, which may be turned to advantage in the management of delirium. Compared to haloperidol, its onset is more rapid, its duration shorter (effects beginning to wane in two to four hours), and its incidence of extrapyramidal symptoms lower. Its onset of action, nearly as rapid after im as after iv administration, usually occurs within five minutes, although some patients may not show a robust response until 15 to 30 minutes after injection. Dosages for acutely agitated patients typically range from 5 to 20 mg, although amounts exceeding 100 mg have been used without adverse effect and may be required in some severely agitated patients. Repeated doses may be given after 30 minutes if the response to the first injection is less than adequate (Ayd 1980; Granacher and Ruth 1979; Hooper and Minter 1983; Neff et al. 1972; Resnick and Burton 1984; van Leeuwen et al. 1977).

Droperidol is available in the United States in parenteral form only, 2.5 mg/ml. Intravenous administration should be slow, spanning several minutes or more, depending on dosage. Because of the large volumes involved, amounts larger than 10 mg should be given iv; im dosages between 5 and 10 mg should be administered at separate injection sites. A summary of medications useful in managing the behavioral manifestations of delirium is presented in Table 4.

Electroconvulsive therapy.   Electroconvulsive therapy (ECT) has been reported to be safe and effective in reducing the clinical manifestations of delirium, including those associated with phencyclidine and with alcohol withdrawal (Dudley and Williams 1972; Kramp and Bolwig 1981; Roberts 1963; Rosen et al. 1984; Taylor 1982). Lipowski (1980) reported that in rare cases, where severe agitation is life threatening and unresponsive to medication, two or three treatments may be highly effective. However, he cautioned that ECT should not be considered as a routine treatment modality in delirium and should be employed only in exceptional circumstances.

Table 4.   Medications Useful in the Management of Behavioral Manifestations of Delirium

Target Behavior	Medication	Initial Dosage[a]	Route	Frequency
Initial insomnia	Triazolam	0.25–0.5 mg	po	hs
Middle or terminal insomnia	Temazepam	15–30 mg	po	hs
	Lorazepam	2–4 mg	po, im, or iv	hs
	Oxazepam	15–45 mg	po	hs
	Chloral hydrate	1–2 g	po	hs
Restlessness, agitation	Lorazepam	0.5–3 mg	po, im, or iv	bid–tid
	Oxazepam	15–30 mg	po	tid–qid
	Temazepam	15–30 mg	po	bid–tid
Severe agitation, psychosis	Droperidol	5–20 mg	im or iv[b]	q 0.5–4 h
	Haloperidol	2–10 mg	po	q 4–6 h
		1–5 mg	im	q 4–6 h

[a]Younger adult dosage. For use in geriatric or debilitated patients, reduce dosage to one-third to one-half of that listed. For pediatric use refer to manufacturer's prescribing information.
[b]im dosages between 5 and 10 mg should be administered at separate injection sites.

Monitoring.   The clinical course of the delirious patient must be closely monitored for two important reasons. First, the effect of therapeutic interventions must be assessed regularly and frequently. Second, by its nature, the course of delirium is unpredictable and extremely variable. The physician and other clinicians must be alert to sudden exacerbations in the clinical state that may endanger the patient or others. Placing the patient in a room next to the nurses' station and using remote video observation, cardiac monitoring, and one-to-one nursing care are, therefore, often essential for this purpose.

Specific Treatments

The number of conditions and disorders causally associated with delirium is far too great to allow detailed consideration of all specific treatments. However, five of the clinical conditions that psychiatrists may expect to encounter in the treatment of psychiatric patients are discussed briefly.

Alcohol Withdrawal Delirium

Clinical features.   Delirium resulting from withdrawal from alcohol is an uncommon but serious and life-threatening complication (Lipowski 1980). The onset of alcohol withdrawal delirium occurs within a few hours to as much as 10 days after the cessation of alcohol consumption, but usually becomes evident in the first two or three days (Greenblatt and Shader 1975; Holloway et al. 1984). This delirium tends to subside spontaneously in one to five days after it becomes clinically manifest (Freemon 1981; Holloway et al. 1984). Alcohol withdrawal delirium has clinical features of a typical delirious state with vivid, often threatening hallucinations, psychomotor hyperactivity (although a hypoactive variant is reported), autonomic hyperactivity (e.g., increased blood pressure, sweating, and increased heart rate), persecutory delusions, coarse tremor, and seizures. Predisposing conditions and complicating intercurrent disease states include malnutrition, fever, dehydration, hypokalemia, hypomagnesemia, hypoglycemia, pneumonia, pancreatitis, liver failure, gastrointestinal bleeding, fracture, and subdural hematoma (Freemon 1981; Goodwin 1982, 1985; Greenblatt and Shader 1975; Holloway et al. 1984). Alcohol withdrawal delirium is usually not seen unless there have been several years of heavy alcohol use.

Treatment.   Treatment principles do not differ appreciably from those for less severe forms of alcohol withdrawal syndrome (i.e., sedation, vitamin and nutrition supplementation, correction of fluid and electrolyte imbalances, and treatment of hypoglycemia and associated medical illnesses). Drugs with cross-tolerance to ethanol may be used for sedation. The benzodiazepines are the most popular because of their excellent sedative properties, low cardiorespiratory toxicity, absence of REM suppression, anticonvulsant effects, and relatively gradual fall in blood levels. The following method of treatment is suggested by Holloway et al. (1984): Using chlordiazepoxide, an oral loading dose of 50 to 100 mg is followed with similar dosages each hour until satisfactory sedation is achieved, repeating the dosage subsequently if signs of withdrawal reappear. Diazepam may be used instead, in a dosage of 10 to 40 mg po. Both chlordiazepoxide and diazepam may be administered iv if necessary but should not be given im because of relatively unreliable absorption. Since long-acting sedatives should be avoided in patients with impairment of drug metabolism or excretion, shorter half-life benzodiazepines (e.g., lorazepam, 1 to 4 mg po every six to eight hours; or oxazepam, 15 to 60 mg po every eight hours) are preferable in patients with hepatic or renal decompensation and in elderly individuals. However, because of their short half-lives, it is important that these drugs be administered at regular intervals and discontinued by gradually decreasing dosages given at these same intervals to avoid withdrawal symptoms (Greenblatt and Shader 1975; Holloway et al. 1984). With the control of the delirium, treatment of the alcohol abstinence syndrome may be continued until withdrawal has been completed. (For additional information on the treatment of alcohol intoxication and withdrawal, see Section 12.)

Sedative, Hypnotic, or Anxiolytic Withdrawal Delirium

Clinical features. The clinical features of delirium secondary to abstinence from barbiturates or similarly acting sedative or hypnotic drugs are very similar to those of alcohol withdrawal delirium, including agitation, apprehension, tremulousness, fever, insomnia, autonomic hyperactivity, hyperreflexia, psychotic manifestations, and, in some cases, seizures. Moreover, as with alcohol withdrawal, delirium in sedative, hypnotic, or anxiolytic withdrawal usually reflects heavy daily use for extended periods of time—for example, the equivalent of 1,000 mg/day of secobarbital for at least one month (Shader et al. 1975; Wikler 1968). The onset of the delirium typically occurs between three and five days after the cessation of drug administration, although with long-acting benzodiazepines (e.g., chlordiazepoxide, diazepam, prazepam) it may not become manifest until two weeks after discontinuing the drug (Liskow 1982; Shader et al. 1975).

Treatment. The appearance of delirium in the sedative, hypnotic, or anxiolytic syndrome, as in alcohol withdrawal, calls for immediate sedation of the patient, using adequate and often large dosages of a sedative agent until a soporific effect is achieved (Jackson and Shader 1973; Liskow 1982; Wikler 1968). While delirium may result from the cessation of virtually any type or combination of sedative, hypnotic or anxiolytic agent(s), the fact that there exists at least partial cross-tolerance among this general class of drugs, including ethanol, obviates the need to identify the specific drug(s) involved. Thus sedation may be accomplished by administration of an intermediate duration barbiturate such as pentobarbital given either parenterally or orally in sufficient amounts to achieve suppression of the delirium, typically 200 to 400 mg every four to six hours (Jackson and Shader 1973; McNichol and Hoshino 1975; Wikler 1968). This regimen should be continued, together with necessary physiologic and nutritional supportive measures, until the patient's total daily sedative, hypnotic, or anxiolytic requirement is established and gradual detoxification can be undertaken. (For further discussion of the treatment of sedative, hypnotic, or anxiolytic dependence, see Section 13.)

Anticholinergic Delirium

Clinical features. Drugs with anticholinergic properties taken in intentional or accidental overdose may cause profound delirium, which may progress to coma. Such drugs include over-the-counter preparations containing belladonna alkaloids, certain antihistamines, antiparkinsonian drugs, gastrointestinal antispasmodics, tricyclic antidepressants, and some neuroleptic agents. The clinical manifestations of the anticholinergic syndrome include mydriasis, fever, flushed facies, anhidrosis, decreased peristalsis, urinary retention, tachycardia, elevated blood pressure, and tachypnea. Spontaneous recovery is the rule, but it may not occur for up to five days after onset. Medical consultation and co-management of the condition may be especially important when cardiac toxicity is present (Berger and Dunn 1982; Duvoisin and Katz 1968; Heiser and Gillin 1971).

Treatment.   The drug of choice in the treatment of delirium induced by anti-cholinergic substances is physostigmine salicylate, a reversible anticholinesterase that easily crosses the blood-brain barrier. In the absence of contraindications (see below), if the history and clinical presentation suggest anticholinergic toxicity, physostigmine serves both as a diagnostic and therapeutic tool in that response is rapid, often with complete resolution of the delirium after an iv dosage of 1 to 2 mg, administered at a rate not faster than 1 mg/minute. If there is no or little response, this dosage may be repeated in 15 minutes. As physostigmine is degraded completely in one to two hours, response tends to be transitory and repeated doses of 1 to 2 mg iv or im every one to three hours are frequently necessary (Berger and Dunn 1982; Duvoisin and Katz 1968; Heiser and Gillin 1971). Alternatively, when numerous administrations are indicated, continuous iv infusion at a rate of 1 to 3 mg/hour may be preferable, titrating dosage against the patient's signs and symptoms and monitoring cardiac parameters continuously (Stern 1983).

Excessive or too rapid administration of physostigmine may produce cholinergic crisis with bradycardia, sialorrhea, nausea and vomiting, diarrhea, and respiratory arrest. This crisis may be counteracted with 0.5 to 1 mg atropine iv (Berger and Dunn 1982; Heiser and Gillin 1971).

Contraindications to physostigmine include asthma, diabetes mellitus, gangrene, mechanical obstruction of the intestinal or urinary tract, and cardiovascular disease. In patients with anticholinergic delirium in whom anticholinesterases are contraindicated, the delirium must be treated by the general methods of sedation and physiologic and psychological support. Phenothiazines and other drugs with significant anticholinergic properties should, of course, be avoided. Berger and Dunn (1982) recommended that comatose patients suspected of having anticholinergic delirium also be given glucose, 50 cc of a 50 percent solution iv, and naloxone, 0.4 mg iv, since hypoglycemia and opiates may contribute to the coma.

Phencyclidine (PCP) Delirium

Clinical features.   The clinical manifestations of intoxication with PCP or other arylcyclohexylamines, such as ketamine, may include delirium, often with marked paranoia and belligerent or assaultive behavior, together with vertical or horizontal nystagmus, increased deep tendon reflexes, myoclonus, tremor, weakness, vertigo, dysarthria, ataxia, analgesia, absent corneal reflexes and other sensory modality impairments, diaphoresis, tachycardia, increased blood pressure, nausea and vomiting, depression of cardiopulmonary function, and seizures, as well as psychotic manifestations that may closely resemble schizophrenia (Berger and Dunn 1982; Castellani et al 1982; Grinspoon and Bakalar 1985; Showalter and Thornton 1977). Although PCP undergoes rapid hepatic detoxification by hydroxylation and conjugation (Showalter and Thornton 1977), detectable levels may remain in the urine and blood for a week or more (Grinspoon and Bakalar 1985), and manifest psychotic effects may persist for weeks (Berger and Dunn 1982).

Treatment. No specific antagonists for PCP intoxication are known. "Talking down" is of little value; placing the patient in a quiet and dimly lit room to decrease stimulation has been found useful. Physiologic support, including maintenance of adequate cardiopulmonary function, is important. For the control and prevention of myoclonus and seizures, diazepam 10 to 30 mg iv is reported to be helpful. For control of hyperactive and psychotic manifestations, butyrophenones are recommended—for example, haloperidol 5 mg im every hour until adequate control is achieved (Berger and Dunn 1982; Showalter and Thornton 1977). Although its efficacy in the treatment of PCP delirium has not been established in the literature, droperidol has been reported to be effective for "bad trips" (Neff et al. 1972) and for drug-induced psychosis (Ayd 1980); it would appear to be the drug of choice in the highly agitated patient because of its sedative properties. Dosages of droperidol should follow the guidelines recommended earlier. In addition, because PCP has central anticholinergic properties, physostigmine employed in a similar manner to that described for anticholinergic delirium above may be effective in PCP-induced delirium (Castellani et al. 1982). Acidification of the urine with ascorbic acid and administration of ammonium chloride may be helpful in promoting excretion of the drug (Grinspoon and Bakalar 1985). Finally, for patients who are refractory to these interventions, ECT may be effective (Rosen et al. 1984). (For additional considerations in the treatment of PCP intoxication, see Section 13.)

ECT Emergence Delirium

Clinical features. In 5 to 10 percent of patients receiving ECT, a typical delirium ensues with emergence from anesthesia before full consciousness is regained. It tends to subside in 10 to 15 minutes but may persist for longer periods (Abrams 1982). Concurrent use of lithium and ECT not only may cause excess morbidity in terms of impairment of memory and cognitive and neurologic abnormalities (Small et al. 1980), but may predispose to the development of emergence delirium, associated with continuing seizure activity on EEG (Weiner et al. 1980). This complication is seen even with serum lithium concentrations well below toxic levels, and it may not clear until lithium is discontinued and blood levels fall over the course of 24 to 72 hours (Mandel et al. 1980).

Treatment. ECT emergence delirium can usually be treated effectively by iv administration of 5 to 10 mg of diazepam (Abrams 1982; Weiner et al. 1980). Abrams (1982) recommended that with all subsequent ECT treatments, this dosage be administered immediately at the cessation of the seizure. He also cautioned that diazepam should not be mixed with other iv solutions because of the formation of insoluble precipitates. Alternatively, recurrence of ECT emergence delirium may be prevented by using nondominant hemisphere unilateral electrode placement and brief-pulse, square wave stimulation (Daniel et al. 1983; Sackeim et al. 1983).

Summary

Delirium is a common organic mental syndrome, especially among children and the elderly, although it is often overlooked or not considered in the differential diagnosis of patients who may appear to have nonorganic psychoses or who have reduced psychomotor activity. Once it is considered as a diagnostic possibility, it can usually be distinguished readily from the other organic mental syndromes, including the dementias. Treatment of underlying conditions and secondary manifestations is usually successful, and specific treatments are available for many deliria that are likely to be encountered by the psychiatrist. The importance of delirium lies in the fact that it carries a significant risk of associated morbidity and mortality, making early identification and effective intervention essential.

Chapter 94

Dementia and Amnestic Syndromes

Of all the psychiatric disorders, the dementia and amnestic syndromes have long been considered the least treatable. Such a reputation is unjustifiably pessimistic. Although specific causes and treatments are lacking for many forms of these syndromes, symptomatic treatments often relieve suffering and improve functioning of even moderately and severely impaired patients. As clinicians await the results of research aimed at identifying etiologies of these often devastating disorders, a clear, systematic approach to both specific and symptomatic treatments will ensure comprehensive and humane care. Because of the many overlaps in the diagnosis and treatment of the dementia and amnestic syndromes, they will be reviewed here in a single chapter.

Definitions and Diagnostic Criteria

Table 1 lists the diagnostic criteria for dementia according to DSM-III-R (American Psychiatric Association 1987). For dementia, several criteria must be present, including: 1) loss of intellectual ability resulting in social or occupational impairment; 2) memory loss; 3) impairment in abstract thinking, judgment, other higher cortical functions, or personality change; 4) clear state of consciousness; and 5) documented or presumed evidence of an organic cause. These criteria differ from earlier ones in several ways. First, the diagnosis is based on behavioral phenomena so that dementia characterizes a clinical syndrome, a cluster of signs and symptoms that should lead to a search for a cause. Second, these criteria avoid reference to reversibility, duration, and rate of onset. This departure from prior definitions may be a wise one. Reversibility and duration are difficult to apply as criteria because they can be established

Table 1. DSM-III-R Diagnostic Criteria for Dementia

A. Demonstrable evidence of impairment in short- and long-term memory. Impairment in short-term memory (inability to learn new information) may be indicated by inability to remember three objects after five minutes. Long-term memory impairment (inability to remember information that was known in the past) may be indicated by inability to remember past personal information (e.g., what happened yesterday, birthplace, occupation) or facts of common knowledge (e.g., past Presidents, well-known dates).

B. At least one of the following:

(1) impairment in abstract thinking, as indicated by inability to find similarities and differences between related words, difficulty in defining words and concepts, and other similar tasks

(2) impaired judgment, as indicated by inability to make reasonable plans to deal with interpersonal, family, and job-related problems and issues

(3) other disturbances of higher cortical function, such as aphasia (disorder of language), apraxia (inability to carry out motor activities despite intact comprehension and motor function), agnosia (failure to recognize or identify objects despite intact sensory function), and "constructional difficulty" (e.g., inability to copy three-dimensional figures, assemble blocks, or arrange sticks in specific designs)

(4) personality change, i.e., alteration or accentuation of premorbid traits

C. The disturbance in A and B significantly interferes with work or usual social activities or relationships with others.

D. Not occurring exclusively during the course of Delirium.

E. Either (1) or (2):

(1) there is evidence from the history, physical examination, or laboratory tests of a specific organic factor (or factors) judged to be etiologically related to the disturbance

(2) in the absence of such evidence, an etiologic organic factor can be presumed if the disturbance cannot be accounted for by any nonorganic mental disorder, e.g., Major Depression accounting for cognitive impairment

Criteria for severity of Dementia:

Mild: Although work or social activities are significantly impaired, the capacity for independent living remains, with adequate personal hygiene and relatively intact judgment.

Moderate: Independent living is hazardous, and some degree of supervision is necessary.

Severe: Activities of daily living are so impaired that continual supervision is required, e.g., unable to maintain minimal personal hygiene; largely incoherent or mute.

only retrospectively. Moreover, they are functions of the state of the art at any one time. Similarly, the rate of onset of illness as a criterion presents difficulties because not all dementias begin insidiously; for example, dementia due to anoxia may have an acute onset, yet may fit DSM-III-R criteria of dementia. Even though these criteria are an improvement over earlier ones, further changes have been suggested. In particular, elimination of the need for "documented or presumed evidence of an organic cause" would allow the inclusion of such disorders as depression as causes of the dementia syndrome (Jarvik 1982b).

Table 2 lists the DSM-III-R diagnostic criteria for amnestic syndrome. The hallmark of the disorder is memory impairment. Patients show deficits in both recent and remote memory with sparing of immediate recall. Short-term (recent) memory, or the ability to learn new material (anterograde amnesia), is usually most severely

Table 2. DSM-III-R Diagnostic Criteria for Amnestic Syndrome

A. Demonstrable evidence of impairment in both short- and long-term memory; with regard to long-term memory, very remote events are remembered better than more recent events. Impairment in short-term memory (inability to learn new information) may be indicated by inability to remember three objects after five minutes. Long-term memory impairment (inability to remember information that was known in the past) may be indicated by inability to remember past personal information (e.g., what happened yesterday, birthplace, occupation) or facts of common knowledge (e.g., past Presidents, well-known dates).

B. Not occurring exclusively during the course of Delirium, and does not meet the criteria for Dementia (i.e., no impairment in abstract thinking or judgment, no other disturbances of higher cortical function, and no personality change).

C. There is evidence from the history, physical examination, or laboratory tests of a specific organic factor (or factors) judged to be etiologically related to the disturbance.

affected. Consequently, these patients are disoriented to place and time. In addition, long-term (remote) memory is impaired so patients with amnestic syndrome have trouble recalling material from the past (retrograde amnesia). Immediate memory or the ability to repeat items (digit span) is not affected. The DSM-III-R criteria, like those for dementia, specify an organic factor as a cause. The frequently associated feature of confabulation (filling in memory gaps with imaginary events) is not included in the DSM-III-R criteria. Amnestic syndrome differs from dementia in that the impairment is limited to memory function. By contrast, dementia is characterized by deficits in memory as well as other areas (e.g., judgment, abstraction, or personality) (Table 1).

Epidemiology

The likelihood of developing the dementia syndrome increases with age. The most widely quoted estimates are that 5 percent of people 65 years of age or older and 20 percent of those 80 years or older experience cognitive impairment of sufficient severity to warrant the diagnosis of dementia (Gurland and Cross 1982; Jarvik et al. 1980; Mortimer and Schuman 1981). Such estimates have been based on limited epidemiologic data and even fewer data are available for rates of cognitive impairment among younger adults. Folstein et al. (1985) studied 3,481 community residents in the Baltimore area. Using DSM-III (American Psychiatric Association 1980) criteria, they found that 6.1 percent of people 65 years of age or older suffered from dementia. Dementia of the Alzheimer type (DAT) was diagnosed in 2.0 percent of them; multi-infarct dementia (MID) comprised 2.8 percent of the group. This frequency for MID is higher than expected from neuropathologic studies, which probably reflects the difficulties in clinically differentiating these two dementias. For the people 75 years of age or above, 11.7 percent were diagnosed as demented: 4.6 percent with DAT and 6.0 percent with MID. Prevalence rates for dementia in the younger adults studied were not reported, although the authors noted that 4 percent of people aged 18 to 64 had Mini-Mental State Examination (MMSE) (Folstein et al. 1975) scores within a range characteristic of dementia (22 or lower out of a possible 30 points) compared to 20 percent in the 65+ age group. The Epidemiologic Catchment Area Program

(Robins et al. 1984) found a similar trend for cognitive impairment, as measured by the MMSE, to increase with age.

Most patients with dementia suffer from illnesses for which no specific treatments exist. Although no large-scale epidemiologic studies have as yet determined the prevalence of reversible dementia in the aged, data from small samples suggest that 10 to 30 percent of demented persons 65 years and older have potentially reversible disorders (Maletta et al. 1982; Marsden and Harrison 1972; Smith and Kiloh 1981). In a review by Cummings and Benson (1983b), 7 percent of patients initially diagnosed as demented had a dementia associated with a psychiatric disorder; 4 percent were later diagnosed as not demented.

By contrast, amnestic syndrome occurs rarely in either the young or the old. The most common type of amnestic syndrome is that due to thiamine deficiency associated with chronic alcohol abuse. Abrupt onset of oculomotor disturbance, cerebellar ataxia, and memory impairment is the acute presentation of thiamine deficiency, known as Wernicke's encephalopathy (Reuler et al. 1985). The diagnostic rate for Wernicke's syndrome is 0.05 percent of general hospital admissions, a marked underestimate of the 1 percent diagnostic rate at autopsy (Nakada and Knight 1984). The prevalence of the chronic form of the disorder, Korsakoff's syndrome, is difficult to estimate. In recent years, investigators have questioned whether Wernicke-Korsakoff's syndrome is as discrete an entity as previously assumed. Some of these patients may be more accurately labeled as suffering from "alcoholic dementia" (Lishman 1981), which confounds epidemiologic estimates.

Clinical Syndromes and Differential Diagnosis

The first step toward treatment of any disorder is accurate diagnosis. A wide variety of conditions can cause memory impairment and other cognitive changes resulting in an amnestic or dementia syndrome. In addition to disorders lacking specific treatment, such as DAT, there are numerous other causes, which are often treatable (Table 3). It is essential first to identify causes for which specific treatments do exist. Common causes, such as drug effects, depression, and physical disease, must be considered initially; less common conditions can then be explored, depending on the individual circumstances of a particular case. Even if no underlying treatable illnesses are found, it is important to differentiate DAT and MID because of the possibility of prophylaxis for the latter.

Primary Degenerative Dementia

When the dementia syndrome has an insidious onset, a gradually progressive course, and no specific identified causes, the DSM-III diagnosis of primary degenerative dementia (PDD) is most likely. Dementia of the Alzheimer type (DAT) is the most common form, although autopsy studies show that clinical diagnosis of this disorder is not always accurate, and the patient may have had some other form of PDD (e.g., Pick's disease). A work group on the diagnosis of Alzheimer's disease was established by the National Institute of Neurological and Communicative Disorders and Stroke and the Alzheimer's Disease and Related Disorders Association (McKhann et al. 1984). Its report specified criteria that provide a guide for the diagnosis of possible, probable, and definite Alzheimer disease and was a much needed addition to the DSM-III criteria. DSM-III-R incorporates criteria for severity of dementia (mild,

Table 3.   Some Conditions Reported to Cause Memory Impairment and Other Cognitive Changes

Benign senescent forgetfulness and normal aging	Severe anemia
Mental retardation and developmental disorders	Thyroid disorders
Dementia of the Alzheimer type	Infections
Multi-infarct dementia	Influenza
Pick's disease	Meningitis
Psychiatric disorders	Pneumonia
Adjustment disorders	Tuberculosis
Depressive disorders	Cardiovascular diseases
Paranoid disorders	Arrhythmia
Delirium	Congestive heart failure
Drugs	Deficiency states
Alcohol	Folate deficiency
Antianxiety agents	Thiamine deficiency
Anticonvulsants	Vitamin B_{12} deficiency
Antidepressants	Collagen vascular disorders
Antihypertensive agents	Systemic lupus erythematosus
Atropine and related compounds	Temporal arteritis
Neuroleptics	Intracranial conditions
Metabolic and endocrine disorders	Normal pressure hydrocephalus
Fluid and electrolyte imbalance	Subdural hematoma
Hepatic failure	Stroke
Parathyroid disorders	Tumor
Renal failure	

Note.   Adapted from Small et al. (1981).

moderate, and severe) and introduces primary degenerative dementia of the Alzheimer type (PDDAT). PDDAT or DAT accounts for an estimated 50 percent of the dementias in the elderly, and the risk of this form of dementia increases steadily through adult life (Heston and Mastri 1982; Tomlinson et al. 1970). The differential diagnosis between Pick's disease and DAT is particularly problematic for middle-aged patients because the frequency of Pick's disease tends to increase until about age 60 and then becomes rare at ages 70 and above (Heston and Mastri 1982). The cause or causes of DAT are unknown. DAT may represent a heterogeneous disorder involving any of several possible causes, including chromosomal abnormalities, immune changes, leukocyte dysmotility, neurotransmitter defects, slow viruses, heavy metals, and human leukocyte antigens (Read et al. 1985).

Amnestic Syndrome

Anything that can damage the diencephalic and medial temporal structures of the brain can result in the amnestic syndrome. Thiamine deficiency may be the most common cause. Moreover, many disorders that can cause the dementia syndrome can also cause the amnestic syndrome, including head trauma, stroke, encephalitis, anoxia, and brain tumors (Benson and Blumer 1982).

Delirium

Because delirium involves cognitive function, it may be confused with dementia. Delirium may often be differentiated from dementia by its abrupt onset, short duration, and accompanying impairment of attention, alertness, and perception. The disorder tends to fluctuate and worsen at night. Many of the conditions causing dementia (Table 3) may also cause delirium, and both syndromes may occur together (Lipowski 1985). Medications frequently cause delirium and should be considered initially in the differential diagnosis. (For a detailed discussion of delirium, please refer to Chapter 93.)

DAT versus MID

In contrast to the insidious onset and gradually progressive course of DAT, MID is characterized by a sudden onset of illness and stepwise decline in intellectual function. Focal neurologic signs and association with hypertension in many patients may also help differentiate MID from DAT. The clinical signs and symptoms, coded and given weighted scores (Hachinski et al. 1975; Rosen et al. 1980), have been used widely to help differentiate MID from DAT (see Table 4), although the validity of these scales has been questioned (Liston and LaRue 1983a, 1983b). An expanded scale aimed at correcting methodological shortcomings of the earlier instrument has been developed (Small 1985). Nonetheless, the frequent coexistence of MID and DAT is bound to impair diagnostic accuracy (Tomlinson et al. 1970).

Dementia Associated with Alcoholism

When a dementia syndrome emerges in a chronic alcoholic, dementia associated with alcoholism is often diagnosed. According to DSM-III-R, the dementia must persist for at least three weeks after drinking has ceased. Other causes, of course, must be excluded, and many years of heavy drinking are apparently necessary. Alcohol amnestic syndrome due to thiamine deficiency is also known as Korsakoff's disease. Lishman (1981) pointed out that the distinction between alcoholic dementia and amnestic syndrome is less clear than previously appreciated. Moreover, other factors contributing to brain damage in alcoholics (e.g., trauma, vascular changes, hepatic damage) complicate diagnostic differentiation. In patients with a history of significant alcohol use, the diagnosis of PDDAT is often particularly difficult.

Drug Effects and Physical Illnesses

In addition to alcohol-related memory disorders, a wide variety of medications can cause cognitive impairment resembling dementia syndrome (see Table 3). For elderly patients, drugs deserve special emphasis as a cause of memory impairment

Table 4. Clinical Features of the Modified Ischemic Score

Feature	Point Values[a]
Abrupt onset	2
Stepwise deterioration	1
Somatic complaints	1
Emotional incontinence	1
History or presence of hypertension	1
History of strokes	2
Focal neurologic symptoms	2
Focal neurologic signs	2

Note. Adapted from Rosen WG et al. (1980).
[a]A score of 4 or more is consistent with multi-infarct dementia.

because of widespread polypharmacy (Chien et al. 1979) and age-related changes in body function and pharmacokinetics (Greenblatt and Shader 1981).

Another important cause of dementia in the elderly is physical illness (see Table 3). An elderly person's brain is extremely sensitive to change in its environment, and almost any physical illness can effect such a change and produce cognitive decline (Small and Jarvik 1982). Disorders of thyroid metabolism (both hyper- and hypothyroidism) are the most frequent endocrinopathies reported to impair cognition. Lethargy and confusion can result from hyperparathyroidism or hypercalcemia from any cause. Impaired cognition has also been reported from numerous causes of cerebral hypoxia, including bilateral coronary artery disease, cardiac dysrhythmias, and pulmonary edema. A wide variety of infections, too, can cause confusion, ranging from acute meningitis to tuberculosis. A variety of intracranial disorders, such as subdural hematoma or neoplasm, also need consideration in the differential diagnosis. Recognition of these conditions is crucial because treatment may reverse the cognitive impairment.

Depression

Depression is rarely confused with dementia in young adults. In the elderly, however, the clinical presentation of depression often mimics dementia. It has been termed "depressive pseudodementia" (Kiloh 1961) and dementia syndrome of depression (Folstein and McHugh 1978). The reported frequency of mistaking depressed for demented patients ranges from 8 to 15 percent (Caine 1981; Duckworth and Ross 1975; Marsden and Harrison 1972; McAllister 1983; Nott and Fleminger 1975; Ron et al. 1979). Apathy, psychomotor retardation, impaired concentration, delusions, and confusion in the depressed patient may be readily taken for dementia, particularly when they are accompanied by complaints of memory loss (Wells 1979). In the dementia syndrome of depression, the complaints of memory loss tend to exceed the actual memory impairment observed on psychological testing (Kahn et al. 1975). The diagnosis is further complicated by the fact that dementia and depression often coexist; recent investigations suggest that 20 to 30 percent of demented patients have concurrent depression (Reifler et al. 1982; Ron et al. 1979). Further knowledge of these disorders will have to come from longitudinal studies.

Other Conditions

In the elderly, age-related deficits in recent and remote memory must be differentiated from the malignant losses of dementia. According to Kral (1978), people with benign senescent forgetfulness have transiently impaired recall of unimportant aspects of remote experiences but remember and relate the essence of the experiences. With increasing public awareness of the symptoms of early DAT, people in their 50s and older often experience anxiety because they associate such benign forgetfulness with the malignant forgetfulness of DAT.

Transient global amnesia (Kane 1983) is an organic condition that can be mistaken for amnestic syndrome. It is characterized by abrupt onset of disorientation and amnesia. The retrograde amnesia diminishes after minutes to hours, and all symptoms are generally gone within 24 hours. It most often occurs in men 50 years of age or older. The underlying pathology is presumed to be vascular in origin.

According to DSM-III-R, psychogenic amnesia is a sudden inability to recall important personal information that is too extensive to be explained by ordinary forgetfulness. The disturbance generally involves memories about personal information so that patients may even be disoriented to self. Recent memory and the ability to learn new information are often unimpaired, in contrast to the amnestic syndrome. A bland lack of concern or la belle indifference has been reported to be associated with psychogenic amnesia, in contrast to the concern patients may express about amnestic episodes associated with transient ischemia. Like other dissociative disorders, psychogenic amnesia is rare in the elderly. An apparent psychogenic amnesia presenting for the first time in a geriatric patient should be evaluated carefully for possible organic causes.

Patient Evaluation

History, Physical, and Mental Status Examination

A detailed history is essential in the comprehensive evaluation of the mentally impaired patient. Because of the patient's memory impairment, the physician needs the cooperation of someone who knows the patient well and who can validate and supplement the information obtained from the patient. The onset of symptoms should be carefully explored with an attempt to distinguish acute from gradual onset. This distinction may be difficult to make because a traumatic event (e.g., retirement, bereavement, illness) may produce a considerable worsening of previously unrecognized insidious intellectual decline. Given the profound effect that medications can have on the mental status of geriatric patients, an inventory of both prescription and over-the-counter drugs is also vital.

A thorough physical examination and careful assessment of neurologic status will help to identify underlying medical conditions. Confusion may be the primary presenting symptom in a variety of illnesses (ranging from a myocardial infarction to Cushing's syndrome) or in any form of delirium. Physical examination may provide pathognomonic information. Asterixis, for example, may indicate liver disease or a metabolic disorder. Neurologic signs may be indicative of stroke or intracranial tumor. Careful attention must be paid to the examination of extraocular movements, cerebellar dysfunction, and gait to identify Wernicke's encephalopathy, which represents a medical emergency. Other signs of chronic alcohol abuse (e.g., hepatomegaly, spider hemangiomas) will point the clinician in the direction of alcohol-related memory disorders. The question of adequate sensory input is too frequently neglected. A patient may appear confused or apathetic because of inadequate sensory input, and inappropriate answers to questions may result from embarrassment about disclosing a hearing impairment. Prolonged hospitalization has also been observed to cause confusion and memory loss, particularly in elderly patients.

Because dementia and amnestic syndromes represent defects in cognition, the mental status examination should focus on memory, retention and recall of new information, the ability to calculate, the quality of judgment, and the patient's emotional state. The physician can evaluate these functions by paying close attention throughout the interview to the patient's verbal and nonverbal communications. The intellectually impaired patient should be approached with respect for his or her sense of dignity and desire to appear competent. Formal testing to confirm or invalidate the diagnosis of memory disorder can often be done subtly, in such a manner as not to discourage the patient. Although such testing is best spread throughout the interview, standardized brief mental status questionnaires are often useful in quantifying the patient's cognitive state, especially for serial examinations aimed at following improvement or decline.

The Mental Status Questionnaire (MSQ) (Kahn 1971) is one scale used widely throughout the country (Table 5). The test consists of 10 questions and takes five to 10 minutes to perform. The results of the MSQ provide a numerical score, ranging from 0 to 10, that estimates the degree of brain dysfunction. Isaacs and Kennie (1970) introduced another simple instrument, the set test, used extensively in geriatrics. The patient is asked to name 10 items in each of four general categories (e.g., towns, colors, animals, fruits). For each different item named, the patient scores one point. A total of less than 15 of the possible 40 points is consistent with moderate to severe dementia. Scores from 15 to 24 are suggestive of dementia. Another popular test is the Mini-Mental State Examination (Folstein et al. 1975) (Table 6). Although longer than the MSQ, it provides more comprehensive data, tapping several areas of cognitive functioning, including orientation, registration, attention, calculation, recall, and language. A number of other useful instruments that provide numerical ratings of the severity of illness are also available (Blessed et al. 1968; Hughes et al. 1982; Reisberg et al. 1982). Although these brief tests are adequate for most situations, more extensive neuropsychological batteries may be needed (Albert 1984).

Laboratory Examinations

Laboratory tests should be obtained as indicated by the history, physical, and psychiatric examinations, with highest priority to the diagnosis of treatable memory impairments. The actual number and order of tests depend on the particular case presentation and the physician's clinical judgment. Table 7 lists the minimum screening tests for evaluating dementia. The Task Force sponsored by the National Institute on Aging (1980) originally included a chest roentgenogram as routine for screening of patients with dementia. A study by Hubbell et al. (1985), however, has raised questions about its usefulness in asymptomatic patients. Computed tomography (CT) scans of the head are used primarily to rule out such intracranial conditions as space-

Table 5. Mental Status Questionnaire

Questions

1. Where are you now? (Name and kind of place)
2. Where is this place? (Address)
3. What month is it?
4. What year is it?
5. What day of the month is it? (Correct is within two days)
6. How old are you? (Age in years)
7. What month were you born?
8. What year were you born?
9. Who is President of the United States?
10. Who was President before him/her?

Answer Interpretation

Total Incorrect Answers Including Unanswered Questions:	*Estimate of Degree of Brain Dysfunction:*
0–2	None or mild
3–8	Moderate
9–10	Severe

Note. Adapted from Kahn (1971).

Table 6. Mini-Mental State Examination

Maximum Score	Score	

Orientation

| 5 | ( ) | What is the (year) (season) (date) (day) (month)? |
| 5 | ( ) | Where are we: (state) (county) (town) (hospital) (floor)? |

Registration

| 3 | ( ) | Name 3 objects: 1 second to say each. Then ask the patient all 3. Give 1 point for each correct answer. Then repeat them until all 3 are learned. Count trials and record. Trials _____ |

Attention and Calculation

| 5 | ( ) | Serial 7s. 1 point for each correct. Stop after 5 answers. Alternatively spell "world" backwards. |

Recall

| 3 | ( ) | Ask for the 3 objects repeated above. Give 1 point for each correct. |

Language

| 9 | ( ) | Name a pencil and watch (2 points) Repeat the following: "No ifs, ands or buts." (1 point) Follow a 3-stage command: "Take a paper in your right hand, fold it in half, and put it on the floor" (3 points) Read and obey the following: Close your eyes (1 point) Write a sentence (1 point) Copy design (1 point) Total score Assess level of consciousness along a continuum _____ |

| | | Alert | Drowsy | Stupor | Coma |

Instructions for Administration of Mini-Mental State Examination

Orientation

(1) Ask for the date. Then ask specifically for parts omitted, e.g., "Can you also tell me what season it is?" One point for each correct.

(2) Ask in turn "Can you tell me the name of this hospital?" (town, county, etc.) One point for each correct.

Registration

Ask the patient if you may test his/her memory. Then say the names of 3 unrelated objects, clearly and slowly, about one second for each. After you have said all 3, ask him/her to repeat them. This first repetition determines the score (0–3) but keep saying them until he/she can repeat all 3, up to 6 trials. If he/she does not eventually learn all 3, recall cannot be meaningfully tested.

(continued)

Table 6. Mini-Mental State Examination (*continued*)

Attention and Calculation

Ask the patient to begin with 100 and count backwards by 7. Stop after 5 subtractions (93, 86, 79, 72, 65). Score the total number of correct answers.

If the patient cannot or will not perform this task, ask him/her to spell the word "world" backwards. The score is the number of letters in correct order. E.g., dlrow = 5, dlorw = 3.

Recall

Ask the patient if he/she can recall the 3 words you previously asked him/her to remember. Score 0–3.

Language

Naming: Show the patient a wrist watch and ask what it is. Repeat for pencil. Score 0–2.

Repetition: Ask the patient to repeat the sentence after you. Allow only one trial. Score 0 or 1.

3-Stage command: Give the patient a piece of plain blank paper and repeat the command. Score 1 point for each part correctly executed.

Reading: On a blank piece of paper print the sentence, "Close your eyes," in letters large enough for the patient to see clearly. Ask him/her to read it and do what it says. Score 1 point only if he/she actually closes eyes.

Writing: Give the patient a blank piece of paper and ask him/her to write a sentence. Do not dictate a sentence, it is to be written spontaneously. It must contain a subject and verb and be sensible. Correct grammar and punctuation are not necessary.

Copying: On a clean piece of paper, draw intersecting pentagons each side about 1 in., and ask him/her to copy it exactly as it is. All 10 angles must be present and 2 must intersect to score 1 point. Tremor and rotation are ignored.

Estimate the patient's level of sensorium along a continuum, from alert on the left to coma on the right.

Note.   Reproduced with permission from Folstein et al. (1975).

Table 7. Screening Tests for Evaluating Cognitive Impairment

1. Complete blood count
2. Urinalysis
3. Serum urea nitrogen and glucose; serum electrolytes (sodium, potassium, carbon dioxide content, chloride, calcium, phosphorus); bilirubin; serum vitamin B_{12}, folic acid, lactate dehydrogenase, alkaline phosphatase, liver enzymes.
4. Thyroid function tests
5. Serologic test for syphilis
6. Electrocardiogram
7. Electroencephalogram
8. Computed tomography scan of the brain

occupying lesions, hydrocephalus, hemorrhage, infarction, and brain edema. CT scan evidence of cortical atrophy is not useful clinically in diagnosing DAT (Hughes and Gado 1981). Because many of the disorders that cause dementia could also cause the amnestic syndrome, these same screening tests are suggested for both syndromes. The electroencephalogram may be helpful in verifying the presence of organic disease, differentiating focal and diffuse lesions, and, by serial study, following the illness course. In primary degenerative dementia, it is often abnormal with generalized slowing.

Treatment

Correction of Underlying Causes

Specific treatments of underlying causes may not reverse cognitive deficits completely, but may arrest dementing processes or alleviate associated symptoms. Often, the treatment of one illness may affect other concurrent illnesses or treatments. For example, treating hypertension with methyldopa in a patient with MID may worsen a concurrent depression or further reduce cerebral blood flow, thus risking recurrent infarction. Even minor medical illnesses can upset a delicately maintained intellectual integrity. The clinician should pay particular attention to pain because many cognitively impaired patients are unable to express it verbally. Careful use of analgesics and nonsteroidal anti-inflammatory agents can improve the patient's level of comfort as well as function. Elderly patients with dementia are especially vulnerable to such complications as falls, bed sores, fecal impactions, and incontinence. Meticulous hygiene and treatment of multiple medical conditions are essential for optimizing the patient's remaining intellectual abilities. For patients with chronic and progressive disorders, regular follow-up appointments allow the clinician to monitor the patient's course and evaluate and treat any intercurrent illnesses or behavioral changes.

Wernicke's encephalopathy is a neuropsychiatric emergency. Prompt treatment with parenteral thiamine is essential; the outcome, however, may still be poor. Although as little as 3 mg of thiamine may be enough to reverse the ocular changes (Cole et al. 1969), larger doses are routinely recommended to maximize adequate treatment of the other neurologic abnormalities (Reuler et al. 1985). Patients suspected of this disorder should be treated with 100 mg of thiamine iv and 50 mg im at once. For the next week, 50 mg/day im or, if possible, po should be given. If Wernicke's disease is treated early with large doses of thiamine, alcohol amnestic disorder may not develop.

For patients suspected of suffering from MID, low dose aspirin has been recommended as a measure to prevent recurrent infarction because of its potential as an antithrombotic agent (Verstraete and Vermylen 1984). Recommended dosages range from 325 mg/day to one "baby aspirin" every third day. A discussion of experimental treatments of MID may be found in Chapter 107.

For most patients with dementia, no specific treatment is available. Although the prognosis is bleak, the comfort and daily functioning of these patients can be improved considerably by the symptomatic treatments discussed below. A discussion of experimental treatments of DAT may be found in Chapter 108.

Pharmacologic Treatments

Antipsychotics. Although antipsychotics have been used widely to treat the agitation, wandering, and paranoid symptoms associated with dementia, the research basis for such use is limited. Of the 21 studies using antipsychotics in patients with dementia, only three have been methodologically sound (Helms 1985). Thiothixene (Rada and Kellner 1976), haloperidol, and loxapine (Barnes et al. 1982; Petrie et al. 1982a) were all found to have at least moderate benefit in treating psychosis and associated symptoms of dementia. The results of such studies do seem to support the judicious use of antipsychotics in managing the behavioral complications of dementia.

Studies demonstrating the advantage or disadvantage of specific agents are lacking, but clinical experience suggests that the guidelines for choosing a particular agent should rest on the differential side effects. Low doses of a high potency neuroleptic drug (e.g., 0.5 to 2 mg of haloperidol or the equivalent dose of another neuroleptic) can be given several times a day in divided doses, or as one dose in the evening. Early evening doses seem to lessen daytime sedation and decrease "sun-downing" (i.e., worsening agitation and confusion at night). Such high potency neuroleptics have low anticholinergic and cardiovascular effects and are thus not likely to cause central anticholinergic confusion or postural hypotension (Baldessarini 1985). Low potency neuroleptic agents such as thioridazine or chlorpromazine are more likely to have these effects. The high anticholinergic effects of such low potency neuroleptics suggest that these agents are less likely to worsen extrapyramidal symptoms of patients with Parkinson's disease (Baldessarini 1985), but could worsen cognitive functioning.

Because of the risk of tardive dyskinesia, neuroleptics should be used judiciously. A study of 57 elderly psychiatric patients showed that the greatest risk for tardive dyskinesia is during the first two years of neuroleptic treatment (Toenniessen et al. 1985). Whether low potency-high anticholinergic and high potency-low anticholinergic neuroleptics differ in eventual risk for tardive dyskinesia remains a controversial issue. In light of the risk of tardive dyskinesia, some clinicians prefer the use of antianxiety agents for treatment of agitation.

Antidepressants. Up to 30 percent of patients with dementia syndrome also suffer from symptoms of depression (Reifler et al. 1982), yet clinical trials using antidepressants for this group are largely lacking. Guidelines for the use of antidepressants in patients with dementia and depression are based on clinical experience as well as data derived from antidepressant trials performed on depressed patients who are not demented (Baldessarini 1985; Jarvik and Gerson 1985).

Antidepressants may be useful for the treatment of insomnia occurring in patients with dementia and depression, aside from the therapeutic trial of antidepressants indicated when depressive "pseudodementia" is suspected. Side effects can be minimized by combining low dosages with gradual increases (e.g., 25-mg increments of doxepin or desipramine with increases every few days). For elderly depressed patients, daily dosages necessary for a therapeutic effect can range from as low as 25 mg to more than 150 mg (Salzman 1982b). Divided doses throughout the day may lessen the common side effects of postural hypotension and anticholinergic symptoms, such as dry mouth or urinary retention. Tricyclic drugs appear to prolong both atrial and ventricular depolarization, an important consideration when treating patients with concurrent impairment of cardiac conduction (Cassem 1982). In general, tertiary amine tricyclic antidepressants (e.g., amitriptyline or imipramine) cause more bothersome and potentially dangerous side effects than tetracyclic (e.g., maprotiline), nontricyclic (e.g., the triazolopyridine trazodone), or secondary amine tricyclic (e.g., desipramine, nortriptyline) agents (Cassem 1982). For elderly patients, it is wise to avoid the use of amitriptyline, imipramine, or trimipramine, except perhaps when the patient has a clear history of favorable response. Doxepin seems better tolerated in nondemented elderly than the other tertiary amines, and in one study caused less postural hypotension than imipramine (Neshkes et al. 1985).

Orthostatic hypotension is an important potential side effect of antidepressant drugs and can lead to noncompliance, stroke, myocardial infarction, or falls. Patients with pretreatment orthostatic hypotension appear to be more likely to develop orthostatic changes during treatment and such changes are not clearly dose related (Glassman and Bigger 1981). The adverse effects of orthostatic hypotension can be minimized in some patients by adjusting the timing and amount of doses, as well as by instructing patients to get up slowly and pause for a few minutes while supporting themselves.

In a group of elderly nondemented depressed patients treated with either imipramine or doxepin, pretreatment systolic orthostatic drop correlated with eventual symptom response (Jarvik et al. 1983). Schneider et al. (1986) also found that pretreatment orthostatic hypotension in depressed elderly outpatients identified patients who responded favorably to nortriptyline. These unexpected and interesting findings suggest that pretreatment orthostatic change may become a clinical predictor of response to some antidepressant medications. It has not yet been assessed in patients with concurrent dementia and depression.

For patients with cognitive impairment and depression unresponsive to initial antidepressant treatment, second-line antidepressants may be useful, especially when there is a high index of suspicion of underlying depressive illness. Monoamine oxidase (MAO) inhibitors, the addition of 25 to 50 mg of triiodothyronine to a tricyclic antidepressant, or electroconvulsive therapy would all be reasonable approaches, although well-controlled studies demonstrating their efficacy in patients with concurrent dementia and depression are lacking. Jenike (1985b) reported on the successful use of the MAO inhibitor tranylcypromine in treating two patients with Alzheimer's disease and depression. As noted in this report, the finding that patients with Alzheimer-type dementia have higher MAO levels than age-matched controls offers a rationale for using MAO inhibitors in this group of patients.

Recent reports suggest that adding lithium to a tricyclic antidepressant will promote a response in some depressed patients who initially fail to respond to a tricyclic alone. Double-blind controlled studies in the elderly, however, have not yet been carried out. In addition, uncontrolled studies indicate that poor response and toxicity to lithium are associated with underlying neurologic disease (Plotkin et al. 1987). Lithium, therefore, should be used with caution in patients with dementia.

Hypnotics and antianxiety agents. Sleep disturbances often accompany dementia syndrome. Specific causes for insomnia should be carefully evaluated, such as restless leg syndrome, obstructive apnea, urinary frequency due to prostatic disease, lack of daytime exercise, or prolonged stays in bed. Before using pharmacologic agents, attempts at reducing daytime sleep, avoiding nighttime stimulants, and regulating timing of meals and activities should be made, although they often prove insufficient. Clinical experience suggests that a short-acting benzodiazepine, such as lorazepam 0.5 to 1 mg, or temazepam 15 mg, an hour before bedtime often relieves early insomnia associated with dementia and avoids the paradoxical excitement more commonly experienced with the barbiturates. Benzodiazepines with longer half-lives (e.g., diazepam) should be avoided in elderly patients because of a tendency to accumulate in the blood (Salzman 1982b). Triazolam, a benzodiazepine with an extremely short elimination half-life, has been reported to cause early morning insomnia after one or two weeks of nightly administration to young adults with chronic insomnia (Kales et al. 1983). Definitive studies using this agent in cognitively impaired elderly patients are unavailable. The sedative action of any of the antianxiety agents may increase withdrawal, worsen cognitive deficits, and/or cause confusion and depression in patients with cognitive impairment and so must be used with caution.

Although rigorous clinical trials of benzodiazepines have not yet been carried out in geriatric patients with concurrent dementia and depression, these agents are often used particularly when a patient's cardiovascular status precludes the use of tricyclic antidepressants. One double-blind controlled study of nondemented, depressed geriatric patients found alprazolam treatment in conjunction with psychotherapy to be effective, but not more so than psychotherapy without pharmacotherapy (Plotkin et al. 1987).

Other pharmacologic approaches.   A wide variety of investigational compounds has been studied; many have been used clinically. As yet, pharmacologic efforts to increase intellectual functioning have been disappointing. Case reports of the efficacy of cerebral vasodilators often fail tests of replication and double-blind study design. Hydergine (dihydrogenated ergot alkaloids), not primarily a cerebral vasodilator, has offered some promise in improving mood and self-care. Although there has been some controversy abut the clinical significance of such improvements (Jarvik 1981), numerous controlled trials suggest that a subgroup of patients do show a favorable response in mood and self-care but not in cognition (Hollister and Yesavage 1984).

Another approach has been to enhance cholinergic activity in the brain. Autopsies of patients with DAT have demonstrated reduced choline acetyltransferase, consistent with central cholinergic deficit (Coyle et al. 1983). Furthermore, preliminary trials of cholinergic agonists have improved memory in young and old normal volunteers. Trials of these agents (including physostigmine, choline, and lecithin), however, in patients with dementia, have shown only mild or no effects on memory in patients with dementia (Plotkin and Jarvik 1986).

The psychostimulant methylphenidate has been reported to cause global improvement in elderly patients with depression and cognitive impairment (Katon and Raskind 1980), although these reports have been criticized on methodological grounds (Small and Mandel 1981). A possible justification for the use of psychostimulants is found in the work of Bondareff et al. (1981), which showed a deficiency of noradrenergic cells in the nucleus locus coeruleus in patients with Alzheimer's disease. Methylphenidate has also been used as a predictor of response to noradrenergic antidepressants (Spar and LaRue 1985).

Attention to the Environment

Intellectually impaired patients are highly sensitive to their surroundings and thus require optimal stimulation. Too much or too little environmental stimulation may result in withdrawal or agitation. Either of these results, when extreme, can make the difference between the need for institutional care or the ability to function in the community.

Empirical approaches to the care of patients with cognitive impairment are often helpful in maximizing functioning (Winograd and Jarvik 1986). Patients with dementia do best in familiar and constant surroundings. Daily routines increase their sense of security, and prominent displays of clocks and calendars, nightlights, checklists, and diaries all aid in their orientation and memory. Medication schedules should be kept as simple as possible. Moves should be avoided but, if a move is necessary, photographs and other familiar objects from the patient's previous home should be placed in the new environment to make it like "home." Frequent family contacts and access to current events through newspapers, radio, and television are also important to maintain the patient's awareness of the environment.

Family Intervention and Psychotherapy

Another essential aspect of treatment is support for and from family members (Schmidt and Keyes 1985; Winograd and Jarvik 1986). Education and counseling about the nature of the patient's illness should begin at the time of diagnosis to encourage family involvement in the patient's treatment. Uninformed relatives may react with anger and puzzlement to the emotional lability characteristic of so many demented patients. The patient's loss of emotional and verbal inhibitions, as well as physical incontinence, may cause embarrassment to the family and be misinterpreted as willful behavior demonstrating lack of love or concern.

Both patient and family seem to benefit from psychotherapy, although no carefully controlled studies of psychotherapy for dementia have been carried out (Winograd and Jarvik 1986). Clinical experience suggests that the psychiatrist can provide information about the nature of the illness and about ways to cope with intellectual deficits. Patients often need help in grieving and accepting their disability as well as support in maximizing remaining abilities and adaptive skills. Psychological support for care givers will lighten their emotional burden. Anger, guilt, shame, frustration, and helplessness are all natural responses to the task of caring for a once vital and now deteriorating loved one. Relatives may need reassurance that such reactions are common and that discussing them can offer relief. Psychodynamic interventions may also be useful for relatives whose earlier unresolved conflicts are reactivated by the patient's illness and need for care.

The family's decision to seek nursing home care is usually a painful one. The psychiatrist can play a crucial role in helping family members understand their feelings about such decisions. Group therapy for family members may provide both educational and emotional support. The Alzheimer's Disease and Related Disorders Association, a national organization of family members with local chapters throughout the country, has been at the forefront in providing such services. Major research and treatment centers also offer services for families.

Memory Training

Although training programs have been shown to improve some memory functions in normal elderly people (Yesavage 1985), attempts at memory training have not been shown to be effective in patients with progressive dementias. Novel learning techniques may offer hope for retrieval of some memory function in selected patients, particularly those with amnesias or nonprogressive dementias. For example, one report suggested the usefulness of a learning technique for chronically amnesic patients who suffered from varied organic causes or amnestic syndrome. This method linked word-list items in a novel manner known as "ridiculously-imaged-stories" (Kovner et al. 1983). Items to be learned might be linked together through a bizarre and perhaps humorous storyline. The technique seemed to provide artificial "chunks" of memory that could be encoded into long-term memory. For severe cognitive impairment, however, memory training in its current forms has not been shown to reverse the deficits.

Conclusion

Dementia and amnestic syndromes may occur in any age group. Although the risk of developing a form of dementia increases with age, it is not a normal consequence of aging. Some 80 to 95 percent of people 65 years and older never develop these disorders. Whenever cognitive impairment develops, therefore, the clinician must pursue an adequate differential diagnosis and focus on a search for treatable disorders. Even if no underlying treatable cause is identified, numerous symptomatic treatments are available. Antianxiety agents, antipsychotics, and antidepressants often relieve many of the secondary symptoms that accompany impairment.

Dementia is defined in terms of graduated decrements in a person's intellectual, social, and occupational functioning. The clinician can maximize the patient's functioning through not only medical and pharmacologic interventions but also through environmental management and support of the patient's family.

Summary

1. Accurate diagnosis is the first step toward comprehensive treatment of the dementia and amnestic syndromes.
2. Treatment of underlying causes should commence before initiating symptomatic treatments.
3. Symptomatic treatments typically include pharmacologic and psychotherapeutic approaches.
4. Dementia is more common among the elderly, who are more sensitive to medication side effects than younger adults. Medications should be prescribed cautiously and with the clinician's full awareness of potential toxicity.
5. Short-acting benzodiazepines may be useful for insomnia associated with cognitive impairment.
6. High potency antipsychotics in low doses are recommended for agitation and psychotic symptoms.
7. Antidepressants may improve depressive symptoms that accompany cognitive impairment.
8. Regular follow-up appointments are useful for monitoring the patient's course and evaluating and treating intercurrent illnesses or behavioral changes.

Chapter 95

Organic Delusional Syndrome and Organic Hallucinosis

Definition and Diagnostic Criteria

Organic delusional syndrome and organic hallucinosis are clinical syndromes characterized by the predominance of delusions or hallucinations that are attributable to some specific organic factor. Three criteria are used in DSM-III-R (American Psychiatric

Association 1987) to make the diagnoses (see Table 1). If the patient manifests features of another disorder (e.g., dementia, delirium, schizophrenia), then the diagnosis of organic delusional syndrome or organic hallucinosis cannot be made. The delusions of organic delusional syndrome may be of any type (e.g., persecutory, somatic). In some patients the delusions are well organized and elaborate; in others they are relatively crude and simple. Similarly, the type of hallucinations of organic hallucinosis can vary (e.g., auditory, visual, tactile) and may be simple or complex.

There is often associated mild general cognitive impairment present (although not sufficient to meet criteria for dementia), as these relatively rare syndromes are seldom seen in pure form (Wells 1985c).

Epidemiology

Epidemiologic studies of organic delusional syndrome or organic hallucinosis as discrete diagnostic entities have not been performed.

Etiology

There is a wide range of causative agents or factors that can produce an organic psychosis. Some of the most common causes of organic delusional syndrome or organic hallucinosis are a variety of drugs (e.g., amphetamines, cocaine, hallucinogens), but physical disorders (e.g., stroke) can also produce an organic psychosis.

Drugs

Of the drugs that can cause these syndromes, perhaps the most common and most studied are the amphetamines. Amphetamines have been known for many years to produce a syndrome not unlike paranoid schizophrenia (Connell 1958). Amphetamine psychosis has been proposed as a model of schizophrenia, the presumed mechanism being excess release of the neurotransmitter dopamine (Snyder 1973). The psychotic state associated with amphetamines generally develops over a long period

---

Table 1.   DSM-III-R Diagnostic Criteria for Organic Delusional Syndrome and Organic Hallucinosis

Organic Delusional Syndrome

A. Prominent delusions.

B. There is evidence from the history, physical examination, or laboratory tests of a specific organic factor (or factors) judged to be etiologically related to the disturbance.

C. Not occurring exclusively during the course of Delirium.

Organic Hallucinosis

A. Prominent persistent or recurrent hallucinations.

B. There is evidence from the history, physical examination, or laboratory tests of a specific organic factor (or factors) judged to be etiologically related to the disturbance.

C. Not occurring exclusively during the course of Delirium.

of time, with repeated drug use. There is usually an evolution over time of behavioral states from euphoria to the delusional state (usually with persecutory delusions) (Ellinwood et al. 1973). The psychosis can appear quickly with repeat drug exposure (Angrist and Gershon 1970; Bell 1973), even after long periods of abstinence (Sato et al. 1983).

Chronic use of cocaine can also result in an organic delusional syndrome with clinical features similar to those found in an amphetamine delusional syndrome (Post 1975), except that the psychosis usually subsides within 48 to 72 hours after cessation of the drug (Resnick and Resnick 1984).

Hallucinogens (e.g., LSD, mescaline, psilocybin) and phencyclidine can also cause a delusional syndrome, although hallucinations rather than delusions are often the predominant psychotic feature and thus warrant a diagnosis of organic hallucinosis.

Marijuana (cannabis) is occasionally associated with a delusional syndrome that can persist up to approximately one month after the last use of the drug (Jones 1984).

DSM-III-R has included separate diagnostic classifications for organic psychoses known to be associated with some of the more commonly used and abused drugs. Thus if an organic delusional syndrome is caused by amphetamines or similarly acting sympathomimetics, cannabis, cocaine, a hallucinogen, or phencyclidine or similarly acting arylcyclohexylamines, then the appropriate diagnostic category should be used (see Table 2). If an organic hallucinosis is caused by alcohol or a hallucinogen, then that diagnosis should be used (see Table 3).

A number of medicinally used drugs are also associated with an organic psychosis, which sometimes satisfies the criteria for organic delusional syndrome or organic hallucinosis. Given the hypothesized link between psychosis and excess dopamine (e.g., as in schizophrenia), one should not be surprised to find that dopamine precursors and agonists are known to be associated with organic psychoses. In particular, L-dopa (Moscowitz et al. 1978), amantadine (Postma and Van Tilburg 1975), and bromocriptine (Parkes 1980) have been implicated. One study (Turner et al. 1984) evaluated patients with no prior psychiatric history who were treated for hyperprolactinemia or acromegaly with either bromocriptine or lisuride. A psychotic process developed in 1 to 2 percent of patients, although a diagnosis of organic delusional syndrome or organic hallucinosis might not be warranted in all patients because of associated affective changes.

Other medications occasionally implicated in an organic psychosis include anticonvulsants such as phenytoin (Tollefson 1980), analgesics such as pentazocine (Miller 1975), and cancer chemotherapeutic agents (Silberfarb 1983).

Alcohol

Alcohol hallucinosis usually occurs within two to three days after the cessation or reduction of drinking in an individual who has been drinking on a chronic basis (Surawicz 1980). Hallucinations may be auditory, visual, or tactile and may be accompanied by paranoid ideation. The hallucinosis may persist for weeks to months and may resemble schizophrenia.

Cerebral Lesions

Cerebral lesions, such as those caused by stroke or trauma, are sometimes associated with a delusional state. This is particularly true of temporal-limbic lesions (Davison and Bagley 1969; Hillbom 1960) as well as lesions affecting subcortical structures (Cummings 1985b). In general, left-sided lesions are more likely to cause schizo-

Table 2.   DSM-III-R Diagnostic Criteria for Delusional Disorders Caused by Amphetamine or Similarly Acting Sympathomimetics, for Cannabis, for Cocaine, for a Hallucinogen, and for Phencyclidine or Similarly Acting Arylcyclohexylamines

Diagnostic criteria for 292.11 Amphetamine or Similarly Acting Sympathomimetic Delusional Disorder

A. Organic Delusional Syndrome developing shortly after use of amphetamine or a similarly acting sympathomimetic.

B. Rapidly developing persecutory delusions are the predominant clinical feature.

C. Not due to any physical or other mental disorder.

Note: When the differential diagnosis must be made without a clear-cut history or toxicologic analysis of body fluids, it may be qualified as "Provisional."

Diagnostic criteria for 292.11 Cannabis Delusional Disorder

A. Organic Delusional Syndrome developing shortly after cannabis use.

B. Not due to any physical or other mental disorder.

Note: When the differential diagnosis must be made without a clear-cut history or toxicologic analysis of body fluids, it may be qualified as "Provisional."

Diagnostic criteria for 292.11 Cocaine Delusional Disorder

A. Organic Delusional Syndrome developing shortly after use of cocaine.

B. Rapidly developing persecutory delusions are the predominant clinical feature.

C. Not due to any physical or other mental disorder.

Note: When the differential diagnosis must be made without a clear-cut history or toxicologic analysis of body fluids, it may be qualified as "Provisional."

Diagnostic criteria for 292.11 Hallucinogen Delusional Disorder

A. Organic Delusional Syndrome developing shortly after hallucinogen use.

B. Not due to any physical or other mental disorder, such as Schizophrenia.

Note: When the differential diagnosis must be made without a clear-cut history or toxicologic analysis of body fluids, it may be qualified as "Provisional."

Diagnostic criteria for 292.11 Phencyclidine (PCP) or Similarly Acting Arylcyclohexylamine Delusional Disorder

A. Organic Delusional Syndrome developing shortly after use of phencyclidine or a similarly acting arylcyclohexylamine, or emerging up to a week after an overdose.

B. Not due to any physical or other mental disorder, such as Schizophrenia.

Note: When the differential diagnosis must be made without a clear-cut history or toxicologic analysis of body fluids, it may be qualified as "Provisional."

phrenic-like psychoses than are right-sided lesions (Cummings 1985b), although certain specific delusional disorders such as Capgras' syndrome have been associated with right hemispheric dysfunction (Quinn 1981). Patients with right-sided lesions often have other cognitive dysfunctions (e.g., spatial neglect, constructional apraxia, anosognosia), but they do not have the diffuse, global deficits of a dementia. Not every cerebral insult will result in a delusional syndrome; in one study of right-sided cerebral infarctions, preexisting cerebral atrophy was required for the development of a delusional state (Levine and Grek 1984).

Table 3. DSM-III-R Diagnostic Criteria for Hallucinogen Hallucinosis and for Alcohol Hallucinosis

Diagnostic criteria for 305.30 Hallucinogen Hallucinosis

A. Recent use of a hallucinogen.

B. Maladaptive behavioral changes, e.g., marked anxiety or depression, ideas of reference, fear of losing one's mind, paranoid ideation, impaired judgment, impaired social or occupational functioning.

C. Perceptual changes occurring in a state of full wakefulness and alertness, e.g., subjective intensification of perceptions, depersonalization, derealization, illusions, hallucinations, synesthesias.

D. At least two of the following signs:

1. pupillary dilation
2. tachycardia
3. sweating
4. palpitations
5. blurring of vision
6. tremors
7. incoordination

E. Not due to any physical or other mental disorder.

Note: When the differential diagnosis must be made without a clear-cut history or toxicologic analysis of body fluids, it may be qualified as "Provisional."

Diagnostic criteria for 291.30 Alcohol Hallucinosis

A. Organic Hallucinosis with vivid and persistent hallucinations (auditory or visual) developing shortly (usually within 48 hours) after cessation of or reduction in heavy ingestion of alcohol in a person who apparently has Alcohol Dependence.

B. No Delirium as in Alcohol Withdrawal Delirium.

C. Not due to any physical or other mental disorder.

Some relatively specific delusions have been observed to occur with specific neurologic deficits. Anton's syndrome (denial of blindness) is often secondary to bilateral occipital lobe lesions, leading to cerebral blindness (Bergman 1957). Denial of hemiparesis is associated with parietal lobe insult, usually right-sided (Cutting 1978). Reduplicative paramnesia (belief that one is in two locations simultaneously) seems to require right parietal dysfunction (Benson et al. 1976). Deja vu and jamais vu phenomena have been correlated with medial temporal lobe damage (Lechtenberg 1982).

Cerebral lesions can also cause hallucinosis. These may be simple formed visual hallucinations associated with a visual field cut (Lance 1976), visual "release hallucinations" secondary to posterior cerebral artery occlusion (Brust and Behrens 1977), or complex visual hallucinations associated with temporal lobe tumors (Teuber 1972).

Sensory Changes

Sensory change (usually loss) has also been associated with psychotic states, such as complex visual hallucinations with blindness (Charles Bonnet Syndrome) (McNamara et al. 1982; White 1980), auditory (musical) hallucinations with deafness (Hammeke et al. 1983; Ross et al. 1975), or poorly formed hallucinations (phosphenes) induced by sound (Lessel and Cohen 1979).

Seizures

Complex partial seizures have for many years been associated with a delusional syndrome. This is often observed in the interictal period (Trimble 1982b) and is thought not to be dependent on seizure activity per se (Lechtenberg 1982). Typically, the psychotic state occurs in individuals with clear-cut left temporal lobe epileptogenic foci on the electroencephalogram (Pritchard et al. 1980), but does not occur until some years after the seizure disorder begins (Slater et al. 1963).

Other Organic Etiologies

A variety of other organic causes of delusional disorder have been reported, mostly in case report format (Miller et al. 1986). In particular, cases of Capgras' syndrome with suspected organic etiology have been reported, including cases of myxedema (Madakasira and Hall 1981), pseudohypoparathyroidism (Hay et al. 1974; Preskorn and Reveley 1978), chickenpox encephalitis (Nikolovski and Fernandez 1978), and folic acid deficiency (MacCallam 1973). Electroencephalographic studies on patients with several different rare delusional syndromes (e.g., intermetamorphosis, subjective doubles) have found a high frequency of associated nonspecific abnormalities, suggesting an organic etiology (Christodoulou and Malliara-Loulakaki 1981). The dermatologic literature reveals the syndrome of monosymptomatic hypochondriasis (delusions of parasitosis, dysmorphosis, bromosis, or others), which has been associated with organic disease (Bishop 1983).

A delusional disorder may also be associated with a number of other disease states, including systemic illnesses, endocrinopathies, vitamin deficiency states, inflammatory and collagen-vascular disorders, and degenerative neurologic diseases (e.g., Huntington's chorea). Oftentimes, however, the delusions are an associated but not predominant clinical feature; therefore, the diagnosis of organic delusional syndrome cannot be made.

Differential Diagnosis

Organic delusional syndrome and organic hallucinosis should be distinguished from psychotic disorders for which there is no known organic etiology, such as schizophrenia, brief reactive psychosis, or delusional (paranoid) disorder. In schizophrenia, deterioration from a previous level of functioning, loosening of associations, blunted or inappropriate affect, insidious onset, and positive family history will enable the clinician to make the correct diagnosis. With brief reactive psychosis, the diagnostic distinction can be difficult to make and may depend entirely on evidence that proves, or strongly suggests, an organic etiology versus a psychological reaction to a stressful event. Delusional (paranoid) disorder will also be difficult to distinguish from an organic delusional syndrome or organic hallucinosis unless there is strong evidence of an organic etiology. Delusional (paranoid) disorder occurring in late life has been termed "late paraphrenia," particularly in the European literature. It is most likely a heterogeneous syndrome rather than a distinct disease entity (Holden 1987) and is not included in DSM-III-R. Recent work has demonstrated an organic etiology in some cases of late paraphrenia (Miller et al. 1986).

Mild cognitive impairment is not unusual in organic delusional syndrome (Wells 1985c), but must be distinguished from the more global, severe impairment and loss of social or occupational functioning found in dementia.

Distinguishing between an organic delusional syndrome (or an organic hallucinosis) and a delirium can be difficult and may depend on subtle clinical findings and
interpretation of whether or not there is clouding of consciousness. The diagnostic
distinction between delirium and organic psychoses is, indeed, somewhat arbitrary,
and is further blurred by the recognition of "chronic confusional states" (Mullaley et
al. 1982) and "quiet delirium" (Adams and Victor 1977). Moreover, certain conditions
(e.g., the reduplicative phenomena) may be viewed as a delusion by some (Benson
et al. 1976) and as a "disorientation" by others (Fisher 1982a).

Organic hallucinosis, organic mood syndrome, and organic personality syndrome
can be distinguished from organic delusional syndrome on the basis of the predominant clinical features.

Patient Evaluation

A thorough psychiatric evaluation is indicated in the workup of all patients with a
delusional syndrome or a hallucinosis. This should be as comprehensive and aggressive as is the recommended workup for a delirium. The diagnosis is made on
clinical grounds and is aided by history (e.g., history of amphetamine abuse), laboratory findings (e.g., toxicology screen positive for amphetamines), and radiologic
findings (e.g., infarct on computed tomography of the head). The investigating psychiatrist should have a high index of suspicion for an organic cause of psychosis in
individuals without a prior psychiatric history who are at least 30 years of age. Prior
to that approximate age, it may be difficult if not impossible to distinguish between
functional and organic psychoses on the basis of a single cross-sectional evaluation.
Thus longitudinal follow-up will often be necessary to make a firm diagnosis. In
elderly individuals, a delusional state may be the initial presentation of a dementia;
again, longitudinal follow-up will be the key to accurate diagnosis.

General Treatment Considerations

Treatment of organic delusional syndrome or organic hallucinosis is dependent on
knowledge of the specific etiologic agent or factor. Thus in delusional syndrome
secondary to amphetamine use, cessation of amphetamines may be enough to allow
the delusional state to resolve. In cases of low thyroid hormone or low folic acid, the
addition of thyroid or folic acid, respectively, may be sufficient to correct the psychopathology. In a psychosis associated with partial complex seizures, adjustment of
anticonvulsant medication may ameliorate the delusional condition.

Sometimes an organic etiology is suspected, but the precise agent cannot be
determined with certainty. Still other times treatment aimed at correcting the underlying problem may not suffice despite knowledge of the presumed etiologic factor(s).
For example, cessation of amphetamine use may not result in a remission in sufficient
time to avoid considerable damage or complications of a delusional state such as
family difficulties, conflicts with the law, or a postpsychotic depression. Thus general
treatments that afford a rapid onset of action are often indicated. These include
hospitalization (particularly if patient compliance with the treatment plan is in doubt)
to provide a safe and structured environment and pharmacotherapy.

Whether for inpatients or outpatients, the most effective medications for treatment of organic delusional syndrome or organic hallucinosis are the neuroleptics. In

general, the short-term administration of a neuroleptic in conjunction with a psychosocial approach (e.g., substance abuse rehabilitation program) will be the treatment of choice. Complex delusions may be more refractory to neuroleptic treatment than are simple, loosely held delusions (Cummings 1985b). In choosing a neuroleptic agent, the physician must be guided by the clinical context and presumed etiology as well as by personal preference and experience. Agents should be used in the lowest effective doses and carefully monitored for side effects (e.g., extrapyramidal symptomatology, orthostatic hypotension).

Specific Treatments

Amphetamine Psychosis

Early attempts to treat amphetamine psychosis made use of common sedative—hypnotics (e.g., barbiturates, chloral hydrate, paraldehyde) without much success (Angrist 1978).

Barbiturates, in particular, are not indicated in the treatment of amphetamine psychosis because of their potentiation of the cardiovascular effects of amphetamines (Bell 1973). Neuroleptics were used as early as 1956 (Hopkin and Jones 1956) and have become the mainstay of treatment (Angrist et al. 1974; Espelin and Done 1968). In choosing a particular agent, one must be mindful of side-effects profiles because the therapeutic action is approximately equal among different agents (Angrist 1978). Low-potency phenothiazines such as chlorpromazine have alpha-adrenergic-blocking properties that may be advantageous in selected patients with sympathomimetic-related hypertension, although dangerous hypotension may be precipitated. Also, chlorpromazine increases amphetamine half-life in brain and blood (Lemberger et al. 1970), making it undesirable compared to a high-potency nonphenothiazine agent such as haloperidol (a butyrophenone). Ascorbic acid may augment the effect of haloperidol in drug intoxication (Giannini 1987; Rebec et al. 1985), although its effect in organic psychoses is not known.

Cocaine Psychosis

The literature is divided on how best to treat cocaine psychosis pharmacologically. Some researchers cite the epileptogenic effect of cocaine and advise against using neuroleptic agents, which are also known to affect seizure threshold. They recommend use of diazepam (Gay 1982) and propranolol (Rappolt et al. 1977). Others note the apparent continuity of bipolar disorder with substance abuse disorders (Flemenbaum 1974) and have success with lithium in cocaine psychoses (Scott and Muhaly 1981) and cocaine "highs" (Cranson and Flemenbaum 1978).

Neuroleptics, however, have been used successfully to treat cocaine psychoses. Some advocate the low-potency phenothiazine chlorpromazine because of its sedative effects (Kleber and Gawin 1984) and its antagonism of lethal cocaine effects in primates (Guinn et al. 1980). Others recommend use of the high-potency butyrophenone haloperidol (Smith 1984). Neuroleptics may increase the craving for cocaine (Gold et al. 1985), lending more support to the notion that these agents should be used for a brief time only (several days) and then followed by rehabilitation.

Psychoses Associated with Seizures

In delusional syndrome or hallucinosis secondary to seizures, one must be particularly mindful of the effects of neuroleptics on the seizure threshold. In general, all neuroleptics are epileptogenic and, even at therapeutic levels, can cause or exacerbate seizures (Itil and Soldatos 1980). Chlorpromazine is considered to be the worst offender; haloperidol and thiothixene occupy a midposition; fluphenazine and thioridazine have low epileptogenic potential; and the less well-studied molindone is also thought to be relatively safe (Mendez et al. 1984; Oliver et al. 1982). If neuroleptics are used in patients with seizures, they should be started at low doses (10 to 50 mg of thioridazine or 0.5 to 2 mg of haloperidol), increased slowly, and used one at a time (Toone and Fenton 1977). Monitoring neuroleptic blood levels as well as the electroencephalogram may be helpful.

Other Specific Treatments

A neuroleptic that has been used with some success in dermatologic presentation of monosymptomatic hypochondriasis is the diphenylbutylpiperidine agent, pimozide (Reilly et al. 1978; Riding and Munro 1975). Of the remaining neuroleptics, haloperidol has been the most effective (Bishop 1983). In general, treatment of organic delusional syndrome or organic hallucinosis should closely follow the treatment plan for delirium, with careful attention to environmental factors, neuroleptic use, and drug-drug interactions.

Chapter 96

Organic Personality Disorder, Explosive Type

Violent and aggressive behaviors are highly prevalent among psychiatric patients in general (Tardiff and Sweillam 1982; Taylor and Gunn 1984) and among patients who suffer from organic brain disorders in specific (Elliott 1976; Silver and Yudofsky 1987a; Tardiff and Sweillam 1980; Yudofsky and Silver 1985). Elliott (1982) reported that 94 percent of 286 patients with histories of recurrent uncontrolled rage attacks that occurred with little or no provocation had objective evidence of developmental or acquired brain defects.

Aggressive episodes related to organic brain disorders may range from moderately distracting verbal expressions to physical outbursts in which severe injury is inflicted. A review of 15 death row inmates who were chosen for comprehensive neuropsychological examination because of the imminence of their executions and not because of neuropsychopathology revealed that all had histories of severe head injury, five had major neurologic impairment, and seven others had other, less serious neurologic problems such as blackouts or "soft" neurologic signs (Lewis et al. 1986).

Each year in the United States, more than one million people suffer brain injury secondary to trauma, stroke, and tumor. Of the 410,000 traumatic brain injuries, 180,000 are secondary to motor vehicle accidents (Kraus et al. 1984). Irritability and aggressiveness occur in as high as 70 percent of people who suffer brain damage from blunt trauma (McKinlay et al. 1981). In the brain-injured population, irritability and aggressiveness—as opposed to physical deficits—are the major source of disability to victims and of stress to families. The psychiatrist is commonly called on by other medical specialists or by families to treat such patients with aggression secondary to organic brain damage.

Definition and Diagnostic Criteria

Explosive rage and violent behavior have long been associated with focal lesions as well as diffuse damage to the central nervous system (Elliott 1976; Lishman 1978). Various investigators and nosologic systems have labeled and described this condition in different ways (Silver and Yudofsky 1987a; Yudofsky and Silver 1985). Names for organic dyscontrol include episodic dyscontrol syndrome, disinhibition syndrome, and explosive personality disorder. DSM-III-R (American Psychiatric Association 1987) calls the condition intermittent explosive disorder and places the category under "Impulse Control Disorders Not Elsewhere Classified" (Table 1).

DSM-III (American Psychiatric Association 1980) also called the syndrome intermittent explosive disorder and maintained that "an underlying physical disorder, such as brain tumor or epilepsy, may in rare cases cause this syndrome" (p. 297). This is inconsistent with the broad range of clinical experience that points to organic etiologies as the most common source of this condition (Elliott 1987; Silver and Yudofsky 1987a, 1987b). DSM-III-R reflects this clinical reality and calls the syndrome organic personality disorder, explosive type (Table 2).

We submit that the condition should be classified as an organic mental disorder and be called organic aggressive syndrome (Table 3), which more accurately describes the condition of dyscontrol of rage and violence secondary to a brain lesion than does organic personality disorder, explosive type, which refers to a multiplicity of emotional

---

Table 1.   DSM-III-R Diagnostic Criteria for Intermittent Explosive Disorder

A. Several discrete episodes of loss of control of aggressive impulses resulting in serious assaultive acts or destruction of property.

B. The degree of aggressiveness expressed during the episodes is grossly out of proportion to any precipitating psychosocial stressors.

C. There are no signs of generalized impulsiveness or aggressiveness between the episodes.

D. The episodes of loss of control do not occur during the course of a psychotic disorder, Organic Personality Syndrome, Antisocial or Borderline Personality Disorder, Conduct Disorder, or intoxication with a psychoactive substance.

Table 2. DSM-III-R Diagnostic Criteria for Organic Personality Syndrome

A. A persistent personality disturbance, either lifelong or representing a change or accentuation of a previously characteristic trait, involving at least one of the following:

    (1) affective instability, e.g., marked shifts from normal mood to depression, irritability, or anxiety

    (2) recurrent outbursts of aggression or rage that are grossly out of proportion to any precipitating psychosocial stressors

    (3) markedly impaired social judgment, e.g., sexual indiscretions

    (4) marked apathy and indifference

    (5) suspiciousness or paranoid ideation

B. There is evidence from the history, physical examination, or laboratory tests of a specific organic factor (or factors) judged to be etiologically related to the disturbance

C. This diagnosis is not given to a child or adolescent if the clinical picture is limited to the features that characterize Attention-deficit Hyperactivity Disorder.

D. Not occurring exclusively during the course of Delirium, and does not meet the criteria for Dementia.

Specify explosive type if outbursts of aggression or rage are the predominant feature.

Table 3. Proposed Diagnostic Criteria for Organic Aggressive Syndrome

A. Persistent or recurrent aggressive outbursts, either of a verbal or physical nature.

B. The outbursts are out of proportion to the precipitating stress or provocation.

C. Evidence from history, physical examination, or laboratory tests of a specific organic factor that is judged to be etiologically related to the disturbance.

D. The outbursts are not primarily related to personality features or disorders such as paranoia, manic disorder, narcissistic personality disorder, or borderline disorder.

E. Not due to Schizophrenia, Antisocial Personality Disorder, or Conduct Disorder.

and behavioral changes that can include impaired social judgment, marked apathy and indifference, paranoid ideation, and so on. The problem with the DSM-III-R classification is that most of the personality changes described in this category are related to deficits in the prefrontal and frontal cortical areas. Although it is true that many patients with damage to these areas of the cortex do show aggressive symptomatologies related to such lesions, violent outbursts are also associated with lesions in other areas of the brain such as the temporal lobes, the midbrain, areas around the third ventricle and cerebral aqueduct, and many other regions of the brain that do not give rise to concomitant disturbances in personality associated with frontal lobe deficits. The classification of organic aggressive syndrome would encompass aggressive outbursts judged to be etiologically related to a central nervous system lesion no matter where it occurs and would not require specific behavioral changes beyond the aggressiveness per se to establish the diagnosis. In this fashion, the classification of organic aggressive syndrome would closely parallel the DSM-III-R classifications organic affective syndrome, organic delusional syndrome, and organic anxiety syndrome, which refer to specific disturbances secondary to an organic factor affecting any region of the brain that is judged to be etiologically related to the disturbance.

A prototypic example of organic aggressive syndrome secondary to chronic organic brain syndrome is the patient whose aggression was first reported to have been treated with propranolol (Yudofsky et al. 1981). This 63-year-old man was transferred to the Neuropsychiatric Service of Columbia Presbyterian Medical Center after he had been struck in the head by a truck tire that exploded while he was filling it with air. He was in a coma for three weeks subsequent to the accident and began to develop agitation and episodic violent behavior on emerging from his coma. Electroencephalogram (EEG) and computed tomography (CT) findings were consistent with diffuse, bilateral structural damage to the patient's prefrontal cortex. Over the year following his injury, the patient's aggressive events intensified to the point that he would become rageful and combative four to 10 times per day, punch angrily and dangerously at family members and nursing staff, and, uncharacteristically, scream profanities. The most modest frustration could result in an explosive discharge of violence. For example, during his inpatient stay, the patient requested a glass of orange juice from the nurse. When the nurse replied that she would go to the pantry and be right back with his orange juice, the patient screamed, "No, I want the orange juice now!" With that, he swung his fist at the nurse, knocked her glasses from her face, and scratched the cornea of her right eye. Later, when the patient was more calm, he expressed remorse and shame over the incident as well as concern for the injured nurse. He stated, "I just can't help myself, I don't know what gets into me."

Epidemiology

The epidemiology of organic aggressive syndrome has yet to be studied systematically. In all likelihood, the incidence of organic aggressive syndrome relates to the overall prevalence of the underlying disorder as well as the frequency of the development of aggression within each specific disorder. For example, because of the widespread use and abuse of alcohol in our society, organic aggressive syndrome is commonly associated with the use of this agent. On the other hand, phencyclidine use is much more likely to produce violence in a given individual than is alcohol use, but the former is, today, far less prevalent than the latter.

In Elliott's (1982) sample of 236 patients with histories of recurrent attacks of uncontrolled rage with little or no provocation, 119 were diagnosed as having minimal brain dysfunction, which Elliott defined as suggestions of organicity from history (learning disability, attention deficit disorder), from neurologic examination, from diagnostic testing (EEG, CT), or formal neuropsychological testing. Of these patients, 51 had head injury, 47 epilepsy, 13 cerebral tumor, 13 encephalitis, 11 stroke, 6 multiple sclerosis, and 3 Alzheimer's disease (Elliott 1982). Only 18 patients in the sample had no demonstrable organicity based on neurologic examination, EEG, neuropsychological testing, and CT. Organic aggressive syndrome is most commonly found in patients with developmental and perinatal central nervous system deficits (including mental retardation), and in patients with histories of head trauma, cerebrovascular accidents, complex partial seizures, Alzheimer's disease, and metabolic disorders (Silver and Yudofsky 1987a). Also to be included on this list are those patients with substance-induced organic mental syndromes comprising those related to alcohol intoxication and withdrawal, as well as those associated with abuse of barbiturates, cocaine, amphetamines or similarly acting sympathomimetics, phencyclidine, hallucinogens, or those caused by toxic reactions and side effects of medications. Those patients whose dyscontrol of rage and violent behavior is associated with seizure disorders or occurs after head trauma tend, in general, to be younger

(30 years of age and younger); those patients whose dyscontrol is secondary to cerebral vascular accidents, Alzheimer's disease, or the central nervous system effects of chronic alcohol abuse tend to be older (above 50 years of age).

Clinical Description

The key features of organic aggressive syndrome are recurrent violent events, either verbal or physical in nature, that are out of proportion to the precipitating stress or provocation and that stem from organic etiologies. Although the subjective experience of rage and anger may be a concomitant of organic mental syndrome, dyscontrol, by definition, implies objective or operational manifestations of angry affects. In an effort to assess and to document aggressive behaviors for research purposes, a scale that measures observable aggressive events was developed and tested for reliability (Silver and Yudofsky 1987b; Yudofsky et al. 1986). To this end, aggression was divided into verbal aggression, physical aggression against objects, physical aggression against self, and physical aggression against others. Efforts were made to quantify aggressive incidents by measuring the relative severity of individual events. Oldham et al. (1983) have shown that serious physical violence is often preceded by verbal and other less damaging expressions of aggression. It is important for clinicians and family members of patients with organic aggressive syndrome to be aware of and respond appropriately to the milder expressions of aggression to help prevent escalation of these behaviors into more severe forms of violence. Table 4 provides a summary of the spectrum of aggressive events.

Although one must be sensitive to the psychosocial interfaces in organic aggressive syndrome, patients with this syndrome may exhibit features that help distinguish the condition from aggressive behaviors with solely functional etiologies. First, if a patient's historical data, neuropsychological testing, or physical or neurologic examinations show evidence of a central nervous system lesion or dysfunction, the index of suspicion of an organic etiology should be raised. Second, organic aggressive disorders are characteristically precipitous in nature. Patients change from states of relative calm to extreme aggression within an instant and often without any objective warning sign. Organic aggressive outbursts are rarely premeditated. Third, the violent outbursts of patients with organic aggressive disorder are characteristically under less control than the aggressive events with solely functional etiologies. The organic outbursts frequently are not structured and disciplined fighting, but have a flaring, slashing quality. Fourth, organic aggressive events, although frequently recurrent, are typically well demarcated. The events often end as abruptly as they begin, with a patient returning from peaks of rage to calm behavior within an instant. Fifth, the aggressive behavior of organic dyscontrol is characteristically ego dystonic. During intercurrent periods, the patients do not seem angry, irritated, or agitated. Patients with organic aggressive syndrome often show embarrassment and deep remorse for the sequelae of their aggressive activity. This is in sharp distinction from aggressive events that stem from functional etiologies, such as sociopathic or borderline personality disorder wherein patients will rationalize and justify their violent acts.

It must be emphasized that patients often exhibit mixtures of functional and organic aggressive activity, and distinctions may be artificial and misleading. Both past and present stress may combine with functional and organic disorders to increase the potential of a patient to exhibit violence. Many clinicians and other people are aware of the time-worn adage that frustration breeds aggression. Dollard et al. (1939) hypothesized that frustration was the most important single cause of aggression.

Table 4.   The Spectrum of Aggressive Behavior

Verbal Aggression

Makes loud noises, shouts angrily.
Yells mild personal insults (e.g., "You're stupid").
Curses viciously, uses foul language in anger, makes moderate threats to others or self.
Makes clear threats of violence toward others or self ("I'm going to kill you") or requests help to control self.

Physical Aggression Against Objects

Slams door, scatters clothing, makes a mess.
Throws objects down, kicks furniture without breaking it, marks the wall.
Breaks objects, smashes windows.
Sets fires.

Physical Aggression Against Self

Picks or scratches skin, hits self, pulls hair (with no or minor injury only).
Bangs head, hits fist into objects, throws self onto floor or into objects (hurts self without serious injury).
Small cuts or bruises, minor burns.
Mutilates self, makes deep cuts, bites that bleed, internal injury, fracture, loss of consciousness, loss of teeth.

Physical Aggression Against Other People

Makes threatening gesture, swings at people, grabs at clothes.
Strikes, kicks, pushes, pulls hair (without injury to them).
Attacks others causing mild to moderate physical injury (bruises, sprains, welts).
Attacks others causing severe physical injury (broken bones, deep lacerations, internal injury).

Note.   Abstracted from Silver and Yudofsky (1987b) and Yudofsky et al. (1986).

Although this assertion is difficult to prove by research in humans, Baron (1985) and others feel that intense frustration increases anxiety, especially when the frustration is perceived as arbitrary or illegitimate rather than when it is viewed as deserved or legitimate. The prototypic example is a violent young adult who was continuously abused physically by an alcoholic father to the point that he suffered brain injury and chronic residual impairment. Certainly, such an individual would exhibit angry affects and, likely, violent activities secondary to emotional reactions to parental abuse. If his angry feelings or violent behavior worsen significantly subsequent to brain injury, one may assume that his psychological and organic predispositions to aggressive behaviors are interacting to increase his potential for violent outbursts (Elliott 1976; Lewis et al. 1986; Lishman 1978; Thomsen 1984).

Because of the high frequency in which the prefrontal and frontal regions of the cortex are damaged in closed head injuries, specific changes in personality known as the frontal lobe syndrome are not uncommon. Table 5 summarizes prototypic personality and cognitive changes in patients with frontal lobe syndrome. Although frontal lobe syndrome is not a DSM-III-R diagnosis, this term is used frequently by neurologists and referred to in neurologic textbooks. Frequently, but not always, patients with frontal lobe syndrome also demonstrate organic aggressive syndrome, which occurs as well in patients with diffuse cortical damage. Other areas of the brain in which lesions may give rise to organic aggressive syndrome include the amygdala,

Table 5.   Frontal Lobe Syndrome

Changes associated with damage to the frontal cortex:

A. Social and behavioral changes

1. Exacerbation of preexisting behavioral traits such as disorderliness, suspiciousness, argumentativeness, disruptiveness, and anxiousness.
2. Apathy, loss of interest in social interactions, global lack of concern for consequences of behavior.
3. Uncharacteristic lewdness with loss of social graces, inattention to personal appearance and to hygiene.
4. Intrusiveness, boisterousness, increased volume of speech, and pervasive, uncharacteristic profanity.
5. Increased risk taking, unrestrained drinking of alcoholic beverages, indiscriminate selection of foods, and gluttony.
6. Impulsivity and distractibility.

B. Affective changes
1. Indifference, shallowness.
2. Lability of affect, irritability, manic states.
3. Dyscontrol of rage and violent behavior.

C. Intellectual changes
1. Reduced capacity to utilize language, symbols, and logic.
2. Reduced ability to use mathematics, to calculate, to process abstract information, and to reason.
3. Diminished ability to focus, to concentrate, and to be oriented to time or place.

Note.   Abstracted from MacKinnon and Yudofsky (1986).

the hippocampus, the hypothalamus, the fornix, the cingulate gyri, the septum pellucidum, and areas around the third ventricle (Elliott 1976).

Patient Evaluation

The evaluation of a patient with organic aggressive syndrome requires a thorough examination of the central nervous system as well as an extensive psychosocial assessment. Evaluation includes a complete medical history and physical examination, with special attention to the review of neurologic symptoms and the neurologic examination. In addition, a comprehensive psychological assessment and a psychiatric mental status examination are essential to differentiate those aggressive disorders that are a result of functional etiologies from those that are primarily related to organic etiologies—when such distinction is possible. Aggressive behaviors secondary to organic etiologies are exquisitely sensitive to psychosocial factors, and failure to be cognizant of such interrelationships will result in incomplete understanding and inadequate control of aggressive symptoms. A discussion of the content and process of conducting a comprehensive psychological assessment and psychiatric mental status examination is beyond the scope of this chapter.

Other components in the evaluation of patients with organic aggressive syndrome include relevant laboratory testing, EEG with nasopharyngeal leads, CT scan, or, where available, magnetic resonance imaging (MRI). Special placement of nasopharyngeal electrodes or sphenoidal electrodes enables the EEG to pick up abnormal electrical activity in the anterior temporal lobes that may otherwise be missed. This is especially important in the diagnosis of temporal lobe epilepsy wherein kindling—or the creation of new or secondary epileptic foci following repeated electrical stimulation—occurs most readily in deeper limbic structures such as the amygdala (Bear et al. 1985; MacKinnon and Yudofsky 1986). As in other medical conditions, there is no such entity as a routine workup for a patient with organic aggressive syndrome. The patient's history, physical examination, and complaints should guide the physician in ordering tests. Attention should also be paid to the benefits of such testing in comparison with the expense and discomfort they bring to the patient. For example, MRI improves resolution and may reveal smaller lesions than can be located by CT; however, this test is expensive and often requires that the patient be maintained immobile for extended periods of time. The latter situation is often difficult to accomplish with patients who suffer from organic aggressive syndrome, and may result in significant stress to the patient or require considerable premedication with sedatives.

Prevention

Many of the common organic etiologies that underly organic aggressive syndrome are potentially preventable. Organic dyscontrol is often secondary to brain trauma caused by motor vehicle accidents. The proper use of seat belts with upper torso restraints is a highly effective measure for the prevention of head injury, but it is used by less than 10 percent of drivers (Haddon and Baker 1981). The proper use of seat belts is 50 to 65 percent effective in the prevention of fatalities and injuries, and this could be translated to 12,000 to 16,000 lives saved per year according to the National Safety Council (1985). In the United States, it is estimated by the National Safety Council that alcohol ingestion is implicated in more than 50 percent of all automobile fatalities (Haddon and Baker 1981). Therefore, in psychiatric and other medical histories, detailed inquiry about alcohol and other drug use, driving patterns, and seat belt use is essential. The use of motorcycles (with or without helmets) and the use of bicycles for commuting purposes are strongly associated with head injury, even when safety precautions are taken and regulations observed (Frankowski et al. 1985; Poleck 1967).

If a practitioner identifies a patient to be a high risk for brain injury, there are some preventive measures that may be taken, such as instruction in the proper use of medications, psychological counseling, family and peer support, specialized treatment groups such as Alcoholics Anonymous, and education related to the use of seat belts. For example, an interstate truck driver suffering from major depressive disorder with insomnia (which he was attempting to "self-treat" with increased alcohol consumption), poor concentration, and diminished energy (for which he was taking amphetamines) would be at high risk for a motor vehicle accident. In this circumstance, the risk could be reduced by counseling and the appropriate antidepressant agents. The clinician should be alert to the possibility that patients may be neglectful, may use poor judgment, or may be directly violent in their treatment of children. For young children, infant seats are found to be 80 to 90 percent effective in the prevention of deaths in severe motor vehicle injuries according to the National Safety Council (1985) and the Insurance Institute for Highway Safety (1983).

Potential preventive measures for cerebral vascular disease should not be ignored. Some of the treatable risk factors for stroke are hypertension, heart disease, diabetes, elevated blood lipid levels, cigarette smoking, alcoholism, and obesity. Among this group, hypertension is the most significant potentially reversible risk factor. The incidence of stroke increases sixfold in patients with hypertension; 50 percent of the cerebral vascular accidents occur in 20 percent of adults who have hypertension (Wolf and Kannel 1982). It has been found that the death rate from cerebral vascular disease in treated hypertension populations is reduced to a level approaching that of the general US population (Hypertension Detection and Follow-Up Program Cooperative Group 1982). Prevention of strokes may be aided by encouraging all adult patients to have regular physical examinations, by carefully monitoring the blood pressure of those patients at high risk, by counseling and other treatments for alcoholism and cigarette smoking (Hillbom and Kaste 1981), and by helping a patient to reduce life stress. Special attention should be paid to patients receiving medications that may affect blood pressure (e.g., monoamine oxidase inhibitors, tricyclic antidepressants, antipsychotic agents) or clotting of blood (e.g., warfarin sodium, aspirin).

Treatment

Patients who suffer from organic aggressive syndrome require a full spectrum of medical and psychiatric treatments, including social, psychological, and biologic interventions, because it is rare that any single treatment will prove effective. Therefore, the psychiatrist must devote adequate time for meeting with the family, coordinating communication with other medical disciplines, and mobilizing community resources, as well as for assessing the psychological and psychopharmacologic management of the patient.

Psychosocial Interventions

Violent and aggressive behaviors are not only highly disabling to patients but are also severely disruptive to families. Often the clinician may detect preliminary indications that a patient suffers from organic aggressive syndrome in the physicians' waiting room solely through the observation of the patient's family. The family members appear to be "walking on eggshells" from fear and concern that they might trigger an aggressive episode in the patient. Families often become frustrated and angry with themselves as well as with the patient who exhibits recurrent dyscontrol of violent behavior. The anger and frustration of family members may, in turn, precipitate further aggression on the part of the patient. Support of the family by the clinician can interrupt this dangerous cycle of accelerating aggression. It is helpful to explain to the family that the patient is not altogether responsible for the aggressive behavior, especially because the behaviors have neuropathologic bases for which the patient has no realistic responsibility. Such explanations can help to reduce the family's tendency to blame the patient for aggressive outbursts.

The family treatment is essential to prevent the previously described destructive cycle in which family members become angry and frustrated with the patient's outbursts, their anger is communicated to the patient, and the patient's angry feelings and violent behavior escalate. The family should be supported by encouragement, by a carefully orchestrated treatment plan, and by suggesting behaviors that reduce rather than increase aggression (Oddy et al. 1978). Family treatment also provides a controlled setting in which, during times of nonviolence, both the patient and the family can express feelings of guilt.

Silver and Yudofsky (1987b) systematically documented 4,600 aggressive events in approximately 40 psychiatric inpatients in state hospital systems. Through the analysis of these data, we found that aggressive events were most likely to occur at times of high stimulation, such as during change of shifts or occupational therapy hours. The lowest incidence of violence was during the most restful times with reduced staff and fewest visitors, such as in the evenings and on weekends. From these and other data related to patients with schizophrenia, one concludes that reducing emotional intensity and stimuli in family and work settings is a valuable intervention for patients with violent behaviors in general and with organic aggressive syndrome in particular.

Psychological Interventions

Psychological interventions in treating patients with organic aggressive syndrome usually revolve around four major issues: 1) understanding and treating psychopathology that preceded the central nervous system dysfunction; 2) treating psychological responses to any traumatic events (e.g., car accident) that may have been involved in the brain injury or lesion; 3) reducing stress and stimuli that precipitate dyscontrol; and 4) preventing the recurrence of the events that led to the initial brain insult. It is important to recognize that some preexisting psychiatric illness is intensified by brain injury. Therefore, the person who is psychologically angry may become much more so after a stroke, brain trauma, the development of Alzheimer's disease, or under the influence of central nervous system depressants such as alcohol (Fordyce et al. 1983; Gold et al. 1985). Although attention, concentration, and intellectual functions are often diminished in patients with organic aggressive syndrome, one must not underestimate the usefulness of psychological and psychotherapeutic approaches. Many of these patients respond to supportive psychotherapy even though they have significant brain dysfunction and recurrent rage outbursts. Insight into physical and interpersonal problems as well as suggestions from the therapist about how to reduce stress and improve self-esteem are often helpful. It is important to be alert for depression, which is often associated with organic aggressive syndrome—either as a response to the syndrome or a concomitant of the brain lesion (Robinson and Szetela 1981; Robinson et al. 1984c, 1985); psychotherapy and/or pharmacotherapy are employed as appropriate.

Behavioral Treatments

Behavioral treatments are important in the care of patients with organic aggressive syndrome (Franzen and Lovell 1987). Such treatments run the gamut from refusing to reinforce aggressive behaviors to arranging behavior modification programs. In general, one should attempt to structure the physical environment as well as interpersonal relationships to be safe, nonthreatening, and not overstimulating. Efforts should be made to reduce the patient's overall frustrations. This is best accomplished in the hospital environment by providing clues to orientation, by delivering brief and clear messages related to the patient's overall care, and by avoiding power struggles. Hospital and home environments with low noise levels, with soft color tones, and with reduced human contact are encouraged. Often people who work successfully with violent patients are, themselves, calm individuals who speak in a quiet but clear fashion. Many studies indicate the clinical benefit of behavior modification techniques in the treatment of organic aggressive syndrome. Behavioral treatments are essential for patients who have suffered severe traumatic brain injury and require careful design and execution by a staff well-versed in behavioral techniques. One study found the behavior modification approach 75 percent effective in dealing with disturbed behaviors after severe brain injury (Eames and Wood 1985). Because these programs are designed for individual patients with specific problems, a full review of such programs is beyond the scope of this chapter. The reader is directed to texts on behavior modification as well as to specific articles on behavioral techniques in the treatment of organic aggressive syndrome (Franzen and Lovell 1987; Liberman and Wong 1984).

Psychopharmacology

Although there is no FDA-approved medication specific for the treatment of rage and violent behavior, psychopharmacologic management of aggression secondary to organic aggressive syndrome is commonplace. Most of the substantiated studies related to treatments of aggression have been done with animal models. The psychopharmacology of aggressive disorders in humans is vastly understudied, and every study in the literature has significant methodologic problems. Because of the disruptive and often dangerous behaviors inherent with aggressive disorders, it is difficult to utilize standard research designs that may include the discontinuation of all medications prior to the initiation of the study. Research on the psychopharmacologic treatment of violence often must be carried out in difficult environments such as in prisons or in special treatment units for aggressive patients within state hospital systems. Therefore, the preponderance of published literature on the psychopharmacology of aggression utilizes series of case reports rather than prospective, double-blind placebo research designs (Yudofsky et al. 1987).

Antipsychotics. The most widely used and misused category of medications for the management of aggression is antipsychotic agents. Antipsychotic drugs are appropriate for the management of aggression secondary to psychotic ideation and are frequently the agents of choice for this clinical condition. However, when aggression related to organic aggressive syndrome is being treated, it is often the sedative side effects of these agents rather than their antipsychotic properties that are being utilized. In cases of organic aggressive syndrome, violence is often a chronic, intermittent-episodic behavior, and patients are frequently managed by chronic sedation with phenothiazines or butyrophenones. The result is the emergence of side effects, including oversedation, parkinsonian symptoms, and akathisia. Frequently, tolerance occurs to the sedative effects of the agents, and doses are continuously increased. Of significant concern in utilizing antipsychotic agents in the management of aggression is the potential emergence of tardive dyskinesia. With a prevalence rate of about 25 percent (Jeste and Wyatt 1982; Jeste et al. 1985), tardive dyskinesia constitutes a significant risk when long-term neuroleptic treatment is used to manage chronic aggression.

A review of the literature revealed that almost all of the patients who were treated with propranolol for aggression had been unsuccessfully treated on previous occasions with antipsychotic agents (Silver and Yudofsky 1985; Yudofsky et al. 1987). Sedative side effects may control acute symptomatology, but the ultimate result is often a patient who is chronically lethargic and dysfunctional. Antipsychotic agents lower seizure thresholds and may exacerbate a patient's organic dyscontrol of rage and violence. The use of antipsychotic agents is, therefore, recommended only for the management of aggression stemming from psychotic ideation or for the intermittent management of brief aggressive events related to organic aggressive syndrome. The use of antipsychotic agents for longer than eight weeks is not recommended to treat aggression secondary to central nervous system lesions because of the frequent emergence of such side effects as akathisias and sedation, because of the possible intensification of violent behavior, and because of the potential emergence of tardive dyskinesias with more prolonged use.

Sedatives and hypnotics.   A second class of medications employed to manage aggression is sedative-hypnotics and minor tranquilizers. Included in this category are the benzodiazepines and their derivatives, barbiturates, antihistamines, and agents such as paraldehyde and chloral hydrate. As with antipsychotics, this category of drugs may be useful in the management of acute aggressive episodes but has many disadvantages in the management of the chronically aggressive patient. Among such disadvantages are oversedation, dependency, aggravation of concomitant depression, and paradoxical induction of rage and violence. The use of these drugs on a chronic basis is not recommended.

Lithium carbonate.   Several studies have suggested that lithium carbonate may have value in treating aggression in specific patient populations (Schiff et al., 1982). In a double-blind placebo-controlled crossover study of severely mentally retarded inpatients with frequent aggressive behaviors (Worrall 1978; Worrall et al. 1975), three of seven patients became less aggressive, and two of these showed significant improvement, as measured by a simple seven-point scale. In an open trial (Dale 1980), 11 of 15 patients with long histories of aggressive behavior and mental retardation showed a sustained decrease in aggressive behavior. The largest studies of lithium in the treatment of aggression have been in prison populations. When 27 inmates were treated in an open fashion (Tupin et al. 1973), prison-rule infractions decreased in 15 of 22 patients who completed the study. In a single-blind crossover study of the effects of lithium and placebo on 12 chronically assaultive male prisoners, Sheard (1975) reported a "significant" reduction in aggressive affect. In a medium security prison, he then studied 66 male inmates who were nonpsychotic, had no evidence of organic brain syndrome, and were on no other psychoactive medication (Sheard et al. 1976). The inmates were randomly assigned to lithium or placebo after a one-month medication-free evaluation. Sheard found a significant reduction in the number of major infractions by those inmates receiving lithium. It is important to note that 80 percent of those inmates assigned to lithium treatment were able to guess that they were receiving active drug. In contrast to these studies, we found that lithium had little effect on the aggression of patients with organic aggressive syndrome in the general hospital neuropsychiatric setting as well as in chronic inpatient psychiatric facilities, except for those whose violence and agitation were secondary to manic affects.

Anticonvulsants.   The fourth class of medications that has been advocated for the treatment of aggressive behaviors is anticonvulsant agents. Three controlled studies (Conners et al. 1971; Gottschalk et al. 1973; Lefkowitz 1969) found diphenylhydantoin to be ineffective in the treatment of aggression. Positive results were obtained in a fourth one (Maletzky 1973), in which 86 percent of the patients (22 men with episodic dyscontrol) had a 75 to 100 percent reduction in the frequency or severity of their violent outbursts on one-year follow-up.

Carbamazepine is an anticonvulsant with proven efficacy in major motor and complex partial seizure disorders. Several studies reviewed by Roy-Byrne et al. (1984) reported that the medication is effective in treating both those aggressive disorders that are associated with temporal lobe epilepsy and those that are not (Folks et al. 1982; Hakoloa and Laulumaa 1982; Luchins 1983a; Tunks and Dever 1977). Doses of carbamazepine recommended for the treatment of aggressive dyscontrol syndromes averaged 600 mg/day in divided doses of 200 mg (see also Chapter 101). There are a few reports of a small number of cases that support its use for organic aggressive syndrome related to other etiologies, and these results are encouraging.

Beta blockers. Beta blockers are a fifth class of medications advocated for the treatment of uncontrolled rage and violent outbursts secondary to organic mental syndromes (Elliott 1977; Ratey et al. 1983; Silver and Yudofsky 1986; Williams et al. 1982; Yudofsky et al. 1981, 1984). Silver and Yudofsky (1985) reviewed the literature of 10 published reports with a total of 59 patients whose uncontrolled rage outbursts responded to propranolol. All reports were case studies or retrospective reviews of patients with some form of brain damage. The doses of propranolol to which the patients responded were generally lower than 640 mg/day, with a median dosage of 400 mg/day. Response time varied from less than two days to more than six weeks. In most of the cases reported, especially in those of patients with chronic central nervous system dysfunction, aggressive behaviors returned with the discontinuation of propranolol. There are a number of reports and discussions of the potential neuropsychiatric side effects of propranolol and other beta blockers (including psychotic symptoms and depression), but they are difficult to evaluate and by no means conclusive. For a more detailed review of these reports, as well as a discussion of potential drug-drug interactions of propranolol with tricyclic antidepressants, monoamine oxidase inhibitors, and antipsychotics, see Chapter 102.

Presently, Silver and colleagues are conducting a prospective, randomized, double-blind discontinuation study to test the efficacy of propranolol in the treatment of aggression in patients with schizophrenia or brain damage who are chronically institutionalized in state hospitals (Silver and Yudofsky 1986). The results of this ongoing study, although encouraging, are not as yet definitive. Nonetheless, from clinical experience involving the "open" treatment of over 300 patients with aggression and violence related to organic brain syndrome, and from the extensive experience of neurologist Frank Elliott (personal communication, 1986), who has also treated hundreds of patients with organic dyscontrol, use of propranolol is a reasonable psychopharmacologic approach in patients with chronic organic aggressive syndrome. Table 6 summarizes the clinical use of propranolol in the management of the aggressive patient. Other beta blockers have also been reported to have beneficial effects on aggressive behavior (Sorgi et al. 1986).

Summary

Violent and aggressive behaviors are common among patients with organic brain disorders and, when they occur, are disabling to patients and disruptive to their families. A multifaceted and multidisciplinary approach to the assessment, treatment, and prevention of rage and violent behavior related to organic brain disorders may include the following:

1. Comprehensive biologic evaluation of the patient in an attempt to diagnose, when possible, the specific etiology and location(s) in the central nervous system of the brain lesion.
2. Assessment of the role of psychosocial factors in the causes of, or in the psychosocial features that result from, organic aggressive syndrome.
3. Treatment that utilizes psychological, behavioral, and psychopharmacologic in-

Table 6.   Clinical Use of Propranolol

1. Conduct a thorough medical evaluation, including electrocardiogram.
2. Exclude patients with the following disorders: bronchial asthma, chronic obstructive pulmonary disease, insulin-dependent diabetes, diabetes mellitus, congestive heart failure, persistent angina, significant peripheral vascular disease, hyperthyroidism.
3. In patients for whom there are clinical concerns about hypotension or bradycardia, begin with a single test dose of 20 mg/day. Increase the dose of propranolol by 20 mg/day every three days.
4. For patients without cardiovascular or cardiopulmonary disorder, initiate propranolol on a 20 mg tid schedule.
5. Increase the dose of propranolol by 60 mg/day, every three days.
6. Increase propranolol until the pulse rate is reduced below 50 bpm, or systolic blood pressure is less than 90 mm Hg.
7. Hold medication dose if severe dizziness, ataxia, or wheezing occurs. Reduce or discontinue propranolol if such symptoms persist.
8. Increase dose to 12 mg/kg or until aggressive behavior is under control. Doses of greater than 800 mg are not usually required to control aggressive behavior.
9. Maintain the patient on the highest dose of propranolol for at least eight weeks prior to determining that the patient is not responding to the medication. Some patients, however, may respond rapidly to propranolol.
10. Utilize concurrent medications with caution. Monitor plasma blood levels of all antipsychotic and anticonvulsant medications. Propranolol has been shown to increase plasma levels of chlorpromazine and thioridazine.
11. Avoid sudden discontinuation of propranolol, particularly in patients with hypertension.
12. Taper a patient's dose of propranolol by 60 mg/day until such time as the patient is on a total daily dose of 60 mg/day. At that point, taper the medication at a rate of 20 mg every other day (or more gradually in patients with hypertension) to avoid rebound hypertension.

terventions that are carefully chosen to treat specific underlying etiologies and discrete symptomatologies. Interventions should be chosen that have the fewest behavioral restrictions, and medications should be selected to treat, as specifically as possible, the underlying etiologies of the organic aggressive syndrome. The chronic use of antipsychotics or hypnotics solely to sedate patients who have episodic dyscontrol is discouraged. Through counseling, treatment, and education of patients who have hypertension, who smoke, who abuse alcohol, and who do not use seat belts and special restraints for their infants and children while driving, it is hoped that common sources of brain injury that lead to organic aggressive syndrome will be reduced.

Chapter 97

Organic Mood Syndrome

Definition and Diagnostic Criteria

Organic mood syndrome is described in DSM-III-R (American Psychiatric Association 1987) as "prominent and persistent depressed, elevated, or expansive mood, resembling either a Manic Episode or a Major Depressive Episode, that is due to a specific organic factor" (p. 111). The diagnostic criteria for organic mood syndrome are listed in Table 1.

Epidemiology

The epidemiology of organic mood syndrome depends on the specific organic etiology. Although epidemiologic studies of organic mood syndromes per se have not been published, mood syndrome secondary to toxic factors is likely to be most prevalent. Other relatively common causes of organic mood syndrome include endocrinologic disorders, such as hypothyroidism, hyperthyroidism, hypoadrenocorticalism, hyperadrenocorticalism, and structural lesions of the brain.

Etiology

Several broad categories of agents have been claimed, on the basis of case reports, to cause organic mood disorder. Whitlock (1982), following extensive critical review of the literature, concluded that medications (and other ingested or injected substances) are most likely to provoke depression, hypomania, or mania in individuals with a prior history of mood disorder; structural lesions of the brain appear to be capable of causing mood syndrome in individuals not so predisposed. Endocrinologic disorders, according to Whitlock, occupy a middle ground between structural lesions of the brain and ingested substances. The role of other organic agents (such as viruses) remains controversial.

Table 1. DSM-III-R Diagnostic Criteria for Organic Mood Syndrome
A. Prominent and persistent depressed, elevated, or expansive mood.
B. There is evidence from the history, physical examination, or laboratory tests of a specific organic factor (or factors) judged to be etiologically related to the disturbance.
C. Not occurring exclusively during the course of Delirium.
Specify: manic, depressed, or **mixed.**

These comments in mind, the organic factors that have been associated with depression include the following:

1. Antihypertensive medications such as reserpine, methyldopa, propranolol, and clonidine; nonsteroidal anti-inflammatory agents; central nervous system depressants such as alcohol, barbiturates, benzodiazepines, and related compounds; and some antineoplastic agents, such as cis-platinum.
2. Endocrinologic disorders including hypothyroidism, hyperthyroidism, hyperparathyroidism, hypoadrenocorticalism, and hyperadrenocorticalism.
3. Neoplasms, particularly carcinoma of the pancreas, and some brain malignancies, mainly in supratentorial locations. Corsellis et al. (1968) described three cases of "limbic encephalopathy," a nonmalignant degenerative and inflammatory disease of limbic structures associated with pulmonary carcinoma; prominent and severe depression was present in one of the three patients.
4. Cerebral infarction, particularly of the left hemisphere. A study by Robinson et al. (1984b) suggested that the likelihood of depressive disorder increases with proximity of the lesion to the anterior, frontal pole of the left hemisphere, although this association contradicts earlier findings (Folstein et al. 1977; Lishman 1968).
5. Cerebral injury (again, particularly if frontal lobes are involved).
6. Certain neurologic syndromes, such as Parkinson's disease, Huntington's chorea, multiple sclerosis, and epilepsy.
7. Other, including some viral illnesses (such as influenza, hepatitis, encephalitis, Dengue fever, Epstein-Barr virus), systemic lupus erythematosus, and other collagen-vascular diseases, vitamin deficiencies (particularly B_{12} and folate), and hypercalcemia secondary to metastatic cancer with bony involvement.

Organic manic or hypomanic syndrome has also been associated with several categories of organic etiology, including:

1. Certain medications, such as amphetamines, methylphenidate, cocaine, tricyclic antidepressants, monoamine oxidase inhibitors, L-dopa, phencyclidine, and exogenous corticosteroids.
2. Endocrinologic disorders, including hyperadrenocorticalism and hyperthyroidism.
3. Other, including multiple sclerosis, brain tumor, and epilepsy. Intermittent explosive disorder, which may share some features (e.g., extreme anger, rapid shifts of mood) with organic manic syndrome, has been associated with brain trauma.

Differential Diagnosis

Severe organic depressive syndrome is distinguished from major depressive episode in which symptoms may be identical but a specific organic etiology is not demonstrable. This distinction may be particularly difficult in patients with a prior history of mood syndrome who are briefly exposed to a medication such as reserpine, and then develop affective symptoms that do not remit when the reserpine is discontinued. Such cases probably represent organically triggered rather than organically caused depression and, according to DSM-III-R guidelines, should not be classified as organic depressive syndrome. On the other hand, if a prior history of mood disorder is not present, organic mood syndrome would be the appropriate diagnosis. Less severe organic depressive syndrome is also distinguished from similarly less severe nonorganic mood disorders, such as dysthymic disorder or cyclothymic disorder, in which an organic cause is not demonstrable.

Organic hallucinosis, organic delusional disorder, and dementia may be accompanied by symptoms of depression, but in these disorders the clinical picture is dominated by other symptoms: hallucinations in organic hallucinosis, delusions in organic delusional syndrome, and cognitive dysfunction in a clear sensorium in dementia.

Symptoms otherwise identical to those of organic depressive syndrome may also be seen in other conditions in which an organic cause is not demonstrable, such as schizophrenia and schizoaffective disorder, in which schizophrenic symptoms are also present; and uncomplicated bereavement, in which the onset of symptoms occurs within two to three months following a major loss, such as the death of a loved one.

Similarly, organic manic syndrome should be distinguished from other organic mental syndromes such as organic hallucinosis, organic delusional disorder, delirium, and dementia. Organic manic syndrome closely resembles manic episode, in which an organic etiology is not demonstrable. Similar symptoms may be seen in other nonorganic psychiatric disorders such as schizophrenia and schizoaffective disorder, in which symptoms of schizophrenia are also present, and cyclothymic disorder, in which characteristic shifts of mood from hypomania to depression occur. The distinction between organic and functional mood syndromes is important in that failure to recognize an organic etiology may delay appropriate treatment and result in unnecessary administration of antidepressant or antimanic agents, all of which are associated with side effects and potentially serious adverse reactions.

Patient Evaluation

When faced with a patient who may have organic depressive, manic, or mixed syndrome, a complete medical and psychiatric history, with emphasis on recent drug ingestion, and complete physical and neurologic examinations are indicated. Serum and urine analyses for toxic agents, assessment of thyroid and adrenal function, and measurement of serum calcium levels should be performed in all cases. Other lab tests (e.g., B_{12}) may be needed, depending on clinical impressions. Roentgenologic examination of the head, electroencephalography, scintillation or computerized tomographic scanning, or nuclear magnetic resonance imaging of the head may also be indicated, depending on the findings from the history, physical examination, and laboratory analyses.

Specific Treatment

Discontinuing medications that can cause organic depressive or manic syndrome may be sufficient in many cases. Replacement therapy in hypothyroidism and hypoadrenocorticalism and appropriate medical and surgical treatment of hyperthyroidism, hyperparathyroidism, hyperadrenocorticalism, hypercalcemia, pancreatic carcinoma, intracranial mass lesion, or stroke are also indicated, and may suffice to reverse mood symptoms.

General Treatment Considerations

Symptoms of organic depressive syndrome that remain following specific treatment (or that necessitate treatment before specific therapy can be administered) may respond to somatic therapies used for "functional" depressive disorder. Indeed, numerous clinical case reports claim efficacy for these therapies, but there are as yet no data from controlled studies to verify these claims. Treatments reported to be effective include cyclic and monoamine oxidase inhibiting antidepressants and electroconvulsive therapy (ECT). Dosage typically compares to that required for nonorganic depression: treatment usually begins with low dosages (i.e., 25 mg for most tricyclics, 10 to 15 mg for monoamine oxidase inhibitors), which are gradually increased until remission occurs or side effects supervene.

In organic mania or hypomania, high-potency neuroleptic agents (e.g., fluphenazine, haloperidol, thiothixine) have been reported to be effective for acute control and for maintenance therapy, in dosages ranging from 0.5 to 10–20 mg/day. Lithium carbonate, in dosages adequate to produce serum lithium levels in the 0.8 to 1.2 meq/L range, has been effective in bringing hypomanic or manic symptoms under control within five to seven days; maintenance dosages should be adjusted to achieve serum levels in the 0.4 to 0.8 meq/L range (Young et al. 1977). In cases refractory to neuroleptic or lithium therapy, carbamazepine has been effective in dosages of 200 to 400 mg/day administered in divided doses. When organic mania is not responsive to any of these agents, ECT may be indicated. Intracranial lesions that occupy space or impede the outflow of cerebrospinal fluid, of course, contraindicate the use of ECT.

Summary

Organic mood syndrome may result from a wide variety of etiologic agents, including exogenous toxins, endogenous hormone imbalances, infections, structural lesions of the brain including neoplasm, contusion, infarction, and others. The precise relationships between mood symptoms and the organic causes discussed in this chapter remain unclear; the literature in this area is entirely case report in nature and is insufficient to clarify issues of pathogenesis until controlled studies are published. Organic mood syndrome generally resembles nonorganic mood disorder. Pending definitive studies, treatment should include removal of the etiologic agents and initiation of conventional therapy for depression, hypomania, or mania, as indicated.

Chapter 98

Organic Personality Syndrome

Definition and Diagnostic Criteria

Organic personality syndrome is described in DSM-III-R (American Psychiatric Association 1987) as "a persistent personality disturbance, either lifelong or representing a change or accentuation of a previously characteristic trait, that is due to a specific organic factor" (p. 114). The diagnostic criteria for organic personality syndrome are listed in Table 1.

The existence of organic personality syndrome as a broadly defined clinical entity appears to be widely accepted by clinicians; however, there is only one systematic study in the literature that supports an association between a specific cluster of clinical features and a particular organic etiology. To be sure, there are remarkably few candidates for study. A review of the English language literature revealed only three relatively well-defined specific organic personality disorders (discussed below), at least one of which remains quite controversial.

Epidemiology

The epidemiology of organic personality syndrome depends on the specific organic etiology. Although epidemiologic studies of organic personality per se have not been published, those associated with neoplasms of the brain, brain damage secondary to

---

Table 1. DSM-III-R Diagnostic Criteria for Organic Personality Syndrome

A. A persistent personality disturbance, either lifelong or representing a change or accentuation of a previously characteristic trait, involving at least one of the following:

   (1) affective instability, e.g., marked shifts from normal mood to depression, irritability, or anxiety

   (2) recurrent outbursts of aggression or rage that are grossly out of proportion to any precipitating psychosocial stressors

   (3) markedly impaired social judgment, e.g., sexual indiscretions

   (4) marked apathy and indifference

   (5) suspiciousness or paranoid ideation

B. There is evidence from the history, physical examination, or laboratory tests of a specific organic factor (or factors) judged to be etiologically related to the disturbance.

C. This diagnosis is not given to a child or adolescent if the clinical picture is limited to the features that characterize Attention-deficit Hyperactivity Disorder.

D. Not occurring exclusively during the course of Delirium, and does not meet the criteria for Dementia.

Specify explosive type if outbursts of aggression or rage are the predominant feature.

trauma or stroke, epilepsy (particularly of the temporal lobe variety), and chronic ingestion of psychoactive substances (e.g., amphetamines, cocaine, cannabis) are probably the most common.

Etiology

Damage to the frontal lobes of the brain, either by neoplasm, stroke, or trauma, has been associated with two specific patterns of organic personality disorder, depending on the location of the pathology. Benson and Blumer (1975) asserted that lesions of the prefrontal convexities tend to produce apathy, indifference, and slowness. Patients with these lesions are reported to lose initiative and interest in previously interesting activities, and are often misdiagnosed as depressed, particularly when the brain damage is otherwise neurologically silent. Lesions of the orbital surface of the frontal lobes are claimed to be more commonly associated with poor impulse control, inappropriate social behavior (particularly relating to sexual matters), and angry outbursts; however, Benson and Blumer also acknowledged that most cases of frontal lobe damage present with admixtures of the two, as damage is rarely localized solely to the frontal convexities or the orbital surfaces.

Another relatively distinct organic personality syndrome has been described in patients with temporal lobe epilepsy (see Chapter 101). These patients are reported to demonstrate reduced sexual interest and reponse, increased religiosity and a heightened sense of the meaning and significance of relatively trivial events, hypometamorphosis (an aversion to change), and viscosity (a tendency to belabor irrelevant details in speech). Occasional outbursts of "pent-up anger" are also described, as are paranoid, depressive, hypomanic, and hypochondriacal symptoms.

Organic personality syndrome has been described in association with chronic, heavy ingestion of cannabis, either as marijuana or hashish. In this syndrome, marked loss of interest in usual activities; diminished capacity to carry out complex, long-term plans; reduced mental concentration; social withdrawal; and a pervasive amotivational state have been reported (McGlothlin and West 1968); however, some authorities question the specific causal role of cannabis in the disorder, suggesting that cultural and personal factors may play a more important role than the cannabis per se.

Less specific organic personality syndromes may also occur in patients with Huntington's chorea, Wilson's disease, Cushing's syndrome, and multiple sclerosis, although in most cases these conditions are accompanied by affective or cognitive changes severe enough to warrant a diagnosis of another organic mental syndrome (e.g., dementia, organic mood syndrome).

Differential Diagnosis

A diagnosis of organic personality syndrome is formally precluded during the course of delirium and if dementia or attention-deficit hyperactivity disorder is present. It must also be distinguished from other organic mental syndromes in which personality changes occur but are not the predominant psychopathology. For example, personality changes are not unusual in organic mood syndrome, organic hallucinosis, and organic delusional syndrome, but are secondary in importance to mood disorder, hallucinations, and delusions, respectively. Organic personality syndrome is also distinguished from nonorganic mental disorders in which personality changes may occur. These include schizophrenia, mood disorder, substance abuse disorder, phobic and panic disorders, hypochondriasis, and certain childhood-onset disorders (e.g., transsexualism). Finally, organic personality syndrome is distinguished from functional personality disorder by the absence of evidence of a "specific organic factor" in the latter condition. Although "organic" features (e.g., impulsivity, temper outbursts) (see Chapter 96) may be present in functional personality disorder (e.g., borderline personality disorder), they typically do not emerge following specific events (e.g., head trauma, intoxication).

Patient Evaluation

A complete medical and psychiatric history, physical and neurologic examination, and laboratory tests (as indicated) should be performed in all cases of suspected organic personality syndrome. Computed tomography or magnetic resonance imaging of the head, electroencephalography, serum measurement of adrenal and thyroid function, and toxicologic screening of serum and urine may be particularly helpful. Neuropsychological testing may complement the clinical mental status examination by ruling out cognitive changes severe enough to warrant a diagnosis of dementia, in addition to helping localize and quantify pathology. Psychometric evaluation of personality (e.g., Minnesota Multiphasic Personality Inventory) may also be of value, particularly if premorbid profiles are available for comparison.

Specific Treatment

Specific treatment of organic personality syndrome is aimed at amelioration of the specific organic factor judged to be etiologic in each case. Surgical and medical treatment of brain neoplasm, trauma, stroke, temporal lobe epilepsy, and the other specific conditions referred to above may lead to a return of the premorbid personality. Similarly, cessation of ingestion of cannabis may also result in the disappearance of abnormal personality characteristics without further treatment.

General Treatment Considerations

There are no systematic data available evaluating the efficacy of nonspecific therapy for organic personality syndrome. On the basis of clinical case reports, somatic therapies, including medications and electroconvulsive therapy, have been claimed to be effective for depressive, hypomanic, or manic symptoms, as have neuroleptic agents for the suspiciousness, paranoia, and impulsivity found in some patients with organic personality syndrome. Lishman (1978) proposed a role for psychostimulants in patients with sluggishness and anergy on the basis of hypothalamic damage. I have treated two patients with marked apathy in association with frontal lobe disease and noted modest increases in motivation and interest following treatment with methylphenidate (10 to 20 mg/day). Insight-oriented psychotherapy, often helpful in nonorganic personality disorder, may also be of value in selected cases of organic personality syndrome, particularly when insight into the more disturbing aspects of the patient's behavior can be attained (Lishman 1978). Psychotherapeutic support in the form of reassurance; an opportunity to ventilate feelings of sadness, frustration, and anger; explanation; and encouragement may provide similar benefit to patients and members of their family.

Summary

Organic personality syndrome may be caused by structural and functional lesions of the brain, chronic drug ingestion, and other less common mental disorders. Accurate diagnosis rests on identification of the specific organic factor that is etiologic in each case. Specific treatment is aimed at removal of the etiologic factor, while selected signs and symptoms may be amenable to conventional psychopharmacologic treatment. Psychotherapy may be useful for the patient with organic personality syndrome and the patient's family.

Chapter 99

The Patient with Parkinson's Disease

The Clinical Syndrome

Parkinson's disease (PD) is a disorder characterized primarily by symptoms of tremor, rigidity, and akinesia. Disturbances of autonomic function, equilibrium, and posture also occur frequently. The prevalence in the United States is about 250 per 100,000 (Mayeux 1984). The disease usually begins between the ages of 50 and 65, with subtle symptoms of loss of agility, a sense of slowness, and feelings of tremulousness. With advancing years, the major symptoms become evident and progressively worsen, with significant deterioration in functioning five to 10 years after onset. The characteristic tremor of PD is a gross, rhythmic tremor at rest with a frequency of 4 to 7 Hz. The alternating movement of thumb and forefinger is usually referred to as pill-rolling. The tremor generally stops with movement of the involved limb. Early in the course of the disease, tremor is frequently asymmetrical, involving distal extremities to a greater extent. With time, however, it tends to spread and involve other segments of the body as well. Postural, intention, and action tremors may also variably develop and complicate the clinical picture. The rigidity initially may be mild and restricted to a few muscle groups, but eventually it intensifies and involves more areas of the body. Rigidity occurs in both agonist and antagonist muscle groups and is present throughout the entire range of motion. On examination, when passively stretched, the involved muscles may display an irregular jerkiness called cogwheel rigidity.

One of the most disabling aspects of PD is akinesia, the marked restriction in performing usual volitional motor activities. All aspects of daily living are slowed down, with ordinary activities like dressing requiring an inordinate amount of time. Patients may become frozen in place while walking. Gait is small-stepped and shuffling, with reduced or absent arm swing. In erect position, body posture is abnormal, with trunk bent forward, head down, and arms flexed at the elbow. There is periodic eye blinking. The voice is monotonous and has a reduced amplitude. Many symptoms indicative of autonomic dysfunction occur: hyperhidrosis, impaired vasomotor control of peripheral blood vessels, hypotension, and bowel and bladder disorders. Sialorrhea and facial seborrhea may also occur. Many patients with PD develop dementia and depression. On physical exam, tendon reflexes are usually unimpaired, and a hyperactive glabellar reflex is found.

Typical pathologic findings are neuronal loss and depigmentation in the substantia nigra; additionally, there is loss of cells and pigment in the locus ceruleus and the dorsal vagal nucleus of the brain stem (Yahr 1984). These three areas also demonstrate an intracellular inclusion body called the Lewy body. Mesolimbic and mesocortical dopamine projections also degenerate (Fibiger 1984). Dopamine depletion occurs in the neostriatum and can be correlated with the degree of degeneration in the substantia nigra. Cortical choline acetyltransferase is reduced in the cortex and hippocampus (Agid et al. 1984).

Although idiopathic PD is of unknown cause, certain cases have been attributed to cerebral arteriosclerosis and encephalitis. Postencephalitic parkinsonism is the result of affliction with encephalitis lethargica, an epidemic that occurred between 1919 and 1926. In addition, there are diseases with associated parkinsonian symptoms that produce secondary parkinsonism. Included in this category are: progressive supranuclear palsy; Shy-Drager syndrome; olivopontocerebellar degeneration; striatonigral degeneration; poisoning with carbon monoxide, manganese, or other heavy metals; Wilson's disease; hypoparathyroidism; brain tumors in the region of the basal ganglia; cerebral trauma; and neuroleptic drugs (Klawans and Tanner 1984; Lishman 1978; McDowell et al. 1978; Yahr 1984). Associated neurologic and systemic features of these disorders that are not typical of primary PD will usually alert the clinician that the disorder is not primary parkinsonism.

Organic Mental Syndrome in Parkinson's Disease

Features of organic mental syndrome are frequently seen in PD. Cognitive changes may represent a degenerative dementia, depression, or a confusional or psychotic state associated with antiparkinson medication. In addition, patients with PD are subject to the many systemic and neurologic disorders that frequently cause organic mental syndromes in elderly people.

Dementia

Reported estimates of dementia in PD range from 20 to 90 percent, reflecting different methodologies and patients (Mayeux 1984). Although many patients have evidence of intellectual dysfunction, only about 30 percent are estimated to have sufficient intellectual dysfunction to meet DSM-III (American Psychiatric Association 1980) criteria for dementia (Mayeux and Stern 1983). Perceptual motor or visuospatial function is frequently disturbed and tends to parallel the severity of the disease (Mayeux 1982).

Two varieties of dementia in PD have been suggested, a cortical type such as dementia of the Alzheimer type (DAT), and a subcortical type based on basal ganglia dysfunction. Behavioral changes in subcortical dementia are different from those found in patients with DAT cortical dementia. Characteristics of subcortical dementia include: involuntary movements, psychomotor retardation, forgetfulness with ability to learn new material preserved, apathy, and the absence of cortical signs such as aphasia, agnosia, or apraxia (Benson 1984; Jeste et al. 1984). Eventually, severe cognitive disturbance does appear in subcortical dementia, but usually not until late in its course (Benson 1983). Others have argued that the neuropsychological impairments in dementia of the Alzheimer type and PD are not distinct and result from a combination of cortical and subcortical degeneration (Mayeux et al. 1983).

Some investigators attribute the dementia to a coincident degenerative process similar to DAT. In one study, the prevalence of pathologically established DAT changes (senile plaques and fibrillary tangles) and dementia among patients with PD was more than six times that found in an age-matched population (Boller et al. 1980). The development of DAT shortened the patients' survival. Despite the similarity, some investigators feel that the dementia of PD is not as severe or rapidly progressing as that of DAT (Portin et al. 1984). There appears to be no relationship between intellectual impairment and duration of illness (Jellinger and Riederer 1984; Loranger et al. 1972a), although a consistent relationship has been found between the severity of parkinsonian signs and the extent of intellectual impairment. In particular, the degree of bradykinesia has correlated with intellectual changes (Mayeux and Stern 1983; Mortimer et al. 1982), although in one study the slowing of thought did not necessarily accompany bradykinesia (Rafal et al. 1984). Despite the fact that advanced age is not the basis of dementia in PD (Rajput et al. 1984), parkinsonian patients with dementia are generally older than those who are not demented (Mayeux and Stern 1983).

Some have claimed that levodopa can cause an organic dementia as a direct effect of the drug (Agnoli et al. 1984), although several studies have substantiated a temporary improvement in cognitive function after starting levodopa (Loranger et al. 1973). This effect will be discussed more fully later. Significant deterioration in intermediate memory may also occur in parkinsonian patients taking anticholinergic drugs (Sadeh et al. 1982).

Depression

Frequently depression will present as a reversible dementia. Distinguishing these two disorders, sometimes occurring concurrently, can be difficult (Feinberg and Goodman 1984; Klerman and Davidson 1984). In PD this is a very important issue because depression and dementia commonly occur. Mayeux et al. (1984) stated that "depression is probably the most frequently encountered mental change, unrelated to medications, associated with PD" (p. 249). Depressive symptoms may be of variable intensity, with 40 to 50 percent of patients reporting symptoms of depression at some point during their illness; in one study, 27.5 percent met DSM-III criteria for a major depression (Mayeux et al. 1984). In this study, there was no correlation between the severity of PD and the presence of depression. They stated that although symptoms such as sleep disturbance may be found in both depression and PD, the patients with major depression were distinguished by having these symptoms only during the period of dysphoric mood. Depressive episodes may occur prior to the development of PD as well as during its course (Celesia and Wanamaker 1972). Intellectual changes involving memory and cognition may be associated with the depression (Mayeux and Stern 1983). Depression has inconsistently been related to sex of patient, severity of disease, type of treatment, or age (Mayeux 1982; Rabins 1982). Occasionally levodopa has been implicated in the development of depression; some have felt that it may also contribute to a recurrence of depression in patients with preexisting affective disorder (Mindham et al. 1976).

Confusional States

Confusional states occur frequently during the course of PD and are usually related to the use of antiparkinson medication. Levodopa, bromocriptine, amantadine, and anticholinergics have all been implicated, although some investigators feel that these episodes are particularly common with anticholinergic drugs (Agid et al. 1984; Serby et al. 1978; Sweet et al. 1976). They argue that anticholinergic drugs further aggravate the already impaired cholinergic function in PD (Agid et al. 1984). Confusional episodes are frequently of sudden onset and are associated with intense anxiety and agitation (Damasio et al. 1971). They are sometimes accompanied by hallucinations and delusions. Frequently the beginnings of the confusional state can be traced to a change in treatment (Rondot et al. 1984). In other cases, the cause may be concomitant systemic illness or subdural hematomas caused by falls. In one study, agitated confusion became increasingly frequent with levodopa treatment and was observed in 60 percent of patients taking levodopa for six years (Sweet et al. 1976). Another report showed a relationship between antecedent electroencephalographic abnormalities and the later development of a confusional syndrome on bromocriptine (Serby et al. 1980).

Psychotic Reactions

Psychotic reactions, sometimes associated with confusion, are a common side effect of treatment with antiparkinson medication (Danielczyk 1984; Lipper 1976; Serby 1980; Serby et al. 1978). Levodopa, bromocriptine, amantadine, and anticholinergics have all been implicated. A couple of reports suggest that psychotic features in patients treated with bromocriptine are more florid and persist longer than those associated with levodopa (Calne et al. 1978; Pearce and Pearce 1978). In one study, 37 percent of patients had hallucinations at some point during treatment; treatment with multiple drugs, especially anticholinergic agents, was felt to be important in the pathogenesis of hallucinations (Tanner et al. 1983). Hallucinations associated with use of amantadine may be potentiated by concurrent use of anticholinergics (McClelland 1981). These psychotic episodes may be especially common in patients with preexisting dementia (Celesia and Wanamaker 1972; Sacks et al. 1972).

The psychoses are frequently stereotyped for any particular individual, although various forms exist (Goetz et al. 1982). They often occur within a clear sensorium. Visual hallucinations are more common than auditory, but other senses may become involved. Hallucinations may seem benign to the individual, representing known people. In other cases, hallucinations may be extremely threatening, with associated paranoid delusions (Rondot et al. 1984; Sweet et al. 1976). Psychotic episodes may occur early in the course of antiparkinson therapy, especially in individuals who have had previous psychotic experiences (Goodwin et al. 1971; Klawans 1978). Patients with preexisting schizophrenia may have an acute exacerbation of their illness on starting treatment; some researchers think that this diagnosis is a contraindication to using levodopa (Klawans 1978). Other investigators think that schizophrenia and idiopathic PD infrequently occur within the same person (Rabins 1982). Nightmares, night terrors, and sleep disruption may occur (Klawans 1978; Nausieda et al. 1984). Hypomanic reactions can be precipitated (Celesia and Wanamaker 1972; Goodwin 1971) and may be associated with inappropriate sexual behavior. Psychotic episodes may also occur later in the course of PD on a steady regimen of antiparkinson medication (Celesia and Barr 1970; Goetz et al. 1982). In some cases, psychosis may represent psychotic depression.

Patient Evaluation

The first step in the evaluation is to take a careful medical and psychiatric history, with special emphasis on the mental status examination. Searching for antecedent or current evidence of systemic and neurologic illness is critical before attributing cognitive change to a primary degenerative dementia or to current drug treatment. The manner of onset and type of progression need to be assessed. A history of drug abuse is important. All of the medications the patient is taking need to be evaluated. History of past psychotic or affective disorder is important in judging potential reactions to antiparkinson medicine. Mental status examination may reveal hallucinations, delusions, affective disturbance, confusion, disorientation, and aphasia, as well as impaired memory, attention, and intellectual ability. Clues for depression that may be masquerading as dementia need to be examined (Spar 1982). On physical examination, evidence of focal neurologic signs other than those usually seen in PD may reveal another pathologic process. Visual and auditory acuity should be carefully examined because disorders in these senses may contribute to apparent cognitive decline. Peripheral signs and symptoms indicative of anticholinergic toxicity need to be assessed (Dysken et al. 1978).

Laboratory screening should include complete blood count, sedimentation rate, blood urea nitrogen, glucose, electrolytes, vitamin B_{12}, folate, liver function tests, thyroid function tests, VDRL, urinalysis, electrocardiogram, and chest X ray (Spar 1982). Formal psychological testing may further clarify the nature of the cognitive decline. A lumbar puncture may be necessary to evaluate the possibility of central nervous system infection, and an electroencephalogram may be helpful in evaluating an epileptogenic or structural disorder underlying the mental deterioration (Benson 1983). Computed tomography (CT) of the head may also be helpful in identifying a focal brain lesion. In one study, the presence of organic mental syndrome in a parkinsonian population was invariably associated with CT signs of cerebral atrophy (Sroka et al. 1981). By contrast, patients without evidence of organic mental syndrome were indistinguishable from an age-adjusted control group regarding structural changes on their scans. Another study demonstrated consistently significant correlations between cognitive impairment and central atrophy, but not with general cortical atrophy (Portin et al. 1984).

Specific Treatments

The treatment of the organic mental syndrome in PD depends entirely on the etiology of the cognitive deficit. As soon as various systemic and neurologic disorders have been ruled out, disorders intrinsic to the disease and side effects of its treatment become the focus. The dementia associated with PD is a progressive degenerative disorder for which there is no cure. Nevertheless, there is evidence that, at least temporarily, levodopa may improve cognitive function (Beardsley and Puletti 1971; Halgin et al. 1977). In some cases, it may improve attention span without increasing overall cognitive ability (Bowen et al. 1975). Some investigators found that levodopa improved intellectual functioning during the first year of treatment, but after 30 months most patients did not maintain the improvement (Loranger et al. 1972b, 1973). There was little or no relationship between physical or affective improvement and intellectual improvement. Others have also found that changes in motor and cognitive function are not necessarily parallel (Marsden 1984; Rafal et al. 1984). The "off" condition, an episodic, akinetic state seen during long-term levodopa treatment, may exacerbate memory problems (Delis et al. 1982). Besides pharmacotherapy, ultimately the mainstay of treatment must be the usual psychosocial approaches used in patients with dementia (Roth 1978).

When the organic mental syndrome is secondary to depression, the treatment is directed toward depression. The initiation of levodopa treatment may alleviate the depressive symptoms frequently seen in PD, although levodopa is generally not an effective antidepressant (Mayeux et al. 1984). In various studies, tricyclic antidepressants have been very effective for depression in parkinsonian patients (Andersen et al. 1980; Damasio et al. 1971; Rondot et al. 1984). Antidepressants with less anticholinergic effect, like desipramine and nortriptyline, are less likely to cause toxic reactions, especially in individuals already on other anticholinergic medications. Many patients improve in mood even though there may be no improvement in their physical condition (Mindham 1970). As with most elderly patients, initiation of treatment should be with low doses, with the dosage gradually increasing over time. Electroconvulsive therapy is another treatment for depression in PD that has been shown to be effective in a number of reports (Holcomb et al. 1983; Young et al. 1985; Yudofsky 1979).

Acute confusional states are frequently caused by antiparkinson drugs. Most of these reactions can be controlled by lowering the dose of medication; sometimes the medication may need to be temporarily stopped (Bianchine 1980; Sroka et al. 1981; Sweet et al. 1976; Yahr et al. 1969). When anticholinergic agents are being used concomitantly with levodopa, lowering or eliminating the anticholinergic drug may be sufficient to eliminate the confusional state (Klawans 1978). After withdrawal, symptoms may persist for up to two weeks (Burton and Calne 1984). Eliminating other psychotropic medications may also alleviate the disorder. Occasionally small doses of neuroleptics may be necessary (Sweet and McDowell 1975), but must be used with caution because of their anticholinergic and extrapyramidal side effects.

Psychosis may be caused by all antiparkinson medications, and will usually respond within several days to lowering or discontinuing the offending agent (Goetz et al. 1982; Mayeux 1984). If the psychosis has confusional elements, anticholinergics or amantadine may be playing a primary role and should be withdrawn before lowering levodopa (Klawans 1978). If the psychosis continues, levodopa may need to be lowered or temporarily discontinued. Hallucinations associated with simultaneous use of anticholinergics and amantadine may disappear with withdrawal of anticholinergics (McClelland 1981). In some cases, the severity and persistence of the psychosis may necessitate use of neuroleptics. Haloperidol and phenothiazines in low doses have been used with success (Hale and Bellizzi 1980; Rondot et al. 1984); sometimes only several days of treatment are necessary (Klawans 1978). Benzodiazepines in low doses may be used to control the agitation associated with such reactions (Burton and Calne 1984; Damasio et al. 1971), but long-acting preparations should be avoided in the older patient. Hypomanic reactions to levodopa usually respond to a lowering of the dose (Celesia and Barr 1970; McClelland 1981). Lithium should be used with caution in manic parkinsonian patients because toxic reactions are common. In one study, 11 of 15 elderly bipolar patients with extrapyramidal syndromes developed neurotoxicity at low serum levels of lithium (Himmelhoch et al. 1980).

Drug-Disease Interactions

Various drugs used to treat psychiatric disturbances in patients with PD may produce side effects possibly related to the altered physiology. Tricyclic antidepressants can usually be used without adverse consequences (Andersen et al. 1980; Damasio et al. 1971; Mayeux 1982); those with low anticholinergic effect should be used. Individuals who have preexisting hypotension as a result of their PD may be susceptible, however, to development of increased orthostatic hypotension. The anticholinergic effects of tricyclics may also cause a worsening in mental status in those patients with dementia. Other anticholinergic effects that must be anticipated are urinary retention and the precipitation of an attack of narrow angle glaucoma. On the positive side, in some patients, tricyclics may actually cause an amelioration of extrapyramidal symptoms, particularly rigidity and akinesia (Andersen et al. 1980; Mayeux 1982). Tremor is less affected and may worsen in some cases (Andersen et al. 1980). Electroconvulsive therapy, another effective modality in the treatment of depression, may also improve parkinsonian symptoms (Holcomb et al. 1983; Young et al. 1985; Yudofsky 1979), even without substantial improvement in affective symptoms (Young et al. 1985).

Neuroleptics must be used cautiously because they may potentiate anticholinergic effects as well as exacerbate orthostatic hypotension. They should be used in low doses because their antidopaminergic effect tends to worsen extrapyramidal symptoms (Bianchine 1980).

Lithium must also be used with caution because it may aggravate parkinsonian symptoms (Himmelhoch et al. 1980; Kelwala et al. 1984), even at relatively low doses. Further deterioration in cognitive function may also occur. Lithium has been reported to improve the "on-off" phenomenon in PD (Coffey et al. 1982). This therapeutic effect, however, remains controversial (Reches and Fahn 1983). In some cases, lithium has been reported to improve levodopa-induced dyskinesias; other reports indicate a worsening (Coffey et al. 1984; Dalen and Steg 1973). There have also been reports of worsening of parkinsonian symptoms with diazepam (Hansten 1985).

Drug-Drug Interactions

The potential effects of drug-drug interactions must always be monitored carefully. Tricyclic antidepressants and neuroleptics have anticholinergic properties that may augment the anticholinergic effects of antiparkinson drugs. This additional anticholinergic effect may cause delayed gastric emptying, leading to decreased absorption of levodopa with decreased therapeutic effect (Bianchine 1976; Hansten 1985; Salzman 1984). Cessation of tricyclics and neuroleptics may then result in altered serum levels of levodopa. Neuroleptics may also negate the therapeutic effect of antiparkinson agents on extrapyramidal symptoms.

Monoamine oxidase inhibitors should not be used in patients on levodopa because there is the great potential for development of severe hypertensive reactions

(Bianchine 1980; Hansten 1985). L-deprenyl, a selective monoamine oxidase-B inhibitor with antiparkinson effects, is being studied for its antidepressant effects. The results of pilot studies on its efficacy for depression are mixed (Mann et al. 1984). Although it has been used with safety in patients on levodopa (Sandler and Stern 1982), some have observed potentiation of cardiovascular effects in patients given tyramine (Simpson and White 1984).

When initiating treatment with levodopa, orthostatic hypotension may occur, although tolerance to this effect is frequently seen (Bianchine 1976, 1980). Levodopa and tricyclics may be combined, however, without blood pressure disturbance (Damasio et al. 1971). In one study, 11 patients were treated with the levodopa-tricyclic antidepressant combination without any blood pressure disturbance (Damasio et al. 1971). In another study, when used in combination, nortriptyline and levodopa caused disabling orthostatic hypotension in two out of 22 patients (Andersen et al. 1980). Tricyclic antidepressants should be started in low doses and increased slowly, with blood pressure carefully monitored.

Chapter 100

The Patient with Stroke

Stroke, the most common manifestation of cerebrovascular disease, is the sudden onset of a focal, nonconvulsive neurologic or behavioral deficit. The diverse symptoms and courses depend on the localization and laterality of the lesion, the extent of brain tissue destruction, distant effects, the underlying pathophysiologic processes, and a number of general factors. The symptoms may be solely behavioral, but more typically include identifiable neurologic signs.

Stroke continues to be the third leading cause of death in the United States (after heart disease and cancer), killing approximately 275,000 and disabling another 300,000 people yearly. Half of those admitted to the hospital acutely die within the first three weeks, and half of the survivors within three years (Goodstein 1983). Overall incidence of stroke is estimated at 150 per 100,000, and the rate more than doubles for each successive decade over 55 years (Kurtzke 1984). Incidence has declined by close to 45 percent over the last 30 years, however, more rapidly than any other component of cardiovascular mortality (Garraway et al. 1979). This has largely been attributed to the treatment of hypertension (Garraway and Whisnant 1987), the prevention of rheumatic heart disease, the recognition and diagnosis of transient ischemic attacks, and anticoagulant, antiplatelet, antiarrhythmic, and myocardium-preserving therapies (Hachinski 1984). Myocardial infarction remains the most common cause of death in survivors of stroke (Adams et al. 1984; Komrad et al. 1984).

Psychiatrists, and particularly those caring for the elderly, are increasingly likely to see patients with cerebrovascular disease, which should be considered in the differential diagnosis of confusion or atypical mental disorder, particularly of acute onset. Recognition of particular patterns of focal cognitive changes may be crucial to the correct diagnosis. More frequent, perhaps, will be consultation on the patient already identified with stroke. The clinical evaluation will require some familiarity with the anatomy of the cerebral vasculature and with some of the treatments for stroke. These will be reviewed briefly before considering the organic mental syndromes per se.

Anatomy

The anatomy of the vascular supply to the brain as well as vessel size determines the manner of clinical presentation. The arterial blood supply to the brain derives from four main vessels that arise from the aortic arch or its major branches. For each hemisphere, the anterior circulation, consisting of the anterior and middle cerebral arteries, derives from the ipsilateral internal carotid artery. The brain stem, cerebellum, and postero-inferior cerebral hemispheres are supplied by the vessels of the posterior circulation. These derive from the vertebral arteries, which unite to form the basilar and then redivide into the posterior cerebral arteries and other major arteries. These territories are crucial to understanding the localization of poststroke deficits (Angevine and Cotman 1981). Variability in development, however, as well as extensive anastomoses, both at the vessels' origin (through the Circle of Willis) and via end branch collateralization, may result in deviation from the expected clinical syndromes outlined here.

Occlusions of the middle cerebral artery lead to a contralateral hemiparesis and hemisensory loss, often with hemianopia. Aphasia is common with lesions in the dominant hemisphere (Benson 1979), and neglect syndromes with lesions in the nondominant hemisphere (Mesulam 1985). Deep infarctions are liable to produce dense, global hemiparesis. Anterior cerebral artery infarction affects the leg more than the arm; incontinence is a frequent finding. Mutism or decreased initiation of speech, personality changes, or abulia may be so prominent as to suggest a global dementia (Lishman 1978).

Occlusion of branches of the posterior cerebral artery lead to a contralateral hemianopia and/or visual agnosias. Memory disturbances due to damaged hippocampal and limbic structures of the inferotemporal surface of the temporal lobes are probably more common than is recognized (Lishman 1978). A wide number of brainstem syndromes have been described with unilateral or bilateral motor findings; these may produce altered consciousness or other mental symptoms (Fisher 1982).

At times the cerebrovascular insult leads not to segmental infarction and one of the classic stroke syndromes, but rather to a more diffuse injury. For example, hypotension (from ruptured aneurysm, cardiac arrest, ventricular fibrillation, or surgery) produces the so-called watershed infarct, with necrosis along the territories between two major arteries. Microembolization can produce widespread damage in a similar distribution (Malone et al. 1981; Torvik 1984). Chronic hypertension sometimes impairs circulation through the vessels penetrating cerebral white matter, resulting in multifocal demyelination known as Binswanger's disease (Cummings and Benson 1983a).

Treatment of Stroke

The pathogenesis and treatment of acute stroke are areas under active investigation that cannot be covered in this chapter. The interested reader is referred elsewhere (Charness 1985; Hass 1983; Millikan and McDowell 1981). Similarly, treatment for disease processes underlying stroke are covered elsewhere (Chapter 102).

The decreasing incidence of stroke has been attributed to the primary and secondary prevention of risk factors. Hypertension is the most significant; the incidence of both atherothrombotic stroke and intraparenchymal hemorrhage is increased proportionate to the elevation of diastolic blood pressure greater than 83 mm Hg and systolic greater than 130 mm Hg. Other risk factors are somewhat stronger for peripheral or coronary vascular disease and become less important with advancing age: smoking, elevated serum cholesterol, low-density lipoprotein-cholesterol complexes, diabetes mellitus, and obesity (Wolf et al. 1983a).

Cardiac impairment is the most important factor after age and hypertension, doubling the risk of stroke for any level of blood pressure. Paroxysmal, intermittent, and recent onset of atrial fibrillation are ominous precursors of stroke; recurrence of embolization seems to cluster in the early months of onset of this disturbance of cardiac rhythm (Wolf et al. 1983b). Other causes of embolus include valvular disease, myocardial infarction, and complications of cardiac surgery. Mitral valve prolapse, a common cardiac abnormality, shows an association with stroke (Barnett et al. 1980).

Oral contraceptives have been associated with thrombosis and subarachnoid hemorrhage, the latter particularly in women older than 35 years who smoke cigarettes (Longstreth and Swanson 1984). An increased hematocrit may lead to increase in blood viscosity that achieves pathologic significance in narrowed small penetrating arteries and in high-grade major artery stenosis (Wolf et al. 1983a).

A transient ischemic attack (TIA) may presage myocardial infarction (MI). Indeed, fatal MI has affected the estimates of the long-term outcome of medical or surgical treatment for TIA and, in one study on carotid endarterectomy, was responsible for twice as many deaths as stroke. The investigation and management of cardiac and vascular disease in the patient with TIA has not been well established (Adams et al. 1984). A proper discussion of antihypertensive, antiarrhythmic, antiatherogenic, and valvular disease treatments can be found elsewhere (Petersdorf et al. 1983); treatments for cardiovascular disease may have their own neuropsychiatric consequences (see Chapter 102).

Blood vessels are not simple conduits but rather structures dependent on the integrity of the endothelial cell layer and hemodynamic factors; desquamation, platelet adhesion, and loss of normal cell orientation can form thrombogenic sites and pathologic changes in the underlying smooth muscle tissue (Grady 1984). Anticoagulation with warfarin reduces the long-term risk of recurrent embolization by up to 80 to 90 percent for those with rheumatic heart disease, atrial arrhythmia, prosthetic heart valves, and MI (Charness 1985; Millikan and McDowell 1981). Bleeding, of course, is the acute hazard. Altered liver metabolism can strongly affect serum levels of many medications, leading to toxicity or decreased effectiveness. Antiplatelet agents including acetylsalicylic acid (ASA), dipyridamole, and sulfinpyrazone have been studied alone and in combination. Three of four studies showed that ASA caused a significant decrease in subsequent MI and death in patients with TIA. Sulfinpyrazone, aside from some trends, did not show a greater effectiveness in reducing recurrent TIA or stroke. Dipyridamole has a different means of action, but as yet several studies have not shown an advantage over ASA (Dyken 1983; Kistler et al. 1984).

Carotid endarterectomy is considered a mainstay of treatment for preventing the recurrence of TIA or stroke from an extracranial carotid artery, although no well-performed, controlled, randomized study has confirmed this. Patients with tightly stenotic lesions of the internal carotid and occlusion of the contralateral system or tandem lesions have had poorer outcome. Although a subgroup (tight lesions less than 1.5 mm) may be in greater danger, there is little evidence in favor of operating on an asymptomatic bruit (Kistler et al. 1984).

Clinical Evaluation

Those few studies on psychopathology due to stroke suggest that neuropsychiatric residuum is common. Coughlan and Humphrey (1982) reported problems with self-care in two-thirds of stroke survivors, with restricted mobility in half; memory deficits and difficulty in oral or written expression comprehension were common. Personality changes, consisting mostly of irritability, loss of self-control, impatience, lower tolerance for frustration, emotional lability, self-centeredness, and decreased initiative occurred in two-thirds of the patients.

The mental status examination is the key to relating stroke deficits and mental and behavioral symptoms. It must, of course, be supplemented by physical examination (especially of the cardiovascular and neurologic systems), laboratory tests, and imaging procedures. These, again, are reviewed elsewhere (Adams and Victor 1981; Bradley et al. 1984; Frakowiak and Wise 1983; Kuhl 1984; Sandok 1980). Full cognitive evaluation is necessary to interpret the symptoms of the stroke patient as the psychiatrist may encounter disturbances of behavior that do not fit well into conventional nomenclature. The deficits may also require the clinician to evaluate the mood, affect, and behavior differently (Strub and Black 1977).

The ability to focus and shift attention underlies all cognitive functions. Tests such as the familiar digit span and a continuous performance task are often useful. Evidence suggests that four regions provide an integrated network for the spatial distribution of directed attention: the posterior parietal lobe, the cingulate gyrus, the frontal lobe, and the reticular activating system (Mesulam 1981).

Failure to identify the inability to use language leads to many pitfalls. The fluent (Wernicke's) aphasic may be called "crazy," the nonfluent (Broca's) dismissed as uncooperative. Fluency, comprehension, repetition, naming, reading, writing, and the ability to perform actions on command, so-called ideomotor apraxia, should all be assessed (Benson 1979).

A variety of visual phenomena may occur. Occipital infarction may produce functional blindness without awareness (Anton's syndrome). Patients may lose the ability to recognize familiar faces or locations. An inability to copy drawings occurs with many lesions and provides a simple bedside test.

Memory may reliably be tested at the bedside if the patient is attentive and if information is presented in a form that the patient can perceive accurately. Both verbal and visual recall should be assessed. An experienced neuropsychologist can be a valuable resource to clarify ambiguous findings and quantify a deficit for future reference.

Diagnostic Categories

The DSM-III-R (American Psychiatric Association 1987) delineates a series of organic mental syndromes, defined as "a constellation of psychological or behavioral signs and symptoms without reference to etiology" (p. 97), but adds, in addition, the concept of organic mental disorder when there is an associated Axis III diagnosis. For a large number of behavioral consequences of stroke, however, the reports of cognitive and affective changes are still at the anecdotal stage. The following account attempts to synthesize this diverse literature. We will discuss the syndromes under neutral headings (e.g., hallucinosis instead of organic hallucinosis) in the belief that it is the role of future studies to clarify criteria, phenomenologic features, and the issue of etiology. The separation of functional and organic syndromes is probably artificial; ultimately it may be more useful to name the former idiopathic (Cummings 1985a) and the latter secondary, recording the phenomenologic syndrome on Axis I and the identified pathology on Axis III.

Delirium

An essential feature of delirium, or confusional state, is the inability to sustain attention, both tonic (the state of consciousness or level of awareness) and phasic (the selective directed flow of thought). The patient may be either hypoactive or hyperactive. The retarded, withdrawn patient may elude identification and the disorder be eventually mistaken for dementia. The reader is referred to Plum and Posner (1980) and Liston (Chapter 93) for a discussion of investigation and treatment of delirium in general. We will discuss particular diagnostic concerns in the patient with cerebrovascular disease.

In acute stroke, alterations of consciousness can occur from the focal injury itself or from mass effects, general metabolic abnormalities, or as secondary effects of medical treatment. Most often, disturbance of consciousness is due to a subcortical or brain-stem lesion, the posterior circulation being, therefore, more frequently implicated. Segarra (1970) outlined two chronic unresponsive states termed *akinetic mutism*: an agitated, attentive-appearing form in which eye movements are preserved, and an apathetic, somnolent, mute form with ophthalmoplegia and loss of pupillary light reflexes. The former is due to anterior cerebral and/or communicating artery infarction; the latter to occlusion in the basilar artery system, with damage to nuclei in the rostral midbrain (Caplan 1980; Graff-Radford et al. 1984). Injury to the posterior hypothalamus causes behaviors that range from those resembling normal sleepiness through to coma (Plum and Posner 1980). In the "locked-in" state, consciousness is preserved despite paralysis of all but oculomotor movements due to interruption of descending motor pathways. Symmetrical destruction of the putamen and globus pallidus results in mutism, extreme hypokinesia, and rigidity. Destruction of the neocortical mantle leaves a patient in the so-called apallic state, reacting in only an elementary fashion, lying mute and immobile with open eyes that may follow objects or roam (Plum and Posner 1980; Segarra 1970). A trial of stimulants or dopamine agonists may benefit the occasional patient.

Reports of disturbance of consciousness due to purely cortical lesions are less common. Severely agitated states have been found with bilateral lesions in the posterior cerebral artery distribution, often with visual field defects. Horenstein et al. (1967) found that infarctions of the undersurface of the temporal and occipital lobes caused restlessness, forced shouting, and easy distractibility with exaggerated responses to visual, auditory, or tactile stimuli. Somewhat similar symptoms appear in a similar group of patients with damage to the medial temporal region (Medina et al. 1977). Infarcts of the nondominant supramarginal and angular gyri have caused confusional states. Mesulam et al. (1976) postulated that sensory information converging on these important secondary and tertiary association areas is interrupted; similar changes may result from the disconnection of neocortical and limbic structures.

Dementia

The hallmark of dementia is acquired global intellectual impairment implying, in general, diffuse brain disease. DSM-III-R specifically requires memory impairment in the absence of delirium plus deficits in cognition, personality, judgment, or one of the so-called higher cortical functions (e.g., aphasia). In DSM-III-R, the diagnosis of multi-infarct dementia is made on the basis of the above features plus the presence of neurologic deficits and a course consistent with multiple strokes. As discussed in Chapter 94 and elsewhere (Read and Jarvik 1984), the diversity of pathologic processes and the varied distribution of lesions result in heterogeneity of dementia due to cerebrovascular disease.

Widely accepted as the second most prevalent cause of dementia, identification may be facilitiated by the use of an Ischemia Scale developed by Hachinski (1983) and validated by cerebral blood flow studies. Fisher (1982) is of the opinion that dementia due to so-called lacunar state is rare, although it is the pathology most frequently conjured up by the term. Tomlinson et al. (1970) found that cortical infarctions were common and that the volume of infarcted tissue was the best predictor of dementia; but small infarcts in the angular gyrus (Benson et al. 1982) or thalamus (Brust 1983; Fisher 1982) have been mistaken for dementia of the Alzheimer type (DAT). In an extensive review, Liston and La Rue (1983a, 1983b) concluded that the concept of multi-infarct dementia had not been rigorously validated. Our experience, however, is that vascular events are the most frequently overlooked causes of dementia in patients who come with presumptive diagnosis of DAT. This misidentification leads to inaccurate predictions of inevitable progression, which can be self-fulfilling. Specific treatments for multi-infarct dementia are in the experimental stage, as reviewed in Chapter 108.

Amnestic Syndrome

Memory is the ability to recall previously learned material. Three sequentially dependent steps are differentiated: registration of information transmitted in one or more modalities; retention or storage; and retrieval. As each can be affected in isolation, they are probably mediated by separate neuroanatomic sites or processes. Clinical distinction is made among immediate recall (repetition), short-term memory (recall) after minutes or hours, and long-term (or remote) memory. Although amnesia classically refers to the inability to learn new information (Benson 1978), the DSM-III-R criteria include impairment of both short- and long-term memory (see also Chapter 94).

Amnesia due to stroke has no specific treatment, but several syndromes may be recognized. Other mental syndromes should be sought out first (e.g., inattention due to delirium interferes with registration); depression or anxiety may contribute to decreased memory either by inattention or by mechanisms similar to other subcortical disturbances with problems in retrieval ("forgetfulness") (Cummings and Benson 1984). Dementias include memory disturbance with global cognitive dysfunction. Patients with aphasia, particularly anomic aphasia, may present with "memory" complaints; however, they have "forgotten" the words for events, not the events themselves.

Transient global amnesia produces an inability to record ongoing information without alteration in the level of alertness. Patients are painfully aware of their problem and ask repeated questions about their environment and themselves. A retrograde amnesia may involve many years but shrinks almost completely with recovery; memory for the episode, which may last many hours, is permanently impaired. Unlike psychomotor epilepsy, the patient can carry on higher cognitive functions, personal identity is intact, and the neurologic examination is within normal limits (Shuping et al. 1980). The cause is assumed to be due to ischemia in the medial temporal lobe structures from posterior cerebral artery occlusion. Two-thirds of patients were found to have one or more of the risk factors for stroke. Recurrence is uncommon, although a few patients are subject to multiple attacks (Rowan and Protass 1979).

Medial temporal lobe infarction may present with a confusional state that clears to a residual amnesia; a variable retrograde amnesia also occurs (the amnestic stroke). Destruction of thalamic nuclei have also produced permanent deficits in new learning (Benson et al. 1974). Severe anoxia with or without hypotension may leave amnesia or a mixed organic mental syndrome. The major lesion again appears to be medial temporal necrosis (Cummings et al. 1984). Confabulation is usually a transient symptom in the setting of an acute amnesia. It does not correlate with suggestibility, disorientation, or the degree of amnesia but is related, however, to the loss of the ability to monitor responses and may be associated with significant bilateral frontal lobe dysfunction in these patients (Benson 1978).

Perceptual Abnormalities

An organic "secondary" hallicinosis is diagnosed when a hallucination attributable to a specific etiologic factor persists in a normal state of consciousness (see Chapter 95). Formed auditory hallucinations may occur with lesions in the superolateral temporal lobe. Unformed (or elementary) ones may result from pontine lesions. Temporal lobe lesions may leave hearing intact but change the quality of perceived sound (Adams and Victor 1981).

Formed and unformed hallucinations have been reported with a variety of lesions in the visual system. Partial deafferentation of the anterior visual pathways may give rise to unformed images with startling auditory stimuli (auditory-visual synesthesia) (Jacobs et al. 1981). Peduncular hallucinations are vivid, well-formed images, occasionally smaller than normal size (Lilliputian), which are usually recognized as not being real. These appear in ischemic episodes affecting possibly the midbrain reticular formation with nonspecific excitation of the cortex or specialized thalamic nuclei. Since the hallucinations are most common in the evening and sleep disorders are present, they may represent intrusions of dreaming (Caplan 1980).

"Release" hallucinations are formed, persistent images with variable content that appear in the visual-field defect (Brust and Behrens 1977); the lesions are more common in the posterior cerebral artery territory on the right (Lance 1976). Injury to the occipital pole of the calcarine cortex produces stationary lights or stars; with more anterior lesions, these seem to move from the periphery to the center. Visions that are stereotyped, lifelike, and use only simple repetitive actions but do not enact a scene may arise from the parieto-occipital cortex (including parastriate area 19) (British Medical Journal 1977).

A wide variety of illusions may be caused by lesions of occipital, occipito-parietal, or occipito-temporal cortex, more frequently again when the nondominant hemisphere is involved. These most often present as change in size, displacement in space, angulation with or without movement, reduplication or perseveration, and/or changes in color. The alterations in size may be limited to half or a quarter of the field, making objects appear bizarre or grotesque (Adams and Victor 1981; Caplan 1980). "Central dazzle," in which there is a painless intolerance to light, has been attributed to infarction in the right posterior cerebral artery territory, involving the thalamus and occipital and posterior inferior medial temporal regions; this may be analogous to the dysesthesia and hyperpathia of the thalamic syndrome (Cummings and Crittinger 1981).

In general, these hallucinations do not require or respond particularly well to neuroleptic treatment. Reassurance and explanation can be surprisingly helpful. Neuroleptics may help the patient who elaborates secondary delusions. Specific treatments are anecdotal. Anticonvulsants may rarely suppress "release" hallucinations. In one report (Caplan 1980), 5-hydroxytryptophan treated both the sleep disorder and peduncular hallucinations. Partial relief was obtained in central dazzle with amitriptyline and perphenazine (Cummings and Crittinger 1981) and in a similar auditory syndrome with amitriptyline. Indoleamine compounds include many psychogens with prominent hallucinatory properties. Pharmacologic manipulation of the serotonergic system may prove useful in disorders of aberrant or annoying sensation or dysaesthesia. Pimozide, a neuroleptic used for monosymptomatic hypochondriacal psychosis, on the assumption that it modulates sensory gating, may also be useful in this regard.

Delusional Syndromes

There are few studies specifically linking delusions with stroke. A study of patients with mixed pathologies (Cummings 1985b) found four general groups of organic delusions: simple persecutory delusions consisting of transient, poorly structured elementary beliefs (e.g., theft, unfaithfulness); complex persecutory delusions (delusional jealousy, Capgras' syndrome, Schneiderian symptoms, elaborate paranoid systems); grandiose delusions; and delusions related to specific neurologic deficits such as neglect. Simple delusions appeared most frequently in demented patients in the early or middle phases of their illness. Left hemisphere lesions were more likely to cause a schizophrenia-like delusion.

Posterior aphasics, unaware of their deficits and unable to comprehend what is happening around them, often show a marked paranoid syndrome similar to that seen with acquired deafness. Serious agitated behavior, including physical attack against medical staff, family, or other patients, is particular common with pure word deafness and Wernicke's aphasia, much less so with other posterior aphasias, and almost unknown with anterior aphasia (Benson 1979).

Capgras' syndrome (the delusion of substitution) has been linked to the disorder of "reduplicative paramnesia." In a small series, this particular delusion was seen with bilateral frontal and nondominant parietal lobe damage (Alexander et al. 1979). Temporal lobe epilepsy patients with lesions on the left are at particular risk for the development of psychosis (Sherwin et al. 1982). Recent studies on the neuropathology of schizophrenia implicate changes in brain-stem and limbic structures (Stevens 1982). There has been a report of focal lesions in the ventral tegmental area producing persecutory psychosis (Trimble and Cummings 1981).

A delusion that results from a structural injury may not remit completely, but the distress, agitation, and behavioral consequences may be lessened with sufficient doses of high-potency neuroleptics. This is particularly important in calming the paranoid syndrome of posterior aphasics. Low doses (e.g., haloperidol 0.5 to 1.0 mg two or three times per day) usually suffice. If high doses are necessary or the sedation that accompanies lower-potency neuroleptics is desired, the effects of the drug on blood pressure should be watched closely (see also Chapter 95).

Mood Disorders

Many workers have presumed that the depression accompanying stroke is re-active to disability, but comparing orthopedic and stroke patients with comparable physical impairment revealed more depression in the latter. Half of the patients with acute stroke have clinically significant depressions, one-quarter with neurovegetative symptoms (Robinson et al. 1983). On follow-up, at least one-third have a persistent depression (Lim and Ebrahim 1983; Robinson and Price 1982; Robinson et al. 1984). While a number of factors adversely affected return to work (older age, greater dis-ability, blue collar or farm worker) (Howard et al. 1985), depression is significantly related to the failure to resume premorbid social or occupational activities (Feibel and Springer 1982).

Treatment of depressed stroke patients with nortriptyline at therapeutic serum levels has been beneficial (Lipsey et al. 1984). Nonsuppression of cortisol in response to dexamethasone was associated with depression, but with a substantial number of both false positives and false negatives (Lipsey et al. 1983). Longitudinal study of poststroke patients, however, suggests a significant incidence of depression emerging months after a stroke and apparently reactive to physical and/or cognitive difficulties (Robinson et al. 1984).

The location of lesions causing depression is not random. Although a syndrome with irritability, loss of interest, and difficulty concentrating in addition to depression has been reported with right hemisphere infarction (Folstein et al. 1977), most studies indicate more frequent and severe depression, including the endogenomorphic syn-drome, with injury on the left (Finklestein et al. 1982). Using DSM-III criteria for major depression and the Hamilton Depression Scale, Lipsey et al. (1983) found the closer the injury to the left frontal pole, the greater was the incidence and degree of depression even with bilateral hemispheric strokes. Impaired communication of or self-awareness of mood may lead to an underidentification of depression with right hemisphere lesions (Gainotti 1983; Ross 1981).

Mania may occur in the patient with stroke, although uncommonly. Krautham-mer and Klerman (1978) outlined a concept of secondary mania as a clinical syndrome resulting from a variety of pathophysiologic pathways. It appeared later than the average age of onset of idiopathic mania, and patients lacked a family history of affective disorder. Focal lesions associated with secondary mania involve the dien-cephalic structures or adjacent areas of the basal forebrain, more often on the right, and affect areas important to the modulation of emotion and neurovegetative func-tions (Cummings and Mendez 1984).

Pharmacologic agents have been advocated for major depression in stroke pa-tients; there are a variety of agents with low anticholinergic side effects (Gerner 1984). The initial dose should be less than that for younger patients or those who have not suffered brain injury. For the confused, severely depressed, or psychotic patient, the addition of low doses of high-potency neuroleptics (e.g., haloperidol, trifluoperazine) may be required, although there is a greater risk of tardive dyskinesia. Electrocon-vulsive therapy has been used safely and successfully in organic depressions (Karliner 1978). Its use is also to be considered when delusions are present with either phase of affective disorder. The indications, pretreatment evaluations, procedures, central nervous system effects, and contraindications have been well reviewed (Crowe 1984; Weiner 1979).

Manic syndromes from a variety of structural etiologies have responded favorably to lithium carbonate (Jampala and Abrams 1983). In the elderly, the therapeutic and toxic side effects appear at lower doses and plasma levels than in younger patients (Friedel 1903). Treatment should be started with 300 mg/day and advanced slowly and carefully. Anecdotal reports support a role for carbamazepine, alone or in combination with other medications, in the treatment of bipolar disorder (Post and Uhde 1985), but its value in patients with structural lesions is not well defined.

Stroke is a major stress ("life-event") for both patients and their families. Factors that affect the patient's reaction to stroke include the personalized meaning of the illness to the patient; loss of dignity; the self-perception of the specific loss of function, control, social standing and role, independence, appearance, and sexuality; the reactions of relatives, friends, and social network; fears of death, cognitive impairment, or disfigurement; rate of lack of improvement; and concurrent medical disorders and their treatments. Family and medical staff reactions of denial, anger, guilt, and unrealistic expectations may exacerbate these problems (Goodstein 1983).

Before undertaking psychotherapy, the patient's ability to comprehend, the degree of denial, and the need for medication should be carefully assessed. A significant number of fully physically restored stroke victims showed marked disturbances in social function (e.g., socialization in and outside the home, hobbies, interests) (Labi et al. 1980). While it is important to discuss and explore the inevitable themes of loss, rage, and narcissistic injury, the patient should be directed to resume rehabilitation and participate in family and social activities to "reengage" the world. Family, peer, and patient-family groups can be helpful in dealing with reactions to the patient's problems (Lezak 1978).

Personality and Psychosexual Problems

Personality change, as an isolated phenomenon, is rarely due to stroke, but may certainly accompany other deficits. Frontal lobe infarcts are most frequently involved. Chronic apathy or assaultiveness are the most troublesome problems (Blumer and Benson 1975; Lishman 1978) and can be refractory to treatments, as discussed above. Partial relief may be obtained when a complicating depression or delusion is treated (see also Chapter 98).

Psychosexual Disorders

Sexual behavior is subject to physiologic, psychological, and pharmacologic variables. Physical mobility, loss of spincter control, and sensory loss interfere greatly with stimulation and the mechanics of intercourse; tact is required to identify these problems. Damage to autonomic centers may cause a decrease in libido, as well as partial erections, impotence, delayed or retrograde ejaculation, impairment of lubrication or orgasm, and, in premenopausal women, transient or persistent amenorrhea (Binder 1984; Renshaw 1975). Further dysfunction may be induced by drugs used in the treatment of hypertension (methyldopa, guanethidine, clonidine, propranolol) (Hogan et al. 1980). Diazepam, barbiturates, neuroleptics (thioridazine), and antidepressants (trazodone) may impair sexual performance, as may the worry that resumption of sexual activity will precipitate a recurrence of the stroke. The perception of oneself as damaged, unattractive, and undesirable impedes sexual relations, as does depression or anxiety about performance. Nonverbal or emotional cues may be misinterpreted; there can be comparable difficulty in behaving in an amorous fashion (Renshaw 1975).

Injury to the frontal lobes may lead to a coarsening of sexual appetite and expression, with disinhibition or lack of concern for the partner (see also Chapter 96).

Paraphilias, especially exhibitionism, and promiscuity can appear with the "pseudo-psychopathic" variety of frontal lobe syndrome (Blumer and Benson 1975). If this is a severe problem, libido-reducing drugs (e.g., progesterone, neuroleptics) may be a consideration. (For further discussion refer to Section 22.)

Summary

Neuropsychiatric syndromes are common in stroke patients. Some appear to be reactive to the consequences of stroke and others to be more direct results of brain damage. Correct diagnosis and management evolve best from a clinical approach derived from neuroanatomic principles.

Firm recommendations for the treatment of organic mental disorders in stroke must await further data, but their correction in many cases plays a major role in improving the level of function regained. Indications for antidepressants and neuroleptics are clear in selected patients. Other treatments should be chosen judiciously but courageously in the face of compromised neuronal metabolism on the one hand and the possibility of reversible psychiatric dysfunction on the other. Innovative studies are needed to identify the key features of mental syndromes in stroke patients to enable better care of this large and growing group of patients.

Chapter 101

The Patient with Epilepsy

The Clinical Syndrome

Epilepsy is a disease characterized by recurrent seizures. Seizures result from synchronized electrical discharges of brain neurons that are expressed as motoric or sensory changes or altered state of consciousness. The clinical presentation of epilepsy is variable. Clinical, electroencephalographic (EEG), etiologic, therapeutic, anatomic, and pathologic criteria have been used to classify epilepsy at various times. By 1970, the International Clinical and Electroencephalographic Classification of Epileptic Seizures had been developed on the basis of both clinical and EEG criteria. This system divides epileptic seizures into the following main categories.

Partial Seizures (Focal Cerebral Epilepsy)

This is the most common type of epilepsy; seizures that first occur in adult life are almost always partial seizures (Solomon et al. 1983). Partial epilepsies are usually the result of acquired focal cerebral pathology including post-traumatic scars, neoplasms, localized degenerative disorders, arteriovenous malformations, and cerebrovascular infarcts. The electrical discharge in these seizures originates from a group of neurons in one of the hemispheres. Partial seizures are classified as follows:

1. Partial seizures with elementary symptomatology (motor, sensory, or autonomic focal seizures). These seizures generally do not affect the state of consciousness and may be expressed as focal motor, sensory, or autonomic, or as compound forms where various symptoms of the elementary subgroups appear at the same time.

2. Partial seizures with complex symptomatology (psychomotor epilepsy). The state of consciousness is almost always affected in these patients, and the clinical presentation of seizures is variable. In most cases, the EEG shows slow waves and spike discharges in the temporal lobe area. Some patients may only have momentary (one or two minutes) loss of awareness (staring spells). Others may have brief periods of stereotyped cognitive disturbances, including a strong sense of familiarity (deja vu) or unfamiliarity (jamais vu) or an experience of forced thinking. Partial complex seizures may present with affective symptomatology expressed as brief attacks of intense emotions. Fear is the most common affect resulting from seizures, although laughter (gelastic epilepsy) frequently occurs. In other cases, characteristic attacks with psychosensory symptomatology occur with illusions (micropsia or macropsia) or olfactory or gustatory hallucinations. Some patients have predominantly psychomotor symptomatology. These seizures begin with an aura, progress into a state of clouded consciousness along with stereotyped activity that may appear almost purposeful (automatisms), last approximately one to two minutes, and are followed by postictal confusion and amnesia. It should be emphasized that partial complex seizures may present as attacks with compound symptomatology, including cognitive, affective, psychosensory, and psychomotor symptoms.

3. Partial seizures secondarily generalized. The epileptogenic focus in these cases is in one of the hemispheres, and seizure episodes begin as partial seizures. The electrical discharge, however, spreads to centrencephalic structures (i.e., the diencephalon, mesencephalon, and reticular formation), and the patients proceed to develop the clinical symptomatology of generalized seizures.

Generalized Seizures

These seizures usually result in transient impairment of consciousness; motor changes, when they occur, are bilateral. The EEG shows bilateral symmetrical discharges from the onset of the attack. In contrast to partial seizures, the etiology of generalized epilepsy remains undetermined in most cases (Solomon et al, 1983). The generalized seizures are divided into: *1) absences* (petit mal), characterized by staring episodes of short duration accompanied frequently by eye blinking, and a characteristic EEG pattern of 3 Hz spike-and-wave discharges (similar EEG abnormalities are common in the relatives of these patients); *2) bilateral massive epileptic myoclonus* (myoclonic seizures), characterized by episodes of generalized myoclonic jerks and an EEG picture of polyspikes and waves; *3) infantile spasms* (salaam spells), which are massive spasms of flexor muscles, and an EEG pattern with high voltage delta waves and multifocal spikes (hypsarrhythmia); *4) generalized clonic seizures; 5) generalized tonic seizures; 6) generalized tonic-clonic seizures* (grand mal), which present with loss of consciousness, a tonic phase with an EEG consisting of rhythmic discharges of approximately 10 Hz, succeeded by a clonic phase with the EEG pattern interrupted by a spike-and-wave pattern, and followed by postictal confusion during which EEG slow waves predominate; *7) generalized atonic seizures* (minor motor epilepsy or epileptic drop attacks); and *8) generalized akinetic seizures* characterized by one-half minute to several minutes duration, an inability to move, falling (although the state of consciousness and the muscular tone remain unaffected), and a rhythmic spike-and-wave EEG pattern with fast and slow waves and polyspikes.

Unilateral Seizures

These seizures are limited to one side of the body, as a rule have the same clinical presentation as the generalized seizures, and show EEG abnormalities limited to the contralateral hemisphere. A characteristic tonic phase succeeded by a clonic phase distinguishes unilateral seizures from partial seizures.

Unclassified Seizures

This category includes seizure disorders that cannot be classified in any other category (e.g., reflex epilepsy, photosensitive epilepsy, communication-evoked epilepsy).

Behavioral Disorders of Epilepsy

Behavioral Disorders Related to Seizures

Some epileptic patients present behavioral changes shortly before, during, and after a seizure.

Prodromal symptoms. These are behavioral changes that build up before the onset of an epileptic discharge and last a few minutes, hours, or several days. Generally, epileptic patients do not complain spontaneously of prodromal symptoms. However, careful interviewing often reveals unpleasant mental experiences before seizures. These patients usually have clouded thinking and an inability to concentrate; they appear apathetic. In most cases, irritability and affective lability are present. Prodromata are more common in children than in adults and are more frequent in partial seizures with complex symptomatology than in other types of epilepsy.

Ictal behavioral changes. Epileptic auras are the initial events signaling the beginning of a seizure; they appear abruptly and last for a few seconds to one minute. The clinical manifestations of auras range from simple sensations to complex emotional or ideational disturbances. The symptoms are fairly specific for the brain region in which the seizure originates and, along with the EEG picture, can be essential for localization of the epileptic focus.

Seizures originating within the frontal lobes sometimes begin without an aura, although, if the focus is in the posterior areas, the head and eyes may briefly turn to the direction opposite the affected hemisphere. If the prerolandic area is affected, involuntary clonic movements of the opposite limb or face or tongue (Jacksonian march) occur.

Partial complex seizures of medial or orbital frontal lobe origin include often bizarre behavioral manifestations leading to erroneous diagnosis of hysteria. Williamson et al. (1985) observed that stereotyped attack patterns helped establish the diagnosis of epilepsy, whereas interictal or ictal EEG was often not helpful and sometimes misleading. Clinical features such as brief duration, high frequency of attacks, complex motor automatisms with kicking and thrushing, sexual automatisms, vocalizations, and frequent development of partial complex status epilepticus often characterize seizures of medial or orbital lobe origin and distinguish them from complex partial seizures originating elsewhere (Williamson et al. 1985).

Parietal lobe seizures often are expressed as transient paresthesias that begin at some point of the body on the contralateral side and spread to the adjacent areas. If the focus is in the posterior area of the parietal lobe, disorders of the body image may result, including neglect of the opposite side, depersonalization, and phantom limb experiences.

Occipital seizures usually present with visual symptoms on the opposite half field that can either be scotomata or hallucinations (e.g., light flashes or colors). Seizures originating from the medial aspect of the hemisphere may present as transient poorly defined unpleasant epigastric symptoms similar to those of patients with a temporal lobe focus. More posterior parietal lesions may result in paresthesias on the contralateral leg and the anogenital areas.

Seizures originating in the temporal lobe have the most variable clinical presentation, including autonomic effects and visceral sensations (epigastric aura), olfactory or gustatory hallucinations, forced thinking, deja vu and jamais vu experiences, overwhelming sense of fear, automatisms, or combinations of these symptoms.

Fugues and twilight states are terms used in the older literature to describe behavioral disturbances that may be related to abnormal electrical discharges in the brain. In some of these patients, an epileptic locus was identified in the inferior medial structures of the temporal lobe (Lishman 1978). During episodes, patients with fugues have the tendency to wander for hours or days and appear perplexed and incoherent, although in some cases they are able to use public transportation or make purchases. In fugues, the abnormal behavior is more organized, consciousness is less affected, and the duration of episodes is longer compared to automatisms. It remains unclear whether fugues are a direct result of epileptic discharges because clinical observation and EEG recording have rarely been done during fugues. A variety of psychogenic disorders may lead to behavior indistinguishable from fugues. Another possible explanation may be that after an epileptic automatism, the patient develops a period of dissociation manifested as fugue. The fugue in this case is a psychogenic disturbance facilitated by the epileptic seizure.

The clinical manifestations of twilight states and their EEG abnormalities have not been classified adequately. Patients with twilight states always have somewhat compromised alertness while the remaining clinical manifestations range from affective and vivid hallucinatory experiences to elaborate delusions. Psychomotor retardation or episodes of irritability culminating in a rage attack may occur. Varying degrees of amnesia accompany all attacks, although sometimes hallucinations may be remembered vividly. In some cases, a twilight state may terminate with a grand mal convulsion. The clinical presentation of twilight states may resemble that of frontal or temporal lobe seizures, but their duration is much longer.

Postictal behavioral changes. Most grand mal convulsions are succeeded by a period of impaired alertness, drowsiness, or sleep. Some partial seizures may be followed by prolonged periods of semipurposeful behavior. The patient appears confused and uncoordinated. Sometimes agitation and paranoia occur, but aggressive behavior develops only in a small minority of cases. Postictal twilight states have also been described and present with motor retardation, vivid hallucinations, and intense affective changes (Landolt 1958). Some authors believe that psychological factors influence the clinical presentation of postictal states because the temporary impairment of high functions permits more primitive behavior to be expressed (Pond 1957). It should be noted, however, that the differentiation between postictal and ictal events remains difficult.

Confusional episodes may sometimes precede an epileptic seizure, but as a rule they occur during the postictal period. In a classic study of 516 epileptic patients, disturbances of awareness were more frequently associated with generalized rather than partial seizures (Dongier 1959). Confusional episodes with generalized spike-and-wave discharges in the EEG do not present any additional symptomatology. They usually occur in children and represent an absence status. Confusional states with diffuse slow waves generally follow tonic-clonic seizures and have shorter duration and milder impairment in the state of alertness, but present agitated behavior more frequently. When confusion was accompanied by visual hallucinations, agitation, and affective changes, it occurred in conjunction with partial seizures.

Behavior Disorders of the Interictal Periods

Various psychiatric syndromes occur at higher frequency in epileptic patients than in the general population. Pond and Bidwell (1960) reported that approximately one-third of epileptic patients recruited from general practices in England and Wales had psychiatric disorders, including impairment in high intellectual functions; low intelligence; schizophreniform, affective or anxiety syndromes; and personality disorders.

A considerable number of epileptic patients present cognitive disturbances resulting from the brain damage responsible for their seizures. Cognitive disturbances are most frequent in patients with partial seizures, especially those with a focus at the temporal lobe (Ounsted et al. 1966; Vislie and Hendriksen 1958). Their deficits include impairment in verbal abilities, concentration, attention, retention, and recall. Epileptogenic loci on the dominant hemisphere are associated with greater impairment in verbal skills, whereas patients with loci in the nondominant hemisphere have more pronounced difficulties in nonverbal performance tests, including tasks of spatial arrangement and construction. Impairment in high intellectual functions is less frequent in patients with tonic-clonic seizures and rare in absences because these patients as a rule have no structural brain damage.

Compared to the general population, epileptic patients score somewhat lower in intelligence tests. Low intelligence in epilepsy has been attributed to anoxia and acidosis occurring during seizures; however, these metabolic changes may be only partly responsible for brain damage of patients with tonic-clonic seizures. Since cognitive deficits are even more frequent in patients with partial seizures, it is likely that the electrical discharge itself may affect intellectual function. Patients with onset of seizures in early life generally have lower intelligence than those with illness onset later in life. There is good evidence that control of seizures and drug toxicity in children reduces the risk and the extent of deterioration of high intellectual functions (Lennox 1960; Rodin 1968).

In a classic paper, Slater et al. (1963) reported that patients with psychomotor seizures or EEG temporal lobe spikes had a higher incidence of schizophreniform syndromes than patients with other forms of epilepsy or the general population. The onset of psychotic syndrome was at approximately 30 years of age, and the patients had low incidence of psychotic disorders in their families. The higher frequency of psychosis in patients with partial complex epilepsy has been corroborated (Gudmundsson 1966; Guerrant et al. 1962; Jensen and Larsen 1979; Slater and Moran 1969; Taylor 1975). Other studies, however, failed to support these findings (Parnas and Korsgaard 1982; Pond and Bidwell 1960; Toone 1981; Trimble 1982a). The prevalence of psychosis in epileptic patients may be influenced by factors such as geographic variations, setting, and interval of time over which data were collected (Cooper and Morgan 1973), making it difficult to establish whether the conditions are significantly associated. There is some evidence that patients who develop psychosis have an epileptogenic focus on the dominant side more frequently than nonpsychotic epileptic patients (Flor-Henry 1969; Trimble 1984); however, a controlled study failed to demonstrate laterality differences between patients with and without psychosis (Kristensen and Sindrup 1978).

There is a complex relationship between mood disorders and epilepsy. Depression of varying degrees of severity occurs in epileptics, but it is unclear whether the incidence of bipolar disorders is higher than in the general population. Epileptic patients have a five times higher risk for suicide than the general population (Barraclough 1981). Patients with epileptogenic focus in the temporal lobe have an even higher incidence of suicide attempts and completed suicides. It has been suggested that epileptic patients with affective syndromes frequently have a focus in the nondominant hemisphere, in contrast to those with schizophreniform syndromes whose focus is often in the dominant hemisphere (Flor-Henry 1969). The antiepileptic drug carbamazepine has been found effective in the treatment and prevention of episodes of bipolar and probably unipolar affective disorders in nonepileptic patients; this suggests that mood disorders and epilepsy may have some common pathophysiologic abnormalities (Ballenger and Post 1980; Post et al. 1984).

Previous reports have noted that depression and anxiety syndromes and personality disorders are the most frequent psychiatric problems among adult epileptic patients (Blumer 1975; Gudmundsson 1966; Pond and Bidwell 1960). Traditionally, epileptic patients have been thought to be argumentative, persistent, suspicious, irritable, egocentric, circumstantial, and religious. This view has not been supported by clinical research, although a small number of patients may have such personality characteristics (Pond and Bidwell 1960). The hypothesis has been advanced that behavior disorders in some epileptic patients result from chronic electrical discharges in the mesial temporal lobe and the limbic structures (Gastaut 1954; Gibbs 1951). This view is supported by clinical findings, suggesting that epileptic patients with a focus in the temporal lobe are overly emotional, irritable, dependent, humorless, and obsessive and have religious preoccupations (Bear and Fedio 1977). In their series, patients with nondominant temporal lobe focus had mood swings ranging from sadness to elation and irritability; those with dominant hemisphere focus had primarily ideational disturbances, including ruminations and religious and philosophical preoccupations. This study, however, used epilepsy clinic patients who are known to have more psychiatric pathology than the overall population of epileptic patients. Epidemiologic studies are needed to compare the incidence of personality pathology in various forms of epilepsy with that in other medical disorders and the medically healthy population. The role of pychosocial factors in the development of abnormal personality features in epileptic patients awaits evaluation. Children with epilepsy have been found to be more socially isolated, inattentive, overactive, and anxious. These behavioral problems are more frequent in children with a focus in the left temporal lobe (Stores 1978).

There is some relationship between violence and epilepsy. Epileptic patients are rarely violent during the interictal periods, and it is unclear whether violence is a result of organic pathology. Prisoners charged with violent crimes, however, have a higher percentage of epilepsy and EEG abnormalities than that found in the general population (Gunn 1969; Gunn and Fenton 1971), although no difference has been found between epileptic and nonepileptic prisoners with regard to violence (Gunn and Bonn 1971). Some authors have described a syndrome characterized by violent outbursts resulting in attacks against people or objects or in self-destructive acts, including suicide attempts (Barraclough 1981; Mark and Ervin 1970). These episodes occurred primarily in young men with low intelligence; were often precipitated by sleep, fatigue, or emotional changes; and were accompanied by various degrees of impairment in alertness. This "organic dyscontrol" syndrome is discussed separately.

Violence is rare during partial complex seizures and practically nonexistent during other types of seizures. When it occurs as part of an epileptic seizure it is nondirected. Patients may strike only if somebody attempts to restrain them. Other symptoms that may accompany violent behavior resulting from a seizure are the presence of typical automatisms such as swallowing or chewing, confusion, fear or anxiety, gustatory or olfactory hallucinations, deja vu experiences, macropsia or micropsia, and complete or relative amnesia for the episode.

Differential Diagnosis

Psychiatric Disorders

The diagnosis of epilepsy is made easily in most cases. Patients seen by psychiatrists, however, present more diagnostic challenges because the usual reasons for psychiatric consultation are behavioral abnormalities that are difficult to classify.

Psychiatric entities that most frequently need to be differentiated from epilepsy are conversion disorder, dissociative disorders, panic disorder, schizophrenia, factitious disorders, malingering, and rage outbursts in patients with severe personality disorders (Lishman 1978). Conversion syndromes do not follow any typical pattern of epileptic presentation, and they usually occur when the patients are distressed and have an audience. Impaired alertness may not be a helpful sign because alertness may be completely preserved in partial epilepsy. In conversion-simulating tonic-clonic seizures, incontinence, tongue biting, and injury from falling are rare, and reflexes remain unaffected. EEG obtained during or immediately after the attack can be helpful, although deep cortical seizures may not manifest abnormalities in EEG using standard scalp electrode application. Videotape monitoring of patients' behavior and EEG telemetry for long periods of time are recently introduced methods that appear useful in differentiating epileptic seizures from conversion. Some patients with generalized seizures or partial complex seizures have an increase in prolactin secretion. Finding elevated serum levels of prolactin 20 to 30 minutes after a seizure strongly supports the diagnosis of epilepsy. Lack of serum prolactin elevation, however, does not exclude an epileptic seizure (Yerby et al. 1987). It is probably a more common error to diagnose conversion in patients with epilepsy rather than the opposite. The diagnosis of conversion disorder does not exclude presence of epilepsy because epileptic patients sometimes also have a conversion disorder.

Dissociative disorders may resemble epileptic automatisms. Behavioral abnormalities are more likely to be part of epilepsy when they have abrupt onset, brief duration, do not appear with regularity, and are out of character for the particular patient (Falconer and Taylor 1970). Patients with factitious disorders may present episodic behavioral abnormalities similar to those of epilepsy. In such cases, the appearance of episodes follows the patient's notion of epileptic seizures.

Partial seizures may present symptoms similar to those of schizophrenia (i.e., posturing, stereotyped movements, thought insertion, thought blocking, sense of unreality, auditory and visual hallucinations) (Karagulla and Robertson 1955). Epileptic seizures, however, are episodic and of brief duration; the state of consciousness is usually compromised; the hallucinatory experiences are hard to recall; and they are followed by postictal confusion. In most cases, longitudinal observation of symptomatology can establish the diagnosis.

There may be a need to distinguish partial seizures from panic disorders with depersonalization. In contrast to panic disorders, partial seizures usually begin with a characteristic pattern of symptom development, consciousness is compromised, and the end is abrupt.

Rage attacks in patients with personality disorders can raise the possibility of an epileptic automatism. EEG abnormalities or amnesia following the attacks may not help with differentiation because they may be found in both conditions. In contrast to rage attacks, automatisms begin and end abruptly without a build-up period of anger; their duration is very brief; alertness is often impaired; the patient's behavior appears purposeless; and motor coordination is compromised.

Seizures may develop in a psychiatric patient as a complication of somatic therapies. It has been reported that patients receiving large doses of phenothiazines (daily doses of chlorpromazine greater than 1,000 mg or equivalent doses of other neuroleptics) may have as high an incidence of seizures as 9 percent, whereas less than 0.5 percent develop seizures on lower doses of phenothiazines (Logothetis 1967). Seizures may develop after an overdose of tricyclic antidepressants, use of the tetracyclic antidepressant maprotiline, or as part of the withdrawal syndrome in patients addicted to alcohol, benzodiazepines, barbiturates, or other central nervous system depressants. Spontaneous seizures have been reported within days or weeks after electroconvulsive therapy, but they are rare and may not even exceed the incidence of seizures in the general population.

Nonpsychiatric Disorders

Various physical conditions need to be differentiated from epilepsy, including bradyarrhythmias, vasovagal attacks, transient ischemic attacks, transient global amnesia, migraine, hypoglycemia, and substance intoxication. Patients with bradyarrhythmias may have repeated episodes of loss of consciousness with or without convulsions. The electrocardiogram usually shows conduction defects, and the diagnosis is finally established by Holter monitoring. Vasovagal attacks ("fainting"), as a rule, can be easily distinguished from epilepsy. In most cases, they follow an emotionally stressful experience and have gradual onset with a feeling of faintness that progresses into loss of consciousness accompanied by muscular flaccidity. Recovery occurs in one or two minutes, and there is no period of confusion or sleep following the attack. In contrast to the paroxysmal electrical discharges observed in epilepsy, the EEG in vasovagal attacks shows slow activity that may even reach silence if the duration is long. On recovery, the EEG becomes normalized and does not have slow wave activity as is seen in patients coming out of an epileptic seizure.

Transient ischemic attacks may resemble partial epilepsy (Gibberd 1973). Patients with transient ischemic attacks typically present motor weakness or dysphasia, with sudden onset and with remission in a few minutes or hours. The most consistent difference from epileptic seizures is the longer duration of attacks (Lishman 1978); the motor weakness may be identified erroneously as akinetic partial seizures (Todd's paralysis). Transient global amnesia may be confused with automatisms because it has sudden onset, brief duration, and is recurrent in some cases. The most important clinical difference from epileptic automatisms is that the patient's symptomatology is limited to memory dysfunction while the other high intellectual functions remain essentially unaffected. Some migraine attacks may be difficult to distinguish from epilepsy, especially when they are accompanied by transient visual experiences, amnesia, and only mild headache. In such cases, longitudinal observation of the patient usually reveals the remaining characteristics of migraine and establishes the diagnosis.

Hypoglycemic attacks can mimic epilepsy. Occasionally, tonic-clonic seizures (and probably even absences) may occur during periods of hypoglycemia and need to be differentiated from idiopathic epilepsy. The clinical characteristics of hypoglycemia, including perspiration, dizziness, anxiety, and tremor, may raise the clinician's suspicion; low blood sugar levels and improvement of symptoms after intravenous infusion of a glucose solution can establish the diagnosis. Finally, the loss of consciousness or behavioral abnormalities resembling epilepsy may be caused by various other metabolic or toxic disturbances, including substance intoxication. History of drug or alcohol abuse and the presence of such substances in the blood or urine can be diagnostic in delirium of toxic etiology.

Patient Evaluation

The history and clinical examination contribute the most valuable information to the diagnosis of epilepsy. The extent of laboratory workup depends on the clinical findings. Onset of epileptic attacks in childhood suggests idiopathic epilepsy; neoplasm is the most frequent cause of seizures, with onset during early adulthood; and cerebrovascular disease accounts for most seizures, with onset after 60 years of age (Solomon et al. 1983). Symptoms and signs suggesting a neurologic or systemic disturbance call for a more rigorous investigation.

There is rarely reason to pursue a workup for structural lesions in patients with absences. It is important, however, to differentiate absences from partial epilepsy with a similar presentation. Contrary to absence, partial epilepsy as a rule results from structural lesions and requires different medication. Generalized seizures are frequently idiopathic; however, they often result from generalization of a partial seizure with underlying structural pathology.

Clinical history should include information about the patient's birth, presence of febrile convulsions during childhood, head injury, and recent history of headache and alcohol and drug abuse. The clinical examination should seek to demonstrate or exclude focal neurologic signs or signs of increased intracranial pressure. Metastatic neoplastic disease must be suspected in older patients. Finally, the examiner should look for signs of metabolic disturbances, endocrinopathy, or infection.

The laboratory workup usually includes hematologic and blood chemistry studies, as well as serologic syphilis tests to exclude hypoglycemia, hypocalcemia, uremia, hepatic failure, or neurosyphilis. Blood or urine drug screen examination is sometimes helpful when substance abuse is suspected. Skull X rays may show fractures or tumors of the skull. Brain computed tomography (CT) is helpful in demonstrating midline shifts, tumors of the brain or the supportive structures, or hemangiomas, and must be part of the workup in all cases of partial epilepsy. Magnetic resonance imaging is particularly useful in identifying lesions in the temporal lobe, atrophy, or demyelination.

The EEG is the most important laboratory test for the diagnosis and management of the patient with epilepsy. The EEG can be helpful in localizing the epileptogenic focus, especially in quickly generalized seizures, in partial seizures without localizing features, or in seizures with multiple foci. Local decrease of background activity or localized slow activity raise the suspicion of a space-occupying lesion. Generalized disorganization or diffuse slow wave activity suggest a metabolic disease. The EEG can aid in the differential diagnosis between epilepsy and psychogenic seizures. Presence of EEG abnormalities strongly supports the diagnosis of epilepsy, but absence of EEG findings does not exclude epilepsy. Activating techniques can be of value. Hyperventilation can elicit a 3 Hz wave absence, and sleep deprivation or sleep can activate a temporal lobe focus. Sphenoidal or nasopharyngeal leads permit recording of discharges originating in the medial aspects of the temporal lobes. It must be emphasized that nonepileptic psychiatric patients have a higher percentage of EEG abnormalities (up to 50 percent) than the general population (15 percent) (Pincus and Tucker 1978). Telemetry recording of EEG over periods of 24 hours or longer combined with videotapes of the patient's behavior are often useful in confirming the diagnosis of epilepsy when EEG records obtained over short periods of time fail to demonstrate epileptic activity.

Cerebral angiography is recommended when a vascular tumor is suspected. Examination of the cerebrospinal fluid should be performed if there is any suspicion of central nervous system infection. However, lumbar puncture should not be performed if there is evidence of increased intracranial pressure since it increases the risk of herniation. Psychometric and projective psychological tests may help in the assessment of the patient's intelligence and psychological profile. Finally, a comprehensive clinical evaluation of the patient's strengths and liabilities is essential for making recommendations for social and vocational rehabilitation.

Treatment

General Considerations

Informing the epileptic patient of the diagnosis, prognosis, and treatment recommendations is a sensitive clinical matter. Often patients deny their condition and either seek other opinions or fail to comply with treatment. It is helpful to explore the patient's rational or irrational fears when the diagnosis of epilepsy is communicated. Concerns about the social stigma of epilepsy and about changes in daily activities should be discussed in an effort to clarify their meaning for the patient. It is extremely important for the physician to develop rapport with the epileptic patient and the patient's family. An open relationship with the physician increases compliance to the antiepileptic regimen.

While in most cases epileptic seizures are well controlled, social adjustment is more of a problem. Underemployment or unemployment of epileptic patients has been ascribed to the concomitant presence of psychiatric disorders or intellectual limitations (Rodin 1978). Vocational rehabilitation of epileptic patients may be a crucial factor in their treatment. A trusting relationship with the physician facilitates resolution of many psychological and social difficulties. Complex cases may require referral to a psychiatrist.

The psychiatrist usually sees epileptic patients with psychopathology. While there is no specific psychiatric treatment for these patients, interactions between antiepileptic and psychotropic drugs may complicate pharmacotherapy. Poor compliance with drug regimens and careless exposure to stimulation known to precipitate seizures frequently represent conscious or unconscious mechanisms used to express certain emotions.

Use of alcohol or sedatives is associated with increased risk for seizures. Generalized tonic-clonic seizures sometimes develop in addicted individuals during withdrawal from alcohol or sedatives. Epileptic patients are at higher risk for developing seizures after a bout of heavy drinking even if they are not addicted to alcohol. As a rule, the seizures occur during the withdrawal phase, usually during the night or the morning following the drinking bout (Solomon et al. 1983). Heavy drinking, development of alcoholism, or drug abuse may be the reason for continuing seizures in an epileptic patient who is receiving antiepileptic treatment. Alcohol or drug abuse should be suspected if seizures develop in a previously well-regulated patient. Counseling, referral to self-help organizations such as Alcoholics Anonymous or Narcotics Anonymous, or referral to a psychiatrist should be considered when problems with alcohol or drugs are identified.

Principles of Antiepileptic Treatment

The decision to begin antiepileptic pharmacotherapy is not always obvious. Many physicians do not recommend antiepileptics after the first seizure because in the presence of a normal EEG, approximately 60 percent of patients may not have a second seizure. Clinicians are more keen to start drugs if the first seizure was generalized because recurrence may endanger the patient. However, this decision also depends on the patient's life-style, occupation, and habits. Absences or some partial seizures represent a smaller risk for the patient's safety, and the decision to begin antiepileptic drugs may be deferred. Repeated subthreshold stimulation of the brain may lead to seizure development (kindling).

With pharmacotherapy, 30 to 50 percent of patients can achieve complete control of seizures (Solomon et al. 1983). The prognosis for seizure control depends on a variety of factors. Approximately half the patients with generalized seizures can achieve complete seizure control, whereas only 30 percent of patients with partial epilepsy are successful. Chronic illness, high frequency of seizures, neurologic abnormalities, and persistent EEG abnormalities are generally predictors of poor outcome of seizure control (Rodin 1968).

Antiepileptic therapy should start with one drug; combinations should follow only if it is demonstrated that one drug alone is either ineffective or intolerable at therapeutic blood concentrations. Systematic trials of single antiepileptic agents permit the clinician to determine treatment response and individual sensitivity to a drug.

Follow-up of epileptic patients should include periodic neurologic examination, EEG, and determination of blood drug levels at least every three to six months for most drugs. Carbamazepine and valproate require monthly examinations of liver function tests, blood count, and blood levels at least during the first six months. Development of new neurologic signs or EEG changes may result from a previously undetected brain space-occupying lesion. Reevaluation, including CT scan, is indicated in such cases. Monitoring of antiepileptic drug levels begins when the patient is expected to have reached a steady state (Table 1). In addition to blood drug levels

Table 1. Pharmacokinetic Parameters of Frequently Used Antiepileptic Drugs

Drugs	Blood Levels Therapeutic Range	Time to Steady State (Days)	Plasma Half-Life (Hours)
Phenytoin	10–20 μg/ml	5–10	15–30
Phenobarbital	20–40 μg/ml	15–30	72–120
Primidone	5–15 μg/ml	2–5	5–12
Phenobarbital	20–40 μg/ml	15–30	2–120
Carbamazepine	6–12 μg/ml	4–6	12–14
Ethosuximide	50–100 μg/ml	7–14	30–60
Valproate	50–100 μg/ml	3–6	6–18
Clonazepam	20–80 ng/ml	5–8	12–24
Diazepam	500–1500 μg/ml	4–8	10–50
Desmethyldiazepam		7–21	24–72

Note. Adapted from Eadie (1980a) and Solomon et al. (1983).

obtained during routine follow-up, blood drug concentrations should be determined if there is a change in the frequency of seizures, if side effects develop, or if another drug is added.

The question of when to stop antiepileptic drugs after seizures have been under control must always be answered on an individual basis. Several authors suggested that an attempt to discontinue drugs should be made after two to three years of good seizure control in children with absence and in two to five years in other types of epilepsy (Emerson et al. 1981; Oller-Daurella et al. 1976; Solomon et al. 1983; Thurston et al. 1982). If these guidelines are followed, approximately 20 to 50 percent of patients are expected to relapse with seizures; factors that increase the risk for relapse include prolonged periods with uncontrolled seizures (over six years), high frequency of seizures (two or more per month), neurologic deficits, markedly abnormal EEG, and seizures with extensive spread (Solomon et al. 1983). Antiepileptic drugs must not be stopped abruptly or status epilepticus may result.

Choice of Antiepileptic Regimen

The choice of a pharmacologic regimen depends on the type of seizures (Table 2), the history of response to treatment, and individual tolerance of drugs.

In partial elementary epilepsy, the drug of first choice is phenytoin or carbamazepine (Mattson et al. 1985), although some clinicians prefer phenobarbital in preschool children. Primidone is also effective, but it causes sedation and may interfere with the patient's functioning. Partial complex seizures are generally more difficult to control than elementary seizures. Carbamazepine is the initial drug of choice in such cases; phenytoin is an alternative choice (Personage 1975). If neither drug alone is effective, combinations of the two may be used or primidone alone can be tried. Approximately 30 percent of patients with partial complex seizures do not respond to these regimens. In these cases, addition of valproate, chlorazepate, or methsuximide may improve the control of seizures (Wilder and Bruni 1981).

Phenytoin is the initial drug of choice in adults and older children with generalized tonic-clonic seizures. Phenobarbital is often used as the drug of first choice in preschool children. Primidone is also effective, but it is used as the first drug infrequently because it is sedating, at least during the initial stages of treatment. Carba-

Table 2. Guidelines for Choosing Antiepileptic Drugs

Classification of Seizures	Antiepileptic Drug
Partial Seizures	
With elementary symptomatology	Phenytoin,* phenobarbital,
With complex symptomatology	carbamazepine,* phenytoin, primidone, valproate, chlorazepate, methsuximide
Generalized Seizures	
Tonic-clonic	Phenytoin,* phenobarbital, primidone, carbamazepine *Adjunct drugs*: valproate, mephenytoin, acetazolamide, methsuximide, bromides
Absences	Ethosuximide,* valproate, trimethadione, clonazepam
Infantile spasms	Corticotropin,* corticosteroids, clonazepam,* diazepam, valproate
Atonic, akinetic, or massive myoclonic seizures	Valproate,* clonazepam, corticotropin, corticosteroids

Note. Adapted from Solomon et al. (1983).
*Drug of first choice.

mazepine is an alternative, but clinicians have been reluctant to use this drug as the first choice because of its hematologic and hepatotoxic effects (Solomon et al. 1983). If seizures are not controlled with phenytoin, barbiturates, or carbamazepine, the addition of valproate has been shown to be effective in approximately half the patients with refractory epilepsy (Wilder and Bruni 1981). This drug, however, may cause severe hepatotoxicity, and it should not be the first choice. Mephenytoin, methsuximide, and bromides have anticonvulsant properties in patients with tonic-clonic seizures, but they are probably less effective than the drugs of first choice. Acetazolamide has been used as an adjunct to antiepileptic therapy, but it is effective only for short periods of time. Acetazolamide is particularly helpful in women with increased seizure frequency before or during the menstrual period. In such cases, acetazolamide may be added for one week prior to or during menstruation (Solomon et al. 1983).

In absence epilepsy, the drugs of choice are ethosuximide or valproate. Acetazolamide and clonazepam, if added to ethosuximide, may control seizures in drug-resistant patients, but their effect lasts only a few months. Methosuximide is effective in absences, but it is avoided because of its frequent toxicity.

Tonic-clonic status epilepticus is a medical emergency. The following are treatment guidelines proposed by Solomon et al. (1983). The first task is to establish an airway and provide adequate ventilation by giving oxygen through a mask or a nasal catheter. Preparations should be made for intubation. An intravenous catheter should then be inserted and blood obtained for determination of glucose, electrolytes, blood urea nitrogen, and drug screens. Since hypoglycemia is always a possibility, 50 ml of 50 percent glucose solution should be injected intravenously with 100 mg of thiamine. Diazepam (5 mg) iv must next be given over a period of two minutes. A loading dose of phenytoin (up to 20 mg/kg) iv can then be given at the rate of 50 mg/minute, while the pulse, blood pressure, and respiration are closely monitored. If seizures are not interrupted, another 5 mg of diazepam can be given (1 to 2 mg/minute). Seizures sometimes stop but start again because of the rapid distribution of diazepam in fat tissues. In this case, diazepam may be repeated, but the total dose should not exceed 30 mg. Lorazepam (2 mg) or amobarbital (250 mg) iv may be used instead of diazepam. Lorazepam has a longer-lasting effect because its redistribution is not as rapid as that of diazepam. Amobarbital has also been used in the past, but it is profoundly sedating. Sedating drugs should be avoided in patients who need monitoring of state of consciousness as in recent head trauma or neurosurgery; in such cases, phenytoin is the drug of choice. If seizures persist despite the use of benzodiazepines, phenobarbital (1 mg/kg) iv may be given (up to 100 mg in one to two minutes). The maximal effect of phenobarbital occurs in approximately 30 minutes because of its slow distribution. If seizures continue for longer than 60 minutes, general anesthesia should be administered with pentothal or halothan. After the seizures are under control, the physician should focus the investigation on diagnosing the cause of status epilepticus.

Antiepileptic Drugs and Drug Interactions

Phenytoin

The main action of phenytoin is to suppress the spread of seizure discharge to normal tissue surrounding the epileptogenic focus (Deupree 1980). Patients on phenytoin should be followed for symptoms and signs of drug intoxication. These correlate with elevated blood drug concentrations; in adults, the first sign is nystagmus and usually appears at blood levels above 20 mcg/ml (Kutt et al. 1964b). Ataxic gait is indicative of more severe intoxication, while confusion and sedation correspond to blood levels in the area of 40 mcg/ml (Eadie 1980b). Other side effects of phenytoin are described in detail elsewhere (Eadie 1980b; Solomon et al. 1983).

Phenytoin is absorbed slowly over four to six hours and approximately 90 percent is bound to plasma albumin (Eadie 1980a). The plasma protein binding of phenytoin is lower in the infant than in the adult (Loughman et al. 1977). It is metabolized in the liver by para-hydroxylation and glycuronidation. The metabolites of phenytoin do not have antiepileptic properties. About 70 percent of the ingested drug is excreted in the urine, 5 percent unchanged and approximately 65 percent as metabolites. Because of its prolonged half-life after oral administration (22 hours), phenytoin, if tolerated, can be used in a once-a-day regimen in adult patients. The usual adult therapeutic daily dose of phenytoin is 300 mg/day and produces blood drug levels ranging from 5 to 15 mcg/ml in approximately one week. If rapid antiepileptic coverage is required, phenytoin can be administered slowly (50 mg/minute) up to a total dose of 1 g.

The absorption of phenytoin may be reduced by calcium, although contradictory reports exist as to whether calcium-containing antacids lower phenytoin's absorption (Kulshrestha et al. 1978; O'Brien et al. 1978). The metabolism of phenytoin is inhibited by a large number of drugs that are metabolized by the liver mitochondria and may increase the phenytoin blood concentration. These include drugs frequently used in psychiatric practice (e.g., phenothiazines, tricyclic antidepressants, benzodiazepines, methylphenidate, disulfiram), antiepileptics (e.g., phenobarbital, ethosuximide), and other frequently used drugs (e.g., digoxin, dicoumarol, isoniazid). A small number of cases have been reported in which phenytoin possibly enhanced lithium toxicity manifested by polyuria, ataxia, tremor, and gastrointestinal symptoms (Hansten 1985). Phenylbutazone, sulfafurazone, salicylates, diazoxide, and valproate displace albumin-bound phenytoin with a resulting increase of free phenytoin. The potentiation of phenytoin is mild because of its high volume of distribution (amount of drug in plasma is small compared with total amount in the body). Since a relatively large number of phenytoin-treated epileptic patients require treatment with other drugs, phenytoin plasma levels should be monitored closely.

Phenobarbital

Phenobarbital is absorbed slowly, and peak blood drug concentration after oral administration is achieved in approximately 16 hours, while it requires only 20 minutes after intravenous injection. Approximately 50 percent of phenobarbital is bound to plasma protein. Phenobarbital is metabolized in the liver by parahydroxylation and is excreted by the kidney. The half-life of phenobarbital is shorter in children (37 to 73 hours) than in adults (72 to 120 hours).

Phenobarbital is a potent inducer of the hepatic microsomal drug-metabolizing enzymes and increases the hepatic metabolism of benzodiazepines, tricyclic antidepressants, and neuroleptics. Because some of these drugs (e.g., amitriptyline, imipramine, doxepin, chlorpromazine) have biologically active metabolites, their overall therapeutic activity cannot be predicted when combined with phenobarbital. Some patients respond while on high concentrations of the parent psychotropic drug, but their psychiatric symptoms may worsen when the level of the parent substance is reduced and its metabolites are increased after the introduction of phenobarbital. Psychiatric symptomatology and blood concentrations of antiepileptic drugs, and psychotropic drugs and their metabolites should be followed closely, especially if changes in the patients' regimen are made. Monoamine oxidase inhibitors potentiate phenobarbital, probably by inhibiting its metabolism (Goodman Gilman et al. 1980), and may lead to phenobarbital intoxication manifested by nystagmus, ataxia, sedation, or hyperkinesis. Phenobarbital potentiates the central nervous system depressant effect of other barbiturates, benzodiazepines, and ethanol.

Phenobarbital increases the hepatic metabolism of several nonpsychotropic drugs, including phenytoin, carbamazepine, warfarin, steroids, digitoxin, and quinidine. Although most interactions result in lower pharmacologic activity of the affected drug, drugs with active metabolites (e.g., digitoxin) may be potentiated. Sodium valproate inhibits the metabolism of phenobarbital. A 30 percent reduction of the phenobarbital dosage may be required to maintain a constant phenobarbital blood concentration when valproate is given to patients receiving phenobarbital (Flachs et al. 1977). Alkalinizing drugs enhance the renal clearance of phenobarbital; urine-acidfying drugs have the opposite effect.

Primidone

Most of the anticonvulsant action of primidone results from its metabolites phenylethylmanolamine and phenobarbital; the parent substance itself has only weak therapeutic potency. Adequacy of antiepileptic coverage with primidone is established by obtaining the blood levels of both primidone and phenobarbital (Table 1). Steady state of anticonvulsant is determined by the blood level of phenobarbital because this metabolite has a long half-life. The blood level of primidone is useful in estimating when the last dose was taken. In patients receiving their medication regularly, the phenobarbital level is two to three times the primidone level (Solomon et al. 1983). Age does not seem to influence the relationship between steady state phenobarbital level and primidone dose (Eadie et al. 1977).

Primidone accelerates the hepatic metabolism of benzodiazepines, tricyclic antidepressants, and neuroleptics. The same precautions should be taken as when these drugs are combined with phenobarbital. Monoamine oxidase inhibitors potentiate primidone, and careful monitoring for signs of intoxication (i.e., nystagmus, ataxia, and sedation) is required when these drugs are combined. The amount of primidone bound to plasma proteins is negligible; therefore, this drug does not interact with drugs that have high affinity for plasma proteins. Primidone induces the liver mitochondrial enzymes and stimulates the metabolism of various drugs (Perucca and Richens, 1980). An example is the induction of carbamazepine metabolism demonstrated by a reduced ratio of carbamazepine to its epoxide metabolite. The reduction of therapeutic activity may be smaller than expected because 10-11-epoxide-carbamazepine is pharmacologically active. Phenytoin stimulates the metabolism of primidone and leads to increased formation of phenobarbital (Reynolds et al. 1975). Since phenobarbital has a long half-life, it accumulates; the end result is potentiation of primidone. Valproate inhibits the metabolism of primidone (Flachs et al. 1977); its addition to a primidone regimen may require up to 30 percent reduction of the original primidone dose. Inhibition of the metabolism of primidone may also occur when sulthiame and isoniazid are prescribed. Renal excretion of phenobarbital is enhanced by urine alkalinizing drugs (Waddel and Butler 1957).

Carbamazepine

The chemical structure of carbamazepine (iminostilvene nucleus) is dissimilar from that of other anticonvulsants and resembles that of tricyclic antidepressants. Despite its chemical structure, carbamazepine has therapeutic and pharmacologic properties comparable to phenytoin (Schauf et al. 1974), which suggests that the action of these drugs may be mediated by the same receptors (Deupree 1980).

Carbamazepine is absorbed rapidly from the gastrointestinal tract and reaches peak blood concentration in four to eight hours. Approximately 70 to 80 percent of carbamazepine is bound to plasma proteins. Carbamazepine is oxidized in the liver and forms an epoxide and a dihydroxy derivative. Carbamazepine-10,11-epoxide has anticonvulsant properties. The usual starting adult antiepileptic dose of carbamazepine is 200 to 400 mg/day. No effect of age has been found on the relationship between plasma level and dose of carbamazepine (Lander et al. 1977).

The most important side effects of carbamazepine are leukopenia and hepatic toxicity. Liver toxicity has been fatal in some cases (Zucker et al. 1977). Central nervous system toxicity is dose related and consists of nystagmus, dizziness, ataxia, diplopia, and slurred speech. Close monitoring of side effects and blood levels (Table 1) is necessary when a patient is started on carbamazepine. Blood count and liver function tests should be obtained initially, monthly, and every three months later (Solomon et al. 1983).

Carbamazepine induces the hepatic enzymes that metabolize several drugs, including benzodiazepines, tricyclic antidepressants, and neuroleptics. Carbamazepine has anticholinergic properties; therefore, when it is combined with tricyclic antidepressants or neuroleptics with anticholinergic action, the additive effect may lead to atropine psychosis, increased intraocular pressure, constipation, or urinary retention. Since carbamazepine has a chemical structure similar to that of tricyclic antidepressants, it is possible that concomitant use of this drug with monoamine oxidase inhibitors may result in a hypertensive crisis, although no clinical reports of this interaction have appeared. Carbamazepine may increase the risk for lithium toxicity (Ghose 1978). In a small number of patients, however, the combination of carbamazepine and lithium has been observed to improve symptoms of mania, while each drug alone failed to produce significant improvement (Lipinski and Pope 1982).

Acceleration of the metabolism of carbamazepine itself occurs (autoinduction) and results in progressive lowering of the serum concentration in the first four to five weeks of treatment (Eichelbaum et al. 1975). The blood concentration of carbamazepine is reduced by concomitant administration of phenytoin, phenobarbital, or primidone (Johannessen and Strandjord 1975), but it is not clear whether the antiepileptic efficacy of the combined regimen is compromised. This interaction is probably a result of acceleration of the metabolism of carbamazepine because the blood levels of carbamazepine-10,11-epoxide are raised. The metabolism of carbamazepine is reduced by propoxyphene (Dam et al. 1977) and triacetyloleandromycin (Dravet et al. 1977), but the clinical significance of this interaction is unclear (Dravet et al. 1977). Carbamazepine stimulates the metabolism of steroid contraceptives and may reduce their efficacy (Stockley 1976). Phenytoin reduces the frequency of the water intoxication syndrome induced by carbamazepine, probably by antagonizing the secretion of inappropriate antidiuretic hormone stimulated by carbamazepine (Sordillo et al. 1978).

Nonpharmacologic Treatments

Surgical Treatment

Surgical treatment is often indicated for patients with epileptogenic structural lesions (e.g., tumors, arteriovenous malformations, cysts), as well as for epileptic patients with seizures unresponsive to antiepileptic drug treatment, provided that they have a consistent epileptogenic focus accessible to surgery (Solomon et al. 1983). The most common epileptogenic lesion of chronic epileptics has been sclerosis of the mesial aspects of the temporal lobe, probably resulting from anoxia during febrile seizures in infancy (Falconer 1973). Removal of the anterior portion of the temporal lobe, including the uncus and anterior hippocampus, results in complete remission of seizures in 50 percent of selected epileptic patients and in some improvement in the remainder. Patients younger than 20 years of age with onset of seizures at young age had the best prognosis. Use of depth EEG (Spencer et al. 1982) and positron emission tomography scan (Engel et al. 1981) has been found helpful in localizing epileptogenic foci and in improving the prognosis of surgery.

More recent surgical procedures include stereotaxic ablation of selected diencephalic areas, callosal commissurotomy, and stimulation of the cerebellum. These procedures are currently under further investigation.

As a rule, the final decision for surgery is made by neurosurgeons specialized in these techniques. The psychiatrist, however, is well equipped to assess the disruption in psychological and social adjustment resulting form uncontrolled epilepsy. A comprehensive treatment approach that addresses the multiple needs of the patient may improve compliance and obviate the need for surgery.

Behavioral Methods

Behavior modification techniques have been applied as a method of reducing frequency of seizures in epilepsy. Relaxation training has been used for the purpose of reducing anxiety and tension, which have been found to increase the probability for seizures in epileptic patients (Mattson et al. 1970). Extinction of response through habituation has been found to improve seizure control in patients whose seizures are triggered by known visual, auditory, or other sensory stimuli (Foster 1977). Finally, a variety of reinforcement techniques have been used (e.g., rewarding the absence of seizures), with the goal of reducing the occurrence of seizures (Mostofsky and Balaschak 1977). The use of behavioral techniques in the hands of specially trained clinicians can be a helpful adjunct to the pharmacologic treatment of epilepsy.

Animal experiments suggest that biofeedback techniques leading to increase of the EEG rhythm over the sensorimotor cortex make the animals partially resistant to chemically induced seizures (Sterman 1973). Biofeedback training in epileptic patients aimed at increasing the frequency of EEG rhythm over the sensorimotor cortex resulted in reduced frequency of seizures (Finley et al. 1975; Lubar 1977; Lubar and Bahler, 1976; Seifert and Lubar 1975); however, this effect was small and was not replicated by other investigators (Quy et al. 1979). Changes in EEG rhythms such as increase in occipital alpha rhythm (Cabral and Scott 1976), increase in fast low voltage activity (Whyler et al. 1976), or enhancement of the naturally occurring Mu rhythm (Kaplan 1975; Kuhlman and Allison 1977) decreased the frequency of seizures. More studies are necessary, however, before biofeedback becomes a conventional treatment of epilepsy. At present, biofeedback techniques applied alone do not appear to be adequate to control epilepsy.

Chapter 102

The Patient with Cardiovascular Disease

The Clinical Syndrome

The patient with both an organic mental syndrome (OMS) and cardiovascular disease poses a number of complex clinical questions because of the variety of ways in which the central nervous system (CNS) and cardiovascular system can interact.

An OMS may occur as a direct result of heart disease, as in the case of severe congestive heart failure associated with changes in cerebral arterial oxygen tension or blood flow. In other cases, an OMS may be the result of secondary complications of cardiovascular disease such as cerebral thromboembolic events, effects of tumor, infection, hypertension, electrolyte and acid-base disturbances, or consequences of drug treatment. In still other patients, an OMS and cardiovascular disease may be present as concurrent, but unrelated, conditions. Whatever the relationship, the presence of one condition may complicate the diagnosis and treatment of the other.

OMS as a Consequence of Cardiovascular Disease

Heart Failure

Heart failure can be defined as a state in which an abnormality of cardiac function results in failure of the heart to pump blood at a rate sufficient to meet the body's needs (Braunwald 1980a). Causes of heart failure may be related to myocardial or extramyocardial factors. Myocardial failure may result from a defect in heart muscle, as in some cardiomyopathies, or from damage secondary to ischemia, infarction, drugs, toxins, infection, or inflammation (Braunwald 1980a; Jefferson and Marshall 1981a).

Extramyocardial causes of heart failure include endocardial disease, pericardial disease (constriction, tamponade), valvular disease (stenosis, insufficiency, rupture), abnormal shunting (atrial or ventricular septal defects, arteriovenous fistulae), certain cardiac tumors, and severe hypertension (systemic or pulmonary).

While they may overlap, it is useful to distinguish the underlying cause of heart failure from precipitating causes (Braunwald 1980a). For example, while certain arrhythmias may produce heart failure even in the absence of underlying myocardial disease, others may precipitate failure only in the presence of an already compromised myocardium. Other common precipitating conditions include anemia, fever, infection, hypertension, pulmonary embolus, thyrotoxicosis, pregnancy, physical or emotional exertion, increased sodium intake, and increased heat or humidity.

Neuropsychiatric sequelae. Symptoms produced by impaired cerebral blood flow and resulting hypoxia will depend on the acuteness of onset and severity of the disturbance. Moderate degrees of hypoxia associated with chronic heart failure may be asymptomatic or may present with a mild confusional state evidenced by inattentiveness, decreased concentration, slowing of thought processes and reaction time, impaired motor coordination, and subtle alterations in judgment. Affective disturbances with anxiety, irritable or labile mood, or depression may also be present (Sandok 1980b).

More acute onset or worsening of hypoxia may present with severe anxiety, psychomotor agitation, or delirium. As oxygen deprivation continues, progressive obtundation ensues, eventually leading to stupor and coma. An important clinical rule is that degrees of hypoxia insufficient to cause loss of consciousness rarely, if ever, produce irreversible neurologic damage (Adams and Victor 1985).

Complete recovery usually occurs if adequate circulation and oxygenation is restored within three to five minutes; beyond this time, neuronal cell death will ensue. Certain brain regions are relatively more sensitive than others to hypoxia, either due to their metabolic requirements or their location in "border zone" regions with marginal collateral circulation. In general, gray matter is more susceptible to hypoxia than white matter. The cerebral cortex (particularly hippocampus and parieto-occipital lobes), striatum, globus pallidus, thalamus, and Purkinje cells of the cerebellum are especially vulnerable regions (Adams and Victor 1985; Sandok 1980b).

Resulting neuropsychiatric sequelae of prolonged hypoxic states may include dementia, amnestic syndromes, extrapyramidal syndromes, hyperkinetic states, and focal cortical disorders such as visual agnosia, apraxias, and aphasias (Sandok 1980b). Some patients who recover from a severe hypoxic episode develop a syndrome of further neuropsychiatric dysfunction known as delayed postanoxic encephalopathy (Adams and Victor 1985). Initial improvement is followed in from one to four weeks by relapse characterized by confusion, apathy, irritability, and agitation. While many patients recover from this second episode, others undergo progressive neurologic deterioration ending in coma and death after several weeks. Postmortem examination in these cases has revealed extensive subcortical demyelination.

Cardiac Tumors

Tumors involving the heart may be classified as primary or secondary, benign or malignant, mural or intracavitary (Jefferson and Marshall 1981a). Cardiac myxomas, although rare, are the most common type of primary heart tumor seen in adults. They are of particular clinical significance because they represent a potentially treatable form of heart disease, but can present with a puzzling array of systemic and neuropsychiatric manifestations. Symptoms may result from mechanical obstruction by the tumor, embolization of tumor fragments, and general constitutional abnormalities (Glick and Braunwald 1980). Embolization of tumor fragments may produce a wide variety of neurologic signs and symptoms, including behavioral disturbance, that may suggest functional illness. Constitutional manifestations may include weight loss, malaise, fever, arthralgias, myalgias, anemia, elevated sedimentation rate, hyperglobulinemia, and abnormal liver function tests (Glick and Braunwald 1980).

Diagnosis requires a high index of suspicion and can be confirmed by echocardiography or angiocardiography. Early surgical treatment is essential because of the morbidity associated with these tumors.

Infective Endocarditis

Infective endocarditis is a microbial infection of the heart valves or of the endocardium. It may occur abruptly and pursue a fulminant course (acute endocarditis) or have a more insidious onset and prolonged course (subacute endocarditis). Symptoms may result from systemic infection, immunologic response, local cardiac damage, and embolic phenomenon. Destruction of the heart valves may precipitate acute heart failure, and metastatic abscesses following septic emobli are common (Pelletier and Petersdorf 1980).

When neuropsychiatric manifestations predominate, diagnosis may be delayed. In one review, neurologic lesions were found in 39 percent of patients with bacterial endocarditis (Pruitt et al. 1978). In nearly half of these, the neurologic sequelae (e.g., cerebral embolism, brain abscess, seizures, hemiparesis, sudden blindness) were the initial manifestations of the illness. Psychiatric symptoms may be those of an OMS, or at times a schizophreniform psychosis (Jefferson and Marshall 1981a) and may also antedate other disease symptoms.

One review found neuropsychiatric symptoms to be the chief complaint or one of the major presenting complaints in as many as 60 percent of patients (Jones et al. 1969) with bacterial endocarditis. Delusions of various types, hallucinations, paranoid ideation, and transient confusion were common and led to direct psychiatric admission and delayed diagnosis in several patients. Severe encephalopathy was the second most common neuropsychiatric presentation of infective endocarditis, occurring in nearly 20 percent of patients.

An echocardiogram may reveal the presence of valvular vegetations, and blood cultures are positive in the majority of cases. They may be negative, however, in patients recently treated with antibiotics or in those with infection by unusual microorganisms. Extended parenteral treatment with appropriate antibiotics is essential, and a high level of suspicion is often necessary to make an early diagnosis.

Hypertensive Encephalopathy

Hypertension, unless severe, is usually a silent disease. Hypertensive encephalopathy refers to a syndrome characterized by severe elevations in blood pressure (diastolic above 130 mm Hg) associated with headache, nausea, vomiting, seizures, visual disturbances, delirium, stupor, and coma (Adams and Victor 1985). The predominant CNS symptoms are severe headache and altered state of consciousness (Chester et al. 1978). These symptoms of diffuse cerebral dysfunction may be accompanied by focal neurologic signs, either transient or lasting, which suggest cerebral hemorrhage or infarct. The etiology of the encephalopathic symptoms is not clear, but may be related to microinfarcts occurring secondary to extensive small vessel damage (Chester et al. 1978).

By the time encephalopathic symptoms occur, prolonged hypertension has usually resulted in retinal, cardiac, and renal damage. Aggressive treatment with antihypertensive agents is important to prevent further damage to the brain and other organ systems.

Conditions that may mimic hypertensive encephalopathy include severe hypertension that may accompany congestive heart failure with pulmonary edema, and an anxiety episode that may markedly elevate blood pressure in a patient with preexisting labile hypertension (Jefferson and Marshall 1981a). History, physical examination, chest X ray, and electrocardiogram (ECG) should help differentiate these disorders. In addition, pheochromocytoma may present with paroxysmal hypertension along with headache, diaphoresis, palpitations, weakness, anxiety, and a variety of other neuropsychiatric symptoms. Measurement of urinary catecholamines and their metabolites will aid in the diagnosis.

Acid-Base Disturbances

Congestive heart failure (CHF) may be associated with hyperventilation and respiratory alkalosis. Excessive diuresis with volume contraction can lead to increased renal absorption of sodium and bicarbonate, with resulting metabolic alkalosis. If circulatory or respiratory failure occurs, metabolic or respiratory acidosis may ensue.

Acid-base disturbances may produce varying degrees of metabolic encephalopathy, with apathy, confusion, depressed level of consciousness, and stupor (Jefferson and Marshall 1981a). Symptoms will depend on the severity and acuteness of onset of the acid-base disturbances, and are often difficult to distinguish from those of the underlying disorder.

Treatment invariably involves correction of the underlying disorder. If metabolic acidosis is severe, administration of sodium bicarbonate may be necessary. Since cerebrospinal fluid (CSF) bicarbonate does not equilibrate rapidly with plasma, too rapid an administration of bicarbonate may lead to a relative CSF acidosis, and hence, a delayed respiratory alkalosis. Metabolic alkalosis may also be superimposed as renal and metabolic compensatory measures continue beyond the immediate correction of the disturbance (Levinsky 1980a), resulting in prolongation or worsening of encephalopathic features. Primary metabolic alkalosis associated with potassium, chloride, and volume depletion requires correction of these disturbances to enable the kidney to excrete bicarbonate and correct the alkalosis.

Electrolyte Disturbances

Hyponatremia. Hyponatremia reflects an excess of water relative to sodium concentration. In most cases there is an associated impairment in the kidney's ability to excrete a dilute urine. It is seen commonly in patients with CHF, who may have a decreased "effective" circulating volume because of decreased cardiac output or sequestration of fluid outside of the intravascular compartment. Hyponatremia will be maintained if there is excessive use of diuretics with further intravascular volume depletion and if the patient has access only to dilute fluids, orally or intravenously.

Other causes of hyponatremia in patients with OMS must also be ruled out. The syndrome of inappropriate antidiuretic hormone secretion (SIADH) results in failure to excrete an appropriately dilute urine despite the hyponatremia. Conditions associated with SIADH include malignancies (especially oat-cell carcinoma of the lung), pulmonary disease, CNS disease (trauma, encephalitis, meningitis, tumors, infarction), and various drugs (including carbamazepine, antidepressants, and antipsychotics). Acute psychosis itself has also been suggested as a cause of SIADH (Jefferson and Marshall 1981a). To date there is no adequate explanation.

Psychogenic polydipsia, when extreme or associated with impairment in renal diluting ability, may result in significant hyponatremia and symptoms of water intoxication. It may be associated with a variety of psychiatric syndromes, including schizophrenia, mania, and major depression with psychotic features.

Neuropsychiatric sequelae of hyponatremia will depend on the acuteness of onset and the severity of disturbance. Rapid reduction of serum sodium to 125 mEq/l may result in headache, nausea, vomiting, myoclonus, asterixis, seizure, and coma. Symptoms are probably related to cerebral edema, and focal as well as diffuse neurologic manifestations may occur (Jefferson and Marshall 1981a).

With more gradual onset, symptoms of hyponatremia are more insidious. Lethargy, sleepiness, weakness, muscle cramps, and a mild confusional state are common early manifestations. At times, a chronic headache may be the only symptom of hyponatremia (Jefferson and Marshall 1981a). If not recognized, further decline in serum sodium will eventually lead to delirium, stupor, and coma.

Treatment of hyponatremia should involve correction of underlying causes when possible. Mild to moderate hyponatremia associated with CHF will usually respond to general measures designed to improve cardiac output. When volume depletion is present, hyponatremia may respond to a reduction in diuretic dosage or cautious volume replacement with isotonic fluid. Conditions due to water overload may require restriction of free water intake. Hypertonic saline should be administered only if the clinical manifestations of hyponatremia are extreme (Levinsky 1980b).

Hypernatremia. Hypernatremia is due to a deficit of water relative to sodium concentration. Since hypertonicity normally leads to thirst and subsequent restoration of sodium balance, severe hypernatremia will persist only in patients who cannot respond to thirst by ingestion of fluid. This may be especially relevant in patients debilitated by cardiac disease, or in patients with OMS whose fluid intake may be limited because of depression, apathy, delusional ideation, or confusion.

Symptoms of hypernatremia, as with hyponatremia, will depend on the rate and severity of change in serum sodium concentration. Rapid elevation of plasma osmolality will result in a shift of fluid out of the intracellular compartment, including the CNS. Contraction of brain volume may result in tearing of venous sinuses with resulting intracerebral and subdural hemorrhage (Jefferson and Marshall 1981a). Focal neurologic abnormalities, seizures, delirium, stupor, and coma may result. More gradual onset of hyponatremia will result in nonspecific symptoms of a metabolic encephalopathy.

Treatment should include gradual correction of sodium balance with hypotonic fluid. Too rapid correction may result in cerebral edema with deterioration in neurologic status (Levinsky 1980b).

Hypokalemia. Hypokalemia may result from gastrointestinal or renal loss of potassium, or from intracellular shift of potassium associated with alkalosis or effects of insulin. In the cardiac patient, it is most often associated with diuretic use in the absence of adequate potassium supplementation. Volume contraction with resultant aldosterone secretion and metabolic alkalosis may exacerbate hypokalemia.

Manifestations of hypokalemia generally appear as serum levels drop below 3 mEq/l and primarily involve the neuromuscular and cardiac systems. Moderate degrees of potassium depletion may be asymptomatic or present with muscle weakness and cramps. More severe degrees of hypokalemia may result in more pronounced muscular weakness, hyporeflexia, lethargy, irritability, and confusion. ECG changes include T-wave flattening or inversion and a prominent U-wave. Digitalis toxicity may be enhanced and result in a variety of disturbances in cardiac rhythm and conduction (Jefferson and Marshall 1981a; Levinsky 1980b).

Treatment should include correction of the underlying disturbance and supplementation of potassium intake. If oral supplementation is not possible or if hypokalemia is severe, intravenous potassium should be administered cautiously.

Hyperkalemia. Hyperkalemia can result from excessive intake of potassium salts, impaired renal excretion of potassium, or shift from intracellular sites in association with trauma, acidosis, or drugs such as succinylcholine or digitalis. In the cardiac patient, hyperkalemia is seen most commonly when potassium-sparing diuretics are used in the presence of progressive renal insufficiency or continued oral potassium supplementation.

The most important effects of hyperkalemia are on the heart. ECG changes include peaked T-waves and prolongation of PR and QRS intervals. Various arrhythmias may occur, including sinus arrest, atrial fibrillation, supraventricular tachycardia, and complete heart block. Ultimately, ventricular fibrillation and cardiac arrest may ensue. Neuromuscular effects of hyperkalemia include weakness, hyporeflexia, and paresthesias. In more severe cases, a flaccid ascending paralysis may occur (Jefferson and Marshall 1981a; Levinsky 1980b).

Mild degrees of hyperkalemia may be treated by elimination of a cause, such as potassium-sparing diuretics. More severe hyperkalemia requires specific measures such as promoting intracellular shift with glucose, insulin, and bicarbonate, and increasing potassium excretion with cation exchange resins or dialysis. Calcium gluconate will help counter the adverse effects of hyperkalemia on cardiac and neuromuscular function (Jefferson and Marshall 1981a; Levinsky 1980b).

OMS Coexisting with Cardiovascular Disease

OMS and cardiovascular disease are both common entities, particularly in the elderly. It is estimated that 40 million Americans have some form of cardiovascular disease, and the prevalence of coronary, cerebrovascular, and hypertensive disease increases markedly with age (Levy 1985).

Similarly, psychotic symptoms from all causes increase significantly beyond age 65 years (Butler and Lewis 1973), and a large proportion of these are secondary to OMS. It is estimated that of the more than 25 million Americans currently older than 65 years, 11 to 12 percent have mild to moderate dementia and 4 to 5 percent moderate to severe dementia (Schneck et al. 1982). This age group is also uniquely prone to develop transient confusional states or delirium, particularly in response to a variety of physical illnesses or drugs (Lipowski 1983). It is, therefore, not surprising that cardiovascular disease and OMS may frequently occur in the same patient.

Coexistence of these conditions may seriously confound diagnosis and treatment. For example, patients with an OMS may be unable to provide an adequate history of symptoms of cardiac disease, and some manifestations of heart disease may go unnoticed or be attributed to the OMS (e.g., vague complaints, nocturnal dyspnea, agitation, increased confusion). Cardiac medications may not be taken as prescribed because of apathy, memory impairment, or delusional ideation. Even when taken properly, there may be a variety of drug side effects or drug interactions that can further impair cognitive function or worsen psychiatric symptoms (see below).

Conversely, symptoms of a new or developing OMS in patients with known cardiac disease may be mistakenly attributed to their heart disease without adequate search for other causes. Psychotropic medication used in treating an OMS may also adversely affect cardiac function (see below).

The diagnostic dilemmas posed by these patients require careful evaluation and continuous vigilance on the part of the physician; effective treatment is often dependent on careful collaboration among physicians, family, and other health care personnel.

While the bulk of this chapter focuses on drug-disease interactions in patients with OMS and cardiovascular disease, it should be noted that psychotherapeutic strategies may often be the initial intervention of choice and may help avoid a number of potentially adverse drug effects and interactions. Even when concomitant pharmacotherapy is required, an understanding and appropriate management of the psychological impact of illness in a given patient is conducive to a favorable outcome.

Patients with both cardiac disease and OMS are in "double jeopardy," facing conflicts relating to loss of physical integrity as well as cognitive decline. Fears of death, prolonged disability, loss of control over bodily functions, forced dependency, and loss of self-esteem with abrogation of prior roles are all common reactions. In addition, cognitive impairment may lessen the efficacy of previously adequate psychological defense mechanisms and coping skills, resulting in even greater degrees of anxiety and distress.

Some knowledge of a patient's premorbid personality is essential in assessing the potential impact of a given illness. For example, a person with rigid obsessional defenses or narcissistic personality traits may have a much more severe reaction to even relatively minor cognitive impairment or cardiac disease than someone with histrionic or dependent traits. Reactions of family members or significant others to the illness is also an important variable.

The type of psychotherapeutic interventions indicated will depend in part on the degree of cognitive impairment, severity of physical illness, and nature of the psychiatric disturbance, as well as premorbid personality characteristics. Patients with relatively minor or focal cognitive impairment and with the capacity for insight may benefit from a brief, dynamically oriented approach focusing on their fears and fantasies about the meaning of their illness in the context of prior life events and goals, and both the conscious and unconscious conflicts that are activated as a result. Those with prolonged depressive symptoms may benefit from cognitive therapy to help restructure persistent negative views of themselves and the world. When anxiety symptoms are prominent, relaxation techniques may be a useful adjunct to other therapeutic modalities.

Patients with substantial cognitive impairment, severe medical illness, or reduced capacity for insight may require a supportive approach, aimed at reinforcing adaptive defense mechanisms and coping strategies, while discouraging those that are less adaptive and more regressive. Moderate cognitive impairment may be helped by memory training techniques and other forms of cognitive rehabilitation.

Patients with advanced dementia or delirium will require environmental manipulation to optimize levels of stimulation and maximize orientation and reality testing. Behavioral techniques and frequent but brief contacts with a consistent therapist may also help diminish anxiety and agitation. The ultimate goal of all these interventions is to help patients cope with physical illness and cognitive decline while preserving a sense of dignity and maximizing remaining functional abilities.

Drug-Disease Interactions

Although I will focus on the cardiovascular and neuropsychiatric side effects of psychotropic and cardiovascular drugs, respectively (drug-disease interactions), it should be noted that cardiac disease itself can produce a number of pharmacokinetic changes (disease-drug interactions).

For example, severe congestive heart failure may result in gastrointestinal edema and hence diminished absorption and decreased effect of certain drugs. On the other hand, diminished renal and hepatic blood flow and chronic passive congestion of the liver may lead to decreased metabolism and increased effect of other drugs. These factors must be balanced against each other as well as a variety of potential drug-drug interactions in arriving at a rational pharmacotherapeutic regimen.

Cardiovascular Effects of Psychotropic Drugs

Tricyclic antidepressants (TCAs). It is important to differentiate cardiac effects of the TCAs at high concentrations (i.e., overdose) from those seen at normal therapeutic levels, and to distinguish side effects in patients with specific types of cardiac disease from those with normal cardiac function.

In general, TCAs have effects on cardiac conduction resembling those of the Type 1 antiarrhythmic drugs quinidine, procainamide, and disopyramide; these include decreased automaticity; decreased conduction velocity; prolonged effective refractory period; prolonged PR, QRS, and QT intervals; and decreased T-wave amplitude. His-bundle studies have shown that the prolonged PR interval on the standard ECG results from slowing of conduction distal to the A-V node (H-V interval), with conduction across the A-V node itself (A-H interval) remaining normal (Glassman and Bigger 1981). The clinical relevance of these effects varies considerably, depending on other characteristics of the particular antidepressant, blood level of the drug, interaction with other drugs, and presence and nature of underlying heart disease.

Among the classic TCAs, significant differences have been found in their effects on cardiac conduction. In patients free from significant conduction delays, therapeutic concentrations of nortriptyline (50 to 150 ng/ml) have little effect on PR or QRS intervals. However, delayed conduction may occur at plasma levels above 200 ng/ml, or only slightly higher than the postulated "therapeutic window" for nortriptyline

(Vohra et al. 1975; Ziegler et al. 1977). Early studies suggesting that doxepin has less effect on cardiac conduction than nortriptyline did not control for blood levels of medication and are not conclusive (Burrows et al. 1977; Luchins 1983b). Imipramine, by contrast, has been shown regularly to increase PR, QRS, and QT intervals at well within therapeutic levels (Giardinia et al. 1979). Higher degrees of heart block are rarely, if ever, produced by therapeutic doses of TCAs alone in the absence of preexisting conduction system disease. Those at greatest risk for development of second- or third-degree heart block are patients with the most severe conduction deficits prior to treatment (Glassman and Bigger 1981).

Most reports examining the effect of TCAs on heart rate have studied imipramine and, to a lesser extent, desipramine (Giardinia et al. 1979; Glassman and Bigger 1981; Veith et al. 1982). They generally reveal a modest tendency to increase heart rate during the first several weeks of treatment, with this effect diminishing over the next several weeks. Less reliable data are available for amitriptyline and nortriptyline, but they may tend to have a greater effect on the heart rate than the former two drugs (Glassman 1984a; Glassman and Bigger 1981). While some investigators report that clinically significant sinus tachycardia is a rare side effect of TCAs, others report this to be a more frequent problem, especially in a medically ill population (Cassem 1982).

A number of studies have confirmed the usefulness of imipramine and other TCAs in reducing the frequency of ventricular premature contractions (Bigger et al. 19787; Giardinia et al 1981; Glassman and Bigger 1981). At therapeutic levels, these drugs are, therefore, not only safe in depressed patients with certain arrhythmias, but may actually be useful in the treatment of the arrhythmias and allow for reduction or discontinuation of the Type 1 antiarrhythmic drugs.

One of the most frequent and troublesome side effects of TCAs is orthostatic hypotension. If severe, it can lead to falls, fractures, myocardial infarction, and other serious complications. The drug most studied for its effect on blood pressure is imipramine, and several important clinical observations have been made. Patients who develop orthostatic hypotension seem to do so early in treatment and show little tendency to accommodate to this effect (Glassman et al. 1979; Hayes et al. 1977). At least one study found that orthostasis was maximal at imipramine blood levels well below those therapeutic for depression (Glassman et al. 1979). While there is some anecdotal clinical evidence to the contrary, these data would suggest that patients with significant orthostatic hypotension on a given dose of imipramine would not benefit from a reduction in dose. Conversely, increasing the dose would not increase orthostasis.

Less information is available for other TCAs, but amitriptyline and desipramine can also produce significant orthostatic hypotension (Hayes et al. 1977; Nelson et al. 1982). The only currently available TCAs for which there is evidence of significantly less orthostatic effect compared to imipramine are nortriptyline (Freyschuss et al. 1970; Roose et al. 1981) and doxepin (Neshkes et al. 1985).

The group of patients at greatest risk for severe orthostatic hypotension with TCAs are those with major depression and CHF (Glassman et al. 1983; Veith et al. 1982). At this point, it is not clear whether this effect is related directly to the impaired left ventricular performance, to interaction of TCAs with other cardioactive drugs, or to a combination of factors. The presence of major depression itself appears related to abnormalities in autonomic and peripheral noradrenergic function, and may be a relevant variable in the development of orthostasis (Friedman 1978; Giardinia et al. 1981; Jarvik et al. 1983; Lake et al. 1982).

Management of orthostatic hypotension should include avoidance of medication that may have additive effects on blood pressure, careful attention to hydration status, use of antigravity support stockings, and, in refractory cases, consideration of the cautious use of sodium chloride fludrocortisone (a mineralocorticoid) or sympatho-mimetics. In some patients, giving the antidepressant medication in divided doses or switching to a different drug may be helpful.

While depressed patients with congestive heart failure may be uniquely prone to develop problems of orthostatic hypotension, studies using radionucleide angiog-raphy have shown that TCAs do not further impair left ventricular performance even in this high-risk group (Glassman et al. 1983; Veith et al. 1982).

When taken in overdoses, TCAs can have a number of adverse cardiac effects resulting in sinus arrhythmias, premature ventricular contractions, ventricular tachy-cardia, ventricular fibrillation, second- or third-degree A-V block, bundle branch block, and refractory hypotension. Serious arrhythmias may occur up to two to three days following ingestion; therefore, continuous cardiac monitoring for this period is es-sential. Type 1 antiarrhythmic drugs are contraindicated because their cardiac effects are similar to those of TCAs. Propranolol should also be avoided because it may further depress myocardial contractility. Molar sodium lactate may be useful in treat-ing ventricular arrhythmias associated with conduction defects. Serious ventricular arrhythmias may necessitate artificial pacemaker insertion. Circulatory collapse is probably secondary to vasodilation and impaired myocardial contractility and may respond to volume expansion and dopamine drip (Bigger et al. 1978).

Use of TCAs following myocardial infarction (MI) poses special clinical problems. Depression is common following an MI and may complicate recovery (Stern et al. 1976; Wishnie et al. 1970). It is generally agreed that TCAs are relatively contraindi-cated in the acute recovery period following an MI, especially in the presence of significant conduction defects or unstable arrhythmias. However, there are scant data available on their use in this population, and the risks must be weighed against those of the psychophysiologic stress of severe depression (Jefferson 1983).

In the stable cardiac patient (i.e., at least four months post-MI and without significant conduction defects or unstable arrhythmia), TCAs can be safely used to treat major depression (Raskind et al. 1982a). A baseline ECG should be obtained, along with assessment of electrolytes, plasma levels of cardiac medications, and pos-tural blood pressure change. A conservative starting dose should be used (25 to 50 mg/day), and the dosage increased by 25 mg every two to three days until a therapeutic dosage is reached (Levenson and Friedel 1985). The ECG should be monitored at least one to two times per week while dosage is being adjusted, along with frequent checks of pulse rate and postural blood pressure change. Because of wide variation in rates of hepatic metabolism of TCAs, monitoring of plasma levels can be useful in this high-risk population. This is especially true of drugs for which therapeutic plasma levels have been fairly well defined, such as nortriptyline, imipramine, and desipra-mine (Task Force on the Use of Laboratory Tests in Psychiatry 1985). In the elderly, therapeutic plasma levels await definition, and doses should generally be even lower.

For patients with significant conduction defects for whom TCAs appear strongly indicated, implantation of a cardiac pacemaker might be considered. Alternative con-siderations include the use of monoamine oxidase inhibitors (MAOIs) or low doses of psychostimulants, although their potential adverse effects on blood pressure and cardiac rhythm must be taken into account. Some newer antidepressants such as trazodone bupropion and fluoxetine may have fewer effects on cardiac conduction than TCAs, but their relative safety in this population requires further substantiation (Levenson and Friedel 1935). Alprazolam has few cardiac side effects, but its efficacy as an antidepressant also remains to be substantiated (Binder 1984). Electroconvulsive therapy (ECT) has been used safely in patients with recent MIs (Pitts 1982), but the risks of transient hypertension, tachycardia, and arrhythmia may be significant. Systematic studies in post-MI patients comparing the safety of ECT to that of antidepressant medication are lacking.

In summary, therapeutic doses of TCAs are generally free from serious cardiovascular side effects in depressed patients without heart disease. Orthostatic hypotension is the most common significant complication of these drugs, and it may be especially troublesome in patients with congestive heart failure. Patients with bundle branch block are at risk for higher degrees of heart block; those with ventricular arrhythmias may show improvement. TCAs at therapeutic levels have minimal negative inotropic effect, even in patients with significant congestive heart failure. TCAs pose certain risks in the acute post-MI setting, and alternative treatments should be considered. However, risks must be weighed against those of depression itself, and TCAs can be safely used in the stable post-MI patient.

Newer antidepressants.   Amoxapine is a demethylated derivative of the antipsychotic loxapine and has significant dopamine-blocking activity, in addition to its noradrenergic and serotonergic effects. The data on cardiovascular effects of amoxapine are limited. Case reports of overdoses suggest relatively few serious cardiovascular sequelae (Bock et al. 1982; Kulig et al. 1982). However, patients taking both therapeutic doses as well as those taking overdoses have manifested a variety of disturbances in cardiac conduction and rhythm including bundle branch block, atrial flutter, and premature atrial contractions (Bock et al. 1982; Oritz and Josef 1983; Zavodnick 1981). Orthostatic hypotension does occur with amoxapine, but its incidence compared with other antidepressants is not clear.

Maprotiline is a tetracyclic compound. Initial claims of a lower incidence of cardiovascular toxicity have not been clearly substantiated. Like TCAs, maprotiline can cause orthostatic hypotension (Burckhardt et al. 1978; Edwards and Goldie 1983), conduction delays at normal therapeutic doses (Edwards and Goldie 1983), and has been associated in overdose with cardiovascular death with heart block and asystole (Crome and Newman 1979).

Trazodone is a triazolopyridine derivative that has a chemical structure and cardiovascular profile distinct from that of other antidepressants (Himmelhoch 1982). One major difference is the virtual absence of anticholinergic effects reported in both in vivo and in vitro studies (Gershon and Newton 1980; Richelson 1983). The other major difference is trazodone's apparently minimal effects on cardiac conduction compared with TCAs (Burgess et al. 1982; Gomoll and Byrne 1979; Hayes et al. 1983). There are now several case reports of trazodone overdoses in which no cardiovascular complications, including conduction delays, occurred (Henry and Ali 1983; Lesar et al. 1983; Lippman et al. 1982). However, there are also a growing number of case reports of conduction delays associated with therapeutic doses of trazodone in patients with varying degrees of cardiovascular disease (Irwin and Spar 1983; McCracken and Kosanin 1984; Rausch et al. 1984). In addition, trazodone has been reported to increase ventricular ectopy in some patients with preexisting ventricular arrhythmias (Janowsky et al. 1983a, 1983b). Trazodone does cause orthostatic hypotension, although further studies are needed to clarify whether the pattern is different from that associated with TCAs (Glassman 1984b). It would, therefore, seem advisable to exercise caution in the use of trazodone for patients with underlying conduction defects, ventricular arrhythmias, or severe congestive heart failure.

Fluoxetine is a newly released antidepressant that selectively inhibits neuronal serotonin uptake. It has minimal affinity for histaminic, muscarinic, noradrenergic and serotinergic receptors which may be related to its low incidence of adverse cardiac effects (Stark et al. 1988). Fluoxetine generally causes a slight slowing of heart rate but no significant change in PR, QRS, or QT intervals (Fisch 1985). The few reported cases of overdose with fluoxetine have also failed to show significant ECG changes (Fisch 1985; Cooper 1988). Incidence of orthostatic hypotension with fluoxetine requires further study but initial data suggest it is relatively infrequent (Wernicke 1985). Thus fluoxetine appears to be a promising new agent for treatment of depression in cardiac patients, but further studies are required in patients with specific types of cardiac disease.

MAOIs. Animal studies have shown that different MAOIs may have very different cardiac effects (Risch et al. 1982). For example, phenelzine has positive inotropic effects; iproniazid has negative inotropic effects. Large doses of MAOIs cause vasodilation of coronary arteries, but this is probably insignificant at usual clinical doses.

Amphetamine-like effects, hypertensive episodes, and onsets of atrial flutter have been associated with tranylcypromine independent of degree of monoamine oxidase (MAO) inhibition. With significant MAO inhibition, ingestion of tyramine or other indirect-acting sympathomimetics may lead to serious hypertensive crisis. The selective MAO-B inhibitor, L-deprenyl, offers the major safety advantage of no significant increase in tyramine sensitivity at low doses, but its relative efficacy as an antidepressant compared with other MAOIs is still under study (Mann et al. 1984).

One of the most common cardiovascular side effects of MAOIs is orthostatic hypotension. The exact incidence is difficult to determine because of anecdotal and often contradictory reports, but estimates range from 1 percent (Rabkin et al. 1985) to 47 percent (Robinson et al. 1978). There may be significant differences between MAOIs and TCAs in the pattern of blood pressure changes produced. Kronig et al. (1983) found that phenelzine, unlike TCAs, caused a decrease in supine systolic pressure, as well as an orthostatic drop. In addition, the blood pressure effects of phenelzine occurred over a different time course than with TCAs. Both the maximum orthostatic drop and maximum decrease in supine systolic pressure occurred after four weeks on phenelzine, compared with a maximum drop by one week with imipramine. This suggests the need for more prolonged monitoring of blood pressure with patients on phenelzine because of the possibility of a delayed onset of significant orthostatic hypotension.

ECG effects of MAOIs include a modest decrease in heart rate and shortening of the QT interval (Robinson et al. 1982) and are independent of the degree of MAO inhibition. Compared with TCAs, MAOIs have significantly fewer anticholinergic effects (Cassem 1982).

In summary, MAOIs can have variable, but usually minimal effects on cardiac rate, rhythm, conduction, and contractility. With appropriate dietary restrictions, they can generally be used safely, even in patients with heart failure or conduction delays. The most frequent serious complication is orthostatic hypotension, the management of which is similar to that described above in the section on TCAs except that monitoring needs to be prolonged.

Lithium carbonate. At therapeutic concentrations in patients without significant cardiovascular disease, lithium produces predominantly benign and reversible effects on the ECG. These include T-wave flattening or inversion and occasional U-waves. These changes resemble the effects of hypokalemia, although they occur with normal serum potassium levels, and may be seen in at least 20 to 30 percent of patients on lithium (Mitchell and Mackenzie 1982).

A number of case reports have also implicated therapeutic levels of lithium in reversible interference with sinoatrial and atrioventricular conduction (Hagman et al. 1979; Risch et al. 1981). This may result in episodic complaints of dizziness or syncopal episodes, which should prompt Holter monitoring.

Lithium has also been noted to diminish the frequency of preexisting premature atrial contractions and supraventricular tachyarrhythmias, but may induce or worsen premature ventricular contractions and ventricular arrhythmias (Risch et al. 1982; Tilkian et al. 1976). These findings have occurred in patients without cardiac disease and at therapeutic lithium levels, and have normalized with discontinuation of lithium.

Lithium may also cause edema and precipitate or aggravate CHF. Therapeutic lithium levels have been associated in several cases with diffuse myocarditis and death (Stancer and Kivi 1971; Swedberg and Winblad 1974).

At toxic levels lithium may cause prolongation and depression of ST and QT intervals and eventually arrhythmias, circulatory collapse, and death. Treatment of lithium intoxication is primarily supportive while attempting to hasten lithium excretion. Severe cases require admission to an intensive care unit and continuous cardiac monitoring. Lithium is excreted by the kidneys, and serum levels drop approximately 50 percent every one to two days after discontinuation of lithium. Osmotic diuresis, aminophylline, urea, mannitol, alkalinization of the urine, and hemodialysis may all hasten excretion. Supportive treatment should include correction of fluid and electrolyte disturbance, maintenance of renal function, and support of blood pressure and respiration (Risch et al. 1982).

The incidence of significant ECG abnormalities associated with lithium therapy appears greatest in patients over age 60, so the ECG should be monitored at least at yearly intervals in this population and more often if there is a history of cardiac disease. Other drugs that prolong intraventricular conduction (e.g., TCAs, phenothiazines, quinidine) should be used with caution (Mitchell and Mackenzie 1982). Arrhythmias may first develop after lithium therapy has continued for over a year, so continued caution over a prolonged period may be required in high-risk patients. Particular caution should also be used in debilitated patients prone to dehydration, those with lithium-induced renal-concentrating defects, and patients on diuretics because they may be especially vulnerable to lithium toxicity.

Antipsychotics. Antipsychotics may have a variety of effects at different levels of the cardiovascular system, such as direct effects on cardiac muscle; peripheral effects, which include cholinergic, alpha adrenergic, histaminergic, and serotonergic blockade, as well as adrenergic agonist activity; and central effects involving dopaminergic, serotonergic, and cholinergic systems, and probably peptide and opiate neurotransmitters as well.

At the level of the myocardium, phenothiazines have been reported to decrease membrane permeability, resulting in decreased myocardial contractility and repolarization abnormalities. They also prolong atrial and ventricular conduction time and refractory periods (Risch et al. 1981). While some of the cardiac effects of neuroleptics, particularly thioridazine, resemble those of the class 1 antiarrhythmics, some reports suggested that other cardiac effects of thioridazine may be due to calcium channel blockade (e.g., Gould et al. 1984). Clinically, these effects may produce a number of ECG changes, as well as cardiac conduction defects, arrhythmias, and aggravation of congestive heart failure (Alexander 1968; Stimmel 1975).

In general, cardiac effects are most pronounced with piperidine phenothiazines such as thioridazine, intermediate with aliphatic phenothiazines such as chlorpromazine, and least common with piperazine phenothiazines, thioxanthenes, and butyrophenones. ECG changes reported with therapeutic doses of phenothiazines include prolongation of the QT interval, lowering of the ST segment, depression or notching of T-waves, and appearance of U-waves (Ban and St. Jean 1964).

Neuroleptics may act centrally to depress vasomotor regulatory centers and peripherally to depress cardiovascular reflexes. Alpha-adrenergic blockade may cause local vasodilation and increased coronary artery blood flow, a factor that may be offset by systemic hypotension. Elevated resting and exercising pulse and a reduction in exercise-induced cardiac output may accompany chronic neuroleptization (Risch et al. 1981).

Antipsychotics may cause orthostatic hypotension, especially the aliphatic and piperidine phenothiazines. There are few controlled studies of this side effect, but available data suggest that significant systolic drops (10 to 40 mm Hg or more) are most common with parenteral administration (greater than 25 to 50 mg) or larger oral doses (greater than 750 mg) of chlorpromazine or thioridazine (Risch et al. 1981). These orthostatic changes, like those occurring with antidepressants, may be particularly prominent and dangerous in patients taking other drugs that may affect blood pressure regulation, in those with intravascular volume depletion, or in those with congestive heart failure.

There are occasional reports that implicate phenothiazines in serious conduction disturbances, arrhythmias, and sudden death. The significance of these reports is often difficult to evaluate because patients may have been taking other cardioactive medications or may have had preexisting cardiac disease. In a few cases they report apparently direct effects of phenothiazines on cardiac conduction or rhythm in otherwise apparently healthy individuals (Aherwadker et al. 1964; Giles and Modlin 1968). In other cases, preexisting ventricular premature contractions in the presence of a prolonged QT interval produced by phenothiazines may have increased the likelihood of an "R-on-T" phenomenon and subsequent ventricular fibrillation.

Neuropsychiatric Effects of Cardiac Drugs

Digitalis. The ability of digitalis preparations to produce neuropsychiatric symptoms has been recognized since the nineteenth century. Digitalis has one of the narrowest therapeutic ratios of any commonly used drug, and estimates of the frequency of intoxication range from 20 percent in the general hospital population (Greenblatt and Shader 1972) to 35 percent of medically hospitalized patients taking digitalis (Smith 1973). Cardiac arrhythmias of various types are the most serious consequence of digitalis toxicity, although gastrointestinal, visual, and CNS symptoms are common and may be the only initial manifestations.

A number of factors may predispose patients to develop digitalis toxicity (Greenblatt and Shader 1972). Old age is commonly cited as one of these. However, it may be that other factors than age per se are responsible, such as changes in volume of distribution due to decline in muscle mass or decline in renal function in the case of preparations like digoxin that are primarily excreted through the kidney. Other factors include acute myocardial ischemia, hypoxia, hypokalemia, magnesium depletion, hypercalcemia, hypothyroidism, and cor pulmonale.

A wide variety of CNS symptoms have been reported in association with digitalis toxicity. Most have been based on retrospective case reports, although some have prospectively correlated clinical signs with serum glycoside level (Greenblatt and Shader 1972). Nonspecific complaints of weakness, fatigue, malaise, drowsiness, lassitude, anorexia, restlessness, irritability, and agitation are the most common and may occur at therapeutic levels. Other neuropsychiatric symptoms attributed to digitalis toxicity include depression, manic-like behavior with euphoria and giddiness, labile mood, belligerence, combativeness, insomnia, nightmares, paresthesias, vertigo, ataxia, memory loss, aphasia, delusions, hallucinations, delirium, and, at very high levels, seizure, stupor, and coma.

The classic visual abnormalities associated with digitalis intoxication are hazy vision, scotomas, flickering halos, and chromatopsia (objects appearing to have yellow-green borders or tints). However, there are also reports of more dramatic and bizarre visual phenomena (including formed hallucinations) occurring as a result of digitalis toxicity (Greenblatt and Shader 1972; Volpe and Soave 1979).

Beta blockers. Since the introduction of propranolol in 1964, the use of and number of indications for beta blockers have steadily increased. The psychopharmacologic aspects of these drugs have been the subject of several reviews (Greenblatt and Shader 1972; Jefferson 1974).

Paykel et al. (1982) examined the incidence of side effects of propranolol in 31 published clinical trials involving 1,773 patients. Dosage varied between 80 and 400 mg/day. Sedation, lethargy, and fatigue were among the most common neuropsychiatric side effects, reported in 3.8 percent of the cases. Light-headedness was reported in 0.7 percent, dizziness in 2 percent, and insomnia in 0.7 percent. Nightmares or bizarre and disturbing dreams were reported in 1.6 percent. Visual hallucinations were found in 0.6 percent, and this number increased considerably if one included hallucinations and perceptual distortions occurring only in the hypnogogic or hypnopompic state. In many instances these side effects appeared dose related, but this was not always the case.

Depression is one of the more talked-about side effects of propranolol, but its actual frequency is difficult to evaluate. Many case reports are retrospective and anecdotal; early reports often confounded symptoms of lethargy and fatigue with depression, and patients with a previous history or family history of major depression are not always distinguished from patients without such histories. In Paykel et al.'s (1982) review, the incidence of significant depression was 1.1 percent. In another study, depression was seen in 0.7 percent of patients on propranolol compared with 0.4 percent on hydrochlorothiazide (Veterans Administration Cooperative Study Group on Antihypertensive Agents 1982). It is generally agreed that the risk is increased for patients with a personal or family history of major depression, and although a positive dose-response relationship is suggested, it is by no means confirmed (Petrie et al. 1982b).

There have now been a number of reports of a variety of psychotic symptoms, including full-blown schizophrenic-like disorders, associated with the use of propranolol or other beta blockers in patients both with and without prior histories or family histories of psychiatric illness (Gershon et al. 1979; Steinert and Pugh 1979; Thompson 1979). Some are associated with varying degrees of cognitive impairment, including delirium (Kuhl 1979; Kurland 1979; Remick et al. 1981; Topliss and Bond 1977); others occur in the presence of apparently normal cognitive function. The effect of dose again appears variable. While some reported abnormal mental status only at high doses (greater than 500 mg) of propranolol (Fraser and Carr 1976; Kuhl 1979), other occurrences have been reported at more usual therapeutic doses (160 mg or less) (Gershon et al. 1979; Remick et al. 1981). Unfortunately, the significance of some of these case reports is difficult to evaluate because of unclear definition of terms, inadequate description of mental status, or the presence of medical conditions or other drugs that might affect mental status.

While this discussion has focused on propranolol, most of these side effects have been reported with other beta blockers as well. There is some evidence that less lipophilic beta blockers such as atenolol and nadolol may have a lower propensity to produce central effects than the more lipophilic beta blockers such as propranolol (McNeil et al. 1982; White and Riotte 1982), although this has not clearly been established.

Calcium channel blockers. The calcium channel blockers, a relatively new class of drugs, are used in cardiology principally to treat supraventricular arrhythmias and angina pectoris, although other uses have also been suggested (McSweeney et al. 1981). Their mechanism of action is believed to involve the blockade of the slow calcium ion channel, which is involved in excitation-contraction coupling of cardiac smooth muscle cells, as well as the activation of sinoatrial and atrioventricular pacemaker cells. Verapamil and diltiazem have relatively greater effects on nodal tissue (slowing conduction), whereas nifedipine has relatively greater effect on arteriolar smooth muscle cells (causing vasodilation) (McSweeney et al. 1983).

Neuropsychiatric side effects reported with verapamil have included dizziness, headache, and fatigue (McSweeney et al. 1982b). It should be used with caution in patients with A-V conduction delays, CHF, and those taking drugs that may further slow A-V conduction (e.g., digitalis) or beta blockers that may result in additive negative inotropic or chronotropic effects. Both verapamil and nifedipine have been shown to increase plasma digoxin levels, thereby increasing risk of toxicity (McSweeney et al. 1982a).

Of interest are several case reports suggesting that verapamil may have antidepressant effects (Höschl 1983) and antimanic effects (Dubovsky et al. 1982; Giannini et al. 1984), as well as a possible role in maintenance therapy for bipolar illness (Gitlin and Weiss 1984). Further studies are needed to confirm these findings. Nifedipine, like verapamil, has also been reported to cause dizziness, headache, and fatigue. Individual case reports have also implicated nifedipine in the development of an acute agitated and anxious state (Freed and Reiner 1984) and of Capgras' syndrome (Franklin et al. 1982).

Antiarrhythmics. Lidocaine, a local anesthetic, is used for acute treatment and prevention of life-threatening ventricular arrhythmias. According to the Boston Collaborative Drug Surveillance Program (Greenblatt 1976), 3.1 percent of patients receiving intravenous lidocaine have CNS complications. Neuropsychiatric manifestations of toxicity have included numbness, tremor, weakness, drowsiness, euphoria, difficulty concentrating, disorientation, dysarthria, agitation, and acute psychotic episodes. High concentrations of lidocaine may cause seizures, but at lower concentrations it has anticonvulsant properties. Toxicity may occur at plasma levels of 5 to 6 μg/ml, but there is considerable individual variation (Lloyd and Greenblatt 1981).

Quinidine is an antiarrhythmic used in the treatment and prevention of atrial fibrillation, as well as certain other supraventricular and ventricular arrhythmias. Rarely, even small doses may produce symptoms of the syndrome known as cinchonism, which includes headache, tinnitus, distorted vision, apprehension, excitement, and confusion (Moe and Abildskov 1975). Of interest is a case report of a dementia-like syndrome developing in a 72-year-old woman over a 14-year period, which coincided with the length of time she had been on quinidine (Gilbert 1977). Dramatic improvement in her condition was noted within 24 hours after discontinuing the drug and was maintained over the next two months.

Procainamide has electrophysiologic effects similar to those of quinidine. Clinically, its principal use is in the treatment and prevention of ventricular tachyarrhythmias. Procainamide has been reported to cause weakness, depression, giddiness, and hallucinations (Moe and Abildskov 1975). Chronic use may induce a systemic lupus erythematosus-like syndrome, which rarely has been associated with CNS manifestations of this disorder. A case suggestive of procainamide-induced psychosis has been reported, although the patient had an underlying bipolar illness, and exacerbation of a developing manic episode could not be ruled out (McCrum and Guidry 1978).

Disopyramide has a mechanism of action similar to that of quinidine and procainamide and is most frequently used for the suppression of frequent ventricular extrasystoles. While the overall incidence of adverse effects has been reported to be less than with quinidine, it has greater anticholinergic effects and hence greater potential for production of a central anticholinergic syndrome. This may have been a factor in the several case reports of acute psychosis associated with the use of this drug (Falk et al. 1977; Padfield et al. 1977). Additional side effects associated with disopyramide have included headache, fatigue, insomnia, anxiety, impotence, and depression, although the incidence is low and a causal relationship has not been documented (Jefferson and Marshall 1981a). Its therapeutic and toxic effects may be potentiated by high plasma potassium concentration (Braunwald 1980b).

Phenytoin, although used primarily as an anticonvulsant, also has an established role as an antiarrhythmic agent. Unlike quinidine, phenytoin does not reduce atrioventricular or intraventricular conduction velocity and does not prolong the ventricular refractory period. It is effective in treating supraventricular and ventricular arrhythmias, particularly those resulting from digitalis toxicity. Adverse neuropsychiatric effects of phenytoin, usually occurring at toxic blood levels (greater than 20 μg/ml), include nystagmus, ataxia, dysarthria, lethargy, confusion, hyperactivity, and hallucinations (Jefferson and Marshall 1981a). Chronic use may be associated with a folate-responsive megaloblastic anemia and peripheral neuropathy (Braunwald 1980b).

Antihypertensive agents.   Reserpine, while still in use today, to a large extent has been replaced by other more specific drugs with fewer side effects. The common clinical observation of depression occurring in patients treated with reserpine and subsequent elucidation of its mechanism of action—depletion of catecholamines and serotonin from presynaptic intraneuronal storage-sites—were major factors in the development of the biogenic amine theory of depression. The average incidence of depression in patients treated with reserpine is reported to be 20 percent, but the definition of depression used in many of the early studies is far from clear. When limited to "severe" depression with prominent "endogenous" features, the incidence is closer to 5 percent (Goodwin et al. 1972). The dosage of reserpine at which depression is reported ranges from 0.25 to 10 mg/day, with most cases occurring at doses over 0.5 mg/day. There is generally a lag period of two to eight months with an average of five months between starting the drug and appearance of depressive symptoms. A past history of affective illness appears to be the single most reliable predictor of who will develop depression on reserpine. This fact, along with the lack of clear dose-response relationship and frequent continuation of depression after stopping the drug, suggests that reserpine may precipitate depression in susceptible individuals rather than inducing it de novo (Goodwin et al. 1972). Other neuropsychiatric side effects reported with reserpine include anxiety, OMS with visual hallucinations and altered sensorium, nightmares, and altered sleep pattern with increased rapid eye movement (REM) and decreased slow-wave sleep.

Methyldopa is a centrally acting antihypertensive with symptomatic effects. Sedation is the most frequently reported neuropsychiatric side effect, and excessive lethargy, drowsiness, or fatigue are reported to occur in at least 32.5 to 51 percent of patients (Paykel et al. 1982). These complaints are usually transient, often beginning with the first dose and diminishing over the next few weeks. Reports of lack of concentration and forgetfulness may be related to the sedative effects (Adler 1974). By contrast, there are several reports of sleep disturbance, nightmares, and insomnia, usually during initiation of treatment. Sleep studies have revealed increased REM sleep and decreased slow-wave sleep (Paykel et al. 1982), a finding similar to that reported with reserpine. Symptoms of dizziness and faintness may be related to central sedation and/or orthostatic hypotension. Depression is an important side effect of methyldopa, although its incidence is difficult to evaluate. As with reserpine, many of the early reports did not clearly define criteria used for depression or differentiate depression from nonspecific symptoms related to sedation. In their review of a series of studies conducted between 1962 and 1975, Paykel et al. (1982) estimated the incidence of depression to be 3.6 percent, occurring with sufficient severity to require complete withdrawal of the drug in slightly less than one-third of the depressed patients. This incidence appears to be lower than that with reserpine, but higher than that reported for most other antihypertensive drugs. As with reserpine, a past history of depression seems to be an important risk factor for development of depression while taking methyldopa. Unlike reserpine, the onset of depression seems to occur relatively early in the course of treatment and often subsides after withdrawal of the drug. While there is not a clear dose relationship, it may be that the relatively lower doses used in recent years explains in part the lower incidence of depression reported in earlier studies (Paykel et al. 1982). There are rare reports of a reversible parkinsonian-like syndrome produced by methyldopa, with onset between three weeks and eight months of treatment at doses varying between 1 and 3 g/day (Paykel et al. 1982). The mechanism is presumed to be drug-induced dopamine depletion, and all cases remitted within one week after withdrawal of the drug.

Clonidine is another centrally acting sympatholytic whose mechanism probably involves stimulation of the inhibitory alpha-2 adrenergic receptors. As with methyldopa, sedation is the most prominent neuropsychiatric side effect, with related complaints of drowsiness, lethargy, fatigue, weakness, or dizziness occurring in 24 to 95 percent of patients (Paykel et al. 1982). Sleep disturbance and nightmares have also been reported. Reports of depression have been relatively infrequent, with a total incidence in one series of 1.5 percent (Paykel et al. 1982). As with beta blockers, reserpine, and methyldopa, most occurrences were in patients with prior history of depression. There are occasional reports of other neuropsychiatric symptoms attributed to clonidine, including anxiety, paranoid hallucinations, hypomania, and confusional states (Paykel et al. 1982). The etiologic role of clonidine in these reports has not been clearly established. Abrupt discontinuation of clonidine may produce a withdrawal syndrome characterized by heightened sympathetic activity (Hunyor et al. 1973); symptoms include hypertension, headache, anxiety, diaphoresis, tremor, restlessness, and vivid dreams. Clonidine has been reported to have antianxiety effects in animals and humans, although its anxiolytic effects in humans are only partially effective and seem to diminish with time (Hoehn-Saric et al. 1981; Liebowitz et al. 1981). It has been suggested that these anxiolytic effects may be secondary to the general effects of clonidine on arousal mediated through the locus ceruleus (Insel et al. 1984). Clonidine has also been found useful in blocking symptoms of sympathetic overactivity during opiate withdrawal (Gold et al. 1978), treatment of Tourette's syndrome (Shapiro et al. 1983), obsessive-compulsive disorder (Knesevich 1982), and mania (Jouvent et al. 1980).

Guanethidine is a peripherally acting sympatholytic drug that blocks post-ganglionic adrenergic neurons. While it does not readily cross the blood-brain barrier, the possibility of central effects has not been excluded. The most troublesome side effect of guanethidine is dose-dependent hypotension, particularly orthostatic and exertional, with consequent risk in some patients of syncope, transient ischemic attack, cerebral infarction, or MI (Paykel et al. 1982). Complaints of dizziness, fatigue, lack of energy, and weakness are not uncommon, but often appear related to the hypotensive effects (Dollery et al. 1960) and are less marked that those reported with methyldopa. Depression is infrequent and in some series absent. Paykel et al. (1982) estimated an overall incidence of 1.9 percent, a figure similar to that for clonidine. There is one report of paranoid psychosis associated with guanethidine, but a causal relationship is far from clear (Evanson and Sears 1960).

Prazosin is also a peripherally acting sympatholytic drug that blocks vascular alpha-adrenergic receptors, resulting in both arterial and venous dilation. It causes less tachycardia that the purely arteriolar vasodilator, hydralazine, but more orthostatic hypotension (McSweeney et al. 1984d). A major side effect of prazosin is the so-called first dose effect. A small percentage of patients will develop profound orthostatic hypotension and syncope one to three hours after the first dose of the drug. This effect can be minimized by giving a small initial dose and having the patient remain supine for several hours (McSweeney et al. 1984d). Complaints of dizziness, light-headedness, drowsiness, weakness, lack of energy, and dry mouth sometimes occur, but often diminish with time and rarely require discontinuation of the drug. They are probably related to the drug's hypotensive and anticholinergic effects (Hammond and Kirkendall 1979; McSweeney et al. 1984d).

Hydralazine acts directly on arteriolar smooth muscle to produce vasodilation. Coadministration of a beta adrenergic blocking agent is often used to diminish sympathetically mediated reflex tachycardia. Doses greater than 200 mg/day increase the risk of developing a systemic lupus erythematosus-like syndrome, which, however, rarely seems to be associated with psychiatric sequelae (Alarcon-Segovia et al. 1967). Anxiety, depression, mania, and psychosis have all been reported in association with hydralazine, but largely in anecdotal fashion (Paykel et al. 1982). Peripheral neuropathy and parathesia secondary to inhibition of pyridoxine metabolism have also been reported (Raskin and Fishman 1965).

Diuretics act primarily by increasing sodium and water excretion and decreasing intravascular volume. Some may also have vasodilating effects. Complaints of fatigue and depression can be found in up to 40 percent of patients taking diuretics (Hammond and Kirkendall 1979), but these often seem to be nonspecific symptoms from uncontrolled case reports. Many factors may play a role, including underlying illness, other medications, volume depletion, and electrolyte disturbance.

Drug-Drug Interactions

There are numerous possible interactions within and between classes of psychotropic and cardiovascular drugs via alterations in absorption, distribution, metabolism, excretion, and action at receptor sites. I will consider here only clinically significant interactions between commonly used psychotropic and cardiovascular drugs.

Heterocyclic Antidepressants

Antihypertensive agents. TCAs can block the neuronal uptake of guanethidine and related adrenergic agents and result in loss of blood pressure control (Mitchell et al. 1970). Conversely, if a TCA is withdrawn from a patient already stabilized on guanethidine, serious hypotension can result. Mianserin and maprotiline have been reported to produce this interaction less often than classic TCAs (Burgess et al. 1978; Smith and Bant 1975). Reserpine and methyldopa do not have significant peripheral interactions with TCAs, but may have central interactions with resultant loss of blood pressure control and possible increase of CNS toxicity (Risch et al. 1982). TCAs can also antagonize the central effects of clonidine with a resulting decrease in blood pressure control (Briant et al. 1973).

Antiarrhythmics. The quinidine-like and anticholinergic effects of TCAs may be additive with those of the Type 1 antiarrhythmic drugs quinidine, procainamide, and disopyramide. Patients receiving one of these drugs who are started on a TCA may, therefore, need to have the antiarrhythmic drug decreased or discontinued (Glassman and Bigger 1981). Diuretics have no significant interaction other than increasing the risk of serious orthostatic hypotension.

Sympathomimetic amines. TCAs can potentiate the pressor effects of direct-acting sympathomimetics (e.g., norepinephrine, epinephrine) by preventing their synaptic reuptake, resulting in hypertensive crisis. Indirect-acting sympathomimetics (e.g., amphetamine, ephedrine, phenylpropanolamine) may be blocked or potentiated, depending on relative timing of administration (Risch et al. 1982).

Digoxin. Digoxin does not interact significantly with classic TCAs. However, one report suggested that trazodone may potentially precipitate digoxin toxicity (Rauch and Jenike 1984). Also, TCAs with strong anticholinergic effects may decrease gastric motility and thereby increase digoxin absorption.

Propranolol. Propranolol can generally be used safely with TCAs. However, increased orthostatic hypotension may occur. TCAs may diminish the cardiovascular effects, but this may be partially offset by TCA-induced inhibition of hepatic microsomal enzyme systems and consequent delayed metabolism of propranolol (Pond et al. 1975). Conversely, one report suggested that propranolol may decrease the metabolism and hence increase the blood level of maprotiline (Tollefson and Lesar 1984).

Oral anticoagulants. TCAs may diminish hepatic metabolism of oral anticoagulants, resulting in fluctuations in prothrombin time when starting or stopping antidepressant therapy (Vessell et al. 1970).

MAOIs

Antihypertensive agents. Guanethidine in combination with MAOIs may result in severe hypotension or hypertension (Gaultieri and Powell 1978). CNS excitation and hypertension have been reported with combined use of methyldopa and MAOIs (Stockley 1973). Additive hypotension may occur with hydralazine and MAOIs (Gaultieri and Powell 1978) and with thiazide diuretics and MAOIs (Moser 1961). Acute administration of reserpine to patients receiving MAOIs may provoke a hypertensive crisis (Davies 1960).

Sympathomimetic amines. Indirect-acting sympathomimetics produce their effects through release of intraneuronal stores of norepinephrine and dopamine, which depend in part on MAO for their metabolism. In contrast, direct-acting sympathomimetics do not cause release of intracellular monoamines, but rather bind directly to postsynaptic receptors. Therefore, the indirect-acting sympathomimetics are much more likely to provoke a hypertensive crisis in patients receiving MAOIs than are the direct-acting agents.

Narcotic analgesics.   Administration of meperidine with MAOIs may provoke a syndrome similar to a hypertensive crisis, with marked elevation in blood pressure, headache, tachycardia, diaphoresis, and hyperpyrexia. In addition, the inhibition of hepatic enzyme systems by MAOIs may delay metabolism of narcotic analgesics, particularly meperidine, resulting in elevated levels and possible hypotension, respiratory depression, and coma (Eade and Penton 1970).

Propranolol.   Beta receptor blockade in patients receiving MAOIs may result in relatively unopposed alpha-adrenergic activity and severe hypertension (Frieden 1967).

Oral anticoagulants.   MAOIs can potentiate the effect of oral anticoagulants (Gaultieri and Powell 1978). Thus the dose of these agents should be adjusted accordingly when starting or stopping MAOIs.

Lithium Carbonate

Antihypertensive agents and diuretics.   Thiazide diuretics and potassium-sparing diuretics decrease renal lithium clearance and increase serum lithium levels. Loop diuretics such as furosemide probably have less effect on lithium level, although the data are somewhat contradictory. Osmotic diuretics and carbonic anhydrase inhibitors increase lithium excretion and decrease serum levels. There have been several case reports of symptoms of neurotoxicity developing in patients on methyldopa and lithium at therapeutic levels (Jefferson et al. 1981).

Digoxin.   While lithium and digoxin can generally be used together safely, there is one case report suggesting that a high lithium level may potentiate digoxin's effect and precipitate a bradyarrhythmia (Winters and Ralph 1977).

Antipsychotics

Antihypertensive agents.   Chlorpromazine can significantly antagonize the effect of guanethidine, probably by inhibiting its synaptic uptake (Fann et al. 1971). Haloperidol and thiothixene have this same effect, but to a lesser degree (Janowsky et al. 1973).

Molindone does not seem to interact with guanethidine (Simpson 1979) and may be the antipsychotic of choice for patients receiving this drug. Phenothiazines may potentiate the hypotensive effects of methyldopa (Chouinard et al. 1973a). Conversely, methyldopa may potentiate the effect of haloperidol (Chouinard et al. 1973b), but also has been reported to cause a marked worsening of symptoms in schizophrenic patients previously well controlled on haloperidol (Nadel and Wallach 1979) and to produce a dementia-like syndrome in combination with haloperidol (Thornton 1976).

Sympathomimetic amines.   The antiadrenergic action of antipsychotics may diminish the pressor effect of alphaadrenergic agonists such as norepinephrine, but this may be offset by other effects of neuroleptics on cardiovascular reflex mechanisms. Patients on phenothiazines may develop severe hypotension if given epinephrine due to unopposed beta adrenergic activity in the presence of alpha adrenergic blockade (Thornton and Pray 1975).

Digoxin.   Antipsychotics with significant anticholinergic activity may decrease gastric motility and increase digoxin absorption, potentially leading to toxicity (Gaultieri and Powell 1978).

Propranolol.   Propranolol and chlorpromazine can inhibit each other's hepatic metabolism (Miller and Rampling 1982; Vestal et al. 1979); therefore, patients receiving both these drugs may be prone to develop symptoms of toxicity of each, and doses must be adjusted accordingly. Combined use may also produce additive orthostatic hypotension. There is one report of severe hypotension and cardiopulmonary arrest occurring on several occasions in association with concurrent haloperidol and propranolol therapy (Alexander et al. 1984).

Antiarrhythmic agents.   Phenothiazines, particularly thioridazine, have quinidine-like effects; therefore, concurrent administration of quinidine and phenothiazines may produce additive effects on cardiac conduction and necessitate a reduction in dosages. Phenothiazines decrease hepatic metabolism and therefore increase plasma levels of phenytoin (Gaultieri and Powell 1978). Of interest is the recent observation that thioridazine and mesoridazine possess calcium channel antagonist activity (Gould et al. 1984). Whether these drugs will have synergistic toxic effects with the known calcium channel blockers such as verapamil, nifedipine, and diltiazem remains to be seen.

Oral anticoagulants.   Antipsychotics have been reported both to increase and decrease oral anticoagulant effect (Gaultieri and Powell 1978).

Sedative-Hypnotics and Minor Tranquilizers

Chronic use of barbiturates, chloral hydrate, and to a lesser extent other sedative-hypnotics can induce hepatic microsomal enzymes and thereby increase metabolism and decrease therapeutic efficacy of a number of drugs, including oral anticoagulants, phenytoin, beta-adrenergic blockers, and digoxin. Conversely, acute administration of barbiturates and other sedative-hypnotics may potentiate the activity of a number of drugs through competition for the same enzyme systems. Reports suggest that digoxin toxicity may be precipitated by alprazolam (Tollefson et al. 1984) and diazepam (Castillo-Ferrando et al. 1980), presumably via decreased renal clearance of digoxin.

Chapter 103

The Patient with Renal Disease

The relationship of renal function to psychiatric symptoms is a complex one. Renal failure can cause psychiatric disturbances requiring psychopharmacologic intervention. Conversely, the use of psychiatric medications in patients with renal disease can be hazardous. Special attention must be given to changes in rates of excretion and binding by plasma protein. The use of modern treatment modalities for renal disease, particularly hemodialysis, has given rise to new forms of organic psychiatric disturbance.

The Clinical Syndrome

Renal disease can produce diminished glomerular filtration with secondary accumulation of toxic metabolites or increased glomerular permeability resulting in loss of plasma protein. Loss of excretory capacity is equivalent to renal failure and can directly result in an organic mental syndrome (OMS). A severe and sustained loss of plasma protein can lead to the nephrotic syndrome (proteinuria, hypoproteinemia, and edema), which alone does not cause organic brain disturbances but which does alter the pharmacokinetics of psychotropic medications.

Renal failure and its neuropsychiatric aspects have been summarized elsewhere (Jefferson and Marshall 1981b). Impaired renal function is indicated by a reduction in the 24-hour urine volume to less than 400 ml and/or creatinine clearance below the normal range of 85 to 104 ml/minute. However, more profound reductions are usually necessary before one sees organic psychiatric disturbance. Renal failure can be acute or chronic, and the associated psychiatric and psychopharmacologic complications are essentially the same in both cases. In the ensuing discussion, I will focus on chronic renal failure, the more common of the two.

Chronic renal failure ultimately results in disturbances of all bodily systems. Abnormalities can include anemia, nausea and vomiting, hyperglycemia, hyperuricemia, secondary hyperparathyroidism with osteomalacia, hypertension, congestive heart failure, electrolyte disturbances with metabolic acidosis, and uremic delirium. Severe impairment has become less frequent with the increased availability of hemodialysis.

Early changes in mental status include a generalized feeling of malaise, apathy, fatigue, and lethargy. The picture is sufficiently similar to depression to result in misdiagnosis (Wise 1974). As renal insufficiency progresses, a frank delirium develops associated with alterations in consciousness, impaired memory, disorientation, and psychotic symptoms. Some investigators have suggested that negativistic combative behavior is common (Stënback and Haapanen 1967); others have classified the delirium into schizophrenic, paranoid, and affective forms (Baker and Knutson 1946). It is difficult to distinguish the contributions of premorbid personality and defensive adaptation to the clinical picture from those of uremic encephalopathy, leading to the conclusion that a specific uremic delirium probably does not exist (Jefferson and Marshall 1981b).

OMS as a Consequence of Renal Disease

Uremic Brain Syndrome

The organic brain syndrome of renal failure results from the accumulation of an as yet unidentified endotoxin. Nitrogenous by-products of protein and amino acid metabolism are the most likely offending agents. These waste compounds include urea, urates, aliphatic amines, and peptides. The diminished brain oxygen utilization that accompanies uremic encephalopathy is thought to increase cortical vulnerability to accumulated uremic toxins (Scheinberg 1954).

Urea accounts for more than 80 percent of urinary nitrogen in chronic renal patients on 40-g low protein diets (Brenner and Lazarus 1983). Although blood levels of urea are an efficient means of representing the degree of renal impairment, high levels of this compound do not appear to cause neuropsychiatric disturbance. Dialysis of patients against solutions containing urea concentrations equal to their own still results in marked clinical improvement (Merrill et al. 1953). Furthermore, the administration of intravenous urea in large quantities does not lead to signs of central nervous system (CNS) toxicity (Javid and Settlage 1956). Nevertheless, serum urea, by providing an index of renal failure, does have value as a laboratory predictor of psychiatric disturbance. In one study, 36 percent of 58 patients with levels over 250 mg/100 ml were found to be delirious compared to 13 percent of 39 renal failure patients with levels between 50 and 199 mg/100 ml (Stenback and Haapanen 1967).

Elevations in blood urea also correlate with disturbances in the electroencephalogram (EEG). Normal recordings are usually seen with levels below 42 mg/100 ml; abnormalities are most common with levels above 60 mg/100 ml (Tyler 1965). Disturbances include a loss of organized alpha activity and progressive slowing. Runs of five to seven waves per second replace other rhythms, a picture resembling that seen in hepatic encephalopathy (Lishman 1978).

Dialysis Disequilibrium Syndrome

The dialysis disequilibrium syndrome refers to an acute brain syndrome occurring during, or soon after, hemodialysis (Arieff and Massey 1976). The clinical picture may range from drowsiness and headache to an acute delirium. In severe cases, signs and symptoms of increased intracranial pressure ensue with muscle irritability, convulsions, and coma, sometimes leading to death (Jefferson and Marshall 1981b; Lishman 1978). The syndrome is thought to result from cerebral edema caused by an imbalance in osmolality (Arieff and Massey 1976). It occurs most frequently when predialysis urea levels are high and the dialysis is carried out rapidly (Lishman 1978). The syndrome can be prevented by utilizing slower and longer dialyses or more frequent brief procedures. Dialysis against a high glucose concentration also prevents the pathogenic rapid osmolal changes (Jefferson and Marshall 1981b).

Pharmacologic treatment of psychotic manifestations of the dialysis disequilibrium syndrome must consider the interdialysis accumulation of medications normally excreted by the kidney and the rapid removal of dialyzable drugs during the dialysis (Levy 1981). Furthermore, most patients who do not have severe biochemical imbalance can be expected to recover spontaneously within 24 hours (Jefferson and Marshall 1981b).

Dialysis Dementia

Patients who have been treated with repeated hemodialysis for a period of years are vulnerable to the progressive and fatal syndrome of dialysis dementia. The syndrome has been reviewed by Jack et al. (1983/1984).

Reports of the incidence of dialysis dementia in patients receiving hemodialysis have ranged from 0.6 to 4.6 percent (Jack et al. 1983/1984). The syndrome is marked by abnormal speech, myoclonus, and global impairment of cognitive functioning. Speech disturbance is an early sign. It usually begins with stuttering that progresses to dysarthria and dysphasia. Periods of muteness can occur. Abnormal motor activity occurs, ranging from myoclonus early in the course to grand mal seizures as a late finding. The dementia is global and includes impaired recent memory in association with a normal level of consciousness.

Dialysis dementia is progressive and usually leads to coma within five years. Improvement in symptoms occurs in 50 percent of patients who receive transplantation, with the remainder having an unchanged course. Abnormalities of trace metals in the brain (including diminished rubidium and increased tin and aluminum) have been implicated in the pathogenesis of this disorder (Alfrey et al. 1976). Aluminum concentration in brains of dialysis dementia patients are more than 30 times those found in normal controls and three and one half times that found in asymptomatic dialysis patients with comparable differences existing in serum (Bates et al. 1985). The theory of aluminum toxicity (Vaisrub 1978) receives support from reports that elimination of antacids containing aluminum and aluminum in dialysate fluid has led to a markedly diminished incidence of dementia (Bates et al. 1985).

Patients receiving hemodialysis may be at increased risk for suffering subdural hematomas (Talalla et al. 1970). Contributing causes include the anticoagulants used to maintain the patency of shunts and the abnormal platelet function seen in chronic renal disease. The clinician must consider the possibility of subdural hematoma when mental status changes develop in patients receiving hemodialysis. The development of focal neurologic abnormalities in association with evidence of increased intracranial pressure are indicative of this diagnosis.

OMS Coexisting with Renal Disease

The concurrence of an OMS and renal disease may have three explanations. First, the OMS can be secondary to the renal failure; this association has been discussed above. Second, the OMS and renal failure can be coincident but not causally related; a patient with delirium tremens can have renal disease that is not physiologically related to the chronic alcoholism. Third, the OMS and renal failure can be due to the same underlying condition; examples of this not infrequent form of concurrence are listed in Table 1. The list is not exhaustive; these examples illustrate that when renal disease and OMS are found to coexist, and the OMS is not clearly secondary to a severe degree of renal insufficiency, the search for and treatment of a possible cause of both conditions must be diligently pursued.

Differential Diagnosis

Differential diagnostic considerations are, for the most part, limited to the organic syndromes of delirium and dementia and to depression. Other forms of organic brain syndrome are unlikely to result from renal disease, although organic personality

Table 1. Conditions Causing Both OMS and Renal Failure

1. Diabetes mellitus	5. Congestive heart failure
2. Hypertension	6. Heavy metal poisoning
3. Connective tissue disease (systemic lupus erythematosus)	7. Miliary tuberculosis
	8. Hepatorenal syndrome
4. Vasculitis (polyarteritis nodosa)	9. Heat stroke

disturbances and dyscontrol can occur secondary to a subdural hematoma related to renal failure.

Mental changes associated with renal insufficiency are roughly proportional to the degree of impairment. Mild elevations of blood urea are associated with fatigue, apathy, and lethargy, which can mimic depression. The presence of anorexia, weight loss, and anhedonia can add to diagnostic confusion. The fact that depression, like uremia, can impair cognitive performance (Folstein and McHugh 1978) can lead to further diagnostic difficulty.

Special attention to the differential diagnosis of apathy and lethargy is required. The "feeling unwell" of chronic medical illness must be distinguished from the dysphoria of depression. Amotivational apathy must be distinguished from lethargy. The demonstration of diminished level of arousal or diminished recent memory should lead the clinician to investigate for the presence of a causative organic disturbance. Elevation of blood urea above the normal range of 10 to 20 mg/100 ml is suggestive of renal failure but can be due to dehydration from depression. Since dehydration does not cause comparable increases in serum creatinine, the normal 10:1 blood urea nitrogen (BUN) to creatinine ratio is likely to be elevated in uremia secondary to fluid loss (Coe 1983). The diagnosis is confounded when uremic encephalopathy and depressive symptoms are both present. In that instance, the patient's thought content has diagnostic relevance. Patients preoccupied with feelings of helplessness and a sense of not having control over even nontreatment life dimensions are more likely to be depressed (Devins et al. 1981).

In situations of profound impairment, a uremic delirium supervenes. Cases of terminal renal failure characterized by the classic skin changes of uremic frost and the uriniferous breath of uremic fetor are rare in contemporary medicine. The picture more commonly seen is one of classic delirium with laboratory evidence of underlying renal failure. Despite the rough correlation between mental status changes and elevations of urea, fluctuations in degree of delirium can occur independently of measurable chemical changes and can lag behind or precede alterations in levels of urea (Jefferson and Marshall 1981b).

The delirium associated with dialysis disequilibrium is best recognized by its temporal association with hemodialysis. Symptoms of increased intracranial pressure are usually present, ranging from headache in mild cases to nausea and vomiting, blurred vision, and elevated blood pressure (Arieff and Massey 1976).

The development of speech disturbance, myoclonus, and signs of an evolving dementia in a patient on chronic hemodialysis suggests the syndrome of dialysis dementia. The presence of disordered speech during dialysis with recovery after treatment occurs early and allows for a prompt diagnosis. Early identification of patients and the subsequent use of alternative treatments could prevent the progression of the dementia, and in some cases lead to its reversal.

Means for preventing or reversing toxic-metabolic features of uremic encephalopathy, dialysis disequilibrium syndrome, and dialysis dementia have been described. The reader is referred to Chapters 93 and 94 for discussions of the treatment of psychiatric features of delirium and dementia.

Patient Evaluation

Previous chapters emphasize the importance of a complete and accurate history to diagnosing the cause of an OMS. Renal disease can contribute to an OMS directly through renal failure, or indirectly through the effects of renal disease on biologic responses to medications. Decreased renal clearance, altered binding by plasma proteins, interactions between psychiatric and renal medications, and abnormal CNS activity of usually nontoxic drugs can all play a role. The clinician must, therefore, carefully search for a history of diseases known to predispose to renal failure (e.g., hypertension, diabetes mellitus) as well as for prior episodes of actual renal insufficiency. Medications taken for kidney illness must be identified and their potential for causing psychiatric disturbances understood.

Acute renal failure caused by hypovolemia, urinary tract obstruction, and toxins can occur without a history of prior illness. In these cases, the presence of recent onset of decreased urine output or conditions causing nephrotoxicity, occurring in association with an OMS, can assist in making the diagnosis.

Physical findings can be helpful in cases of severe renal insufficiency. Signs of malnutrition, severe anemia, and poor skin turgor with uremic frost are end-stage findings and rarely necessary for accurate diagnosis. Physical examination is of greater value in identifying the underlying cause of decreased renal function. For example, ophthalmologic examination can establish the presence of diabetic retinopathy, which is often associated with chronic glomerulonephritis.

Laboratory measures are critical for identifying the presence and severity of renal failure. Oliguria (urine output of less than 400 ml/day) is diagnostic, although non-oliguric acute renal failure can occur (Anderson and Schrier 1983). Elevations of BUN and creatinine are of greater diagnostic import. The EEG can also be contributory if the triphasic spikes seen in both hepatic and renal failure are present.

In summary, the elucidation of preexisting kidney disease or use of renal medications and the application of appropriate laboratory investigations as well as the application of a knowledge of the pharmacologic aspects of renal dysfunction (discussed below) are required for the clinician to identify a renal contribution to an OMS.

Drug-Disease Interactions

Drug toxicity accounts for nearly one-third of cases of CNS dysfunction in patients with renal disease. Nearly half of these present with psychiatric disturbance (Richet et al. 1970). Psychiatric symptoms can occur at nontoxic concentrations of centrally acting drugs, suggesting a pharmacodynamic interaction: uremic toxins are thought to render the CNS vulnerable to therapeutic quantities of medication (Bennet 1975; Richet et al. 1970).

Pharmacokinetic interactions of medications and renal disease are multiple. They affect volume of distribution, binding by plasma proteins, metabolism, and excretion. Specific alterations depend on both the nature of the renal disease and the characteristics of the particular medication. The effects of pharmacokinetic changes due to renal disease differ, depending on whether a medication is lipid soluble (lipophilic) or water soluble (hydrophilic).

Lipophilic Agents

The majority of psychotropic agents are highly fat soluble. This property facilitates their entry into the CNS. Lipophilic agents require metabolism into a water soluble form prior to renal excretion. If the hydrophilic form is pharmacologically inactive and the metabolic pathway (primarily hepatic conjugation) is intact, patients with compromised renal function should not be at high risk for adverse CNS reactions to medications. Nevertheless, an understanding of alterations in the various dimensions of pharmacokinetics by renal disease will assist the clinician in achieving an effective dose while minimizing the risk of toxicity.

Pharmacokinetic factors that can be influenced by renal disease are outlined in Table 2. Bennet et al. (1980) have reviewed pharmacokinetic issues in the treatment of renal patients and provided clinical recommendations. The changes are complex and interactional: changes in one pharmacokinetic variable will affect others. For example, diminished binding by plasma protein increases the percentage of unbound drug available for metabolism and excretion.

Absorption

Systematic studies of the effect of renal failure on drug absorption are scant. The gastrointestinal disturbances seen in cases of profound uremia can be expected to diminish absorption. Whether similar changes occur in less severe renal failure is uncertain. Rates of absorption of the benzodiazepine lorazepam are comparable for chronic renal patients and healthy controls (Morrison et al. 1984).

The use of antacids to treat gastrointestinal symptoms and diminish metabolic acidosis is part of the conservative management of renal failure (Carpenter and Lazarus 1983). Aluminum hydroxide gel is specifically utilized to bind dietary phosphate and prevent secondary hyperparathroidism (Brenner and Lazarus 1983). The use of antacids would be expected to diminish the absorption of phenothiazines, tricyclic antidepressants, and benzodiazepines by delaying gastric emptying; however, aluminum hydroxide may actually increase the bioavailability of diazepam (Harvey 1980). Despite the expectation that absorption of psychotropic agents in renal disease will be diminished by gastrointestinal disturbance and use of antacids, systematic studies are required to clarify this question. This is particularly relevant for the effect of specific antacids on specific psychotropic medications.

Table 2. Pharmacokinetic Interaction of Renal Disease with Lipophilic Agents

Disease Action	Drug Reaction
1. Decrease in absorption due to use of antacids and/or uremic gastrointestinal symptoms	1. Decrease in available drug
2. Change in volume of distribution	1. Decrease in percentage of body fat

	2. Changes in plasma proteins
	    a. decrease in albumin (benzodiazepines)
	    b. increase in alpha-l-acid glycoprotein (tricyclics and phenothiazines)

	3. Corresponding decrease or increase in renal clearance and increase or decrease in plasma levels
3. Increase in glucuronidation	1. Prevents accumulation of active drug
	2. Increase in levels of inactive (?) glucuronide
4. Decrease in renal clearance of unbound parent drug	1. No significant effect for lipophilic agents

Volume of Distribution

The volume of distribution determines the amount of an administered dose of medication available for pharmacodynamic activity. The smaller the volume of distribution, the greater the percentage that is free, resulting in an increased rate of clearance and decreased plasma level of active drug at steady state conditions. This pharmacokinetic dimension is largely the contribution of drug storage in tissues and at binding sites on plasma proteins. Chronic renal failure is thought to alter the volume of distribution of lipophilic agents in three principal ways. First, less adipose tissue relative to total body weight results in decreased available storage sites. This change may be particularly relevant for highly lipid soluble substances such as diazepam and the principal metabolite of chlordiazepoxide, desmethyldiazepam (Ochs et al. 1984). Second, the accumulation of endogenous compounds associated with uremia may decrease the binding of active drug to plasma protein through competitive displacement (Gulyassy and Depner 1983; McNamara et al. 1981). Third, changes occur in the quantities of circulating albumin and alpha-l-acid glycoprotein, the two major plasma binding sites for psychotropic medications (Abel et al. 1980; Piafsky and Borga 1977; Piafsky et al. 1978; Sellers et al. 1981). Since more than 90 percent of circulating benzodiazepines, phenothiazines, and tricyclic antidepressants are bound to plasma proteins, changes in amounts of these proteins due to renal disease lead to large differences in quantities of free drug; thus doubling the amount of plasma protein will halve the concentration of free medication.

Malnutrition and glomerular damage due to chronic kidney disease contribute to loss of albumin. Hypoalbuminemia is most severe in patients with nephrotic syndrome. Since diazepam and most other benzodiazepines are strongly bound to albumin (Abel et al. 1980; Grossman et al. 1982; Sellers et al. 1981), the free fraction of these medications increases in the presence of renal insufficiency (Greenblatt et al. 1983; Ochs et al. 1984).

Data from kinetic studies in patients with kidney failure treated with standard doses of oxazepam, lorazepam, and diazepam are consistent with a decreased volume of distribution for these agents. Decreased protein binding is associated with reduced plasma concentrations, but with increased free fraction and faster clearance of parent drug. Marked steady state increments of the inactive glucuronide occur due to intact hepatic metabolism (Greenblatt et al. 1983; Morrison et al. 1984; Ochs et al. 1984). This process, summarized in Table 3, prevents the toxic accumulation of administered medication. The clinician must consider the possibility that some uremic patients,

Table 3. Pharmacokinetic Effects of Decreased Binding Protein

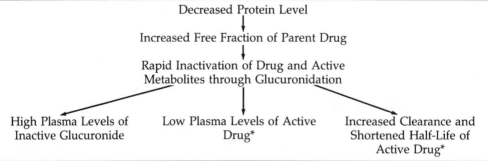

*Standard plasma measurements of active drug include both free and bound portions.

due to increased CNS pharmacodynamic sensitivity, may be unable to tolerate usual quantities of free drug, although systematic studies of this question have not been carried out with psychotropic agents.

The phenothiazines and tricyclic antidepressants are preferentially bound by alpha-l-acid glycoprotein (Piafsky and Borga 1977; Piafsky et al. 1978). Changes in this plasma protein in patients with kidney disease are more complex. As an acute phase reactant, alpha-l-acid glycoprotein was thought to increase when chronic renal disease was associated with concurrent inflammatory process (Piafsky et al. 1978). A study by Docci et al. (1985) demonstrated a positive correlation between levels of alpha-l-acid glycoprotein and serum creatinine in patients with renal failure, indicating that renal impairment alone leads to an accumulation of this protein. An increase in alpha-l-acid glycoprotein due to renal failure contrasts to the assumption that levels would fall due to glomerular leakage (Curry 1981).

If plasma binding of tricyclic antidepressants and phenothiazines increases in renal failure, a process opposite to that for the albumin-bound benzodiazepines takes place. Decreased clearance of active drug due to increased plasma-binding leads to elevation of plasma levels. This process has been documented with imipramine when alpha-l-acid glycoprotein levels were raised by an inflammatory process (Kragh-Sørenson et al. 1981). Since only free drug is pharmacodynamically active, increased binding leads to a diminished quantity of free drug for any given plasma level (Piafsky et al. 1978). At steady state, the quantity of free drug is therefore unaltered. Here, too, plasma levels do not reflect quantities of active drug.

Studies comparing the pharmacokinetics of tricyclic antidepressants in patients with renal failure to those of controls have found comparable rates of clearance (Dawling et al. 1982; Lieberman et al. 1985). Large interindividual differences and intraindividual fluctuations were identified and attributed to other unexplained alterations in volume of distribution. Two studies of steady state plasma concentrations found renal patients to have levels comparable to (Lieberman et al. 1985) or lower than (Sandoz et al. 1984) those of controls. Thus despite elevations in the alpha-l-acid binding protein, decreased clearance and increased concentrations of tricyclics do not occur. Investigators explain this by invoking the suggestion of Piafsky et al. (1978) that the apparently unchanged total binding of these drugs in uremic patients is the net result of increased levels of alpha-l-acid glycoprotein and the displacement from protein by endogenous substances present in uremic plasma.

In summary, the changes in volume of distribution in uremia lead to diminished blood levels of benzodiazepines due to hypoalbuminemia. Levels of tricyclic antidepressants, and presumably phenothiazines, are comparable to those found in nonuremic patients due to increased binding protein, which counteracts the displacing effects of uremic compounds. These multiple pharmacokinetic changes make blood levels an unreliable assay of active free drug and poor indicators of the need for adjusting dosage so long as glucuronidation is intact (Dawling et al. 1982; Sandoz et al. 1984).

Drug Metabolism and Excretion

Inactivation of lipophilic agents is principally achieved through hepatic conjugation with glucuronic acid. This mechanism remains intact in patients with severe renal failure, contributing to profound accumulation of glucuronide. Subjects with sufficient impairment to require dialysis have conjugated tricyclic levels that are 500 to 2,000 percent higher than those of controls (Dawling et al. 1982; Lieberman et al. 1985). Comparable increases in glucuronide have been found with the benzodiazepines and tricyclic antidepressants. Glucuronidation of the pharmacodynamically active hydroxy metabolites appears to be unaffected by renal insufficiency (Dawling et al. 1981). Since large quantities of the unconjugated form of these metabolites are excreted unchanged in the urine, their accumulation would be expected to result from renal failure (Potter et al. 1984). Special concern, therefore, arises when factors that could impair hepatic function are present, resulting in diminished conjugation of both parent compounds and active metabolites (Dawling et al. 1981; Verbeeck et al. 1981).

Although the glucuronide is thought to be pharmacodynamically inert, controversy exists as to whether elevated concentrations of this metabolite can affect biotransformation of the parent compound through regeneration of the active drug by systemic deconjugation or enterohepatic recycling. The possibilities of feedback inhibition of metabolism and displacement of the parent compound from protein binding sites have also been proposed (Verbeeck 1982). Changes in volume of distribution associated with renal failure render these mechanisms difficult to assess, but their contribution to clearance of the active compound appears to be negligible (Verbeeck et al. 1981). Since direct urinary excretion accounts for less than 10 percent of the elimination of lipophilic psychotropic drugs, and glucuronidation is unimpaired in renal failure, alterations in dosage of these agents is usually not required (Bennet et al. 1980).

Hydrophilic Agents and Lithium

Hydrophilic agents are excreted unchanged by the kidneys. Decreased renal function reduces clearance of these agents, resulting in toxic accumulations. This factor contributes to the increased risk of delirium in patients with reduced renal function treated with amantadine, a dopaminergic agent (Postma and Van Tilburg 1975). The injudicious prescription of standard doses of lithium carbonate to patients with impaired glomerular filtration will have analogous effects. The importance and complexity of renal-lithium interaction merits special consideration.

Indications for lithium use in patients with OMS have been discussed earlier in this volume. General indications include the occurrence of brain disease in patients with bipolar disorder and the development of "secondary mania" (Krauthammer and Klerman 1978) subsequent to a cortical insult. An increased frequency of adverse CNS reactions to therapeutic concentrations of lithium in patients with OMS (Himmelhoch et al. 1980) suggests increased pharmacodynamic vulnerabiity in these patients. Furthermore, cognitive deficits resuting from the OMS can lead to poor compliance and fluctuations in lithium levels. Special attention must be given to concurrent renal disease, which could lead to the toxic accumulation of lithium and exacerbation of the OMS. Several authors (e.g., Amdisen 1977; Davis et al. 1981; Schou 1976) described lithium pharmacokinetics. Jefferson and Greist (1979) provided a comprehensive review of interactions between lithium and kidney. A thorough understanding of these issues will enable the psychiatrist to prescribe lithium in the doubly precarious clinical context of coexisting renal and brain impairment.

Pharmacokinetic Considerations

Between 80 and 95 percent of orally administered lithium is recovered in the urine; oral absorption of most preparations is nearly complete, and excretion is almost entirely dependent on renal excretion (Davis et al. 1981). Lithium is not protein bound and the volume of distribution is between 50 to 100 percent of total body weight (Mason et al. 1978). Lithium passes freely through the glomerular membrane. Only

20 percent of filtered lithium is excreted; 80 percent is reabsorbed, predominantly in the proximal-tubule at the site of sodium reabsorption (Jefferson and Greist 1979). Under normal circumstances, renal lithium clearance is the same as that for sodium and approximately 20 percent of the glomerular filtration rate (Shou 1976). Factors that decrease filtration should, therefore, lead to a higher lithium level for a given dose. Studies demonstrating a decrease in glomerular filtration as a function of age (Rowe 1980) suggest that lower doses should be used in elderly patients.

Filtered sodium load is a second factor influencing renal excretion of lithium. Since lithium is reabsorbed at the same proximal site as sodium, the delivery of a greater load of sodium will reduce the quantity of lithium reabsorbed. Conversely, sodium depletion due to dehydration leads to a compensatory increase in reabsorption of sodium proximally with a concomitant increase in reabsorbed lithium. A variation of this process occurs when thiazide diuretics are used to treat kidney-related disease. Jefferson and Greist (1979) reviewed and summarized this literature. Thiazides act by blocking sodium reabsorption early in the distal tubule. The resulting sodium depletion leads to the delivery of a lower sodium load to the proximal tubule, where an increased reabsorption of both sodium and lithium takes place. The net effect is increased lithium retention, which is proportional to the dose of thiazide used. Diuretics that block sodium reabsorption in the Loop of Henle (furosemide and ethycrynic acid) appear to have little potential for causing lithium retention, whereas the potassium-sparing diuretics (spironolactone, triamterene, amiloride) do appear to possess this property. Carbonic anhydrase inhibitors and xanthine diuretics cause increased lithium excretion. The reason for differences in effect on lithium retention by various sodium reuptake blocking diuretics remains uncertain, but presumably arises from different mechanisms acting at different sites within the kidney. Future investigations are required to clarify the potential for different types of diuretics to produce lithium retention and the mechanism by which this occurs. It is already clear that even thiazide diuretics can be used with relative safety in combination with lithium so long as appropriate dosage adjustments are made, the treatment regimens are stable, and consistent lithium levels for a given dosage have been established (Jefferson and Greist 1979).

Lithium and Nephrotoxicity

A thorough discussion of lithium as a potential cause of kidney damage is beyond the scope of this chapter. Several excellent reviews are available (Jenner 1979; Ramsey and Cox 1982; Vestergaard 1980). The literature is best summarized by dividing the nephrotoxic effects of lithium into those thought to be caused by elevated blood levels and those attributed to prolonged exposure to "therapeutic" concentration of lithium. It should be remembered that the term *renal damage* condenses a number of different putative nephrotoxic effects: glomerular damage, tubular dysfunction with decreased concentrating ability, and actual tissue damage due to interstitial fibrosis and tubular sclerosis. To what extent lithium causes any or all of these disturbances and how they relate to each other remains to be clarified.

Acute Intoxication and Renal Damage

The suggestion that elevated lithium levels can cause renal damage arises from two sources. First, animal studies demonstrate that exposure to toxic amounts of lithium can cause oliguria and azotemia. Interstitial fibrosis and atrophy of distal tubules has been the most consistent finding (Jefferson and Greist 1979). Second, numerous case reports demonstrate an association between elevated lithium levels and impaired kidney function. Histopathologic confirmation of tissue damage in these reports has been variable, ranging from limited to substantial (Jefferson and Greist 1979). In the most severe cases, lithium use has been associated with both uremia and histopathologic evidence of profound tubular damage (Hestbech and Aurell 1979; Olsen 1976).

Few studies utilizing systematically obtained data from series of lithium-intoxicated patients are available. One early investigation of eight toxic patients found no evidence of renal impairment in seven, with the eighth demonstrating a mild and transient azotemia (Schou et al. 1968). A study of 23 lithium-intoxicated patients, 21 of whom became toxic during maintenance treatment, revealed 16 to have a creatinine clearance of less than 45 ml/minute, with anuria developing in two patients (Hansen and Amdisen 1978). The study does not provide sufficient data to determine precisely the extent to which underlying renal disease was a cause rather than an effect of the lithium intoxication. The authors did suggest a renal etiology in at least three cases. Although data on long-term renal damage are not available, creatinine clearance returned to normal before discharge in 11 of the 16 patients who received hemodialysis. The paucity of case reports of either acute or permanent renal insufficiency occurring after intoxication, relative to the frequency with which elevations in lithium levels presumably occur, raises questions about the strength of the causal connection. However, given lithium's known nephrotoxic effects in animals, the clinical reports in humans, and the literature suggesting that long-term use can cause tissue damage, the clinician is urged to monitor renal function closely in all cases of lithium intoxication.

Prolonged Lithium Use and Renal Damage

Polyuria and diminished ability to concentrate urine are the most frequent consequences of long-term use of lithium. Between 10 and 40 percent of patients have 24-hour urine volumes in excess of 3 l/day (Jefferson et al. 1983). Nearly 50 percent have impaired maximal concentrating ability (Wallin et al. 1982). Both are thought to result from lithium-induced decreased tubular responsiveness to antidiuretic hormone, causing a syndrome analogous to nephrogenic diabetes insipidus (NDI) (Reisberg and Gershon 1979). These side effects were considered benign and transient results of a pharmacodynamic disturbance, without associated histopathologic changes that would indicate permanent damage (Schou 1976). The publication of case reports demonstrating irreversible NDI-like disturbances and studies demonstrating morphologic changes in kidney tissue (Burrows et al. 1978; Hestbech et al. 1977) has raised concerns that chronic lithium use can lead to permanent kidney damage with consequent disruption of function.

Bendz (1983) reviewed the findings and issues. Conclusions and unresolved controversies can be summarized as follows. First, an association does apparently exist between the degree of lithium-induced NDI and the extent of histopathologic damage (Bucht et al. 1980; Hansen et al. 1979). Second, the use of untreated affectively ill controls is necessary for conclusions to be valid because both untreated affective illness and use of other psychotropic medications can be associated with a concentrating defect (Coppen et al. 1980; Wahlin et al. 1980) and renal tubular damage (Kincaid-Smith et al. 1979; Walker et al. 1982). Third, it is difficult to assess the contribution of either duration of treatment or transient episodes of toxic lithium concentrations to renal effects. The former is confounded by duration of illness and the latter by the absence of continuous monitoring. Fourth, although the prolonged use of lithium is not usually associated with diminished glomerular filtration, it does occur in some patients (Depaulo et al. 1981; Vestergaard et al. 1979). The absence of documented cases of renal failure caused by long-term use of lithium suggests that the risk of significant glomerular damage is minimal (Ramsey and Cox 1982). Nevertheless, the evidence for lithium's effect on the kidney is sufficiently strong to require that special precautions be taken in patients with cognitive impairment and CNS vulnerability due to an OMS and concomitant renal disease. More frequent assessments of lithium levels to avoid episodes of toxicity and more careful monitoring of renal function are required.

Since lithium is effectively removed by both peritoneal and hemodialysis (Thomsen and Schou 1975), it can also be used in patients with end-stage renal disease. It can be administered through the dialysis bath (Oakley et al. 1974) or after each treatment (Port et al. 1979). Thus the use of lithium in patients with varying degrees of renal impairment is not contraindicated and may be preferable to disruption of the medical regimen caused by an unstable affective disturbance (Jefferson and Greist 1979).

Lithium Interactions with Other Medications

Diuretics increase sodium excretion as part of their mechanism of action. Since loss of sodium leads to increased reabsorption of both sodium and lithium in the proximal tubule, sodium depletion caused by diuretics would be expected to result uniformly in lithium retention. This is not the case. Furosemide and ethacrynic acid are powerful diuretics acting at the Loop of Henle that do not, during acute administration, lead to diminished lithium excretion (Thomsen and Schou 1975). The site of action within the kidney appears to be the critical factor. Thiazide diuretics, acting proximally within the distal tubule, do decrease lithium clearance by upwards of 40 percent, with the effect in part determined by thiazide dose (Jefferson and Greist 1979). Potassium-sparing diuretics appear to have an intermediary effect on lithium retention (Jefferson and Greist 1979).

The thiazide-lithium interaction need not have adverse consequences if the physician is aware of the regimen and closely monitors the patient's blood level. The interaction has been safely utilized to reduce polyuria in patients with NDI and is posited to have a synergistic effect in some patients with an otherwise lithium-refractory mood disorder (Himmelhoch et al. 1977).

Nonsteroidal antiinflammatory agents are used to control rheumatoid symptoms in patients with inflammatory illnesses. They may be used in patients with lupus erythematosus-caused renal disease who cannot tolerate steroids. Many of these agents inhibit synthesis of renal prostaglandin, leading to diminished excretion of lithium. This interaction has been demonstrated for indomethacin, phenylbutazone, and diclofenac, but not for aspirin. Indomethacin can raise lithium levels by more than 40 percent compared to ibuprofen, which has inconsistent effects, and aspirin, which does not change lithium clearance (Ragheb et al. 1980; Reimann et al. 1983). Until more precise information becomes available about specific drug interactions, the clinician should use caution in prescribing any nonsteroidal antiinflammatory drug in combination with lithium.

Drug-Drug Interactions of Lipophillic Agents

Antihypertensives

Hypertension can be a cause or consequence of kidney disease. Patients receiving psychotropic drugs to treat manifestations of an OMS may also require antihypertensive agents because of a concurrent renal disorder. Both psychiatric and antihypertensive agents act by modulating catecholaminergic function. Their interaction can lead to potentiation or inhibition of pharmacodynamic effects.

Guanethidine exerts its antihypertensive effect by depleting norepinephrine from peripheral adrenergic neurones and blocking the release of stored catecholamines after sympathetic stimulation (Woosley and Nies 1976). Guanethidine must first be taken up into the adrenergic terminals by the same amine pump that is blocked by tricyclics and phenothiazines (Mitchell et al. 1970). The use of these psychotropic medications, and perhaps haloperidol, thiothixine, and monoamine oxidase inhibitors, in combination with guanethidine antagonizes the latter's antihypertensive effects (Hansten 1976). Monoamine oxidase inhibitors can also cause a hypertensive crisis resulting from an initial guanethidine-induced release of norepinephrine. Data on other neuroleptics and tricyclics are less substantial than information about chlorpromazine and imipramine, but less potent phenothiazines (perphenazine and trifluoperazine) and doxepin may cause less inhibition of guanethidine's antihypertensive activity (Hansten 1976).

Clonidine, unlike guanethidine, does cross the blood-brain barrier. Clonidine produces its antihypertensive effects by stimulating the inhibition of alpha 2 presynaptic receptors within the CNS, resulting in a decreased adrenergic outflow (Blaschke and Melmon 1980). Desipramine reduces the sensitivity of these alpha 2 receptors and reverses clonidine's antihypertensive effects (Charney et al. 1981b). This alpha 2 down-regulating property has been postulated as the primary mode of desipramine's antidepressant action (Charney et al. 1981b). Although all antidepressants are proposed to act through a "final common pathway" of reducing postsynaptic amine sensitivity, the mechanism by which this occurs appears to vary among different drugs (Charney et al. 1981a). Only those antidepressants that have this effect by presynaptic down-regulation would be expected to reverse clonidine's antihypertensive effects.

Methyldopa exerts its antihypertensive effect by a mechanism similar to that of clonidine. The parent drug is metabolized within the CNS into alpha methylnorepinephrine, a potent presynaptic alpha 2 agonist (Blaschke and Melmon 1980). The interaction between tricyclic antidepressants or phenothiazine and alpha methyldopa is less clear than their interaction with clonidine. Despite the suggestion that the sympatholytic properties of these agents would antagonize alpha methyldopa's hypotensive effects (Van Zwieten 1977), studies in humans using chlorpromazine (Rankin et al. 1982) and desipramine (Reid et al. 1979) do not demonstrate this interaction. In the absence of further information, the use of any centrally acting antihypertensive agent in conjunction with psychotropic drugs having adrenergic activity should be carried out cautiously.

Orthostatic Hypotension

The use of antihypertensives such as hydralazine and prazosin that act through peripheral vasodilatation is associated with the side effect of orthostatic hypotension (Blaschke and Melmon 1980). Tricyclic antidepressants and low-potency phenothiazines also cause orthostatic hypotension, presumably through peripheral alpha-adrenergic blockade (U'Prichard et al. 1978). The vasodilatory action of monoamine oxidase inhibitors frequently produces significant orthostatic hypotensive changes (Kronig et al. 1983). The combined use of these antihypertensive and psychiatric medications would be expected to increase the risk. An analogous interaction should occur when sodium-depleting diuretics, coronary vasodilators, or beta blockers are used. These physiologic mechanisms offer a partial explanation for the increased risk of clinically significant orthostatic hypotension in cardiac patients who receive diuretics or vasodilators in combination with imipramine (Glassman et al. 1982).

Summary

Renal factors complicate the diagnosis and treatment of patients who have both OMS and kidney disease. Renal failure can lead to a toxic metabolic delirium through the accumulation of endogenous waste products and electrolyte imbalance. The treatment of renal insufficiency by hemodialysis carries the risk of causing new forms of OMS: dialysis disequilibrium syndrome and dialysis dementia. Systemic processes, whether inflammatory, toxic, or infectious, can lead to concurrent damage of both kidney and brain.

The use of psychotropic medications to treat OMS-related phenomena is confounded in the presence of renal failure. Most psychiatric medications are lipophilic and require metabolism into a water soluble glucuronide form prior to excretion. Diminished glomerular filtration will not lead to toxic accumulations of these medications. Nevertheless, a conservative approach is recommended, beginning with smaller dosages than usual and a longer interval between doses. Dosage should be titrated carefully against patient response. Given the heightened CNS vulnerability of the uremic patient, increased sensitivity to normally well-tolerated concentrations can be a problem. The major impact of the pharmacokinetic changes of renal failure is on the value of plasma levels in assessing adequacy of treatment. Alterations in protein binding and other aspects of drug distribution produce profound alterations in the ratio of free to bound medication. Plasma levels do not reflect this phenomenon and can be easily misinterpreted. A total drug concentration in the usually recommended range does not indicate appropriateness of dosage when renal failure profoundly alters the ratio of free and active to bound drug.

Lithium is the principal hydrophilic drug utilized in psychiatry. Because more than 90 percent is excreted in the urine, renal failure leads to toxic accumulations unless dosage is reduced and blood levels carefully monitored. Although controversy persists as to the nature and extent of lithium's nephrotoxic effects, the use of this agent in patients with severe renal failure is preferable to the destabilization of a precise medical regimen because of a labile affective illness.

Taking renal issues into consideration in the patient with OMS requires the clinician to be aware of renal physiology and the pharmacology of psychiatric drugs. A consideration and understanding of these issues enables the physician to treat the renal patient adequately and safely.

Chapter 104

The Patient with Hepatic Disease

Hepatic encephalopathy, an organic mental syndrome (OMS), is characterized by the presence of psychiatric symptoms, personality changes, disturbances in consciousness, and fluctuating and variable neurologic signs. The syndrome, also referred to as hepatic coma, may occur in the presence of acute or chronic hepatocellular disease or portal-systemic venus shunting (LaMont et al. 1983). The course of the illness may be "acute or chronic, mild or severe, intermittent or progressive, or self-limiting" (Jefferson and Marshall 1981a, p. 114).

The Clinical Syndrome

Hepatic encephalopathy secondary to acute or chronic hepatocellular disease has been subdivided into four clinical stages (see Table 1), which are defined by the progressive appearance of central nervous system (CNS) signs (Davidson and Gabuzda 1969).

Prodrome

The onset of this stage is usually so subtle that it is recognized only in retrospect. However, family members may report changes or accentuation of personality traits, mild cognitive deficits, and shifts in the affective or motoric spheres ranging from irritability to assaultiveness and from apathy to euphoria. The duration of these states varies from days to weeks. Sleep disturbances have been reported, ranging from daytime drowsiness to episodes of sleep. Eventually day-night reversal of the sleep cycle may be noted along with nighttime wandering and confusion typical of OMS patients with nocturnal delirium (Jefferson and Marshall 1981a; Kornfeld 1973).

Impending Hepatic Coma (Precoma)

This stage is characterized by more specific OMS signs and symptoms, including disorientation to time, place, and person; perceptual distortions; and paranoid ideation and responses. Asterixis ("liver flap") may begin in this stage and may persist for days or even months after recovery from the final stage of coma (Adams and Foley 1953). However the liver flap is not specific for hepatic encephalopathy and has been noted occasionally in cases of chronic pulmonary insufficiency, uremia, and arteriosclerotic cardiovascular disease (Conn 1960). Liver flap is a nonrhythmic assymetric flapping tremor of the extremities. These are best noted when the patient is asked to extend the hands or dorsiflex the wrists. During this stage, a characteristic abnormal electroencephalogram (EEG) is present (Adams and Foley 1953). The EEG has been

Table 1. Clinical Stages of Hepatic Encephalopathy

Stage	Mental Status	"Liver Flap"	Electroencephalogram
1. Prodrome	Confusion (absent or minimal) Depression/ euphoria Slurred speech Slight slowing of mentation Sleep disturbance	May be present or absent	Usually normal
2. Impending coma (precoma)	Confusion Euphoria Inappropriate behavior Drowsiness	Usually present	Abnormal with characteristic changes
3. Stupor	Marked confusion Incoherent speech Sleeps frequently but is arousable	Usually present	Abnormal
4. Coma	Unconscious	Absent because of lack of muscle tone	Abnormal

Note.   Adapted from Davidson and Gabuzda (1975) and LaMont et al. (1983).

reported as "paroxysms of bilaterally synchronous symmetrical high voltage slow waves in the delta range, 1½ to 3 cycles per second, interspersed with or superimposed on relatively normal alpha waves" (Adams and Foley 1953). However, the EEG findings are not specific for impending hepatic coma nor are they consistently found in all patients in this phase of the illness (Kornfeld 1973).

The presence of an OMS, asterixis, and characteristic EEG in a patient with diagnosed liver disease strongly portends hepatic encephalopathy. However, appropriate medical intervention at this stage can prevent the onset of coma and its associated high mortality rate (Jefferson and Marshall 1981a; Kornfeld 1973).

Stupor and Coma

Confusion and disorientation are common, as is drowsiness that eventually yields to a state of coma of varying depth. Within a relatively short period of time, the patient's consciousness can fluctuate widely from a state of alertness to one of stupor. Common neurologic findings include abnormal reflexes and convulsions. However, in deep coma the patient may be areflexic and unresponsive to stimuli. This stage may be terminated by death secondary to complications or may continue as an unabating chronic illness (Jefferson and Marshall 1981a; Kornfeld 1973).

Etiology of Hepatic Encephalopathy

The OMS of hepatic encephalopathy can occur in a variety of advanced or decompensated liver diseases.

Fulminating Hepatic Failure

This is defined as "hepatic failure with encephalopathy developing in less than eight weeks in a patient without preexisting liver disease" (Scharschmidt 1985). It occurs most commonly in type B or nonA nonB viral hepatitis. However, it may be precipitated by ingesting prescribed or nonprescribed hepatotoxic drugs or being exposed to certain anesthetic agents. Fulminating hepatic failure may also be associated with liver disorders and infections such as acute hepatic vein occlusion and herpes simplex, respectively (Scharschmidt 1985).

Chronic Hepatic Failure

Patients with chronic hepatic failure are prone to encephalopathy. The most common liver disease associated with the syndrome is cirrhosis with portal systemic shunting. Factors frequently reported to precipitate encephalopathy include medications, gastrointestinal hemorrhage, increased dietary protein, azotemia, hypokalemia, infection, constipation, anesthesia, surgery, hypoxia, and diuretics (Scharschmidt 1985).

Hepatic cirrhosis is the most common form of chronic liver disease. Etiologic factors frequently associated with cirrhosis include malnutrition, alcoholism, hepatitis, repeated and chronic exposure to hepatotoxins, ulcerative colitis, congenital syphilis, and parasitic infestations (LaMont et al. 1983).

Biliary cirrhosis, another type of chronic disease of the liver, occurs very frequently as the end result of obstruction of the bile flow by calculus, neoplasm, scarring, or congenital atresia. Intrahepatic obstruction of bile flow may occur in viral hepatitis or exposure to toxins and is generally progressive (LaMont et al. 1983).

Acute Porphyria

A variety of types of porphyria have been reported (Lishman 1978). Acute porphyria, the most common type, is due to an inborn error of porphyrin biosynthesis and is inherited as a dominant autosomal gene with incomplete penetrance. The illness occurs from puberty to a peak incidence in the third decade and is characterized by attacks of acute abdominal pain, nausea, vomiting, headache, and convulsion. A peripheral motor neuropathy with weakness, numbness, paresthesias, and pain is common. During the attack, the patient may be restless, agitated, and belligerent, and may exhibit marked emotional lability. Confusion and clouding of consciousness may ensue and progress to delirium with hallucinations and delusions (Lishman 1978). The diagnosis is confirmed by the presence of porphobilinogen and d-amino levulinic acid in the urine. Since there is no unequivocal specific treatment, psychiatric intervention may be required to avert further attacks (Lishman 1978).

Alcoholic Liver Disease

Alcoholic liver disease refers to a number of different hepatic diseases associated with acute and chronic alcoholism and includes alcoholic fatty liver, alcoholic hepatitis, and alcoholic cirrhosis (LaMont et al. 1983). These three may occur independently or concomitantly. Alcoholic cirrhosis, which is the most common in the United States, is a progressive disease but with the potential of functional improvement on cessation of alcohol consumption. With chronic, excessive alcohol intake, progressive liver deterioration, fluid retention, and portal hypertension may develop. There is increasing weakness, anorexia, weight loss, jaundice, ankle edema, and ascites. Spider angioma, gynecomastia, testicular atrophy, menstrual irregularity, palmar erythema, purpura, parotid gland enlargement, clubbing of fingers, loss of body hair, and so on become evident. Eventually, over a period of time, hepatic coma, which is often precipitated by infections or bleeding from esophageal varices, may develop (LaMont et al. 1983).

Alcoholics often manifest a dementia, the pathophysiology of which is not unequivocally clarified (Strub and Black 1981). The alcoholic who has drunk excessively and chronically for a number of years manifests a progressive loss of interest in the environment, personal appearance, and hygiene. In addition to poor concentration, poor judgment, and relative lack of insight, the thinking processes are retarded. In various studies, patients had difficulty with recent memory, disorientation, mild aphasia, and perseveration (Horvath 1975; Kleinknecht and Goldstein 1972; Tarter 1973).

The progression of the dementia is accelerated with the continuation of excessive intake of alcohol. On sudden cessation or reduction in alcohol consumption, delirium tremens (DTs) is to be anticipated and an appropriate withdrawal treatment regimen instituted immediately (see Chapter 93) (Greenblatt and Shader 1975). The patient with chronic hepatic disease secondary to alcoholism will require ongoing psychiatric treatment.

Cancer of the Liver

Carcinoma of the liver may be hepatocellular, cholangiocellular, or mixed in origin. The hepatocellular type accounts for 80 to 90 percent of the liver carcinomas (Alpert and Isselbacher 1983). Metastases to the liver are not uncommon. Chronic liver disease of any type, including metabolic, alcoholic, and viral, can predispose to liver cell carcinoma (Alpert and Isselbacher 1983). However, alcoholic and postnecrotic cirrhosis are the most common types of liver disease associated with hepatocellular carcinoma that may induce hepatic encephalopathy.

Liver Transplantation

Liver transplants have been performed in patients with tumors, all types of cirrhosis, sclerosing cholangitis, and metabolic disorders including antitrypsin deficiency, Wilson's disease, glycogen storage disease, galactosemia, and hemochromatosis (Scharschmidt 1985). In one study, 25 percent of the transplants were for neoplastic disease with a three-year survival rate of 12 percent (Scharschmidt 1984). Forty-four percent of the patients received transplants for end-stage cirrhosis. The three-year survival rate was lowest for alcoholic cirrhosis. In another study, preoperative "psychiatric" difficulties were noted in virtually every patient (19 of 20) (House et al. 1983). Although 50 percent of the patients manifested a fluctuating encephalopathy prior to surgery, postoperatively eight patients had an OMS. Depression, anxiety, insomnia, and dependency were common findings. Psychosis from postoperative use of immunosuppressants, such as steroids in high dosage, is a familiar phenomenon.

Wilson's Disease (Hepatolenticular Degeneration)

This rare, recessively inherited illness is due to an abnormality in copper metabolism, with the metal being subsequently deposited primarily in the liver, the putamen, and globus pallidus (Strub and Black 1981). The illness usually has its onset early in the young adult years but cases occurring in later years have been reported

(Goldstein et al. 1968; Walker 1969). The illness presents with tremors, involuntary grimacing, choreoathetosis, dysarthria, rigidity, and posturing (Strub and Black 1981). Inappropriate social behavior and delusions have been reported. Cognitive difficulties, including decreased concentration, memory difficulty, and inappropriate judgment, have been reported (Goldstein et al. 1968; Scheinberg et al. 1968). With progression of the disease, severe dementia eventually ensues. The presence of low serum ceruloplasmin, low serum copper, and high levels of urinary copper confirm the diagnosis. Treatment with penicillamine is effective in ameliorating the behavioral and neurologic symptoms (Strub and Black 1981).

OMS Coexisting with Liver Disease

An OMS may coexist in patients with liver disease. However, as with any syndrome, the underlying etiologic factors must be elucidated. Various categories of causes of OMS are known and include vascular, infectious, neoplastic, degenerative, congenital, traumatic, endocrine-metabolic, and those due to intoxication or vitamin deficiencies (Scharschmidt 1984). The contribution of each (i.e., the preexisting OMS and the liver disease) to the complicated clinical picture must be assessed. The observed OMS may be due solely to the preexisting OMS, to the combined processes, and/or the proper or improper treatment of the hepatic disease.

Differential Diagnosis

The differentiation of hepatic precoma from the complications of alcoholism (i.e., DTs) is critical for treatment. Sedatives are indicated for alcohol withdrawal and impending DTs, whereas in hepatic precoma, these drugs can accelerate the process to the end stage of hepatic coma (Jefferson and Marshall 1981a).

The delirium of hepatic precoma may suggest DTs. However DTs follow the abrupt discontinuation of alcohol and are characterized by a state of agitation, fear, visual hallucinations, and a coarse rhythmic tremor (not a liver flap) (Jefferson and Marshall 1981a). The patient in a hepatic precoma commonly manifests a liver flap and characteristic EEG pattern. Vivid visual hallucinations are usually not present. The liver function tests—including serum glutamic-oxaloacetic transaminase (SGOT), serum glutamic-pyruvic transaminase (SGPT), ammonia, and prothrombin time—may be abnormal in both hepatic precoma and DTs (Jefferson and Marshall 1981a). At times, the differentiation of hepatic encephalopathy from alcohol intoxication may be difficult because the two may coexist.

Head trauma and the consequences of such must be differentiated from hepatic coma. Subdural hematomas are common in alcoholics who not infrequently have either an acute or chronic liver disease (Jefferson and Marshall 1981a). An EEG and computed tomography (CT) scan will be useful in this situation. The EEG pattern will be characteristic in hepatic precoma, and the CT scan will reveal the structural lesion in the patient with head trauma. However, the presence of head trauma does not rule out hepatic encephalopathy, and various tests for liver function may be of great importance.

The distinction from Wilson's disease may be important. In this disease, the neurologic disturbance is relatively stable and consistent, the tremor is choreoathetoid (nonflapping tremor), and a characteristic Kayser-Fleischer corneal ring is present.

The diagnosis of Wilson's disease can be established in the presence of low serum ceruloplasmin, low serum copper, and high level of urinary copper (Jefferson and Marshall 1981a; Lishman 1978).

Patients with liver disease being treated with diuretics or a low sodium diet may become hyponatremic (Chatton 1979). The resulting metabolic encephalopathy can easily be misconstrued as hepatic encephalopathy. Hyponatremia may induce mental confusion with disorientation, delusions, and hallucinations (Lishman 1978). The condition may progress to coma and is associated with apathy, weakness, anorexia, nausea, vomiting, muscle cramps, and occasionally seizures (Lishman 1978). The sodium levels in these patients are very low, and the syndrome dissipates on salt repletion and fluid restriction.

Schizophrenic and manic and dementia syndromes have been reported after portal-systemic surgical shunting (Havens and Child 1955; Kornfeld 1973; Read et al. 1967). When they occur, functional psychoses of an affective or schizophrenic type are usually seen in the early postoperative period.

Depression must be differentiated from hepatic encephalopathy, which not infrequently is associated with a fixed facial expression, psychomotor retardation, and moods of sadness and apathy. Patients with a history of depression may also have personal and family histories of excessive alcohol ingestion. However, the presence of liver disease, characteristic EEG pattern, and asterixis should assist in making the diagnosis.

Catatonic schizophrenia may be considered in the differential diagnosis because of the presence of mutism and stupor (Lishman 1978). However, in the absence of symptoms such as waxy flexibility, posturing, auditory hallucinations, and past history of schizophrenic episodes, this diagnosis can be easily disregarded.

Not uncommonly, many patients in the early stages of hepatic encephalopathy are incorrectly diagnosed as neurotic anxiety, hysterical ataxia, psychomotor epilepsy, narcolepsy, frontal lobe tumor, multiple sclerosis, cerebral arteriosclerosis, and Parkinson's disease (Sherlock et al. 1954; Summerskill et al. 1956).

Patient Evaluation

The diagnosis of hepatic encephalopathy is made primarily on the basis of history, physical examination, and laboratory findings. The history taking includes interviews with the immediate family and support system, in addition to the patient, and encompasses a comprehensive psychosocial and drug-substance abuse evaluation. The focus should be on precipitating factors such as the use and abuse of sedative-hypnotics, infections, recent gastrointestinal bleeding, fluid and electrolyte disturbances, constipation, and increased ingestion of dietary protein (McClain 1980).

The assessment of liver disease emphasizes the history of alcohol ingestion, drug use, jaundice, hepatitis, and exposure to hepatotoxins or blood transfusion (McClain 1980).

The physical examination focuses on signs of underlying liver disease: jaundice, hepatosplenomegaly, ascites, dilated abdominal veins, spider angioma, palmar erythema, asterixis, gynecomastia, Dupuytren's contractures, testicular atrophy, and possibly hypothermia (McClain 1980). The latter has been correlated with the poor prognosis of hepatic encephalopathy (Margolis 1979). Probably the most specific sign of this syndrome is fetor hepaticus (i.e., an odor of garlic).

Neuropsychiatric examination is an invaluable component of a comprehensive evaluation of hepatic encephalopathy. It includes a psychiatric assessment focusing on mental alertness, speech patterns, content and form of thoughts, mood, and motoric activity. A mental status examination assessing cognitive functioning is to be included.

Neurologic examination usually reveals a flapping tremor, dysarthria, ataxia, hyperreflexia, and clonus. Perseverative speech disturbances, diplopia, and nystagmus may also be present (Lishman 1978). These neurologic signs and symptoms are variable and may wax and wane from one day to the next. Serial handwriting may be used to follow the course of the illness (Sherlock 1981).

Laboratory tests may or may not be of assistance in establishing the diagnosis of hepatic encephalopathy. Liver function tests including serum bilirubin, SGOT, SGPT, and prothrombin activity may be abnormal. Although these parameters are useful reflectors of liver disease, the degree of abnormality of these tests is not an accurate predictor of the diagnosis or prognosis of hepatic encephalopathy (Jefferson and Marshall 1981a). However, negative laboratory tests do not rule out encephalopathy completely. Arterial blood ammonia levels usually correlate fairly well with the intensity of the coma (Chen and Chen 1977). However, routine blood ammonia levels are not recommended (Sherlock 1981).

The EEG pattern as described is a useful diagnostic test in the presence of liver disease. However, it is also found in diverse conditions as uremia, hypokalemia, anoxia, hypoglycemia, vitamin B_{12} deficiency, and in early states of increased intracranial pressure (Kennedy et al. 1973; Lishman 1978). More recently, automated EEG analysis has been suggested as a means of classifying stages of hepatic encephalopathy (Van der Rijt et al. 1984). The visual evoked potential technique has been reported as being a helpful method for differentiating the stages of hepatic encephalopathy, including identification of the preclinical stage, which is usually diagnosed only retrospectively (Zeneroli et al. 1984).

Treatment of Hepatic Encephalopathy

The treatment of hepatic encephalopathy is directed toward the underlying cause of the liver disease. In acute or fulminant hepatic failure, treatment depends on the proper identification of the specific etiologic factor. Specific medical treatment measures are detailed elsewhere (Chatton 1979; Maddrey and Weber 1975).

Treatment for chronic hepatic failure consists of regulated dietary intake consisting of a modest (30 to 40 g) protein restriction, salt restriction, bed rest, complete abstinence from alcohol, and avoidance of narcotics and sedatives metabolized by the liver (Chatton 1979). The treatment of hepatic encephalopathy includes immediate control of gastrointestinal bleeding, discontinuation of drugs containing ammonium or amino groups, restriction of dietary protein, removal of fecal material from the colon through enemas, administration of lactulose, administration of neomycin, control of infections, and correction of electrolyte abnormalities (Chatton 1979).

L-Dopa and bromocriptine have been reported useful in the therapy of hepatic encephalopathy (Lunzer et al. 1974; Morgan et al. 1977; Parkes et al. 1970). However, the use of these drugs is still equivocal at this time (Schenker and Hoyumpa 1984).

The treatment of ascites and edema involves salt and water restriction, use of diuretics, bed rest, salt-free albumin, and peritoneovenous shunt for resistant non-infected ascites (Chatton 1979).

Treatment of Psychotic Symptoms and Behavior

The treatment of psychotic symptoms and behavior that not uncommonly accompany the syndrome of hepatic encephalopathy is best directed at the precipitating factors and the underlying liver disease. With this approach, the psychotic symptoms and behavior will abate. The use of sedative-hypnotics such as barbiturates, antianxiety agents such as chlordiazepoxide, and antipsychotic drugs such as chlorpromazine, which are metabolized by the liver, may enhance the progression of hepatic encephalopathy. However, if a psychotropic medication is to be used, it is generally agreed that lorazepam or oxazepam be administered in small doses (Kraus et al. 1978; Shull et al. 1976).

Drug Use Precautions in Liver Disease

A major role of the liver is to render ingested chemicals water soluble so that they can be eliminated by the kidneys or the biliary system. The liver plays a major role in drug metabolism through the microsomal oxidizing system (Hoyumpa and Schenker 1982). In severe liver disease, enzymatic induction is markedly reduced, which in turn affects the metabolism of various drugs (Farrell et al. 1979; Hoyumpa and Schenker 1982).

Psychotropic Medications

Benzodiazepines are metabolized primarily in the liver, have a low clearance, and are highly bound to plasma proteins with a variable elimination in the presence of liver disease (Hoyumpa and Schenker 1982). However, the presence of liver disease virtually had no effect on the metabolism of oxazepam and lorazepam (Klotz et al. 1977; Kraus et al. 1978). Of the two, oxazepam is preferred in patients with parenchymal liver disease (Jefferson and Marshall 1981a). If a parenteral route of dosing is necessary, then lorazepam rather than diazepam or chlordiazepoxide is indicated. However, it is advised that very low doses should be given because they all may cause excessive drowsiness.

The antipsychotics have not been adequately studied in various liver diseases. The only drug studied to any extent has been chlorpromazine. The elimination of this drug in compensated cirrhotics was not any different from the controls (Maxwell et al. 1972). There are currently no data to substantiate the impression that patients with preexisting liver disease are more susceptible to hepatotoxicity of psychotropic drugs (Dujovne 1977). However chlorpromazine has been associated with reports of hepatotoxicity in patients presumably without preexisting liver disease. The incidence for chlorpromazine associated hepatotoxicity ranges from 0.1 to 2 percent (Ebert and Shader 1970; Jefferson and Marshall 1981a). The hydrazine monoamine oxidase inhibitors have also been reported to cause severe hepatocellular damage, whereas the nonhydrazine monoamine oxidase inhibitor tranylcypromine appears to have a much lower incidence of inducing liver disease (Ebert and Shader 1970).

There are no data on the pharmacokinetics of antidepressants or lithium in patients with liver disease (Jefferson and Marshall 1981a). However, since antidepressants are metabolized in the liver, caution is suggested with frequent monitoring of plasma levels, side effects, and possibility of cardiotoxicity.

In severe liver diease with or without ascites, the use of diuretics and salt-restricted diets might hinder the ease with which lithium is prescribed. Moreover, the massive shifts in fluid compartments in patients with ascites would portend difficulty in controlling the lithium levels. In these patients, a superimposed lithium toxicity might be expected. Whether or not lithium should be used in these patients is equivocal. However, if the psychiatric condition is life threatening, and if such a patient fails to respond to other measures, lithium treatment may be undertaken with extreme caution. In such instances, hospitalization may be necessary.

The hepatic disposition and elimination of barbiturates are markedly reduced in liver disease with the potential of accumulation. Barbiturates as a class generally are to be avoided in hepatic encephalopathy (Hoyumpa and Schenker 1982).

Analgesics

Patients with stable cirrhosis have received morphine and showed no mental or EEG changes suggestive of encephalopathy (Hoyumpa and Schenker 1982; Laidlaw et al. 1961). However, the elimination of methadone in patients with severe parenchymal liver disease is prolonged (Novick et al. 1980). This drug should be monitored carefully when used in heroin addicts who not uncommonly have an associated liver disease. It is not uncommon to find increased levels of analgesics such as acetaminophen, pentazocine, salicylates, and phenylbutazone in liver disease (Hoyumpa and Schenker 1982).

Cardiovascular Drugs

Digoxin and digitoxin in the presence of liver disease are eliminated relatively normally. There is only a slight impairment of elimination of quinidine and procainamide. However, the clearance of lidocaine is markedly reduced in patients with liver disease (Hoyumpa and Schenker 1982). The beta blocker propranolol is metabolized in the liver to various inactive agents and appears to be highly bound to plasma protein (Shand 1976). In the presence of liver disease, its clearance may be decreased, and the elimination half-life markedly increased (Patterson et al. 1970; Shand 1976).

Diuretics

Spironolactone and furosemide pharmacokinetics have been studied in the presence of liver disease. Spironolactone elimination is not impaired in severe liver disease (Abshagen et al. 1977), whereas the half-life of furosemide is prolonged (Verbeeck et al. 1982).

Steroids

Liver disease has been reported to impair the reduction of prednisone, with resulting lower plasma levels of prednisolone (Davis et al. 1978; Madsbad et al. 1980). Both drugs have been used in patients with liver disease (Cook et al. 1971). However, the use of prednisolone may yield higher and relatively more consistent plasma levels (Davis et al. 1978; Madsbad et al. 1980).

Diphenylhydantoin

On therapeutic doses of diphenylhydantoin, patients with liver disease have been reported to have higher plasma concentrations of the drug and manifested signs of toxicity such as ataxia and nystagmus (Kutt et al. 1964a).

Summary

The patient with hepatic disease may present with an OMS characterized by medical, neurologic, and psychiatric signs and symptoms. The course of the syndrome may be "acute or chronic, mild or severe, intermittent or progressive or self limiting" (Jefferson and Marshall 1981a). Patients with hepatic encephalopathy frequently are incorrectly diagnosed. Treatment is directed at the etiology of the liver disease. If psychotropic medications are to be used to control psychotic symptoms and behavior, they must be prescribed cautiously and judiciously, with frequent monitoring of the patient. After the resolution of the acute medical-psychiatric problem, many of these patients will require continuous psychiatric treatment to deal with a variety of issues (e.g., substance abuse and addiction, chronic illness, dying, and death).

Chapter 105

The Patient with Lung Disease

A number of organic mental syndromes (OMS) are associated with lung diseases and the medications frequently used to treat these disorders. Some of these syndromes are secondary to hypoxia, hypercapnia, brain metastases, paraneoplastic syndromes or remote effects of lung tumors, or pulmonary emboli. Medications used to treat asthma, chronic obstructive pulmonary disease (COPD), tuberculosis, and lung neoplasia may all produce mental syndromes. Anxiety, depression, and psychosis occur in patients with lung disease, and certain precautions are required in treating these psychiatric disorders in pulmonary patients.

The Clinical Syndromes

OMS Secondary to COPD

Chronic respiratory disease. A number of psychologic and neuropsychologic alterations occur with COPD. Depression, anxiety, and excessive bodily preoccupation coupled with fears of certain behaviors such as sexual activity are common among these patients (Agle and Baum 1977; Agle et al. 1973; DeCencio et al. 1968; Fletcher and Martin 1982; Greenberg et al. 1985; Lester 1973). Such findings are found in other chronically ill patients, however, and are not specific to COPD (Lester 1973). One study did find that those patients with COPD with the greatest degree of pulmonary obstruction produced the most elevated neurotic scales on the Minnesota Multiphasic

Personality Inventory (Lester 1973). It is not known whether the emotional concomitants of COPD are a manifestation of biologic alterations secondary to hypoxia or hypercapnia or are secondary psychologic reactions to a chronic debilitating disease.

Cognitive dysfunction in patients with COPD has been documented (Fix et al. 1982; Grant et al. 1980, 1982; Huppert 1982; Greenberg et al. 1985; Nocturnal Oxygen Therapy Trial Group 1980; Prigatano et al. 1983). Over half of mildly hypoxemic patients reportedly have some impairment in abstract reasoning, in complex tactual-spatial motor skills, and in language function (Fix et al. 1982; Grant et al. 1980, 1982; Prigatano et al. 1983). Again, it is difficult to determine if chronic illness per se, rather than just COPD, may account for some of the dysfunction. Secondary changes from chronic hypoxia, such as elevated hematocrit, have been demonstrated to result in impaired memory (Bornstein et al. 1980; Willison et al. 1980). Generally, overall intelligence testing of patients with COPD places them in the average range; cognitive changes appear to be subtle and may be most evident during times of stress (Greenberg et al. 1985). There are no prospective studies on the cognitive effects of persistent hypoxia.

Cognitive alterations in the hypoxic patient do not appear to be permanent and may be reversed by supplemental oxygen treatment (Block et al. 1974; Heaton et al. 1983; Krop et al. 1973); the amount of supplemental oxygen is related to the degree of cognitive improvement (Heaton et al. 1983; Nocturnal Oxygen Therapy Trial Group 1980). After 12 months of treatment, patients receiving continuous oxygen therapy improved more on a number of neuropsychological parameters than did those receiving only nocturnal oxygen. Cognitive tests were administered after all subjects had been breathing room air for several hours in an attempt to eliminate differential acute effects.

Considerable evidence suggests that quality of life is directly related to neuropsychologic function and that correction of hypoxic states facilitates both emotional health and life quality (Greenberg et al. 1985; McSweeney et al. 1980). The relationship between emotional disturbance and neuropsychologic dysfunction may indicate that some of the emotional effects of hypoxemia may be the result of an inadequate supply of oxygen to the limbic system and other portions of the brain that mediate emotional behavior (McSweeney et al. 1980).

Respiratory failure. Most of the studies on OMS secondary to respiratory failure have been done in patients with COPD (Arieff and Buckingham 1970; Austen et al. 1957; Dulfano and Ishikawa 1965; Krop et al. 1973). Acute respiratory failure is diagnosed by finding hypoxemia with or without elevated CO_2 on arterial blood gas examination (Rogers 1977) and may be caused by intrinsic lung disease or by extrapulmonary causes such as myasthenia gravis, respiratory depressant drugs, upper airway obstruction, and head or chest trauma. The secondary delirium may be caused by hypoxemia, hypercapnia, or both (Lipowski 1980; Rogers 1977).

The mental effects of hypoxia differ depending on the rate of its development. With chronic hypoxia, oxygen saturation as low as 60 percent may cause few changes, whereas abrupt falls in this level will generally result in a delirious state (Austen et al. 1957; Lipowski 1980) (see also Chapter 93). Similarly with hypercapnia, acute elevations of pCO_2 to 70 mm Hg will produce mental confusion; patients with chronic hypercapnia may remain alert at a level of 90 mm Hg (Dulfano and Ishikawa 1965). Carbon dioxide produces anesthetic-like changes that resemble barbiturate intoxication. Hypercapnia lowers pH, and the severity of neuropsychiatric symptoms correlates with the intensity of cerebrospinal fluid (CSF) acidosis (Plum and Posner 1972). In patients with chronic pulmonary insufficiency, delirium may result from acute exacerbation of respiratory failure induced by respiratory infection or by sedating drugs (Lipowski 1980). Patients with elevated pCO_2 (usually above 70 mm Hg) may exhibit confusion, headache, lethargy, tachycardia, and diaphoresis. One study reported that seven of 50 patients with acute pulmonary decompensation developed hallucinations, delusions, and excitability (Dulfano and Ishikawa 1965).

OMS Secondary to Lung Malignancies

Metastatic disease.   It is clear that metastatic lung disease in the central nervous system (CNS) can produce neuropsychiatric symptoms. Lung carcinoma is the most frequent malignancy to spread to the brain; such metastases are usually multiple and grow rapidly (Lishman 1978). Occasionally, however, single nodules, which can be surgically removed, are found. Intracranial masses will sometimes produce focal neurologic signs and symptoms before the parent lung tumor is identified (Lishman 1978).

Meningeal carcinomatosis, with diffuse metastatic deposits to the leptomeninges, may produce a clinical syndrome similar to bacterial meningitis with fever, headache, and neck stiffness (Lishman 1978). In some cases, neuropsychiatric symptoms of dementia, mutism, or mania may be the presenting features (Fischer-Williams et al. 1955). The diagnosis can be made when carcinomatous cells are found in the CSF.

Multiple cerebral infarctions and multi-infarct dementia can occur in association with systemic malignancies as a result of intravascular coagulation (Collins et al. 1975; Reagan and Okazaki 1974).

Nonmetastatic disease.   Some patients develop neuropsychiatric symptoms secondary to lung carcinoma that has not spread; patients with these well-described but poorly understood syndromes develop clear CNS pathology while the carcinoma remains confined to its original site (Lishman 1978). The prevalence of these syndromes is unknown. Mental symptoms are often reported to antedate clinical evidence of the primary lung tumor by up to several years. These syndromes may even progress after the lung tumor has been removed and may occasionally begin some time after a primary tumor has been excised when there is no evidence of recurrence (Lishman 1978). Lishman elaborated on the work of earlier authors and described a number of syndromes, which will be briefly discussed (Brain and Adams 1965; Lishman 1978). These syndromes are sometimes distinct but frequently merge into one another.

Subacute cerebellar degeneration, one of the first nonmetastatic syndromes to be identified, is manifested by ataxia and dysarthria and is sometimes associated with dysphagia, diplopia, muscle weakness, and sensory symptoms. Almost all of these patients develop some degree of dementia (Brain and Henson 1958); agitation and depression may occur concomitantly (Brain and Wilkinson 1965). The course of the illness may be very rapid, leading to a bedridden state within a few weeks, or may progress over many months (Lishman 1978). There are prominent pathologic changes in the cerebellum (loss of Purkinje cells and neuronal degeneration), cerebral white matter (microglial proliferation), and the spinal cord (long tract degeneration) at autopsy.

An *encephalopathy* may be associated with lung carcinoma. In some cases, a dementing illness may be superimposed on varied neurologic signs, including ataxia, bulbar palsy, disordered extraocular movements, limb muscle weakness, extensor plantar responses, involuntary movements, and sensory loss (Lishman 1978). This syndrome may precede the overt development of lung carcinoma by a number of years. In some cases, neurologic abnormalities are not present until late in the course, and the initial presentation is largely psychiatric. Mental disturbances include a rapidly progressive dementia or depression or agitation (Brain and Adams 1965; Lishman 1978).

Carcinoma of the lung has also been associated with fluctuating disturbances of consciousness and intermittent lucidity (delirium) and occasionally with depression. These mental changes may arise over many months prior to death, may not be associated with neurologic abnormalities, and may have no demonstrable brain pathology at autopsy (Charatan and Brierley 1956; McGovern et al. 1959). Lishman (1978) suggested that these cases may be due to some *metabolic disturbances*; the autopsy findings that many of these patients had no brain lesions but did have livers that were full of metastases helps support his idea (Charatan and Brierley 1956). Similar cases have been reported, however, where both the liver and brain were free of lesions at autopsy (McGovern et al. 1959).

Lung carcinoma of bronchial origin, without CNS metastases, is sometimes associated with pathologic changes primarily limited to the limbic gray matter of the brain. The clinical picture has been called *limbic encephalopathy*. Patients present with marked alterations of recent memory, and more generalized loss of intellectual function often follows (Corsellis et al. 1968). Severe anxiety or depression is not uncommon; hallucinations and seizures have been reported (Corsellis et al. 1968; Lishman 1978). Analysis of CSF may show a raised lymphocyte count with elevated protein, and the electroencephalogram may reveal temporal abnormalities (Lishman 1978). Tumor cells, however, have not been identified within the CNS (Brierley et al. 1960; Yahr et al. 1965). Limbic encephalitis has a course of one to two years (Cummings and Benson 1983a), occurs usually in the sixth to eighth decade, and affects men more often than women. In a few patients, amnesia is virtually the only neuropsychologic abnormality. As the encephalopathy progresses, gradual dilapidation of other cognitive abilities may occur (Corsellis et al. 1968; Daniels et al. 1969; Dorfman and Forno 1972; Glaser and Pincus 1969).

A special form of myasthenia is occasionally observed with oat-cell carcinoma of the lung (Adams and Victor 1981; Eaton and Lambert 1957). This form of myasthenia, the *Eaton-Lambert syndrome*, differs in some ways from myasthenia gravis but is also associated with muscular weakness exacerbated by exercise. Some of the earlier described mental changes associated with lung neoplasia may also occur concomitantly.

Mechanism. Two main themes predominate concerning the cause of nonendocrine nonmetastatic neuropsychiatric syndromes associated with lung carcinoma. The tumor may be secreting some as yet unidentified neurotoxin, or the changes may reflect an abnormality in the patient's immune system that has led to a viral infection. The rarity of these syndromes makes systematic study difficult.

If a toxic agent were produced by a tumor, one would suspect that removal of the tumor would lead to improvement, or at least no further advancement in the neuropsychiatric manifestations. In fact, improvement is rare, and progression is the rule. It is well documented that lung tumors may indeed secrete a number of active agents such as parathormone-like and adrenocorticotropic hormone (ACTH)-like substances and, in addition, may produce hypoglycemia from an insulin-like agent or low sodium from secretion of antidiuretic hormone (ADH) (Lishman 1978).

Examination of affected brain tissue has led to speculation that a viral pathogen may be involved. Lishman (1978) noted that in addition to degenerative changes in the brain, there are inflammatory reactions that are also found in nondegenerating areas of afflicted brains. In addition, the presence of a virus would be consistent with the typical finding of a lack of any predictable relationship between the course of the neuropsychiatric complications and the progression of the tumor. Unfortunately, no viral agent has yet been identified.

Endocrine abnormalities. As mentioned above, a number of endocrine abnormalities have been associated with lung carcinoma, including hypoglycemia, inappropriate ADH production with hyponatremia, parathormone secretion with hypercalcemia, and ectopic ACTH production with Cushing's syndrome (Cummings and Benson 1983a). Oat-cell carcinoma of the lung has frequently been associated with the inappropriate secretion of ADH (Leaf 1971; Martin et al. 1977) and also ectopic ACTH production, although ACTH may also be secreted by bronchial carcinomas (Martin et al. 1977). Hypercalcemia, with resultant changes in mental status ranging from delirium to psychosis, can be produced by bone metastases or by ectopic parathormone elaborated by the lung tumor (Odell 1968).

OMS Secondary to Pulmonary Embolism

About 60 percent of patients develop mental changes after a pulmonary embolism (Plum and Posner 1972). Patients typically look and feel anxious, often with superimposed delirium. There may be decreased cerebral blood flow secondary to lowered cardiac output. Often the initial presentation is a loss of consciousness with or without an associated seizure; on awakening, the patient usually complains of dyspnea (Lipowski 1980). Whenever a patient suddenly becomes delirious, tachypnic, or faints without apparent reason, pulmonary embolism should be considered and blood gases (showing lowered arterial pO_2 with a reduced pCO_2) should be determined (Lipowski 1980; Plum and Posner 1972). A lung scan may confirm the diagnosis.

Drug-Induced OMS

Drugs for COPD and Asthma

A number of drugs that are commonly used to treat pulmonary disorders may be associated with mental symptoms. Theophylline may cause withdrawal, mutism, hyperactivity, and delirium (McSweeney et al. 1984c; Nolke 1956; Wasser et al. 1981). These changes almost always occur at high serum concentrations of the drug.

Between 1 and 2 percent of patients taking prednisone develop a psychosis (Boston Collaborative Drug Surveillance Program 1972; Villareal et al. 1974). Cortisone and ACTH produce a higher incidence of psychosis, about 4 percent (Lipowski 1980; Ritchie 1956). When high doses of prednisone are used (greater than 80 mg/day), the incidence of psychiatric side effects rises to almost 10 percent (Boston Collaborative Drug Surveillance Program 1972). Most often the psychoses involve a confusional state with superimposed manic symptoms and occasional paranoid features and hallucinations (Lipowski 1980). Even though delirium is more likely with high doses, there is no consistent relationship between dosage and symptom appearance (Lipowski 1980). The onset of the psychosis is typically sudden, occurring about two to four weeks after therapy is begun. Treatment involves gradual steroid reduction when possible. Haloperidol (Lipowski 1980) and electroconvulsive treatment (Villareal et al. 1974) have been recommended in refractory cases, and lithium carbonate has been demonstrated to provide prophylaxis against the development of corticosteroid-induced mania (Falk et al. 1979).

A number of beta 2-receptor agonists are used in the treatment of asthma to relax bronchial smooth muscle; all have been reported to sometimes cause nervousness, weakness, and drowsiness (Innes and Nickerson 1975). Drugs of this type include metaproterenol, salbutamol, terbutaline, fenoterol, ritodrine, isoetharine, albuterol, and ephedrine. There are also several reports of hallucinations and paranoia with albuterol (McSweeney et al. 1984c; Ray and Evans 1978) and with ephedrine (Herridge and A'Brook 1968).

Antituberculosis Agents

Four antituberculosis drugs may produce organic mental disorders: iproniazid, isoniazid, ethionamide, and cycloserine (Lipowski 1980; Shader 1972). Isoniazid may produce schizophreniform psychosis or delirium (Pleasure 1954; Shader 1972) or may cause euphoria or agitation. Patients may exhibit marked paranoia, sometimes with auditory and visual hallucinations (Kiersch 1954), which may last for weeks (Lipowski 1980; Shader 1972). Delirium, reportedly responsive to nicotinamide (Shader 1972), may result from drug-induced pellagra. Iproniazid only rarely produces a delirium (Crane 1956; Shader 1972), as does cycloserine. Cycloserine has, however, been reported to cause irritability, excitement, drowsiness, nightmares, concentration problems, insomnia, and depression (Bankier 1965). Ethionamide may induce psychosis (Lansdown et al. 1967; Shader 1972).

Antineoplastic Agents

The majority of patients with lung tumors require treatment with cytotoxic drugs sometime during the course of their illness. Since many of these agents may produce OMS, it may be difficult to determine which drug is the offending agent. Use of single-agent chemotherapy is not usually helpful, while combinations of three to five drugs produce objective responses in a majority of patients with oat-cell carcinomas and in nearly half of those with non-oat-cell types (Rosenberg 1984). A frequently used combination consists of cyclophosphamide, methotrexate, and vincristine. Other agents that are commonly used include procarbazine, nitrosureas, bleomycin, and doxorubicin.

Although the main toxicity of most of these agents is to the bone marrow and gastrointestinal system, OMS is occasionally reported. Methotrexate does not usually cross the blood-brain barrier except when given after craniospinal radiotherapy (Lipowski 1980). Encephalopathy may occur when it is given intrathecally (Holland 1981; Pizzo et al. 1976; Pochedly 1977; Weiss et al. 1974). Delirium with diffuse electroencephalogram slowing has been reported (Norell et al. 1974; Pizzo et al. 1976; Weiss et al. 1974) and an irreversible dementia, which may be a manifestation of leukoencephalopathy, may rarely follow methotrexate therapy (Fusner et al. 1977).

Less than 5 percent of patients on vincristine develop hallucinations, usually at high doses (Holland et al. 1973). It is unclear whether these patients become delirious (Holland 1981; Lipowski 1980; Weiss et al. 1974). Procarbazine may induce somnolence, confusion, agitation, hallucinations, depression, and psychosis (Weiss et al. 1974). Drowsiness or disorientation occurs in about 10 percent of those treated with typical oral doses (Weiss et al. 1974). Procarbazine is also known to inhibit brain monoamine oxidase and has synergistic sedative effects with narcotics, antidepressants, barbiturates, and neuroleptics (Lipowski 1980). It must be emphasized that Lipowski reports that procarbazine-induced delirium should not be treated with phenothiazines because severe orthostatic hypotension may result. Occasional patients manifest hallucinations, agitation, poor attention, and lassitude (Weiss et al. 1974).

There is one case report of procarbazine-induced mania (Carney et al. 1982). Other cytotoxic agents are occasionally associated with delirium but not in any consistent manner that would indicate cause and effect.

Drug Treatment of Psychiatric Symptoms in the Patient with Lung Disease

Agitation and combativeness on the part of an asthmatic patient may suggest severe hypoxemia and hypercapnia or could be due to excessive CNS stimulation from toxic levels of theophylline. Appropriate treatment of asthma or reduction of theophylline dosage is the required therapy, not the use of sedating agents (Fishman 1982). In delirious or depressed patients with Cushing's syndrome secondary to ectopic production of ACTH, the primary treatment would be to remove the tumor or to block the production of cortisol with metyrapone (Kramlinger et al. 1985). Many patients, however, will have a primary psychiatric illness as well as lung disorders, and special considerations that apply in choosing an appropriate anxiolytic, antidepressant, or neuroleptic drug are discussed below.

Treatment of Anxiety

In general, benzodiazepines are the drugs of choice in patients with lung disease; they cause fewer respiratory depressant effects than earlier agents like meprobamate, ethclorvynol, and the barbiturates (Cohn 1983; Jenike 1985a). A number of studies, however, have shown that the longer-acting benzodiazepines, such as diazepam and chlordiazepoxide, do have significant respiratory-depressant effects (Catchlove and Kafer 1971; Cohn 1983; Huch and Huch 1974; Jenike 1985a; Kronenberg et al. 1975; Rao et al. 1973; Utting and Pleuvry 1975). By contrast, the short-acting agents, such as oxazepam and lorazepam, seem to be much less likely to depress respiration. Steen et al. (1966) gave intravenous oxazepam (approved by the Food and Drug Administration for oral use only) to four volunteers and could show no statistically significant change in the response to breathing elevated carbon dioxide levels. Others report actual respiratory stimulation after oral doses of lorazepam (Dodson et al. 1976) and triazolam (Elliott et al. 1975). Temazepam in oral doses of 40 mg, but not 20 mg, significantly depressed the ventilatory response to carbon dioxide in 12 healthy volunteers (Pleuvry et al. 1980).

Denaut et al. (1975) compared the respiratory effects of lorazepam and diazepam in 20 patients with COPD and found that both drugs induced a respiratory depression with slight respiratory acidosis, but only lorazepam caused no significant hypoxemia. At the present time, the bulk of the data support the choice of lorazepam in the anxious patient with significant lung disease (Jenike 1985a).

There are a number of anecdotal reports that benzodiazepines can interfere with memory (Angus and Romney 1984; Barclay 1982; Bixler et al. 1979; George and Dundee 1977; Kothary et al. 1981; McKay and Dundee 1980; Pandit et al. 1976; Peterson and Ghoneim 1980; Roth et al. 1980; Scharf et al. 1983). Both short-term and long-term memory effects are reported, but the most profound documented effects are on the consolidation process (i.e., the transfer from short-term to long-term memory) (Angus and Romney 1984). Clinicians can test for these difficulties by giving the patient a few items to remember (e.g., clock, keys, quarter, comb) and seeing if the patient can retain them more than five minutes. To interpret such tests, baseline tests of memory must be on record so that abnormalities after the drug is begun can be compared to pre-drug results. When patients become less compliant and more forgetful, the possibility of drug-induced forgetfulness should be considered.

Treatment of Depression

Depression (Shershow et al. 1973, 1976) and grief (Jellinek et al. 1985) can depress the ventilatory response to inhaled CO_2 in patients without lung disease. At least theoretically, these emotional states can contribute to decrements in pulmonary function that could be clinically significant in the patient with COPD.

There have been no studies on the respiratory effects of different antidepressant agents. Since most of the patients with clinically significant pulmonary disease are elderly and many have multisystem disease, a few generalizations about choice of antidepressant medication can be made (Jenike 1985a). Tertiary amines such as amitriptyline and imipramine are more likely to cause hypotension than the secondary amines such as desipramine, protriptyline, and nortriptyline (Salzman 1982a) and are best avoided in the elderly. Recent evidence, however, indicates that the tertiary amine doxepin is safe in elderly patients in terms of orthostatic changes (Neshkes et al. 1985). Amitriptyline is also the most anticholinergic antidepressant (150 mg corresponds to about 7.5 mg of atropine) and is generally regarded as the tricyclic most likely to cause a clinically hazardous tachycardia (Cassem 1982).

The treatment of depression in the patient with pulmonary disease and OMS, therefore, does not differ from that of depression in general. If a patient has had a prior positive response or if the patient has a relative who had a good outcome from a particular drug, it may be best to begin treatment with that drug. Also, agents with high anticholinergic potency should be avoided in elderly patients.

Treatment of Psychosis

The need to control severe agitation or psychosis in the patient with severe respiratory distress poses a difficult clinical problem. Neuroleptics are best avoided in the agitated nonpsychotic patient; short-acting benzodiazepines may be effective. In patients with severe respiratory disease who are extremely agitated or psychotic, neuroleptics may be required; they may dramatically improve mental status, but may worsen respiratory dysfunction (Hollister 1974; Young and Patel 1984). The less sedating antipsychotic drugs (haloperidol, thiothixene, and fluphenazine) have been advocated for use in patients who are predisposed to respiratory difficulty (Dudley and Sitzman 1979).

Besides neuroleptic-induced oversedation, other mechanisms may be involved in respiratory failure (Solomon 1977; Von Brauchtisch and May 1968). Antipsychotic drugs may decrease respiratory motility through action on the brain stem directly (Masm and Granacher 1980). These actions may represent a dystonic reaction that generally responds to discontinuing medication or adding an anticholinergic agent like benztropine. Long-term use of neuroleptics rarely may produce a pure tardive respiratory dyskinesia (Faheem et al. 1982; Masm and Granacher 1980; Portnoy 1979; Young and Patel 1984), which may induce respiratory depression sufficiently extensive to affect pulmonary function tests (Weiner et al. 1978).

Respiratory dystonias may predispose to aspiration; the careful evaluation and monitoring of the gag reflex during neuroleptic treatment has been suggested as a useful guideline to the possibility of impaired laryngopharyngeal neuromuscular mechanisms (Young and Patel 1984).

Drug-Disease and Drug-Drug Interactions

Many elderly patients with lung disease have multisystem illnesses and are on numerous medications. Theophylline clearance can be decreased by cirrhosis, heart failure, and severe obstructive pulmonary disease (McSweeney et al. 1984a; Powell et al. 1978). Some drugs are known to slow theophylline metabolism regularly, including cimetidine (Campbell et al. 1981; Jenike 1982), propranolol, allopurinol, and the macrolide antibiotics such as erythromycin (Parish et al. 1983). Influenza vaccine has also been reported to slow theophylline metabolism, although reports are conflicting (Fischer et al. 1982; Renton et al. 1980). Phenytoin (Marquis et al. 1982), the barbiturates (McSweeney et al. 1984a), and carbamazepine (McSweeney et al. 1984b) all produce an increase in theophylline metabolism with a resultant decrease in effect. Serum concentrations of theophylline should be followed closely in patients taking any of these agents concurrently, especially when the potentially interacting drug is introduced or discontinued. For example, the patient with COPD on stable theophylline levels may become rapidly toxic when cimetidine is added.

Summary

Not only pulmonary diseases themselves but also some of the drugs commonly used to treat these illnesses are associated with organic mental symptoms. Lung tumors, the most frequent malignancies to spread to the brain, can cause a number of neuropsychiatric effects by direct invasion or by the production of a number of hormones. Nonmetastatic psychiatric manifestations of lung carcinoma are very interesting but poorly understood concomitants of some tumors. These are relatively rare, and large-scale studies have not been performed to determine their prevalence.

Mental symptoms including delirium, delusions, and hallucinations occur predictably with respiratory failure as pO_2 is lowered with or without elevated pCO_2. Asthma and COPD are frequently associated with depression, anxiety, bodily preoccupation, and avoidance behaviors. Reversible cognitive alterations have been documented, and it appears that emotional health and life quality are enhanced by improved oxygenation. Pulmonary emboli with resultant hypoxia (with possible decreased cerebral blood flow) may produce a classic reversible delirium.

Some drugs that are used to treat pulmonary disease may produce mental symptoms. Theophylline is usually well tolerated except at high doses; a number of drugs and medical illnesses can raise theophylline levels and thereby cause mental symptoms.

Corticosteroids produce mental symptoms, which occur more frequently as dosage is raised. Treatment involves decreasing steroid dosage, haloperidol, or electroconvulsive therapy. Lithium may be of use prophylactically in patients who have had a previous episode of steroid psychosis or mania.

Beta-agonists commonly produce tension and anxiety and occasionally paranoia and hallucinations. Four of the commonly used antituberculosis agents may produce mental symptoms, which may range from simple insomnia or drowsiness to depression or frank schizophreniform psychosis. Some of the cytotoxic agents used to treat primary lung tumors may cause CNS symptoms. Because these agents are usually given in multiple-drug regimens, it may be difficult to identify the offending agent. Encephalopathy and dementia have been reported with methotrexate when it is given intrathecally or after craniospinal radiation. Vincristine and procarbazine may produce a psychosis along with other changes in mental status.

Treatment of anxiety, depression, and psychosis in a patient with lung disease may require special considerations. The short-acting benzodiazepines, especially lorazepam, may be the least toxic antianxiety agents. Longer-acting agents are more likely to induce hypoxia than the shorter-acting drugs. Anterograde amnesia occurs rarely with the benzodiazepines.

Imipramine and highly anticholinergic antidepressants, such as amitriptyline, are best avoided in elderly patients with lung disease. Initial choice of drug can be based on the clinical picture (e.g., a sedating agent for the patient with insomnia, an activating drug for the hypersomnic or lethargic depressed patient). Even though any antidepressant may eventually improve depression-induced insomnia and fatigue, patients may be more comfortable during the first few weeks of therapy if insomnia is relieved or if lethargy is improved early in treatment.

Neuroleptics can affect respiration through mechanisms of sedation, dystonia, or tardive dyskinesia; when used in a patient with severe respiratory disease, careful monitoring of respiratory status is required.

Chapter 106

The Patient with Sensory Impairment

The Clinical Syndrome

It has been clear for centuries that an association exists between impairment of sensory organs and the development of psychiatric disturbances. From Beethoven (1802) we learn that he experienced periods of classic depression, social withdrawal, and feelings of isolation as a result of his hearing loss. In addition, we know that the sensory organs are vulnerable to disease processes, which because of the large sensory pathways and cerebral cortical representation can result in neuropsychiatric syndromes that present with mixed features. These may include psychiatric symptoms, sensory impairment, motor involvement, and vegetative changes. Thus mental disturbance in the sensory-impaired population may result from peripheral sensory loss, intracranial lesions, or both. The challenge to the clinician, therefore, is to determine if the sensory impairment is causative of mental changes in the patient, or if the sensory impairment and mental changes are concurrent findings resulting from other patho-logic processes.

There is little help available from the literature, which is neither extensive nor recent. The early literature is hampered by methodological shortcomings and con-fusing terminology, and the dozen or so publications since 1980 include textbook references, case reports, and only a handful of actual studies of sensory and psychiatric disturbances.

Types of Onset

Mental status changes in the sensory-impaired patient population can present acutely (as in delirium secondary to bilateral eye patching, hallucinosis following sudden loss of hearing, or amnesia associated with loss of smell following head injuries) or insidiously (as in patients with progressive hearing loss, optic atrophy, brain tumor, or degenerative disease such as multiple sclerosis).

Types of Manifestations

Traditionally, the diagnostic terminology regarding most psychiatric presenta-tions in sensory-impaired patients has been descriptive and comes from earlier lit-erature, making it difficult to use DSM-III-R (American Psychiatric Association 1987) classifications. The manifestations of organic mental syndromes (OMS) in this patient population include delirium, depression, hallucinosis, delusional syndromes, and personality changes. A few points about their presentations are noteworthy:

1. Transient, reversible OMS (delirium) associated with paraesthesias, tinnitus, and visual changes can be seen in metabolic states such as hypoglycemia and hypo-calcemia.
2. OMS associated with intracranial lesions does not have a predictable sequence, and the mental changes may precede, accompany, or follow the sensory, motor, and vegetative changes. Also, the specific manifestations in such conditions will vary according to the nature, extent, and location of the lesion.
3. Personality changes in OMS can be of sudden or gradual onset. If insidious in onset, the personality change could go unnoticed. Often, the patient's premorbid personality structure is retained while individual traits are enhanced or dampened (Benson and Geschwind 1975). For example, an aggressive trait becomes exag-gerated or a passive characteristic is lost.
4. The varied and sometimes subtle presentations of mental disturbances arising from or associated with sensory impairment emphasize the importance of alertness and sensitivity in the clinical evaluation of these patients.

I will provide an elaboration of the clinical manifestations according to OMS 1) as a consequence of sensory impairment and 2) coexisting with sensory impairment.

OMS as a Consequence of Sensory Impairment

Loss of Smell or Taste

Loss of sense of smell or taste is not known to produce any psychiatric disorder.

Visual Loss

Psychiatric sequelae to sudden visual loss are described in several case reports and a few organized studies. Fitzgerald (1970) reported from an investigation of 66 adults with visual loss that two-thirds of the group exhibited protracted depression accompanied by insomnia and social withdrawal. The symptoms persisted up to 18 months after onset of the blindness. He also noted serious suicide attempts in two of the sample patients. In describing his work with blind patients, Schulz (1977) noted that many pass through a phase of clinical depression with weight loss, sleep disturbance, and suicidal preoccupation.

Much disagreement exists over whether or not paranoid illnesses can be attributed to loss of vision. Three studies reported an increased frequency of blindness in patients with paranoid delusions (Cooper and Porter 1976; Moore 1981; Roth and McClelland 1971); two others (Kay and Roth 1961; McClelland et al. 1968) found no significant difference when such patients are compared to those with affective disorders. In a study of 340 elderly psychiatric patients with and without sensory deficits (22 deaf, 12 blind, 14 blind and deaf, 281 without sensory deficit), Moore (1981) noted that among her blind patients delusions of persecution were also associated with sexual delusions and poor memory. However, she attributed this increased frequency of delusion to age rather than to sensory impairment.

Temporary deprivation of visual stimuli may produce a picture of transient delirium, well known in the ophthalmologic patient following bilateral eye patching. Referred to as "black patch psychosis," the mental changes include disorientation, confusion, agitation, and visual hallucinations (Heiman 1977; Weisman and Hackett 1958). The mental changes typically begin 12 to 24 hours after surgery and may persist for several days. Although the exact prevalence of this condition remains unclear, a prospective study done by Karhunen and Orko (1982) of 1,505 patients undergoing cataract extraction revealed that only 50 patients (3.3 percent) developed postoperative psychosis. This finding contrasts sharply with the earlier finding of Linn et al. (1953), who noted postoperative psychosis in 20 of their 21 patients (95 percent).

Visual hallucinations may also present as solitary symptoms in the patient with a clear sensorium. In their survey of 150 elderly patients, Berrios and Brook (1984) noted visual hallucinations in 30 percent of the sample. Some of the patients described picturesque hallucinations referred to as complex visual hallucinations. Decreased visual acuity was reported in one-half of the patients who had experienced hallucinations. Complex visual hallucinations are vivid, static or moving, colorful or pale images that involve animals, humans, or complex scenes. Complex hallucinations are seen also in hemianopias caused by lesions of the occipital pathway. In a sample of 120 patients with hemianopias, Kolmel (1985) noted that 16 patients with lesions involving the occipital lobe were reporting complex hallucinations, which in some cases were reduced in size and did not fit the entire visual field.

Hearing Loss

The patient's age at onset of hearing loss and the degree of hearing impairment are important variables in the development of psychiatric symptoms. Severe deafness can begin prior to the development of language and communication skills (prelingual) or after their development (postlingual).

Prelingual deafness. Because of the importance of language in early growth and development, the prelingually deaf patient typically presents with developmental retardation (Denmark 1966; Rainer et al. 1963; Remvig 1969), which is generally attributed to the early, abnormally low to absent input of auditory stimuli. The majority of the prelingually deaf have severe linguistic and literary problems, impaired ability to develop speech, and a reduced ability to develop normal thought processes, the latter deficit being characterized by concrete thought processes with little development of abstract concepts and ideas (Cooper 1979). There is a retardation of the whole process of emotional and personality growth, with the most predominant presenting symptom being impulsive or aggressive behavior or temperament instability that is attributed to the severe sensory deprivation (Denmark 1966; Remvig 1969). Given the disruptive and stressful nature of prelingual deafness, Altshuler and Sarlin (1963) investigated its relationship to schizophrenia but failed to find a significant increase.

Postlingual deafness (hard of hearing).   The conclusions that can be drawn from studies of the "hard of hearing" patient are restricted by: 1) methodological difficulties, 2) factors related to the duration and severity of deafness, and 3) the influence of other physical diseases. Depression is the most frequent problem encountered when hearing loss is sudden. It can be severe and often is associated with suicidal ideation. In a prospective, partially blind study of 49 bilaterally deaf patients, Mahapatra (1974) reported that depression was present in 23 (46.9 percent) of the patients.

The methodological difficulties alluded to earlier pervade most of the studies on the relationship between paranoid symptoms and hearing impairment. Although no firm conclusion can be drawn, the role of hearing loss as a contributory factor in paranoid symptomatology cannot be ruled out. In a study involving two large groups of patients who were described as having late paraphrenia and who were compared to control groups of patients with affective psychosis, Kay and Roth (1961) reported that hearing impairment was present in twice as many patients with paraphrenia as in the control group. The term *paraphrenia* is used in their study to describe patients who display paranoid psychosis without evidence of degenerative brain disease or a primary affective psychosis. Similar findings were reported by Post (1968) and by Roth and McClelland (1971).

In another well-controlled study that attempted to overcome methodological shortcomings, Cooper et al. (1974) noted a higher incidence of long-standing, bilateral deafness in patients with paranoid psychosis when compared to a control group of patients with affective illness. In further studying the same group of patients (Kay et al. 1976), the authors reported that social deafness at the onset of psychosis and schizoid traits were independent factors contributing significantly to the development of paranoid psychosis.

The popular notion of increased suspicion as a personality trait among the deaf has not found support in the literature. A study by Mykleburst (1964) described failure of the Minnesota Multiphasic Personality Inventory to demonstrate the presence of paranoid traits among the hard of hearing, but noted that the participants scored high on the schizophrenia scale, a finding that he attributed to the social isolation experienced by the deaf.

Although systematic studies are not available, several case reports (Miller and Crosby 1979; Ross et al. 1975) described auditory hallucinations in deaf patients. The patients described in these reports usually had long-standing hearing loss that had rapidly accelerated prior to the onset of hallucinations.

OMS Coexisting with Sensory Impairment

Numerous conditions of varied etiology present with sensory impairment and mental syndromes.

Smell

Loss of the sense of smell (anosmia) is usually a result of head injury or intracranial tumor. The sensory loss can be unilateral or bilateral, partial or complete. In studying 1,167 patients with head injuries, Sumner (1964) noted anosmia in 7.5 percent of the group—2.9 percent of those without amnestic periods and 31.5 percent of patients who had periods of amnesia (duration: one to seven days). Anosmia following head injury results from division or compression of the olfactory nerve fibers as they pass through the cribriform plate of the ethmoid bone. Such patients come to the attention of psychiatrists when psychiatric evaluation is sought for the management of behavioral manifestations of closed head injury, or in compensation settings when anosmia is evaluated to eliminate those who feign it in the hope of material gain.

Compression of the olfactory tract may result from a tumor in the olfactory groove (meningiomas), from a tumor of the frontal lobe, or from the distension of cerebral hemispheres in obstructive hydrocephalus. In all of these cases, the patient also may present with psychiatric symptoms. Systematic studies of psychiatric presentation in the above syndromes are unavailable.

Vision

Viral infectious agents of the herpes and arbovirus groups produce a picture of encephalitis with psychiatric symptoms (lethargy, confusion, and psychosis) and visual changes including decreased vision and retinitis (Newell 1982). A measles (rubeola)-like virus is associated with subacute sclerosing panencephalitis, a rare, progressive illness afflicting children and young adults. It develops within a few weeks to months after a measles-like infection and initially manifests with intellectual decline, withdrawal, behavioral changes, and poor school performance (Lehrich 1979). It is at this stage that behavioral manifestations of the disease are likely to be mistaken for a functional illness, early neurologic signs being ignored or improperly interpreted (Himmelhoch et al. 1970). Manifestations that facilitate proper diagnosis are usually not seen until a later stage of the illness. These signs include seizures, myoclonic jerks, apraxia, and visual impairment including chorioretinitis, cortical blindness, and optic atrophy (Robb and Watters 1970).

Systemic lupus erythematosus (SLE) is a collagen vascular disease with central nervous system (CNS) involvement in up to 59 percent of cases (Estes and Christian 1971). Psychiatric symptoms commonly antedate the better-known manifestations of the disease (Bennett et al. 1972). In a study of patients with neuropsychiatric manifestations, Feinglass et al. (1976) noted that 63 percent of the patients developed neuropsychiatric changes within one year prior to the establishment of the diagnosis of SLE. Psychotic episodes, confusional episodes, hypomania, and depression were the more common psychiatric manifestations of the disease and were noted by the authors in 92 percent of the patients with psychiatric symptoms. In a study by Brandt et al. (1975), it was found that between 5 and 33 percent of patients with CNS lupus presented with cranial nerve involvement that began unexpectedly. Visual changes were the most common presentation and involved visual-field defects, formed and unformed visual hallucinations, scotomas, and cortical blindness. Corticosteroids are the mainstay of treatment, and these often produce additional mental changes due to the high doses in which they are prescribed (Bennett et al. 1972).

Neoplasms produce a diffuse picture of mental changes and visual impairment, including visual-field cuts and diminished acuity. Anterior pituitary tumors that characteristically occur in the middle years produce remote effects from excess secretion of hormones, or a picture of panhypopituitarism and visual-field cuts from the effects of pressure on the optic chiasm (Scheie and Albert 1977). Craniopharyngiomas are tumors of the epithelial remnants of Rathke's pouch. They are usually supracellar and produce compression of the superior aspect of the optic chiasm, resulting in inferotemporal field cuts. They also may involve the third ventricle, resulting in internal hydrocephalus, papilledema, and secondary optic atrophy.

Hearing

Central deafness is caused by lesions of the CNS at locations between the auditory nuclei and the cortex. The lesions may be neoplastic or result from vascular accidents. Although peripheral hearing is preserved, patients with central deafness have difficulty perceiving and interpreting complex information, as in pure word deafness. A detailed discussion of these presentations is beyond the scope of this chapter.

Taste

Little is known of central lesions causing loss of sense of taste (ageusia), although it is seen in conjunction with anosmia in cases of head injury. Hallucinations of taste or smell are also seen in irritative lesions of the uncinate gyrus (uncinate fits).

Differential Diagnosis

The differential diagnosis in the sensory-impaired patient with mental syndrome would entail: 1) organic sensory impairment versus functional sensory impairment and 2) OMS versus functional psychiatric disorders.

Sensory Impairment

Numerous organic causes result in sensory impairment. Their discussion is beyond the scope of this chapter. When psychiatric consultation is sought, psychological symptoms are evident, or the sensory impairment is believed to be "functional," or a "functional overlay" is thought to accompany a known sensory impairment.

Smell. Factitious anosmia and alleged memory disturbances usually follow a head injury, and typically the patient is involved in litigation. Testing for smell (discussed under physical examination) helps differentiate the factitious patients from the true anosmic (Doueck 1974).

Delusional symptoms involving smell are seen in schizophrenic patients who also have olfactory hallucinations (Doueck 1974), and often mimic OMS.

Olfactory reference syndrome (Doueck 1974) is an extremely rare condition of true olfactory hallucination in the nonschizophrenic patient. If afflicts young men, and an attempt to mask or wash away the odor becomes habitual. Social withdrawal, shame, anxiety, and a preoccupation with the foul body odor are other features of the syndrome.

Vision. Factitious visual loss can be monocular or binocular and usually involves the entire visual field. The patient typically is involved in litigation (Smith et al. 1983) and presents with a history of trauma and mild neurologic or ophthalmologic insult.

Visually impaired patients may experience exaggeration of their impairment as a functional disturbance (functional overlay). The patient characteristically shows a lack of concern for the progression of symptoms ("la belle indifference"). The history usually reveals interpersonal or intrafamilial conflicts, the symptom exaggeration representing a means of escape for the patient.

Hearing. The hearing-impaired patient can present with exaggerated hearing loss as a functional manifestation. Exaggerations or fluctuations in hearing loss (as witnessed in patient description such as, "he hears what he wants to hear") are encountered when sensitive subject matters are discussed, or denial and organic mental symptoms (inattentiveness, decreased concentration) complicate the clinical presentation and lead to an erroneous assumption of accelerated sensory impairment. Surprisingly, this aspect of functional hearing loss has not been studied adequately.

Patient Evaluation

Information gathering is challenging in patients with both sensory and communication difficulties. The evaluation is best carried out in a quiet, well-lit environment. The necessity of such an environment is emphasized by the reliance of deaf patients on nonverbal cues, such as facial expressions and lip movements, which require the interviewer's face to be clearly visible. Allotment of extra time may be necessary for interviewing the hearing impaired, and the presence of a family member or an interpreter skilled in sign language is helpful when evaluating a profoundly deaf patient. Interviewing becomes more difficult when hostility or suspicion limits the deaf patient's ability to communicate. Hence interviewing significant others as well as the patient becomes crucial when dealing with the sensory-impaired patient with an OMS. Giving attention to subjective feelings and observations may be the key to obtaining relevant diagnostic information. In addition, multiple sensory losses commonly occur in the elderly; they often tend to compound each other and prevent compensatory activities. For example, the older person with impaired hearing and impaired vision together with some impairment of fine motor activity can have major problems adapting to or adjusting a hearing aid. Furthermore, multiple relatively minor sensory impairments may lead to impaired mobility and predisposition to falling because depth perception and balance may be affected. In these situations, no one disability is major.

History Taking

The chronology of sensory impairment, organic mental changes, and other symptoms, if any, should be established by actively seeking information on their temporal relationship. If the presenting complaint is deafness or visual impairment and the onset is in middle or late life, the patient may regard the sensory deficit as a symptom of aging. The use of denial may result in deemphasizing the problem. Conversely, depression may be so overwhelming in some patients that the sensory impairment is missed on history taking.

Patient Examination

For maximum results, evaluation of the sensory system is carried out when the patient's mental acuity is at its best. However, mental status examination is repeated often, to determine the interrelationship between mentation and varying patient behavior.

Physical examination. A general impression of the patient's attitude should be noted. Body language can alert the interviewer to the presence of a visual-field defect when the patient 1) takes no notice of people or objects on one side of the room or 2) relies on auditory cues and turns the head to accommodate for the visual-field defect. A thorough evaluation of the sensory system should be done when indicated but is likely to be exceedingly difficult (and at times nearly impossible) in the patient with OMS who also has sensory impairment. Results of examination of sensory function are greatly determined by patient cooperation, attentiveness, and cognitive functioning; therefore, sensory examination of a patient with OMS may need to be repeated at frequent intervals at times (e.g., early morning) and under conditions (e.g., drug free) when the patient is best able to cooperate. Newer methods of assessment of visual and auditory functions incorporate technological advances and include tests such as visual and auditory evoked potentials (Desmedt 1984), electroretinography (Carr and Siegel 1982), and electrocochleogram (Davis 1978). However, their use in patients with OMS remains poorly documented.

The help of a care giver during the examination not only may relieve some of the patient's anxiety about being examined, but also may facilitate communication between the doctor and the patient by translating instructions into phrases or cues familiar to the patient. The help of such a person is vital when sign language or other nonverbal communication is needed.

When testing smell, several important considerations are kept in mind: 1) few odorous substances stimulate the trigeminal (V cranial) nerve to a greater or lesser degree; 2) test substances should be familiar to the patient, with the following four suggested: coffee, oil of lemon, benzaldehyde (almond), and crude tar; 3) each nostril is tested separately; and 4) failure to identify any one of the four is suggestive of a disturbance in olfaction (Sumner 1972). In evaluating factitious anosmia, a weak solution of ammonia is used and the patient asked to identify the odor. Ammonia usually stimulates areas of the nasopharynx (innervated by the V cranial nerve) and is readily identified by the true anosmic but often missed by the factitious patient (Doueck 1974).

An evaluation of the visual field can usually be accomplished on routine examination, but requires great skill and acumen in the patient with OMS. The visual field is tested using the examiner's visual field for comparison. The patient is asked to identify the approaching "moving finger" while looking straight into the examiner's eye and keeping the other eye closed. The right eye of the patient is tested using the left eye of the examiner and vice versa. When visual loss is functional, it is monocular or binocular and usually involves the entire visual field. Several neuro-ophthalmologic tests help differentiate functional from organic visual impairment (Keane 1982; Smith et al. 1983). Test procedures involve afferent and efferent visual system and monocular and binocular vision. Although the distinction between factitious and hysterical visual loss is important in patient management, a clear separation may not always be possible on examination. A review of the test procedures is beyond the scope of this text.

To test hearing in the patient with OMS may be clinically most challenging. The routine procedure is as follows: After forming a rough estimate of hearing in either ear (an impression that is usually gathered during the course of conversations), a tuning fork is used to differentiate middle ear disease from neural deafness. In middle ear disease, air conduction is impaired while bone conduction is preserved. In neural deafness, both bone and air conduction are affected. In Weber's test, a vibrating tuning fork is placed on the midline of the forehead, or vertex, and the patient asked to report the location of the sound that is heard. With normal hearing, the sound is reported to be on the midline; in middle ear disease, the sound is localized to the affected ear; in nerve deafness, localization is to the normal ear. In Rinne's test, a vibrating tuning fork is placed first on the mastoid process of one ear to test bone conduction. The patient is asked to report when the sound ceases. The fork is then placed at the external meatus to test air conduction. In middle ear disease, the sound is not heard by air conduction. In nerve deafness, the reverse is true. In functional deafness, the absence of any pattern of hearing loss is noteworthy, as is the day-to-day variation. Characteristically, there are inconsistencies in the patient's responses to sound signals. The audiograms tend to vary from one day to the next without any pathologic pattern (Sataloff, 1966).

Sense of taste is tested using weak solutions of sugar, table salt, quinine, and vinegar. The patient's protruded tongue is dried and drops of each solution applied to separate areas of the tongue (the lateral side of each half anteriorly and posteriorly). The patient is asked to identify each taste as the solution is applied. Answers are selected from a card on which all four tastes are recorded.

Mental status examination.   In evaluating the patient with sensory impairment, attention is additionally directed to the following. First, patient and family attitudes toward the sensory impairment and the patient's level of acceptance should be evaluated. Responses such as "I hear as well as I used to," "People don't talk clearly anymore," or "My loss of vision is merely a nuisance" enable the interviewer to pursue and determine the level of acceptance or denial of impairment. Second, the effects of organic mental symptoms (cognitive impairment) on the patient's ability to retain previously acquired knowledge or learn the advantages and limitations in use of mechanical aids should be determined, including proper use and maintenance, knowledge of control features, and the constant practice with hearing aids of adjusting volume control (i.e., turning it up in quiet environments and reducing gain in noisy conditions). Such information on patient limitations is of much value for the otolaryngologist or audiologist. Third, it should be determined if organic mental symptoms in a patient are attributable to more than one causative agent (e.g., delirium in a patient with hearing loss and dementia). Determining the role of individual causative agents which can be an extremely difficult task, is an area that has received little support from the literature. Fourth, is there a loss of higher cortical functions (aphasias producing communication difficulties or loss of sense of touch in blind patients)?

Specific Treatment

Special Aids

Special aids include hearing aids, visual aids, and communication aids. There is no known literature on the effects of OMS on the sensory-impaired patient's ability to use these aids. Some authors acknowledge the problem in a sentence or less, but offer no discussion or elaboration.

Hearing aids.   As the name implies, a hearing aid is designed not to correct the disorder but to assist the user in sensing auditory stimuli. A hearing aid amplifies all acoustic stimuli within the instrument's frequency response, and it amplifies meaningful sound as well as background noise. This can be disconcerting to the new user who has to become familiar with its use. Both verbal explanation and demonstration are usually given by an audiologist, and the patient will initially need to practice in a quiet environment with familiar people. The volume (gain) control of the instrument needs frequent manipulation by the user to permit auditory signals to be heard consistently. Additional adjustments are needed as the intensity of input varies or the batteries weaken. Many hearing-impaired patients also lack confidence in their ability to distinguish auditory signals that pertain to communication, as every uttered word in conversation is not heard verbatim by the patient. After an initial period of anxiety and with frequent practice, the patient learns to perceive the "gist" of the conversation and thus learns to respond and gain confidence. As experience increases, the hearing aid user learns to identify situations that are "difficult listening situations." Situations with high ambient noise or a significant distance between speaker and listener are common problems and solutions remain tenuous.

When perceptual (poor attention span) or cognitive (memory loss) deficits exist, difficulties are experienced by the organic mental patient in learning and practicing successful hearing aid use. Poor use or rejection of the hearing aid results, secondary to the improper amplification accompanying inadequate regulation of gain control. Further limitations in hearing aid use develop, with exacerbations of perceptual and cognitive deficits. (Delirium is an extreme example.) Paradoxically, hearing aids therefore seem least effective at a time when sensory input seems most beneficial to the patient.

Communication aids.   There are two types of communication aids for deaf patients: 1) auditory amplifiers that enhance signal-to-noise ratio, and 2) acoustic substitutes with signal converters (Riko and Alberti 1984) such as teletypewriters and television decoders. Many patients who are using a hearing aid for the first time are not ready for such devices. They seem to be used most successfully by those who have mastered hearing aid use and are eager to improve their communication skills (Riko and Alberti 1984). Their use by patients with OMS is restricted by the severity and extent of symptoms.

Visual aids.   A variety of devices is presently available for the blind patient. The American Foundation for the Blind publishes catalogs of tools and devices, including items such as audio calculators and braille typewriters. As with communication aids, their use is restricted in patients with OMS.

Pharmacologic Agents

Little is known about the psychopharmacologic treatment of psychiatric disturbances in the sensory-impaired patient. The use of psychotropic drugs in this patient population is well accepted, although systematic studies are not available. When treatment involves the use of psychotropic agents, their effect on the sensory impairment and their interactions with medications used in sensory organ disease must be carefully considered.

Drug-Disease Interactions

Two types of drug-disease interaction should be considered when pharmacologic management is indicated: drugs that are known 1) to produce or accelerate sensory impairment when introduced systemically and 2) to produce organic mental changes when used topically in treating sensory organ disease.

Psychotropic drugs including neuroleptics and cyclical antidepressants produce mydriasis and myopia that are reversible. However, piperidine derivatives of phenothiazine (thioridazine and mesoridazine) in high doses may produce retinal pigmentary changes that can be irreversible. A comprehensive list of drugs and their effects on sensory organs is provided in Tables 1 and 2. Caution is necessary in using some of these drugs on a long-term basis in any patients, and alertness for additional organ damage that can occur with the sensory impaired is essential.

Topically applied drugs producing mental changes include anticholinergic agents and beta-adrenergic blocking eye preparations. Anticholinergic preparations of atropine, homatropine, scopolamine, and cyclopentolate are used as cycloplegic or mydriatric agents. The CNS effects produced by the anticholinergic agents have included visual hallucinations, restlessness, and delirium (Newcomb and Ranson 1984). Although epidemiologic studies of mental changes produced by drugs used in ophthalmologic practice are unavailable (Newcomb and Ranson 1984), precautionary measures are known.

Hoefnagel (1961) commented on drugs draining via the nasolacrimal duct into the nasopharynx, thereby resulting in their absorption and the possibility for systemic side effects. He and several others recommended that, following the instillation of

Table 1.   Drugs Contributing to Ocular Pathology

Drug	Ocular Effects
Antimalarials 　Chloroquine 　Hydroxychloroquine 　Amodiaquine	Decreased accommodation, bull's eye pigmentary retinopathy, visual-field changes, color vision disturbances, optic atrophy
Corticosteroids	Myopia, posterior subcapsular cataracts, increased intraocular pressure, visual-field defects
Phenothiazines	Mydriasis, myopia, narrow angle glaucoma, retinal pigmentary changes, visual-field defects, night blindness, optic atrophy
Nonsteroidal antiinflammatory agents	Retinal hemorrhages, color vision disturbances, visual-field defects, optic neuritis
Digitalis glycosides	Decreased vision, scotomas, retrobulbar neuritis
Oral contraceptives	Myopia, visual-field defects, optic neuritis, papilledema
Chloramphenicol	Optic neuritis
Tricyclic antidepressants	Narrow angle glaucoma
Anticholinergics	Narrow angle glaucoma

Table 2. Drugs Contributing to Auditory Pathology

Drug	Auditory Effects
Aminoglycoside antibacterials Streptomycin Dihydrostreptomycin Neomycin Kanamycin Gentamycin Tobramycin Amikacin	The auditory effects produced by these drugs include tinnitus and hearing loss.
Diuretics Furosemide Ethacrynic acid	
Cytotoxic agents N-Mustard Cis-Platinum Bleomycin	

drops into the conjunctival sac, light pressure be applied to the region over the lower puncta and nasolacrimal duct to minimize the overflow of drugs into the nasopharynx.

Timolol is a beta-adrenergic agent used in the treatment of glaucoma. In a study of 165 patients treated with timolol (McMahon et al. 1979), 17 (10.3 percent) developed CNS side effects, including lightheadedness, fatigue, sedation, depression, dissociative behavior, and memory loss. Similar findings including disorientation and visual hallucination have been reported by others (Van Buskirk 1980; Wilson et al. 1980).

Drug-Drug Interactions

A variety of drugs used in the treatment of eye and ear diseases are known to interact with psychotropic agents. The net effect can be increased anticholinergic or sympathomimetic activity.

Anticholinergic Effects

Antipsychotics, antidepressants, and anticholinergic agents react synergistically with anticholinergic (mydriatic) eye preparations, producing an increase in the total muscarinic effects. When psychotropics are prescribed for patients receiving anticholinergic eye preparations, a dose adjustment of either or both agents may be required.

Sympathomimetic Effects

Monoamine oxidase inhibitors impede the breakdown of sympathomimetic drugs. Mydriatic preparations of sympathomimetic drugs (phenylephrine eye drops) may, therefore, result in an increase in blood pressure (Hansten 1985).

Renal Effects

Reabsorption of lithium can be impaired by acetazolamide, a carbonic anhydrase inhibitor used in treating glaucoma. Even though acetazolamide acts as a proximal tubule diuretic, no clinical significance has been established for the interaction (Hansten 1985).

Summary

Among the sensory-impaired patient population, a variety of organic mental symptoms are seen. Before determining that the sensory impairment is a preexisting handicap, the clinician needs to decide if the sensory impairment is causative of the organic mental symptoms, or if the impairment and mental changes are concurrent findings resulting from other pathologic processes. Patient evaluation based on such an approach gives the sensory impairment and mental symptoms equal attention, sets the path for proper diagnosis (including that of other disease processes), and facilitates prompt evaluation and treatment for the sensory impairment, organic mental symptoms, and other disease processes, if any.

Accomplishment of these objectives depends on a thorough history taking, which in these patients is doubly challenging because of the cognitive impairment and communication difficulties (e.g., hearing loss). Adequate time needs to be allotted to interview these patients, and it is critical to have a second informant. Frequent assessment is sometimes the only way to obtain a reliable measure of sensory impairment, and it facilitates understanding interrelationships between OMS, sensory impairment, and other disease processes.

Prompt correction of the sensory impairment can result in amelioration of the organic mental symptoms in some cases, usually those in which the mental symptoms are a result of the sensory impairment. Numerous sensory and communication aids exist today; their use by the organic mental patient is restricted by the presence of cognitive and perceptual impairment.

When pharmacologic agents are used for treating sensory organ disease or organic mental symptoms, adequate attention must be given to the interaction between illness symptoms (OMS, sensory disease) and drug toxicity (additional organic mental symptoms or acceleration of sensory impairment). The dose and choice of pharmacologic agents should receive careful consideration to keep drug-drug and drug-disease interactions to a minimum and yet provide maximum patient benefit.

Chapter 107

Multi-Infarct Dementia

Research Problems

Few experimental treatment studies have focused on multi-infarct dementia (MID) as a distinct entity. In most studies of the treatment of dementing disorders in late life, the patient population was poorly defined according to current nosology. Patients with MID were not distinguished from those with dementia of the Alzheimer type; therefore, their response to treatment was not examined separately.

One problem with research in the treatment of MID, even today, is the limitation of diagnostic reliability and validity (see also Chapter 94). The criteria on which the clinical diagnosis is based depend heavily on historical information, such as "abrupt onset." The Ischemia Score, as originally proposed by Hachinski et al. (1975) and as modified by Rosen et al. (1980), is intended to assist in diagnosis. This instrument has been criticized, however. Small (1985) proposed improvements in the scale. A low Ischemia Score can help to exclude MID, but a high score can occur in cases of MID or dementia of mixed degenerative and vascular type.

The limits of the relationship between premorbid clinical diagnosis and postmortem findings were emphasized by Liston and LaRue (1983a, 1983b). Treatment studies have not included postmortem findings. As these authors pointed out, brain computed tomography scans, although more frequently showing infarctions in MID than in senile dementia of the Alzheimer type, are often negative in MID. Magnetic resonance imaging may remedy that situation. Focal electroencephalographic abnormalities, too, are often absent in MID. While regional cerebral blood flow (rCBF) measurements (Hachinski et al. 1975; Yamaguchi et al. 1980) using 133 Xenon inhalation and other techniques may prove useful, the relationship of rCBF to the clinical diagnosis of MID is tenuous; changes in rCBF following CO_2 inhalation (Yamamoto et al. 1980) may provide more specific information; so may emission tomography.

Presumably, MID is a clinically, anatomically, and biochemically heterogeneous group of disorders. There has been, however, no work validating subgroups defined by either clinical features or laboratory measures. Besides imaging techniques, neurotransmitter metabolite measures and neuroendocrine challenge tests are examples of laboratory measures that might be useful in this effort. Recent preliminary examples of their application in MID are the work of Meyer et al. (1977), Jonker (1983), and Charles and Rush (1985).

There are many other methodologic difficulties in the existing literature. One important issue, for example, is the inadequacy of the clinical rating instruments used, including lack of assessment of severity of illness and lack of standardized, valid ratings for depressive symptomatology. Another major deficiency is the lack of long-term reassessments in most studies, which would allow further validation of diagnosis and evaluation of treatment outcome.

Prophylaxis

The major risk factor for MID is hypertension. Additional risk factors include diabetes mellitus, hyperlipidemia, heart disease, smoking, obesity, and history of stroke in a parent (Meyer 1981). There have been no studies assessing the degree to which control of such risk factors alters the progression of MID or prevents MID from occurring in patients at risk.

Somatic Interventions

Treatments Directed at Presumed Pathogenetic Mechanisms

Anticoagulation, reduction of blood viscosity. One report (Ratner et al. 1972) suggesting benefits of anticoagulation in an apparently mixed group of demented patients did not describe the sample using any operational diagnostic criteria. A potential risk of this approach is hemorrhage (Rabins et al. 1983). The potential benefits of reduction of platelet cohesion (e.g., through chronic acetylsalicylic acid administration) have not been tested in MID. Some vasodilators share this effect (Table 1).

Vasodilators. These agents were originally studied in elderly demented patients based on the old assumption that vascular phenomena were pathogenetic in all senile dementias. Interestingly, they have received little study in MID. Using them in MID has apparent face validity. On the other hand, rCBF reportedly decreases during CO_2 inhalation in patients with MID (Yamamoto et al. 1980). The literature concerning cerebral vasodilators has been reviewed by Yesavage et al. (1979) and Cook and Jones (1981). Some of these drugs produce systemic hypotension; the incidence of this has not been well studied. Furthermore, they may reduce rather than enhance rCBF.

One review (Yesavage et al. 1979) distinguished those drugs with vasodilator effects alone from those with mixed vasodilator and "metabolic" effects. Those in the first category include cyclandelate, papaverine, isoxsuprine, and cinnarizine (Table 1). Their therapeutic effects in undifferentiated groups of demented elderly patients have been equivocal.

Drugs with mixed vasodilation and metabolic effects have more consistently shown effects in undifferentiated demented populations. These have been small effects, generally on subjective reports or affective symptoms, as discussed in Chapter 108. These drugs include dihydroergotoxine (Hydergine), nafronyl, pyritinol (a derivative of pyridoxine), and pentoxifylline (Trental), a xanthine derivative (Table 1).

Newer classes of drugs, little studied in the dementias, have vasodilatory effects. Among these are calcium channel blockers (e.g., nifedipine, nimodipine).

Other pharmacotherapy for presumed pathophysiology. Many different brain neurotransmitter systems, including catecholamines and indoleamines, can be disrupted by vascular damage in MID. Enhancing or reducing the efficacy of remaining neurotransmitter systems through drug administration might have therapeutic benefits. One report (Meyer et al. 1977) noted abnormally low cerebrospinal fluid concentrations of the dopamine metabolite homovanillic acid and the serotonin metabolite 5-hydroxyindoleacetic acid in some MID patients before and after probenecid pretreatment, suggesting low brain turnover of these neurotransmitters. Interestingly, in a trial of amino acid precursor (tyrosine and L-dopa) administration in 10 demented

Table 1. Vasodilators

	Effect on Cerebral Blood Flow (oral administration)	Receptor Effects	Metabolic Effects	Platelet Aggregation/ Viscosity
Cyclandelate	small ↑			
Papaverine	small ↑		Inhibits phosphodiesterase ↑ intracellular cyclic adenosine monophosphate	
Isoxsuprine	—	α antagonist; β agonist		↓
Cinnarizine	—	histamine antagonist		
Betahistine	small ↑	histamine agonist		
Nylidrin	large ↑	β agonist		
Dihydroer- gotoxine	—	α antagonist	Inhibits phosphodiesterase ↓ adenosine triphosphate?	
Nafronyl	0		↑ pyruvate/lactate ratio ↑ intracellular adenosine triphosphate	
Pyritinol				
Pentoxifylline	↑		Inhibits phosphodiesterase ↑ adenosine triphosphate	↓
Vincamine	—		Inhibits phosphodiesterase	
Niacin	0		Source of nicotinamide	
Hexobendine	0			
Tinofedrine	↑			
Clophenoxate				

patients with MID, senile dementia of the Alzheimer type, or mixed Alzheimer-type and MID, the two patients who improved had either MID or mixed dementia. These preliminary findings require further assessment.

Drugs with alpha noradrenergic receptor antagonist properties can be vasodilators (e.g., isoxsuprine, dihydroergotoxine), as can beta noradrenergic receptor agonist drugs (e.g., isoxsuprine, nylidrin). These drugs, therefore, may have both neuronal-synaptic and vascular effects.

Enhancement of central cholinergic neurotransmission can have vasodilatory effects (Roberts 1982). This important experimental therapeutic strategy for senile dementia of the Alzheimer type may also be relevant to treatment of MID, but this has not as yet been investigated.

Surgical interventions.   It has been suggested that surgical procedures, being investigated as treatment for cerebrovascular disease, might alter the symptoms or course of MID. Carotid endoarterectomy can be used in cases of extracranial stenosis of the internal carotid artery. Bypass grafts from the superficial temporal to the middle cerebral artery can be performed for intracranial occlusion or stenosis of the internal carotid or middle cerebral arteries. Data assessing benefits and risks in MID are not available.

Somatic Treatment of Specific Clinical Features

Various other treatments are available to clincans treating patients with presumed MID who have particular associated signs and symptoms, including anxiety, depressive syndrome, hallucinations or delusions, or agitation. Minor tranquilizers, antidepressant drugs, convulsive therapy, or neuroleptics may be helpful when used carefully in these situations. However, there is once again a need for systematic data concerning the optimal use, effectiveness, and toxicity of these agents in patients with MID.

Other Treatment Approaches

In addition to the paucity of data concerning somatic treatments, there is also essentially no information on other interventions available to clinicians treating patients with MID. These include periodic contact with a supportive health professional, structured daily routine, specific social and individual activities, changes in aspects of the physical environment, and intervention with family members.

Summary

This discussion highlights the lack of available information concerning both benefits and risks of various interventions in MID. If current trends in experimental treatment of senile dementia of the Alzheimer type are used as a model for future studies of MID, several directions are suggested. Slowing of progression of illness and reduction in associated signs and symptoms, such as depressive features or psychosis, may be the most realistic focus of immediate attention rather than improvement in cognitive function per se, especially where moderately severe dysfunction already exists. Studies need especially to target early or mild cases or individuals at risk. Treatment effects need to be examined in subgroups of patients defined by clinical features and laboratory measures, and combined treatment regimens need to be studied.

Chapter 108

Dementia of the Alzheimer Type

Research Problems

The DSM-III-R (American Psychiatric Association 1987) Axis I diagnosis of primary degenerative dementia of the Alzheimer type (DAT) refers to a disorder having an insidious onset and a progressively deteriorating course. Patients with this organic mental disorder are diagnosed as suffering from Alzheimer's disease on Axis III. This diagnostic category was developed because DAT represents nearly all cases of primary degenerative dementia. DAT is diagnosed by exclusion, requiring a comprehensive clinical and laboratory evaluation to detect other known causes of dementia. Chapter 94 describes diagnostic criteria for dementia as well as treatment approaches to the frequently associated disturbances of affect and behavior. In this chapter, we will describe current experimental strategies for the treatment of the generalized intellectual deterioration DAT.

The increasing numbers of individuals surviving into the decades of greatest risk and an explosion of information about the nature of DAT have focused public and scientific interest on this disorder. Over 1.8 million Americans are estimated to suffer from DAT (Plum 1979), with one million of these incapacitated (Crook 1985). More than 100,000 are said to die of it each year (Wurtman 1985). The financial cost is staggering: In 1982, 10 billion of the 21 billion dollars spent on nursing care in the United States was spent on the care of these patients (Terry and Katzman 1983). The acceleration in research activity has, nevertheless, an attendant problem: scientific inquiry has frequently outpaced the resolution of basic methodological questions involving diagnosis, classification, staging of illness, and measurement of change.

Problems of Diagnosis and Classification

The validity and replicability of treatment outcome studies depend on homogeneity of the patient sample and soundness of the research method. Early clinical trials suffered from numerous problems, including the mixing of DAT with multi-infarct patients, the absence of placebo-controlled double-blind designs, and inattention to dose-response relationships.

Table 1 outlines ongoing research difficulties that are, in part, related to the nature of DAT. Although the use of valid diagnostic criteria is crucial to evaluating treatment efficacy, studies carried out as recently as the 1970s found that 10 to 50 percent of "DAT patients" received a false positive diagnosis (Marsden and Harrison 1972; Ron et al. 1979; Wells 1977). The presence of depressive signs or symptoms and a history of affective illness have been identified as factors increasing the risk of misdiagnosis (Crook 1985; Reisberg 1981). The development and application of generally agreed on research diagnostic criteria (Eisdorfer and Cohen 1980; McKhann et al. 1984) will increase the validity of results.

Table 1. Research Problems in the Treatment of DAT

Cause	Effect
1. Limits of diagnostic criteria	Inclusion of patients with false positive diagnoses alters outcome
2. Heterogeneity of disorder	Different responses in patients with different pathophysiologies
3. Lack of staging criteria	Difficult to compare studies; patients with early disease may be more treatment responsive than those at later stages
4. Variation in psychometric tests of cognitive function used across studies	Difficult to compare studies; difficult to identify functional specificity of treatment effect
5. Disease does not occur in animals	Precludes many controlled experiments to study etiologic factors and pharmacologic effects

Unfortunately, even diagnosis by histopathology remains imperfect (Blass and Barclay 1985). Some individuals who die without evidence of dementia meet neuropathologic criteria for the disorder (Terry 1978). Moreover, the original data of Blessed et al. (1968) demonstrated a histopathologic overlap between patients dying with DAT and age-matched cognitively normal controls; some patients with degenerative dementia have fewer plaques than normal controls. The existence of pathologic outliers, although of research interest, can be a confounding factor in treatment trials. With the combined use of biochemical analyses and histopathologic findings, it is hoped that postmortem diagnostic certainty will be increased (Blass and Barclay 1985).

Experimental treatment trials are also confounded by the unresolved question of heterogeneity of the disorder. Bondareff's (1983) suggestion that patients with an onset of the disease during middle age suffer massive losses of noradrenergic in addition to cholinergic neurons, demonstrate more severe clinical symptoms, and have a more rapid course exemplifies the augmentation of interindividual differences in treatment outcome.

A systematized and generally utilized staging system is critically needed for DAT research. Drug responsiveness can be related to severity of illness (Leber 1983); patients in the early stages of disease can be presumed to have greater neuronal integrity and, therefore, to be more drug responsive. This situation has been considered as analogous to that in Parkinson's disease, in which L-dopa is most effective early in the illness (Blass and Weksler 1983). Indeed, some have suggested that only patients in early stages be included in therapeutic trials (Davies 1981). The development and utilization of reliable and valid clinical rating scales (Hughes et al. 1982; Reisberg et al. 1982) should improve future studies.

An equally serious problem results from the absence of a widely accepted and used psychometric instrument in treatment efficacy studies (Mohs et al. 1983). Criteria for such a scale include: sensitivity to subtle yet clinically meaningful changes in cognition and behavior; a sufficiently wide range between ceiling and floor; multiple equivalent versions with test-retest reliability; and validation of the scale against neuropathologic and neurochemical abnormalities. An additional problem is the wide range of changes in mood, behavior, and memory encompassed by the mild to severe stages of the disorder; most existing instruments can provide the needed sensitivity for only a portion of the range (Ferris and Crook 1983; Mohs et al. 1983). Treatment studies have had to rely on a variety of scales ·or sets of scales sensitive to various symptomatic changes and stages of the disease.

The number of inaccurate recalls or intrusion errors provides a measure of memory dysfunction that has had neuropathologic verification (Fuld et al. 1982). The use of memory testing is especially relevant because memory impairment is considered the most reliable sign of DAT (Brinkman and Gershon 1983). Commonly used assessments focus on recognition memory for either words or pictures (Brinkman and Gershon 1983). Many of these tests are variations of a selective reminding procedure (Buschke 1973; Fuld 1981). Tests requiring recognition may be easier to perform for patients with DAT and, therefore, more sensitive to medication effects than those requiring free recall. This explanation has been used to explain negative results in physostigmine treatment studies utilizing measures of recall (Johns et al. 1985). The use of instruments with different psychometric properties that measure different aspects of cognitive functioning has been another limiting factor in understanding and comparing the results of specific pharmacologic interventions.

The fact that animals do not develop a disease analogous to DAT contributes to these problems. An animal model would permit control of diagnostic, staging, and measurement issues in systematic studies of the effect of pharmacologic interventions.

The Cholinergic Hypothesis

The cholinergic hypothesis proposes that disruption of the acetylcholine (Ach) neurotransmitter system is a major factor contributing to the memory deficits seen in normal senescence and in DAT (Bartus et al. 1982; Drachman 1977). The basis for this hypothesis is outlined in Table 2.

The anticholinergic drug scopolamine produces forgetfulness when used as a preanesthetic (Weiner 1980). Various centrally acting anticholinergic drugs have also been found to disrupt memory functioning while producing varying degrees of delirium (Safer and Allen 1971). Scopolamine evokes a pattern of cognitive deficits in young adult volunteers that is similar to that found in normal aging (Drachman and Leavitt 1974). The reversibility of these effects by physostigmine, a cholinomimetic agent, but not by the stimulant amphetamine demonstrates that the cognitive dysfunction is specifically caused by the anticholinergic property of scopolamine (Drachman 1977).

Although aged animals do not develop the neuropathologic lesions of DAT, diminished memory does frequently accompany senescence in primates (Bartus et al. 1976), providing a means for assessing the influence of pharmacologic inhibition or enhancement of the cholinergic system. Cholinergic disruption has been found to impair short-term memory (Bartus and Johnson 1976), while physostigmine enhances memory in aged nonhuman primates (Bartus 1979). Similar transient improvements in memory functioning after treatment with physostigmine have been found in young adults (Davis et al. 1978) as well as in normal elderly volunteers (Drachman and Sahakian 1980).

Neurochemical studies of the cholinergic hypothesis have complemented work done with pharmacologic probes. Choline acetyl transferase (CAT), the enzyme that catalyzes the synthesis of acetylcholine from acetyl coenzyme A and choline (Mayer 1980), has been the most extensively studied potential biologic marker. Investigations of CAT activity are particularly important because: 1) this enzyme is exclusively found

Table 2. Research Basis for the Cholinergic Hypothesis

Clinical studies	
Scopolamine causes temporary "dementia"	Drachman and Leavitt (1974)
	Safer and Allen (1971)
Physostigmine improves memory in normals	Davis et al. (1978)
	Drachman and Leavitt (1974)
Physostigmine reverses scopolamine dementia	Drachman (1977)

Neurochemical studies	
Cholinergic activity is lower in the brains of DAT patients than in those of age-matched controls	Bowen et al. (1976)
	Davies and Maloney (1976)
	White et al. (1977)
	Perry et al. (1977a)
Cholinergic deficits are greatest in brain areas with the neuropathology of DAT	Perry et al. (1978)
Cholinergic deficits correlate with degree of dementia	Perry et al. (1978)
Cholinergic pathways degenerate in DAT	Whitehouse et al. (1981)
Lesioning the presynaptic cholinergic pathway in rats causes memory deficits that partially respond to physostigmine	Johns et al. (1985)

in neurons that release acetylcholine (Davies 1981); 2) CAT is far from saturated under normal conditions (Bartus et al. 1982); and 3) decreased CAT activity has been consistently found in the brains of patients with DAT compared to normal elderly controls (Bartus et al. 1982; Bowen et al. 1979; Davies 1981). Furthermore, deficiencies in CAT activity are greatest in brain areas that show the most neuropathologic change in DAT, and diminished activity is correlated with both plaque count and degree of dementia (Perry et al. 1978). These findings, combined with data suggesting that DAT is not associated with a loss of postsynaptic cholinergic receptors beyond that due to normal aging (Bartus et al. 1982), form the theoretic framework for the treatment strategies designed to increase cholinergic activity. Its foundation has been strengthened by the finding that the nucleus basalis of Meynert, the major extrinsic source of cholinergic innervation to the cortex, undergoes profound degeneration in patients with DAT (Price et al. 1982; Whitehouse et al. 1981), leading to the proposal that the selective loss of cholinergic neurons from the nucleus basalis of Meynert "is a major specific pathologic mechanism" (Johns et al. 1985) in DAT. The identification of this cholinergic nucleus has allowed the development of a hypocholinergic animal model based on its chemical destruction. Lesioning of the nucleus basalis in rats causes impairment in learning and memory that improves after the administration of physostigmine (Johns et al. 1985). These results suggest that medications with cholinergic activity may improve cognitive function in patients with DAT.

Attempts to measure levels of brain Ach have been limited by the instability of this neurotransmitter. An uncontrolled study found Ach levels in cerebrospinal fluid (CSF) of DAT patients to be highly correlated with cognitive performance (Johns et al. 1985).

Treatments Based on the Cholinergic Hypothesis

Pharmacotherapeutic strategies designed to facilitate cholinergic transmission can be separated into four approaches (Table 3). The goal of each is to maximize functioning of intact cholinergic neurons and thereby diminish clinical signs and symptoms presumably resulting from the putative deficiency. A second theoretical benefit is to increase available transmitter and thereby diminish a postulated process of cell self-destruction in which neurons break down their own walls to increase available choline (Wurtman 1985).

Precursor loading. Treatment trials utilizing supplemental choline in an attempt to increase central cholinergic activity and thereby reverse the DAT-caused cognitive deficits have been unsuccessful (Bartus et al. 1982; Crook 1985; Davis et al. 1981; Reisberg et al. 1981). Negative findings have occurred despite the ability of investigators to administer large quantities of choline efficiently through its usual dietary source, lecithin. The failure of precursor loading treatment is particularly important because it is the approach most consistent with normal physiology: it is based on increasing neurotransmitter available for the normal temporal sequence of neuronal firing and not on either increasing the duration of neurotransmitter action by inhibiting degradation or on artificially stimulating postsynaptic receptors by administering a cholinergic agonist.

Attempts to explain the failure of the precursor strategy have focused on the biochemical nature of the cholinergic dysfunction, and this in turn has given rise to a new generation of studies (Bartus et al. 1982; Davies 1985). The administration of precursors to animals does increase Ach levels, suggesting that CAT is not operating maximally under normal conditions (Cohen and Wurtman 1976). However, for increased choline to allow CAT to synthesize more Ach, the second substrate, acetyl coenzyme A, must also be available (Davies 1981). This is especially relevant because acetyl coenzyme A is synthesized through oxidative metabolism, and the synthesis of Ach is very sensitive to decreases in this metabolic process (Peterson and Gibson 1983). Quantities of available coenzyme could be increased by facilitating transport into the cytoplasm from the mitochondria, a process that appears to be calcium dependent (Davies 1985). Investigations with 4-aminopyridine, which enhances entry of calcium into presynaptic nerve terminals, suggest that this compound improves cholinergic activity under hypoxic conditions. Administration of 4-aminopyridine to hypoxic mice partially reversed deficits in behavior. A cholinergic contribution to the deficits was demonstrated in that pretreatment with physostigmine improved performance and this effect was blocked by atropine (Gibson et al. 1983). Analogous combination studies have been carried out with piracetam, a metabolic enhancer. Piracetam also facilitates Ach release and improves neuronal function under hypoxic

Table 3. Treatment Approaches to Correct Cholinergic Deficiency

Type of intervention	Example
1. Precursor loading	Choline, lecithin
2. Inhibit acetylcholine degradation	Physostigmine
3. Substitute cholinergic agonist	Arecholine
4. Combination of cholinergic agent with metabolic enhancer	Lecithin plus piracetam

conditions. The administration of choline alone did not reverse age-related memory impairment in mice, whereas choline plus piracetam resulted in a marked improvement (Bartus et al. 1982). A preliminary study in patients with DAT demonstrated that lecithin and piracetam led to substantially greater improvement in recall than lecithin alone (Smith and Reisberg 1984).

Cholinesterase inhibitors. Therapeutic trials with cholinesterase inhibitors such as physostigmine and tetrahydroaminoacidine are based on the premise that interfering with the enzymatic degradation of Ach will correct the dysfunctions in this system seen in DAT. Results of this strategy have been encouraging but complex. Physostigmine is the most frequently investigated agent of this type. Its use has been hampered by potent peripheral activity and a short plasma half-life (Davies 1985).

Davis and Mohs (1982) demonstrated a U-shaped dose response to physostigmine that may explain the inconsistent results of many studies. Improved memory occurred in some patients after receiving an individualized optimal dose; functioning diminished in response to higher or lower dosages. These investigators recommend a "two-phase strategy" with dose finding and therapeutic stages (Davis and Mohs 1982). The use of this two-phase approach in a second study with oral physostigmine plus supplemental lecithin demonstrated improved memory performance in six of eight patients (Thal et al. 1983); the number of intrusion errors was also significantly decreased. A strong correlation between diminished error score and reduced CSF cholinesterase activity is consistent with the hypothesis that therapeutic effect occurred through inhibition of Ach degradation within the central nervous system (CNS). Oral administration does not obviate the problem of physostigmine's short half-life; however, the finding that cognitive functioning did not return to baseline until 36 hours after the last dose led these investigators to suggest that physostigmine may be biologically active longer than previously thought (Thal et al. 1983).

Even if cholinesterase inhibitors can produce transient memory task improvement in some patients, their usefulness as a definitive treatment has theoretic limitations (Davies 1981). Decreased Ach availability due to neuronal degeneration would impair physostigmine efficacy, and increasing duration of Ach receptor-site activity could lead to postsynaptic subsensitivity, resulting in decreased effectiveness of physostigmine or toxicity. Finally, the potent peripheral effects of present cholinesterase inhibitors limit the maximum possible dosage of these agents.

A report by Summers et al. (1986) on the efficacy of tetrahydroaminoacridine (THA), another centrally acting anticholinesterase, is encouraging. Improvement in global functioning and performance on a names learning test was noted in 14 subjects during the placebo-controlled crossover phase of the study. The potential palliative effects of THA for some of the deficits caused by DAT are currently being investigated in a multicenter study.

Agonist therapy. The cholinergic agonist model is based on the apparently normal number and function of postsynaptic cholinergic receptors. Both precursor and cholinesterase inhibitor strategies require presynaptic neuronal functioning and Ach release. Since these approaches theoretically depend on the presence of a sufficient number of functionally intact neurons, their effectiveness should be greater in patients at early stages of dementia (Thal et al. 1983). Cholinergic agonists bypass the presynaptic neuron entirely and could have clinical effects at a later stage of illness. This conceptualization is as yet untested. Arecoline, the most widely studied cholinergic agonist, enhances learning in normal volunteers (Sitaram et al. 1978) and in aged monkeys (Bartus 1981). Arecoline has been used in patients suffering from

DAT. Seven of 11 patients who received 4 mg iv of arecoline showed brief improvement in memory function that achieved statistical significance (Christie et al. 1981); however, in only two of the seven was the response clear-cut and reproducible. Unfortunately, arecoline suffers from the same problem of a short half-life as physostigmine.

Issues of dose schedule and bioavailability have been overcome by the neurosurgical technique of continuous intracranial infusion utilizing bethanechol, a pure muscarinic agonist that is not degraded by cholinesterases (Harbaugh et al. 1984). In a preliminary open study of four patients with biopsy-confirmed diagnoses of DAT, decreased confusion and increased social functioning were noted by family members; this finding was not reported after placebo infusion. Interestingly, these patients all had moderate to severe dementia, which is consistent with the notion that if agonist therapy does have a role, it will be with patients who have severe disruption of the presynaptic system. The issue of patient selection is especially relevant when a treatment strategy requires neurosurgical intervention.

Any cholinergic agonist therapy would confront significant theoretic difficulties (Davies 1981). The flooding of postsynaptic receptors would appear to be quite different from the sensitive physiologic temporal sequence of neuronal transmission and could lead to receptor desensitization, to tolerance, and ultimately to toxic effects. One possible mechanism for a therapeutic effect of agonist treatment posits the binding of an optimal number of unsaturated receptor sites so that receptor cells can become sensitive to subnormal quantities of physiologically released Ach (Davies 1981). Carefully controlled investigations would be required to document the validity of this model as well as the efficacy of agonist treatment.

Combination treatment. As has been described earlier in this chapter, precursor loading alone does not improve memory functioning in patients with DAT. Since Ach synthesis is known to be very sensitive to decreases in oxidative metabolism (Gibson and Blass 1976; Gibson and Peterson 1983), and since the diminished glucose metabolism of normal aging is exaggerated in DAT (Ferris 1981), agents that improve oxidative metabolism could be expected to increase Ach synthesis. Furthermore, Ach synthesis is tied to Ach release (Davies 1985).

A treatment approach that provides both precursor and a drug that improves neuronal function in a hypoxic environment would, therefore, be expected to yield better results than precursor loading alone (Bartus 1981). This phenomenon has been clearly demonstrated in aged rats: administration of choline in combination with the metabolic enhancer piracetam was several times more effective in improving memory than either agent alone (Bartus et al. 1981). Similarly, drugs such as 4-aminopyridine when administered with physostigmine appear to enhance cholinergic function during hypoxia (Gibson et al. 1983). Further studies utilizing combined treatment to correct what may be an "interactive neurochemical dysfunction" are required to assess whether this hypothesized multipathway deficiency is accessible to pharmacologic intervention in humans (Bartus et al. 1982).

Vasodilators

Although drugs with vasodilatory action have been used to treat geriatric cognitive decline for most of this century, their efficacy remains unproven (Crook 1985). Furthermore, the original basis for this use of vasodilators has been eroded by studies demonstrating that the preponderance of late-life dementias yield neuropathologic findings of neuronal degeneration rather than cerebral infarction (Blessed et al. 1968; Corsellis and Evans 1965). Those dementias caused by cerebral infarction are subsumed by the diagnosis of multi-infarct dementia, and experimental treatments of this condition are described in Chapter 107.

Findings that the diminished glucose metabolism of normal aging is further reduced in patients with DAT has provided a new rationale for the use of vasodilators. Increasing blood supply could improve oxidative metabolism, thereby enhancing Ach synthesis and release as described above. This argument is supported by the finding of diminished cerebral blood flow in DAT, which responds to the vasodilatory effects of inhaled CO_2 (Yamaguchi et al. 1980).

Vasodilator drugs can be classified into "primary" and "mixed" categories outlined in a recent review (Yesavage et al. 1979). Since cerebral blood flow is diminished in DAT and drugs that reverse this diminution thereby improve oxidative metabolism, the arbitrary distinction between primary vasodilators and those that are also metabolic may be misleading (Reisberg 1981). Furthermore, many primary vasodilator drugs have been found to possess direct metabolic effects (Reisberg 1981). Additional drugs from both categories are being investigated, but there is no evidence yet that these agents are more effective than those currently available (Crook 1985; Reisberg 1981).

Subclassification of vasodilators by their ability to enhance oxidative metabolism does gain validity from studies suggesting that drugs with this property have more therapeutic efficacy than primary vasodilators (Yesavage et al. 1979). Papaverine, a smooth muscle relaxant with the documented ability to increase cerebral circulation (Reisberg 1981), is the most extensively studied of the three primary vasodilator drugs available for this use in the United States. Only nine papaverine studies were placebo controlled and double blind. A review of these investigations led to the conclusion that papaverine's usefulness is uncertain (Yesavage et al. 1979). Fewer studies exist for cyclandelate and isoxsuprine, with even less evidence for effectiveness (Yesavage et al. 1979). The lack of documented efficacy has led to controversy over whether these agents should be approved treatments for DAT (Crook 1985).

Dihydroergotoxine (Hydergine) is the best studied of the mixed vasodilators and has demonstrated the most evidence for therapeutic benefit. This agent has a number of beneficial effects on cerebral metabolism, including the ability to increase cerebral oxygen utilization and to reverse partially electroencephalographic changes caused by temporary ischemia (Hollister and Yesavage 1984; Reisberg 1981). Unfortunately, most dihydroergotoxine treatment studies were carried out prior to the application of modern diagnostic criteria and did not include specific assessments of memory function (Crook 1985). Investigations demonstrating clinical improvement have relied on behavioral variables including alertness, mood, and attitude (Crook 1985; Jarvik 1981; Reisberg 1981; Yesavage et al. 1979). Dihydroergotoxine studies have frequently used the Sandoz Clinical Assessment Geriatric scale, which includes a number of measures for changes in mood but lacks any tests for memory (Reisberg 1981). However, studies utilizing standardized tests of cognition have generally failed to demonstrate improvement (McDonald 1982). Although it would appear that dihydroergotoxine's beneficial effects occur by increasing motivation and improving mood rather than by directly affecting cognition (Crook 1985), the possibility remains that systematic studies utilizing higher doses (at least 6 mg/day) for longer periods (a minimum of six months) will demonstrate a beneficial clinical effect in treating or preventing the progression of memory impairment in DAT (Crook 1985; Hollister and Yesavage 1984; Kugler et al. 1978; Reisberg 1981; Spiegel et al. 1983).

Other mixed drugs include nafronyl, pentoxifylline, and vincamine. These drugs are not approved for use in the United States. The research status of these agents is preliminary, and more studies are necessary to establish if they are of any benefit to patients with DAT (Reisberg 1981; Yesavage et al. 1979). Further description of vasodilator agents is provided in Chapter 107.

Metabolic Enhancers

The pure metabolic enhancers include drugs such as piracetam and its analogs, centrophenoxine, and newer drugs that improve cerebral oxidative metabolism (Table 4).

Piracetam is the prototype of a new class of drugs, termed nootropics, with central but not peripheral effects (Giurgea 1976). Piracetam is an analog of gamma-aminobutyric acid (GABA), without GABA activity, that in animals has been found to enhance learning and protect against memory impairment caused by hypoxia. Unfortunately, despite piracetam's unique ability to increase brain energy stores without toxic peripheral effects (Reisberg et al. 1981), its efficacy in treating age-related cognitive decline has not been proven (Crook 1985). The possible benefit of using this agent in combination with cholinergic precursors remains to be explored. Centrophenoxine appears to facilitate oxidative metabolism by activating the pentose shunt pathway (Nandy 1978). Equivocal and contradictory results of its efficacy in treating cognitive impairment due to aging or DAT have been reported (Ferris 1981).

Both 4-aminopyridine and 3,4-diaminopyridine have multiple pharmacologic effects, including the stimulation of calcium influx into the nerve terminal, which improves Ach release under hypoxic conditions (Peterson and Gibson 1983). A combination of 4-aminopyridine and physostigmine improves hypoxia-induced behavioral effects in mice (Gibson et al. 1983). Clarification of whether these drugs will have therapeutic efficacy in DAT awaits further research.

Active lipid, a combination of neutral lipids, phosphatidylcholine, and phosphatidylethanolamine, appears to reverse tissue aging by fluidizing all membranes (Crook 1985). Research with this compound is extremely preliminary, but it is representative of an approach to improving function by altering basic cellular processes.

Biogenic Amines

Animal experiments have supported a role for the brain catecholamine neurotransmitters noradrenaline (NE) and dopamine (DA) as well as the indoleamine serotonin (5-hydroxytryptophan; 5-HT) in learning and memory. These experiments include inducing intracerebral neurochemical lesions with relatively specific neurotoxins such

Table 4. Investigational Metabolic Enhancers

1. Nootropics, piracetam, and its analogs (annuracetam, oxiracetam, piracetam)
2. Centrophenoxine
3. 4-Aminopyridine and 3,4-diaminopyridine
4. Active lipid

Note. Dihydroergotoxine, a medication with metabolic enhancer properties and approved for use in the United States, is described with the vasodilators.

as 6-hydroxydopamine, and establishing the effects of drugs that disrupt or enhance neurotransmission, such as reserpine and amphetamine (Fibiger 1984).

Scandinavian workers and others have reported differences in amine neurotransmitter-related markers in postmortem brains of patients with DAT compared to controls. Low concentrations of DA and of its major metabolite homovanillic acid (HVA) have been reported in basal ganglia, particularly in younger patients (Adolfsson et al. 1979; Gottfries et al. 1968, 1969, 1976; Winblad et al. 1982). An inverse correlation, stronger in younger patients, has been noted between tissue HVA concentrations and degree of dementia-rated postmortem (Gottfries 1980; Gottfries et al. 1968; Winblad et al. 1982). Similarly, low postmortem brain concentrations of NE have been reported. Mann et al. (1980) noted loss of locus ceruleus cell bodies, as have Bondareff and Mountjoy (1985), particularly, again, in those patients with younger age of onset. Adolfsson et al. (1979) found that brain concentrations of NE were inversely correlated with a retrospective estimate of degree of dementia. Elevations in tissue concentrations of the NE metabolite 3-methoxy-4-hydroxyphenylethylene glycol (MHPG) have been described (Carlsson 1979), particularly in early onset cases (Francis et al. 1985); normal (Francis et al. 1985) or low concentrations have been noted in older patients (Cross et al. 1983). Significant positive correlations of tissue MHPG concentrations with motor impairment and negative correlation with degree of depression have been noted in some brain regions (Winblad et al. 1982). Major reductions of 5-HT concentrations were also reported by Carlsson (1981); levels of the 5-HT metabolite 5-hydroxyindoleacetic acid (5-HIAA) were normal. Furthermore, some investigators have found increased activity of monoamine oxidase (MAO) B, but not of MAO-A, in tissue from hippocampus, caudate, and cortex (Adolfsson et al. 1980; Carlsson 1981).

Indirect measures of brain biogenic amine neurotransmitter function have been studied in patients with DAT and in controls. CSF metabolite concentrations of HVA and 5-HIAA are reportedly reduced in DAT (Gottfries 1980; Gottfries and Roos 1973, 1976; Gottfries et al. 1968, 1974; Pinessi et al. 1984; Soininen et al. 1981). Bowen et al. (1981) reported low CSF HVA in an elderly patient with a progressive dementia who lacked Alzheimer histopathology postmortem, suggesting some biochemical heterogeneity in the disorder. There have also been negative reports in patients with DAT (Growdon and Logue 1982; Mann et al. 1981). CSF concentrations of MHPG have not been extensively studied in DAT. Normal values have been reported (Pinessi et al. 1984; Raskind et al. 1984) in some patients; Raskind et al. (1984) also noted increased concentrations in a subgroup of younger patients.

Peripheral MAO activity has been studied as a marker and as a possible index of brain MAO activity. Several groups have found platelet MAO activity to be increased in DAT (Adolfsson et al. 1980; Alexopoulos et al. 1984b; Smith et al. 1982), although Mann et al. (1981) did not.

Neuroendocrine challenge tests provide another indirect measure of brain neurotransmitter function. For example, resistance to dexamethasone suppression, an index of hypothalamic pituitary adrenocortical hyperfunction, is noted in a subgroup of patients with DAT (Alexopoulos et al. 1984a; Balldin et al. 1983; Coppen et al. 1983; Jenike 1983a; Jenike and Albert 1984; Katona and Aldridge 1984; McKeith 1984; Raskind et al. 1982b; Spar and Gerner 1982).

Treatment Strategies

Precursor loading. Several groups have explored the treatment of DAT with large doses of metabolic precursor amino acids, on the model of L-dopa treatment of Parkinson's disease (Table 5). Some positive effects of L-dopa on behavior, including

Table 5. DAT Treatment Strategies Focused on Biogenic Amine Neurotransmitter Dysfunction

Mechanism	Pharmacologic agent	Reference
1. Precursor loading	L-Dopa	Adolfsson et al. (1982) Kristensen et al. (1977) Lewis et al. (1978)
	Tryptophan	Lehmann et al. (1981)
2. Enhanced presynaptic release	D-Amphetamine	Crook (1979) Crook et al. (1977)
	Methylphenidate Yohimbine	Loew and Singer (1983)
3. Reuptake blockade	Tricyclic antidepressants Alaproclate	Reding et al. (1983) Bergman et al. (1983)
4. Degradative enzyme inhibition	Nonspecific MAO inhibitors Selective MAO inhibitors	
5. Postsynaptic receptor agonists and antagonists	Bromocriptine Clonidine Propranolol	Adolfsson et al. (1978) Jenike (1983b) Petrie and Ban (1981)
	Isoproterenol	
6. Postreceptor mechanisms		

motor activity, have been noted. Lehmann et al. (1981) reported in an open study that tryptophan produced beneficial clinical effects, in particular in those patients with poor absorption of that amino acid from the gut. Whether such treatment altered brain neurotransmitter metabolism or synaptic function in these patients is not clear.

Enhanced presynaptic release.   Indirect sympathomimetic agents such as D-amphetamine and methylphenidate enhance presynaptic neuronal release of catecholamines and indoleamines. Reports concerning their effects in demented elderly populations have been disappointing (Crook 1979; Crook et al. 1977; Loew and Singer 1983). Although yohimbine, which blocks noradrenergic alpha$_2$ presynaptic receptors, enhances NE release, its cardiovascular and other side effects may limit any possible utility in patients with DAT.

Reuptake blockade.   The tricyclic antidepressant drugs are a model for blockade of presynaptic reuptake mechanisms, but there has been little investigation of these agents in DAT. Reding et al. (1983) reported no enhancement of Mini-Mental State Examination scores by moderate doses of amitriptyline in a group of patients with DAT who were not depressed. Potential problems with the use of these drugs are their relative lack of specificity for particular neurotransmitter systems and their concomitant anticholinergic and other receptor antagonist effects. Alaproclate, a 5-HT reuptake inhibitor with a narrow pharmacologic spectrum of action, has been tested in DAT; preliminary results have been negative (Bergman et al. 1983).

Degradative enzyme inhibition.   Although combined MAO-A and MAO-B inhibitors have long been in clinical use as antidepressants, their effects in DAT have not been studied. More recently MAO inhibitors with more pharmacologic specificity for MAO-A or MAO-B have become available; some of these may have additional practical advantages of reversible tissue binding or lack of requirement for dietary restriction.

Postsynaptic receptor agonists and antagonists.   Catecholamine and indole-amine neurotransmitter systems can also be manipulated at postsynaptic receptors in DAT. Receptor agonists and antagonists for these systems remain to be tested. In one study (Adolfsson et al. 1978), the dopamine agonist bromocriptine improved psychomotor activity. Uncontrolled studies of propranolol suggesting reduction of agitated, aggressive behavior in elderly patients have been reported (Jenike 1983b; Petrie and Ban 1981).

Postreceptor mechanisms.   In the future, postreceptor mechanisms may provide opportunities for therapeutic intervention in DAT. For example, Walaas et al. (1983), who have been characterizing neuronal phosphoproteins, found that certain of these may be specific to particular monoamine neurotransmitter systems.

Neuropeptides

Animal studies have indicated that analogues of adrenocorticotropic hormone (ACTH) enhance performance of learning tasks. Their behavioral effects are independent of effects on the adrenal gland. Some reviews (de Wied 1974; de Wied et al. 1976; Sandman and Kastin 1977) have concluded that the ACTH analogues enhance attention, motivation, or both. Some studies have also suggested improved memory consolidation (Flood et al. 1976; Gold and McGaugh 1977).

Initial human studies of ACTH analogues used single doses or relatively short administration periods; findings with respect to memory tasks were largely negative (e.g., Branconnier et al. 1978). Berger and Tinklenberg (1981) did note, however, improved psychomotor reaction time following acute administration in elderly outpatients. Improvement in measures of depression, anxiety, and sociability have been described after repeated administration in elderly patients (Ferris et al. 1981; Martin et al. 1983; Pigache and Rigter 1981). Tinklenberg et al. (1984) suggested that repeated administration is the strategy most likely to yield positive effects, and that modest improvements in performance with peptide treatment may be primarily related to changes in attention, motivation, and mood.

Alpha melanocyte-stimulating hormone (MSH), a peptide structurally related to ACTH, enhances performance of tasks requiring attention or cognitive flexibility in rodents (Kastin et al. 1981). Enhanced attention has been reported in normal human subjects (Kastin et al. 1981). In mentally retarded patients and normal subjects, MSH enhances response to novel stimuli while preserving discrimination of relevant from irrelevant information (Sandman et al. 1976, 1980; Walker and Sandman 1979). Tests of the effectiveness of MSH in DAT are being conducted by these investigators.

Vasopressin (VP), contained in the posterior lobe of the pituitary gland, is also localized in brain neurons. Animal studies indicate that VP facilitates retention of a passive avoidance task and also improves performance in other experimental paradigms (Berger and Tinklenberg 1981). The effects of lysine vasopressin and 1-desamino-8-d-arginine vasopressin (DDAVP) have therefore been studied in human subjects.

Reports of positive effects of DDAVP in amnesias related to trauma or alcohol

(LeBoeuf et al. 1978; Oliveras et al. 1978) or electroconvulsive therapy (Weingartner et al. 1981b), in learning task performance in Lesch-Nyhan syndrome (Anderson et al. 1979), and in verbal learning in major depression (Gold et al. 1979) have led to an interest in its use in DAT. Berger and Tinklenberg (1981) reported positive effects of DDAVP on verbal learning in the least cognitively impaired among a small group of subjects, some of whom had DAT with presenile onset. Their report was consistent with others in which subjects with mild cognitive impairment improved (Gold et al. 1979; Weingartner et al. 1981b), and with negative findings in subjects with more severe deficits (Jenkins et al. 1979, 1981; Koch-Henriksen and Nielsen 1981; Reichert and Blass 1982). Weingartner et al. (1981a) reported enhancement of semantic memory by DDAVP in patients with DAT. Positive findings encourage further study, including use of different analogues of VP. For example, desglycinamide-arginine vasopressin may have fewer side effects, such as water retention, than DDAVP. Other reports regarding learning and memory tasks in DAT patients have been negative (Durso et al. 1982; Jenkins et al. 1982; Reding and DiPonte 1983). However, Durso et al. (1982) noted increased reaction time, and Tinklenberg et al. (1984) noted reduced depression ratings and increased ratings of vigor. The latter group (Tinklenberg et al. 1984) concluded that VP administration may alter mood, attention, or other memory-modulating processes in DAT that may enhance cognitive performance in less severely impaired patients.

Animal experimental data again suggest that endogenous opiates influence learning and memory. Enkephalin and its analogues excite hippocampal neurons, an effect that is blocked by naloxone (Gahwiler 1980; Martinez et al. 1979; Taylor et al. 1979); the hippocampus may be involved in consolidation of long-term from short-term memory (Kastin et al. 1981). Disruptive effects on memory of exogenous enkephalin and beta endorphin, and facilitative effects of low dose naloxone on learning, have been described in rodents; however, under certain conditions, enkephalins can also have facilitative effects on memory. Kastin et al. (1981) reported that plasma levels of beta endorphins may be increased in DAT.

Reisberg et al. (1983) noted improvement in cognitive function in DAT following naloxone administration; however, others have not replicated such an effect (Blass et al. 1983). Naloxone may enhance attentional processes (Arnsten 1984). The effects of exogenous opiates on DAT have not been examined.

Other peptides have been examined in DAT brain postmortem, and some have been found to be decreased compared to age-matched controls. Somatostatin is localized with intrinsic neurons in the neocortex and hippocampus. Davies et al. (1982) noted decreases in somatostatin-like immunoreactivity (SLI) in seven of nine brain regions sampled. In some regions with decreased SLI, the SLI was correlated with CAT activity. Rossor et al. (1982) also noted significantly decreased SLI in temporal cortex in DAT, but reductions were not statistically significant in other regions examined. Decreased concentrations of substance P-like immunoreactivity in hippocampus, superior temporal gyrus, and midfrontal cortex in DAT compared to controls were reported by Davies et al. (1982). Therapeutic agents directed at such deficiencies might prove beneficial in DAT.

Preliminary studies of concentrations of other peptides in DAT suggest that cortical neuronal losses do not involve all neuronal populations. Vasoactive inhibitory peptide, also intrinsic to cortical neurons, is apparently unchanged in DAT (Rossor et al. 1982). Similarly, these workers found normal cholecystokinin (CCK)-like immunoreactivity in cortical tissue in DAT (Rossor et al. 1981). Sanders et al. (1982), however, noted increased CCK immunoreactivity in cortical white matter in DAT, while there was no difference from controls in cortical gray matter.

GABA

GABA is one putative neurotransmitter intrinsic to cortical neurons. Reduced concentrations of the synthetic enzyme glutamic acid decarboxylase (GAD) have been reported in postmortem cortical brain areas in DAT (Bowen et al. 1976; Davies 1979; Perry et al. 1977b). Rossor et al. (1982) noted that GAD may be very sensitive to agonal factors, however, and therefore measured GABA itself in DAT brain; reductions in GABA were noted in cortex and hippocampus. Piracetam, a model nootropic, is a GABA agonist. Studies of treatment with piracetam alone in DAT have been disappointing, but its effect in combination with other agents is being investigated (Crook 1985).

Summary

Experimental research strategies in DAT have emphasized the replacement of hypothesized deficiencies in neurotransmitter systems. The model of Parkinson's disease has been used because replacement therapy with L-dopa or DA agonists has led to symptomatic improvement in patients with that deficiency illness.

Cholinergic strategies have received the most attention; the Ach neurotransmitter system is the most generally affected, and anticholinergic drug toxicity produces memory disturbances that mimic those of patients with DAT. Although early treatment trials based on this model were ineffective, recent studies utilizing more sophisticated methodology, more stringent patient selection criteria, attention to dose-response relationships, and combined treatment regimens have reported clinical benefits in some, but not all, patients treated. The results are frequently subtle and manifested by statistically significant improvement on memory performance tests when group scores are compared. It is not clear that cholinergic treatment will ever provide sufficiently robust or long-standing clinical benefit to justify widespread use, but this research has provided preliminary clinical confirmation for the hypothesis that some of the disturbances in DAT result from a hypofunctioning cholinergic system.

Investigations of other neurotransmitter systems are at a more rudimentary stage. Transmitter deficiencies must be identified before means of augmentation can be developed and clinical trials begun. It does appear that at least some patients with DAT have diminished noradrenergic function; DA and 5-HT may also be involved. Varying degrees of catecholamine and indoleamine dysfunction have been suggested by postmortem studies and by indirect measures in subgroups of patients with DAT. Preliminary experimental treatment efforts directed at such deficits have been unsuccessful, but the number of such studies is limited and only a few of the number of potential strategies have been tested adequately. In testing such treatments, it will be critical to define subgroups of patients with different profiles and neurotransmitter function-related markers. The number of peptides known to be present in the brain has continued to increase at a staggering rate in recent years. Some may serve as neurotransmitters, neuromodulators, or neurohormones (Berger and Tinklenberg 1981). Excess or deficiency of such peptides might be part of the pathogenesis of DAT; but even if they are not, modulation of such systems might have therapeutic effects by enhancing or suppressing function of intact neuronal systems.

As discussed by Kastin et al. (1981), there are several levels at which pharmacologic manipulation of peptide systems could be focused. These include inhibition of enzymes involved in synthesis of prohormones, in conversion (cleavage) of prohormones to active peptides, or in degradation of peptides. Furthermore, receptor sites can be saturated with peptide analogues or antagonists.

Peptide studies have focused on analogues of vasopressin and somatostatin. The use of the former is based on vasopressin's capacity to increase some forms of learning in animals, while somatostatin has been found to be decreased in some patients with DAT. Attempts to replicate a preliminary report of benefits from naloxone have been discouraging. Here, as in earlier studies with agents such as dihydroergotoxine (Hydergine), mood-altering effects must be distinguished from real improvement in cognition.

In conclusion, experimental treatments of DAT have, thus far, had greater heuristic than clinical value. The elucidation of the multiplicity of neurotransmitter deficiencies implies a complex and heterogeneous disorder. Treatment approaches are confounded by the possible influence of changes in one neurotransmitter system on the functioning of others. Future research will be required to identify neurochemical subtypes and possible clinical correlates. The theme of recent research data suggests that an individualized treatment approach may be necessary, with the combination and dosage of medications tailored to the particular patient. The clinician is currently limited to utilizing psychological intervention, environmental manipulation, and pharmacotherapy to manage secondary psychiatric symptomatology as ways to optimize patient functioning.

Chapter 109

Economic Issues

Issues in Treatment

Economic issues in the treatment of all psychiatric patients have received a great deal of attention in recent years, particularly with the introduction of prospective payment systems for Medicare inpatient admissions (Iglehart 1982). In this chapter, I will discuss these economic issues in relation to the treatment of patients with organic mental syndromes. Those interested in a more general discussion should refer to review articles (e.g., Goldman et al. 1984).

Other chapters in this section have discussed various organic mental syndromes that may affect patients of all ages. However, the vast majority of those with delirium and dementia (the most common syndromes) are over the age of 65. For that reason, this chapter will be written largely from the perspective of geriatric patients. It should be clear that the discussion relates to the United States because the issues are different in countries with different health and social welfare programs (Liptzin 1984).

Patient Issues

Data from the US Bureau of the Census (American Association of Retired Persons 1987) indicate that the median income of older persons in 1986 was $11,544 for men and $6,425 for women. Families headed by persons 65 years and older had a median income of $19,932 in 1986. About 15 percent of families headed by an older person had incomes less than $10,000. Nearly half of the elderly persons living alone or with nonrelatives reported incomes of $7,000 or less. Using the official 1986 definition of poverty (i.e., $6,630 for a couple or $5,255 for an older individual living alone), about 3.5 million elderly people were living below the poverty level. The poverty rate for persons 65 and older was 12.4 percent, which is substantial although lower than the rate for persons under 65 (15.4 percent).

The above data indicate that many older people have limited income. If an older person develops a health problem or functional disability, that person or the person's spouse may be forced to choose between medical treatment, supportive services, and basic needs (e.g., food, clothing, heat, electricity, telephone). Fortunately, people over 65 are able to pay for many of their medical care needs with Medicare, the only National Health Insurance program in the United States. However, even with Medicare, older people pay out-of-pocket one-fourth of their average health care expenditures of $4,000 per year per person. Concern about rising federal expenditures has led to proposals to increase the amount of cost sharing to be borne by Medicare beneficiaries.

Younger patients with organic mental syndromes may receive Medicare health insurance benefits if they qualify for Social Security Disability or have received Supplemental Security Income for two years. Alternatively, they may qualify for Medicaid health benefits if their income is below the cutoff level in their state. Patients of any age with organic mental syndromes may have special difficulty understanding how to apply for or use these government benefits.

Provider Issues

In the last few years, economic issues have come to be a major focus of provider concerns about services for the elderly, in contrast to the 1960s and 1970s when the issues were those of availability, accessibility, and quality of care.

There has been a revolutionary change for inpatient reimbursement from a retrospective cost-based reimbursement system to a prospective payment system based on diagnosis-related groups (DRGs) (Iglehart 1982). This prospective payment system puts hospitals at financial risk if the care they provide uses more resources than the care provided on the average in all similar hospitals. As of this writing, most psychiatric units in general hospitals and all psychiatric hospitals are exempt from prospective payment (Widem et al. 1984). However, the future implications of the changing reimbursement system are unclear, and this has created considerable uncertainty and anxiety (Goldman et al. 1984). Even before the introduction of the prospective payment system, hospitals generally received lower reimbursement for their services from Medicare than from private health insurance payers. Utilization review programs could also disallow payment for the admission of a patient with an organic mental syndrome or insist that the patient be discharged because he or she was not likely to benefit from the services. Retrospective reviews could lead to determinations that care was not "medically necessary," and therefore, should not be reimbursed. There has been an additional limit of 190 lifetime days of coverage under Medicare for inpatient treatment in a psychiatric hospital.

Economic issues have also been important for outpatient care. From its inception, the Medicare program has specifically limited reimbursement for the treatment of mental and nervous disorders. Outpatient psychiatric treatment has been reimbursed at one-half the usual and customary fee allowed by Medicare in contrast to the 80 percent reimbursement of the allowable fee for other medical services. There has also been an annual limit of $250 on the outpatient treatment of mental and nervous disorders. These limits have undoubtedly created economic disincentives for practitioners to treat geriatric patients because many younger patients have better insurance coverage or are better able to pay for care. The Secretary of the Department of Health and Human Services (DHHS) recognized that these arbitrary limits were inappropriate for patients with organic mental syndromes, particularly patients with dementia of the Alzheimer type. A DHHS Task Force (US Department of Health and Human Services 1984) recommended that for patients with dementia of the Alzheimer type and related disorders, psychiatric services (other than psychotherapy) be reimbursed at the 80 percent level without a specified maximum (just as all other medical disorders and treatments are reimbursed). In 1987, Congress agreed to extend this reimbursement change to the "medical management" of all psychiatric disorders. Psychotherapy is still reimbursed at 50 percent but the limit has been raised to $1,100. While the services of psychiatrists to such patients may now be more adequately reimbursed, nonphysician mental health practitioners in private practice are still not reimbursed under the Medicare program.

Community mental health centers were established and eligible for federal staffing grants from the mid 1960s. It was hoped that these centers would provide care to those communities and individuals who were not being served. In 1975, amendments were passed specifically to require that services be provided to elderly persons, including those with organic mental syndromes (Sharfstein 1978). Community mental health centers were also supposed to facilitate the placement of those patients leaving state mental hospitals and to provide follow-up services to the nursing homes where many patients with organic mental syndromes were transferred. Many centers did set up elderly service teams in the late 1970s. However, cutbacks in federal funding since 1981 have led to a sharp reduction in the staffing of these teams. Even harder hit than direct services were the consultation services to nursing homes, which were not readily reimbursed.

Most patients with organic mental syndromes, including those with dementia, continue to reside in the community. However, a substantial number require institutional care. This is provided largely in intermediate-care facilities or nursing homes. Few patients can afford to pay for nursing home care from their own savings and income. Those who can afford to pay are more financially attractive to nursing homes because the private fee is generally twice as high as that paid by the Medicaid program for indigent patients in most states. Private patients have a wider choice of homes that will accept them because of the financial incentive for nursing homes, most of which are proprietary. Patients with organic mental syndromes who have behavior problems and have no private resources can be very difficult to place in an adequate nursing home. Even nursing homes with substantial numbers of private patients are reluctant to hire psychiatric consultants except to provide direct services that can be billed to individual patients.

Societal Issues

As noted above, the number one priority in health care at the present time is cost containment. Health care expenditures currently account for more than 10 percent of the gross national product, and this proportion has been rising steadily for the last 20 years. Increased cost sharing by patients and prospective payment systems including prepaid health maintenance organizations (HMOs) are attempts to slow down or reverse the trend of rising costs.

In addition to cost containment efforts, questions are being asked about the cost-benefit and cost effectiveness of various health interventions (Weinstein and Stason 1977). Although attempts to put a dollar value on a human life raise ethical questions, it is appropriate to ask if expenditures are being properly allocated. How much is it worth to assess thoroughly an elderly person with moderate to severe cognitive deficits? When can heroic life-saving treatments be abandoned or denied to such patients (Wanzer et al. 1984)? As uncomfortable as these questions are for health care providers, in a world with finite resources, allocation decisions have to be made. As an example, public expenditures are overwhelmingly skewed toward institutional care. Would more people be better helped if the balance were shifted somewhat to provide home care, day care, respite care, or other noninstitutional services (see Chapter 111)?

Issues in Treatment Research

There are many important issues that apply to mental illness treatment research in general. One editorial, for example, highlighted the need for a greatly increased national commitment to research on mental and addictive disorders (Barchas et al. 1985). The potential effects of prospective payment on clinical research in psychiatry have also been examined (Pincus et al. 1985). The reader interested in a more detailed discussion of the issues in funding research on mental illness should refer to the report of the Institute of Medicine (1985). The focus here is on the specific issues in treatment research on organic mental syndromes.

Funding for treatment research on organic mental syndromes is available from various sources. These include: the National Institute on Aging; the National Institute on Neurological, Communicative Disorders and Stroke; and the National Institute of Mental Health (all of which are part of the US Public Health Service); special research allocations in certain states; private foundations; and pharmaceutical companies. The federal government has provided by far the largest share of funding for treatment research. Support from this source has increased substantially in the last 10 years from almost nothing to more than 10 million dollars a year including funding for Alzheimer's Disease Research Centers at 10 medical schools. The increased funding has been achieved largely by intense lobbying by organizations such as the Alzheimer's Disease and Related Disorders Associations, which has helped to educate the public and its elected representatives in federal and state legislatures to the huge financial and personal costs associated with organic mental syndromes.

Although there has been a substantial increase in expenditures for treatment research on organic mental syndromes, there is still an enormous discrepancy between these modest amounts and the billions of dollars spent on health care, including custodial care for patients with these disorders. Furthermore, Medicare guidelines specifically prohibit payment for experimental treatments of any condition. In the short run, this policy may limit expenditures, but it is clear that in the long run an intervention that effectively treats or prevents the common organic mental syndromes will save substantial money and greatly reduce the suffering of patients and their families.

Summary

Many patients suffering from organic mental syndromes are over the age of 65 years. Despite Medicare, the elderly as a group have higher medical expenses than the younger population. Regardless of age, patients with organic mental syndromes may have particular difficulty understanding what services and benefits are available and how to obtain them. Moreover, the evolving nationwide change from a cost-based retrospective to a prospective payment system, while not yet generally applied to psychiatric services, is a potential threat to equitable reimbursement and service availability, especially when added to the lower payment scales of Medicare compared to private health insurance payers, and the long-standing prejudicial reimbursement rates for psychiatric treatments. The recent recommendations that psychiatric care (other than psychotherapy alone) be reimbursed according to the same guidelines as other medical treatments is a long overdue step in the right direction, but inequities remain. Problems of funding for community mental health centers and reimbursement for nursing home services continue to limit severely the services available to patients with organic mental syndromes.

With the national focus on cost containment, cost-benefit, and cost effectiveness of health care, difficult ethical questions are being raised about allocation of resources.

Although funding for research on treatment of organic mental syndromes has increased substantially, it still constitutes only a fraction of 1 percent of the dollar amounts spent to provide care for the patients. The prohibition of Medicare payment for experimental treatment of any condition is, perhaps, justifiable as a short-term cost containment measure, but the long-term cost in delayed solutions to the treatment dilemmas presented by the organic mental syndromes may prove to be exceedingly high.

Chapter 110

Legal Aspects

Traditionally, the law has presumed that adults are competent, knowledgeable, and act voluntarily (Mills et al. 1980). Whether the matter being considered was a medical treatment decision, a will, or a contract, this presumption has led to considerable stability where such decisions are concerned (Slovenko 1973).

During the last 30 years, however, the law has been more carefully examining issues surrounding treatment decisions. There are numerous reasons for this heightened legal scrutiny. One is the enhanced potency of frequently used technologies: as the risks associated with treatment or palliation multiplied, public policy supported the perspective that they should be disclosed (Katz 1972). Another is the advances in medical technology making it possible to preserve life even where cognitive capacity was seriously impaired. Additionally, the great interest in minority rights that began with the Brown (1954) decision inspired specific consideration of mental patients' capacities to accept and refuse treatment. For these and other reasons, the courts have become more involved with assessing capacity to consent, developing standards of competence for consent, and making provisions for those who no longer have (or never had) the requisite capacity (Roth et al. 1977).

Patients with organic mental disorders have, by definition, particular problems learning, retaining, and recalling information (Jarvik 1982a). Axiomatically, they have problems with judgment, and therefore may lack the capacity to make informed medical decisions (Comfort 1980). Thus the treatment of such patients raises problematic legal issues. Is the patient competent to consent to evaluation or treatment (Appelbaum and Roth 1982)? What about confidentiality (Jonsen et al. 1982)? Is the physician responsible for advising the patient and the family to consider making a will when the clinical evidence suggests that the patient's course will be one of increasing incapacity? How should the patient who starts to wander or to become combative be managed (Lennard and Kaufman 1985)? These are some of the issues considered in this chapter.

Caveats

Given society's present litigiousness, it may seem prudent to practice with one eye on the patient and another on evolving legal developments. We believe that this is neither desirable nor necessary (Mills 1984). The public and the courts prefer that clinicians become more expert in their arena of chosen expertise, not that they become quasi-attorneys. In the majority of cases, common sense and good clinical practice will not only provide the patient with good care, but will greatly reduce the physician's exposure to liability. Nevertheless, a certain cognizance of some legal (and medical) minima for adequate clinical care is desirable (Stone 1984). Most of these caveats are sufficiently obvious that they hardly warrant restating; yet inattention to these fundamentals costs clinicians needless lawsuits each year and sometimes their licenses.

First, avoid the obvious breaches: practicing while intoxicated, becoming addicted to illicit substances, or having sexual relationships with patients. Second, practice within your area of competence; when practicing near the metaphoric periphery, or whenever questions arise, obtain consultation. Third, recount all significant transactions in the medical record. Fourth, respect patient confidentiality unless there are compelling reasons to the contrary (e.g., elder-abuse reporting laws). Fifth, refine your skills by attending continuing medical education courses and doing appropriate journal reading. Finally, treat patients with courtesy and respect. This is a limited but not inconsequential list that is solidly within the grasp of most physicians.

Clinical Vignettes

The patient with an organic mental syndrome may present challenges in management, both clinically and legally, from the moment of contact. The clinical vignettes that follow illustrate some of the most frequently encountered legal issues arising in the context of evaluating and treating patients with organic mental syndromes.

Difficult Evaluation

Consider the patient brought to an emergency room by the local police after being found wandering on a nearby expressway. The patient is oriented only to his name and carries no identification so that even that fact cannot be verified. Previous attempts at questioning, according to the police report, resulted in angry striking out; thus the police transported him to the medical center. On approach, the patient yells obscenities and demands to be released, claiming that he is being held against his will. What is the appropriate legal and clinical course for the patient who refuses to consent to a medical evaluation?

On the basis of the fragmentary history and brief clinical description, it is not evident what is transpiring, although a preliminary differential diagnosis would include organic mental syndromes, functional mental disorders, and malingering. Because of the patient's history of walking on the expressway and being combative, further investigation is warranted. Legally, this would ordinarily be accomplished by initiating civil commitment (Roth 1979). State laws and procedures would dictate whether the police themselves initiated commitment prior to bringing the patient to the medical center, or transported the patient directly, awaiting the physician's assessment. Similarly, local procedures and laws would determine whether commitment was to be initiated before the physician continued the medical evaluation, or whether it occurred only if, following the initial examination, the patient was deemed to require commitment. However, the legal authority is clear: when an emergency arises or when the patient is acting in a fashion that is dangerous to himself or others, or when he appears incapable of taking care of himself, medical evaluation can take place even over the patient's objections.

Suppose that the patient is in a jurisdiction that requires initiation of commitment even prior to evaluation if the patient expresses a clear wish to leave. Further, suppose that when asked to remain, he strikes out. Since the patient is not yet committed, are there legal grounds to restrain the patient, at least pending the completion of the commitment forms? The commonsense answer is the correct one: the patient may be lawfully detained while the forms initiating civil commitment are completed.

With the patient legally detained, the evaluation would continue. Suppose that mental status examination reveals little more than known before: the patient is oriented to what he claims is his name, but not to place or date. Worse, following a scuffle with the evaluating staff, the patient becomes mute and refuses all further communication. Given the patient's apparent disorientation, he has a presumptive organic mental syndrome; therefore, a thorough medical, neurologic, and laboratory evaluation needs to be undertaken. Assume that this process is begun with the patient being generally uncooperative. When the patient is approached with a syringe to have blood drawn, however, he very clearly articulates he does not wish any further medical evaluation or treatment, that he knows the law, and that commitment only provides physicians with the authority to administer psychiatric, not medical, treatment.

This utterance, although overdrawn legally, is helpful clinically in providing more information about the patient's background and degree of impairment and points correctly to a truth about commitment laws. In general, such laws do not authorize emergency medical treatment, only emergency psychiatric treatment. The emergency evaluation of a seriously disturbed patient, however, is not treatment. Thus it would be appropriate, from the legal viewpoint, for the physician to explain the rationale for seeking the sample of blood and to proceed with obtaining it. Since the patient was being legally detained and the diagnosis included a number of organic conditions, even forcibly restraining the patient during venipuncture would be appropriate if necessary. Similarly, if the patient required an emergency computed tomography (CT) scan or lumbar puncture, those procedures could be administered in the context of performing the emergency evaluation; unnecessary laboratory and other tests would not qualify as emergency evaluation.

Meanwhile, during this complex and thus protracted evaluation, the patient again becomes assaultive. Given the now-existing medical presumption that the patient's diagnosis is organic, is it still appropriate legally to restrain or sedate him under the authority of the civil commitment law? The answer is generally yes: functional illness has not been definitively ruled out, and until that occurs, the civil commitment statute is a valid legal vehicle for restraining or sedating the patient to complete the diagnostic assessment. Even if the patient's diagnosis is known to be organic, he can be briefly sedated under the authority of the state's police power (civil commitment statutes).

Questionable Consent

A different hypothetical case illustrates the other frequently encountered legal problem: the compliant patient who is willing to sign any form but who, from the medical perspective, is so cognitively impaired that informed consent cannot be deemed to have occurred (Stanley et al. 1985). How should the physician proceed to maximize that patient's welfare, while respecting the law and minimizing the risk of lawsuits alleging the inappropriate failure to obtain informed consent (Eth 1985)? As with the combative patient previously discussed, problems may occur at the outset.

An elderly female patient is brought to the medical center by her middle-aged children. They report that her family physician suggested a comprehensive evaluation for what appeared to be an increasingly serious organic mental syndrome. Prior to making this suggestion, the physician had not seen the patient for five years because she had refused all medical contact. However, when the children perceived that her home was ever more untidy and that she appeared to have lost considerable weight, they insisted on medical evaluation. At the medical center admission office, the patient is asked, per the center routine, to sign the admission form authorizing admission and providing blanket approval of routine laboratory procedures. The patient complies. Now the patient has been admitted to the neurobehavioral ward. On initial evaluation, it is apparent to the physician that she has no idea of where she is nor what efforts are being considered on her behalf; further, she has no recollection of having signed anything.

The physician has completed the physical examination and is about to continue the workup with venipuncture and lumbar puncture, but is curious about the legal status of the patient's consent. Adult patients are, in the eyes of the law, presumed competent. Since the patient has not been declared incompetent by a court (this information was learned from the patient's children whom the physician considers reliable), her consent for low-risk evaluative procedures generally would be considered valid.

Still, suppose that the examination and tests reveal no metabolic abnormalities, but demonstrate masses in both the lung and brain. Both masses appear resectable, but because of the patient's frailty, the surgeon and the oncologist recommend biopsying both masses before contemplating further treatment. The patient willingly consents. However, in the context of the much greater risk to the patient posed by these procedures, the physician is concerned about the propriety of considering the consent valid.

Given the risks associated with these biopsies, the prudent legal course would be to request that the probate court appoint a guardian or conservator with the power to make treatment decisions. In the context of needing to choose between surgery, chemotherapy, radiotherapy, some combination of these, or no treatment, the appointment of a guardian or conservator makes particular sense because of the potential importance of the decision. In most states, however, that process takes weeks, and although an emergency does not exist, it might not be medically prudent to wait that long. Depending on the state where the evaluation and treatment are occurring, several options are available to the physician. Some states have probate courts that provide a 24-hour "hotline" service in which a judge can authorize urgent treatment that does not allow for a routine court hearing but falls outside the implied consent doctrine that authorizes treatment in emergencies. Because the risks of the procedure are material in the instant case, having the court authorize the biopsies would be preferable to performing them without such approval. In a number of states without hotline services, urgent treatment can be authorized by the probate court within 48 hours. In this hypothetical case, that time frame would probably suffice. Unfortunately, there are some states where such rapid judicial access is uncertain; in those states, other mechanisms for ratifying the patient's consent would need to be found.

Most clinicians are reasonably familiar with these mechanisms: they include authorization for treatment by the medical center's chief of staff or by the risk manager (Mills et al. 1984). Such consent, often termed vicarious consent, is useful when the need for diagnostic evaluation or treatment is too urgent to allow access to the court. Appropriately, however, courts do not consider such vicarious consent ideal. Most troubling to the law is the awareness that the standard employed by hospitals in such circumstances is typically that of what a reasonable patient would desire if faced with a similar set of conditions and alternatives. The problem with this benign sounding standard is that it generally does not adequately consider the individual patient's own, potentially idiosyncratic beliefs about what the patient would have wanted under the present circumstances. Because family members often have considerable knowledge about such preferences, when such occasions arise, it is important that they be queried about the patient's past expression of preference. The results of such discussion should be documented in the medical record to provide support for the treatment decision. This is most important where there are several equally acceptable clinical alternatives, and the treatment choice is determined in deference to the patient's past statements of intent.

On the other hand, for physicians to assume that the patient's rights had been fully respected, so long as family members (including spouses) authorized the proposed intervention, would be a mistake. The law recognizes that for a variety of reasons family members may not have the patient's interest fully in mind. In the present case, if one assumes that the clinical matter is too urgent for the probate court to determine, a senior colleague (chief of staff or medical director) should write a note detailing why the procedure is urgent and why the proposed intervention is the medically preferable one. Further, if time allows, the primary physician should write a note indicating that the family was consulted and that they approved the proposed plan.

Consider the course that should be followed where the family objects to the proffered intervention. They claim that, well prior to the onset of her organic mental syndrome, the patient had repeatedly stated that if she were ever old with diminished faculties, that she wished to be allowed to die without any heroic measures. This complicates matters, although the extreme cases are relatively straightforward. If sufficient time has elapsed that the patient's condition is now emergent, the medical center should proceed with the necessary evaluation or treatment because in emergencies, as noted above, the law recognizes the doctrine of implied consent—that the prudent patient would rather be saved than have concern for the niceties of consent diminish the chance of recovery. This point merits emphasis: in emergencies physicians should not believe themselves constrained by the ordinary requirements about obtaining informed consent. By the nature of the emergent situation, consent is legally implied.

At the other extreme, when there is sufficient time, prudence would suggest that another attempt be made to reconcile the family and, if that fails, to obtain a court order. If both prove impossible, the medical center's legal counsel should be consulted. Presumably, this has already occurred, as it would be the attorney who indicated that there was insufficient time to apply to the probate court. Depending on the gravity of the situation, the attorney might conclude that having the chief of staff authorize treatment was sufficient; however, detailed and complete documentation in the medical record would be necessary.

This hypothetical case can present a more complex, but not unrealistic, situation if one further assumes that the patient objects to hospitalization and, while on the ward, endeavors to leave the hospital. In most jurisdictions, such a patient would be civilly committed, although civil commitment is not an ideal legal vehicle for detaining this patient because her diagnosis is organic. In states with a hotline, the probate court could authorize continued diagnostic evaluation or treatment because of the urgent nature of her condition. In emergencies, hospitalization, evaluation, and treatment can be initiated with no formal legal mechanism other than the doctrine of implied consent; however, given the gradual onset of the patient's condition, it is doubtful that an emergency exists (yet). The consent of the family alone would not constitute sufficient legal grounds to detain the patient unless there were concurrent legal grounds such as commitment or the presence of a medically defined emergency.

Finally, consider a situation that simplifies, rather than complicates, matters. Suppose that the patient lived in a jurisdiction that recognizes so-called durable powers of attorney. Such powers of attorney allow for an individual to give to another enduring authorization to make certain kinds of decisions. In some states, those decisions include the power to authorize hospitalization, diagnostic evaluation, and treatment. If the patient, realizing her advancing age and the increased risk of cognitive impairment, were to have created such a durable power of attorney, many of the issues outlined above would recede. Because such powers of attorney do not carry with them a formal declaration of incompetence around a specific issue, they are becoming more frequently used. (In most instances, before a probate court will appoint a guardian, it generally must find that the patient is incompetent to make the specific types of decisions that the guardian is being proposed to make.) Durable powers of attorney do not, however, provide a comprehensive resolution to the clinicolegal difficulties presented here because they do not have the same procedural safeguards that probate court decisions do. Thus it might be possible for an ardent family member and a careless attorney to draft a durable power of attorney without adequate attention being paid to the fact that the client-patient was already severely cognitively impaired. When the physician believes that this has occurred, the physician should consult the medical center's attorney or, if the center has none, his or her own.

Confidentiality of Diagnosis

The treatment of patients suffering from dementia in particular, as contrasted with those suffering from delirium, raises important issues of confidentiality. As the following case illustrates, such issues range from nettlesome to profound.

A middle-aged couple seeks medical assistance: over the last few months they have both noticed that the husband has become more forgetful. Although he still recalls many events from earlier in his life, he can only rarely recall what he ate at the previous meal. He often needs prompting to perform the routine activities of ordinary life, although earlier in life he had been remarkably fastidious. Preliminary mental status examination suggests cognitive limitations; the medical and neurologic examinations reveal no focal deficits. The physician arranges for comprehensive psychometric evaluation, lumbar puncture, and CT scan. While these arrangements are being made, the patient's wife quietly indicates that she would like to speak with the physician privately.

Once in private, she expresses her deep concern, noting that her husband's parents both died of Alzheimer's disease in late middle age. She is, not inappropriately, deeply worried that her husband has this condition, wonders about the prognosis, what she should tell their children, and whether she should contact the family lawyer. She then bursts into tears, indicating that, unbeknownst to her husband, she has noticed increasing difficulties with her own memory (e.g., even when she makes a shopping list, she often forgets some items when shopping for groceries), and is terrified that she, too, has a dementing disease, for which her family history is positive. She is also distressed about whether, and how, to tell her husband any of this (Clark 1985).

With her, particularly at this point in her husband's assessment and given her emotional distress, reassurance is appropriate; many people with a positive family history of dementia do not develop that condition and because her symptoms may reflect only her anxiety and depression over her husband's condition (Cobe 1985). Further, given the relatively brief interval between initiating her husband's diagnostic workup and the anticipated results, if makes sense to defer an in-depth discussion of her fears for both of them until his test results are available. In the meantime, it is prudent and compassionate to tell the patient, first alone and then with his wife present if he agrees, that your preliminary investigation suggests that he has some cognitive deficits (this should be expressed in language that the patient can understand, for example, that as he knows, he has problems with memory, language, or calculations—whichever is appropriate), and that is the rationale for your having ordered more tests. Further, one would attempt to preserve hope on the part of the patient and his wife by noting that problems with memory have many causes, some of which are eminently treatable (Butler 1984).

It might make sense to suggest to the wife privately that, given her concerns about her own health, she should be formally evaluated (while reassuring her that some memory loss, particularly during times of stress, is normal). Further, one might explore with her the kinds of family and social supports she has. Given the tentativeness of her concerns, the stress she is under, and the presence of her husband's deficits, counseling disclosure of her concerns to her husband would generally be premature. So far, then, the confidentiality of each party would have been largely preserved, although in describing the patient's condition to his wife, given that the patient may not be able to weigh the risks of such disclosure fully, the physician has somewhat stretched confidentiality to aid the wife's understanding of her husband's condition. One would do this out of the hope that such disclosure would reassure her and enhance the likelihood of her taking good care of her husband.

Several weeks later, with tests completed, the couple returns. On the basis of information then available, the physician believes that the patient has dementia of the Alzheimer type. Given his relatively intact mental state, it would be appropriate to ask the patient in private if he wishes his condition discussed with his wife or if he wishes that his condition remain confidential. Considering the hypothetical case in which the condition is found relatively early in its course, excessive pliancy on the patient's part is much more likely than obstinateness; thus it is likely that the patient will accept the physician's suggestion that both parties learn what the tests have revealed. We believe that unless there are obvious reasons to the contrary (e.g., the physician knows independently that the wife is interested in learning of the patient's disease so that she can use their assets to her own ends), it is best to assume that the patient has the capacity to consent meaningfully to the wife's learning about his illness, especially when there are many practical reasons for her being informed.

Suppose, however, that the patient is atypically truculent and that he enjoins the physician from disclosing the results of the evaluation to the wife (Reisberg et al. 1985). Because physicians are trained clinically, not legally, it is wise for them to consider the clinical options first. The obvious clinical approach would be to reassure the patient that his wishes will be respected, but to inquire into the rationale for them. This should be accomplished while gently commenting that it is apt to make the wife's care for the patient less certain, while increasing her anxiety. Thoughtful examination of the patient's reasons for not wishing his wife to be included in the discussion of his condition should be undertaken. Aside from its value in illuminating the immediate impasse, it would also further the physician's knowledge of the patient's thought processes and cognitive functioning. Additionally, discussion of the patient's concerns would, in some instances, allow the patient to be reassured and perhaps then change his mind regarding disclosure.

If the patient remains adamant, the physician should explain to the wife that the patient has expressed the wish that, at least temporarily, diagnostic impressions remain confidential, and that the physician is concerned about this but will respect the patient's wishes for the present. Further, the physician should reassure the wife that he is sufficiently troubled by the patient's wish in this regard that he will continue to discuss the matter with the patient and has scheduled another appointment to do just that. Still, where the situation requires it (when the patient's condition appears to be rapidly evolving and requires immediate in-hospital evaluation), the physician should, we believe, explain the nature of his condition, even over the patient's objection.

Suppose that during the next several visits the patient recants and expresses his willingness to have his diagnosis, prognosis, and treatment plan discussed with his spouse. From the academic perspective one could question whether this expression reflects the patient's greater comprehension of his situation; therefore it would make clinical sense to assess this by discussing with the patient his reasons for changing his mind. We believe, however, that there are so many practical benefits from an open discussion of these matters that reasonable ambiguity should be construed in favor of disclosure. With that settled, how far should the physician go in discussing the probable course of the disease and in encouraging the couple to seek legal counsel?

Again, no firm rules can be enunciated. A number of guidelines, however can be presented (Winslade et al. 1984). At least insofar as discussion with the patient's spouse or family is concerned, the most important guideline is that disclosure should be keyed to the patient's wishes. Since dementing patients are likely to be ambivalent, as are the rest of us, when it comes to learning information about their illness, it is wise to proceed gradually. Given the nature of the illness, the patient is apt, even fairly early in the course of the disease, to forget much of what is revealed. Given the disease's ominous nature, such forgetting may reflect, at least in part, the successful operation of an ego defense. When it comes to the spouse, however, we believe that fairly complete although gradual disclosure will be helpful in allowing for reasonable plans to be made. Since the spouse may be frail, effective planning for the patient's needs is essential and may be time consuming. Thus we believe that it is also appropriate to suggest that the spouse discuss the matter with the children. We encourage that it be suggested to both the patient and his wife that an attorney be contacted to consider the changing legal situation represented by the husband's disease. This need not take the form of counseling the patient to make or revise a will, but rather the expression that chronic illness often has far-reaching ramifications, and that the legal ones, among others, need to be considered.

Assuming that the patient's wife had a dementia syndrome of depression occasioned by her husband's condition, with sufficient therapy and support there is a reasonable chance that she will be able to help him, at least during the early phases of the illness. To the extent that this is the case, and that the couple has sufficient resources to have competent professional assistance, their lives will be much more comfortable. The point worthy of underscoring is, that with dementing conditions that have a fairly certain clinical trajectory, it makes good sense to initiate the necessary legal and dispositional arrangements early in the course of the illness. This allows the patient to have a much greater say in the ultimate arrangements and reduces the chances that major issues will remain unattended. Thus, the provision of a durable power of attorney or a guardianship-conservatorship relatively early in the course of the illness will serve to resolve many of the potential legal ambiguities outlined above. Issues left unresolved are likely to increase greatly the discomfort of the patient's spouse, the physician, and the treatment team.

Combative Patients

While the moribund demented patient is characteristically docile, between the onset of the illness and the terminal phase there may be a protracted period of disinhibition in which combative and/or sexually provocative behavior is fairly common. When such behaviors occur, it is not uncommon for physicians to express doubts as to the appropriate legal intervention and to request legal consultation. In our experience, many such requests are metaphoric: the physician is more expressing a discomfort with the patient's behavior than seeking specific legal advice (Perl and Shelp 1982).

From the legal perspective, the combative patient presents relatively few issues. However, recent statutory changes have tended to increase the physician's work load by requiring careful documentation when seclusion and restraint are used. Still, within the context of first some and later many procedural guarantees, the common law has generally expressed the notion that the private right ends where the public peril begins. To a considerable extent, this notion underpins contemporaneous criminal codes and provides a fundamental rationale for detaining mentally disordered patients who are perceived as being dangerous to others. Nevertheless, the organically impaired patient does not have a "mental" illness insofar as the medical profession is concerned (because commitment statutes narrowly define mental illness so as to limit the range of involuntary treatment), and thus commitment does not provide the appropriate long-term legal authority for seclusion or restraint. What does, then, provide for such authority?

Ironically, and accounting for physicians' discomfort in this regard, there is little comprehensive statutory authority in most states. Instead, there is considerable overlapping of common law and statutory authority. Some authority comes from the emergency treatment doctrine of implied consent, some from the guardianship-conservatorship process (where the patient has substitute decision makers in place), and some from the state's civil commitment authority (that often fails to distinguish organic from functional illness, but always reflects the viewpoint that the public should be protected). Thus, while the precise location for the authority to seclude and/or restrain the patient is sometimes unclear, the authority itself is not so.

Changes in commitment laws and the near plethora of regulations enacted to prevent the perceived mistreatment of patients with cognitive or emotional disabilities, however, require that the rationale for seclusion and restraint be carefully described in the medical record. Some states, moreover, limit the amount of time that a patient can be secluded or restrained, or require additional documentation if the amount goes beyond a statutorily defined maximum. In the context of treating a combative and demented patient, these requirements, while often experienced as burdensome, are relatively minor and straightforward. Additionally, when the patient has a guardian or conservator, such requirements are sometimes vitiated because of the legal fiction that the patient is consenting to the treatment (including seclusion and restraint) per the legal authority of the conservator. Seclusion and restraint are, nonetheless, extreme remedies, and the clinician should consider (and document that consideration) other clinical interventions such as medication that are arguably less intrusive.

Discussion

The clinical vignettes underscore that while the patient with an organic mental syndrome poses important clinical issues for the physician, many of the so-called legal issues can be dealt with in a relatively straightforward manner. Still, it should be evident that some of the clinicolegal problems raised by delirious and demented patients require particular sensitivity to the law (Mills et al. 1984). Such problems have been, traditionally, analyzed along thematic lines such as informed consent, confidentiality, civil commitment, seclusion and restraint, the rights to treatment and to refuse treatment, termination of treatment, elder abuse, and testamentary capacity. Many of these issues have been presented by the clinical vignettes. Others have merely been mentioned because their relationship to routine clinical practice is peripheral. It is noteworthy that these issues, whether concerning patients with organic mental syndromes or patients generally, are quite similar from the legal perspective.

The essential issues in consent involve knowledge (of the proposed procedure), competence (the ability to determine rationally and with good judgment which of the proffered treatments best suits one's predilictions and needs), and voluntariness. For organically impaired patients, the issue is what degree of impairment in the patients' ability to make sensible judgments regarding their interests is sufficient to trigger legal intervention. Two practically oriented guidelines may be useful here. For patients who appear genuinely incapable of determining what is best for them, substitute decision makers should be found (although this may occasion the arguably stigmatizing process of guardianship or conservatorship). Also, when the risks associated with the proffered diagnostic or therapeutic procedure are high, particularly if the risks are high in comparison to the anticipated benefits, the physician should be particularly attentive to the formalities of consent (Wolfensberger 1967). Such heuristics, although not entirely foolproof, will adequately deal with most dilemmas posed by the organically impaired patient.

Confidentiality is simultaneously the most obvious of the legal themes and the most recondite (Jonsen et al. 1982). Nearly every physician agrees that, barring major extraneous circumstances, it is respectful and prudent to preserve the patient's confidences. The issue, of course, is what precisely constitutes such circumstances. Slovenko (1973) perceptively although churlishly pointed out that it is whatever the courts deem it to be: an analytically correct but heuristically limited position. To make matters more complex, the courts and legislatures frequently erode the remaining vestiges of the privilege by creating or discovering new laws. Yet, as the clinical vignettes illustrate, the core principle is obvious: the private privilege ends where the public peril begins (Tarasoff 1974, 1976). This principle can be stated more affirmatively: if confidentiality is to be breached, there should be a palpable reason, either clinical (such as contributing to the patient's welfare) or legal (such as protecting the welfare of another). With this concept in mind, the physician should be able to deal effectively with most problems of confidentiality, reserving consultation for those that present especially troublesome issues.

Most of the remaining legal issues mentioned at the beginning of this chapter are sufficiently complex that they require separate and detailed consideration. Thus the reader should turn to more focused sources when issues arise involving consent (Meisel et al. 1977), civil commitment (Roth 1979), seclusion or restraint (Tardiff 1984), rights to treatment, (Mills 1982), rights to refuse treatment (Mills et al. 1983), and termination of treatment (Meyers 1985; Wanzer et al. 1984; Younger et al. 1985). (Termination of treatment is also examined in Chapter 111.) That leaves elder abuse and testamentary capacity as issues with which the physician who treats patients with organic mental syndromes should have some familiarity.

As societal awareness of child, spouse, and elder abuse (Kosberg 1982) has grown, state legislatures have intervened to proscribe such conduct. It is necessary for physicians to familiarize themselves with the relevant reporting laws in the state in which they practice. Some statutes are mandatory; others are discretionary. Discretionary statutes allow reporting and indemnify the physician from suit for violating the patient's confidentiality. A number of states have made reporting mandatory and enacted significant penalties for failing to report. Since elderly patients fall within the purview of such statutes, physicians who routinely treat geriatric patients should be well versed in local law and procedure (e.g., to whom does one make a report when one suspects abuse). Local professional societies are a good source for such information.

Testamentary, or will-making, capacity is another issue that can routinely be expected to arise in the course of treating geriatric patients, and periodically with nongeriatric, organically impaired patients. Although the specific components of testamentary capacity are controlled by state law and thus vary slightly across jurisdictions, the general themes are sufficiently common and logical that physicians should know them. Essentially, patients are deemed to have testamentary capacity if at the time of making their will they know what their estates contain, who their natural heirs are, and to whom they would like to leave what. As the law has evolved, it has come to appreciate that mental states may change over time; hence it is the capacity at the time that the will was signed that is critical. Further, the law accepts, as common sense would dictate, that there are various degrees of knowing. Thus, the patient does not need to know the precise magnitude of the estate nor every potential heir.

The patient with an organic mental syndrome may well have the requisite capacity; the patient's periodic disorientation or combativeness does not per se suggest that the patient lacks the relevant capacity.

Conclusion

This chapter has a central thesis: that reasonable sensitivity to legal issues is not unduly burdensome and often promotes high quality care and treatment. When specific legal issues arise, the physician should determine whether the issue is of such import or complexity that consultation is advisable. The answer may be no. Either way, a general understanding of legal issues makes clinical practice better informed and less anxiety provoking. Even in this "belegaled" age, conscientious practice remains the most important principle of good treatment.

Chapter 111

Ethical Issues

General Concerns

Biopsychosocial Aspects of Old Age

Organic mental syndromes afflict people of all ages and general health conditions. However, as illustrated throughout this book, these disorders are most commonly found in the old and sick. About 85 percent of all people over 65 years of age have chronic health problems. While 4 percent of the 65- to 74-year age group may be diagnosed as suffering from an organic mental syndrome, the percentage almost triples to 11 percent for those over 75 (Jarvik 1982a). Likewise, the 65- to 74-year age group comprises about 15 percent of nursing home patients, while the over-75 group represents 80 percent despite its smaller proportion of the population. Further, at least 60 percent of these patients have a psychiatric diagnosis (Busse 1981). These facts have contributed to the public perception that old age and one of the organic mental syndromes, dementia, are virtually synonymous. Consequently, any analysis of the ethical issues associated with organic mental syndromes must include an explicit discussion of ethics and the elderly.

If biologic aging is a progressive loss of functional capacity, at what point along the continuum is old age? Complicating this vexing question is our understanding that functional capacity is not a solitary measure, but is itself composed of a multitude of capabilities, each varying across the human life span (Benton et al. 1981). A subjective sense of becoming old may not be experienced until the relative failure of an organ system, regardless of chronological age (Grotjohn 1982). For others, old age itself is an illness (senectus ipsa morbus, Terentius). There does not appear to be a unique or specific biologic marker of the state of old age. The process of aging is continuous, and the demarcation of senescence is uncertain and arbitrary. Perhaps that is why the age of entitlement for Social Security, Medicare, retirement, and the like has been set by political forces. In effect, the decision of what is old is based on value judgments concerning average expectable function.

The ethnosocial contribution to the perception of old age is considerable. In a Los Angeles study of adults, more than 30 percent of Mexican Americans identified themselves as old at age 57, the same percentage of blacks at 63 and whites at 70 (Bengtson 1983). Acceptance of the self-definition of old, at whatever age, may coincide with an identification with negative stereotypes of the elderly. Especially in contemporary society, the aged are seen as senile, dirty, and disabled. This prejudice has been termed *gerontophobia* and implies a "rejection of the old, their exclusion from work and their accustomed social space, their premature burial by society as 'unpeople,' and a rich and erroneous folklore of mental decline, infirmity, asexuality, ineducability, and the normality of causeless mental disorder in the old" (Comfort 1980, p. 2).

The existence of a negative stereotype prompts consideration of the elderly as a minority group deserving compensatory special treatment. Affirmative action programs have been established for blacks, Hispanics, the handicapped, and others. It may be argued that the elderly constitute such a group for similar reasons. The over-65-year-olds are recognizably distinct, looking older and being predominantly female. Although the class contains only 10 percent of the total population, they account for 20 percent of all the poor. The prevailing conscious and unconscious prejudice (ageism) tends to be shared by the elderly themselves and may result in "youth creep"—the desperate attempt to look and act younger to escape minority status.

For complex reasons, being old has a disadvantageous impact on health care. While the average medical patient with a psychiatric diagnosis has a 40 percent chance of seeing a psychiatrist, the probability for an otherwise comparable elderly patient is only 3 percent (Schurman et al. 1985). There are a variety of ethnic subgroups within the elderly minority group, with many bearing a double burden of social disadvantage. The interaction of ethnicity and age produces a fascinating blend of characteristics that awaits investigation (Myerhoff 1978). This serves as a reminder that the elderly are not homogenous; each person must be considered individually. Despite this chapter's focus on those suffering from organic mental syndromes, most of the elderly do not. However, the presence of a brain syndrome or other major illness compounds the need for special consideration. Careful scrutiny of relevant ethical issues is, therefore, a priority concern.

Role of Ethics

Ethics is that branch of philosophy whose domain encompasses the analysis of moral value judgments and their justification. Ethics has been studied and taught as an academic discipline for millennia, but only within the last 50 years has it captured widespread public and professional interest. Several forces account for the conspicuous emergence of ethics in medicine, as reflected in the proliferation of books and articles devoted to this topic (Jonsen et al. 1982; Redlich and Mollica 1976). A significant influence has been the repeated exposure of unethical experimentation by physicians, as documented in Beecher's (1966) landmark article. These revelations led directly to the creation of the National Commission for the Protection of Human Subjects of Biomedical and Behavioral Research and to the mandated formation of local institutional review boards.

Another factor promoting the awareness of medical ethics has been the discovery of new technologies. The development of hemodialysis stimulated debate over the rightful allocation of this scarce and expensive life-preserving treatment. Similar questions are now being asked about the totally implantable artificial heart. Although acknowledged experts in establishing diagnoses and formulating treatment, doctors have no moral hegemony in deciding, for instance, who is most deserving of an extraordinary procedure or whether to give electroconvulsive therapy over an involuntary patient's objection. These are ethical and not medical dilemmas.

The public has also influenced the growth of professional interest in medical ethics. The social phenomenon of consumerism has increased attention paid to medical activities, coinciding with a rise in the prevalence of malpractice actions. Patients are becoming more assertive in their interactions with physicians and are insisting on quality service. The ethical dimension of medical care delivery is recognized for its powerful contribution to patient satisfaction.

Diagnostic Concerns

Uncertainty and Limitations of the Workup

"Ethical dilemmas in medical care arise when a particular course of action involves a conflict between competing moral values" (Perl and Shelp 1982, p. 618). With regard to the organic mental syndromes and elderly patients, moral difficulties are encountered from the start of the diagnostic process and extend through treatment and research activities. The importance of establishing a definitive diagnosis is usually stressed as the foundation of patient care. There is no question that the identification of a treatable organic mental syndrome is a priority consideration. However, as with all interventions, attention must be paid both to the anticipated benefits and to the possible harm associated with the action. Although diagnostic evaluations are generally considered to be low-risk procedures, the balance may be shifted somewhat in this population, raising significant ethical issues.

Modern medicine has witnessed the introduction of a variety of expensive tests, the use of which over time becomes customary. The incremental value of each additional procedure may go unexamined. Leaf (1984) defined the problem succinctly: "Decisions by physicians determine between 70 and 80 percent of all personal medical expenditures, but nothing in medical tradition, training, or experience gives them any expertise to act wisely in making these hard choices" (p. 718). For instance, ought a computed tomography (CT) scan of the brain be performed on every patient demonstrating a deterioration of cognitive function? In this as in every case the potential for obtaining important information must be weighed against the cost. Because the risk of physical injury is small for this procedure, the therapeutic advantage is seen to favor performing the test whatever the likelihood of producing a useful finding (Task Force sponsored by the National Institute on Aging 1980). However, the aggregate price to society for making a CT scan routine may indeed be quite large and may necessitate funding cutbacks in other areas. The physician is then torn between a clinical duty to the patient and a fiscal responsibility to society. For an expensive, low-yield procedure, the interest of society at large may outweigh the needs of individual patients. Some argue that the actual financial cost ought to take precedence over the hypothetically useful results of a diagnostic procedure. If this principle were accepted, then the components of a standard dementia evaluation would be dictated jointly by the salient clinical issues and by the competing concerns of interested third parties. This conflict will inevitably intensify in the current climate of diagnosis-related groups (DRGs) (Griffin and Thomasma 1983).

Truth-Telling

The dilemma of whether or not to reveal a catastrophic diagnosis has long plagued the medical profession. Both conventional wisdom and common practice have evolved over the years from a policy of deception to one of disclosure. Worcester (1935) advised his colleagues that a physician finding an asymptomatic intestinal tumor in an aged patient should not "mention his discovery. The patient will not live so long or happily if told of it" (p. 14). Worcester quoted Oliver Wendell Holmes in support of this position: "It is no kindness for science to reveal what Nature is kindly concealing" (p. 14). The argument is essentially utilitarian: more good is served by keeping the diagnosis a secret than by divulging it to the unsuspecting patient. Further, if confiding a horrifying diagnosis causes immediate psychological injury, then the physician is specifically enjoined from doing so by the ethical principle of *primum no nocere* (first do no harm). For generations, physicians have routinely avoided telling their patients of a fatal illness in the sincere belief that it was in their patients' best interest not to know.

For a number of reasons, the situation has changed radically in the last 20 years. It has become increasingly accepted that lying is a prima facie wrong and that physicians are not exempt from the moral duty to tell the truth (Bok 1978). This position implies that the injury to the patient's moral integrity perpetrated by lying takes precedence over any apparent advantage achieved by the falsehood. Others have defended truthfulness by its utility, by questioning whether there is much to be gained by lying about a diagnosis anyway. Empirical evidence seems to indicate that patients in general want to be told their diagnosis and may on some level already know the truth (Katz 1984). There are also the benefits accrued to patients who can use the facts about their conditions to make informed life plans. It has become clear that concealment tends to sabotage the very foundation of the doctor-patient relationship and society's trust of health professionals. Loss of belief in physician honesty would be detrimental to patient care. Finally, as psychiatrists we must be alert to the extent to which avoidance of truth-telling represents a countertransference reaction to an uncomfortable task. The legally prudent practice is for the physician to share with the patient the diagnosis and its significance unless specifically asked not to do so.

Recognizing that doctors should and do disclose grave diagnoses, are any modifications indicated for the patient with an organic mental syndrome? It is apparent that delirious patients should not be immediately presented with cognitive material that is impossible for them to assimilate. A delay until the patient's sensorium has cleared seems appropriate. However, the patient with dementia raises serious ethical difficulties. The fragility of ego defenses in dementia has been well described (MacKinnon and Michels 1971). When organic patients are forced to contend with cognitive tasks they cannot perform, they may respond with agitation, panic, and expansion of their deficits. This response is termed a *catastrophic reaction*. These patients may be overwhelmed by being told of a diagnosis of Alzheimer's disease, or cancer, or some other dread illness. The preceding discussion of honesty presupposed a fully competent adult for whom the risk of psychiatric decompensation is remote. Patients with dementia are least able to cope and are generally deemed in need of protection. "The welfare of the patient should be the paramount consideration in determining just how much should be told, when, and by whom" (Gordon 1984, p. 90).

Thus if a physician has the well-substantiated conviction that informing the patient of the diagnosis of Alzheimer's disease would precipitate serious deterioration, the physician is justified in withholding that information as part of "therapeutic privilege." However, the physician has the moral obligation to confide the diagnosis when and if it is safe to do so, assuming no specific patient instruction prohibiting disclosure. Substituting a euphemism represents a partial solution, which may begin a process of communication with some apprehensive patients.

Treatment Concerns

Consent

The overriding importance of consent is widely recognized (Ramsey 1970). The ethical priority ascribed to consent derives from the natural right of human beings to freedom and liberty. Autonomy signifies this concept of self-determination that is a necessary attribute for the full status of personhood. In a medical context, autonomous persons retain the right to information about their condition and the right to accept or refuse treatment. Another strongly held positive value is beneficence, which expresses the Hippocratic tradition of altruistic service. Doing good by helping others is a potent ethical justification for intrusive action. The model for medical paternalism is the caring parent who nurtures and protects a child without waiting for permission. Conflicts arise from disagreements over what the physician believes the patient needs and what the patient actually claims to want (Brody 1980).

The commonly held view is that patient autonomy takes precedence over physician beneficence, even if that results in a patient declining to consent to lifesaving treatment. This moral rule applies except when autonomy is compromised. Autonomy presupposes a mentally competent moral agent. Incompetency negates autonomy and deprives the individual of free choice. Under these circumstances, beneficent intervention is an appropriate infringement on impaired self-determination. From a clinical perspective, the critical concerns of the psychiatrist are the diagnosis and treatment of conditions affecting mentation, including the organic mental syndromes. The extent of any cognitive deficits will be delineated during that process. The decision as to whether that particular degree of impairment constitutes incompetency is left to the courts. But the question of where to define the border of mental competence is a matter of ethics and social policy (Fredman 1981; Roth et al. 1977).

The standard for competency must be finely tuned to balance society's dual desires to ensure personal freedom and to protect human life. The problem is where exactly to draw the line between allowing organically impaired patients to make their own medical decisions and giving that responsibility to someone else. Commentators have voiced opinions ranging from an extreme libertarian position, which holds that patients need only evidence a choice or voice assent in order for their wishes to be obeyed, to those biased in favor of permitting beneficent action by physicians.

Abernethy (1984) proposed that "the standard for finding a patient not competent to refuse treatment should be no less than generalized incompetence, including clear evidence that a patient is uninformable on emotionally neutral issues and cognitively incapable of making ordinary decisions on matters unrelated to the crisis at hand"

(p. 53). This test would seem to require that the patient with an organic mental syndrome be unable to function in activities of daily living in order to establish incompetence. Its application would seem to imply that most demented patients could not, for example, be compelled to have a gangrenous foot amputated. Patient rights organizations and some court decisions have vigorously supported this broad definition of competence, to the frustration of many physicians.

Other standards demand that the patient show an actual understanding of relevant medical information or be able to base a conclusion on logical reasoning. Drane (1984) advocated a test that requires an appreciation of the nature and consequences of the decision, consistent with a mental capacity that is technical and personal, cognitive and affective, and subjectively critical and rational. Although these standards facilitate beneficent action by physicians, they may deprive persons of their autonomy because of deviant life-styles or selective incapacities.

Culver et al. (1980) and Drane (1984) advised a sliding scale such that a more stringent test of competency would be in force for critical medical decisions. Although this approach would tend to allow paternalistic action in urgent situations, it seems inconsistent to change the rules according to the gravity of the decision. Eventually the burden to prove competency falls on the patient rather than on the physician to prove incompetency (Eth 1985). Because of the enduring tension between patient autonomy and physician beneficence, no consensus has been reached on an ethical standard for determining competency to consent. Each patient with an organic mental syndrome presents with a unique array of pertinent clinical issues that must be analyzed with a sensitivity to intelligent and compassionate compromise.

Confidentiality and Family Involvement

Confidentiality has a long tradition in medicine. The Hippocratic Oath states: "Whatsoever things I see or hear in any attendance on the sick I will keep silent thereon, counting such things to be professional secrets." The enduring quality of this duty is apparent in the current *Principles of Medical Ethics*: "A physician shall safeguard patient confidences within the constraints of the law" (American Psychiatric Association 1985, p. 2). Confidentiality is no less important to the organically impaired patient, however complicated the issue may become.

The window of disclosure of patient information can be opened in three ways. Patients can consent to the release, the law may require the reporting of certain facts, and the therapist may have the duty to violate confidentiality in order to protect life. The usual method by which patient infomation is shared is through consent. The signing of a release form permits dissemination of material to a third party, often another physician. Ideally the person receiving the information will similarly hold it in confidence. Concern has been raised about the sanctity of data given to insurance companies. Potentially devastating consequences could ensue if, for instance, an employer were to learn of an employee's diagnosis of dementia.

The concept of implied consent has been applied to the practice of providing access to the medical record to all of the health care team. Hospitalized patients understand that their chart is available to nurses, physicians, technicians, students, and others involved in their treatment, all of whom are morally bound to respect the patient's confidentiality. It has been argued that psychiatric findings should be handled differently, perhaps even to the extent of separate psychiatric records. A problem may develop when a psychiatric consultation is requested by the treating physician. Under these circumstances, it is ambiguous whether the psychiatrist is an agent of the physician or owes primary allegiance to the patient (Engelhardt and McCullough

1979). At the start of the examination, the psychiatrist ought to inform the patient of the extent to which confidentiality can be honored. For example, if the patient is being evaluated for a transplant, then the psychiatrist should warn the patient that the patient's responses will be conveyed to the surgeon. The presence of an organic mental syndrome or other serious psychopathology could well be an exclusion criterion for the transplant protocol (Berenson and Grosser 1984).

The physician's moral duty to obey the law may justify a selective breach of confidentiality. There is the legal obligation to notify the health department of cases of certain communicable diseases. A recent development in some states is the passage of mandatory reporting laws for elder abuse (Kosberg 1982). As with child abuse reporting statutes, the therapist is compelled to violate confidentiality in cases of abusive injury to elderly patients. Psychiatrists will also need to document some confidential clinical data for the purpose of instituting civil commitment proceedings or in processing guardian or conservator actions. Under these circumstances, a patient's insistence on secrecy may be overruled to comply with the local regulations. An increasingly recognized priority is the duty to protect others or the so-called *Tarasoff* warning. If there is no alternative means to prevent serious harm, a therapist may be morally and legally bound to breach confidentiality to warn an intended victim of a threatened attack by a patient. However, because the range of possible options is so broad (e.g., a change in treatment strategy, civil commitment), this step is rarely necessary.

By far the most common way for problems with confidentiality to surface is in the context of contacts with the patient's family. Open discussion with family members forces the psychiatrist to reconcile the wish to maintain confidences with the clinical need to share information. Even in the first interview with an organically impaired patient, the psychiatrist may need to question reliable relatives to supplement or confirm the medical history. As a dementing illness progresses, the role of the caretaking family grows. The desirability of eliciting patient consent to include concerned family members is evident. The consent is best obtained in writing in the first session and flexibly extended throughout the entire treatment unless specifically withdrawn. Working with the family will also enhance their support, benefiting the patient.

Unfortunately, many patients will not cooperate with a psychiatrist's recommendation to involve the family in treatment. One study of older adults found that the most frequently reported moral problem concerned relationships with family members (Rybash et al. 1983). Many elderly persons resent the social changes that follow infirmity. Physical and mental incapacity is often associated with a role reversal such that the adult children come to provide care for their parents. This situation can be rife with conflict. The organically impaired patient may insist on strict secrecy as a way to feel more in control. The secret information can be unknown to the entire family or may be shared with some but not all family members (Karpel 1980).

Of course, certain facts confided to the psychiatrist may be private material of no great relevance to anyone else. But other information may be significant and confront the psychiatrist with the uncomfortable role of secret-holder. Karasu (1980) identified this dilemma: "each communication with the family [of less healthy patients] not only complicates the treatment but also raises serious ethical questions about breaches of confidentiality and whose interests the therapist is serving" (p. 1507). Physician loyalty lies with the patient's desire for secrecy, despite another family member's vital interest in discovering medical information. For example, the psychiatrist should respect the wish of the newly diagnosed patient with Huntington's disease not to share this diagnosis with the children, while attempting to work through the patient's psychological reaction to the illness.

As with the issue of consent, the psychiatrist seeks to preserve confidence and patient autonomy except in those situations where physician beneficence takes priority. When a patient's life is threatened, information disclosure is permissible and may be obligatory. After a patient's death, the restraints of confidentiality are eased and appropriate information may be divulged to family members (Eth 1983).

Institutional and Community Care Constraints

A majority of the elderly and of the persons with organic mental syndromes live in the community. About half of the aged in the community tend to be "relatively satisfied with their lot and managing adequately, while nearly all of the chronic brain syndrome group were dissatisfied or managing poorly" (Fisch et al. 1968, p. 742). As long as the organic mental syndrome does not cause offensive behavior, social integration can persist despite objective evidence of intellectual decline. Retaining the freedom and dignity of noninstitutional living is highly desirable. However, employees suffering from organic mental syndromes may perform poorly; for example, pilots with dementia may have an increased frequency of accidents, and physicians with cognitive deficits may harm their patients.

Psychiatrists occasionally come into contact with a colleague who demonstrates noticeable organicity. In the ensuing moral dilemma, "special consideration should be given to those psychiatrists who, because of mental illness, jeopardize the welfare of their patients and their own reputations and practices. It is ethical, even encouraged, for another psychiatrist to intercede in such situations" (American Psychiatric Association 1985, p. 4). Although intervention is encouraged, it is not clear what form the intervention should take. For instance, what should a psychiatrist do on noticing that a colleague seems disoriented in an informal gathering or conspicuously confused at a meeting, or when discussing a patient referral manifests major memory deficits? Psychiatric societies and licensing boards rarely receive complaints from psychiatrists about physicians who may be manifesting signs of organicity. The opportunities for support and supervision available to impaired physicians are of benefit only to those accepting these services. Compassionate referral mechanisms are needed to assist colleagues and to protect patients.

Another unquestionably difficult decision is to refer a patient or place a relative with an organic mental syndrome into an institution offering long-term care. Although the intention is to secure appropriate treatment, the result may be iatrogenic morbidity and mortality for the more than one million Americans in nursing homes. Nursing homes have been characterized as the halfway house between society and the cemetery. One-third of those entering a nursing home die in the first year, many succumbing to "transfer mortality" (Butler and Lewis 1977). Residents who survive begin to experience the impact of institutionalization. The need to surrender self-determination to obtain total care carries with it a corresponding erosion of autonomy. The seemingly arbitrary institutional rules and loss of privacy combine to produce feelings of frustration, powerlessness, hopelessness, and lowered self-confidence and self-esteem (Mercer 1982). Family visits steadily decline as relatives contend with their own reactions of anger and guilt. Eventually depression and despair emerge, along with a learned helplessness as the nursing home patients' cognitive and emotional deficits render them unable to appreciate any effect of their actions. This deterioration in mental functioning and emotional responsiveness is the first "psychological" death (Butler 1984). Within three years, more than 70 percent of the residents experience the second and final physical death.

Two-thirds of nursing home residents exhibit some form of behavioral disturbance, frequently related to their cognitive impairment. In addition, many demented patients also develop secondary psychiatric disorders. These frequently treatable conditions, including major depression, may be entirely overlooked while attention is focused on the disruptive behaviors that interfere with institutional routine (Rovner and Rabins 1985). Concern has been expressed about the physician's role in overtranquilization of unruly nursing home residents (Waxman et al. 1985). Consultant psychiatrists, who may be in the employ of the institution, are often called on to medicate "agitated" patients. Psychiatrists must be alert to the possible sacrifice of the patient's interests in order to facilitate the efficient operation of the institution. Psychiatrists ought not to intervene with the sole intention of suppressing annoying behavior and lessening appropriate demands on staff time. Similarly at issue is the use of behavior modification to ensure patient conformity to nursing home rules. These techniques may be applied without the patient's consent in a milieu where the staff has full control of all reinforcers (Steuer 1982).

The prevailing conditions of most institutional placements confer an ethical agenda on the psychiatric profession. Psychiatrists are morally bound to ensure that each patient with an organic mental syndrome in the community obtains a multidimensional assessment, including activities of daily living, to prevent premature confinement (Skigen and Solomon 1978). If the ethical preference for outpatient treatment is unworkable, then other community alternatives should be considered first. The guiding principle is that the patient is to remain in the least restrictive environment for as long as possible to maximize autonomy and to avoid the perils of institutionalization. Adult day-care, home health service, or congregate housing may represent viable options for particular patients (Szekais 1985). Some have argued that social and political activism is a moral imperative for physicians seeking to improve patient care in long-term facilities (Cassel and Jameton 1981). Certainly, neglect of this major public health problem is a moral wrong.

Terminal Care

Certain of the organic mental syndromes, especially primary degenerative dementia, can be progressive and severely incapacitating. Depending on other medical factors, these patients may enter a terminal phase, the treatment of which is beset by ethical controversy. Consider the following case history (Veatch 1976): Mr. B, a 79-year-old Alzheimer's patient, was transferred from a nursing home to a hospital to replace the battery in his cardiac pacemaker. His wife refused permission for the surgery complaining to the effect: "What has he got to live for? Nothing! He knows nothing, he has no memory whatsoever. He is turning into a vegetable. Isn't death better?"

An analysis of the issues in this case depends on clarifying the moral distinction between intended termination of a patient's life and withholding treatment. The death of a human being brought about on purpose as part of the medical care is euthanasia (Working Party 1982). Although withholding treatment has been labeled "passive euthanasia," that term is fundamentally misleading. There are clear differences in intent, in cause of death, in the underlying nature of commission and omission, and in the legal ramifications. Developing a plan of no treatment is congruent with the role of physician, while instituting a lethal treatment plan is not. Thus in theory a decision to forego battery replacement may be ethical, whereas a fatal injection of potassium would not be. But other factors relevant to Mr. B must be considered as well. Death is the inevitable end point of life. Everyone will die. Does this fact signify that death is "natural" and "not the enemy" (Landau and Gustafson 1984)? Reasoning that the existence of X implies that X ought to be or that X is good is an example of the naturalistic fallacy (Frankena 1973). Nonetheless, there is a growing tendency to perceive benefit to the individual and society in the rapid demise of old, sick patients. The corollary is that it may be inappropriate for a physician to provide expensive treatment to the aged and intellectually deteriorated (Gilson 1985). For instance, the variable of mental state was significantly associated with the decision not to treat fever in an extended-care facility (Brown and Thompson 1979).

It has been advocated that "severely and irreversibly demented patients be given only the care needed to make them comfortable" (Wanzer et al. 1984). Thus it is deemed ethically permissible to withhold artificially administered nutrition and the usual medical treatment of intercurrent illness. Although that may be so in particular cases, there is a danger in premature generalization to the entire class of severely and irreversibly demented patients. In an era of scarce resources, we may be forced to ask if expenditures on dying patients are disproportionate, unreasonable, or unjust (Bayer et al. 1983). Various US courts have considered requests to reduce the level of care for organically impaired patients. In the absence of laws and precedents to guide their decisions, judges rely on their perception of society's wisdom (Jonsen 1984). In 1978, a Massachusetts Appeals Court upheld the validity of a no code order for a 67-year-old widow with advanced Alzheimer's disease (Matter of Dinnerstein). The justices ruled that death is a process with which physicians are not obligated to interfere. By the same reasoning, the Massachusetts Supreme Court held in 1979 that a 78-year-old person suffering from dementia and renal failure need not be dialyzed (Matter of Spring). For patients in permanent coma or persistent vegetative states, decisions have been fairly consistent in approving the physician's and family's desire to discontinue active treatment efforts (Beresford 1984).

Several justices have relied on a document produced by the President's Commission for the Study of Ethical Problems in Medicine and Biomedical and Behavioral Research (1983). This position paper proposed a revision of the traditional concept of ordinary and extraordinary means of care. Instead it distinguished proportionate treatment, in which the benefits to the patient outweigh the burdens, from disproportionate treatment, where the opposite occurs. Hence, the sophistication of the treatment is irrelevant; the focus is on its effectiveness to the patient, as a function of the prognosis and the associated risks of the procedure. For a patient with advanced dementia, a pacemaker battery replacement may be disproportionate care, whereas for another patient a heart transplant might not be. For at least one ethics commentator, all medical interventions for patients in irreversible coma are disproportionate because there can be no benefit to a body lacking the capacity to appreciate (Jonsen 1984).

The most conspicuous ethical quandry in the treatment of terminal organic mental syndrome patients is whether it is morally acceptable to discontinue fluids and nutritional support. When the spoon-feeding of an aged patient with dementia becomes impossible, the choices are tube-feeding or allowing the patient to die from dehydration (Bexell et al. 1980). A study of about 100 geriatric patients in chronic care for dementia found that "infusions and tube-feeding prescribed in such cases were given not for the patient's benefit but to relieve anxiety in care workers and relatives. Permitting the patient a natural, painless death from water deficiency may be preferable to prolonging pain and discomfort by intervening" (Norberg et al. 1980, p. 378). However, the "anxiety" generated by watching a patient starve to death cannot be easily dismissed. Nourishment intuitively seems rather more like a basic necessity of life than a medical treatment. As such it falls within that minimum level of care that any person has a right to expect from society. Our dignity as moral agents commands us to provide at least that much to a fellow human being (Meyers 1985). As physicians, we are held to a higher moral standard: "to cure sometimes, to relieve occasionally, to comfort always" (Siegler and Weisbard 1985, p. 130). By ordering the removal of food and water, isn't the physician causing the patient's death, regardless of the underlying medical illness?

A dispassionate assessment of these conflicting sentiments finds little room for compromise. Yet a preponderance of the evidence appears to be accumulating in support of one of the dichotomous positions. It is clear that nutrition is a basic necessity of life, but so is oxygen. Mechanical ventilation is recognized as a medical procedure and serves an analogous purpose. If that is so, we should accept the statement that "physicians should administer nutritional support according to the same guidelines they follow in judging the propriety of other forms of medical treatment for a particular patient" (Dresser and Boisaubin 1985, p. 122). The critical issue then becomes whether the benefits of this treatment outweigh the burdens. It is reasonable, although emotionally distressing, to conclude that "tube feedings are not indicated when the life-threatening medical problems are irreversible, the quality of life is poor, and the family agrees that the appropriate goal is to provide comfort rather than deliver calories or try to prolong life" (Lo and Dornbrand 1984, p. 403). That is how the New Jersey Supreme Court ruled in a case involving the removal of a feeding nasogastric tube from a severely organic 84-year-old woman. For a terminally ill patient, the court found that administering food and fluid is no different from other procedures, and that there is no legal distinction between agreeing not to start a particular treatment and agreeing to terminate the treatment once it has begun (Paris and Rearden 1985).

Consistent with the themes developed in this and the consent sections, physicians have a duty to respect patients' autonomy over their own bodies. Clearly, the rule of beneficence precludes a request to kill a patient. But a demand to terminate treatment is a morally legitimate request, which ought to be validated when the benefits of the treatments are disproportionate to burdens (Dyck 1984). Mrs. B's surgeon petitioned for a court order. The court named the hospital director as guardian, authorizing the hospital to perform whatever medical and surgical procedures were necessary to protect or to sustain health and life. That case was adjudicated in 1973 at a time of enthusiasm for medical progress and trust in the infallibility of physicians. The ability to create life-sustaining biomedical technology does not automatically confer the wisdom to employ the devices appropriately. That wisdom depends as much on ethical sensitivity as it does on scientific sophistication and clinical expertise. We realize today that we have come far in these matters, but still have much further to go.

Countertransference

Psychiatric work with organically impaired patients is often perceived as difficult or unpleasant, which may contribute to the relative unpopularity of psychogeriatrics as a subspecialty. Although this patient population does tend to have more incapacitating illnesses and to be less affluent, it offers abundant diagnostic and therapeutic challenges. "Unrecognized emotional factors," countertransference reactions (Bibring 1956) underlying ethical problems associated with the care of the elderly, and prejudice may be the sources of the discomfort for some physicians.

According to Cassel and Jameton (1981), Alzheimer's patients become undesirable when their deteriorated cognitive function changes the conventional doctor-patient interaction. Therapeutic hopelessness is captured in the designation of "veterinary medicine" applied to the care of demented patients. This book attests to the fact that the organic mental syndromes are fundamentally similar to other disease categories. Even dementia of the Alzheimer type resembles many chronic illnesses where the emphasis of treatment is on symptom management and palliative care rather than cure. The value judgment is indefensible that patients with progressive dementia or those who are near death do not deserve the time investment required for psychiatric treatment. "A physician shall be dedicated to providing competent medical service with compassion and respect for human dignity" (American Psychiatric Association 1985, p. 2).

It is useful to consider the sources of the physician's emotional needs and conflicts as expressed in work with organically impaired patients. Indeed, such patients have diminished restitutive capacity, but physicians can be inspired by their rescue fantasies. The admonishment of "what do you expect in your condition?" is inappropriate; it may explain why treatable causes of dementia are routinely missed (Butler 1984). The exposure of medical students to positive psychogeriatric role models and satisfying experiences early in their education (Woolliscroft et al. 1984) is bound to contribute to the eradication of this countertherapeutic stance, to the benefit of physician and patient alike.

Research Concerns

Vulnerability to Selection

The importance of clinical research in the organic mental syndromes is obvious: "If research is not carried out then increase in knowledge will be slow and sporadic, to the detriment of care of the patient" (Denham 1984, p. 322). Although there is agreement on the need for research on dementia, there is no ethical consensus how best to perform it (Ratzan 1980). As a function of their cognitive deficits and age, these patients, especially if they reside in institutions, have diminished capacity for informed consent. The frequently cited example of exploitation of the uninformed elderly is the Jewish Chronic Disease Hospital Study, in which live cancer cells were injected into disabled patients without their knowledge. The investigators' defense was that since the risk was felt to be low, a full explanation of the study would frighten the patients unnecessarily (Katz 1972). This project produced no valuable scientific findings, but did alert the profession and the public to the dangers of unbridled research.

Because patients with organic mental syndromes are uniquely qualified to participate in studies of these conditions, there is a legitimately compelling reason to include them in research activities. Further, since those with more serious disease tend to cluster in institutions, they will be overrepresented without implying bias. However, there are other factors that render these patients more vulnerable to prejudicial selection. It must be remembered that regardless of how important the research endeavor may be, the patient has no moral duty to participate. Although it is certainly praiseworthy for the patient to volunteer, it is not blameworthy to decline or withdraw.

As mentioned previously, these patients are at risk for coercion, however well intended the investigator may be. They are less able to understand the nature of the experiment and to appreciate the possible dangers. They may have the self-perception of being powerless, especially if poorly educated, foreign born, or nonwhite. A general reluctance to offend authority figures by being noncompliant is also prevalent among these patients, particularly those in institutions. They are highly susceptible to inadvertent exploitation, constituting a ready pool of available subjects whose environment and diet can be easily controlled and who can be conveniently studied.

There is also the incentive of significantly better care for those in a study. This problem was a source of major ethical accusations against the Willowbrook hepatitis investigation involving retarded children (Rothman 1982). A similar issue is the perceived threat of a loss of medical care for refusal to cooperate with research. Seriously ill patients may, rightly or wrongly, feel in jeopardy were they to decline to participate or withdraw from a study valued by the institution. The frightened, passive, or suggestible subject does not give full meaning to voluntary consent.

A final issue concerns the patients' motivation to volunteer for research: Is it the altruistic desire to derive a measure of personal satisfaction by helping others? Or is it the desire to prove themselves still important and needed, participation in research appearing the sole remaining avenue to prove their present worth?

Participation Versus Protection

The inevitable catch-22 predicament for those studying the organic mental syndromes is that conducting research using demented patients is objectionable because they are not competent to consent, but performing it on competent subjects is impossible because they do not have dementia (Ratzan 1980). Resolving this bind by terminating research efforts dooms these disorders to the status of scientific orphans. No further progress will be made, and the care of future patients will suffer. The psychiatrist investigator must attempt to balance the need to recruit suitable subjects with the obligation to guard against inappropriate inclusion. To err on the side of paternalistic overprotection stigmatizes the demented as incapable of an altruistic contribution to medical progress. Erring by permitting unrestrained participation violates the physician's responsibility to ensure that no patient is unknowingly exposed to harm by being a research subject.

It is possible to distinguish two broad categories of research activities that have qualitatively different moral implications. The first category is often referred to as "therapeutic" research. In these studies there is the intent and reasonable probability of improving the health or well-being of the subject. These medically beneficial investigations may involve an experimental drug or procedure designed to augment the patient's treatment. It would seem counterproductive to deny an incompetent, organic mental syndrome patient the opportunity to receive a potentially lifesaving therapy. However, there must also be some mechanism to allow for the patient's representative to consider the alternatives before deciding to offer voluntary informed consent on behalf of the patient. Fortunately, court-appointed representatives may be empowered to permit patient participation in therapeutic research.

The issue of the entry of dementia patients into therapeutic research protocols may become complicated by the study design. For instance, the comparison of a placebo control group to patients receiving an active agent is ethical only when there is no established or effective treatment to offer. Similarly the ethical use of randomized trials requires the new treatment to be considered comparable to the standard treatment. It is unethical to withhold treatment for the purpose of research where a safe and efficacious treatment is readily available.

The second category of research, the nontherapeutic type, is ethically problematic for patients with organic mental syndromes. These studies have no direct medical benefits for the subject and are performed principally to advance knowledge in the field. They may be subdivided into three groups. First, studies that carry only minimal risk. Entry into these investigations affords the patient the opportunity to contribute to science without incurring harm. It seems unnecessarily overprotective to exclude patients with organic mental disorders who have consenting representatives.

Second, studies where the hazard of participating exceeds the threat of daily living, but presents essentially only minimal danger. Does the exposure of patients with organic mental syndromes to the real risk of harm, however slight, solely to benefit others exceed the bounds of ethical conduct? It would certainly be unethical to involve patients in this type of research if there were any reason to believe that nondemented persons could substitute, or if there were any reason to suspect that patients would not agree to participate if they were competent to consent. The more vexing situation is where there is evidence that the demented patient would have consented prior to the incapacitating illness. Ought we to deprive patients of the opportunity to enter a study because they are no longer able to voice their desire to participate? If, and only if, it can be established that the patient's former personal values are known to be altruistic, then it should be permissible to allow the representative to consent to the patient's inclusion in the study. This rule would not apply to children since their values are, by definition, still unformed.

Third, the final category of nontherapeutic research includes all of the studies that carry a greater than minor possibility of harm. These are frequently important investigations whose results depend on the assumption of significant risk by the subject. If the research protocol is approved by the local institutional review board, any competent individual can freely consent to be part of the study. A person may agree to face some degree of danger in order to further scientific knowledge. That decision must be made by the potential subject alone; not by a substitute. The right to protection of bodily integrity should not be compromised by a representative. Patients with organic mental syndrome who are incompetent cannot be included in dangerous nontherapeutic research, however damaging that may be to scientific progress.

Because of their peculiar vulnerability, research subjects with organic mental syndrome, especially those in institutions, are candidates for close ethical scrutiny (Reich 1978). The first and most critical intervention is to ensure that all patients who are no longer competent receive the watchful supervision of a patient representative. Accepting the consent of an incompetent patient is unethical. Whenever there is doubt regarding a patient's ability to authorize treatment or research, legal consultation should be solicited. There are other measures that may afford additional protection to patients with organic mental syndromes. The insitutional review board, which reviews all research protocols involving human subjects, can seek to include patients as full members and can implement procedures designed to safeguard patients recruited for research. It has been proposed that potential subjects be routinely screened for competence with a cognitive test (Denham and Jefferys 1972). Another suggestion involves the use of a two-stage consent form requiring the subject to demonstrate an understanding of the content of the consent form before being accepted into the study (Miller and Willner 1974). Some commentators have advocated the creation of consent monitors to guard against inappropriate persuasion or motivation (Eth and Eth 1981). The desirability for an impartial monitor is conspicuous in those cases where the treating physician is also the investigator (the so-called double agent dilemma). By analogy, institutionalized subjects may need an independent patient advocate to oversee the research process in that closed setting.

The preceding comments all would have the effect of imposing obstacles to conducting research. Research is already difficult to perform. The investigator must obtain institutional review board approval, secure funding, find suitable subjects, and seek their consent—all of which needs to be accomplished before the data can actually be collected (Ratzan 1981). Unfortunately, investigators are recognizing that the balance of forces has tilted away from participation and in favor of protection, and can be expected to shift even further. Within this ethically sensitive framework, there may still be some latitude for creative facilitation of research endeavors. One possibility is the pursuit of future consent (Schneiderman and Arras 1985). It may be conceivable to obtain a consent for a later experiment from a patient early in the course of a dementing illness. These patients would have competently agreed to be subjects at a distant time when they will no longer be competent (Kolata 1982). Although there are some problems with withdrawal of consent in this model, it is a promising and innovative approach. Closer collaboration of researchers and ethicists may help end the adversarial relationship between participation and protection.

Conclusion

Psychiatrists have a responsibility to recognize the vulnerabilities associated with the organic mental syndromes. These conditions affect the patient's moral integrity as well as cognitive function. Special precautions must be assumed by the psychiatrist to ensure the adequacy of informed consent and to protect patients from the hazards of institutionalization and the risks of nontherapeutic research. Clinical work with these patients is often difficult; however, the capacity of these patients for improved function and enhanced quality of life confers a priority for psychiatrists to become actively involved in this field.

References

Section 11
Organic Mental Syndromes

Abel JG, Sellers EM, Naranjo CA, et al: Inter- and intrasubject variation in diazepam free fraction. Clin Pharmacol Ther 26:247–255, 1980

Abernethy V: Compassion, control, and decisions about competency. Am J Psychiatry 141:53–58, 1984

Abrams R: Technique of electroconvulsive therapy, in Electroconvulsive Therapy: Biological Foundations and Clinical Applications. Edited by Abrams R, Essman WB. New York, Spectrum Publications, 1982

Abshagen U, Rennekamp H, Luszpinski G: Disposition kinetics of spironolactone in hepatic failure and single doses and prolonged treatment. Eur J Clin Pharmacol 11:169–176, 1977

Adams HP, Kassell NF, Mazuz H: The patient with transient ischemic attacks: is this the time for a new therapeutic approach? Stroke 15:371–375, 1984

Adams RD, Victor M: Principles of Neurology, New York, McGraw-Hill, 1977

Adams RD, Victor M: Principles of Neurology, 2nd ed. New York, McGraw-Hill, 1981

Adams RD, Victor M: Principles of Neurology, 3rd ed. New York, McGraw-Hill, 1985

Adams RO, Foley JM: The neurological disorder associated with liver disease. Res Publ Assoc Res Nerv Ment Dis 32:198–237, 1953

Adler S: Methyldopa-induced decrease in mental activity. JAMA 230:1428–1429, 1974

Adolfsson R, Aquilonius SM, Gottfries CG: Substitution therapy with L-dopa and dopamine agonist in dementia disorders of Alzheimer type. The 11th International Congress of Gerontology, Tokyo, 1978

Adolfsson R, Gottfries CG, Roos BE: Changes in the brain catecholamines in patients with dementia of Alzheimer type. Br J Psychiatry 135:216–223, 1979

Adolfsson R, Gottfries CG, Oreland L, et al: Increased activity of brain and platelet monoamine oxidase activity in dementia of Alzheimer type. Life Sci 27:1029–1034, 1980

Adolfsson R, Brane G, Bucht G, et al: A double-blind study with levodopa in dementia of Alzheimer's type, in Alzheimer's Disease: A Report of Progress (Aging, vol 19). Edited by Corkin S, Davis KL, Growdon JH, et al. New York, Raven Press, 1982

Agid Y, Ruberg M, Dubois B, et al: Biochemical substrates of mental disturbances in Parkinson's disease, in Advances in Neurology, vol 40. Edited by Hassler RG, Christ JF. New York, Raven Press, 1984

Agle DP, Baum GL: Psychological aspects of COPD. Med Clin North Am 61:749–758, 1977

Agle DP, Baum GL, Chester EH, et al: Multidiscipline treatment of chronic pulmonary insufficiency: 1. Psychologic aspects of rehabilitation. Psychosom Med 35:41–49, 1973

Agnoli A, Ruggieri S, Meco G, et al: An appraisal of the problem of dementia in Parkinson's disease, in Advances in Neurology, vol 40. Edited by Hassler RG, Christ JF. New York, Raven Press, 1984

Aherwadker SJ, Eferdigil MC, Coulshed MN: Chlorpromazine therapy and associated acute disturbances of cardiac rhythm. Br Heart J 36:1251–1252, 1964

Alarcon-Segovia D, Wakim KG, Worthington JW, et al: Clinical and experimental studies on the hydralazine syndrome and its relationship to systemic lupus erythematosus. Medicine 46:1–33, 1967

Albert M: Assessment of cognitive function in the elderly. Psychosomatics 25:310–317, 1984

Alexander CS: Cardiotoxic effects of phenothiazines and related drugs. Circulation 38:1014–1015, 1968

Alexander HE, McCarty K, Giffen MB: Hypotension and cardiopulmonary arrest associated with concurrent haloperidol and propranolol therapy. JAMA 252:87–88, 1984

Alexander MP, Stuss DT, Benson DF: Capgras syndrome: a reduplicative phenomenon. Neurology 29:334–339, 1979

Alexopoulos GS, Young RC, Haycox JA, et al: DST in geriatric depression and dementia (abstract), in New Research Abstracts. Washington, DC, American Psychiatric Association, 1984a

Alexopoulos GS, Lieberman KW, Young RC: Platelet monoamine oxidase in degenerative dementia. Am J Psychiatry 141:97–99, 1984b

Alfrey AC, LeGendre GR, Kaehny WD: The dialysis encephalopathy syndrome. N Engl J Med 294:184–188, 1976

Alpert E, Isselbacher KJ: Tumors of the liver, in Harrison's Principles of Internal Medicine, 10th ed. Edited by Petersdorf RG, Adams RD, Braunwald E, et al. New York, McGraw-Hill, 1983

Altshuler KZ, Sarlin MB: Deafness and schizophrenia: a family study, in Family and Mental Health Problems in a Deaf Population. Edited by Rainer JD, Altshuler KZ, Kallmann FJ, et al. New York, Columbia University Press, 1963

Amdisen A: Serum level monitoring and clinical pharmacokinetics of lithium. Clin Pharmacokinet 2:73–92, 1977

American Association of Retired Persons: A profile of older Americans. Washington, DC, American Association of Retired Persons, 1987

American Psychiatric Association: The Principles of Medical Ethics. Washington, DC, American Psychiatric Association, 1985

American Psychiatric Association: Diagnostic and Statistical Manual of Mental Disorders, 3rd ed, revised. Washington, DC, American Psychiatric Association, 1987

Andersen J, Aabro E, Gulmann N, et al: Anti-depressive treatment in Parkinson's disease: a controlled trial of the effect of nortriptyline in patients with Parkinson's disease treated with L-dopa. Acta Neurol Scand 62:210–219, 1980

Anderson LT, David R, Bonnet K: Passive avoidance learning in Lesch-Nyhan disease: effect of 1-desamino-8-arginine vasopressin. Life Sci 24:905–910, 1979

Anderson RJ, Schrier RW: Acute renal failure, in Harrison's Principles of Internal Medicine, 10th ed. Edited by Petersdorf RG, Adams RD, Braunwald E, et al. New York, McGraw-Hill, 1983

Angevine JB, Cotman CW: Principles of Neuroanatomy. New York, Oxford University Press, 1981

Angrist BM: Toxic manifestations of amphetamine. Psychiatric Annals 8:443–445, 1978

Angrist B, Gershon S: The phenomenology of experimentally-induced amphetamine psychosis. Biol Psychiatry 2:95–107, 1970

Angrist B, Lee HK, Gershon S: The antagonism of amphetamine-induced symptomatology by a neuroleptic. Am J Psychiatry 131:817–819, 1974

Angus WR, Romney DM: The effect of diazepam on patients' memory. J Clin Psychopharmacol 4:203–206, 1984

Appelbaum PS, Roth LS: Competency to consent to research: a psychiatric overview. Arch Gen Psychiatry 39:951–958, 1982

Arieff AJ, Buckingham WB: Fluctuating "acute dementia" due to emphysema with pulmonary insufficiency. Transactions of the American Neurological Association 95:203–205, 1970

Arieff AJ, Massey SG: Dialysis disequilibrium syndrome, in Clinical Aspects of Uremia. Edited by Massey SG, Sellers AL. Springfield, Ill, Charles C Thomas, 1976

Arnsten AFT: Behavioral effects of nalozone in animals and humans: potential for treatment of aging disorders, in Alzheimer's Disease: Advances in Basic Research and Therapies. Edited by Wurtman RJ, Corkin SH, Growdon JH. Cambridge, Mass, Center for Brain Sciences and Metabolism Charitable Trust, 1984

Austen FK, Charmichael MW, Adams RD: Neurologic manifestations of chronic pulmonary insufficiency. N Engl J Med 257:579–590, 1957

Ayd FJ Jr: Parenteral (IM/IV) droperidol for acutely disturbed behavior in psychotic and non-psychotic individuals. International Drug Therapy Newsletter 15:13–16, 1980

Baldessarini RJ: Chemotherapy in Psychiatry, revised. Cambridge, Mass, Harvard University Press, 1985

Balldin J, Gottfries CG, Carlsson I, et al: Dexamethasone suppression test and serum prolactin in dementia disorders. Br J Psychiatry 142:277–285, 1983

Ballenger JC, Post RM: Carbamazepine in manic-depressive illness: a new treatment. Am J Psychiatry 137:782–790, 1980

Ban TA, St. Jean A: The effects of phenothiazines on the electrocardiogram. Can Med Assoc J 91:537–540, 1964

Bankier RG: Psychosis associated with cycloserine. Can Med Assoc J 93:35–37, 1965

Barchas JD, Elliott GR, Berger PA, et al: The ultimate stigma: inadequate funding for research on mental illness and addictive disorders. Am J Psychiatry 142(suppl):6–7, 1985

Barclay J: Variations in amnesia with intravenous diazepam. Oral Surg 53:329–334, 1982

Barnes R, Veith R, Okimoto J, et al: Efficacy of antipsychotic medication in behaviorally disturbed dementia patients. Am J Psychiatry 139:1170–1174, 1982

Barnett HJM, Boughner DR, Taylor DW, et al: Further evidence relating initial-valve prolapse to cerebral ischemic events. N Engl J Med 302:139–144, 1980

Baron RA: Aggression, in Comprehensive Textbook of Psychiatry, 4th ed, vol 1. Edited by Kaplan HI, Sadock BJ. Baltimore, Williams and Wilkins, 1985

Barraclough B: Suicide and epilepsy, in Epilepsy and Psychiatry. Edited by Reynolds EH, Trimble MR. Edinburgh, Churchill Livingstone, 1981

Bartus RT: Physostigmine and recent memory: effects in young and aged non-human primates. Science 206:1087–1089, 1979

Bartus RT: Age-related memory loss and cholinergic dysfunction: possible directions based on animal models, in Strategies for the Development of an Effective Treatment for Senile Dementia. Edited by Crook T, Gershon S. New Canaan, Conn, Mark Powley Associates, 1981

Bartus RT, Johnson HR: Short-term memory in the rhesus monkey: disruption from the anticholinergic scopolamine. Pharmacol Biochem Behav 5:39–40, 1976

Bartus RT, Flemming DL, Johnson HR: Aging in the rhesus monkey: debilitating effects on short-term memory. J Gerontol 33:858–871, 1976

Bartus RT, Dean RL, Sherman KA, et al: Profound effects of combining choline and piracetam on memory. Neurobiol Aging 2:105–111, 1981

Bartus RT, Dean RL, Beer B, et al: The cholinergic hypothesis of geriatric memory dysfunction. Science 217:408–417, 1982

Bayer R, Callahan D, Fletcher J, et al: The care of the terminally ill: morality and economics. N Engl J Med 309:1490–1494, 1983

Bear D, Fedio P: Qualitative analysis of interictal behavior in temporal lobe epilepsy. Arch Neurol 34:454–467, 1977

Bear D, Freeman R, Schiff D, et al: Interictal behavior changes in patients with temporal lobe epilepsy, in American Psychiatric Association Annual Review, vol 4. Edited by Hales RE, Frances AJ. Washington, DC, American Psychiatric Press, 1985

Beardsley JV, Puletti F: Personality (MMPI) and cognitive (WAIS) changes after levodopa treatment: occurrence in patients with Parkinson's disease. Arch Neurol 25:145–150, 1971

Beecher HK: Ethics and clinical research. N Engl J Med 274:1354–1360, 1966

Beethoven L Von: Heiligenstadt Document. Hamburg, Stadtbibliothek, 1802

Bell DS: The experimental reproduction of amphetamine psychosis. Arch Gen Psychiatry 29:35–40, 1973

Bendz H: Kidney function in lithium-treated patients: a literature survey. Acta Psychiatr Scand 68:303–324, 1983

Bengtson VL: Ethnicity and perceptions of aging, in Aging: A Challenge to Science and Society, vol 3. Edited by Birren JE, Munnichs JMA, Thomal H, et al. New York, Oxford University Press, 1983

Bennet WM: Principles of drug therapy in patients with renal disease. West J Med 123:372–379, 1975

Bennet WM, Muther RS, Parker RA, et al: Drug therapy in renal failure: dosing guidelines for adults. Ann Intern Med 93:286–325, 1980

Bennett R, Hughes CRV, Bywaters EGL: Neuropsychiatric problems in systemic lupus erythematosus. Br Med J 4:342–343, 1972

Benson DF: Amnesia. South Med J 71:1221–1228, 1978

Benson DF: Aphasia, Alexia, and Agraphia. New York, Churchill Livingstone, 1979

Benson DF: Subcortical dementia: a clinical approach, in The Dementias, vol 38. Edited by Mayeux R, Rosen WG. New York, Raven Press, 1983

Benson DF: Parkinsonian dementia: cortical or subcortical?, in Advances in Neurology, vol 40. Edited by Hassler RG, Christ JF. New York, Raven Press, 1984

Benson DF, Blumer D (eds): Psychiatric Aspects of Neurologic Disease. New York, Grune & Stratton, 1975

Benson DF, Blumer D: Amnesia: a clinical approach to memory, in Psychiatric Aspects of Neurologic Disease. Edited by Benson DF, Blumer D. New York, Grune & Stratton, 1982

Benson DF, Geschwind N: Psychiatric conditions associated with focal lesions of the central nervous system, in American Handbook of Psychiatry, vol 4. Edited by Reiser M. New York, Basic Books, 1975

Benson DF, Marsden CD, Meadows JC: The amnesic syndrome of posterior cerebral artery occlusion. Acta Neurol Scand 50:133–145, 1974

Benson DF, Gardner H, Meadows JC: Reduplicative paramnesia. Neurology 26:147–151, 1976

Benson DF, Cummings JL, Tsai SY: Angular gyrus syndrome simulating Alzheimer's disease. Arch Neurol 39:616–620, 1982

Benton AI, Eslinger PJ, Damasio AR: Normative observations on neuropsychological test performances in old age. J Clin Neuropsychol 3:33–42, 1981

Berenson CK, Grosser BI: Total artificial heart implantation. Arch Gen Psychiatry 41:910–916, 1984

Beresford HR: Severe neurological impairment: legal aspects of decisions to reduce care. Ann Neurol 15:409–414, 1984

Beresin E: Delirium, in Inpatient Psychiatry: Diagnosis and Treatment. Edited by Sederer LI. Baltimore, Williams and Wilkins, 1983

Berger PA, Dunn MJ: Substance induced and substance use disorders, in Treatment of Mental Disorders. Edited by Greist JH, Jefferson JW, Spitzer RL. New York, Oxford University Press, 1982

Berger PA, Tinklenberg JR: Neuropeptides and senile dementia, in Strategies for the Development of an Effective Treatment for Senile Dementia. Edited by Crook T, Gershon S. New Canaan, Conn, Mark Powley Associates, 1981

Bergman I, Brane G, Gottfries CG, et al: Alaproclate: a pharmacokinetic and biochemical study in patients with dementia of Alzheimer type. Psychopharmacology 80:279–283, 1983

Bergman PJ: Cerebral blindness. Arch Neurol Psychiatry 78:568–584, 1957

Berrios GE, Brook P: Visual hallucinations and sensory delusions in the elderly. Br J Psychiatry 144:662–664, 1984

Bexell G, Norberg A, Norberg B: Ethical conflicts in long-term care of aged patients. Ethics in Science and Medicine 7:141–145, 1980

Bianchine JR: Drug therapy of parkinsonism. N Engl J Med 295:814–818, 1976

Bianchine JR: Drugs for Parkinson's disease, in The Pharmacological Basis of Therapeutics, 6th ed. Edited by Goodman Gilman A, Goodman LS, Gilman A. New York, Macmillan, 1980

Bibring GL: Psychiatry and medical practice in a general hospital. N Engl J Med 254:366–372, 1956

Bigger JT Jr, Giardinia EG, Perel JM, et al: Cardiac antiarrhythmic effect of imipramine hydrochloride. N Engl J Med 296:206–208, 1977

Bigger JT Jr, Kantor SJ, Glassman AH, et al: Cardiovascular side effects of antidepressant drugs, in Psychopharmacology: A Generation of Progress. Edited by Lipton MA, DiMascio A, Killian KF. New York, Raven Press, 1978

Binder LM: Biological Therapies in Psychiatry 7:26–27, 1984

Binder LM: Emotional problems after stroke. Stroke 15:174–177, 1984

Bishop ER Jr: Monosymptomatic hypochondriacal syndromes in dermatology. J Am Acad Dermatol 9:152–158, 1983

Bixler EO, Scharf MB, Soldatos CR, et al: Effects of hypnotic drugs on memory. Life Sci 25:1379–1388, 1979

Blaschke TF, Melmon KL: Antihypertensive agents and the drug therapy of hypertension, in The Pharmacological Basis of Therapeutics, 6th ed. Edited by Goodman Gilman A, Goodman LS, Gilman A. New York, Macmillan, 1980

Blass JP, Barclay LL: New developments in the diagnosis of the dementias. Drug Dev Res 5:39–58, 1985

Blass JP, Weksler ME: Toward an effective treatment of Alzheimer's disease. Ann Intern Med 98:251–252, 1983

Blass J, Reding MJ, Drachman D, et al: Cholinesterase inhibitors and opiate antagonists in patients with Alzheimer's disease. N Engl J Med 309:555–556, 1983

Blessed G, Tomlinson BE, Roth M: The association between quantitative measures of dementia and of senile change in the cerebral grey matter of elderly subjects. Br J Psychiatry 114:797–811, 1968

Block AJ, Castle JR, Keitt AS: Chronic oxygen therapy: treatment of COPD at sea level. Chest 65:279–288, 1974

Blumer D: Temporal lobe epilepsy and its psychiatric significance, in Psychiatric Aspects of Neurological Disease. Edited by Benson DF, Blumer D. New York, Grune & Stratton, 1975

Blumer D, Benson DF: Personality changes with frontal and temporal lobe lesions, in Psychiatric Aspects of Neurologic Disease. Edited by Benson DF, Blumer D. New York, Grune & Stratton, 1975

Bock JL, Cummings KC, Jatlow PI: Amoxapine overdose: a case report. Am J Psychiatry 139:1619–1620, 1982

Bok S: Lying: Moral Choice in Public and Private Life. New York, Pantheon, 1978

Boller F, Mizutani T, Roessmann U, et al: Parkinson disease, dementia, and Alzheimer disease: clinicopathological correlations. Ann Neurol 7:329–335, 1980

Bondareff W: Age and Alzheimer's disease. Lancet 1:447, 1983

Bondareff W, Mountjoy CQ: Subtypes of Alzheimer's disease. Presented at the Annual Meeting of the American Psychiatric Association. Dallas, 1985

Bondareff W, Mountjoy CQ, Roth M: Selective loss of neurones of adrenergic projection to cerebral cortex (nucleus locus coeruleus) in senile dementia. Lancet 1:782–783, 1981

Bornstein R, Menon D, York E, et al: Effects of venesection on cerebral function in chronic lung disease. Can J Neurol Sci 7:293–296, 1980

Boston Collaborative Drug Surveillance Program: Acute adverse reaction to prednisone in relation to dosage. Clin Pharmacol Ther 13:694–698, 1972

Bowen DM, Smith CB, White P, et al: Neurotransmitter-related enzymes and indices of hypoxia in senile dementia and other abiotrophies. Brain 99:459–496, 1976

Bowen DM, Spillane JA, Curzon G, et al: Accelerated aging or selective neuronal loss as an important cause of dementia. Lancet 1:11–14, 1979

Bowen DM, Benton S, Curzon G, et al: Biochemical changes in cortical brain biopsies and cerebrospinal fluid from demented patients including some with Alzheimer's disease (AD). International Society of Neurochemistry 8:339, 1981

Bowen FP, Kamienny RS, Burns MM, et al: Parkinsonism: effects of levodopa treatment on concept formation. Neurology 25:701–704, 1975

Bradley WG, Waluch V, Yadley RA, et al: Comparison of CT and MR in 400 patients with suspected disease of the brain and cervical spinal cord. Radiology 152:695–702, 1984

Brain WR, Adams RD: Epilogue: a guide to the classification and investigation of neurological disorders associated with neoplasms, in The Remote Effects of Cancer on the Nervous System, Contemporary Neurology Symposia, vol 1. Edited by Brain WR, Norris FH. New York, Grune & Stratton, 1965

Brain WR, Henson RA: Neurological syndromes associated with carcinoma. Lancet 2:971–975, 1958

Brain WR, Wilkinson M: Subacute cerebellar degeneration in patients with carcinoma, in The Remote Effects of Cancer on the Nervous System, Contemporary Neurology Symposia, vol 1. Edited by Brain WR, Norris FH. New York, Grune & Stratton, 1965

Branconnier RJ, Cole JO, Gardos G: ACTH 4-10 in the amelioration of neuropsychological symptomatology associated with senile organic brain syndrome. Psychopharmacol Bull 14:27–30, 1978

Brandt KD, Simmons L, Cohen AS: Cerebral disorders of vision in systemic lupus erythematosus. Ann Intern Med 83:163–169, 1975

Braunwald E: Heart failure, in Principles of Internal Medicine, 9th ed. Edited by Isselbacher KJ, Adams RD, Braunwald E, et al. New York, McGraw-Hill, 1980a

Braunwald E: Pharmacologic treatment of cardiovascular disorders, in Principles of Internal Medicine, 9th ed. Edited by Isselbacher KJ, Adams RD, Braunwald E, et al. New York, McGraw-Hill, 1980b

Brenner BM, Lazarus JM: Chronic renal failure: pathophysiologic and clinical considerations, in Harrison's Principles of Internal Medicine, 10th ed. Edited by Petersdorf RG, Adams RD, Braunwald E, et al. New York, McGraw-Hill, 1983

Briant RH, Reid JL, Dollery CT: Interaction between clonidine and desipramine in man. Br Med J 1:522–523, 1973

Brierley JB, Corsellis JAN, Hierons R, et al: Subacute encephalitis of later life: mainly affecting the limbic areas. Brain 83:357–368, 1960

Brinkman SD, Gershon S: Measurement of cholinergic drug effects on memory and Alzheimer's disease. Neurobiol Aging 4:139–145, 1983

British Medical Journal: Localisation of visual hallucinations. Br Med J 2:147–148, 1977

Brody DS: The patient's role in clinical decision-making. Ann Intern Med 93:718–722, 1980

Brown v Board of Education, 347 US 483, 74 S Ct 686, 98 L Ed 873 (1954)

Brown NK, Thompson DJ: Nontreatment of fever in extended care facilities. N Engl J Med 300:1246–1250, 1979

Brust JCM: Dementia and cerebrovascular disease, in The Dementias. Edited by Mayeux R, Rosen WG. New York, Raven Press, 1983

Brust JCM, Behrens MM: "Release hallucinations" as the major symptoms of posterior cerebral artery occlusion: a report of 2 cases. Ann Neurol 2:432–436, 1977

Bucht G, Wahlin A, Wentzel T, et al: Renal function and morphology in long-term lithium and combined lithium-neuroleptic treatment. Acta Med Scand 208:381–385, 1980

Burckhardt D, Raeder E, Mueller V, et al: Cardiovascular effects of tricyclic and tetracyclic antidepressants. JAMA 239:213–216, 1978

Burgess CD, Turner P, Wadsworth J: Cardiovascular responses to mianserin hydrochloride: a comparison with tricyclic antidepressant drugs. Br J Clin Pharmacol 5(suppl 1):215–285, 1978

Burgess CD, Hames TK, George CF: The electrocardiographic and anticholinergic effects of trazodone and imipramine in man. Eur J Clin Pharmacol 23:417–421, 1982

Burrows GD, Vohra J, Dumovic P, et al: Tricyclic antidepressant drugs and cardiac conduction. Prog Neuropsychopharmacol 1:329–334, 1977

Burrows GD, Davies B, Kincaid-Smith P: Unique tabular lesion after lithium. Lancet 1:1310, 1978

Burton K, Calne DB: Pharmacology of Parkinson's disease, in Neurologic Clinics, vol 2. Edited by Jankovic J. Philadelphia, WB Saunders, 1984

Buschke H: Selective reminding for analysis of memory and learning. Journal of Verbal Learning and Verbal Behavior 12:543–550, 1973

Busse EW: Therapy of mental illness in late life, in American Handbook of Psychiatry, 2nd ed, vol 7. Edited by Arieti S, Brodie HKH. New York, Basic Books, 1981

Butler RN: Old Age: Right to privacy and patient's right to know. Mt Sinai J Med (NY) 51:86–88, 1984

Butler RN, Lewis MI: Aging and Mental Health. St. Louis, CV Mosby, 1973

Butler RN, Lewis MI: Aging and Mental Health, 2nd ed. St Louis, CV Mosby, 1977

Byerley B, Gillin JC: Diagnosis and management of insomnia. Psychiatr Clin North Am 7:773–789, 1984

Cabral RJ, Scott DF: Effects of two desensitization techniques, biofeedback and relaxation, on intractable epilepsy: follow-up study. J Neurol Neurosurg Psychiatry 39:504–507, 1976

Caine ED: Pseudodementia. Arch Gen Psychiatry 38:1359–1364, 1981

Calne DB, Williams AC, Neophytides A, et al: Long-term treatment of parkinsonism with bromocriptine. Lancet 1:735–737, 1978

Campbell MA, Plachetka JR, Jackson JE, et al: Cimetidine decreases theophylline clearance. Ann Intern Med 95:68–69, 1981

Caplan LR: "Top of the basilar" syndrome. Neurology 30:72–79, 1980

Carlsson A: The impact of catecholamine research on medical science and practice, in Catecholamines: Basic and Clinical Frontiers. Edited by Usdin E, Kopin IJ, Barchas J. New York, Pergamon Press, 1979

Carlsson A: Aging and brain neurotransmitters, in Strategies for the Development of an Effective Treatment for Senile Dementia. Edited by Crook T, Gershon S. New Canaan, Conn, Mark Powley Associates, 1981

Carney MWP, Ravindran A, Lewis DS: Manic psychosis associated with procarbazine. Br Med J 284:82–83, 1982

Carpenter CB, Lazarus JM: Dialysis and transplantation in the treatment of renal failure, in Harrison's Principles of Internal Medicine, 10th ed. Edited by Petersdorf RG, Adams RD, Braunwald E, et al. New York, McGraw-Hill, 1983

Carr RE, Siegel IM: Visual Electrodiagnostic Testing. Baltimore, Williams and Wilkins, 1982

Cassel CR, Jameton AL: The elderly: an analysis of medical responsibility. Ann Intern Med 94:802–807, 1981

Cassem NH: Cardiovascular effects of antidepressants. J Clin Psychiatry 43:22–28, 1982

Castellani S, Giannini AJ, Adams PM: Physostigmine and haloperidol treatment of acute phencyclidine intoxication. Am J Psychiatry 139:508–510, 1982

Castillo-Ferrando JR, Garcia M, Carmona J: Digoxin levels and diazepam. Lancet 2:368, 1980

Catchlove RFH, Kafer ER: The effects of diazepam on respiration in patients with obstructive pulmonary disease. Anesthesiology 34:14–18, 1971

Celesia GG, Barr AN: Psychosis and other psychiatric manifestations of levodopa therapy. Arch Neurol 23:193–200, 1970

Celesia GG, Wanamaker WM: Psychiatric disturbances in Parkinson's disease. Diseases of the Nervous System 33:577–583, 1972

Charatan FB, Brierley JB: Mental disorders associated with primary lung carcinoma. Br Med J 1:765–768, 1956

Charles GA, Rush AJ: Dexamethasone suppression test in dementia (abstract). Presented at the New Research Section, 138th Annual Meeting, American Psychiatric Association. Dallas, 1985

Charness ME: Controversies in the medical management of stroke. West J Med 142:74–78, 1985

Charney DS, Heninger GR, Sternberg DE, et al: Presynaptic adrenergic receptor sensitivity in depression. Arch Gen Psychiatry 38:1334–1340, 1981a

Charney DS, Menkes DB, Heninger GR: Receptor sensitivity and the mechanism of action of antidepressant treatment. Arch Gen Psychiatry 38:1160–1180, 1981b

Chatton MF (ed): Handbook of Medical Treatment. Greenbrae, Calif, Jones Medical Publishing, 1979

Chen TS, Chen PS: Essential Hepatology. Boston, Butterworths, 1977

Chester EM, Agamanolis DP, Banker BQ, et al: Hypertensive encephalopathy: a clinicopathologic study of 20 cases. Neurology 28:928–939, 1978

Chien CP, Townsend EJ, Ross-Townsend A: Substance use and abuse among the aged, in Drug Use Among the Aged. Edited by Peterson DM. Spectrum Publications, 1979

Chouinard G, Pinard G, Prenoveau Y, et al: Alphamethyldopa-chlorpromazine interaction in schizophrenic patients. Current Therapy Research 15:60–72, 1973a

Chouinard G, Pinard G, Serrano M, et al: Potentiation of haloperidol by alpha methyldopa in the treatment of schizophrenic patients. Current Therapy Research 15:473–483, 1973b

Christie JE, Shering A, Ferguson J, et al: Physostigmine and arecoline: efforts of intravenous infusions in Alzheimer presenile dementia. Br J Psychiatry 138:46–50, 1981

Christodoulou GN, Malliara-Loulakaki S: Delusional misidentification syndromes and cerebral dysrhythmia. Psychiatr Clin 14:245–251, 1981

Clark EO: Evaluation of the elderly and their familes: clinical and ethical issues, in Geriatric Psychiatry: Ethical and Legal Issues. Edited by Stanley B. Washington, DC, American Psychiatric Press, 1985

Cobe GM: The family of the aged: issues in treatment. Psychiatric Annals 15:343–347, 1985

Coe FL: Proteinuria hematuria azotemia and oliguria, in Harrison's Principles of Internal Medicine, 10th ed. Edited by Petersdorf RG, Adams RD, Braunwald E, et al. New York, McGraw-Hill, 1983

Coffey CE, Ross DR, Ferren EL, et al: Treatment of the "on-off" phenomenon in parkinsonism with lithium carbonate. Ann Neurol 12:375–379, 1982

Coffey CE, Ross DR, Massey EW, et al: Dyskinesias associated with lithium therapy in parkinsonism. Clin Neuropharmacol 7:223–229, 1984

Cohen EL, Wurtman RJ: Brain acetyl choline: control by dietary choline. Science 191:561–562, 1976

Cohen GD: Mental health services and the elderly: needs and options. Am J Psychiatry 133:65–68, 1976

Cohen GD: Prospects for mental health and aging, in Handbook of Mental Health and Aging. Edited by Birren JE, Sloane RB. Englewood Cliffs, NJ, Prentice-Hall, 1980

Cohen GD: Toward an interface of mental and physical health phenomena in geriatrics: clinical findings and questions, in Aging 2000: Our Health Care Destiny, vol 1. Edited by Gaitz CM, Samorajski T. New York, Springer-Verlag, 1985

Cohn MA: Hypnotics and the control of breathing: a review. Br J Clin Pharmacol 16:2455–2505, 1983

Cole M, Turner A, Frank O, et al: Extraocular palsy and thiamine therapy in Wernicke's encephalopathy. Am J Clin Nutr 22:44–51, 1969

Collins RC, Al-Mondhiry H, Chernik NL, et al: Neurologic manifestations of intramuscular coagulation in patients with cancer. Neurology 25:795–806, 1975

Comfort A: Practice of Geriatric Psychiatry. New York, Elsevier, 1980

Conn HD: Asterixis in non-hepatic disorders. Am J Med 29:647–661, 1960

Connell PH: Amphetamine Psychosis (Maudsley Monographs No 5). London, Oxford University Press, 1958

Connors CK, Kramer R, Rothschild GH, et al: Treatment of young delinquent boys with diphenylhydantoin sodium and methylphenidate: a controlled comparison. Arch Gen Psychiatry 24:156–160, 1971

Cook GC, Mulligan R, Sherlock S: Controlled prospective trial of corticosteroid therapy in active chronic hepatitis. Q J Med 40:159–185, 1971

Cook P, Jones I: Cerebral vasodilators. N Engl J Med 305:1508–1513, 1560–1564, 1981

Coopen A, Biship ME, Bailey JE, et al: Renal function in lithium and non-lithium treated patients with affective disorders. Acta Psychiatr Scand 62:343–355, 1980

Cooper AF: Deafness, psychiatric illness, and the role of hearing loss in schizophrenia, in Hearing and Hearing Impairment. Edited by Bradford LJ, Hardy WG. New York, Grune & Stratton, 1979

Cooper AF, Porter R: Visual acuity and ocular pathology in the paranoid and affective psychosis of later life. J Psychosom Res 20:107–114, 1976

Cooper AF, Curry AR, Kay DWK, et al: Hearing loss in the paranoid and affective psychoses of the elderly. Lancet 2:851–854, 1974

Cooper B, Morgan HG: Epidemiological Psychiatry. Springfield, Ill, Charles C Thomas, 1973

Cooper G: The safety of fluoxetine—an update. Br J Psychiatry 153 (suppl. 3): 77–86, 1988

Coppen A, Abou-Saleh M, Milln P, et al: Dexamethasone suppression test in depression and other psychiatric illness. Br J Psychiatry 142:498–504, 1983

Corsellis JAN, Evans PH: The relation of stenosis of the extracranial cerebral arteries to mental disorder and cerebral degeneration in old age, in Proceedings of the Fifth International Congress of Neuropathology. The Hague, Netherlands, Mouton and Co, 1965

Corsellis JAN, Goldberg GJ, Norton AR: 'Limbic encephalitis' and its associations with carcinoma. Brain 91:481–496, 1968

Coughlan AK, Humphrey M: Pre-senile stroke: long-term outcome for patients and their families. Rheumatology Tindall 21:115–122, 1982

Coyle JT, Price DL, Delong MR: Alzheimer's disease: a disorder of cortical cholinergic innervation. Science 219:1184–1190, 1983

Crane GE: The psychiatric side effects of iproniazid. Am J Psychiatry 112:494–501, 1956

Cranson A, Flemenbaum A: Antagonism of cocaine highs by lithium. Am J Psychiatry 135:856–857, 1978

Crome P, Newman B: Fatal tricyclic antidepressant poisoning. J R Soc Med 72:649–653, 1979

Crook T: Central-nervous-system stimulants: appraisal of use in geropsychiatric patients. J Am Geriatr Soc 27:476–477, 1979

Crook T: Geriatric psychopathology: an overview of the ailments and current therapies. Drug Dev Res 5:5–23, 1985

Crook T, Ferris S, Sathananthan G, et al: The effect of methylphenidate on test performance in the cognitively impaired aged. Psychopharmacology 52:251–255, 1977

Cross AJ, Crow TJ, Johnson JA: Monoamine metabolism in senile dementia of Alzheimer type. J Neurol Sci 60:383–392, 1983

Crowe RR: Electroconvulsive therapy: a current perspective. N Engl J Med 311:163–167, 1984

Culver CM, Ferrell RB, Green RM: ECT and the special problem of informed consent. Am J Psychiatry 137:586–591, 1980

Cummings JL, Benson DF: Dementia: A Clinical Approach. Boston, Butterworths, 1983a

Cummings JL, Benson DF: Dementia: definition, prevalence, classification, and approach to diagnosis, in Dementia—A Clinical Approach. Edited by Cummings JL, Benson DF. Boston, Butterworths, 1983b

Cummings JL: Clinical Neuropsychiatry. New York, Grune & Stratton, 1985a

Cummings JL: Organic delusions: phenomenology, anatomical correlations, and review. Br J Psychiatry 146:184–197, 1985b

Cummings JL, Crittinger JW: Central dazzle: a thalamic syndrome. Arch Neurol 38:372–374, 1981

Cummings JL, Mendez MF: Secondary mania with focal cerebrovascular lesions. Am J Psychiatry 141:1084–1087, 1984

Cummings JL, Tomiyasu U, Read S, et al: Amnesia with hippocampal lesions after cardiopulmonary arrest. Neurology 34:679–681, 1984

Curry SH: Binding of psychotropic drugs to plasma protein and its influence on drug distribution, in Clinical Pharmacology in Psychiatry. Edited by Usdin E. New York, Elsevier-North Holland, 1981

Cutting J: Study of anosognosia. J Neurol Neurosurg Psychiatry 41:548–555, 1978

Dale PG: Lithium therapy in aggressive mentally subnormal patients. Br J Psychiatry 137:469–474, 1980

Dalen P, Steg G: Lithium and levodopa in parkinsonism. Lancet 1:936–937, 1973

Dam M, Kristensen CB, Hansen BS, et al: Interaction between carbamazepine and propoxyphene in man. Acta Neurol Scand 56:603–607, 1977

Damasio AR, Lobo-Antunes J, Macedo C: Psychiatric aspects in parkinsonism treated with L-dopa. J Neurol Neurosurg Psychiatry 34:502–507, 1971

Daniel WF, Weiner RD, Crovitz HF, et al: ECT-induced delirium and further ECT: a case report. Am J Psychiatry 140:922–924, 1983

Danielczyk W: Pharmacotoxic psychoses in patients with neurological disorders in old age, in Advances in Neurology, vol 40. Edited by Hassler RG, Christ JF. New York, Raven Press, 1984

Daniels AC, Chokroverty S, Barron KD: Thalamic degeneration, dementia, and seizures. Arch Neurol 21:15–24, 1969

Davidson CS, Gabuzda GJ: Hepatic coma, in Diseases of the Liver, 3rd ed. Edited by Schiff L. Philadelphia, JB Lippincott, 1969

Davidson CS, Gabuzda GJ: Hepatic coma, in Diseases of the Liver, 4th ed. Edited by Schiff L. Philadelphia, JB Lippincott, 1975

Davies P: Neurotransmitter related enzymes in senile dementia of the Alzheimer type. Brain Res 171:319–327, 1979

Davies P: Theoretical treatment possibilities for dementia of the Alzheimer's type: the cholinergic hypothesis, in Strategies for the Development of an Effective Treatment for Senile Dementia. Edited by Crook T, Gershon S. New Canaan, Conn, Mark Powley Associates, 1981

Davies P: Is it possible to design rational treatments for the symptoms of Alzheimer's disease? Drug Dev Res 5:69–76, 1985

Davies P, Katz DA, Crystal HA: Choline acetyltransferase, somatostatin and substance P in selected cases of Alzheimer's disease, in Alzheimer's Disease: A Report of Progress (Aging, vol 19). Edited by Corkin S, Davis KL, Growdon JH, et al. New York, Raven Press, 1982

Davies TS: Monoamine oxidase inhibitors and rauwolfia compounds. Br Med J 2:739–740, 1960

Davis H: Audiometry—other auditory tests, in Hearing and Deafness. Edited by Davis H, Silverman SR. New York, Holt Rinehart and Winston, 1978

Davis JW, Blumenthal MD, Robinson-Hawkins S: A model of risk of falling for psychogeriatric patients. Arch Gen Psychiatry 38:463–467, 1981

Davis KL, Mohs RC: Enhancement of memory processes in Alzheimer's disease with multiple dose intravenous physostigmine. Am J Psychiatry 139:1421–1424, 1982

Davis KL, Mohs RC, Tinklenberg JR, et al: Physostigmine: improvement of long-term memory processes in normal humans. Science 201:272–274, 1978

Davis KL, Mohs RC, Davis BM, et al: Cholinomimetic agents and human memory: clinical studies in Alzheimer's disease and scopolamine dementia, in Strategies for the Development of an Effective Treatment for Senile Dementia. Edited by Crook T, Gershon S. New Canaan, Conn, Mark Powley Associates, 1981

Davis M, Williams R, Chakraborty J, et al: Prednisone or prednisolone for the treatment of chronic active hepatitis? A comparison of plasma availability. Br J Clin Pharmacol 5:501–505, 1978

Davison K, Bagley CR: Schizophrenia-like psychoses associated with organic disorders of the central nervous system: a review of the literature. Br J Psychiatry (spec issue no 4):113–184, 1969

Dawling S, Lynn K, Rossner R, et al: The pharmacokinetics of nortriptyline in patients with chronic renal failure. Br J Clin Pharmacol 12:39–45, 1981

Dawling S, Lynn K, Rossner R, et al: Nortriptyline metabolism in chronic renal failure: metabolite elimination. Clin Pharmacol Ther 32:322–329, 1982

DeCencio DV, Leshner M, Leshner B: Personality characteristics of patients with chronic obstructive pulmonary emphysema. Arch Phys Med Rehabil 49:471–475, 1968

Delis D, Direnfeld L, Alexander MP, et al: Cognitive fluctuations associated with on-off phenomenon in Parkinson's disease. Neurology 32:1049–1052, 1982

Denaut M, Yernault JC, DeCoster A: A double-blind comparison of the respiratory effects of parenteral lorazepam and diazepam in patients with COLD. Curr Med Res Opin 2:611–615, 1975

Denham MJ: Ethics of research in the elderly. Age Aging 13:321–327, 1984

Denham MJ, Jefferys PM: Routine mental testing in the elderly. Modern Geriatrics 2:275–279, 1972

Denmark JC: Mental illness and early profound deafness. Br J Med Psychol 39:117–124, 1966

Depaulo JR Jr, Correa EI, Sapir DG: Renal glomerular function and long term lithium therapy. Am J Psychiatry 138:324–327, 1981

Desmedt JE: Clinical use of evoked potentials. Rinsho Shinkeigaku 12:1198–1210, 1984

Deupree JD: The mode of action of anticonvulsant drugs: membrane effects, in The Treatment of Epilepsy. Edited by Tyrer JH. Philadelphia, JB Lippincott, 1980

Devins GM, Binik YM, Hollomby DJ: Helplessness and depression in end-stage renal disease. J Abnorm Psychol 90:531–545, 1981

dc Wied D: Pituitary-adrenal system hormones and behavior, in The Neurosciences, Third Study Program. Edited by Schmitt FO, Worden FG. Cambridge, Mass, MIT Press, 1974

de Wied D, Bohies B, Gispen WH: Hormonal influences on motivational, learning and memory processes, in Hormones, Behavior and Psychopathology. Edited by Sachar EJ. New York, Raven Press, 1976

Docci D, Bilancioni R, Pistocchi E, et al: Serum alpha-1-acid glycoprotein in chronic renal failure. Nephron 39:160–163, 1985

Dodson ME, Yousseff Y, Madison S, et al: Respiratory effects of lorazepam. Br J Anaesth 48:611–612, 1976

Dollard J, Dobb L, Miller N, et al: Frustration and Aggression. New Haven, Conn, Yale University Press, 1939

Dollery CT, Emslie-Smith D, Milne MD: Guanethidine in the treatment of hypertension. Lancet 2:381–387, 1960

Dongier S: Statistical study of clinical and encephalographic manifestations of 536 psychotic episodes occurring in 516 epileptics between clinical seizures. Epilepsia 1:117–142, 1959

Dorfman LJ, Forno LS: Paraneoplastic encephalomyelitis. Acta Neurol Scand 48:556–574, 1972

Doueck E: The Sense of Smell and Its Abnormalities. Edinburgh, Churchill Livingstone, 1974

Drachman DA: Memory and cognitive function in man: does the cholinergic system have a specific role? Neurology 27:783–790, 1977

Drachman DA, Leavitt J: Human memory and the cholinergic system: a relationship to aging? Arch Neurol 30:113–121, 1974

Drachman DA, Sahakian BJ: Memory and cognitive function in the elderly: a preliminary trial of physostigmine. Arch Neurol 37:674–675, 1980

Drane JF: Competency to give an informed consent: a model for making clinical assessments. JAMA 252:925–927, 1984

Dravet C, Mesdjian E, Cernand B, et al: Interaction between carbamazepine and triacetyloleandramycin. Lancet 1:810–811, 1977

Dresser RS, Boisaubin EV: Ethics, law, and nutritional support. Arch Intern Med 145:122–124, 1985

Dubovsky SL, Franks RD, Lifschitz M, et al: Effectiveness of verapamil in the treatment of the manic patient. Am J Psychiatry 139:502–504, 1982

Duckworth GS, Ross H: Diagnostic differences in psychogeriatric patients. New York, and London, England. Can Med Assoc J 112:847–851, 1975

Dudley DL, Sitzman J: Psychosocial and psychophysicologic approach to the patient. Seminars in Respiratory Medicine 1:59–83, 1979

Dudley WHC Jr, Williams JG: Electroconvulsive therapy in delirium tremens. Compr Psychiatry 13:357–360, 1972

Dujovne CA: A clinical pharamcologist's view of drug hepatotoxicity. Pharmacol Res Commun 9:1–15, 1977

Dulfano MJ, Ishikawa S: Hypercapnia: mental changes and extrapulmonary complications. Ann Intern Med 63:829–841, 1965

Durso P, Fedio P, Browers K, et al: Lysine vasopressin in Alzheimer disease. Neurology 6:674–677, 1982

Duvoisin RC, Katz R: Reversal of central anticholinergic syndrome in man by physostigmine. JAMA 206:1963–1965, 1968

Dyck AJ: Ethical aspects of care for the dying incompetent. J Am Geriatr Soc 32:661–664, 1984

Dyken ML: Anticoagulant and platelet-anti-aggregating therapy in stroke and threatened stroke. Neurologic Clinics 1:223–242, 1983

Dysken MW, Merry W, Davis JM: Anticholinergic psychosis. Psychiatric Annals 8:452–456, 1978

Eade NR, Penton KW: The effect of phenelzine and tranylcypromine on the degradation of meperidine. J Pharmacol Exp Ther 173:31–36, 1970

Eadie MJ: Pharmacokinetics of the anticonvulsant drugs, in The Treatment of Epilepsy. Edited by Tyrer JH. Philadelphia, JB Lippincott, 1980a

Eadie MJ: Unwanted effects of anticonvulsant drugs, in The Treatment of Epilepsy. Edited by Tyrer JH. Philadelphia, JB Lippincott, 1980b

Eadie MJ, Tyrer JH, Smith GA, et al: Pharmacokinetics of drugs used for petit mal absence epilepsy. Clin Exp Neurol 14:172–183, 1977

Eames P, Wood R: Rehabilitation after severe brain injury: a follow-up study of a behavior modification approach. J Neurol Neurosurg Psychiatry 48:613–619, 1985

Eaton LM, Lambert EH: Electromyography and electric stimulation of nerves and diseases of motor unit: observations on myasthenic syndrome associated with malignant tumors. JAMA 163:1117–1123, 1957

Ebert MH, Shader RI: Hepatic effects, in Psychotropic Drug Side Effects: Clinical and Theoretical Perspectives. Edited by Shader RI, DiMascio A. Baltimore, Williams and Wilkins, 1970

Edwards JG, Goldie A: Mianserin, maprotiline, and intracardiac conduction. Br J Pharmacol 15(suppl)249s–254s, 1983

Eichelbaum M, Ekbom K, Bertilsson L, et al: Plasma kinetics of carbamazepine and its epoxide metabolite in man during single and multiple dosing. Eur J Clin Pharmacol 8:337–341, 1975

Eisdorfer C, Cohen D: Diagnostic criteria for primary neuronal degeneration of the Alzheimer's type. J Fam Pract 11:553–557, 1980

Ellinwood EH, Sudilovsky A, Nelson LM: Evolving behavior in the clinical and experimental (model) psychosis. Am J Psychiatry 130:1088–1092, 1973

Elliott FA: The neurology of explosive rage. Practitioner 217:51–59, 1976

Elliott FA: Propranolol for the control of belligerent behavior following acute brain damage. Ann Neurol 5:489–491, 1977

Elliott FA: Neurological findings in adult minimal brain dysfunction and the dyscontrol syndrome. J Nerv Ment Dis 170:680–687, 1982

Elliott HW, Navarro G, Kokka N, et al: Early phase I evaluation of sedatives, hypnotics, or minor tranquilizers, in Hypnotics, Methods of Development and Evaluation. Edited by Fred Kagan. New York, Spectrum, 1975

Emerson R, D'Souza BJ, Vining EP, et al: Stopping medication in children with epilepsy: prediction of outcome. N Engl J Med 304:1125–1129, 1981

Engel J Jr, Kuhl DE, Phelps ME, et al: Pathological correlates of focal temporal lobe hypometabolism in partial epilepsy. Epilepsia 22:236, 1981

Engelhardt HT, McCullough LB: Confidentiality in the consultation-liaison process. Psychiatr Clin North Am 2:403–413, 1979

Espelin DE, Done AK: Amphetamine poisoning effectiveness of chlorpromazine. N Engl J Med 278:1361–1365, 1968

Estes D, Christian CL: The natural history of systemic lupus erythematosus by prospective analysis. Medicine 50:85–95, 1971

Eth S: I want to see my mother's picture! Hastings Cent Rep 13:21–22, 1983

Eth S: Competency and consent to treatment. JAMA 253:778–779, 1985

Eth S, Eth C: Can a research subject be too eager to consent? Hastings Cent Rep 11:20–21, 1981

Evanson JM, Sears HTN: Comparison of bretylium tosylate with guanethidine in the treatment of severe hypertension. Lancet 2:387–389, 1960

Faheem AD, Brightwell DR, Burton GC, et al: Respiratory dyskinesia and dysarthria from prolonged neuroleptic use: tardive dyskinesia. Am J Psychiatry 139:517–518, 1982

Falconer MA: Reversibility by temporal-lobe resection of the behavioral abnormalities of temporal-lobe epilepsy. N Engl J Med 289:451, 1973

Falconer MA, Taylor DC: Temporal lobe epilepsy: clinical features, pathology, diagnosis, and treatment, in Modern Times in Psychological Medicine. Edited by Price JH. London, Butterworth Scientific, 1970

Falk RH, Nisbet PA, Gray TJ: Mental distress in patient on disopyramide. Lancet 1:858–859, 1977

Falk WE, Mahnke MD, Poskanzer MD: Lithium prophylaxis of corticotropin-induced psychosis. JAMA 241:1011–1012, 1979

Fann WE, Janowsky DS, Davis JM, et al: Chlorpromazine reversal of the antihypertensive action of guanethidine. Lancet 2:236–237, 1971

Farrell GC, Cooksley WGE, Powell LW: Drug metabolism in liver disease: activity of hepatic microsomal metabolizing enzymes. Clin Pharmacol Ther 26:483–492, 1979

Feibel JH, Springer CJ: Depression and failure to resume social activities after stroke. Arch Phys Med Rehabil 63:276–278, 1982

Feinberg T, Goodman B: Affective illness, dementia, and pseudodementia. J Clin Psychiatry 45:99–103, 1984

Feinglass EJ, Arnett FC, Dorsch CA, et al: Neuropsychiatric manifestations of systemic lupus erythematosus: diagnosis, clinical spectrum and relationship to other features of the disease. Medicine 55:323–339, 1976

Ferris SH: Empirical studies in senile dementia with central nervous system stimulants and metabolic enhancers, in Strategies for the Development of an Effective Treatment for Senile Dementia. Edited by Crook T, Gershon S. New Canaan, Conn, Mark Powley Associates, 1981

Ferris SH, Crook T: Cognitive assessment in mild to moderately severe dementia, in Assessment in Geriatric Psychopharmacology. Edited by Crook T, Ferris S, Bartus R. New Canaan, Conn, Mark Powley Associates, 1983

Ferris SH, Reisberg B, Gershon S: Neuropeptide effects on cognition in the elderly, in Aging in the 1980's: Selected Contemporary Issues in the Psychology of Aging. Edited by Poon L. Washington, DC, American Psychological Association, 1981

Fibiger HC: The neurobiological substrates of depression in Parkinson's disease: a hypothesis. Can J Neurol Sci 11:105–107, 1984

Fink M, Green M, Bender MB: The face-hand test as a diagnostic sign of organic mental syndrome. Neurology 2:46–58, 1952

Finklestein S, Benowitz LI, Baldessarini RJ, et al: Mood, vegetative disturbance, and dexamethasone suppression test after stroke. Ann Neurol 12:463–468, 1982

Finley WW, Smith HA, Etherton MD: Reduction of seizures and normalization of the EEG in a severe epileptic following sensori-motor biofeedback training: preliminary study. Biol Psychol 2:189–203, 1975

Fisch C: Effect of fluoxetine on the electrocardiogram. J Clin Psychiatry 46:42–44, 1985

Fisch M, Goldfarb AI, Shahinian SP, et al: Chronic brain syndrome in the community aged. Arch Gen Psychiatry 18:739–745, 1968

Fischer RG, Booth BH, Mitchell DQ, et al: Influence of trivalent influenza vaccine on serum theophylline levels. Can Med Assoc J 126:1312–1313, 1982

Fischer-Williams M, Bosanquet FD, Daniel PM: Carcinomatosis of the meninges. Brain 78:42–58, 1955

Fisher CM: Disorientation for place. Arch Neurol 39:33–36, 1982a

Fisher CM: Lacunar strokes and infarcts: a review. Neurology 32:871–876, 1982b

Fishman AP: Update: Pulmonary Diseases and Disorders. New York, McGraw-Hill, 1982

Fitzgerald RG: Reactions to blindness. Arch Gen Psychiatry 22:370–379, 1970

Fix AJ, Golden CJ Daughton D, et al: Neuropsychological deficits among patients with COPD. Int J Neurosci 16:99–105, 1982

Flachs H, Wurtz-Jorgensen A, Gram L, et al: Sodium di-n-propylacetate: its interaction with other antiepileptic drugs, in Pharmacokinetics and Metabolism of the Antiepileptic Drug Sodium Valproate. Edited by Vree TB, Vander Kleijn E. Ultrect, Scheltema and Holkema, 1977

Flemenbaum A: Affective disorders and 'chemical dependence': lithium for alcohol and drug addiction? A clinical note. Diseases of the Nervous System 35:281–285, 1974

Fletcher EC, Martin RJ: Sexual dysfunction and erectile impotence in COPD. Chest 81:413–421, 1982

Flood JF, Jarvik ME, Bennet EL: Effects of ACTH peptide fragments on memory formation. Pharmacol Biochem Behav 5(suppl 1):41–51, 1976

Flor-Henry P: Psychosis and temporal lobe epilepsy: a controlled investigation. Epilepsia 10:363–395, 1969

Folks DG, King LD, Dowdy SB, et al: Carbamazepine treatment of selective affectively disordered inpatients. Am J Psychiatry 139:115–117, 1982

Folstein MF, McHugh PR: Dementia syndrome of depression, in Alzheimer's Disease: Senile Dementia and Related Disorders, vol 7: Aging. Edited by Katzman R, Terry RD, Bick KL. New York, Raven Press, 1978

Folstein MF, Folstein SE, McHugh PR: "Mini-Mental State": a practical method for grading the cognitive state of patients for the clinician. J Psychiatr Res 12:189–198, 1975

Folstein MF, Maiberger R, McHugh PR: Mood disorder as a specific complication of stroke. J Neurol Neurosurg Psychiatry 40:1018–1020, 1977

Folstein MF, Anthony JC, Parhad I, et al: The meaning of cognitive impairment in the elderly. J Am Geriatr Soc 33:228–235, 1985

Fordyce DJ, Roueche JR, Prigatano GP: Enhanced emotional reactions in chronic head trauma patients. J Neurol Neurosurg Psychiatry 46:620–624, 1983

Foster FM: Reflex epilepsy. Behaviour Therapy and Conditional Reflexes. Springfield, Ill, Charles C Thomas, 1977

Frakowiak RSJ, Wise RJS: Positron tomography in ischemic cerebrovascular disease. Neurologic Clinics 1:183–200, 1983

Francis PT, Palmer AM, Sims NR, et al: Neurochemical studies of early-onset Alzheimer's disease: possible influence on treatment. N Engl J Med 313:7–11, 1985

Frankena WK: Ethics, 2nd ed. Englewood Cliffs, NJ, Prentice Hall, 1973

Franklin GS, Brown JW, Freedman ML: Shared Capgras syndrome and nifedipine. Lancet 2:222, 1982

Frankowski RF, Annegers JF, Whitman S: Epidemiological and descriptive studies part 1: The descriptive epidemiology of head trauma in the United States, in Central Nervous System Trauma Status Report. Edited by Becker DP, Povlishock JT. Washington, DC, National Institutes of Health, 1985

Franzen MD, Lovell MR: Behavioral treatments of aggressive sequelae of brain injury. Psychiatric Annals 17:389–396, 1987

Fraser HS, Carr AC: Propranolol psychosis. Br J Psychiatry 129:508–509, 1976

Fredman B: Competence, marginal and otherwise: concepts and ethics. Int J Law Psychiatry 4:53–72, 1981

Freed JS, Reiner MA: Nifedipine-induced acute psychosis. J Am Geriatr Soc 32:408, 1984

Freemon FR: Organic Mental Disease. New York, Spectrum Publications, 1981

Freyschuss U, Sjoqvist F, Tuck D, et al: Circulatory effects in man of nortriptyline, a tricyclic antidepressant drug. Pharmacological Clinic 2:68–71, 1970

Friedel RO: Affective disorders in the geriatric patient, in Psychiatry Update, vol 2. Edited by Grinspoon L. Washington, DC, American Psychiatric Press, 1983

Frieden J: Propranolol as an antiarrhythmic agent. Am Heart J 75:283–285, 1967

Friedman MJ: Does receptor supersensitivity accompany depressive illness? Am J Psychiatry 135:107–109, 1978

Fuld PA: The Fuld Object Memory Evaluation. Chicago, Stoelting Instrument Co, 1981

Fuld PA, Katzman R, Davies P, et al: Intrusions as a sign of Alzheimer's dementia: chemical and pathological verification. Ann Neurol 11:155–159, 1982

Fusner JE, Poplack DG, Piazzo PA, et al: Leukoencephalopathy following chemotherapy for rhabdomyosarcoma: reversibility of cerebral changes demonstrated by computed technology. J Pediatr 9:77–79, 1977

Gahwiler BH: Excitatory action of opioid peptides and opiates on cultured hippocampal pyramidal cells. Brain Res 194:193–203, 1980

Gainotti G: Laterality of affect: the emotional behavior of right- and left-brain-damaged patients, in Hemisyndromes: Psychobiology, Neurology, Psychiatry. Edited by Myslobodsky MS. New York, Academic Press, 1983

Garraway WM, Whisnant JP: The changing pattern of hypertension and the declining incidence of stroke. JAMA 258:214–217, 1987

Garraway WM, Whisnant JP, Furlan AJ, et al: The declining incidence of stroke. N Engl J Med 300:449–452, 1979

Gastaut H: Interpretation des symptoms de l'epilepsie "psychomotrice" en fonction des donnees de la psychologie rhinen-encephalique. Presse Medicale 62:1535–1537, 1954

Gaultieri CT, Powell SF: Psychoactive drug interactions. J Clin Psychiatry 39:720–729, 1978

Gay GR: Clinical management of acute and chronic cocaine poisoning. Ann Emerg Med 11:562–572, 1982

George K, Dundee J: Relative amnesic actions of diazepam, flunitrazepam and lorazepam in man. Br J Clin Pharmacol 4:45–50, 1977

Gerner RH: Antidepressant selection in the elderly. Psychosomatics 25:528–535, 1984

Gershon ES, Goldstein RG, Moss AJ, et al: Psychosis with ordinary doses of propranolol. Ann Intern Med 90:938–939, 1979

Gershon S, Newton R: Lack of anticholinergic side effects with a new antidepressant: trazodone. J Clin Psychiatry 41:100–104, 1980

Ghose K: Effect of carbamazepine in polyuria associated with lithium therapy. Pharmacopsychiatria 11:241–245, 1978

Giannini AJ: Augmentation of haloperidol by ascorbic acid in phencyclidine intoxication. Am J Psychiatry 144:9, 1987

Giannini AJ, Houser WL, Loiselle RH, et al: Antimanic effects of verapamil. Am J Psychiatry 141:1602–1603, 1984

Giardinia EG, Bigger JT Jr, Glassman AH, et al: The electrocardiographic and antiarrhythmic effects of imipramine hydrochloride at therapeutic plasma concentrations. Circulation 60:1045–1052, 1979

Giardinia EG, Bigger JT Jr, Johnson LL: The effect of imipramine and nortriptyline on ventricular depolarizations and left ventricular function (abstract). Circulation 64:316, 1981

Gibberd FB: The diagnosis and investigation of epilepsy. Br J Hosp Med 9:152–158, 1973

Gibbs FA: Ictal and non-ictal psychiatric disorders in temporal lobe epilepsy. J Nerv Ment Dis 11:522–528, 1951

Gibson GE, Blass JP: Impaired synthesis of acetylcholine in brain accompanying mild hypoxia and hypoglycemia. J Neurochem 27:37–42, 1976

Gibson GE, Peterson C: Pharmacologic models of age related deficits, in Assessment in Geriatric Psychopharmacology. Edited by Crook T, Ferris S, Bartus R. New Canaan, Conn, Mark Powley Associates, 1983

Gibson GE, Pelmas CJ, Peterson C: Cholinergic drugs and 4-aminopyridine alter hypoxic-induced behavioral deficits. Pharmacol Biochem Behav 18:909–916, 1983

Gilbert GJ: Quinidine dementia. JAMA 27:2093–2094, 1977

Giles TO, Modlin RK: Death associated with ventricular arrhythmias and thioridazine hydrochloride. JAMA 205:108–110, 1968

Gilson SB: The trick is to live. JAMA 253:17–21, 1985

Gitlin MJ, Weiss J: Verapamil as maintenance treatment in bipolar illness: a case report. J Clin Psychopharmacol 4:341–343, 1984

Giurgea C: Piracetam: nootropic pharmacology of neurointegrative activity. Curr Dev Psychopharmacol 3:221–273, 1976

Glaser GH, Pincus JH: Limbic encephalitis. J Nerv Ment Dis 149:59–67, 1969

Glassman AH: Cardiovascular effects of tricyclic antidepressants. Annu Rev Med 35:503–511, 1984a

Glassman AH: The newer antidepressant drugs and their cardiovascular effects. Psychopharmacol Bull 20:272–279, 1984b

Glassman AH, Bigger JT Jr: Cardiovascular effects of therapeutic doses of tricyclic antidepressant drugs. Arch Gen Psychiatry 38:815–820, 1981

Glassman AH, Bigger JT, Giardinia EV, et al: Clinical characteristics of imipramine-induced orthostatic hypotension. Lancet 1:468–472, 1979

Glassman AH, Walsh BT, Roose SP, et al: Factors related to orthostatic hypotension associated with tricyclic antidepressants. J Clin Psychiatry 43:35–38, 1982

Glassman AH, Johnson LL, Giardinia EG, et al: The use of imipramine in depressed patients with congestive heart failure. JAMA 250:1997–2001, 1983

Glick G, Braunwald E: Cardiac tumors and other unusual forms of heart disease, in Principles of Internal Medicine, 9th ed. Edited by Isselbacher KJ, Adams RD, Braunwald E, et al. New York, McGraw-Hill, 1980

Goetz CG, Tanner CM, Klawans HL: Pharmacology of hallucinations induced by long-term drug therapy. Am J Psychiatry 139:494–497, 1982

Gold ME, Washton AM, Wackis CA: 'Cocaine Abuse': Neurochemistry, Phenomenology, and Treatment. NIDA Research Monograph Series No 61. Publication ADM 130-150. Rockville, MD, US Department of Health and Human Services, 1985

Gold MS, Redmond DE Jr, Kleber HD: Clonidine blocks acute opiate-withdrawal symptoms. Lancet 2:599–602, 1978

Gold MS, Estroff TW, Pottash ALC: Substance induced organic mental disorders, in American Psychiatric Association Annual Review, vol 4. Edited by Hales RE, Frances AJ. Washington, DC, American Psychiatric Press, 1985

Gold PE, McGaugh JL: Hormones and memory, in Neuropeptide Influences on the Brain. Edited by Miller LH, Sandman CA, Kastin AJ. New York, Raven Press, 1977

Gold PW, Ballenger JC, Weingartner H, et al: Effects of 1-desamino-8-arginine vasopressin on behavior and cognition in primary affective disorders. Lancet 2:992–994, 1979

Goldman HH, Pincus HA, Taube CA, et al: Prospective payment for psychiatric hospitalization: questions and issues. Hosp Community Psychiatry 35:460–464, 1984

Goldman HH, Cohen GD, Davis M: Expanded Medicare outpatient coverage for Alzheimer's disease. Hosp Community Psychiatry 36:939–942, 1985

Goldstein NP, Ewert JC, Randall RV, et al: Psychiatric aspects of Wilson's disease: results of psychometric tests during long term therapy. Am J Psychiatry 124:1555–1561, 1968

Gomoll AW, Byrne JE: Trazodone and imipramine: comparative effects on canine cardiac conduction. Eur J Pharmacol 57:335–342, 1979

Goodman Gilman A, Goodman LS, Gilman A: The Pharmacological Basis of Therapeutics, 6th ed. New York, Macmillan, 1980

Goodstein RK: Overview: cerebrovascular accident and the hospitalized elderly: a multidimensional clinical problem. Am J Psychiatry 140:141–147, 1983

Goodwin DW: Substance induced and substance use disorders: alcohol, in Treatment of Mental Disorders. Edited by Griest JH, Jefferson JW, Spitzer RL. New York, Oxford University Press, 1982

Goodwin DW: Alcoholism and alcoholic psychoses, in Comprehensive Textbook of Psychiatry, 4th ed, vol 4. Edited by Kaplan HI, Sadock BJ. Baltimore, Williams and Wilkins, 1985

Goodwin FK: Psychiatric side effects of levodopa in man. JAMA 218:1915–1920, 1971

Goodwin FK, Murphy DL, Brodie HKH, et al: Levodopa: alterations in behavior. Clin Pharmacol Ther 12:383–396, 1971

Goodwin FK, Ebert MH, Bunney WE Jr: Mental effects of reserpine in man: a review, in Psychiatric Complications of Medical Drugs. Edited by Shader RI. New York, Raven Press, 1972

Gordon MA: Rabbinic comment: old age: right to privacy and patient's right to know. Mt Sinai J Med (NY) 51:89–91, 1984

Gottfries CG: Levels of monoamines, monoamine metabolites and activity in related enzyme systems correlated to normal aging and in patients with dementia of Alzheimer type, in Proceedings of the Symposium "Clinical Pharmacology of Apomorphine and Other Dopaminomimetics." Cagliari, Sardinia, Italy, 1980

Gottfries CG, Roos BE: Acid monoamine metabolites in cerebrospinal fluid from patients with presenile dementia (Alzheimer's disease). Acta Psychiatr Scand 49:257–263, 1973

Gottfries CG, Roos BE: Monoamine metabolites in cerebrospinal fluid (CSF) in patients with organic presenile and senile dementias. Aktuel Gerontol 6:37–42, 1976

Gottfries CG, Gottfries I, Roos BE: Disturbances of monoamine metabolism in the brains from patients with dementia senilis and Mb Alzheimer. Excerpta Medica International Congress Series 180:310–312, 1968

Gottfries CG, Gottfries I, Roos BE: The investigation of homovanillic acid in the human brain and its correlation to senile dementia. Br J Psychiatry 115:563–574, 1969

Gottfries CG, Kjallquist A, Ponten U: Cerebrospinal fluid pH and monoamine and glucolytic metabolites in Alzheimer's disease. Br J Psychiatry 124:280–287, 1974

Gottfries CG, Roos BE, Winblad B: Monoamine and monoamine metabolites in the human brain post mortem in senile dementia. Aktuel Gerontol 6:429–435, 1976

Gottschalk LA, Coui L, Uliana R, et al: Effects of diphenylhydantoin on anxiety and hostility in institutionalized prisoners. Compr Psychiatry 14:503–511, 1973

Gould RJ, Murphy KMM, Reynolds IJ, et al: Calcium channel blockade: possible explanation for thioridazine's peripheral side effects. Am J Psychiatry 141:352–357, 1984

Grady PA: Pathophysiology of extracranial cerebral artery stenosis: a critical review. Stroke 15:224–236, 1984

Graff-Radford NR, Esbinger PJ, Damasio AR, et al: Nonhemorrhagic infarction of the thalamus: behavioral, anatomic, and physiologic correlates. Neurology 34:14–23, 1984

Granacher RP Jr, Ruth DD: Droperidol in acute agitation. Current Therapeutic Research 25:361–365, 1979

Granick S, Patterson RD: Human Aging II: An Eleven-Year Followup Biomedical and Behavioral Study. Publication HSM 71-9037. Rockville, Md, US Department of Health, Education, and Welfare, 1971

Grant I, Heaton RK, McSweeney AJ, et al: Brain dysfunction in COPD. Chest 77:308–309, 1980

Grant I, Heaton RK, McSweeney AJ, et al: Neuropsychologic findings in hypoxemic COPD. Arch Intern Med 142:1470–1476, 1982

Greenberg GD, Ryan JJ, Bourlier PF: Psychological and neuropsychological aspects of COPD. Psychosomatics 26:29–33, 1985

Greenblatt DJ: Antiarrhythmic agents, in Drug Effects in Hospitalized Patients: Experiences of the Boston Collaborative Drug Surveillance Program, 1966–1975. Edited by Miller RR, Greenblatt DJ. New York, John Wiley and Sons, 1976

Greenblatt DJ, Shader RI: Treatment of the alcohol withdrawal syndrome, in Manual of Psychiatric Therapeutics. Edited by Shader RI. Boston, Little, Brown, 1975

Greenblatt DJ, Shader R: Pharmacokinetics in old age: principles and problems of assessment, in Clinical Pharmacology and the Aged Patient. Edited by Jarvik LF, Greenblatt DJ, Harman D. New York, Raven Press, 1981

Greenblatt DJ, Murray TG, Audet PR, et al: Multiple-dose kinetics and dialyzability of oxazepam in renal insufficiency. Nephron 34:234–238, 1983

Griffin A, Thomasma DC: Pediatric critical care: should medical costs influence clinical decisions? Arch Intern Med 143:325–327, 1983

Grinspoon L, Bakalar JB: Drug dependence: nonnarcotic agents, in Comprehensive Textbook of Psychiatry, 4th ed, vol 4. Edited by Kaplan HI, Sadock BJ. Baltimore, Williams and Wilkins, 1985

Grossman SH, Davis D, Kitchell BB, et al: Diazepam and lidocaine plasma protein binding in renal disease. Clin Pharmacol Ther 31:350–357, 1982

Grotjohn M: The day I got old. Psychiatr Clin North Am 5:233–234, 1982

Growdon JH, Logue M: Choline, HVA and 5-HIAA levels in cerebrospinal fluid of patients with Alzheimer's disease, in Alzheimer's Disease: A Report of Progress (Aging, vol 19). Edited by Corkin S, Davis KL, Growdon JH, et al. New York, Raven Press, 1982

Gudmundsson G: Epilepsy in Iceland: a clinical and epidemiological investigation. Acta Neurol Scand [Suppl] 25:1–124, 1966

Guerrant J, Anderson WW, Fisher A, et al: Personality in Epilepsy. Springfield, Ill, Charles C Thomas, 1962

Guinn MM, Medford JA, Wilson MC: Antagonism of intravenous cocaine lethality in nonhuman primates. Clin Toxicol 16:499–508, 1980

Gulyassy PF, Depner TA: Impaired binding of drugs and endogenous ligands in renal diseases. Am J Kidney Dis 2:578–601, 1983

Gunn J: The prevalence of epilepsy among prisoners. Procedings of the Royal Society of Medicine 62:60–63, 1969

Gunn J, Bonn J: Criminality and violence in epileptic prisoners. Br J Psychiatry 118:337–343, 1971

Gunn J, Fenton GW: Epilepsy, automatism and crime. Lancet 1:1173–1176, 1971

Gurland BJ, Cross PS: Epidemiology of psychopathology in old age: Some implications for clinical services. Psychiatr Clin North Am 5:11–26, 1982

Hachinski V: Multi-infarct dementia. Neurologic Clinics 1:27–36, 1983

Hachinski V: Decreased incidence and mortality of stroke. Stroke 15:376–378, 1984

Hachinski VC, Iliff LD, Zilhka E, et al: Cerebral blood flow in dementia. Arch Neurol 32:632–637, 1975

Haddon JW, Baker SP: Injury control, in Prevention and Community Medicine. Edited by Clark D, McMahn B. Boston, Little Brown, 1981

Hagman A, Arnman K, Ryden L: Syncope caused by lithium treatment. Report on two cases and a prospective investigation of the prevalence of lithium-induced sinus node dysfunction. Acta Med Scand 205:467–471, 1979

Hakoloa HP, Laulumaa VA: Carbamazepine in treatment of violent schizophrenics. Lancet 1:1358, 1982

Hale MS, Bellizzi J: Low dose perphenazine and levodopa/carbidopa therapy in a patient with parkinsonism and a psychotic illness. J Nerv Ment Dis 168:312–314, 1980

Halgin R, Riklan M, Misiak H: Levodopa, parkinsonism, and recent memory. J Nerv Ment Dis 164:268–272, 1977

Hammond JJ, Kirkendall UM: Antihypertensive agents, in Neuropsychiatric Side Effects of Drugs in the Elderly (Aging, vol 9). Edited by Levenson AJ. New York, Raven Press, 1979

Hansen HE, Amdisen A: Lithium intoxication. Q J Med 186:123–144, 1978

Hansen HE, Hestbech J, Sorenson JL, et al: Chronic interstitial nephropathy in patients on long-term lithium treatment. Q J Med 48:577–591, 1979

Hansten PD: Drug Interactions. Philadelphia, Lea and Febiger, 1976

Hansten PD: Drug Interactions, 5th ed. Philadelphia, Lea and Febiger, 1985

Harbaugh RE, Roberts DW, Coombs DW, et al: Preliminary report: intracranial cholinergic drug infusion in patients with Alzheimer's disease. Neurosurgery 15:514–518, 1984

Harvey SC: Hypnotics and sedatives, in The Pharmacological Basis of Therapeutics, 6th ed. Edited by Goodman Gilman A, Goodman LS, Gilman A. New York, Macmillan, 1980

Hass WK: The cerebral ischemic cascade. Neurologic Clinics 1:345–353, 1983

Havens LL, Child CG: Recurrent psychosis associated with liver disease and elevated blood ammonia. N Engl J Med 252:756–759, 1955

Hayes JR, Born GP, Rosenbaum AH: Incidence of orthostatic hypotension in patients with primary affective disorders treated with tricyclic antidepressants. Mayo Clin Proc 52:509–512, 1977

Hayes RL, Gerner RH, Fairbanks L, et al: ECG findings in geriatric depressives given trazodone, placebo, or imipramine. J Clin Psychiatry 44:180–183, 1983

Heaton RK, Grant I, McSweeney AJ, et al: Psychologic effects of continuous and nocturnal oxygen therapy in hypoxemia COPD. Arch Intern Med 143:1941–1947, 1983

Heiman J: Psychiatric experiences associated with eye surgery and trauma requiring patching, in Psychiatric Problems in Ophthalmology. Edited by Pearlman JT, Adams GL, Sloan SH. Springfield, Ill, Charles C Thomas, 1977

Heiser JF, Gillin JC: The reversal of anticholinergic drug-induced delirium and coma with physostigmine. Am J Psychiatry 127:1050–1054, 1971

Helms PM: Efficacy of antipsychotics in the treatment of the behavioral complications of dementia: a review of the literature. J Am Geriatr Soc 33:206–209, 1985

Henry JA, Ali CJ: Trazodone overdosage: experience from a poisons information service. Hum Toxicol 2:353–356, 1983

Herridge CF, A'Brook MF: Ephedrine psychosis. Br Med J 2:160, 1968

Hestbech J, Aurell M: Lithium-induced uraemia. Lancet 1:212–213, 1979

Hestbech J, Hansen HE, Amdisen A, et al: Chronic renal lesions following long-term treatment with lithium. Kidney Int 12:205–213, 1977

Heston LL, Mastri AR: Age at onset of Pick's and Alzheimer's dementia: implications for diagnosis and research. J Gerontol 37:422–424, 1982

Hillbom E: After-effects of brain injuries. Acta Psychiatrica et Neurologica Scandinavica 142:1–135, 1960

Hillbom M, Kaste M: Ethanol intoxication: a risk factor for ischemic brain infarction in adolescents and young adults. Stroke 12:422–425, 1981

Himmelhoch JM: Cardiovascular effects of trazodone in humans. J Clin Pharmacol 1(suppl):76s–81s, 1982

Himmelhoch J, Pincus J, Tucker G, et al: Sub-acute encephalitis: behavioral and neurological aspects. Br J Psychiatry 116:531–538, 1970

Himmelhoch JM, Forrest J, Neil JF, et al: Thiazide-lithium synergy in refractory mood swings. Am J Psychiatry 134:149–152, 1977

Himmelhoch JM, Neil JF, May SJ, et al: Age, dementia, dyskinesias, and lithium response. Am J Psychiatry 137:941–945, 1980

Hoefnagel D: Toxic effects of atropine and homatropine eye drops in children. N Engl J Med 264:168–171, 1961

Hoehn-Saric R, Merchant AF, Keyser ML, et al: Effects of clonidine on anxiety disorders. Arch Gen Psychiatry 38:1278–1282, 1981

Hogan MJ, Wallin JD, Baer RM: Antihypertensive therapy and male sexual dysfunction. Psychosomatics 21:234–237, 1980

Holcomb HH, Sternberg DE, Heninger GR: Effects of electroconvulsive therapy on mood, parkinsonism, and tardive dyskinesia in a depressed patient: ECT and dopamine systems. Biol Psychiatry 18:865–873, 1983

Holden NL: Late parapherenia or the paraphrenias? A descriptive study with a 10-year follow-up. Br J Psychiatry 150:635–639, 1987

Holland J: Psychologic aspects of cancer, in Cancer Medicine, 2nd ed. Edited by Holland JF, Frei E. Philadelphia, Lea and Febiger, 1981

Holland JF, Scharlau C, Gailani S, et al: Vincristine treatment of advanced cancer: a cooperative study of 392 cases. Cancer Res 33:1258–1264, 1973

Hollister LE: Adverse reactions to phenothiazines. JAMA 189:143–145, 1974

Hollister LE, Yesavage J: Ergoloid mesylates for senile dementias: unanswered questions. Ann Intern Med 100:894–898, 1984

Holloway HC, Hales RE, Watanabe HK: Recognition and treatment of acute alcohol withdrawal syndromes. Psychiatr Clin North Am 7:729–743, 1984

Hooper JF, Minter G: Droperidol in the management of psychiatric emergencies. J Clin Psychopharmacol 3:262–263, 1983

Hopkin B, Jones CM: Dextroamphetamine poisoning. Br Med J 1:1044, 1956

Horenstein S, Chamberlain W, Conomy J: Infarction of the fusiform and calcarine regions: agitated delirium and hemianopsia. Transactions of the American Neurological Association 92:85–89, 1967

Horvath TB: Clinical spectrum and epidemiological features of alcoholic dementia, in Alcohol, Drugs and Brain Damage: Proceedings of a Symposium on Effects of Chronic Use of Alcohol and Other Psychoactive Drugs on Cerebral Function. Edited by Rankin JG. Toronto, Alcoholism and Drug Addiction Research Foundation of Ontario, 1975

Höschl C: Verapamil for depression? Am J Psychiatry 140:1100, 1983

House R, Dubovsky SL, Penn I: Psychiatric aspects of hepatic transplantation. Transplantation 36:146–150, 1983

Howard G, Till JS, Toole JF, et al: Factors influencing return to work following cerebral infarction. JAMA 253:226–232, 1985

Hoyumpa AM, Schenker S: Major drug interactions: effects of liver disease, alcohol and malnutrition. Annu Rev Med 33:113–149, 1982

Hubbell FA, Greenfield S, Tyler JL, et al: The impact of routine admission chest x-ray films on patient care. N Engl J Med 312:209–213, 1985

Huch R, Huch A: Respiratory depression after tranquilizers. Lancet 1:1267, 1974

Hughes CP, Gado M: Computed tomography and aging of the brain. Neuroradiology 139:391–396, 1981

Hughes CP, Berg L, Danziger WL, et al: A new clinical scale for the staging of dementia. Br J Psychiatry 140:566–572, 1982

Hunyor SN, Hansson L, Harrison TS, et al: Effects of clonidine withdrawal: possible mechanisms and suggestion for management. Br Med J 2:209–211, 1973

Huppert FA: Memory impairment associated with chronic hypoxia. Thorax 37:858–860, 1982

Hypertension Detection and Follow-Up Program Cooperative Group: Five-year findings of the hypertension detection and follow-up program, III: reduction in stroke incidence among persons with high blood pressure. JAMA 247:633–638, 1982

Iglehart JK: The new era of prospective payment for hospitals. N Engl J Med 307:1288–1292, 1982

Innes IR, Nickerson M: Norepinephrine, epinephrine, and the sympathomimetic amines, in The Pharmacologic Basis of Therapeutics, 5th ed. Edited by Goodman LS, Gilman A. New York, Macmillan, 1975

Insel TR, Ninan PT, Aloi J, et al: A benzodiazepine receptor-mediated model of anxiety. Arch Gen Psychiatry 41:741–750, 1984

Institute of Medicine: Research on mental illness and addictive disorders: progress and prospects. Am J Psychiatry 142(suppl):8–41, 1985

Insurance Institute for Highway Safety: Children in crashes. Washington, DC, Insurance Institute for Highway Safety, 1983

Irwin M, Spar JE: Reversible cardiac conduction abnormality associated with trazodone administration. Am J Psychiatry 140:945–946, 1983

Isaacs B, Kennie AT: The set test as an aid to the detection of dementia in old people. Br J Psychiatry 123:467–470, 1970

Itil TM, Soldatos C: Epileptogenic side effects of psychotropic drugs. JAMA 244:1460–1463, 1980

Jack R, Rabin PL, McKinney TD: Dialysis encephalopathy: a review. Int J Psychiatry Med 13:309–326, 1983/1984

Jackson AH, Shader RI: Guidelines for the withdrawal of narcotics and general depressant drugs. Diseases of the Nervous System 34:162–166, 1973

Jacobs L, Karpik A, Bozian D, et al: Auditory-visual synesthesia: sound-induced photisms. Arch Neurol 38:211–216, 1981

Jampala VC, Abrams R: Mania secondary to left and right hemisphere damage. Am J Psychiatry 140:1197–1199, 1983

Janowsky DS, El-Yousef MK, Davis JM, et al: Antagonism of guanethidine by chlorpromazine. Am J Psychiatry 130:808–810, 1973

Janowsky D, Curtis G, Zisook S, et al: Trazodone-aggravated ventricular arrhythmias. J Clin Psychopharmacol 3:372–376, 1983a

Janowsky D, Curtis G, Zisook S, et al: Ventricular arrhythmias possibly aggravated by trazodone. Am J Psychiatry 140:796–797, 1983b

Jarvik LF: Hydergine as a treatment for organic brain syndrome in late life. Psychopharmacol Bull 17:40–41, 1981

Jarvik LF: Aging and psychiatry. Psychiatr Clin North Am 5:5–9, 1982a

Jarvik LF: Dementia in old age: reflections on nomenclature. Psychiatr Clin North Am 5:105–106, 1982b

Jarvik LF, Bank L: Aging twins: longitudinal psychometric data, in Longitudinal Studies of Adult Psychological Development. Edited by Schaie KW. New York, Guilford Press,1983

Jarvik LF, Gerson S: Outcome of drug treatment in depressed patients over the age of fifty, in Treatment of Affective Disorders in the Elderly. Edited by Shamoian CA. Washington, DC, American Psychiatric Press, 1985

Jarvik LF, Ruth V, Matsuyama SS: Organic brain syndrome and aging: a six year follow-up of surviving twins. Arch Gen Psychiatry 37:280–286, 1980

Jarvik LF, Read SL, Mintz J, et al: Pretreatment orthostatic hypotension in geriatric depression: predictor of response to imipramine and doxepin. J Clin Psychopharmacol 3:368–372, 1983

Javid M, Settlage P: Effect of urea on cerebrospinal fluid pressure in human subjects. JAMA 160:943–949, 1956

Jefferson JW: Beta-adrenergic receptor blocking drugs in psychiatry. Arch Gen Psychiatry 31:681–691, 1974

Jefferson JW: Treating affective disorders in the presence of cardiovascular disease. Psychiatr Clin North Am 6:141–155, 1983

Jefferson JW, Greist JH: Lithium and the kidney, in Psychopharmacology Update: New and Neglected Areas. Edited by Davis JM, Greenblatt D. New York, Grune & Stratton, 1979

Jefferson JW, Marshall JR (eds): Neuropsychiatric features of medical disorders. New York, Plenum, 1981a

Jefferson JW, Marshall JR: Renal disorders, in Neuropsychiatric Features of Medical Disorders. Edited by Jefferson JW, Marshall JR. New York, Plenum, 1981b

Jefferson JW, Griest JH, Baudhuin M: Lithium: interactions with other drugs. J Clin Psychopharmacol 1:124–134, 1981

Jefferson JW, Greist JH, Ackerman DL: Lithium Encyclopedia for Clinical Practice. Madison, Wisc, Lithium Information Center, 1983

Jellinek MS, Goldenheim PD, Jenike MA: The impact of grief on ventilatory control. Am J Psychiatry 142:121–123, 1985

Jellinger K, Riederer P: Dementia in Parkinson's disease and (pre) senile dementia of Alzheimer type: morphological aspects and changes in the intracerebral MAO activity, in Advances in Neurology, vol 40. Edited by Hassler RG, Christ JF. New York, Raven Press, 1984

Jenike MA: Cimetidine in elderly patients: review of uses and risks. J Am Geriatr Soc 30:170–173, 1982

Jenike MA: Dexamethasone suppression test as a clinical aid in elderly depressed patients. J Am Geriatr Soc 31:45–48, 1983a

Jenike MA: Treating the violent elderly patient with propranolol. Geriatrics 38:29–30, 34, 1983b

Jenike MA: Handbook of Geriatric Psychopharmacology. Littleton, Mass, PSG Publishing, 1985a

Jenike MA: Monoamine oxidase inhibitors as treatment for depressed patients with primary degenerative dementia (Alzheimer's disease). Am J Psychiatry 142:763–764, 1985b

Jenike MA, Albert MS: The dexamethasone suppression test in patients with presenile and senile dementia of the Alzheimer's type. J Am Geriatr Soc 32:441–444, 1984

Jenkins JS, Mather HM, Coughlan AK, et al: Desmopressin in posttraumatic amnesia. Lancet 2:1245–1246, 1979

Jenkins JS, Mather HM, Coughlan AK, et al: Desmopressin and desglycinamide vasopressin in posttraumatic amnesia. Lancet 1:39, 1981

Jenkins JS, Mather HM, Coughlan AK: Effect of desmopressin on normal and impaired memory. J Neurosurg Psychiatry 45:830–831, 1982

Jenner FA: Lithium and the question of kidney damage. Arch Gen Psychiatry 36:888–890, 1979

Jensen I, Larsen JK: Mental aspects of temporal lobe epilepsy: follow up of 74 patients after resection of a temporal lobe. J Neurol Neurosurg Psychiatry 42:256–265, 1979

Jeste DV, Wyatt RJ: Understanding and treating tardive dyskinesia. New York, Guilford Press, 1982

Jeste DV, Karson CN, Wyatt RJ: Movement disorders and psychopathology, in Neuropsychiatric Movement Disorders. Edited by Jeste DV, Wyatt RJ. Washington, DC, American Psychiatric Press, 1984

Jeste DV, Grebb JA, Wyatt RJ: Psychiatric aspects of movement disorders and demyelinating diseases, in American Psychiatric Association Annual Review, vol 4. Edited by Hales RE, Frances AJ. Washington, DC, American Psychiatric Press, 1985

Johannessen SI, Strandjord RE: The influence of phenobarbitone and phenytoin on carbamazepine serum levels, in Clinical Pharmacology of Antiepileptic Drugs. Edited by Schneider H, Janz D, Gardner-Thorpe C, et al. Heidelberg, Springer, 1975

Johns CA, Haroutunian V, Greenwald BS, et al: Development of cholinergic drugs for the treatment of Alzheimer's disease. Drug Dev Res 5:77–96, 1985

Jones HR, Siekert RG, Geraci JE: Neurologic manifestations of bacterial endocarditis. Ann Intern Med 71:21–28, 1969

Jonker C: VII Work Congress of Psychiatry (abstract). Vienna, 1983

Jonsen AR, Siegler M, Winslade WJ: Clinical Ethics. New York, Macmillan, 1982

Jouvent R, Lecrubier Y, Puech AJ, et al: Antimanic effect of clonidine. Am J Psychiatry 137:1275–1276, 1980

Kahn RL: Psychological aspects of aging, in Clinical Geriatrics. Edited by Rossman I. Philadelphia, JB Lippincott, 1971

Kahn RL, Goldfarb AI, Pollack M, et al: Brief objective measures for the determination of mental status in the aged. Am J Psychiatry 117:326–328, 1960

Kahn RL, Zarit SH, Hilbert NM, et al: Memory complaint and impairment in the aged. Arch Gen Psychiatry 32:1569–1573, 1975

Kales A, Soldatos CR, Bixler EO, et al: Early morning insomnia with rapidly eliminated benzodiazepines. Science 230:95–97, 1983

Kane CA: Transient global amnesia: A common benign condition. West J Med 138:725–727, 1983

Kaplan B: Biofeedback in epileptics: equivocal relationship of reinforced EEG frequency to seizure reduction. Epilepsia 16:477–485, 1975

Karagulla S, Robertson EE: Physical phenomena in temporal lobe epilepsy and the psychoses. Br Med J 1:748–752, 1955

Karhunen U, Orko R: Psychiatric reactions complicating cataract surgery: a prospective study. Ophthalmic Surg 13:1008–1012, 1982

Karliner W: ECT for patients with CNS disease. Psychosomatics 19:781–783, 1978

Karpel MA: Family secrets. Fam Process 19:295–306, 1980

Kastin AJ, Olson GA, Sandman CA, et al: Possible role of peptides in senile dementia, in Strategies for the Development of an Effective Treatment for Senile Dementia.

Edited by Crook T, Gershon S. New Canaan, Conn, Mark Powley Associates, 1981

Katon W, Raskind M: Treatment of depression in the medically ill elderly with methylphenidate. Am J Psychiatry 137:963–965, 1980

Katona CL, Aldridge CR: The dexamethasone suppression test and dementia. Br J Psychiatry 144:333, 1984

Katz J: Experimentation with Human Beings. New York, Russel Sage Foundation, 1972

Katz J: The Silent World of Doctor and Patient. New York, Free Press, 1984

Kay DWK, Roth M: Environmental and hereditary factors in the schizophrenias of old age and their bearing on the general problem of causation in schizophrenia. J Ment Sci 107:649–686, 1961

Kay DWK, Cooper AF, Garside RF, et al: The differentiation of paranoid from affective psychoses by patient's premorbid characteristics. Br J Psychiatry 129:207–215, 1976

Keane JR: Neuro-ophthalmic signs and symptoms of hysteria. Neurology (NY) 32:757–762, 1982

Kelwala S, Pomara N, Stanley M, et al: Lithium-induced accentuation of extrapyramidal symptoms in individuals with Alzeheimer's disease. J Clin Psychiatry 45:342–344, 1984

Kennedy J, Parbhoo SP, MacGillwray B, et al: Effects of extracorporeal liver perfusion on the electroencephalogram of patients in coma due to acute liver failure. Q J Med 42:549–561, 1973

Kiersch TA: Toxic organic psychoses due to isoniazid therapy. US Armed Forces Medical Journal 5:1353–1359, 1954

Kiloh LG: Pseudo-dementia. Acta Psychiatr Scand 37:336–351, 1961

Kincaid-Smith P, Burrows GD, Davies DM, et al: Renal biopsy findings in lithium and prelithium patients. Lancet 2:700–701, 1979

Kistler JP, Ropper AH, Heros RL: Therapy of ischemic cerebral vascular disease due to atherothrombosis: part II. N Engl J Med 311:100–105, 1984

Klawans HL: Levodopa-induced psychosis. Psychiatric Annals 8:447–451, 1978

Klawans HL, Tanner CM: Movement disorders in the elderly, in Clinical Neurology of Aging. Edited by Albert ML. New York, Oxford University Press, 1984

Kleber HD, Gawin FH: The spectrum of cocaine abuse and its treatment. J Clin Psychiatry 45(suppl):18–23, 1984

Kleinknecht RA, Goldstein SC: Neuropsychological deficits associated with alcoholism: a review and discussion. Quarterly Journal of Studies on Alcohol 33:999–1019, 1972

Klerman GL, Davidson JM: Memory loss and affective disorders. Psychosomatics 25:29–32, 1984

Klotz U, Antonin KH, Brugel H, et al: Disposition of diazepam and its major metabolite, desmethyl diazepam, in patients with liver disease. Clin Pharmacol Ther 21:430–436, 1977

Knesevich JW: Successful treatment of obsessive-compulsive disorder with clonidine hydrochloride. Am J Psychiatry 139:364–366, 1982

Koch-Henriksen H, Nielsen H: Vasopressin in posttraumatic amnesia. Lancet 1:38–39, 1981

Kolata G: Alzheimer's research poses dilemma. Science 215:47–48, 1982

Kolmel HW: Complex visual hallucinations in the hemianopic field. J Neurol Neurosurg Psychiatry 48:29–38, 1985

Komrad MS, Coffey CE, Coffey KS, et al: Myocardial infarction and stroke. Neurology 34:1403–1409, 1984

Kornfeld DS: Psychiatric aspects of liver disease, in Emotional Factors in Gastrointestinal Illness. Edited by Lindner AE. Amsterdam, Excerpta Medica, 1973

Kosberg JI (ed): Abuse and Maltreatment of the Elderly. Boston, John Wright, 1982

Kothary S, Brown A, Pandit M, et al: Time course of antirecall effect of diazepam and lorazepam following oral administration. Anesthesiology 55:641–644, 1981

Kovner R, Mattis S, Goldmeier E: A technique for promoting robust free recall in chronic organic amnesia. J Clin Neuropsychol 5:65–71, 1983

Kragh-Sørensen P, Gram LF, Larsen NE: Routine use of plasma concentration measurement of tricyclic antidepressant drugs: indications and limitations, in Clinical Pharmacology in Psychiatry. Edited by Usdin E. New York, Elsevier-North Holland, 1981

Kral VA: Benign senescent forgetfulness, in Alzheimer's Disease: Senile Dementia and Related Disorders (Aging, vol 7). Edited by Katzman R, Terry RD, Bick KL. New York, Raven Press, 1978

Kramlinger KG, Peterson GL, Watson PK, et al: Metyrapone for depression and delirium secondary to Cushing's syndrome. Psychosomatics 26:67–71, 1985

Kramp P, Bolwig TG: Electroconvulsive therapy in acute delirious states. Compr Psychiatry 22:368–371, 1981

Kraus JF, Black MA, Hessol N, et al: The incidence of acute brain injury and serious impairment in a defined population. Am J Epidemiol 119:186–201, 1984

Kraus JM, Desmond PV, Marshall JP, et al: Effects of aging and liver disease on disposition of lorazepam. Clin Pharmacol Ther 24:411–419, 1978

Krauthammer C, Klerman GL: Secondary mania: manic syndromes associated with antecedent physical illness or drugs. Arch Gen Psychiatry 35:1333–1339, 1978

Kristensen O, Sindrup EH: Psychomotor epilepsy and psychosis. Acta Neurol Scand 57:361–379, 1978

Kristensen V, Olsen M, Theilgaard A: Levodopa treatment of presenile dementia. Acta Psychiatr Scand 55:41–51, 1977

Kronenberg RS, Cosio MG, Stevenson JE, et al: The use of oral diazepam in patients with obstructive lung disease and hypercapnia. Ann Intern Med 83:83–84, 1975

Kronig MH, Roose SP, Walsh BT, et al: Blood pressure effects of phenelzine. J Clin Psychopharmacol 3:307–310, 1983

Krop HD, Block AJ, Cohen E: Neuropsychologic effects of continuous oxygen therapy in chronic obstructive pulmonary disease. Chest 64:317–322, 1973

Kugler J, Oswald WD, Herzfeld U, et al: Long-term treatment of the symptoms of senile cerebral insufficiency: a prospective study of hydergine. Dtsch Med Wochenschr 103:456–462, 1978

Kuhl DE: Prolonged delirium with propranolol. J Clin Psychiatry 40:194–195, 1979

Kuhl DE: Imaging local brain function with emission computed tomography. Radiology 150:625–631, 1984

Kuhlman WM, Allison T: EEG feedback training in the treatment of epilepsy: some questions and answers. Pavlov J Biol Sci 12:112–122, 1977

Kulig K, Rumack BH, Sullivan JB, et al: Amoxapine overdose: coma and seizures without cardiotoxic effects. JAMA 248:1092–1094, 1982

Kulshrestha VK, Thomas M, Wadsworth J, et al: Interaction between antacids and phenytoin. Br J Clin Pharmacol 6:177–179, 1978

Kurland ML: Organic brain syndrome with propranolol. N Engl J Med 300:366, 1979

Kurtzke JF: Neuroepidemiology. Ann Neurol 16:265–277, 1984

Kutt H, Winters W, Scherman R, et al: Diphenylhydantoin and phenobarbital toxicity. Arch Neurol 11:649–656, 1964a

Kutt H, Winters W, Kokenge R, et al: Diphenylhydantoin metabolism, blood levels and toxicity. Arch Neurol 11:642–648, 1964b

Labi MLC, Phillips TF, Gresham GE: Psychosocial disability in physically restored long-term stroke survivors. Arch Phys Med Rehabil 61:561–565, 1980

Laidlaw J, Read AE, Sherlock S: Morphine tolerance in hepatic cirrhosis. Gastroenterology 40:389–396, 1961

Lake CR, Pickar D, Ziegler MG, et al: High plasma norepinephrine levels in patients with major affective disorder. Am J Psychiatry 139:1315–1318, 1982

LaMont JT, Koff RS, Isselbacher KJ: Cirrhosis, in Harrison's Principles of Internal Medicine, 10th ed. Edited by Petersdorf RG, Adams RD, Braunwald E, et al. New York, McGraw-Hill, 1983

Lance JW: Simple formed hallucinations confined to the area of a specific visual field defect. Brain 99:719–734, 1976

Landau RL, Gustafson JM: Death is not the enemy. JAMA 252:2458, 1984

Lander CM, Eadie MJ, Tyrer JH: Factors influencing plasma carbamazepine concentrations. Clin Exp Neurol 14:184–193, 1977

Landolt WG: Serial electroencephalographic investigations during schizophrenic attacks, in Lectures on Epilepsy. Edited by De Haan L. Amsterdam, Elsevier, 1958

Lansdown FS, Beran M, Litwak T: Psychotoxic reaction during ethioamide therapy. Am Rev Respir Dis 95:1053, 1055, 1967

Leaf A: Posterior pituitary, in Textbook of Medicine, 13th ed. Edited by Beeson PB, McDermott W. Philadelphia, WB Saunders, 1971

Leaf A: The doctor's dilemma: and society's too. N Engl J Med 310:718–720, 1984

Leber P. Establishing the efficacy of drugs with psychogeriatric indications, in Assessment in Geriatric Psychopharmacology. Edited by Crook T, Ferris S, Bartus R. New Canaan, Conn, Mark Powley Associates, 1983

LeBoeuf A, Lodge J, Eames PG: Vasopressin and memory in Korsakoff syndrome. Lancet 2:1370, 1978

Lechtenberg R: The Psychiatrist's Guide to Disease of the Nervous System. New York, John Wiley and Sons, 1982

Lefkowitz MM: Effects of diphenylhydantoin on disruptive behavior: study of male delinquents. Arch Gen Psychiatry 20:645–651, 1969

Lehmann J, Persson S, Walinder J, et al: Tryptophan malabsorption in dementia: improvement in certain cases after tryptophan therapy as indicated by mental behaviour and blood analysis. Acta Psychiatr Scand 64:123–131, 1981

Lehrich JR: Measles like virus: subacute sclerosing panencephalitis, in Principles and Practice of Infectious Disease. Edited by Mandell GL, Douglas RG, Bennett JE. New York, John Wiley and Sons, 1979

Lemberger L, Sernantin E, Kuntzman R: The effects of haloperidol and chlorpromazine on amphetamine metabolism and amphetamine stereotype behavior in the rat. J Pharmacol Exp Ther 174:428–433, 1970

Lennard C, Kaufman BS: Legal issues in geriatric psychiatry, in Geriatric Psychiatry: Ethical and Legal Issues. Edited by Stanley B. Washington, DC, American Psychiatric Press, 1985

Lennox WG: Epilepsy and Related Disorders, vol 2. Boston, Little Brown, 1960

Lesar T, Kingston R, Dahms R, et al: Trazodone overdose. Ann Emerg Med 12:221–223, 1983

Lessel S, Cohen MM: Phosphenes induced by sound. Neurology 29:1524–1526, 1979

Lester DM: The psychological import of COPD, in Pulmonary Care. Edited by Johnson RF. New York, Grune & Stratton, 1973

Levenson JL, Friedel RO: Major depression in patients with cardiac disease: diagnosis and somatic treatment. Psychosomatics 26:91–102, 1985

Levine DN, Grek A: The anatomic basis of delusions after right cerebral infarction. Neurology 34:577–582, 1984

Levinsky NG: Acidosis and alkalosis, in Principles of Internal Medicine, 9th ed. Edited by Isselbacher KJ, Adams RD, Braunwald E, et al. New York, McGraw-Hill, 1980a

Levinsky NG: Fluids and electrolytes, in Principles of Internal Medicine, 9th ed. Edited by Isselbacher KJ, Adams RD, Braunwald E, et al. New York, McGraw-Hill, 1980b

Levy NB: Psychological reactions to machine dependency: hemodialysis. Psychiatr Clin North Am 4:351–363, 1981

Levy RI: Prevalence and epidemiology of cardiovascular disease, in Cecil's Textbook of Medicine, 17th ed. Edited by Wyngaarden JB, Smith LH. Philadelphia, WB Saunders, 1985

Lewis C, Ballinger BR, Presly AS: Trial of levodopa in senile dementia. Br Med J 1:550, 1978

Lewis DO, Pincus JH, Feldman M, et al: Psychiatric, neurological, and psychoeducational characteristics of 15 death row inmates in the United States. Am J Psychiatry 143:838–845, 1986

Lezak MD: Living with the characterologically altered brain injured patient. J Clin Psychiatry 39:592–598, 1978

Liberman RP, Wong SE: Behavior analysis and therapy procedures related to seclusion and restraint, in The Psychiatric Uses of Seclusion and Restraint. Edited by Tardiff K. Washington, DC, American Psychiatric Press, 1984

Lieberman JA, Cooper TB, Suckow RF: Tricyclic antidepressant and metabolite levels in chronic renal failure. Clin Pharmacol Ther 37:301–307, 1985

Liebowitz M, Fryer AJ, McGrath P, et al: Clonidine treatment of panic disorder. Psychopharmacol Bull 17:122–123, 1981

Lim ML, Ebrahim SBJ: Depression after stroke: a hospital treatment survey. Postgrad Med J 59:489–491, 1983

Linn L, Kahn RL, Coles R, et al: Patterns of behavior following cataract extraction. Am J Psychiatry 110:281–289, 1953

Lipinski JF, Pope HG Jr: Possible synergistic action between carbamazepine and lithium carbonate in the treatment of three manic patients. Am J Psychiatry 139:948–949, 1982

Lipowski ZJ: Delirium: Acute Brain Failure in Man. Springfield, Ill, Charles C Thomas, 1980

Lipowski ZJ: Transient cognitive disorders (delirium, acute confusional states) in the elderly. Am J Psychiatry 140:1426–1436, 1983

Lipowski ZJ: Delirium (acute confusional state), in Handbook of Clinical Neurology. Edited by Vinken PJ, Bruyn GW, Klawans HL. New York, Elsevier, 1985

Lipper S: Psychosis in patient on bromocriptine and levodopa with carbidopa. Lancet 2:571–572, 1976

Lippman G, Bunch S, Abuton J, et al: A trazodone overdosage. Am J Psychiatry 139:1373, 1982

Lipsey JR, Robinson RG, Pearlson GD, et al: Mood change following bilateral hemisphere brain injury. Br J Psychiatry 143:266–273, 1983

Lipsey JR, Robinson RG, Pearlson GD, et al: Nortriptyline treatment of post-stroke depression: a double-blind study. Lancet 1:297–300, 1984

Liptzin B: Canadian and U.S. systems of care for the mentally ill elderly. Gerontologist 24:174–178, 1984

Lishman WA: Brain damage in relation to psychiatric disability after head injury. Br J Psychiatry 114:373–410, 1968

Lishman WA: Organic Psychiatry: The Psychological Consequences of Cerebral Disorder. Oxford, Blackwell Scientific, 1978

Lishman WA: Cerebral disorder in alcoholism: syndromes of impairment. Brain 104:1–20, 1981

Liskow B: Substance induced and substance use disorders: barbiturates and similarly acting sedative hypnotics, in Treatment of Mental Disorders. Edited by Greist JH, Jefferson JW, Spitzer RL. New York, Oxford University Press, 1982

Liston EH: Delirium in the aged. Psychiatr Clin North Am 5:49–66, 1982

Liston EH: Diagnosis and management of delirium in the elderly patient. Psychiatric Annals 14:109–118, 1984

Liston EH, La Rue A: Clinical differentiation of primary degenerative and multi-infarct dementia: a critical review of the evidence: part I. Biol Psychiatry 18:1451–1465, 1983a

Liston EH, La Rue A: Clinical differentiation of primary degenerative and multi-infarct dementia: a critical review of the evidence: part II. Biol Psychiatry 18:1467–1484, 1983b

Lloyd BL, Greenblatt DJ: Neuropsychiatric sequelae of pharmacotherapy of cardiac arrhythmias and hypertension. J Clin Psychopharmacol 1:394–398, 1981

Lo B, Dornbrand L: Guiding the hand that feeds: caring for the demented elderly. N Engl J Med 311:402–404, 1984

Loew DM, Singer JM: Stimulants and senility, in Stimulants: Neurochemical, Behavioral, and Clinical Perspectives. Edited by Creese I. New York, Raven Press, 1983

Logothetis J: Spontaneous epileptic seizures and electroencephalographic changes in the course of phenothiazine treatment. Neurology 17:869–877, 1967

Longstreth WT, Swanson PD: Oral contraceptives and stroke. Stroke 15:747–750, 1984

Loranger AW, Goodell H, McDowell FH, et al: Intellectual impairment in Parkinson's syndrome. Brain 95:405–412, 1972a

Loranger AW, Goodell H, Lee JE, et al: Levodopa treatment of Parkinson's syndrome: improved intellectual functioning. Arch Gen Psychiatry 26:163–168, 1972b

Loranger AW, Goodell H, McDowell FH, et al: Parkinsonism, L-dopa, and intelligence. Am J Psychiatry 130:1386–1389, 1973

Loughman PM, Greenwald A, Purton WW: Pharmacokinetic observations of phenytoin disposition in the newborn and young infant. Arch Dis Child 52:302–309, 1977

Lubar JF: Electroencephalographic methodology and the management of epilepsy. Pavlov J Biol Sci 12:147–185, 1977

Lubar JF, Bahler JF: Behavioural management of epileptic seizures following EEG biofeedback training of the sensori-motor rhythm. Biofeedback Self Regul 1:77–104, 1976

Luchins DJ: Carbamazepine for the violent psychiatric patient. Lancet 2:766, 1983a

Luchins DJ: Review of clinical and animal studies comparing the cardiovascular effects of doxepin and other tricyclic antidepressants. Am J Psychiatry 140:1006–1009, 1983b

Lunzer M, James IM, Weinman JJ, et al: Treatment of chronic hepatic encephalopathy with levodopa. Gut 15:555–561, 1974

MacCallam WAG: Capgras symptoms with an organic basis. Br J Psychiatry 123:639–642, 1973

MacKinnon RA, Michels R: Psychiatric Interview in Clinical Practice. New York, Saunders, 1971

MacKinnon RA, Yudofsky SC (eds): The Psychiatric Evaluation in Clinical Practice. Philadelphia, JB Lippincott, 1986

Madakasira S, Hall TB III: Capras syndrome in a patient with myxedema. Am J Psychiatry 138:1506–1508, 1981

Maddrey WC, Weber FL: Chronic hepatic encephalopathy. Med Clin North Am 59:937–944, 1975

Madsbad S, Bjerregaard B, Henriksen JH, et al: Impaired conversion of prednisolone in patients with liver cirrhosis. Gut 21:52–56, 1980

Mahapatra SB: Deafness and mental health: psychiatric and psychosomatic illness in the deaf. Acta Psychiatr Scand 50:596–611, 1974

Maletta GJ, Pirozzolo FT, Thompson G, et al: Organic mental disorders in a geriatric outpatient population. Am J Psychiatry 139:521–523, 1982

Maletzky BM: The episodic dyscontrol syndrome. Diseases of the Nervous System 34:186–189, 1973

Malone M, Prior P, Scholtz CL: Brain damage after cardio-pulmonary bypass: correlations between neurophysiological and neuropathological findings. J Neurol Neurosurg Psychiatry 44:924–931, 1981

Mandel MR, Madsen J, Miller AL, et al: Intoxication associated with lithium and ECT. Am J Psychiatry 137:1107–1109, 1980

Mann DMA, Lincoln J, Yates PO: Changes in the monoamine containing neurons of the human CNS in senile dementia. Br J Psychiatry 136:533–541, 1980

Mann JJ, Stanley M, Neophytides H, et al: Central amine metabolism in Alzheimer's disease: in vivo relationship to cognitive deficit. Neurobiol Aging 2:57–60, 1981

Mann JJ, Aarons SF, Frances AJ, et al: Studies of selective and reversible monoamine oxidase inhibitors. J Clin Psychiatry 45:62–66, 1984

Margolis J: Hypothermia, a grave prognostic sign in hepatic coma. Arch Intern Med 139:103–104, 1979

Mark VH, Ervin FR: Violence and the Brain. New York, Harper and Row, 1970

Marquis JF, Carruthers SG, Spence JD, et al: Phenytoin-theophylline interaction. N Engl J Med 307:1189–1190, 1982

Marsden CD: Function of the basal ganglia as revealed by cognitive and motor disorders in Parkinson's disease. Can J Neurol Sci 11:129–135, 1984

Marsden CD, Harrison MJG: Outcome of investigation of patients with pre-senile dementia. Br Med J 2:249–252, 1972

Martin JB, Reichlin S, Brown GM: Clinical neuroendocrinology. Philadelphia, FA Davis, 1977

Martin JC, Ballinger BR, Cockram LL, et al: Effect of a synthetic peptide, ORG 2766, on inpatients with severe senile dementia: a controlled clinical trial. Acta Psychiatr Scand 67:205–207, 1983

Martinez JL Jr, Jensen RA, Creager R: Selective effects of enkephalin on electrical activity of the in vitro hippocampal slice. Behav Neural Biol 26:128–131, 1979

Masm AS, Granacher RD: Clinical Handbook of Antipsychotic Drug Therapy. New York, Brunner/Mazel, 1980

Mason RW, McQueen EG, Keary PJ, et al: Pharmacokinetics of lithium: elimination half-life, renal clearance and apparent volume of distribution and schizophrenia. Clin Pharmacokinet 3:241–246, 1978

Mattson RH, Heninger GR, Gallagher BB, et al: Psycho-physiological precipitants of seizures in epileptics. Neurology 20:407, 1970

Mattson RH, Cramer JA, Collins JF, et al: Comparison of carbamazepine, phenobarbital, phenytoin, and primidone in partial and secondarily generalized tonic-clonic seizures. N Engl J Med 313:145–151, 1985

Maxwell JD, Carella M, Parkes JD, et al: Plasma disappearance and cerebral effects of chlorpromazine in cirrhosis. Clin Sci 43:143–151, 1972

Mayer SE: Neurohumoral transmissions and the autonomic nervous system, in The Pharmacological Basis of Therapeutics, 6th ed. Edited by Goodman Gilman A, Goodman LS, Gilman A. New York, Macmillan, 1980

Mayeux R: Depression and dementia in Parkinson's disease, in Movement Disorders, vol 2. Edited by Marsden CD, Fahn S. London, Butterworth Scientific, 1982

Mayeux R: Behavioral manifestations of movement disorders: Parkinson's and Huntington's disease, in Neurologic Clinics, vol 2. Edited by Jankovic J. Philadelphia, WB Saunders, 1984

Mayeux R, Stern Y: Intellectual dysfunction and dementia in Parkinson disease, in The Dementias. Edited by Mayeux R, Rosen WG. New York, Raven Press, 1983

Mayeux R, Stern Y, Rosen J, et al: Is "subcortical dementia" a recognizable clinical entity? Ann Neurol 14:278–283, 1983

Mayeux R, Williams JBW, Stern Y, et al: Depression and Parkinson's disease, in Advances in Neurology, vol 40. Edited by Hassler RG, Christ JF, New York, Raven Press, 1984

McAllister TW: Overview: pseudodementia. Am J Psychiatry 140:528–533, 1983

McClain CJ: When liver disease causes brain damage. Geriatrics 35:74–89, 1980

McClelland HA: Psychiatric disorders, in Textbook of Adverse Drug Reactions, 2nd ed. Edited by Davies DM. Oxford, Oxford University Press, 1981

McClelland HA, Roth M, Neubauer H, et al: Some observations on a case material based on patients with common schizophrenic symptoms. Proceedings of the IV World Congress of Psychiatry 4:2955–2957, 1968

McCracken J, Kosanin R: Trazodone administration during ECT associated with cardiac conduction abnormality. Am J Psychiatry 141:1488–1489, 1984

McCrum ED, Guidry JR: Procainamide-induced psychosis. JAMA 240:1265–1266, 1978

McDonald RJ: Drug treatment of senile dementia, in Psychopharmacology of Old Age. Edited by Wheatly D. London, Oxford University Press, 1982

McDowell FH, Lee JE, Sweet RD: Extrapyramidal diseases, in Clinical Neurology, 3rd ed, vol 2. Edited by Baker AB, Baker LH. Maryland, Harper and Row, 1978

McGlothlin WH, West LJ: The marijuana problem: an overview. Am J Psychiatry 125:1126–1134, 1968

McGovern GP, Miller DH, Robertson EE: A mental syndrome associated with lung carcinoma. Arch Neurol Psychiatry 81:341–347, 1959

McKay AC, Dundee JW: Effect of oral benzodiazepines on memory. Br J Anaesth 52:1247–1257, 1980

McKeith IG: Clinical use of the DST in a psychogeriatric population. Br J Psychiatry 145:389–393, 1984

McKhann G, Drachman D, Folstein M, et al: Clinical diagnosis of Alzheimer's disease: report of the NINCDS-ADRDA Work Group under the auspices of Department of Health and Human Services Task Force on Alzheimer's Disease. Neurology 34:939–944, 1984

McKinlay WW, Brooks DN, Bond MR, et al: The short-term outcome of severe blunt head injury as reported by the relatives of the injured person. J Neurol Neurosurg Psychiatry 44:527–533, 1981

McMahon CD, Shaffer RN, Hoskins HD, et al: Adverse effects experienced by patients taking timolol. Am J Ophthalmol 88:736–738, 1979

McNamara ME, Heros RC, Boller F: Visual hallucinations in blindness: the Charles Bonnet syndrome. Int J Neurosci 17:13–15, 1982

McNamara PJ, Lalka D, Gibaldi M: Endogenous accumulation products and serum protein binding in uremia. J Lab Clin Med 98:730–740, 1981

McNeil GN, Shaw PK, Dock DS: Substitution of atenolol for propranolol in a case of propranolol-induced depression. Am J Psychiatry 139:1187–1188, 1982

McNichol RW, Hoshino AY: Therapy for deliria, in Current Psychiatric Therapies, vol 15. Edited by Masserman JH. New York, Grune & Stratton, 1975

McSweeney AJ, Heaton RK, Grant I, et al: COPD: socioemotional adjustment and life quality. Chest 77:309–311, 1980

McSweeney AJ, Heaton RK, Grant I, et al: Med Lett Drugs Ther 23:29–30, 1981

McSweeney AJ, Heaton RK, Grant I, et al: Med Lett Drugs Ther 24:39–41, 1982a

McSweeney AJ, Heaton RK, Grant I, et al: Med Lett Drugs Ther 24:56–58, 1982b

McSweeney AJ, Heaton RK, Grant I, et al: Med Lett Drugs Ther 25:17–18, 1983

McSweeney AJ, Heaton RK, Grant I, et al: Med Lett Drugs Ther 26:1–4, 1984a

McSweeney AJ, Heaton RK, Grant I, et al: Med Lett Drugs Ther 26:11–14, 1984b

McSweeney AJ, Heaton RK, Grant I, et al: Med Lett Drugs Ther 26:75–78, 1984c

McSweeney AJ, Heaton RK, Grant I, et al: Med Lett Drugs Ther 26:107–112, 1984d

Medina JL, Chokroverty S, Rubino FA: Syndrome of agitated delirium and visual impairment: a manifestation of medial temporo-occipital infarction. J Neurol Neurosurg Psychiatry 40:861–864, 1977

Meisel A, Roth LR, Lidz CW: Toward a model of the legal doctrine of informed consent. Am J Psychiatry 134:285–289, 1977

Mendez MF, Cummings JL, Benson DF: Epilepsy: psychiatric aspects and use of psychotropics. Psychosomatics 25:883–893, 1984

Mercer SO: Consequences of institutionalization of the aged, in Abuse and Maltreatment of the Elderly, Edited by Kosberg JI. Boston, John Wright, 1982

Merrill JP, Legrain M, Hoigne R: Observations on the role of urea in uremia. Am J Med 14:519–520, 1953

Mesulam MM: A cortical network for directed attention and unilateral neglect. Ann Neurol 10:309–325, 1981

Mesulam MM: Attention, confusional states and neglect, in Principles of Behavioral Neurology. Edited by Mesulam MM. Philadelphia, FA Davis Co, 1985

Mesulam MM, Waxman SG, Geschwind N, et al: Acute confusional states with right middle cerebral artery infarction. J Neurol Neurosurg Psychiatry 39:84–89, 1976

Meyer JS: Strategies for drug development in multi-infarct dementia, in Strategies for the Development of an Effective Treatment for Senile Dementia. Edited by Crook T, Gershon S. New Canaan, Conn, Mark Powley Associates, 1981

Meyer JS, Welch KM, Deshmukh VD, et al: Neurotransmitter precursor amino acids in the treatment of multiinfarct dementia and Alzheimer's disease. J Am Geriatr Soc 25:289–298, 1977

Meyers DW: Legal aspects of withdrawing nourishment from an incurably ill patient. Arch Intern Med 145:125–128, 1985

Miller BL et al: Late-life paraphrenia: an organic delusional syndrome. J Clin Psychiatry 47:4, 1986

Miller FA, Rampling D: Adverse effects of combined propranolol and chlorpromazine therapy. Am J Psychiatry 139:1198–1199, 1982

Miller RR: Clinical effects of pentazocine in hospitalized medical patients. J Clin Pharmacol 15:198–205, 1975

Miller R, Willner HS: The two-part consent form: a suggestion for promoting free and informed consent. N Engl J Med 290:964–966, 1974

Miller TC, Crosby TW: Musical hallucinations in a deaf elderly patient. Ann Neurol 5:301–302, 1979

Millikan CH, McDowell FH: Treatment of progressing stroke. Stroke 12:397–409, 1981

Mills MJ: The right to treatment: little law, but much impact, in Psychiatry 1982. Edited by Grinspoon L. Washington, DC, American Psychiatric Association, 1982

Mills MJ: Legal issues in psychiatric practice, in Psychiatric Medicine, vol 2. Edited by Hall RCW. New York, Spectrum, 1984

Mills MJ, Hsu LC, Berger PA: Informed consent: psychotic patients and research. Bull Am Acad Psychiatry Law 8:119–132, 1980

Mills MJ, Yesavage JA, Gutheil TG: Continuing case law development in the right to refuse treatment. Am J Psychiatry 134:715–719, 1983

Mills MJ, Winslade WJ, Lyon MA, et al: Clinicolegal aspects of treating demented patients. Psychiatric Annals 14:209–211, 1984

Mindham RHS: Psychiatric symptoms in Parkinsonism. J Neurol Neurosurg Psychiatry 33:188–191, 1970

Mindham RHS, Marsden CD, Parkes JD: Psychiatric symptoms during L-dopa therapy for Parkinson's disease and their relationship to physical disability. Psychol Med 6:23–33, 1976

Mitchell JE, Mackenzie TB: Cardiac effects of lithium therapy in man: a review. J Clin Psychiatry 43:47–51, 1982

Mitchell JR, Cavanaugh JH, Arias L, et al: Guanethidine and related agents, III: antagonism by drugs which inhibit the norephinephrine pump in man. J Clin Invest 49:1596–1604, 1970

Moe GK, Abildskov JA: Antiarrhythmic drugs, in the Pharmacologic Basis of Therapeutics, 5th ed. Edited by Goodman LS, Gilman A. New York, Macmillan, 1975

Mohs RC, Rosen WG, Greenwald DS, et al: Neuropathologically validated scales for Alzheimer's disease, in Assessment in Geriatric Psychopharmacology. Edited by Crook T, Ferris S, Bartus R. New Canaan, Conn, Mark Powley Associates, 1983

Moore DP: Rapid treatment of delirium in critically ill patients. Am J Psychiatr 134:1431–1432, 1977

Moore NC: Is paranoid illness associated with sensory defects in the elderly? J Psychosom Res 25:69–74, 1981

Morgan MY, Jakobovits A, Elithorn A, et al: Successful use of bromocriptine in the treatment of a patient with chronic portal-systemic encephalopathy. N Engl J Med 296:793–794, 1977

Morrison G, Chiang ST, Koepke HH, et al: Effect of renal impairment and hemodialysis on lorazepam kinetics. Clin Pharmacol Ther 35:646–652, 1984

Morse RM, Litin EM: The anatomy of a delirium. Am J Psychiatry 128:111–116, 1974

Mortimer JA, Schuman LM (eds.): The Epidemiology of Dementia. New York, Oxford University Press, 1981

Mortimer JA, Pirozzolo FJ, Hansch EC, et al: Relationship of motor symptoms to intellectual deficits in Parkinson disease. Neurology 32:133–137, 1982

Moscowitz C, Moses H, Klawans HL: Levodopa-induced psychosis: a kindling phenomenon. Am J Psychiatry 135:669–675, 1978

Moser M: Experience with isocarboxazid. JAMA 176:276–290, 1961

Mostofsky DI, Balaschak BA: Psychobiological control of seizures. Psychol Bull 4:723–759, 1977

Mullaley W, Huff K, Ronthal M, et al: Chronic confusional state with right middle cerebral artery occlusion (abstract). Neurology 32:96, 1982

Myerhoff B: Number Our Days. New York, Touchstone, 1978

Mykleburst HR: The Psychology of Deafness. New York, Grune & Stratton, 1964

Nadel I, Wallach M: Drug interaction between haloperidol and methyldopa. Br J Psychiatry 135:484, 1979

Nakada T, Knight RT: Alcohol and the central nervous system. Med Clin North Am 68:121–131, 1984

Nandy K: Centrophenoxine: effects on aging mammalian brain. J Am Geriatr Soc 27:74–81, 1978

National Safety Council: Accident Facts. Chicago, National Safety Council, 1985

Nausieda PA, Glantz R, Weber S, et al: Psychiatric complications of levodopa therapy of Parkinson's disease, in Advances in Neurology, vol 40. Edited by Hassler RG, Christ JF. New York, Raven Press, 1984

Neff KE, Denney D, Blachy PH: Control of severe agitation with droperidol. Diseases of the Nervous System 33:594–597, 1972

Nelson JC, Jatlow PI, Bock J, et al: Major adverse reactions during desipramine treatment, relationship to plasma drug concentrations, concomitant antipsychotic treatment, and patient characteristics. Arch Gen Psychiatry 39:1055–1061, 1982

Neshkes RE, Gerner R, Jarvik LF, et al: Orthostatic effects of imipramine and doxepin in depressed geriatric outpatients. J Clin Psychopharmacol 5:102–106, 1985

Newcomb RD, Ranson FG: Adverse systemic effects of ocular drug therapy, in Clinical

Ocular Pharmacology. Edited by Bartlet JD, Jaanus SD. Boston, Butterworths, 1984

Newell FW: Ophthalmology: Principles and Concepts. St. Louis, CV Mosby, 1982

Nikolovski OT, Fernandez JV: Capgras syndrome as an aftermath of chickenpox encephalitis. Psychiatric Opinion 15:39–43, 1978

Nocturnal Oxygen Therapy Trial Group: Continuous or nocturnal oxygen therapy in hypoxemic chronic obstructive lung disease. Ann Intern Med 93:391–398, 1980

Nolke AC: Severe toxic effects from aminophylline and theophylline suppositories in children. JAMA 161:693–697, 1956

Norberg A, Norberg B, Gippert H, et al: Ethical conflicts in long-term care of the aged: nutritional problems and the patient-care worker relationship. Br Med J 1:377–378, 1980

Norell H, Wilson CB, Slagel DE, et al: Leukoencephalopathy following the administration of methotrexate into the CSF in the treatment of primary brain tumors. Cancer 33:923–932, 1974

Nott PN, Fleminger JJ: Presenile dementia: the difficulties of early diagnosis Acta Psychiatr Scand 51:210–217, 1975

Novick D, Kreek MJ, Fanizza A, et al: Methadone disposition in maintained patients with chronic liver disease (abstract). Clin Res 28:622A, 1980

Oakley WF, Clarke WF, Parsons V: The use of dialysis bath fluid as a vehicle for a drug with a narrow therapeutic index. Postgrad Med J 50:511–512, 1974

O'Brien LS, Orine ML, Breckenridge AM: Failure of antacids to alter the pharmacokinetics of phenytoin. Br J Clin Pharmacol 6:176–177, 1978

Ochs HR, Rauh HW, Greenblatt DJ, et al: Clorazepate dipotassium and diazepam in renal insufficiency: serum concentrations and protein binding of diazepam and desmethyldiazepam. Nephron 37:100–104, 1984

Oddy M. Humphrey M, Uttley D: Stresses upon the relatives of head-injured patients. Br J Psychiatry 133:507–513, 1978

Odell WH: Humoral manifestations of nonendocrine neoplasm, in Textbook of Endocrinology, 4th ed. Edited by Williams RH. Philadelphia, WB Saunders, 1968

Oldham JM, Russakoff LM, Prusnofsky L: Seclusion: patterns and milieu. J Nerv Ment Dis 171:645–650, 1983

Oliver AP, Luchins DJ, Wyatt RJ: Neuroleptic-induced seizures. Arch Gen Psychiatry 39:206–209, 1982

Oliveras JC, Jandali MK, Timsit-Berthier M, et al: Vasopressin in amnesia. Lancet 1:42, 1978

Oller-Daurella L, Ramies R, Oller L: Reduction or discontinuance of antiepileptic drugs in patients seizure-free for more than 5 years, in Epileptology. Edited by Janz D. Stuttgart, George Thieme, 1976

Olsen S: Renal histopathology in various forms of acute anuria in man. Kidney Int [Suppl] 10:S2–8, 1976

Oritz A, Josef NC: Premature atrial contractions and amoxapine therapy: a case report. J Clin Pharmacol 3:246–249, 1983

Ounsted C, Lindsay J, Norman R: Biological Factors in Temporal Lobe Epilepsy. London, William Heinemann Medical Books, 1966

Owens WA: Age and mental abilities: a longitudinal study. Genet Psychol Monogr 48:3–54, 1953

Owens WA: Age and mental abilities: a second follow-up. J Educ Psychol 57:311–325, 1966

Padfield PL, Smith DA, Fitzsimmons EJ, et al: Disopyramide and acute psychosis. Lancet 1:1152, 1977

Palmore E: The social factors in aging, in Handbook of Geriatric Psychiatry. Edited by Busse EW, Blazer DG. New York, Van Nostrand Reinhold Co., 1980

Pandit SK, Heisterkamp DV, Cohen PJ: Further studies of the antirecall effect of lorazepam. Anesthesiology 45:495–500, 1976

Paris JJ, Rearden FE: Court responses to withholding or withdrawing artificial nutrition and fluids. JAMA 253:2243–2245, 1985

Parish RA, Haulman NJ, Burns RM: Interaction of theophylline with erythromycin base in a patient with seizure activity. Pediatrics 72:828–830, 1983

Parkes D: Mechanisms of bromocriptine-induced hallucinations. N Engl J Med 302:1479, 1980

Parkes JD, Sharpstone P, Williams R: Levodopa in hepatic coma. Lancet 2:1341–1343, 1970

Parnas J, Korsgaard S: Epilepsy and psychosis. Acta Psychiatr Scand 66:89–99, 1982

Patterson JW, Conolly ME, Dollery CT: The pharmacodynamics and metabolism of propranolol in man. Pharmacol Clin 2:127–133, 1970

Paykel E, Fleminger R, Watson JP: Psychiatric side effects of antihypertensive drugs other than reserpine. J Clin Psychopharmacol 2:14–39, 1982

Pearce I, Pearce JMS: Bromocriptine in parkinsonism. Br Med J 1:1402–1404, 1978

Pelletier LL Jr, Petersdorf RG: Infective endocarditis, in Principles of Internal Medicine, 9th ed. Edited by Isselbacher KJ, Adams RD, Braunwald E, et al. New York, McGraw-Hill, 1980

Perl M, Shelp EE: Psychiatric consultation masking moral dilemmas in medicine. N Engl J Med 307:618–621, 1982

Perry EK, Perry RH, Blessed G, et al: Necropsy evidence of central cholinergic deficits in senile dementia. Lancet 1:189, 1977a

Perry EK, Gibson PH, Blessed G, et al: Neurotransmitter enzyme abnormalities in senile dementia. J Neurol Sci 34:247–265, 1977b

Perry EK, Tomlinson BE, Blessed G, et al: Correlation of cholinergic abnormalities with senile plaques and mental test scores in senile dementia. Br Med J 2:1457–1459, 1978

Personage M: Treatment with carbamazepine: adults, in Advances in Neurology, vol 2. Edited by Penry JK, Dely DD. New York, Raven Press, 1975

Perucca E, Richens A: Anticonvulsant drug interactions, in The Treatment of Epilepsy. Edited by Tyrer JH. Philadelphia, JB Lippincott, 1980

Petersdorf RG, Adams RD, Braunwald E, et al: Harrison's Principles of Internal Medicine, 10th ed. New York, McGraw-Hill, 1983

Peterson C, Gibson GE: Amelioration of age-related neurochemical and behavioral deficits by 3, 4-diaminopyridine. Neurobiol Aging 4:25–30, 1983

Peterson R, Ghoneim M: Diazepam and human memory: influence on acquisition, retrieval, and state-dependent learning. Prog Neuropsychopharmacol 4:81–89, 1980

Petrie WM, Ban TA: Propranolol in organic agitation. Lancet 1:324, 1981

Petrie WM, Ban TA, Berney S, et al: Loxapine in psychogeriatrics: a placebo- and standard-controlled clinical investigation. J Clin Psychopharmacol 2:122–126, 1982a

Petrie WM, Maffucci RJ, Woolsey RL: Propranolol and depression. Am J Psychiatry 139:92–94, 1982b

Piafsky KM, Borga O: Plasma protein binding of basic drugs, II: importance of alpha 1-acid glycoprotein for interindividual variation. Clin Pharmacol Ther 22:545–549, 1977

Piafsky KM, Borga O, Odar-Cederlof I, et al: Increased plasma protein binding of propranolol and chlorpromazine mediated by disease-induced elevations of plasma alpha 1-acid glycoprotein. N Engl J Med 299:1435–1439, 1978

Pigache RM, Rigter H: Effects of peptides related to ACTH on mood and vigilance in man. Frontiers of Hormone Research 8:193–207, 1981

Pincus JH, Tucker G: Behavioral Neurology, 2nd ed. New York, Oxford University Press, 1978

Pincus HA, West J, Goldman H: Diagnosis-related groups and clinical research in psychiatry. Arch Gen Psychiatry 42:627–629, 1985

Pinessi L, Rainero I, Bianco C, et al: CSF and plasma dopamine levels in dementia of Alzheimer type, in Program of the 14th Collegium Internationale Neuro-Psychopharmacologicum Congress, Florence, Italy, 1984

Pitts F: Medical psychology of ECT, in Electroconvulsive Therapy: Biological Foundations and Clinical Applications. Edited by Abrams R, Essman WB. New York, SP Medical and Scientific Books, 1982

Pizzo PA, Bleyer WA, Poplack DG, et al: Reversible dementia temporally associated with intraventricular therapy with methotrexate in a child with acute myelogenous leukemia. J Pediatr 88:131–133, 1976

Pleasure H: Psychiatric and neurological side effects of isoniazid and iproniazid. Arch Neurol Psychiatry 73:313–320, 1954

Pleuvry BJ, Madison SE, Odeh RB, et al: Respiratory and psychological effects of oral temazepam in volunteers. Br J Anaesth 52:901–905, 1980

Plotkin DA, Jarvik LF: Cholinergic dysfunction in Alzheimer disease: cause or effect? in Perspectives in Aetiology of Psychiatric Disorders: Brain Neurotransmission and Neuropeptides, vol 65. Edited by van Ree JM, Matthysse S. Amsterdam: Elsevier, 1986

Plotkin DA, Gerson SC, Jarvik LF: Antidepressant drug treatment in the elderly, in Psychopharmacology, the Third Generation of Progress: The Emergence of Molecular Biology and Biological Psychiatry. Edited by Meltzer HY. New York, Raven Press, 1987, pp 1149–1158

Plum F: Dementia: an approaching epidemic. Nature 279:372–373, 1979

Plum F, Posner JB: Diagnosis of Stupor and Coma, 2nd ed. Philadelphia, FA Davis, 1972

Plum F, Posner JB: The Diagnosis of Stupor and Coma, 3rd ed. Philadelphia, FA Davis Co, 1980

Pochedly C: Neurotoxicity due to CNS therapy for leukemia. Med Pediatr Oncol 3:101–115, 1977

Poleck DG: The body: what happens to it in a crash. Traffic Safety Magazine April 1967

Pond DA: Psychiatric aspects of epilepsy. Journal of the Indian Medical Profession (Bombay) 3:1441–1451, 1957

Pond DA, Bidwell BH: A survey of epilepsy in 14 general practices, II: social and psychological aspects. Epilepsia 1:285–299, 1960

Pond SM, Graham GG, Birkett DJ, et al: Effects of tricyclic antidepressants on drug metabolism. Clin Pharmacol Ther 18:191–199, 1975

Port FK, Kroll PD, Rosenzweiz J: Lithium therapy during maintenance hemodialysis. Psychosomatics 20:130–131, 1979

Portin R, Raininko R, Rinne UK: Neuropsychological disturbances and cerebral atrophy determined by computerized tomography in parkinsonian patients with long-term levodopa treatment, in Advances in Neurology, vol 40. Edited by Hassler RG, Christ JF. New York, Raven Press, 1984

Portnoy RA: Hyperkinetic dysarthria as an early indicator of impending tardive dyskinesia. J Speech Hear Disord 44:214–219, 1979

Post F: Persistent Persecutory States of the Elderly. London, Pergamon Press, 1968

Post RM: Cocaine psychoses: a continuum model. Am J Psychiatry 132:225–231, 1975

Post RM, Uhde TW: Are the psychotropic effects of carbamazepine in manic depressive illness mediated through the limbic system: Psychiatr J Univ Ottawa 10:205–219, 1985

Post RM, Uhde TW, Wolff EA: Profile of clinical efficacy and side effects of carbamazepine in psychiatric illness. Acta Psychiatr Scand [Suppl] 313:104–117, 1984

Postma JU, Van Tilburg W: Visual hallucinations and delirium during treatment with amantadine (Symmetrel). J Am Geriatr Soc 23:212–215, 1975

Potter WZ, Rudorfer MV, Lane EA: Active metabolites of antidepressants: Pharmacodynamics and relative pharmacokinetics. Adv Biochem Psychopharmacol 39:373–390, 1984

Powell JR, Vozeh S, Hopewell P, et al: Theophylline disposition in acutely ill hospitalized patients: the effect of smoking, heart failure, severe airway obstruction, and pneumonia. Am Rev Respir Dis 118:227–238, 1978

President's Commission for the Study of Ethical Problems in Medicine and Biomedical and Behavioral Research: Deciding to Forego Life-Sustaining Treatment. Washington, DC, Government Printing Office, 1983

Preskorn SH, Reveley A: Pseudo-hypoparathyroidism and Capgras syndrome. Br J Psychiatry 133:34–37, 1978

Price DL, Whitehouse PJ, Struble RD, et al: Basal forebrain cholinergic systems in Alzheimer's disease and related dementias. Neuroscience Comment 1:84–92, 1982

Prigatano GP, Parsons OA, Wright E, et al: Neuropsychological test performance in mildly hypoxemic patients with COPD. J Consult Clin Psychol 51:108–116, 1983

Pritchard PB, Lombroso CT, McIntyre M: Psychological complications of temporal lobe epilepsy. Neurology 30:227–232, 1980

Pruitt AA, Rubin RH, Karchmer AW: Neurologic complications of bacterial endocarditis. Medicine 57:329–343, 1978

Quinn D: The Capgras syndrome : two case reports and a review. Can J Psychiatry 26:126–129, 1981

Quy RJ, Hutt SJ, Forrest S: Sensorimotor rhythm feedback training and epilepsy. Biol Psychol 9:129–149, 1979

Rabins PV: Psychopathology of Parkinson's disease. Compr Psychiatry 23:421–429, 1982

Rabins PV, Folstein MF: Delirium and dementia: diagnostic criteria and fatality rates. Br J Psychiatry 140:149–153, 1982

Rabins PV, Mace NL, Lucas MJ: Improvement of dementia. JAMA 249:353, 1983

Rabkin JG, Quitkin FM, McGrath P, et al: Adverse reactions to monoamine oxidase inhibitors, part II: treatment correlates and clinical management. J Clin Pharmacol 5:2–9, 1985

Rada RT, Kellner R: Thiothixene in the treatment of geriatric patients with chronic organic brain syndrome. J Am Geriatr Soc 24:105, 1976

Rafal RD, Posner MI, Walker JA, et al: Cognition and the basal ganglia: separating mental and motor components of performance in Parkinson's disease. Brain 107:1083–1094, 1984

Ragheb M, Buchanan D, Frolich JC: Interaction of indomethacin and ibuprofen with lithium in manic patients under a steady-state lithium level. J Clin Psychiatry 41:397–398, 1980

Rainer JD, Altshuler KZ, Kallmann FJ, et al: Family and Mental Health Problems in a Deaf Population. New York, Columbia University Press, 1963

Rajput AH, Offord K, Beard CM, et al: Epidemiological survey of dementia in parkinsonism and control population, in Advances in Neurology, vol 40. Edited by Hassler RG, Christ JF. New York, Raven Press, 1984

Ramsey P: The Patient as a Person. New Haven, Yale University Press, 1970

Ramsey TA, Cox M: Lithium and the kidney: a review. Am J Psychiatry 139:443–449, 1982

Rankin GO, Watkins BE, Sawutz DG: Chlorpromazine interactions with guanethidine

and a-methyldopa: effects on arterial pressure control and heart rate in renovas-
cular hypertensive rats. Arch Int Pharmacodyn Ther 260:130–140, 1982

Rao S, Sherbaniuk RW, Prosad K, et al: Cardiopulmonary effects of diazepam. Clin
Pharmacol Ther 14:182–184, 1973

Rappolt TR, Gay GR, Inaba DS: Propranolol: a specific antagonist to cocaine. Clin
Toxicol 10:265–270, 1977

Raskin NH, Fishman RA: Pyridoxine-deficiency neuropathy due to hydralazine. N
Engl J Med 273:1182–1185, 1965

Raskind M, Veith R, Barnes R, et al: Cardiovascular and antidepressant effects of
imipramine in the treatment of secondary depression in patients with ischemic
heart disease. Am J Psychiatry 139:1114–1117, 1982a

Raskind MA, Peskind ER, Rivard MF, et al: Dexamethasone suppression test and
cortisol circadian rhythm in primary degenerative dementia. Am J Psychiatry
139:1468–1471, 1982b

Raskind MA, Peskind ER, Holter JB, et al: Norepinephrine and MHPG levels in CSF
and plasma in Alzheimer's disease. Arch Gen Psychiatry 41:343–346, 1984

Ratey JS, Morrill R, Oxenkrug G: Use of propranolol for provoked and unprovoked
episodes of rage. Am J Psychiatry 140:1356–1357, 1983

Ratner J, Rosenberg G, Kral V, et al: Anticoagulant therapy for senile dementia. J Am
Geriatr Soc 20:556–559, 1972

Ratzan RM: Being old makes you different: the ethics of research with elderly subjects.
Hastings Cent Rep 10:32–42, 1980

Ratzan RM: The experiment that wasn't: a case report in clinical geriatric research.
Gerontologist 21:297–302, 1981

Rauch PK, Jenike MA: Digoxin toxicity possibly precipitated by trazodone. Psychosomatics 25:334–335, 1984

Rausch JL, Pavlinac DM, Newman PE: Complete heart block following a single dose
of trazodone. Am J Psychiatry 141:1472–1473, 1984

Ray I, Evans CJ: Paranoid psychosis with Ventolin (salbutamol tablets B.P.). Canadian
Psychiatric Association Journal 23:427, 1978

Read AE, Sherlock S, Laidlaw J, et al: The neuropsychiatric syndrome associated with
chronic liver disease and an extensive portal-systemic collateral circulation. Q J
Med 36:135–150, 1967

Read SL, Jarvik LF: Cerebrovascular disease in the differential diagnosis of dementia.
Psychiatric Annals 14:100–108, 1984

Read SL, Small GW, Jarvik LF: Dementia syndrome, in American Psychiatric Association Annual Review, vol 4. Edited by Hales RE, Frances AJ. Washington, DC,
American Psychiatric Press, 1985

Reagan TJ, Okazaki H: The thrombotic syndrome associated with carcinoma. Arch
Neurol 31:390–395, 1974

Rebec GV, Centore JM, White LK, et al: Ascorbic acid and the behavioral response
to haloperidol: implication for the action of antipsychotic drugs. Science 227:438–
440, 1985

Reches A, Fahn S: Lithium in the "on-off" phenomenon. Ann Neurol 14:91–92, 1983

Redick RW, Taube CA: Demography and mental health care of the aged, in Handbook
of Mental Health and Aging. Edited by Birren JE, Sloane RB. Englewood Cliffs,
NJ, Prentice-Hall, 1980

Reding MJ, DiPonte P: Vasopressin in Alzheimer's disease. Neurology (NY) 33:1634–
1635, 1983

Reding M, DiPonte P, Young RC: Amitriptyline in dementia. Neurology 33:522–523,
1983

Redlich F, Mollica RF: Overview: ethical issues in contemporary psychiatry. Am J
Psychiatry 133:125–136, 1976

Reich WT: Ethical issues related to research involving elderly subjects. Gerontologist 18:326–337, 1978

Reichert WH, Blass JP: A placebo-controlled trial shows no effect of vasopressin on recovery from closed head injury. Ann Neurol 12:390–392, 1982

Reid JL, Porsius AJ, Zamboulis C, et al: The effects of desmethylimipramine on the pharmacological action of a-methyldopa in man. Eur J Clin Pharmacol 16:75–80, 1979

Reifler BV, Larson E, Hanley R: Coexistence of cognitive impairment and depression in geriatric outpatients. Am J Psychiatry 139:623–626, 1982

Reilly TM, Jopling WH, Beard AW: Successful treatment with pimozide of delusional parasitosis. Br J Dermatol 98:457–459, 1978

Reimann IW, Diener U, Frolich JC: Indomethacin but not aspirin increases plasma lithium ion levels. Arch Gen Psychiatry 40:283–286, 1983

Reisberg B: Empirical studies in senile dementia with metabolic enhancers and agents that alter the blood flow and oxygen utilization, in Strategies for the Development of an Effective Treatment for Senile Dementia. Edited by Crook T, Gershon S. New Canaan, Conn, Mark Powley Associates, 1981

Reisberg B, Gershon S: Side effects associated with lithium therapy. Arch Gen Psychiatry 36:879–887, 1979

Reisberg B, Ferris SH, Gershon S: An overview of pharmacologic treatment of cognitive decline in the aged. Am J Psychiatry 138:593–600, 1981

Reisberg B, Ferris SH, deLeon MJ, et al: The Global Deterioration Scale for assessment of primary degenerative dementia. Am J Psychiatry 139:1136–1139, 1982

Reisberg B, Ferris SH, Anand R, et al: Effects of naloxone in senile dementia: a double-blind trial. N Engl J Med 308:721–722, 1983

Reisberg B, Gordon B, McCarthy M, et al: Insight and denial accompanying progressive cognitive decline in normal aging and Alzheimer's disease, in Geriatric Psychiatry: Ethical and Legal Issues. Edited by Stanley B. Washington, DC, American Psychiatric Press, 1985

Remick RA, O'Kane J, Sparling TG: A case report of toxic psychosis with low-dose propranolol therapy. Am J Psychiatry 138:850–851, 1981

Remvig J: Deaf mutism and psychiatry. Acta Psychiatr Scand (Suppl) 210:9–64, 1969

Renshaw DC: Sexual problems in stroke patients. Medical Aspects of Human Sexuality 9:68–74, 1975

Renton KW, Gray JD, Hall RI: Decreased elimination of theophylline after influenza vaccination. Can Med Assoc J 123:288–290, 1980

Resnick M, Burton BT: Droperidol vs. haloperidol in the initial management of acutely agitated patients. J Clin Psychiatry 45:298–299, 1984

Resnick RB, Resnick EB: Cocaine abuse and its treatment. Psychiatr Clin North Am 7:713–728, 1984

Reuler JB, Girard DE, Cooney TG: Wernicke's encephalopathy. N Engl J Med 312:1035–1039, 1985

Richelson E: Antimuscarinic and other receptor-blocking properties of antidepressants. Mayo Clin Proc 58:40–46, 1983

Richet G, de Novales EL, Verroust P: Drug intoxication and neurological episodes in chronic renal failure. Br Med J 2:394–395, 1970

Riding J, Munro A: Pimozide in the treatment of monosymptomatic hypochondriacal psychosis. Acta Psychiatr Scand 52:23–30, 1975

Riko K, Alberti PW: Rehabilitation of the hearing impaired adult. Otorhinolaryngol Clin North Am 17:641–651, 1984

Risch SC, Groom GP, Janowsky DS: Interfaces of psychopharmacology and cardiology—part one. J Clin Psychiatry 42:23–24, 1981

Risch SC, Groom GP, Janowsky D: The effects of psychotropic drugs on the cardiovascular system. J Clin Psychiatry 43(sec 2):16–31, 1982

Ritchie EA: Toxic psychosis under cortisone and corticotropin. J Ment Sci 102:830–837, 1956

Robb RM, Watters GV: Ophthalmic manifestations of subacute sclerosing panencephalitis. Arch Ophthalmol 83:426–435, 1970

Roberts AH: The value of ECT in delirium. Br J Psychiatry 109:653–655, 1963

Roberts E: Potential therapies in aging and senile dementias. Ann NY Acad Sci 396:165–178, 1982

Robins LE, Helzer JE, Weissman MM, et al: Lifetime prevalence of specific psychiatric disorders in three sites. Arch Gen Psychiatry 41:949–958, 1984

Robinson DS, Nies A, Ravaris CL, et al: Clinical pharmacology of phenelzine. Arch Gen Psychiatry 35:629–635, 1978

Robinson DS, Nies A, Corcella J, et al: Cardiovascular effects of phenelzine and amitriptyline in depressed outpatients. J Clin Psychiatry 43(sec 2):8–15, 1982

Robinson RG, Price TR: Post-stroke depressive disorders: a follow-up study of 103 patients. Stroke 13:635–641, 1982

Robinson RG, Szetela B: Mood changes following left-hemispheric brain injury. Ann Neurol 9:447–453, 1981

Robinson RG, Starr LB, Kubos KL, et al: A two-year longitudinal study of post-stroke mood disorders: findings during the initial evaluation. Stroke 14:736–741, 1983

Robinson RG, Starr LB, Lipsey JR, et al: A two-year longitudinal study of post-stroke mood disorders: dynamic changes in associated variables over the first six months of follow-up. Stroke 15:510–517, 1984a

Robinson RG, Kubos KL, Starr LB, et al: Mood disorder in stroke patients: importance of location of lesion. Brain 107:81–93, 1984b

Robinson RG, Starr LB, Price TR: A two-year longitudinal study of mood disorders following stroke: prevalence and duration at six months followup. Br J Psychiatry 144:256–262, 1984c

Robinson RG, Lipsey JR, Bolla-Wilson F, et al: Mood disorders in left-handed stroke patients. Am J Psychiatry 142:1425–1429, 1985

Rodin EA: The Prognosis of Patients with Epilepsy. Springfield, Ill, Charles C Thomas, 1968

Rogers RM (ed): Respiratory Intensive Care. Springfield, Ill, Charles C Thomas, 1977

Romano J, Engel GL: Physiologic and psychologic considerations of delirium. Med Clin North Am 28:629–638, 1944

Ron MA, Toone BK, Garralda ME, et al: Diagnostic accuracy in presenile dementia. Br J Psychiatry 134:161–168, 1979

Rondot P, deRecondo J, Coignet A, et al: Mental disorders in Parkinson's disease after treatment with L-dopa, in Advances in Neurology, vol 40. Edited by Hassler RG, Christ JF. New York, Raven Press, 1984

Roose SP, Glassman AH, Siris S, et al: Comparison of imipramine- and nortriptyline-induced orthostatic hypotension: a meaningful difference. J Clin Psychopharmacol 1:316–319, 1981

Rosen AM, Mukherjee S, Shinbach K: The efficacy of ECT in phencyclidine-induced psychosis. J Clin Psychiatry 45:220–222, 1984

Rosen WG, Terry RD, Fuld PA, et al: Pathological verification of ischemic score in differentiation of dementias. Ann Neurol 7:486–488, 1980

Rosenberg SA: The common cancers encountered in clinical practice, in Scientific American Medicine. Edited by Rubenstein E, Federman DD. New York, Scientific American, 1984

Ross ED: The aprosodias: functional-anatomic organization of the affective components of language in the right hemisphere. Arch Neurol 38:561–569, 1981

Ross ED, Jossman PB, Bell B, et al: Musical hallucinations in deafness. JAMA 231:620–622, 1975

Rossor MN, Rehfield JF, Emson PC, et al: Normal cortical concentrations of cholecystokinin-like immunoreactivity with reduced choline acetyl transferase activity in senile dementia of Alzheimer's type. Life Sci 29:405–410, 1981

Rossor MN, Emson PC, Iversen LL, et al: Neuropeptides and neurotransmitters in cerebral cortex in Alzheimer's disease, in Alzheimer's Disease: A Report of Progress (Aging, vol 19). Edited by Corkin S, Davis KL, Growdon JH, et al. New York, Raven Press, 1982

Roth LH: A commitment law for patients, doctors, and lawyers. Am J Psychiatry 136:1121–1127, 1979

Roth LH, Meisel A, Lidz CW: Tests of competency to consent to treatment. Am J Psychiatry 134:279–284, 1977

Roth M: The management of dementia. Psychiatr Clin North Am 1:81–99, 1978

Roth M, McClelland HA: Sensory defects, physical deformity and somatic illness in schizophrenics. Vestn Akad Med Nauk SSSR 5:77–79, 1971

Roth T, Hartse KM, Saab PG, et al: The effects of flurazepam, lorazepam, and triazolam on sleep and memory. Psychopharmacology 70:231–237, 1980

Rothman DJ: Were tuskegee and willowbrook "studies of nature?" Hastings Cent Rep 12:5–8, 1982

Rovner BW, Rabins PV: Mental illness among nursing home patients. Hosp Community Psychiatry 36:119–128, 1985

Rowan AJ, Protass LM: Transient global amnesia: clinical and electroencephalographic findings in 10 cases. Neurology 29:869–872, 1979

Rowe JW: Aging and renal function. Annual Review of Gerontology and Geriatrics 1:161–179, 1980

Roy-Byrne PP, Uhde TW, Post RM: Carbamazepine as a treatment for aggression, schizophrenia and non-affective syndromes. International Drug Therapy Newsletter 19:9–12, 1984

Rybash JM, Roodin PA, Hoyer WJ: Expressions of moral thought in later adulthood. Gerontologist 23:254–260, 1983

Sackeim HA, Decina P, Malitz S, et al: Postictal excitement following bilateral and right-unilateral ECT. Am J Psychiatry 140:1367–1368, 1983

Sacks OW, Kohl MS, Messeloff CR, et al: Effects of levodopa in parkinsonian patients with dementia. Neurology 22:516–519, 1972

Sadeh M, Braham J, Modan M: Effects of anticholinergic drugs on memory in Parkinson's disease. Arch Neurol 39:666–667, 1982

Safer DJ, Allen RP: The central effects of scopolamine in man. Biol Psychiatry 3:347–355, 1971

Salzman C: A primer on geriatric psychopharmacology. Am J Psychiatry 139:67–76, 1982a

Salzman C: Key concepts in geriatric psychopharmacology: Altered pharmacokinetics and polypharmacy. Psychiatr Clin North Am 5:181–190, 1982b

Salzman C: Psychotropic drug dosages and drug interactions, in Clinical Geriatric Psychopharmacology. Edited by Salzman C. New York, McGraw-Hill, 1984

Sanders DJ, Zahedi-Asl S, Marr AP: Glucagon and CCK in human brain controls and patients with senile dementia of Alzheimer type, in Progress in Brain Research, vol 55, Chemical Transmission in the Brain. Edited by Buigs RM, Pevest P, Swaab DF. New York, Elsevier, 1982

Sandler M, Stern GM: Deprenyl in Parkinson's disease, in Movement Disorders, vol 2. Edited by Marsden CD, Fahn S. London, Butterworth Scientific, 1982

Sandman CA, Kastin AJ: Pituitary peptide influences on attention and memory, in

Neurobiology of Sleep and Memory. Edited by Drucker-Colin RR, McGaugh JL. New York, Academic Press, 1977

Sandman CA, George J, Walker B, et al: The heptapeptide MSH/ACTH 4-10 enhances attention in the mentally retarded. Pharmacol Biochem Behav 5(suppl 1):23–28, 1976

Sandman CA, Walker BB, Lawton CA: An analogue of MSH/ACTH 4-9 enhances interpersonal and environmental awareness in mentally retarded adults. Peptides 1:109–114, 1980

Sandok BA: Clinical evaluation of patients with cerebrovascular disease, Cerebrovascular Survey Report. Edited by Siebert RG. Bethesda, MD, Joint Council Subcommittee on Cerebrovascular Disease, 1980

Sandok BA: Organic mental disorders associated with circulatory disturbances, in Comprehensive Textbook of Psychiatry/III, 3rd ed, vol 2. Edited by Kaplan HI, Freedman AM, Sadock BJ. Baltimore, Williams and Wilkins, 1980b

Sandoz M, Vandel S, Vande B: Metabolism of amitriptyline in patients with chronic renal failure. Eur J Clin Pharmacol 26:227–232, 1984

Sataloff J: Functional hearing loss, in Hearing Loss. Philadelphia, JB Lippincott, 1966

Sato M, Chen CC, Akiyama K, et al: Acute exacerbation of paranoid psychotic state after long-term abstinence in patients with previous methamphetamine psychosis. Biol Psychiatry 18:429–440, 1983

Scharf MB, Khosla N, Lysaght R, et al: Anterograde amnesia with oral lorazepam. J Clin Psychiatry 44:362–364, 1983

Scharschmidt BF: Human liver transplantation: analysis of data on 540 patients from four centers. Hepatology 4:955–1015, 1984

Scharschmidt BF: Acute and chronic hepatic failure with encephalopathy, in Cecil's Textbook of Medicine, 17th ed. Edited by Wyngaarden JB, Smith LH. Philadelphia, WB Saunders, 1985

Schauf CL, Davis FA, Marder J: Effects of carbamazepine on the ionic conductance of myxicol giant axons. J Pharmacol Exp Ther 189:538–543, 1974

Scheie HG, Albert DM: Textbook of Ophthalmology. Philadelphia, WB Saunders, 1977

Scheinberg IH, Sternlieb I, Richman J: Psychiatric manifestations in patients with Wilson's disease, in Wilson's Disease: Birth Defects (Original Article Series, vol 4, no 2). Edited by Bergsma D. New York, The National Foundation, 1968

Scheinberg P: Effects of uremia on cerebral blood flow and metabolism. Neurology 4:101–109, 1954

Schenker S, Hoyumpa AM: Pathophysiology of hepatic encephalopathy. Hospital Practice 19:99–121, 1984

Schiff HB, Sabin TD, Geller A, et al: Lithium in aggressive behavior. Am J Psychiatry 139:1346–1348, 1982

Schmidt GL, Keyes B: Group psychotherapy with family caregivers of demented patients. Gerontologist 25:347–350, 1985

Schneck M, Reisberg B, Ferris SH: An overview of current concepts of Alzeheimer's disease. Am J Psychiatry 139:165–173, 1982

Schneider LS, Sloane RB, Staples FR, et al: Pretreatment orthostatic hypotension as a predictor of response to nortriptyline in geriatric depression. J Clin Psychopharmacol 6:172–176, 1986

Schneiderman LJ, Arras JD: Counseling patients to counsel physicians on future care in the event of patient incompetence. Ann Intern Med 102:648–693, 1985

Schou M: Pharmacology and toxicology of lithium. Annu Rev Pharmacol Toxicol 16:231–243, 1976

Schou M, Amdisen A, Trap-Jensen J: Lithium poisoning. Am J Psychiatry 125:520–527, 1968

Schulz PJ: Reaction to loss of sight, in Psychiatric Problems in Ophthalmology. Edited by Perlman JT, Adams GL, Sherwin HS. Springfield, Ill, Charles C Thomas, 1977

Schurman RA, Kramer PD, Mitchell JB: The hidden mental health network. Arch Gen Psychiatry 42:89–94, 1985

Scott M, Muhaly R: Lithium therapy for cocaine-induced psychosis: a clinical perspective. South Med J 74:1475–1477, 1981

Segarra JM: Cerebral vascular disease and behavior, I: the syndrome of the mesencephalic artery (basilar artery bifurcation). Arch Neurol 22:408–418, 1970.

Seifert AR, Lubar TF: Reduction of epileptic seizures through EEG biofeedback training. Biol Psychol 3:156–184, 1975

Sellers EM, Abel JG, Romach MK, et al: Sources of variation in binding of psychotherapeutic drugs to plasma proteins, in Clinical Pharmacology in Psychiatry. Edited by Usdin E. New York, Elsevier-North Holland, 1981

Serby M: Psychiatric issues in Parkinson's disease. Compr Psychiatry 21:317–322, 1980

Serby M, Angrist B, Lieberman A: Mental disturbances during bromocriptine and lergotrile treatment of Parkinson's disease. Am J Psychiatry 135:1227–1229, 1978

Serby M, Angrist B, Lieberman A: Psychiatric effects of bromocriptine and lergotrile in parkinsonian patients, in Advances in Biochemical Psychopharmacology, vol 23. Edited by Goldstein M, Calne DB, Lieberman AN, et al. New York, Raven Press, 1980

Shader RI (ed): Psychiatric Complications of Medical Drugs. New York, Raven Press, 1972

Shader RI, Caine ED, Meyer RE: Treatment of dependence on barbiturates and sedative-hypnotics, in Manual of Psychiatric Therapeutics. Edited by Shader RI. Boston, Little, Brown, 1975

Shand DG: Pharmacokinetics of propranolol: a review. Postgrad Med J 52(suppl 4): 22–25, 1976

Shapiro AK, Shapiro E, Eisenkraft GJ: Treatment of Gilles de la Tourette's syndrome with clonidine and neuroleptics. Arch Gen Psychiatry 40:1235–1240, 1983

Sharfstein SS: Will community mental health survive in the 1980's? Am J Psychiatry 135:1363–1365, 1978

Sheard MH: Lithium in the treatment of aggression. J Nerv Ment Dis 160:108–118, 1975

Sheard MH, Marium JL, Bridges CI, et al: The effects of lithium in impulsive aggressive behavior in man. Am J Psychiatry 133:1409–1413, 1976

Sherlock S: Diseases of the Liver and Biliary System, 6th ed. London, Blackwell Scientific Publications, 1981

Sherlock S, Summerskill WHJ, White LP, et al: Portal-systemic encephalopathy, neurological complications of liver disease. Lancet 2:453–457, 1954

Shershow JC, King A, Robinson S: Carbon dioxide sensitivity and personality. Psychosom Med 35: 155–160, 1973

Shershow JC, Kanarek DJ, Kazemi H: Ventilatory response to carbon dioxide in depression. Psychosom Med 38:282–287, 1976

Sherwin I, Peron-Magnan P, Bancaud J, et al: Prevalence of psychosis in epilepsy as a function of the laterality of the epileptogenic lesion. Arch Neurol 39:621–625, 1982

Showalter CV, Thornton WE: Clinical pharmacology of phencyclidine toxicity. Am J Psychiatry 134:1234–1238, 1977

Shull HJ, Wilkinson GR, Johnson R, et al: Normal disposition of oxazepam in acute viral hepatitis and cirrhosis. Ann Intern Med 84:420–425, 1976

Shuping JR, Rollinson RD, Toole JF: Transient global amnesia. Ann Neurol 7:281–285, 1980

Siegler M, Weisbard AJ: Against the emerging stream: should fluids and nutritional support be discontinued? Arch Intern Med 145:129–131, 1985

Silberfarb PM: Chemotherapy and cognitive defect in cancer patients. Annu Rev Med 34:35–46, 1983

Silver JM, Yudofsky SC: Propranolol for aggression: literature review and clinical guidelines. International Drug Therapy Newsletter 20:9–12, 1985

Silver JM, Yudofsky SC: Propranolol in the treatment of chronically hospitalized violent patients, in proceedings of the IVth World Congress of Biological Psychiatry, September 1985. Edited by Shagass C, Josiassen RC, Bridger WH, et al. New York, Elsevier, 1986, pp 174–176

Silver JM, Yudofsky SC: Aggressive behavior in patients with neuropsychiatric disorders. Psychiatric Annals 17:367–370, 1987a

Silver JM, Yudofsky SC: Documentation of aggression in the assessment of the violent patient. Psychiatric Annals 17:375–384, 1987b

Simpson GM, White K: Tyramine studies and the safety of MAOI drugs. J Clin Psychiatry 45:59–61, 1984

Simpson LL: Combined use of molindone and guanethidine in patients with schizophrenia and hypertension. Am J Psychiatry 136:1410–1414, 1979

Sitaram N, Weingartner H, Gillian JC: Human serial learning: enhancement with arecoline and choline impairment with scopolamine. Science 261:274–276, 1978

Skigen J, Solomon JR: Community resources and facilities for the elderly patient with organic mental disease. Psychiatr Clin North Am 1:169–177, 1978

Slater E, Moran EA: Schizophrenia-like psychoses of epilepsy: relation between ages of onset. Br J Psychiatry 115:599–600, 1969

Slater E, Beard AW, Glithero E: The schizophrenia-like psychosis of epilepsy. Br J Psychiatry 109:95–150, 1963

Slovenko R: Psychiatry and Law. Boston, Little, Brown, 1973

Small GW: Revised ischemic score for diagnosing multi-infarct dementia. J Clin Psychiatry 46:514–517, 1985

Small GW, Jarvik LF: The dementia syndrome. Lancet 2:1443–1446, 1982

Small GW, Mandel MR: The medically ill elderly, tricyclic response, and ECT. AM Psychiatry 137:963–965, 1981

Small JC, Kellams JJ, Milstein V, et al: Complications with electroconvulsive treatment combined with lithium. Biol Psychiatry 15:103–112, 1980

Small GW, Liston EH, Jarvik LF: Diagnosis and treatment of dementia in the aged. West J Med 135:469–481, 1981

Smith AJ, Bant WP: Interactions between post-ganglionic sympathetic blocking drugs and antidepressants. J Int Med Res 3:55–60, 1975

Smith CH, Beck RW, Mills RP: Functional disease in neuroophthalmology. Neurol Clin 1:955–971, 1983

Smith DE: Diagnostic, treatment, and aftercare approaches to cocaine abuse. Journal of Substance Abuse Treatment 1:5–9, 1984

Smith JS, Kiloh LG: The investigation of dementia: results in 200 consecutive admissions. Lancet 1:824–827, 1981

Smith RC, Reisberg B: Pharmacologic treatment of Alzheimer's-type dementia: new approaches. Psychopharmacol Bull 20:542–545, 1984

Smith RC, Ho BT, Kralik P: Platelet monoamine oxidase in Alzheimer disease. J Gerontol 37:572–574, 1982

Smith TW: Digitalis glycosides. N Engl J Med 288:719–722, 1973

Snyder SH: Amphetamine psychosis: a "model" schizophrenia mediated by catecholamines. Am J Psychiatry 130:61–67, 1973

Soininen H, MacDonald E, Rekenon M, et al. Homovanillic acid levels in cerebrospinal fluid of patients with senile dementia of Alzheimer type. Acta Neurol Scand 64:101–107, 1981

Solomon GE, Kutt H, Plum F: Clinical management of seizures, 2nd ed. Philadelphia, WB Saunders, 1983

Solomon K: Phenothiazine bulbar palsy-like syndrome and sudden death. Am J Psychiatry 134:308–311, 1977

Sordillo P, Sagransky DM, Mercado R, et al: Carbamazepine-induced syndrome of inappropriate antidiuretic hormone secretion. Reversal by concomitant phenytoin therapy. Arch Intern Med 138:299–301, 1978

Sorgi PJ, Ratey JJ, Polakoff S: B-adrenergic blockers for the control of aggressive behavior in patients with chronic schizophrenia. Am J Psychiatry 143:775–776, 1986

Spar JE: Dementia in the aged. Psychiatr Clin North Am 5:67–86, 1982

Spar JE, Gerner R: Does the dexamethasone suppression test distinguish dementia from depression? Am J Psychiatry 139:238–240, 1982

Spar JE, LaRue A: Acute response to methylphenidate as a predictor of outcome of treatment with TCAs in the elderly. J Clin Psychiatry 46:466–469, 1985

Spencer SS, Spencer DD, Williamson PD, et al: The localizing value of depth electroencephalography in 32 patients with refractory epilepsy. Ann Neurol 12:248–253, 1982

Spiegel R, Huber F, Koeberle S: A controlled long-term study with ergoloid mesylates (Hydergine) in healthy, elderly volunteers: results after 3 years. J Am Geriatr Soc 31:549–555, 1983

Sroka H, Elizan TS, Yahr MD, et al: Organic mental syndrome and confusional states in Parkinson's disease: relationship to computerized tomographic signs of cerebral atrophy. Arch Neurol 38:339–342, 1981

Stancer HC, Kivi R: Lithium carbonate and edema. Lancet 2:985, 1971

Stanley B, Stanley M, Pomara N: Informed consent and geriatric patients, in Geriatric Psychiatry: Ethical and Legal Issues. Edited by Stanley B. Washington, DC, American Psychiatric Press, 1985

Stark P, Fuller RW, Wong DT: The pharmacologic profile of fluoxetine. J Clin Psychiatry 46:7–13, 1985

Steen SM, Amaha K, Martinez LR: Effect of oxazepam on respiratory response to carbon dioxide. Anesthesia and Analgesia Current Researchers 45:455–458, 1966

Steinert J, Pugh CR: Two patients with schizophrenia-like psychosis after treatment with beta-adrenergic blockers. Br Med J 1:790, 1979

Steinhart MJ: Treatment of delirium: a reappraisal. Int J Psychiatry Med 9:191–197, 1978/1979

Stenback A, Haapanen E: Azotemia and psychosis. Acta Psychiatr Scand 43:30–38, 1967

Sterman MB: Neurophysiologic and clinical studies of sensorimotor EEG biofeedback training: some effects of epilepsy, in Biofeedback: Behavior Medicine. Edited by Birk L. Boston, Grune & Stratton, 1973, pp 507–526

Stern MJ, Pascale L, McLoone JB: Psychosocial adaptation following an acute myocardial infarction. J Chronic Dis 29:513–526, 1976

Stern TA: Continuous infusion of physostigmine in anticholinergic delirium: case report. J Clin Psychiatry 44:463–464, 1983

Steuer J: Psychotherapy with the elderly. Psychiatr Clin North Am 5:199–213, 1982

Stevens JR: Neuropathology of schizophrenia. Arch Gen Psychiatry 39:1131–1139, 1982

Stimmel B: The effects of mood altering drugs on the heart, in Drugs in Cardiology, Part 1. Edited by Donoso E. New York, Grune & Stratton, 1975

Stockley IH: Monoamine oxidase inhibitors, part 2: interactions with antihypertensive agents, hypoglycemics, CNS depressants, narcotics, and antiparkinsonian agents. Pharm J 211:95–98, 1973

Stockley I: Interactions with oral contraceptives. Pharmacology Journal 216:140–143, 1976

Stone AA: Law, Psychiatry, and Morality. Washington, DC, American Psychiatric Press, 1984

Stores G: School children with epilepsy at risk for learning and behavioral problems. Dev Med Child Neurol 20:502–508, 1978

Strub RL, Black FW: The Mental Status Examination in Neurology. Philadelphia, FA Davis Co, 1977

Strub RL, Black FW: Organic Brain Syndromes: An Introduction to Neurobehavioral Disorders. Philadelphia, FA Davis, 1981

Summers WK, Majovski LV Marsh GM, et al: Oral tetrahydroaminoacridine in long-term treatment of senile dementia, Alzheimer type. N Engl J Med 315:1241–1245, 1986

Summerskill WHJ, Davidson EA, Sherlock S, et al: The neuropsychiatric syndrome associated with hepatic cirrhosis and an extensive portal collateral circulation. Q J Med 25:245–266, 1956

Sumner D: Post traumatic anosmia. Brain 87:107–120, 1964

Sumner D: Clinical aspects of anosmia, in Scientific Foundations of Neurology. Edited by Critchley M, O'Leary JL, Jennett B. London, William Heinemann Medical Books, 1972

Surawicz FG: Alcohol hallucinosis: a missed diagnosis. Can J Psychiatry 25:57–63, 1980

Swedberg K, Winblad B: Heart failure as a complication of lithium treatment. Acta Med Scand 196:279–280, 1974

Sweet RD, McDowell FH: Five years' treatment of Parkinson's disease with levodopa: therapeutic results and survival of 100 patients. Ann Intern Med 83:456–463, 1975

Sweet RD, McDowell FH, Feigenson JS, et al: Mental symptoms in Parkinson's disease during chronic treatment with levodopa. Neurology 26:305–310, 1976

Szekais B: Adult day centers: geriatric day health services in the community. J Fam Pract 20:157–161, 1985

Talalla A, Halbrook H, Barbour BH, et al: Subdural hematoma associated with long-term hemodialysis for chronic renal disease. JAMA 212:1847–1849, 1970

Tanner CM, Vogel C, Goetz CG, et al: Hallucinations in Parkinson's disease: a population study. Ann Neurol 14:136, 1983

Tarasoff v Regents of the University of California, 118 Cal Rptr 129 (1974), reargued, 17 Cal 3d 425 (1976)

Tardiff K (ed): The Psychiatric Use of Seclusion and Restraint. Washington, DC, American Psychiatric Press, 1984

Tardiff K, Sweillam A: Assault, suicide and mental illness. Arch Gen Psychiatry 37:164–169, 1980

Tardiff K, Sweillam A: Assaultive behavior among chronic inpatients. Am J Psychiatry 139:212–215, 1982

Tarter RE: An analysis of cognitive deficits in chronic alcoholics. J Nerv Ment Dis 157:138–147, 1973

Task Force Sponsored by the National Institute on Aging: Senility reconsidered: treatment possibilities for mental impairment in the elderly. JAMA 244:259–263, 1980

Task Force on the Use of Laboratory Tests in Psychiatry: Tricyclic antidepressants: blood level measurements and clinical outcome: an APA Task Force report. Am J Psychiatry 142:155–162, 1985

Taylor DC: Factors influencing the occurrence of schizophrenia-like psychoses in patients with temporal lobe epilepsy. Psychol Med 5:249–254, 1975

Taylor D, Hoffer B, Ziegigansberger W, et al: Opioid peptides excite pyramidal neurons and evoke epileptiform activity in hippocampal transplants in oculo. Brain Res 176:135–142, 1979

Taylor MA: Indications for electroconvulsive treatment, in Electroconvulsive Therapy: Biological Foundations and Clinical Applications. Edited by Abrams R, Essman WB. New York, Spectrum Publications, 1982

Taylor PJ, Gunn J: Violence and psychosis, I: risk of violence among psychotic men. Br Med J 288:1945–1949, 1984

Terry RD: Senile dementia. Fed Proc 37:2837–2840, 1978

Terry RD: Katzman R: Senile dementia of the Alzheimer's type. Ann Neurol 14:497–506, 1983

Teuber HL: Prospects for research on schizophrenia: effects of focal brain lesions. Neuroscience Research Program Bulletin 10:381–396, 1972

Thal LJ, Fuld PA, Masur DM, et al: Oral physostigmine and lecithin improve memory in Alzheimer disease. Ann Neurol 13:491–496, 1983

Thompson MK: Schizophrenia-like psychosis after treatment with beta-blockers. Br Med J 1:1084–1085, 1979

Thomsen K, Schou M: The treatment of lithium poisoning, in Lithium Research and Therapy. Edited by Johnson FN. New York, Academic Press, 1975

Thomsen IV: Late outcome of very severe blunt head trauma: a 10-15 year second follow-up. J Neurol Neurosurg Psychiatry 47:260–268, 1984

Thornton WF: Dementia induced by methyldopa with haloperidol. N Engl J Med 294:1222, 1976

Thornton WF, Pray BJ: Combination drug therapy in psychopharmacology. J Clin Pharmacol 15: 511–517, 1975

Thurston JH, Thurston DL, Hixon BB, et al: Prognosis of childhood epilepsy: additional following of 148 children 15 to 35 years after withdrawal of anticonvulsant therapy. N Engl J Med 306:831–836, 1982

Tilkian AG, Schroeder JS, Kao J: Effect of lithium on cardiovascular performance: report on extended ambulatory monitoring and exercise testing before and during lithium therapy. Am J Cardiol 38:701–708, 1976

Tinklenberg JR, Thornton JE, Yesavage JA: Clinical geriatric psychopharmacology and neuropeptides, in Dementia in the Elderly. Edited by Shamoian CA. Washington, DC, American Psychiatric Press, 1984

Toenniessen LM, Casey DE, McFarland BH: Tardive dyskinesia in the aged. Arch Gen Psychiatry 42:278–284, 1985

Tollefson G: Psychiatric implications on anticonvulsant drugs. J Clin Psychiatry 41:295–302, 1980

Tollefson G, Lesar T: Effect of propranolol on maprotiline clearance. Am J Psychiatry 141:148–149, 1984

Tollefson G, Lesar T, Grothe D, et al: Alprazolam-related digoxin toxicity. Am J Psychiatry 141:1612–1614, 1984

Tomlinson BE, Blessed G, Roth M: Observations on the brains of demented old people. J Neurol Sci 11:205–242, 1970

Toone B: Psychoses of epilepsy, in Epilepsy and Psychiatry. Edited by Reynolds EH, Trimble MR. New York, Raven Press, 1981

Toone BK, Fenton GW: Epileptic seizures induced by psychotropic drugs. Psychol Med 7:265–270, 1977

Topliss D, Bond R: Acute brain syndrome after propranolol treatment. Lancet 2:1133–1134, 1977

Torvik A: The pathogenesis of watershed infarcts in the brain. Stroke 15:221–223, 1984

Trimble MR: Psychosis and epilepsy, in a Textbook of Epilepsy. Edited by Laidlaw J, Richens A. Edinburgh, Churchill Livingstone, 1982a

Trimble MR: The interictal psychoses of epilepsy, in Psychiatric Aspects of Neurologic Disease, vol II. Edited by Benson DF, Blumer D. New York, Grune & Stratton, 1982b

Trimble MR: Interictal psychoses of epilepsy. Acta Psychiatr Scand [Suppl] 313:9–18, 1984

Trimble, MR, Cummings JL: Neuropsychiatric disturbances following brainstem lesions. Br J Psychiatry 138:56–59, 1981

Tunks ER, Dever SW: Carbamazepine in the dyscontrol syndrome associated with dysfunction. J Nerv Ment Dis 164:56–63, 1977

Tupin JP, Smith DB, Clanon TL, et al: Long-term use of lithium in aggressive prisoners. Compr Psychiatry 14:311–317, 1973

Turner TH, Cookson JC, Wass JAH, et al: Psychotic reactions during treatment of pituitary tumors with dopamine agonists. Br Med J 289:1101–1103, 1984

Tyler R: Neurological complications of acute and chronic failure, in The Treatment of Renal Failure. Edited by Merrill JP. London, William Heinemann Medical Books, 1965

U'Prichard D, Greenberg D, Sheehan P, et al: Tricyclic antidepressants: therapeutic properties and affinity for a-noradrenergic receptor binding sites in the brain. Science 199:197–199, 1978

US Department of Health, Education, and Welfare: Statistical Reports on Older Americans: 3: Some Prospects for the Future Elderly Population. Publication OHDSO 78-20288. Rockville, Md, US Department of Health, Education, and Welfare, 1978

US Department of Health and Human Services Task Force on Alzheimer's Disease: Alzheimer's Disease: Report of the Secretary's Task Force on Alzheimer's Disease. DHHS Publication ADM 84-1323. Rockville, Md. US Department of Health and Human Services, 1984

US Senate Special Committee on Aging in Conjunction with the American Association of Retired Persons: Aging America: Trends and Projections, 1984

Utting HG, Pleuvry BJ: Benzoctamine: a study of the respiratory effects of oral doses in human volunteers and interactions with morphine in mice. Br J Anaesth 47:987–992, 1975

Vaisrub S: Dangerous waters. JAMA 240:1630, 1978

Van Buskirk EM: Adverse reactions from timolol administration. Ophthalmology 87:447–450, 1980

Van der Rijt CCD, Schalm SW, De Groot GH, et al: Objective measurement of hepatic encephalopathy by means of automated EEG analysis. Electroencephalogr Clin Neurophysiol 57:423–426, 1984

van Leeuwen AMH, Molders J, Sterkmans P, et al.: Droperidol in acutely agitated patients: a double blind placebo-controlled study. J Nerv Ment Dis 164:280–283, 1977

Van Zwieten PA: Reduction of the hypertensive effect of clonidine and a-methyldopa by various psychotropic drugs. Clinical Science and Molecular Medicine 51(suppl):411s–413s, 1976

Veatch RM: Death, Dying, and the Biological Revolution: Our Last Quest for Responsibility. New Haven, Yale University Press, 1976

Veith RC, Raskind MA, Caldwell JH, et al: Cardiovascular effects of tricyclic antidepressants in depressed patients with chronic heart disease. N Engl J Med 306:954–959, 1982

Verbeeck RK: Glucuronidation and disposition of drug glucuronides in patients with renal failure: a review. Drug Metab Dispos 10:87–89, 1982

Verbeeck RK, Branch RA, Wilkinson GR: Drug metabolites in renal failure: pharmacokinetic and clinical implications. Clin Pharmacokinet 6:329–345, 1981

Verbeeck RK, Patwardhan RV, Villeneuve JP, et al: Furosemide disposition in cirrhosis. Clin Pharmacol Ther 31:719–725, 1982

Vessell ES, Passananti T, Green FE: Impairment of drug metabolism in man by allopurinol and nortriptyline. N Engl J Med 283:1484–1488, 1970

Vestal RE, Kornhauser DM, Hollifield JW, et al: Inhibition of propranolol metabolism by chlorpromazine. Clin Pharmacol Ther 25:19–24, 1979

Vestergaard P: Renal side-effects of lithium, in Handbook of Lithium Therapy. Edited by Johnson FN. Lancaster, Engl, MTP Press, 1980

Vestergaard P, Amdisen A, Hansen HE, et al: Lithium treatment and kidney function. Acta Psychiatr Scand 60:504–520, 1979

Veterans Administration Cooperative Study Group on Antihypertensive Agents: Comparison of propranolol and hydrochlorothiazide for the initial treatment of hypertension, II: results of long-term therapy. JAMA 28:2004–2011, 1982

Villareal SU, Escande M, Levet C: A propos des psychoses cortisoniques. Ann Med Psychol (Paris) 14:523–530, 1974

Vislie H, Hendriksen GF: Psychic disturbances in epileptics, in Lectures on Epilepsy. Edited by De Haas L. Amsterdam, Elsevier, 1958

Vohra J, Burrows GD, Sloman G: Assessment of cardiovascular side effects of therapeutic doses of tricyclic antidepressant drugs. Aust NZ J Med 5:7–11, 1975

Volpe BT, Soave R: Formed visual hallucinations as digitalis toxicity. Ann Intern Med 91:865–866, 1979

Von Brauchtisch K, May W: Deaths from aspiration and asphyxiation in a mental hospital. Arch Gen Psychiatry 18:129–136, 1968

Waddel WJ, Butler TC: The distribution and excretion of phenobarbital. J Clin Invest 36:1217–1226, 1957

Wahlin A, Bucht G, von Knorring L, et al: Kidney function in patients with affective disorders with and without lithium therapy. Int Pharmacopsychiatry 15:253–259, 1980

Walaas SI, Aswad DW, Greengard P: A dopamine- and cyclic AMP-regulated phosphoprotein enriched in dopamine-innervated brain regions. Nature 301:69–71, 1983

Walker BB, Sandman CA: Influence of an analog of the neuropeptide ACTH 4-9 on mentally retarded adults. Am J Ment Defic 83:346–352, 1979

Walker RG, Davies BM, Holwill BJ, et al: A clinical-pathological study of lithium nephrotoxicity. J Chronic Dis 35:685–695, 1982

Walker S: The psychiatric presentation of Wilson's disease (hepatolentricular degeneration) with an etiologic explanation. Behavioral Neuropsychiatry 1:38–43, 1969

Wallin L, Alling C, Aurell M: Impairment of renal function in patients on long-term lithium treatment. Clin Nephrol 18:23–28, 1982

Wanzer, SH, Adelstein SJ, Cranford RE, et al: The physician's responsibility toward hopelessly ill patients. N Engl J Med 310:955–959, 1984

Wasser WG, Bronheim HE, Richardson BK: Theophylline madness. Ann Intern Med 95:191, 1981

Waxman HM, Klein M, Carner EA: Drug misuse in nursing homes: an institution addiction. Hosp Community Psychiatry 36:886–887, 1985

Wechsler D: The Measurement of Adult Intelligence. Baltimore, Williams and Wilkins, 1944

Weiner N: Atropine, scopolamine, and related antimuscarinic drugs, in The Pharmacological Basis of Therapeutics, 6th ed. Edited by Goodman Gilman A, Goodman LS, Gilman A. New York, Macmillan, 1980

Weiner RD: The psychiatric use of electrically induced seizures. Am J Psychiatry 136:1507–1517, 1979

Weiner RD, Whanger AD, Erwin CW, et al: Prolonged confusional state and EEG seizure activity following concurrent ECT and lithium use. Am J Psychiatry 137:1452–1453, 1980

Weiner WJ, Goetz CG, Nausieda PA, et al: Respiratory dyskinesia: Extrapyramidal dysfunctions and dyspnea. Ann Intern Med 88:327–331, 1978

Weingartner H, Kaye W, Ebert M, et al: Effects of vasopressin on cognitive impairments in dementia. Life Sci 29:2721–2726, 1981a

Weingartner H, Gold P, Ballenger JC, et al: Effects of vasopressin on memory. Science 211:601–603, 1981b

Weinstein MC, Stason WB: Foundations of cost-effectiveness analysis for health and medical practices. N Engl J Med 296:716–721, 1977

Weisman AD, Hackett TP: Psychosis after eye surgery. N Engl J Med 258:1284–1289, 1958

Weiss HD, Walker MD, Wiernik PH: Neurotoxicity of commonly used antineoplastic agents. N Engl J Med 291:75–81, 127–133, 1974

Wells CE: Diagnostic evaluation and treatment in dementia, in Dementia. Edited by Wells CE. Philadelphia, FA Davis, 1977

Wells CE: Pseudodementia. Am J Psychiatry 136:895–900, 1979

Wells CE: Organic syndromes: delirium, in Comprehensive Textbook of Psychiatry, 4th ed, vol 4. Edited by Kaplan HI, Sadock BJ. Baltimore, Williams and Wilkins, 1985a

Wells CE: Other organic brain syndromes, in Comprehensive Textbook of Psychiatry/ IV, 4th ed. Edited by Kaplan HI, Sadock BJ. Baltimore, Williams and Wilkins Co, 1985b

Wells CE, McEvoy JP: Organic mental disorders, in Treatment of Mental Disorders. Edited by Griest JH, Jefferson JW, Spitzer RL. New York, Oxford University Press, 1982

Wernicke JF: The side effect profile and safety of fluoxetine. J Clin Psychiatry 46:59–67, 1985

White NJ: Complex visual hallucinations in partial blindness due to eye disease. Br J Psychiatry 136:284–286, 1980

White P, Goodhardt MJ, Keet JP, et al: Neocortical cholinergic neurons in elderly people. Lancet 1:688–670, 1977

White WB, Riotte K: Propranol and white rabbits. N Engl J Med 307:558–559, 1982

Whitehouse PJ, Price DL, Clark AW, et al: Alzheimer disease: evidence for selective loss of cholinergic neurons in the nucleus basalis. Ann Neurol 10:122–126, 1981

Whitlock FA: Symptomatic Affective Disorder. New York, Academic Press, 1982

Whyler AR, Lockard JS, Ward AA, et al: Condition EEG desynchronization and seizure occurrence in patients. Electroencephalogr Clin Neurophysiol 41:501–512, 1976

Widem P, Pincus HA, Goldman HH, et al: Prospective payment for psychiatric hospitalization: context and background. Hosp Community Psychiatry 35:447–451, 1984

Wikler A: Diagnosis and treatment of drug dependence of the barbiturate type. Am J Psychiatry 125:758–765, 1968

Wilder BJ, Bruni J: Seizure Disorders: A Pharmacological Approach to Treatment. New York, Raven Press, 1981

Williams DT, Mehl R, Yudofsky S, et al: The effect of propranolol on uncontrolled rage outbursts in children and adolescents with organic brain dysfunction. J Am Acad Child Psychiatry 21:129–135, 1982

Williamson PD, Spencer DD, Spencer SS, et al: Complex partial seizures of frontal lobe origin. Ann Neurol 18:497–504, 1985

Willison JR, Thomas DJ, duBoulay GH, et al: Effect of high hematocrit on alertness. Lancet 1:846–848, 1980

Wilson RP, Spaeth GL, Poryzees E: The place of timolol in the practice of ophthalmology. Ophthalmology 87:451–454, 1980

Winblad B, Adolfsson R, Carlsson A, et al: Biogenic amines in brains of patients with Alzheimer's disease, in Alzheimer's Disease: A Report of Progress (Aging, vol 19). Edited by Corkin S, Davis KL, Growdon JH, et al. New York, Raven Press, 1982

Winograd CH, Jarvik LF: Physician management of the demented patient. J Am Geriatr Soc 34:295–308, 1986

Winslade WJ, Lyon MA, Levine ML, et al: Making medical decisions for the Alzheimer's patient; paternalism and advocacy. Psychiatric Annals 14:206–208, 1984

Winters WD, Ralph DD: Digoxin-lithium drug interaction. Clin Toxicol 10:487–488, 1977

Wise TN: The pitfalls of diagnosing depression in chronic renal disease. Psychosomatics 15:83–84, 1974

Wishnie HA, Hackett TP, Cassem NH: Psychological hazards of convalescence following MI. JAMA 215:1292–1298, 1970

Wolf P, Kannel W: Controllable risk factors for stroke: preventive implications of trends in stroke mortality, in Diagnosis and Management of Stroke and TIA's. Edited by Meyer JS, Shaw T. Menlo Park, Calif, Addison-Wesley, 1982

Wolf PA, Kannel WB, Verter J: Current status of risk factors for stroke. Neurologic Clinics 1:317–344, 1983a

Wolf PA, Kannel WB, McGee DL, et al: Duration of atrial fibrillation and imminence of stroke: the Framingham study. Stroke 14:664–667, 1983b

Wolfensberger W: Ethical issues in research with human subjects. Science Study 155:47–51, 1967

Woolliscroft JO, Calhoun JG, Maxim BR, et al: Medical education in facilities for the elderly. JAMA 252:3382–3385, 1984

Woosley RL, Nies AS: Guanethidine. N Engl J Med 295:1053–1057, 1976

Worcester A: Care of the Aged, the Dying, and the Dead. Springfield, Ill, Charles C Thomas, 1935

Working Party: Euthanasia and Clinical Practice. London, Linacre Center, 1982

Worrall EP: The antiaggressive effects of lithium, in Lithium in Medical Practice. Edited by Johnson FN, Johnson S. Lancaster, Engl, MTP Press, 1978

Worrall EP, Moody JP, Naylor GT: Lithium in non-manic depressives: antiaggressive effect and red blood cell lithium values. Br J Psychiatry 126:464–468, 1975

Wurtman RJ: Alzheimer's disease. Sci Am 252:62–74, 1985

Yahr MD: Parkinsonism, in Merritt's Textbook of Neurology, 7th ed. Edited by Rowland LP. Philadelphia, Lea and Febiger, 1984

Yahr MD, Duvoisin RC, Cowen D: Encephalopathy associated with carcinoma. Transactions of the American Neurology Association 90:80–86, 1965

Yahr MD, Duvoisin RC, Schear MJ, et al: Treatment of parkinsonism with levodopa. Arch Neurol 21:343–354, 1969

Yamaguchi F, Meyer JS, Yamamoto M, et al: Noninvasive regional cerebral blood flow measurements in dementia. Arch Neurol 37:410–418, 1980

Yamamoto M, Meyer JS, Sakai F: Aging and cerebral vasodilator response to hypercarbia. Arch Neurol 37:489–496, 1980

Yerby MS, Van Belle G, Friel PN, et al: Serum prolactins in the diagnosis of epilepsy. Neurology 37:1224–1226, 1987

Yesavage JA: Nonpharmacologic treatments for memory losses with normal aging. Am J Psychiatry 142:600–605, 1985

Yesavage JA, Tinklenberg JR, Hollister LE, et al: Vasodilators in senile dementia: a review of the literature. Arch Gen Psychiatry 36:220–223, 1979

Young LD, Patel MM: Respiratory complication of antipsychotic drugs in medically ill patients. Resident and Staff Physician 30:73–80, 1984

Young LD, Taylor I, Holmstrom V: Lithium treatment of patients with affective illness associated with organic brain symptoms. Am J Psychiatry 134:1405–1407, 1977

Young RC, Alexopoulos GS, Shamoian CA: Dissociation of motor response from mood and cognition in a parkinsonian patient treated with ECT. Biol Psychiatry 20:566–569, 1985

Younger SJ, Lwandowski W, McClish DK, et al: Do not resuscitate orders. JAMA 253:54–57, 1985

Yudofsky SC: Parkinson's disease, depression, and electroconvulsive therapy, a clinical and neurobiologic synthesis. Compr Psychiatry 20:579–581, 1979

Yudofsky SC, Silver JM: Psychiatric aspects of brain injury: trauma, stroke, and tumor, in American Psychiatric Association Annual Review, vol 4. Edited by Hales RE, Frances AJ. Washington, DC, American Psychiatric Press, 1985

Yudofsky SC, Williams D, Gorman J: Propranolol in the treatment of rage and violent behavior in patients with chronic brain syndromes. Am J Psychiatry 138:218–220, 1981

Yudofsky SC, Stevens L, Silver J, et al: Propranolol in the treatment of rage and violent behavior associated with Korsakoff's psychosis. Am J Psychiatry 141:114–115, 1984

Yudofsky SC, Silver JM, Jackson W, et al: The Overt Aggression Scale: an operationalized rating scale for verbal and physical aggression. Am J Psychiatry 143:35–39, 1986

Yudofsky SC, Silver JM, Schneider SE: Psychopharmacologic treatment of aggression. Psychiatric Annals 17:397–407, 1987

Zavodnick S: Atrial flutter with amoxapine: a case report. Am J Psychiatry 138:1503–1504, 1981

Zeneroli MI, Pinelli G, Gollini G, et al: Visual evoked potential: a diagnostic tool for the assessment of hepatic encephalopathy. Gut 25:291–299, 1984

Ziegler VE, Co BT, Biggs JT: Plasma nortriptyline levels and ECG findings. Am J Psychiatry 134:441–443, 1977

Zucker, P, Daum F, Cohen M: Fatal carbamazepine hepatitis. J Pediatr 91:667–668, 1977

Psychoactive Substance Use Disorders (Alcohol)

Chapter 112

Introduction

Considerations in Diagnoses

Few if any patient groups present the consulting psychiatrist with treatment options as puzzling as do alcoholics. The settings in which such patients are treated vary greatly, as do the professional backgrounds of the care givers involved in treatment. In addition, although the full complement of approaches available, as represented in this book, provides excellent options for multimodality care, it is not always clear how the practitioner should select the appropriate one from those available.

It is now well established that a large portion of alcoholic patients do have some encounter with mental health professionals at any point in time. In the multicenter epidemiologic Catchment Area Program, for example, 14 percent of alcohol and drug abusers were reported to have made mental health visits in the past six months (Shapiro et al. 1980). In 1980, in fact, more than 1.7 million alcoholics received treatment for alcoholism in medically based facilities across the country (Vischi et al. 1980).

What role psychiatrists play in such treatment is not always clear. In federally assisted alcoholism programs, for example, only 1 percent of full-time equivalent clinical staff were psychiatrists; the majority (66 percent) of the remainder were social workers and counselors. Altogether, the number of alcoholics seeing private practitioners for treatment is less well known, but the role of the private practitioner is certainly vital to ensuring care for large numbers of alcoholics who seek care.

It is therefore important to consider how alcoholism is diagnosed, and which treatments may be integrated into a practical approach to alcoholism, particularly for the office practitioner. Importantly, this latter care giver often confronts the alcoholic patient with relatively little experience in such treatment, and with the knowledge that the mental health field has often experienced only modest success in this area. Training for physicians in this field is far from well established (Galanter 1980; Pokorny et al. 1978).

Issues related to proper diagnosis will be reviewed here first, primarily in relation to DSM-III-R (American Psychiatric Association 1987). We will also consider the patient's evaluation in a pragmatic fashion, specifically related to choosing a strategy for treatment options.

DSM-III (American Psychiatric Association 1980) introduced a number of important innovations into the nomenclature of alcoholism. In the first place, it did not use the term *alcoholism* per se. DSM-III introduced the terms *alcohol dependence* and *alcohol abuse*, thereby indicating two independent patterns of alcohol-related problems, each meriting attention, and thereby acknowledging that alcohol-related problems do not conform to one continuous or necessarily progressive sequence of illness.

In addition, substance abuse disorders were treated by DSM-III, and no longer grouped together with personality disorders, as they previously had been. This lent recognition to the growing appreciation that addictive behavior was not necessarily the product of character disorder or psychological conflict. The current diagnostic nomenclature for psychoactive substance dependence and abuse are described in DSM-III-R (Table 1). Alcohol dependence may be mild, moderate, or severe.

Table 1. DSM-III-R Diagnostic Criteria for Psychoactive Substance Dependence and Psychoactive Substance Abuse

Psychoactive Substance Dependence

A. At least three of the following:

   (1) substance often taken in larger amounts or over a longer period than the person intended

   (2) persistent desire or one or more unsuccessful efforts to cut down or control substance use

   (3) a great deal of time spent in activities necessary to get the substance (e.g., theft), taking the substance (e.g., chain smoking), or recovering from its effects

   (4) frequent intoxication or withdrawal symptoms when expected to fulfill major role obligations at work, school, or home (e.g., does not go to work because hung over, goes to school or work "high," intoxicated while taking care of his or her children), or when substance use is physically hazardous (e.g., drives when intoxicated)

   (5) important social, occupational, or recreational activities given up or reduced because of substance use

   (6) continued substance use despite knowledge of having a persistent or recurrent social, psychological, or physical problem that is caused or exacerbated by the use of the substance (e.g., keeps using heroin despite family arguments about it, cocaine-induced depression, or having an ulcer made worse by drinking)

   (7) marked tolerance: need for markedly increased amounts of the substance (i.e., at least a 50% increase) in order to achieve intoxication or desired effect, or markedly diminished effect with continued use of the same amount

   Note: The following items may not apply to cannabis, hallucinogens, or phencyclidine (PCP):

   (8) characteristic withdrawal symptoms (see specific withdrawal syndromes under Psychoactive Substance-induced Organic Mental Disorders)

   (9) substance often taken to relieve or avoid withdrawal symptoms

B. Some symptoms of the disturbance have persisted for at least one month, or have occurred repeatedly over a longer period of time.

Psychoactive Substance Abuse

A. A maladaptive pattern of psychoactive substance use indicated by at least one of the following:

   (1) continued use despite knowledge of having a persistent or recurrent social, occupational, psychological, or physical problem that is caused or exacerbated by use of the psychoactive substance

   (2) recurrent use in situations in which use is physically hazardous (e.g., driving while intoxicated)

B. Some symptoms of the disturbance have persisted for at least one month, or have occurred repeatedly over a longer period of time.

C. Never met the criteria for Psychoactive Substance Dependence for this substance.

Chapter 113

Typologies

Progress in the practice of medicine has traditionally followed the development of valid diagnostic criteria for etiologically, therapeutically, and prognostically clear categories of syndromes, diseases, and pathologic subtypes. Classification and treatment in the field of alcoholism has vacillated between a simple binary system (alcoholic versus nonalcoholic) and efforts to differentiate meaningful subtypes of alcoholic patients. For the most part, alcoholism treatment currently is based on a simple binary classification system in which all patients in any given treatment program receive the same package of services. The effort to identify meaningful subtypes dates back to the Ebers Papyrus (McKinlay 1949) and includes several classification schemes developed in the 19th century. When Bowman and Jellinek attempted their review of alcoholic typologies in 1941, there were at least 23 classifications of abnormal drinkers that they were able to identify. In 1960, Jellinek advanced his own typology based on differences in drinking pattern and pathologic consequences. Jellinek's approach to classification was based on a comprehensive knowledge of members of Alcoholics Anonymous. Since the 1960s, advances in statistical methodology have resulted in two distinct approaches to classification (Meyer et al. 1983). The first approach consists of classifying two or more groups of alcoholics according to a priori criteria, and then comparing them on a number of empirical measures representing relevant variables and constructs. The criteria employed have varied considerably from one formulation to another, and have included gender (Rimmer et al. 1971), nationality (Babor et al. 1974), psychopathology (Winokur et al. 1971), drinking pattern (Tarter et al. 1977), drinking history (Cahalan et al. 1969), and family history of alcoholism (Penick et al. 1978). Table 1 describes some representative typologies, as well as relevant hypotheses evolving from these classification schemes.

In general, these typologies have been theory-based in that the statistics that have been employed have been applied for hypothesis testing. Typologies have also been derived from atheoretical correlational methods designed to find the commonalities within homogeneous subgroups of patients or among sets of variables. In these retrospective descriptive studies, factor analysis is generally applied to a large data base representing concomitants and/or consequences of alcoholism. Then the patient population is divided into subtypes by cluster analysis or discriminant function analysis. In general, these multivariate correlational studies have not offered a rationale for the selection of variables. For the most part, they have differed in the use of assessment instruments and have generally failed to replicate specific clusters between studies. Skinner (1980) criticized the use of factor analysis in studies on alcohol, arguing that many studies fail to employ this technique appropriately. Moreover, the derived clusters have not usually been clinically relevant and have not been used by clinicians on a prospective basis.

One area in which cluster analysis has produced some replicated findings has involved the Minnesota Multiphasic Personality Inventory (MMPI) (Goldstein and Linden 1969; O'Leary et al. 1980; Skinner et al. 1974). Goldstein and Linden divided

Table 1. Operational Definitions and Research Hypotheses Associated with Some Typological Formulations of Alcoholism

Primary Source	Subtypes Postulated	Operational Criteria	Research Hypotheses
Jellinek (1960) Negrete (1973)	Gamma Delta	American alcoholics scoring high on "loss of control" scale, low on "inability to abstain" scale items French alcoholics scoring low on loss of control items and high on inability to abstain items	Gamma alcoholics will report more frequent intoxication, more severe withdrawal symptoms, more psychological "escape" reasons for drinking. Delta alcoholics will manifest greater social and psychological adjustment, and drink with greater frequency, less variability, and more for social reasons. Gamma alcoholics are expected to have a better prognosis.
Levine and Zigler (1973)	Essential-reactive	STEN scores on the 16 Personality Factor Inventory measuring high (essential) and low (reactive) emotional stability	Reactive alcoholics will manifest more variable drinking patterns, drink more for psychological escape reasons, manifest more current and past psychopathology, respond better to treatment.
Tomosovic (1974)	Binge-steady	Self-report measure of quantity, frequency, and variability of consumption; previous month, previous 6 months, lifetime	Binge drinkers will indicate more social consequences, drink more for escape reasons, manifest more current and past psychopathology, relapse more rapidly after reinitiation of drinking.
Winokur et al. (1971)	Primary-secondary	Age of onset of alcoholism and other psychopathology	Primary alcoholics will drink more for social reasons, manifest fewer social consequences, begin drinking earlier, and come into treatment at a later age.
Schuckit et al. (1969)	Depressed-antisocial personality	Psychiatric diagnosis	Secondary (and depressed-antisocial personality) alcoholics will report more loss of control, more escape drinking.
Penick et al. (1978)	Positive-negative family history of alcoholism	Family History Interview	Patients with positive family history will tend to have an earlier age of onset, indicate more psychopathology; female alcoholics, especially binge drinkers, should have more family history.
Shelly and Goldstein (1976)	Positive-negative organic brain dysfunction	Halstead-Reitan Neuropsychological Evaluation	Positives will report a longer history of heavy alcohol consumption, and indicate more numerous physical dysfunctions.
Smart (1979)	Male-female	Gender identification	Males will report higher average daily intake, a longer history of daily drinking, greater tolerance and dependence, more social consequences. Females will drink more for psychological reasons, and indicate a greater prevalence of depression and a lower prevalence of antisocial personality.

Note. Reprinted with permission from *The International Journal of the Addictions*

alcoholics into neurotic and personality disorder groups based on cluster analysis of MMPI data from 513 male alcoholics. They differentiated between subjects with primary and secondary psychopathic traits and subjects with a depressive-anxiety pattern on the MMPI. O'Leary et al. (1980) and Morey and Blashfield (1981) reviewed various studies that utilized cluster analysis of MMPI data to categorize alcoholic patients. In general, there seems consistent support for the existence of one or more subtypes scoring high on psychopathic personality, a passive-dependent personality type, and a more depressed-anxious group. Unfortunately, the subjects in these studies were disproportionally male from state hospital and Veterans Administration (VA) hospital treatment settings. This is clearly a limited sample of the universe of alcoholic individuals inside and outside of treatment settings.

Apart from studies utilizing the MMPI, a number of investigators have noted the possible importance of specific kinds of associated psychopathology in alcoholic patients, including primary and secondary antisocial personality (Schuckit 1973), primary and secondary depression (Hesselbrock et al. 1983a, 1983b; Schuckit 1979), cognitive impairment (Eckhardt et al. 1980; Shelly and Goldstein 1976), and disturbances in family functioning (Finney et al. 1980; Orford et al. 1976b). At this juncture, with the introduction of DSM-III (American Psychiatric Association 1980), a new standard approach to the diagnosis of alcoholism and coexisting psychopathology was proposed. It offered the prospect for defining psychopathologically discrete subtypes of alcoholic patients whose clinical relevance can be examined in prospective research. Diagnoses associated with alcohol-related problems are described in both the "organic mental syndromes and disorders" and the "psychoactive substance use disorders" sections of DSM-III-R (American Psychiatric Association 1987). In the organic mental disorders section, alcohol-related pathology has been described in seven discrete categories: alcohol intoxication, alcohol idiosyncratic intoxication, uncomplicated alcohol withdrawal, alcohol withdrawal delirium, alcohol hallucinosis, alcohol amnestic disorder, and dementia associated with alcoholism. The categories are clear, with reasonably definite etiological, therapeutic, and prognostic implications. This is consistent with the traditional importance of diagnosis in the practice of medicine.

Current DSM-III-R criteria for substance use disorders are based on three dimensions: pathologic use, substance use associated with social impairment, and physiologic tolerance and withdrawal. These three dimensions result in two categories: alcohol abuse and alcohol dependence. The latter requires the presence of tolerance or withdrawal symptoms and either of the other two criteria. To qualify for a diagnosis of alcohol abuse, an individual must show evidence of both pathologic alcohol use and impaired social functioning associated with use. Data indicate that most patients with alcohol use disorders who come in for inpatient treatment are in fact alcohol dependent (Hesselbrock et al. 1985). DSM-III-R does not differentiate levels of severity of alcohol dependence. Yet some studies suggest that some aspects of alcohol dependence may have prognostic significance (Babor et al. in press; Polich et al. 1981). Edwards and Gross (1976) proposed the existence of a behaviorally defined alcohol dependence syndrome. The syndrome is described in Table 2. Edwards et al. (1976) recommended that alcohol dependence and disabilities be viewed separately along a continuum of severity. The disabilities cluster involves those psychological, physiologic, and/or social disorders that are associated with excessive alcohol use. The dependence syndrome (Table 2) specifically refers to a core set of symptoms characterized by diminished capacity for control over alcohol intake, tolerance, and the presence of withdrawal symptoms.

Several reports provided empirical evidence in support of Edwards et al.'s (1970) biaxial classification (Babor et al. in press; Hodgson et al. 1979; Skinner 1981; Skinner

Table 2. Constituent Elements of the Alcohol Dependence Syndrome

Elements	Interpretation/Examples
Narrowing of the drinking repertoire	A tendency for the drinking pattern to become stereotyped around a regular schedule of almost continuous daily consumption
Salience of drink-seeking behavior	Drinking given higher priority than other activities despite its negative consequences
Increased tolerance to alcohol	More and more alcohol required to produce behavioral, subjective, and metabolic changes; large amounts of alcohol can be tolerated
Repeated withdrawal symptoms	Tremulousness, sweatiness, nausea, etc. after short periods of abstinence
Relief drinking	Relief or avoidance of withdrawal symptoms by further drinking, especially in morning
Compulsion to drink	Subjective awareness of craving for alcohol, as well as impaired control over quantity and frequency of intake
Readdiction liability	A tendency for the syndrome to be reinstated rapidly when drinking is recommenced after a period of abstinence

Note. Adapted from Edwards et al. (1976, 1981). Reprinted with permission from "Treatment 1982—State of the Art and Research Needs" by T.F. Babor, R. Kadden, and R.E. Meyer. In Fifth Special Report to Congress on Alcohol and Health.

and Allen 1982). In addition, a number of research instruments have been developed to quantify alcohol dependence (Chick 1980; Hesselbrock et al. 1985; Skinner 1981; Stockwell et al. 1979). The study by Hesselbrock et al. indicated that alcohol-related psychosocial disabilities correlated with the lifetime prevalence of psychopathology—including antisocial personality disorder, major depression, and obsessive-compulsive disorder—while severity of alcohol dependence was positively related to the quantity and frequency of alcohol consumption. At this juncture it appears that severity of dependence predicts attendance at a treatment clinic (Skinner and Allen 1982), craving for alcohol after a drink (Hodgson et al. 1979), responsivity to alcohol cues and placebo alcohol (Kaplan et al. 1983), and relapse to problem drinking (Polich et al. 1981) and reinstatement of dependence after drinking (Babor et al. in press). There is some evidence suggesting that cognitive-behavioral intervention with non-dependent heavy drinkers was associated with modification of drinking behavior and improved well-being (Chick et al. 1980; Miller and Hester 1980; Orford et al. 1976a). The data support the need for careful assessment of severity of alcohol dependence in the evaluation of alcoholic patients.

DSM-III encouraged the listing of all psychiatric diagnoses (Axis I); personality disorders (Axis II); medical disorders (Axis III); life stress (Axis IV); and adaptive functioning (Axis V) in assessing psychiatric patients. These dimensions appear especially relevant in assessing the treatment needs of alcoholic patients. Three reports highlight the heterogeneity of DSM-III psychopathology found in samples of such patients (Hesselbrock et al. 1985; Penick et al. 1983; Rounsaville et al. in press). Penick et al. studied the prevalence of psychiatric syndromes and their age of onset in 565 male alcoholics in five VA treatment programs. Slightly more than one-third of the patients fulfilled diagnostic criteria for alcoholism only; 63 percent were positive for at least two syndromes. Twenty-nine percent fulfilled criteria for one additional syndrome; 14 percent for two additional syndromes; 14 percent for three to four additional syndromes; and 6 percent for five or more additional syndromes. Depression was the most frequent (42 percent), followed by mania (22 percent) and antisocial personality disorder (20 percent). Between 10 and 15 percent of the sample were positive for drug abuse, panic attacks, phobia, and obsessive-compulsive disorder. Other conditions occurred in less than 5 percent of the sample. Patients who had no other DSM-III psychopathology apart from alcoholism reported a significantly later onset of problem drinking than those patients who had at least one other syndrome in addition to alcoholism. Antisocial alcoholics were younger and less educated and had experienced greater work instability than other patient groups. They also reported the earliest onset of problem drinking. Similar data on antisocial alcoholics were reported by Hesselbrock et al. (1984), who found that antisocial male and female alcoholics began problem drinking at a significantly earlier age and progressed more rapidly to problems associated with drinking. Babor et al. (in press) found a similar course in those alcoholics in France who carried the additional diagnosis of antisocial personality disorder.

The traditional clinical literature on psychopathology and alcoholism has tended to presume that the presence of addictive behavior was a consequence of psychopathology. In contrast, data from long-term longitudinal studies of individuals who became alcoholic (Vaillant 1983), as well as studies of chronic alcohol intoxication in the clinical research laboratory (Davis 1971; Mendelson and Mello 1966; Nathan et al. 1970), indicate that the relationship may not simply be cause and effect. Epidemiologic data suggest that psychopathology is most clearly a risk factor for alcoholism in those societies and subcultures where heavy drinking is not normative (Robins 1977). The psychiatric disorder that has been most consistently identified as a risk factor for both alcoholism and substance abuse is antisocial personality disorder. The latter condition is not found in all addicts or alcoholics. However, among males, it is one of the most prevalent associated psychiatric disorders, with frequencies of occurrence in alcoholic samples ranging from 16 to 49 percent across a variety of studies. The frequency of occurrence of antisocial personality disorder varies depending on the type of sample and the diagnostic criteria used (Hesselbrock et al. 1985). The DSM-III criteria for antisocial personality disorder are fairly "broad" and may result in higher prevalence rates of this disorder in alcoholic patients than have been previously reported. The DSM-III criteria for antisocial personality disorder are based in large measure on the longitudinal data of. Robins et al. (1962), who found that antisocial behaviors among boys seen at a child guidance clinic tended to predict subsequent alcoholism. Jones (1968) found that boys who later became problem drinkers tended to be more assertive, extroverted, rebellious, and impulsive in childhood. While most alcoholics do not manifest antisocial personality disorder, the association between antisocial personality disorder and alcoholism may represent one subtype of addictive disorder with major implications for research, prevention, and treatment. As described above, Hesselbrock et al. found that the presence of antisocial personality disorder in alcoholic individuals appeared to affect the age of onset, course, and alcoholism symptomatology. Both men and women with antisocial personality disorder began drinking at a much earlier age, progressed from regular drinking at a much earlier age, and progressed from regular drinking to alcoholism much faster than did subjects without antisocial personality disorder. They also reported substantially greater psychosocial disability symptoms in the last six months of drinking. No other psychiatric diagnosis had as significant an effect on the course of alcoholism. Rounsaville et al. (in press) reported that antisocial personality disorder is also associated with a poorer prognosis in treatment.

Rada (1980) described some treatment implications of the diagnosis of antisocial personality disorder in alcoholics. Like Schuckit (1973), he differentiated between the alcoholic sociopath, the sociopathic alcoholic, and the primary alcoholic. The latter two groups are said to manifest sociopathic features secondary to their alcohol addiction and may show remission of sociopathic features with cessation of drinking behavior. In contrast, the primary sociopath who becomes alcoholic requires treatment of the antisocial personality disorder. Rada reviewed a number of suggested treatment approaches, including efforts at ego building (Draughon 1977; Yochelson and Samenow 1976, 1977), socialization through peer confrontation (Rubin and Lawlis 1970), and behavior modification in a contingency contracting (Cohen et al. 1971; Miller et al. 1974). He concluded with a number of "general principles" derived from clinical experience. As with nonsociopathic alcoholics, the primary goal of treatment is control of addictive behavior. Outpatient medications, particularly benzodiazepines, represent a special risk of cross-addiction and pathologic drug intoxication in the antisocial alcoholic. On the other hand, such patients tend to disrupt standard inpatient milieu therapy programs; they appear to do better in programs that emphasize personal responsibility for behavior via peer confrontation groups or contingency management. Finally, court-ordered treatment may be a useful mode of entry for such patients into the treatment system. This may be of particular importance in arranging ambulatory care, especially when disulfiram is employed.

A second typological construct based on the presence of specific psychopathology in the alcoholic is depression. This diagnosis in the alcoholic appears to have multiple variations. The Washington University group has emphasized the distinction between primary and secondary depression, wherein the latter occurs in individuals who have another primary psychiatric and/or medical condition (Woodruff et al. 1973). Alcoholism is one disorder in which secondary depression is believed to occur (Winokur et al. 1971). Depression also occurs in sociopathic individuals who become alcoholic (Cadoret 1981). In a cohort of 321 alcoholic inpatients in the Hartford, Connecticut, area, Hesselbrock et al. (1985) found a lifetime prevalence rate of major depression in 32 percent of male and 52 percent of female alcoholics. Two-thirds of the depressed female alcoholics became depressed (primary depression) before they began to use alcohol, whereas primary and secondary depression were equally prevalent in the male alcoholics who carried an additional lifetime diagnosis of major depression. The data are consistent with the hypothesis that depression may contribute to risk for alcoholism in some women, and possibly some men.

In a series of classic studies on the subjective and behavioral effects of chronic ethanol intoxication in alcoholics, Mendelson and Mello (1966) found that subjects became more withdrawn, less self-confident, more depressed, and more anxious during states of chronic intoxication than when sober. These findings were confirmed by Davis (1971) and Nathan et al. (1970). The acute withdrawal period is also marked by depressive symptoms in many patients. Depressive symptoms during chronic intoxication and withdrawal do not constitute an Axis I diagnosis of affective disorder. As Jaffe (1984) pointed out, the postdetoxification affective symptoms observed in a significant percentage of patients are probably etiologically heterogeneous. Alcoholic individuals sustain real object and material losses as a consequence of their addictive behavior. Their drug of choice modifies synaptic transmission and metabolism. Chronic heavy drinking is associated with significant cognitive impairment, which may be associated with depressive affect. The decision about whether to treat depression in the alcoholic is not clear-cut. The dexamethasone suppression test, which continues to be controversial in the assessment of melancholic depression in the nonalcoholic individual, is false positive in the immediate postalcohol-withdrawal period. After three weeks of abstinence, the incidence of escape from dexamethasone suppression is not greater among nondepressed alcoholics than among normal controls (Khan et al. 1984).

Cognitive impairment in the alcoholic is a significant consequence of chronic alcohol use. Shelly and Goldstein (1976) postulated that the impairment consequent to chronic alcoholism can have a major impact on treatment response and recovery of social and occupational functioning. In general, chronic alcoholics show three kinds of cognitive impairment: deficits in abstraction, short-term memory, and visuospatial performance (Eckhardt et al. 1980). Meyer et al. (1983b) reported that 60 percent of alcoholics in their inpatient settings found some impairment on the Halstead-Reitan neuropsychological test battery (principally on the categories test), the Tactual Performance Task, performance measures on the Wechsler Adult Intelligence Scale, and the Trails B. A derived impairment index, the Brain Age Quotient, was positively correlated with certain parameters on the computerized electroencephalogram. Cognitively impaired alcoholics manifested a paucity of alpha activity, and abnormalities in synchrony and coherence (Kaplan et al. in press). Computed tomography scan studies indicated ventricular enlargement and frontal cortical shrinkage (Wilkinson and Carlen 1980), but these studies did not demonstrate a relationship between X-ray data and cognitive performance. As the number of studies of alcohol and brain function increases, it is likely that the clinician will be able to differentiate the cognitive impairment across a variety of parameters. While cognition may improve over the course of a year of abstinence (Meyer et al. 1983b), it is possible that more persistent and subtle cognitive deficits may make it difficult for some individuals to continue successfully in their usual occupations. Of special concern is the impact of cognitive impairment on treatment response. Insight-oriented therapies may be of limited usefulness for some of these patients (Rosett 1976). Becker and Jaffe (1984) found alcoholics have limited recall for the content of alcohol education films compared with nonalcoholic individuals. It is possible that the education and psychotherapy programs that are now part of most inpatient alcoholism treatment programs should be delayed for patients with alcohol-related cognitive impairment until they have the skills to benefit from such interventions.

Finally, McLellan et al. (1981) questioned the value of the categorical approach to the diagnosis of associated psychopathologies in alcohol- and drug-dependent individuals. They have found that a global measure of severity of psychological disability associated with addictive disorders was a better predictor of treatment outcome than any specific diagnostic category of psychopathology. In contrast, Rounsaville et al. (in press) argued for a categorical approach; in their study specific diagnoses were associated with different prognoses in men and women. Alcoholic males without other psychopathology did better at one year than did males with any additional psychiatric diagnoses, whereas female alcoholics with a diagnosis of major depression had a better prognosis than did other female patients. This work, as well as studies on the comparative usefulness of the primary-secondary distinction, requires further study in other settings.

In summary, at this writing, the concept of therapeutically and prognostically valid patient subtypes within the general class of individuals with alcoholism remains an area in need of further study. Previous efforts to subclassify alcoholics using cluster analysis or discriminant function analysis have not resulted in the definition of clinically useful typologies that have treatment or prognostic implications. Typologies developed from one data set have not generally been replicated in other data sets. Typologies based on the MMPI have divided alcoholics into neurotic and personality-disordered groups, and there has seemed to be support for subtypes of male alcoholism based on the MMPI, in some settings. Some studies have suggested that the presence of other DSM-III diagnoses (particularly antisocial personality disorder) may represent a useful classification scheme. There is further support for this approach to classification from studies based on an analysis of data of Swedish adoptees (Cloninger et al. 1981), by investigators in Sweden and St. Louis, and on analyses of data of cohorts of alcoholic probands and offspring by investigators at the University of Connecticut.

Cloninger et al. proposed the existence of two types of familial alcoholism. Type I alcoholism occurs in both male and female children of alcoholics and appears to be influenced (in terms of severity) by environmental factors (e.g., socioeconomic class). Type 2 alcoholism is male limited and is associated with a history of criminality. Hesselbrock et al. (1985) described an earlier onset and more rapid course of alcoholism in individuals with antisocial personality disorder. With reports of electrophysiologic differences in some sons of alcoholics (Begleiter et al. 1984) and diminished sensitivity to moderate doses of ethanol in males with a family history of alcoholism (Schuckit 1984), we may be moving to a time when typologies of alcoholism will be defined on the basis of different factors (i.e., genetic and environmental) associated with risk of developing the disorder. At this time, Cloninger et al.'s (1981) proposal describing two types of alcoholism represents an important direction for future research on typologies.

Chapter 114

Goals of Treatment

General Factors Impacting on Treatment Goals

In this chapter, I will discuss general goals appropriate for alcoholism treatment. The comments are aimed at helping the reader to understand better the more detailed discussions of specific approaches given in the other chapters of this section. The ideas given here are, by necessity, global, but specific examples are offered whenever possible.

All types of programs need to consider the following:

1. Treatment goals for any disorder must be based on considerations of fiscal and political, as well as therapeutic, realities. The amount of monies available compared

to the number of patients seeking care establishes a ratio that dictates the type of facility, the therapeutic regimen, the number of staff, the length of contact with patients, the number of hours that the facility can be open, and so on. The source of this funding also dictates political realities that impinge on treatment goals. For instance, for a city-funded skid row facility, probable low one-year rate of abstinence for homeless alcoholics entering rehabilitation makes it unwise to judge the program by the number of patients who abstain over long periods of time (Powell et al. 1985; Schuckit 1984). A more appropriate goal might address severe medical problems that require active treatment because efforts here can be lifesaving and outcomes more easily documented.

2. In any treatment setting, it is important that the program recognize the scarcity of financial and staff resources. In general, treatment approaches should be kept simple, avoiding potentially expensive or potentially dangerous additions until controlled studies have demonstrated that these more costly approaches are justified.

3. The philosophy and training of the program directors influence other goals by dictating the staff chosen to carry out the day-to-day treatment.

4. No treatment is totally safe. Patients can have adverse reactions to medications or diagnostic procedures, may act on bad advice, and run the risk of exhausting scarce resources of time and money. Therefore, all programs should attempt to do the most possible good with the least possible harm. This cost-benefit ratio depends on knowledge of the probable course of the disorder (i.e., is the danger of intervening of more or less risk than the probable future course if the patient is left alone?) weighed against the balance between the intervention's chances for success and its risks. One way to estimate the probable course with and without treatment is through carefully establishing the diagnosis (Goodwin and Guze 1984).

5. Once a clear label has been assigned, clinicians must determine if the diagnosis is primary or secondary to another disorder to understand the prognosis (Schuckit 1983, 1984, 1985a). Secondary illness tends to run a complex course heavily influenced by the primary problem (Schuckit 1983, 1986). For example, a patient appearing for treatment with alcohol on his breath, signs of autonomic overactivity, and a tremor could be demonstrating physiologic symptoms of withdrawal from alcohol, but could also be a "social drinker" with diabetes who had not followed his diet during an evening on the town. This diagnostic distinction can mean the difference between life and death. Similarly, a patient presenting with alcohol intoxication, suicidal ideas, insomnia, and feelings of guilt may have primary alcoholism with depressions occurring only in the midst of heavy drinking. The primary alcoholic with secondary depression might require antisuicidal precautions for several days but will not need antidepressant medications and is usually ready to begin alcohol rehabilitation within a week of abstinence.

6. A related treatment goal is the need to address relevant primary psychiatric disorders. About one in four alcoholics entering an alcohol treatment program have a major preexisting psychiatric disorder (i.e., they have secondary alcoholism) (Schuckit 1983, 1986). For example, a patient with serious affective episodes antedating the alcoholism or demonstrating severe depression during long periods of abstinence probably has primary affective disorder and secondary alcoholism and might require appropriate medications (e.g., lithium or antidepressant medications) and psychotherapy before the depression will clear. Also, the schizophrenic with thought disorders antedating alcohol-related problems must be recognized and treated with antipsychotic drugs or psychotic symptoms will not improve (Alterman et al. 1984). This is different from the primary alcoholics de-

scribed above because dangerous psychiatric symptoms that occur only in the midst of heavy drinking usually disappear with abstinence.

7. Alcohol adversely affects almost all body systems so that even apparently well-nourished middle-class alcoholics are at high risk for serious medical problems (Ashley 1981; Schuckit 1984, 1987). These encompass the gamut of medical diseases, including alcohol-related hypertension and other cardiac disorders, an increased risk for cancers, alcohol-related gastrointestinal abnormalities, and neurologic degenerations. Proper care of the alcoholic requires that these disorders be recognized and treated.

These seven general goals apply to all alcoholics.

General Goals for Addressing Substance-Induced Organic Mental Disorders

This diagnostic category covers a diverse group of problems, including simple intoxication, withdrawal, and psychotic symptoms in the midst of alcoholism. No matter what the specific diagnosis, the factors outlined above must be considered.

Some of these general treatment rules have special relevance to organic disorders. Even more than other alcoholics, those with signs of organic impairment are at high risk for physical problems that could lead to death during withdrawal if not corrected (e.g., heart failure, pneumonia, subdural hematomas). Patients with what appear to be substance-induced organic mental disorders should be evaluated to determine if the hallucinations or delusions, for example, began prior to age 40 and occurred independent of periods of heavy drinking because primary schizophrenia carries its own prognoses and treatment needs.

Patients who are confused and agitated (e.g., some alcoholic withdrawal states and alcoholic idiosyncratic reactions) carry a risk for violence that must be addressed (Coid 1979, 1982). A commonsense approach to dealing with violent patients includes the use of a "show of force" when necessary, making no sudden moves without explaining them first to the patient, using appropriate antianxiety or antipsychotic medications to control the behavior, and rarely using physical restraints (Lewis and Senay 1981). Similarly, confused and agitated patients, even if primary alcoholics, must be carefully evaluated for suicidal thoughts and plans, if present, with appropriate actions taken (Fowler et al. 1986).

Finally, it is important that interventions in patients with alcohol-related organic impairment be viewed as only a first step in treatment. After addressing acute medical, psychiatric, and substance-related problems, each alcoholic must be considered as a potential candidate for alcoholic rehabilitation. While some alcoholics requiring emergency care for organic disorders or withdrawal are not ready to address rehabilitation (Annis and Smart 1978), the possibility should be considered.

Goals of Alcoholic Rehabilitation for Alcohol Abuse and Dependence

All of the goals outlined earlier apply to rehabilitation programs. The comments here assume that the proper psychiatric and medical diagnoses have been established and that the patient has been confronted with the problem and has agreed to consider rehabilitation.

Complete abstinence from alcohol is the major goal for most programs (Armor et al. 1976). However, not all alcoholics will agree to work for total abstention (Elal-Lawrence et al. 1986). Temporary periods of controlled drinking are part of the natural history of alcoholism, and a small percentage of alcoholics do appear to be able to achieve moderate, nonproblematic drinking over extended periods of time (Ludwig 1972; Orford et al. 1976; Popham and Schmidt 1976). Some workers have used these observations to develop experimental programs to help alcoholics who refuse abstinence by attempting to teach them to control their drinking (Sobell and Sobell 1976). Unfortunately, the studies to date have been small and follow-ups may have been incomplete (Pendery et al. 1982), with the result that no solid conclusions on the effectiveness of this approach can be reached. Therefore, it is best to view controlled drinking as an area worthy of investigation but inappropriate for routine clinical use in clinical settings until better data are available.

Abstinence alone, however, may not yield significant improvement in some patients' lives (Polich et al. 1980) and most programs recognize the need to improve overall level of health and psychological and behavioral functioning (Pattison 1976). This is accomplished by a series of maneuvers that fall into two general categories (Schuckit 1984). The first is an effort to help the patient develop a high level of motivation toward abstinence through education about the disorder given to patients and their significant others and the possible use of medications like disulfiram to decrease the chance of a spur-of-the-moment return to drinking (Schuckit 1985b). The second series of maneuvers helps the patient rebuild his or her life without alcohol through 1) counseling, dealing with problems with family and social interactions; 2) constructive use of free time; 3) job functioning; 4) learning how to improve impairment in a psychological state, for example, periods of sadness and anxiety (Schuckit 1983); and 5) dealing with impaired physical functioning.

There are also a number of goals rehabilitation programs are likely to exclude. It may be difficult or impossible to determine the patient's basic personality structure, mood swings, general levels of anxiety, and so on until the patient has been abstinent for a period of months (Mandel and Melisaratos 1985). Patients are likely to come for help at a time of crisis and may experience autonomic nervous system dysfunction as part of a protracted abstinence syndrome for many months after the acute withdrawal has passed (Kissen 1979). Programs should focus on maneuvers to achieve and maintain abstention and *not* attempt to change lifelong personality patterns (or even assess them) until patients can be evaluated in a stable sober state (Berger 1983).

Similarly, while attempting to help a patient achieve and maintain abstinence as well as to develop a life-style free of alcohol, it is unwise to treat insomnia or anxiety with medications. With the exception of depressants (e.g., benzodiazepines) for the *treatment of withdrawal* and possibly disulfiram-type drugs during rehabilitation, there is little evidence that benzodiazepines, lithium, antipsychotic medications, or tricyclic antidepressants will help the alcoholic maintain abstinence (Armor et al. 1976; Florenzano 1983; Schuckit 1984; Viamontes 1972). For the primary alcoholic, symptoms of anxiety and depression are likely to disappear on their own, and any of these drugs can be dangerous if the patient mixes them with alcohol. Of course, carefully defined secondary alcoholics with primary unipolar affective disorders may benefit from antidepressants; primary bipolar patients with secondary alcohol-related problems may benefit from lithium; and the primary schizophrenic with secondary alcoholism entering alcoholism rehabilitation will almost certainly require antipsychotic medication.

Summary: The Goals in Alcoholism Treatment

First, perhaps 15 to 30 percent of general psychiatric patients presenting with symptoms of depression or anxiety have primary alcoholism and need to be recognized and appropriately treated (Schuckit 1983). The clinician can help cull out the secondary alcoholic with primary affective disorder, primary schizophrenia, and so on, and treat the primary disorder. The clinician has to carry out confrontation of the alcoholic skillfully, emphasizing the patient's responsibility for his or her own actions and beginning proper intervention or referring the patient to an adequate facility (Schuckit 1984). The clinician can also help reach out to disturbed families of alcoholics and see that they get adequate care (Steinglass 1981).

Abstinence is the only appropriate goal for primary or secondary alcoholism once identified. Counseling or individual and/or group therapy and involvement with Alcoholics Anonymous aimed at helping patients achieve abstinence and readjust to life without alcohol are very important.

Psychiatrists have to monitor medications during rehabilitation. For the average primary alcoholic, psychotropic drugs serve no purpose once detoxification has been completed (with the possible exception of disulfiram). The psychiatrist monitoring rehabilitation must ensure that such inappropriate and potentially dangerous drugs are not given.

We can also help patients through offering behavior modification techniques. These include nonmedicinal efforts to improve sleep and to control anxiety during the first months of sobriety, using such techniques as biofeedback, systematic muscle relaxation, and meditation (Schuckit 1984).

Chapter 115

Treatment of Organic Mental Disorders

Treatment of Alcohol Intoxication

Differential Diagnosis

Because of the widespread use of alcohol in our society, both physicians and laypersons are frequently too hasty in attributing unusual behavior or difficulty with coordination to alcohol. When a patient arrives in a physician's office or an emergency room with symptoms of slurred speech, difficulty with coordination, ataxia, loquaciousness, and difficulty with attention, there may be a natural tendency for the physician to attribute the patient's symptoms to alcohol intoxication. However, similar symptoms may be caused by certain neurologic diseases such as multiple sclerosis, cerebellar dysfunction, or intoxication due to other sedative substances (e.g., barbiturates or benzodiazepines). Metabolic diseases such as diabetes mellitus may also be associated with impairment of central nervous system function and subsequent development of these signs and symptoms. Even if the diagnostic impression is supported by a relatively high blood level of alcohol, it would be wise for the physician to follow the patient carefully to be sure that these symptoms clear as the alcohol disappears from the blood. It should be emphasized that the alcohol intoxication may be masking underlying physical sequelae of alcoholism. A careful history and physical examination should evaluate the possibility of trauma.

If the patient is cooperative, careful inquiry into recent meals and the amount of alcohol ingested may help the physician to formulate an educated guess about the present level of blood alcohol. Food inhibits alcohol absorption. If the patient has started drinking less than one hour after the last heavy meal, the blood alcohol level should be somewhat modified as compared to drinking on an empty stomach (Lin et al. 1976). The blood alcohol peaks within 30 minutes to three hours after rapid ingestion ceases. Each ounce of whiskey, glass of wine, or 12-ounce bottle of beer raises the blood level by approximately 15 to 25 mg percent.

Severity of the symptoms of intoxication depends on the rapidity of the blood alcohol level ascent and on the peak level of blood alcohol concentration attained, as well as the patient's acquired tolerance and the presence of other drugs. It has been demonstrated that women become intoxicated more rapidly than men, exhibiting an increase of blood alcohol levels between 20 to 45 percent higher than men, after receiving the same amount of alcohol per unit of weight, regardless of body build (Jones and Jones 1975; Sutker et al. 1983). However, it does appear that the differences in the peak levels of blood alcohol may be explained by differences in body water content between the sexes. Evaluation of women ingesting alcohol during the premenstrual phase indicates that peak blood alcohol levels may occur even more rapidly during this time with higher absorption rates as compared to other phases of the menstrual cycle (Jones and Jones 1975). It should be noted that oral contraceptives contain compounds such as estrogen that inhibit the metabolism of alcohol, resulting in higher peak levels and more sustained blood alcohol levels (Hatcher and Jones 1977).

If the patient does not show typical signs and symptoms of alcohol intoxication (as detailed in Table 1) at blood alcohol levels of 150 mg percent, this display of very high tolerance indicates a strong possibility of alcohol dependence. If the blood alcohol level is 300 mg percent and the patient is still ambulatory, the diagnosis of alcohol dependence can be confirmed.

From a medical and legal viewpoint, it is essential for the physician to obtain a blood alcohol level because the unreliability of the alcoholic's history of alcohol consumption has been well established. In one study, only 17 percent of the alcoholic patients in a medical clinic were consistently honest about their drinking; these data were confirmed by the evaluation of 24-hour urine collections for alcohol content prior to the day of clinical appointment (Orrego et al. 1979). The patients did not realize that their urine was being surveyed for the presence of alcohol. The denial mechanism utilized by patients, who fool themselves as well as the people around them, can be grossly exaggerated when they are intoxicated, particularly as to the amount that they drank prior to the clinic visit.

Table 1. Signs and Symptoms of Alcohol Intoxication and Overdose

Signs	Symptoms	Diagnostic Aids
Mild to moderate intoxication • Impaired attention • Poor motor coordination • Dysmetria • Ataxia • Nystagmus • Slurred speech • Prolonged reaction time • Flushed face • Orthostatic hypotension • Hematemesis • Stupor	**Mild to moderate intoxication** • Alcohol on breath • Loquacity • Impaired judgment • Inappropriate behavioral responses • Inappropriate emotional responses • Euphoria • Dizziness • Blurred vision	• In low-dose intoxication, blood alcohol level is about 100 mg percent or higher. (If level is greater than 300 mg percent and patient is alert and relatively well-coordinated, then this highly tolerant person may be an alcoholic and experience withdrawal symptoms as the blood alcohol level decreases.)
Severe intoxication and overdose • Respiratory rate decreased • Bruises or scars from analgesia and lacks coordination • Shock • Coma	**Severe intoxication** • Irrational, angry outbursts with violent acts • Progressively sluggish responses to environmental stimuli • "Dry heaves"	• In high-dose coma, the blood alcohol level should be greater than 300 mg percent. • Otherwise, the etiology of the coma may not be alcohol. • Diabetic acidosis and hypoglycemia may be easily ruled out.

Note. Adapted with permission from Gallant (1982c).

Early Clinical and Physical Signs of Alcoholism

A sensitively performed clinical history is essential if the physician is to make an early diagnosis of alcoholism before gross evidence of chronic alcohol-induced damage develops. The chemical use history should begin with questions about the least threatening or safest subjects. Thus one should begin by inquiring about substances that are legal or culturally acceptable, such as the number of cups of caffeinated beverages per day, progress to the number of cigarettes filtered or unfiltered, and then to the daily number of glasses of wine and beer and/or ounces of liquor per day. In addition to the type and amount of drug, the interviewer should try to assess the pattern of use. The interviewer must be very sensitive in handling the transition to questions about marijuana and then to the "harder" drugs because polydrug misuse has become more common in alcoholic patients and can confuse the clinical presentation as well as the formulation of a treatment plan (Gallant 1982b). Attention to type, amount, and pattern of drug use will result in more reliable information. Use of the Diagnostic Questions for Early or Advanced Alcoholism and the Michigan Alcoholism Screening Test may enable patients to take a more objective look at themselves (Gallant 1982a). The Brief Alcoholism Screening Test is a highly reliable index of the presence of alcoholism (Woodruff et al. 1976). The questions are simple and easy to remember:

1. Has your family ever objected to your drinking?
2. Did you ever think you drank too much in general?
3. Have others (such as friends, physicians, clergy) ever said you drink too much for your own good?

These three questions correctly identified about 96 percent of alcoholic patients and misidentified only 10 percent of nonalcoholics, using the Michigan Alcoholism Screening Test (Woodruff et al. 1976) as the comparison diagnostic instrument.

Frequent headaches, recurring gastrointestinal complaints, recent absences from work or school based on vague physical complaints, and/or sudden unexplained mood changes are possible early symptoms of alcohol abuse. Somewhat more advanced symptoms may be the continued use of the same amounts of alcohol even after having sustained alcohol-related injuries or being charged with driving while intoxicated. Increased frequency of use despite "blackouts," antisocial or belligerent behavior while under the influence of chemicals, or confrontation by spouse or friends about the use are often symptoms of loss of control. Frequent injuries or cigarette burns due to drowsiness may be other symptoms of alcohol misuse. Later stages of alcoholism are associated with evidence of acne rosacea (dilation of vessels with thickening of skin), palmar erythema, spider nevi, cheilitis, skin bruises, evidence of multiple trauma, and poor nutrition.

Management of Acute Alcohol Intoxication

The Attitude of the Physician

Many physicians, when recalling their days in medical school, may remember a number of negative experiences with alcoholic patients. It is the chronic treatment failure who repeatedly returns to the emergency room and walk-in clinic at the general hospital where the students spend most of their clinical time. In these surroundings, it is quite unusual to see a successful treatment case. As a result, the future physician not only develops a distasteful attitude toward alcoholic patients, but also may acquire very pessimistic opinions about the prognosis. This type of attitude can become part of an unconscious negative orientation toward alcoholic patients and may interfere with the development of an adequate therapeutic relationship.

In most cases of mild alcohol intoxication, it is essential for physicians to remember that their attitudes will be most important in determining whether or not patients follow up with therapy. Physicians must show their concern about their patients' welfare, but be nonjudgmental and genuine in their statements to the patients. Although intoxicated patients may be revealing some of their innermost sober feelings, these feelings are usually expressed inappropriately while they are under the influence of alcohol. Any anger or defensiveness on the part of physicians will usually result in the patients' discontinuing efforts at follow-up therapy for their drinking problems. A firm but kind therapeutic approach offers patients some confidence in developing a trusting relationship, which is the key for future constructive efforts in follow-up treatment.

Criteria have been developed for medical audits for acute alcoholism to justify medical intervention, patient outcome, and management of complications (West 1978). As noted in Table 2, the medical audit for acute alcoholism includes justification for the diagnosis of acute alcoholism, the measurable symptoms and signs of psychomotor agitation, tremulousness, tachycardia, hypertension, hallucinations, delirium, or seizure activity. Admission criteria for acute alcoholism or alcohol intoxication include the DSM-III (American Psychiatric Association 1980) criteria for alcohol intoxication associated with an injury or accompanying medical disorders such as diabetes, dehydration, or other medical complications. Classification of the withdrawal states, as outlined in Table 2, enables the physician to be more specific about the

Table 2. Audit Criteria for Acute Alcoholism

Criteria Number Elements	Standard 100%	0%	Exceptions	Instructions and Definitions for Data Retrieval
Diagnosis				
1. (a) Psychomotor agitation and tremors or	X			Psychomotor agitation = shakes
(b) Hallucinations or				Acute intoxication = blood alcohol 150 mg/100 ml
(c) Delirium or				
(d) Seizures				
Admission				
2. (a) Acute intoxication or stage I with other disease or injury or	X		Admission criteria, if not noted on emergency room record, may be found on progress notes, history, physical, and discharge summary	Stage I = psychomotor agitation, tachycardia (pulse 90) tremulousness, sweating, hypertension (150/-)
(b) Stage II, III, or IV acute withdrawal syndrome				Stage II = above with hallucinations
(c) Acute intoxication with history of stage II, III, or IV withdrawal symptoms				Stage III = above with delirium (disorientation)
				Stage IV = above with seizures or history of seizures
				Either the stage number or the symptoms may be recorded
Above to be noted on emergency room AC record				
Treatment: stages I–IV and acute intoxication				
3. Sedatives and	X			Sedatives include the use of benzodiazepines
4. Therapy	X			Therapy (individual counseling, group therapy, Alcoholics Anonymous meeting) criteria met if any of the above is ordered and nurses' notes document participation
5. No restraints	X		Restraints in stage III if threat to self or others	
6. Anticonvulsants if stage IV	X			

		Critical preventive and responsive management	
Discharge status (outcome)			
7. Ambulatory and	X		
8. All psychoactive drugs (sedatives) discontinued and	X		
9. On solid diet			
10. Mortality			
11. Length of stay two to 10 days	X	Complications in length of stay below	
12. Other iv if dehydration is not documented	X		
Complications (indicators)			
13. Dehydration	X	Fluid (iv) replacement	Dehydration as documented in record
14. Hyperpyrexia	X	Hypothermia machine, fluids	Hyperpyrexia = temperature 103°
15. Renal shutdown	X	Fluids, steroids, hypothermia machine	Renal shutdown = no urinary output
16. Esophageal hemorrhage	X	Blood replacement, portocaval shunt or sclerosing of veins	
17. Gastric hemorrhage	X	Blood replacement if hematocrit below 30	Gastric hemorrhage = any vomiting of blood
18. Pancreatitis	X	Antibiotics, pain medication	

Note. Adapted with permission from West (1978).

criteria for admitting the patient to a general hospital. The majority of patients who arrive at a general hospital in a state of acute intoxication are uncomplicated cases or in a mild state of withdrawal (stage I in Table 2). These patients can be detoxified in a nonmedical setting as outpatients (Whitfield 1980).

For those patients requiring admission for the syndrome of alcohol intoxication, one medical audit established the length of stay from two to 10 days, with discontinuation of all psychopharmacologic habituating drugs as one of the criteria for ambulatory discharge status (West 1978). In this study of 100 consecutive cases, the inappropriate use of intravenous (iv) fluids for acute withdrawal appears to be the most common problem, occurring in 12 percent of these cases. In every one of these specific mismanagement problems, the fluids were ordered by the emergency room personnel.

In more severe cases of alcohol intoxication, particularly in those individuals who have been on a poor diet with a resulting glycogen-depleted liver and impaired gluconeogenesis, hypoglycemia may be an additional medical problem. If the patient is semicomatose or comatose, immediate steps should be taken to sustain the airway, assure a regular respiratory rate, and maintain the circulatory system. Besides checking vital signs every 15 to 30 minutes, the physician must explore the possibility of occult bleeding and other causes of coma, such as central nervous system disturbances. In patients with very poor nutrition, severe pulmonary infection can occur with little increase in white blood cell count or temperature, indicating a deficit in the patient's immune response.

In comatose patients who are showing impairment of respiration on admission, several emergency steps can be initiated while awaiting the results of the laboratory tests. To rule out severe hypoglycemia, 50 ml of 50 percent glucose solution iv can be given with 10 mg of thiamine. If the patient's skin shows needle marks indicative of narcotic drug use, the administration of naloxone in a dosage of 0.4 to 2.0 mg iv and repeated at two- to three-minute intervals, two or three times, may prove to be lifesaving.

In conscious patients, medical observation and adequate nursing care should be sufficient after other causes of intoxicated behavior have been ruled out. The patient should be placed on the side with the head down to avoid aspiration of vomitus. An infusion should not be started unless the patient is dehydrated from vomiting or diarrhea; routine use of infusions in this type of patient may offer more iatrogenic risks than benefits.

The use of gastric lavage and activated charcoal are not indicated on a routine basis unless the ingestion of alcohol has taken place shortly before the patient's admission to the emergency room. The rapid absorption of alcohol is a contraindication for using these procedures in a routine manner. However, if the blood alcohol level is greater than 600 mg percent, hemodialysis may then be useful in patients with impaired liver function. The use of analeptics is of no value.

The Syndrome of Alcohol Idiosyncratic Intoxication (291.40)

The criteria for the diagnosis of this disorder stress the behavioral changes displayed by the patient while under the influence of a relatively small amount of alcohol and considered to be unusual or atypical behavior for the patient. The lay diagnosis of "alcoholic blackout" and the DSM-II (American Psychiatric Association 1968) diagnosis of pathological intoxication have been assigned to this category despite the fact that these episodes may also occur under the influence of large amounts of alcohol.

This diagnostic category may have important legal implications when the patient has committed a criminal offense during these unusual episodes that are associated with the ingestion of alcohol. The alcoholic blackout would be defined as an incident that occurs while the patient is drinking moderately or heavily and one that the patient cannot recall when sober. In obtaining carefully detailed histories, it is not unusual to find that the amnesic behavior was only routine insignificant speech or action that the patient cannot recall. However, those incidents in which the patients become assaultive or violent are so impressive to the interviewer that many physicians believe that the typical incident of an alcoholic blackout involves very peculiar or very unusual behavior. When one sees a patient during an alcoholic blackout, it is impossible to determine if this is an episode for which the patient will be amnesic the next day. In fact, some patients actually appear to act less intoxicated during these episodes. It should be emphasized that although the patient is responsible for attaining the state of intoxication in which this type of amnesic behavior occurs, the patient may not be responsible for his or her actions or words during the actual incident. If the patient has had a previous history of violent behavior during an alcoholic blackout (i.e., pathological intoxication), the patient is much more likely to repeat this behavior during another blackout. In episodes of pathological intoxication it has been shown that there is a very high incidence of abnormal electroencephalograms during the period of dangerous behavior (Maletzky 1978).

In an extensive evaluation of 220 alcoholics admitted to a treatment program, it was found that 43 percent had a history of psychotic symptomatology, usually during heavy alcohol or drug use and associated with a prior history of antisocial problems or drug abuse (Schuckit 1980). The severely abnormal episodic behavior often displayed by these patients during alcohol consumption can be confused with other neuropsychiatric diagnoses such as temporal lobe epilepsy, schizophrenia, and drug intoxication. Complaints of numbness, cerebellar dysfunction with ataxia and slurring of speech, nausea, and diaphoresis can all be seen with phencyclidine intoxication as well as with alcohol intoxication. Therefore, careful elicitation of drug history as well as urine survey for phencyclidine may be necessary, particularly in young intoxicated patients who come into the emergency room with assaultive or suicidal behavior.

Management

As mentioned before, it is sometimes quite difficult to know when a patient is in the middle of an alcohol idiosyncratic intoxication or pathological intoxication episode and thus not fully responsible for his or her actions at this time. If aggression or extreme anger is part of the patient's clinical presentation during this rather sudden behavioral change, the clinician should regard the patient as dangerous and approach the patient as carefully as one would any totally incompetent and potentially violent patient. The guidelines for this type of situation follow:

1. One should never disagree with the patient about anything the patient says. An individual who is on the verge of an explosion can be set off by any discord in the environment.
2. One should use the voice and body movements as therapeutic tools. The voice should always be calm, with slow speech in a monotone and no sudden changes of pitch. The motor movements should be kept to a minimum and initiated in a very slow manner. Thus both voice and movement should serve as instruments of therapy.

3. Although in most situations the patient should be addressed by his or her title and last name out of respect for the person, in this type of precarious situation it may be wise to learn the patient's first name and start using it in a calm, familiar, and friendly manner. The familiar form of address will usually help the patient to feel more comfortable.

4. In talking to the patient, one should always remember that there is little likelihood of violence while the dialogue is going on. At the same time, one must try to find out personal facts about the patient that have a positive affective charge, such as the names of one or two persons to whom the patient feels closest and for whom the patient has positive feelings. If this type of information can be elicited, the next step is to attempt to get the patient's permission to telephone them in order to bring someone with a positive affective charge in contact with the patient. The longer the conversation progresses, the less chance there is for violence. Also, having the patient verbalize about positive affective relationships in the past or talk to a close friend or relative on the telephone may help bring the patient out of this partial amnestic episode by recalling events that are familiar.

It may be necessary to use iv benzodiazepine sedation if the patient's assaultive behavior continues. If required, the benzodiazepine should be administered quite slowly: 10 mg of diazepam over a period of one to two minutes, repeated if necessary in 10 minutes, or lorazepam, 1 to 2 mg over a period of one to two minutes, repeated if necessary in 10 minutes.

Alcohol Withdrawal Syndromes

Mild to Moderate Alcohol Withdrawal (Uncomplicated Alcohol Withdrawal—291.80)

Diagnostic criteria and differential diagnosis. Diagnostic criteria of this syndrome include such symptoms as gastrointestinal distress, asthenia, anxiety, irritability, and autonomic hyperactivity. According to DSM-III-R (American Psychiatric Association 1987) the patient should show at least one of these symptoms within the first several hours after cessation or reduction of heavy, prolonged ingestion of alcohol. Other diagnoses that may resemble this syndrome are hypoglycemia, ketoacidosis, short-acting sedative withdrawal syndromes, and familial or essential tremor.

Management. For the majority of patients with uncomplicated alcohol withdrawal, outpatient treatment can be sufficient. The blood alcohol can be used as one of the more reliable guidelines for making decisions about placing the patient on an alcohol withdrawal unit with specialized care, placing the patient on a medical ward for more intensive treatment of severe withdrawal symptoms, or following the patient at home with proper supervision. For example, if the blood alcohol level is 150 to 200 mg percent and the patient appears to be alert and not dysarthric, then the physician should be on guard about the possible appearance of withdrawal symptoms as the blood alcohol level decreases. In this type of patient, the tolerance for alcohol is far too high and suggests chronic alcohol abuse with an increased predisposition to develop withdrawal symptoms on cessation of the alcohol.

In one study of 564 acute alcohol outpatient admissions, only 45 (8 percent) required hospitalization (Pattison 1977). In another extensive study of alcohol detoxification, less than 10 percent required medical detoxification, and the remainder of the 1,024 patients in the study received nondrug detoxification (Whitfield 1980). Seizures occurred in only 1 percent, hallucinations in 3.7 percent, and delirium tremens in less than 1 percent. In this study, however, the treatment team was specially trained to deal with nondrug detoxification and instructed on how to "talk the patient down" and provide reality testing in a therapeutic manner. The use of benzodiazepines was required in less than 10 percent of the entire patient population. The psychological approach was reassurance and reality orientation. These two studies suggest that the majority of alcoholic patients could be withdrawn from alcohol without the use of potentially habituating minor tranquilizers.

Therapeutic management of acute withdrawal is not necessarily the first step in treatment. The physician may help the patient to titrate the decrease of alcohol with family aid and then to change over to a short-acting hypnotic (e.g., chloral hydrate) for sleep for the next five to seven days. The use of relaxation techniques such as reality orientation, the use of mild pleasurable sensory stimulations such as appropriate music, the availability of friends and relatives, attempts to keep the patient active, and reassurance may help to decrease discomfort as the patient goes through the process of a mild withdrawal stage. In this manner, it may be possible to avoid the automatic pharmacologic approach used by some detoxification units in the place of psychological management. Thiamine, 50 to 100 mg/day, in addition to multivitamins and folic acid, 1 to 3 mg/day, should be given to all patients experiencing mild to severe alcohol withdrawal, with oral vitamins for patients in the mild to moderate stages, and subcutaneously or intravenously to those with poor gastrointestinal absorption or those who are in a severe stage of withdrawal. Short-term administration of high dosages of vitamins should not result in any serious side effects. The signs and symptoms of alcoholic withdrawal are detailed in Tables 2 and 3.

If the patient shows a combination of symptoms that suggest that the withdrawal stage is associated with too much discomfort, a benzodiazepine may be used on a temporary basis and administered by relative or friend to be sure the patient does not misuse the medication. Of course, the more severe the signs and symptoms of withdrawal, the more difficulty the patient will experience in abstaining from alcohol and the more frequently the patient should be seen at the office. It is not unusual to have patients come in on a daily basis when they have started on disulfiram and to give only enough tranquilizers to last until they return to the clinic the next day. Dependency-producing medication such as benzodiazepines should not be used for longer than one to two weeks because patients with problems of alcohol abuse are more likely to misuse these tranquilizers as well.

In those alcoholic patients displaying tremor, the physician must learn how to distinguish between the "alcoholic tremor" of withdrawal and the benign essential or familial tremor that is readily relieved by alcohol and seen frequently among alcoholics. In the latter case, the patient's drinking to relieve the tremor may have subsequently led to increased alcohol consumption. The benign essential tremor is rhythmic, usually at a rate of four to 10/second, and worsens with fatigue, extreme cold, and social stress. Adrenergic blockers such as propranolol or metoprolol are most efficacious in treating this condition. Many alcoholic patients who use this essential tremor as a reason for increasing alcohol consumption show an impressive positive personality change after the tremor has been inhibited by propranolol.

If the patient continues to drink sporadically during this outpatient treatment of the mild to moderate alcohol withdrawal syndrome, it may be necessary to institute inpatient detoxification even though the patient may not be experiencing severe withdrawal symptoms. From a therapeutic viewpoint, it may be necessary to interrupt the self-destructive cycle of heavy drinking followed by withdrawal symptoms, which are then relieved through resumption of alcohol intake.

Table 3. Signs and Symptoms of Alcohol Withdrawal

Signs	Symptoms	Diagnostic Aids
Mild to moderate signs	**Mild to moderate symptoms**	• Electroencephalogram showing bursts of high amplitude slow waves with random spikes
• Malaise or weakness	• Fluctuation of symptoms during the course of a day	
• Muscle tension		
• Tremor	• Irritability	• Electrolyte depletion
• Hyperreflexia	• Anxiety and agitation	• Hypoglycemia may be present
• Elevated blood pressure	• Extreme fatigue	
• Tachycardia	• Disturbance of sleep-wakefulness cycle	• Association of high laboratory values commonly found in alcoholics (e.g., macrocytosis, elevated levels of uric acid, SGPT, alkaline phosphatase, bilirubin, and triglycerides) without any other known cause
• Diaphoresis		
• Hyperacuity of all sensory modalities	• Anorexia	
	• Vomiting	
• Flushed face	• Headache	
	• Diarrhea	
	• Expressions of strong craving of alcohol	
Severe withdrawal signs	**Severe withdrawal symptoms**	
• Respiratory alkalosis with hyperventilation	• Incoherent speech	
• Fever	• Global confusion with clouding of consciousness	
• Grand mal seizures	• Illusions	
	• Hallucinations with lack of insight	

Note. SGPT = serum glutamic-pyruvic transaminase. Adapted with permission from Gallant (1982c).

Severe Withdrawal (Alcohol Withdrawal Delirium—291.00)

Indications for hospitalization. Diagnostic criteria for alcohol withdrawal delirium include a clouding of consciousness, difficulty in sustaining attention, disorientation, and autonomic hyperactivity, with these symptoms occurring within the first several days after complete cessation of drinking or reduction of extremely heavy alcohol ingestion. These signs and symptoms indicate the need for hospitalization. With adequate treatment, these symptoms should disappear by the end of the first week.

A diagnostic problem arises when the history of alcohol intake is unknown and there is no family available to offer additional information. Such diagnoses as schizophrenia, schizophreniform disorder, other psychotic disorders, or dementia can be confused with the diagnosis of withdrawal delirium if there is no history of alcohol intake. Although the visual hallucinations usually associated with this type of delirium may be quite impressive, the occurrence of auditory hallucinations is more frequent than expected when a careful detailed history is obtained. If unaware of the relative frequency of these auditory hallucinations in this syndrome, the clinician may mistakenly diagnose the patient as having another type of psychosis. The clinician also has to be very much aware that the illusions and hallucinations that frequently occur in alcohol withdrawal delirium may be masking head trauma, space-occupying lesions, metabolic abnormalities, or even hypoxia associated with congestive heart failure in a person who has a diagnosis of alcoholism. In one study of this type of delirium, 13 of 27 patients referred to a psychiatric clinic in a delirious state after prolonged intoxication were found to have chronic subdural hematomas (Reisner 1979).

The Use of Benzodiazepines and Other Hypnotics

If the diagnosis of alcohol withdrawal delirium is correct, then immediate hospitalization is indicated; this diagnosis infers that patients are unable to care for themselves and are seriously ill. The use of benzodiazepines on a temporary basis may be of considerable help in alcoholics who have experienced recent alcohol withdrawal convulsions because these compounds possess anticonvulsant activity as well as sedative properties. If the patient is suspected of having a moderate amount of liver damage, the most appropriate benzodiazepines may be oxazepam or lorazepam, which do not require hydroxylation by the liver and therefore do not accumulate. Chlordiazepoxide, diazepam, and chlorazepate are all metabolized in the liver and thus can accumulate in the patient who has a fair degree of liver damage, particularly since these agents have a relatively long half-life. Hydroxyzine is a safer sedative from the viewpoint of dependence, but its anticholinergic activity may confuse the patient if the drug is administered in high dosages. Unlike the benzodiazepines, it has no anticonvulsant properties. The adequate use of sedative-hypnotic therapy for severe withdrawal symptoms, good nursing care, the absence of restraint, a well-lighted room, and the use of thiamine and multivitamins can help to alleviate the symptomatology.

The use of antipsychotic agents or neuroleptics for the withdrawal syndrome is contraindicated because these agents can lower the convulsive threshold as well as potentiate orthostatic hypotension or cause uncomfortable atropine-like side effects. Some alcoholic patients receiving neuroleptics have been reported to develop prolonged unconsciousness following the use of these medications (Holzbach and Buhler 1978). These compounds can potentiate seizure activity; benzodiazepines can control and prevent the development of withdrawal seizures.

The dosage range for benzodiazepines should vary with the duration and intensity of the alcohol consumption prior to withdrawal, the weight of the patient, and other pharmacokinetic variables if the data are available. In mild to moderate cases of uncomplicated alcohol withdrawal syndrome without delirium, the dosage of oxazepam may vary from 15 to 30 mg qid; the dosage of chlordiazepoxide may vary from 25 to 50 mg qid (Gallant 1982c). In severe cases of Alcohol Withdrawal Delirium, a dosage of oxazepam as high as 45 mg qid may be needed, and the dosage of chlordiazepoxide may have to be as much as 100 mg qid. In one double-blind comparison of lorazepam and diazepam in the treatment of patients displaying moderate alcohol withdrawal symptoms, 6 mg of lorazepam showed no significant differences in efficacy from 30 mg of diazepam, except for a significant drop in blood pressure in the diazepam-treated patients. Lorazepam is a benzodiazepine with a relatively short half-life compared with diazepam; thus it may be simpler and more predictable in its pharmacologic effects for patients presenting the alcohol withdrawal syndromes (O'Brien et al. 1983).

It is extremely important to decrease and then discontinue the benzodiazepines prior to discharge from the hospital. It appears that those patients discharged on benzodiazepines are more likely either to become habituated to the medication or else to return to alcohol (Gallant 1982c). An interesting analogy of this experience has been reported as occurring in mice. After chronic involuntary administration of alcohol, mice have been shown to have an increased tendency to continue self-administration of the alcohol when offered free choice between alcohol and tap water (Deutsch and Walton 1977). Diazepam administered during the period of withdrawal served to maintain the alcohol self-administration. Without diazepam, the tendency toward self-administration of alcohol returned to control levels. The similarity of the examples in mice and human subjects concerning the return to alcohol consumption after using diazepam as a means of withdrawal is noteworthy.

Concerning the use of benzodiazepines im, the clinician should be aware that compounds such as chlordiazepoxide and diazepam absorb quite poorly. If the patient is vomiting profusely and unable to tolerate oral medication, then the use of lorazepam or prochlorperazine im is indicated with possible use of 25 mg of prochlorperazine as a suppository. It should be stressed that iv infusions should be used only in patients who are definitely dehydrated from excessive vomiting or diarrhea. Even in these cases, the clinician has to be cautious with glycogen-depleted patients who might be thiamine-deficient because the patient may be converted to Wernicke's encephalopathy by a glucose infusion. These patients should be weighed daily to evaluate the hydration state.

Management of Potential Withdrawal Convulsions

If the patient has had a recent history of alcohol withdrawal seizures or other type of seizures, the use of benzodiazepines possessing effective anticonvulsant activity is indicated. Since diazepam is rapidly absorbed after oral ingestion, a safe anticonvulsant blood level is more rapidly reached with this medication than with phenytoin. In addition, experimental studies in animals suggest that phenytoin may be ineffective in the treatment of alcohol withdrawal convulsions (Gessner 1979). In both animal and human research related to alcohol withdrawal seizures, diazepam has been shown to be a most effective anticonvulsant (Guerrero-Figueroa et al. 1970). When seizures develop or are present on admission to the hospital, diazepam iv may be given at a dosage of 10 mg over a period of one to two minutes and then repeated until seizures cease, but no more than a total of 30 mg should be administered over a period of 15 to 20 minutes. The diazepam should be administered slowly to avoid laryngospasm. If this effort fails, then iv amobarbital can be given at a rate of 100 to 150 mg/minute unless respiration is compromised. At that point, anesthesiology assistance may be required for a systemic inducement of muscle relaxation with succinylcholine and ventilation.

Management of Multiple Drug Users

There are an increasing number of patients who abuse habituating drugs in association with alcohol. Patients combining alcohol and barbiturates present an additional medical problem in the treatment of withdrawal because they are more likely to have seizures. A fairly reliable method of calculating the dosage of medication to be used during withdrawal in this type of patient is the substitution of 15 mg of phenobarbital for an ounce of 100 proof alcohol. Administration of 200 mg of pentobarbital may help the physician determine the extent of the addiction. The appearance of ataxia with slurred speech at this dose suggests that the patient is not severely physically dependent and should not require too large a dosage of a long-acting barbiturate for withdrawal purposes. If the patient is addicted, a relatively safe treatment procedure for the barbiturate-type of addiction has been detailed (Robinson et al. 1981). Phenobarbital is administered at a dosage of 120 mg every hour until the patient develops three of the five following symptoms: dysarthria, ataxia, nystagmus, confusion, and drowsiness. The urine is maintained at a pH of less than 6.5, which slows the excretion of the phenobarbital, thus allowing the patient to follow a "smooth" withdrawal from the combination alcohol-barbiturate drug addiction. In a series of 54 cases, not one convulsion developed with the use of this technique (Robinson et al. 1981).

Although propranolol has been used to decrease the clinical manifestation of the alcohol withdrawal syndromes, inhibiting delirium tremens and modifying the blood pressure increase, the clinician should proceed cautiously with the use of this drug because it may potentiate the hypoglycemia that can occur in the first 36 hours after ingestion of large amounts of alcohol by malnourished alcoholics (Gallant 1982c). Since alcoholics do seem to have an increased incidence of chronic obstructive airway disease with bronchospasm as well cardiomyopathy, precautions about the use of propranolol should be further emphasized. Without a specific negative history of asthma, propranolol should not be administered to severely ill patients.

Management of Alcohol Hallucinosis (291.30)

Alcohol hallucinosis can be a very confusing diagnosis if there is no history of alcohol intake and no family available to give a history. The patient will usually show an effect that correlates with the type of hallucination, and there is no clouding of consciousness as in delirium tremens. These symptoms may be quite dramatic and the patient can be misdiagnosed as a schizophrenic if there is no adequate history available, which is frequently the case in the hospital emergency room. An evaluation of the hallucinations of functional psychotics and alcoholics found a higher incidence of only auditory and taste hallucinations in the functional group (Deiker and Chambers 1978). In regard to visual, olfactory, tactile, and sexual aspects of the hallucinatory material, there were no significant differences in the two groups.

Usually the onset of this type of withdrawal syndrome occurs only after many years of heavy drinking; the average age of onset is approximately 40. This diagnosis cannot be applied to those individuals who have had prior psychotic episodes without any relationship to alcohol or drug intake. Even when the patient is displaying paranoid delusions as well as hallucinations, the sensorium still has to be clear in relation to orientation for one to make a definitive diagnosis.

The development of these hallucinatory symptoms is due solely to the phenomenon of alcohol withdrawal and should not persist beyond two weeks. Therefore, the use of neuroleptics is not indicated because they will only confuse the diagnostic problem. The appearance of extrapyramidal side effects with masked facies secondary to neuroleptic drug administration can only result in the patient's appearing even more "schizophrenic" to the interviewer. Temporary sedation with the use of short-acting hypnotics, such as the benzodiazepines, which have a relatively short half-life, may be necessary. Follow-up evaluation of these patients does not show any evidence of a trend toward development of a chronic hallucinatory process (Gallant 1982c).

The Protracted Withdrawal Syndrome

Although the protracted withdrawal syndrome is not listed in DSM-III or DSM-III-R, it has been adequately described in the literature (Gallant 1982c; Kissin 1979, 1981). Symptoms attributable to the protracted withdrawal syndrome include such physiologic variations as respiratory irregularity, labile blood pressure and pulse, impairment of slow-wave sleep, decrease in cold-stress response, persistence of tolerance to sedative effects, and tremor. Subjective complaints of spontaneous anxiety, depressive episodes for no reason, and even transient psychotic reactions have been reported in relation to this syndrome, which apparently persists in some patients after the acute withdrawal syndrome has terminated. Biochemical changes may include diminished tryptamine metabolism and lowered norepinephrine and testosterone levels. This syndrome has been described as lasting anywhere from one to several months. To diagnose this syndrome, the therapist should be certain that the patient has not had a combination of these symptoms prior to alcohol abstinence. No other metabolic, physiologic, or psychological cause for these behavioral and emotional abnormalities should be apparent other than abstinence from alcohol.

It does appear that the syndromes of mild to moderate acute withdrawal, as well as those of severe withdrawal (see Tables 2 and 3), can gradually blend into the protracted withdrawal syndrome. It has been shown that the drug-free alcoholic tested at seven days, 17 days, and 21 days after the last drink exhibited very little improvement in neuropsychological testing of cognitive performance (Gallant 1982c). The therapist should, therefore, move more slowly in therapy with such patients; abrupt confrontation therapy should be avoided until cognitive abilities show maximal improvement. Instead, during this stage, stress should be placed on the therapeutic approaches that are used in developing a trusting relationship with the patient.

In addition to the physiologic and behavioral changes already described, the patient shows an increased irritability and impatience with family members and friends, often complaining of fatigue and lower stress tolerance. Some patients can panic, believing that they are slipping back, and may suddenly resort to the use of alcohol in an attempt to alleviate these symptoms. Complaints of emotional lability are not unusual. Forgetfulness occurs with periods of loss of concentration, and minor problems become major crises. There is a high level of distractibility, and patients may be unconsciously setting themselves up for return to alcohol because of these symptoms, feeling that sobriety results in misery.

The major therapeutic approach for this problem is a fully detailed explanation to the patient and the family, helping them to understand that these symptoms may be a part of the withdrawal phase of alcohol. This explanation can help the alcoholic to accommodate temporarily to the discomfort and maintain abstinence. The therapist has to remember that during this state, the patient is unable to make any plans concerning the future and is, therefore, present-oriented, as well as impulsive with a low frustration tolerance. Use of psychopharmacologic agents during these periods may cause uncomfortable reactions such as anticholinergic or sedative side effects, which may further confuse the patient. Full explanation of the possibility of protracted withdrawal may help psychologically to alleviate some of these symptoms and to enable the family to provide more knowledgeable assistance to the patient. It can also help to decrease the anxiety of the unknown and to aid the patient in surviving and surmounting the symptoms of this syndrome. It is important to emphasize that the emotional and physical reactions during this phase are not unusual; patients will do well as long as they realize that these symptoms are not a sign of relapse or of psychological illness.

While antianxiety agents may be helpful during the acute phase of the withdrawal syndrome, the use of psychopharmacologic agents during this phase of abstinence is rarely indicated. If the restlessness, severe insomnia, anxiety, or depression become intolerable, minor tranquilizers, such as the shorter-acting benzodiazepines or antidepressants when indicated, may be used on a temporary basis.

Alcoholics Anonymous (AA) can be of tremendous help at this time. The reader is referred to Chapter 125 for an understanding of the help that can be rendered to the patient and the family during this crucial period of time. AA uses the term "dry drunk" to refer to some of these symptoms. Inclusion of the spouse in couples or married couples group therapy, as well as in Al-Anon, is crucial during this phase (Gallant 1982c). It is all-important for the spouse and family to understand the implication of these symptoms and to be in a position to help the patient modify them. The physician should try to avoid unnecessary use of sedative-hypnotics because these patients already have difficulty with distractibility and attention span associated with their physiologic lability. By increasing the attention problems and impairing daytime cognition, the benzodiazepines can only hinder the patients' attempts to rehabilitate themselves in therapy.

Alcohol-Related Irreversible Organic Mental Disorders

Alcohol Amnestic Disorder (291.10)

The diagnoses that must be considered in the differential diagnoses of alcohol amnestic disorder are delirium of metabolic or other causes, dementia of the Alzheimer type, and discrete cerebrovascular lesions, secondary to thrombotic episodes. This syndrome is a result of circumscribed neuropsychiatric symptomatology characterized by anterograde and retrograde amnesia, with fairly good preservation of other intellectual abilities. The former diagnosis known as Korsakoff's syndrome falls in this category; it is characterized by an anterograde amnesic deficit greater than retrograde amnesia. If the patient is using a great deal of denial about the drinking problem or other problems prior to the onset of this discrete neurophysiologic dysfunction, the patient may then tend to deny the memory defects in a rather pathetic way. For example, the patient may make an inappropriate guess about the month or year to try to cover up a memory deficit. While trauma and anoxia as well as cerebral accidents can cause this type of syndrome, the most common cause is alcoholism. The major pathology appears to be in the diencephalon or mesial temporal structures (Gallant 1982c). There is no clouding of consciousness as in delirium and intoxication, and no general loss of intellectual abilities as in dementia associated with alcoholism or Alzheimer's disease.

Dementia Associated with Alcoholism (291.20)

Diagnostic problems. Alcoholic dementia is difficult to classify as a distinct disorder (Lishman 1986). The differential diagnoses of this disorder are Alzheimer's disease or senile dementia of the Alzheimer type (SDAT); alcohol amnestic disorder, which does not include loss of intellectual abilities for social and occupational functioning; and chronic subdural hematoma, which has been frequently misdiagnosed as either chronic dementia or acute mental disorder (Reisner 1979). The state of consciousness is not clouded in this chronic organic mental disorder. The prognosis of alcoholic dementia is obviously better than that of SDAT, which is one of progressive deterioration; unlike SDAT, this syndrome does not include aphasia. In association with moderate to severe amnesia, functional deficits are somewhat more specific, with constructional difficulty in drawing, stick design, copying geometric designs, and behavioral disturbances. If the alcoholic dementia patient is able to maintain abstinence, it is not unusual to see improvement occurring as long as six to 12 months after the patient has initiated sobriety. The same observations are valid for alcohol amnestic disorder, which is a more circumscribed illness, structurally and functionally, and less incapacitating since the remaining intellectual functions are relatively intact except for memory changes.

Wernicke's encephalopathy appears to be associated with progressive neuronal degeneration, particularly in the periventricular area of the brain. Wernicke's encephalopathy is a diagnosis that may first be made at autopsy. In an extensive autopsy review, 1.7 percent of all autopsies showed Wernicke's encephalopathy to be present (Harper 1979). Of the 51 patients with this disease at death, 45 were alcoholics and only seven had been diagnosed as alcoholics prior to death. Many of the patients died suddenly as a result of hemorrhage into the brain stem, involving the cardiac and respiratory nuclei. Cerebral atrophy and ventricular dilatation were commonly associated with the autopsy findings. One major recommendation resulting from the data of this study was the routine use of large dosages of prophylactic thiamine in alcoholic patients, particularly those with clinical evidence of cerebral damage. Recent research into the etiology of the Wernicke-Korsakoff's syndrome has indicated that thiamine pyrophosphatase-dependent transketalase activity may be decreased in those patients who develop the syndrome (Blass and Gibson 1979). Transketalase activity was evaluated in five patients with this illness; four of them showed a low transketalase activity in the blood cells. It was suggested that some alcoholics may have more of a genetic-metabolic tendency than others for development of the Wernicke-Korsakoff's syndrome. It should be reemphasized that the safest precaution in the treatment of alcoholics is the routine administration of thiamine in dosages of 100 mg, either po or iv, whichever is appropriate at the time, to all alcoholics entering detoxification and rehabilitation treatment programs.

Prognosis and rehabilitation.   Although the brain damage that is associated with alcoholism resembles premature aging of adaptive abilities, the alcohol-induced atrophy may be partially reversible with improvement of functional impairment as abstinence is maintained (Gallant 1982c). Tests that may detect long-term residual central nervous system damage after 12 months of abstinence are the trail making test and block design of the Wechsler Adult Intelligence Scale (Parsons 1977).

It is important to realize that approximately 35 to 50 percent of alcoholics in different rehabilitation settings showed demonstrable neuropsychological impairment on the previously mentioned tests as well as on the Halstead-Reitan category subtest and Wisconsin Scoring Test. The degree of impairment appears to be associated with the duration of drinking history (Parsons 1977).

The types of brain damage described in the alcoholic dementias are more widespread than generally thought. In an evaluation of the extent of alcoholic brain damage in Ireland, it was estimated that 2,000 or more of approximately 6,000 alcoholic admissions to Irish psychiatric hospitals each year have brain damage (Draper 1978). If this one-third figure were applied to the US psychiatric hospitals, then more than 10 percent of all admissions (33 percent of all psychiatric admissions are for alcoholism) to these hospitals each year would have neuropsychological impairment due to alcohol abuse. Early brain damage has to be recognized by the physician and the family and treated appropriately or else relapse will almost certainly occur as a result of impaired judgment.

Realizing the nature and degree of impairment can help the therapist to establish realistic guidelines and goals for the patient, thus avoiding early failure in treatment. The type of neuropsychological impairment in dementias associated with alcoholism as measured by such tests as the Halstead-Reitan category subtest and picture arrangement indicate a deficit in ability to adapt to new situations and new abstraction problems. Therefore, vocational rehabilitation and other aspects of therapeutic guidance should not involve any marked departure from the patient's former occupation or social habits.

An invaluable part of treatment of the organic mental disorder is helping the patient and the family to recognize the problem and meaning of alcohol-induced brain damage. It is important for them to realize that there is a possibility that many of the organic mental changes are reversible with time, abstinence, and adequate nutrition. It is essential to give them an optimistic viewpoint and appropriate instructions on how to manage the daily behavior of the patient while waiting for some of the organic symptoms to resolve. Short training sessions concentrating on visual-motor coordination with appropriate exercises of attention span can be performed on a daily basis. Since the patient has problems with attention span, these sessions should probably not last more than 20 minutes, but they can be repeated twice daily. Abstract thinking tasks, such as creating three-dimensional figures and abstracting from categories, should be included in these training sessions. For memory tasks, the use of mnemonics can be a most useful technique for those patients displaying moderate to marked memory impairment. Utilizing these procedures to help the patient develop routine habits has proved most useful. Encourage the patient to get out of bed at the same time every day, to eat meals at the same time every day, and try to stay with the same schedule, including sleep time, on a daily basis. In addition, have the patient keep a little notebook with time of appointments for that day, times for telephone calls, times for other types of social engagements, and professional or work schedules. The patient should be encouraged to use these notes to compensate for the short-term memory deficit, the major problem in most patients with alcohol-induced brain damage when they are admitted to a rehabilitation program.

Chapter 116

Individual Management and Psychotherapy

Individual therapy is an effective treatment for alcoholism if applied to the appropriate alcoholic patient with an understanding of the psychodynamics of alcoholism. Of course, before this or any other therapy can be given to an alcoholic patient, a diagnosis of alcoholism must be established and a differential diagnosis in relation to other psychiatric disorders must be made.

It is essential to realize that alcoholics are not a homogeneous population. They sometimes present with a variety of acute and chronic behavioral, mood, and thought disorders and age-related developmental problems along with the alcoholism. To treat the alcoholic person effectively, these possible coexisting problems must be evaluated and the problem elucidated in regard to whether the alcoholism came before or after the psychiatric disorder.

There are a number of psychiatric disorders that have existed in individuals prior to their becoming alcoholic. Therefore, a complete psychiatric history and a mental status examination are both important in evaluating all alcoholic patients (Zimberg 1982). Some alcoholics have been found to have a history of attention-deficit hyperactivity disorder when they were children and continued with the disorder into adulthood. As adults they developed alcoholism but retained the disorder in a modified form characterized by defects in attention and impulsivity. The diagnosis can be established by taking a careful history (including a developmental history) and determining if hyperactivity as well as attention defects and impulsivity were present in the individuals as children. The diagnosis is established by history and observation of the patient alcohol-free six to eight weeks.

Patients with schizophrenia have been noted to use and abuse alcohol as self-medication. Such patients when observed alcohol-free three to four weeks can be noted to have persistent functional psychotic symptoms and usually give a history of prolonged duration of these symptoms and psychiatric hospitalization prior to their drinking problem.

A significant number of patients with borderline syndrome abuse alcohol and become alcoholics. The borderline patients give a history of mood and behavioral disturbances preexisting the alcoholism, including impulsive behavior, very poor interpersonal relationships, inappropriate and intense anger, poor self-identity, physical self-mutilation, and long-term feelings of depression, emptiness, boredom, loneliness, and intense anxiety.

Anxiety is a common symptom among alcoholics. However, in primary alcoholics, it generally clears up within four weeks of detoxification with the maintenance of abstinence. In some alcoholics it will persist longer as part of the protracted withdrawal syndrome. Some alcoholic patients will present themselves with a long history of episodic bouts of intense anxiety characterized as panic reactions. Such patients have panic-anxiety disorder and are secondary alcoholics.

Alcoholism can coexist with other neurotic or personality disorders. In such situations, the alcoholism must be addressed initially until sobriety is well established six months to one year before any uncovering therapy is attempted for the existing neurotic or personality disorder.

Depression is a common symptom in alcoholics. In most cases the feelings of depression will lessen or disappear with four weeks of abstinence. However, in a substantial number of alcoholics, the depression will persist in the alcohol-free state.

One must be able to provide an effective differential diagnosis and appropriate treatment for coexisting major psychiatric disorders. Most alcoholics are *primary* alcoholics and may not require psychiatric treatment. For those that do, however, such a multitreatment approach is essential.

Psychodynamics of Primary Alcoholism

There is considerable evidence that conflict with dependent needs is a major psychological factor that contributes to alcoholism (Bacon et al. 1965; Blane 1968; Knight 1937; McCord and McCord 1962; Tahlka 1966; Tiebout 1961). This conflict may have developed because of childhood rejection by one or both parents, overprotection, or forcing premature responsibility on a child, particularly if a parent is alcoholic.

The psychological conflict observed in alcoholics consists of low self-esteem along with feelings of worthlessness and inadequacy (Zimberg 1985). These feelings are denied and repressed and lead to unconscious needs to be taken care of and accepted. Since these dependent needs cannot be met in reality, they lead to anxiety and compensatory needs for control, power, achievement, and elevated self-esteem. Alcohol tranquilizes the anxiety; more importantly, it creates pharmacologically induced feelings of power, omnipotence, and invulnerability in men (McClelland et al. 1972) and enhanced feelings of womanliness in women (Wilsnack 1976). When alcoholics wake up after a drinking episode, they experience guilt and despair because they have not achieved anything more than before they drank and their problems remain. Thus their feelings of worthlessness are intensified and the conflict continues in a vicious circle, often with a progressive downward spiral (see Figure 1).

Alcohol provides an artificial feeling state of power, control, and elevated self-

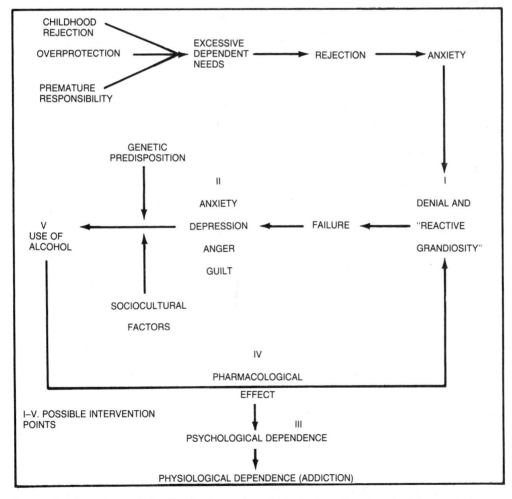

Figure 1. Paradigm of the Psychodynamics of Alcoholism. Reprinted with permission from Zimberg (1985).

esteem that cannot be achieved in reality. The very act of producing this feeling of power at will feeds the alcoholic's grandiose self-image.

An individual with such a psychological conflict will become an alcoholic if there is a genetic predisposition to alcoholism and if the individual lives in a society in which the use of alcohol is sanctioned as a way to feel better or in which there is considerable ambivalence regarding the use of alcohol. In any particular individual, one or more of these etiologic factors may predominate and lead to alcoholism. This paradigm can also be used to understand currently existing treatment approaches (Figure 1). Alcoholic Anonymous (AA) has been one of the most successful treatment approaches for alcoholism; it is also the model for other successful self-help movements. How does the effectiveness of AA relate to the psychodynamic understanding of alcoholism just presented?

Tiebout (1961) described a similar psychodynamic understanding of alcoholism in his paper discussing the process by which an alcoholic becomes involved in AA. The process occurs in four steps: 1) the need to hit bottom, 2) the need to be humble, 3) the need to surrender, and 4) the need for ego reduction. These steps were based on Tiebout's observation of an excessive amount of narcissism in the alcoholic's ego, which gives rise to feelings of omnipotence. These steps in the rehabilitation process are necessary to produce a reduction in narcissism, which perpetuates the self-destructive drinking behavior and the coexisting denial. Tiebout did not indicate, however, what happens to the excessive narcissism of the alcoholic's ego. Clearly, the narcissism is sublimated toward the goal of AA to rescue other alcoholics. Thus the grandiosity becomes fulfilled and socially useful, and much of their dependent needs are met by the group. AA members recognize that their support of other alcoholics helps themselves maintain sobriety. Therefore, the successful development of AA was based on an intuitive understanding of the alcoholic's psychological conflict and needs.

Other treatment approaches can be understood by looking at Figure 1 in relation to possible intervention points on this paradigm. Intervention point I represents the traditional psychoanalytic approach to treating alcoholism. In this case, the therapist attempts to work from the defenses to uncover the underlying psychological conflicts. The very technique of uncovering therapy produces anxiety, which results in the need to drink and this is ineffective. Also, insight alone cannot affect physiologic addiction.

Intervention point II represents an area in which mood-altering drugs might reduce the need to use alcohol to reduce dysphoric feelings. After many studies, there is no evidence that the major tranquilizers, the antidepressants, or the minor tranquilizers (antianxiety drugs) are of benefit in the treatment of chronic alcoholism. Subpopulations of alcoholics who were clinically depressed have been noted to have benefited from lithium treatment (Merry et al. 1976). Such patients most likely represent secondary alcoholism rather than primary alcoholism.

Intervention point III represents the use of drugs or other modalities that would alter the effect of alcohol on the brain and result in a reduced craving for alcohol, a lessening of the pleasant effect of alcohol or reduction in the degree of physiologic dependence. With our understanding of the mechanisms of how alcohol affects the brain, we may be able to alter the adverse effects selectively. This area probably represents the future of alcoholism treatment. Considerable research effort is underway to determine the acute and chronic effects of alcohol on the opiate and benzodiazepine receptors and neurotransmitters.

Intervention at point IV can interrupt the pleasurable feelings associated with alcohol consumption that become reinforced by repetitive drinking leading to alcoholism. Lovibond and Caddy (1970) applied aversive conditioning with electric shocks to enable alcoholics to discriminate their blood alcohol levels and to maintain low levels characterized by controlled social drinking. They reported considerable success with this approach. Ewing and Rouse (1976) utilized a similar approach in an attempt to replicate Lovibond and Caddy's work. Ewing and Rouse reported that although the alcoholic patients were able to learn to recognize their levels of blood alcohol and develop controlled drinking patterns while in the program, all relapsed into loss-of-control drinking during the 27- to 55-month follow-up period. Sobell and Sobell (1976) reported high rates of success with electric aversion therapy leading to controlled drinking in addicted alcoholics. However, a study by Pendery et al. (1982) on the same patients studied by the Sobells found that none of the patients were able to maintain controlled drinking. They all either had relapsed into alcoholic drinking, died, or recovered with the maintenance of abstinence. The literature is replete with such equivocal results in various controlled drinking conditioning approaches. Aversive conditioning leading to abstinence with a nausea-producing drug, emetine, has been used in a number of European countries and the United States. Neuberger et al. (1982) reported high rates of abstinence for one year with this aversive conditioning approach. This area remains an important area for treatment research.

The fifth point of possible intervention represents the current approach to individual psychotherapy. This method involves eliminating the use of alcohol by directive approaches (including detoxification, disulfiram use, and AA attendance) and helping the alcoholic learn to live without alcohol in the face of stress and unpleasant feelings.

The central problem in the psychotherapy of the alcoholic is breaking through the reactive grandiosity that produces the massive denial of profound feelings of inferiority and dependence that permit the pattern of self-destructive drinking to continue. Alcoholics destroy not only themselves, but also their loved ones without perceiving their lack of control of their behavior pattern. The typical response of an alcoholic without insight into this behavior is, "I can stop drinking any time I want to," despite overwhelming evidence to the contrary. This self-deception must be penetrated if rehabilitation is to succeed.

Indications for Individual Psychotherapy

The directive psychotherapy approach requires a thorough knowledge of the patient's childhood and developmental history, drinking history, and current interpersonal and adaptive functioning. This knowledge permits targeted interventions to help the patient adjust to sobriety and most importantly to avoid making suggestions or interventions that will create severe anxiety in the patients, leading to resumption of drinking or leaving therapy. Individual therapy also encourages a dependent relationship with the therapist that can be useful in influencing the patient toward sobriety. Individual therapy is of particular value when treating patients with a coexisting psychiatric disorder.

Establishing the Treatment Contract

The treatment contract with alcoholic patients should indicate that the goal of treatment is abstinence. Some patients, particularly not-addicted alcoholics and secondary alcoholics, may be able to return to social drinking. It is clinically impossible, however, to predict at the beginning of treatment which patient might be able to accomplish this. The most practical clinical approach to alcoholism at our present level of knowledge is to indicate to all patients that abstinence has to be the goal of treatment.

The early stages of treatment should deal with the issues of how the patient can maintain abstinence by using the tools of treatment, AA, disulfiram, and directive psychotherapy, rather than why the patient became alcoholic. Patients who are unable to maintain sobriety but continue to drink should not be allowed to remain in treatment indefinitely; limits should be placed on the continuation of treatment in such circumstances. When patients should be terminated from treatment for continued drinking should depend on the individual situation, but it should be borne in mind that successful psychotherapy of alcoholism cannot take place in an actively drinking patient. If termination does occur, the patient should be referred to an inpatient treatment facility for more intensive treatment or to another therapist, with the door left open to return for treatment when the patient is more willing or able to utilize the tools of psychotherapy.

Stages of Recovery with Psychotherapy

Patients have been observed to progress through several stages as they recover from alcoholism. These stages reflect increasing capacity to control the impulse to drink.

The first stage can be characterized as the stage of "I can't drink." This is the initial stage when patients enter treatment. They don't really want to give up alcohol, but would rather continue drinking in a social, controlled manner without all the problems that they have encountered. The external pressure of the job situation or a spouse, or an alcohol-related medical problem is forcing them to the realization that they can't drink. At this stage, external control over the impulse to drink in the form of detoxification, disulfiram maintenance, peer pressure of AA, and observation by the therapist are necessary. This stage is very unstable. Patients can easily resume drinking unless leverage is found that will produce very undesirable consequences if the patient resumes drinking in the form of threat of the loss of a job, loss of a spouse, or a serious adverse medical condition.

With directive psychotherapy used to help the patient adjust his or her life and feelings to sobriety, and with a significant change in attitude about the necessity of alcohol consumption, the patient, after an average of about six months to one year, enters the stage of "I won't drink."

The "I won't drink" stage represents internalized control over the impulse to drink and is fairly stable. There is no insight into psychological factors that contribute to the alcoholism but there is no longer any conscious conflict about whether to drink or not. This is the stage that successful AA participants have achieved. They may still have no insight into their psychological conflicts and may have serious interpersonal problems and problems with feelings, but they have experienced the fact that alcohol is no longer necessary for their lives or even for feeling good. At this stage, discontinuation of disulfiram can be considered, but continued AA participation is recommended.

After about one-and-a-half to two years, the second stage has been well established and one can consider discontinuing psychotherapy. However, if serious interpersonal problems or problems with feelings and functioning persist, one should offer the patient the option to try to achieve the third stage of recovery: "I don't have to drink." This stage requires psychoanalytically oriented psychotherapy and can result in insight and conflict resolution. Because not all alcoholic patients can or need to achieve this stage, this option should be left for mutual decision of patient and therapist.

The fourth stage of "I can return to social drinking" is a theoretical stage and should not be offered to patients because our limited knowledge cannot determine which patients might be able to achieve this. The reality of alcohol use is that alcohol is not necessary for life or even for being happy, and its loss does not produce any significantly adverse reaction in anyone. This reality is accepted by alcoholic patients who have achieved a significant degree of recovery and period of time without drinking.

Techniques of Individual Directive Psychotherapy

During the first two stages of recovery, psychotherapy should be directive and supportive rather than uncovering. Efforts should be directed at helping the alcoholic to retain sobriety and to see and feel the advantages of not drinking. Problems, conflicts, unpleasant feelings, difficult interpersonal relationships, and difficulty with feelings, (particularly anger) will become apparent to the alcoholic once the anesthetic effects of alcohol are absent. Directive psychotherapy should help the alcoholic deal with these difficulties with advice, encouragement, anticipatory guidance, and direct suggestions that involve the lending of the therapist's ego in the form of the therapist's own life experiences, judgment, and wisdom. Alcoholics are receptive to directive psychotherapy if they have established a dependent relationship to the therapist. This relationship should be encouraged and should not be interpreted. The defenses should be left intact and redirected in the service of remaining abstinent. Staying sober and avoiding drink-precipitating situations should be the focus of therapy.

The transference established by the alcoholic patient will be dependent, but also ambivalent and testing. There may be provocative episodes of drinking to test whether the therapist cares for the patient. These provocations should be dealt with in a nonpunitive, nonjudgmental way by instituting the use of disulfiram, urging greater AA attendance, or considering possible referral to inpatient treatment if the patient continues to drink.

The countertransference will be also difficult for therapists. Alcoholics can make therapists feel helpless, frustrated, and angry. Therapists must not try to be onmipotent in regard to the alcoholics' drinking but realize that they or anyone else cannot stop an alcoholic determined to drink. The therapist can only offer the tools of treatment to the alcoholic, who will use them in his or her own self-determined effort to abstain. The therapist's self-esteem should never be on the line regarding a patient's recovery or the therapy will fail.

Another important principle is the use of "therapeutic leverage" in the treatment of alcoholics. This involves finding something in the alcoholic's life that is valued very highly and is directly threatened by continued drinking (e.g., the threat of losing one's job or the breakup of a marriage). Manipulating this possible loss can be extremely beneficial in the early stages of treatment until the alcoholic has developed internalized control over the impulse to drink.

Individual therapy carried out with these techniques to achieve a stage II level of recovery will take about one to one-and-a-half years of treatment for most patients. A few patients can achieve this in as little as six months with intensive AA involvement, but some patients are unable to achieve more than a stage I level of tenuous sobriety.

Patients who have achieved a stage II level of recovery and appear to have continued interpersonal problems and problems with feelings should be offered an opportunity for uncovering psychotherapy. Some patients will accept this; others will not. This is a decision that should be arrived at mutually. As far as a well-established abstinence, psychoanalytically oriented psychotherapy to achieve a stage III level of recovery is not necessary.

Rationale and Use of Disulfiram

Disulfiram is a drug that inhibits the enzymatic breakdown of ethyl alcohol at the step of acetaldehyde production. Acetaldehyde is a toxic substance that produces the adverse reaction of facial flushing, tachycardia, hypotension, nausea and vomiting, and severe discomfort. Therefore, the alcohol-disulfiram reaction is dose related. No alcohol consumption, no reaction. The more alcohol consumed, the greater the disulfiram-alcohol reaction. The reaction is life threatening only in individuals who have cardiac decompensation or liver decompensation. The disulfiram-alcohol reaction can be treated with intravenous diphenylhydramine, intravenous ascorbic acid (oxidation-reduction agent), and vasopressors if severe hypotension results. In most cases, the reaction requires only that the patient sleep for a period of time, and it will spontaneously remit.

The maintenance dose of disulfiram is 250 mg/day. Patients who have had a history of myocardial infarction without cardiac decompensation can be maintained on 125 mg/day. A physical examination to provide medical clearance is necessary to start a patient on the drug.

Adverse Reactions

Side effects from disulfiram alone are generally minor and rare. There can be an acneform eruption, allergic dermatitis, urticaria, lassitude, tremors, restlessness, reduced sexual potency, headache, dizziness, a garlic-like or metallic taste, and a mild gastrointestinal disturbance. These side effects usually can be eliminated by reducing the dosage to 125 mg/day.

A few cases of toxic hepatitis associated with disulfiram use have been reported. This side effect, however, is quite rare.

Disulfiram can produce a toxic psychosis on rare occasions. Such a reaction produces anxiety, confusion, disorientation, agitation, paranoid reaction, and visual or auditory hallucinations.

Sometimes only a mild organic mental syndrome will be noted without psychotic symptoms. This rare reaction may be due to disulfiram's inhibition of the central nervous system enzyme dopamine beta-dehydroxylase. Minor tranquilizers can be used to control the anxiety. Phenothiazines may be used cautiously if there are severe agitation and overt psychotic symptoms. The reaction usually subsides within a few days after disulfiram is discontinued.

A significant number of toxic psychotic reactions have been reported when disulfiram has been used along with the antitubercular drug isoniazid or the antiprotozoal drug metronidazole (Flagyl). Disulfiram also potentiates the efforts of diphenylhydantoin (Dilantin) and coumadin anticoagulants by increasing the concentration of these drugs by inhibiting their liver metabolism. Individuals on amitriptyline (Elavil) may experience an enhanced disulfiram-alcohol reaction if alcohol is ingested. A history of the concurrent use of other medication must be obtained for all patients who are to be placed on disulfiram.

Clinical Use of Disulfiram

Most alcoholics can benefit from disulfiram during the first two stages of treatment. However, many will initially refuse to take disulfiram, preferring not to rely on a "crutch." A contract should be established with such resistant patients indicating that if the patient can maintain sobriety without disulfiram, that is fine; however, if the patient has a slip, then disulfiram becomes mandatory. Most patients will accept this contract; if they resume drinking, it becomes apparent to them that they cannot control the impulse to drink and that an external control is necessary.

Some patients will agree to take disulfiram, but stop it at times and drink. In such situations, disulfiram should be administered by a spouse or in an industrial alcoholism program by a nurse on a daily basis until the patient has become more committed to abstinence. An occasional patient will drink while taking disulfiram and have a reaction. If the reaction is mild and not a sufficient deterrent, the maintenance dose of disulfiram can be increased to 500 mg/day.

When the patient has achieved a well-established stage II level of recovery, one can consider discontinuing disulfiram. If the disulfiram is discontinued, it should be available for use by the patient intermittently for certain conflict-ridden situations as a trial before discontinuing it completely.

Other Ancillary Medications

The benzodiazepines are the drugs of choice for detoxification from alcohol for both inpatients and outpatients. Chlordiazepoxide is more useful on an inpatient basis because it is more sedating. Diazepam is more useful for an outpatient detoxification because it is less sedating and has a longer half-life. Benzodiazepines should never be used for maintenance treatment in alcoholics because they will be subject to abuse and will stimulate craving for alcohol.

Antidepressants, lithium carbonate, and the major tranquilizers have no place in the treatment of primary alcoholism. However, they can be useful 1) to treat a major psychiatric disorder that coexists with the alcoholism, 2) when the differential diagnosis establishes the alcoholism as a secondary disorder, and 3) where the signs and symptoms of the major psychiatric disorder have been established by observations of the alcoholic patient, alcohol free for four to six weeks. In all cases of secondary alcoholism, efforts to treat the alcoholism should be undertaken as well as treating the major coexisting psychiatric disorders.

Role of AA in Alcoholism Treatment

AA can be helpful to all alcoholics in their recovery. It can be an important adjunct to most alcoholics. Those patients who would not recover without AA involvement are patients who manifest the highest levels of denial about their alcoholism and the greatest degree of grandiosity. Such patients can be characterized as having all the answers but none of the solutions to their problems. These patients generally need the peer pressure and peer support of AA for their recovery.

All alcoholic patients should be encouraged to go to AA, but many will resist going. They should be informed that AA is not a religious group but a spiritual one. They should be told that they don't have to say a word or even "confess" that they are alcoholics. They only have to listen to the speakers and try to identify with their experiences with alcohol. AA is the best place to learn about alcoholism, to learn how people can live in our drinking society without drinking, and to learn that there is hope for their own recovery. With this "soft" sell of AA, most patients will attend at least some meetings. They should be cautioned to look for groups made up of people who are similar to themselves so that they will feel comfortable.

Patients who are taking disulfiram should be cautioned about the fact that some AA members will disapprove. The reality is that this is not AA's viewpoint since officially AA takes no position regarding medical treatment. If disulfiram helps sobriety, that is the most important thing.

Secondary alcoholics taking psychiatric medication should also be forewarned about meeting considerable disapproval. The patient should be told that there is no drug treatment for alcoholism and that the drug they are taking is being used to treat a coexisting psychiatric problem, not the alcoholism. With these precautions, most patients can avoid conflicting messages between the psychiatrist and AA members.

Outpatient Versus Inpatient Treatment of Alcoholism

Many clinicians who initiate treatment with alcoholics suggest the patient be hospitalized for detoxification and then spend three to six weeks in inpatient treatment for alcoholism. This approach is used because it is felt that the more intensive exposure to alcoholism treatment will increase motivation for treatment and result in better outcomes. Research has not established this to be the case comparing inpatient and outpatient treatment outcomes (Baekeland et al. 1975).

Outpatient treatment tried intially has been successful in a high percentage of patients, using inpatient treatment only if patients do not respond to ambulatory approaches. Individual therapy has been particularly valuable in assessing patient progress and establishing the necessary support to have patients referred to inpatient treatment if they are unable to stop drinking. When such patients finish the inpatient stay, they return for aftercare to the referring therapist with a generally better prognosis for recovery.

Contraindications to Individual Therapy

There are no significant contraindications to individual therapy. Patients who refuse to attend AA and who have inadequate peer or family support for sobriety might do better, however, in group therapy. Group therapy is also a better approach in inpatient programs where the normal attrition rate of group therapy is less likely to occur and the peer group influence is maximized.

Individual therapy is the treatment of choice if there are coexisting major psychiatric problems in the patient. It is also the treatment of last resort if the patient refuses participation in a group. This refusal of group participation is a fairly frequent occurrence in alcoholic patients. The ideal and most effective treatment approach for ambulatory alcoholics is individual therapy with AA participation, thus combining an intensive therapeutic and supportive relationship with peer support and influence.

Controlled Drinking as Outcome in Primary and Secondary Alcoholics

The primary-addicted alcoholic's return to controlled drinking for any significant period of time (more than four to six weeks) is extremely rare. Usually, the patient will lose control and begin drinking alcoholically. However, there have been secondary alcoholics and alcohol abusers (not addicted) who seemed able to drink in a controlled manner for long periods of time. The problem has been, however, the impossibility to predict which alcohol abuser or secondary alcoholic could accomplish this. Therefore, for practical clinical reasons, all alcoholics should be encouraged to attain the goal of abstinence, which is attainable in a large percentage of patients and is generally associated with recovery in other areas of functioning.

Conclusion

The field of alcoholism treatment is deficient in the availability of controlled outcome studies, particularly as it may relate to the value of specific modalities of therapy. The recent focus of evaluation of alcoholism treatment has been an attempt to determine which particular subpopulation of the heterogeneous alcoholic population will respond best to which particular type of treatment (Ewing 1977; Pattison 1979). This attempt at defining more specific treatment is still too new to determine definite conclusions. Most alcoholism treatment clinicians have found what Baekeland et al. (1975) concluded to be valid, that is, that patient factors such as stable relationships, and employment and higher socioeconomic levels will more likely determine a prognosis rather than type of treatment. They also concluded that multidisciplinary and multimodality treatment approaches were more effective than any one specific type of treatment. The issue of which type of treatment for a particular alcoholic will have to wait for more definitive studies.

The individual therapy along with disulfiram maintenance, AA involvement, joint therapy for couples, and Al-Anon participation for spouses proved to be effective for a majority of addicted alcoholics treated in private practice.

Chapter 117

Psychodynamic Psychotherapy

Paralleling the success of the disease concept of alcoholism, many arguments have been advanced that alcoholic drinking should not be treated as a symptom of underlying emotional illness. Indeed, some psychiatrists have argued that psychodynamically oriented psychiatry is dangerous and contraindicated with such patients (Vaillant 1981). However, alcoholism is frequently encountered coexisting with other problems or as a central problem presented by patients and families who will not or cannot accept Alcoholics Anonymous (AA) or other treatments. Psychodynamically oriented psychiatrists and psychotherapists need to consider the conditions that are necessary to conduct psychotherapy with alcoholics, the timing and appropriateness of the psychotherapeutic interventions they employ, and the need to combine or substitute creatively other approaches based on the patients' needs and responses to the treatment that has been adopted.

A survey of 1,700 American Psychiatric Association members' treatment of alcoholism by Miller and Frances (1986) found that although 60 percent frequently do individual supportive psychotherapy, only 33 percent often and 28.3 percent sometimes use insight-oriented psychotherapy, down from an earlier report of 84 percent (Hayman 1967). This suggests a downward trend in the use of dynamically oriented therapy in patients with alcoholism.

All too often, the baby has been thrown out with the bathwater, with many therapists underutilizing a dynamic understanding of the alcoholic patient. Both patients and therapists have experienced frustration with analytic treatments that did not work, partly because of a lack of a requirement for abstinence during therapy, a lack of flexibility in approach techniques in the initial phases of recovery, and lack of integration with other approaches (Frances 1983). A central valuable feature of dynamically oriented treatment is an awareness and utilization of the dynamics of the therapist-patient relationship, which is so often complicated in working with the alcoholic. Alcoholics present in a deteriorated, out-of-control, helpless fashion that may lead to responses in the therapist ranging from overinvolvement to therapeutic nihilism and burnout of the therapist.

The study of the right combination of treatments tailored to each patient's needs is relatively new, and outcome research evidence in this area is sparse (Frances et al. 1984). Patients with alcoholism have additional psychiatric diagnoses 60 to 70 percent of the time, which will increase the technical complexity of treatment due to the interaction of other Axis I, II, and III disorders (Penick 1984; Weissman and Myers 1980). Chapter 116 emphasizes the importance of careful psychiatric diagnosis and sorting out primary and secondary problems, which can best be done as part of an individual dynamically informed treatment. The dynamically oriented therapist needs to integrate and utilize a wide range of advances in the field of alcoholism that have taken place in the last 15 years and find the right treatment or combination of treatments for each specific case. The individual dynamic therapist accepts a role as part of a treatment team that utilizes other modalities such as AA, family therapy, group therapy, Al-Anon, disulfiram (Antabuse), and adoption of more flexible parameters of treatment suited to this category of patient (Frances and Alexopoulos 1982). The team approach and the biopsychosocial model includes a sophisticated understanding of child development, careful history taking, and assessment of ego functions such as object relations, impulse control, reality testing, and defenses.

The Contribution of Applied Psychoanalytic Ideas

Advances in psychoanalysis that have led to psychoanalytically oriented therapies for borderline and narcissistic character disorders (Kernberg 1967, 1975; Kohut 1971, 1977) that take into account object relations theory, self-psychology, advances in ego psychology, and a sophisticated understanding of transference and countertransference issues are helpful when applied to patients with alcoholism. Mack (1981) and Khantzian (183) emphasized self-care governance impairment in alcoholics based on an ego psychological and object relations focus that has been a valuable contribution to theory in this area. Silber (1970, 1974) emphasized the alcoholics' pathologic identification with destructive or psychotic parents. Balint (1968) and Kohut (1977) described alcoholics' "faults" or "defects" in obtaining harmony or comfort.

Although certain kinds of personality disorders (e.g., borderline, narcissistic, antisocial) have increased alcoholism, it is important not to mistake regression due to drinking as part of underlying character disorders. Alcoholics often function on a higher level for years prior to their drinking, and they have spent years prone toward regression, influenced by both the toxic and psychosocial effects of chronic alcohol use on the brain and personality (Khantzian et al. 1974). Typically, alcoholics appear at intake to be sociopathic, impulsive, dependent, and depressed. This regression may relate to the toxic effects of alcohol on ego, disuse atrophy of ego functions, and major social disruption. Addictions contribute to denial as well as result from it. When the superego, skills in interpersonal relations, and reality testing are not used for long periods of time, they deteriorate.

In the initial phase of treatment, in addition to allowing the brain to recover from alcohol's effects, an active program of rehabilitation involving resocialization, education, and external ego and superego supports are needed until the patient is able again to be his or her own police officer and social director. During treatment, functioning improves and alcohol is given up. This helps self-esteem through both pleasure in functioning and gratification of meeting ego ideals. Patients sometimes experience a rebound "high" analogous to Mahler et al.'s (1975) practicing subphase of development in the second year of life, when there is a burst of autonomous development (e.g., walking and talking). Patients get enthusiastic about being able to function again. This should not be confused with manic denial, which can also occur.

Alcohol-induced regression in id, ego, and superego functions and a history of highest past development is important. Passivity, homosexual behavior, child abuse, and unfocused aggression may be the result of id as well as ego-regression. Primitive defenses such as denial, splitting, projection, and projective identification are likely to be more prominent in the initial stages of treatment and are similar to those frequently seen in borderline patients. Object relations regression is seen in the selfish use of others as part objects, or need-satisfying objects. There are greater problems in individuation and separation from parents and spouse. Reality testing is affected, and there may be temporary psychotic episodes.

Cognitive impairment is marked, especially in temporal and spatial functions. The superego is inconsistent, alternating between little restraint on impulses and a primitive, punitive, rigid need for self-punishment. The self-destructiveness may result from superego regression, the weakening of the ego's defenses against the superego, and impaired control of impulses.

Psychodynamic therapists have too often looked for single explanations for complex phenomena. In fact, alcoholism may be related to a variety of neurotic problems and personality disorders, not just one addictive personality, and may be primary or secondary to other problems, as well as be an attempt to escape from them. In any case, psychodynamic underpinnings and psychoanalytic theory may be useful, both in individual therapy and in rehabilitation programs, as well as other treatment modalities.

Indications

The indications for individual dynamically oriented psychotherapy for patients with alcoholism are similar in many respects to those for other psychiatric disorders. If a patient is unable, through embarrassment or need for privacy, to accept AA, group, or family treatment, individual work may be required. This is especially true for adolescents and young adults sorting out identity issues, problems in individuation, and need for independence. The principal indication is a firmly structured intrapsychic conflict at any psychosexual level that leads to a repeated negative pattern beyond an immediate crisis (Frances et al. 1984). Dynamic therapy is best suited for patients who have a capacity for insight, intimacy, identification with the therapist, average or superior intelligence, time, money, and high motivation to understand and change, not just the drinking but other undesirable aspects of themselves. As found with most modalities, patients who do best have greater socioeconomic and marital stability, less psychopathology, and less sociopathy.

One initial impediment to dynamically oriented treatment in addicts is what Krystal (1982) called "alexithymia," a problem in identifying and verbalizing feelings, which leads to somatization of them. The therapists' active, open, supportive, emphatic stance, combined with an understanding of alcoholic patients' experience of alexithymia and anhedonia, is important in preparing these patients to explore their inner lives. An effort is made to instruct the patient about these issues and to help them express and tolerate their painful feelings of anger or depression instead of avoiding them or acting them out (Khantzian 1986).

Relative contraindications to outpatient individual insight-oriented therapy include patients who continue to drink while in treatment and will not accept abstinence as a precondition for treatment (Dodes 1984). These patients may need hospitalization or crisis work to prepare them for treatment. Patients who tend to regress in individual treatment, and whose severe masochism leads to frequent negative therapeutic reactions, should be in group or family treatments and AA. Patients whose principal problems are family-related should be in family treatment. Traditional, unmodified psychoanalytic approaches utilizing a couch, daily sessions, analytic neutrality, and a lack of specific goals are contraindicated in all cases of alcoholism in the initial phases, but may become possible in carefully selected cases after one or two years of sobriety.

Treatment Setting

Dynamically oriented treatment may occur in an office practice, with inpatients, or in a day hospital. The treatment takes place one to three times per week, can be brief or long-term, and may last three to five years or longer. In an inpatient setting, treatment usually is brief and preparatory for longer-term therapy with the same or another therapist; it can be used to determine whether or not the patient is suitable for insight-oriented work.

Choice of setting depends mainly on whether adequate personal and social supports exist for maintaining sobriety as an outpatient. The capacity to treat more patients in outpatient settings depends partly on good use of networks of support (see Chapter 121) and on the skill of the therapist in titrating a mixture of supportive and expressive measures. Some patients are more safely confronted in a hospital setting, in which there are greater supports. Inpatient treatment, although often necessary and helpful, is the treatment of last resort: outpatient and day hospital programs are effective for a majority of patients.

Technique

The application of psychoanalytic thinking to alcoholism treatment, although requiring some modification of technique, basically depends on the established aspects of modern dynamic understanding. There is an emphasis on increasing understanding of intrapsychic conflicts and developmental impairments through interpretations. These conflicts may be at any psychosexual level. A hysteric may drink to reach orgasm or as a way of avoiding intercourse. An obsessional may use alcohol as a means of exerting control, as an excuse for losing control, or as a means of distancing from or expressing angry feelings (Khantzian 1977). A careful developmental history, with attention to important figures of identification, is part of the approach. Exploration of alcohol and drug effects sought and experienced may reveal how these effects are used to permit, augment, or obliterate affects that are otherwise absent or overwhelming (Khantzian 1981). Dreams, slips, and free association may be used to help the patient understand unconscious derivatives of behavior (e.g., the unconscious wish to drink) or to avoid other means of meeting dependency needs (Lorand 1948). With the alcoholic patient, dynamically oriented therapy works through resistance and defense, as with other patients, with sensitivity to the importance of drinking as a way out of facing these issues.

Patients may enter what can become insight-oriented treatment as a result of coercion by family, employer, physician, or a probation officer. In the beginning, trust and a working alliance may be difficult to achieve. As the patient feels helped and understood in the course of treatment, and as positive transference develops, more open expression may become possible. In the early stages, confrontation of lying as well as denial is important. Meeting with family and use of laboratory aids may be needed to confront dishonesty. Dishonest patients with multiple substance abuse can fool the doctor for long periods of time unless the therapist employs a combination of careful observation and weekly or biweekly laboratory testing. Use of a breathalyzer and regular monitoring of urine and blood for other substances of abuse (e.g., cocaine) are helpful when there is a suspicion of possible intoxication and when there may be reason to distrust a patient's account of any substance use. Recently, laboratory tests have advanced in sensitivity, reliability, and availability and have decreased in cost.

Having patients involved with AA while in psychotherapy can be helpful in many ways. AA provides the patient with education and auxiliary ego and superego support, and may help diffuse some of the powerful negative transferences that patients will bring to treatment. The patient and the therapist can together look at the process of projection and introjection that may go on in relationship to other AA members who may remind the patient of alcoholic relatives.

In dynamically oriented treatment, the emphasis is on getting the patient to tell how he or she feels rather than showing the therapist through acting-out. The therapist needs to help the patient reestablish controls and boundaries between thought and action. This is especially a problem in alcoholism, where patients have for a long time acted out their fantasies.

For most patients, the focus of treatment will initially be on issues surrounding the addiction, with conflicts including acceptance of the problem, acceptance of dependency needs for help, and conflicts around loss of people, jobs, health, and even alcohol. Soon, other issues such as problems in self-care, self-esteem, and specific conflicts over assertiveness, problems handling aggression, alcohol's role in either allowing or distancing from a sexual life, and issues around control may become prominent. For most patients, support will be needed at first, with gradual increase in clarification, confrontation, and interpretation of denial, lying, splitting, and projective defenses. Some patients may need to be more directly confronted early on in order for them to see a need for change. Many alcoholics are affectively constricted, and dynamically informed treatment aims at aiding patients understand the conscious basis for problems in expressing feelings openly and appropriately in a sober state.

Analysts were traditionally not very successful in treating alcoholics with psychoanalysis, perhaps partly because they rarely insisted that patients remain abstinent during treatment. This parameter makes possible dynamically oriented psychotherapy with suitable patients. Dodes (1984) found that the empathic exploration of alcoholics' impairment in self-care may be the pathway to help alcoholics adopt abstinence. If a patient repeatedly returns to drinking within the course of treatment, addition of AA, disulfiram, or other modalities may be needed, or inpatient therapy should be recommended. Without abstinence, attempts at working through underlying conflicts in an effort to remove alcoholism as a symptom are likely to fail. Of course, alcoholism is a chronic relapsing illness. The therapist must be prepared for relapses and be neither punitive nor avoidant of confrontation if needed (Tamerin and Mendelson 1969).

The therapist needs to be keenly aware of the therapist-patient relationship, aware of those situations in which neutrality needs to be guarded and those times in which greater activity may be required as compared with other categories of patients. Therapists may find themselves in extremes of enabling patients or overly battering patients with interpretations that the patient will not hear (Moore 1965). There may be times when it may be appropriate for the therapist to telephone the patient or family in a crisis.

Exploratory techniques, such as clarification, interpretation, and genetic reconstruction, especially at early stages, may be combined with directive approaches (e.g., assertiveness training, modeling, positive reinforcement, suggestion, and cognitive awareness). Establishing empathy through careful listening, combined with a sound knowledge of typical problems related to alcoholism and the alcoholic family, will be extremely valuable.

Transference and Countertransference Issues

An understanding of how patients tend to make the therapist feel and what kinds of responses the patient is trying to evoke in the therapist are often of value when interpreted to the alcoholic patient. For example, patients with alcoholism may expect that a therapist is going to be critical of them or of their having had a slip or a drink and will avoid talking about this because of an expectation that the therapist will be critical in the way that they felt that their spouses or parents were. Interpretation by the therapist being placed in this role may be very helpful to the patient.

A second kind of countertransference is one that develops out of lack of knowledge of the field and the disease entity. The less a therapist knows about anything, the more likely the therapist is to project his or her own difficulties onto the situation. A broad knowledge of alcoholism and substance abuse and a familiarity with diagnostic, etiologic, and treatment issues in a biopsychosocial context will go far toward reducing attitudinal problems in working with this category of patients (Tamerin and Neumann 1974). Therapists are less frightened when they know what they are dealing with and how to approach it. This has certainly been true of those who get a good education in the alcohol and substance abuse field. Just as interest in character pathology and borderline personality have made it possible to treat a wider number of patients who stimulate strong countertransference responses, an understanding of these principles in combination with an understanding of alcoholism is also very useful.

The social network in which the treatment takes place influences countertransference, especially in hospital treatment. Our experience is that structured and informed programs have fewer countertransference problems. A consultant may help diagnose systems problems that interfere with optimal patient care. There can be institutional pressures that might affect or corrupt the attitudes of the practicing therapist when the therapist is part of a team or hosptial structure. A hospital that has traditionally not accepted alcoholic patients may make it difficult for the therapist to go against such a team approach. If the institution's practice is to make special arrangements in the treatment of patients with a VIP status, it may be difficult for a therapist to set appropriate limits for the VIP patient who has problems with substance abuse. In these cases, understanding of dynamic principles may be helpful to the treatment team or organization.

A third source of major countertransference, and one that is often more deeply unconscious, is the particular kind of problem that the therapist is likely to have with any patient with substance abuse or one that relates to problems in the therapist that get projected onto patients. A therapist's own wishes and fears concerning addiction or chronic pain can be projected onto the patient and warded off. The therapist may have a fear of contracting addiction or chronic pain, and countertransference may lead to extremes of underprescription, overprescription, overinvolvement, avoidance, hopelessness, zealousness, a search for magical solutions, and burnout. These reactions are often parallel to the extremes that are typical of addictive patients' transferences. Whereas early analysts saw countertransference purely as an impediment, recently there has been controversy as to whether, how, and with what frequency therapists' reactions can be used to help the patient. In our experience, a lot depends on the style, tact, and training of the particular therapist.

In the substance abuse field, this is especially important because some therapists are attracted to the field because they are either recovering from addiction themselves or have had experience with a relative who has had a problem. For this group especially, collusion between patient and therapist may lead them both to avoid certain unconscious, painful issues. Sometimes, these therapists use the same interpretation for every patient. The recovering therapist must be careful when the patient says, "I won't tell you my problem unless you tell me yours first." Once the therapist does reveal an instance of abusive behavior in the therapist's own family in attempt to model, the patient may use this to reject help, asserting that the therapist's problems are a lot worse than the patient's own and that the therapist is not to be trusted. Once learning the weaknesses of the therapist, the patient will be able to find a way to take advantage of the therapist. On the positive side, the experience of having been an adult child of an alcoholic may have led to long experience and strength in caring for family members, which later may be expressed in interest in Twelve Step work or in becoming a therapist.

A typical example of a countertransference problem is the therapist who has more difficulty meeting the dependency needs of an alcoholic person as compared with a patient with a medical problem such as diabetes, both of whom may be highly dependent but having a hard time accepting their own dependency needs. Being sensitive to the projective mechanisms of patients and therapists' reactions to them can be very helpful.

Silber (1974) emphasized the therapist's fear with regard to aggression of patients, which plays an important role in problems that many beginning therapists have in working with alcoholic patients. Becoming more aware of reactions to the patient's anger often had an almost magical affect on the therapist's doing better work with the patients. Silber directed efforts to helping therapists quickly recognize and appreciate the essential helplessness of their patients by attempting to modify the therapists' preconceived attitudes, which were often antagonistic. It was possible to facilitate successful treatment outcome in many patients by this kind of awareness.

All too often in training, young clinicians may get the sense that unacceptable feelings on the part of the therapist should be pushed away or dealt with in their own treatment and are not open to discussion even in the supervisory process. It is very helpful for the therapist to have a trusted group of colleagues to discuss reactions to patients comfortably, in an open way. Seminars devoted to transference and countertransference issues are especially helpful in allowing therapists to learn to use their feelings in ways that are helpful to the treatment.

The Experience of Being the Adult Child of an Alcoholic

Recently, an expanding body of literature has been developed on children of alcoholics (COAs) and adult children of alcholics (ACOAs), who have been called "the hidden tragedy" and the neglected problem. Understanding of children's reactions to parents' alcoholism can be helpful, both in understanding adults' resistance to individual therapy and some of the ways in which group treatment and AA are effective and used in conjunction with individual treatment. As children, the ACOAs are exposed to both genetic and environmental factors that put them at higher risk (Cloninger et al. 1981). Intervention with COAs at early ages may be beneficial. Costs of early intervention and primary prevention at this level unfortunately are staggering, due to the millions of children possibly involved. Fortunately, some COAs do well despite adversity and genetic vulnerability. Understanding protective factors may be helpful (Wolin et al. 1980).

More needs to be learned about the nature of the connection between disorganization, alcoholism, and emotional disturbance in children (Woodside 1982). It is in the early years that we see the beginning of emotional stigma, alienation, estrangement, and a sense of difference from others who have a more normal family life. The nonalcoholic parent is also affected by the alcoholism and may have difficulty protecting the child from abuse by the alcoholic parent. These children often are expected to take on parental roles with respect to the alcohol-dependent parent. Problems with sexual identity, loss, abandonment, and neglect occur frequently in these families.

An empathic approach to understanding the experience of a COA or ACOA is useful in efforts at psychotherapy of the substance abuse patient. Growing up in an inconsistent household in which parents may sometimes be wonderful and other times terrible leads to a distrust of authority figures and a greater tendency to depend on peers or on no one. Siblings have to care for each other, as well as take care of their parents, and tend to pick friends who also have problems themselves and have similarly troubled families. They are afraid to bring friends home who do not have families with problems similar to their own. This peer group grows up protesting their parents' behavior, attempting to be different but often developing the same problems.

It is this lack of trust that is brought into the treatment situation with a therapist and has been experienced with teachers, nurses, or other professionals who represent authority figures. Interpretation of this resistance may help in forming a therapeutic alliance. Understanding of this pattern helps explain why self-help groups, group therapy, and family approaches are especially helpful alone or in conjunction with individual therapy in that the person with the problem can turn to peer support, this time with friends and family working at obtaining sobriety together. This model explains why AA, Alateen, Drugs Anonymous, school-based support groups, and groups for ACOAs have wide appeal and effectiveness. The individual therapist may share an understanding of the patient's childhood experiences and use some of the natural group settings that the patient will be involved with as an adjunct to the individual dynamically oriented treatment. For some patients, working through issues at a peer level may be important before the patient is able to deal with authority issues in individual therapy.

Chapter 118

Family Therapy

In the past two decades, three factors have played a prominent role in stimulating the growing awareness of the importance of family factors in alcoholism. The first factor has been the emergence of survey data indicating that the extent of alcoholism as a public health problem has been grossly underestimated. Furthermore, these data conclusively demonstrated that only a small percentage of alcoholics were homeless individuals living in the skid row settings of our large cities (the popular perception up to that point of the "average" alcoholic person). Instead, these survey data told us the vast majority were living in intact nuclear family units. As a second factor, compelling evidence has emerged regarding the familial nature of alcoholism. Whether or not one accepts a genetic hypothesis as the best explanation for these familial incidence rates, the evidence is now quite clear that having alcoholic parents vastly increases one's own chance of developing alcoholism. Third, it has become increasingly clear that alcoholism is associated with other phenomena of dire consequences for families—foremost among them family violence and incest.

The increased focus on the family stimulated by the above three factors has, in turn, led to a desire to understand better how the family environment differentially influences the course of alcoholism (Jacob and Seilhamer 1987; Jacob et al. 1978; Moos et al. 1979; Steinglass 1980; Steinglass et al. 1987) and how treatment interventions aimed at the family might be integrated into a comprehensive treatment program for alcoholism (Anderson and Henderson 1983; Kaufman 1985; Lawson et al. 1983; Steinglass 1977).

Indications for Family Therapy

No generally accepted criteria currently exist regarding indications for family-oriented treatment of alcoholism. At the same time, however, family therapy in one form or another has been applied with increasing frequency to this condition. This is true both for alcoholism treatment programs that deal extensively with this condition and for family-oriented treatment programs serving a more heterogeneous clientele.

Family-Oriented Diagnosis of Alcoholism

Although there is widespread acknowledgment of the importance of family factors in the onset and course of chronic alcoholism, thus far no widely accepted schema exist for integrating a family prospective with either the Axis I criteria (American Psychiatric Association 1987) sets for diagnosing alcohol abuse and alcohol dependence or with other popular diagnostic criteria sets such as those suggested by the National Council on Alcoholism (1972). Instead, family clinicians have offered a variety of descriptive typologies thought to be clinically useful in differentiating families with alcoholic members. Two examples are detailed below.

The systems approach model.   One typological scheme, based on family systems theory, centers on the concept of the alcoholic system, defined as a behavioral system in which alcohol acquisition and/or consumption is a major organizing principle for patterns of interactional behavior within the system (Steinglass et al. 1971). Bottle-gangs are perhaps the purest examples of such drinking systems. But families can also become alcoholic systems in that chronic alcoholism occupies a central position as a core identity issue for many families dealing with chronic alcoholic problems. The term *alcoholic family* has been suggested to describe such a situation. The family systems typology contrasts the alcoholic family with a second type of family, the *family with an alcoholic member*, the latter subtype being a family still faced with the challenges of chronic alcoholism but one that has not reorganized in substantive ways to accommodate these challenges.

Thus the basic distinction being made in this typology centers around the extent to which the family has become altered in its behavior patterns by the presence of a chronic alcoholic member. Three areas of family life have been suggested as foci for assessing this question: daily routines (Steinglass 1981); family rituals (e.g., holidays, vacations, dinnertime) (Wolin et al. 1980); and short-term problem-solving strategies (Steinglass et al. 1977). For each area, the central question is the extent to which family behavior patterns have been organized and/or altered to accommodate the unique demands generated by the family's alcoholic member.

Clinicians using this systems approach have recommended family therapy as the treatment of choice whenever this reorganization around the alcoholic symptom has occurred in the family. Further, it has been suggested that this reorganization process may substantively increase the likelihood of cross-generational transmission of alcoholism, whether or not a genetic predisposition is concurrently present.

It should also be noted that the family systems approach to alcoholism also draws links between alcoholism and other conditions, emphasizing that the alcoholic family is an example of a more general phenomenon characteristic of all chronic illnesses. That is, families dealing with such chronic conditions as diabetes, end-stage renal disease, heroin addiction, traumatic injuries leading to permanent disabilities, mental retardation, or chronic psychosis all have this capacity to become organized around strategies for accommodating to or maintaining the chronic illness process.

The family functioning model.   A second classification system offered by family-oriented alcoholism clinicians places greater emphasis on the overall functionality of the family system (Kaufman and Pattison 1982). Four family types are described: 1) the functional family system, in which alcoholic drinking is thought to be the product primarily of personal neurotic conflict or individual social strains, but not of family systemic malfunction; 2) the neurotic, enmeshed family system, in which drinking behavior interrupts normal family tasks, causes conflict, shifts roles, and demands adjustive and adaptive responses from family members who do not know how to respond appropriately; 3) the disintegrated family system, in which family functioning has largely collapsed as the result of failure to cope adequately with drinking behavior; and 4) the absent family system, thought of as a final severing of the bonds between the family and the alcoholic member, either as a result of extrusion or of family dissolution.

Once again, this system (which bears obvious analogous features to the first model described) has been proposed as a useful tool for treatment planning. Thus, for example, functional family systems are thought to respond well to treatment plans that engage them in a supportive plan aimed mainly at the identified alcoholic member, such as the use of disulfiram (Antabuse), group therapy for the alcoholic member, and Alcoholics Anonymous (AA). The neurotic, enmeshed family system, on the other hand, usually is in need of a treatment program that aims at restructuring of the entire family system, and may call for hospitalization of the drinking member as an initial step in order to involve the family in therapy. In the disintegrated family system, separate but concurrent treatment programs for the identified alcoholic and the family are often recommended. Here the family might be engaged in supportive treatment and/or Alanon, while a largely independent, individually oriented treatment program is instituted for the alcoholic member. Finally, the absent family system is, by definition, usually not available to the therapist, and treatment centers entirely on the individual alcoholic.

Family Therapy Methods

Unique Aspects of the Alcoholic Family

Family-oriented clinicians attempting to work with alcoholism problems must keep in mind four aspects of the condition that impact on family life in unique ways. These are:

1. *Its chronicity.* Clinicians usually encounter alcoholism problems many years after they have reached pathologic proportions. Relationships between the condition itself, the alcoholic family member, and the rest of the family have usually reached some steady state. The precipitating event leading to a request for treatment is often a crisis that has temporarily disrupted this steady state (e.g., a medical crisis, a drunk driving arrest, a confrontation by an employer because of deterioration in work functioning). However, therapy, to be successful, must combat and overcome long-standing patterns of behavior that have become rigidified over time. These obviously include family interaction patterns.
2. *The use of a psychobiologically active drug.* Because the family's alcoholic member is chronically ingesting a psychobiologically active drug that is both a depressant and a drug that significantly impairs cognition and verbal communication, family behavior patterns have gradually been adopted to accommodate for these defects. These patterns are often not immediately apparent and therefore represent a challenge to the family therapist during the initial phases of treatment.
3. *Sober-intoxicated cycling.* Direct observations of interactional behavior of alcoholic families have indicated that these families manifest two quite distinct interactional

styles—one that occurs when the alcoholic member is sober and another that occurs when the alcoholic member is intoxicated. It has been suggested, therefore, that a unique feature of the alcoholic family is its dual-state interactional style. It has further been suggested that family therapists must develop strategies for accessing information about the intoxicated interactional state in order to appreciate fully the interrelationships between alcohol use and interactional behavior that have developed in these families.

4. *Intergenerational transmission of alcoholism.* Alcoholism is a familial condition. Most likely, both genetic and psychosocial factors contribute to the intergenerational transmission of alcoholism. Family therapists must appreciate that their interventions are appropriately directed not only at containing alcoholic behavior as it is currently being manifested, but also in attending to the needs of children within the family toward the goal of disrupting possible intergenerational transmission of the condition.

Different Therapy Approaches

The above unique aspects of chronic alcoholism have presented family therapists with multiple challenges. Not surprisingly, responses to these challenges have taken many forms. Although difficult to categorize because many of these treatment approaches must still be considered experimental or developing, one can roughly divide the field into two major divisions dependent on whether the underlying conceptual rationale for treatment is based on a family systems model or on a social network-support system model. In addition, it is important to take account of self-help approaches for families with alcoholic members, especially Al-Anon.

Family systems therapy. Treatment approaches utilizing a family systems model have the following distinctive characteristics:

1. The therapist views the whole family, not the alcoholic member alone, as the primary patient. (However, the family in this case definitely includes the identified alcoholic as well.) The working assumption is that families with alcoholic members have often restructured internal relationships and patterns of family behavior to accommodate the chronic demands of alcoholism. This restructuring has led to a reorganization, with alcoholism now dictating and shaping important aspects of family life. This is the alcoholic system concept described earlier. In such instances, it is argued, the whole family should be viewed as the patient.
2. Given this conceptual orientation, the focus of the treatment is on correction of dysfunctional patterns of interactional behavior rather than on individual psychodynamics.
3. Outcome measures include improvement in the functioning of the family as a unit in addition to traditional goals regarding cessation of drinking.
4. Treatment goals are determined by careful assessment of family functional characteristics as well as assessment of alcoholism parameters. For example, for some families treatment goals are focused on restabilization of family behavior postcessation of drinking; for other families cessation of drinking permits major reorganization and the development of new patterns of behavior. However, it is important to underscore that family systems therapy shares with every other psychotherapeutic approach to alcoholism a conviction that the first step in the treatment process must be the cessation of drinking (including the use of inpatient detoxification where necessary).

Social network therapy.   The second major approach, based on a social systems model, utilizes a variety of family interventions in support of a treatment plan targeted at the alcoholic individual as the primary patient. Here, the involvement of the family is undertaken with one or more of the following goals in mind:

1. To obtain more accurate and complete historical data regarding alcoholism history of the identified patient;
2. To increase the likelihood of engagement of the patient in the treatment process;
3. To increase compliance rates, especially as regards disulfiram (Antabuse) therapy and detoxification strategies;
4. To increase the social supports available to the alcoholic individual, especially during the postdetoxification period; and
5. To provide independent counseling to family members regarding their own coping strategies and psychological sequelae attendant to the impact of chronic alcoholism on family life.

Typically, these goals are achieved by establishing a concurrent program for family members parallel to and integrated with the treatment program for the identified alcoholic member of the family. For example, family sessions (often without the alcoholic member present) might occur on a regular basis during the time when the alcoholic member is engaged in a residential detoxification program. Another popular approach has been the use of multiple family group psychotherapy, groups that focus on issues presumably relevant to the nonalcoholic members of the family, including supportive approaches geared to assist families in dealing with common difficulties they face as a result of having an alcoholic member. In some instances these are established for spouses and/or children that meet concurrently with groups for the alcoholic family members. In other instances the alcoholic members are included in the group, but the focus remains a social systems one.

Al-Anon groups.   Although in many instances the above family-oriented interventions are designed and implemented by professionals (usually an alcoholism specialist, but occasionally a family therapy specialist as well), by far the most active family-oriented program for alcoholism is a self-help one: the Al-Anon family group. Al-Anon is an indigenous self-help movement that arose spontaneously as a parallel but separate movement to AA in the 1940s. Al-Anon family groups are modeled after AA (i.e., a group fellowship of peers sharing a common problem). In the case of Al-Anon, the peers are spouses, children, and close relatives of alcoholics who are usually, but not necessarily, part of an AA group.

Ablon (1974), who has extensively studied the Al-Anon movement, suggested that successful Al-Anon members must accept one basic didactic lesson and three principles for operating in the groups themselves. The didactic lesson is the acceptance of the AA concept of alcoholism as "an obsession of the mind and an allergy of the body," implying that the alcoholic is suffering from a disease that is totally outside his or her control. The three operating principles are: first, a "loving detachment from the alcoholic," in which family members accept as a given that they are powerless to intervene constructively in the behavior of the alcoholic family member; second, the reestablishment of self-esteem and independence; and third, a reliance on a "higher power," a spiritual emphasis that, of course, also closely parallels AA.

Family therapists are divided in their opinions about the combining of traditional family therapy approaches with concurrent involvement in AA or Al-Anon groups. Some have argued that the two approaches work at cross-purposes in that AA and

Al-Anon clearly see the alcoholic person, not the family, as the "patient." The prevailing view, however, is that participation in self-help groups is a useful adjunctive experience to family therapy for many families (Berenson 1976).

Conclusion

A modest literature now exists examining the efficacy of a wide variety of family therapy approaches for the treatment of alcoholism. Although somewhat artificial, it is possible to divide the studies that have been published into a four-step sequence, with stages that roughly build on one another. The first stage focused on an examination of the marital dynamics of male alcoholics and their wives (Edwards et al. 1973). The second stage comprised a series of treatment outcome studies focusing on concurrent group psychotherapy as a treatment approach for alcoholism (Ewing et al. 1961; Gliedman 1957). The third stage was more a stage of theory and model-building than of final outcome studies. These systems approaches were also pivotal in stimulating the growing application of family therapy techniques to the treatment of alcoholic families. These techniques included conjoint family therapy (Esser 1970; Kaufman and Pattison 1981; Usher et al. 1982), marital group therapy (Arieli 1981; Gallant et al. 1970; Sands and Hanson 1971), and conjoint hospitalization of marital couples (Paolino and McCrady 1976; Steinglass 1979). The fourth stage, a natural outgrowth of the increasing experimentation with family therapy approaches, has been the formal testing of these treatments in a small series of case history treatment outcome studies and controlled clinical trials carried out during the 1970s and 1980s (e.g., Cadogan 1973; McCrady et al. 1982; Meeks and Kelly 1970).

The following generalizations about this treatment evaluation literature seem warranted:

1. Both clinical reports and controlled studies are overwhelmingly favorable to the use of family therapy for the treatment of alcoholism. However, with rare exception, all studies published to date must be characterized as pilot in nature. Sample sizes are small, random assignment of patients has been carried out in only a few studies, and details regarding treatment programs and qualifications of therapists tend to be scanty. On the other hand, there are no reports in the literature suggesting that family therapy is either less effective than an alternative treatment approach to which it has been compared, or that inclusion of family members in a treatment program has had detrimental effects. Nevertheless, we have yet to see a treatment outcome study carried out by experienced family therapists incorporating sound research principles. Nor do we have any data at this point about the comparative efficacy of the different family therapy approaches one against the other.

2. A wide variety of family treatment approaches have been tried, including conjoint family therapy, behavioral marital therapy, concurrent group therapy, multiple couples therapy, and multiple family therapy. All have been reported to be efficacious; none has occupied a dominant position in the field.

3. Compelling evidence does exist that the involvement of a non-alcoholic spouse in a treatment program significantly improves the likelihood that the alcoholic individual will participate in treatment as well. Although this finding would also benefit from large scale replication, given the consistency of data from multiple studies, involvement of nonalcoholic spouses (at the very least) should be incorporated into all alcoholism treatment programs for patients still living in intact families.

4. There is little evidence in the treatment outcome literature that clinicians are approaching alcoholism with a sophisticated sense of family dynamics or family systems principles. Nor is there evidence that clinicians appreciate the heterogeneity of this interesting group of families. Instead, the dominant model in clinical practice remains heavily influenced by the AA–Al-Anon philosophy of "separate but equal" treatment. For example, it would be unusual to find an alcoholism treatment program that incorporates a sophisticated family assessment as a mandatory part of its workup and then designs a treatment program based on the findings of such a workup. Much more likely, a standard program exists and the alcoholic individual and family are pushed and squeezed to fit the preconceived notions, treatment schedule, and goals of this already established program.

5. Overall, therefore, the alcoholism field is receptive to the notion that family intervention has an appropriate place in the overall treatment process, but is still struggling to define the scope and form this intervention should take.

Chapter 119

Group Therapy

Group treatment has emerged as a dominant method in the treatment of alcoholism (Allman and Crocker 1982; Blume 1978; Doroff 1977; Kansas 1982; Zimberg 1982). This has occurred despite only a small amount of empirical research demonstrating its efficacy (Brandsma and Pattison 1985; Colson and Horwitz 1983). Rather, the widespread utilization of group methods has come from clinical experience with alcoholics. Several factors have contributed to the assumption that group approaches are particularly salient for alcoholism.

First, the historical importance of Alcoholics Anonymous (AA) as a leaderless group experience demonstrated the efficacy of peer pressure and peer support. This became a model for the field.

Second, practicality, efficiency, and economy are virtues that are seen also as attributes of group therapy. However, these obvious advantages are mitigated somewhat by time spent with patients and families before and after group and by record keeping.

Third, dependency issues include both dependency on alcohol and deep-seated dependent personality traits. Groups teach interdependence (not dependence on a therapist) and foster a better social network. Groups reduce the emotional isolation of the alcoholic, but identify superficial and manipulative relationships. The "oral equation" works with alcoholics—that is, the more you talk about your problems, the less you drink for them.

Fourth, group identity often works powerfully and cohesively to change the valence of self-identity from the negative "alcoholic" to the positive "recovering alcoholic"—a more supportable, even heroic posture.

Fifth, there is an interactional relationship between drinking and contextual interpersonal cues. The group provides a congenial setting to observe these relations, to compare them to self-report, to confront denial, and then to use the group as a laboratory for training in new responses and new skills in interpersonal behaviors.

Sixth, groups provide a way to channel and socialize an alcoholic's narcissistic need to feel powerful by providing a place in the group and being helpful to others.

Seventh, the sharing of mutual problems, conflicts, and the life situation of "being alcoholic" reduces the ubiquitous emotional flooding of shame and guilt observed in almost all alcoholics.

The above indicate the personal "needs" of alcoholic patients that are addressed in groups. We can complement this picture by looking at general group attributes. Yalom (1985) detailed eight therapeutic elements in group therapy. The relationship to alcoholism is briefly stated:

1. Information. Groups provide concepts of alcoholism, family dynamics, behavioral alternatives, and availability of community resources.
2. Hope. Groups provide positive expectations that problems can be solved, needs met.
3. Universality. Patients find that they are not unique in their wretchedness or overwhelming emotions. On the other hand, those striving for perfection become more mellow about being "just human."
4. Catharsis. Patients learn that feelings can be expressed and handled, rather than turned into anxiety. They find these experiences are likely to bind people to you rather than drive them away if done in a relatively constructive way. Shared problem identification reduces inappropriate guilt and shame.
5. Altruism. Reciprocal helping relationships in the group increase a person's sense of value and power.
6. Imitation and Learning New Social Skills. Patients model and practice coping behaviors and acquire revised social identity.
7. Cohesiveness. Groups provide a sense of solidarity, identity, perhaps even the sense of a "new family." The alcoholic finds people in caring relationships oriented toward positive change and coping without alcohol.
8. Interpersonal Learning. Patients find out how they are perceived by others, how they largely create or maintain their own problems, how they can become responsible for their feelings and their lives without self-perpetuating, self-destructive "games of alcoholism."

Compared to other kinds of patients in group therapy, the following special questions will need to be addressed by the therapist conducting group therapy with alcoholics (Allman and Crocker 1982; Vannicelli 1982).

1. During initial sessions (and later), how much information and other kinds of structure must be provided to reduce anxiety and to facilitate therapy? Most therapists agree that more is better than less initially.
2. Alcoholics test and evade limits. A leader must provide limits for the group work.
3. How much active outreach should a therapist provide to nonattenders who may be drinking?

4. What are the limits of confidentiality for group members and outsiders, where alcoholismic behavior involves significant others?
5. What are the expectations of this group as compared to other groups, such as Alcoholics Anonymous (AA) or education groups?
6. How will requests for information on the therapist's drinking behavior and values or attitudes be handled?
7. How will slips be dealt with in the group?
8. What will be done with the group member that arrives intoxicated?
9. Alcoholics defuse focus on feelings and issues. The leader faces problems of keeping the group "on target."
   - How will talking about drinking to avoid group work be handled?
   - What about patients who refuse to talk about their drinking?
   - What about patients who are dishonest about their drinking or honestly have no intentions of changing?

Group therapy techniques in alcoholism are multifaceted, influenced by setting, concepts of alcoholism, group methods, and goals. Major goals of various group formats include management, support, education, behavior change, or intrapsychic change. What follows is a brief description of the various clinical types of groups used in treating alcoholics. Not included are AA groups, inpatient therapeutic community groups, family therapy, and patient-government groups on alcoholism wards. Perhaps the group formats discussed below could be organized by theoretical orientation in categories such as social-systems, interpersonal-interactional, intrapsychic-dynamic, and behavioral, but many groups combine multiple theories and techniques.

Intake-Orientation Groups

There are many kinds of intake groups used to orient and educate patients to larger programs. The time frame is variable but usually short. For example, Sands and Hanson (1971) described a group in which a patient's motivation is assessed, information on alcoholism and their program is provided, and the patient's suitability for other groups and treatments in their program is evaluated. In another variant, groups of five to eight patients meet without a therapist to orient new patients and to discuss topics given to them by the staff. Pattison et al. (1965) used diagnostic intake groups to orient wives to the treatment of their spouses. Extending these concepts, Gallant and his colleagues (Gallant 1964; Gallant et al. 1966) conducted intake groups with both staff and new patients as participants in assessment and treatment planning. Galanter and Panepinto (1980) developed a group program to enhance engagement of inpatients into the outpatient clinic.

Marital Couples Group

Marital conflict is intimately related to drinking behavior (Pattison and Kaufman 1981). It is not surprising that many emphasize that spouses must be active participants in treatment. Group therapy with couples where one or both members have problems with alcohol has proven effective in outpatient, inpatient, and aftercare settings (Arieli 1981; Berman 1968; Cadogan 1973). Usually there are five couples per group, with a range of four to seven reported; sometimes single alcoholics are allowed in these groups as well. Often they begin when the husband is on an inpatient alcoholism rehabilitation unit. Content foci are on the expression of feelings, communication problems, confrontation of rationalizations, the process of problem solving, and the dominant spouse (Kaufman and Pattison 1982). These groups run from one to two hours once or twice per week for at least three months and often up to a year. At times the therapist must do supportive therapy with the spouse outside the group. These are to be distinguished from spouse-support groups, where only spouses attend. In these groups, spouses ventilate, share experiences, and discuss how they participate in the maintenance of the alcoholic's problem. Hopefully they define better lines of responsibility for the drinking behaviors (Ablon 1974; Bailey 1965).

Behavioral Couples Group

Here groups of couples attempt to modify their interactions through "contingency contracting" and communication skills (O'Farrell and Cutter 1984). Communication is broken down into support giving, problem solving, and assertiveness training. These are demonstrated and practiced, especially with regard to those interactions that are identified as relating to alcohol ingestion. Before the group begins, educational videotapes are used to show the reciprocal dependency of alcoholic couples, and a list of marital problems for each couple is compiled. Daily phone calls to the couple for 10 days are used to collect baseline data. In the group, only a present or future tense focus is allowed by the leader. Couples report on their progress, negotiate assignments, and discuss problems. Each couple must negotiate an agreement on how to manage daily disulfiram (Antabuse) for the alcoholic spouse (Greenbaum 1954). Discussions are conducted around pleasing behaviors, planning recreation, and behaviors that lead to drinking. The last part of the program is training the couple on how to maintain their gains; then the group terminates. This type of treatment does not seem to be "enough" for crisis-prone families.

Supportive Groups for Teenagers

Alcoholism is hard on families, especially the children. Some treatment programs for alcoholic patients offer a supportive, educational group experience for the teenage children (McElfresh 1970). These sessions are once per week for two hours in a four-week cycle. Audiovisual materials are used for educational purposes and to trigger discussion. Content involves how alcohol has affected their lives, how to cope with it, and whether alcoholism is hereditary. Information and referral to other resources is often provided. Another self-help group variant of recent vintage concerns adult children of alcoholics (ACOA).

Interactional Psychotherapy Groups

This kind of group usually meets long-term on an outpatient basis for one and one-half hours once per week. It may involve both male and female alcoholics. These groups work on the alcoholic's personality problems by focusing on the interpersonal pathology in the current group relationships. AA is seen as a useful adjunct. Therapists encourage honesty and emotional expression, facilitate a personal and direct level of exchange, and at the same time ask for a self-reflective posture from the participants. When anxiety becomes too intense, supportive structure can be provided by putting an interpersonal agenda on a blackboard, didactic teaching about the group, or videotape playback of problematic events that have occurred (Feeny and Dranger 1976; Yalom 1974).

Gestalt Groups

The techniques and philosophies of Gestalt therapy have been applied to alcoholics, both in the hospital and on an outpatient basis (Boylin 1975). The emphasis is on a growth of self-awareness and self-support in responsible ways. Therapists tend to work with patients one at a time, but involve the other group members as participants in role playing and for feedback. There is an emphasis on experimentation to try out new or risky behaviors as well as "staying with their feelings" until some form of resolution can occur. Questions are discouraged, dialogue encouraged, and dreams or fantasies are often played out (much like in psychodrama) in the group. A balance between action, affect, and reflection is sought.

Encounter Groups

Although not as popular as a decade ago and more often used with drug addicts, the sensitivity-training movement has had an impact on group therapy and has been tried with alcoholics with reported good results (Tomsovic 1976). Closed groups are formed in inpatient settings with 10 to 16 members for two to three months of daily meetings. Leaders use the method of sensitivity training to structure the groups (Blagooyen 1974). Most report a greater cohesion, trust, and intensity of feeling expression in such groups. An important variant is the Marathon Encounter group, which uses aggressive confrontation to break down denial and rationalization. These groups for eight to 12 members with three to five therapists can run as long as 60 hours. This type of group should be optional and only for patients with good ego functions and average intelligence.

Psychodrama Groups

Psychodrama seems to have many benefits to alcoholics as an adjunct to a larger treatment program. It is action-oriented, stressing catharsis and role playing rather than other more verbal psychotherapies (Blume 1977). Psychodrama cuts directly into the alcoholic's isolation from others and from his or her own feelings. In the hands of a well-trained director, structured enactment involves the group around the significant events in an individual's life, which are played out. There is not much confrontation, but feedback, role reversal, and alter egos are utilized as techniques. These groups are often intense and high on the variable of immediacy, thus requiring a well-trained leader. Results in modifying habitual reactions and emotions are reported to be good.

Rogerian Groups

Although more popular in earlier decades, group therapy run according to the principles of client-centered therapy is often a part of alcoholism treatment programs. Clients provide the material, and the leader empathically reflects the process of the group as well as the content and feeling tone of the communications (Ends and Page 1957).

Rational Groups

Suitable for inpatient or outpatient groups, the teaching of the principles of rational thinking and problem solving can be done in groups with lay or professional leaders (Brandsma et al. 1980). These groups emphasize how cognition (self-talk) controls feelings and behavior, and helps alcoholics retrain themselves to think rationally through written, behavioral, and imagery homework assignments. Videotapes and extensive group discussions are also utilized. A meld of rational thinking techniques plus self-applied behavioral methods help alcoholics to change their self-destructive patterns.

Reality Therapy Groups

Reality therapy attempts to help alcoholics fulfill their basic needs for love and worth in more realistic ways. Therapists and groups members attempt to "get involved" with each other to "face reality" and then work out behavioral contracts in order to become more responsible (Bratter 1974).

Group Behavioral Therapy

This is an educational kind of group involving 10 members for 10 weeks, 90 minutes per week. Significant others are invited to attend. A 10-chapter textbook has been developed as a guide to weekly teaching and discussion. Before the program begins, there is an intake interview, an orientation meeting, and two weeks of keeping baseline data. The outcome goal is moderation (controlled drinking); the content of the program is oriented toward self-reinforcement, stimulus control, functional analysis, relaxation, and behavioral alternatives (Miller et al. 1981b). Important adjuncts or programs in their own right are group assertiveness training (Adinolfi et al. 1976) and social skills training (Frye et al. 1981), which teach alcoholics to resist social pressure to drink. The group provides a more realistic modeling, peer pressure, and better generalization effects (Hedberg and Campbell 1974).

Institutionally-Based Self Help

It has also been demonstrated that a self-help model can be incorporated into an institutional treatment regimen, and that these can in turn complement AA involvement. Patient-led self-help groups thereby become part of the treatment regimen. Institutionally-based large groups in the self-help modality serve to induce behavioral changes in the patient by providing the alcoholic with a sense of affiliation and a new system of beliefs (Galanter 1984; Galanter et al. 1987).

Aftercare Groups

Many inpatient programs provide supportive aftercare groups for their discharged alcoholic patients with mixed results. These groups facilitate the transition back into the community and may be a place for referral to other resources (Dubourg 1969; Hunt and Azrin 1973). In Europe, community or industry "clubs" are quite popular and seem to fulfill much the same role (Despotovic and Milosavcevic 1967).

The Outcome Issues

Group psychotherapy as a treatment modality for alcoholics has become exceedingly popular in the past three decades, but there are unresolved issues:

> Many treatment agencies continue to employ pedestrian and poorly described group techniques as a primary treatment approach. The pervasive dominance of these eclectic group techniques, whose superiority as a treatment approach in alcoholism has never been satisfactorily demonstrated, remains unexplained. They are part of the rich folklore of alcoholism and appear to possess an internal dynamic provocative of unquestioning loyalty in both therapist and alcoholic. (Swinner 1979)

Although there is much literature consisting of descriptive and anecdotal reports, some with process or attendance data, there is much less with outcome or follow-up data and very few studies with adequate research design. From a scientific perspective, there are several problems of inadequate specification, control, standardized measurements, and replication. Beyond these problems, the research often suffers from the conceptual problem of viewing alcoholism as a unitary phenomenon. However, with regard to scientific merit, group therapy research with the alcoholic population is very similar to critiques of group therapy research in general (Bednar and Kaul 1978; Parloff and Dies 1977).

All reviews echo the same refrain:

1. Patient variables should be specified in more detail.
2. Multiple measures of therapeutic change should be employed.
3. Control techniques and follow-up procedures are lacking.
4. Treatments should be specified and not combined with components of other aspects of a program.
5. Outcomes must be related in some way to drinking behavior.

No sweeping generalizations can be made about the efficacy of any specific group treatment method for alcoholism. However, we can point to clinical issues that are highlighted in the specific research on group treatment with alcoholic populations (Brandsma and Pattison 1985).

1. Group therapy is usually embedded with other programmatic aspects of treatment, which makes it impossible to evaluate in itself. Does it add anything to treatment programs? Kish and Hermann (1971) would strongly suggest that it does not. Adding 16 hours of group therapy to their two-month inpatient program did not add to their improvement rates significantly. Nor when they looked at other Veterans Administration programs having 64 or 120 hours of group therapy did it seem to increase the overall abstinence rates significantly over a 12-month follow-up. The other programs they refer to are Pokorny et al. (1968) and Tomsovic (1976). However, Gerard and Saenger (1966) found that a group facilitated maintenance of contact with an outpatient clinic and that long-term patients that received either group or individual therapy were equal in their therapeutic outcome.
2. Does group therapy appear to increase intake compliance? Both Gallant et al. (1966) and Levinson (1979) reported better dispositions and compliance when intake groups were employed.
3. Is group therapy success an artifact of having better motivated and activated patients at the outset? A patient's ability to tolerate more intensive therapy and the

patient's capacity to participate may be responsible for the positive results rather than group effect per se (Browne-Mayers et al. 1978; Wood et al. 1978; Yalom et al. 1978).

4. Do certain types of groups have specific positive effects? The answer to this is a resounding yes for marital couples groups (Arieli 1981; Cadogan 1972; Corder et al. 1972); for assertion training (Adinolfi et al. 1976; Hirsch et al. 1978); for self-control (Miller et al. 1981); for ego strength (McGinnis 1963); for self-concept (Ends and Page 1957, 1959; Tomsovic 1976), although also predictive of relapse to drinking (Heather et al. 1975); and for mood problems, such as anxiety and depression (Forrest 1975; Hoy 1969). It seems clear that group therapy targeted toward specific behavioral referents has a high probability of improving those specific problem areas.

5. Does group therapy affect drinking behavior? The data are equivocal. A number of studies reported abstinence or improvement rates of between 15 and 53 percent (Fisher et al. 1979; Pokorny et al. 1968, 1973; Westfield 1972; Wolff 1968). This is within the range reported for other inpatient and outpatient programs. Whether or not group therapy adds to drinking improvement is still open to question because the design of these studies cannot partial out these effects. The comparative study by Ends and Page (1957) indicated that certain types of group therapy do better than others on this variable after an 18-month follow-up.

6. Does group therapy have multiple effects on drinking, work, and social functioning? Pokorny et al. (1968, 1973) and Rathod et al. (1966) indicated that this is a good possibility.

7. Should patients be selected for group psychotherapy? We would answer this in the affirmative, citing a negative selection example wherein only 8 percent of a skid row population were successful (Gallant et al. 1968) and targeted behavioral groups with prisoners acquiring a good self-image as a positive selection example (Annis 1979; Annis and Chan 1983).

To reiterate, we briefly restate the clinical problems in this research:

1. Group therapy methods are not separated from other treatment modalities.
2. Single outcome measures are most often employed.
3. Investigators fail to distinguish between process, outcome, and follow-up measures.
4. There is a notable lack of controls.
5. There is generally a lack of specification of the type of group method employed.
6. There is generally a lack of comparison of types of groups.
7. The relationship to drinking behavior is usually not identified.

In sum, despite the scientific problems, we would like to state that considering the state-of-the-art of empirical research, there seems to be decent clinical, face, and some empirical validity to group therapy as a valuable addition to treatment or as a part of a program. The preponderance of evidence is in a positive direction and supports clinical, anecdotal conclusions but lacks robust and substantive empirical validation.

Group therapy may not be the treatment of choice for alcoholism, but seems to have relevant efficacy for specific target areas of dysfunction.

Conclusion

It is obvious that there are a wide variety of group methods that can and are being used. In the initial stages of detoxification, many alcoholics have neuropsychological deficits and thus cannot engage in intense psychotherapy; management-supportive groups are most useful at this point. Later many alcoholics view alcohol as "the problem" and are resistant to individual self-exploration. In behavioral groups, the focus of content will be on the problem, so it may be a more acceptable treatment modality to alcoholics. Since alcoholism problems are always embedded in a social context, the problematic social cues are often difficult to elicit in individual psychotherapy, whereas psychodynamic and interactional group therapy may evoke the drinking cues and problematic personal and interpersonal behaviors. No doubt, certain kinds of alcoholics are amenable to individual forms of psychotherapy, but group methods offer a larger panorama of access approaches to therapy for the individual alcoholic. There are insufficient research data to discuss the relative benefits or liabilities of any of the group methods described herein. Nevertheless, more than 30 years of clinical experience with group methods has demonstrated the clinical viability and utility of group treatment.

Chapter 120

Behavior Therapy

Simplistically defined, behavior modification is the systematic application of principles derived from learning theory to the rational modification of undesirable behavior. Therefore, the application of learning principles concentrates on the behavior itself and attempts to attack deviant behavior directly, focusing primarily on current behavior patterns rather than underlying dynamics or past history. Basic to this approach is that all behaviors, no matter how diverse, are subject to the same psychological principles of learning.

Within the context of the behavioral approach, excessive drinking is seen as a learned response that is acquired according to the same principles as any other response and that is shaped and maintained because of its rewarding consequences. Since the emphasis is on current behavior rather than historical causes, regardless of why excessive drinking originated, the therapeutic intervention is concentrated mainly on patients' current behavior when they present for treatment. The emphasis is on changing the behavior rather than understanding it.

Behavioral techniques share with more dynamic forms of therapy detailed history taking, the expectancy of the patient, the relationship between therapist and patient, suggestion, persuasion, and encouragement. In addition, the emphasis is on a precise and detailed behavioral analysis of the immediate circumstances that relate to drinking, carefully graded training programs, and specific schedules of positive or negative reinforcement, all of which are discussed with the patient and carried out as a joint venture between therapist and patient, rather than imposed on the patient.

Aversion Therapy

In this form of treatment, a conditioned stimulus (CS), alcohol, is presented with an unconditioned stimulus (UCS), electric shock or noxious chemical, until a conditioned response (CR), pain, nausea, or anxiety, follows when the conditioned stimulus is presented alone.

Electrical Aversion Treatment Procedures

Patients are presented with slides or pictures of alcoholic drinks, and with the actual sight of bottles of spirits, wine, or beer, and asked to smell and taste these beverages. Electric shock is administered during the tasting and smelling on the premise that the subsequent smelling or tasting of alcohol will become associated with the pain. Some experimenters have used slightly different procedures where the patient is asked to drink the alcohol but can terminate the shock if the alcohol is spit out; in other cases the patient may avoid shock altogether.

Electrical aversion therapy originally seemed a reasonable procedure both on theoretical grounds and on the grounds that it was technically superior to other forms of aversion therapy because the technique enabled greater precision both in the control of the subjective pain threshold of the patient and the time between the administration of alcohol and the subsequent shock. While the theoretical basis could not be demonstrated in the clinical trials using these procedures, there were interesting aspects in that some patients who had undergone this form of treatment reported changes in their perception of their problems and motivation to stop drinking. However, if these cognitive changes are produced in some patients by the use of electrical aversion, it might be better to develop strategies for eliciting these changes in ways other than subjecting patients to the kind of pain and distress inherent in electrical aversion procedures.

There are at least 22 studies that indicate that the addition of electrical aversion therapy does not enhance the results of a treatment program (e.g., Caddy and Lovibond 1976; Miller 1977; Vogler et al. 1975).

Both on ethical grounds and on the practical grounds it appears that treatment efficacy has not been demonstrated when electrical aversion is used as the main modality of treatment or as part of a broad spectrum treatment program.

Chemical Aversion

Chemical agents have also been used as the noxious stimulus in the aversive control of excessive drinking behavior. In contrast to electrical aversion, these drugs present particular problems when applied in the treatment situation.

Disulfiram—a drug that leads to nausea, vomiting, tachycardia, marked drop in blood pressure, and other symptoms of massive autonomic arousal if followed by the ingestion of alcohol—is widely used as a treatment agent, with varying degrees of effectiveness. Some mild conditioned aversion to alcohol consequent on disulfiram treatment has been reported. However, the process involved is not a matter of establishing associations between stimulus and response where none existed before, but results as a direct pharmacologic action of the drug. One of the problems in the use of disulfiram therapy is ensuring that patients who have been prescribed this course of treatment actually take their tablets. A method of behavioral contracting (Bigelow et al. 1976), which will be discussed more fully later, has been used successfully in connection with disulfiram treatment. Outpatient alcoholics were required to deposit funds with a clinic. They were repaid in small installments when they attended the clinic to receive their disulfiram. During the course of their contracts, patients not only showed substantial increase in clinic attendance but also showed substantial decrease in their drinking.

Emetine and apomorphine as aversive stimuli are much more difficult to control than electrical shock. Because of variable and fluctuating differences in individual response, there is considerable difficulty in controlling the timing between the administration of the drug and the onset of the nausea. Despite these theoretical considerations and practical considerations such as the distress to patients undergoing this form of treatment and such undesirable side effects as cardiac arrest and myocardial failure, some of the trials using these techniques have indicated surprisingly successful outcomes.

The research evidence indicates that with a group of highly motivated, well-educated, middle-class patients, emetic aversion therapy, in conjunction with a therapeutic milieu, community involvement, and regular booster sessions, can be extremely effective in modifying excessive drinking (Lemere 1947; Lemere and Voegtlin 1950; Wiens et al. 1976). However, with individuals whose drinking history is relatively short, who are under 30 years of age, or who are not educated nor of high socioeconomic status, chemical aversion techniques produce discouraging results (Boland et al. 1978; Cannon and Baker 1981; Lemere 1947; Lemere and Voegtlin 1950; Neuberger et al. 1980).

Verbal Aversion: Covert Sensitization

In covert sensitization, the noxious stimulus is aversive verbal imagery rather than electrical shock or chemical agents. The patient is first taught relaxation, and then asked to visualize very clearly alcohol and scenes involving alcohol. As each scene is visualized, the patient is instructed in very graphic and explicit terms to imagine step-by-step the onset of violent nausea and vomiting, so that the scenes involving alcohol become strongly associated with nausea.

Practically, there seem to be advantages to using covert sensitization as a form of aversion therapy because it does not require elaborate equipment, it is less traumatic than electrical aversion, and it does not involve the possible serious consequences to health as do chemical aversion techniques. Then too, patients are taught a technique that may be practiced and used outside the treatment situation and thus may be self-administered. However, the powerful visual imagery that is required may be difficult for some patients to create at will as may be the appropriate intensity of emotional response required.

There is insufficient evidence to assess the efficacy of covert sensitization either alone or in conjunction with other procedures. Four studies (Ashem and Donner 1968; Elkins 1977; Elkins and Murdoch 1977; Maletzky 1974) indicated covert sensitization procedures were more effective than other treatments, whereas two others (Fleiger and Zingle 1973; Piorkowsky and Mann 1975) reported no differences. In those studies where significant results were obtained, one consistent finding is that patients treated with covert sensitization were more likely to resume controlled drinking rather than abstinence.

Contingency Management and Contingency Contracting

Contingency management procedures are based on the assumption that the consequences of any given behavior govern the probability of continuing that behavior. The first step is to identify the target behavior to be controlled. The second is to find effective reinforcers that are sufficiently powerful not only to modify that behavior but also to diminish the value of the reinforcers that are maintaining that behavior. Essentially, this is a scientific reiteration of the simple, but apparently correct, principle that people will act in such a way as to maximize the rewards and minimize either the punishments or loss of rewards in their lives. This is what makes the continuation of excessive drinking so difficult to understand. Well before they come into treatment, alcoholics have usually been subject to powerful contingencies associated with their drinking behavior. Yet it is surprising how ineffective such serious consequences as marital breakdown, loss of job, social isolation, and even imprisonment can be in the modification of alcohol abuse.

The most interesting application of contingency-management procedures has been developed in a "community reinforcement" program in Baltimore (Hunt and Azrin 1973). The inpatient treatment consisted of specific behavior training focused on the improvement of long-standing vocational, interpersonal, and family problems. Role playing, behavioral rehearsal, and cognitive restructuring of perceptions, attitudes, and beliefs about the appropriateness of certain behavior were among the techniques used. In addition, an experienced behavioral clinician contracted with each patient in setting specific goals, helped them to find jobs (and trained them in letter writing and interview behavior), aided in restructuring rewarding social activities, and was directly involved in marital counseling and other means of improving family relationships. Once the patient could deal more effectively with family, job, and friends and experienced these as rewarding, these newfound reinforcers were incorporated into a contingency-management program. A six-month aftercare phase was then introduced, during which time frequent home visits were made to help the alcoholic strengthen the value of these rewarding gains, access to hospital facilities was made available, and so on, all made contingent on sobriety.

In a further modification (Azrin 1976), disulfiram was given to all clients to reduce the likelihood of impulsive drinking, which would dilute the effectiveness of the contingency contract. Behavioral efforts were made to teach clients to view the use of disulfiram as a positive step in helping them maintain the gains of treatment. An "early warning" system was introduced so that clients' family, friends, and employers reported regularly to the counselor, particularly if there were drinking or other incipient problems. A neighborhood "buddy" was elected and trained for peer counseling for continuing social support before and after professional counseling stopped. Finally, to reduce the amount of professional time involved, small groups were set up to include two to four clients, their spouses, and their peer counselors.

Contingency contracting has also been applied to a group of chronic, debilitated alcoholics, who were selected from a group of "public drunkenness offenders" while they were still in prison (Miller 1975). These men were provided with a broad range of goods and services in exchange for their demonstration of successful attempts to control their drinking when they were released from prison. Special arrangements were made to house and feed the men; efforts were made to get them work; medical assistance was provided where needed; coupons were provided for clothing, cigarettes, and meals; and the men received counseling sessions geared to practical advice. During the time these contingencies were in force, the men were tested for blood alcohol level at unpredictable intervals in their natural environment. If their blood alcohol level exceeded 10 mg/100 ml at any time, the goods and services were withheld for five days. The giving and withdrawing of goods and services contingent on blood alcohol level was far more effective than simply supplying these services without making them contingent on appropriate drinking behavior.

Hunt and Azrin (1973) found that patients who had gone through a community reinforcement program spent significantly less time drinking, unemployed, or in institutional care than patients in a control group who had received the standard hospital program. Using the modified program, Azrin (1976) reported similar results. Miller (1975) reported that the 10 debilitated, chronic alcoholics who received goods and services on a contingency basis significantly reduced their rate of drinking and number of arrests, while significantly increasing time spent in employment.

Bigelow et al. (1973, 1976) found substantial improvement in drinking behavior, job performances, and clinic attendance using contingency contracting in connection with disulfiram.

The apparent success of contingency management and contingency contracting begins to shed some light on why alcoholics continue to drink when faced with the dire consequences of their behavior. Spouses, employers, and others rarely adhere to the contingencies as rigorously or as consistently as they should for maximum effectiveness. Contingencies are effective only when they are specifically articulated, based on mutual agreement between the patient and the clinician, carefully observed, and rigorously carried out.

Broad-Spectrum Treatment Approaches

With the growing realization of the complexities of alcoholism and the recognition that no single form of treatment was going to provide clinicians with the "magic cure," broad-spectrum or multimodel behavioral treatment programs have been developed in the last decade. These broad-spectrum programs include a variety of behavioral techniques designed to change intrapersonal and interpersonal behavior as well as drinking. The community reinforcement program described above is one example of the broad-spectrum approach. Other broad-spectrum "packages" have included the following: 1) sessions where prior circumstances precipitating excessive drinking are defined and the individual is trained in alternative, socially acceptable responses to these situations; 2) aversion therapy administered contingent on appropriate drinking behavior (i.e., diluting, sipping, spacing drinks, and stopping after three drinks); 3) video tape confrontation while sober and while drunk; 4) education sessions to teach basic facts about alcohol consumption and to explain a treatment rationale based on drinking as learned behavior; 5) social skills training; 6) assertiveness training, and 7) relaxation training. Some broad-spectrum programs have included also a form of contingency contracting that required outpatients to pay all treatment fees in advance and also to pay a "commitment fee," which could be earned back if the patients rigorously adhered to treatment instructions, regularly attended all treatment sessions, and committed themselves to follow-up procedures.

Broad-spectrum behavioral treatment programs have been shown to reduce ethanol consumption significantly (Pomerleau 1978; Sobell and Sobell 1978; Vogler et al. 1975) over conventional treatment programs. Caddy et al. (1978) and Alden (1978) found multimodal treatment programs more effective than behavioral self-control training (below) or narrower versions of the same program (Caddy and Lovibond 1976). However, Vogler et al. (1977) reported that patients given only alternative training, behavioral counseling, and alcohol education were as successful as groups given the multimodal package, which required twice the length of treatment time.

While these broad-spectrum behavioral treatment programs have in general showed superior results to conventional forms of treatment, the cost effectiveness of expensive broad-spectrum treatments over streamlined programs has not yet been demonstrated. Tailoring the package to the individual rather than vice versa may yet prove the most effective means of achieving successful treatment.

Behavioral Self-Control and Other Cognitive Therapies

This approach is based specifically on the theory that cognition governs emotions. Thus by altering cognitions, perceptions, attitudes, and beliefs, the cognitive control over drinking behavior will lead to long-term treatment effectiveness. Programs utilizing this model concentrate on goal setting; specific information about the effects of varying levels of alcohol consumption on the body; external cue blood alcohol concentration training (i.e., teaching the behavioral effects of various quantities of alcohol); self-monitoring of alcohol consumption by the client; training to teach diluting, sipping, spacing, and stopping; and training designed to teach coping skills other than using alcohol.

Behavioral self-control training and other cognitive therapies have been successful in moderating the drinking of problem drinkers, particularly where controlled drinking may be an alternative goal of therapy rather than abstinence only (Alden 1978; Miller 1978; Miller et al. 1980, 1981; Pomerleau et al. 1978; Vogler et al. 1977).

Miller and Joyce (1979) found that individuals who attained controlled drinking successfully 1) had lower alcohol consumption at intake, 2) had less family history of alcoholism, 3) had less severe problem drinking, 4) were more likely to be female, and 5) were less likely to identify themselves as alcoholics. Sanchez-Craig et al. (1983) compared a cognitive behavioral program, with early-stage problem drinkers assigned randomly to abstinence or controlled drinking. Their results indicated that no significant differences were found between the two groups on alcohol consumption over a two-year follow-up. They suggested that controlled drinking is a more suitable goal for early problem drinkers.

Relapse Prevention: Cue Exposure and Coping Skills Training

With the recognition that while treatment in the short term may be effective, it is the high rate of relapse subsequent to treatment that is of ultimate concern. There has been recent emphasis on relapse prevention strategies. Among these strategies is the teaching of alternative coping behaviors to prevent relapse. Litman et al. (1978, 1983) found that the strongest discriminator between relapses and survivors in the group they studied was the use of cognitive control as an effective coping behavior. Sanchez-Craig (1975, 1976) described methods for teaching coping skills that included cognitive restructuring and covert rehearsal. Chaney et al. (1978) and Intaglia (1978) reported success in coping skill training with alcoholic patients.

Cue Exposure

Cue exposure is based on a conditioning model that suggests that drinking in the alcoholic is frequently reinforced by the avoidance of unpleasant consequences and that these avoidance responses are triggered by certain cues, particularly alcohol itself. The technique consists of prolonged exposure to alcohol cues (e.g., sight, smell), with the patient prevented from drinking alcohol and thus prevented from achieving the effect of the drug. Theoretically, this should extinguish craving and reduce the likelihood of relapse.

Hodgson and Rankin (1976) reported successful use of this technique in a single case study. Cooney et al. (1983) reported the use of this technique along with coping skills training (see above) but no outcome results were given. Blakely and Baker (1980) described cases in which patients were gradually exposed to a variety of cues, including trips to pubs. At the end of treatment, which involved as many as 40 exposure trials, patients reported no desire to drink. Five of the six patients continued to be abstinent at two to nine months follow-up.

Conclusion

When appropriately applied, behavioral programs appear to be effective and cost efficient.

Chapter 121

Office Management

The Target Population and the Choice of Clinical Approach

Once the diagnosis of alcohol abuse or dependence has been made, the clinician must next consider whether a patient falls into a large class of alcohol-dependent patients whose treatment may be undertaken in office practice by a practical multimodality approach to management. I will describe the approach below. This class of patients is characterized by the following clinical hallmarks of addictive illness, which are specifically relevant to the treatment model to be described. First, when they initiate consumption, these patients frequently cannot limit intake to a reasonable and predictable level, a problem that has been termed loss of control; although their drinking may be moderate on many occasions, at other times it becomes excessive and damaging, despite their desire for moderation. Second, if they have even attempted to decrease or terminate their drinking, they have consistently relapsed to heavy use; often the relapse is entirely unexpected, while at other times it may be foreseen by the patient, even planned and rationalized. Clearly these patients are best assured of stability when their abstinence from alcohol is assured for the long-term.

From this group of patients, whose treatment is considered here, we exclude both the less severe and the profoundly disabled abusers. An aggressive treatment approach, one directed at abstinence, is therefore not necessary for those abusers who can, in fact, learn to set limits on their alcohol use. For them, abuse may be treated as a behavioral symptom in a more traditional fashion using insight or behavioral therapy. For some, nonabstinent goals may be considered if a sound therapeutic contact is achieved (Pattison 1976).

Office management is also not the best way to initiate treatment for those patients whose addictive pattern is unmanageable from the outset, such as those with a history of long and frequent binges, those who cannot make an initial commitment to initiate abstinence, or others with unusual destabilizing circumstances (e.g., homelessness, severe character pathology, psychosis). These patients may need special inpatient supportive care, such as detoxification and intensive residential rehabilitation (see Chapter 122).

For the population whose treatment is discussed below, it is essential to rely on acquired clinical experience, but it is equally important, when necessary, to depart from the usual mode of psychotherapeutic treatment. For example, activity rather than passivity is essential when a problem of alcohol dependence is likely; the concept of therapist and patient enclosed in an inviolable envelope must be modified. Immediate circumstances that may expose the patient to alcohol must always take precedence over issues of long-term understanding and insight. These principles are applicable within the multimodality technique to be outlined, one that represents a viable approach (but certainly not the only one) to office treatment of most alcohol-dependent patients.

This approach is directed at assisting the patient in maintaining abstinence because the weight of clinical experience supports the view that abstinence is the most practical goal to propose for rehabilitation of the person addicted to alcohol (Gitlow and Peyser 1980; Zimberg 1982). Although many patients will accept this option initially, the therapist must assure the provision of necessary social supports for a stable abstinence to be achieved. I will describe here how a long-term support network is initiated for this purpose, by means of integrating a number of modalities, including the availability of the therapist, significant others, Alcoholics Anonymous (AA), and disulfiram use.

Establishing a Support Network

The issue of assuring abstinence should be addressed from the outset of treatment. Active engagement in a social support network constitutes one way of stabilizing this, and the technique described here offers one approach to assuring the success of this component of treatment (Galanter 1984). There are certain considerable advantages in introducing the participation of members of the patient's natural support network from the outset of the therapeutic contact because a well-orchestrated support for abstinence over time can lead the network to serve as an agent for negative reenforcement of the urge to drink, as well as for the provision of practical assistance. For example, the patient can be asked to bring his or her spouse or a close friend to the first or second session. Since alcoholic patients may deny or rationalize even if they have voluntarily sought help, input from a significant other is invaluable in both history taking and drawing up a viable treatment plan. A close relative or friend can often cut through the patient's denial in the way that an unfamiliar therapist cannot and can thereby be invaluable in setting a standard of realism in dealing with the addiction.

Some patients make clear that they wish to come to the initial sessions on their own. This is often associated with their desire to preserve the option of continued alcohol use and is born out of the fear that an alliance will be established independent of them to prevent this. While a delay is acceptable for a session or two, there should be no ambiguity when using this approach that effective treatment will be undertaken on the basis of a therapeutic alliance that includes the support of significant others and that a network of family and/or close friends will be brought in within a session or two at the most.

Establishing the full support network is a task that requires the active collaboration of patient and therapist. Both may be aided by those parties who join the network initially and must search for the right balance of members. This process is not without problems, and the therapist must think in a strategic fashion, carefully promoting the choice of appropriate network members. Heavy alcohol or drug use in a network member, for example, may lead that member to deny the patient's problems along with his or her own. The patient's spouse, roommate, close relatives, and friends are among the candidates. Membership ranges from one to several persons close to the patient.

It is important that the network be forged into a working group to provide necessary support for the patient between the initial sessions. Contacts between network members at the early stages typically include telephone calls (usually at the patient's initiative) and social contacts and should be preplanned as indicated by the patient's relative stability during the initial joint sessions. These encounters are therefore most often undertaken at a time when alcohol use is likely to recur. In planning together, however, it should be made clear to network members that relatively little undue effort will be required for the long term and that after the patient is stabilized, their participation will come to little more than attendance at joint sessions with the patient and therapist.

A pattern of network sessions closely tied to the patient's clinical status must be established. At the outset of therapy, it is important to see the patient with the family or network on a weekly basis, for at least the first month. Unstable circumstances may demand more frequent contacts with the network. Sessions can be tapered off to biweekly and then monthly or bimonthly intervals after a time and take place in the context of ongoing individual contacts.

This approach raises the issues of confidentiality. The terms of this aspect of the therapeutic contract should be made clear. They include open communication on matters regarding alcohol, but the therapist must set the proper tone of mutual trust and understanding so that the patient's right to privacy is not otherwise compromised. Full confidentiality, therefore, applies to all other (i.e., nonalcohol-related) communications between therapist and patient.

Introducing AA and Disulfiram

AA has been shown to be a successful adjunct to professional care (Emrick et al. 1977). Use of this important self-help modality is desirable, whenever possible. One approach is to tell patients at the outset that they are expected to attend at least two AA meetings a week for a trial period of one or two months, so as to familiarize themselves with that program. During this period, more active ongoing involvement is encouraged for continuing membership. The therapist may also solicit assistance from the support network in order to continue encouraging patient involvement with AA.

It often takes a considerable period of time, but ultimately many patients become closely associated with AA; they adopt the group ethos and express a deep commitment to abstinence, a measure of commitment rarely observed in alcoholic patients who experience psychotherapy alone. When this occurs, the therapist may assume that a good portion of the network's support function has been taken up by AA, but the therapist should still continue with network meetings at intervals.

For the alcoholic, disulfiram (Antabuse) may also be a very useful tool in assuring abstinence, but it is valuable only when it is carefully integrated into an ongoing therapeutic process (Fuller and Wilford 1980). The therapist may use the initial telephone contact to engage the patient's agreement to be abstinent from alcohol for the day immediately prior to the first session. The therapist then has the option of prescribing or administering disulfiram at the first session. For a patient who is in earnest about seeking assistance for alcoholism, this brief period of abstinence is usually not difficult if some time is spent on the phone helping the patient make plans to avoid the contexts in which the patient drinks during that period. If it is not feasible to undertake this on the phone, it may be addressed at the first session. Such planning with the patient will almost always involve organizing time with significant others, and therefore may serve as a basis for developing the patient's support network. Strategically, it is advantageous to specify the period of time for taking disulfiram at the outset of the therapy; this may be one year and may then be renewable if thought helpful by both therapist and patient.

The administration of disulfiram under observation during the initial months is another treatment option that is easily adapted to work with a family of social networks. A patient who takes disulfiram cannot drink; one who agrees to be observed by a responsible party, a family or network member, when taking disulfiram each morning will not miss the dose without the observer's knowing. This may take a measure of persuasion and, above all, the therapist's commitment to the idea that such an approach can be reasonable and helpful. The observer should be instructed to notify the therapist if more than one dose is missed.

Disulfiram is typically initiated with one dose of 500 mg, and then 250 mg every morning (when the urge to drink is generally least). Particulars of administration and the nature of the disulfiram-alcohol reaction should be carefully reviewed with the patient (Ewing 1982).

The Ongoing Treatment and Relapse Prevention

Most individual (Heyman 1956) and family (Steinglass 1976) therapists see the alcohol- or drug-abuser as a patient with poor prognosis. This is largely because, in the context of traditional psychotherapy, there are no intrinsic behavioral controls to prevent the recurrence of alcohol use; limited resources are available to the therapist if a recurrence takes place, which it often does at some point or points after treatment is initiated. Unlike neurotic disorders and character pathology, in alcoholism unanticipated conditioned cues may trigger craving or drinking at unexpected times (Wikler 1973). Unlike psychotic disorders, the prodromal symptoms of relapse typically lead the patient to avoid help from the therapist, rather than turn to the therapist for relief.

A system of impediments to the emergence of relapse, resting heavily on both the actual and symbolic role of the support network, must therefore be established. The therapist must have assistance in addressing any minor episode of use or temptation to assure that this ever-present problem does not lead to an unmanageable relapse or an unsuccessful termination of therapy. The patient's abstinence is therefore supported and monitored by the therapist, patient, and selected family (or network) members, as a group. AA and disulfiram are also used. Finally, the patient is engaged concomitantly in a more traditional individual therapy.

Let us consider the network's ongoing role, and then the place of individual therapy. As conceived here, the therapist's relationship to the family or network is like that of a good manager rather than that of a family therapist. The network is established to implement a straightforward task, that of aiding the therapist to sustain the patient's abstinence. Competing and alternative goals must be suppressed or circumvented, but at the least prevented from interfering with the primary task. Active reworking of relationships in the network is rarely advisable, particularly if it detracts in any way from the primary task.

Unlike patients involved in traditional family therapy, network members are not led to expect symptom relief or self-realization. This prevents the development of competing goals for the network's meetings. It also assures the members' protection from having their own motives scrutinized, and thereby supports their continuing involvement without the threat of an assault on their own psychological defenses. Since network members have volunteered to participate, their motives must not be impugned; their constructive behavior should be commended. It is useful to acknowledge appreciation for the contribution they are making to the therapy. There is always a counterproductive tendency on their part to minimize the value of their contribution. The network must, therefore, be structured as an effective working group with good morale.

Each network session should begin with a review by the patient of all alcohol-related events since the last session. Patient, therapist, and network members should be charged with discussing together alcohol-related issues (e.g., dealing with upcoming events that might precipitate drinking) or changes in disulfiram regimen. The patient should come to internalize, as it were, the image of the collaboration with the network in thinking about alcohol. With the passage of time, this serves as a suppressant of alcohol-seeking behavior.

Since network sessions are generally scheduled on a weekly basis at the outset of treatment, this may compromise the number of individual contacts at first. Indeed, if therapy sessions are scheduled once a week, the patient may not be seen individually for a period of time. This may be perceived as a deprivation by the patient unless the individual therapy is presented as an opportunity for further growth predicated on achieving stable abstinence assured through work with the network.

When the individual therapy does begin, the traditional objectives of therapy must be prioritized so as to accommodate the goals of the alcohol treatment. Of first importance is the need to address exposure to substances of abuse, or exposure to cues that might precipitate alcohol or drug use (Galanter 1984). Both patient and therapist should be sensitive to this matter, label the cues to drinking behavior, and explore the related situations as they arise; the patient must be trained to recognize cues and contexts that precipitate drinking or craving. Second, a stable social context in an appropriate social environment—one conducive to abstinence with minimal disruption of life circumstances—should be encouraged. Considerations of even minor disruptions in place of residence, friends, or job cannot go untended with recovering addicted patients. For a considerable period of time, the alcoholic is highly vulnerable to recurrence of addictive behavior and must be viewed with considerable caution.

In addition to these priorities, the patient's rehabilitation and readaptation become increasingly important as stability is achieved. In the case of insight-oriented therapy, clarification of unconscious motivations is a primary objective; for supportive therapy, the bolstering of established defenses is primary.

Chapter 122

Inpatient Programs

Detoxification

Admission Criteria

Although many individuals spontaneously withdraw from chronic alcohol abuse without medical assistance, a significant number of persons require medically oriented detoxification. These include persons who: 1) have experienced severe withdrawal signs and symptoms following previous drinking episodes; 2) have increased volume and frequency of alcohol consumption during the current episode of drinking in comparison to past drinking history; 3) have alcohol- or nonalcohol-related intercurrent illness; 4) have a history of seizure disorders following cessation of drinking; 5) have affective disorders antecedent to or consequent on alcohol abuse where suicide may occur.

It is often difficult to predict the potential severity of alcohol withdrawal states by observation of the patient's behavior and health status during intoxication or shortly following cessation of drinking. Single or even multiple blood alcohol determinations during early withdrawal are not reliable predictors of severity and duration of withdrawal syndromes. Theoretically, patients with a high blood alcohol level should experience more severe withdrawal states than persons with relatively low blood alcohol levels, but this relationship is often not observed.

Demographic factors such as age, gender, ethnicity, or socioeconomic status are not strongly correlated with specific behavioral or biologic disorders associated with the withdrawal syndrome. Therefore, exclusionary admission criteria based on these factors are not medically justifiable. Finally, although most alcohol withdrawal syndromes are at maximal intensity eight to 24 hours following cessation of drinking, the most severe alcohol withdrawal states (delirium tremens) may peak 72 hours following induction of abstinence; seizure disorders (most frequent, 24 hours following abstinence) may occur at any time.

Since many medical problems may be initiated or exacerbated during alcohol withdrawal, relatively short-term hospitalization for alcohol detoxification may not only attenuate patient discomfort but may also result in prompt cost-effective intervention for potentially serious illness.

Pharmacotherapy

During the past two decades, major advances have been made in perfecting safe and effective pharmacotherapeutic regimens for alcohol withdrawal. These procedures, which have been described in detail elsewhere, will not be recapitulated in this brief overview. However, three controversial but important topics relating to pharmacotherapy for alcohol withdrawal will be discussed.

First, relatively new data indicate that many patients may be successfully treated without use of any pharmacotherapy procedures during alcohol withdrawal. These studies have been carried out in carefully monitored inpatient hospital settings, and it is quite clear that pharmacotherapy may not be required for a number of patients. But these data, which have probabilistic value, are often difficult to interpret when individual patient treatment decisions are necessary. Thus use of pharmacotherapy during detoxification should always be based on individualized case evaluation. Moreover, it should be appreciated that the efficacy of pharmacotherapy in alcohol withdrawal states should not be judged solely on drug-induced suppression of withdrawal signs (e.g., tremulousness). Equally important is the efficacy of pharmacotherapy for reducing subjective symptoms, which often include severe apprehension and anxiety during withdrawal.

The safety and efficacy of the benzodiazepines for treatment of symptoms and signs of alcohol withdrawal have been amply demonstrated in a variety of studies. Although there is some evidence that programmed alcohol administration can also effectively suppress withdrawal signs and symptoms, this form of pharmacotherapy has not achieved wide popularity. Perhaps the most important reason for not using alcohol to detoxify patients is the adverse effect of high-dosage alcohol administration on hepatic function, hematologic status, and gastrointestinal function. Present evidence indicates that judicious use of benzodiazepine drugs is probably superior to detoxification with alcohol because benzodiazepine dosage sufficient to attenuate withdrawal signs and symptoms does not produce tissue damage de novo or enhance derangements of organ function due to antecedent alcohol intake.

Decisions to initiate antidepressant therapy during or immediately following alcohol detoxification requires very careful and difficult judgments. Generally, administration of antidepressants should not be attempted until patients have been able to abstain from alcohol for a two- to four-week period. There is increasing evidence that severe depression may occur either antecedent to or following long-term alcohol abuse. Severely depressed patients may have a remission as a function of abstaining from alcohol. It is extremely difficult to ascertain the causal factors in depression when patients are acutely intoxicated or during the early phases of alcohol abstinence. The dexamethasone suppression test for the diagnosis of affective disorder may be compromised by the effects of alcohol and alcohol withdrawal on the hypothalamic-pituitary-adrenal axis.

As a general rule, pharmacotherapy for withdrawal symptoms per se should involve judicious use of benzodiazepines. As will be discussed later, pharmacotherapy for intercurrent medical disorders may also be necessary during detoxification, and overzealous or injudicious use of drugs during alcohol withdrawal states may impede adequate diagnostic evaluation of psychiatric and other medical disorders.

Adjunctive Medical Care

A major national survey carried out with more than 10,700 first hospital admissions for alcoholism treatment (most frequently for initial detoxification) revealed that a large number of patients had serious alcohol-related intercurrent illnesses that obviously require adjunctive medical care.

Facilities that provide detoxification services may not possess the full range of treatment modalities or adequate resources for basic diagnostic procedures for detecting serious medical disorders. All patients who enter detoxification should have a thorough physical examination, basic laboratory studies (biochemistry and hemograms), an electrocardiogram, and a urine drug screen to facilitate diagnosis of potential polydrug abuse. The detoxification unit should also have ready access to X-ray and other diagnostic procedures that are necessary. It is reasonable to assume that a majority of patients entering treatment for alcohol detoxification will have at least one other significant medical or psychiatric disorder that will require diagnostic exploration and prompt treatment.

Adjunctive Psychosocial Care

It is essential to begin psychosocial evaluations and intervention procedures early during detoxification because patients may be more willing to cooperate and participate actively during this time in contrast to later phases of treatment.

Two psychosocial factors have been found to be positively correlated with successful outcome for alcoholism treatment. The first favorable condition is one in which the patient has a spouse or another significant person who is directly concerned about and committed to support and help. Thus treatment facilities should establish contact and good rapport with this individual (or individuals) and initiate plans for programs of future patient care. A second important predictor for favorable outcome relates to the patient's employment status and work resources. Early during detoxification, plans should be formulated to facilitate job counseling or communication with potential employment resources. Although the duration of hospitalization for detoxification may be relatively short, good progress toward both of these goals is possible.

Discharge and Follow-Up

Because many patients admitted for detoxification will also have associated psychiatric disorders or intercurrent medical illness, it is essential to arrange for adequate follow-up treatment and consultation after discharge. In many instances, the most optimal and cost-effective medical strategy will involve direct transfer of the patient to an appropriate hospital or ambulatory treatment program. Although geographic contiguity between the detoxification and follow-up treatment facility is ideal, absence of this circumstance should not be used as a rationalization for lack of adequate follow-up procedures.

It is extremely important to recognize that patients often express the greatest motivation for affecting change in their drinking behavior and life-style during alcohol detoxification. During detoxification, patients tend to abandon (at least in part) denial, rationalization, and intellectualization previously employed to support their perpetuation of alcohol abuse.

While arrangements for follow-up procedures should always involve informed participation of the patient, full responsibility for making appropriate contacts for follow-up should not be delegated to the patient. The staff of the detoxification facility should attempt to make appropriate one-to-one contacts with other agencies and treatment resources to facilitate a smooth transition from detoxification to long-term aftercare assistance. Whenever possible, the detoxification facility should solicit informed consent from the patient for permission to obtain information on a periodic follow-up basis. Although economic and work-force constraints often make frequent periodic follow-ups difficult, even occasional recontact with the patient may be of great value.

Multimodality Treatment Programs

Admission Criteria

Although the range and scope of multimodality treatment programs are not necessarily dependent on where these programs are based (e.g., inpatient or ambulatory care facilities), some special considerations are necessary for selection of hospital versus residential facility care. Ideally, admission criteria for inpatient care should not be based on economic considerations nor should fiscal frugality constitute a major factor for recommending ambulatory care assistance. Admission criteria for inpatient or outpatient care must involve a thorough assessment of the patient's total life situation along with judgments about the risks, and benefits of hospitalization.

The admission criteria for inpatient care of patients with alcoholism and the selection of specific treatment modalities or combination of such is as difficult as any decision-making process in medical practice. For example, all patients with chest pain should not be hospitalized. All patients with recurrent angina should not be hospitalized. But the diagnostic and decision-making process that affords the greatest probability of reducing suffering and prolonging life for such patients and for patients with alcohol-related problems requires a combination of skill, experience, and compassion.

The major admission criteria for multimodality hospital or residential treatment for alcoholism should be based on a decision by the physician in concert with informed communication with the patient that this treatment plan would be of immediate best interest to the patient. Although there are a number of strong inclusion factors to support this decision (e.g., hospitalization essential for adequate treatment of intercurrent medical or psychiatric disorders), the establishment of exclusion criteria that have uniform applicability are virtually impossible.

Formulation of Therapeutic Programs

Many of the best inpatient treatment programs offer the widest range of therapeutic options. However, it could not be argued that all patients require all programs or that breadth may compensate for lack of program depth. The formulation of a therapeutic plan can only be accomplished after an adequate diagnostic evaluation of the patient's physical and mental status plus communication with clinical, social, and interpersonal resources for the patient (e.g., employer, spouse, significant other, and family and social network).

A major problem often encountered in current multimodality alcoholism treatment programs is the notion that some components of the program are absolutely essential. "Absolute essentials" of many programs become specific contingencies for patient care. For example, some programs insist on enrollment and participation in Alcoholics Anonymous meetings, interaction with other peer self-help groups, or disulfiram (Antabuse) therapy. It is assumed that some or all of these basics are minimum necessities that will not harm the patient even if they do not help.

At the present time, we should acknowledge that we do not know which therapy or which combination of therapies is the best for many patients. There are patients who will benefit from interaction with Alcoholics Anonymous, but there are also those who may not. There are patients who will benefit from group or individual psychotherapy and those who may be harmed. There are patients for whom didactic presentation of information about alcohol abuse and its problems will be beneficial;

for others, this activity will be virtually useless. How to decide what, for whom, and for how long involves development of consensus by the treatment team and the patient, a process that is regularly utilized in the best systems of psychiatric therapy. In short, the formulation of therapeutic programs for patients with alcoholism should be based on data derived from a comprehensive diagnostic workup, the availability of professional and technological resources for institution of therapy, and the patients' willingness to participate in treatment.

Coordination of Therapeutic Programs

There should be ongoing conferences, consultations, and meetings among the staff. While this situation undoubtedly causes some waste of valuable time, better coordination of resources will not only ultimately benefit the patient, but also improve the quality of resources themselves.

Open and honest coordination and interchange of information by treatment personnel can often uncover and obviate redundant endeavors. Finally, but no less important, coordination of therapeutic programs makes possible constructive critical input of members from the various disciplines contributing to the treatment network and also involves creative critical participation by patients themselves.

Discharge and Follow-Up Assessments

Much better criteria need to be developed for determining when and under what conditions discharge from inpatient facilities should take place. Currently, many hospital and residential care programs mandate that the patient remain in treatment for a specified period of time. The time specified is usually the same for all patients and determinants of the predetermined temporal interval appear to be related to the most optimal cost-reimbursement arrangements. Our current knowledge does not permit an a priori selection of the best contiguous time period for hospitalization. Judgment about severity of illness remains the best practical guide for predicting duration of hospitalization.

Residential Facilities Other Than Hospitals

Admission Criteria

Admission to half-way houses, day-care, or night-care programs usually follows detoxification and hospital treatment. Transitional care may be accomplished in many facilities without personnel or technological systems of medical or psychiatric hospitals. But initial admission to these units should take place only after very careful diagnostic screening to rule out serious medical and psychiatric illnesses. Unfortunately, decisions to admit to half-way houses, day-care, or night-care facilities may be based on history of recrudescence of illness. Recidivism or recrudescence should not mitigate against admission to full-care hospital units when such care is necessary.

Programmatic Features of Partial-Care Facilities
(Day-Care, Night-Care, Half-Way Houses)

Many of these units were originally developed for provision of quasi-custodial care for persons with limited fiscal and social resources. A more appropriate model should be based on the chronic care and rehabilitation hospitals, which have proved extremely valuable to American medicine. These facilities do much more than provide custodial care. They have been designed to facilitate the rehabilitation of patients with severe chronic illness, and their accomplishments are noteworthy.

Partial-care treatment programs for alcohol-related disorders should formulate and carry out treatment plans in a manner analogous to those utilized in full-care units. While these treatment plans may require fewer modalities and less complex intervention programs, they nevertheless should be carefully thought through and periodically reviewed and updated. Ongoing utilization review is a prerequisite for successful operation of these facilities, and requirements for humane care and professionalism should be no less stringent than those expected for the general or psychiatric hospital. In short, the ideals and goals of partial-care facilities should be more similar to the chronic rehabilitation hospitals for stroke victims rather than the soup kitchen or alms house model.

"Free-Standing" Alcoholism Treatment Facilities

A hybrid treatment facility that is neither hospital nor half way house is currently under development by a number of institutions, particularly proprietary health care providers. These units contain elements found in hospitals (e.g., medical evaluation, detoxification employing pharmacotherapy, and psychosocial counseling) as well as peer, occupational, and social assistance programs, which have often been utilized in aftercare programs. One major advantage of "free-standing" alcoholism treatment programs is their relatively low cost. However, the cost effectiveness of these facilities has yet to be determined. For example, although day-care costs may be less than hospitals, admission criteria may be more lax. In some free-standing facilities, the decision for patient admission is made by an alcoholism counselor. Clinical evaluation may occur only after admission; therefore, both biologic and psychological criteria, which ordinarily govern admission policies, may be compromised. These statements should not be interpreted as a condemnation of free-standing facilities for alcoholism treatment. Rather, it is suggested that these facilities receive careful professional and public scrutiny to ensure that their patients receive efficacious assistance.

Cost Effectiveness of Alcoholism Treatment

Among the many important factors that should be considered for assessing cost effectiveness of alcoholism treatment is the economic burden of untreated alcoholism. Conservative estimates indicate that alcoholism and alcohol-related problems cost Americans more than 50 billion dollars annually. This staggering impact on our nation's economy has no real counterpart in present-day public health economics. If infectious disease wrought the same degree of personal and economic havoc, public outcry would demand research and vigorous treatment programs to combat the problem.

Within the alcoholism field, there is good general consensus that alcohol abuse and alcoholism can be successfully treated. Although there are differences of opinion about the most efficacious procedures for alcoholism treatment, treatment of some kind has been judged to alleviate suffering and to save lives and money.

Virtually all studies to determine efficacy of alcoholism treatment based on assessment of outcome have been flawed by serious conceptual and methodological inadequacies. Because of these problems and because superiority of one form of alcoholism treatment (e.g., inpatient, outpatient) has not been demonstrated in limited studies, it has been erroneously assumed that less costly modes of treatment are as effective as more costly interventions.

At present, we should consider cost effectiveness for alcoholism treatment within the context of the best criteria for admitting patients into specific treatment modalities. By analogy, intensive care units are much more costly than general hospital wards, but it would be absurd to argue that intensive care units should be closed because they are not cost effective.

There is good evidence that cost effectiveness is achieved through most forms of alcoholism treatment and that the economic benefits derived impact not only on the patient but also on large segments of society. It should also be remembered, however, that it has only been three decades since the American Medical Association formally declared that alcoholism is an illness that deserves treatment by medical specialists and hospitals. The decriminalization of alcoholism per se occurred slowly and painfully. The stigmatization of the alcoholic never really disappeared.

It is essential that we continue to explore ways and means for achieving the most efficacious and least costly treatments for alcohol abuse and alcoholism. While we do possess some information that permits enlightened judgments, our general data base is poor. Research on outcome of alcoholism treatments must be improved and expanded. Objective and systematic assessments of existing and new treatment modalities must be carried out.

Chapter 123

Employee Assistance Programs

Prior to the 1940s, there were no employee assistance programs for those who had problems with alcohol or drug abuse. When these individuals could no longer conceal their alcohol or drug abuse problems, their employment was simply terminated. With the growing recognition that these problems were amenable to treatment and the realization of the cost to companies caused by wastage of trained workers through job termination, many companies set up employee assistance programs. The basic design of these programs was developed at the Yale Center of Alcohol Studies and became known as the Yale Plan. The Yale Plan was designed to discover the nature, extent, and cost of the problem within a given organization; to determine what proportion of those affected could be helped efficiently; to provide means for rehabilitation; and to develop increasingly sensitive measures to detect cases in earlier stages and, if possible, at the time of employment.

Employee assistance programs are specifically concerned with the rehabilitation of employees only where alcohol or drug abuse problems are impairing their job performance. An employee's choice of whether or not to drink or to use drugs is a personal matter with which the employer is not generally concerned. However, when drinking or drug abuse directly affects work performance, this then becomes relevant to the employer and suitable for official company intervention.

The Yale Plan design has been implemented in several ways. The most widely used approach is to set up a program to train management and union officials to identify employees with problems and to make proper use of the referral network that has been specified as part of company policy.

In the attempt to avoid the possibility of value judgments and social stigmatization, indications for referral are based on behavioral observations of work performance. Some of these indications include the following.

Work Performance

The supervisor is trained to look for such possible indications as lowered productivity or sporadic productivity, and mistakes due to carelessness or errors of judgment resulting in an increase in spoilage. Absence and poor time keeping will also have a bearing on the decrease in work output.

Absenteeism

Frequently, absenteeism may be the first indication that an employee may have a problem. Some of the signs are recurrent and unexplained absences; absences for trivial or inadequate reasons; frequent lateness; and repeated medical certificates for gastroenteritis or dyspepsia.

Personality Changes

Some of the indicators for referral are disruptive behavior, lethargy, frequent arguments with colleagues, general irritability, signs of confusion, or difficulties with concentration.

Accidents

Other indications of alcohol or drug problems may be frequent minor accidents both at and away from work, resulting in lost time. Others may be carelessness in handling or maintenance of equipment that results in accidents, breakdowns, and spoiled materials; a distinct lack of safety sense, which may be a threat not only to the individual concerned but also to others; and risk taking to increase work output after a period of poor achievement.

It is apparent that any of the above may be due to problems other than alcohol or drug abuse. The supervisor is trained to make a referral, but is cautioned *not* to make a diagnosis. Before the referral is made, the supervisor is asked to make careful observations of performance levels and to document accurately and specifically significant behavioral declines and changes in an employee's work pattern.

Once the supervisor has produced such a behavioral documentation indicating decline in work performance, subsequent action varies slightly, depending on the size of the company and its policies. However, the general procedure is for the immediate supervisor to confront the individual with evidence of poor performance to ascertain whether work performance can be corrected through their joint efforts. If this is not accomplished within a reasonable period of time, the employee is again confronted and at this point given the choice of referral to a treatment program or the risk of dismissal if there is no evidence of improved work performance.

If the company's structure is such that it has both an employee relations department and a medical department, the supervisor's first referral will usually be to the employee relations department, who screen those employees needing further care and refer them on to the medical department. If there is evidence of an alcohol or drug problem, the medical department will then refer the employee to a specially trained counselor who is either directly employed within the company or, more likely, acts as a consultant to the company. In some cases, employees may be given the option of receiving treatment from their own doctor.

Within this referral system, there are certain rules that should generally be followed. The first is that employees are made responsible for complying with referral and cooperating with the prescribed treatment, and are specifically notified that if they refuse referral or do not comply with treatment and if this lack of cooperation continues to affect job performance adversely, then they will be dismissed. On the other hand, employees must be assured of complete confidentiality. Supervisors must not discuss employees' problems except with members of the referral sources. Information concerning referral and counseling must be kept separately and should not be part of the employee's job records. While cooperation with referral and counseling procedures does not include special privileges or exemption from standard job performance requirements, employees must be assured that they will not jeopardize their jobs or promotional opportunities because they have undergone treatment.

One of the major advantages of occupational alcoholism and drug abuse programming is that individuals who have alcohol and drug abuse problems are no longer able to deny or manipulate. The "constructive confrontation" based on work deterioration generally precipitates a crisis that may serve to increase motivation for seeking help. Impressive progress has been made in the design, development, and implementation of these programs over the past years so that detection of early problem drinkers is more extensive.

However, there are still areas that need attention if employee assistance programs are to reach their full potential. One key concern is the gap between company policy and its implementation. The central individual in the referral system is the supervisor, who is trained to detect problems, confront the worker, and subsequently make the referral. Even after training, supervisors may be ambivalent and vacillate about whether or not to take action because of feelings about protecting individuals under their supervision or misguided responsibility in that referral to a program is somehow an admission of their own failure as supervisors. They may even be threatened because of their own alcohol abuse or drug taking. Union officials involved in referral programs may also be ambivalent because of what they may perceive as infringements of workers' rights. They may also find themselves in the ambiguous position of wanting to help the employee through referral to the program, while the possibility exists that they may also have to represent the employee is subsequent grievance procedures. Another reason for vacillation in referral may be the skid row stereotype of the alcoholic or drug-dependent individual. In their zeal to be seen to be doing their best for employees, companies may make available high status, medically based activities, with emphasis on detoxification, inpatient treatment, and medical management, which inadvertently propagates the stereotype of the alcoholic as one who is severely and obviously damaged. Thus the program is not seen as applicable to the less damaged, early problem drinker.

Another weak link in these programs is the identification and referral of individuals at the management and executive levels of organization. While theoretically the programs are meant to cover all employees, the position of the program coordinator within the organizational hierarchy determines who will be referred. If the individual who acts as program coordinator holds a job in the middle or lower levels of this hierarchy, the probability that anyone superior in rank will be identified officially or referred sharply decreases. Then too, the specification of impaired performance at the managerial and executive levels is far more ambiguous than for rank-and-file workers. Since there is some evidence to show that there is an association between higher corporate rank and increased problems with drinking (Roman 1975), this is becoming an increasingly serious problem. One solution proposed is to set up a two-tier system, with one program directed toward the workers below a certain rank in the organization and the other specialized program directed toward managers and executives.

Finally, there is some concern about whether employees are actually informed officially that such programs exists within their organization. Although research indicates there is little difference in outcome between self-referrals and those constructively confronted, one study of alcoholics from four industrial alcoholism programs indicated that only half of the 180 patients had actually heard of the program before they were referred and only four knew of it through such official channels as training or company-distributed materials (Heyman 1976).

Outcome Issue

The relative success of constructive confrontation versus self-referral has been reported in three studies, with conflicting results. Maberg (1974) found that at three-month follow-up individuals who had been coerced by their supervisors to accept rehabilitation referral were not associated with as much abstinence as the self-referred, although these results were not statistically significant. On the other hand, Smart (1974) found that there were no differences in the subsequent drinking behavior of voluntary and coerced patients at the rehabilitation units. To further obfuscate matters, Heyman (1976) found that although programs having the highest coercion score had only 59 percent of persons stating their performance had improved, when she looked at the combined results of four industrial alcoholism programs, significantly more of the highly coerced (67 percent) showed work improvement.

It is estimated that problems with alcohol affect 4 to 8 percent of the entire labor force (Roman 1975). While outcome results generally concur with the findings of Heyman (1976) in that about two thirds of those treated show improvement in job performance, it is obvious as well that recovery rates are not accurate measures of program success in that the true measure of program effectiveness is penetration. That is, what percentage of the employee population is being identified and referred to treatment? To date, there is no definitive research in this area.

Chapter 124

Community-Based Treatment

In this chapter, we will discuss community-based treatment resources for alcohol abuse and dependence and review selected studies on matching patient characteristics to particular services. The importance for the psychiatrist of maintaining a flexible approach is emphasized, with selection of the psychiatrist's role dependent on individual patient needs. The types of community service that we will review include outpatient treatment, drunken driver diversion, detoxification, shelter care facilities, half-way houses, therapeutic communities, and other self-help groups.

The distinction between the medical and psychiatric models of treatment and consideration of significant social factors can clarify the choice of community treatments for the alcoholic patient. Research data support a view of alcoholism treatment that broadens the disease model to include important interpersonal and social factors such as family adjustment, employment, and social stability. In addition, the sociology of patient selection of various treatment options has important implications for prognosis. The skilled therapist must appreciate where he or she is more accurate in predicting treatment outcomes and where the patient's preference represents the most effective selection of treatment alternatives.

An appreciation of the dichotomy between the addiction (medical) and psychodynamic (psychiatric) models is important for understanding the limitations of either approach. The addiction model defines alcoholism as a primary disorder in its own right. The therapist treats the addiction directly, is confrontational, and strictly against continued substance abuse. The responsibility for the treatment lies with the patient, who is encouraged or required to participate in self-help groups. Surveillance for compliance often is included, and coercion at times seems to be useful. Treatment goals include rehabilitation, but do not include a concept of cure. In contrast, the psychodynamic model defines alcoholism as a symptom of an underlying psychiatric disorder. The primary goal is to treat the underlying disorder with an individualized approach and some permissiveness. The professional is responsible for the treatment and may not encourage participation with self-help groups. Surveillance for compliance is avoided, and coercion is used only as a last resort (Atkinson 1984). An integrated model should include all relevant biopsychosocial factors and should give careful attention to individual patient needs. Hopefully, an integrated approach will avoid the risks of applying recipe treatment from the limitations of a narrower addiction or psychodynamic approach.

Outpatient Treatments

Within the past decade there has been significant growth of the variety of outpatient treatments for alcoholic patients. It is important to realize that our ability to prescribe precisely the most effective type of outpatient treatment for alcoholism is limited.

Therefore, our decisions often have been made in reference to the context for care rather than for a specific treatment approach. Furthermore, the most powerful argument for outpatient treatment lies with the lack of convincing results for additional effectiveness of inpatient treatment. Miller and Hester (1986) reviewed 26 controlled comparisons of inpatient alcoholism treatment and concluded that the results have consistently shown no overall advantage for residential over nonresidential settings, for longer over shorter inpatient programs, or for more intensive over less intensive interventions in treating alcohol abuse. However, many of the studies comparing outpatient with inpatient treatments have not controlled for patient choice, medication, and level of alcoholic dependence.

Various outpatient treatments include alcohol programs, community mental health centers, private outpatient and hospital clinics, and the office of the private practitioner. The type of service delivery system available to a patient may depend more on how the patient's alcoholism initially is identified by the community than on the patient's specific problem area. The entry into a particular system also is determined by socioeconomic class, patient preference for treatment programs with a specific cultural orientation, and unanticipated random events (e.g., an intoxicated driving offense). The Rand report of treatment history confirmed the general effectiveness of community treatment with a 70 percent improvement rate (Armor et al. 1976). However, in a review of 384 studies of psychologically oriented alcoholism treatment, Emrick (1975) demonstrated that specific differences in treatment methods did not significantly affect long-term outcome. He showed that more treated than nontreated alcoholics improved, suggesting that any formal treatment increased an alcoholic's chance of reducing drinking problems. Edwards et al. (1977) evaluated alcoholism rehabilitation by comparing a controlled trial of treatment to advice. In this study, two groups of alcoholics received either one counseling session or several months of inpatient and outpatient treatment. One year later there were no significant differences in outcome between the two groups. Obviously these and other surveys of outpatient services have demonstrated a wide variation in philosophy, treatment goals, staffing, and outcome.

Reliable case finding is a critical component of community treatment. Beginning in the emergency outpatient setting, it is essential for psychiatrists and other physicians to address case finding with careful history taking. Rund et al. (1981) reported that 20 percent of a general emergency room patient population were alcoholic. Solomon et al. (1980) demonstrated that emergency room physicians recognized alcohol misusers in less than half of the patients who were subsequently identified as alcoholics by the alcohol abuse scale or the brief version of the Michigan Alcoholism Screening Test (MAST). Biggs and Huettner (1983) discovered that 46 percent of a patient sample with a positive MAST score did not receive physician documentation of a drinking history. The physicians failed to document the history in 66 percent of a general hospital population where 19 percent of the patients, including previous alcoholics, surfaced as having potential for alcohol abuse.

Murphy (1980) discussed the hidden barriers to the diagnosis and treatment of alcohol abuse using patients from a general practitioner's office. He demonstrated that patients were not likely to raise the subject of problem drinking spontaneously. Only two of 51 alcoholics asked their physicians for aid, although 18 mentioned their drinking problem. Physicians spontaneously suggested specific treatment for the alcoholic in only eight of these cases. Most patients felt their physician should have recognized and broached the subject of their condition before it had become critical. This profile of inconsistent case finding has important implications for the psychiatrist's role as a case finder-diagnostician and as a consultant to nonpsychiatric physicians on the community treatment of alcoholism.

The medical role of the psychiatrist in the outpatient and community treatment of the alcoholic is essential. In some communities, physicians are more likely initially to refer alcoholics to a psychiatrist than to any other treatment resource (Smith and Barnes 1982). In these cases, the psychiatrist becomes the portal of entry into the array of outpatient treatments. While a careful substance abuse history would seem to be an absolute essential in a comprehensive evaluation, studies indicate that psychiatric history taking is inconsistent. Jones (1979) studied the recognition of alcoholic admissions to the emergency clinic of the Maudsley Hospital in London. The psychiatrist recognized 59 percent of the patients at the intake interview. The missed cases initially were diagnosed as having a wide variety of psychiatric problems, including affective and personality disorder, psychoses, and dementia.

In addition, the psychiatrist must search diligently for unrecognized cases of multiple drug abuse. In a comprehensive literature review, Kaufman (1982) reported that the percentage of multiple drug abuse by alcoholics was at least 50 percent in numerous studies.

Drunken Driver Diversion

In addition to voluntary community services, programs for drunken driver diversion currently are the focus of significant public and political concern. Development of scientific models for alcoholism treatment and the widespread utilization of disulfiram (Antabuse) have led to optimistic public policy initiatives utilizing judicial interventions to facilitate referral and compliance with community outpatient treatment for drunken driving offenders. In an extensive review of the literature, the outcome evaluation of first-time offender programs and repeated offender programs were compared (Shore and Kofoed 1984). The programs consisted of a wide range of educational and treatment approaches and included: "Don't Drink and Drive" classes, home study, mandated group therapy or Alcoholics Anonymous (AA), individual counseling, motivational groups, and disulfiram. There are few dramatically positive results in these studies. However, they vary widely in evaluation methods and illustrate the difficulties inherent in such research. Choice of outcome measures is difficult. Alcohol consumption, driving while intoxicated (DWI) arrests, and accident rates appear surprisingly unrelated in the study populations, perhaps because of the low likelihood of arrest and the even lower chance of conviction or accident per drunken driving event. Attitudes and knowledge have an uncertain relationship to drinking behavior. Legal and ethical considerations limit use of completely unpunished or untreated control groups. Follow-up length varies, although it appears that longer research follow-up usually demonstrates poorer results. Finally, the introduction of the 55 mph speed limit, which dropped highway fatalities significantly, occurred in the middle of many of the program evaluations and complicated interpretation of the data.

Evaluation of these same drunken driver diversion programs also focuses attention on the effectiveness of disulfiram, which has become widely used in these programs. A major limitation in generalizing the evaluation of disulfiram treatment programs to other community settings is that most studies include only patients voluntarily taking medication. Some studies show that patients mandated to treatment do better than untreated controls or volunteer patients, but that disulfiram use alone accounted for little of the outcome variance. In a cooperative study of disulfiram treatment, the Veterans Administration evaluated 605 men in a controlled, blinded, multicenter design and found that there were no significant differences among the groups in total abstinence, time to first drink, employment, or social stability (Fuller et al. 1986). However, there was a significant relationship between adherence to the treatment regimen and fewer drinking days, indicating that disulfiram may help reduce drinking frequency after relapse. Obviously, while disulfiram remains a popular treatment option both in voluntary and coercive treatment programs, its individual effectiveness needs further research.

Outpatient and Social Detoxification

With an increasing emphasis on outpatient treatment and cost effectiveness, many arguments can be made for the expansion of outpatient and social detoxification. Two different types of nontraditional detoxification treatments have been evaluated. Both avoid the reinforcement of secondary gain and the expense of hospitalization from inpatient treatment. Outpatient medical detoxification does not provide the secondary gain of hospitalization and is less expensive. Social detoxification encourages the replacement of the drugs with interpersonal relearning in the ambulatory setting and may offer a psychological advantage in drug-free rehabilitation treatments. The evaluation of these approaches suggests that even in groups of relatively low socioeconomic status patients, outpatient and social detoxification can be highly effective and safe. In several studies evaluating more than 1,600 patients, there was no mortality, and less than 5 percent of the combined samples required a subsequent hospitalization (Shore and Kofoed 1984).

Obviously, hospital-based treatment is an essential backup for all community-based treatment, especially detoxification. In fact, predictor data clearly suggest that intensive treatment is differentially beneficial for the more severely deteriorated and less socially stable individuals (Miller and Hester 1986). However, the success of the outpatient approaches provides enough reassurance to consider an expansion of their availability and to challenge our excessive reliance on hospital-based treatment for alcoholism.

Shelter Care Facilities, Half-Way Houses, and Therapeutic Communities

There are more than 1,000 alcoholism half-way houses in the United States and a large number of shelter care facilities. These institutions have grown out of the social movement and are committed to sobriety as a first step in alcoholism treatment, with the provision of group living in the rehabilitation process. The length of stay for shelter facilities often ranges from three to six months, with some lengths of stay in half-way houses exceeding a year. In addition to these community services, a number of longer-term therapeutic communities had developed by the mid-1970s from influences of the general alcohol inpatient rehabilitation center and the guru-style drug-addiction facility. The therapeutic community included long-term residential rehabilitation, focusing predominately on the young adult male alcoholic with patterns of polydrug abuse. The orientation was strongly AA, with skilled counselors, often nondrinking alcoholics themselves, as primary therapists.

With rapidly changing patient demographics, it is likely that residents of the shelter and half-way houses will have a larger subgroup that can be identified as the new chronic patient (Shore 1983). These alcoholics, predominantly younger males, are suffering from major mental illnesses and have drifted to a lower socioeconomic status, with a pattern of alcohol addiction often associated with a history of frequent arrests. This subgroup is especially high risk and needs the comprehensive resources of community treatments, including a psychiatric diagnostic assessment and continued care. Follow-up studies in these populations are difficult. For these types of services, improvement in postdischarge outcome is significantly linked to length of stay. Katz (1966) studied two patient groups with a six-month follow-up and demonstrated that only 34 to 37 percent could be located and interviewed, emphasizing the nomadic characteristics of the population. For those interviewed, however, there was a reduction in binge drinking during the follow-up period, with 25 percent of the respondents reporting total abstinence and 55 percent abstinent for more than three months. In a study of chronic alcoholics in a half-way house, Walker et al. (1982) observed generally poor outcome for both men and women. However, in a predictive analysis, intake characteristics were found to be relatively strong predictors of drinking and employment outcomes. The best predictor of postdischarge drinking was level of chronicity at admission. The best predictor of work at follow-up was the subject's prior work history.

Chapter 125

Alcoholics Anonymous

Alcoholics Anonymous [AA] is a fellowship of men and women who share their experience, strength, and hope with each other that they may solve their common problem and help others to recover from alcoholism.

The only requirement for membership is a desire to stop drinking. There are no dues or fees for AA membership; we are self-supporting through our own contributions.

AA is not allied with any sect, denomination, politics, organization, or institution; does not wish to engage in any controversy; neither endorses nor opposes any causes.

Our primary purpose is to stay sober and help other alcoholics to achieve sobriety. (The AA Preamble is reprinted with permission of AA Grapevine, Inc.)

This often-quoted introductory statement of AA sets out the primary purpose, requirement for membership, and general operational policy of an organization that has just recently celebrated its 50th anniversary. The intent of this chapter is to survey various aspects of AA—its history, therapeutic mechanisms of change, and effectiveness—as well as the associated organizations of Al-Anon and Alateen. Although

I hope to give the reader an understanding of the role of AA in alcoholism theory and treatment, adequate comprehension of the organization can be achieved only by attending several meetings and becoming familiar with the official literature of AA and its associated organizations.

Before embarking on a brief recounting of the history of AA, a comment regarding the nature of the requirement of anonymity is appropriate. Anonymity was considered necessary to avoid the potential stigma of alcoholism and the associated threat of ostracism by family, friends, and employers. When there were only a few members in the organization in the early days, there was concern that the demand for help from suffering alcoholics would be so great that its members could not carry on their occupations. Anonymity would protect the members from being inundated with requests for help (Robinson 1979). Despite there being less need in the 1980s for concern with public reaction to the admission of alcoholism and despite the enormous growth of AA, which has produced an ample cadre of those who can help new members, anonymity has been preserved because it discourages the abuse of AA membership by the "big ego" that emerges from a member's infantile narcissism, encouraging instead the development of a more mature, humble self (Tiebout 1961). In addition, anonymity promotes the confidentiality among the membership that is requisite for candid problem discussion.

History and Development of AA

AA was founded in Ohio in 1935 at a time when professional treaters were often unhelpful, let alone unresponsive to the needs of alcohol-dependent individuals. Convinced that he needed to help other alcoholics in order to keep sober himself, Bill W, a New York stockbroker, aided Dr. Bob S, an Akron, Ohio surgeon; together they embarked on helping other alcoholics. Some months later, Bill started building another self-help group in New York, and a third group was formed in Cleveland. Several ideas stemming from the founders' contacts with moral rearmament (Cantril 1963) guided them. In 1938 and 1939 these ideas were translated into the Twelve Step structure and philosophy of the AA program (Table 1).

Growth was very slow until around 1940, when several national articles about AA were published. Since then, AA has developed rapidly, having an average annual growth of about 8 percent since 1968, with a reported active membership in 1986 of 804,000 in 43,000 groups in the United States and Canada (Alcoholics Anonymous 1987). The actual membership is estimated to be much larger than that reported to the General Service Office of AA—more than 1,000,000 in 114 countries throughout the world (Alcoholics Anonymous World Service Center, personal communication, 13 February 1986). Despite its tremendous size, AA remains a movement of non-professionals, resisting the pressure of some to turn it into a worldwide professional organization (Norris 1970).

Membership Characteristics of AA

Contrary to popular opinion, AA members are often middle-class, married, and employed. Over the course of surveys conducted every three years from 1968 to 1986 by the General Service Office of AA, the membership has undergone some changes in composition. The percentage of women members has increased from 22 percent

Table 1. The Twelve Steps of AA

1. We admitted we were powerless over alcohol . . . that our lives had become unmanageable.
2. Came to believe that a Power greater than ourselves could restore us to sanity.
3. Made a decision to turn our will and our lives over to the care of God *as we understood Him*.
4. Made a searching and fearless moral inventory of ourselves.
5. Admitted to God, to ourselves, and to another human being the exact nature of our wrongs.
6. Were entirely ready to have God remove all these defects of character.
7. Humbly asked Him to remove our shortcomings.
8. Made a list of all persons we had harmed and became willing to make amends to them all.
9. Made direct amends to such people wherever possible, except when to do so would injure them or others.
10. Continued to take personal inventory and when we were wrong promptly admitted it.
11. Sought through prayer and meditation to improve our conscious contact with God *as we understood Him*, praying only for knowledge of His will for us and the power to carry that out.
12. Having had a spiritual awakening as the result of these Steps, we tried to carry this message to alcoholics, and to practice these principles in all our affairs.

Note. Reprinted with permission of AA World Services, Inc.

in 1968 to about 34 percent in 1986; the percentage of members who are 30 years old and younger jumped from about 7 percent at the beginning of the time period to about 20 percent in 1986; more members report being addicted to drugs in addition to alcohol with 38 percent in the 1986 survey being so addicted (Alcoholics Anonymous 1987).

Early research indicated that alcohol-dependent individuals who affiliate with AA are not representative of the total population of alcoholics (Bean 1975b; Leach 1973; Ogborne and Glaser 1981; Trice and Roman 1970). Compared to alcohol-dependent persons who did not join AA but who often received other forms of treatment, AA members were observed to be more sociable and affiliative, guilty over past behavior, field dependent in perceptual style, cognitively simplistic, more chronically and severely problemed, more often middle class, physically healthier, and more socially stable. These findings possess a certain amount of face validity inasmuch as the variables that were found to relate to AA involvement match the role demands AA appears to place on its members. For example, consistent with members' sociability and affiliativeness, AA meetings call for members to interact with others in a group.

Several findings regarding the AA affiliation process—drawn largely from treatment samples of alcohol dependent individuals—raise doubts about our ability to identify which alcoholics are most likely to affiliate actively with AA (e.g., O'Leary et al. 1980a, 1980b; Vaillant 1983). More often than not, the variables that have been studied have been found to be unrelated consistently with membership or to be unrelated in some samples and positively or negatively associated in others. Consistent with early research, the majority of pertinent samples did find a positive relationship between AA membership and loss of control of behavior when drinking as well as measurement of the severity of alcohol dependence and related problems. Notwithstanding this trend in the data, the general lack of systematic differences between AA affiliates and nonaffiliates suggests that the philosophy and program of

AA does not uniformly exclude from membership any particular type of alcohol-dependent individual.

Despite the lack of systematic exclusion of certain types of alcohol-dependent individuals from AA, only some alcoholics will choose this organization as a form of help. It is therefore appropriate to regard AA as a resource of important although not unlimited applicability to the population of alcohol-dependent individuals who seek treatment.

Therapeutic Procedures in AA

Alcoholics who affiliate with AA generally make their initial contact during a crisis, although some alcohol-dependent people are required to attend by court systems, treatment programs, and employee assistance programs. Once a member, the individual may choose one or more "older" members to be a sponsor. By sharing their experience with the newcomer, these sponsors facilitate the alcoholic's participation in AA. Initially, a sponsor may stress means by which sobriety can be achieved. As members become more established in the program, a sponsor may emphasize ways to work through the Twelve Steps and to make behavioral and psychological changes (Alibrandi 1978). AA participants frequently become identified with a particular group. Besides attending the meetings of their "home" group, which commonly occur weekly, AA members may go to meetings of other groups. An estimated 25 percent of active members go to at least three meetings per week (Norris 1974a). Between meetings, members may call on others at any time for assistance. Actively involved AA members appear to participate in the program for about four or five years before "graduating" (Bohince and Orensteen 1950; Edwards et al. 1966, 1967; Robinson 1979). Many members, of course, stay for longer periods of time, some for a lifetime. By following these therapeutic procedures, the alcohol-dependent individual obtains a chance to benefit from the therapeutic processes and mechanisms of change that are operative in AA.

Therapeutic Processes and Mechanisms of Change in AA

In AA change occurs through: 1) the Twelve Step program of self-help, 2) assistance by individual members in one-to-one relationships, and 3) help in group meetings. Each modality entails different processes and mechanisms of change.

Self-Help Process

The Twelve Step program requires members to do most of the work by themselves, although support is received from others in group meetings and in one-to-one encounters. The mechanisms of change involved can be analyzed from a variety of theoretical frameworks, including the philosophical theories of existentialism (Kurtz 1982) and stoicism (Brundage 1985), cybernetic epistemology (Bateson 1971), and ego-analytic (Mack 1981) or cognitive-behavioral (Mahoney 1974) theories of psychology. Although the steps are stated in numerical order, it is understood that members do not always proceed sequentially through them (Bean 1975a).

Initially the newcomer changes the conception of self from one who controls his or her drinking to one who cannot (Step One). Avoidance is abandoned as is denial of the drinking problem and adherence to the belief that all challenges can be met

(Bateson 1971). The belief that regulation of the self requires the use of resources (a "Power") beyond the self is adopted (Step Two), and the member agrees to utilize these resources (Step Three). The particular conceptualization of the Power beyond the self is left to the individual.

The AA member then moves to a specific and complex activity (Step Four), which entails self-analysis of character traits and associated unpleasant emotional experiences—especially fear, guilt, and anger—which are hypothesized to foster alcoholismic drinking. Responsibility for managing these antecedents to drinking is shifted from others to oneself. The defects or weaknesses in character that have been identified are then acknowledged to the Power beyond the self and to another person, such as another AA member, member of the clergy, friend, or professional therapist (Step Five). This confession can be very cathartic and ameliorative of guilt and anxiety.

Pessimism toward the permanence of catharsis-induced change is dealt with by taking the next two steps. Members first ready themselves (Step Six) and then ask (Step Seven) the Power to "remove [their] shortcomings." If the belief in the healing effects of the Power is sincerely adopted, the AA members will feel and act as if their faults can be corrected. As with Step Two, an alteration in an individual's conception of the self operates as a central mechanism of change in these steps.

In the next two steps the participant initiates change by making restitution to those the member has hurt in the past. After making a list of everyone the individual can remember harming (Step Eight), action is taken to make amends and to undo the harm caused (Step Nine), unless doing so would hurt the member or others. By perceiving oneself to be engaged in prosocial behavior, the individual may come to think of himself or herself as a caring, loving person (Bem 1970)—a more positive self-perception that can reinforce the behavioral changes made. Of course, improvement in self-esteem may also emerge from the reduction of guilt that accompanies the making of amends.

The member continues to identify problems and admit them to himself or herself, others, and the Power (Step Ten). Prayer and meditation are practiced to reinforce the decision to allow the Power to help (Step Eleven). These steps are regarded as helpful in maintaining the changes already accomplished in the first nine steps.

The member then strives to maintain these changes in thoughts, feelings, and actions (i.e., "spiritual awakening") by helping other alcohol-dependent people acquire and maintain sobriety and by working to sustain individual AA groups as well as AA organization at local, district, and national levels (Step Twelve). One-to-one relationships are formed in helping other alcoholics and have much in common with the relationship between a patient and the patient's individual professional therapist.

One-to-One Therapeutic Relationships

The majority of AA members join the organization during a crisis, when a suffering, alcohol-dependent individual reaches out to AA participants who are engaged in Twelfth Step work. If the person in need seems responsive to the AA program, the individual may be invited to accompany one or more members to an AA meeting. This continues the care initiated during the crisis contact.

Once having joined AA, the alcohol-dependent person may become a sponsoree of one or more "older" members (or sponsors). The importance of this sponsor-sponsoree relationship has been inconsistently assessed. According to Bales (1962), the relationship is "the heart of the therapeutic process" (p. 575). Edwards et al. (1967) believed the importance of the sponsor "can be exaggerated" (p. 203). Regardless of this importance, the sponsor functions variously as a father-confessor or priest, psychotherapist, social companion, and, sometimes, financial helper. However, the sponsor does not actually solve problems and thereby avoids the "rescue" game alcoholics typically wish to play in order to escape responsibility for stopping drinking (Steiner 1971). Not only is the sponsoree aided by this interaction: functioning as a sponsor in AA has been found to be associated with successful sobriety (Bohince and Orensteen 1950; Kammeier and Anderson 1976; Patton 1979), apparently reflecting beneficial effects that accrue to the helper for his or her efforts.

Group Structure and Function

AA meetings follow one of two basic formats: 1) the discussion meeting, in which the chairperson may "tell his or her story" of alcoholism and the road to recovery and then open the meeting to general discussion about alcoholism or problems related to alcoholism, or 2) the speaker's meeting, in which two or three speakers "tell their stories" of alcoholism and recovery from it. Meetings may be open where anyone interested in alcoholism is welcome, or closed, where only alcoholics are present. Both types are noninteractionally focused. During meetings, members focus on alcoholism and related problems rather than on their reactions to one another.

In an effort to understand the conditions for change and therapeutic mechanisms of change operative in AA groups meetings, Emrick et al. (1977) reviewed the available literature describing AA groups, searching for direct and indirect references to the 12 "curative factors" Yalom (1970, 1975) identified as essential to the therapeutic process in professionally led psychotherapy groups. The findings of the review indicated that AA groups rely to a large extent for their therapeutic impact on members' providing help to one another, perceiving closeness among group members who share a common problem as well as a method for dealing with the problem, identifying with other members when they recount their struggles with alcoholism and the efforts to overcome the malady with the help of AA, fostering hope for recovery when successful members are observed, receiving guidance from others who offer suggestions for recovery that are based on personal experience, and creating the experience of not being alone in suffering from alcoholism and associated difficulties.

Treatment Effectiveness of AA

A dispassionate scientific approach to AA has not always been taken, with many unsubstantiated claims having been made about the organization's success. Mendelson and Mello (1985) stated that "at present we do not possess scientific data that either support or refute the relative efficacy of AA for the treatment of alcoholism" (p. 340). In the review to follow, tendentious claims give way to empirical data that are organized around the four approaches that have been most often taken in evaluating the effectiveness of AA: 1) large-scale questionnaire surveys of members attending meetings, 2) studies of the effects of AA as an adjunct to professional treatment, 3) investigations of members' psychological and spiritual functioning, and 4) outcome evaluations in which AA is the only known intervention for most alcoholics. None of these sources allows for unequivocal conclusions regarding AA's effectiveness because methodological problems plague them all (Bebbington 1976) yet they do provide some glimpses into how alcoholics function when they are actively involved in AA.

Evaluation Studies

Among the many methodological weaknesses of AA surveys (Alcoholics Anonymous 1981, 1984, 1987; Bailey and Leach 1965; Edwards et al. 1966, 1967; Kiviranta 1969; Norris 1970, 1974a, 1974b, 1978; Robinson 1979) are highly biased sampling (e.g., more active members are more likely to be studied) and the confounding of the effects of AA with those of professional treatment (i.e., a significant portion of respondents have had professional treatment before or during AA). Overall, the surveys found that 33 to 40 percent of the respondents had reported being abstinent less than a year (Alcoholics Anonymous 1981, 1984, 1987; Norris 1970, 1974a, 1978), 26 to 40 percent had been abstinent one to five or six years and another 20 to 30 percent had been abstinent five or six years or more (Alcoholics Anonymous 1981, 1984, 1987; Bailey and Leach 1965; Edwards et al. 1966, 1967; Norris 1970, 1974a, 1974b, 1978). Thus from 46.5 percent (Edwards et al. 1966, 1967) to 67 percent (Alcoholics Anonymous 1987) of the active members had had at least one year of continuous sobriety behind them.

Numerous studies have evaluated the relationship between AA involvement and outcome after some form of professional treatment for alcoholism. The basic strategy of these studies has been to compare the outcome of alcoholics who have participated in AA before, during, or after some type of professional treatment with the outcome of patients who have not participated in AA or who have attended meetings less frequently. Outcome assessment has usually been limited to drinking behavior or an adjustment measure with drinking as a principal component. Prominent among the methodological flaws of these evaluation efforts is the confounding of AA participation with patient variables, inasmuch as only self-selected AA members have been assessed. Since methodological problems preclude the drawing of definitive conclusions about AA's effectiveness as an adjunct to professional treatment, the results are only summarized. The data suggest that attendance at AA prior to entering a treatment experience is often not related to outcome, but when a relationship is observed it is usually positive (i.e., those who attend AA prior to treatment have a more favorable outcome). Attending AA during, or after treatment is more often positively related to treatment outcome, with the majority of results showing the patients who attend AA during or after other treatment for alcoholism enjoy better outcome status. On the other hand, several studies (e.g., Ogborne and Bornet 1982; Polich et al. 1980) reported finding a negative association between AA attendance during or after treatment and the outcome of reduced drinking. Overall, this body of data suggests that patients who are involved in AA before, during, or after professional treatment may or may not function better. If they do not, they will probably do no worse than patients who are not involved with AA or who go to meetings less frequently, that is unless they continue to drink. Then, AA membership may be associated with symptomatic drinking, perhaps through the mechanism of the self-fulfilling prophecy: AA members believe that they are unable to control their drinking and are thus likely to drink problematically should they drink at all (Ogborne and Bornet 1982; Rudy 1980).

Other studies have examined the psychological and spiritual functioning of AA members. Given that each project suffers from design deficiencies, only a few examples of the findings are noted. Among the changes that have been found to be associated with AA involvement are a decrease in dependence on others and an increase in an intrapsychic sense of well-being (Cohen 1962), greater acceptance of oneself as an alcohol-dependent person and in need to help (Bell 1970; Bell et al. 1969), a decrease in self-ideal self-concept discrepancy (Carroll and Fuller 1969), and an increase in ethical concern for others as well as oneself (Eckhardt 1967). Whether or not AA participation is causally related to these changes remains, of course, undemonstrated by these studies.

Several projects have evaluated the adjustment of members of one or more AA groups when this was the only help received for most, if not all, the members. Projects such as these are capable of providing the most valid indices of AA's effectiveness because the effects of AA are not confounded with the results of professional treatment for at least a majority of subjects, and samples, if properly constructed, include (or are representative of) all members of the group(s) under study. Such samples lend themselves to interpretable comparisons with other treatment efforts. The data from these studies lead to the following tentative conclusions. A large percentage of alcoholics who go to AA drop out of the organization, some very quickly (Bohince and Orensteen 1950; Brandsma et al. 1980; 1965). About 40 to 50 percent of alcoholics who join AA and become long-term, active members may have several years of total abstinence while involved with the program; and 60 to 68 percent of active members improve to some extent, drinking less or not at all during AA participation (Bohince and Orensteen 1950; Brown 1963; Thorpe and Perret 1959). Although AA membership is associated with abstinence or reduction in drinking for a large portion of alcohol-dependent individuals, it is no more effective than are comparison treatment methods in helping court-ordered patients recover from alcoholism (Brandsma et al. 1980; Ditman et al. 1967).

Comparison with Professional Treatment

AA's failure to demonstrate relative effectiveness with the unmotivated alcoholic is certainly no surprise to anyone at all familiar with AA, particularly since the organization is designed to help only those alcoholics who "desire to stop drinking." Perhaps AA is relatively more effective than other intervention methods with more motivated alcohol-dependent individuals, but this hypothesis has not yet been adequately tested through clinical trials. At present we are left with making a coarse comparison between AA outcomes and a handful of data from the professional treatment literature that used methodology similar to those evaluation studies in which AA was the only known intervention for most alcoholics (Emrick et al. 1977). The comparison leads to two impressions: 1) apparently, AA is associated more often with the outcome of total abstinence than is professional treatment and 2) professional treatment appears to be associated more often with the outcome of reduced drinking than does AA.

Although AA appears to be associated more often with the outcome of total abstinence than does professional treatment, AA is not necessarily more effective in "causing" abstinence. This is because alcoholics who choose to go to AA versus those selecting professional treatment probably have, on the whole, greater motivation to work toward the goal of total abstinence, which is AA's sole and unequivocal goal. Professionally treated alcoholics may, on the other hand, seek professional treatment in the hope of receiving help to reduce rather than eliminate drinking completely.

Given the variant nature of alcohol-dependent individuals, it seems prudent to view AA as most appropriate at certain times or for particular individuals while professionals may provide a more suitable response to other alcoholics or at different times in the course of the disorder and its treatment. Still for other alcoholics, or at certain times, a combination of AA and professional treatment may prove to be the most appropriate.

Patient Referral to and Professional Linkage with AA

In recent years, professionals have played an increasingly important role in alcoholics' finding their way to AA. The 1986 survey of AA members (Alcoholics Anonymous 1987) found that 36 percent had listed counselors and rehabilitation programs as a major factor in their joining the organization. In England in 1976, 56 percent of AA members indicated that psychiatrists, general practitioners, or social workers had been involved in the decision to go to their first meeting (Robinson 1979).

Professionals would do well to help appropriate patients become interested in AA while they are actively involved in treatment. Once a patient has expressed a willingness to explore membership, the professional is advised to be involved actively in seeing to it that the patient gets to a meeting. For residential settings that offer AA meetings, this is an easily accomplished step. However, more effort needs to be expended by the outpatient professional to effect a linkage with AA. Outpatient staff need to arrange for a contact between the patient and an active member, ensuring that someone will take the patient to a meeting and introduce the patient to others. A small sample size clinical trial by Sisson and Mallams (1981) demonstrated that when a therapist at an outpatient mental health alcoholism treatment program made arrangements for patients to be escorted to an initial AA meeting and the therapist showed continued interest in the patient's progress in AA, 100 percent of the individuals attended compared to none of the patients who were merely encouraged to attend AA and were given information about meeting times and locations ($p < .001$). Once patients initiate involvement in AA, professionals are wise to encourage them to remain in constant contact for at least the first three months since it is during this time that dropping out is most likely to occur (Norris 1982). When alcoholics are in professional treatment and AA simultaneously, the professionals need to monitor patients' potential for splitting the two activities, which can vitiate the benefits of both (Davis 1980).

Another situation arises when alcoholics initiate professional treatment after long-term, successful involvement in AA. Clinicians need to be sensitive to the issues involved in the patient's efforts to become more separate from AA as greater autonomy is established. A narrow path should be followed by the clinician between encouraging the patient to separate too much or too quickly from AA versus ignoring the patient's dependence on the organization. If done skillfully, this approach can facilitate the patient's experience and expression of self beyond that of a recovering alcoholic (Brown 1985; Rosen 1981).

Professionals can enhance their patients' utilization of AA and its associated organizations by familiarizing themselves with groups in the community. Their attendance at open meetings can help foster working relationships with AA members as can an invitation from them for members to hold meetings at their facility or to volunteer at their agency for the purpose of introducing patients to AA. The influence of AA can be augmented further by their hiring appropriately trained and skilled members as alcoholism counselors; although careful attention must be paid to preserving the distinction between the individual as a counselor and as an AA participant.

Besides attending meetings and becoming knowledgeable about the Twelve Step program of recovery, professionals are advised to familiarize themselves with the Twelve Traditions of AA. These policy statements can guide the professional in ensuring that his or her dealings with AA will respect and preserve the integrity of the organization at all times (Alcoholics Anonymous 1976; Patrick 1980).

Al-Anon and Alateen

Two organizations that emerged from AA,—Al-Anon and Alateen—have extended AA's self-help program of recovery to spouses, other adult relatives, children, and friends of alcoholics. The importance of these groups in the treatment of those who have been affected by alcoholism warrants their being studied considerably more than has been the case to date.

Al-Anon History, Therapeutic Principles, Composition, and Effectiveness

Al-Anon was founded in 1951 as an outgrowth of spouses and relatives of AA members meeting to share their problems in living with an alcoholic. Its treatment procedures and therapeutic mechanisms of change parallel those of AA with adaptation to relatives and friends of alcoholics. More than 26,000 groups averaging 15 to 20 members in size from 84 countries in the world have been registered at the World Service Office of Al-Anon (J. Johnson, personal communication, 6 February 1986). Approximately 13,000 of these groups are in the United States. Reflecting a recent trend toward greater awareness by and identification of adults who were children of alcoholics, a significant number of Al-Anon groups are now being registered as adult children Al-Anon Family Groups. More than 1,100 such groups have been registered, mostly within the last few years. Although these groups are intended to help those who have grown up in families that have been affected by alcoholism, Al-Anon has taken care to ensure the integrity of its organization by requiring such groups to use only Al-Anon approved literature during meetings, to be independent and not registered with any other organization, and to welcome in the group anyone who has been affected by someone else's drinking, even if the individual has not been reared in an alcohol-involved family.

Three principles guide the Al-Anon member's efforts to achieve psychological and spiritual growth: "loving detachment" from the alcoholic with a shift in focus to self-care, improvement in self-care, improvement in self-esteem and autonomy through self-improvement and self-analysis, and enhancement of the capacity for self-regulation through reliance on resources outside the self (i.e., the "Higher Power") (Ablon 1977).

Two surveys of Al-Anon groups in the United States and in Canada recently conducted under the auspices of the World Service Office (Al-Anon 1984, 1988) found that active Al-Anon members were mostly Caucasian, urban or suburban, middle-aged females who were married and employed. Most female members were the spouse of an alcoholic whereas only a little more than half of the males were married to an alcoholic. The majority of active members attended one or two meetings a week. Nearly half had recieved treatment or counseling either prior to joining or since joining Al-Anon. More than a third reported that professionals had played a contributing role in their first meeting.

With regard to the effectiveness of Al-Anon, two studies of wives of alcoholics have reported a positive association between Al-Anon membership and better functioning. In one project (Bailey 1967), Al-Anon membership (versus nonmembership) was observed to be associated significantly ($p < .001$) with less psychophysiologic impairment, regardless of the husband's drinking status. In the other study (Gorman and Rooney 1979), this one of Al-Anon members only, duration of Al-Anon membership was found to be associated with reduced negative coping behavior with respect to the spouse's drinking.

Alateen History, Composition, and Effectiveness

Alateen was founded "in 1957 by a 17-year-old son of an AA father and an Al-Anon mother" (Ablon 1977, p. 281). This organization is modeled after AA and Al-Anon and is primarily geared to 12- to 20-year-olds, although younger children sometimes do attend.

There are about 3,500 Alateen groups registered with the World Service Office of Al-Anon (J. Johnson, personal communication, 6 July 1986). Each group is sponsored by an Al-Anon member and, perhaps, an AA participant. Alateen participants appear to come from families that are less healthy than the norm (Petersen-Kelley 1985).

Research on the therapeutic effectiveness of Alateen has been quite sparse. The most pertinent data come from a study by Hughes (1977) in which she, among other things, matched established Alateen members with teenagers who had one or two alcoholic parents and who were, for the most part, attending their first Alateen meeting. Matching was done by age, sex, grade level, and father's occupational level. Hughes found that Alateen members scored more positively than did the non-Alateen teenagers on measures of mood states and self-esteem, concluding that Alateen appears to help teenagers from alcoholic homes improve their mood and associated self-esteem. Inasmuch as this researcher attempted to control for the "patient" motivation variable by using as a comparison group those who were investigating Alateen for first time, these findings appear to be more valid than those which have typically been obtained for the assessment of AA's effectiveness.

The more recently conducted Al-Anon surveys (Al-Anon, 1984, 1988) provided information about Alateen members as well as those of Al-Anon. The 1987 survey found that 58 percent of Alateens were females, with 54 percent of the membership being 14 or under. The 1984 survey found that most Alateens were students. The majority of participants attended one or two meetings a week and nearly half had an Al-Anon or Alateen sponsor. In both surveys, about a third of the respondents reported that they had received treatment or counseling prior to or since joining Alateen; however, only 6 percent of the 1987 respondents reported that a professional had facilitated their initial contact with the organization. In both surveys, the majority of respondents were children of alcoholics.

Conclusion

AA has been and remains to this day a major influence in the field of alcoholism and its treatment, and there are no signs that its significance is waning. The philosophy of AA permeates most professional treatment programs. For example, it is typical for patients to be introduced to the AA program of recovery while in treatment. Often patients in residential alcoholism treatment programs attend several AA meetings a week and are guided by the treatment staff in taking the first three to five steps of the Twelve Step program before they are discharged. On termination of the intensive phase of treatment (whether offered on an inpatient or outpatient basis), patients and their families are encouraged to maintain and enhance progress primarily through reliance on AA, Al-Anon, and Alateen as aftercare resources.

Of course, AA is not for everyone (Young and Lawson 1984). A large number of alcoholics appear to recover without AA, stopping drinking instead with the help of professionals or without any type of formal treatment (e.g., Vaillant 1983). Also, as has been indicated in this chapter, some alcohol-dependent individuals may be more likely to drink problematically, should they drink anything at all, if they affiliate with AA than if they do not. Nevertheless, the professional who comes in contact with alcohol-dependent individuals should become familiar with AA and its associated organizations and strive to utilize these self-help resources whenever appropriate.

References

Section 12
Psychoactive Substance Use Disorders (Alcohol)

Ablon J: Alanon family groups: impetus for change through the presentation of alternatives. Am J Psychother 28:30–38, 1974

Ablon J: Perspectives on Al-Anon family groups, in Alcoholism: Development, Consequences, and Interventions. Edited by Estes NJ, Heinemann ME. St Louis, CV Mosby Co, 1977

Adinolfi AA, McCourt WF, Geoghegan S: Group assertiveness training for alcoholics. J Stud Alcohol 37:311–320, 1976

Al-Anon: An Al-Anon/Alateen Member Survey. New York, Al-Anon Family Group Headquarters, Inc, 1984

Al-Anon: Who Are the Members of Al-Anon and Alateen? 1987 Survey in the US and Canada. New York, Al-Anon Family Group Headquarters, Inc, 1988

Alcoholics Anonymous: The Story of How Many Thousands of Men and Women Have Recovered from Alcoholism, 3rd ed. New York, Alcoholics Anonymous World Services, Inc, 1976

Alcoholics Anonymous: Analysis of the 1980 Survey of the Membership of A.A. New York, Alcoholics Anonymous World Services, Inc, 1981

Alcoholics Anonymous: Analysis of the 1983 Survey of the Membership of A.A. New York, Alcoholics Anonymous World Services, Inc, 1984

Alcoholics Anonymous: Analysis of the 1986 Survey of the Membership of A.A. New York, Alcoholics Anonymous World Services, Inc, 1987

Alden L: Evaluation of a preventive self-management program for problem drinkers. Canadian Journal of Behavioral Science 10:258, 1978

Alibrandi LA: The folk psychotherapy of Alcoholics Anonymous, in Practical Approaches to Alcoholism Psychotherapy. Edited by Zimberg S, Wallace J, Blume SB. New York, Plenum, 1978

Allman M, Crocker R (eds): Social Group Work and Alcoholism. New York, Haworth Press, 1982

Alterman AI, Ayre FR, Williford WO: Diagnostic validation of conjoint schizophrenia and alcoholism. J Clin Psychiatry 45:300–303, 1984

American Psychiatric Association: Diagnostic and Statistical Manual of Mental Disorders, 2nd ed. Washington, DC, American Psychiatric Association, 1968

American Psychiatric Association: Diagnostic and Statistical Manual of Mental Disorders, 3rd ed. Washington, DC, American Psychiatric Association, 1980

American Psychiatric Association: Diagnostic and Statistical Manual of Mental Disorders, 3d ed, revised. Washington, DC, American Psychiatric Association, 1987

Anderson SC, Henderson DC: Family therapy in the treatment of alcoholism. Soc Work Health Care 3:79–84, 1983

Annis HM: Group treatment of incarcerated offenders with alcohol and drug problems: a controlled evaluation. Canadian Journal of Criminology 21:3–15, 1979

Annis HM, Chan D: The differential treatment model: empirical evidence from a personality typology of adult offenders. Criminal Justice Behavior 10:159–173, 1983

Annis HM, Smart RG: Arrests, readmissions and treatment following release from detoxication centers. J Stud Alcohol 39:1276–1283, 1978

Arieli A: Multi-couple group therapy of alcoholics. Int J Addict 16:773–782, 1981

Armor DJ, Polich JM, Stambul HB: Alcoholism and Treatment. Santa Monica, Calif, Rand Corp, 1976

Ashem B, Donner L: Covert sensitization with alcoholics: a controlled replication. Behav Res Ther 6:7, 1968

Ashley M: The physical disease characteristics of inpatient alcoholics. J Stud Alcohol 42:4, 1981

Atkinson RM: Persuading alcoholic patients to seek treatment. Unpublished manuscript, 1984

Azrin NH: Improvements in the common reinforcement approach to alcoholism. Behav Res Ther 14:339, 1976

Babor TF, McCabe T, Mansanes P, et al: Patterns of alcoholism in France and America: a comparative study, in Alcoholism: A Multilevel Problem. Proceedings of the 3rd Annual Alcoholism Conference of NIAAA. Edited by Chafetz ME. Washington, DC, 1974

Babor TF, Martinay C, Benard JY, et al: Homme alcoholique, Femme alcoholique: Etude comparative et emperique. (Male alcoholic, female alcoholic: An empirical and descriptive study). Bulletin de la Societie Francaise d'Alcohologie, in press

Bacon MK, Barry H, Child IL: A cross-cultural study of drinking, II: relation to other features of culture. Quarterly Journal of Studies on Alcohol 3:29–48, 1965

Baekeland F, Lundwall L, Kissin B: Methods for the treatment of chronic alcoholism: a critical appraisal, in Research Advances in Alcohol and Drug Problems, vol 2. Edited by Gibbins RJ, Israel Y, Kalant H, et al. Toronto, John Wiley and Sons, 1975

Bailey M: Al-Anon family groups as an aid to wives of alcoholics. Social Work 10:68–79, 1965

Bailey MB: Psychophysiological impairment in wives of alcoholics as related to their husbands' drinking and sobriety, in Alcoholism: Behavioral Research, Therapeutic Approaches. Edited by Fox R. New York, Springer, 1967

Bailey MB, Leach B: Alcoholics Anonymous Pathway to Recovery: A Study of 1,058 Members of the AA Fellowship in New York City, New York, National Council on Alcoholism, 1965

Bales RF: The therapeutic role of Alcoholics Anonymous as seen by a sociologist, in Society, Culture, and Drinking Patterns. Edited by Pittman DJ, Snyder CR. New York, John Wiley and Sons, 1962

Balint M: The Basic Fault. London, Tavistock Publications, 1968

Bateson G: The cybernetics of self: a theory of alcoholism. Psychiatry 34:1–18, 1971

Bean M: Alcoholics Anonymous I. Psychiatric Annals 5:7–61, 1975a

Bean M: Alcoholics Anonymous II. Psychiatric Annals 5:7–57, 1975b

Bebbington PE: The efficacy of Alcoholics Anonymous: the elusiveness of hard data. Br J Psychiatry 128:572–580, 1976

Becker JT, Jaffe JH: Impaired memory for treatment-relevant information inpatient male alcoholics. J Stud Alcohol 40:339–343, 1984

Bednar RL, Kaul TJ: Experimental group research: current perspectives, in Handbook of Psychotherapy and Behavior Change, 2nd ed. Edited by Garfield SL, Berger AE. New York, John Wiley and Sons, 1978

Begleiter H, Porjesz B, Bihari B, et al: Event-related brain potentials in boys at risk for alcoholism. Science 225:1493–1495, 1984

Bell AH: The Bell Alcoholism Scale of Adjustment: a validity study. Quarterly Journal of Studies on Alcohol 31:965–967, 1970

Bell AH, Weingold HP, Lachin JM: Measuring adjustment in patients disabled with alcoholism. Quarterly Journal of Studies on Alcohol 30:634–639, 1969

Bem DJ: Beliefs, Attitudes, and Human Affairs. Monterey, Calif, Brooks-Cole, 1970

Berenson D: Alcohol and the family system, in Family Therapy: Theory and Practice. Edited by Guerin PJ. New York, Gardner Press, 1976

Berger F: Alcoholism rehabilitation: a supportive approach. Hosp Community Psychiatry 34:1040–1043, 1983

Berman K: Multiple Conjoint Family Groups in the Treatment of Alcoholism. J Med Soc NJ 65:6–8, 1968

Bigelow G, Liebson I, Lawrence C: Prevention of alcohol abuse by reinforcement of incompatible behavior. Presented at Association for Advancement of Behavior Therapy, 1973

Bigelow G, Strickler D, Liebson I: Maintaining disulfiram ingestion among outpatient alcoholics: a security-deposit contingency contracting procedure. Behav Res Ther 14:378, 1976

Blagooyen TJ: Comparison of the effect of Synanon "game" verbal attack therapy and standard group therapy practice on hospitalized chronic alcoholics. Journal of Community Psychology 2:54–58, 1974

Blakely R, Baker R: An exposure approach to alcohol abuse. Behav Res Ther 18:319–325, 1980

Blane HT: The Personality of the Alcoholic: Guises of Dependence. New York, Harper and Row, 1968

Blass JP, Gibson GE: Genetic factors in Wernicke-Korsakoff syndrome. Alcoholism: Clinical and Experimental Research 3:126–134, 1979

Blume SB: Psychodrama in the treatment of alcoholism, in Alcoholism: Development, Consequences, and Interventions. Edited by Estes N, Heinemann E. St Louis, CV Mosby, 1977

Blume SB: Group psychotherapy in the treatment of alcoholism, in Practical Approaches to Alcoholism Psychotherapy. Edited by Zimberg S, Wallace J, Blume SB. New York, Plenum, 1978

Bohince EA, Orensteen AC: An Evaluation of the Services and Program of the Minneapolis Chapter of Alcoholics Anonymous. Master's thesis. University of Minnesota, 1950

Boland BJ, Meller CS, Revusky S: Chemical aversion treatment of alcoholism: lithium as the aversive agent. Behav Res Ther 16:401, 1978

Bowman KM, Jellinek EM: Alcohol addiction and its treatment. Quarterly Journal of Studies on Alcohol 2: 98–176, 1941

Boylin ER: Gestalt encounter in the treatment of hospitalized alcoholic patients. Am J Psychother 29:524–534, 1975

Brandsma JM, Pattison EM: The outcome of group psychotherapy for alcoholics: an empirical review. Am J Drug Alcohol Abuse 11: 151–162, 1985

Brandsma JM, Maultsby MC Jr, Welsh RJ: Outpatient Treatment of Alcoholism: A Review and Comparative Study. Baltimore, University Park Press, 1980

Bratter TE: Reality therapy: a group psychotherapeutic approach with adolescent alcoholics. Ann NY Acad Sci 233:104–114, 1974

Briggs TG, Huettner J: The alcoholism task force. Minn Med 66:245–248, 1983

Brown RF: An aftercare program for alcoholics. Crime and Delinquency 9:77–83, 1963

Brown S: Treating the Alcoholic: A Developmental Model of Recovery. New York, John Wiley and Sons, 1985

Browne-Mayers AN, Galdreux JR, Seelye EE, et al: Participation in group therapy:

outcome in treatment, in Currents in Alcoholism, vol 4. Edited by Seixas FA. New York, Grune & Stratton, 1978

Brundage V: Gregory Bateson, Alcoholics Anonymous, and stoicism. Psychiatry 48:40–51, 1985

Caddy GR, Lovibond SH: Self-regulation and discriminated aversive conditioning in the modification of alcoholics' drinking behavior. Behav Res Ther 7:223, 1976

Caddy GR, Addington HJ, Perkins D: Individualized behavior therapy for the alcoholic. Behav Res Ther 16:345, 1978

Cadogan DA: Marital group therapy in the treatment of alcoholism. Quarterly Journal of Studies on Alcohol 34:1187–1194, 1973

Cadoret R: Depression and alcoholism, in Evaluation of the Alcoholic: Implications for Research, Theory, and Treatment. NIAAA Research Monograph No. 5. Publication ADM 81-1033. Edited by Meyer RE, Babor TF, Glueck B, et al: Washington, DC, US Department of Health and Human Services, 1981

Cahalan D, Cisen I, Crossley H: American Drinking Practices. Piscataway NJ, Rutgers Center of Alcohol Studies, 1969

Cannon DS, Baker TB: Emetic and electric shock alcohol aversion therapy: assessment of conditioning. J Consult Clin Psychol 49:20, 1981

Cantril H: The Psychology of Social Movements. New York, John Wiley and Sons, 1963

Carroll JL, Fuller GB: The self and ideal-self concept of the alcoholic as influenced by length of sobriety and/or participation in Alcoholics Anonymous. J Clin Psychol 25:363–364, 1969

C B: The growth and effectiveness of Alcoholics Anonymous in a southwestern city, 1945–1962. Quarterly Journal of Studies on Alcohol 26:279–284, 1965

Chaney EF, O'Leary MR, Marlatt GA: Skill training with alcoholics. J Consult Clin Psychol 46:1092, 1978

Chick J: Alcohol dependence: methodological issues in its measurement: reliability of the criteria. Br J Addict 75:175–186, 1980

Chick J, Lloyd G, Crombie E: Natural history and effect of minimal intervention in newly identified problem drinkers in a general hospital. Proceedings of Conference on Early Identification of the Problem Drinker. Washington, DC, National Institute on Alcohol Abuse and Alcoholism, 1980

Cloninger C, Bohman M, Sigvardsonn S: Inheritance of alcohol abuse: cross fostering analysis of adopted men. Arch Gen Psychiatry 38:861–868, 1981

Cohen F: Personality changes among members of Alcoholics Anonymous. Mental Hygiene 46:427–437, 1962

Cohen M, Liebson I, Faillace LA, et al: Alcoholism: controlled drinking and incentives for abstinence. Psychol Reports 28:575–580, 1971

Coid J: Mania a potu: a critical review of pathological intoxication. Psychol Med 9:709–719, 1979

Coid J: Alcoholism and violence. Drug and Alcohol Abuse 9:1–13, 1982

Colson DB, Horwitz L. Research in group psychotherapy, in Comprehensive Group Psychotherapy, 2nd ed. Edited by Kaplan HI, Sadock BJ. Baltimore, Williams and Wilkins, 1983

Cooney N, Baker L, Pomerleau OF: Cue exposure for relapse prevention in alcohol treatment, in Advances in Clinical Behavior Therapy. Edited by McMahon R, Craig K. New York, Brunner/Mazel, 1983

Corder BF, Corder RF, Laidlow N: An intensive treatment program for alcoholics and their wives. Quarterly Journal of Studies on Alcohol 33:1144–1146, 1972

Davis D: Mood changes in alcoholic subjects with programmed and free choice drinking, in Recent Advances in Studies of Alcoholism. Publication HSM 719045.

Edited by Mello NK, Mendelson JH. Washington, DC, US Public Health Service, 1971

Davis DI: Alcoholics Anonymous and family therapy. Journal of Marital and Family Therapy 6:65–73, 1980

Deiker T, Chambers HE: Structure and content of hallucinations in alcohol withdrawal and functional psychosis. J Stud Alcohol 39:1831–1840, 1978

Despotovic A, Milosavcevic V: Clubs of treated alcoholics in dispensary conditions of work. Anali Bolnics "Dr. M. Stojanovic" 6:316–321, 1967

Deutsch JA, Walton NY: Diazepam maintenance of alcohol preference during alcohol withdrawal. Science 198:307–309, 1977

Ditman KS, Crawford GG, Forgy EW, et al: A controlled experiment on the use of court probation for drunk arrests. Am J Psychiatry 124:160–163, 1967

Dodes L: Abstinence from alcohol in long-term individual psychotherapy with alcoholics. Am J Psychother 38:248–256, 1984

Doroff DR: Group psychotherapy in alcoholism, in Treatment and Rehabilitation of the Chronic Alcoholic. Edited by Kissin B, Begleiter H. New York, Plenum, 1977

Draper RJ: The extent of alcoholic brain damage in the Republic of Ireland. Journal of the Irish Medical Association 71:356–360, 1978

Draughon M: Ego building: an aspect of the treatment of psychopaths. Psychol Reports 40:615–626, 1977

Dubourg GD: After-care for alcoholics: a follow-up study. Br J Addict 64:155–163, 1969

Eckhardt M: Alcoholic values and Alcoholics Anonymous. Quarterly Journal of Studies on Alcohol 28:277–288, 1967

Eckhardt M, Ryback R, Paulter C: Neuropsychological deficits in alcoholic men in their mid-30s. Am J Psychiatry 137:932–936, 1980

Edwards G, Gross MM: Alcohol dependence: provisional description of a clinical syndrome. Br Med J 1:1058–1061, 1976

Edwards G, Hensman C, Hawker A, et al: Who goes to Alcoholics Anonymous? Lancet 2:382–384, 1966

Edwards G, Hensman C, Hawker A, et al: Alcoholics Anonymous: The anatomy of a self-help group. Soc Psychiatry 1:195–204, 1967

Edwards G, Gross MM, Keller M, et al: Alcohol-related problems in the disability perspective. J Stud Alcohol 37:1360–1382, 1976

Edwards G, Orford J, Egert S, et al: Alcoholism: a controlled trial of "treatment" and "advice." J Stud Alcohol 38:1004–1031, 1977

Edwards G, Arif A, Hodgson R: Nomenclature and classification of drug- and alcohol-related problems: a WHO memorandum. Bull WHO 59:225–242, 1981

Edwards P, Harvey C, Whitehead PC: Wives of alcoholics, a critical review and analysis. Quarterly Journal of Studies on Alcohol 34:112–132, 1973

Elal-Lawrence G, Slade PD, Dewey ME: Predictors of outcome type in treated problem drinkers. J Stud Alcohol 47:41–47, 1986

Elkins RL: A therapeutic phoenix emergent normal drinking by failures in an abstinence oriented program: verbal aversion therapy for alcoholism. Scandinavian Journal of Behavioral Therapy 6:55, 1977

Elkins RL, Murdock RP: The contribution of successful conditioning to abstinence maintenance following covert sensitization (verbal aversion) treatment of alcoholism. IRCS Medical Science 5:167, 1977

Emrick CD: A review of psychologically oriented treatment in alcoholism. J Stud Alcohol 36:88–108, 1975

Emrick C, Lassen CL, Edwards MT: Nonprofessional peers as therapeutic agents, in Effective Psychotherapy: A Handbook of Research. Edited by Gurman AS, Razin AM. New York, Pergamon Press, 1977, pp 120–161

Ends EJ, Page CW: A study of three types of group psychotherapy with hospitalized male inebriates. Quarterly Journal of Studies on Alcohol 18:263–277, 1957

Ends EJ, Page CW: Group psychotherapy and concomitant psychological change. Psychological Monographs 73, Whole 480, 1959

Esser PH: Conjoint family therapy with alcoholics: a new approach. Br J Addict 64:275–286, 1970

Ewing J: Matching therapy and patients: the cafeteria plan. Br J Addict 72:13–18, 1977

Ewing JA: Disulfiram and other deterrent drugs, in The Encyclopedic Handbook of Alcoholism. Edited by Pattison EM, Kaufman E. New York, Gardner Press, 1982, pp 1022–1042

Ewing JA, Rouse BA: Failure of an experimental treatment program to inculcate controlled drinking in alcoholics. Br J Addict 71:127–134, 1976

Ewing JA, Long V, Wenzel GG: Concurrent group psychotherapy of alcoholic patients and their wives. Int J Group Psychother 11:329–338, 1961

Feeny DJ, Dranger P: Alcoholics view group therapy: process and goals. J Stud Alcohol 37:611–618, 1976

Finney JW, Moos RH, Mewborn CR: Posttreatment experiences and treatment outcome of alcoholic patients six months and two years after hospitalization. J Consult Clin Psychol 48:17–29, 1980

Fisher B, Wieman RJ, Bechtel JE: Independence House: a specialized program. Alcohol Health Research World 4:18–23, 1979

Fleiger DL, Zingle HW: Covert sensitization treatment with alcoholics. Canadian Counseling 7:269, 1973

Florenzano, R: A therapeutic trial of lithium carbonate in ambulatory alcohol patients (abstract). JAMA 249:3367, 1983

Forrest G: The Diagnosis and Treatment of Alcoholism. Springfield, Ill, Charles C Thomas, 1975

Fowler RC, Rich CL, Young D: San Diego suicide study, II: substance abuse in young cases. Arch Gen Psychiatry 43:962–968, 1986

Frances A, Clarkin J, Perry S: Differential therapeutics: psychiatry. New York, Brunner/Mazel, 1984

Frances R: The application of psychoanalytic concepts in alcoholism treatment, in Social Work Treatment of Alcohol Problems. (NIAAA-RUCAS Alcoholism Treatment Series No. 5.) Edited by Cook D, Fewell C, Riolo J. Piscataway, NJ, Rutgers Center of Alcohol Studies, 1983

Frye FV, Hammer MF, Burke G III: The confrontation-sensitivity (C-S) group, in Drug Dependence and Alcoholism. Edited by Schechter AJ. New York, Plenum, 1981

Fuller RK, Wilford WO: Life-table analysis of abstinence in a study evaluating the efficacy of disulfiram. Alcoholism: Clinical and Experimental Research 4:298–301, 1980

Fuller R, Branchey L, Brightwell D, et al: Disulfiram treatment of alcoholism: a Veterans Administration cooperative study. JAMA 256:1449–1455, 1986

Galanter M (ed): Alcohol and Drug Abuse in Medical Education. Washington, DC, US Government Printing Office, 1980

Galanter M: Self-help group therapy for alcoholism: a controlled study. Alcoholism Clin Exp Res 8:16–23, 1984a

Galanter M: The use of social networks in office management of the substance abuser, in Advances in the Psychosocial Treatment of Alcoholism. Edited by Galanter M, Pattison EM. Washington, DC, American Psychiatric Press, 1984, pp 97–114

Galanter M, Castaneda R, Salamon I: Institutional self-help therapy for alcoholism: clinical outcome. Alcohol Clin Exp Res 11:424–429, 1987

Galanter M, Panepinto W: Entering the alcohol outpatient service: Application of a systems approach to patient dropout, in Currents in Alcoholism, Vol VII. Galanter M (ed.). New York, Grune & Stratton, pp 307–314, 1980

Gallant DM: Group staffing in an alcoholism treatment service. Int J Group Psychother 19:218–221, 1964

Gallant DM: Alcohol and Drug Abuse Curriculum Guide for Psychiatry Faculty. Publication ADM 82–1159. Rockville, Md, US Department of Health and Human Services, 1982a

Gallant DM: The new breed of alcoholics. Alcoholism: Clinical and Experimental Research 6:536–537, 1982b

Gallant DM: Psychiatric aspects of alcohol intoxication, withdrawal, and organic brain syndromes, in Alcoholism and Clinical Psychiatry. Edited by Solomon J. New York, Plenum, 1982c

Gallant DM, Bishop MP, Stoy B, et al: The value of a "first contact" group intake session in an alcohol outpatient clinic: statistical conformation. Psychosomatics 7:349–352, 1966

Gallant DM, Bishop MP, Faulkner MA, et al: A comparative evaluation of compulsory and voluntary treatment of the chronic alcoholic municipal court offender. Psychosomatics 9:306–310, 1968

Gallant DM, Rich A, Bey E, et al: Group psychotherapy with married couples: a successful technique in New Orleans alcoholism clinic patients. J LA Med Soc 122:41–44, 1970

Gerard DL, Saenger G: Outpatient Treatment of Alcoholism. Toronto, University of Toronto Press, 1966

Gessner PK: Treatment of the alcohol withdrawal syndrome. Substance Abuse 1:2–5, 1979

Gitlow SE, Peyser HS (eds): Alcoholism: A Practical Treatment Guide. New York, Gardner Press, 1980

Gliedman LH: Concurrent and combined group treatment of chronic alcoholics and their wives. Int J Group Psychother 7:414–424, 1957

Goldstein SG, Linden JD: Multivariate classification of alcoholics by means of the MMPI. J Abnorm Psychol 74:661–669, 1969

Goodwin DW, Guze SB: Psychiatric Diagnosis. New York, Oxford University Press, 1984

Gorman JM, Rooney JF: The influence of Al-Anon on the coping behavior of wives of alcoholics. J Stud Alcohol 40:1030–1038, 1979

Greenbaum H: Group psychotherapy with alcoholics in conjunction with Antabuse treatment. Int J Group Psychother 4:30–45, 1954

Guerrero-Figueroa R, Rye NM, Gallant DM, et al: Electrographic and behavioral effects of diazepam during alcohol withdrawal in cats. Neuropharmacology 9:143–150, 1970

Harper C: Wernicke's encephalopathy: a more common disease than realized: a neuropathological study of 51 cases. J Neurol Neurosurg Psychiatry 42:226–231, 1979

Hatcher R, Jones BM: Inhibition of alcohol dehydrogenase with estrogen. Alcohol Technical Report 6:39–41, 1977

Hayman M: Current attitudes toward alcoholism of psychotherapists in southern California. Am J Psychiatry 112:485–685, 1967

Heather N, Edwards S, Hore BD: Changes in construing and outcome of group therapy for alcoholism. J Stud Alcohol 36:1238–1253, 1975

Hedberg AG, Campbell L III: A comparison of four behavioral treatments of alcoholism. J Behav Ther Exp Psychiatry 5:251–256, 1974

Hesselbrock MN, Hesselbrock VM, Tennen HR, et al: Methodological consideration in assessment of depression in alcoholics. J Consult Clin Psychol 51:399–405, 1983a

Hesselbrock MN, Babor TF, Hesselbrock VM, et al: "Never believe an alcoholic"? on the validity of self-report measures of alcohol dependence and related constructs. Int J Addict 18:593–609, 1983b

Hesselbrock MN, Hesselbrock VM, Babor TF, et al: Antisocial behavior, psychopathology and problem drinking in the natural history of alcoholism, in Longitudinal Studies of Antisocial Behavior. Edited by Mednick SA, Van Dusen K. Hingham, Mass, Kluwer Academic Publishers, 1984

Hesselbrock MN, Meyer RE, Keener JJ: Psychopathology in the alcoholic patient. Arch Gen Psychiatry 42:1050, 1985

Heyman MM: Referral to alcoholism programs in industry: coercion, confrontation and choice. J Stud Alcohol 37:7, 900–907, 1976

Hirsch SM, Von Rosenberg R, Phelam C, et al: Effectiveness of assertiveness training with alcoholics. J Stud Alcohol 39:89–97, 1978

Hodgson R, Rankin H: Modification of excessive drinking by cue exposure. Behav Res Ther 14:305–307, 1976

Hodgson RJ, Rankin JJ, Stockwell TR: Alcohol dependence and the priming effect. Behav Res Ther 17:379–387, 1979

Holzbach E, Buhler KE: Die behandlung des Delirium Tremens mit Haldol. Nervenarzt 49:405–409, 1978

Hoy RM: The personality of inpatient alcoholics in relation to group psychotherapy: as measured by the 16PF. Quarterly Journal of Studies on Alcohol 30:401–407, 1969

Hughes JM: Adolescent children of alcoholic parents and the relationship of Alateen to these children. J Consult Clin Psychol 45:946–947, 1977

Hunt GM, Azrin NH: A community-reinforcement approach to alcoholism. Behav Res Ther 11:91–104, 1973

Intaglia JC: Increasing the interpersonal problem solving skills of an alcoholic population. J Consult Clin Psychol 46:498, 1978

Jacob T, Seilhamer RA: Alcoholism and family interaction, in Family Interaction and Psychopathology. Edited by Jacob T. New York, Plenum, 1987

Jacob T, Favorini A, Meisel SS, et al: The alcoholic spouse, children and family interactions: substantive findings and methodological issues. J Stud Alcohol 39:1231–1251, 1978

Jaffe JH: Alcoholism and affective disturbance: current drugs and shortcomings, in Pharmacological Treatments for Alcoholism. Edited by Edwards G, Littleton J. New York, Beckenham, Kent, Methuen, 1984

Jellinek EM: The Disease Concept of Alcoholism. Highland Park, NJ, Hillhouse Press, 1960

Jones BM, Jones MK: Alcohol effects in women during the menstrual cycle. Ann NY Acad Sci 576–587, 1975

Jones GH: The recognition of alcoholism by psychiatrists in training. Psychol Med 9:789–791, 1979

Jones MC: Personality correlates and antecedents of drinking patterns in adult males. J Consult Clin Psychol 32:2–12, 1968

Kammeier ML, Anderson PO: Two years later: posttreatment participation in AA by 1970 Hazelden patients. Presented at the 27th Annual Meeting of Alcohol and Drug Problems Association of North America. New Orleans, September 1976

Kansas N: Alcoholism and group psychotherapy, in Encyclopedic Handbook of Alcoholism. Edited by Pattison EM, Kaufman E. New York, Gardner, 1982

Kaplan RF, Meyer RE, Stroebel CF: Alcohol dependence and responsivity to an ethanol stimulus as predictors of ethanol consumption. Br J Addict 78:259–267, 1983

Kaplan RF, Glueck BC, Hesselbrock MN: Spectral and coherence analysis of the EEG in alcoholics and matched controls. J Stud Alcohol (in press)

Katz L: The Salvation Army men's social service center, II: results. Quarterly Journal of Studies on Alcohol 27:636–647, 1966

Kaufman E: Alcoholism and the use of other drugs, in Encyclopedic Handbook of Alcoholism. Edited by Pattison EM, Kaufman E. New York, Gardner Press, 1982, pp 696–708

Kaufman E: Family systems and family therapy of substance abuse: an overview of two decades of research and clinical experience. Int J Addict 20:897–916, 1985

Kaufman E, Pattison EM: Differential methods of family therapy in the treatment of alcoholism. J Stud Alcohol 42:951–971, 1981

Kaufman E, Pattison EM: Family and network therapy in alcoholism, in Encyclopedic Handbook of Alcoholism. Edited by Pattison EM, Kaufman E. New York, Gardner Press, 1982

Kernberg O: Borderline personality organization. J Am Psychoanal Assoc 15:641–685, 1967

Kernberg O: Borderline conditions and pathological narcissism. New York, Aronson, 1975

Khan A, Ciraulo D, Nelson W, et al: Dexamethasone suppression test in recently detoxified alcoholics. J Clin Psychopharmacol 4:94–97, 1984

Khantzian E: Psychodynamics of drug dependence: an overview, in Psychodynamics of Drug Dependence. Research Monograph No. 12. Rockville, Md, National Institute on Drug Abuse, 1977, pp 11–25

Khantzian E: Some treatment implications of the ego and self disturbances in alcoholism, in Dynamic Approaches to the Understanding and Treatment of Alcoholism. Edited by Bean MH, Zinberg NE. New York, Macmillan, 1981, pp 163–188

Khantzian E: Self-preservation and the care of the self: ego instincts reconsidered. Psychoanal Study Child 38:209–232, 1983

Khantzian E: A contemporary psychodynamic approach to drug abuse treatment. Am J Drug Alcohol Abuse 12:213–223, 1986

Khantzian E, Mark J, Schatzberg A: Heroin use as an attempt to cope: clinical observations. Am J Psychiatry 131:160–164, 1974

Kish GB, Hermann HT: The Fort Mead Alcoholism Treatment Program: a follow-up study. Quarterly Journal of Studies on Alcohol 32:628–635, 1971

Kissin B: Biological investigations in alcohol research, in Research Priorities on Alcohol. Edited by Keller M. Piscataway, NJ, Rutgers Center of Alcohol Studies, 1979a, pp 168–173

Kissin B: Biological investigations in alcohol research. J Stud Alcohol [Suppl] 8:146–181, 1979b

Kissin B: The role of physical dependence and brain damage in the protracted alcohol abstinence syndrome. Advances in Alcohol 2:1–3, 1981

Kiviranta P: Alcoholism Syndrome in Finland. Helsinki, Finnish Foundation for Alcohol Studies, 1969

Knight RF: The psychodynamics of chronic alcoholism. J Nerv Ment Disord 8:538–543, 1937

Kohut H: The Analyses of the Self. New York, International Universities Press, 1971

Kohut H: Restoration of the Self. New York, International Universities Press, 1977

Krystal H: Alexithymia and the effectiveness of psychoanalytic treatment. Int J Psychoanal Psychother 9:353–338, 1982

Kurtz E: Why A.A. works: the intellectual significance of Alcoholics Anonymous. J Stud Alcohol 43:38–80, 1982

Lawson G, Peterson JS, Lawson A: Alcoholism and the Family. Rockville, Md, Aspen, 1983

Leach B: Does Alcoholics Anonymous really work?, in Alcoholism: Progress in Research and Treatment. Edited by Bourne PG, Fox R. New York, Academic Press, 1973

Lemere F: Psychological factors in the conditioned-reflex treatment of alcoholism. Quarterly Journal of Studies in Alcohol 8:261, 1947

Lemere F, Voegtlin WL: An evaluation of the aversion treatment of alcoholism. Quarterly Journal of Studies on Alcohol 11:199, 1950

Levine J, Zigler E: The essential-reactive distinction in alcoholism: a developmental approach. J Abnorm Psychol 81:242–249, 1973

Levinson UR: The decision group: beginning treatment in an alcoholism clinic. Health Soc Work 4:199–221, 1979

Lewis DC, Senay EC: Treatment of Drug and Alcohol Abuse. New York, State University of New York, 1981

Lin Y-J, Weidler DJ, Garg DC: Effects of solid food on blood levels of alcohol in man. Res Common Chem Pathol Pharmacol 13:713–722, 1976

Lishman WA: Alcoholic dementia: a hypothesis. Lancet 1:1184–1186, 1986

Litman GK, Eiser JR, Rawson SB, et al: Differences in relapse precipitants and coping behavior between alcoholic relapsers and survivors. Behav Res Ther 17:89, 1978

Litman GK, Stapleton J, Oppenheim AN, et al: Coping behaviors, their perceived effectiveness and alcoholism relapse and survival. Br J Addict 78:269–276, 1983

Lorand S: A summary of psychoanalytic literature on problems of alcoholism bibliography. Yearbook of Psychoanalysis 1:359–378, 1948

Lovibond SH, Caddy G: Discriminated aversive control of alcoholics' drinking behavior. Behavior Therapy 1:437–444, 1970

Ludwig AM: On and off the wagon. Quarterly Journal of Studies on Alcohol 33:91–96, 1972

Maberg D: Follow-up study of persons referred for inpatient treatment from an industrial alcohol program. Presented at the Occupational Programs Section, Alcohol and Drug Problems Association of North America. San Francisco, 1974

Mack JE: Alcoholism, A.A., and the governance of the self, in Dynamic Approaches to the Understanding and Treatment of Alcoholism. Edited by Bean MH, Zinberg NE. New York, Free Press, 1981

Mahler M, Pine R, Bergman A: The Psychological Birth of the Human Infant: Symbiosis and Individuation. New York, Basic Books, 1975

Mahoney MJ: Cognition and Behavior Modification. Cambridge, Mass, Ballinger, 1974

Maletzky BM: Assisted covert sensitization for drug abuse. Int J Addict 9:411, 1974

Maletzky BM: The alcohol provocation test. J Clin Psychiatry 39:407–411, 1978

Mandel W, Melisaratos N: Protracted alcohol withdrawal syndromes. Presented at the Annual Meeting of the Research Society on Alcoholism. South Carolina, May 29–June 1, 1985

McClelland DC, Davis WN, Kalin R, et al: The Drinking Man. New York, Free Press, 1972

McCord W, McCord J: A longitudinal study of the personality of alcoholics, in Society, Culture and Drinking Patterns. Edited by Pittman J, Snyder CR. New York, John Wiley and Sons, 1962

McCrady BS, Moreau J, Paolino TJ, et al: Joint hospitalization and couples therapy for alcoholism: a four-year followup. J Stud Alcohol 43:1244–1255, 1982

McElfresh O: Supportive groups for teenagers of the alcoholic parent: a preliminary report. Med. Ecol. Clinical Research 3:26–29, 1970

McGinnis CA: The effect of group therapy on ego-strength scale scores of alcoholic patients. J Clin Psychol 19:346–347, 1963

McKinlay AP: Ancient experience with intoxicating drink: nonclassical peoples. Quarterly Journal of Studies on Alcohol 9:388–414, 1949

McLellan AT, Erdlen FR, Erdlen DL, et al: Psychological severity and response to alcoholism rehabilitation. Drug Alcohol Depend 8:23–35, 1981

Meeks DE, Kelly C: Family therapy with the families of recovering alcoholics. Quarterly Journal of Studies on Alcohol 31:399–413, 1970

Mendelson JH, Mello NK: Experimental analysis of drinking behavior of chronic alcoholics. Ann NY Acad Sci 133:828–845, 1966

Mendelson JH, Mello NK: Alcohol Use and Abuse in America. Boston, Little, Brown and Co, 1985

Merry J, Reynolds CM, Bailey J, et al: A prophylactic treatment of alcoholism by lithium carbonate. Lancet 2:481–482, 1976

Meyer RE, Babor TF, Hessenbrock MN, et al: New directions in the assessment of the alcoholic patient. Presented at International Research Seminar. Washington, DC, November 1983a

Meyer RE, Babor TF, Mirkin PM: Typologies in alcoholism: an overview. Int J Addict 18:235–249, 1983b

Miller PM: A behavioral intervention program for chronic public drunkenness offenders. Arch Gen Psychiatry 32:915, 1975

Miller PM, Hersen M, Eisler RM, et al: Contingent reinforcement of lowered blood alcohol levels in an outpatient clinic. Behav Res Ther 12:261–263, 1974

Miller S, Frances R: Psychiatrists and the treatment of addiction: perception and practices. Am J Drug Alcohol Abuse 12:187–199, 1986

Miller WR: Behavioral self-control training in the treatment of problem drinkers, in Behavioral Self Management: Strategies, Techniques and Outcomes. New York, Brunner/Mazel, 1977, pp 154–175

Miller WR: Behavioral treatment of problem drinkers: a comparative outcome study of three controlled drinking therapies. J Consult Clin Psychol 46:74, 1978

Miller WR, Hester RK: Treating the problem drinker: modern approaches, in Addictive Behaviors. Edited by Miller WR. New York, Pergamon Press, 1980

Miller W, Hester R: Inpatient alcoholism treatment: who benefits? Am Psychol 41:794–805, 1986

Miller WR, Joyce MA: Prediction of abstinence, controlled drinking and heavy drinking outcome following behavioral self-control training. J Consult Clin Psychol 41:773–775, 1979

Miller WR, Taylor CA, West JB: Focused versus broad-spectrum behavior therapy for problem drinkers. J Consult Clin Psychol 48:590–601, 1980

Miller WR, Gribskov CJ, Martell AL: Effectiveness of a self-control manual for problem drinkers with and without therapist contact. Int J Addict 1981a

Miller WR, Pechocek TF, Hamburg S: Group behavior therapy for problem drinkers. Int J Addict 16:829–839, 1981b

Moore R: Some countertransference reactions in the treatment of alcoholism. Psychiatry Digest 26:35–43, 1965

Moos RH, Bromet E, Tsu Z, et al: Family characteristics and the outcome of treatment for alcoholism. J Stud Alcohol 40:78–88, 1979

Morey LC, Blashfield RK: Empirical classifications of alcoholism: a review. J Stud Alcohol 42:925–937, 1981

Murphy HBM: Hidden barriers to the diagnosis and treatment of alcoholism and other alcohol misuse. J Stud Alcohol 41:417–428, 1980

Nathan PE, Titler NA, Lowenstein LM, et al: Behavioral analysis of chronic alcoholism. Arch Gen Psychiatry 22:419–430, 1970

National Council on Alcoholism: Criteria Committee: criteria for the diagnosis of alcoholism. Am J Psychiatry 129:127–135, 1972

Negrete JC: Cultural influences on social performance of alcoholics: a comparative study. Quarterly Journal of Studies on Alcohol 34:905–916, 1973

Neuberger OW, Matarazzo JD, Schmitz RE: One year follow-up of total abstinence in chronic alcohol patients following emetic counterconditioning. Alcoholism: Clinical and Experimental Research 4:304, 1980

Neuberger OW, Miller SI, Schmitz RE, et al: Replicable abstinence rates in alcoholism treatment program. JAMA 248:960–963, 1982

Norris JL: Alcoholics Anonymous, in World Dialogue on Alcohol and Drug Dependence. Edited by Whitney ED. Boston, Beacon Press, 1970

Norris JL: A.A.'s 1974 membership survey. Presented at the North American Congress on Alcohol and Drug Problems. San Francisco, December 1974a

Norris JL: General survey: General Service Board of Alcoholics Anonymous, Inc. Presented at the North American Congress on Alcohol and Drug Problems. San Francisco, December 1974b

Norris JL: Analysis of the 1977 survey of the membership of A.A. Presented at the meeting of the 32nd International Congress on Alcoholism and Drug Dependence. Warsaw, Poland, September 1978

Norris JL: Bridging the gap between active treatment and normal living—AA involvement. Alcohol Health and Research World 6:6–9, 1982

O'Brien JE, Meyer RE, Thoms DC: Double-blind comparison of lorazepam and diazepam in the treatment of the acute alcohol syndrome. Current Therapy Research 34:825–830, 1983

O'Farrell TJ, Cutter HS: Evaluating behavioral marital therapy for alcoholics: procedures and preliminary results, in Essentials of Behavioral Treatments for Families. Edited by Hamerlynch LA. New York, Brunner/Mazel, 1984

Ogborne AC, Bornet A: Brief report: abstinence and abusive drinking among affiliates of Alcoholics Anonymous: are these the only alternatives? Addict Behav 7:199–202, 1982

Ogborne AC, Glaser FB: Characteristics of affiliates of Alcoholics Anonymous: a review of the literature. J Stud Alcohol 42:661–675, 1981

O'Leary DE, Haddock DL, Donovan DM, et al: Alcohol use patterns and Alcoholics Anonymous affiliation as predictors of alcoholism treatment outcome. Research Communications in Substance Abuse 1:197–209, 1980a

O'Leary MR, Calsyn DA, Haddock DL, et al: Differential alcohol use patterns and personality traits among three Alcoholics Anonymous attendance level groups: further considerations of the affiliation profile. Drug Alcohol Depend 5:135–144, 1980b

O'Leary R, Donovan DM, Chaney EF, et al: Relationship of alcoholic personality subtypes to treatment follow-up measures. J Nerv Ment Dis 8:475–480, 1980

Orford J, Oppenheimer E, Edwards G: Abstinence or control: the outcome for excessive drinkers two years after consultation. Behav Res Ther 14:409–418, 1976a

Orford J, Oppenheimer E, Egert S, et al: The cohesiveness of alcoholism complicated marriages and its influence on treatment outcome. Br J Psychiatry 128:318–339, 1976b

Orrego H, Blake JE, Blendis LM: Reliability of assessment of alcohol intake based on personal interviews in a liver clinic. Lancet 2:1354–1356, 1979

Paolino TJ, McCrady BS: Joint admission as a treatment modality for problem drinkers: a case report. Am J Psychiatry 133:222–224, 1976

Parloff MB, Dies RR: Group therapy outcome research, 1966–1975. Int J Group Psychother 27:281–319, 1977

Parsons OA: Neuropsychological deficits in alcoholics: facts and fictions. Alcoholism: Clinical and Experimental Research 1:51–56, 1977

Patrick GM: Alcoholics Anonymous—Competitive or complementary to occupational consultants, in Association of Labor-Management Administrators and Consultants on Alcoholism, Inc. Proceedings of the eighth annual meeting of ALMACA,

Detroit, MI, 1–5 October 1979. Compiled by Marsha Moran-Sackett. Arlington, VA, ALMACA, 1980

Pattison EM: A conceptual approach to alcoholism treatment goals. Addict Behav 1:177–192, 1976a

Pattison EM: Nonabstinent drinking goals in the treatment of alcoholism: a clinical typology. Arch Gen Psychiatry 33:923–930, 1976b

Pattison EM: Management of alcoholism in medical practice. Med Clin North Am 61:797–809, 1977

Pattison EM: The selection of treatment modalities for the alcoholic patient, in Diagnosis and Treatment of Alcoholism. Edited by Mendelson JH, Mello N. New York, McGraw-Hill, 1979

Pattison EM, Kaufman E: Family therapy in the treatment of alcoholism, in Family Therapy and Major Psychopathology. Edited by Lansky MR. New York, Grune & Stratton, 1981

Pattison EM, Courlas PG, Patti R, et al: Diagnostic-therapeutic intake groups for wives of alcoholics. Quarterly Journal of Studies on Alcohol 26:605–616, 1965

Patton MQ: The Outcomes of Treatment: A Study of Patients Admitted to Hazelden in 1976. Center City, Minn, Hazelden Foundation, Inc, 1979

Pendery ML, Maltzman IM, West JL: Controlled drinking by alcoholics? New findings and reevaluation of a major affirmative study. Science 217:169–174, 1982

Penick E: Familial alcoholism and other psychiatric disorders. (Abstract APA Summary Syllabus). Presented at the Annual Meeting of the American Psychiatric Association. Dallas, 1984

Penick EC, Read MR, Crowley PA, et al: Differentiation by alcoholics by family history. Quarterly Journal of Studies on Alcohol 3:1944–1948, 1978

Penick EC, Powell BJ, Othmer E, et al: Subtyping alcoholics by co-existing psychiatric syndromes: course, family history, outcome, in Longitudinal Research in Alcholism. Edited by Goodwin DW, Van Dusen KT, Mednick SA. Hingham, Mass, Kluwer Academic Publishers, 1983

Petersen-Kelley A: Family environment and Alateens: A note on alcohol abuse potential. Journal of Community Psychology 13:75–76, 1985

Piorkowsky GK, Mann ET: Issues in treatment efficacy research with alcoholics. Percept Mot Skills 41:695, 1975

Pokorny AD, Miller BA, Cleveland SE: Response to treatment of alcoholism. Quarterly Journal of Studies on Alcohol 29:364–381, 1968

Pokorny AD, Miller BA, Kansas T, et al: Effectiveness of extended aftercare in the treatment of alcoholism. Quarterly Journal of Studies on Alcohol 34:435–443, 1973

Pokorny A, Putnam P, Fryer J: Drug abuse and alcoholism teaching in the U.S. medical and osteopathic schools. J Med Educ 53:816–824, 1978

Polich JM, Armor DJ, Braiker HB: The Course of Alcoholism: Four Years after Treatment. Santa Monica, Calif, Rand Corp, 1980

Pomerleau OF, Pertschuk M, Adkins D: A comparison of behavioral and traditional treatment for middle income problem drinkers. Behav Res Ther 9:187, 1978

Popham RE, Schmidt W: Some factors affecting the likelihood of moderate drinking by treated alcoholics. J Stud Alcohol 37:868–882, 1976

Powell B, Penick EC, Read MR, et al: Comparison of three outpatient treatment interventions. J Stud Alcohol 46:309–312, 1985

Rada RR: Sociopathy and alcoholism: diagnostic and treatment implications, in The Treatment of Antisocial Syndromes. Edited by Reid WH. New York, Van Nostrand Reinhold, 1980

Rathod NH, Gregory E, Blows P, et al: A two year follow-up study of alcoholic patients. Br J Psychiatry 112:683–692, 1966

Reisner H: Das chronische subdurale Hamatom-Pachymeningeosis haemorrhagica interna. Nervenarzt 50:74–78, 1979

Rimmer J, Pitts FN Jr, Reich T, et al: Alcoholism, sex, socioeconomic status and race in two hospitalized samples. Quarterly Journal of Studies on Alcohol 32:942–953, 1971

Robins LN: Estimating addiction rates and locating target populations, in The Epidemiology of Heroin and Other Narcotics. NIDA Monograph No. 16. Edited by Rittenhouse JD. Washington, DC, National Institute on Drug Abuse, 1977

Robins LN, Bates WM, O'Neil P: Adult drinking patterns of former problem children, in Society, Culture and Drinking Patterns. Edited by Pittman DJ, Snyder CR. New York, John Wiley and Sons, 1962

Robinson D: Talking Out of Alcoholism: The Self-Help Process of Alcoholics Anonymous. London, Croom Helm, 1979

Robinson GM, Sellers EM, Janacek E: Barbiturate and hypnosedative withdrawal by multiple oral phenobarbital loading dose techniques. Clin Pharmacol Ther 28:71–76, 1981

Roman PM: Spirits at work revisited: needed priorities in occupational alcoholism programming, in Proceedings of the Fourth Annual Conference on Alcoholism of NIAAA. Edited by Chafetz M. Washington, DC, US Government Printing Office, 1975

Rosen A: Psychotherapy and Alcoholics Anonymous: can they be coordinated? Bull Menninger Clin 45:229–246, 1981

Rosett H: How the alcoholic's brain makes it hard to treat his mind. Presented at Symposium, Psychoanalytic Society and Institute, November 1976

Rounsaville BJ, Dolinsky ZS, Babor TF, et al: Psychopathology as a predictor of treatment outcome in alcoholics. Arch Gen Psychiatry (in press)

Rubin SE, Lawlis GF: A model for differential treatment of alcoholics. Rehabilitation Research Practice Rev 1:53–59, 1970

Rudy DR: Slipping and sobriety: the functions of drinking in Alcoholics Anonymous. J Stud Alcohol 41:727–732, 1980

Rund DA, Summers WK, Levin M: Alcohol use and psychiatric illness in emergency patients. JAMA 245:1240–1245, 1981

Sanchez-Craig BM: A self-control strategy for drinking tendencies. Ontario Psychology 7:25, 1975

Sanchez-Craig BM: Cognitive and behavioral coping strategies in the reappraisal of stressful social situations. Journal of Counseling Psychology 23:7, 1976

Sanchez-Craig M, Annis H, Barnet AR, et al: Random Assignment to Abstinence and Controlled Drinking: Evaluation of a Cognitive Behavioral Program for Problem Drinkers. Toronto, ARF Internal Document No. 15. Addiction Research Foundation, 1983

Sands PM, Hanson PG: Psychotherapeutic groups for alcoholics and relatives in an outpatient setting. Int J Group Psychother 21:23–33, 1971

Schuckit M: Alcoholism and sociopathy: diagnostic confusion. Quarterly Journal of Studies on Alcohol 34:157–164, 1973

Schuckit M: Alcoholism and affective disorder: diagnostic confusion, in Alcoholism and Affective Disorders. Edited by Erickson CK. New York, Spectrum Publications, 1979

Schuckit MA: The history of psychotic symptoms in alcoholics. Presented at the Annual Meeting of the American Psychiatric Association. San Francisco, May 1980

Schuckit MA: Alcoholism and other psychiatric disorders. Hosp Community Psychiatry 34:1022–1027, 1983

Schuckit MA: Drug and Alcohol Abuse: A Clinical Guide to Diagnosis and Treatment, 2nd ed. New York, Plenum, 1984a

Schuckit M: Subjective responses to alcohol in sons of alcoholics and control subjects. Arch Gen Psychiatry 41:879–884, 1984b

Schuckit MA: The clinical implications of primary diagnostic groups among alcoholics. Arch Gen Psychiatry 42:1043–1049, 1985a

Schuckit MA: A one-year follow-up of men alcoholics given disulfiram. J Stud Alcohol 46:191–195, 1985b

Schuckit MA: Genetic and clinical implications of alcoholism and affective disorder. Am J Psychiatry 143:140–147, 1986

Schuckit MA: Alcohol and alcoholism, in Harrison's Principles of Internal Medicine, 11th ed. Edited by Petersdorf RG, Adams RD, Braunwald E, et al. New York, McGraw-Hill, 1987, pp 2106–2111

Schuckit M et al: Alcoholism: two types of alcoholism in women. Arch Environ Health 20:301–306, 1969

Shapiro S, Skinner EA, Kessler LG, et al: Utilization of Health and Human Services, 1980

Shelly CH, Goldstein G: An empirically derived typology of hospitalized alcoholics, in Empirical Studies of Alcoholism. Edited by Goldstein D, Heuringer CC. New York, Ballinger, 1976

Shore JH: The epidemiology of chronic mental illness, in Effective Aftercare for the 1980's. Edited by Cutler D. San Francisco, Jossey-Bass, 1983

Shore JH, Kofoed L: The treatment of alcoholism in the community, in Psychosocial Treatment of Alcoholism. Edited by Gallanter M. Washington, DC, American Psychiatric Press, 1984

Silber A: An addendum to the technique of psychotherapy with alcoholics. J Nerv Ment Dis 150:423–437, 1970

Silber A: Rationale for the technique of psychotherapy with alcoholics. Int J Psychoanal Psychother 3:28–47, 1974

Sisson RW, Mallams JH: The use of systematic encouragement and community access procedures to increase attendance at Alcoholic Anonymous and Al-Anon meetings. Am J Drug Alcohol Abuse 8:371–376, 1981

Skinner HA: Factor analysis and studies on alcohol: a methodological review. J Stud Alcohol 41:1091–1101, 1980

Skinner HA: Primary syndromes of alcohol abuse: their management and correlates. Br J Addict 76:63–76, 1981

Skinner HA, Allen BA: Alcohol dependence syndrome: measurement and validation. J Abnorm Psychol 91:199–209, 1982

Skinner HA, Jackson DN, Hoffman H: Alcoholic personality types: identification and correlates. J Abnorm Psychol 83:658–666, 1974

Smart RG: Employed alcoholics treated voluntarily and under constructive coercion: a follow-up study. Quarterly Journal of Studies on Alcohol 35:196–209, 1974

Smart RG: Female and male alcoholics in treatment: characteristics at intake and recovery rates. Br J Addict 74:275–281, 1979

Smith CM, Barnes GM: Alcohol and drug problems in medical patients. NY State J Med 82:947–951, 1982

Sobell MB, Sobell LC: Second year treatment outcome of alcoholics treated by individualized behavior therapy: results. Behav Res Ther 14:195–215, 1976

Sobell MB, Sobell LC: Behavioral Treatment of Alcohol Problems. New York, Plenum, 1978

Solomon J, Vanga N, Morgan JP: Emergency-room physicians' recognition of alcohol misuse. J Stud Alcohol 41:583–586, 1980

Steiner C: Games Alcoholics Play: The Analysis of Life Scripts. New York, Ballantine, 1971

Steinglass P: Experimenting with family treatment approaches to alcoholism 1950–1975: a review. Fam Proc 15:97–123, 1976

Steinglass P: Family therapy in alcoholism, in The Biology of Alcoholism, vol 5. Edited by Kissin B, Begleiter H. New York, Plenum, 1977

Steinglass P: An experimental treatment program for alcoholic couples. J Stud Alcohol 40:159–182, 1979

Steinglass P: A life history model of the alcoholic family. Fam Process 19:211–226, 1980

Steinglass P: The alcoholic family at home: patterns of interaction in wet, dry, and transitional phases of alcoholism. Arch Gen Psychiatry 38:578–584, 1981

Steinglass P, Weiner S, Mendelson JH: A systems approach to alcoholism: a model and its clinical application. Arch Gen Psychiatry 24:401–408, 1971

Steinglass P, Davis DI, Berenson D: Observations of conjointly hospitalized "alcoholic couples" during sobriety of intoxication: implications for theory and therapy. Fam Process 16:1–16, 1977

Steinglass P, Bennett LA, Wolin SJ, et al: The Alcoholic Family. New York, Basic Books, 1987

Stockwell T, Hodgson R, Edwards G, et al: The development of a questionnaire to measure severity of alcohol dependence. Br J Addict 74:79–87, 1979

Sutker PB, Tabakoff B, Goist KC, et al: Acute alcohol intoxication, mood states, and alcohol metabolism in women and men. Pharmacol Biochem Behav 18:349–354, 1983

Swinner P: Treatment Approaches, in Alcoholism in Perspective. Edited by Grant M, Swinner P. Baltimore, University Park Press, 1979

Tahlka V: The Alcoholic Personality. Helsinki, Finnish Foundation for Alcohol Studies, 1966

Tamerin J, Mendelson J: The psychodynamics of chronic inebriation: observations of alcoholics during the process of drinking in an experimental group setting. Am J Psychiatry 125:886–899, 1969

Tamerin J, Neumann C: The alcoholic stereotype: clinical reappraisal and implications for treatment. Am J Psychoanal 34:315–323, 1974

Tarter R, McBride H, Buonpane N, et al: Differentiation of alcoholics according to childhood history of minimal brain dysfunction, family history, and drinking pattern. Arch Gen Psychiatry 34:761–768, 1977

Thorpe JJ, Perret JT: Problem drinking: a follow-up study. Archives of Industrial Health 19:24–32, 1959

Tiebout HM: Alcoholics Anonymous—an experiment of nature. Quarterly Journal of Studies on Alcohol 22:52–68, 1961

Tomsovic M: "Binge" and continuous drinkers: characteristics and treatment follow-up. Quarterly Journal of Studies on Alcohol 35:558–564, 1974

Tomsovic M: Group therapy and changes in the self-concept of alcoholics. J Stud Alcohol 37:53–57, 1976

Trice HM, Roman PM: Sociopsychological predictors of affiliation with Alcoholics Anonymous: a longitudinal study of "treatment success." Soc Psychiatry 5:51–59, 1970

Usher ML, Jay J, Glass DR: Family therapy as a treatment modality for alcoholism. J Stud Alcohol 43:927–938, 1982

Vaillant G: Dangers of psychotherapy in the treatment of alcohol, in Dynamic Approaches to the Understanding and Treatment of Alcoholism. Edited by Bean MH, Zinberg NE. New York, Macmillan, 1981, pp 36–54

Vaillant GE: The Natural History of Alcoholism: Causes, Patterns, and Paths to Recovery. Cambridge, Mass, Harvard University Press, 1983

Vannicelli M: Group psychotherapy with alcoholics: special techniques. J Stud Alcohol 43:17–37, 1982

Viamontes JA: Review of drug effectiveness in the treatment of alcoholism. Am J Psychiatry 128:1570–1571, 1972

Vischi T, Jones KR, Shank E, et al: Alcohol Drug Abuse and Mental Health National Data Book. DHHS #ADM80983, 1980

Vogler RE, Compton JU, Weissbach TA: Integrated behavioral change technique for alcoholism. J Consult Clin Psychol 43:233, 1975

Vogler RE, Weissbach TA, Compton JU: Learning techniques for alcohol abuse. Behav Res Ther 15:31, 1977

Walker K, Sanchez-Craig M, Bornet A: Teaching coping skills to chronic alcoholics in a coeducational halfway house, II: assessment of outcome and identification of outcome predictors. Br J Addict 77:185–196, 1982

Weissman M, Myers J: Clinical depression in alcoholism. Am J Psychiatry 137:372–373, 1980

West JW: A medical audit of acute alcoholism and chronic alcoholism. Alcoholism: Clinical and Experimental Research 2:287–291, 1978

Westfield DR: Two years experience of group methods in the treatment of male alcoholics in a Scottish mental hospital. Br J Addict 67:267–276, 1972

Whitelock PR, Overall JE, Patrick JH: Personality patterns of alcohol abuse in a state hospital population. J Abnorm Psychol 78:9–16, 1971

Whitfield CL: Nondrug detoxification, in Phenomenology and Treatment of Alcoholism. Edited by Whitfield C. New York, Spectrum Publications, 1980

Wiens AN, Montague JR, Maraugh TS: Pharmacological aversive counterconditioning to alcohol in a private hospital: one year follow-up. J Stud Alcohol 37:1320, 1976

Wikler A: Dynamics of drug dependence. Arch Gen Psychiatry 28:611–616, 1973

Wilkinson DA, Carlen PL: Relation of neuropsychological test performance in alcoholics to brain morphology measured by computed tomography, in Biological Effects of Alcohol. Edited by Begleiter H. New York, Plenum, 1980

Wilsnack JC: The impact of sex roles and women's alcohol use and abuse, in Alcoholism Problems in Women and Children. Edited by Greenblatt M, Schuckit MA. New York, Grune & Stratton, 1976

Winokur G, Rimmer J, Reich T: Alcoholism, IV: is there more than one type of alcoholism? Br J Psychiatry 118:525–531, 1971

Wolff K: Hospitalized alcoholic patients, III: motivating alcoholics through group psychotherapy. Hosp Community Psychiatry 19:206–209, 1968

Wolin S, Bennet L, Noond D, et al: Disrupted family rituals: a factor in the intergenerational transmission of alcoholism. J Stud Alcohol 41:214, 1980

Wood D, Del Nuovo A, Bucky SF, et al: Psychodrama with an alcohol abuser population. Group Psychotherapy and Psychodrama 31:75–88, 1978

Woodruff RA, Guze SB, Clayton PJ: Alcoholism and depression. Arch Gen Psychiatry 28:97–100, 1973

Woodruff RA, Clayton PJ, Cloninger CR, et al: A brief method of screening for alcoholism. J Clin Psychiatry 37:434–435, 1976

Woodside M: Children of Alcoholics. Albany, New York State Division of Alcoholism and Alcohol Abuse, 1982

Yalom ID: The Theory and Practice of Group Psychotherapy. New York, Basic Books, 1970

Yalom ID: Group therapy and alcoholism. Ann NY Acad Sci 233:85–103, 1974

Yalom ID: The Theory and Practice of Group Psychotherapy, 2nd ed. New York, Basic Books, 1975

Yalom ID: The Theory and Practice of Group Psychotherapy, 3rd ed. New York, Basic Books, 1985

Yalom ID, Bloch S, Bond G, et al: Alcoholics in interactional group therapy. Arch Gen Psychiatry 35:419–425, 1978

Yochelson S, Samenow SE: The Criminal Personality, vol. 1, A Profile for Change. New York, Jason Aronson, 1976

Yochelson S, Samenow SE: The Criminal Personality, vol. 2, The Change Process. New York, Jason Aronson, 1977

Young TJ, Lawson GW: A.A. referrals for alcohol related crimes: the advantages and limitations. International Journal of Offender Therapy and Comparative Criminology 28:131–139, 1984

Zimberg S: The Clinical Management of Alcoholism. New York, Brunner/Mazel, 1982

Zimberg S: Principles of alcoholism psychotherapy, in Practical Approaches to Alcoholism Psychotherapy, 2nd ed. Edited by Zimberg S, Blume SB, Wallace J. New York, Plenum Press, 1985

SECTION 13

Psychoactive Substance Use Disorders (Not Alcohol)

Chapter 126

Clinical Assessment of Drug Abusers

Spitzer and Williams (1980) pointed out that the purposes of diagnosis are communication, control, and comprehension. In clinical settings, these functions translate into the ability to convey pertinent information to other clinicians and facilities, to guide in the choice of appropriate treatments, and to provide information on the determinants of drug abuse in the individual being assessed.

Clinicians charged with assessing drug abusers are typically faced with special problems resulting from administrative and geographic separation of drug treatment units from general psychiatric or medical clinics as well as from complex diagnostic issues posed by the patients themselves. In this chapter, I will address four questions most pertinent to the clinical assessment of this special population: What should a clinical assessment of substance abusers include? How should assessments be made? How should drug-induced mental states be handled? How can the veracity of drug abusers' self-reports be maximized?

What Should a Clinical Assessment of Substance Abusers Include?

To alert clinicians to the range of relevant problem areas presented by drug abusing patients, the assessment needs to be multidimensional. Although curtailment or substantial reduction of drug use must be the primary goal of a drug treatment program, rehabilitation and prevention of relapse often cannot take place without attending to associated social, psychological, or medical impairment, which frequently contributes to the onset or perpetuation of the drug abuse. Regarding the issue of multidimensionality, clinical investigators have repeatedly demonstrated that drug abusers present to treatment with abuse of multiple classes of substances, legal problems, social disruption, occupational impairment, psychiatric syndromes, and a range of drug and life-style-related medical problems (Babor et al., in press; Kosten et al. 1987b; McLellan et al. 1981; Rounsaville et al. 1982a). Moreover, impairment in these "ancillary" areas has been shown to be associated with poorer treatment outcome, including relapse to substance abuse (Kosten et al. 1986, 1987; McLellan et al. 1981; Rounsaville et al. 1982a, 1986). In addition, the posttreatment course of drug abusers has also been shown to be characterized by multidimensionality so that improvement in one area may be largely independent of improvement in other areas. Thus, for example, reduction in drug use is not powerfully associated with a comparable improvement in psychological impairment, social functioning, or occupational performance. The exception to this trend with opioid addicts is the relatively close association between relapse to opioid use and resumption of criminal activities (McGlothlin 1985).

The major function of clinical assessment is to guide treatment. In this chapter, I will briefly outline the clinical relevance for assessing multiple areas of the drug abuser's problems.

Type and Severity of Drug Abuse

Given the increasing trend for patients to seek treatment with abuse of multiple substances, clinical assessment needs to include specific inquiry into the major classes of drugs commonly used in this country: opioids, cocaine, amphetamines or similarly acting sympathomimetics, cannabis, hallucinogens, inhalants, phencyclidine (PCP) or similarly acting arylcyclohexylamines, sedatives-hypnotics-anxiolytics, and alcohol. Inquiry should be guided by a questionnaire listing these classes of drugs and giving examples of them because patients frequently present to specialized programs emphasizing the current primary drug of abuse (e.g., cocaine) while deemphasizing the concurrent abuse of other, equally important substances (e.g., alcohol, tranquilizers). Knowledge of the range of substances abused by patients is vital at all phases of treatment. During detoxification, co-dependence on additional drugs can greatly increase the complexity and risk involved in the withdrawal process, as is seen with alcohol dependence in patients seeking treatment for cocaine abuse. During the ongoing phase of treatment, abuse of nontargeted substances frequently continues or increases even though the patient has curtailed use of the primary drug of abuse. Important examples of this are use of alcohol, anxiolytics, or cocaine by opioid addicts enrolled in methadone maintenance or narcotic antagonist programs (Gawin and Kleber 1985; Jackson and Richman 1973; Jackson et al. 1983; Kosten et al. 1985, 1987a; Rounsaville et al. 1982b; Stimmel et al. 1982; Stitzer et al. 1981). It is noteworthy that onset of abuse of nontargeted substances usually has begun prior to treatment seeking. Hence, initial assessment of the full range of drugs used can alert clinicians to the possibility that nontargeted drugs may be abused when use of the principal drug of abuse is controlled. During the posttreatment phase, continued use of nontargeted substances is often the route for relapse to the primary substance of abuse. Use of the nontargeted substance can simultaneously act as a cue for drug abuse (e.g., drinking at bars may bring a cocaine abuser back to his or her typical site of cocaine use), and the intoxicated state may decrease a patient's ability to resist the impulse to return to drug use. For many patients, this means that achievement of long-standing abstinence from the primary drug of abuse is predicated on abstinence from use of all psychoactive substances. This is less likely to take place if treating clinicians are not aware of the range of a patient's drug use.

In addition to assessment of the range of drugs abused, it is useful to assess the severity of drug use of the different classes. Severity of alcohol dependence, measured in accordance with the alcohol dependence syndrome concept (Edwards and Gross 1976; Edwards et al. 1981) has been repeatedly shown to predict poorer prognosis in alcoholics (Edwards 1986; Rounsaville et al. 1987). While similar empirical findings are unavailable for abusers of other classes of psychoactive substances, dependence severity is likely to be an important factor with them as well. As a method for rating drug use severity, the DSM-III-R (American Psychiatric Association 1987) dependence criteria include guidelines that can be readily used in clinical settings.

Psychopathology

Several reports have demonstrated high rates of psychiatric co-morbidity in patient groups seeking treatment for alcoholism (Hesselbrock et al. 1985; Schuckit 1985), opioid dependence (Khantzian and Treece 1985; Rounsaville et al. 1982c), or cocaine dependence (Gawin and Kleber 1986; Mirin 1984; Weiss et al. 1986). Nondrug syndromes diagnosed most frequently are depressive, anxiety, and antisocial personality disorders. Presence of psychiatric impairment or coexistent psychiatric syndromes has been shown to reduce a substance abuser's chances of succeeding in treatment (Rounsaville et al. 1982a, 1982d, 1986). Given the treatability of depressive and anxiety disorders with pharmacotherapy and psychotherapy (Weissman et al. 1987), detection of these syndromes can have significant treatment implications. Although there are no reports of demonstrably effective treatment of antisocial personality, Woody et al. (1985) showed that this diagnosis need not be a predictor of negative treatment outcome if it is also associated with a diagnosis of major depression, a common pattern in treatment-seeking opioid addicts (Rounsaville et al. 1982c).

Medical Problems

A wide range of medical problems is commonly seen in treatment-seeking drug abusers. These may relate to chronic or acute effects of the drugs themselves; adulterants in the drug preparations used; use of dirty or shared needles or injection equipment; chronic irritation to the site of preferred drug use (e.g., nasal septum in cocaine insufflation, surface veins in iv use); or a hazardous life-style associated with chronic drug abuse (e.g., injuries or venereal disease secondary to prostitution). A complete physical examination, with special emphasis on systems likely to be affected by drug abuse, is an essential part of routine treatment of this population. Because iv drug abusers are a group at very high risk for HIV infection and acquired immune deficiency syndrome (AIDS), screening for seropositivity to HIV infection should be available to patients entering drug treatment. Although detailed description of methods for protecting patients' confidentiality and for AIDS counseling for drug abusing patients is beyond the scope of this chapter, a responsible testing program must include these procedures.

Legal Problems

Given the illicit nature of commerce in abused drugs, many patients are motivated to seek treatment by current or impending legal problems. While legal counseling is not a typical function of a drug treatment program, knowledge of a patient's status in this area can provide information about motivation to continue in treatment or about possible interruptions of the treatment process (McGlothlin 1985; McLellan 1983).

Occupational and Social Functioning

Social crisis is a common precipitant of entering treatment (Kosten et al. 1983, 1986; Prusoff et al. 1977) for drug abusers, and enlistment of significant others in the treatment process has been frequently recommended (see Chapter 139). Improvement of deficiencies in social and occupational functioning is important to the long-range prognosis of drug abusers; numerous follow-up studies have shown that integration into a nondrug-using social support system is a positive factor in preventing relapse (Maddux and Desmond 1986).

Although some evaluation of all of the areas listed above is likely to be useful for any drug treatment program, the thoroughness of assessment in any given area should be determined by actual services available at the particular treatment setting. For example, detailed evaluation of family functioning is of greater importance in a program offering family therapy compared with one not offering this treatment modality. However, it should be remembered that the drug treatment program may be a drug abuser's primary entry into the health care and social services systems. Hence, even when the drug treatment program does not offer services needed by the patient (e.g., financial assistance for unemployed drug abusers, legal assistance), it is incumbent on program staff to be alert to related problems and to provide referral to appropriate agencies. Even when services to address the range of drug abusers' problems are not readily available, knowledge of multiple problems can guide the choice of modality (e.g., inpatient versus outpatient) or the length of treatment to be recommended (i.e., longer treatment for those with multiple problem areas).

How Should Assessments Be Made?

In devising an assessment system, the clinician can choose between self-reports versus clinician interviews, structured versus unstructured interviews, paraprofessional versus professional interviewers, and screening versus diagnostic evaluations.

Self-Reports

When patients do not have trouble with literacy, use of self-reported assessments saves considerable staff time and can frequently be accomplished during a time period when the patient is waiting for an appointment. While self-reported instruments may yield inadequate information because of patients' misunderstanding the forms, omission of items, and so on, these drawbacks can be avoided if the clinical evaluator reviews the patient's answers with the patient after the forms have been completed. Self-reported forms are most acceptable if they are brief and simple. These properties are most common in measures that are conceived as screening tests, such as the Beck Depression Inventory, which is useful to screen for depression (Beck et al. 1961; Rounsaville et al. 1979) or the Michigan Alcoholism Screening Test, which can detect unsuspected alcoholism in a drug abusing patient group (Rounsaville et al. 1983; Selzer 1971).

Structured Versus Unstructured Interviews

Structured interviews have the disadvantage of allowing less time for spontaneous exploration of a patient's problems. This is far outweighed, however, by the advantages of increased reliability, avoidance of significant omissions, and efficiency.

Paraprofessional-Professional Interviewers and Screening-Diagnostic Interviews

Because professional time is usually a scarce resource in most drug treatment programs, it is desirable to develop an assessment system that can be largely conducted by paraprofessional staff. This is facilitated by the use of structured interview scales, which ensure uniformity in areas assessed and in ways questions are phrased (Rounsaville et al. 1980).

The use of a paraprofessional assessment staff is particularly justified when evaluations are conceived of as a two-stage process, with the first stage consisting of screening and the second stage comprised of more definitive diagnosis.

In the screening phase, the purpose is to provide a highly sensitive, if less specific, assessment of areas in which the drug abuser is likely to have clinically significant problems. For example, initial screening with the Beck Depression Inventory is highly sensitive to the presence of possible depression in opioid addicts (Rounsaville et al. 1979). In the diagnostic phase, a more thorough, professional evaluation can be made on those with high screening scores to determine whether the screening results were indicative of a clinically significant problem, such as a current diagnosis of major depression.

To facilitate a multidimensional, structured evaluation system that can be conducted by paraprofessionals in drug treatment programs, McLellan et al. (1980) developed the Addiction Severity Index (ASI), a clinician-administered instrument that elicits information about a drug abuser's problems in six areas: drug use, medical, psychological, legal, social, and occupational. The ASI can be administered in 30 to 45 minutes and provides reliable ratings that agree well with longer assessments of the six problem areas and are highly correlated with treatment outcome (McLellan et al. 1980, 1983). Moreover, it is useful as a method for assessing a patient's progress in treatment by comparing later reevaluations of the six problem areas with those made on entrance into the program. Given its clinical utility, this instrument has gained increasingly widespread acceptance both in the United States and abroad. In the area of psychopathology, it is useful as a screening tool, with more extensive psychiatric evaluation reserved for those whose ASI ratings of psychological problems are high.

How Should Drug-Induced Mental States Be Handled?

The defining characteristic of drug abusers is that they engage in frequent or excessive use of substances that induce alterations in mental states. In obtaining information in any of the areas described above, the patient is required at minimum to remember events. For many areas, the patient is asked to make complex judgments or evaluations about his or her current and past life. The extent to which validity and reliability of information obtained is reduced because of drug-induced states has been inadequately studied. In evaluating drug abusers, the clinician should take the subject's substance-induced state into account when the two domains in which decisions need to be made relate to 1) the timing of the assessment and 2) the time period to be covered by the assessment.

Regarding the patient's ability to provide an accurate history, there are four general states in relationship to psychoactive substance use: 1) acute intoxication, which is usually limited to less than 24 hours following drug ingestion, 2) steady-state use of the drug, during which time the subject has ingested sufficient amounts of a drug to which the subject is tolerant to avoid withdrawal symptoms but not enough to induce an acute intoxicated state, 3) withdrawal states, which result from abstinence from a drug to which the subject has become dependent, and 4) extended abstinence, during which the subject has curtailed substance use for a sufficient time that the subject is no longer experiencing noticeable or persistent withdrawal symptoms. Ideally, all patients should be evaluated during a period of extended abstinence, in which drug-induced impairment in cognitive acuity or motivation to cooperate and drug-induced mood changes are not factors in conducting and interpreting examinations. However, for most treatment settings, patients in extended periods of abstinence are rare. For example, a typical pattern for opioid abusers is to use opioids more or less steadily for a period of years. After entering treatment, the most likely form of therapy is methadone maintenance, which involves moving the subject from steady-state use (albeit at often irregular dosing) of one powerful opioid to steady-state use of another. The most typical patients are available to be evaluated comparatively shortly after cessation of drug use or during a steady-state use of one or more drugs. To examine subjects during steady-state use requires careful consideration of the type of influence the current drug state will have on the evaluations to be conducted.

In developing assessment guidelines, the clinician needs to consider not only the four drug-related states described above but the type of direct drug effects and abstinence syndromes for the type of drug the subject may be using and the pharmacodynamics (e.g., half-life) of the substances. Regarding pharmacodynamic properties of the drugs vis-à-vis their effect on evaluations, the most important feature is the half-life, or the amount of time required to reduce blood levels of the substance by half. As a rule of thumb, the shorter the half-life, the more intense and the briefer the duration of the "high" or intoxication state. Likewise, the intensity of the abstinence syndrome is proportionately higher and the duration briefer for drugs with a shorter half-life.

When the clinician takes into consideration the four drug-related states, the five general classes of substances inducing these states, the variability in half-life for substances within these categories, and the fact that most drug abusers use a variety of agents regularly, development of guidelines for timing of evaluations and for the time period on which to base evaluations may appear impossibly complex. However, several steps can be taken to reduce the distortion of findings by variability in drug-induced states across subjects and across evaluations:

1. Before evaluation, the investigator should determine the amount and types of substances that have been used both in the past week and the past 30 days. The more detailed one can be about the actual substances used (e.g., heroin versus methadone), the more accurate can be the judgment about whether the examination should take place at this time.
2. Before evaluation, the investigator should perform at least a cursory evaluation of the subject's current subjective status regarding drugs. At its simplest, this can be a 100-mm line with "high" or "intoxicated" at one end and "crashing" or "withdrawing" at the other, or a similarly designed 7-point Likert-type item. Subjects who are determined to be either acutely intoxicated or in a significant withdrawal state should ideally be rescheduled for evaluation at a later time.
3. In instances in which the length of evaluations require that patients be seen in more than one sitting, the investigator may group together evaluations that are likely to be unaffected by variations in the drug state and administer them separately from those likely to be influenced by this factor. Thus, for example, demographic data and legal history are less likely to be influenced by mild intoxication or withdrawal states than cognitive functioning or current mood. The former evaluations can be given to everyone with less regard to recency of drug use, whereas the latter may be given only in a state of extended abstinence or steady-state use.

To illustrate the use of these guidelines and to provide suggestions for clinicians while evaluating psychopathology in substance abusers, I will present the decisions of the Yale research team made in evaluating psychiatric disorders in opioid addicts seeking treatment (Rounsaville et al. 1982c).

The setting in which most evaluations were made was the screening and evaluation unit of a substance abuse treatment center. Opioid-abusing clients were ambulatory at the time of the evaluations, which needed to take place at least within two weeks of first contact with screening staff. Hence most patients to be evaluated were seeking treatment during a time of regular (usually daily) opioid use or at a time when they had recently curtailed regular opioid use. From the screening and evaluation unit, clients could be referred to psychiatric hospitalization for inpatient detoxification, a residential therapeutic community, outpatient drug-free programs that used narcotic antagonists, or methadone maintenance. Hence there was little value in waiting until clients had entered into their more permanent treatment setting because this would lead to significant attrition and would still not enable the staff to evaluate subjects in the same status in relation to recency of opioid use.

The major task of the evaluations was to take a current and lifetime history of psychiatric symptoms using the structured interview schedule, the Schedule for Affective Disorders and Schizophrenia, Lifetime version (Endicott et al. 1978). This involved asking about lifetime history of symptoms that are diagnostic of a wide range of mental disorders, including schizophrenia, mania, depression, anxiety disorders, and personality disorders. The researchers were interested in determining 1) the types and rates of mental disorders in addition to drug abuse presented by opiate addicts seeking treatment and 2) the lifetime history of mental disorders that may have preceded drug abuse or complicated the course of drug abuse. However, the history of symptoms taken was not entirely related to the direct acute effects of the substances themselves or the acute effects of withdrawal from the substances. Hence, in inquiring about lifetime history of psychiatric symptoms, there was a need to develop rules for determining whether they would consider a given symptom as a part of a mental disorder in addition to drug abuse. Thus a number of potential drug effect-diagnosis interactions were identified.

1. Direct effects of substances. There are two kinds of direct effects: acute direct effects (i.e., "high" or intoxication) and chronic effects of regular heavy use.

   Acute effects.   These effects are typically short lived (usually less than 24 hours) and are directly linked to the ingestion of the drug. All drugs of abuse produce a disinhibition state that may be described by the subject as similar to the euphoria and grandiosity of mania, especially in response to the probe questions in the section on affective disorders. Other important acute intoxication effects are psychotic symptoms (e.g., hallucinations, delusions), which are commonly the effect of large doses of stimulants, hallucinogens, marijuana, alcohol, and barbiturates-sedatives.

   Chronic effects.   For many individuals, including most opioid addicts seeking treatment, drugs are used daily or almost daily for a period of weeks, months, or years. There are often no clear periods of six months or more in which drugs are not used. During these periods of steady-state use, a decision was made not to ignore significant psychopathology if mental symptoms occurred during steady-state use. However, this decision did not hold for all drugs that may be used regularly. The depression that seemed to occur during long runs of heavy stimulant use, paranoia or psychosis occurring during heavy stimulant use, and psychoses occurring during long periods of hallucinogen or PCP use were most likely to be attributable to the effects of the drugs.

2. Withdrawal effects. For many classes of drugs, including opioids, there is a substantial withdrawal syndrome characterized by symptoms that may mimic those produced by mental disorders. As with acute drug effects, the withdrawal syndromes may be divided into acute and chronic phases and are related to the half-life of the drug (shorter half-life = shorter withdrawal syndrome).

Acute phases.   During the acute withdrawal phase, the person typically experiences withdrawal symptoms that are somewhat the opposite of the direct drug effect. Although the withdrawal symptoms are somewhat dissimilar for the different classes of drugs, they all share the similarity of producing symptoms of anxiety disorders and affective disorders.

Protracted withdrawal states.   Following the acute withdrawal state that may be only a few days and is usually identified by the clients as being "sick," there may be a period of one to two weeks in which the individual has a syndrome that is indistinguishable from a depressive episode. This is particularly likely to occur following withdrawal from alcohol-sedatives or from stimulants. However, if the syndrome persists for more than a few weeks, then it is not likely to be simply the result of a protracted withdrawal state.

The two major areas in which there was a need to develop guidelines for evaluating psychiatric symptoms in opiate addicts seeking treatment were 1) timing of interviews and 2) time periods in which symptoms elicited by the interview were considered to be most likely to be related to drug effects.

For timing of the interviews, the following decisions were made: 1) interviews of psychiatric history were conducted only after history of recent drug use had been obtained; 2) subjects were not given a psychiatric history if they indicated that they were either acutely "high" or "kicking" on a 7-point scale (only subjects receiving a 3, 4, or 5 were interviewed); 3) urine specimens were obtained on a subsample to evaluate veracity of subjects' reports regarding recency of use and recency of opiate use; 4) recency of drug use and subjects' self-ratings on the 7-point "high" scale were included as possible determinants of symptomatology in the data analysis, and the relationship was found to be minimal; and 5) both patients who had recently ingested opiates but who were comfortable during the interview and those who had recently curtailed opiate use but were not experiencing substantial withdrawal symptoms during the interview were included.

To handle the issue of psychiatric symptoms being solely caused by intoxication or withdrawal effects, each interviewer was given a detailed sheet that showed, drug by drug, the symptoms likely to be caused by it. In addition, three general rules were developed:

1. If the individual is a substance abuser, do not give another diagnosis if the symptoms of the other disorder occur only during the acute intoxication or acute withdrawal phase.
2. Do not give a diagnosis of a psychotic disorder or affective disorder if the symptoms of these disorders only occur during extended periods of stimulant, hallucinogen, or PCP use.
3. All other diagnoses can be made as if they were not drug induced either if the

symptoms were present during a drug-free period lasting at least six months, or if the symptoms were present during a steady-state period in which the drugs were used regularly.

How Can the Veracity of Drug Abusers' Self-Reports Be Maximized?

A perennial concern in evaluating drug abusers is that they will intentionally distort or falsify information about type and severity of drug use along with other clinically significant drug-related problems. In a clinical setting, patients may be motivated either to minimize or exaggerate various types of drug use. Patients who are pressured to enter treatment may wish the program to give them a "clean bill of health" and may give low estimates of drug consumption. Patients presenting to an alcoholism treatment program may be unwilling to admit abuse of other drugs, and those in drug treatment programs may not admit to alcohol abuse. Once the treatment process has started, continued drug abuse may be denied to avoid sanctions that are part of the treatment contract. At other times, patients may exaggerate drug use either out of a desire to be placed on methadone or to receive a minimal sentence for criminal activities that are claimed to be drug-related. To maximize the accuracy of sensitive information obtained from drug abusers, the following guidelines should be observed:

1. Clearly ensure confidentiality. All states protect the confidentiality of treatment records. Explaining the procedures for protecting confidentiality in that setting is often reassuring.
2. Use more than one informant where possible. For patients who deny the extent of substance abuse, more accurate information may be obtained from a family member or significant other. However, in the case of illicit substances, the patient may have taken successful precautions to hide illicit drug use from others so that information from a significant other may underestimate the extent of the problem (Rounsaville et al. 1981). When the patient and significant other disagree about the extent of a problem, the clinician has the dilemma of determining to which informant to give credence. As a rule of thumb, the informant reporting the most severe problem level is likely to be the one who is most accurate.
3. Provide a measure that is not simply based on the patient's self-report where possible. The most obvious instance of this procedure is to screen urine or blood specimens for the presence of substances under question. An important limitation of this is that absence of substances in the specimen does not rule out intermittent abuse because many substances are not detectable in blood or urine for more than a day or two. Conversely, presence of abused substances in body fluids confirms only use, not abuse or dependence on the substances. Hence the clinician must rely on patient reports to determine the pattern and severity of drug use. The exceptions to this are the barbiturates and sedatives, in which degree of tolerance can be determined via a test dose, and the opioids, in which a naloxone challenge can confirm physical dependence. When resources are not available to test all patients, veracity of self-reported use can be increased by the "bogus pipeline" approach, which involves informing patients that they may be tested later to verify reports, spot-checking a portion of patients, or collecting urine specimens on all patients even though only a portion are analyzed.

Conclusion

Methods are now available to assess the full range of substance abusers' problems, including multiple patterns of drug use, legal difficulties, medical problems, social and occupational impairment, and psychopathology. Assessing a range of areas is important because outcome in this population is multidimensional and related to many factors beyond presenting patterns of drug use. To maximize efficiency, most evaluations can be made in a two-step process, consisting of initial screening with self-reports or paraprofessional interviews, while reserving more definitive, professional diagnosis for those with initially positive findings. Although information obtained from substance abusers may be intentionally distorted or biased as a result of substance-induced mental states, guidelines that have been successful in maximizing the validity of information obtained from this patient population are described.

Chapter 127

Substance Abuse Etiology

As an introduction to theories of substance abuse, it is neither necessary nor possible to cover, in detail, the many theories that have been proposed to explain substance abuse. For an extensive comparison of 43 different theories, the reader is referred elsewhere (Lettieri et al. 1980).

It is no longer uncommon to hear both researchers and clinicians discuss adolescent drug use as a generic problem of chemical dependency rather than as addiction per se. In fact, the concept of dependence disorders is broadening to encompass a variety of habitual behaviors, such as hyperobesity, gambling, risk-engendering activities, polysurgery, promiscuity, in addition to substance use and abuse (Farberow 1980). The view that the premier criteria of addiction are withdrawal and tolerance is waning.

It has been the observation of practitioners that adolescents who use alcohol and illicit drugs abusively do not seem to fit the classic molds of alcoholics or drug addicts. Others have cautioned against labeling youth as alcoholics or addicts for fear of instituting a self-fulfilling prophecy.

For whatever reasons, the net effect has been to study chemical use among adolescents from a broader and more generic framework. This is not to imply that all chemical users are alike (for clearly they are not), but rather that at the early stages of use, the similarities among users may be more evident than the contrasts. It is only with repeated use and maturation into a chemical dependency life-style that distinct subtypes of chemical users emerge. For those for whom dependency becomes a life-style, differential treatment is de rigeur.

For discursive purposes, it may be helpful to distinguish at least four gross subgroupings, as depicted in Figure 1. Substance abuse or chemical dependency is not a unidimensional disorder. The drug dependence field early dismissed the search for a singular addictive personality, model, or syndrome. What is becoming more commonly accepted is the notion that the serious, chronic user of one class of drugs (e.g., stimulants) has needs, life themes, characteristics, coping styles, and motives different from the user of another class of drugs (e.g., depressants). These differences are in addition to whether they are acute or chronic, episodic or continuous users.

In short, this alternative view would stress that we garner the phenomenologic perspective of what a particular drug offers the user. Thus with heavy, chronic users, it is essential to differentiate users of different classes of drugs. The pioneering work of Spotts and Shontz (1980, 1982) vividly highlighted the major "personological" differences between heavy abusers of different classes of drugs. The more refined the categories and typologies become, the more necessary it is that clinicians find individualized (i.e., patient-specific) and distinct (pure rather than eclectic) implementations of particular treatment regimens (Luborsky et al. 1985; Woody et al. in press). It is becoming apparent that clients receiving treatment for heavy, chronic substance abuse should be matched to the class of drug they abuse, as well as to a particular therapeutic regimen commensurate with their ability (both cognitively and behaviorally) to profit from such regimens. Selecting the appropriate treatment for the substance user becomes immensely more complex if the user is now seen as multi-typed on several axes (viz., style of use, duration of use, drug class, phenomenologic experience).

Symptoms Versus Syndromes

There are two general schemata for substance abuse. One is to view the behavior in question as a function of some underlying tension or dynamic; thus substance-abusing behaviors can be seen as symptoms of other underlying elements. Alternatively, one can regard substance abuse as a syndrome, an orderly, albeit complex, admixture of

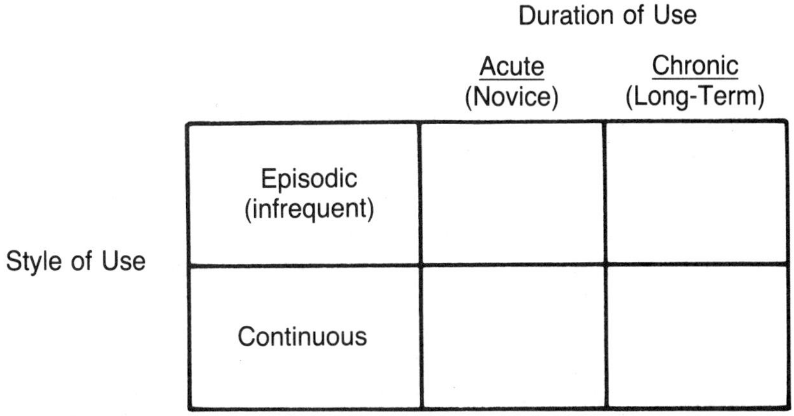

	Duration of Use	
	Acute (Novice)	Chronic (Long-Term)
Episodic (infrequent)		
Continuous		

Style of Use

Figure 1.   Duration and Style of Use

elements that move the organism to some predictable (predisposing) behavior. The roots of the latter approach may be traced to Aristotle's notion of entelechy (viz., the predictable "unfolding" of certain predetermined dispositions). For instance, if one were to examine a hen's egg by opening it, one should observe a yolk and a white. The entelic or unfolding is that within that yolk and white resides the potential for a chicken. Therefore, the search for genetic markers may be akin to seeking the predispositions or unfolding potential for substance abuse. Although genetic markers are of pronounced interest in medicine today, there is no firm evidence of such with substance abusers. Jonas and Jonas (1977) speculated that the marker may be akin to a gene for "hyperstimulation." They proposed that such a trait may have been useful in our distant past when it was necessary to be ever vigilant to predators. It could be argued that in modern technological society, already replete with stimulus overloads, users of depressants may be driven to lessen the stimulus overload their systems experience in their daily business of living.

It is probably premature, and not essential, at this juncture to resolve the symptom versus syndrome issue. Addiction can be seen as a life-style, a style of coping with the world, a mode of interpreting experience. Because both symptom and syndrome are inextricably intertwined, it is of lesser priority to discern the proportions attributable to entelic versus social factors.

Dependence Cycle

Throughout this chapter, the term *theories* is used somewhat interchangeably with explanations, perspectives, and models. The focal question becomes: What are the components of a theory or theoretic explanation of substance abuse?

In Figure 2, substance abuse is depicted as cyclical and progressive, with five essential stages, each addressing a particularly relevant set of inquiries:

1. Initiation: why, how does one begin using?
2. Continuation: why does one continue to use?
3. Escalation: when, why does use escalate to abuse?
4. Cessation: why does one cease use?
5. Relapse: why, how, and when does relapse occur?

Explanatory Models

It is difficult to select the best theory. The ripeness of an idea is rarely the direct consequence of the thinking of the thinker. The adequacy of an explanation is infrequently appraised solely on its scientific merit, but rather on the ripeness of the idea within its particular social, political, and epistemological climate.

Theories of substance abuse are many. It is no coincidence that this is so. Human behavior abounds in its variety, and one's view of and response to the world is related to the kind of blinders or rose-colored glasses one wears. Some years ago, Floyd Allport commented that if one were to ask a watch (a timepiece) to explain itself, the timepiece would do so by continuing to tick. For the timepiece, this would be a most acceptable explanation and exposition of its essence or meaning. For the human observer, however, such exposition should likely be less than satisfactory.

Throughout Western thought, a handful of methods have been used to reach

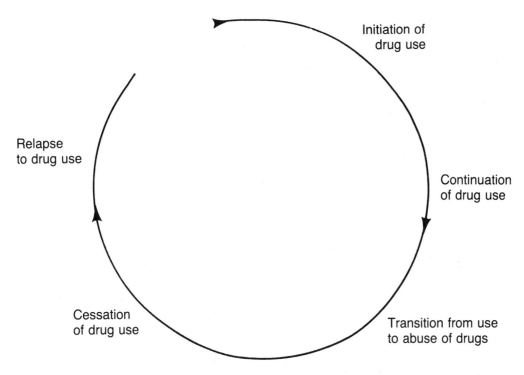

Figure 2.   The Drug Dependence Cycle

knowledge and explanations. These include: 1) recourse to reference and authority; 2) classification (Aristotle); 3) induction (Bacon); 4) deduction (Descartes); 5) experimental approach; 6) mathematical approach; and 7) model building. Each has drawbacks, and many of these are used in combination (Lettieri 1985). For example, recourse to reference and authority, the most commonly used method, entails citing quotations from many authorities. It is a definition of scholarship in some circles. Yet it is equally fallacious to presume that merely because many great minds have thought that way, then the matter must indeed be so. On the other hand, in the social sciences, the experimental approach has proven less than optimal due to the difficulties in disaggregating complex social variables, and the impracticability of experimentally isolating key variables. At base, its primary weakness is that while it relies on hypotheses, we have no definite way of generating them. A hypothesis can be suggested by data, but for the hypothesis to be more than a mere summarization of the data, it is the human mind that must generate the major part of it as an idea. In sum, nothing is any more powerful than an idea in the mind of a single person.

Some readers will likely select that theoretic perspective most consonant with their preferred level of abstraction and their prior disciplinary training.

Interdisciplinary Focus

In light of these provisos, how then can we compare, contrast, select, or favor certain theoretic explanations to the exclusion of others? I would argue that different disciplines or fields seem better suited to explain certain parts of the chemical dependency or addiction cycle (i.e., the cycle from initiation to cessation of substance use). Should one seek to account for why persons continue in their use of drugs, then biomedical disciplines are most germane; in contrast, however, if one wishes to explain the initiation of substance use, clearly social psychological explanations seem most pertinent. For an understanding of the escalation of use to abuse, sociological elements combined with biomedical factors may be optimal. Psychological, political, and economic factors are necessary for understanding the cessation of use. In sum, one must be cognizant of the need to incorporate variables from diverse scientific disciplines to understand fully the substance abuse dependence cycle. No single discipline has adequately accounted for the multifaceted phenomenon of substance dependence.

Motives and Uses of Substances

As a framework for understanding the various actual and potential uses of substances, it is noteworthy to examine the science fiction literature and discern what those authors have envisioned. Silverberg (1974) reviewed that literature and summarized nine uses of substances (Table 1).

Obviously it is important to understand the user's phenomenologic perceptions of and motives for substance use. The choice of treatment must be predicated on this understanding. Once the motives for use are determined, alternative behaviors can be suggested. For instance, if persons whose primary use of drugs was recreational and peer-pressure influenced, implementation of alternative recreational activities or independence training, as well as the ability to resist peer pressure, might be therapeutically appropriate. In contrast, if the user's prime motivation is escapism or retreatism, then social skills training, stress management, and enhanced self-acceptance might be an optimal therapeutic approach. In sum, it is perhaps best to understand substance abusers as seeking out and testing various coping strategies; in a sense they act as their own psychopharmacologist (Lettieri 1978). Sterling-Smith (1978) aptly posited drug use as a matter of toys versus therapy.

Table 1.   Potential Uses of Drugs

Euphorics	give pleasure in simple unstructured ways, through release from depression and tension
Mind expanders	provide psychedelic visions of other times or places or offer a sensation of oneness with the cosmos
Panaceas	calm the mind, through tranquilizing or neutralizing effects, without necessarily inducing euphoria
Mind controllers	enable one entity to limit or direct activities or desires of another (analogous to brainwashing)
Intelligence enhancers	extend or amplify the rational processes of the mind
Sensation enhancers	extend or amplify bodily sensation-response (perhaps analogous to marijuana in our society)
Reality testers	permit the user to penetrate the "real" realities beyond the surface manifestations of daily life
Means of communications	open hitherto unknown channels of communication between minds

Theory Variables and Domains

Although the terms used to describe various theories may differ, there are more similarities among the concepts than differences. As the founder of social psychology, McDougall once opined about that aborning discipline as old wine in new bottles; likewise there are many explanatory variables (Lettieri et al. 1980).

It would be an understatement to note that it is complex to find terms sufficiently general to capture the essence of the variables employed by these theorists. A brobdingnagian attempt at classifying these concepts into a few categories has produced seven major domains of substance abuse theories: 1) euphoria-pleasure, 2) drug knowledge, 3) cognitive factors, 4) tension and anxiety reduction, 5) interpersonal variables, 6) "personological" features, and 7) social and environmental factors.

Table 2 embeds the variables within each of the substance abuse theory domains. Within each of the broad domains, variables have been further subclustered. It is noteworthy that there appears to be significant synonymy and consonance within the subclusters—a further indication that essentially the same phenomena are consistently recognized by diverse scientific disciplines.

In addition, one can peruse an extensive listing of the names of theorists and their theory titles, and where each falls along a continuum that distinguishes theories relevant to humans 1) in relationship to the self, 2) in relationship to others, 3) in relationship to society, and 4) in relationship to nature (Lettieri 1985).

Initiation

A number of prime concepts pervade the explanatory perspectives relevant to the initiation of substance abuse. Although various theorists bring slightly different emphases to particular variables, it is evident that there is a unifying thread to the dominant explanatory themes underlying initiation of substance abuse. What becomes clear is that the different emphases can be accounted for, in part, by the particular class or type of drug user under discussion (e.g., opiate addict versus novice marijuana user) as depicted in Figure 1. At this point it is appropriate to embed and discursively highlight several nuances among theories within a discussion of the initiation of use. The field has not yet reached full consensus on these matters, but it is suggested that the reader ponder each of these variables while also considering the user's style and duration of use, the class of drug abused, and the motivations or phenomenologic meanings of such use for the user.

Personality Deficiency

Drug abuse is generally initiated as a result of an individual's involvement with drug-using age-mates. Adolescents who are motivationally immature, have ready access to drugs, and live in a milieu attitudinally tolerant of drug use quickly appreciate the adjustive value of drug use (Ausubel 1958, 1961).

Disruptive Environment

Among juvenile users who became addicts, Chein et al. (1964) found that they had personality disturbances prior to the onset of drug use and shared a special orientation to life consisting of general pessimism, unhappiness, a sense of futility,

Table 2.   Variables Within Substance Abuse Domains

1. **Euphoria-pleasure**
   A.   Biologic systems
   - biologic drive, pleasure as a biologic preference system, biologic rhythms
   - metabolic disease
   - genetic susceptibility or predisposition, phylogeny, species viability or survival
   - sensory overload, quality of sensory experiences, impaired somatic feedback, hypersensitivity to stimuli, stimulation seeking or avoidance
   - narcotic hunger, physical dependence, narcotic blockade
   - opioid receptors, endorphins, enkephalins

   B.   Intrapsychic system
   - pain relief, discomfort relief, pain modulation, euphoria, dysphoria, hypophoria reduction, sense of well-being, pleasure-pain balance, abstinence syndrome, withdrawal avoidance
   - pursuit of altered consciousness
   - immediate gratification needs
   - sensation seeking, stimulation seeking, relief from boredom

2. **Drug knowledge**
   - knowledge about drugs, prior drug use, perceived drug effects, values, beliefs, attitudes toward drugs, controlled drug use, cognitive awareness of dependence

3. **Cognitive factors**
   A.   Cognitive variables
   - social sanctions, nonnormative group expectations
   - impaired feedback
   - search for meaning
   - cognitive style, habit, cognitive set, life themes
   - self-medication
   - religiosity

   B.   Learning and reinforcement
   - learning, social learning, conditioning, reinforcement, dependence as a memory function, intermittent reinforcement, automedication

4. **Tension and anxiety reduction**
   A.   Anxiety-pain-tension
   - anxiety reduction, pain relief, hypophoria reduction, stimulation avoidance, discomfort relief, stress or tension reduction

   B.   Coping
   - cognitive conflict, conflict-aggression-rage reduction
   - coping strategies, behavioral styles, affective defense, adaptive or defense function, coping abilities and mechanisms
   - life-style enhancement, risk-taking
   - humorless life-style

5. **Interpersonal variables**
   A.   Interpersonal influence
   - social pressure, drug-using culture, social control, social acceptance, addict-peer-family-social influence
   - normative systems, social rituals, social deviance, conduct norms, cultural modes of decorum
   - social orientation, conformity or nonconformity, conventionality or unconventionality, problem-behavior proneness, independent will
   - population density or control
   - social isolation

Table 2.   Variables Within Substance Abuse Domains   (continued)

   B. Family factors
- family isolation, parental and family relations, family systems, family homeostatic model, parent-child overinvolvement, disrupted family life, middle-class parent culture

   C. Interpersonal loss and trauma
- death-separation-loss, traumatic loss
- role strain, role deprivation, social constriction or entrapment

   D. Interpersonal factors
- achievement orientation-performance-competition, fear of failure

6.   **"Personological" features**
   A. Personality characteristics or deficiencies
- curiosity, risk taking
- claustrophobia
- guilt
- low self-esteem, self-concept, self-deprecation, narcissism
- autonomy or independence, locus of control, externalization
- rebelliousness, obedience
- retreatism, escapism

   B. Affective states
- emptiness, alienation, fear of separation
- hopelessness, powerlessness, helplessness, depression
- hypersensitivity to stimuli
- rage, apathy, affective regression, emotional or affective deprivation
- feelings of inferiority or superiority

   C. Personality syndromes and characterologic features
- personality deficiency, inadequate personality syndrome, self-pathology, superego deficits and splits, self versus ideal self, arrested crisis resolution, ego deficiency, developmental disturbance, ego-state alterations, pseudo-individuation
- self-destructiveness, impaired self-care or self-preservation, self-rejecting styles
- delinquency, sociopathy, tolerance of deviance, antisocial personality, psychopathology
- present versus future orientation
- phobic core
- self-perceived behavioral pressures

7.   **Social and environmental factors**
- drug availability, drug distribution
- socioeconomic status, social class, social location

---

mistrust, negativism, and defiance. These attributes often stemmed from parents who were of low socioeconomic status and had little hope of a better future. There was lack of love and support for the children, and no clear standards of behavior, with inconsistent application of rewards and punishments.

Coleman (1979) and Coleman and Stanton (1979) depicted drug use as indicative of a functional imbalance in the family. Drug use is seen not as a linear, cause-and-effect model, but rather as part of a cycle in the family. Opiate addiction is viewed as a means of coping with (traumatic) family experience.

Using a refined typology of life themes based on early learned styles in the family,

Spotts and Shontz (1982) characterized the mother of the amphetamine user as manipulative, and the father as passive, weak, and psychologically castrated by the mother. The male user attempts to deny feelings of helplessness and impotence through engagement in hypermasculine activities. These can include displays of sexual prowess over women, high achievement needs, and aggressive and violent acts. The barbiturate user typically lacks good parental relationships, feels unloved, and wishes to escape from these feelings of failure, frustration, and distress. The narcotic user's father is usually tyrannical or absent, the mother is weak and passive, and the user sees himself as lonely, isolated, and vulnerable, thus wishing to withdraw from life's burdens rather than confront them constructively.

Adaptive Difficulties

Drug use grows out of adaptive difficulties. What is important is not that the adolescent tries drugs, but what adaptive significance does the adolescent attribute to the experience of drug use (Hendin 1973, 1974, 1975).

In a related vein, Gorsuch and Butler (1976) suggested that initial drug use may occur 1) to respond to a state of physical pain, 2) to deal with mental anguish, or 3) to provide relief from boredom through sensation seeking.

Peer Pressure

The bulk of theorists attribute major importance to peer pressure as a key element in the initiation, continuation, and relapse of substance use. At one extreme, Huba et al. (1980) asserted that initiation of drug use, particularly in adolescents, is almost entirely derived from self-perceived behavioral pressure resulting from the individual's intimate support system (viz., peer values, models, reinforcers, and inadequate alternative healthy behaviors). Although personality plays a role, it is a lesser role through such dimensions as extroversion, leadership or autonomy strivings, and rebelliousness.

Developmental Stages of Use

One of the leading theorists (Kandel 1973, 1975, 1978, 1980) has empirically shown that different social-psychological factors predict adolescent initiation into different stages of drug use, thus affording strong evidence for the existence of stages. She has shown that there are three sequential stages of adolescent drug use: hard liquor, marijuana, and other illicit drugs. Four clusters of predictor variables were isolated: 1) parental influence, 2) peer influence, 3) adolescent involvement in various behaviors, and 4) adolescent beliefs and values. What is important is that each cluster has differential importance for the various developmental stages of use. In particular, prior involvements in a variety of activities, such as minor delinquency and use of cigarettes, beer, and wine, are most important for predicting hard liquor use. Adolescent's beliefs and values favorable to the use of marijuana and association with marijuana-using peers are the strongest predictors of initiation into marijuana. Poor relations with parents, feelings of depression, and exposure to drug-using peers are most important for predicting initiation into illicit drugs other than marijuana. Thus at the earliest levels of involvement, adolescents who have engaged in a number of minor delinquent or deviant activities, who enjoy high levels of sociability with their peers, and who are exposed to peers and parents who drink start to drink themselves. The relationship with parental use of hard liquor suggests that these youths learn drinking patterns from their parents. The use of marijuana is preceded by acceptance of a cluster of beliefs and values that are favorable to marijuana use and in opposition to many standards upheld by adults, by involvement in a peer environment in which marijuana is used, and by participation in the same minor forms of deviant behavior that precede the use of hard liquor. By comparison, use of illicit drugs other than marijuana is preceded by poor relationships with parents; by exposure to parents and to peers who themselves use a variety of legal, medical, and illegal drugs; by psychological distress; and by a series of personal characteristics somewhat more deviant than those that characterize the novice marijuana or hard liquor user (Kandel 1980, p. 322).

Self-Rejecting, Self-Derogating Attitudes

For some theorists (e.g., Kaplan 1975, 1976, 1980), drug use or abuse is seen as a response to intense self-rejecting attitudes resulting from a history of being unable to forestall or assuage the self-evaluating experiences in normative groups (e.g., family, school, peers). As a result of distressful negative self-attitudes, the person loses motivation to conform to group patterns and seeks alternative (deviant) patterns in the hope of reducing negative self-attitudes.

Ego Deficits and Impaired Coping Strategies

From a psychoanalytic perspective, Khantzian (1978, 1980) highlighted deficiencies in affect defence (shaky or rigid defenses), poor self-esteem, and an impaired sense of self-care. For persons who progress to extreme dependency, this theorist argued that they have failed to develop internal mechanisms for coping and consequently use drugs to heighten a sense of well-being, security, and pleasure. But perhaps the central theme is that fully dependent persons have deficient self-care functions in that they seem unconcerned about the possible dangers of drugs. This tendency is present before addiction and persists even after detoxification and stabilization.

Steffenhagen (1974) considered drug use a compensatory mechanism, an excuse for life's failures, a preservation of "self," and an insulator from social responsibility. It may stem from the Adlerian view of "pampered" (and hence ill-prepared) lifestyles.

Stress and Tension Reduction

Among the major concepts commonly invoked in explanations for substance abuse, one of the most common is that of stress, anxiety, or tension reduction. Although widely cited, it has not proved to be a very useful research term. In substance abuse research, accepting that stress may be the cause of the behavior has not yet allowed us fully to understand, predict, or treat that behavior. Stress is a term with excess meanings. It has signified antecedent, concomitant, and consequent factors. It has been used tautologically to refer both to the external stimulus that produces a reaction and to the reaction itself. Consequently, a basic difficulty in working operationally with the term has been how to define it independently of the effects it produces.

Differentiating stressors that are internal versus external to the organism has proved difficult. For example, while drinking or drug taking may diminish an external stressor (i.e., the user's perception or recognition of it), drug use may in fact augment and increase internal physiologic stressors (Pohorecky 1981). We have yet to understand adequately how substance abuse may both reduce and increase stress or tension.

What if an individual does not respond to stressors? Does this mean the individual is resistant to stress or that the particular stressor was not idiosyncratically stressful? Maher (1966) has shown that when subjects are allowed to define stress in their own way, there are none who do not react to stressors with a stress reaction. Noteworthy is the conclusion that no persons are immune to stress—the differences are presumably phenomenologic, idiotropic, and socioenvironmentally determined.

It has been found that some persons with high sensation-seeking needs consume more substances than those with low sensation-seeking needs, and that there may be no clear relationship between anxiety and consumption (Schwarz et al. 1982). Hull's (1981) self-awareness model proposed that some drugs (viz., alcohol) are inhibitors of self-awareness processing and as such offer the individual a feeling of psychological relief. His model proposed that certain drugs interfere with the individual's recognition of cues regarding appropriate behavior and the self-evaluative nature of feedback about past behaviors. It is plausible to suggest that if feedback processing is impaired, then sensation-seeking needs may also be affected.

At base, if chemical abuse is a coping strategy, then it may well be that coping can be assessed by contrasting the number of perceived stressors before, during, and after substance abuse episodes. Bry et al. (1982) reported that higher substance use was associated with increased numbers of perceived stressors. If one assumes substance users act as their own psychopharmacologist, then one could contend they select particular drugs at certain times to achieve specific effects, malleations, or realignments in perceived needs and mood states.

Relapse

The variables implicated in explaining initiation of use are also relevant in accounting for relapse, with the important addition of the role of learning. In sum, learning, conditioning, habit, stimulus generalization, the strength of the reinforcers and their slowness to extinguish, and the removal of the social controls or sanctions that brought about cessation in the first place hallmark the explanations for relapse. Theorists have merely posited that relapse will occur when there is a recurrence of those conditions formerly present at onset of use. It is understood that the chronic, continuous user will have developed strong, less extinguishable behavior patterns than the acute or episodic user, and hence relapse is more likely with the former type of substance abuser, thus signaling that once acquired, a reinforcement history remains a permanent part of the user's makeup (McAuliffe and Gordon 1980).

Conclusion

Addiction is a person problem, not a chemical problem. The ultimate resolutions will rest with demand reduction, not supply reduction. Abstinence without personal reorientation cannot be touted as a viable cure for addiction. The fact that some individuals (polydrug users) switch from one substance to another merely hallmarks that use is determined, in large measure, by the phenomenologic experience that the drug creates for the user.

Chapter 128

The Hallucinogens

The hallucinogens (psychotomimetics, psychedelics) are an unusual series of drugs in that they produce thought, mood, and perceptual disorders that resemble naturally occurring disorders such as schizophrenia and mania. Depending on dosage, expectation, and environment, they also induce euphoria and a state similar to a transcendental experience.

While none of the hallucinogenic agents are recognized for use in medicine, they will be encountered by physicians when they evoke behavioral dysfunction resulting from their mind-altering effects.

Classification

The commonly used typical hallucinogens include:

1. Indolealkylamine derivatives
   a. LSD (D-lysergic acid diethylamide, acid). Synthesized from lysergic acid from the fungus, ergot (*claviceps purpurea*).
   b. DMT (dimethyltryptamine). Found in cohaba snuff from the seeds of *Piptadenia peregrina*, but made synthetically for street sales.
   c. Psilocybin (dimethyl-4-phosphoryltryptamine, mushrooms). Found in *Psilocybe mexicana* and related mushrooms.
2. Phenylalkylamine derivatives
   a. Mescaline (3,4,5-trimethoxyphenylethylamine). Found in the buttons of the peyote cactus (*Lophophora Williamsii*). Peyote is the only hallucinogen that can be legally used in this country. Members of the Native American Church use it during certain religious ceremonies in a number of states and in Canada.
   b. A series of ring-substituted amphetamines including MDMA and MDA (Marquardt et al. 1978). MDMA was also known as DOM and STP (2,5-dimethoxy-4-methylamphetamine). It is currently being employed experimentally as a psychotherapeutic adjunct just as LSD, mescaline, and psilocybin were a quarter century ago.

      Although other drugs, tetrahydrocannabinol (THC) and phencyclidine (PCP), for example, can evoke similar hallucinatory-delusional states in appropriate dosage, they are not typical hallucinogens nor do they produce cross-tolerance to the above-mentioned drugs.

In equivalent dosages, LSD, mescaline, and the methoxylated amphetamines are long acting, (eight to 24 hours), whereas DMT and psilocybin are shorter acting (two to six hours). Since a large series of the substituted amphetamines can have euphoro-hallucinogenic properties, it can be expected that analogues with slight modifications of structure will be synthesized to evade legal controls. They fit into the concept of "designer drug" agents that produce mood alterations but are legal because of minor molecular manipulations (Shafer 1985). Because LSD is the most widely used and researched of the hallucinogens, it will serve as a model for all of them.

Psychosocial Aspects

The original purposes for ingestion of the synthetic hallucinogenic series was to provide a chemical transcendental experience. Indeed, the practice of using naturally occurring substances like peyote, psilocybe mushrooms, caapi, and other theobotanicals is ancient. Many societies have used these plants to achieve out-of-the-body religious and mystical states in their priests or congregations. It is likely that our current upsurge of drug abuse was initiated with LSD during the 1960s. The difference between the employment of crude plants to alter consciousness and self-concept and the more modern use of highly potent synthetics is the very intense states that emerge, with subsequent potential disturbances of psychological homeostasis, particularly in vulnerable, unprepared populations.

As the psychedelic "revolution" developed and LSD, mescaline, and similar agents became widely available and popular, the motivation to consume these drugs shifted to a desire for hedonic experience and sensory stimulation.

Initially, the hallucinogens were tried by college students and their young professors. As the practice of "dropping acid" spread, the age level decreased to high school and junior high school students. It can be said that what was once a young adult, white, middle-class practice eventually came to involve most age groups, races, and classes.

The prevalence of hallucinogenic drug use on the college campuses of the 1960s is difficult to determine because adequate surveys are not available. Estimates that between one-third and one-half of students had experimented with LSD were commonly heard. It is certain that the use of the hallucinogens has substantially decreased. In the reliable high school senior survey for 1982 (Johnston et al. 1982), about 10 percent of high school seniors have ever tried LSD, 6 percent have used LSD during the past year, and 2 percent within the past month. Future outbreaks of hallucinogenic drug use are fairly likely because the state is usually enjoyable and intriguing, and the adverse effects are forgotten and must be rediscovered by subsequent generations.

Most studies of the character structure of hallucinogen users have reported preexisting psychiatric problems (Bakkar 1969). This is especially true when the heavy, consistent user group is studied.

Symptomatology

Physiologic

The typical hallucinogens all dilate the pupils, increase the heart rate, and produce slight hypertension and hyperthermia. While under the influence, the face may be flushed, and the deep reflexes quicken. On occasion, piloerection, salivation, nausea, a fine tremor, and lacrimation may be noted. In addition, a minor degree of incoordination, restlessness, and visual blurring might occur. A stress response with elevation of 17-hydroxycorticoids and free fatty acids is present.

Psychological

When the hallucinogens are taken orally, there may be a delay of 20 to 60 minutes before any psychic phenomena are noted. These can vary considerably, depending on the amount consumed and the setting and the set of both the subject and of the observer. Hypersuggestibility and distractibility are notable, perhaps because the critical functions of the ego are diminished or absent.

The perceptual alterations are most notable. The first subjective effect may be a colorful, mobile display of geometrical patterns slanting past one's closed eyes. Later, complex human, animal, or other forms may be projected onto the visual field. With eyes open, the color of perceived objects becomes more saturated and intense. The afterimage is remarkably prolonged. Fixed objects undulate and flow. Such illusions are common and assume a personal meaning; for example, a spot on the wall may be seen as a peering eye. Pseudohallucinations, images seen for which no external cue exists, are apprehended as "not really there" by the subject. True hallucinations of various senses are less frequent but occur at high doses, and no insight into their hallucinatory character is recognized. Auditory hallucinations are seldom described, but hyperacusis is commonly reported. Greater sensitivity of touch sensation is regularly noticed, and sometimes taste and smell are altered. An interesting synesthesia may be described: the overflow from one sense modality into another. Colors are heard, and music will change the visual percepts. Concepts, percepts, and emotions may fuse into a single theme and be impossible to distinguish. Subjective time is invariably affected, usually in the direction of subjective time "standing still."

The emotional responses to the hallucinogens can vary markedly. Initial apprehension is common, but the most frequent response is one of euphoria. Elation, ecstacy, and a blissful calm have been described. Less frequently, tension and anxiety culminating in panic has occurred. The mood is labile, shifting easily from gaiety to depression and back again. Prolonged laughter or tears and a general loosening of the emotions may seem inappropriate to the situation. Complete withdrawal and paranoid rage reactions have been encountered. An interesting phasic intensification and fading of the experience is present, with the subject cyclicly going deeply into the state and later coming out appearing to be recovered.

The thought processes are significantly altered under the influence of psychotomimetic drugs. A loosening of associations with unusual content is regularly noted. Thought sequences are nonlogical, fantasy laden, and eidetic. The thinking aberration has been called "knight's move" mentation, with jumps in the orderly rational processing of information. Thoughts flood consciousness; on the other hand, a complete absence of thought is mentioned on occasion. Intelligence testing is worsened, but this may be due to a lack of motivation to perform or a preoccupation with the unusual experience. Orientation is ordinarily not impaired, but judgments are, by no means, reliable. Paranoid grandiosity, and less frequently persecutory ideation, can be readily elicited.

Changes of ego functioning may be imperceptible at the lower dosage ranges, or they can be completely disrupted when large amounts of the hallucinogens have been taken. At first one can observe the usual ego defense mechanisms come into play to cope with the peculiar, unsettling mental state. Eventually, they are overwhelmed to the point that depersonalization and derealization might emerge. External events and memories may not be capable of differentiation. The body image is distorted, with parts of the body becoming larger, smaller, or completely disappearing. Multiple selves have been reported. The self-concept undergoes considerable alteration, usually in the direction of self-enhancement, but the opposite is possible.

Diagnosis

The diagnosis of hallucinogen exposure is normally made from the patient's or accompanying person's report. The diagnosis can be made clinically when an individual is actively hallucinating; delusional; and describing illusions, changes in body size or shape, slowing of time, and a waxing and waning of these and other symptoms. Ordinarily, the individual is able to report having taken a substance prior to the acute onset of the symptoms. The presence of dilated pupils, tachycardia, and quickened deep tendon reflexes increases the possibility that an hallucinogen has been consumed.

The routine drug screen does not include testing for the hallucinogens. They can be detected in blood, and for longer periods in urine, by thin-layer chromatography, flame ionization gas chromatography, fluorometry, or gas chromatography-mass spectrometry (Basalt 1982). A radioimmunoassay for LSD is available. Testing for the currently popular hallucinogens should be done if a history of recent ingestion is available and if future medicolegal problems are anticipated. Shifts in body metabolism are insufficient to induce specific abnormalities of blood chemistries, blood counts, or urine analyses.

The differential diagnosis of the psychotomimetic state would include consumption of deliriant drugs such as the atropine-like agents or the atypical hallucinogens PCP and THC. Many drugs can produce a toxic psychosis, but this state should be readily differentiated from the psychotomimetic picture. In the former condition, confusion and loss of some aspects of orientation are present. In the latter state, the perceptual and associative changes occur in clear consciousness and with retention of orientation. In addition, the hallucinogens produce electroencephalogram (EEG) arousal while drugs that cause delirial changes result in EEG slowing (Fink and Itil 1968). The THC psychosis often occurs with drowsiness rather than the hyperalertness of the LSD state. PCP psychosis is accompanied by marked neurologic signs, (e.g., nystagmus, ataxia) and more pronounced autononic effects than are seen with the psychotomimetics.

A young person arriving at a health care center in an acute psychotic state must be studied to determine whether an acute schizophrenic reaction or a hallucinogen-induced psychosis has occurred. The differentiation is not always readily made. It should be recalled that initial interest in LSD arose because of the possibility that it might be a model of schizophrenia. The brief reactive schizophrenic psychosis is also of sudden onset, but usually following psychosocial stressors and associated with emotional turmoil. Hallucinations in psychosis are usually auditory in contrast to hallucinations from psychotomimetics, which are predominantly visual.

Treatment of Complications

The Acute Psychotomimetic Reactions

The acute dysphoric reaction. These are commonly known as "bummers" or "bad trips." They are caused by loss of control, the inability to cope with ego dissolution, or marked environmental dissonance. The result is anxiety and, in some instances, panic. These are best managed by using the hypersuggestibility of the hallucinogen state to calm and assure the individual that he or she will be protected and that the condition will soon subside.

The acute paranoid state.   These adverse responses result from the hypervigilant state, overreading of external cues, and the unusual thoughts that occur in the course of the hallucinogenic experience. Although likely to be grandiose or megalomaniacal, they sometimes are in the direction of suspiciousness and persecution.

Since the anxiety and paranoid reactions may last for an hour or a few days, the patient requires unobtrusive protection. Reassurance and support, the "talkdown," is combined with a quiet environment, usually in a home-like setting. Since closing the eyes intensifies the state, the patient should sit up or walk about. Reminding the patient that a drug has produced the extraordinary ideas and feelings and that they will disappear may be helpful. The time sense distortion that makes minutes seem like hours should be explained. If drugs are needed, a benzodiazepine can be given for continuing panicky feelings. Phenothiazines are helpful in extreme anxiety, but paradoxical reactions have been reported (Schwartz 1968).

Overdose.   Overdose with the psychotomimetic drugs is rare. Instances are known of people surviving 10,000 mg of LSD, 100 times the average dose. On the other hand, a few deaths have been reported from large amounts of methoxylated amphetamines.

The Chronic Psychotomimetic Reactions

A number of protracted untoward reactions can occur following the use of hallucinogenic drugs. In addition, the consistent use of these substances has been claimed to cause brain damage, although the evidence for this is inconclusive. Instead, it is more likely that such use can lead to an attenuation of acceptable social behaviors.

Schizophreniform reactions lasting weeks or much longer periods have followed the psychotomimetic experience. Following on a dysphoric experience or developing shortly after a positive one, the manifestations of psychosis may emerge. These reactions are supposed to be precipitated in characterologically predisposed individuals who decompensated due to the upsurge of repressed material that overwhelmed their ego defenses.

The management of these prolonged psychotic reactions does not differ from that of schizophrenia. Neuroleptics are used, sometimes in a residential setting when behavioral dysfunction makes it necessary. Efforts at self-treatment may be made by these patients, and serious polydrug abuse patterns have been seen (Wesson and Smith 1978). The prognosis of these states is usually favorable; however, a few remain recalcitrant to treatment for years. It has been empirically found that a series of electroconvulsive treatments can help those who are resistant to other antipsychotic measures.

Depression.   Immediately following a hallucinogenic experience or after a brief, symptom-free interval, a depression of varying severity can develop. The lowered mood state might result from the coming down from a state of "bliss" to deal with an imperfect and stressful world. Some of the unconscious material that came to awareness may have been very upsetting and guilt provoking. Disappointment at the lack of personal change after one or more revelatory experiences can also prove depressing.

Usually the depressive mood responds to brief psychotherapy. On the other hand, suicidal attempts and a few completed suicides have been reported. A trial of the tricyclic antidepressants may be indicated.

Chronic anxiety states. It is evident that to some people, perhaps to all people under adverse circumstances, the LSD type of experience can be an unsettling one. In general, the psyche is capable of reconstituting itself surprisingly well within a reasonable period of time. A few people continue to experience anxiety and tension states for unusually long periods of time and attribute their "shook up" feelings to the mescaline, LSD, or some other psychotomimetic that they took. It is difficult to know how much of the anxiety or phobic state that sometimes occurs is due to a disruption of psychological homeostasis, and how much was because a fragile personality who should never have taken or been given the hallucinogen was exposed to it. At any rate, the anxiety persists indefinitely, and one wonders what would have happened if the person had never encountered LSD.

The management of such individuals is similar to that of other anxiety states. Pharmacotherapy in the form of antianxiety agents and nondrug techniques such as relaxation exercises and behavioral therapy are helpful. One should not accede to the magical thinking of the patient that maybe another psychedelic session might reshuffle the psychological fragments back into their premorbid pattern.

Flashbacks. A phenomenon unique to the hallucinogens has emerged during the past quarter century. This is the flashback, the apparently spontaneous recrudescence of effects that were experienced during the psychotomimetic state. These are usually brief visual, temporal, or emotional recurrences that may appear days or months after the last drug exposure. Since flashbacks appear suddenly, unexpectedly, and inappropriately, the emotional responses may be foreboding or dread. Fear of going mad may arise because no external cause for the strange, often recurrent phenomena is apparent. Other people seem to enjoy the "flash."

It is possible that these recurrences represent a response learned during a state of hyperarousal (Cohen 1981). Stress, fatigue, and certain drugs like marijuana and antihistamines may precipitate the event.

The most important aspect of treatment consists of reassurance that the condition will pass, that the brain is not damaged, and that the hallucinogen is not retained in the brain. If the person is agitated because of repeated flashbacks, an anxiolytic drug is indicated. The physical and mental status should be improved with appropriate hygienic measures, and marijuana or other hallucinogens must be avoided. If no flashbacks have occurred for a year since the last ingestion of the hallucinogen, it is most unlikely that any more will occur.

Shared paranoid disorder. A number of instances of folie à deux have been noted in connection with the use of psychotomimetic drugs. The best known of these is that of Charles Manson and his "family" (Watkins and Soledad 1979). Manson, a schizophrenic long before his arrival at the Haight-Ashbury in California had consumed considerable LSD. These episodes apparently crystallized previously held vague feelings of grandiosity that he was "The Son of Man" as his name implied. His "family" also had experienced frequent LSD sessions. In the closed information loop, at their remote ranch, Manson's pronouncements had an overwhelming validity for them, a further instance of the drug's hypersuggestibility. From records, they derived the message that a race war had to be provoked between blacks and whites so that Manson could finally assume his ordained role as Messiah. The multiple insanity was not easily dissolved; after the trial, some of the members still persisted in their deluded thinking.

Treatment is difficult. Group psychoses rarely come to medical attention, and when they do, the members are resistant to an alteration of their delusional system.

Individual, reality-based psychotherapy would seem to offer the best possibility of reorienting their ideas.

Neurologic and Other Reactions

Convulsions.   Grand mal convulsions are a rare complication of LSD exposure. Baker (1985) mentioned five major seizures occurring in the treatment of 150 patients, one of whom went into status epilepticus. Other mentions of this adverse reaction are few and scattered.

Permanent brain damage.   A quarter century ago, when the nonmedical use of LSD was underway, the opinion was expressed that irreversible brain damage resulted for consistent high-dose use. Even the users themselves would speak of "acid heads" whose brains were "fried" by the drug. Today, it is still not possible to confirm or deny that histopathologic changes are possible. The purity of illicit LSD is certainly open to question, and nothing is known about the neurotoxicity of its common contaminants.

Chromosomal damage.   During the late 1960s, a flurry of articles appeared indicating that LSD did or did not cause chromosomal damage. It now appears that whatever significant mutagenic alterations occurred were more likely to be due to the life-style of the user or to impurities. LSD, itself, appears to be a weak mutagen (Dishotsky et al. 1971).

Detoxification.   Detoxification is completely unnecessary even when the psychedelic drugs are used daily, which would be unusual. Total tolerance develops to large doses within days; unless substantial increments in dosage are taken daily, no mental effects may be discernable (Siva Sankar 1975). No signs of an abstinence syndrome have been recognized. Abrupt stoppage of these drugs is not associated with any autonomic neurologic or clear-cut psychiatric symptoms.

Chapter 129

Phencyclidine Abuse and Dependence

Phencyclidine

Phencyclidine (1-[1-phencyclohexyl] piperidine monohydrochloride) (PCP) was synthesized in the late 1950s. It was the first of a new class of general anesthetics known as cataleptoid anesthetics or dissociative anesthetics. PCP can be manufactured easily in unsophisticated laboratories from simple materials. Other arylcyclohexylamines include N-ethyl-1-phencyclohexalamine (PCE), 1-(1-2-thienyl-cyclohexyl) piperidine (TCP), 1-(1-phencyclohexyl) pyrrolidine (PHP), 1-piperidinocyclohexane carbonitrile (PCC), and ketamine. These products have been found as contaminants in samples of PCP sold on the street (Schnoll 1980).

PCP was originally described as a drug of abuse in both New York and San Francisco in the mid-1960s, but rapidly disappeared as a popular drug of abuse because of the unexpected reactions that often occurred following use of the drug. In the late 1960s and early 1970s, PCP emerged as a frequent contaminant of other drugs sold on the illicit market, most often in samples of hallucinogens and tetrahydrocannabinol (THC). In the past few years, PCP has once again become a sought after drug of abuse as well as being a contaminant in other drugs of abuse.

PCP can be taken through several routes of administration: oral, intravenous, smoking, or insufflation (snorting). As a frequent contaminant of street drugs, it is often used in conjunction with other drugs. Although the absorption with oral administration usually takes more than one hour, the effect is almost immediate after smoking. This crystalline, water-soluble, and lipophilic substance penetrates easily into fat stores and other cells, resulting in a long half-life. Metabolism takes place primarily in the liver by oxidation, hydroxylation, and conjugation with glucuronic acid. Ony a small amount of the active drug is excreted directly in the urine.

PCP has been demonstrated to interact with numerous central nervous system (CNS) neurotransmitter systems, including 5-hydroxytryptamine, norepinephrine, acetylcholine, dopamine, and glutamic acid. It has dopamine and acetylcholine agonistic properties and depresses cell firing in several brain centers, including the locus ceruleus. Its sympathomimetic action increases CNS catecholamines, with a subsequent rise in blood pressure, heart rate, and respiratory rate. This may also be a cause of the panic reaction sometimes seen in users of PCP. Its effect on reflexes probably leads later to muscle rigidity. Its cholinergic effects lead to increased CNS acetylcholine, with resulting sweating, flushing, drooling, and pupillary constriction. Its serotonergic effects cause dizziness, incoordination, slurred speech, and nystagmus. PCP has been shown to bind to specific receptors in the liver, kidney, lung, heart, and brain. In addition, it binds to muscarinic and opiate receptors (Weinstein et al. 1981).

PCP produces brief dissociative psychotic reactions similar to schizophrenic psychoses. These are characterized by changes in body image, thought disorder, depersonalization, and autism. At higher doses, subjects have great difficulty differentiating between themselves and their surroundings. Other users will experience hostility, paranoia, violence, and preoccupation with death. The differences in the response to PCP may be dose related or based on the individual response of the user (National Institute on Drug Abuse 1979).

Tolerance to the disruptive effects of PCP on operant behavior has been reported. PCP withdrawal has been observed in animals within four to eight hours after the drug is discontinued. In humans, because of a longer half-life, the withdrawal may not be seen for several days if at all. Increased neuromuscular activity and bruxism are common. Diarrhea and abdominal pain have also been described (Balster and Woolverton 1981).

PCP is used primarily by adolescents and young adults. First use is usually between the ages of 13 and 15. Three percent of young people in the 12- to 17-year age group have taken PCP. PCP users are usually polydrug abusers, with more than 90 percent of PCP users reporting use of other substances, mainly marijuana and alcohol. In the past, PCP was often found as a contaminant in other street drugs.

However, at the present time, samples of PCP are often contaminated by other drugs. The lack of knowledge of PCP's interactions with other drugs has led to problems in treating PCP reactions (Schnoll 1980).

On the street, PCP has been known by many names, including: angel dust, cadillac, dummy mist, dust, embalming fluid, green, hog, horse, jet, K, mist, peace pill, purple, rocket fuel, Sherman, THC, and whack. The abundance of street names for this substance is probably related to the initial lack of popularity of the oral route of PCP use. As a rule, it has been suggested that a new drug with a bizarre name that is smoked or snorted can be assumed to be PCP until proven otherwise.

Phencyclidine Intoxication (305.90)

DSM-III-R (American Psychiatric Association 1987) diagnostic criteria for PCP or similarly acting arylcyclohexylamine intoxication are listed in Table 1. A diagnosis of PCP intoxication should be confirmed with toxicologic analysis of blood or urine. Without this confirmation, the diagnosis can only be presumptive at best.

Although not discrete from each other, three stages for PCP intoxication have been described depending on the dose taken: behavioral toxicity, stuporous stage, and comatose stage. The behavioral toxicity presents with the symptoms described in the criteria noted above. The stuporous stage is characterized by a stupor with open eyes and a wakeful appearance. The patient may fluctuate between the stuporous stage and the stage of behavior toxicity in one- to two-hour periods. While in the stuporous condition, the patient will respond appropriately to deep pain and show purposeless movements, myoclonus, and exaggerated deep tendon reflexes. In the comatose stage, the patient is rigid and may show repetitive stereotyped movements and profuse sweating. The gag and corneal reflexes may be absent. This stage

Table 1. DSM-III-R Diagnostic Criteria for Phencyclidine (PCP) or Similarly Acting Arylcyclohexylamine Intoxication.

A. Recent use of phencyclidine or a similarly acting arylcyclohexylamine.

B. Maladaptive behavioral changes, e.g., belligerence, assaultiveness, impulsiveness, unpredictability, psychomotor agitation, impaired judgment, impaired social or occupational function.

C. Within an hour (less when smoked, insufflated ["snorted"], or used intravenously), at least two of the following signs:

    (1) vertical or horizontal nystagmus
    (2) increased blood pressure or heart rate
    (3) numbness or diminished responsiveness to pain
    (4) ataxia
    (5) dysarthria
    (6) muscle rigidity
    (7) seizures
    (8) hyperacusis

D. Not due to any physical or other mental disorder, e.g., Phencyclidine (PCP) or Similarly Acting Arylcyclohexylamine Delirium.

Note: When the differential diagnosis must be made without a clear-cut history or toxicologic analysis of body fluids, it may be qualified as "Provisional."

may last from one to four days, depending on the dose of PCP taken and rate of excretion of the drug. The electroencephalogram (EEG) shows delta wave activity followed by theta activity.

The differential diagnosis for PCP intoxication should include head trauma, schizophrenia or acute psychosis, organic brain syndrome, mania, cardiovascular accident, and stupor and/or coma (of metabolic origin, from drug overdose, or from other unexplained etiology).

The clinical picture that should lead the physician to consider the possibility of PCP abuse in patients presenting with an unusual behavior includes cerebellar symptoms (nystagmus, "Groucho eyes," ataxia and dysarthria), elevation of pulse and blood pressure, reduced sensitivity to pain, increased deep tendon reflexes, excessive salivation, and nausea. This constellation of signs and symptoms should be utilized along with urine and blood toxicology to differentiate PCP intoxication from acute psychosis or schizophrenia.

Emergency rooms should have available laboratory techniques to detect the presence of PCP in body fluids to assist in making an accurate diagnosis. Although further confirmation is necessary, a study at the Los Angeles County Psychiatric Hospital emergency room found that 43 percent of patients were positive for PCP (Yago et al. 1981). PCP should also be tested for in the body fluids in arrests associated with impulsive bizarre behavior or unexplained assaultive acts. As in all instances of toxicologic analysis, a positive urine for PCP should be verified by using a second analytical technique because diphenhydramine may produce a false positive result (Gallant 1981).

The presence of ataxia and nystagmus and the absence of dilated pupils are useful in ruling out the CNS stimulants and D-lysergic acid diethylamide (LSD) when evaluating the acutely agitated and confused patient. The presence of hyperreflexia and hypertension differentiate PCP intoxication from sedative-hypnotic intoxication (National Institute on Drug Abuse 1979), although these signs may be present in acute withdrawal from sedative-hypnotic medications or ethanol.

Management of PCP Intoxication

Due to poor judgment, the patient usually will require protective supervision in a nonstimulating environment that should include protection from self-injury. When possible, a careful history should be taken, including drugs taken, duration of use, time of last dose, adverse reactions to drugs, and psychiatric history. Obtaining history from companions or family members may be useful. Belongings should be carefully searched for the presence of drugs or paraphernalia that should be analyzed to assist in making the diagnosis.

A thorough physical and neurologic examination should be performed. Vital signs need to be monitored for laryngeal stridor or respiratory depression, and a respirator may be required. Restraints are to be avoided. Lahmeyer and Stock (1983) reported that the use of restraints may cause rhabdomyolysis and acute renal failure.

Although the "talking-down" technique has been used to treat acute hallucinogen reactions, this approach should be avoided in PCP-intoxicated patients because it may intensify agitation.

To establish the diagnosis, other types of obtundation should be ruled out. Naloxone may be given to rule out opioid intoxication. Toxicology screen on blood (10 ml) and urine (50 ml) samples is important, although reliance on blood levels is hazardous because the active substance may be repeatedly released from fat stores. The serum concentration of PCP is a less accurate indicator of a patient's level of intoxication than a fat biopsy. Test kits for PCP preparations are now available through law enforcement agencies (Gallant 1981), although reliance on the results of unverified tests may be misleading.

There is no specific antagonist for PCP. If PCP is taken orally, a gastric lavage performed with a liter or more of half normal saline could be done. Following this, the patient could be placed on continuous gastric suction using a nasogastric tube.

The concentration of PCP in the body fluids and tissues is profoundly influenced by pH. Some PCP is retained in fatty tissues and in the brain, where it escapes hepatic metabolism. Acidification of urine increases the excretion rate of PCP roughly 100-fold because the drug is a weak base. If acidification is done prior to toxicologic screens of urine and blood for the presence of other drugs, excretion and analysis for other drugs (e.g., barbiturates or salicylates) may be adversely affected.

In cases of coma secondary to acute PCP intoxication, residual drug should be removed from the stomach and sent off for analysis. Before the nasogastric tube is removed, ammonium chloride 2.75 mEq/kg dissolved in 60 ml of saline could be given through the nasogastric tube every six hours until the urine pH is 5 or less. Another approach to urine acidification is to administer vitamin C (ascorbic acid) with iv fluids at the rate of 2 g in 500 ml every six hours. Urine pH needs to be checked two to four times each day. When the pH is 5, diuresis could be enforced by using furosemide (Lasix) 20 to 40 mg iv. After consciousness returns, urine acidification should continue for a week, giving cranberry juice along with ammonium chloride, 500 mg orally qid or ascorbic acid 1 g orally tid. Throughout the initial treatment, electrolytes should be maintained, and blood gases should be monitored periodically. Acidification is contraindicated in severe liver disease and in the presence of renal insufficiency. Other than the use of acidifying agents, medication should be avoided in the patient who is comatose from PCP intoxication. The exception to this rule is a patient who is hypertensive secondary to PCP. In this case, antihypertensive medications should be administered to reduce the blood pressure. If the patient is severely agitated and poses a potential threat to self or others, haloperidol has been demonstrated to be effective in controlling the agitation. When there is doubt about the drug the person has taken or when a combination of drugs may be present, diazepam 5 to 20 mg iv slowly or orally could be used.

Complications of PCP Intoxication

1. *Undetected PCP overdose.* This usually follows oral ingestion, which has a later onset of action. This should be suspected in children, as well as in patients who fail to improve after three hours of observation or in those whose level of confusion seems to increase rather than decrease with time. In any case where there is suspicion of PCP ingestion, urine, blood, or gastric contents should be collected and sent for toxicologic analysis to confirm or rule out the diagnosis.
2. *Seizure and status epilepticus.* No medication is necessary to treat a single seizure; however, if there are repeated seizures or if the patient is in status epilepticus, use diazepam 10 to 20 mg iv.
3. *Hypertension.* Use hydralazine (Apresoline) or phentolamine iv drip (2 to 5 mg over five to 10 minutes).
4. *Hyperthermia.* Use hypothermic blankets or ice.
5. *Opisthotonus and acute dystonia.* This usually clears as blood levels of the drug decrease. If the problem persists, diazepam iv to relax the musculature is often effective.

6. *Cardiac arrhythmia.* In the case of a severe arrhythmia that does not clear, a cardiology consultation should be called.
7. *Rhabdomyolysis, myoglobinuria, and acute renal failure.* When acute renal failure is present, a nephrology consultation should be obtained.
8. *Phencyclidine psychosis.* See the following on PCP delirium.

PCP Delirium (292.81)

PCP is considered one of the most common causes of emergency room admissions for drug-induced psychoses (Yago et al. 1981). Intravenous PCP has produced schizophrenic-like symptoms in subjects with no previous history of psychotic behavior (Gallant 1981). Initially, alterations of body image occur, with a loss of body boundaries and a sense of unreality. Feelings of estrangement and loneliness follow, sometimes associated with an intensification of dependency needs. Progressive disorganization of thought, negativism, and hostility can also develop. Some subjects become catatonic with dream-like experiences. Distortion of body image and depersonalization are universal reactions. Attention and cognitive deficits are often present.

The psychosis can persist in some individuals anywhere from 24 hours to several months or even years after the cessation of active PCP use. Whether this is a direct effect of PCP or the drug exacerbating an underlying psychotic disorder is not clear; administration of PCP to schizophrenic patients has been reported to exacerbate schizophrenic-psychotic symptoms acutely.

A PCP psychosis in the presence of a clear sensorium is rare. It is important to examine the patient for the presence of horizontal or vertical nystagmus, ataxia, or slurred speech. These signs indicate PCP intoxication rather than PCP psychosis. Preexisting psychiatric disorders should be ruled out. Daghestani (1987) emphasized the importance of a thorough diagnostic workup with all patients who present with acute psychotic decompensation. Anticholinergic drug intoxication must be ruled out before initiating treatment with an antipsychotic agent.

The clinical picture is dominated by insomnia, restlessness, and behavior that is purposeless, hyperactive, bizarre, aggressive, or agitated. The mental state may fluctuate to include paranoia, mania, grandiosity, rapid thought, and speech with emotional lability. The degree of psychosis usually relates to the amount of drug used.

Three phases for PCP psychosis have been described, each lasting approximately five days: 1) agitated phase, 2) mixed phase, and 3) resolution phase. Factors reported to reduce the duration of each phase are individual susceptibility, degree of exposure to the drug, dosage of antipsychotic, and urine acidification.

Luisada and Brown (1976) observed that "about one fourth of the patients originally treated for phencyclidine psychosis return about a year later with schizophrenia in the absence of drug use. These later episodes have lacked the characteristic violence of the phencyclidine-induced psychosis, and they respond quickly to antipsychotic drugs."

Management of PCP Delirium

The guidelines for treatment approaches discussed in the management of PCP intoxication apply here to a large extent. The goals of treatment should include prevention of injury, facilitation of the excretion of PCP from urine, and the amelioration of psychosis. The patient should be hospitalized in a closed psychiatric unit and assigned to a quiet room. If agitated, the patient could be restrained by trained personnel. All efforts should be made to avoid physical restraints. Because of the intense physical exertion often associated with the agitation seen in PCP delirium, the patient should be given adequate hydration.

The principles of urine acidification discussed above are the same, although the acidifying agents should be given orally: cranberry juice (8 to 16 oz qid), ascorbic acid (1 g qid) or ammonium chloride (liquid solution 500 mg/5 ml with an initial loading dose of 15 to 20 ml of ammonium chloride followed by 10 ml qid).

Once the urine pH is 5.5 or less, diuresis may be encouraged by the administration of furosemide 40 mg bid. Oral potassium supplement will be necessary to avoid potassium depletion, and serum electrolytes should be monitored daily. Improvement could be expected six to eight hours after diuresis. Urine acidification should continue for at least three days after all evidence of psychosis has disappeared, and most patients will require a three- to 10-day course of acidification.

The use of antacids, which act as alkalinizing agents, should be avoided while attempts are being made to enhance excretion of PCP by acidifying the urine. The antacids significantly reduce the ability of ammonium chloride and other acidifying drugs to lower the urine pH, resulting in retention of PCP in the serum.

The use of psychoactive drugs should be undertaken carefully and judiciously. Both benzodiazepines and haloperidol have been described as being useful in the treatment of delirium caused by PCP. Pitts (1984) suggested that a standard dose of a benzodiazepine, a neuroleptic, and a beta blocker given together will resolve the delirious psychotic state within minutes. The reseacher conceived of this approach because all neurotransmitter effects are aggravated by PCP use. It was thought that blockers or competitors would blunt the responses seen in these patients. According to Pitts, few patients who maintain confusional symptoms will require long-term therapy. Additional reports of the effectiveness of this approach will help to substantiate usefulness of this technique.

Rosen et al. (1984) described four patients who had a history of PCP abuse, prolonged psychosis, and poor neuroleptic response. Three of these patients were given electroconvulsive therapy (ECT); all showed a dramatic response after the third or fourth treatment. The authors recommended that ECT be tried in psychotic patients who have used PCP if they fail to respond to antipsychotic medications after one week of inpatient treatment. Further reports on the improvement of PCP-associated psychosis with ECT were made by Grover et al. (1986).

Following the resolution of the acute confusional psychotic state, a referral to long-term therapy would be important.

PCP Organic Mental Disorder Not Otherwise Specified (292.90)

The DSM-III-R diagnostic criteria for this category are listed in Table 2. This chronic mental impairment is believed to result from chronic PCP use. This condition is characterized by memory deficits and a state of confusion or decreased intellectual functioning with associated assaultiveness. There are also visual disturbances and speech difficulty, such as a blocking or an inability to retrieve the proper words. A differential diagnosis should rule out other possible causes of organicity. The course of the disorder may be quite variable. The reasons for this variability are not clear but may be related to residual drug being released from adipose tissues of the chronic user. The confusional state may last four to six weeks. The condition may improve

Table 2. DSM-III-R Diagnostic Criteria for Phencyclidine (PCP) or Similarly Acting Arylcyclohexylamine Organic Mental Disorder Not Otherwise Specified.
A. Recent use of phencyclidine or a similarly acting arylcyclohexylamine.
B. The resulting illness involves features of several Organic Mental Syndromes or a progression from one Organic Mental Syndrome to another, e.g., initially there is Delirium, followed by an Organic Delusional Syndrome.
C. Not due to any physical or other mental disorder.
Note: When the differential diagnosis must be made without a clear-cut history or toxicologic analysis of body fluids, it may be qualified as "Provisional."

with time if PCP exposure does not recur and if residual PCP is excreted by acidifying the patient's urine as described above.

Management of PCP Organic Mental Disorder Not Otherwise Specified

The basic management plan is that of protecting the patient from injury and helping the patient deal with disorientation by utilizing a simple, structured, and supportive approach. Sensory input and stimuli have to be kept to a minimum. Nonthreatening environment and nonjudgmental staff are of paramount importance. Excessive stimulation can result in agitation and violent and aggressive behavior.

PCP Abuse (305.90) and PCP Dependence (304.50)

The DSM-III-R diagnostic criteria for PCP or similarly acting arylcyclohexylamine abuse include the following:

A. Pattern of pathologic use: intoxication throughout the day; episodes of phencyclidine or similarly acting arylcyclohexylamine delirium or mixed organic mental disorder;
B. Impairment in social or occupational functioning due to substance use, for example fights, loss of friends, absence from work, loss of job or legal difficulties (other than due to a single arrest for possession, purchase, or sale of the substance);
C. Duration of disturbance of at least one month.

The criteria stated above should be supported by the presence of PCP or other arylcyclohexylamines in the blood or urine.

In addition to the listed criteria, Smith et al. (1978) reported that a significant number of users experience profound depression from chronic use of PCP.

Management of PCP Abuse and Dependence

Therapists should be cognizant of the fact that PCP users display a wide range of behaviors, including flattened affect, belligerence, depression, and anxiety. They are often unable to cope with the demands and expectations of a structured intensive confrontive environment of the type often found in the traditional therapeutic community. Bolter (1980) suggested that the following management strategies may be effective at the beginning of treatment: 1) establish clear ground rules that are enforced; 2) keep decision making to a minimum; 3) accept some absentmindedness initially, directions may have to be repeated; 4) develop a short list of tasks with a regular routine; 5) avoid stressful situations; and 6) set realistic consequences for both positive and negative behavior and be consistent in the application of these consequences.

Because of the cognitive impairments associated with PCP abuse, the therapeutic environment should provide a supportive structure. All staff members must be aware of the treatment plan to prevent any splitting of staff members by the patient. The treatment staff should be well trained in the effects of PCP so they can work effectively with the types of problems presented.

Caracci et al. (1983) described three cases of PCP-induced depression. Many of the patients had poor compliance with regular clinic attendance, making it difficult to engage them in a meaningful therapeutic alliance. Individual and group therapies appear to have a weak impact. Because of these problems and because of the high suicide risk, Caracci et al. recommended hospitalization for treatment of PCP-induced depression and suicidal potential.

For the treatment of PCP withdrawal, Tennant et al. (1981) suggested the use of desipramine 50 to 150 mg in the first day to be decreased over the following two weeks. The use of this technique has not been verified in additional studies.

Some differences exist between long-term narcotic-dependent individuals and chronic PCP abusers, making the therapeutic community approach inappropriate for those individuals needing long-term treatment for chronic PCP abuse. The PCP abusers tend to be younger, more immature, and do not tolerate the usual confrontation techniques employed in therapeutic communities (De Angelis and Goldstein 1978).

Chronic PCP abusers exhibit characteristics similar to a child with so-called learning disabilities. They generally show emotional lability, social incompetence, overt impulsiveness, poor social judgment, poor attention span and concentration, poor interpersonal relationships, and social maladjustment. These characteristics may be reversible if PCP use stops and appropriate treatment is provided.

During the course of outpatient therapy, educational and nutritional awareness will enhance the level of self-care of the patient. Vocational counseling and training may prove to be beneficial in enhancing the self-esteem of the patient.

Using self-help groups has become an established and essential part of any successful treatment of PCP and other drug dependence. Narcotics Anonymous (NA) groups have begun to gain increasing acceptance of PCP users, and many patients have been able to utilize NA as part of a recovery program.

Outpatient follow-up treatment is aimed at keeping the patient away from resuming drug use. It is important to assist staff in being realistic about their expectations for treatment.

PCP abusers may not be expected initially to join extensively in group therapy, individual therapy, or school or recreation programs. They may be belligerent toward treatment, especially on program entry.

The following are important considerations when structuring a program responsive to PCP abusers. First, there should be minimal confrontation or hostility-provoking behavior on the part of staff. Second, patients should be provided with a nonthreatening, supportive environment in which they can begin to feel comfortable. Third, minimal patient involvement in specific therapeutic intervention should be anticipated initially.

De Angelis and Goldstein (1978) found that chronic PCP abusers stay in treatment longer than occasional PCP users. Individual, family, couples, and group therapies have been used with some success. Body awareness therapy, yoga, and progressive relaxation techniques help patients to focus and help to improve attention span and concentration.

Many PCP abusers have a sense of a loss of contact with their bodies. These exercises can be helpful in restoring a healthy body image. Consistent with this, patients should be encouraged to seek out athletic activities.

Treatment of PCP abuse and dependence, like all other chemical dependence problems, requires long-term treatment. Persistence and patience on the part of staff are necessary to achieve a satisfactory outcome.

Chapter 130

Stimulants

In this chapter, we describe stimulant abuse and its treatment. Treating the stimulant abuser requires broad understanding, including the understanding of: recent cultural changes and older historical forces; the characteristics of acute stimulant euphoria and acute post-use dysphoria; the significance of administration route, of neurochemical effects, and of medical consequences; and the clinical characteristics of the transition to dependence, of abstinence phases and symptoms, and of interactions with psychiatric disorders. All of these require understanding before the clinical presentation of any stimulant abuser can be adequately interpreted and before effective treatment for that individual can be implemented. Consequently, the initial pages of this chapter provide brief reviews of recent history and epidemiology, acute stimulant effects, medical morbidity, clinical descriptions of phases in dependence, and clinical psychiatric presentations in order to provide a foundation for the discussion of stimulant abuse treatment.

Recent History and Epidemiology

A stimulant-use epidemic is now underway. Cocaine users number almost half as many as marijuana users. Cocaine "addiction," although different from opiate dependence, exists in one to five million individuals, compared to half a million heroin addicts. After a decade of decreased use, more recent reports indicate methamphetamine abuse is again increasing, perhaps becoming the "poor man's cocaine." For the first time, smokable ("freebase" or "crack") cocaine, in ready-to-smoke form, is freely available on the streets of all major cities. Smoking cocaine has the abuse liability of intravenous injection without the stigma of injection and may be the most dangerous change in substance abuse to appear in the 1980s.

Surprisingly, much of the public and the medical community considered cocaine a safe, nonaddictive euphoriant, different from amphetamine or methamphetamine, less than 10 years ago. Psychiatric texts stated "cocaine creates no serious problems" (Grinspoon and Bakalar 1980). Two national drug abuse commissions determined that cocaine created minimal morbidity or societal costs (National Commission on Marihuana and Drug Abuse 1973; Strategy Council on Drug Abuse 1973). Clinical reports of adverse cocaine effects from the beginning of the century were considered exaggerations, similar to exaggerated marijuana reports from the same era. Societal acceptance of all drug use had reached unprecedented levels. No systematic clinical cocaine abuse research existed. The absence of objective systematically derived data in humans was misinterpreted as meaning that cocaine use had no adverse consequences. Paradoxically, animal research demonstrated very close similarity between cocaine and amphetamine, and pharmacologists warned that historical reports might not be exaggerated.

By 1985, cocaine abuse exploded. Increased social acceptance of drug use, the illusion of safety, increased availability, and a new, powerful route of administration (cocaine smoking) all combined to produce an explosion of cocaine use and abuse, which in turn led to obvious harm from cocaine and beginning medical and public awareness of cocaine's dangers. Sadly, this reenacted cyclical "discovery" of old knowledge. In the 1890s and 1920s, cocaine use surged and was temporarily considered safe. In the 1930s, a potent, allegedly "safe" stimulant was synthesized: amphetamine. But in the early 1950s and late 1960s, amphetamine abuse epidemics proved amphetamine was as dangerous as cocaine (Byck 1986).

Stimulant epidemics run consistent, predictable courses (Ellinwood 1974). After an epidemic reemerges, adverse consequences first slowly change the perception of drug users themselves, decreasing the glamour associated with stimulant abuse. (For example, "speed kills" became a common slogan in the drug subculture after widespread methamphetamine or "speed" abuse appeared.) The incidence of new users diminishes, and the clinical consequences for those already exposed run their course. Decreasing the stimulant supply also sometimes limits epidemics; decreased production and prescription of amphetamines a decade ago contributed to the waning of that epidemic. After an epidemic wanes, stimulant use quiesces for five to 15 years, then a misperception of stimulant safety again appears. Initial clinical statements recorded in each stimulant epidemic uniformly describe illusory safety; perhaps because one to four years usually intervenes between first stimulant use and abuse (Schnoll et al 1985; Siegel 1985b), and because we forget or ignore history.

By 1984, more than 10 percent of the US population had tried cocaine, with almost 50 percent in some age groups (Abelson and Miller 1985). A sevenfold increase occurred between 1976 and 1983 in emergency room visits attributed to cocaine, in cocaine-related deaths (> 2 per 1,000 deaths), and in public treatment admissions for cocaine (Adams and Durell 1984; Blanken et al. 1986). These data do not include private treatment contacts and thus underrepresent actual morbidity. Cocaine use was still increasing at the time of the last national household survey in 1983, and more recent data show sharper increases in use and treatment contacts, decreased prices, and decreased age at first use (Adams et al. 1987; Adams and Kozel 1985). Cocaine trafficking has become the leading source of income from any illicit activity.

The incidence of first time use of cocaine had recently peaked and may be leveling (Abelson and Miller 1985), but the advent of inexpensive smokable cocaine ("crack") in 1986 could reverse this trend. In the Bahamas, smokable cocaine was introduced in 1983 and resulted in greater than sevenfold increases in hospital and outpatient admissions for cocaine abuse by the end of 1984. Moreover, in the United States, there is no indication of any decrease in cocaine importation. Since 18 to 48 months intervene between first intranasal use and appearance for treatment, adverse health effects and clinical treatment demands probably have not peaked. Finally, because total use and exposure to cocaine is now many times higher than ever before, the current stimulant epidemic may leave a legacy of high endemic use, continued human distress, and continued demands for treatment.

Acute Actions

The most extensively abused psychomotor stimulants, cocaine and amphetamine, are also the best understood, although major gaps in our knowledge do exist. All high abuse stimulants share very similar neurochemical and clinical characteristics, but other centrally stimulating agents, such as caffeine or xanthines, have very different use patterns, less abuse potential, and different neurochemical actions (Goodman and Gilman 1985). These "mild" stimulants do not present major abuse or management problems. The different stimulants and their abuse liabilities are listed in Table 1. The remainder of this review describes high abuse stimulants like cocaine and amphetamine.

Stimulants create an activated euphoria. Cocaine, amphetamine, and many other similar stimulants are self-administered in pursuit of intensified pleasure. Acutely, stimulants produce profound subjective well-being with alertness. Normal pleasures are magnified. Anxiety is decreased. Self-confidence and self-perceptions of mastery increase. Social inhibitions are reduced and interpersonal communication is facilitated. All aspects of the personal environment take on intensified qualities, but without hallucinatory perceptual distortions. Emotionality and sexual feelings are enhanced (Freud 1884; Gawin 1978; Lasagna et al. 1955; Lewin 1924; Nathanson 1937; Van Dyke et al. 1982). While stimulant use is initially enjoyable and seemingly easily controlled, repeated use gradually produces obsessions over recapturing stimulant-induced euphoria and extreme, compulsive urges for more use. This alters behavior and often causes severe psychological distress.

Stimulants with high abuse potential activate mesolimbic or mesocortical dopaminergic pathways to produce euphoria (Goeders and Smith 1982; Yokel and Wise 1983). In animals, electrical self-stimulation of these pathways mirrors stimulant self-administration. Increases in behavioral and physiologic reward indices are produced by either electrical stimulation of these dopaminergic reward regions or by stimulants. Such increases in reward are decreased by pharmacologic dopamine receptor blockade or lesions in dopaminergic reward pathways. Substantial preclinical research gener-

Table 1.   Stimulants

High Abuse Stimulants	Low Abuse Stimulants
1. Cocaine	1. Caffeine
2. Amphetamine	2. Nicotine
3. Methamphetamine	3. Phenylpropanolamine
4. Methylenedioxyamphetamine	4. Ephedrine
5. Phenmetrazine	5. Pseudoephedrine
6. Phendimetrazine	6. Theophylline
7. Dietylpropion	7. Fenfluramine
8. Methylphenidate	8. Strychnine

ated over the past two decades supports the central role of dopamine in stimulant reward (reviewed in Wise 1984), and there is minimal contradictory evidence (Gawin 1986b; Reith et al. 1983; Spyraki et al. 1982). The neurochemical and neuroanatomic localization of stimulant euphorigenic effects in dopaminergic reward regions is extremely important because it provides new avenues toward understanding and researching both stimulant withdrawal and potential treatments (Gawin and Ellinwood 1988). In contrast to other abused substances like heroin, activation of opiate receptors or endorphinergic-enkephalinergic pathways are not necessary to support stimulant reward or euphoria (Ettenburg et al. 1982; Pettit et al. 1982).

Cocaine, the amphetamines, methylphenidate, and other stimulants are structurally dissimilar but neuropharmacologically alike. On acute, blind laboratory administration in humans, abused stimulants are indistinguishable (Brown et al. 1978; Fischman et al. 1976). In animals, they produce cross-tolerance and stimulus generalization to each other as well as very rapid learning of self-administration (Colpaert et al. 1979; Leith and Barrett 1976, 1981). Table 2 summarizes known neurochemical actions of stimulants. None of the single neurochemical actions is responsible for stimulant euphoria; each known action is also produced by other pharmacologic agents that have not been reported to produce euphoria, are not self-administered by animals, and are not abused by humans. Thus euphorigenic stimulant central nervous system (CNS) activation clearly occurs in dopaminergic pathways, but the neurochemical mechanisms responsible for this activation are unclear. In addition, the relative contribution of direct stimulant actions on dopaminergic neurones, as opposed to actions on dopaminergic systems by nondopaminergic collateral neuronal systems that are also affected by stimulants, cannot be easily differentiated at this time.

There are no proven distinctions, pertinent to abuse, between individual stimulants except for differences in half-life. Other differences in activity (e.g., varied local anesthetic properties) do not have known drug abuse consequences. Cocaine's half-life is less than 90 minutes, but tachyphylaxis reduces the half-life of single-dose euphoria to 30 minutes (Van Dyke et al. 1982). Amphetamine half-life is more than four hours, and euphoria from single doses can last several hours (Gunne and Anggard 1973). This may produce different patterns of administration and influences the likelihood of adverse sequelae. Cocaine binges are characterized by up to 10 readministrations of the drug per hour. Rapid and frequent changes in mood occur as a last dose wears off and a new dose is administered. Although cocaine binges can last as long as seven consecutive days or more, it is more common for them to last less than 12 hours (Gawin and Kleber 1985a). Amphetamine binges are characterized by several hours between readministrations, less variability of mood, generally more sustained and intense abuse, and longer total duration, often lasting more than 24

Table 2.　Neurochemical Actions of Stimulants

Stimulant	Catecholamine Reuptake Blockade	Serotonin Release or Reuptake Blockade	Local Anesthesia	Dopamine Release	Monoamine Oxidase Inhibition
Amphetamine	Marked	Moderate	Mild	Moderate	Mild
Cocaine	Marked	Moderate	Marked	Moderate	None
Methylphenidate	Marked	Unknown	Unknown	Moderate	None

Note.　See Gawin and Ellinwood (1988) for reviews.

hours (Kramer et al. 1967). It is not certain that differences in morbidity occur, but it is our impression that amphetamines' less frequent readministrations and decreased total dosage required, combined with lower cost and the relatively larger personal amphetamine supplies available to the abuser (amphetamine is about 10 times as potent as cocaine but is sold for equivalent prices in similar amounts) all make amphetamines more likely to produce prolonged high-intensity abuse. When the intensity and duration of cocaine abuse approximates high-dose amphetamine abuse, as can occur with cocaine smoking or with large cocaine supplies, then the two do not appear clinically distinguishable. Because of the basic similarity between these agents in all areas except those just noted, the term *stimulants* in the remainder of this chapter refers jointly to amphetamine and cocaine.

Clinical Characteristics and Treatment

Multiple, consistent clinical reports on the characteristics of stimulant abusers appearing for treatment exist in the literature. Observations from the beginning of this century (Lewin 1924; Maier 1926), through the latest US amphetamine epidemic of 1967 to 1972 (Connell 1970; Ellinwood 1967; Kramer et al. 1967; Smith 1969), and the current surge in cocaine abuse (Gawin and Kleber 1986a; Gold et al. 1985; Siegel 1982) all indicate that 1) predictable psychiatric complications can occur acutely during or after individual episodes or "binges" of stimulant abuse, and 2) chronic abuse might be associated with separate chronic psychiatric sequelae, particularly mood dysfunctions. Clinical presentations often include a mixture of acute and chronic symptoms, with differing intensities of each. Separation of these dimensions requires ongoing longitudinal assessments. Descriptions of specific components of psychiatric presentations in stimulant abusers follow, along with guidelines for clinical management.

Acute Stimulant Use Sequelae and Their Treatment

Stimulant Intoxication

Stimulant euphoria is phenomenologically distinct from opiate-, alcohol-, or other substance-induced euphorias. As noted earlier, qualities of acute intoxication in usual street dosages include euphoria, activation, decreased anxiety (initially), disinhibition, heightened curiosity and increased interest in the personal environment, feelings of increased competence and self-esteem, and a clear sensorium without hallucinations or cognitive confusion. Adverse consequences of stimulant intoxication reflect atypical reactions or exaggerations of these sought-after components of the stimulant euphoria. Exaggerations include euphoric disinhibition, impaired judgment, grandiosity, impulsiveness, irresponsibility, atypical generosity, hypersexuality, hyperawareness, compulsive repetitive actions, and extreme psychomotor activation. Adverse sequelae include the psychosocial and economic consequences of actions undertaken while intoxicated—such as abrogation of responsibilities, loss of money, sexual indiscretions, or atypical illegal activities—but can also include physical injury that results from dangerous acts performed while judgment is impaired.

If intoxication is uncomplicated, no treatment is indicated other than observation through a return to baseline. Observation is also always indicated because complications such as acute psychiatric disorders or medical emergencies can occur. It should be noted that treatable medical emergencies are not common because of rapid stimulant actions; effective emergency intervention occurs only if administration of the drug is in close temporal proximity to medical attention, usually within one half-life, or if absorption is delayed (e.g., through oral cocaine or amphetamine use). Marked stimulant intoxication strongly resembles the mania or hypomania or bipolar psychiatric disorder and can sometimes trigger mania. If stimulant activation is not self-remitting within less than 24 hours in an observed, stimulant-free setting, then mania is probably present and treatment for mania may be required.

Stimulant Delirium

Euphoric stimulation can become dysphoric as the dosage and duration of administration increase. In most stimulant intoxications, an admixture of anxiety and irritability soon accompany the desired euphoric effects. Anxiety ranges from mild dysphoric stimulation to extreme paranoia or to a panic-like delirium. In moderate form, a state of global sympathetic discharge occurs, which strongly resembles a panic anxiety attack and is often associated with a fear of impending death from the stimulant. Disorientation is not usually present but may develop. In more severe forms, an organic psychosis with disorientation occurs. When frank delirium exists, neuroleptics and restraints may be needed. However, extreme caution is indicated in treating stimulant delirium because such symptoms may indicate impending stimulant overdose. In this circumstance, emergency medical management and monitoring should absolutely take precedence over psychiatric management.

Stimulant Delusions

Delusional psychoses occur after prolonged and intense stimulant binges. These have been experimentally induced by amphetamine in unselected normals and appear related to the amount and duration of stimulant administration rather than to predisposition to psychosis (Bell 1970). Identical experiments have not been done with cocaine, but similar clinical reports exist for cocaine. The delusional content is usually paranoid, and, if mild, the stimulant abuser may retain awareness that induced fears are a consequence of the immediately preceding stimulant intake (Ellinwood 1967). If severe, however, reality testing is completely impaired and caution is required. Case reports of homicides with stimulant psychoses exist (Ellinwood 1970).

Cocaine delusions are usually transient and usually remit following sleep normalization. Amphetamine delusions are most often similarly brief, but clinicians more frequently report longer episodes, lasting several days. Even longer episodes, however, have been described after very prolonged stimulant binges or in individuals having preexistent schizophrenic or manic psychoses. Short-term neuroleptic treatment is routinely used to ameliorate delusional symptomatology. Observation is essential until the delusions remit. Flashback phenomena or delayed reemergence of symptoms have not been described for stimulant-induced psychoses.

Poststimulant Dysphoria

If a stimulant use episode involves several serial readministrations or substantial doses, even in a naive, nondependent user, then mood does not return to baseline when use ceases but instead rapidly descends into dysphoria. This dysphoria, called the "crash" by abusers, is usually self-limited and resolves following one or two nights of sleep. Clinically, the crash fully mimics unipolar depression with melancholia, except for its comparatively brief duration. It is a regular accompaniment of the recurrent binges that occur in stimulant dependence and will be discussed more fully later. However, since emergency presentations of the crash are clinically common, require specific acute interventions, and can occur in nondependent individuals, we discuss treatment for the "crash" itself here.

The depression of the crash can be extremely intense and may include potentially lethal, but temporary, suicidal ideation, which remits completely when the crash is over. This transient suicidal ideation can occur in individuals who have no prior history of depression or of suicidal ideation or suicide attempts. True unipolar depression (which is not self-remitting and requires antidepressant treatment) may also occur in a subpopulation, as discussed later in this chapter. Usual clinical management occurs in two stages. First, observation is indicated to prevent self-harm and to provide an opportunity for sleep and recovery of mood. Second, evaluation after sleep is needed to ensure that neurovegetative symptoms and suicidal ideation have remitted. In most cases, this can be done in an emergency room setting, and hospital admission is most often not necessary to manage the crash.

Stimulant Morbidity

The full extent of morbidity caused by chronic stimulant abuse is not known with certainty. Many different types of adverse consequences have been identified, ranging from medical complications including overdose, to pathology due to administration route, to neurotoxicity, to interactions with major psychiatric disorders, and to psychosocial disruption without clear physiologic or psychiatric insult. Preclinical and clinical assessment of stimulant abuse has been far from exhaustive. Surprisingly, there are no human data that rigorously define the chronic medical or psychiatric consequences of long-term stimulant abuse, and few animal studies have been designed to reflect chronic human abuse. Most of what is known is based on survey data such as Drug Abuse Warning Network (DAWN) reports (or telephone surveys with inherent limitations based on sample self-selection), or on clinical observations of single cases or small samples, or on animal data with questionable generalizability. Such research helps define the range, or types, of confirmed or suspected adverse stimulant sequelae but does not specify the extent or quantity of the sequelae, nor their likelihood for a given abuser. They therefore provide a starting point for treatment design, but not detailed guidelines.

Chronic Stimulant Abuse: Medical Complications

Death can result from stimulant-induced sympathomimetic storms that can cause hypertensive cerebrovascular accidents, hyperpyrexia, or myocardial infarction and cardiorespiratory collapse; more than 50 case reports now exist in the world literature (Cregler and Mark 1985; Kalant and Kalant 1979; Roberts et al. 1984). Plasma cholinesterases metabolize cocaine. Pseudocholinesterase deficiency should produce hypersensitivity (Jatlow et al. 1979), but this has not yet been clinically reported. Emergency medical treatment of cocaine and amphetamine largely involves providing routine countermeasures for toxic symptoms, such as cardiac arrythmias or seizures. It should be noted that acid loading facilitates amphetamine excretion and that propranolol, often used previously to reduce adrenergic tone with cocaine overdose, has been shown to cause some toxic interaction. Details of overdose management have been reviewed elsewhere (Gay 1982) and will not be covered here.

Nonlethal cardiovascular or cerebrovascular injury can also follow overdose. Gross cerebrovascular injury and diffuse microinfarctions have been reported (Rumbaugh et al. 1971, 1980). No systematic outcome data on treatment for such complications exist. Cocaine hepatotoxicity has been described in animals (Rauckman et al. 1982), but not as yet in humans. Colitis, pseudomediastinum, and bullous disease have been reported (Bush et al. 1984; Fishel et al. 1985). Neonatal complications in children of stimulant-addicted mothers have also been reported (Chasnoff et al. 1985). Lack of other documented medical problems caused by stimulants may not reflect their absence, but may instead indicate a lack of systematic clinical investigations. For example, we are not aware of any studies of physiologic functioning, excluding pulmonary function in cocaine smokers, in any population of chronic stimulant abusers.

Other medical complications are consequences of administration route. Complications of intravenous stimulant administration include thrombosis, hepatitis, acquired immunodeficiency disorder, local sepsis, abscess, angiitis, endocarditis, and septicemia. Cocaine smoking causes pulmonary dysfunction (Itkonen et al. 1984; Weiss et al. 1981), and intranasal stimulant use can be associated with rhinitis and mucosal excoriation. Treatment for stimulant-related medical disease does not differ from routine management.

Chronic Stimulant Abuse: Psychiatric Complications and Treatment

Knowledge About Stimulant Abuse Treatment

Current clinical understanding and management of chronic stimulant abuse are largely based on research and clinical experience gained treating users of other abused substances and on nonsystematic, descriptive reports of treatment for stimulant abusers. Few large-scale clinical investigations of either the clinical psychiatric consequences of stimulant abuse or their treatment exist. We are only now witnessing the appearance of systematic observations of abuse and abstinence patterns, of well-designed treatment experiments, and of refined conceptualizations of stimulant abuse and dependence. Further, rigorous substantiation is needed in all areas. A substantial proportion of the following discussion is therefore based on clinical consensus, not on the precise, scientific observation or experimentation available for some other psychiatric and substance abuse disorders.

The Spectrum of Stimulant Use and Abuse

Early stimulant use.   Stimulant use occurs across a wide spectrum. In the early 1960s, millions of individuals were prescribed chronic amphetamines for depression or weight loss, and yet millions of amphetamine abusers clearly did not result. Most patients were successfully and relatively easily weaned from stimulants when restrictions were applied because use became uncontrolled in small subgroups. Similarly, the National Institute on Drug Abuse estimated that of 30 million persons who have tried cocaine in the United States six million are regular users, and one-fourth of those are in immediate need of treatment. These data indicate that most individuals use cocaine intermittently and that controlled low-intensity regular use may occur, as with amphetamine in the preceding stimulant epidemic (NIDA National Household Survey 1986).

Development of stimulant dependence takes place within a social-occupational matrix (Gawin and Ellinwood 1988). Initially, low doses enhance interactions with the environment, facilitating performance and confidence to enable productive increases in interpersonal or occupational industry and adventurousness (Connell 1970; Ellinwood and Petrie 1977; Gawin and Kleber 1985a; Siegel 1985a). Euphoria in early stimulant use is thus primarily due to increasingly positive external feedback to the user, instead of direct pharmacologic effects; it is often misperceived by the user as originating in the environment rather than in the drug (Gawin and Ellinwood 1988). Combined with absent or scarcely apparent negative contingencies, such early stimulant experiences are seductive (Ellinwood and Petrie 1977; Kleber and Gawin 1984a).

Perhaps the most fundamental and important treatment questions for stimulant abuse are: what distinguishes those who can easily cease stimulant use from those who cannot, and how can the capacity to cease use be restored? With the exception of one study of recreational cocaine users by Siegal (1985a), no detailed data on controlled stimulant users exist. Telephone hot-line surveys provide little information on controlled use because these lack clinical detail. Further, caller characteristics (Gold et al. 1985) are similar to treatment samples, rather than to community survey populations. Detailed abuse reports are, however, available from patients in treatment, and retrospective data from abusers who develop dyscontrol and appear for treatment, combined with judicious application of animal data, provide a preliminary answer to the questions posed.

The "High-Intensity Transition."   Animals given free access to stimulants engage in continuous self-administration. Death from cardiorespiratory collapse or infection follows, usually within 14 days (reviewed in Johanson 1984). Stimulants are chosen over food, sex, opiates, alcohol, sedatives, hallucinogens, and phencyclidine. In limited stimulant-administration paradigms, animals can be kept alive, but they generally adjust self-administration to maintain maximum effects within the limits of the paradigm (Gay 1982). Humans appear to be similar. Abusers who are severely impaired report virtual exclusion of all nonstimulant-related thoughts during stimulant binges. Sex, nourishment, sleep, safety, survival, money, morality, loved ones, and responsibility all become immaterial when juxtaposed with the desire to reexperience stimulant euphoria (Ellinwood and Petrie 1977; Gawin and Kleber 1986a; Lasagna et al. 1955; Lewin 1924; Siegel 1982). Supplies of money or stimulants are drawn on until they are exhausted. Abuse is limited only by access, and human abusers appear to function like the nonhumans in preclinical studies. Only the extreme monetary cost of cocaine and legal limitations on distribution appear to limit this human street "paradigm."

Paradoxically, heavy human abusers report being similar to the millions of noncompulsive users during their early stimulant use (Gawin and Kleber 1985a). No animal studies reported a similar low-intensity use. We believe a phenomenon, the "high-intensity transition" to compulsive use, underlies this paradox. Abusers describe that compulsive use begins when administration route changes, or availability and dosage increases markedly (e.g., increased resources, improved supply sources, engaging in cocaine commerce). Our experience suggests that stimulant use is controlled until episodes of extremely intense euphoria have occurred. Such episodes produce what become "persecutory" memories of intense euphoria. These memories are later contrasted to any immediate dysphoria to become the fount of stimulant craving. Early in stimulant use, high-intensity episodes are precluded by price, availability, and concerns over safety that limit the amounts used or that preclude experimenting with rapid administration routes. Intravenous or smoking stimulant administration uniformly produces very intense euphoria. Consistent with this explanation, noncompulsive use has not been described for these administration routes (Kleber and Gawin 1984a; Siegel 1982, 1985a). Intranasal or oral administration produces "intense" euphoria if initial doses are large enough, but they are less likely to produce the transition because of slower absorption.

Chronic animal studies on stimulants employ substantial boluses and usually intravenous administration. In effect, they begin after the high-intensity transition, explaining the lack of animal data on the transition itself or on low-intensity use. Systematic clinical studies to examine the high-intensity transition, or any other explanation of the apparent dichotomy of stimulant use and abuse, have not been done. Both animal and clinical studies are clearly needed.

Popular misconception has held that intranasal cocaine use does not lead to abuse and that severe abuse requires daily administration. Both of these conceptions appear to be wrong. Treatment data from multiple sources show more than 50 percent of abusers seeking treatment are exclusively intranasal users, with no differences in impairment between administration routes (reviewed in Kleber and Gawin 1984a). Preliminary reports indicate that as many as 90 percent of abusers appearing for treatment use cocaine in extended binges, which disrupt sleep (Gawin and Kleber 1985a), duplicating a pattern previously observed in amphetamine abusers (Connell 1970; Kramer et al. 1967). Several days of abstinence often separate binges, and abusers reported limited daily use patterns precede binge abuse (Connell 1970; Gawin and Kleber 1985a). In contrast to nonstimulant substance abuse, daily stimulant use is not a maximal abuse pattern if normal sleep patterns are maintained, and severe abuse can exist without incessant daily administration. Some abusers with unlimited access do develop an unceasing binge lasting weeks or months with severely disrupted functioning (Siegel 1982), but such cases are rare.

No personality variables predisposing individuals to stimulant abuse have been demonstrated, but major psychiatric mood and attention disorders, where stimulants are used as self-medication, appear to be overrepresented in treatment samples (reviewed below). Genetic predispositions to stimulant abuse may exist; alcohol abuse in family members has been extensively commented on by clinicians but not systematically studied. Studies of genetic factors similar to those reported in alcohol abuse have not been done in stimulant-abusing populations. Taken together, the animal and clinical data presently available clearly support only three clinically applicable predictors of abuse susceptibility or severity: use patterns, availability, and impairment of self-control. More circumscribed categorizations of stimulant abuse are being proposed and evaluated, but are as yet arbitrary and inconclusive. These are discussed elsewhere (Gawin and Kleber 1986a; Gold et al. 1985; Kleber and Gawin 1984a; Siegel 1982, 1985a).

Abstinence Phases

The existence and characteristics of stimulant withdrawal are subjects of current controversy. This reflects dissimilarity between cocaine and opiates or alcohol. Classic pharmacologic drug abuse constructs—such as withdrawal, dependence, and tolerance—do not provide models that can be easily applied to cocaine or other stimulants. Dependence and withdrawal reflected by gross physiologic indices verge on being imperceptible in stimulant abusers. This accounts for the common perception that cocaine and amphetamine are only "psychologically" addictive. DSM-III (American Psychiatric Association 1980) reflected the belief that cocaine abuse does not lead to dependence or withdrawal; consequently, there was no diagnostic category for cocaine dependence. DSM-III-R (American Psychiatric Association 1987) does contain this category for cocaine.

Chronic stimulant abuse regularly produces cyclical reoccurrences of use, as well as time-dependent evolution of abstinence symptoms. We have recently described a triphasic cocaine abstinence pattern, which dispels the recent perceptions that cocaine use produces no withdrawal. Stimulant abstinence is schematized in Figure 1 and described below (see Gawin and Kleber 1986a).

In the discussion that follows, we will first describe all the stages of abstinence, accompanied by pertinent data from the animal literature, to describe an emerging conception of neurophysiologically based stimulant dependence. We then review treatment for chronic dependence, which treaters should adapt according to the needs, progress, and phase of abstinence of the individual stimulant abuser. Finally, special treatment implications of possible coexistence of DSM-III Axis 1 psychiatric disorders will be discussed.

Crash: Acute Dysphoria (Phase One)

As noted under acute sequelae, when euphoria decreases during a binge of stimulant use, anxiety, fatigue, irritability, and depression increase. This usually leads to stimulant readministration and prolongs binges. However, supplies are eventually exhausted, or a state of extreme acute tolerance occurs, in which further high-dose administration produces little euphoria and instead augments anxiety or paranoia, and self-administration ends. The crash is initially a descent into depressed mood with continued stimulation and anxiety. Then a desire for rest and escape from the hyperstimulated dysphoria often cause use of anxiolytics, sedatives, opiates, or al-

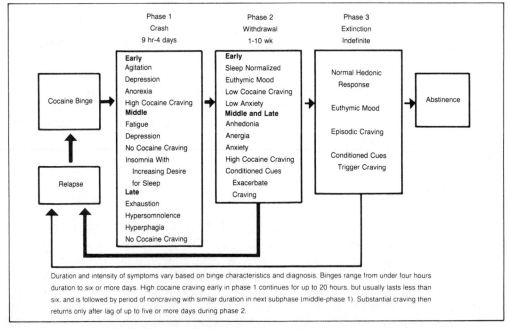

Figure 1. Stimulant Abstinence Phases. Reprinted with permission from Gawin and Kleber 1986a.

cohol to induce sleep. Whether or not sleep is pharmacologically induced, a later period of hypersomnolence and hyperphagia (during brief awakenings or after the hypersomnolence) eventually occurs. The duration of these periods is related to the duration and intensity of the preceding binge (Gawin and Kleber 1986a).

Following week-long stimulant binges, hypersomnolence may last several days (Kramer et al. 1967; Siegel 1982). Awakening from the hypersomnolence is usually associated with markedly improved mood, although some residual dysphoria may occur, particularly in high-intensity abusers. The exhaustion, depression, and hypersomnolence of the crash probably result from acute neurotransmitter depletion secondary to the preceding stimulant binge. Such depletion has been demonstrated directly in animal experiments (Ho et al. 1977) and in experiments using indirect peripheral indices in humans (reviewed in Gawin and Ellinwood 1988). Clinical recovery from the crash probably depends on sleep, diet, and time for new dopamine and norepinephrine synthesis. One report of precursor loading with tyrosine indicates that tyrosine decreases crash symptoms (Gold et al. 1983), but this report has not been replicated or extended to clinical treatment.

Clinical management of the crash was discussed earlier. The crash has sometimes been equated with a withdrawal state (Gold et al. 1983; Siegel 1982; Smith 1969). Acute tolerance to stimulant effects, occurring within a binge, has been clearly described clinically and in laboratory experiments (reviewed in Gawin and Ellinwood 1988). Furthermore, changes in peripheral catecholamine indices and sleep electroencephalogram (EEG) immediately after stimulant administration have been used as support for the existence of a dependent state, at least for amphetamines (Watson et al. 1972). However, unlike opiates and alcohol, stimulant abuse usually does not occur daily; chronic tolerance has not been experimentally proven, and clinical consensus is that it is much less substantial; craving is usually absent immediately after the crash and is episodic only later on (Connell 1970; Gawin and Kleber 1986a; Kramer et al. 1967; Siegel 1982). In opiate or alcohol withdrawal, craving for the abused substance to alleviate withdrawal symptoms is rapid, marked, and continuous. Relapse follows such craving directly. With the exception of the beginning of the stimulant crash, however, craving occurs only for sleep or rest, and further stimulant use is often strongly rejected in the hope that sleep rest may be attained (Gawin and Kleber 1986a).

Further, the crash appears in first-time users if the dose and duration of stimulant administration are large. It thus appears that the crash may be similar to immediate high-dose alcohol aftereffects (hangover) rather than to alcohol or opiate withdrawal. The crash thus appears to be a self-limiting acute state that does not itself require active treatment. It apparently does not contribute to chronic relapse and abuse, but only to prolonging stimulant binges (Gawin and Kleber 1986a).

Withdrawal: Poststimulant Mood Dysfunction (Phase 2)

Assessing the stimulant withdrawal is a crucial focus of current treatment research. The nervous system's usual response to persistent, drug-induced neurochemical perturbation is compensatory adaptation in the perturbed systems. Dysregulation occurs when the drug is not present. Despite the recent perception that stimulants may only be "psychologically" addictive, it is illogical to assume neuroadaptation does not occur in stimulant abuse. This does not mean a classic drug abstinence syndrome uniformly occurs; instead, chronic high-dose stimulant use could generate sustained neurophysiologic changes in brain systems that regulate psychological processes only. Changes in these neurophysiologic systems produce a true physiologic addiction and withdrawal, but one whose clinical expression is psychological.

Both extensive experimental data in animals and clinical evidence, summarized in Table 3, support this view. Briefly, animal experiments using electrical stimulation at brain reward sites show a decrease in sensitivity after chronic stimulant use (Colpaert et al. 1979; Kokkinidis and Zacharko 1980; Leith and Barrett 1976; Simpson et al. 1977) that is reversible with antidepressant administration (Kokkinidis et al. 1980; Simpson et al. 1977). Human stimulant abusers display a symptom constellation, described below, that is consistent with a decreased capacity to perceive reward or pleasure. Further, chronic stimulants produce long-term animal neurotransmitter and neuroreceptor changes (Banerjee et al. 1979; Borison et al. 1979; Chanda et al. 1979; Ricuarte et al. 1980; Taylor et al. 1979), animal behavioral changes (Utena 1966; Yagi 1963), and human neuroendocrine and sleep EEG changes (Gawin and Kleber 1985b; Watson et al. 1972). Combined, these data support the presence of a neuroadaptive process. The data are complex and are critically reviewed in more detail elsewhere (Gawin and Ellinwood 1988).

Protracted dysphoria, occurring long after the crash, has been clinically identified in stimulant abusers (Connell 1970; Gawin and Kleber 1986a). Protracted dysphoric symptoms are frequent antecedents of stimulant craving, often leading to unceasing cycles of recurrent binges. These chronic symptoms are not quickly self-remitting and therefore have great importance to treatment. They thus have greater clinical similarity to "withdrawal" in other substances of abuse than other abstinence symptoms, such as the crash.

In most heavy stimulant abusers, a regular symptom progression follows the resolution of intoxication and crash symptoms. On awakening from hypersomnolence, a euthymic interval with normal mood and little stimulant craving occurs. In abusers attempting to cease use, this interval is usually associated with vivid memories of the misery of the crash and acute awareness of the psychosocial costs of continued stimulant abuse. This lasts from several hours to several days (Gawin and Kleber 1986a). It is slowly supplanted by increasing inactivation, amotivation, and restricted pleasurable responses to the environment. These symptoms have been variously labeled anergia, depression (Connell 1970; Kramer et al. 1967), anhedonia (Gawin

Table 3.   Evidence for Protracted Stimulant Adaptation and Anhedonia

Animal	Human
1. ICSS brain reward indices decreased after chronic stimulants; catecholamine-receptor supersensitivity after chronic stimulants	1. Clinical observations of anhedonia
2. ICSS normalization after chronic antidepressant treatment; catecholamine-receptor subsensitivity with chronic antidepressants	2. Decreased craving and abstinence after chronic antidepressants
3. Experimentally induced behavioral depression lasting two to eight weeks	3. Similar time course for clinical observations
4. Neuroreceptor and neurotransmitter alterations	4. Neuroendocrine and sleep electroencephalogram alterations
5. Tolerance and cross-tolerance between abused stimulants	5. Tolerance to euphoria

and Kleber 1984, 1986a), or psychasthenia (Ellinwood and Petrie 1977) by different clinical observers.

The dysphoric symptoms wax and wane; they are often not constant or severe enough to meet psychiatric diagnostic criteria for major affective disorders. The abusers' limited hedonic reactions to existence, contrasted with memories of stimulant-induced euphoria, nonetheless makes resumption of use compellingly seductive. Furthermore, the symptom intensity is responsive to environmental cues—the same stimuli that trigger memories of stimulant euphoria and craving for stimulants also intensify awareness of an abuser's baseline dysphoria. During the experience of craving there is a remarkable lack of memory of the crash or the adverse psychosocial consequences of abuse. Such negative memories often reemerge only when the episode of craving, and possibly relapse, has passed.

Stimulant abusers often describe amelioration of anhedonic symptoms within days to weeks if they can sustain abstinence (Connell 1970; Ellinwood and Petrie 1977; Gawin and Kleber 1986a; Smith 1969). Animal studies administering sufficiently chronic and high-dose stimulants report behavioral depression on withdrawal for a similar time period (Utena 1966; Yagi 1963). Both the severity and duration of these symptoms depend partially on the intensity of the preceding chronic abuse. Predisposing mood disorders may also amplify these symptoms. Conversely, in intermittent controlled stimulant users without psychiatric disorders, an anhedonic-psychasthenic phase may not occur at all. We speculate that the high-intensity transition and coinciding neuroadaptation may be required before psychasthenia and anhedonia emerge.

Extinction: Postwithdrawal Conditioned Dysfunction (Phase 3)

Following successful initiation of abstinence and the resolution of early anhedonia and craving, intermittent stimulant craving continues to be reported (Ellinwood and Petrie 1977; Gawin and Kleber 1986a; Maier 1926). Such craving is not accompanied by the baseline dysphoria of the second phase, and there is no known neurophysiologic mechanism for these episodes. Cravings appear in the context of such divergent factors as particular mood states (positive as well as negative); specific persons, locations, events, or times of year; intoxications with other substances; interpersonal strife; or abuse objects (e.g., money, white powder, pipes, mirrors, syringes, single-edged razor blades). These factors vary; none are uniformly associated with craving. They appear to be conditioned cues, varying according to the abuse habits of the individual abuser. Stimulants are the most potent reinforcing agents known (Johanson 1984), and as such can be expected to produce classical and operant conditioning. Animal experiments have clearly established that strong conditioning to stimulants occurs. The craving is intense and can reemerge months or even years after last stimulant use (Gawin and Kleber 1986a). Conditioned craving is also reported during abstinence from other substances, although our impression is that conditioned cravings are more unpredictable and intense in former stimulant abusers than in abusers of other drugs.

No systematic studies of the reemergence of craving have been carried out, but clinical impressions indicate that the craving is episodic, lasting only hours with, in long abstinent abusers, very long periods free of craving. The magnitude and episodic nature of the craving, the variety of the cues, and their temporal contiguity to stimulant abuse episodes support the view that this craving is conditioned.

By far the most common clinical example of a conditioned cue is alcohol. Alcohol disinhibition can overcome early hesitancies toward trying stimulants based on their extreme expense or illegality. Mild alcohol intoxication often precedes initial stimulant use or early repetitions of use. If this association occurs regularly, alcohol intoxication then becomes a conditioned cue for stimulant craving. Such abusers report little craving except immediately after alcohol intake. Relapse in such patients often follows prolonged abstinence, but occurs with regularity when social contacts are reestablished, following weeks of relative social isolation imposed to initiate abstinence, and occurs only after one or two drinks. In such cases, individuals with years of non-problematic recreational alcohol use and a total weekly alcohol intake of less than half a dozen drinks may require total alcohol abstinence to become stimulant-free.

The conditioning hypothesis is testable and has important research and treatment implications. Psychodynamic, behavioral, interpersonal, and psychosocial explanations for craving and relapse have all also been offered (Anker and Crowley 1982; Rounsaville et al. 1985; Wurmser 1974). Contributions from each of these areas may exist, but have less immediate treatment relevance and often have limited scientific testability.

Chronic Stimulant-Induced Psychiatric Disorders

Do permanent neurotoxic changes occur as a consequence of stimulant abuse? Since most clinical reports indicate that anhedonic symptoms decrease weeks to months after stimulant use ceases, these changes appear reversible. However, permanent dopaminergic neuronal degeneration has been documented in animal studies (Seiden 1984) and is complemented by disturbing clinical observations. Reports from Scandinavia, Japan, and rare cases in the United States (Schuster et al. 1985; Utena 1966), describe chronic high-dose stimulant users, primarily intravenous amphetamine users, who have persistent anhedonia, anergia, and craving that do not remit even after abstinence as long as 10 years. Systematic long-term follow-up studies in abstinent former abusers are thus clearly needed.

Chronic stimulant-induced paranoid psychoses have also been intermittently reported; in the context of how widespread stimulant use has been over the last two decades, however, they occur infrequently. It is not clear whether reported cases had preexistent psychiatric disorder. Persistent schizophreniform psychoses, induced by chronic rather than acute stimulant administration, have been expected on theoretical grounds (Post et al. 1976). Data from one retrospective analysis (McLellan et al. 1979) indicate that long-term psychoses caused by chronic stimulant use may occur, but selection flaws in that study, lack of attempts at replication, and the absence of other supportive data preclude any general conclusions at this time.

Treatment of Chronic Stimulant Abuse

Current stimulant abuse treatment as practiced in the United States is usually alcohol or opiate abuse treatment, applied without adaptation for specific problems associated with stimulant abuse (Kleber and Gawin 1984). Specialized treatments are, however, being explored. Interventions employed have included adaptations of most major types of psychotherapy as well as pharmacotherapeutic trials (Anker and Crowley 1982; Connell 1970; Gawin and Kleber 1984, 1986a; Gold et al. 1985; Khantzian and Khantzian 1984; Kleber and Gawin 1984a; Maier 1926; Rounsaville et al. 1985; Siegel 1982; Wurmser 1974).

Treatment should be subdivided into two parts—cycle disruption and relapse prevention—which correspond to the second and third phases of chronic poststimulant sequelae.

Cycle Disruption

The paramount immediate treatment goal is breaking cycles of recurrent stimulant binges or of daily use. Immediate relapse is a strong possibility as long as anergic and anhedonic symptoms are present. Multiple outpatient approaches have been employed to initiate abstinence. Because stimulant dependence has until recently been considered psychological, established treatments have consisted of psychological strategies aimed at modifying addictive behaviors. Almost all psychotherapeutic treatment of cocaine abusers can be organized around three dimensions: behavioral, supportive, and psychodynamic (Kleber and Gawin 1984).

Behavioral therapy.   Behavioral methods help the abuser to recognize and experience the deleterious effects of cocaine and accept the need to stop use. For the vast majority of people who need treatment, cocaine use has become a central part of their lives. Some seek treatment with a strong internal conviction that they have lost control of their drug use, and pay too heavy a price for it, both financially and personally. Most have more ambivalent feelings. While they recognize that stimulant use harms them, they still hope they can control their drug use and do not want to give up drug-induced euphoria. Often powerful external pressure from family members, employers, or the law pushes them to enter into treatment. If these abusers are to remain in treatment, psychotherapy must have an impact on this ambivalence early in the treatment process.

The most systematized behavioral method, contingency contracting, emphasizes this area by focusing and magnifying the particular harmful effects of drug use. This technique has a long history of use in amphetamine abuse (Boudin 1972) and has been applied to cocaine (Anker and Crowley 1982). According to Anker and Crowley (1982), contingency contracting has two basic elements; agreement to participate in a urine monitoring program and attachment of an aversive contingency to either a positive sample or a failure to appear to deliver a urine sample. The aversive contingencies are derived from the patient's own statements of the adverse consequences expected to result from continued cocaine use. This adverse effect is then scheduled to occur at their very next use of cocaine. The patient may be requested to write a letter of irrevocable personal consequences, such as a letter admitting to cocaine abuse addressed to his or her employer or professional licensing board. This letter is then held by the therapist and mailed to the addressee in the event of positive or missed urinalysis. Such contracts, coupled with supportive psychotherapy, appear to be effective as long as patients are willing to take part in the treatment and the contract remains in effect.

Anker and Crowley (1982) reported 48 percent of an outpatient sample were willing to engage in this treatment, with more than 80 percent cocaine abstinent during the duration of the contract, which averaged three months. However, more than one-half of these patients relapsed following completion of the contract. Patients refusing to enter into contracts (52 percent) were treated with supportive psychotherapy only; more than 90 percent of noncontract patients dropped out and/or resumed cocaine abuse within two to four weeks. Anker and Crowley presented no comparisons of severity of cocaine use, and thus ignored the possibility that cocaine abusers with severe craving and problems of control recognize their inability to comply with such treatment and consequently avoid it. In addition to problems of long-term efficacy and possible inapplicability to more severe cocaine abuse, there are obvious ethical problems existing in those cases in which the procedure could have been based on positive reinforcement or on less aversive techniques.

The major lesson from this treatment approach is straightforward: contingency contracting focuses on and magnifies the actual harm to the self that can result from cocaine abuse. The clear emphasis this method gives to the deleterious effects of cocaine abuse can also be repeatedly reinforced in psychotherapy using individual, group, and family techniques in a less potentially harmful manner than the contingency contracts. Less severe contingencies can be used as well in a graduated fashion. The technique also requires that the patient has something to lose; when patients come to treatment only after they have lost everything, therapists may be hard-pressed to find appropriate contingencies.

Further, positive contingencies can be employed—for example, starting with a sum of money taken from a patient and returning part of that sum each week in exchange for clean urines. Most treatment programs suggest that control over funds should be abrogated to a responsible significant other to initiate abstinence. Gradual return of monetary control occurs, but it is often unrecognized that this is a positive contingency. In most treatment programs, positive and negative contingencies are numerous, but they are not clearly identified or prospectively planned. Contingency contracting demonstrates the therapeutic benefit of such identification and planning. It is our opinion that patients maximally benefit from an overt, individualized, planned combination of both positive and negative contingencies and reinforcements that are under continuous scrutiny throughout treatment. The relative efficacy of emphasizing negative contingencies without formal contracts, with formal contracts, with graduated contingencies, and with positive contingencies has not yet been subject to direct, systematic treatment studies.

Supportive therapy.   This approach initially separates the user from the use-fostering environment by way of external controls, and then gradually facilitates internalization of controls through psychotherapy. Siegel (1982) described using frequent supportive psychotherapy sessions, self-control strategies, "exercise therapy," and liberal use of hospitalization during initial detoxification. One-half of his sample of 32 heavy cocaine smokers dropped out of treatment, but 80 percent of those remaining were cocaine-free at nine-month follow-up.

Anker and Crowley (1982) described key points in their supportive therapy as encouraging increased contact with nonusing friends, eliminating paraphernalia and drug caches, terminating relationships with dealers or drug-using friends, changing telephone numbers or even residences if there is a need to stop drug-related telephone calls and visits, counseling and education of spouse and family, and examining related problem areas in the patient's life. Such commonsense interventions, often overlooked, can be crucial and simple contributions to abstinence.

Because it is not uncommon for heavy users to become dealers to support their habits (and for dealers to become heavy users as a consequence of easy access to large, inexpensive quantities of stimulants), it is important to emphasize that all commerce in stimulants, as well as use of stimulants, must cease. Further, there are some professions, such as entertainment or commodities trading, that require a manic level of intensity and activity, where success may have been contingent on pharmacologic stimulation. It is very unlikely that stimulant abusers can abstain from stimulant use while continuing to sell the drug or using the drug to sell themselves. Sooner or later, most likely sooner, heavy use will begin again. This issue needs to be raised early in therapy and should be kept in the forefront because the large sums of money obtained relatively easily are often as hard or harder to give up than the drug itself. Drastic changes in life-style and socioeconomic status are often required.

Supportive self-help groups such as Alcoholics Anonymous (AA), Narcotics

Anonymous (NA), and Cocaine Anonymous (CA) are widely used in the United States. They provide structure and limits as well as group support, a helping network, and an important spiritual dimension (Ehrlich and McGeehan 1985). They employ behavioral as well as supportive techniques. Although users and clinicians have described them as effective, and clinical consensus strongly supports the usefulness of self-help groups, they have not yet been the subject of outcome studies for stimulant abuse.

In general, such programs insist on the cessation of all mood-altering drugs on the reasonable grounds that the patient has already demonstrated addictive tendencies and thus is likely to become addicted to another drug or relapse if he or she continues any drug use. Often, however, patients have to learn this lesson firsthand by relapsing before they are willing to give up their use of other drugs.

Regular urinalysis is also a supportive mechanism. It is a deterrent to use as well as a means of detection of early relapses. Since cocaine can be detected consistently in the urine by way of its principal metabolite, benzoylecgonine, for only one to two days, random testing at least one to three times weekly is important. Regular urines are sufficient to detect amphetamine, but since most users will abuse either agent, random urinalysis for amphetamine abusers is also necessary to detect cocaine abuse. Early in treatment, the knowledge that urinalysis will occur precludes an internal struggle over whether the abuser can hide use and forms an external support to promote abstinence.

Psychodynamic therapy.   Psychodynamic treatment approaches aim at making the stimulant abuser aware of the needs that stimulants have satisfied in the abuser's life and to help the abuser meet these needs without drugs (Wurmser 1974). Stimulant use meets a variety of needs. Narcissistic needs are often met by the glamour associated with cocaine use. The need for a sense of identity is often met by becoming part of a stimulant-using subculture. Anaclitic needs can be met by way of stimulant-heightened intimate interactions. Stimulants may be used to compensate for interpersonal or professional failures, as well as for inadequate rewards perceived from achieved success. Pursuit, acquisition, and sale of stimulants may help to deal with inadequate time-structuring and leisure skills. Stimulants may also be used to cope with an existential sense of inner emptiness and for self-medication of many other psychological symptoms. Perhaps most importantly, understanding these needs may provide an increased sense of control for the abuser, which often limits the need to turn to stimulant use for an illusory sense of power and control (Rounsaville et al. 1985).

A combination of all three orientations—behavioral, supportive, and psychodynamic—is probably the most common form of both early and long-term treatment in both inpatient and outpatient settings. The optimal combination of these orientations is best determined by a careful evaluation of the abuser, and by the development of an individualized treatment plan, rather than by simple program structure. For example, severe cocaine abusers attempting abstinence may not respond to psychodynamic interventions until abstinence is long substantiated, whereas moderate abusers seem readier to utilize them earlier. Also, the mild abuser may need little more than clarification of the consequences of abuse, perhaps using mild contingency methods, in order to stop cocaine use. Therefore, choice of primary therapeutic orientation might shift from behavioral to psychodynamic to supportive as abuse severity increases, and in the opposite direction as length of abstinence increases (Kleber and Gawin 1984). These notions have not yet received any empirical testing.

Escalating interventions.   If abstinence does not closely follow initiation of outpatient treatment, then escalating interventions become necessary. Two types of additional interventions are clinically employed to facilitate abstinence: hospitalization and experimental pharmacotherapies.

Hospitalization ensures removal from the stimulant-available environment. Some consider it appropriate as an initial treatment (reviewed in Kleber and Gawin 1984a). When used routinely, regardless of abuse severity, this may be excessive. Many treaters strongly favor hospitalization for initial detoxification. However, in recent studies using pharmacologic agents (Gawin and Kleber 1984a) as well as in non-pharmacologic studies by Anker and Crowley (1982), need for hospitalization was infrequent. The differing impressions may be the result of treatment variables. For example, Siegel treated heavy cocaine smokers with minimal pharmacotherapy; pharmacotherapy in other studies may have controlled symptoms that would otherwise have required hospitalization.

Individual cases of severe abuse where hospitalization is the only way to separate the user from stimulants and to ensure safety do exist. The only clearly accepted factors indicating need for inpatient cocaine abuse treatment are severe neurovegetative depression or psychotic symptoms lasting beyond one to three days of the postcocaine crash as well as repeated outpatient failures. Other factors remain controversial. The decision to hospitalize should be based on estimations of the user's support network, stimulant availability, severity of abstinence symptoms, ego strength, motivation, concurrent medical problems, and prior responses to treatment. Length of hospitalization varies but should provide for ensured abstinence through the resolution of phase 2 symptoms.

The only outcome data on inpatient-alone treatment suggest it is less successful than outpatient-alone treatment (Rawson et al. 1986). This could be due to the absence of relapse prevention treatment techniques (detailed below) when hospitalization is not followed by outpatient therapy. Our clinical impressions, gained from work with both severe amphetamine and cocaine abusers, lead us to favor outpatient treatment whenever possible. Since the stimulant abuser must resume everyday life at some point, hospitalization merely defers this point. Studies of animal behavior (Goldberg et al. 1979) as well as clinical work with humans (Maddux and Desmond 1982; Wikler 1973) concur with our opinion, highlighting the importance of environment in conditioning and drug-taking behavior. We have observed that a period of abstinence, akin to a period of "extinction" within the context of everyday life and stressors, is necessary before long-term reduction in craving can occur. This cannot occur purely in the hospital environment, which is devoid of cues and which may simply delay this important task.

The second type of intervention for patients who continue to abuse stimulants, pharmacotherapy, is currently experimental. Open clinical trials of the tricyclic antidepressant, desipramine, produced abstinence in 90 percent of a group given desipramine, compared to less than 50 percent in comparison groups given other agents (lithium and methylphenidate) or continued in psychotherapy without medication (Gawin and Kleber 1984, 1985a). The trials were conducted primarily in nondepressed, psychotherapy-resistant outpatient stimulant abusers to ensure that assessment occurred in severe abusers and that efficacy was not limited to abusers with major affective disorders. These studies were based on two observations. First, changes in animal intracranial self-stimulation indices and neuroreceptor sensitivity after chronic treatment with tricyclic antidepressants are opposite to those demonstrated from chronic stimulants (Gawin and Kleber 1984). Second, antidepressants facilitated abstinence in psychasthenic-anhedonic amphetamine abusers, according to anecdotal reports (Ellinwood and Petrie 1977). A simultaneous open trial with imipramine also demonstrated facilitated abstinence (Rosecan 1983). Short-term tricyclic courses (Tennant et al. 1984), which are not associated with the neurophysiologic changes of longer courses (Charney et al, 1981), do not facilitate abstinence. While encouraging, these findings must be considered tentative. Two larger scale, double-blind, placebo-controlled studies now underway have demonstrated the same trends (Gawin et al. 1985a; Giannini et al. 1986), and further trials are beginning at additional centers, but these studies have assessed too few subjects to be definitive.

If antidepressants are to be used in patients undergoing stimulant withdrawal, the patients should be advised that this is not a use approved by the Food and Drug Administration and their informed consent to this use should be recorded in the progress notes.

Other pharmacologic treatment strategies are at stages of pilot investigation (Gawin and Kleber 1984, 1986b; Jonsson et al. 1969; Rosecan and Klein 1986; Rowbotham et al. 1984). Possible stimulant blockade has been tried using lithium, alpha-methyl-paratyrosine, trazadone, imipramine, or neuroleptics. These have either not demonstrated greater than partial blockade or present side effects that preclude compliance. Pilot attempts to increase dopaminergic neurotransmission using L-dopa, tyrosine, amantadine, trihexylphenidyl, bromocriptene, and methylphenidate have reported short-term decreases in craving, but longer-term assessments are needed to assure these effects are not transient (Dackis and Gold 1985; Gawin et al. 1985b; Gold et al. 1983; Khantzian 1983; Tennant and Tarver 1986). Monoamine oxidase (MAO) inhibitors have also been reported to be useful in preventing relapse (Resnick and Resnick 1985). The dangers of using MAO inhibitors while concurrent stimulant use might occur, however, are unclear. Potentially lethal interaction could occur. Almost half of the initial reports of death due to amphetamine involved MAO inhibitor interactions (Kalant and Kalant 1979); it is not clear if interactions with cocaine are less dangerous. Potential dangers have consequently limited trials with these agents. No systematic pharmacotherapy outcome trials were reported during the previous amphetamine epidemic.

It should be noted that experimental pharmacotherapies are included here under treatments for cycle disruption. No long-term pharmacotherapy conferring enduring immunity to stimulant abuse is being tested in humans. While some blocking agents have been tried clinically without evident blockade and preclinical trials of new blocking agents are underway, there does not yet appear to be a naltrexone-like agent to block relapse in stimulant abusers.

Relapse Prevention

Relapse prevention techniques are introduced gradually at treatment onset. They become central after abstinence has been initiated. While the techniques described for abstinence initiation also promote long-term abstinence, other relapse prevention measures include specific, additional techniques, described in detail by Marlatt and Gordon (1980) and Washton et al. (1985), to facilitate enduring abstinence.

All outpatient treatments provide prolonged support to help abusers withstand craving without relapse. Most often, long-term group psychotherapy is used, modeled on self-help support groups like those of AA. Groups are often combined with individualized peer support, family or couples therapy, behavioral contracts with aversive contingencies (Anker and Crowley 1982), or individual psychotherapies that actively focus on relapse issues like slips, cognitive factors, and the development of tools to manage future episodes of craving without relapse (Khantzian and Khantzian 1984; Rounsaville et al. 1985; Washton et al. 1985).

The techniques used are largely the same as those used postwithdrawal in other substance abuse treatments (Marlatt and Gordon 1980). As noted, extinction of conditioned cues may be the most important relapse prevention measure for stimulant abusers. Stimulant abusers face a situation similar to the cigarette smoker or alcoholic, where the drug must become "psychologically unavailable" because it cannot, with certainty, be made physically unavailable (Kleber and Gawin 1984a). Abusers must eventually sustain abstinence within the setting where abuse developed. Under a conditioning model, abstinence in the context of everyday cues and stressors—an opportunity for extinction to occur with controlled cravings, without relapse—is a prerequisite to consistent long-term amelioration of stimulant craving (Kleber and Gawin 1984a).

No systematic studies have compared relapse prevention approaches. All approaches claim success. It is our opinion that all are partially successful, producing sustained reductions in stimulant craving, despite divergent techniques, through the common mechanism of supporting abstinence while extinction of conditioned craving is allowed to proceed.

Four treatment stages for extinction of craving occur in these treatments. First, during abstinence initiation, enforced abstinence from drug use is linked to strict avoidance of conditioned cues. Second, stimuli and cues are reintroduced psychologically in the context of developing strategies for managing stimulant temptation. Third, reentry into the cue-rich environment gradually occurs under controlled conditions. Fourth, successful abstinence is supplemented with maintenance therapies (continuous self-help and aftercare groups, resumptions of treatment) to counteract the long-term, episodic reemergence of stimulant craving.

Current research is beginning to assess specific psychotherapeutic techniques in relapse prevention. Systematic desensitization, used originally to extinguish conditioned anxiety, is beginning to be researched in conditioned stimulant craving. This technique initially uses imaging and relaxation techniques to induce manageable craving and then proceeds to a graded series of actual craving-inducing situations. Research tools, such as manual-guided therapies, are now being used for the first time to determine what techniques are most useful, and in what subpopulations, among stimulant abusers.

Stages in Recovery and Treatment

The stage of recovery on seeking treatment varies in stimulant abusers seeking treatment. Some abusers break cycles of abuse themselves, appearing after numerous prolonged periods of abstinence could not be sustained. Such abusers clearly require a treatment focus on relapse prevention. Because craving is intermittent after abstinence has been consolidated, there is often a tendency to leave treatment prematurely as episodes between cravings prolong. This must be countered in treatment. Some abusers appear after multiple unsuccessful attempts to sustain any abstinence and have never attained more than a few days free of stimulants. The abuser's recent history of abuse and the past treatment history are thus crucial to determining appropriate treatments, which can differ widely for different abusers.

Outcome Studies

Data from multiple programs using different psychotherapeutic approaches indicate outpatient treatment regularly initiates abstinence. From 50 to 90 percent of abusers remaining in outpatient treatment programs cease stimulant use (Anker and

Crowley 1982; Kleber and Gawin 1984; Rawson et al. 1986; Siegel 1982; Washton et al. 1985). Samples and methods are not comparable between these treatment programs, however, and there is no evidence to suggest any one treatment approach is superior. Further, those abusers who remain in treatment probably comprise the less-impaired portion of the abuse spectrum, and drop-outs are ignored in most reports. Thus far, collective experience can be simply summarized: staying in treatment is the single most important determinant of successful outcome. Further, it is our impression that the recent generation of cocaine abusers is more treatment responsive than prior amphetamine abusers. This could reflect 1) cocaine's greater cost, causing comparatively less abuse at treatment seeking, or 2) the positive correlate of 1, that cocaine abusers in the studies cited come from socioeconomic strata providing increased psychosocial resources, and thus have improved outcome similar to high socioeconomic class opiate abusers. Most probably, these factors combine to produce the high success reported in cocaine abuse treatment. It is not clear whether the advent of "crack" abuse among the socioeconomically less fortunate will also bring the increased treatment resistiveness generally found in opiate abuse to outcome findings for "crack" abuse.

Diagnostic Considerations

A presentation of stimulant use does not always indicate a diagnosis of stimulant abuse. The wide spectrum of stimulant use is reflected in the impression that a wider severity spectrum exists in stimulant abusers seeking treatment than in other substance abusers (Kleber and Gawin 1984). Because of cocaine's now adverse reputation, its great expense, and the substantial amount of nonaddictive (or not-yet-addictive) use that exists, severe psychosocial disruption can lead to treatment seeking despite use in almost homeopathic amounts. When stimulant use is itself minor, it may serve as a symptom of other primary problems (e.g., family discord), and alternative or adjunctive treatment may be indicated.

Excluding coexistent psychiatric disorders is a clinical necessity in stimulant abuse treatment. Psychiatric patients with major affective disorders, atypical depressive disorders, adult attention deficit disorder (ADD), bipolar or cyclothymic disorder, or narcolepsy have all been reported to cease illicit stimulant use when appropriate medications are substituted (Gawin and Kleber 1984; Khantzian et al. 1984; Weiss et al. 1983). Schizophrenic patients have also been known to abuse stimulants. In four systematic studies using DSM-III criteria, chronic affective disorders were present in almost 50 percent of stimulant abusers seeking treatment (Gawin 1986a; Gawin and Kleber 1985a; Weiss et al. 1983). Because acute aftereffects of a stimulant binge can mimic delusional or depressive disorders, and acute intoxication can mimic mania, it is crucial to separate out effects of acute stimulant use in clinical presentations. In practice, this involves careful clinical interviewing—searching for family history of psychiatric disorder as well as searching personal histories for psychiatric symptoms during intervals free of substance abuse.

Since substance abuse and psychiatric disorder often both become evident in young adulthood, establishing a primary diagnosis in this way is often difficult. Tentative diagnoses, warranting appropriate pharmacotherapies, therefore usually must be made based on symptom presentation, provided that several nights of sleep normalization and ensured abstinence (hospitalization or urinalysis) have occurred, if depressive, manic, or psychotic symptoms have not remitted. If abstinence is maintained, whether the diagnosis is primary or secondary can then be determined based on the subsequent clinical course. In many cases, continued, sporadic, stimulant use makes it impossible to determine whether stimulant abuse or another Axis 1 disorder is primary or secondary.

Two groups of pilot efforts that reflect diagnosis in the context of cocaine abuse treatment have been reported. The studies were all nonblind, nonplacebo, preliminary examinations. Seven cocaine abusers with diagnoses of ADD have been reported on (Khantzian 1983; Khantzian et al. 1984; Weiss et al. 1983, 1985). Six responded to appropriate stimulant medications, methylphenidate, and pemoline. None of the successfully treated subjects abused the substitute stimulants, and all remained abstinent at least at six-month follow-up. In an open trial, however, methylphenidate was ineffective in five non-ADD subjects treated (Gawin and Kleber 1985b). Hence, current clinical data indicate that substitute stimulant medication is reasonable only where cocaine is used as self-medication for clearly substantiated ADD.

In a structured open trial of lithium in subjects who had not responded to psychotherapy-only treatment (Gawin and Kleber 1984), we found that lithium administration was associated with cessation of cocaine abuse and with diminished cocaine craving in nine cyclothymic patients. Five noncyclothymic cocaine abusers did not appear to benefit from lithium.

These preliminary data, as well as collective clinical experience, indicate that important subpopulations with Axis I diagnoses exist that are responsive to specific pharmacotherapies. However, larger samples and double-blind comparisons are needed to substantiate these preliminary findings before clinical conclusions can be drawn. Our current clinical approach is to adhere strictly to maximal diagnostic criteria for ADD-residual type, requiring both a childhood diagnosis of ADD and a treatment trial with stimulants during childhood, before employing stimulant treatment in the context of cocaine abuse. We also require that DSM-III-R criteria for cyclothymia be fully met before using lithium.

Research Considerations

The percentage of patients who ceased cocaine use in pharmacotherapy research programs (greater than 80 percent) is similar to the percentage who did well in the reports on patients who remained in treatment in specialized psychotherapy-alone programs for cocaine abusers. It is probably premature, however, to compare treatments across centers unless sample similarity has been clearly demonstrated. When compared to psychotherapy within the same treatment setting, however, pharmacologic approaches have resulted in substantial increases in patient retention, approaching twice that in nonpharmacologic treatment (Gawin and Kleber 1984; Tennant and Rawson 1984; Tennant and Tarver 1986). More such comparisons are needed. For example, compared to treatment of depression, both psychotherapy and pharmacotherapy data for stimulant abuse are at a primitive developmental stage. In this chapter, we have summarized current knowledge and treatment strategies. We would like to conclude with the hope that more scientific stimulant abuse treatment will evolve, by summarizing important methodological points for future stimulant abuse research. These points will all require clarification and consensus. Then, more definitive research might create a coherent, scientifically acceptable body of outcome data on treatment for cocaine abusers. The points include:

1. *Severity*. No treatment studies reported thus far have stratified samples according to any criteria of abuse severity, and no generally accepted indices of severity of abuse exist that would allow comparisons across samples to be made.

2. *Self-selection artifacts.* Most of the treatment studies described have a substantial proportion of early drop-outs or patients eliminated at screening who have not been contrasted to those remaining in treatment. Data characterizing the populations that find particular treatments aversive or inadequate are obviously needed.

3. *Recovery.* There is no consensus regarding how long abstinence must be maintained before recovery occurs or treatment can end. Outcome criteria are widely variable across the studies conducted thus far and, as of this writing, no studies have reported outcome in terms of changes in indices of psychosocial functioning.

4. *Heterogeneity.* Multiple sources of sample heterogeneity exist in cocaine treatment populations, including variations in sociodemographics, psychiatric symptomatology, psychosocial resources, patterns and duration of use, degree of impairment, treatment history, and other substances abused, among many others. Do such factors differ among treatment populations, and do they differentially affect outcome?

5. *Course and neuroadaptation.* There are few data available on the natural history of stimulant abuse, and few data available regarding which patients are likely to deteriorate and which may be expected to maintain stable states of dysfunction, and which will improve. This issue is related to the relative importance of preexisting psychopathology versus neuroadaptation. Although improved characterizations of abstinence symptoms have emerged, more systematic assessments of clinical course are needed, and the contribution of neuroadaptation to continuation of human abuse requires further clarification.

On balance, a number of treatment approaches are in current use and are demonstrating good results. Others are being investigated and promise even further improvements. It now appears no more likely that any single treatment will arise as a definitive treatment for all cocaine abusers than it has for opiate or alcohol abusers. Today, treatment for cocaine abusers should be based on a flexible integration of various approaches, based on the clinical assessment of the characteristics and needs of the individual patient.

Chapter 131

Cannabis Abuse and Dependence

Given the remarkable prevalence of marijuana use in our society, it is not surprising that psychiatrists and other health professionals are asked to evaluate and treat a large number of people with diverse psychiatric and behavioral problems who also use cannabis. In some cases, patients are referred because they have a problem clearly related to the drug, or other drugs of abuse that are used in association with cannabis. In other situations, the psychiatric or behavioral disorders for which the patients are referred are not clearly related to the cannabis use. It is the task of the clinician to provide a comprehensive evaluation of the patient to assess the patterns of abuse of cannabis and other drugs, to define psychopathology and behavioral patterns that exist, to characterize the relationship of the drug-taking patterns to the psychopathology, and to provide treatment or to effect a referral. As with other substance abuse disorders, the provision of appropriate treatments and referrals depends on an appreciation of the varying determinants of the drug-taking patterns as well as their consequences. With marijuana in particular, it continues to be difficult to assess the extent to which the psychopathology or behavioral problems noted in individual patients was a result of the marijuana use or dependence, or preceded it and was a determinant of the drug use.

Epidemiology

Marijuana is the most frequently abused illicit psychoactive drug in our society. The prevalence of marijuana use increased dramatically during the mid to late 1960s, peaked in the period 1979 to 1980, and has decreased significantly since then. In 1987 the annual prevalence of marijuana use in young adults one to 10 years beyond high school had dropped to 34.8 percent. According to the High School Senior Survey (Johnston et al. 1988), lifetime prevalence of marijuana use increased from 20 percent in the class of 1969 to 60.4 percent in the class of 1979 and fell to 54.9 and 50.2 percent in the classes of 1984 and 1987, respectively. Use in the last 30 days declined from a high of 36.5 percent in the class of 1979 to 21 percent in the class of 1987. Daily users, the group presumably most at risk, declined from a high of 10.7 percent in the class of 1978 to 3.3 percent in 1987. Whereas daily use in young adults also declined during the last few years, it is no lower among the older age groups than it is among high school seniors. The proportion of males who have ever used marijuana is only slightly higher than females, although daily use of marijuana is more than twice as frequent among males. Other indices of marijuana use (e.g., emergency room visits and admissions to treatment programs) have also declined.

The reasons for the general decline in marijuana use in recent years are unclear but may in part be attributed to changing perceptions toward the drug. According to the High School Senior Survey (Johnston et al. 1988), the proportions of students perceiving regular marijuana use as involving significant risk increased from 35 percent in 1978 to 73.5 percent in 1987. Those who disapproved of regular use increased from a low of about 65 percent in the class of 1977 to 89 percent in the class of 1987. In the class of 1985, 55 percent of the respondents believed that their friends would disapprove of even experimental use, and 81 percent would disapprove if they smoked marijuana regularly; this trend has continued to the present. It is possible that these trends are based in part on the adverse effects many people have noted in their peers, on the strongly antidrug parents' movement, and on national and local media campaigns.

These well-documented changes in attitudes and beliefs may also be based on broad cultural trends. The Protean style of the 1960s and 1970s with its loss or dishonoring of the traditional symbols of religion, government, family, and authority has given way to a more conventional style. A view of reality that depended on set and setting, that allowed marked shifts in personal involvement and beliefs, and that encouraged multiple images of how one is to live was congruent with the use of marijuana. The more conservative and more controlled style of the late 1970s and 1980s, in which people recognized that they must survive in a relatively unchanging world, may render the altered consciousness sought from marijuana less attractive.

In addition to the decreases in the number of marijuana users reported, there has been a considerable decrease in the use per individual over time that has not been well appreciated. Surveys that rely on large samples of relatively superficially collected data do not recognize decreased usage patterns within broad classifications, such as use in the past 30 days or even daily use. Whereas previously many people identified themselves with respect to society as marijuana users, the drug has now become one of many drugs taken for a variety of purposes, and the behavior has lost much of its symbolic value (Millman and Sbriglio 1986).

Natural History of Cannabis Use

This decreased involvement with the drug may also relate to a natural history of cannabis use in a proportion of adult smokers that has been described (Millman and Sbriglio 1986). Given the vast number of people who began smoking marijuana heavily in the mid-1960s to the early 1970s, moreover, it is surprising that more people have not developed problems related to use of the drug and sought treatment. In a five-year follow-up of regular marijuana users, Weller and Halikas (1982) reported that continued use of the drug was associated with a diminution of the earlier reported positive feelings of peacefulness, relaxation, enhanced sensitivity, self-confidence, and subjective impressions of heightened mental powers.

Whereas a group of successful white middle-class men and women were formerly habitual and daily marijuana smokers who previously described themselves with some pride as "potheads," in a descriptive study they related with some embarrassment and chagrin that they became uncomfortable, anxious, or paranoid when smoking the drug in high concentrations and that they didn't like these feelings (Millman and Sbriglio 1986). Some of them found themselves drinking much more alcohol; several of the group have had problems with cocaine or heroin. They claimed that they still liked marijuana, although they use it much less often and in lower doses.

Marijuana intoxication is marked by an altered time sense, during which time seems to pass slowly, concentration is altered, and little may be accomplished. We have postulated that this experience may be appreciated when one is young and does not understand the limits of his or her time or when people feel powerless to alter their situations or their society. People who have come to understand the aging process and value productivity and ambition may find the passivity and lassitude induced by the drug anxiety provoking (Millman and Sbriglio 1986). The impairment of short-term memory associated with cannabis may contribute to these dysphoric feelings as well (Relman 1982). It is interesting that drugs that promote the illusion of power, energy, or productivity (e.g., cocaine, alcohol) are preferred by these people. The actual level of productivity is not the issue; it is possible that these people get less done after drinking alcohol than after using marijuana. Rather the issue is the sense of power and control. Then too, although marijuana smoking is most often done in groups, individuals remain somewhat solitary, reminiscent of the parallel play of young children. Conversation is disjointed and often aimless. Palpable achievement, power, and satisfaction associated with involvement in the real world may render this behavior less attractive.

Patterns of Abuse

There is a continuum of cannabis use, from occasional or experimental use of the drug to compulsive use patterns. Marijuana is generally the first illicit drug used by young people, although experiences with beer, wine, and cigarettes generally precede its use. Social, cultural, and geographic considerations determine whether a person will use cannabis; personality characteristics and psychopathology, interacting with the psychoactive effects of the drug, are important in determining the patterns and frequency of use (Jessor et al. 1980).

Occasional users generally smoke in groups where the ritual of preparation and smoking of the "joint" is an integral part of social interaction. The drug may be peripheral to the life of the occasional user and there may be no other drug use except intermittent alcohol. Persistent adverse effects have not been described in this group.

More frequent users may use the drug on a daily basis after school or work to relax or listen to music. Other people, particularly adolescents, describe compulsive use patterns where the drug is used all day, every day, and the goal is to remain intoxicated ("stoned") all day long. Acquisition, evaluation, and use of the drug come to dominate the activities of daily living, and the drug use becomes a major source of identity and even pride in some people. Most people who use the drug frequently take a variety of other drugs, when they are available, although a few are purists who pride themselves on their exclusive use of cannabis preparations.

Marijuana and Stronger Drugs

Controversy persists as to whether marijuana use leads to the use of stronger drugs, the so-called stepping stone hypothesis (O'Donnell and Clayton 1979). It has been well demonstrated that there is a hierarchy of drug use and that marijuana is generally used before depressants, hallucinogens, cocaine, or heroin (Jessor 1975). Moreover, the frequency of use of cannabis correlates with the use of stronger drugs. It has been shown in one nationwide study that of those young men who had never used marijuana, less than 1 percent subsequently used heroin or cocaine; of those who had used marijuana 1,000 times or more, 73 percent used cocaine and 33 percent used heroin (O'Donnell et al. 1976). In another study of young men in Manhattan, no nonusers of marijuana had used psychedelics, whereas 37 percent of marijuana users had used psychedelics. Similarly, whereas only 1 to 5 percent of nonusers had used prescription stimulants, sedatives, or opiates, 34 to 36 percent of the marijuana users had used these drugs (Clayton and Voss 1981). National survey data confirmed this association (O'Malley et al. 1985). Of people who have ever tried cocaine, 98 percent have used marijuana and 93 percent used marijuana first. Of those people who have used cannabis at least 100 times, 75 percent have used cocaine. Of high school students who are current cocaine users, 84 percent are also current marijuana users (O'Malley et al. 1985).

Causality is not necessarily proven by demonstrating previous use because most of these people had used cigarettes, wine, beer, coffee, tea, and even milk for that matter. It is likely, however, that the use of marijuana, a so-called gateway drug, is a major determinant of whether someone will go on to use the stronger drugs. Positive experiences with one psychoactive drug or the recognition that the drug experience was not as dangerous as one had been led to believe by the media or parents may certainly encourage experimentation with other mind-altering chemicals. Since marijuana use is illegal, deviant behavior, the barriers to use of the so-called harder drugs even more frowned on by conventional authority may be lowered. Then too, the acquisition and use of marijuana usually encourages association with people who use or have access to other drugs. The increase in the use of heroin by middle- and upper-class people, mostly young adults, who had presumably been using marijuana and cocaine for the past five to 10 years may reflect this phenomenon.

It should be appreciated, however, that the experimental or intermittent use of marijuana or even cocaine is very different from a situation of compulsive use and dependence. Dependence is importantly determined by psychosocial factors in addition to pharmacologic ones. Cannabis use then does lead to experimentation with other drugs, and these drugs may in fact be more difficult to control.

Diagnosis

Evaluation Procedures

Evaluation of all patients with behavioral disorders, particularly those in whom the use of psychoactive drugs is suspected, requires a comprehensive history, physical examination, and psychiatric assessment. Physical examination of the chronic cannabis user may reveal conjunctival vascular injection, a swollen uvula, and chronic bronchitis. A complete history of all psychoactive drug taking, including alcohol, should be obtained, detailing the chronology of use, the psychoactive effects sought and obtained, the circumstances under which the drugs were used, the combinations of the drugs used, and the routes of administration. The relationship of the drugs to mood states and psychiatric symptomatology should be determined. It is important to attempt to determine whether the drug use preceded psychiatric symptomatology or aberrant behavior or followed it. A supportive, interested stance should be assumed, in the recognition that many drug abusers will deny or minimize the extent or impact of the drugs, consciously or otherwise. Patients with severe drug problems often believe that their drug use is similar to that of their friends and has not caused any problems. When the accuracy of the data is in question, it is useful to attempt gently to clarify the issues. It is generally not effective to confront a patient too strongly in initial interviews; data of questionable veracity can be followed up in succeeding contacts.

Marijuana is generally used in association with other drugs. The relationship of the various substances should be clarified. For example, a cocaine abuser may use marijuana to alleviate some of the anxiety or "wired" feelings from the cocaine; a heroin abuser may be seeking to extend the high. Marijuana is also used in association with alcohol to potentiate the feelings of intoxication.

Chronic cannabis abusers, particularly adolescents, often affect styles of dress and carriage that may be quite characteristic and are reminiscent of the styles of the 1960s. They may appear sullen and uninterested in the evaluation process or even openly hostile. To facilitate the evaluation process, it may be necessary to find areas of common interest and then move to the health-related issues. For example, discussing popular music with a teenager may produce useful data. Discussing how patients integrate cannabis into their lives and how the various drugs work will often lead to productive conversation. Many of these people pride themselves on their knowledge of psychoactive substance pharmacology and sociology, and they enjoy talking about their abiding interest.

With youthful patients, it is often useful to ask the parents to accompany the patient to the first interview. Have the parents sit in for the first few minutes of the interview to describe why they are concerned and what they think the problem is. Subsequently, ask them to wait outside and then devote the major portion of your time to conversation with the patient. It is often helpful to explain to the patient that you are working with him or her and that you will not disclose any confidences to the parents. The two of you will attempt to come up with a workable plan of action that can be presented to the parents. If you should determine that the patient is in imminent danger and the patient is unwilling or unable to follow appropriate recommendations, after explaining what you are going to do, you must apprise the parents of the situation. When a few minutes remain, ask the parents to return and either arrange for a subsequent meeting or make the appropriate treatment provisions.

Diagnosis of Cannabis Abuse and Dependence

There is no sharp line that distinguishes appropriate use of any substance from abuse and dependence. These characterizations are based on social, legal, and medical perspectives and are subject to varied interpretations, depending on the perspectives of the observer and prevailing attitudes.

According to DSM-III-R (American Psychiatric Association 1987), the diagnosis of cannabis dependence is determined by the presence of clinically significant behaviors, thoughts, and symptoms that indicate a substantial degree of involvement with cannabis as well as some degree of impairment in physical, social, and occupational functioning. Compared to DSM-III (American Psychiatric Association 1980), in DSM-III-R the diagnosis of abuse is made when the disturbances do not meet the criteria for dependence yet the use of the substance is maladaptive. It is suggested that since most cases of abuse under DSM-III will be classified as dependence under DSM-III-R, early detection and treatment will be encouraged before the drug has caused significant life problems. This line of reasoning posits that the earlier the diagnosis is made, the more successful the intervention is likely to be. It should be noted that this conceptualization has not been well documented. At the same time, since marijuana use is so prevalent in our society and is considered a normative experience by some observers, characterizing intermittent although regular use with no obvious sequelae as dependence may represent overdiagnosis and may be a disservice to many reasonably well-adjusted people (Jessor et al. 1986).

Laboratory Diagnosis

As part of the initial evaluation procedure with a reluctant patient, it is generally useful to obtain an observed urine for toxicologic analysis. This obviates the need to rely on self-report data. It is recognized that it may be difficult for many psychiatrists to accomplish this because of logistics or because of an unwillingness to be so intrusive. They may believe that testing may hinder the development of a therapeutic alliance. Many experienced therapists who were initially unwilling to seek these data have ruefully come to the conclusion that it significantly facilitates the evaluation process.

Analyses of urine and less often of blood for marijuana and the other major drugs of abuse should be performed under a variety of other circumstances as well. Certainly the tests should be performed on patients where there is other evidence suggesting marijuana or other drug use. During the treatment process, it is often useful to obtain drug screens at intervals. Testing should also be performed to clarify the diagnosis of any acute intoxications; to evaluate a sudden change in mental status, mood, or behavior; and to perform "under the influence" evaluations for use at the scene of accidents. Given the widespread use of marijuana and its relationship to psychiatric disorders, testing for marijuana and the other drugs of abuse should be performed on all psychiatric admissions and probably at intervals on inpatients who have had unsupervised contact with society (Verebey et al. 1986).

Much controversy exists as to whether testing should be performed as part of preemployment screens and at random intervals while people are on the job. The intrusiveness of the tests and the abrogation of the rights to privacy must be balanced against the danger of drug use. Critics of widespread drug testing on the job believe that a voluntary program on the employee assistance model is more appropriate. There has been a move to increased use of drug screening tests on individuals who have jobs that put others or themselves at risk. It has also been suggested that drug testing be done in schools (Schwartz and Hawks 1985).

It should be noted that there is poor correlation between the amounts in body fluids and the level of intoxication or performance impairment and it is quite difficult to estimate the time when the drug was last smoked. Although the psychoactivity of cannabis lasts only a few hours, residual effects such as changes in mood (Chait et al. 1985) and fine motor control (Yesavage et al. 1985) may be measured for a substantially longer period, and the metabolites can be detected for weeks. The size of the dose, the method of administration, and the extent of behavioral or metabolic tolerance all influence the level of drug or metabolite determined. Undue reliance on these tests to explain behavior is not warranted.

Approximately 17 percent of the tetrahydrocannabinol (THC), the major psychoactive component in a marijuana cigarette, becomes bioavailable after smoking. Blood levels are therefore quite low. Peak plasma levels of 3 to 50 ng/ml THC are seen in occasional smokers for up to 20 minutes; these levels drop to 1 to 2 ng/ml 24 hours after smoking. Therefore, analytic techniques to determine the immediacy of marijuana smoking must be quite sensitive.

THC and its metabolites are cleared more slowly from the body than most other psychoactive drugs, probably related to high lipid solubility and storage for long periods of time in lipid tissue. The major urinary metabolite of THC is 11-nor-delta-9-THC-9-carboxylic acid (THCA). The average time of detection in the urine of THCA is four to six days in acute users and 20 to 30 days in chronic users. When a 100 ng/ml cutoff is used, positives might be expected from one to 72 hours after smoking. Therefore a positive urine test for marijuana confirms use of the drug at any time between hours and weeks. Salivary analysis, an experimental procedure, may determine whether marijuana use has occurred in the previous four to eight hours (Schwartz and Hawks 1985).

Despite a proliferation of legal cases questioning the reliability of procedures, current testing technology is quite accurate. When the tests are performed correctly, the incidence of false negatives according to various studies is two to three percent, whereas the incidence of false positives, which is more critical from the legal standpoint, is considered to be negligible (Verebey et al. 1985). In practice, by virtue of the markedly variable quality of commercial laboratories, the incidence of false results could be considerable.

Treatment of Acute Psychiatric Reactions

Intoxication

Intoxication is defined by DSM-III-R as a syndrome that occurs after recent use of marijuana and is marked by tachycardia, the development of particular psychological symptoms within two hours of use, and at least one of the following physical symptoms within two hours of use: conjunctival injection, increased appetite, or dry mouth. There may also be maladaptive behavioral effects as noted below. Psychological symptoms are remarkably variable and depend on the dose, the route of administration, the personality of the user, previous experience with the drug, personal expectations, and the environmental and social setting in which the drug is used.

Perceptions of sounds, colors, tastes, textures, and patterns are commonly altered. Ideas may flow rapidly in a disconnected manner and be altered in emphasis and importance. Individuals may become withdrawn or more talkative. Mood changes vary profoundly; a mild euphoria may be experienced, although anxiety and depression may occur as well. Problems may be experienced as either more or less pressing. Drowsiness or hyperactivity and hilarity may be noted. Time is experienced as passing slowly with little activity needed and no sense of boredom. People often spend long periods of time listening to music or reading. Users describe the unique ability to be able to observe their own intoxication, including dysphoric effects (Grinspoon 1983). Intermittent or occasional users are often attempting to facilitate concentration at a concert or movie or to enhance sensitivity in sensual situations.

Adverse Reactions

The most frequently reported adverse reactions to cannabis include anxiety reactions and frank panic attacks. Depressive episodes of varying intensity have also been reported. These generally occur during the period of intoxication and abate within minutes to hours, rarely persisting for more than 24 hours (Knight 1976).

These reactions are more likely to occur in naive users who are unfamiliar with the drug's effects and who take it in an unfamiliar or threatening setting (Khantzian and McKenna 1979). They are quite variable in intensity and characteristics and range from mild discomfort to frank hysteria, often associated with the sensation of being unable to move or breathe or of an impending heart attack. It is unlikely that psychologically predisposed people are more susceptible to these reactions and may be vulnerable to the persistence of symptoms, the development of a cannabis delusional disorder, or even the development of a psychotic reaction.

Treatment consists of calm and gentle reassurance in a warm and supportive atmosphere ("talking down"). These people are often brought to emergency rooms, and the attempt should be made to find an appropriate, quiet place out of the mainstream of traffic. It is useful to remind the patient continually that the symptoms being experienced are related to the drug, are quite common, and will wane rapidly. When necessary, an anxiolytic should be administered, preferably one with a rapid onset of effects and long duration of action (diazepam 10 to 30 mg).

Cannabis Delusional Disorder

According to DSM-III-R, the cannabis delusional disorder is defined as the development of delusional ideation within two hours of use of cannabis with no clouding of consciousness, no significant loss of intellectual abilities, and no predominant hallucinations; it does not persist beyond six hours following cessation of substance use. The delusions are often persecutory, although they may be marked by jealousy, the idea that there is some physical disorder, or appearance abnormality or grandiosity. There is often associated reactive anxiety, depersonalization, derealization, and rarely visual and auditory hallucinatory events.

This disorder is difficult to distinguish from the panic and anxiety states that often occur with cannabis intoxication and may in large part be precipitated by these affective events. As with the adverse sequelae of marijuana intoxication, the delusional disorder appears to be influenced by the dose of the drug, the premorbid psychopathology of the user, and the environment. In predisposed people, the delusional disorder may be a prelude to a persistent psychotic reaction.

Treatment includes close observation in a warm and supportive environment with gentle and continual reassurance provided to the effect that these thoughts and feelings are due to the drug and will defervesce. When necessary, an anxiolytic should be administered (diazepam 10 to 30 mg). In cases with persistent and severe symptoms, it may be necessary to administer neuroleptic medication (haloperidol 2 to 4 mg).

Delirium

A toxic delirium occurs most often incident to the oral ingestion of a large amount of cannabis in one of its many forms. It is marked by clouding of consciousness, confusion, depersonalization, impaired and sluggish thinking, and motor imbalance. There may be memory impairment, visual and auditory hallucinations, paranoia, and violent or bizarre behavior. Speech is disconnected; nystagmus is often present. Four cases of mutism in addition to symptoms of delirium have been reported (Marcotte 1972). The syndrome lasts from a few hours to a few days. The syndrome is undistinguishable from other acute reactions that have been described variously as acute toxic psychoses, ganga psychoses, or acute organic brain syndromes (Keup 1970; Stone 1985; Talbott and Teague 1969). The relationship of this syndrome to a schizophreniform psychosis remains unclear. Treatment is symptomatic. Both anxiolytics and neuroleptics have been used with varying success.

Flashback Syndrome

A flashback is the transitory recurrence of feelings and perceptions originally experienced while under the influence of a psychedelic drug, although they do occur after cannabis use as well. Marijuana smoking at some time after the use of a psychedelic drug is the most common cause of flashbacks, although they may occur in the context of emotional stress, fatigue, or altered ego functioning. They are quite variable in character, intensity, and duration and may last from seconds to hours and may be pleasant or horrifying. Most flashbacks are episodes of visual distortion, reexperienced intense emotion, depersonalization, or physical symptoms. They generally decrease in number and intensity over time; in rare cases they have become more frequent repetitions of frightening images or thoughts (Grinspoon and Bakalar 1986).

Frequent cannabis or psychedelic use may increase the incidence of these occurrences. Whereas the etiology is unclear, they have been variously explained as similar to traumatic neuroses, as based on persisting neurochemical change, and as a kind of visual seizure.

Treatment consists of reassurance and, rarely, anxiolytic medication if the flashback is severe. Individuals should be cautioned against the continued use of marijuana or psychedelic drugs. Psychotherapy might be indicated to relieve the anxiety or to resolve the conflicts that may precipitate these episodes, although there is no good evidence to confirm this. Chronic neuroleptic medication might also be indicated in severe cases.

Treatment of Chronic Psychiatric Disorders Associated with Cannabis

Chronic psychopathology noted in chronic marijuana users as with all other drug abusers is determined by the interaction of the psychobiology of the user with the pharmacology and psychoactive effects of the drug. It remains difficult in individual patients to distinguish what came before the drug use from what is seen after, to distinguish the correlates of abuse and dependence from the consequences. Chronic marijuana use may reflect impaired premorbid social or occupational functioning and psychopathology as well as be a cause of psychiatric symptomatology and behavioral disability.

Psychosocial Correlates

Surveys performed during the early 1970s were compared to studies carried out from the mid-1970s to the early 1980s; these demonstrated a relatively invariant pattern over time, and from adolescence to adulthood, or psychosocial unconventionality that continues to be associated with variations in marijuana use. This pattern includes placing less value on academic achievement, higher value on independence relative to achievement values, greater social criticism and tolerance of deviant behavior, and lower religiosity. Social measures that relate to marijuana use include less perceived control from friends, less compatibility between the expectations of friends and of parents, greater influence of friends relative to parents, and greater involvement in other problem behaviors such as problem drinking, delinquency, and precocious sexual behavior. These findings demonstrate that marijuana use and cocaine use are associated with a larger network of personal, social, and behavioral attributes (Jessor et al. 1986).

The drug use in many young people may represent purposive, goal-directed behavior; they may feel older, more mature, or more in control in association with their drug use. The drug is used to cope with dysphoric feelings of boredom, anxiety, frustration, and inadequacy in relation to the demands or expectations of peers, parents, and school authorities. Marijuana may serve to alter perceptions sufficiently such that these feelings are experienced as less intense, and the situations attendant to these feelings may be perceived as less important (Jessor et al. 1980). Compulsive marijuana use may facilitate a regressive avoidance of distress.

Cannabis as Self-Medication

Cannabis dependency is often associated with significant premorbid psychopathology ranging from personality and affective disorders to psychotic disorders. In some of these disorders, the drug is used as self-medication. It is necessary to define the meaning of the drug in individual patients (Milkman and Frosch 1973). The anxiolytic and sedative properties of the drug may serve to reduce painful affects of depression, rage, shame, and loneliness in people who are postulated to have major defects in affect defense (Khantzian 1985). The drug may alleviate the symptomatology associated with the personality disorders.

A variety of workers have reported on patients with schizophrenic and manic or hypomanic disorders who self-medicated their psychotic symptoms with high doses of marijuana, with a consequent deterioration of the clinical picture. Because cannabis weakens perceptual cues and is itself psychotomimetic, it has been difficult to understand why cannabis would be used as self-medication by these people. Certainly alcohol, depressants, and particularly the opiates would be more effective as self-medication for these disorders. In one study, four schizophrenic patients reported that the antipsychotic medication they were taking produced feelings of emptiness; they felt uninspired, passive, and subdued. With cannabis, patients reported a two-phased experience with initial feelings of relaxation, increased energy, and improved mood followed by a deterioration marked by increased severity of auditory hallucinations and disorganization. It has been postulated that the anticholinergic effects of cannabis may diminish the therapeutic efficacy of neuroleptic agents (Bernhardson and Gunne 1972; Knudsen and Vilmar 1984). The manic and hypomanic patients described may have been attempting to control their symptomatology and experienced a worsening of symptoms leading to a transient marijuana-induced schizophreniform phase of their manic illness (Harding and Knight 1973; Knight 1976). Some of these patients seem to have been trying to distance themselves from threatening symptomatology, in any direction. Perhaps if more effective antipsychotic or antimanic drugs were available, they would have preferentially used them. Interestingly, there are also anecdotal reports of psychosis occurring incident to cessation of cannabis use.

A related phenomenon may be the attempt on the part of some people, particularly adolescents, to rationalize their psychopathology, abnormal or bizarre behavior, and inability to relate to their peers. Their strange thoughts and feelings are attributed to the drug and not to their own psychopathology. The deviant subculture of "pot-heads" and "druggies" is certainly more tolerant of their strange ways than conventional society would be. Some of these people become expert in acquiring, selling, and using drugs such that they have an honored role in society, albeit an antisocial role in a bizarre society.

Treatment of patients with premorbid psychopathology depends on the characterization of their disorder when they have ceased marijuana use. It is often necessary to institute treatment presumptively based on the clinical picture. Psychotic symptoms associated with cannabis use should be treated as functional psychotic symptoms would be. Patients should be carefully educated with respect to issues such as their attempt at self-medication and at rationalization of their psychopathology. Patients on neuroleptics must be specifically cautioned against the use of cannabis.

Cannabis as a Cause of Psychotic Disorders

Reports from all over the world suggest that prolonged or chronic psychotic disorders have been precipitated by high dose and prolonged cannabis use (Bernhardson and Gunne 1972; Chopra and Smith 1974). Whereas many workers have attempted to distinguish the disorders associated with marijuana use from schizophrenic disorders, present evidence suggests that the syndrome is indistinguishable from classic schizophrenia. It is likely that premorbid psychopathology or vulnerability is necessary for the development of this disorder. In most cases, the psychotic symptoms defervesce after days or weeks; in other situations the disorders have proven to be chronic (Keup 1970; Stone 1985). It is unclear whether this symptom picture can be precipitated de novo in normal individuals, although anecdotal reports suggest that prolonged psychotic disorders can occur in nonpredisposed people given high enough doses of the drug as by ingestion. It is possible that the disorder may be shorter lived than that induced in a predisposed patient. Although not well documented, our clinical impression is that after patients recover from a cannabis-precipitated psychotic episode, there is residual psychopathology, including paranoid thoughts and low-level auditory hallucinations that persist for long periods of time. These may be a function of anxiety, a form of flashback or evidence of a persisting neurochemical deficit. Perhaps a "kindling" phenomenon is occurring in some of these people. It has been suggested that some of these people may represent a new group of chronic psychiatric patients; they are typically young males who are highly transient and prone to depression, anger, and aggressive, self-destructive acts (Schwartz and Goldfinger 1982). The chronic drug use in association with psychopathology may produce the clinical picture.

Psychotic episodes precipitated by marijuana should be treated as functional psychotic disorders if they persist. Early on, if anxiety is prominent and seems to be a determinant of the clinical picture, some clinicians suggest anxiolytic therapy to attempt to abort the psychotic episode rapidly (diazepam 40 to 60 mg/day in divided doses). Subsequently, neuroleptic agents without prominent anticholinergic effects (e.g., haloperidol) should be administered in appropriate doses to control symptoms. These patients require a great deal of support and reassurance during this period. When symptoms are brought under control and if patients can tolerate the involvement, the cannabis or other drug dependence should be addressed.

Chronic Cannabis Syndrome

An amotivational syndrome has been described in chronic, high-dose users of marijuana in various parts of the world, marked by apathy, diminished goal-directed activity, and an inability to master new problems. Personal habits deteriorate; users are described as withdrawn, passive, and easily distracted with poor judgment and impaired communication skills (Stefanis et al. 1976). The syndrome has been invoked to explain poor school performance and personality deterioration in adolescents particularly. These reports are compromised by the absence of controls and the inability to distinguish the pharmacologic effects of the drug from antecedent psychological and social conditions. Other reports of chronic users have subsequently failed to demonstrate the existence of this syndrome (Carter 1980; Rubin and Comitas 1975). These reports are also flawed in that they focused on low-level workers doing relatively minimal tasks. The syndrome has not been demonstrated in controlled laboratory studies (Brady et al. 1986).

Given the pharmacologic actions of cannabis—including sedation, disruption of concentration, impairment of short-term memory, even alleviation of performance-related anxiety—it seems likely that the drug does stifle ambition and drive and impair school performance, but only in some people, perhaps those who are in some way vulnerable. In other young people, chronic heavy cannabis use has been associated with profound changes in perspective, dress, and behavior, although they have demonstrated laudable energy and ambition in the pursuit of their particular goals, such as intense involvement with popular music or identification with drug-using cults such as the Rastafarians. The term *aberrant motivational syndrome* has been suggested as a more precise description of the phenomenon (Millman and Sbriglio 1986).

The pharmacologic effects of cannabis, interacting with psychological and social factors, may be responsible for the clinical picture seen. In other highly motivated, productive people, the drug is reported to facilitate performance and productivity, perhaps as self-medication of incapacitating anxiety. It is likely that the dose of drug used is lower than that used by some severely disabled young people.

The chronic cannabis syndrome may be considered to be a variant of the cannabis dependence disorder that has been described. Cessation of the cannabis use in the absence of severe psychopathology and committed involvement to a treatment program frequently results in a marked and rapid improvement in mental clarity and energy levels. In addition to being a result of the waning of drug effects, the often remarkable behavioral changes seen may be a function of decreased feelings of isolation and demoralization that many previously chemically dependent people experience on rejoining the ranks of consensual society, however hated it previously was.

Treatment of Cannabis Abuse and Dependence

As with all other drug-taking syndromes, the treatment of cannabis-related disorders requires an appreciation of the psychosocial characteristics of the patient as well as the pharmacology and patterns of abuse of marijuana. Treatment should be conceptualized as including initial and extended phases. During the initial phases, acute medical or psychological reactions must be dealt with and withdrawal from the drug effected. The extended phase must include provisions to maintain the abstinent state, relapse prevention techniques, and the treatment of associated psychosocial pathology. As in the treatment of other drug-dependent patients, much attention is directed toward what they should not do. It may be critical to remember that they also need help to determine what they *should* do. A major element in any treatment program must be the attempt to provide realistic and rewarding alternatives to the drugs and the associated life-style (Millman and Botvin 1983).

As noted earlier, whereas some people abuse marijuana exclusively, most others use the drug in association with the various other drugs of abuse. The treatment of cannabis dependence should therefore be considered in the context of treating patients who are more eclectic in their tastes and behaviors.

Cessation of Cannabis Use

Patients must be helped to recognize that the drug use is significantly interfering with aspects of their lives. All drug use must cease, and patients should be encouraged to make a commitment to abstinence. There is often significant denial and sometimes open hostility present during this stage, and considerable skill and tact may be necessary to "break through" the denial and motivate the patient to comply with the program. Many programs adhere to a disease model of chemical dependency, where much emphasis is placed on the patient recognizing that he or she has the disease of chemical dependency, is an addict, and must have help to control, never cure, the cannabis or other drug dependency. Some programs use written contracts to concretize the treatment requirements. Patients should be seen on a frequent basis, perhaps even daily; if possible, both group and individual therapies should be provided.

During this phase, a comprehensive drug education component should be provided for the patient and the patient's family. Regular family sessions and attendance at Twelve Step or other self-help program meetings should be strongly encouraged if appropriate. Patients must be helped to terminate drug-related associations and activities and to develop a productive support network comprised of a carefully selected group of family and friends. It has proven useful to formalize this support network by means of regular meetings.

Regular urine drug testing for the major drugs of abuse should be a routine element in the treatment process. Despite the development of a good relationship with the patient, toxicologic data provide an objective measure of treatment progress, enhance the patient's own control over drug-seeking behavior, and may prevent the reemergence of denial that is common to the drug treatment process (Swatek 1984). Patients often do not reveal the presence of a relapse because they do not want to disappoint the therapist. At the same time, by virtue of guilt or anger, if they remain undetected they may lose faith in the therapist or the program and leave treatment. The most experienced clinicians have sometimes been unable to recognize a relapse to drug use in the absence of these data.

Most patients are referred for treatment of drug problems other than cannabis. At the same time, most of them used marijuana before they progressed to other drug use and most continue to use the drug in addition to their primary drug(s) of abuse. They often do not consider it a problem. Different treatment programs approach this issue in different ways. Use of any drug, including alcohol and marijuana, often provides the conditioned associations or disinhibition necessary to resume use of the more destructive substances. Current practice suggests that viewing all drugs as chemical dependency and requiring across-the-board abstinence from all psychoactive drugs promises the best results. In some cases, people with a primary cocaine or heroin dependence have been able to use cannabis or alcohol, intermittently or rarely, and do not relapse to more destructive drug use patterns.

Abstinence Syndrome

Controversy persists as to whether cessation of regular use of cannabis produces a stereotyped withdrawal syndrome of clinical significance. A syndrome marked by nausea, myalgias, irritability, restlessness, nervousness, depression, and insomnia has been reported to occur in animals and humans after abrupt cessation of chronic use of high doses, although it is not well defined and may not occur for days to a week after the drug was discontinued (Jones 1983). Animal studies have variously suggested that the endogenous opioid, the catecholamine, and the serotonergic systems may be implicated in this withdrawal syndrome (Kumar et al. 1984). Whereas most people have few withdrawal symptoms, others will experience signs and symptoms that are quite variable in nature and severity. These seem to be importantly dependent on the premorbid personality of the user and the associations that have been conditioned by environmental cues or expectations.

In general, reassurance and firm support and an attempt to reduce the availability of the drug are sufficient to facilitate the withdrawal process. Medication is not generally indicated. Experiments in animals and humans suggest that since the drug reduces noradrenergic activity and endogenous opioids, desipramine, a potent blocker of the reuptake of norepinephrine, and tyrosine, a norepinephrine precursor, may be indicated as withdrawal agents (Tennant 1986). Anecdotal reports suggest that certain patients dropped out of treatment if they did not receive medication. It is also possible that nonspecific alteration of internal feeling states with medication may allay withdrawal symptoms, decrease the reinforcement properties of dysphoric symptoms, and so promote abstinence. If extreme anxiety occurs, a long-acting benzodiazepine may be indicated. Psychopathology that is present, precipitated, or unmasked by the withdrawal process should be treated appropriately.

Early Recovery

This phase of treatment may require approximately two to 12 months and focuses on relapse prevention and the development of new modes of living. Whereas many of the relapse prevention strategies were developed using a social learning theory model, these techniques may also be adapted to treatments adhering to the disease model (Marlatt 1980). It has proven useful to structure the relapse prevention techniques in group and individual encounters. Some of the critical elements that should be covered include helping the patient to recognize the earliest warning signs of relapse; combating "euphoric recall," the tendency to remember only the positive aspects of the drug experience, often from early on in the drug user's career; overcoming the inevitable desire to attempt to regain control over the drug use; reinforcement of the negative aspects of the drugs ("thinking through the drug"); avoiding situations that have become powerful conditioned stimuli for the resumption of drug-taking behavior ("people, places, and things"); insulating "slips" so that they do not become full-blown relapses; learning new methods to cope with dysphoric symptoms, including the identification of internal feeling states that had become the conditioned stimuli for drug craving; and developing pleasurable and rewarding alternatives to drugs (Galanter 1983; Schnoll and Daghestani 1986; Washton 1986).

Some young people in particular do not have the skills to develop healthy relationships or productive life-styles. They often do not know how to have fun without drugs. Structured activities and exercises are often quite valuable in this regard.

Relapses are common during this phase and often occur in well-known states. Initially patients feel proud and happy at how well they are doing and may decide that treatment is no longer indicated. They may then experiment with cannabis or another drug to demonstrate that they have become stronger and can now control the drug use. Intermittent, careful use then occurs, then escalates, until the control is lost and relapse is complete.

Long-Term Treatment

During this phase, treatment contacts may be reduced to once-weekly group sessions to maintain the commitment to abstinence, to enhance interpersonal skills, to combat renewed denial and overconfidence, and to work toward goals and aspirations. Continued participation in self-help groups should be encouraged. In programs based on Twelve Step principles, participants are encouraged to continue to think of themselves as addicts, albeit in a recovering stage. This has proven to be quite useful for adults who are drug dependent. With respect to youthful marijuana abusers, it may not be necessary to maintain this identification so powerfully. After a year or more of abstinence and appropriate social adjustment, young people might be encouraged to think of themselves as similar to their peers though with the recognition that they continue to be at increased risk. Treatment of psychopathology should be continued as needed.

During this phase, evaluative procedures should continue to characterize more precisely the psychopathology that may have antedated the drug use or may be a result of it. Psychotherapy and pharmacotherapy should be provided as needed.

Treatment Facilities and Procedures

There are few programs that focus primarily on marijuana abusers. Most of the inpatient and outpatient treatment programs are primarily focused on the people who abuse the so-called harder drugs. Recently, in part in response to the increased prevalence of cocaine use in youthful populations, a large number of programs have developed adolescent divisions, which are often appropriate for adolescent cannabis abusers. Whenever possible, these patients should be treated as outpatients and encouraged to remain at work or in school.

Inpatient Programs

It will sometimes be necessary to treat some cannabis users as inpatients. This is an important clinical decision. The criteria for institutionalization include: 1) the inability to cease drug use despite appropriate outpatient maneuvers; 2) psychologic or (rarely) medical conditions that require close observation and treatment such as severe depressive symptoms, psychotic states, or extreme debilitation, 3) the absence of adequate psychosocial supports that might be mobilized to facilitate the cessation of drug use; 4) the necessity to interrupt a living situation that reinforces continued drug taking; and 5) the need to enhance motivation or break through denial.

Since institutions vary considerably in their organizing principles and methods, an appropriate referral attempts to match the program to the needs of the patient. There are three primary referral options. The first is the psychiatric hospital. This modality is generally indicated when severe psychopathology is present, although these facilities often lack an organized drug treatment program and may be insensitive to the needs of drug abuse patients, particularly those who are young and demonstrably rebellious. Too often adversarial relationships are set up between patient and staff over stylistic differences. There may be insufficient structure, and patients often break the rules. Then too, cannabis-dependent adolescents may be less obviously symptomatic than other patients and may feel uncomfortable in this milieu. The second, rehabilitation programs, are based on the disease model of chemical dependency and generally have a strong Twelve Step program component. They are often effective, particularly if they have well-defined adolescent units that encourage the patient to identify strongly with the program. In other cases, cannabis abusers with severe adjustment problems may find little in common with other-drug patients (e.g., alcoholics) and may "go through the motions" with little real change effected. These programs often have inadequate psychiatric backup to treat some of the severely disturbed cannabis abusers; others are too intensely confrontational. The third, therapeutic communities, originally developed to treat heroin addicts. In recent years these facilities have developed programs geared for polydrug abusers, particularly adolescents. These vary considerably with respect to the characteristics of positive and negative reinforcements offered and also with respect to the availability of psychiatric evaluation and the treatments available. Severely disturbed patients often find these programs too confrontational and may panic or leave prematurely.

It should be appreciated that there are little data available on which programs are effective for which patients. Referrals must often be made on relatively tenuous grounds. For example, there is anecdotal evidence to suggest that some cannabis or polydrug abusers with severe personality disorders do better in rehabilitation programs or therapeutic communities than in psychiatric hospitals; they seem to thrive in a milieu that is tightly structured, relies predominantly on group techniques, and encourages strong identification and pride in the program. Difficult transferential issues that occur in individual therapy situations are diffused and diminished by the group identification.

Innovative programs have been developed that provide a variety of experiences and meet particular needs. For example, half-way houses have proven to be useful for some youthful cannabis abusers where they may sleep and eat in the facility but also resume or maintain contacts with school or work.

Outpatient Programs

These are generally organized according to the perspectives of the three major inpatient modalities described above and have many of the same strengths and weaknesses. These provide a range of services from day-long programs to group or individual sessions on a weekly basis.

Optimally, during the early phases of treatment, provision is made for intensive group; individual contacts and the program should be a major focus of the patient's life. With continued progress, the degree of involvement is reduced and the program becomes more peripheral to the life of the patient.

Psychotherapy

Psychotherapeutic intervention may be a crucial treatment option for patients with psychopathology who have cannabis-related problems. In later treatment stages, in particular, treatment of symptoms and resolution of the conflicts that may have led to or are associated with the drug use may be an effective tool to prevent relapse. It should be understood, however, that the primary goal of treatment should be abstinence; resolution of psychological conflicts is not a necessary condition for the achievement or maintenance of abstinence (Blume 1984).

It is often quite difficult to develop a therapeutic alliance with marijuana abusers, particularly those who are young and who have assumed a rebellious, antisocial stance. They may deny the presence or the extent of the problem; they may have had repeated treatment failures, and they have lost control of the drug use. They are often quite controlling and provocative; their behavior may be perceived as self-indulgent, primitive, or uncivilized by the therapist (Imhoff et al. 1984). It is generally agreed on by most workers that during the early treatment stages, the therapist must be quite active in fostering the relationship and should adopt an attitude of empathy and acceptance (Blane 1977). It obviously cannot be unquestioning acceptance; a good deal of tact and discipline should be used as well.

Positive transference should be encouraged, particularly in the early stages of treatment. It is probably only necessary to interpret negative transference if it threatens the therapeutic relationship (Blane 1977). Patients will often develop powerful dependencies on the therapist. This should be accepted, although it may require some fortitude. As with most patients, it is critical that the patient believes that the therapist is perceiving him or her accurately.

It is also critical that the therapist have a good understanding of the pharmacology and psychoactive effects of marijuana and the other drugs of abuse. Patients are instantly aware of the sophistication of the therapist and often find it difficult to place trust in this admittedly well-meaning person who does not know whether you buy an ounce or gram of the substance (Millman 1986).

There are no data suggesting that specific psychotherapeutic techniques for patients with cannabis-related disorders are better than others or that marijuana-dependent patients should be treated differently from other drug-dependent patients in this regard. Clinical experience and some controlled studies do suggest that certain psychotherapeutic methods may be most useful. With patients dependent on narcotics and cocaine, there is evidence that cognitive-behavioral, supportive, expressive, and interpersonal psychotherapeutic techniques may be effective (Rounsaville et al. 1985; Woody et al. 1983). Perhaps these experiences can be extrapolated to apply to cannabis dependence as well.

At the outset, the focus of treatment should be on the drug use and difficulties in interpersonal functioning. As with other substance-abuse patients, an emphasis on consistency of focus, problem solving, and brevity has proven useful.

Whereas during the initial stages an active, educative, sometimes confrontative role is assumed, the therapist should attempt to assume a stance of more neutrality and make efforts slowly to wean the patient off the powerful dependency created as treatment progresses and as the drug becomes less of an imminent danger. Involvement of the patient with peer support groups or the Twelve Step programs may facilitate the process.

Patients who are receiving psychotherapy as an element of a treatment program for dependency on drugs other than marijuana may wish to continue to use marijuana. They may not have had a problem with its control, and they may ascribe increased insight into the world or their personal problems to the drug experience. Rather than challenge their contention, it may be useful to suggest to them that chronic alterations in consciousness with any drug is likely to reduce or negate the value of psychotherapeutic intervention. Growth or learning through psychotherapy requires the recognition of anxiety, other symptomatology, or maladaptive behaviors and acceptance of the need to change these (Millman 1986).

Family Therapy

Since many people with problems relating to marijuana use still reside in family groups and are dependent on parental resources, family therapy may be a critical adjunct to other treatment modalities. Issues such as improved communication patterns, parental expectations, and parental or sibling drug use are important issues to deal with. At times, the marijuana user may be using the drug to cope with intolerable family conflicts that might be resolved through skilled family therapy. Increasingly, inpatient and outpatient drug treatment programs are mandating family involvement in the treatment process (Kaufman and Kaufman 1979). The concept of family therapy has been expanded by some therapists to include selected friends and business associates. The therapist and the patient attempt to develop a unit that will function as a source of support during the early stages of treatment.

Group Therapy

Group therapy has become the most frequently used modality for all classes of drug abusers, including those who primarily abuse cannabis. In distinction to more analytically oriented group techniques for psychiatric patients, drug treatment groups generally encourage strong identification with the group and utilize behavioral techniques and coercion to reinforce abstinence. Education in regard to the determinants and consequences of drug use is often included, and some programs include audiovisual aids and reading materials to supplement the group process. Groups are useful in teaching socialization and problem-solving skills and may reduce the sense of isolation that drug abusers often feel. Groups may be more or less confrontational in their approach. Many groups encourage members to maintain contact with each other outside of the group.

Patients sometimes appear for group meetings intoxicated or may regale the group with stories of their continued drug taking. If the group is unable to take the initiative, group leaders must be prepared to ask a group member to leave a session if his or her behavior is inappropriate. In other cases, group members may be asked to drop out of the group until their drug-taking ceases or their behavior is more conducive to the group process. It is the group leaders' responsibility to make other arrangements for these patients.

Twelve Step Programs

Whereas Twelve Step programs modeled after Alcoholics Anonymous have proven useful for many drug abusers, to date people who are primarily dependent on cannabis have not participated extensively in these groups. In the past this has been due in large part to cultural and stylistic differences between the programs and the people. Many of these predominately young people believed that the groups were too conventional ("straight") and were not sensitive to their concerns, or appreciative of their tastes (e.g., in music, clothing, and language). In fact, many of the groups are comprised of older people as well as those who have "hit bottom." Recently, many meetings of Drugs Anonymous and other self-help groups have become more sensitive to the styles and value systems of these people, and the programs are likely to become a more prominent part of the rehabilitation process in the future. Then too, most cannabis-dependent people abuse other drugs as well.

Many patients will resist attending self-help group meetings; they may feel they have nothing in common with the people who attend, or they may not be in the habit of discussing themselves and their problems publicly. At the same time, patients should be strongly encouraged to participate in appropriate meetings. Psychiatrists and other mental health professionals often find themselves at odds with their patients over these programs. Members of the groups accept dependence on a "higher power" and are encouraged to adhere to steps, traditions, and value systems based primarily on sobriety. It has been suggested that these groups may strengthen the fixation of patients at symbiotic levels of development; they do not encourage analytic self-examination, they may be infantilizing, and they may reduce complex psychological issues to the issue of chemical dependence. These characteristics may appear to be antithetical to professional therapeutic objectives and procedures (Zinberg 1977).

At the same time, it should be appreciated that dependence on these groups is often essential if patients are to abandon primitive methods of coping and drug taking. These groups often reduce the sense of isolation most compulsive drug abusers feel; they enhance self-esteem and provide a powerful structure within which many of these demoralized, dispirited people can find solace. Patients often become disenchanted with professionals and their programs, and many drop out of treatment, sometimes with the encouragement of their sponsors or other members of the self-help fellowship. Therapists may feel threatened by the groups and sometimes assume an adversarial stance with respect to them. Great caution must be exercised by the treatment team; it should be recognized that it is difficult for a patient to transfer the powerful dependence on the group to a therapist. The therapeutic issues involved relate to separation and individuation, and splitting, classic issues dealing with character pathology. When the patient loses the group, there is a tendency to feel extreme anxiety and to experience a powerful recurrence of the need to resume cannabis and other drug use. Then too, the difficult transference problems that a patient with character pathology might have relating to an individual therapist may be diffused by the relationship to the groups.

A frequent although quite effective progression often entails initial evaluation and early intensive treatment by a psychiatrist. The therapist effects the referral to the self-help fellowship, which may result in decreased intensity or even cessation of professional therapeutic contacts during the early stages of sobriety and until stability is achieved. Some patients then come to believe that there are issues and symptoms that should be worked on with the psychiatrist or mental health professional and seek to reestablish or intensify the therapeutic relationship. They may recognize that their psychopathology or their difficulties with realizing aspirations need to be considered according to psychiatric perspectives. Many others will not.

Behavioral Therapy

Although there are no good studies demonstrating efficacy, many of the techniques currently utilized by drug treatment programs are informed by behavioral therapeutic perspectives. These include skill-building techniques (e.g., relaxation exercises assertiveness training) and positive reinforcement for the attainment and maintenance of sobriety or other approved behaviors. Contingency contracting has proven useful with abusers of other classes of drugs and is used in the treatment of marijuana users as well. Aversive conditioning has produced modest results in promoting abstinence in controlled situations with other drugs, although the value of these primarily experimental techniques usually fails to generalize to settings outside the research center, and positive effects appear to erode over time.

The Need for No Treatment

It should be well recognized that for many people, particularly adolescents, intermittent or experimental marijuana use is normative for their peer group, has had no impact on their psychosocial adjustment, and may have little impact on their health. Coercing them into treatment, particularly inpatient treatment, may serve to disrupt their lives and school careers, reinforce the insecurity that many young people feel about their abilities or even their sanity, and stigmatize them. The problem may be complicated by well-meaning although understandably anxious parents or relatives who have learned through the media or from friends that the presumed patient should be forced into one program or another. On the other hand, it should be recognized that most drug abusers minimize their involvement with drugs and deny any impact the drugs might be having. Then too, marijuana use, even that which is intermittent or experimental, may presage more dangerous drug abuse at a later date.

This is often a difficult clinical problem, and intense pressure may be brought to bear on the practitioner. Clinicians must provide a careful evaluation to determine that the marijuana use is peripheral to the identity of the user, is appropriate to that of the individual's peers, is intermittent or rare, and has not had any impact on the social, occupational, or medical status of the user. In these cases, the attempt should be made to educate them as to the possible adverse effects of the drug use, and provisions should be made to follow these people at intervals. Whenever possible and appropriate, parents and relatives should be helped to feel that they are part of the evaluative process.

Chapter 132

Tobacco Withdrawal and Tobacco Dependence

The mounting evidence linking cigarette smoking with serious illness and premature death has placed increasing demands on the medical and mental health community to respond to this problem. Viewed as an addictive behavior, cigarette smoking can be treated from psychosocial, behavioral, and pharmacologic perspectives. A mental health professional in a clinical setting can play an important role in preventing and treating this psychological and/or physiologic addiction.

The DSM-III-R (American Psychiatric Association 1987) and the World Health Organization (1978) recognize tobacco dependence as an addiction. It deserves attention as a serious problem not only because of the health risks involved, but also because nicotine is a psychoactive substance that may control significant aspects of an individual's behavior. Tobacco shares a number of common factors with the other recognized euphoriants (i.e., cocaine, opiates, alcohol). It produces centrally mediated effects on mood and feeling states; is a reinforcer for animals; leads to drug-seeking behavior with deprivation; and shows similar patterns of social mediation and persistence in the face of evidence that it is damaging (Henningfield 1984). Individual variability in the intensity of the dependence is wide, and despite the large number of smokers who successfully quit on their own, many others can and do benefit from formal interventions. As with any behavior change process, patients will have individual needs that will require different approaches to achieve "maximum effect" during treatment.

In this chapter, we examine the current strategies available to the mental health professional and offer guidelines for initial and long-term intervention. We also discuss the smoking patient who presents special clinical problems: the alcoholic, the marijuana smoker, and the patient with other serious psychiatric problems.

Definition: DSM-III-R Criteria

Nicotine dependence is classified as an addiction in DSM-III-R and is considered an organic mental disorder. The difficulty in tobacco cessation may be due to the unpleasant nature of the withdrawal syndrome, the deeply engrained nature of the habit, the repeated effects of nicotine, and the likelihood that a desire to use nicotine is elicited by environmental cues (e.g., presence of other smokers and widespread availability of cigarettes). When efforts to give up smoking are made, nicotine withdrawal may result.

The DSM-III-R diagnostic criteria for nicotine withdrawal syndrome are listed in Table 1. Smokers who experience "withdrawal symptoms" during their cessation attempts have a much more difficult time stopping smoking than those who do not

Table 1.   DSM-III-R Diagnostic Criteria for Nicotine Withdrawal (292.00)

A. Daily use of nicotine for at least several weeks.

B. Abrupt cessation of nicotine use, or reduction in the amount of nicotine used, followed within 24 hours by at least four of the following signs:

   (1) craving for nicotine
   (2) irritability, frustration, or anger
   (3) anxiety
   (4) difficulty concentrating
   (5) restlessness
   (6) decreased heart rate
   (7) increased appetite or weight gain

experience them. The symptoms begin within 24 hours of cessation or reduction of tobacco use and decrease in intensity over a period of a few days to several weeks. The more addictive smoking patterns are generally associated with higher rates of smoking and the experience of withdrawal symptoms, and are inversely related to the likelihood of cessation.

Impact of Cigarette Smoking: Why Should People Stop?

Unlike the other addictions considered in this section, heavy use of tobacco has not been widely recognized as producing significant psychological disturbance, other than craving and difficulty in stopping. Only recently has the powerful addictive nature of nicotine been more thoroughly investigated and better understood (US Department of Health and Human Services 1988). Jaffe (1979) noted in a review of the psychiatric literature that prior to publication of the DSM-III in 1980, virtually no attention had been paid to excessive tobacco use as a psychological problem worthy of treatment. Only in the last few years have social disapproval and even legal sanctions become factors in curbing tobacco use; these may become increasingly important reasons for individuals to seek treatment.

The medical problems arising from cigarette smoking have led to the need to take smoking seriously as an addictive disorder; thus it is appropriate to review first the health risks of smoking. Since the first Surgeon General's Report on Smoking and Health (US Department of Health, Education, and Welfare 1964), smoking has been recognized as a serious medical problem and, in the last 10 years, has been linked irrefutably to many serious diseases, including cancer, heart disease, lung disease, complications of diabetes, and ulcers. Comprehensive discussions of health risks are available in the Surgeon General's reports (e.g., US Department of Health and Human Services 1983, 1985; US Department of Health, Education, and Welfare 1964, 1979). A much briefer summary is presented by Fielding (1985).

Physiologic Effects of Cigarette Smoke

Carbon monoxide and other gases.   The health consequences and symptoms of smoking have been attributed to the many noxious substances found in cigarette smoke, including carbon monoxide and other toxic gases. Carbon monoxide develops a strong bond with hemoglobin, causing smokers to lose as much as 15 percent of the oxygen-carrying capacity of their red blood cells. The loss of this oxygen can have a deleterious effect on the heart and circulatory system and may be a significant causal factor for the increased risk of cigarette smokers for coronary heart disease (CHD). Although levels of tar and nicotine have declined in cigarettes manufactured in recent years, the level of carbon monoxide has not decreased.

Inhaled along with carbon monoxide in cigarette smoke are other toxic gases such as hydrogen cyanide, ammonia, hydrogen oxide, and nitrogen oxide, all of which have been shown to produce toxic effects. These gases are most immediately responsible for coughing and narrowing of the bronchial tubes and, over time, paralysis of the cilia, thickening of the mucus-secreting membranes, and eventually chronic obstructive pulmonary disease (COPD).

Tar. Tar is considered a "complete carcinogen," not only causing but promoting malignant changes. The smoke from the burning end of the cigarette, "side stream" smoke, contains considerably higher amounts of the carcinogenic aromatic amines than does mainstream smoke and has been implicated as having an effect on individuals in the smoker's environment (passive smoking).

Nicotine. Nicotine causes the release of catecholamines, epinephrine, and norepinephrine, causing an increase in the following: heart rate, blood pressure, cardiac output, oxygen consumption, coronary blood flow, arrhythmias, peripheral vasoconstriction, and mobilization and utilization of free fatty acids. Nicotine is thought to contribute to heart disease through the acute strain placed on the cardiovascular system while smoking and, over time, as an irritant in the blood vessels, increasing the build up of plaque and promoting arteriosclerosis. Thus nicotine and carbon monoxide appear to produce the major adverse effects leading to CHD. In the diabetic patient, nicotine is a factor in both acute and chronic reduction of blood flow to the limbs, contributing to death of tissue and amputation. Nicotine as the primary psychoactive substance in tobacco will be discussed later.

Medical impact. The impact of cigarette smoking on morbidity and mortality from chronic disease is great. The occurrence of lung cancer is 10 times more likely for smokers than nonsmokers and 15 to 25 times greater for heavy smokers (two or more packs per day). Smokers have two to four times greater risk of dying from CHD than nonsmokers, depending on their rate of smoking (US Department of Health and Human Services 1983). Of as much concern is its effect on major respiratory ailments; smoking accounts for 90 percent of the development of chronic bronchitis and emphysema (Fielding 1985). Babies of smoking mothers weigh somewhat less at birth compared to those of nonsmoking mothers and are at higher risk for stillbirth and neonatal death, possibly through absorption of lead, cadmium, and cyanide from cigarette smoke (Kuhnert and Kuhnert 1985). Of more immediate concern to many smokers are troublesome symptoms such as morning cough; shortness of breath; fatigue; sputum production; hoarseness; increased pulse; skin and teeth stains; and increased incidence, severity, and duration of colds.

Assessment of a smoking patient also necessitates a consideration of other risk factors that act synergistically to cause CHD, COPD, and cancer. The risk for individuals with hypercholesterolemia and hypertension is greater than just the additive effect of each risk factor. Similarly, smoking, when coupled with exposure to asbestos and other occupationally encountered substances, greatly increases the smoker's risk of cancer of the lung when compared to smokers who are not so exposed.

Smokers sometimes believe that the damage has been done and there is little value in quitting. It is important to inform the patient that for most diseases this is not so. Life expectancy is longer among patients who stop smoking after the diagnosis of CHD than in those who continue to smoke. The risk of heart disease attributable to smoking drops 50 percent in the first year of abstinence and with the next year returns to that of someone who has never smoked (Rosenberg et al. 1985). Similarly, with certain lung diseases and circulation problems, cessation of smoking greatly improves the prognosis; symptoms may reverse quickly following cessation (Fielding 1985), although risk of mortality does not drop as quickly as for heart disease.

In summary, the constituents of cigarette smoke in both the gas and particulate phases have been found to affect almost every organ of the body and to cause excess mortality and morbidity for all of the major diseases. The symptoms of smoking are often obvious, and the more the mental health professional and other health care providers are able to relate these "personally relevant" effects to smoking, the greater the likelihood that the smoker will be motivated with personal reasons to attempt cessation. The provider's knowledge of these health risks is important but must be used skillfully to educate patients without frightening them unnecessarily, which may be counterproductive if it leads to increased denial or resistance.

Factors Supporting Smoking Behavior

Etiology and Stages of Smoking

Cigarette smoking is a complex behavior pattern that, like most behavior patterns, is affected by many psychosocial factors and goes through a sequence of stages. During the initiation phase, individuals start experimenting with cigarettes, generally before they are 20, and then move into the transition phase, where environmental and psychological factors influence their becoming smokers or nonsmokers. The sequence then proceeds through the stages of maintenance (of the habit), cessation, and maintenance of cessation. Since relapse occurs at very high rates among those who have stopped smoking (often as high as 70 to 80 percent return to smoking within one year), the cessation phase is also a transition phase that influences whether a smoker remains an ex-smoker or becomes a recidivist who returns to the old behavior of smoking.

Initiation of smoking is strongly associated with social forces, or forces extrinsic to the individual (e.g., peer pressure) as well as with psychological variables (e.g., self-esteem, status needs, other personal needs). The sociological variables that are so important during the formation of the habit seem to play a minor role in the maintenance stage once smoking has become part of the life-style of the individual. As the habit continues, it becomes more and more tied to psychological and physiologic needs and becomes an intrinsic part of the person's life, having many functions. Cessation and maintenance of cessation are affected by a combination of social, psychological, and physiologic variables acting on and within the individual (Leventhal and Cleary 1980). One study (Salber et al. 1968) suggested that 85 to 90 percent of those who smoke four cigarettes become regular smokers, making smoking as highly addictive as other substances such as heroin or cocaine.

Physiologic Factors

As evidence currently stands, it is likely that cigarette smoking is maintained by at least three physiologic processes: avoidance of nicotine withdrawal effects; desire for the immediate peripheral and central effects of nicotine; and the anticipation of the conditioned reinforcement consequences associated with smoking (Pomerleau and Pomerleau 1984; US Department of Health and Human Services 1988). The first process largely interferes with immediate attempts to withdraw from cigarettes. The second process involves active effects of nicotine, such as the anorexic impact, arousal from norepinephrine activity, increased improvement in concentration, and euphoriant effects possibly mediated by beta-endorphin release. The third process, the conditioning of these effects, is probably responsible for relapse under stress during the maintenance phase of cessation. The presence of this last process is still somewhat hypothetical, but has been implicated in relapse processes in other drug abuse patterns (Pomerleau 1981). The extent of the physiologic addiction is most easily indirectly quantified in a clinical setting using the Fagerstrom Nicotine Addiction Scale (Fagerstrom 1978) (Appendix A), which will be discussed more fully later. The Fagerstrom scale is sensitive to amount of nicotine intake and to smoking to avoid immediate withdrawal effects (e.g., smoking immediately on awakening); lower scores tend to predict greater ability to stop smoking.

Although pharmacologic and physiologic factors play a role in smoking behavior change, they fail to explain the great variability observed in individual responses. There is a greater likelihood that lighter smokers will be more successful at cessation, but there are light smokers who cannot stop just as there are heavy smokers who quit easily. Most of the effects of nicotine are short-term, and therefore it is difficult to understand how they can explain relapse after a somewhat extended period of cessation except as a learned anticipation of the euphoriant effect under stress.

Psychological Factors

Tomkins' (1966) model of smoking and affect, one of the most widely accepted theories of smoking maintenance, proposed that smoking, like other behaviors, is maintained because it provides a way of minimizing negative affects (e.g., distress, anger, fear, shame, contempt) and evokes the positive affects of excitement, enjoyment, and surprise.

Similarly, other investigators noted that a smoker's primary use of cigarettes is to regulate emotional states. Laboratory studies have supported this conclusion that smoking significantly reduces fluctuations or changes in mood or affect during stress (Schachter 1978). For many it also becomes a habitual pattern with little conscious forethought. The cigarette serves as an artificial aid that serves to reinforce smoking behavior.

Smokers who experience more stress in their lives or who have few resources for handling the stress have greater difficulty in the process of smoking cessation and in the maintenance of recently initiated nonsmoking behavior than those who have less stress or more effective resources. Aside from the physiologic effects, many smokers use cigarettes functionally as a way to provide a sanctioned "break" in their routine. The more addictive smoking patterns—which embrace a craving or compulsion, a need to control or prevent high levels of negative affect, or a belief that the cigarette can help control or stabilize troublesome situations—seem well outside the realm of conscious control. Thus some smokers' behavior fits the description of addiction as obsessive behavior centered around obtaining and using a substance. Heavier smokers generally have been found to experience more feelings of negative affect and more withdrawal symptoms than lighter smokers. The more excessive the habit, the less dependent it is on external cues and the more it shows a relationship to internal experiences and negative affect (Ockene et al. 1981).

Individuals who have had more positive past experience with regard to behavior change have good resources for dealing with stress; have an expectation that they can stop smoking or, as Bandura (1977) called it, self-efficacy; and have a greater likelihood of successful cessation than those with negative experiences (Condiotte and Lichtenstein 1981; Yates and Thain 1985). This will be discussed more fully later.

Social and Demographic Factors

The social and cultural environments of smokers have also been shown to affect their ability to stop smoking. Individuals who experience more social support for cessation and have fewer smokers in their environment are more successful at cessation attempts (Ockene et al. 1982). Likewise, smokers who are older and better educated and are at a higher occupational level are more likely to be able to stop smoking than the younger, less educated smoker who is at the lower end of the occupational scale (Ockene et al. 1982, 1985). While approximately 40 percent of blue collar workers presently smoke, only about 27 percent of white collar individuals do so (US Department of Health and Human Services 1988). Because of the demonstrated effect of the cultural and social environment on smokers, an area now under more intensive investigation is the use of work-site smoking intervention programs. These programs offer the premise of creating a more favorable environment and support for nonsmokers while at the same time providing the smoker with skills and resources necessary to become and remain a nonsmoker (Ockene and Camic 1985).

In summary, individuals who have been found to be most successful in cigarette smoking cessation are those who are older, more educated, have good personal resources to help them mediate and implement change, and receive support for the change from individuals in their environment.

General Issues in Treating Smoking in a Mental Health Facility

Treatment is available for smoking cessation from many sources. Mental health professionals who offer such treatment have a responsibility to recognize that other psychiatric problems may exist along with the presenting problems and that the addiction to smoking, both physiologic and psychological, may be of a magnitude to require additional professional attention. Mental health practitioners may also be functioning as part of a health care team, where knowledgeable attention to broader health issues is important. These responsibilities may be summarized as follows:

1. To assess psychiatric issues that may be present (current status; history; use of other addictive substances, especially alcohol and marijuana).
2. To evaluate the impact of these other problems on the patient's ability to stop smoking. Other problems may seriously complicate the course of the patient's ability to stop smoking or to maintain abstinence, resulting in a decision to treat such problems either prior to or concurrently with smoking. On the other hand, the best professional recommendation may be that, despite other problems, the patient can pursue a standard smoking cessation program because the smoking appears relatively disassociated from the other difficulties.
3. To offer treatment or make appropriate referrals for other problems that may become apparent. If a mental health facility or hospital offers a smoking cessation program, individuals may use their smoking as a safer and more acceptable route through which to gain help for other problems.

4. To be familiar with the physiologic processes to which smoking is related and the physiologic aspects of nicotine addiction.
5. To offer treatment sensitive to individual needs. This recommendation in no way precludes offering a standardized treatment program. However, alternative or supplementary treatment should be available.

We will discuss these issues in relation to specific clinical problems in the last part of this chapter.

Diagnosis and Assessment

Most of the evaluation of a smoker is assessment- rather than diagnosis-oriented. Two important diagnostic questions, however, are the extent to which nicotine addiction is present and the coexistence of other addictive or psychiatric problems. Frequently, a medical diagnosis has led to the urgency of treatment. In such an instance, the practitioner would benefit by communicating with the treating physician, with the patient's permission; if the patient is complaining of physical symptoms (e.g., shortness of breath, chest pain) that have not been evaluated, arranging a medical referral is necessary.

The assessment covers the three areas outlined earlier: physiologic components of addiction, psychological components, and social factors. Within these areas, the evaluation of psychological components is the broadest, including behavioral patterns, cognitive or attitudinal aspects, and the emotional significance of smoking for the patient.

How extensive the evaluation is depends on the setting, the apparent needs of the patient, and the types of treatment available. In some settings, patients can be asked to complete a standardized assessment battery prior to the initial interview, including material related to smoking patterns; screening for psychiatric difficulties using a self-report questionnaire, such as the SCL-90-R (Derogatis 1977); and any other special requirements, such as the evaluation of the patient as a subject for hypnosis. Any areas of special concern can be followed up in that interview or in a subsequent one. A standardized assessment might be appropriate when large numbers of individuals are being screened for a standard group treatment in a clinical setting or at a work-site treatment program. If the treatment offered is individual sessions, then the assessment process can be incorporated more appropriately into the initial two sessions.

The distinction between assessment and intervention is usually blurred within a cognitive-behavioral framework; gathering information about the external contingencies supporting smoking or about cognitions related to motivation increases self-awareness in a way that facilitates behavior change. Figure 1 is a flowchart of the major assessment issues discussed below, in relation to possible treatment choices.

Assessment of Physiologic Addiction

There are two primary ways to evaluate the extent of nicotine addiction and the likelihood that the individual will need special assistance during the withdrawal phase. One of the best indications is the reported difficulty of previous quit attempts. The second is the score on the aforementioned Fagerstrom Nicotine Addiction Scale (Fagerstrom 1978), which is psychometrically reliable and predictive of the value of

Figure 1. Flow Chart of Assessment and Treatment Decisions

Assessment Variables	Assessment Outcome	Treatment Choice
1. *Physiologic Factors*	LOW (Hx of few withdrawal symptoms-relapses after two wks; low Fagerstrom score)	Nicotine gum not recommended
Nicotine Dependence	UNKNOWN/UNCLEAR (No previous attempts or moderate symptoms)	Nicotine gum negotiable
	HIGH (Hx of withdrawal symptoms; relapses within one week; high Fagerstrom score)	Nicotine gum, Nicotine fading
2. *Psychosocial Factors*		
	High	
Self-efficacy	Low	Explore; educate; cognitive restructuring
Motivation to Quit	High	Health education; explore issues
	Low	
	Habit	Behavioral modification
Pattern of Psychological Dependence	Use as relaxor	Relaxation training
	Crisis management	Stress management training
	Social crutch	Assertiveness training
	High enjoyment	Aversion therapy
	Good social support for nonsmokers	Assertiveness training; increase contact with nonsmokers
Social Support	Significant others smoke	Assertiveness training; engage others in treatment
	Significant others unsupportive	More therapy contact; consider group treatment
	Few social supports	

nicotine substitutes (e.g., gum containing nicotine) during treatment (see Appendix A).

If the smoker reports having had intense withdrawal symptoms in the past, has a pattern of relapsing within a few hours or days, and scores high on the addiction scale, then nicotine addiction probably plays an important role in maintaining the behavior. Not all heavy smokers (> one pack/day) report intense withdrawal symptoms, and some relatively light smokers appear more susceptible.

If nicotine addiction is a significant problem, a number of treatment options are available (to be discussed in more detail later). Some individuals simply require more reassurance and support. Others may benefit from nicotine fading; the data are fairly clear that prescription of nicotine gum will benefit the addicted smoker more than the nonaddicted smoker. The degree of addiction, given identical nicotine intake, appears to be highly variable and many ex-smokers or relapsed smokers report that withdrawal symptoms lasted longer than might be predicted from what is known of the pharmacology of nicotine because for some individuals psychological stimuli cue physiologic reactions that mimic withdrawal symptoms (Pomerleau and Pomerleau 1984).

Finally, while evaluating nicotine addiction patterns, it is important to assess the use of other addictive substances, in particular alcohol, caffeine, and marijuana.

Psychological Assessment

Behaviorial assessment.   Much can be learned from a simple smoking history questionnaire (Appendix B). In addition to basic descriptive information, the smoker should also be asked about past attempts at quitting, resources that helped, factors that hindered, experience with other behavioral changes, and factors that may have led to relapse.

In addition to the collection of this information, the smoker can be introduced to behavioral self-monitoring, which requires the smoker to record the time, place, mood, need, and thoughts associated with each cigarette smoked (Appendix C). This is best accomplished by the smoker carrying around a sheet of paper wrapped around a cigarette pack, a "wrap sheet" the smoker is instructed to fill out before smoking each cigarette because delayed recall is very unreliable. After one week, it is possible to graph the pattern of cigarettes smoked during the course of one week. These records give the patient and provider an understanding of what behaviors, cognitions, and environmental factors are related to smoking. Following self-monitoring, the smoker is asked to identify any patterns observed; the clinician can then examine the sheets further with the smoker. Some people are uncomfortable keeping behavioral records and should not be pushed to do so. An attempt at a 24-hour recall of cigarettes smoked can be a reasonable replacement for this, or some individuals may just want to stop "cold turkey" at this point.

If a patient is seen only once for an initial evaluation before referral to a treatment group, then self-monitoring can be incorporated into the early group sessions. Otherwise, self-monitoring between the first and second individual session is an effective way to gather more information, engage the patient immediately in the treatment process, and assess level of motivation. Most patients will also find that monitoring in this way assists them in cutting back, particularly on cigarettes smoked automatically.

Assessment of attitudes and cognitions.   The individual's reasons for smoking can be assessed with the Why Do You Smoke? self-test, consisting of 18 questions that assess the aspects of the smoking habit that predominate for that person: stimulation, handling, accentuation of pleasure-relaxation, reduction of negative feelings, psychological addiction, and habit (Appendix D). These dimensions are similar to those provided by Tomkins (1966) and identified by a number of investigators in factor-analytic studies (Kozlowski 1979). Although not evaluating attitudes per se, this scale provides a convenient way to assess a patient's perception of his or her smoking, and the responses can be used quite effectively to introduce the need for a multicomponent approach to treatment. For example, suggestions for behavioral substitution can be tied specifically to those dimensions ranked highest.

More central to assessment of attitude is an evaluation of the patient's commitment to cessation and sense of self-efficacy in reaching a goal of abstinence. A 14-

item self-efficacy questionnaire developed by Yates and Thain (1985) and derived from research by Condiotte and Lichtenstein (1981) was able to predict with a high degree of accuracy who would relapse by six months (Appendix E). A cognitive approach to behavior change emphasizes two types of self-efficacy expectations that mediate the decision to change and the eventual behavior change (Bandura 1977). The first type is a response-outcome expectancy that a given course of action will lead to a particular outcome. For example, how firmly does the patient expect that stopping will improve health? These cognitions must be favorable if the decision to change is to occur. If they are not favorable, then intervention and education must begin at this level.

The second type of self-efficacy has to do with an individual's belief in his or her ability to make the desired change—an expectation of success. A positive belief that one has the necessary tools and resources to live comfortably and effectively without cigarettes leads to a greater commitment to change and to a persistence of efforts. Research in smoking cessation strongly supports the idea that expectation of success is an important factor in changing this behavior. For smokers with little expectation of their ability to quit due either to perceived or actual deficits in personal skills or environmental supports, treatment will begin with enhancing mastery expectations or skills. Once treatment is initiated, expectation enhancement can occur with the use of self-monitoring, successful performance accomplishments, cognitive restructuring, physiologic feedback, and mastery of physiologic or emotional arousal leads.

Emotional meaning of cigarettes.   In some cases, it may become apparent that strong symbolic issues arise in relation to smoking for certain patients. This should be pursued, particularly if there are many unsuccessful attempts at quitting; if the smoker has serious health problems related to smoking; if the cigarettes appear closely tied to self-image; or if a family member has had severe health problems as a smoker. The use of cigarettes probably always had some special meaning to the individual. This meaning need not always be explored in an initial evaluation. Even in a group setting, imagery work or hypnosis may facilitate the uncovering of this meaning in a powerful way. In other cases, the smoker may be aware of the connection but needs encouragement to explore it fully.

The clinician can also consider the impact of other issues in the smoker's life on the smoker's ability to stop smoking. In what way do other psychiatric issues appear to affect the ability to stop smoking? Are there any unusual life stressors occurring so that treatment for smoking might be more successful at another time? Stopping smoking during periods of moderate stress may help the patient realize that alternative coping strategies can be available and may protect against relapse at a future period of higher stress.

Social Assessment

Three aspects of social support are important: 1) the number of smokers among the patient's friends, family and co-workers; 2) the quality of support for cessation that can be expected by the smoker; and 3) the extent to which the smoker is able to be assertive in resisting social pressures to smoke. These can be assessed either in a questionnaire or in the assessment interview. The latter is preferable if time is available.

Assessment of Other Covariants of Smoking

Carbon monoxide, as mentioned above, varies directly with amount of tobacco smoked. Carbon monoxide analyzers are available as small hand-held devices designed to provide a means of sampling alveolar air to measure carbon monoxide levels in the breath in the range of 0 to 500 parts per million. The carbon monoxide test can provide a baseline for the patient prior to tapering or cessation and then can be used as feedback during the cessation process and help to provide positive reinforcement for meeting behavioral goals because it is a measure directly related to health benefits from smoking cessation or tapering.

Heart rate, although not as powerful a measure of physiologic impact of smoking as carbon monoxide, is much easier to monitor, is higher in smokers, and can be expected to decrease after cessation of smoking (US Department of Health and Human Services 1983). Within a multisession treatment program, changes in heart rate from baseline through follow-up can serve as a concrete reminder of the impact of decreased tobacco use at a physiologic level.

Intervention

A wide variety of interventions have been shown to be effective in helping people stop smoking, and many show long-term outcome at six or 12 months to be better than in an untreated comparison group. Investigations evaluating smoking cessation interventions have indicated that those treatments that incorporate behavioral and cognitive behavioral approaches have been the most effective (Lichtenstein 1982). Nicotine-containing chewing gum, a pharmacologic intervention for smoking cessation, has recently become available and has been successfully integrated with these cognitive-behavioral approaches. The methods and treatment program proposed here are based on a cognitive-behavioral model of smoking behavior with incorporation of the physiologic factors. Figure 1 relates selected treatment options back to assessment outcomes.

Smoking cessation has three stages, which various researchers have identified as: 1) contemplation and commitment to change; 2) an action phase for actual change; and 3) maintenance of change (Marlatt and Gordon 1985; Prochaska and DiClemente 1983). The second stage or period of initial change has tended to be the major focus of smoking treatment programs, although of late it has become increasingly evident that it is as important to understand the process of developing a commitment to change and how to prevent relapse once change occurs. Prevention of relapse has gained most of its attention in the alcoholism field. In a natural history study of almost 1,000 smokers, Prochaska and DiClemente found that most individuals cycle through these three stages several times before being abstinent for one year. The clinician may feel less frustrated in attempts to promote change by recognizing that many smokers quit several times before successful maintenance occurs. Strategies corresponding to the stages of change will be presented below, although these strategies and stages are in fact not clearly separated and blend into each other during treatment.

Stage I: Commitment to Change and Goal Setting

The ambivalent patient is the norm. The patient may be attempting to quit for the first time, or may have a history of numerous frustrating attempts and relapses. The patient may be expecting the clinician to perform some "magic" to remove all ambivalence. Without offering such a promise, the smoker needs to be helped to become aware of, understand, and accept these mixed feelings. Before entering this cycle, there is a "pre-contemplation" period in which the smoker is actively resistant to new input that encourages change. The need to work with patients who are actively resistant may increase as social and medical pressures to stop smoking increase, and smokers who are resistant to stopping feel coerced into doing so.

Four steps that utilize the information gathered during the assessment process are suggested to help the provider work with the smoker in the process of developing a commitment to change:

1. To examine the risks of smoking and benefits of quitting in relation to the patient's medical, psychological, and social status. Results from the physical examination can be used effectively here. Smokers who have already experienced the onset of disease have a greater likelihood of quitting (Pederson 1982). As noted in the discussion of assessment of motivation, a positive response-outcome efficacy is necessary before the patient will be willing to initiate change. If this is lacking, then it may be that the smoker has a distorted or erroneous view of the effects of smoking and of cessation on his or her health or may be denying the seriousness of the disease. A pamphlet or other written material about the relationship between smoking and disease can reinforce the verbal message to the patient. The National Cancer Institute (1984) pamphlet "Quit for Good" has a list of useful suggestions. The clinician may have to help the smoker explore other reasons for cessation that may be more important or personally relevant. For example, an individual may be more concerned about the effects of smoking on his or her children than the effects on his or her own health.

2. To review past efforts at behavior change and current smoking patterns. It should be made clear to the patient that the pattern of repeated attempts leading to eventual success at smoking cessation is a common one. Focusing on a past history of even short successes or of successful change in other behaviors can be used to help facilitate self-confidence. Relabeling of past cessation periods (no matter how short) as successes rather than failures is important.

3. To determine the patient's strengths and weaknesses that can help facilitate change or interfere with change. As previously noted, factors that contribute to successful smoking cessation are:

   • a belief in the efficacy of the change
   • a belief in one's ability to change
   • a strong sense of personal security
   • a low level of stress or life changes
   • good social support
   • low levels of negative affect (e.g., depression, anger, anxiety)

   The first two factors were noted to develop during the initial stages of intervention. If there are deficits in the other factors (e.g., a low sense of personal security, high levels of stress, poor social supports, or high levels of negative affect), interventions will be needed to decrease these deficits. Some of these changes may need to occur before an attempt at complete cessation is realistic.

4. To establish specific goals that are important to the patient and within the patient's current abilities. The three main alternatives for the patient are to make no immediate change in smoking, to reduce the amount smoked, or to quit. Some patients will need time to think over the information they have been given; others

prefer to taper, going through a gradual retraining process in order to believe they are capable of making the desired change; and others may be ready to set a quit date at this point.

The aforementioned series of steps can be generally accomplished during the first visit with a smoker who does not have other psychological or substance abuse problems.

Stage II: Initial Change

Once the patient has made the commitment to stop smoking, a number of treatment options are available in the physiologic, psychological, and social domains. These options may be more limited in any given setting, but the full range will be reviewed here. In addition to the treatment modalities, other structural considerations must be made. These include number of sessions, individual versus group treatment, setting the quit date, cost of treatment, use of a written contract, and plans for follow-up.

Each of the above domains and structural considerations will be discussed briefly here. Figure 2 presents an outline of an eight-week multimodal group treatment program incorporating a number of these treatment components. The group protocol suggested incorporates group support, nicotine fading, behavioral management techniques, physiologic feedback, contracting, relaxation training, and relapse prevention, with follow-up arranged on an individual basis. This program is illustrative rather than prescriptive, as many different types of treatment have been shown to be effective for both initial change and maintenance of change.

With few exceptions, adequate evidence does not exist to recommend which approaches might be more effective for given patients. One exception is the better response of more highly addicted patients to treatment directly addressing nicotine addiction (e.g., nicotine fading, use of nicotine gum). Adequate hypnotizability for hypnosis programs is another individual characteristic of significance.

Techniques to Decrease Physiologic Addiction

Nicotine fading

Nicotine fading (Foxx and Brown 1979) has two components: brand switching to a lower nicotine level cigarette, and gradual reduction of number of cigarettes (tapering). Despite laboratory evidence that smokers will compensate for decreased nicotine content by puffing more heavily or more often (Benowitz 1985), brand switching in the context of a treatment program can be effective if patients are instructed to guard against such behavioral compensation. Encouraging patients to switch to a less preferred brand also helps to weaken pleasant associations attached to smoking. Tapering the number of cigarettes before quitting not only reduces the probability of severe withdrawal, but allows more dependent smokers to learn how to suppress smoking urges as well as to develop other skills that are helpful in quitting. A nicotine fading or dosage-reduction program is also helpful for smokers who may have a difficult time with immediate cessation. A partial list of brands and their tar and nicotine contents is included in Appendix F. A complete list can be readily obtained from the Federal Trade Commission. Smokers should not plan to taper to nothing, but should plan to set a quit date after a level of five to 10 cigarettes/day has been

Figure 2. Smoking Cessation Group Treatment Protocol

Session		
1	A.	Introduction of staff and patients
	B.	General overview of program
	C.	Discuss reasons for quitting
	D.	Introduce self-monitoring and concepts of behavioral analysis
	E.	Introduce concept of nicotine fading
	F.	Distribute contract forms
	G.	Measure weight, carbon monoxide (CO) in expired air
2	A.	Collect contract forms and discuss
	B.	Review self-monitoring data and concept of high and low need cigarettes
	C.	Begin nicotine fading by assigning next lower cigarette
	D.	Introduce use of "substitutes" for low need cigarettes
	E.	Discuss personal meaning of smoking and common reasons for smoking (addiction, learning, psychodynamic, social)
	F.	Continue self-monitoring and set weekly goal
	G.	CO monitoring
3	A.	Review self-monitoring
	B.	Introduce and discuss managing environmental stimuli for smoking
	C.	Relaxation training: introduce use of diaphragmatic breathing
	D.	Set weekly goal for nicotine fading and elimination of lower need cigarettes
	E.	CO monitoring
4	A.	General problem solving from self-monitoring sheets
	B.	Relaxation training: add simple meditation component to diaphragmatic breathing
	C.	Discuss availability of social support in system
	D.	Quit date preparation
	E.	Set final goals for fading to minimum number of cigarettes and nicotine level by quit date
	F.	CO monitoring
5	A.	Quit date!
	B.	Discuss concerns over loss of cigarettes (loss of pleasure, anticipation of withdrawal symptoms)
	C.	Review progress and problems from self-monitoring records
	D.	Relaxation training: practice combined relaxation exercises
	E.	Begin relapse prevention: continue discussion of high- and low-risk situations, and monitoring of urges to smoke
	F.	CO monitoring, weight
6	A.	Review progress, problems, slips, withdrawal symptoms
	B.	What's worked; what hasn't
	C.	Introduce aversive imagery
	D.	Relaxation training: review relaxation exercises
	E.	Relapse prevention: coping rehearsal
	F.	CO monitoring
7	A.	Review progress, slips
	B.	Relapse prevention: undermining self-statements
	C.	Assertiveness training
	D.	Review relaxation training: breathing, meditation, and imagery
	E.	CO monitoring

(Skip one week before last session)

Figure 2. Smoking Cessation Group Treatment Protocol (continued)

Session		
8	A.	Review progress, slips
	B.	Relapse prevention: the Abstinence Violation Effect and dealing with unexpected stressors
	C.	Setting long-term maintenance goals
	D.	Relaxation exercise
	E.	CO monitoring, weight
9+		Individual follow-up schedule (to be arranged)

reached. As numbers of cigarettes smoked decrease, carbon monoxide levels in expired air can be measured to provide feedback on dosage reduction.

Nicotine substitutes

Over-the-counter (OTC) drugs purported to aid in smoking cessation have been available for some time, but have generally been found to be no more effective than placebo. In 1984 the Food and Drug Administration (FDA) approved the use of nicotine-containing chewing gum (Nicorette, Lakeside Pharmaceuticals) as a prescription treatment for tobacco dependency to be used in combination with behavioral treatment. Nicorette has been shown to be effective in aiding cessation (Schneider et al. 1983). Most patients using this gum are able to withdraw from it easily within six months, partly because the delivery of nicotine is slow and gradual, rather than the sharp spike of nicotine from cigarettes, which may account for much of their psychoactive appeal. This is the first time that the FDA has approved the use of a physiologically addictive drug for treatment of addiction to that same substance.

Some patients, however, reject the gum because of the purposefully unappealing flavor, dislike for chewing, lack of a nicotine "high," or concern for replacing one drug or addiction with another. The inadequate instruction offered by providers in the use of the gum in many instances also limits the efficacy of this approach. It is important to instruct patients on the need to stop smoking cigarettes completely before the gum is used and to provide the necessary instructions in its correct use. Patients are more likely to use too little gum for too short a time than to abuse it. The instructions can be found on the drug insert. There are also certain contraindications for using Nicorette:

- recent heart attack,
- increasing angina,
- severe arrhythmia,
- pregnancy,
- lactation, or
- severe jaw problems.

All of these conditions, except for the last, are sensitive to the ingestion of nicotine. Although the gum may be safer than continued use of cigarettes, such individuals should explore other means to stop smoking. Alpha adrenergic agonists (e.g., clonidine) have been found to decrease both nicotine withdrawal symptoms and craving (Glassman et al. 1984), but such use is still considered experimental. Jarvik and Henningfield (1988) wrote an excellent review of the theoretical and clinical issues in the pharmacologic treatment of tobacco dependence.

Psychological Dependency: Treatment Modalities

Cognitive-behavioral

Cognitive-behavioral treatment of smoking has been developed from treatment techniques used to intervene with a wide range of behavioral and addictive disorders. Rather than review these interventions extensively here, only illustrative examples are offered. The reader is directed to primary treatment texts such as Bandura (1969) and Goldfried and Davison (1976); the discussions of behavioral treatment of smoking in Marlatt and Gordon (1975) or Lichtenstein and Brown (1985); or to treatment manuals such as *Taking Charge of Your Smoking* (Nash 1981).

Behavior change strategies. Patients can be helped to develop specific strategies to employ to stop smoking. These strategies can be grouped under the following categories of behavioral methods:

- Avoidance of specific situations or events that bring on a desire or urge to smoke.
- Substitution of alternative behaviors incompatible with smoking cigarettes when urges arise (e.g., use of deep muscle or mental relaxation, exercise, low-calorie snacking).
- Cognitive restructuring to help reduce positive associations with cigarettes; to develop alternative thought responses to stressful situations; or to develop the belief that other methods can help reduce anxiety, depression, or other uncomfortable affects.
- Activating social support of friends, family, and/or co-workers.

These strategies can be introduced in conjunction with review of the patient's self-monitoring form (Appendix C), which provides a means to identify higher and lower need cigarettes. The patient then begins to use behavior change strategies to eliminate first low need cigarettes and then higher need cigarettes.

Rewards. Planning rewards throughout the change process will help sustain patient motivation over what may be a long road toward permanent cessation. Advise patients to plan periodic rewards not associated with smoking for successes in meeting goals for a week, a month, and so on (e.g., make a special purchase or a special phone call, treat yourself to an evening out, set time aside for a hobby). As a provider, you can reward signs of progress and reinforce the belief in the patient's ability to change.

Contracts. A behavioral contract can serve as an aid to the provider and patient in establishing realistic goals and steps by which to accomplish them. For a sample contract, see Appendix G. The contract should include specific information about whether the patient will taper or stop smoking, a quit date, reasons for stopping, steps to follow in response to situational factors that could interfere with efforts to stop smoking, and a plan for follow-up. Its purpose is to make explicit the specific ways in which the patient will attempt to change the smoking behavior. The methods listed should be as specific as possible. For example, the patient who chooses exercise as a substitution activity for smoking should identify the type of activity, when it will be done, where it will be done, how it will be done, and with whom. It is also advisable to have alternative strategies written down in case the first choice of coping methods cannot be accomplished (e.g., carrying sugarless candy in your pocket while at a business meeting where it would be inappropriate to start physical activity). The provider and patient can design an appropriate contract, either verbal or written. Written contracts seem to be more effective in sealing the commitment of both parties.

Another aspect of contracting is to set weekly goals for specific changes, an exercise that can be particularly valuable in a group setting. Members can gain feedback on whether their goals are appropriate and support for achieving them. Group members who are on the periphery may be encouraged to focus more attention on specific tasks.

Aversive techniques

The use of aversive stimuli to promote desired behavior change has a strong theoretical foundation in behavioral interventions (within both operant and classical conditioning models). These techniques have included electric shock, covert sensitization (aversive imagery), and aversive manipulation of smoke intake (rapid smoking, satiation smoking, and smoke holding). In addition, maintenance plans may include forfeiture of money (perhaps to a charity) if relapse occurs.

Most of these techniques appear to be relatively weak if utilized alone. Electric shock, in particular, appears to fail in generalizing to outside therapy (Pechacek 1979) and is not often used. Covert sensitization, the use of vivid imagery of unpleasant sensations (e.g., nausea) paired with the behavior of smoking, is one variation on imagery techniques. Use of cigarette smoke as the aversive stimulus is intuitively appealing. Aversion to the smoke itself characterizes many ex-smokers. Rapid smoking (inhaling every six seconds) and satiation (doubling or tripling daily consumption) may help a smoker weaken a positive attachment to cigarettes. Smoke holding (holding smoke in the mouth while continuing to breathe) is also promising because it contains aversive aspects without the medical risks of rapid smoking. It has been shown to be an effective adjunct in combination with other components (Lando and McGovern 1985).

Hypnosis

Broadly defined, there are two basic approaches to the use of hypnosis in the treatment of smoking. In the first, hypnosis is the focus of a single session treatment, instructions are often standardized, and the therapy may be offered in a group format (Barabasz et al. 1986). The best-known version of this approach, developed by Spiegel (1970), focuses on health-promoting suggestions ("For your body smoking is a poison . . . you need your body to live . . . you owe your body respect") and includes the use of self-hypnosis. With a well-motivated patient group, this approach has been shown to produce six-month abstinence rates in the range of 20 to 40 percent, with higher success rates associated with individualized induction, greater clinical experience, and greater patient hypnotizability (Barabasz et al. 1986; Holroyd 1980; Nuland and Field 1970; Spiegel 1970).

The second approach utilizes hypnosis to explore individual motives more fully and to overcome resistance and usually incorporates other adjunctive techniques as indicated. An excellent discussion of the use of hypnobehavioral and hypnoprojective techniques in treatment of smoking is found in Brown and Fromm (1987). When a multimodal approach is taken that may include multiple sessions, self-hypnosis, hypnoprojective techniques, and follow-up, six-month abstinence rates have been reported in the range of 50 to 68 percent (Holroyd 1980; Nuland and Field 1970).

Degree of hypnotizability, whether measured directly with the Stanford Hypnotic Clinical Scale (Morgan and Hilgard 1975) or indirectly with the Tellegan Absorption Scale (Tellegan and Atkinson 1974), helps to predict six-month abstinence from smoking after treatment with hypnosis (Barabasz et al. 1986).

Relaxation techniques

Relaxation training can be a valuable adjunct to smoking cessation treatment. One of the most common reasons given for relapse is inability to handle stressful situations (Shiffman 1982). Habitual smokers may report having few, if any, alternative ways to manage stress (other than avoidance of it).

Certain types of relaxation training (e.g., deep breathing, brief meditation, visualization exercises) can serve as effective functional equivalents to smoking. Once well learned, they can be used for a few moments at a time, under almost any circumstances, and may provide two of the benefits associated with smoking: a brief break from ongoing activity and a physiologically active relaxation effect. Training in diaphragmatic breathing, use of a personal positive relaxing image, or a simple focused mantra meditation technique can be done relatively quickly and then strengthened with home practice and a few minutes of use in treatment sessions.

An intervention related to both relaxation and hypnosis techniques, Restricted Environmental Stimulation Therapy (REST), has been shown to be a promising treatment for smoking, with high maintenance rates when used in combination with self-management techniques (Best and Suedfeld 1980). This use of REST in treatment of smoking involves sensory isolation for 24 hours, with the optional addition of taped messages. A more extensive review of the use of REST in behavioral medicine is found elsewhere (Suedfeld and Kristeller 1982).

Social Support and Number of Contacts

Patient contact should be of high frequency during the initial withdrawal period. The American Lung Association program uses one week of daily contact. Although this frequency of contact has been effective, it is usually not realistic for the patient or provider. For individual treatment, we have found weekly contact for approximately four weeks and then bi-weekly contact for another four weeks a reasonable frequency and one that provides the tapering of contact necessary for the patient to internalize control. This frequency allows the provider to give reinforcement directly and to alter the plan as needed. For the more dependent smoker or one who has other problems, a longer program may be indicated. A follow-up plan is important for helping the patient to maintain the changed behavior and allows the provider to detect the possibility of relapse. The group protocol outlined in Figure 2 has eight weekly sessions with a two-week interval before the final eighth session to wean the participants from dependence on the group. One or more follow-up sessions are scheduled individually. Most relapse occurs within three months, although it continues at a slower rate thereafter (Ockene 1983). The smoking relapse curve appears to be similar to that of other addictive disorders (Hunt et al. 1971).

In addition, regular phone contacts during the first three months of intervention might be arranged with the original therapist or other staff member. Patients can be instructed to call any time they encounter a problem in maintaining the smoking behavior change. Smokers can be helped and encouraged to build up social support systems of individuals in their natural environment. Some individuals have a difficult time asking others for help; the provider can facilitate the development of this ability. Significant others may also be invited to participate in the intervention sessions if this seems appropriate. A patient whose natural support system is weak and cannot be strengthened may need more frequent contacts.

It should be noted that if another member of the health care team is going to participate in follow-up, this information should be conveyed to the patient and spelled out in the contract.

Other Structural Considerations

Individual versus group treatment.   Group treatment is recommended for social support and sharing of strategies and problems by group members. Group programs usually are cognitive-behavioral in orientation (see Figure 2 for outline) and should incorporate tapering, nicotine fading, or use of nicotine gum for the more dependent smoker. The American Cancer Society and American Lung Association sponsor such treatment programs, and they are often offered through clinics or worksites. Hypnosis can also be effectively offered in a group format, either as a single session (Holroyd 1980) or as part of a multimodal treatment program (Brown and Fromm 1987).

Individual treatment is more appropriate when a provider has few smokers in his or her practice and for patients who have other problems that complicate treatment, or for those who refuse a group. Some techniques, such as acupuncture or hypnosis, are more commonly offered individually. All of the noted cognitive-behavioral techniques may be used either individually or in a group. Some clinicians who use the nicotine gum with selected patients have found it useful to insist that these patients attend a cognitive-behavioral group such as the one offered by the American Lung Association before prescribing the gum. Individualized sessions can then be devoted to specialized problems.

Setting the quit date.   In group treatment, all patients are advised to use the same quit date. In the eight-week program we outline here, the quit date is set as the fifth session, providing a tapering phase before and a relapse prevention phase following. Other group programs may set it earlier or later. In any case, the patient should prepare for the quit date, removing environmental signals to smoke (e.g., cigarettes or ashtrays), and take social pressures into mind (the initial three days of withdrawal are the most difficult). In individual treatment, more flexibility is possible. Some patients appear for a first session planning to quit at that point and should not be discouraged if the decision is judged appropriate. The first session must then include a brief review of withdrawal symptoms and an initial development of strategies to be used in lieu of smoking. Quitting immediately may need to be reconsidered, however, if an initial assessment indicates that the patient has an unrealistic view of what can be accomplished or appears to have few resources available. As mentioned above, other patients may hope to taper gradually to nothing, but such a plan is usually unrealistic and further exploration of feelings of loss related to "giving up" cigarettes may be necessary.

Stage III: Maintenance of Nonsmoking: Monitoring and Evaluating Patient Progress

A major difficulty in smoking cessation, as with other substance abuse behaviors, is maintenance of the changed behavior. As many as 70 percent of those who stop smoking relapse within a year. Changing smoking patterns takes time, and a focus on relapse prevention is necessary during the behavior change phase and the maintenance phase. Preparation for coping with withdrawal symptoms may begin with the initial interview and then become more focused and personalized after the actual quit date. The following strategies facilitating maintenance of nonsmoking behavior can be used in the last two sessions of a smoking intervention program as well as during follow-up.

Coping with Withdrawal Effects

Almost all smokers who use a "cold turkey" approach to quitting cigarettes will experience some withdrawal distress (Gunn 1986). Informing patients and preparing them to cope with some of the possible symptoms and side effects of cessation, as described in the DSM-III-R tobacco withdrawal syndrome, can add to the success of the smoking intervention. Additional symptoms may include excess sputum production as the bronchial tubes regain their ability to clean out the lungs; increase in appetite as the anorexic effect of nicotine wears off; and difficulty concentrating. These symptoms will go away with time and can be partly eased by exercise or relaxation or the use of nicotine-containing chewing gum.

Many smokers express concern about gaining weight when they stop smoking. Although the average weight gain of three to 11 pounds cannot be equated to the medical risk of smoking a pack of cigarettes a day, it is a factor that is important to many people and provides a common excuse for people to return to smoking. Several factors have been implicated, including changes in metabolism (cigarettes may raise metabolic rate) (Hofstetter et al. 1986) and decreased preference for sweets while smoking (Grunberg 1982). These biologic factors, in combination with the common use of food as a behavioral substitute, make it quite important to address weight management explicitly in most treatment programs. An excellent discussion of the relationship between smoking and weight reduction is found elsewhere (Wack and Rodin 1982).

Relapse Prevention

Relapse prevention as a treatment technique was originally developed by Marlatt and Gordon (1980) to deal with preventing the relapse of alcohol abuse and has been extrapolated to use with smokers (Lichtenstein and Brown 1985). It has been demonstrated that ex-smokers who learn relapse prevention skills maintain cessation longer and smoke fewer cigarettes if they relapse than their counterparts who do not receive such training (Davis and Glaros 1986). An excellent discussion of relapse prevention from a self-management approach is presented by Shiffman et al. (1985) in a text on relapse prevention edited by Marlatt and Gordon (1985). Four key elements summarized below can provide preparation for maintaining nonsmoking behavior.

1. Identifying high-risk situations

Identification of high-risk situations is the first step to relapse prevention. A high-risk situation is any situation in which a slip or lapse is very likely to occur. It is important for the patient to anticipate high-risk situations as it is difficult to deal with a potential slip at the last moment. Situations formerly associated with smoking can trigger urges to smoke and intense craving even though initial cessation and nicotine withdrawal have occurred. Research studies have revealed three types of situations in which ex-smokers are most likely to slip (Schiffman 1982): 1) situations involving negative emotional states (e.g., anger, frustration, stress); 2) situations involving positive emotional states (being relaxed, in a good mood) and often involving the consumption of alcohol; and 3) situations where others are observed to be smoking cigarettes.

Using this information as a guide, patients can be helped to try to predict specific situations that might cause difficulty and then anticipate various means to cope with them. The initial self-monitoring can be a guide to this process, and group support can be particularly valuable. An important reason to continue either group or individual sessions past the quit date and the nicotine withdrawal period is to allow time for such high-risk situations to occur.

2. Coping rehearsal

The outcome of exposure to a high-risk situation is determined by whether the ex-smoker produces a coping response (Shiffman et al. 1985). Once the patient has identified a situation in which the risk of resuming smoking is high, the patient can do the following to help prepare for the actual situation when it arises:

- Vividly imagining the high-risk situation. Patients are asked to imagine themselves in an identified high-risk situation: where, when, with whom? Visualization creates details of the people, the place, and what the patient is feeling, thinking, and doing in the situation.
- Developing and rehearsing specific coping strategies. Once the high-risk situation has been visualized in sufficient detail, the ex-smoker specifies what could be done to cope with events surrounding this high-risk scene, other than smoking. Such strategies might include excusing yourself briefly from a party to take a walk; carrying gum as substitute; calling a friend if feeling tense; or identifying yourself as a nonsmoker when offered a cigarette. The goal is to develop and mentally to rehearse specific strategies to prevent a slip, which could lead to a full-blown relapse.

3. Identifying and combating undermining self-statements

The cognitive aspects of relapse prevention are equally important. The smoker can think about self-statements as thoughts that can undermine the goal to remain an ex-smoker. Certain self-statements can be a setup for possible slips, which could lead to relapse if one is not prepared for them. Such thoughts, or rationalizations to resume smoking, often develop without really being aware of them, and the smoker needs to learn how to respond to them. Examples of resumptive thinking include:

- Nostalgia: "I remember how nice it was when . . . I smoked at parties."
- Testing oneself: "I'll bet I could smoke just one and then put it down!"
- Crisis: "I think I can handle this better with a cigarette."
- Self-doubts: "I'm one of those people who doesn't have any self-control."

Combating resumptive thinking.   There are various ways that the patient can respond to these thoughts about smoking. The following list of four methods provides convenient strategies.

- Challenging. This involves a direct mental confrontation with the logic of the thoughts. Training and rehearsal of positive responses can help the patient feel that there are choices available and that they need not inevitably lead back to smoking. Such responses would include: "Taking just one cigarette may be an excuse for returning to smoking. I do not need to test myself."

- Visualization of benefits of nonsmoking. It is useful at this point to remind the ex-smoker to think about emerging personal benefits. Thoughts about these benefits can help against rationalizations to resume smoking.
- Visualization of unpleasant smoking experiences. Another strategy is specific recollection of smoking's unpleasant aspects. For example, have the patient think back to how he or she felt the morning after smoking heavily.
- Distractions. Rather than confronting thoughts directly, the ex-smoker can simply divert attention from smoking to pleasant, enjoyable subjects (e.g., vacation spot, relaxation) that help the patient take his or her mind off smoking.

4. Avoiding the abstinence violation effect

If a slip or lapse occurs while a person is committed to abstinence, many people will have a highly emotional reaction known as the abstinence violation effect (AVE) (Marlatt and Gordon 1980), which includes guilt and feelings of low self-esteem or depression. The individual often feels weak and lacking in willpower, leading to such thoughts as "I blew it" and "I might as well keep on smoking." Patients need to be reminded to remember the following points:

- Just knowing about the AVE will help considerably. Help the patient realize that the AVE is a common reaction to a slip, and it is natural to feel guilty and lacking in willpower if one slips. The important point is that the feeling will pass. The challenge is to let the AVE reaction subside without smoking another cigarette to cope with the associated stress.
- A slip is different from a relapse. A slip is nothing more than an error or mistake—everyone makes mistakes—and smoking one cigarette need not imply personal weakness or lack of willpower. A relapse involves a complete resumption of smoking.
- You can learn from your slips. A slip can be a learning experience. Patients can retrace their steps to determine what might be done differently next time to avoid another slip.
- How the individual chooses to interpret the slip is critical. Emphasize that one slip does not make a smoker, unless the person chooses to make it so.

If relapse occurs

In the event of relapse, providers can emphasize the positive aspects of having stopped even briefly and be prepared to recommend another strategy to achieve cessation, rather than focusing on the image of failure. To decide on the future of the intervention process will call for a realistic appraisal of progress so far and willingness to rethink the cessation strategy, if necessary.

Summary of Treatment Recommendations

To stop smoking, a smoker must perceive this change as being beneficial; a smoking cessation program needs to be seen by the smoker as efficacious. The smoker must thus be helped to develop self-confidence and a belief that he or she can become a nonsmoker. The smoker must also learn new skills or enhance old skills that can be used in place of cigarettes to deal with problems as they arise. The individual needs also to be able to attribute changes in smoking behavior to personal abilities and skills rather than to will power or to the external aspects of treatment (Bandura 1977). Finally, the patient will benefit from relapse prevention training, including anticipation of the AVE, and ways to recognize and manage resumptive thinking. In referring back to Figure 1, it becomes clearer how assessment outcome may point the way toward different treatment choices, allowing the clinician to tailor a multicomponent treatment program to the needs of each patient.

Additional Treatment Issues

Smokeless Tobacco

The use of smokeless tobacco, particularly dipped snuff, has been increasing rapidly in the last few years, especially among adolescent boys. Tobacco companies, taking advantage of the lack of a ban on TV advertising for snuff (Blum 1983), often promote it by well-known athletes as a "safe" form of tobacco intake. Unfortunately, the potential for nicotine addiction is as serious as for cigarettes, leading to high usage and all the health risks associated with nicotine (e.g., heart disease, vascular damage, ulcers). In addition, users of smokeless tobacco are at high risk for cancers of the oral cavities. Leukoplakia in the mouth (10 percent of which become cancerous) develop rapidly; these are largely due to the presence of large amounts of nitrosamines in tobacco (Craddock 1983). One study found damage to oral tissue in 48 percent of users, who averaged less than two years of use (Fielding 1985). Treatment of the use of smokeless tobacco must therefore take the presence of nicotine addiction seriously. Given that the use of smokeless tobacco is increasing most among adolescent boys, addressing the social pressures for the habit is also important.

Other Substance Abusers

There is little information on the treatment of use of tobacco in conjunction with other drugs. What research exists has mostly been directed at the incidence of use (Burling and Ziff 1988) rather than issues of interaction of pharmacology, or the impact on other drug intake after the reduction or cessation of smoking, the primary clinical concern. Most of this research investigates the concurrence of alcohol intake and tobacco, with a limited set of studies also looking at marijuana. Because the presence of a second addiction in a patient requires much more complex treatment decisions, we will briefly summarize what is known and will then highlight possible treatment considerations, drawn both from the literature and from clinical experience.

Smoking and alcohol. A significant number of individuals who present for help with stopping smoking may also have problems with alcohol abuse. Tobacco use and alcohol abuse are moderately to strongly related (Istvan and Matarazzo 1984). Among identified alcoholics, the incidence of smoking has been more than 90 percent in all studies; alcoholics are also more likely to be heavy smokers. A study (Burling and Ziff 1988) comparing abusers of other drugs (heroin, amphetamine, and cocaine) to alcoholics found as high a prevalence of smoking (90 percent) among other abusers, but the alcoholics smoked significantly more cigarettes per day. Although there have been attempts to explore various hypotheses regarding this relationship, evidence is inconclusive. For example, the oral drive hypothesis would be supported by the finding that either smoking or alcohol consumption increases if the other decreases (a common concern raised by clinicians), but this pattern has not been found to exist (Maletsky and Klotter 1974; Mello et al. 1980). In a highly structured time analysis of five individuals, Mello et al. found that although smoking and alcohol intake did covary on an hourly basis, particularly among the heavier smokers, overall smoking did not increase with greater alcohol consumption.

The significance of this strong relationship between smoking and alcohol intake is clear. Most patients seen in an alcohol treatment program will be smokers, many of them at a level that is acutely health endangering. Furthermore, a higher proportion than expected of individuals seeking treatment for smoking will also have problems with alcohol intake. It should also not be assumed that heavy drinkers who smoke will not seek out treatment. Some may be referred by physicians because of heart or lung disease; others may be denying alcohol as a problem and feel more comfortable considering giving up smoking.

The common clinical lore makes several assumptions: 1) that smoking should not be treated in active alcoholics (Bobo and Gilchrist 1983); 2) that smoking is an "easier" addiction to treat; and 3) that alcoholics who wish to stop smoking are "denying" the more serious addiction, with the corollary that clinicians who respond to such a request are supporting the denial. A common rule-of-thumb has been to avoid addressing the smoking for six months to one year after drinking ends. The clinician needs to question these assumptions when faced with a smoker who also may have an alcoholism problem. One of the most obvious reasons to treat this smoker may be health. Someone who is drinking in excess may not yet have serious health problems related to alcohol abuse but may have cardiac or lung disease, for which smoking is a recognized risk factor. For example, many physicians will refuse cardiac bypass surgery to a smoker; although the physician may recognize that person's drinking is also undesirable, the immediate health concern is the smoking. Another reason to consider treating smoking in the alcoholic is more controversial. The patient may feel more prepared to stop smoking, a behavior less connected to social patterns and less psychologically addictive, than to stop drinking. In some cases it may be that a successful experience with overcoming the smoking habit may enable that patient to consider changing the drinking habit. Of note to the clinician who is treating smoking in an ex-drinker is the increasing availability of smoke-free Alcoholics Anonymous meetings in many communities. These are often based at medical hospitals.

Smoking and marijuana. The habitual use of marijuana in a smoking patient poses several problems to the practitioner: 1) marijuana has similar effects as cigarettes on lung function, and 2) regular (daily) use of marijuana raises the need to question the patient's psychological resources more closely. Mello et al. (1980) suggested that both drugs may be used in close temporal proximity, although increased marijuana use did not affect overall tobacco intake. Adolescents who begin marijuana use earlier or use it more heavily are also more likely to begin earlier use of tobacco, along with alcohol.

Marijuana carries with it some of the same health risks as tobacco: marked short-term effects on the cardiovascular system (increased heart rate, lowered oxygen delivery) even greater than from cigarettes, and significant respiratory and pulmonary effects. Cannabis deposits more tar than an equivalent amount of tobacco. Marijuana smoke, after even a few joints per day for six to eight weeks, has been demonstrated to produce notable worsening of pulmonary functioning. Marijuana smoke impairs the lung's defense mechanisms and produces changes that are precancerous. There has not been adequate time elapsed to evaluate the chronic impact of marijuana on lung function, but there is some suggestion that many users of marijuana will show serious pulmonary effects 15 years earlier than those seen in smokers (Peterson 1980).

The importance of assessing marijuana use for the clinician lies in conveying the message of health risks to the patient, particularly if the patient is presenting to stop smoking because of health-related concerns. It is also unlikely that a regular marijuana user will gain the immediate motivating benefits of easier breathing and reduction of bronchitis from tobacco cessation if they do not also change their marijuana intake. Other issues related to psychological functioning are similar to those raised by alcohol abuse or other indicators of maladaptive coping mechanisms.

Smoking and Psychiatric Disorders

As discussed above, the relaxing effects of cigarette smoking are well documented and appear to have both physiologic and psychological components. One of the most challenging patients who can present for treatment is the very heavy smoker (three or four packs/day) who is also suffering from an anxiety disorder, clinical depression, or psychosis. Several studies show a much higher incidence of smoking in psychiatric populations (Mathew et al. 1981; O'Farrell et al. 1983). Although there is some confirmation in the literature that heavier smokers tend to have somewhat more psychological distress (e.g., Billings and Moos 1983) or use maladaptive coping strategies (Revell et al. 1985), there has been little consideration of the role of very heavy smoking in the seriously troubled patient. Khantzian (1986) discussed the tendency of some patients to have addictions of choice in order to self-medicate selectively. As the psychoactive impact of nicotine is better understood, it may also become apparent that some psychiatric patients are actively self-medicating through their use of cigarettes (Hall 1980). There is also limited evidence that smoking may interact with commonly used psychoactive medication, including antipsychotics (Pantuck et al. 1982; Wright et al. 1983) and minor tranquilizers (Ochs and Otter 1981) and imipramine, primarily by increasing clearance rates, an effect that is more evident in young adults (Jusko 1981).

One of the most striking types of patients presenting with very high tobacco dependence is the person with panic attacks, post-traumatic stress syndrome, or generalized anxiety disorder. If smokers, such patients may describe intense feelings of dependence on smoking to manage feelings of panic and have little sense of being able to cope without them. If such patients need to stop smoking due to medical problems, they may require highly individualized treatment, long-term follow-up and support, and often a modified goal of reduction of intake.

Depressed patients present a somewhat different picture. For the very needy patient, cigarettes may represent a primary source of attachment. They will talk about cigarettes as a primary source of pleasure, may feel relatively unmotivated by health concerns, and be unable to gather sufficient resources to learn alternative coping strategies. The focus of intervention would then be to increase alternative sources of gratification and to use of social support as a motivating factor.

Treating smoking in hospitalized psychiatric patients presents unusual problems. First of all, they live in a subculture in which cigarettes may have unusual value because relatively few other privileges exist and because access to cigarettes may be a part of a token economy program in some settings (Gaston 1982). Nevertheless, in long-term settings, smoking may become an acute medical risk for patients who develop lung or heart disease; in other settings, it is questionable whether any medical team can condone the use of cigarettes.

There have been few investigations into cigarette use in an inpatient psychiatric setting. In the few studies that have been done, the prevalence of smoking among hospitalized psychiatric patients has ranged from 60 to 88 percent (O'Farrell et al. 1983). When smoking has been restricted (Dawley et al. 1980), it is usually to protect other inmates from the dangers of accidental fires rather than to protect the health of the smokers. The problem of smoking for ward management has been addressed at greater length by Gaston (1982) in a manner that appeared to also reduce the reliance on cigarettes. However, given that the hospital stay of chronic patients may be quite lengthy, management of physical health would also seem to fall under the responsibility of any chronic mental health facility.

It is also highly likely that chronic psychiatric patients who are between admissions are smokers (Dawley et al. 1980). These are often the patients who have highest contact with a mental health center, and the therapist may have an added responsibility to advise such individuals to stop smoking. Although physicians are taking more responsibility for advising their medical patients to stop smoking, they may avoid advising psychiatric patients to do so because of uncertainty in the face of their unusual behavior, or they may believe that the patient's therapist or counselor is the appropriate carrier of such a message.

In summary, the extensive research examining treatment options for smoking in the general population has yet to be extended to treatment of smoking in alcoholics, other drug users, or psychiatric populations, even though it is well documented that tobacco dependence has a very high incidence among them. We have speculated as to what some of the significant treatment issues may be. One of them will involve better understanding of drug interactions between nicotine and common psychoactive medications, and the likelihood that many of these patients are self-medicating through their use of cigarettes. While further clinical research is needed to treat smoking in these populations adequately, we recommend that when working with such individuals serious attention should be given to all of the costs and benefits of smoking cessation. We maintain that the benefits can often outweigh the costs.

Appendix A

Fagerstrom Nicotine Addiction Scale

1. How many cigarettes a day do you smoke?

   0–15   16–25   26 +

2. What is the nicotine yield per cigarette of your usual brand?

   0.3–0.8 g   0.9–1.5 g   1.6–2.2 g

   (Low to medium)   (Medium)   (Medium to high)

3. Do you inhale?

   Never   Sometimes   Always

4. Do you smoke more during the morning than during the rest of the day?

   No   Yes

5. How soon after you wake up do you smoke your first cigarette?
   More than 30 min   Less than 30 min

6. Of all the cigarettes you smoke during the day, which would you most hate to give up?

7. Do you find it difficult to refrain from smoking in places where it is forbidden (e.g., in church, at the library, in a no-smoking cinema)?
   No   Yes

8. Do you smoke even if you are so ill that you are in bed most of the day?
   No   Yes

Scoring: Add up the scores as follows:

1. 0–15, 0; 16–25, 1; 25+, 2
2. Low to medium, 0; Medium, 1; Medium to high, 2
3. Never, 0; sometimes, 1; always, 2
4. No, 0; Yes, 1
5. Less than 30 min, 1; more than 30 min, 0
6. Score one point if you answered: The first cigarette of the day; all others, 0
7. Yes, 1; no, 0
8. Yes, 1; no, 0

This questionnaire measures the degree of physical dependence on the nicotine in cigarettes: 0–3, light dependence; 4–7, medium dependence; 8–11, heavy dependence.

Appendix B

Smoking History Interview

Motivation

1. Would you like to stop smoking? _____

2. Why do you want to stop smoking now? _____

3. Do you have any current medical problems? _____

   If yes to 3: Do you feel these problems are in any way affected by your smoking? _____

Current Smoking Patterns

4. How many cigarettes a day do you smoke? _____

5a. Do you smoke a pipe or cigars? _____ How much? _____

  b. Do you use smokeless tobacco (snuff dipping, chewing tobacco)? _____
How much? _____

6. What brand do you smoke currently? _____

7. How long have you smoked that brand? _____

History and Quit Attempts

8a. What is the most you have smoked on a regular basis? _____

  b. When was that? _____

9. When did you start smoking? _____

10. Have you ever quit? _____

11. What is the longest time you have quit for? _____

12a. When was the last time you stopped smoking? _____

  b. What happened (e.g., request details as to why, under what circumstances, what coping techniques were successful) _____

  c. How long were you off cigarettes? _____

  d. What was the experience like for you? _____

13. Have you ever sought treatment or help for quitting smoking before? _____

Social Support

14a. Will people at work or home be supportive of your present efforts to quit? _____

  b. Who can you count on to be the most supportive? _____

Appendix C

Daily Smoking Record

No.	Time	Need*	Place or Activity	With Whom	Mood or Reason
1					
2					
3					

4					
5					
6					
7					
8					
9					
10					
11					
12					
13					
14					
15					
16					
17					
18					
19					
20					

*Need: How important that particular cigarette is to you at that time

   1 = Extremely important (can't function without it)
   2 = Important (would be difficult to do without it)
   3 = Uncertain about importance (not sure if it is necessary)
   4 = Not important (could do without it)
   5 = Least important (not really aware I wanted it or I know I could do
       without it)

Appendix D

Why Do You Smoke?

Here are some statements made by people to describe what they get out of smoking cigarettes.

How often do you feel this way when smoking? For each statement circle one number that applies best.

Important: ANSWER EVERY QUESTION.

5 = always, 4 = frequently, 3 = occasionally, 2 = seldom, 1 = never

A.	I smoke cigarettes in order to keep myself from slowing down.	5	4	3	2	1
B.	Handling a cigarette is part of the enjoyment of smoking it.	5	4	3	2	1
C.	Smoking cigarettes is pleasant and relaxing.	5	4	3	2	1
D.	I light up a cigarette when I feel angry about something.	5	4	3	2	1
E.	When I have run out of cigarettes I find it almost unbearable until I can get them.	5	4	3	2	1
F.	I smoke cigarettes automatically without even being aware of it.	5	4	3	2	1
G.	I smoke cigarettes to stimulate me, to perk myself up.	5	4	3	2	1
H.	Part of the enjoyment of smoking a cigarette comes from the steps I take to light up.	5	4	3	2	1
I.	I find cigarettes pleasurable.	5	4	3	2	1
J.	When I feel uncomfortable or upset about something, I light up a cigarette.	5	4	3	2	1
K.	I am very much aware of the fact when I am not smoking a cigarette.	5	4	3	2	1
L.	I light up a cigarette without realizing I still have one burning in the ashtray.	5	4	3	2	1
M.	I smoke cigarettes to give me a 'lift.'	5	4	3	2	1
N.	When I smoke a cigarette, part of the enjoyment is watching the smoke as I exhale it.	5	4	3	2	1
O.	I want a cigarette most when I am comfortable and relaxed.	5	4	3	2	1
P.	When I feel 'blue' or want to take my mind off cares and worries, I smoke cigarettes.	5	4	3	2	1
Q.	I get a real gnawing hunger for a cigarette when I haven't smoked for a while.	5	4	3	2	1
R.	I've found a cigarette in my mouth and didn't remember putting it there.	5	4	3	2	1

Scoring

1. Enter the number you have circled for each question in the spaces below, putting the number you have circled to question A over line A, to question B over line B, etc.

2. Add the 3 scores on each line to get your totals. For example, the sum of your scores over lines A, G, and M gives your score on Stimulation; lines B, H, and N give the score on Handling.

Totals

A _____ + G _____ + M _____ = _____ Stimulation

B _____ + H _____ + N _____ = _____ Handling

C _____ + I _____ + O _____ = _____ Pleasurable Relaxation

D _____ + J _____ + P _____ = _____ Crutch: Tension Reduction

E _____ + K _____ + Q _____ = _____ Craving: Psychological Addiction

F _____ + L _____ + R _____ = _____ Habit

Scores can vary from 3 to 15. Any score 11 and above is high; any score 7 and below is low.

Appendix E

Self-Efficacy Questionnaire

Instructions: Please rate each of the following items on the scale on the right to indicate how sure you are that you would be able to resist smoking in that situation.

Item	Completely Unsure						Completely Sure
1. When you feel impatient	1	2	3	4	5	6	7
2. When you are waiting for someone or something	1	2	3	4	5	6	7
3. When you feel frustrated	1	2	3	4	5	6	7
4. When you are worried	1	2	3	4	5	6	7
5. When you want something in your mouth	1	2	3	4	5	6	7
6. When you want to cheer up	1	2	3	4	5	6	7
7. When you want to keep yourself busy	1	2	3	4	5	6	7
8. When you are trying to pass time	1	2	3	4	5	6	7
9. When someone offers you a cigarette	1	2	3	4	5	6	7
10. When you are drinking an alcoholic beverage	1	2	3	4	5	6	7
11. When you feel uncomfortable	1	2	3	4	5	6	7
12. When you feel embarrassed	1	2	3	4	5	6	7

13. When you are in a situation in which   1   2   3   4   5   6   7
you feel smoking is a part of your self-
image

14. When you want to feel more mature   1   2   3   4   5   6   7
and sophisticated

Scoring: Add up all points. Maximum score = 98. Minimum score = 14.

Appendix F

Examples of Tar and Nicotine Content of 28 Selected Cigarettes[1]
(In Increasing Order of Nicotine Value)

Brand	Type	Tar (mg/cig)	Nicotine (mg/cig)
Carlton	King size, filter (hard pack)	<0.5	<.05
Now	King size, filter (hard pack)	1	0.1
Benson & Hedges	Reg. size, filter (hard pack)	1	0.1
Now 100	100 MM, filter, menthol (hard pack)	2	0.2
Kent III	King size, filter	3	0.3
Triumph	King size, filter, menthol	3	0.3
True	King size, filter	5	0.4
Doral II	King size, filter, menthol	4	0.4
Merit	King size, filter, menthol	8	0.5
Parlament Lights	King size, filter	9	0.6
Pall Mall Extra Lights	King size, filter	7	0.6
Camel Lights	King size, filter	8	0.7
L & M Lights	King size, filter	8	0.7
Marlboro Lights	King size, filter	10	0.7
Vantage	King size, filter	10	0.7
Raleigh Lights	King size, filter	10	0.8
Viceroy Rich Lights 100	100 MM, filter	11	0.8
Old Gold Lights	King size, filter	9	0.8
Lark Lights	King size, filter	13	0.9
L & M	King size, filter (hard pack)	13	0.9
Tareyton	King size, filter	13	0.9
Lark	King size, filter	14	0.9
Pall Mall	King size, filter	17	1.1
Winston	King size, filter (hard pack)	16	1.1
Camel	King size, filter	16	1.1

[1]A complete list of 207 cigarettes is available from the Federal Trade Commission, Washington, DC 20580. Ask for FTC Report of "Tar, Nicotine, and Carbon Monoxide of the Smoke of 207 Varieties of Domestic Cigarettes," January 1985. Note: The formulation of some cigarettes listed here may have changed since the report was issued.

Old Gold Filters .... King size, filter	17	1.3
Pall Mall .... King size, nonfilter	23	1.3
Chesterfield............... King size, nonfilter	22	1.5

Appendix G

Smoking Contract

Name: _____ Date of Evaluation: _____

Number of cigarettes now smoking: _____

My reasons for stopping are: 1. _____

2. _____ 4. _____

3. _____ 5. _____

After discussion with _____ (clinician),

I plan to engage in the following treatment program: _____

_____

After careful consideration, I have decided to:

☐ TAPER, by _____ cigarettes per _____ until I reach _____ cigarettes

   AND/OR

☐ STOP, on _____, my quit date.

Steps I will take on my own to achieve stopping are:

1. _____

2. _____

3. _____

4. _____

_____	_____	_____
Signature of Patient	Signature of Therapist/Physician	Date

I agree to the following follow-up plan: _____

_____

_____	_____	_____
Signature of Patient	Signature of Therapist/Physician	Date

Chapter 133

Barbiturate, Sedative, Hypnotic Agents

The sedative-hypnotic group of psychoactive medications is the most widely prescribed psychoactive drugs in the United States, and indeed the world. This is not surprising given the enormous range of treatment indications for these drugs. The sedative-hypnotic group is one of the major divisions of psychoactive drugs, including the benzodiazepines and barbiturates. These drugs represent major tools for the medical management of anxiety, alcohol withdrawal, anesthesia, amnesia, insomnia, convulsions, status epilepticus, epilepsy, spasm, and other medical and psychiatric problems. However, the sedative-hypnotics, like all psychoactive drugs, can play a role as an agent of addictive disease and other psychoactive substance use and dependence disorders, sedative-hypnotic intoxication, withdrawal, withdrawal delirium, amnestic disorders, overdose, dependence, low-dose dependence, abuse, and drug switching.

The DSM-III-R (American Psychiatric Association 1987) describes six separate types of substance use problems related to the use of sedative-hypnotics:

1. Sedative, hypnotic, or anxiolytic intoxication (305.40);
2. Uncomplicated sedative, hypnotic, or anxiolytic withdrawal (292.00);
3. Sedative, hypnotic, or anxiolytic withdrawal delirium (292.00);
4. Sedative, hypnotic, or anxiolytic amnestic disorder (292.83);
5. Sedative, hypnotic, or anxiolytic dependence (304.10);
6. Sedative, hypnotic, or anxiolytic abuse (305.40).

In this chapter we will describe these and other problems related to the sedative-hypnotics.

Intoxication

Intoxication with the barbiturates, the benzodiazepines, and other sedative-hypnotics is qualitatively similar to intoxication with alcohol, which is best described as a sedative-hypnotic itself. Sedative-hypnotic intoxication may vary from time to time, even within the same individual. The desired effect is generally one of "disinhibition euphoria," a state in which mood is elevated; self-criticism, anxiety, and guilt is reduced; and energy and self-confidence increased. While euphoria may occur with sedative-hypnotics, the mood may be quite labile. The individual may experience sadness, rapidly fluctuating mood shifts, irritability and hypochondriacal concerns, increased anxiety, and agitation. The euphoria of the shorter-acting barbiturates and some of the benzodiazepines makes them particularly appealing as intoxicants. The state of disinhibited euphoria is not necessarily synonymous with intoxication.

Individuals intoxicated with sedative-hypnotics commonly show unsteady gait, slurred speech, incoordination, sustained vertical and horizontal nystagmus, and possible memory or attention impairment. The subjective state frequently is reported to be unpleasant or dysphoric. The perception of a drug effect as pleasurable is in part a learned response and in part the pharmacology of the drug, but always influenced greatly by expectation and environmental stimuli. In most cases, disinhibition occurs at dosages above those commonly prescribed.

Regardless of the mood effects, intoxication produces a reduction in the ability to make accurate judgments and markedly impairs motor coordination. Barbiturates and benzodiazepines are generally well absorbed from the stomach, but short-acting ones are absorbed more quickly than the longer-acting ones. Alcohol enhances absorption and produces an added sedative-hypnotic effect.

Drug combination involving the sedative-hypnotics may include alcohol and an alcohol, sedative-hypnotic, and stimulant combination. A current drug combination involves cocaine (perhaps the freebase or "crack" cocaine) and benzodiazepines. The central nervous system (CNS) depressant effects of the sedative-hypnotic depress the self-described negative stimulant effects that accompany stimulant euphoria. This CNS depressant-stimulant combination often leads to an "upper-downer" syndrome, which invariably results in an increased amount of each drug being used, often to lethal levels (Smith 1986). Also, as different drugs metabolize at different rates, the accompanying mood and behavior may change as well. For instance, a person ingesting a long-acting benzodiazepine to counteract the stimulant side effects of cocaine (e.g., anxiety, panic) may become intoxicated as the effects of the shorter-acting cocaine diminish, perhaps while driving home after a party.

Another drug combination of some worry is the combined use of benzodiazepines and opiates. Woody et al. (1975) described a phenomenon where addicts maintained on methadone ingest 40 to 80 mg of diazepam shortly before or immediately after taking their daily methadone dose, accentuating the normal mild sedative-hypnotic effect of the methadone dose.

The DSM-III-R criteria for sedative, hypnotic, or anxiolytic intoxication (305.40) are:

A. Recent use of a sedative, hypnotic, or anxiolytic.
B. Maladaptive behavioral changes (e.g., disinhibition of sexual or aggressive impulses, mood lability, impaired judgment, impaired social or occupational functioning).
C. At least one of the following signs:
   (1) slurred speech
   (2) incoordination
   (3) unsteady gait
   (4) impairment in attention or memory
D. Not due to any physical or other mental disorder.

Withdrawal

The reversal of cellular adaptation to sedative-hypnotics involves withdrawal symptoms that can be uncomfortable and even dangerous to the patient. The detoxification process is designed to accomplish this task both safely as well as in a manner that is tolerable to the patient. However, it is unreasonable to expect symptom-free withdrawal. Both the physician and the patient (as well as significant others) should be educated and prepared for these symptoms and, it is hoped, avoid overreaction to symptom development. The two principles that assist in this process are avoiding the abrupt discontinuance of sedative-hypnotics and substituting longer-acting sedative-hypnotics for rapidly metabolized or excreted ones (Wesson and Smith 1982).

The sedative withdrawal syndrome can be conceptualized as a spectrum of signs and symptoms occurring after stopping the sedative. Symptoms do not follow a specific sequence, but can include anxiety, tremors, nightmares, insomnia, loss of appetite, nausea, vomiting, postural hypotension, seizures, delirium, and hyperpyrexia. The syndrome is similar for all sedative-hypnotics; however, the time course depends on the particular drug involved. With pentobarbital, secobarbital, meprobamate, and methaqualone, withdrawal symptoms may begin 12 to 24 hours after the last dose, and peak in intensity between 24 to 72 hours. The withdrawal reactions to phenobarbital, diazepam, and chlordiazepoxide develop more slowly and peak on the fifth to eighth day.

There are two major methods of detoxifying the sedative-hypnotic patient: 1) gradual withdrawal of the addicting agent on a short-acting barbiturate (Isbell et al. 1950), and 2) the substitution of long-acting phenobarbital for the addicting agent and gradual withdrawal of the substitute drug (Smith and Wesson 1971, 1983; Smith et al. 1978). Either method uses the principle of stepwise withdrawal. Abruptly discontinuing sedative-hypnotics in an individual who is physically dependent on them is poor medical practice and has resulted in death (Fraser et al. 1952), as well as malpractice suits (American Medical Association 1971). Although Isbell et al. recommended that sufficient amounts of barbiturates be used during withdrawal to produce mild toxicity, we do not believe that production of toxicity is necessary to prevent emergence of severe withdrawal signs.

The pharmacologic rationale for phenobarbital substitution technique is similar to the rationale for substituting methadone for heroin during withdrawal. The longer-acting drug permits a withdrawal characterized by fewer fluctuations in blood levels of the drug throughout the day and thus enables the safe use of smaller doses. The safety factor for phenobarbital is greater than that for shorter-acting barbiturates; lethal doses of phenobarbital are several times greater than toxic doses, and the signs of toxicity (e.g., sustained nystagmus, slurred speech, ataxia) are easy to observe. Finally, because phenobarbital intoxication usually does not produce disinhibition euphoria, the behavioral problems commonly associated with shorter-acting barbiturates seldom occur.

A phenobarbital substitution technique (Smith and Wesson 1970) is preferred for withdrawal from any of the benzodiazepines for two reasons. First, none of the patients have had a withdrawal seizure when phenobarbital was used for withdrawal, whereas two patients being withdrawn using gradual reduction of the benzodiazepine have had withdrawal seizures. Second, in the treatment of drug dependence, it is best not to administer the drug of dependence to the patient during treatment.

An estimate of the patient's daily benzodiazepine use during the month before treatment is used to compute the detoxification starting dose of phenobarbital. The benzodiazepine is converted to phenobarbital withdrawal equivalence by using Table 1. The computed phenobarbital equivalence is given daily, divided into three or four doses. If other sedative-hypnotics (including alcohol) are used, the phenobarbital conversion for the other sedative-hypnotic is added to the amount computed for the benzodiazepine. However, regardless of the total computed conversion, the maximum

Table 1. Phenobarbital Withdrawal Conversion for Benzodiazepines and Other Sedative-Hypnotics

Generic Name	Dose (mg)	Phenobarbital Withdrawal Conversion (mg)*
Benzodiazepines		
alprazolam	1	30
chlordiazepoxide	25	30
clonazepam	2	15
clorazepate	15	30
diazepam	10	30
flurazepam	15	30
halazepam	40	30
lorazepam	1	15
oxazepam	10	30
prazepam	10	30
temazepam	15	30
Barbiturates		
amobarbital	100	30
butabarbital	100	30
butalbital	50	15
pentobarbital	100	50
secobarbital	100	30
Glycerols		
meprobamate	400	30
Piperidinediones		
glutethimide	250	30
Quinazolones		
methaqualone	300	30

*Withdrawal doses of phenobarbital are sufficient to suppress most withdrawal symptoms, but are not the same as therapeutic dose equivalency.

phenobarbital dose is 500 mg/day. After two days of stabilization on phenobarbital, the patient's daily phenobarbital dose is then decreased 30 mg each day.

Before each dose of phenobarbital, the patient is checked for the presence of sustained horizontal nystagmus, slurred speech, and ataxia. If sustained nystagmus is present, the scheduled dose of phenobarbital is withheld. If all three signs are present, the next two doses of phenobarbital are withheld, and the total daily dose of phenobarbital for the following day is cut in half.

Figure 1 shows the sequence of pharmacologic treatment when both a sedative-hypnotic and low-dose syndrome are expected. Table 2 gives a comparison of the different withdrawal syndromes.

The physiologic signs we attribute to low-dose benzodiazepine withdrawal (e.g., dilated pupils, increased pulse rate, increased blood pressure) are the same as those observed in human subjects when beta-carboline-03-carboxylic acid is injected. Since these symptoms of beta-carboline are blocked by the benzodiazepine antagonist Ro 15-1788, it may be that the antagonist would be the treatment of choice for low-dose withdrawal—perhaps more specific than propranolol. Antagonists have two different roles, depending on the state of the receptor site when given. If given while ben-

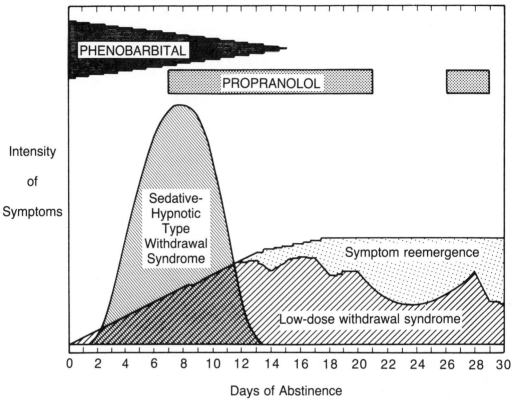

Figure 1. Treatment of Benzodiazepine Withdrawal Syndromes.

zodiazepines (agonists) were still on the receptor sites, the result would be to precipitate withdrawal. If given after the receptor sites were clear (but perhaps hypersensitive to effects of endogenous agonists), the antagonist, by binding to the receptor site, may decrease sensitivity. Further research in the area of benzodiazepine receptor-antagonist interaction is urgently needed and until then the above needs to be considered experimental.

In assessing the length of the withdrawal regimen, one must take into consideration patient variables such as concomitant chronic somatic or psychiatric disorders, evidence of addictive disease, presence of severe stress, family and social support, finances, and history of seizures. Patients who have no somatic or psychiatric disorders, no history of addictive disease, little stress, good family and social support, no history of seizures, and an absence of financial difficulties can be withdrawn somewhat more rapidly (i.e., 3 weeks), unless the dosage was substantially more than the therapeutic range or if the exposure can be measured in years.

However, some (perhaps many) patients may indeed have a chronic somatic or psychiatric disorder, high levels of dysfunctional stress, a poor family and social support system, previous documented failures at chemical dependency treatment for sedative-hypnotic or other drug dependence, a family or personal history of addictive disease, or previous history of seizure. Such a patient should be treated as per the protocol on low-dose sedative-hypnotic dependency syndromes. In general, the more complicating factors, the slower the withdrawal and the greater the need for adjunctive support.

Table 2. Comparison of Syndromes Related to Benzodiazepine Withdrawal

	Sedative-Hypnotic Type Withdrawal	Low-Dose Benzodiazepine	Symptom Reemergence
Symptoms	anxiety insomnia nightmares seizures psychosis hyperpyrexia death	anxiety, including somatic manifestations insomnia muscle spasms psychosis	Variable, but should be the same as symptoms present prior to taking benzodiazepines.
Time Course	Begins one to two days after stopping short-acting benzodiazepines and two to four days after stopping long-acting benzo-diazepines.	Begins one day after stopping. Symptoms may continue weeks to months but improve with time.	Emerge when benzodiazepine is stopped. Continue unabated with time.
Response to Reinstitution of Benzodiazepine	Reversal of symp-toms two to six hours after rein-stituting hypnotic-level doses.	Reversal within 45 to 90 minutes of low dose of benzodiazepine.	Responsive in 45 to 90 minutes to usual therapeutic doses of benzodiazepine.

Note: Reprinted with permission from Smith and Wesson (1983).

During the detoxification process, the patient should be introduced to therapeutic adjuncts to recovery. The term *recovery* in the chemical dependency field refers to the process of psychosocial, familial, spiritual, and sexual restructuring, which is conceptualized as a lifelong event. The patient should be exposed to supportive (i.e., not psychodynamic) therapy and counseling, especially during the worst periods of the withdrawal symptoms and during early recovery. The use of Pills Anonymous, Narcotics Anonymous, and, for the polydrug dependent person, Alcoholics Anonymous and Cocaine Anonymous are of particular value and should be strongly encouraged. These so-called Twelve Step groups provide the specific kind of group support for the establishment and maintenance of sobriety that an individual physician or psychiatrist cannot provide. This is especially true relative to the patients reintegrating back into their society and probably coming into contact with their primary and secondary drugs of abuse. Alternatives to the self-medication of anxiety should be encouraged, including various stress reduction techniques, biofeedback, acupuncture, regular aerobic exercise, hypnosis, and other forms of relaxation and even recreation.

The DSM-III-R describes two types of withdrawal reaction. The criteria for uncomplicated sedative, hypnotic, or anxiolytic withdrawal (292.00) are:

A. Cessation of prolonged (several weeks or more) moderate or heavy use of a sedative, hypnotic, or anxiolytic, or reduction in the amount of substance used, followed by at least three of the following:
(1) nausea or vomiting
(2) malaise or weakness
(3) autonomic hyperactivity (e.g., tachycardia, sweating)
(4) anxiety or irritability
(5) orthostatic hypotension

   (6) coarse tremor of hands, tongue, and eyelids
   (7) marked insomnia
   (8) grand mal seizures
B. Not due to any physical or other mental disorder, such as sedative, hypnotic, or anxiolytic withdrawal delirium.

Withdrawal Delirium

During the first one to five days of untreated sedative-hypnotic withdrawal, the electroencephalogram (EEG) may show a paroxysmal burst of high-voltage, slow-frequency activity, which precedes the development of seizures. The withdrawal delirium may include disorientation to time, place, and situation, as well as visual and auditory hallucinations. The delirium generally follows a period of insomnia. Some individuals may have only delirium, others only seizures, and some may have both delirium and convulsion.

   In using the phenobarbital substitution and withdrawal technique, if the patient is in acute withdrawal and in danger of having seizures, one may administer the initial dose of phenobarbital by injection. We recommend 200 mg im for stabilization. If nystagmus and other signs of intoxication develop following the im dosage, it is doubtful that the individual is barbiturate dependent. Based on the phenobarbital dosage calculated using the withdrawal equivalence, the patient is maintained on the oral dose schedule for two days and then withdrawn with a graded reduction not to exceed 30 mg/day. Regardless of the calculated dosage, doses of phenobarbital should not exceed 500 mg/day.

   The DMS-III-R criteria for sedative, hypnotic, or anxiolytic withdrawal delirium (292.00) are:

A. Delirium developing after the cessation of heavy use of a sedative, hypnotic, or anxiolytic, or a reduction in the amount of substance used (usually within one week).
B. Autonomic hyperactivity (e.g., tachycardia, sweating).
C. Not due to any physical or other mental disorder.

Amnestic Disorder

The essential feature of an amnestic disorder caused by prolonged and heavy use of a barbiturate or similarly acting sedative or hypnotic is an amnestic syndrome. This is characterized by impairment of short-term and long-term memory occurring during normal states of consciousness. The impairment includes inability to learn new information (short-term) and inability to remember information that was known in the past (long-term). The age at onset is earlier than that of alcohol amnestic disorder, usually in the 20s, and full recovery may occur with abstinence.

   The DSM-III-R criteria for sedative, hypnotic, or anxiolytic amnestic disorder (292.83) are:

A. Amnestic syndrome following prolonged heavy use of a sedative, hypnotic, or anxiolytic.
B. Not due to any physical or other mental disorder.

Overdose

Patients who have overdosed on barbiturates or other sedative-hypnotics arrive at emergency units with a variety of signs and symptoms that must be interpreted quickly and accurately. A sedative-hypnotic overdose is a life-threatening emergency that cannot be treated definitively by nonmedical personnel.

Signs and symptoms of sedative-hypnotic overdose are on the same spectrum with those of intoxication. They include slurred speech, staggering gait, sustained vertical or horizontal nystagmus, slowed reactions, lethargy, progressive respiratory depression characterized by shallow and irregular breathing leading to coma, and, in sufficient dosage, death. Figure 2 outlines the ways in which an acute sedative-hypnotic overdose can be treated in an emergency.

Most patients who require treatment for sedative-hypnotic overdose are acutely intoxicated or in a coma following the ingestion of a single large dose. They are usually not physically dependent. Unless the drug has been used daily for more than a month in an amount equivalent to 400 to 600 mg of short-acting barbiturates, a severe withdrawal syndrome should not develop (Seymour et al. 1982).

Dependence

The recent changes in DSM-III-R represent a major shift away from forming a substance use diagnosis on the basis of physical tolerance and physical dependence. DSM-III-R uses the word *dependence* more in line with the concept of chemical dependence or more precisely, chemical dependency. The phrase *chemical dependency* in turn denotes the process of chemical addiction and not simply the development of physical tolerance and dependency. In 1987, the American Medical Association passed a resolution stating that all chemical dependencies were disease, much as alcoholism has been conceptualized as a disease since 1956.

In general, addiction or chemical dependency can be described as a disease that is progressive and potentially life-threatening and that has the characteristic symptoms of 1) compulsion, 2) loss of control over the drug, and 3) continued use despite adverse consequences (Smith et al. 1985). Drug abuse on the other hand is often referred to as the use of any psychoactive drug that impairs a person's ability to function adequately, whether in the psychiatric, psychological, social, financial, medical, or even spiritual context.

Although the sedative-hypnotics provide very useful clinical assistance, they can also be agents of psychoactive substance abuse disorders. In some cases, the sedative-hypnotic use is frankly illicit, such as the nonprescription use of a barbiturate, but in many cases a psychoactive substance use disorder is the product of a legitimate physician-patient relationship. Relative to the latter, there are situations where a person experiences iatrogenic dependency problems because of improper prescribing practices and sometimes as the result of a coexisting psychiatric or other drug problem. The national trend in drug abuse is very clearly in the direction of polysubstance abuse and polysubstance addiction (i.e., people who use one psychoactive drug tend to use another), or perhaps a combination of other psychoactive drugs. Often the use of psychoactive drugs occurs in certain patterns, such as the "upper-downer" syndrome, where CNS stimulant use is followed by CNS depressant use. The most obvious example of the upper-downer syndrome would be a cocaine-alcohol combination, where the alcohol was used as a drug to reduce or eliminate the noxious

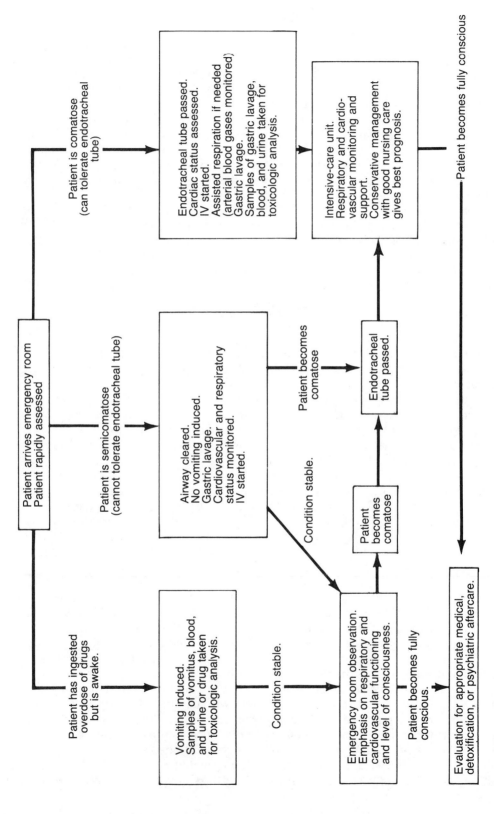

Figure 2. Barbiturate and Other Sedative-Hypnotic Overdose Acute Treatment Diagram (Smith et al. 1979).

Table 3.   Benzodiazepine Duration of Action

Long-Acting: more than 40 hours
   Chlorazepate
   Flurazepam
   Alazepam
   Prazepam
	Short-Acting: six to 20 hours
	   Alprazolam
	   Lorazepam
	   Oxazepam
	   Temazepam

Intermediate-Acting: 20 or more hours
   Diazepam
   Clorazepam
   Chlordiazepoxide
   Triazolam
	Ultra Short-Acting: Less than six hours
	   Triazolam

stimulant properties of cocaine, especially if the cocaine is used in high doses or with a rapid delivery system such as smoking. For many people, the choice of drugs is a culturally influenced decision. A person working in an office or similar setting may find the use of alcohol impossible because of its easy detectability on the breath. However, this person might turn to the use of a barbiturate or a benzodiazepine to self-medicate the dysphoric stimulant effects of cocaine, thus participating in a benzodiazepine-cocaine pattern.

The sedative-hypnotics can be described by way of many of their properties, including the duration of action (Tables 3 and 4) (e.g., long, intermediate, short, or ultra-short). The long-acting barbiturates are often used in the medical management of epilepsy, as a daytime sedative, or in the treatment of sedative-hypnotic withdrawal. The intermediate-acting barbiturates are often used for daytime sedation. The short-acting barbiturates are often used as preoperative hypnotic sedation, or by injection for rapid seizure control. The ultra-short acting barbiturates are used for anesthetic induction.

The benzodiazepines can also be described via their duration of action, from long-acting to ultra-short acting. However, the clinical indications for the benzodiazepines do not relate solely to their duration of action. The benzodiazepines are indicated for the management of anxiety disorders or for the short-term relief of the symptoms of anxiety. For example, oral chlordiazepoxide or diazepam are often used for treatment of preoperative apprehension and anxiety. Alprazolam, lorazepam, and oxazepam are also indicated for the adjunctive management of anxiety associated with depression. Alprazolam is also being used as pharmacologic management of panic disorders and panic attacks. Chlordiazepoxide, chlorazepate, diazepam, and oxazepam are used for the relief of acute alcohol withdrawal symptoms such as acute agitation, tremor,

Table 4.   Barbiturate Duration of Action

Long-Acting: 10 to 12 hours
   Mephobarbital
   Metharbital
   Phenobarbital
	Short-Acting: three to four hours
	   Pentobarbital
	   Secobarbital

Intermediate-Acting: six to eight hours
   Amobarbital
   Aprobarbital
   Butabarbital
   Talbutal
	Ultra Short-Acting: 15 minutes to three hours
	   Tripental

impending or acute delirium tremens, and hallucinosis. Flurazepam, temazepam, and triazolam are often used for the treatment of insomnia, associated with difficulty in falling asleep, frequent nocturnal awakening, or early morning awakening. Lorazepam is often prescribed for insomnia due to anxiety or transient situational stress.

The primary site of action for the sedative-hypnotics is the CNS, where they produce depression ranging from mild sedation to coma. The degree of depression is dependent on the particular sedative-hypnotic, the individual's level of tolerance, the dose, the route of administration, and the state of excitability. Individuals who have ingested amphetamines tolerate large amounts of sedative-hypnotics without sedation (Greenwood and Peachy 1957), as do those in the manic phase of a bipolar disorder (Sapira and Cherubin 1975).

It has been recognized that sedative-hypnotics, taken at doses several times the therapeutic dose or for long periods of time, could lead to the development of sedative-hypnotic dependence. Similarly, sedative-hypnotics, when taken in combination with other psychoactive drugs having similar properties (e.g., alcohol), would more likely be associated with a sedative-hypnotic type dependence. It has been shown that sedative-hypnotics, even when taken at therapeutic doses, can produce a sedative-hypnotic type dependence (Smith et al. 1985). In this situation, the low-dose sedative-hypnotic dependence is best understood as a drug-person interaction and not just a pure result of pharmacologic properties. Low-dose benzodiazepine dependency, for example, is often associated with people who have a past or a family history of alcoholism or other psychoactive substance abuse disorder even though they may not be currently using alcohol or any other sedative-hypnotic.

High-Dose Dependency

Hollister et al. (1961, 1963) demonstrated that after diazepam or chlordiazepoxide had been taken for 30 days in dosages two to three times the maximum recommended daily therapeutic doses, a withdrawal syndrome of the barbiturate type occurred when they were abruptly stopped. Meprobamate, glutethimide, methyprylon, alcohol, methaqualone, and other sedative-hypnotics have a withdrawal syndrome similar to the barbiturates. Currently, the phrase *sedative-hypnotic withdrawal syndrome* is used over the previous *barbiturate-type withdrawal syndrome*.

The severity of these withdrawal syndromes is a function of both time and dose, especially in the case of high-dose dependency. The time to develop physical dependency is inversely related to dose. If barbiturates are given to patients in sufficient quantity to produce continuous sleep, one week is a sufficient period to induce profound physical dependence. For people who are ambulatory at least some of the time, several weeks of daily dosing with a barbiturate is required. The same is true with the benzodiazepines.

The sedative-hypnotic withdrawal syndrome is traditionally divided into major and minor. Minor withdrawal consists of anxiety, insomnia, tremor, and nightmares. A major withdrawal syndrome includes the symptoms of minor withdrawal and in addition may include grand mal seizures, psychosis, hyperpyrexia, and death. There is cross-tolerance between benzodiazepines, alcohol, barbiturates, and other sedative-hypnotics and, as such, benzodiazepines can suppress alcohol and the other sedative-hypnotic withdrawal syndromes. The mechanisms for the development of CNS tolerance and physical dependency for these agents are not completely known. Benzodiazepines are now known to occupy specific receptor sites in many CNS nerve cells; however, the effects of barbiturates do not appear to be produced by direct receptor site binding since specific binding sites for these drugs have not been demonstrated.

Untreated, the high-dose sedative-hypnotic withdrawal syndrome peaks in intensity as blood levels of the sedative-hypnotic drop. Symptoms subside over a few days.

Low-Dose Dependency

While it was believed that a significant benzodiazepine withdrawal syndrome did not occur at usual therapeutic dosage levels, the publication of case studies describing such signs and symptoms after patients abruptly stopped long-term use led to a reevaluation of the concept (e.g., Bant 1975; Berlin and Conell 1983; Lader 1983; LeBellec et al. 1980; Levy 1984; Pevnick et al. 1978). Several review articles describing low-dose benzodiazepine withdrawal have now been published (MacKinnon and Parker 1982; Owen and Tyrer 1983; Schöph 1983).

Symptoms that have been attributed to benzodiazepine withdrawal include anxiety, tension, agitation, restlessness, irritability, tremor, nausea, insomnia, panic attacks, impairment of memory and concentration, perceptual alterations (hyperacusis, hypersensitivity to touch, pain), parathesias, feelings of unreality, visual hallucinations, psychosis, tachycardia, and increased blood pressure. Unfortunately, there are no pathognomonic signs or symptoms, and such a broad range of nonspecific symptoms could be produced by a number of illnesses, including agitated depression, generalized anxiety disorder, panic disorder, partial complex seizures, and schizophreniform disorders.

The validity of the low-dose withdrawal syndrome is controversial. Many people who take benzodiazepines in therapeutic doses for months to years can abruptly discontinue taking the benzodiazepine without developing symptoms. Other people who take similar amounts of a benzodiazepine believe themselves to have developed physical dependency on the benzodiazepine, and they cannot tolerate the symptoms that develop following cessation or dosage reduction of the benzodiazepine. Some physicians believe that the symptoms that emerge during the immediate withdrawal period can be explained solely on the basis of symptom return, whereas other physicians propose that at least some of the symptoms are the product of a withdrawal reaction.

There are four possible etiologies for the symptoms that emerge when benzodiazepines are stopped: symptom reemergence, symptom emergence, symptom generation, and symptom overinterpretation.

1. Symptom Reemergence (or Recrudescence): The patient's symptoms of anxiety, insomnia, or muscle tension abate during benzodiazepine treatment, and the patient forgets how severe the symptoms were before beginning benzodiazepine treatment. As discomfort in the present seems more real than that experienced in the past, present discomfort may be believed to be more severe when, in fact, symptoms are of equal severity to those experienced before treatment.
2. Symptom Emergence: If the patient's initial symptoms were secondary to a progressive disease, symptom progression may have been masked during benzodiazepine therapy. When the benzodiazepine is stopped, the symptoms that emerge are, in fact, more severe in intensity than the symptoms experienced before taking the benzodiazepine, but the etiology of the symptom intensification is due to progression of disease.
3. Symptom Generation or True Withdrawal Syndrome: Signs or symptoms may develop as a result of receptor site alterations due to the benzodiazepine exposure.
4. Symptom Overinterpretation: Everyone on occasion experiences anxiety, varia-

tions in sleep pattern, and musculoskeletal discomfort. Most people accept such symptoms as reasonable consequences of everyday stresses, overexertion, or minor viral infections. They may self-medicate their symptoms with over-the-counter medications or alcohol, but they do not generally go to a physician for treatment of the symptoms. In contrast, people who are stopping benzodiazepines may expect the development of withdrawal symptoms because of the widespread publicity about diazepam (Valium) withdrawal. These patients may assume that any symptoms occurring during the withdrawal period are due to benzodiazepine withdrawal and that they require medical attention. Merz and Ballmer (1983) studied the frequency with which symptoms and symptom combinations attributed to minor barbiturate or low-dose benzodiazepine withdrawal occur in an untreated, healthy population. They reported that many of the nonspecific symptoms attributed to withdrawal are common among "nonpatients" who do not use drugs.

Clearly, assigning causality to a patient's symptoms that emerge after discontinuance of a benzodiazepine is subject to uncertainty. This is especially the case when a patient is evaluated after "dependence" is already established. Unfortunately, this is the usual clinical situation and is the circumstance of most reported case studies of benzodiazepine dependence.

The time course of symptom resolution is the primary differentiating feature between symptoms generated by withdrawal and symptom reemergence, emergence, or overinterpretation. Withdrawal symptoms subside with continued abstinence, whereas symptoms of other etiologies persist. Figure 1 compares the intensity of symptoms in the barbiturate-type withdrawal and the low-dose benzodiazepine withdrawal. The intensity label on the ordinate axis of Figure 1 indicates a global measure of symptoms. The time course shown is for a long-acting benzodiazepine.

Short-acting benzodiazepines have an accelerated time course for the sedative-hypnotic type withdrawal syndrome, and the peak intensity of sedative-hypnotic type withdrawal for the short-acting benzodiazepines (e.g., oxazepam, alprazolam, triazolam) occurs in two to four days. The fluctuation of symptom intensity of the low-dose withdrawal syndrome illustrates the waxing and waning of symptoms that often occurs without apparent psychological cause. The time of emergence is variable, and it may not coincide with the time course illustrated in Figure 1.

We believe that the waxing and waning of symptoms is an important marker to distinguish low-dose withdrawal from symptom reemergence. Table 2 shows salient features of benzodiazepine withdrawal, anxiety disorders, and symptom reemergence.

Chronicity of use, dosage, concurrent drug use, and individual susceptibility all interact in the development of low-dose physical dependency. Continuous exposure to the benzodiazepine fosters development of physical dependence of the sedative-hypnotic type and probably also fosters the development of low-dose dependency. Thus short-acting benzodiazepines are no less prone to development of physical dependence if taken on a daily basis than are long-acting benzodiazepines. Once physical dependence develops, the sedative-hypnotic type withdrawal syndrome produced by short-acting benzodiazepines would be expected to be more intense because of the more rapid drop in tissue levels of these drugs (Hollister 1980).

Since the reports of specific benzodiazepine binding sites in rat brain by Mohler and Okada (1977) and Squires and Braestrup (1977), attempts to characterize the benzodiazepine receptor site have been the subject of intense research. Localized in synaptic contact regions in the cerebral cortex, cerebellum, and hippocampus in association with gamma-aminobutyric acid (GABA) receptor sites, the benzodiazepine receptor sites affect GABA's affinity for binding to its specific site and modify the permeability of the cell membrane to the chloride ion. We have hypothesized that low-dose benzodiazepine withdrawal is receptor-site mediated (Wesson and Smith 1982). A receptor-site-mediated withdrawal syndrome would offer a plausible explanation why symptom resolution takes more time than for nonbenzodiazepine sedative-hypnotic withdrawal.

The specific benzodiazepine antagonist (Ro 15-1788) will precipitate withdrawal reactions in animals dependent on benzodiazepines (Cumin et al. 1982). The availability of a specific benzodiazepine antagonist opens the possibility of testing the benzodiazepine low-dose withdrawal syndrome by inducing withdrawal in the same way that naloxone can be used to test for opiate dependence.

The development of physical dependence may also be influenced by exposure to drugs or medications other than the benzodiazepine. For example, pentobarbital has been shown to increase affinity of diazepam to benzodiazepine receptors (Olsen and Loeb-Lundberg 1981; Skolnick et al. 1981). Pretreatment with barbiturates may affect the development of withdrawal symptoms, as demonstrated in a study by Covi et al. (1973). They randomly assigned 92 patients to a 10-week pre-chlordiazepoxide treatment with either phenobarbital or diphenylhydantoin. During the subsequent two weeks, subjects were given 15 mg chlordiazepoxide three times per day, then switched to an identical-appearing placebo for two weeks, and then returned to a final two-week treatment period of 15 mg chlordiazepoxide three times a day. Although the mean distress levels during chlordiazepoxide treatment were no different in the two groups, the mean distress levels while on placebo were significantly greater for the phenobarbital-pretreated group than the diphenylhydantoin-pretreated group.

Drug Switching

One of the more troubling areas concerning sedative-hypnotic dependence involves the alteration of prescribing practices based on a decision other than a logical, pharmacologic indication. There are a growing number of physicians who utilize the shorter-acting benzodiazepines for their longer-acting benzodiazepine-dependent patients in the hope that the shorter-acting drugs are somehow less dependency producing. The stereotypical example is a patient who was prescribed therapeutic-range diazepam for six months or more for an anxiety disorder. The physician becomes concerned about dependency and switches from diazepam to alprazolam. The physician often believes that the shorter-acting benzodiazepines are not addicting or are less addicting than, say, diazepam. Very often, the physician may also lower the dosage equivalence, leaving the patient with a more rapidly metabolized benzodiazepine, producing fluctuating plasma concentrations of the drug and often troubling symptoms as plasma levels drop throughout the day.

In short, physicians should make prescribing practice decisions based on the pharmacologic indications and clinical utility of the sedative-hypnotics, not based on fear of dependency. The use of all psychoactive medications carries certain risks, and one of them is the risk of dependency. Profound agoraphobia that prohibits a client from going outside, going to work, and carrying on normal duties and responsibilities clearly would benefit from a benzodiazepine. The risk of dependence to that drug is overshadowed by that person's preexisting dysfunctional life-style. However, to prescribe sedative-hypnotics for a person with a history of addictive disease in order to medicate normal life stressors carries with it a very clear risk of dependency and little benefit that could not be obtained through the use of alternative stress and anxiety reduction.

Recovery

The physician often conceptualizes dependence to psychoactive drugs as being equivalent to physical dependence and tolerance. In fact, the person who has developed physical tolerance and dependence to a drug may not display signs and symptoms of addiction (e.g., compulsion, loss of control over the drug, continued use despite adverse consequences). Conversely, a person can use a psychoactive drug compulsively and addictively in the absence of tissue tolerance and dependence (e.g., the binge drinker). These concepts are appropriate for the study and treatment of sedative-hypnotic use, abuse, and addiction.

The point is simple. Addiction and tissue dependency to sedative-hypnotics are distinct and separate terms and processes. Tissue dependency and tolerance to barbiturates and benzodiazepines can be established via a test dose and a substitution of phenobarbital and the subsequent elimination and reduction of withdrawal symptoms. The management of simple sedative-hypnotic dependence may be, for some patients, little more than a gradual reduction of the sedative-hypnotic over a period of a few weeks. The management of addiction to sedative-hypnotics, on the other hand, simply begins with the detoxification process and consists of a full program of adjunctive stress reduction, supportive counseling, and peer support groups such as Narcotics Anonymous, Pills Anonymous, and even Alcoholics Anonymous—groups that provide support for abstinence from all psychoactive drugs.

The role of the physician in the management of the simple sedative-hypnotic withdrawal is as a primary treatment professional. The role of the physician in the management of the more complex sedative-hypnotic withdrawal and for the management of addictive disease where sedative-hypnotics are involved is that of a pivotal player within a team approach utilizing professionals, paraprofessionals, and peer support groups. The physician manages the medical aspects of a disease that also has profound psychosocial, familial, sexual, financial, and even spiritual aspects.

Chapter 134

Opioids: General Issues and Detoxification

Incidence and Prevalence

In the 1985 National Household Survey on Drug Abuse (National Institute on Drug Abuse 1986), 1.2 percent of young adults (ages 18 to 25) reported using heroin at some point in their lives, but less than 0.5 percent reported use during the preceding month. Lifetime experience with nonmedical use of analgesics (presumably opioids other than heroin) was far more common and was reported by 11 percent in this age group. Since the National Household Survey does not sample individuals without fixed residences or those in jails and hospitals (who are believed to have higher levels of psychopathology and drug abuse), it is likely that these percentages underestimate the true prevalence of opioid use and dependence. Nevertheless, the number of opioid addicts seeking treatment in any given year has consistently been far smaller than even these very conservative estimates of the prevalence of opioid use.

Opioid Pharmacology

The term *opioid* is now used to refer to a large number of chemically diverse substances that have in common the capacity to bind specifically and to produce actions at several distinct types of receptors (opioid receptors). Drugs that bind specifically at any of the opioid receptors but produce no actions are referred to as opioid antagonists.

There is now good evidence for more than five types of opioid receptors, and some of these appear to be further differentiated into subtypes. The various receptor types, designated with Greek letters, include the mu (μ) receptor, where the classic opioids such as morphine and methadone show high binding affinity and produce actions such as analgesia, euphoria, and respiratory depression. The kappa (κ) receptor is named for the drug ketocyclazocine. Drugs such as butorphanol (Stadol) and nalbuphine (Nubain) are presumed to exert their major agonistic effects at this receptor. It is now generally accepted that kappa activation produces analgesia, but other effects of kappa activation are not as clearly understood. Some individuals experience euphoria after receiving pentazocine, butorphanol, and nalbuphine. How these individuals differ from those who do not find such drugs pleasurable is not yet clear. After chronic administration, these drugs do produce withdrawal syndromes that are similar to but less distressing than those of typical mu agonists. The endocrine effects of kappa activation are distinct from those of mu activation. The latter is associated with decreases in release of luteinizing hormone (LH), follicle-stimulating hormone (FSH), adrenocorticotropic hormone (ACTH), and beta-endorphin, and increases in release of prolactin and growth hormone (Jaffe and Martin 1985).

The delta (Δ) receptor is the site of preferential binding for certain endogenous peptides, as well as for several synthetic peptides. Delta receptor activation produces analgesia and some endocrine effects, but other delta actions in humans are less well established. Still additional opioid receptor types have been identified. The sigma (Σ) receptor, named for the drug SKF 10,047, is related but not identical to the receptor for the drug phencyclidine (PCP). The actions of SKF 10,047 and PCP are not similar to those of morphine, neither are they antagonized by naloxone. It has been argued, therefore, that the sigma receptors should not be considered members of the opioid receptor family.

Because none of the agonists or antagonists available for use in humans are sufficiently selective, it has been difficult to establish the normal physiologic role of any given receptor type and its endogenous ligands (see below). Thus although in animal tissues morphine has about 10-fold greater affinity for the mu than for delta or kappa receptors, after high doses of morphine mu, delta and kappa receptors may all be activated to some degree.

Endogenous Opioids

Three distinct opioid peptide systems or families—the enkephalins, the endorphins, and the dynorphins—have been described. Each system has a genetically distinct precursor polypeptide. Although there is considerable overlap, the anatomic distribution of the neurons expressing each of the precursor polypeptides is also distinct. The precursor molecules are now commonly designated pro-enkephalin, pro-opiomelanocortin (POMC), and pro-dynorphin (also pro-enkephalin B). Each precursor molecule can be processed by the actions of peptidases into a number of biologically active peptides that vary considerably in their affinity for various opioid receptor types. In all, more than a dozen distinct opioid peptides (e.g., leu- and met-enkephalin, beta-endorphin, dynorphin) have been characterized. Each of these peptides may coexist within the same neurons that contain other peptide and nonpeptide neurotransmitters. Further, even among cells that make the same precursor molecules, there are differences in the activity of the enzymes that break down the pro-peptides, resulting in different mixtures of active opioid peptides stored and released (Akil et al. 1984; Goldstein 1984; Way 1986). These complexities help to explain why it has been so difficult to establish the physiologic role of the endogenous opioid peptides in normal and abnormal states.

Despite the explosion of research in this area, no definite linkages have been established between the biology of any of the endogenous systems, and either the probability of developing opioid dependence or that of relapsing to dependence after a period of abstinence (O'Brien et al. 1982).

Opioid Tolerance and Physical Dependence (Opioid Neuroadaptation)

Tolerance does not develop uniformly to all of the actions of opioid drugs. There can be remarkable tolerance to the analgesic, respiratory depressant, and sedative actions of the mu receptor opioids in the presence of persistent miotic, endocrine, and constipating effects. In animal models, there is little cross-tolerance between opioids that act at different receptor types (i.e., between mu and kappa receptors) (Imerek and Woods 1986; Jaffe 1985).

Opioid neuroadaptation is a drug-induced state manifested by a characteristic response pattern, withdrawal phenomena, when the drug is removed from its receptor. In general, the withdrawal phenomena are opposite in direction to the acute agonistic effects of the drugs (e.g., in the case of the opioids, bowel hypermotility in contrast to the constipation caused by the drugs). The adaptive changes probably begin as soon as the receptors are occupied by agonists, although some period of continuous occupation is required before the changes can be detected by clinical means. Withdrawal phenomena are more intense when the agonists are rapidly displaced, as by the use of an antagonist. As with tolerance, neuroadaptive changes appear to be receptor-type specific (Jaffe 1985). Distinct anatomic sites may be involved in mu receptor-induced analgesia for the reinforcing effects of opioids and for the adaptive changes responsible for classic withdrawal phenomena (Bozarth and Wise 1984; Ling et al. 1984). Tolerance and neuroadaptive changes can be induced locally, as well as in the whole organism. For example, infusions of opioids into the spinal cord can induce tolerance and withdrawal phenomena limited to spinal cord structures (Yaksh et al. 1977).

The cellular mechanisms underlying opioid neuroadaptive changes may involve alterations in receptor number, receptor affinity, activity of intracellular enzymes regulating calcium and/or cyclic adenosine monophosphate (cAMP), and transmitter supersensitivity in those neural systems whose activities are reduced by indirect actions of opioids (Way 1986). Supersensitivity of noradrenergic neurons in the locus coeruleus and other noradrenergic nuclei appears to be responsible for some components of the mu agonist withdrawal syndrome. Reduction of the activity of these neurons by the alpha$_2$ agonists, such as clonidine and lofexidine, forms the basis for the clinical utility of these drugs in managing opioid withdrawal (Redmond and Krystal 1984).

Clinical Characteristics of the Opioid (Mu Agonist) Withdrawal Syndrome

Withdrawal from classic opioids (mu agonists) varies greatly in intensity. Among the factors determining severity are the specific drug used, its daily dose, the degree to which opioid effects were continuously exerted on the central nervous system (CNS), the rate at which the drug is removed from its receptors, and factors that are best described as individual sensitivity. For example, some individuals using heroin complain primarily about stomach cramps, others about backaches or muscle aches. The syndrome induced by the use of an antagonist such as naloxone can be quite intense, but it will subside when the antagonist is metabolized and the opioids still in the body reoccupy the opioid receptors. Rapidly metabolized drugs are generally associated with more severe withdrawal phenomena. Conversely, if the opioid is one that binds tightly to the receptor (e.g., buprenorphine) or is slowly excreted from the body (e.g., methadone, L-acetylmethadol), the withdrawal syndrome, while qualitatively similar in character, will be generally slower in onset and less intense but also more protracted, often lasting several weeks. Using opioid antagonists, it is possible to demonstrate low levels of opioid neuroadaption in humans (as evidenced by withdrawal phenomena) after a single therapeutic dose of morphine.

When short-acting drugs such as morphine and heroin have been given chronically, the onset of withdrawal symptoms occurs about eight to 10 hours after the last dose. Common symptoms are craving, anxiety, dysphoria, yawning, perspiration, lacrimation, rhinorrhea, restlessness, and broken sleep. In more severe syndromes, there may be waves of gooseflesh, hot and cold flashes, aching of bones and muscles, nausea, vomiting, diarrhea, abdominal cramps, weight loss, and low-grade fever. While the acute phase generally passes in seven to 10 days, there is some evidence for a more protracted syndrome, with subtle disturbances of mood and sleep persisting for weeks or months. There is also a protracted withdrawal syndrome following withdrawal of drugs that are longer acting or that bind more firmly to receptors, such as methadone (Martin et al. 1973) and probably following withdrawal of L-alpha-acetylmethadol (L-AAM).

Etiology of Opioid Dependence

Multiple factors play a role in the development of opioid dependence, with some more dominant in certain cases than others. Some factors may play greater roles in determining who will experiment with opioids; others may be more important in influencing the patterns of use, the development of chronic dependence, complications, and response to treatment.

Social Factors

Generally, the use of drugs such as alcohol, tobacco, and (increasingly) marijuana precedes use of illicit opioids (Clayton and Voss 1981; Kandel and Faust 1975). Those persons who go on to experiment with the most socially unacceptable drugs (e.g., heroin) generally come from disrupted families or have disturbed relationships with parents, and they often have a low sense of self-worth (Kandel and Faust 1975). Illicit opioids are often more easily obtained in the inner cities of the large urban centers than in other parts of the country. Commonly, these areas are also characterized by high crime, high unemployment, and demoralized school systems—all of which contribute to the loss of hope and self-esteem that are associated with resistance to use and good prognosis once dependence develops. Availability, in turn, can influence not only initial and continued use but also relapse after treatment. When a significant number of opioid users reside in one area, a subculture supportive of experimentation and of continued use develops (Clayton and Voss 1981).

In Vietnam, about half of those soldiers who tried heroin became dependent; they developed withdrawal symptoms when they attempted to stop using it. Of those soldiers who used the drug at least five times, 73 percent developed dependence. The background factors that were predictors of addiction as a soldier in Vietnam, being young and black, were not the factors that best predicted relapse after return to the United States. Relapse was related to being white, older, and having a parent who had a history of alcoholism or criminality (Robins et al. 1975).

Opioids as Reinforcers

It is not clear which of the multiple actions of opioid drugs (described above) are responsible for their reinforcing properties. The sites involved in reinforcement and drug self-administration are probably distinct from those related to opioid analgesia.

Single doses of opioids reduce anxiety, increase self-esteem, and increase ability to cope with everyday problems. When given intravenously, opioids produce a "rush" or "flash"—a sudden, brief, exceedingly pleasurable sensation.

Heroin addicts self-administering the drug in a research setting developed tolerance to its anxiety-relieving and euphorigenic effects. Despite this tolerance, single injections continued to produce brief periods of mood elevation for 30 to 60 minutes after each dose. After several weeks, subjects reported increasing anxiety and dysphoria, and developed various somatic complaints (Meyer and Mirin 1979). The loss of mood-elevating effects and the appearance of hypophoria and hypochondriasis has also been observed with chronic administration of methadone in a research setting (Martin et al. 1973).

For the intravenous drug user, avoidance of withdrawal is not the sole factor in continued drug use after the development of tolerance. Interviews with dependent heroin users who were tolerant indicated that, despite some tolerance to many of the drug effects, users continued to experience a brief euphoric effect immediately following an injection (McAuliffe and Gordon 1974).

Psychopathology and Psychodynamic Factors

More recent psychoanalytic formulations postulate that opioid addicts suffer from severe ego defects and view the psychopathology of opioid dependence as part of the broad group of narcissistic character disorders. Most analysts agree that users also experience problems with affect, often intense anger and rage, and have weak or ineffective ego defenses against these affects. The psychodynamic perspective is that the use of opioids, pharmacologically and symbolically, aids the ego in controlling these emotions, and that psychopathology is the underlying motivation for initial use, dependent use, and relapse after period of abstinence (Khantzian and Schneider 1986; Wurmser 1979).

Formal Diagnoses

Opioid addicts seeking treatment commonly meet the DSM-III or RDC criteria for several psychiatric disorders in addition to opioid dependence. The most common RDC diagnoses among those seeking admission to the Substance Abuse Treatment Unit of the Connecticut Mental Health Center in New Haven, Connecticut, were affective disorders, alcoholism, antisocial personality, and anxiety disorders (Table 1). Seventy percent met criteria for a current additional diagnosis; 87 percent met the criteria for at least one additional diagnosis at some point in their lives. Multiple additional diagnoses (e.g., alcoholism and antisocial personality) were common. Had DSM-III criteria been used, 54 percent of the patients would have received a diagnosis of antisocial personality (Rounsaville et al. 1982c). Similar findings have been obtained at other treatment programs in the United States. (Mirin et al. 1986; Woody et al. 1983). The relationship of this additional psychopathology to the etiology of opioid dependence remains unclear. The influence of specific psychiatric disorders on the course of the dependence has been a subject of intense research. There is a growing consensus that global severity of psychopathology influences both the natural history of the dependence disorder and the response to treatment. Those who have severe psychopathology do poorly in all treatment modalities. However, with the possible exception of major depression, it is global severity rather than specific diagnosis that influences outcomes (Kosten et al. 1986b; McLellan et al. 1983; Rounsaville et al. 1986a). Treatment may expect its greatest benefits by helping those addicts with depression and other recent losses and adverse life effects (Kosten et al. 1986c).

Biologic Factors

Although it was once postulated that antecedent metabolic deficiency, such as endogenous opioid dysregulation or a metabolic deficiency induced by chronic opioid use, could increase vulnerability to opioid dependence (Dole and Nyswander 1967),

Table 1. Lifetime Rates for Psychiatric Disorders Using Research Diagnostic Criteria

Type of Disorder	Male (N = 403) (%)	Female (N = 130) (%)
Affective disorder		
Major depression	48.9	69.2
Minor depression	9.4	5.4
Intermittent depression	18.1	20.8
Cyclothymic personality	2.5	6.9
Labile personality	17.1	14.6
Manic disorders	0.5	0.8
Hypomanic disorder	5.5	10.0
Bipolar 1 or 2	3.7	10.8
Any affective disorder	70.7	85.4
Schizophrenic disorders		
Schizophrenia	0.7	0.8
Schizoaffective, depressed	2.2	0.0
Schizoaffective, manic	0.5	0.0
Anxiety disorders		
Panic	0.5	3.9
Obsessive-compulsive	1.7	2.3
Generalized anxiety	4.7	7.7
Phobic	8.2	13.9
Any anxiety disorder	13.2	25.4
Alcoholism	37.0	26.9
Personality disorders		
Antisocial personality	29.5	16.9
Briquet's syndrome	0.0	0.7
Schizotypal features	8.7	7.7
Other psychiatric disorders	5.7	10.0

Note. Modified from Rounsaville et al. 1982.

there is little direct evidence of any specific biologic vulnerability to opioid dependence. Individuals who become opioid users are more likely than controls to have antisocial personality and to develop alcoholism and are more likely to have biologic relatives with these disorders (Cadoret et al. 1986). In view of the growing consensus that there are genetic factors in the vulnerability to alcoholism and to antisocial personality, research in these areas is likely to continue.

Family Factors

More than 50 percent of urban heroin addicts come from single-parent families. Even those from two-parent families have disturbed family relationships, with one parent (typically the one of the opposite sex) intensely involved with the addict and the other distant, absent, or punitive. The addict's disability frequently serves as a focal point for family communication and sometimes is the main motive for their remaining together. Thus the family equilibrium may be threatened by the addict's recovery. Alcoholism, drug abuse, or both are common in the families of heroin users. Despite the disturbed interactions, opioid users often remain dependent on and in close communication with their families well into adulthood and view their families of origin or their in-laws as those most likely to provide the most help to them in their efforts to give up drugs. Family therapy can be an important adjunct to other forms of intervention and, in less severe cases, the major approach (Kaufman 1986; Stanton 1982).

Learning

Whether occasional or compulsive, drug use can be regarded as behavior maintained by its consequences; consequences that strengthen a behavior pattern are reinforcers. As noted previously, opioids are positive reinforcers of drug self-administration and can also reinforce antecedent behaviors by terminating some aversive state, such as pain, anger, anxiety, or depression. The use of the drug, apart from its pharmacologic effects, can be reinforcing in some social situations if it results in the approval of friends or conveys special status. Once neuroadaptation occurs, opioid use can produce rapid reinforcement (drug-induced euphoria—a "rush"), alleviation of disturbed affect, alleviation of withdrawal, or any combination of these effects. Because short-acting opioids (e.g., heroin) can cause such reinforcement several times a day, day after day, a powerfully reinforced habit pattern is formed. Even the paraphernalia and hustling associated with drug use become reinforcers (McAuliffe and Ch'ien 1986; McLellan et al. 1986; Meyer and Mirin 1979; Wikler 1980).

Other learning mechanisms also can play a role in dependence and relapse. Opioid withdrawal phenomena can be conditioned, in the classic sense, to environmental or interoceptive stimuli. This has been demonstrated both in laboratory animals and in methadone-maintained human volunteers. For a long time after withdrawal, the addict may experience conditioned withdrawal or conditional craving when exposed to environmental stimuli previously linked with drug use or withdrawal and may interpret the feeling as a need for opioids or an increase in craving. The conditions that elicit the most intense craving are those associated with the availability or use of an opioid, such as watching someone else use heroin or being offered the drug by a friend. Apparently the subjective states of "craving," "high," and withdrawal can be elicited independently by different stimuli. Although the role of these conditioned phenomena in relapse or perpetuation of opioid use is still uncertain, several studies suggest that they are more common and more diverse than previously believed and the therapy directed at the extinction can play a useful role in overall treatment (Childress et al. 1986; McLellan et al. 1986).

Treatment

General Considerations

There is currently no single accepted standard of treatment for opioid dependence. Indeed, opioid dependence is now rarely the sole presenting problem; most patients with opioid dependence abuse drugs other than opioids and commonly have psychopathology in addition to drug dependence. In some programs, more than 70 percent of patients seeking admission have a history of cocaine abuse (Kosten et al. 1986). Treatment of each individual may involve inpatient, residential, day-care, or outpatient settings, and the qualifications of "therapists" may range from advanced degrees in medicine followed by residency training in a specialty to a personal history of recovery from dependence and on-the-job training in a residential program. Programs may emphasize group, family, or individual interaction. All drugs may be proscribed, or the program can be built with the use of a drug as its centerpiece (e.g., methadone or naltrexone). The numerous possible combinations of environments, staffing patterns, and treatment rationales have been categorized into four major program types: 1) opioid maintenance programs, primarily methadone and primarily outpatient; 2) detoxification programs, acute treatment for withdrawal; 3) residential programs, usually "therapeutic communities"; and 4) outpatient drug-free programs. In the United States, 75 percent of opioid users treated annually are treated in one of these four major types of programs.

Many self-help groups such as Alcoholics Anonymous (AA), Narcotics Anonymous (NA), and Cocaine Anonymous (CA) are now active in cities across the United States. It is not uncommon to find opioid users participating in such groups, sometimes in conjunction with other varieties of treatment but often as their sole attempt to deal with their drug problem.

Treatment of opioid addicts employing insight-oriented or supportive psychotherapy also occurs in private hospitals and in professional offices. The clinical availability of clonidine (Catapres), a nonnarcotic, nonscheduled agent that can facilitate detoxification; naltrexone (Trexan), an adjunct to relapse prevention; and the recognition of the influence of psychopathology on the response to treatment may encourage more frequent treatment by psychiatrists in private settings in the future.

In selecting a treatment approach, consideration must be given to available groups, professional skills and facilities, the patient's willingness to accept a given treatment approach, previous treatment experiences, and any associated psychopathology. Psychopathology, whether antecedent or subsequent to the onset of drug use, merits attention. There is general consensus, however, that opioid dependence, once established, must be treated as a disorder sui generis. Since the various treatment types are covered in detail in separate chapters (except detoxification), only a brief overview of them will be given in this chapter.

Detoxification

Patients can be withdrawn from opioids on either an inpatient or an outpatient basis. The techniques used vary considerably. The use of opioid drugs to treat withdrawal or to stabilize patients while they are awaiting admission to a treatment program is regulated by federal and state governments. At the federal level these regulations have been revised. New regulations permit the use of decreasing doses of opioids (as of this writing, methadone is the only approved drug) in outpatient programs over a period as long as six months. Two types of detoxification with differing requirements are described: short-term (up to 30 days) and long-term (30 to 180 days). Patients in long-term detoxification may be given a one-day take-home supply. Under these proposed guidelines, detoxification falls technically under the category of "maintenance treatment." Since not all states are making comparable revisions in regulations, physicians should contact their state agencies to learn what is considered legal and acceptable. Patients who require opioids chronically for the treatment of pain are not considered addicts within the framework of these regulations, but patients with iatrogenic dependence are not exempt. Physicians wishing to treat such patients may apply to the Food and Drug Administration (FDA) for a one-patient program approval.

The most common objective in managing withdrawal is suppression of severe withdrawal symptoms. It is usually impossible to reduce symptoms so completely that patients will perceive no discomfort, but discomfort and associated craving can be reduced by very gradual reduction in opioid dosage. Hospitalized patients are generally able to tolerate more rapid dosage reductions and more withdrawal symptoms than ambulatory patients, who often start using other drugs if symptoms are too severe. In hospitalized patients who have been using heroin, an oral dose of 10 to 20 mg of methadone is given initially. This is repeated after two to four hours if withdrawal symptoms are not suppressed or if they reappear. If withdrawal symptoms are not present initially, the patient should be observed for drowsiness or depressed respiration. Generally, a stabilization dose at which no serious withdrawal is observed (usually not more than 40 mg/day) can be found within a day or two. (Except in cases where there is *documented* evidence of use of opioids in excess of 40 mg methadone, or an equivalent amount per day [see Table 2], the initial dose of methadone should never exceed 30 mg and the total 24-hour dose should never exceed 40 mg.) At this point, dosage reduction of about 20 percent/day (usually 5 to 10 mg) can be started and the entire process completed in a week or two. Some low-level withdrawal symptoms (e.g., sleep and mood disturbances) may persist for weeks after the last dose. Patients who have been maintained on high doses of methadone or professionals with access to pure opioids may have a more severe degree of physical dependence. They may require higher stabilization doses and may be unwilling to tolerate so rapid a withdrawal. If the dose of opioid used is known, the data in Table 2 may aid in deciding the initial dose. More rapid inpatient detoxification techniques using clonidine and naltrexone are discussed below.

Experts disagree about using opioid drugs to treat withdrawal symptoms before there are observable withdrawal signs. Unless one waits for signs and symptoms to develop or gives naloxone to provoke withdrawal, there is no way to know if an opioid user has a clinically significant degree of physical dependence (neuroadaptation). The presence of opioids in urine and current or old needle marks may indicate opioid use, but do not prove tolerance and dependence. To prevent nonaddicts from being given opioids, some clinicians insist on the presence of withdrawal signs, either naturally occurring or antagonist-precipitated. Two arguments can be made for the opposite position. First, most of those who seek treatment do so in the hope that treatment will prevent or ameliorate the withdrawal syndrome. Second, it is generally unlikely that nonaddicts would submit to extensive examinations merely to get a few doses of oral opioids for a few days or weeks. Logic and compassion notwithstanding, some countries, and some localities within the United States, may insist that doctors document evidence of physical dependence before administering opioids to addicts.

Length of Withdrawal

Ideally, the total dose necessary to stabilize the patient in the first 24 hours should be repeated on the second day, or corrections should be made up or down if the dose either excessively sedates the patient or fails to suppress the abstinence syndrome

Table 2.   Comparison of Methadone and Other Opioids in Suppressing Opioid Withdrawal

For purposes of suppressing withdrawal, 1 mg of oral methadone is approximately equivalent to:

Heroin: 1 to 2 mg
Morphine: 3 to 4 mg
Dihydromorphine (Dilaudid): 0.5 mg
Codeine: 30 mg
Meperidine (Demerol): 20 mg
Paregoric: 7 to 8 ml
Levorphonol (Levo-Dromoran): 0.5 mg
Anileridine (Leritine): 8 mg

sufficiently. After the patient is stabilized for 48 hours (several days in outpatients), the dose can then be gradually withdrawn. One common pattern is to decrease the dose by 5 mg/day. A second method is to decrease the dose by 5 mg/day until a level of 10 to 15 mg/day is reached and then decrease it more slowly. Typical daily patterns may then look like this:

Day	1	2	3	4	5	6	7	8			
Dose	30	30	25	20	15	10	5	0			

Day	1	2	3	4	5	6	7	8	9	10	11
Dose	30	30	25	20	15	12	10	8	5	3	0

In general, inpatient, residential withdrawal takes place over five to 10 days; outpatient withdrawal may be stretched out longer to minimize any symptoms. Some clinicians find that allowing the patient to help regulate the duration and speed of his or her withdrawal results in a better outcome. In practice, length of stay in a hospital or outpatient program may be governed by factors other than patient comfort, and clinicians may feel pressured to accelerate the process.

Other Drugs and Supportive Measures

All withdrawal symptoms may not be totally suppressed with the treatment described above, and sometimes for days after treatment has been completed certain symptoms may persist, albeit in a rather mild form. There is no consensus as to the use of other drugs during these periods when very mild symptoms persist. The use of tranquilizers or bedtime sedation can help allay the patient's anxiety and minimize the craving for morphine-like drugs, but nonnarcotic medications are generally ineffective in relieving the specific symptoms of opioid abstinence. If insomnia and other withdrawal symptoms are unusually severe, especially in older patients, relief can be provided by an increment in the next dose of methadone and, therefore, a slower withdrawal schedule.

Insomnia is one of the more debilitating withdrawal symptoms because it is not only difficult to tolerate in and of itself, but it also weakens the addict's ability to deal with other withdrawal problems. There is general agreement that barbiturates, because of their dependence potential, should not be used to treat insomnia. Drugs that have been advocated include flurazepam, diphenhydramine, and the tricyclic antidepressents (e.g., amitriptyline and doxepin). All of these have been used in withdrawal, although objective comparisons are not available. Flurazepam appears preferred by most patients; because of its cumulative nature, it should not be continued for longer than two weeks.

During the inpatient detoxification period, nonpharmaceutical supports can also play an important and useful role. Most helpful is a warm, kind, and reassuring attitude of the treatment staff. Involvement of patients in their own detoxification schedule has been found to be of positive value and usually is not abused. It is, therefore, not necessary most of the time to have an adversary role develop around the issue of medication dose. Staff members do need to take a firm stand about visitors, however, because it is not uncommon to have them attempt to smuggle in drugs. Visitors should be limited to only immediate family (parents or spouse) who are not known to be drug abusers themselves. However, even parents have been known to smuggle in drugs under the pressure of entreaties from patients who claim that the staff does not understand their needs and distress. A watchful presence may be necessary, therefore, for all visitors. Such attempts at deception are less likely to occur if there are family meetings and patient involvement.

Other measures that have been advocated include warm baths, exercise when the patient feels up to it, and various diets. Unless there are specific nutritional deficiencies, there is no evidence of the usefulness of one or another dietary regime. However, because addicts are often malnourished, general vitamin and mineral supplements should be given.

Mixed Addictions

Unrecognized concomitant sedative dependence can produce serious hazards. Not only can seizures occur, but in addition sedative-hypnotic withdrawal can cause delirium, hallucinations, hyperthermia, and even death. Abrupt withdrawal from stimulant-type drugs is much less of a physical hazard, but can be associated with severe depression and, rarely, suicide. If sedative dependence is present, it is often useful first to stabilize the patient on methadone, to withdraw the sedative gradually, and then to withdraw the methadone.

On an outpatient basis, successful completion of withdrawal using methadone is more difficult to achieve (Senay et al. 1977). Patients tend to revert to opioid use or to discontinue treatment as the dose is reduced to less than 10 mg/day. Some clinicians, therefore, recommend very slow dose reductions (e.g., 10 percent of dose/week, then 3 percent/week, when the dose is below 20 mg) (Senay et al. 1977). New FDA regulations are expected to permit such extended detoxification schedules.

Other Detoxification Agents and Methods

The alpha-2 agonist drug, clonidine (Catapres), now marketed as an antihypertensive, has been used to facilitate opioid withdrawal in both inpatient and outpatient settings (Charney et al. 1986; Gold et al. 1978; Kleber et al. 1985a; Washton and Resnick 1981). Clonidine in doses of 0.6 to 2 mg/day reduces many of the autonomic components of the opioid withdrawal syndrome, although craving, lethargy, insomnia, restlessness, and muscle aches are not well suppressed (Charney et al. 1981b; Jasinski et al. 1985). Clonidine is believed to exert its ameliorative actions by binding to alpha-2 auto-receptors in the brain (e.g., locus coeruleus) and spinal cord. Both opioids and clonidine can suppress the activity of the locus coeruleus, which is hyperactive during opioid withdrawal.

Inpatients stabilized up to 50 mg/day or less of methadone can be abruptly switched to clonidine. Doses reaching 2.5 mg/day have been used. Sedation and hypotension have been the major side effects.

Clonidine has also been used for outpatient detoxification. Patients maintained on 20 mg/day or less of methadone and who have developed a relationship with the staff are about as successful after abrupt substitution of clonidine as after reduction of methadone by 1 mg/day (Kleber et al. 1985). Clonidine is less useful for detoxifying addicts directly "from the street." Other alpha-2 adrenergic agonists such as lofexidine and guanabenz also appear to ameliorate aspects of the opioid withdrawal syndrome (Washton and Resnick 1981). Although available as an antihypertensive agent, the use of clonidine as an agent for controlling withdrawal has not yet been given official FDA approval.

Techniques of Withdrawal from Opiates with Clonidine Hydrochloride

On the day before clonidine detoxification is started, the usual dose of opioid is given. The following day (day 1) the opioid is withdrawn completely, and clonidine is given in divided doses as shown in Table 3. Clonidine is to be used with caution in patients with hypotension or patients receiving antihypertensive medications. Use of tricyclic antidepressants within three weeks precludes use of clonidine because these agents render the alpha-2 receptors hyposensitive to the clonidine. Other exclusions include pregnancy, history of psychosis, cardiac arrhythmias, or other medical conditions in which use of clonidine might aggravate the associated medical problem. As clonidine can cause sedation, patients should be cautioned about driving and operating equipment.

Table 3. Clonidine-Aided Detoxification

Schedule for methadone maintained patients (20 to 30 mg/day methadone):

Outpatients	Total dose/day in three divided doses of clonidine (mg)
Day 1	0.3
2	0.4 to 0.6
3	0.5 to 0.8
4	0.5 to 1.2
5 through 10	Maintain on above dose
11 until completion	Reduce by 0.2 mg/day; give in two or three divided doses; the nighttime dose should be reduced last. If the patient complains of side effects, the dose can be reduced by one-half each day, not to exceed 0.4 mg/day.

Inpatients	
Day 1	0.4 to 0.6
2	0.6 to 0.8
3	0.6 to 1.2
4 through 10	Maintain or increase if any withdrawal signs occur
11 to completion	Reduce 0.2 mg/day or by one-half each day, not to exceed 0.4 mg/day.

Schedule for heroin, morphine, oxycodone HCl, meperidine HCl, and levorphanol patients:

Outpatient/Inpatient	Total dose/day (mg) in three divided doses of clonidine (mg)
Day 1	0.3 to 0.6
2	0.4 to 0.8
3	0.6 to 1.2
5	Maintain above
6 through completion	Reduce 0.2 mg/day; give in divided doses; the nighttime dose should be reduced last, or reduce by one-half each day not to exceed 0.4 mg/day.

Precautions for outpatients.   Do not give more than two days' supply. The patient should not drive during the first few days. Blood pressure should be checked when the patient is seen. If dizziness occurs, instruct the patient to cut back on dose or to lie down.

Lower clonidine doses are used on day 1 because narcotic withdrawal is less severe at that point, and the patient usually needs time to adjust to the sedative effects of clonidine. It is useful to give 0.1 mg clonidine as the initial dose and observe the patient's reaction and blood pressure at least over the next hour. The total daily dose should be divided into three parts given at six-hour intervals. Unless the patient is either very thin or very obese, standard doses are used rather than basing dose on patient's body weight. However, the doses from days 2 to 10 should usually not exceed 17 μg/kg/day.

During withdrawal from long-acting opioids such as methadone, clonidine doses can be increased over several days. In treating withdrawal from short-acting opioids, doses of clonidine are increased (titrated to symptoms) as rapidly as is consistent with concern for side effects because serious withdrawal symptoms appear earlier. However, the duration of clonidine dosing is shorter.

Anti-withdrawal effects usually begin within 30 minutes and peak at two to three hours. For inpatients, blood pressure should be checked before each dose; if 85/55 mm Hg or lower, subsequent doses are withheld until the pressure stabilizes. Dizziness between doses is best handled by monitoring blood pressure and having the patient lie down. If the pressure is too low, dosage should be reduced. It may be useful to have tolazoline (Priscoline), a clonidine antagonist, available for hypotensive crises.

Clonidine side effects.   Sedation is commonly experienced, especially within the first few days, but usually remits by day 3 or 4. Dry mouth and facial pain are less common.

Insomnia and other reactions to withdrawal.   With methadone withdrawal, insomnia is not usually a problem until day 3 or 4 but occurs by day 2 or 3 with short active opiates. Paradoxically, clonidine may worsen the insomnia associated with detoxification even while causing sedation during the day. Other withdrawal symptoms not relieved by clonidine are primarily muscle aching, nervousness, and irritability. Benzodiazepines may be used both for the muscle aching and the insomnia, but they should be given with caution because many addicts abuse this class of drugs. Diazepam 10 mg/day tid for muscle spasm and flurazepam 30 mg at bedtime have been commonly employed.

Analgesic effects of clonidine.   Clonidine is known to have mild analgesic effects. Thus in withdrawing "medical opiate addicts" there may be no need for analgesia during the withdrawal period, even though the original painful condition persists to some extent. Pain usually returns 24 to 48 hours after the last clonidine dose; if naltrexone is to be used, pain needs to be treated with nonnarcotic analgesics.

Clonidine detoxification has been used to facilitate the initiation of naltrexone because it avoids the extra seven- to 10-day wait required after the last methadone dose if methadone has been used as the withdrawal agent. An ultra-rapid detoxification technique using a combination of clonidine and naltrexone has been used experimentally both to facilitate naltrexone reduction and to shorten withdrawal generally. Of 40 patients stabilized on methadone up to 50 mg/day (mean dose 32 mg) for periods up to several years (mean duration 46 months), 38 were successfully transferred to oral naltrexone within a period of six days (Charney et al. 1986). The technique involved using clonidine beginning with 5 μg/kg of clonidine and simultaneously starting naltrexone 1 mg orally. The naltrexone dose was repeated every four hours in gradually increasing doses; the clonidine was also given every four hours, with dosage adjusted on the basis of severity of withdrawal. By the sixth hospital day, 38 of 40 patients were able to take 50 mg of naltrexone without significant withdrawal discomfort. Charney et al. estimated that many patients could be discharged on naltrexone and clonidine after the fourth hospital day, thereby significantly shortening the usual 10- to 14-day period of hospitalization.

Opioid Antagonists

The use of opioid antagonists in treating opioid dependence was originally based on the hypothesis that classically and operantly reinforced drug-seeking behaviors contribute to the high relapse rate following detoxification. It was postulated that by blocking the reinforcing effects of opioids, antagonist use would lead to extinction of the operant behavior and that conditioned reinforced withdrawal symptoms, no longer reinforced by cycles of dependence, would also be extinguished (McNicholas and Martin 1984; Resnick et al. 1980). Several different opioid antagonists have been tried clinically. In double-blind studies, results have not been dramatic. For the most part, opioid addicts at public clinics do not continue to take the drugs long enough or consistently enough to obtain the postulated extinction. Six to eight weeks is about the average duration of treatment (Capone et al. 1986; Resnick et al. 1980).

Naltrexone (Trexan) is a long-acting orally effective agent that, when given daily (50 mg) or three times weekly in doses of 100 mg on weekdays and 150 on weekends, produces substantial blockade of the effects of large doses of injected opioid drugs (e.g., 25 mg of heroin iv) (Resnick et al. 1980). In a large double-blind multiclinic study, the attrition rate was so high that it was not possible to demonstrate significant clinical benefits attributable to naltrexone (National Research Council 1978). However, these studies generally required detoxification from either heroin or methadone over a period of a week or two. A more rapid induction to naltrexone may have yielded different results. Patients transferred from long-term methadone to naltrexone over a period of two to three days using clonidine to control withdrawal experienced less protracted withdrawal than patients gradually withdrawn from methadone. It is postulated that the use of naltrexone may reduce protracted withdrawal by accelerating the restoration of normal CNS function (Charney et al. 1986).

Despite the low levels of compliance observed in double-blind studies involving opioid addicts with few social supports and occupational skills, experienced clinicians report that naltrexone is beneficial when prescribed for patients who are well motivated and who have family support and intact legitimate careers (e.g., addicted physicians and other professionals). Such patients are far more likely to take the drug for several months, and those who do so are far more likely to be free of opioid dependence at the one-year follow-up period. One-year abstinence rates of up to 70 percent among such individuals have been reported (Washton et al. 1984a). Those public programs that combine naltrexone with high levels of rehabilitative service have higher compliance and retention rates than those observed in double-blind studies and have also noted that patients taking the drug for more than two months are less likely to be opioid-dependent at follow-up (Capone et al. 1986; Resnick et al. 1980).

In clinical trials with heroin addicts, toxicity was generally low. However, when it was given to nonaddict obese subjects at doses of 300 mg/day, some of the subjects developed elevated transaminase values—for example, serum glutamic-pyruvic transaminase (SGPT) values three to 19 times higher than baseline—indicating that naltrexone at such dosage can produce hepatocellular injury. Naltrexone is therefore contraindicated in acute hepatitis or liver failure. It was previously held that patients must be free of opioid dependence before the use of naltrexone and should be tested first with naloxone. However, new special techniques for use of naltrexone with clonidine are exceptions to this generalization.

Opioid Maintenance

Methadone maintenance is a major modality for treating opioid dependence. The modern maintenance approach, as initiated in 1964 by Dole and Nyswander (1967), postulated that high doses of methadone, a typical μ agonist opioid that tends to bind nonspecifically to tissues, would alleviate "drug hunger" and simultaneously block, by means of cross-tolerance, the euphoria produced by self-administered heroin. Patients would be less preoccupied with drug-seeking behavior and could channel their energies into more productive avenues with help and rehabilitation. The first several hundred chronic heroin addicts treated with this approach showed little tendency to discontinue treatment, dramatic decreases in use of illicit opioids, decreased criminal activity, and increased legitimate, productive work. On the basis of these results, Dole and Nyswander further postulated that opioid dependence is unrelated to antecedent psychological difficulties and that most of the traits of instability and unreliability found in addicts are the consequence, rather than the cause, of their opioid addiction. As other programs utilizing methadone were established, and more disturbed and less motivated patients were admitted, the results were often less dramatic than those seen by Dole and Nyswander (Hubbard et al. 1983; Sells 1979).

Opioid maintenance programs and programs using opioids for detoxification are required to follow detailed federal, state, and sometimes local regulations. Under federal regulations for maintenance treatment, individuals must be actively dependent, have a history of one year of "physiologic dependence," and (unless special approval from FDA and state agencies is obtained) be at least 16 years of age. If otherwise qualified, those recently released from prison need not be actively "physiologically dependent." Regulations also govern dosage. For example, maximum first-day dosage cannot exceed 40 mg of methadone.

Methadone maintenance programs vary with respect to dosage, acceptance of continued antisocial behavior, and long-term goals. Many early programs viewed continued heroin use as a response to an inherent or acquired metabolic deficiency that caused a persistent "drug hunger." These programs used doses of methadone (usually 80 to 120 mg/day) high enough to suppress this drug hunger and to block the effects of illicit opioids.

Other programs found that lower doses of methadone (20 to 60 mg) were adequate to suppress drug-seeking behavior, even if they did not produce adequate cross-tolerance to large doses of heroin. These programs see methadone as a transitional stage to eventual detoxification. They emphasize behavioral change and are less tolerant of continued use of illicit drugs.

Disruptive patients pose problems for methadone maintenance programs because these patients would probably do worse if discharged. However, permitting them to remain in the treatment program demoralizes both staff and the other patients.

Long-term effects.   In terms of organic toxicity, the relative safety of methadone is established. Tolerance to many of its opioid agonist actions, however, is incomplete, and continuing pharmacologic effects are seen in some patients (Kreek 1983). Not all patients develop tolerance to the mood-elevating effects of methadone. In double-blind studies, patients report a greater sense of well-being a few hours after ingesting their daily dose (McCaul et al. 1982).

In-treatment outcome.   The majority of patients treated in methadone programs show significant decreases in opioid and nonopioid drug use, criminal behaviors, and depressive symptoms, as well as increases in gainful employment (Dole and Joseph 1978; Hubbard et al. 1983; Simpson et al. 1982). Some programs seem to be more effective than others in retaining patients in treatment and in helping patients achieve positive outcomes on various measures. During the first year, retention rates in methadone programs vary from 85 percent to well under 50 percent. Programs espousing the view that methadone is more of a transitional treatment on the way to total abstinence, those utilizing only lower methadone doses (20 to 40 mg), or those utilizing more confrontational techniques with their patients tend to have lower retention rates than those favoring indefinite treatment, those utilizing high or flexible doses of methadone, or those using support rather than confrontation (Brown et al. 1982). Not only do maintenance programs seem more effective for patients with severe psychiatric symptomatology than therapeutic communities (McLellan 1986), but many opioid users with low levels of symptomatology and more criminality choose detoxification over maintenance (Kosten et al. 1986c). Further, those with low levels of psychiatric symptomatology may drop out only to re-enter at some later period at which time they are often functioning better than at initial administration.

Detoxification and long-term outcome.   For some methadone maintenance patients, successful withdrawal is extremely difficult because of withdrawal symptoms or return of drug craving; a very slow, gradual tapering of the dosage seems to be the most acceptable approach. Even for those patients who successfully detoxify after a period of maintenance, the ability to remain abstinent over the short-term is uncertain. The percentage of patients remaining abstinent for one to three years after detoxification ranges from 12 to 28 percent for unselected samples of patients—some of whom were detoxified for violation of clinic rules—to 83 percent when analysis is restricted to those who elect to be withdrawn with staff and patient agreement that the treatment is complete (Dole and Joseph 1978; Stimmel et al. 1977). Predictors of retention and positive outcome in treatment do not necessarily predict success in achieving long-term positive outcome or long-term abstinence once withdrawal is completed.

In general, patients with shorter drug histories, less criminality, and more stable work histories who have been maintained in the program for longer periods of time but at lower dosages seem more successful that other patients in detoxifying. Those patients with families are also more successful. A study of a sample of methadone programs included in a national, multiclinic follow-up found that 40 percent of former methadone patients interviewed were abstinent from all illicit opioids and did not have any other significant drug problems six years after completing their initial treatment (Simpson et al. 1982).

Reentry into treatment may not represent treatment failure. Many opioid users drop out when they have achieved an improved social adjustment and have this opioid use under control. Quite often at reentry there exist less opioid dependence, physical disability, and criminality than did on initial admission, suggesting a positive impact for intermittent treatment (Kosten et al. 1986).

Other opioid maintenance drugs. L-AAM is similar to methadone in its pharmacologic actions. Because it is converted into active metabolites that have very long biologic half-lives, L-AAM can be given as infrequently as three times per week (Jaffe and Martin 1985). This reduces the inconvenience of daily clinic attendance to ingest the drug and simultaneously reduces concerns about illicit diversion. Over the past 15 years, L-AAM has been shown to be equivalent to methadone in suppressing illicit opioid use and in encouraging productive activity in both double-blind and large-scale multicenter open studies (Ling et al. 1978; Tennant et al. 1986; Zangwell et al. 1986). However, it has been found consistently that treatment retention rates are lower with L-AAM than with methadone when the latter is used at dosage of 80 to 100 mg/day. A small percentage of patients complain of side effects (e.g., nervousness and stimulation) not commonly seen with methadone (Zangwell et al. 1986). Nevertheless, in two studies, some patients who had taken both L-AAM and methadone reported L-AAM to be preferable at least in some respects (Tennant et al. 1986; Trueblood et al. 1978). Because different patients form and metabolize the various active metabolites at different rates, the pharmacology of L-AAM is more complex than that of methadone. Treatment with L-AAM is more difficult to initiate than treatment with methadone, and its use demands a more skilled clinician (Ling et al. 1984; Tennant et al. 1986).

Buprenorphine

Buprenorphine (Temgesic) is available as an analgesic in Europe and Australia. It is considered a partial mu-receptor agonist, producing morphine-like effects at low doses, but exhibiting a ceiling effect, so that the intensity of its actions does not seem to exceed that achieved with 30 to 60 mg of morphine. Because of this ceiling, risk of overdose may be limited. Given chronically, buprenorphine blocks the subjective effects of parenterally administered morphine or heroin (Jasinski et al. 1978). In experimental settings, chronic heroin users given access to iv heroin sharply reduced their heroin intake when maintained on subcutaneous buprenorphine (Mello and Mendelson 1980). It is unclear whether the blocking action is due to cross-tolerance or to antagonist-like actions. Given to subjects on high doses of opioids, buprenorphine precipitates abstinence; with subjects on low doses, it suppresses withdrawal. The drug binds quite firmly to receptors. Doses of naloxone up to 4 mg do not precipitate withdrawal, although higher doses may do so. Buprenorphine has been proposed as an alternative to methadone in opioid maintenance programs (Jasinski et al. 1978), but in outpatient settings buprenorphine appears to be as effective as low doses of methadone for detoxifying heroin users over a period of weeks (Bickel et al. in press). However, no systematic studies of its value as a maintenance agent have been carried out.

Heroin Versus Methadone

Only one study has compared legitimately prescribed iv heroin to methadone in a random assignment study (Hartnoll et al. 1980). At a London clinic, subjects assigned to legally prescribed heroin continued to inject heroin and stayed involved with the drug culture. Some of the subjects assigned to oral methadone maintenance refused to participate and left treatment immediately. At the one-year follow-up period, 29 percent of oral methadone patients were still at the clinic; 40 percent had left the clinic and were no longer using opioids regularly. Over the 12-month period, more patients assigned to heroin than to oral methadone died or were admitted to hospitals for drug-related problems. Differences in baseline rates of criminality make it difficult to evaluate the net impact of the two types of treatment on crime.

Therapeutic Communities

The dominant perspective of the hundreds of therapeutic communities that have evolved over the past 25 years is that the drug addict is emotionally immature and requires a total immersion in a specialized social structure to modify lifelong destructive behavioral patterns. The addict is expected to live in the therapeutic community for approximately 12 to 18 months. Group sessions, called encounters, usually involving harsh confrontations and mutual criticisms, remain a key element in present-day therapeutic communities. The community also acts in many respects as a surrogate family. Deviation from community expectations in terms of behavior or attitude frequently results in harsh criticisms by staff or by the entire community. Assumption of responsibility within the community is rewarded with increased personal freedom, material comfort, and status. Expulsion from the community is the ultimate punishment, but many addicts who are referred by the criminal justice system may face trial and/or incarceration if they leave the therapeutic community before completing treatment.

Most therapeutic communities were once quite selective, forcing applicants to show a high degree of motivation before they were accepted. Despite this selectivity, drop-out rates were high, with about 50 percent dropping out in the first 90 days, 70 percent within six months, and up to 90 percent by 12 months (DeLeon 1985). Criteria for entry have been modified. Now a substantial proportion of entrants are referred by the courts, and external pressure to stay in treatment has been increased. In addition, the average entrants to therapeutic communities have shown increasing symptoms of depression, poorer performance on IQ tests, and increased tendencies toward suicidal and aggressive behavior (DeLeon et al. 1986).

Therapeutic communities now vary considerably in attitudes toward professionals and in actual staffing patterns (Bale et al. 1984; DeLeon 1985). In every community, at least a few ex-addicts are key personnel on the staff; they serve as role models and visible signs that recovery and acceptance are possible and expected. Some therapeutic communities (e.g., Phoenix House, Odyssey House) are directed by psychiatrists and employ a number of health professionals in key positions. Some federally supported programs have begun to develop individualized treatment plans and to use health care professionals (e.g., physicians, psychologists, master's level counselors, or social workers).

For the average opioid user, residence in a therapeutic community leads to major decreases in drug-related problems; indicators of depression decrease as well. Follow-up studies of "graduates" and drop-outs indicate that patients remaining 90 days or longer exhibit significant decreases in self-reported antisocial behavior, illicit drug use, and recorded arrests, as well as significant increases in legitimate employment. Patients who stay longer have better outcomes on all dimensions at both one- and five-year follow-up intervals (Bale et al. 1984; DeLeon 1985). However, the work of McLellan, O'Brien, Woody, and their co-workers suggests that those opioid users with high levels of psychiatric symptomatology do less well in therapeutic communities than in other forms of therapy (e.g., methadone maintenance); for some, improvement correlates negatively with duration of therapeutic community residence

(McLellan 1986). Therapeutic communities have little appeal to those opioid addicts who have stable and gainful employment and satisfactory marital relationships.

Outpatient Drug-Free Programs

These treatment programs have the same goals as residential therapeutic communities, but they attempt to achieve them in an outpatient setting. The programs vary widely in philosophy, staffing patterns, and program content. They range from highly organized daytime therapeutic communities to drop-in centers offering conversational ("rap") sessions and recreational activities. Outpatient drug-free programs tend to deal mostly with multiple-drug abusers. One of the few outpatient drug-free approaches to relapse prevention that has been subjected to any form of controlled evaluation is built around evidence of stimuli that elicit conditioned craving and withdrawal.

Counseling and Psychotherapy

NA is a self-help group of abstinent drug addicts modeled on AA. While not subjected to formal analysis, there do appear to be benefits from group support. McAuliffe and co-workers developed support groups built on the premise that opioid dependence involves complex learned patterns of behavior and that the prevention of relapse requires the avoidance of those stimuli that have become operantly and classically conditioned to opioid craving, opioid highs, and opioid withdrawal. Controlled studies in the United States and in Hong Kong have shown this new self-help group approach, which differs substantially from the Twelve Step approach of AA, to have significant value (McAuliffe and Ch'ien 1986).

Patients in methadone programs derive significantly greater benefit from individual psychotherapy than from drug counseling alone. Individual, cognitive, and behaviorally oriented therapy or analytically oriented and supportive-expressive therapies were both superior to counseling alone (Woody et al. 1984). Once patients have been in treatment for a while, they appear to be reluctant to engage in psychotherapy (Rounsaville et al. 1983c). To engage patients in individual therapy, it should be started early and be an integral part of the program. Patients who usually do poorly in treatment (i.e., those with more severe psychiatric symptomatology) appear to benefit most from this added help, and with such help their prognosis approaches that of less severely symptomatic patients (McLellan 1986; Woody et al. 1984).

One controlled study with methadone maintained patients suggested that, if urinalysis results are available to monitor drug use, skillful family therapy is superior to standard drug counseling in fostering decreased illicit drug use (Stanton 1982). Family therapy is also used with patients who are not in methadone programs, but controlled studies are lacking (see Kaufman 1986).

Associated and Special Problems

Medical Complications and Life Expectancy

Among older opioid addicts, the mortality rate is two- to threefold higher than that of nonaddicts; for younger addicts, it is up to 20-fold higher than that of age-matched controls. The overall death rate for opioid addicts who have sought treatment is about 1 to 1.5 percent a year. Contributing to the increased mortality rate are deaths from overdose, homicide, infections, and suicide (Simpson et al. 1982; Stimson and Oppenheimer 1982). Over a period of five years, heroin overdose deaths reported by medical examiners in large urban areas ranged from 0.5 to 17 per 100,000 population; fluctuations in this rate were due in part to changes in drug purity. It has been postulated that casual use of heroin combined with quinine (a dilutant) and ethanol also contributes to the likelihood of overdose death (Ruttenberg and Luke 1984).

Although oral opioids are relatively nontoxic, those who inject opioids, even doctors and nurses with access to pure drugs and sterile materials, often neglect to follow hygienic precautions. Infections of skin and internal organs are common. Addicts who filter drugs through cotton or cigarette filters, or who use drugs intended for oral use, introduce starch, talc, and other particulates into the bloodstream, thereby producing embolic and septic phenomena in multiple organs. Other complications related to sharing of injection equipment or life-style include transmission of diseases such as hepatitis, malaria, and the human immunodeficiency virus (HIV), which is responsible for acquired immune deficiency syndrome (AIDS). Testing of patients at drug treatment clinics in the Northeastern United States indicated that as many as 50 percent of patients have positive reactions for HIV antibodies; on the West Coast less than 5 percent of opioid users had positive reactions (Lange et al. unpublished data). It is unclear at present how many of these addicts will develop clinical manifestations of AIDS (Landesman et al. 1985).

Other Complications

Other complications associated with drug effects or contaminants include a variety of pathologic changes in the CNS ranging from transverse myelitis and peripheral neuropathy to severe parkinsonism. The latter syndrome has been produced by a toxic impurity 1-Methyl-4-phenyl-1,2,3,6-Tetrahydropyridine (MPTP) found in synthetic opioids (related to fentanyl) produced in clandestine laboratories (Langston et al. 1984).

Special Problems of Women

Opioid-dependent women are more likely than men to cite medical problems (infections, toxemia) for seeking treatment. They are also more likely to exhibit depression and decreased self-esteem and less likely to have personal resources or vocational skills.

The pregnant opioid addict presents very special problems; opioid withdrawal is far more hazardous to the fetus than to the healthy adult. Many clinicians believe that low-dose methadone maintenance (10 to 40 mg/day) combined with good prenatal care is preferable to continued heroin use or to higher dosage methadone regimens that carry the risk of severe neonatal withdrawal. Reductions in dose levels should be slow (1 mg every three days), and complete withdrawal should be accomplished if deemed necessary during the second trimester (Finnegan 1979). Even with low doses of methadone, the neonatal opioid withdrawal syndrome will frequently require intervention. Oral opioids, such as paregoric, are superior to sedatives (Finnegan et al. 1984).

Alcoholism

Lifetime diagnosis rates of alcoholism of 25 to 40 percent have been reported from various clinic populations. Many of those diagnosed as alcoholic also meet criteria for some form of affective disorder as well (Mirin et al. 1986; Rounsaville et al. 1982). There is a general belief that active alcoholism among patients treated with methadone reduces the likelihood of a good treatment outcome (Green and Jaffe 1977). Special treatment is often provided, but it has been difficult to demonstrate in controlled studies that special programs, special AA counselors, or even the use of disulfiram (Antabuse), which can be combined with methadone without adverse effects, improves retention in treatment or reduce alcohol-related problems (Ling et al. 1983; Stimmel et al. 1983).

Affective Disorders

As shown in Table 1, some form of affective dysregulation is the most common additional psychiatric disorder found among opioid addicts in treatment. The lifetime prevalence rates for any affective disorder criteria exceed 70 percent. Women and those abusing sedative agents seem especially likely to exhibit depressive symptoms. Without any specific treatment directed at depressive symptoms, a substantial percentage of patients reporting depressive symptoms report less depression within the first several months after entry into treatment. Depression among opioid addicts is usually secondary. There is disagreement about the severity of depression typically found among opioid addicts. Some clinicians report that it is generally mild to moderate; others find it often reaches levels where suicide is attempted (Kleber 1983; Rounsaville et al. 1983b). When data are uncorrected for psychiatric severity, depressed patients entering methadone maintenance, therapeutic communities, or outpatient drug-free clinics appear to show about equal degrees of improvement (Ginzburg et al. 1984).

Those patients with manic, hypomanic, or bipolar disorders can benefit from treatment with lithium, which can be combined with either methadone or naltrexone without adverse interactions. For those patients continuing to experience symptoms of depression, efforts at more specific pharmacologic intervention or psychological treatment would appear logical. Several controlled studies of tricyclic antidepressants have been completed. Over a four-week period, doxepin 100 mg/day mixed with methadone produced a more rapid improvement in depressive symptoms than did placebo, but the magnitude of the difference was not great. Imipramine 140 mg/day was not superior to placebo, both groups showing significant improvement (Kleber 1983; Kleber et al. 1983). Patients with severe depression should, nevertheless, be given whatever benefits are to be derived from pharmacotherapy for depression.

It is conceivable that with monitoring of plasma drug levels to assure adequate therapeutic levels, more pronounced effects of antidepressants might have been seen. Because severity of psychiatric problems is a major predictor of overall treatment success (McLellan 1986; McLellan et al. 1983; Woody et al. 1984), clinicians should pay particular attention to persistent depression. It is likely that research in this area will continue despite relatively disappointing findings to date.

Schizophrenia and anxiety disorders rarely receive specific attention in opioid dependence treatment programs. Only one study has been done. Since many of those with anxiety disorders may also have affective disorders, tricyclic antidepressants such as doxepin may be the drugs of choice. Frank schizophrenia is uncommon (less than 1 percent) among patients treated for opioid dependence. Dopaminergic blockers should be useful and can be combined with methadone or naltrexone. Opioids, including methadone, appear to exert some antipsychotic and antimanic effects in some drug users. It has been postulated that these beneficial effects are due to the interactions of the opioids with dopaminergic systems (Kleber 1983).

Opioids and Crime

In the United States, more than 50 percent of heroin addicts have been arrested prior to first use of opioids, and from 30 to 50 percent of illicit opioid users seeking treatment at clinics meet DSM-III criteria for antisocial personality. For many users of illicit opioids, criminal activity after onset of drug use is merely a continuation of a criminal life-style; but it is also true that while they are addicted to illicit opioids, the rate of criminal activity is one-and-a-half- to threefold higher than it is during periods of abstinence or of less than daily use (Anglin and McGlothlin 1984; Nurco et al. 1984). Among individuals without a history of antisocial behavior, chronic use of opioids supplied at low cost or through legitimate channels does not usually result in criminal behavior. Because chronic criminal activity often antedates opioid use, it is unrealistic to expect successful treatment of opioid dependence to eliminate criminal behavior entirely. Treatment in a therapeutic community for periods of several months is frequently associated with long-term decreases in criminal behavior. How this is achieved, whether by an alteration of personality or a selection process by which only the less violent, angry, and unstable addicts remain for more than a few months, is still unclear. Research on the biologic antecedents and correlates of sociopathy and violence is proceeding rapidly. Conceivably, treatments aimed at underlying processes could alter both drug use and criminality.

Prognosis and Natural History

Those who become dependent in the context of medical treatment may experience little interference with normal functioning if they use opioids orally and if their pain is controlled by the amount of drug physicians are willing to prescribe. If pain is not controlled or if more drug or altered schedules are demanded, patients may find themselves involved with repeated diagnostic procedures, attempts at withdrawal, and treatment for depression.

It is likely that many of those who go on to develop some degree of opioid dependence recover without having ever sought formal treatment. Certainly, the number of experimenters and chronic opioid users in the United States over the last 10 years is far larger than the total number who have ever entered treatment programs.

Most of those who persist in using illicit opioids for any substantial period are very likely to come to the attention of the police or to seek treatment for the addiction. For the past decade, the time from addiction to illicit opioids to first treatment has been about two to three years. In general, those who do not seek treatment have fewer legal problems, less psychopathology (especially depression), and more social supports (jobs and family), but, surprisingly, not a lesser degree of dependence (Rounsaville and Kleber 1985).

Opioid addicts who seek treatment in the United States and in England are quite diverse in their attitudes toward conventional values, life-styles, and degree of criminality. They range from the conventional, who hold jobs and are generally law-abiding citizens ("comformists" or "stables"), to those who are highly identified with an addict subculture and subsist exclusively on the proceeds of illicit activities ("hustlers" or "junkies"). Others seem to be "loners," living on welfare rather than by illicit activities; some engage in some criminal activities while living primarily on legitimate earnings (Stimson and Oppenheimer 1982).

The early stages of dependence are often marked by repeated efforts (voluntary or involuntary) to achieve abstinence followed by relapse, often after only a few months. Typically, when no adjuvant treatment such as naltrexone is used, two-thirds of patients will relapse to opioid use within six months following treatment for withdrawal. Repeated relapse is not inevitable, however. For example, 88 percent of US Army enlisted men who became addicted to heroin in Vietnam did not become readdicted any time in the three years following their return to the United States; 56 percent did not use opioids at all during that time (Robins et al. 1975).

Follow-up Studies of Treated Opioid Dependence

Opioid addiction is a disorder that eventually remits for a significant proportion of addicts who survive. Those heavily involved in crime and illicit drug sales are least likely to "mature out" of addiction (Anglin et al. 1985). In a multiprogram study including major treatment modalities, men who were daily heroin users when they entered treatment in 1972 and 1973 were followed up six years later. Patients had been out of initial treatment programs for an average of four years, but many had subsequently reentered the same or other programs or had been incarcerated at some point. Twenty-nine percent were not located or could not be interviewed. Five percent were known to be dead. Of those interviewed, about 5 percent were in jail; 23 percent were using illicit opioids regularly; 3 percent had been abstinent but had relapsed; 12 percent were receiving methadone from clinics; 8 percent were abstinent from opioids but using alcohol or other drugs heavily; and 49 percent were entirely abstinent from opioids and were not abusing other drugs. Over shorter follow-up periods, methadone maintenance, therapeutic communities, and drug-free programs were significantly superior to detoxification programs, but by the sixth year there were no longer any important differences between groups (Simpson et al. 1982).

A seven-year follow-up of addicts who initially received injectable heroin at several clinics in London in 1969 revealed an equally diverse outcome: 12 percent were dead; 5 percent were in prison; 5 percent were using illicit opioids regularly; 43 percent were still receiving opioids from clinics (90 percent of those were still injecting); 24 percent were entirely abstinent and using no other drugs; and the status of 4 percent was uncertain (Stimson and Oppenheimer 1982).

In general, the various measures of outcome, work, crime, drug use, and psychological adjustment are best predicted by different pretreatment variables. Thus pretreatment stable employment predicts posttreatment employment; high pretreatment crime levels predict posttreatment criminal activity (Rounsaville et al. 1986). However, severity of psychiatric symptoms (psychiatric severity) appears to be a more general predictor of outcome. Those with least severe psychiatric problems appear to respond better to all treatments on all outcome measures (McLellan et al. 1983; Rounsaville et al. 1986); those with the most severe symptoms do more poorly in all treatments.

In a 2.5-year outcome study of 361 opioid addicts with a 76 percent follow-up rate (Kosten et al. 1986b; Rounsaville et al. 1986), length of time in drug abuse treatment during the 2.5 years was associated with a significantly greater percentage of time abstinent from drug abuse. Life crises, especially arguments and "exits," were significant risk factors for continued drug abuse as was depression; treatment was shown to ameliorate these factors and lead to a better outcome.

Taken together, recent work suggests that patients who can benefit from different kinds of psychotherapeutic interventions can be identified and that outpatient treatment, mainly methadone maintenance in these cases, when combined with such interventions, can increase the effectiveness of treating the opiate addict.

Chapter 135

Antagonist Treatment: Naltrexone

Seldom does a distinctly new and different treatment become available for general use. However, this was the case in 1985, when naltrexone, a specific opioid antagonist, was approved by the Food and Drug Administration. This new drug specifically blocks opioid receptors; while the drug is present, it prevents re-addiction to heroin and other opioid drugs. Since it is so different from available treatments, naltrexone is commonly misunderstood. Clinicians tend to confuse it with disulfiram (Antabuse) in the treatment of alcoholism or methadone for maintenance of opioid addicts. As an antagonist, naltrexone's mechanism is different and, to use this tool effectively, these differences must be clearly understood.

Although pharmacologically distinctive, naltrexone does not change the fundamental requirements of good treatment for addiction. Rehabilitation still requires a comprehensive treatment program with attention to the nonpharmacologic variables that play a critical role in the complex problem of addiction. Thus the prescription of naltrexone alone will not work. It should be part of an overall treatment program that includes individual or group psychotherapy, family therapy, contingency contracting, and possibly behavioral extinction of drug-conditioned responses.

In considering this new treatment, it should be recognized that naltrexone will not appeal to the majority of opioid-dependent persons. Of street heroin addicts presenting for treatment, not more than 10 to 15 percent show any interest in a drug that "keeps you from getting high" (Greenstein et al. 1984). The vast majority prefer methadone treatment, but for those highly motivated patients who prefer to be opioid-free, naltrexone is an excellent alternative. Certain patients such as health care professionals, middle-class addicts, and former addicts given an early parole from prison may find naltrexone to be the treatment of choice.

It should also be emphasized that naltrexone is helpful only in the treatment of opioid dependence. Cocaine has become a common problem in recent years. Those patients dependent on both opioids and cocaine may be treated with naltrexone, but they will need additional therapy for cocaine dependence.

The Antagonist Concept

The opiates such as heroin and morphine as well as the synthetic opioids such as methadone and meperidine act through specific opioid receptors; these drugs are referred to as agonists (Jaffee and Martin 1985). Antagonists such as naloxone (Narcan) or naltrexone (Trexan) also bind to these receptors but they do not interact with the receptor in such a way that initiates the chain of cellular events that produce so-called opiate effects. Naloxone and naltrexone are relatively "pure" antagonists in that they produce little or no agonist activity at usual doses. This is in contrast to mixed agonist-antagonists such as nalorphine, which produce significant agonist effects. Not only do pure antagonists fail to produce opioid effects, but their presence at the receptor also prevents opioid agonists from binding to the receptor and producing "opiate effects." All of the effects of opioids are thus antagonized or blocked. There can be no opioid-induced euphoria, respiratory depression, pupillary construction, and so on (Martin et al. 1973; O'Brien et al. 1975).

Antagonist Effects

If a person not currently dependent on an opioid agonist receives an antagonist, there are usually no discernible effects. Theoretically, something should happen because the antagonist blocks endogenous opioids (endorphins), which may serve to regulate mood. In fact, there have been reports of dysphoric reactions and endocrine changes in experimental subjects given naltrexone (Ellingboe et al. 1980; Mendelson et al. 1980). Hollister et al. (1982) found adverse mood effects in normal volunteers given naltrexone. Crowley et al. (1985) noted similar effects in recently detoxified opioid addicts. These dysphoric effects of naltrexone were reported after brief treatment (one day to three weeks), and the number of subjects was very small. In contrast, one study of normals reported no differences in mood effects between naltrexone and placebo (O'Brien et al. 1978). Moreover, most large-scale studies in recovering opiate addicts have not found dysphoria or other mood changes to be a problem in the clinical use of naltrexone (Brahen et al. 1984; Greenstein et al. 1984; Tennant et al. 1984; Washton et al. 1984). It may be that blocking endogenous opioids with naltrexone produces mood problems in some patients, and this may explain part of the early drop-out phenomenon. Those who continue on naltrexone for months or even years report no mood effects.

There have been occasional reports (Sideroff et al. 1978) of reduced drug-craving in naltrexone-maintained patients, but it is not clear that this is a pharmacologic effect. It may simply be a reduction in craving caused by the security that patients feel knowing that they are protected from potential opiate effects by the pharmacologic blockade (Meyer et al. 1975).

On the other hand, persons currently dependent on opioids are exquisitely sensitive to antagonists. Even a very small dose of naloxone or naltrexone will rapidly displace enough opioid from receptors to precipitate a withdrawal syndrome. Thus in the clinical use of naltrexone, it is important to be certain that an opioid-dependent person is fully detoxified prior to starting antagonist treatment.

Naloxone and naltrexone differ in several important ways. Naloxone is poorly absorbed from the gut; when given parenterally, it is rapidly metabolized. Naloxone, therefore, is useful only for the emergency treatment of opioid overdoses and in the diagnosis of physical dependence. If the presence of physical dependence is in question, a small (0.4 to 0.8 mg) injection of naloxone can be given. In a dependent person, a withdrawal syndrome would immediately occur, but it would be short-lived (20 to 60 minutes).

In contrast, naltrexone is well absorbed when given by mouth, and it is a long-acting drug. It too could be used to reverse an overdose, but it is usually more practical to use a short-acting drug like naloxone administered by an iv drip, which can be titrated as needed. In this way, an overdose can be reversed by a short-acting drug without the danger of precipitating a withdrawal reaction in an opioid-dependent person. However, a long-acting drug such as naltrexone is ideal for use in preventing relapse to opioids. In the presence of naltrexone, heroin self-administration is no longer rewarding, and the behavior is observed to stop (Mello et al. 1980b). It has been shown to be effective in antagonizing or at least attenuating the effects of opioids for 72 hours. Patients have reported even longer activity against the relatively weak heroin purchased on the street. While daily ingestion would provide the most secure protection against opioid effects, naltrexone can be given as infrequently as two or three times per week with good protection against re-addiction. Tolerance does not appear to develop to this antagonism even after more than a year of regular naltrexone ingestion (Kleber et al. 1985b).

Naltrexone, then, can permit recently detoxified addicts to return to their usual environments secure in the knowledge that they cannot succumb to an impulsive wish to "get high." For many patients, this may be the first time in years that they have been able to exist outside of a hospital or prison in an opioid-free state. The physiologic effects of opioid dependence are known to persist for months (Martin and Jasinski 1969). During this protracted abstinence, the patient's autonomic nervous system is unstable, and symptoms such as anxiety and sleep disturbances are common. Conditioned responses to environmental cues produced by previous drug use (Wikler 1965) also may contribute to relapse. Maintenance on naltrexone provides an ideal situation to extinguish these conditioned responses (O'Brien et al. 1979, 1984) and permit the protracted abstience syndrome to subside.

For a recovering addict who works in a field such as nursing, pharmacy, or medicine, there is an added benefit to naltrexone maintenance: it reduces suspicion about relapse. Since these medical occupations often require working with opioid drugs, there is a daily temptation to resume drug use. Of course, return to work is very important to rehabilitation, but it presents problems in a medical setting. Those colleagues who are aware of the patient's struggle with addiction tend to regard any hint of unusual behavior as a sign that relapse to addiction has occurred. However, with a program of verified naltrexone ingestion as part of a comprehensive treatment program, the professional can return to work. Physicians who are recovering addicts often cite this reduction of suspicion from colleagues as an important reason to continue naltrexone; some for five years or more. Of course, the opiate-free period also permits the use of psychotherapy to deal with underlying or superimposed psychosocial problems.

Comparison to Other Treatment Approaches

Like other treatments for addiction, naltrexone works best within a comprehensive program that deals with all aspects of the patient's problems (Resnick et al. 1979). Naltrexone is similar to methadone in this sense; both are medications that can reduce relapse to illicit drug use. There are significant differences, however. Methadone has been found to be an excellent treatment for the majority of street heroin users because it satisfies their drug craving. It also enables them to stop committing crimes because they no longer have an expensive drug habit to support. They can thus stabilize their lives, take care of their families, and find legal employment. Methadone does not "block" heroin's effects, however. There is cross-tolerance between heroin and methadone, and because street heroin is relatively weak, the methadone-maintained person will get little reward from the usual dose of heroin. In addition to satisfying opioid craving, methadone may produce beneficial psychoactive effects. In contrast, naltrexone cannot be given until all the opioids are out of the system. It does not produce opioid effects or any psychoactive benefits; patients are, therefore, without the feeling of opioids in their systems. Naltrexone will effectively block the effects of any subsequent opioid; thus the patient cannot experience euphoria or calming from the use of heroin.

Another important distinction from methadone is the absence of dependence on naltrexone. It can be stopped abruptly at any time without concern about withdrawal. In a sense, this lack of dependence is a drawback to naltrexone because no drug effect is perceived. Thus there is no built-in "reward," and there is no immediate penalty for stopping. Some clinicians have actually experimented with small monetary payments contingent on ingesting naltrexone in an effort to provide an external reward (Grabowski et al. 1979). Frequently patients feel so good and overconfident at being opioid-free that they may prematurely assume they no longer need naltrexone. They can stop naltrexone abruptly, but several days later they are again at risk for relapse to opioid use.

Another treatment strategy that is often confused with naltrexone is disulfiram (Antabuse). The drugs are similar only in that they are both taken to prevent relapse, and they are both nonaddicting. Disulfiram blocks the metabolism of alcohol, not its effects. If a person receiving disulfiram ingests alcohol, the normal degradation of alcohol is inhibited and acetaldehyde accumulates. Acetaldehyde produces flushing, nausea, and other noxious symptoms. These effects, of course, can be prevented by avoiding alcohol while taking disulfiram. In contrast, no such noxious effects result from the use of opioids in association with naltrexone treatment. The opioid effects are simply blocked or neutralized in the naltrexone pretreated person.

Patients Suited for Naltrexone

Physicians and Others in Medically Related Fields

The best results with naltrexone treatment have been found in studies of physicians and other medical professionals. For example, Washton et al. (1984) found that 74 percent of opioid-dependent physicians completed at least six months of treatment with naltrexone and were opioid-free and practicing medicine at one year follow-up. Ling and Wesson (1984) treated 60 health care professionals for an average of eight months. Forty-seven were rated as "much improved" or "moderately improved" at follow-up. Both of these studies involved comprehensive treatment programs, with naltrexone providing a kind of structure.

The comprehensive treatment program should involve a full medical evaluation, detoxification, psychiatric evaluation, family evaluation, and provision for ongoing therapy along with confirmed regular ingestion of naltrexone. Ongoing therapy usually involves marital therapy and individual therapy. Using this approach, the physician, whose drug use may have been discovered during a crisis, can be detoxified, started on naltrexone, and can be back at work practicing medicine in as little as two weeks. Of course, therapy including naltrexone may continue for several years, but the disruption of family life and medical practice is minimized.

Middle-Class or Suburban Addicts

In any treatment program, patients coming into treatment with the greatest assets tend to respond best to treatment. Thus it is not surprising that patients with a history of recent employment and good educational backgrounds do well on naltrexone. Some of these patients prefer not to be treated with methadone because it ties them to the clinic with daily visits, whereas with naltrexone there is greater flexibility. These patients may be strongly motivated to be drug-free, but they are still susceptible to impulsive drug use. Using naltrexone as a kind of insurance is often a very appealing idea.

Another practical reason that naltrexone has been successful in this population is that it can be prescribed by any licensed physician. Its use is not restricted to a special program for the treatment of addiction. It is recommended, however, that naltrexone be prescribed only by physicians who are familiar with the psychodynamics and behavior patterns of the addicted person. Patients may appreciate the opportunity for treatment by an experienced practitioner from a private office rather than being restricted to a drug treatment clinic.

Tennant et al. (1984) described a group of suburban practitioners treating opioid dependence in a wide range of socioeconomic groups in southern California. They reported on 160 patients with an average history of opioid use of 10.5 years. The majority (63.8 percent) were employed; all expressed a desire for abstinence-oriented treatment. Treatment was on an outpatient basis, and a naloxone challenge was given after completion of detoxification. After a graduated dose increase, naltrexone was given three times per week. Patients paid a fee or had the treatment covered by insurance. Each week the patients were subjected to a urine screen for all drug classes and an alcohol breath test. Counseling sessions were held weekly.

The 160 addicts remained in treatment a mean of 51 days with a range up to 635 days, but the majority were in short-term treatment. Only 27 (17 percent) remained longer than 90 days. Tests for illicit drug or alcohol use were only 1 to 3 percent positive. Tennant et al. (1984) considered the program, which is still in operation, to be successful. However, they pointed out that despite long remissions on naltrexone, relapse to opioid use can still occur after naltrexone is stopped. Based on follow-up results of naltrexone patients, Greenstein et al. (1983) found that while treatment with naltrexone tends to be short-term, even as little as 30 days of treatment is associated with a significant improvement in overall rehabilitative status at six-month follow-up.

Another study of middle-class patients in a higher socioeconomic group found predictably better results. Washton et al. (1984) treated 114 business executives addicted for at least two years on heroin, methadone, or prescription opioids. They were mainly white males about 30 years of age with a mean income of $42,000 per year. A critical feature of this group was that there was considerable external pressure for them to receive treatment and almost half were in jeopardy of losing their jobs or suffering legal consequences.

The Washton et al. (1984) treatment program was oriented toward complete abstinence. It began with four to 10 weeks of inpatient treatment, during which detoxification and induction onto naltrexone was accomplished. There were also intensive individual psychotherapy and involvement in self-help groups. The importance of the posthospital phase was stressed, and all patients signed a contract for aftercare treatment.

All 114 patients succeeded in completing naltrexone induction; 61 percent remained on naltrexone for at least six months with no missed visits or positive urines. An additional 20 percent took naltrexone for less than six months, but remained in the program with drug-free urines. Of the entire group, at 12- to 18-month follow-up, 64 percent were still opioid-free. Those who had stipulated pressure from their employers to get treatment did significantly better than the group without a clear-cut risk of loss of job.

Probationers and Parolees

It is well known that a large proportion of the inmates of prisons throughout the country have been convicted of drug-related crimes. Of course, relapse to drug use and consequent crime is common among these prisoners after they are released. One way to approach this recidivism and perhaps also alleviate some of the overcrowding of our prison system is to utilize a work-release or half-way house program enabling prisoners to obtain an early release with the stipulation that they work in the community and live in a prison-supervised house. Naltrexone can be prescribed for those prisoners who are former heroin addicts. A pioneering model of such a program has been in existence in Nassau County, Long Island, since 1972.

Dr. Leonard Brahen, the founder and director of this program, has reported on the results of 691 former inmates whom he treated with naltrexone (Brahen et al. 1984). The treatment is set within a work-release program during which the members live in a transitional house outside the prison and obtain employment in the community. Prior to the introduction of naltrexone, the success of former opioid addicts in the program was limited because of their high relapse rate on placement in an environment where drugs were freely available.

An inmate with a history of opioid addiction who wishes to volunteer for the program must first be stabilized on a narcotic antagonist. Random urine tests are also used to monitor the participants. Uncashed paychecks must be turned in as proof that attendance at work has been regular; a portion of the salary is applied to the cost of room and board. The participants are given supervision and counseling for problems that develop during this reentry period. Some try to use street heroin to "get high" despite the naltrexone, but because this fails they eventually abandon this behavior. Participants are also offered continuance in treatment after their sentences have been served.

Since the introduction of naltrexone, the rehabilitation success rate of the former addicts is equal to that of inmates without a drug history. Although a controlled study with random assignment to naltrexone was not conducted, the staff of the work-release program are enthusiastic about the benefits of naltrexone. Follow-up data suggest that even after completing their terms and leaving the program, the group treated with naltrexone had fewer drug arrests than did addict inmates who did not receive naltrexone treatment.

Street Heroin Addicts

Theoretically, any detoxified former opioid-dependent person can be treated with naltrexone. Success, however, requires that the person genuinely wish to remain drug-free. Unfortunately, most patients who assert strongly that they want to give up drugs have not really thought through the consequences of their statements. Once they find themselves on a medication that makes it physically impossible for them to "get high," they often change their minds.

The majority of street heroin addicts and participants in methadone maintenance programs are generally not interested in naltrexone treatment after learning how effectively it antagonizes opioids. Studies of the use of naltrexone in public drug treatment clinics have found that no more than 10 to 15 percent of patients are willing to try naltrexone, and they have observed high drop-out rates during the first month of naltrexone treatment (Greenstein et al. 1983; Hollister 1978; Judson and Goldstein 1984; O'Brien et al. 1975).

Among street heroin users involved in crime to support their drug habit, it is difficult to predict who will respond well to treatment with naltrexone, but certainly the proportion of appropriate cases is low. Publicly funded treatment programs may be discouraged by the cost of naltrexone (about three dollars per tablet), although the main cost of the treatment is the counseling required to support patients after detoxification. Most treatment programs have focused on patients who are employed or who have good employment prospects, have a stable relationship with spouse or family, and express willingness to enter into long-term psychotherapy or family therapy. Surprisingly, even short-term (30 days or more) treatment with naltrexone has been shown to be associated with improved outcome at six-month follow-up (Greenstein et al. 1983). Of course, those willing to remain on the antagonist for six to 12 months generally do well, but it is difficult to know to what degree the success is influenced by the patient's strong motivation as evidenced by remaining in treatment. Probably there is an interaction of several factors that produce a good outcome, and any single factor might not have been adequate by itself.

How to Use Naltrexone in a Comprehensive Treatment Program

Detoxification

An opioid abstinence-oriented program must begin with detoxification. This process facilitates the performance of a complete medical evaluation and the determination of what additional health problems may be present. Detoxification, which preferably should be accomplished on an inpatient basis, also allows opportunity for family and individual psychological evaluations.

There are several pharmacologic options for detoxification. Gradually reducing doses of methadone for five to 10 days constitutes one approach. At the other end of the spectrum, a rapid detoxification assisted by clonidine can have the patient ready for naltrexone in as little as 48 hours after being opioid-dependent (Kleber and Kosten 1984). The choice depends on the type of opioid agonist the patient was using (short-acting versus long-acting), the motivation of the patient, and the need for speed in returning the patient to work. See Chapter 134 for a discussion of the different types of withdrawal techniques.

Naloxone Testing for Residual Dependence

There are various methods for beginning treatment with naltrexone (Kleber and Kosten 1984). In all cases, it is important to make certain that there is no residual physical dependence on opioid agonists. If the patient has been using a long-acting opioid such as methadone, it may be necessary to wait seven to 10 days after the last dose before initiating treatment with naltrexone. With dependence on short-acting drugs such as heroin or hydromorphone, the time between detoxification and starting naltrexone can be much shorter. If naltrexone is started too soon, precipitated withdrawal will occur. Even mild withdrawal, consisting only of abdominal cramps or periods of nausea, may be enough to discourage the patient from further treatment. On the other hand, the eagerness of some patients to be protected by naltrexone and to return to work results in their willingness to tolerate mild withdrawal symptoms.

Most clinicians working with naltrexone have found that it is helpful to perform a naloxone test to determine if there is any residual physical dependence prior to giving the first dose of naltrexone. Naloxone can be given parenterally, 0.4 to 1.4 mg subcutaneously or intramuscularly. It can also be used intravenously if very rapid results are desired. A positive test indicating physical dependence consists of symptoms of opioid withdrawal such as nausea or cramps. If present, the symptoms, which would last only 20 to 40 minutes, indicate that the patient should wait at least another day before starting naltrexone.

Some clinicians prefer to use a very small oral dose of naltrexone rather than a naloxone injection to test for residual opioid dependence. They recommend a half or a quarter of a tablet (12.5 to 25 mg) as a safe dose. Certainly this approach is safe, but if even a mild withdrawal syndrome is precipitated, it will be of long duration (at least several hours and perhaps more than a day) and will possibly discourage the patient from further naltrexone treatment.

It is better to wait a longer time between the end of detoxification and the beginning of naltrexone rather than to risk evoking a precipitated withdrawal reaction. This time period is critical, however, because the patient is vulnerable to relapse, as yet unprotected by naltrexone. Thus the clinician must exercise judgment in balancing the benefits of rapid transition to naltrexone against the risks of discouraging the patient with a recurrence of physical withdrawal symptoms.

Naltrexone Maintenance

When the naloxone challenge is negative, naltrexone can be started with an initial dose of 25 mg (one-half tablet). If there are no side effects after an hour, another 25 mg may be administered. The recommended dose subsequently is 50 mg/day. After the first one to two weeks, it is usually possible to graduate to three doses per week (e.g., 100, 100, and 150 mg given on Monday, Wednesday, and Friday, respectively). It is critical that psychotherapy sessions be initiated early in treatment and that these involve family members and other significant figures in the patient's life.

It is important that ingestion of naltrexone be monitored rather than left to the patient's "willpower." Confirmed dosing can occur in the clinic, but it is usually disruptive to the patient's rehabilitation to have to come to the clinic for every dose. For this reason it is important to involve significant figures in the patient's life to observe the ingestion of naltrexone and to report periodically to the therapist. In the case of physicians, for example, a colleague may have already confronted the patient with the problem and helped steer the patient into therapy. This has sometimes been the chief of staff of a hospital or the chairperson of the patient's department. A family member or co-worker can be enlisted after determining the existence of a constructive relationship.

When therapy is progressing well as determined by engagement in psychotherapy, performance on the job, and absence of drug abuse as confirmed by urine analysis, a schedule of only two doses of naltrexone per week may be employed. This reduces the patient's dependence on the therapist and decreases the treatment's interference with the patient's life. Although the degree of pharmacologic block is reduced by the third or fourth day after receiving the drug, at this stage of therapy the patient is unlikely to be testing the degree of blockade.

Side-Effects

Considering that naltrexone is a very specific and potent drug that acts on opiate receptors throughout the body, it is surprising that there are so few side effects. Most patients report no symptoms at all; however, when the drug was first introduced in clinical trials, a variety of effects were reported. These included abdominal pain, headache, and mild increases in blood pressure. Many of these symptoms were probably related to precipitation of withdrawal. Because of the more recent recognition of naltrexone's potency in producing withdrawal in newly detoxified patients, these side effects have now become much less common.

Since naltrexone blocks endogenous opioids in addition to those that are injected, one would expect to find multiple symptoms related to the wide-ranging functions of the endorphin systems. In fact, endocrine changes have been reported, although these are less dramatic than those provided by opioids themselves. Ellingboe et al. (1980) reported a prompt rise in luteinizing hormone and a delayed rise in testosterone after naltrexone.

Most patients do not report subjective effects that can be related to naltrexone. Of course, these patients have just discontinued a drug that has altered endocrine patterns, libido, mood, and pain thresholds, possibly for years. They could be expected to experience some rebound phenomena. Some patients and their spouses report that the use of naltrexone increased sex drive, a finding that has also been reported in rodents. Others report decreased appetite; still others tend to gain weight. Thus the effects of naltrexone are probably confounded with those of protracted opioid withdrawal. Even in patients who have been maintained on naltrexone for several years, consistent subjective effects have been lacking. Certainly the fear that long-term blocking of opioid receptors will lead to problems such as depression has not been realized.

Changes in laboratory tests have also been researched in more than 2,000 patients involved in clinical trials with naltrexone (Hollister 1978; Judson et al. 1981). Despite the fact that addicts are generally unhealthy to begin with, the studies in addiction treatment programs have not turned up significant laboratory abnormalities resulting from naltrexone treatment. Liver function tests are a matter of great concern due to the high frequency of hepatitis among addicts. As many as 70 to 80 percent of addicts in methadone programs have some abnormalities, usually ascribed to past or present hepatitis.

Studies of nonaddict groups at high-dose levels have noted dose-related increments in transaminase levels that were all reversible when the drug was stopped. These subjects generally received 300 mg of naltrexone per day, or about six times the therapeutic dose for prevention of relapse to addiction (Pfohl et al. 1986). This finding raises cautions in the treatment of addiction, although in practice transaminase elevations have not been observed at the lower dose levels used in recovering addicts (Arndt et al. 1986).

Opioid addicts in liver failure should not be treated with naltrexone, although those with minor abnormalities in liver function tests may receive naltrexone. Baseline laboratory tests must include a full battery of liver function studies and monthly retesting should occur for the first three months. If there is no evidence of rising enzymes, the tests can be repeated at three- to six-month intervals. Some clinicians have used as a guideline that naltrexone not be started if the serum glutamic-oxaloacetic transaminase (SGOT) level or the serum glutamic-pyruvic transaminase (SGPT) level is greater than two times normal.

Another set of issues regarding the safety of any new drug concerns its use in pregnant women and in children. There have been no clinical trials in these populations; thus no definitive statements can be made. Studies of naltrexone in animals have generally not shown signs of potential risks to humans at clinical doses (Christian 1984), but there is always the possibility of teratogenic effects specific to humans. Also, ongoing treatment should be stopped if the enzyme levels become greater than three times normal unless, of course, an alternative cause is found. Frequently, the alternative cause is excessive alcohol intake; when this is stopped, the enzyme levels usually return to normal.

Drug Interactions

There have been no systematic studies of nonopioid drug interactions with naltrexone, but with more than 14 years of clinical experience, much anecdotal information is available. Naltrexone has been safely used in combination with disulfiram, lithium, and tricyclic antidepressants; if these agents are indicated, they apparently can be used in their normal way at their usual doses.

One adverse interaction that has been reported is that between thioridazine (Mellaril) and naltrexone. Maany et al. (1987) reported that sedation occurred when naltrexone was added to the regimens of two patients stabilized on thioridazine. No thioridazine plasma levels were available, but a likely explanation is that naltrexone impaired the degradation of thioridazine, resulting in increased plasma levels and increased sedation. If a neuroleptic is required in combination with naltrexone, a nonsedating neuroleptic might be preferable.

Conclusion

Naltrexone is a specific opioid antagonist that is safe and relatively nontoxic when administered properly. It provides an important new treatment option to well-motivated addicts who desire to become drug-free. It must be used within a comprehensive treatment program, including individual or family psychotherapy and urine testing for illicit drugs. The optimum duration of naltrexone therapy has not yet been established, but motivated and consenting patients should probably take it for at least the first three months following detoxification.

Chapter 136

Methadone Maintenance

The concept of using legal opioids in the treatment of opioid dependence dates back at least 100 years. In the 19th century, the king of Siam is said to have decreed that opium should be dispensed by the state to opium-dependent persons. At the turn of the century, the Spanish dispensed legal opioids to indigenous Chinese in the Philippines, a practice not continued by the United States after it took control of the Philippines in the Spanish-American War (Musto 1973). The system appears to have been terminated not because of any examination of its costs and benefits but because legal provision of opioids was ideologically repugnant to policymakers in the United States. In the early 1920s, American use of morphine in maintenance clinics was terminated when American courts ruled that doctors could not treat opioid-dependent persons for their opioid dependence. Again, ideology and politics rather than a reasoned examination of the system appear to have been responsible for termination of the effort. In England, the Rolleston Commission in 1924 ruled that English physicians could dispense opioids to treat opioid dependence if they saw fit. There appears to be little public recognition of the fact that the English changed this policy in 1967 to limit use of opioids in the treatment of opioid-dependent persons to a relative handful of specially licensed practitioners. The English changed because poor prescribing procedures had led to epidemics of heroin (May 1973).

In the 1950s, in the United States, a Joint Commission of the New York State Medical Society and the American Bar Association called for an evaluation of legal narcotics substitution therapy for heroin addicts. This paved the way for the work of Dole and Nyswander (1965, 1968) at Rockefeller University in New York City in the mid 1960s. In their original work, patients were admitted to a hospital for a period of weeks. During this time, methadone was given daily, and the dose increased to the point at which most street doses of heroin would have no effect (i.e., a "blockade"). Patients were then discharged to the community and attended outpatient clinics. Dole and Nyswander found that some 80 percent of theretofore unreachable heroin addicts were markedly improved by methadone maintenance therapy.

Success rates have not continued to be as high as those reported initially by Dole and Nyswander (1965, 1968). They, quite rightly, excluded complicated clinical cases from their early studies, and these cases had to be treated when the method became standardized and in widespread use. But the preponderance of evidence indicates that methadone maintenance treatment has desirable outcomes both for individuals and communities. In the past 20 years, hundreds of thousands of patients have been treated. It is not generally recognized that this method of treatment has been evaluated as much as any human service modality in history.

Methadone has been used in varied social, economic, and cultural settings. The United States and Hong Kong have acquired many years of experience with the therapeutic use of methadone, both for maintenance and for withdrawal in opioid-dependent persons. Canada, Australia, Holland, England, Sweden, France, Switzerland, Italy, Thailand, Burma, and Pakistan have acquired a less extensive experience with methadone. The evaluation studies carried out on methadone, impressive in their quality, number, and breadth, indicate, with a few exceptions, that there are positive gains from use of this agent. But despite the positive results indicated by the data, methadone does not enjoy a good reputation. The general attitude of ambivalence about the use of legal opioid substitution therapy continues to be uninfluenced by the data on outcome.

Evaluation Studies

Critics have called rightfully for studies of methadone under rigorous experimental conditions, with random assignment to no therapy, methadone maintenance, placebo, or to a different treatment modality such as a therapeutic community. Attempts to study methadone maintenance under such conditions in Illinois failed because patients would not accept random assignments to therapeutic communities, and insisted on getting methadone maintenance. Newman and Whitehill (1979), however, succeeded in carrying out a scientific research protocol. They recruited, with informed consent, 100 heroin addicts from Hong Kong for a 32-week study. Subjects were all hospitalized for two weeks and, during this time, were stabilized on methadone 60 mg/day. Then two groups were formed by random assignment and studied under double-blind conditions. Both groups received the same counseling and the same treatment by an identical staff. One group was withdrawn from methadone at a rate of 1 mg/day and then was maintained on daily placebo for the remainder of the study; the second group received methadone either in constant dose or was given dose adjustment as would occur in regular practice. Retention in treatment was 76 percent for the methadone group and 10 percent for the placebo group. Use of illicit heroin, as tested for by frequent urinalyses utilizing thin layer chromatography, decreased sharply for all subjects who stayed in the study. The rate of conviction for criminal activity was more than twice as great for placebo subjects when compared to methadone subjects.

The findings of the study by Newman and Whitehill (1979) reflect those of the Drug Abuse Reporting Project (DARP) and the Treatment Outcome Prospective Study (TOPS), large federally funded evaluations of the national treatment system in the United States (Craddock et al. 1982; Sells 1979). The General Accounting Office (GAO) of the United States Congress examined the data contained in the treatment evaluation studies and recommended to Congress that it direct the National Institute on Drug Abuse to shift more patients into methadone maintenance and therapeutic communities and away from drug-free and detoxification treatment modalities (Comptroller General of the United States 1980).

The National Institute on Drug Abuse in the United States has sponsored large nationwide evaluation studies. The largest of these, DARP, has been carried out by Sells (1979) and co-workers at Texas Christian University. The data base consists of approximately 44,000 drug abuse treatment clients admitted to treatment between 1969 and 1973. Studies on this cohort have been extended to a six-year period and longer periods of follow-up are projected for the future (Simpson 1981; Simpson et al. 1982). Stratified random samples taken from the cohort have been studied. Given the large size of the cohort, at least a moderate degree of generalizability can be inferred. Basic DARP findings have been that more than 50 percent of methadone maintenance clients were retained in treatment for one year or more, and rates of illicit opioid use and criminality decreased sharply in comparison to pretreatment rates. Employment rates improved in methadone maintenance clients; 39 percent were employed before treatment and 62 percent were employed in the year after leaving treatment (National Institute on Drug Abuse 1981).

A second independent evaluation of a large nationwide cohort was carried out by the National Institute on Drug Abuse on 12,000 patients entering treatment in 1979, 1980, and 1981 (Craddock et al. 1982). Again, substantial changes were noted in illicit drug use and criminality when pre- and posttreatment periods were compared. Employment rates improved a little, but because employment was affected negatively by the recession, even modest positive changes are significant. This study added a feature not present in DARP; namely, evaluation of the psychological status of patients. Depression indicators, found to be high in addicts coming for treatment, improved during treatment in this study. Another finding, of both clinical and administrative importance, was that clients received many social, vocational, legal, and educational services, and clients were in general quite satisfied with the treatment that they received.

Another large evaluation study was carried out on veterans who were treated for drug abuse in the Veterans Administration hospital system in the United States (McLellan et al. 1982). Results of this study essentially mirror the findings of DARP and TOPS: illicit drug use and criminality decreased during treatment, and gains were made in social function both during and following treatment. The findings of these nationwide studies complement those of many city and state reports, e.g., Newman's (1977) report in New York City, Judson et al. (1980) in Palo Alto, Senay et al. (1973) in Illinois, Maddox and Bowden (1972) in San Antonio, Burt Associates (1977) in New York and in Washington, DC, and others (Bewley et al. 1972; Blachly 1970; Bloom and Sudderth 1970; Brown et al. 1973; Cushman 1977; DuPont and Green 1973; Gearing and Schweitzer 1974; Gunne 1983; Kleber 1970; Knowles et al. 1970; Maslansky 1970; National Institute on Drug Abuse 1981; Scott et al. 1973; Sheffet et al. 1980; Simpson 1981; Simpson et al. 1982; Tuason and Jones 1974).

In the United States, the national, state, and city results of methadone maintenance are basically favorable. Although not all reports are favorable (Dobbs 1971; Hallgrimsson 1980; Harms 1975; Henderson 1982; Lennard et al. 1972; McLeod and Priest 1973; Perkins and Bloch 1970), the preponderance of data suggests that the positive results observed in the United States are achievable in widely different cultural and social settings. At present, the data gathered on tens of thousands of patients who have been studied by independent evaluators appear to establish that the method works for some addicts.

One of the common questions asked—"Is methadone maintenance superior to therapeutic community treatment?"—is not answerable because to date it has not been possible to assign addicts randomly to these two methods. Bale et al. (1980) studied groups of addicts randomly assigned to therapeutic communities or to methadone maintenance and found that compliance with random assignments was poor.

A better question for the clinician and policymaker is, "How do the two methods complement each other?" or "For whom is each method most appropriate?" The methods appear to serve two different populations of addicts and to serve them in different ways. An addict who has active ties to a relatively healthy family and who possesses a good job is not an appropriate candidate for a therapeutic community because engagement with a therapeutic community would mean possible loss of two major assets: job and family. Methadone maintenance or slow detoxification may be a better treatment in such an instance. Conversely, a heroin addict with no employment, with no family ties, and with social relationships only in the drug culture may be an appropriate candidate for a therapeutic community.

There are many methodological problems inherent in outcome research. Regression toward the mean, the inevitable drop-out problem, and inadequate comparison criteria all need to be considered. Maddox and Bowden (1972) pointed out that dropouts need to be counted all through the evaluation statistical process so that one is not dealing with "remaining samples." Outcome criteria must be clear and comparison data adequate. In a study of methadone maintenance patients, Maddox and McDonald (1973) found that results were still favorable after correcting for these methodological problems.

Why, in the face of truly massive data acquired on thousands of patients studied over many years, is there such a disparity between what the data say and public attitudes about this method of treatment? The GAO report cited lack of dissemination of the outcome data as the chief culprit, and certainly it is an important factor (Comptroller General of the United States 1980). But there are other factors equally potent and as yet apparently insuperable. One is the factionalism in the field of drug abuse treatment. The judgment that providing legal opioids is unethical or sinful and, in any event, ineffective ("it's like giving an alcoholic bourbon") is widespread, particularly in the alcoholism treatment community and among therapeutic community workers. The funding structure frequently reinforces the divisions caused by this philosophical split by pitting methadone programs against therapeutic communities in the struggle for economic survival.

Since, historically speaking, methadone is relatively new and regulatory efforts sometimes too weak and sometimes too strong, a few clinics have been poorly operated and have created justifiable concern. This has sometimes created a local image that all methadone programs are ineffective and poorly organized. Usually the parties involved are not aware that nationwide studies on evaluation have been carried out and that the results are favorable. The disparity between data and opinion is so wide that some communities in the United States have banned methadone programs (McGlothlin and Anglin 1981b).

There are many other factors related to the disparity in question. Most methadone clinics in the United States are located in severely deprived communities. Many people have no experience with the dynamics of disadvantaged communities and therefore do not know how easy it is for the best of efforts to be affected by needs for local autonomy. These needs can create sometimes severe tensions between funding agencies and local communities. These tensions can affect maintenance of standards, acceptability of treatment, ability to carry out evaluation studies, as well as practically every facet of the operation of a clinic.

Another set of problems stems from an occasional clinic whose operator is so exclusively concerned with profit that the patients and surrounding communities are antagonized by the dehumanization that accompanies the "profit is all" entrepreneurial approach. A more serious systemic problem arises from the failure to create adequate standards for training of all personnel involved in treatment of drug abusers. In the United States, the drug abuse field shares this problem with the alcoholism treatment field, although the alcoholism field currently is working on the problem more effectively than the drug abuse field.

Another set of problems with the image of methadone stems from the nature of the relationship between opioid dependence and criminality (McGlothlin 1979). There are some countries in the world that have yet to see a major link between heroin and crime, but the number of such countries is dwindling as heroin is coming to be used intravenously instead of by insufflation and oral ingestion, and the whole complex of drugs and crime and prostitution follows the ascendance of "pop" culture.

The issue of coercion of treatment, which is inherent in the relationship between opioid dependence and crime, is as controversial as the use of legal opioids in therapy.

The concern usually is that addicts' rights are violated by the fact of legal coercion to enter treatment. Experience with this issue, both clinically and administratively, indicates that while it is a substantive legal and philosophical question, it is often irrelevant clinically. Coerced patients seem to do as well as voluntary patients and the issue of coercion does not seem to interfere with standard clinical procedures. Policymakers and legal philosophers sometimes forget that some criminals are just as happy as everyone else that they do not have to commit crimes. Further, even John Stuart Mill, in his essay on freedom, recognized that addicted individuals are not free. Still another hurdle for legal opioid substitution is the notion of "cure." While it is true that there are heroin experimenters and, in some instances, occasional users, it is also true that heroin use is associated with large numbers of dysfunctional abusers whose use becomes chronic, who are criminally active, and whose activities and health needs have a large impact on the quality of life for the communities in which they are imbedded. There are, to put it another way, large numbers of heroin users who develop careers with heroin or frequently with heroin and multiple other intoxicants. The fact—true in every part of the world—is that there is no way to do anything other than to try to engage them in careers of treatment that will reduce crime, improve health, shorten runs of heroin use, reduce time in jail, and lessen contact with the criminal justice system. To demean what can be done because it is not a cure is destructive and has serious negative consequences for public health because careers untreated are much more pathologic than careers treated, both for the addict and for the communities concerned. A report from Sweden illustrated nicely the social and political problems with legal opioid substitution treatment (Gunne 1983). The story has been enacted in communities in many parts of the world.

There are then many reasons for the disparity between the data concerning methadone and public perception. The foregoing analysis implies that this disparity will not be reduced soon and perhaps never, if institutions, national and international, do not improve communication about the data and take action to reduce the impact of the other factors that contribute to the disparity.

One action that can be taken is to institute training standards for workers in the field. The continued contribution of legal opioid substitution therapy must be based on licensing standards for all clinicians and administrators of substance abuse programs. As they currently operate, medical, nursing, social work, psychology, and pharmacy schools do not adequately prepare clinicians to work with substance abusers. Training standards and training institutions must be created. If, as recent data indicate, spending a dollar to treat substance abusers saves two to three dollars of inappropriate future use of the standard health care system, then it becomes all the more sensible to integrate substance abuse care with both the existing psychiatric care system and with standard health care delivery systems.

The medical cost of addiction, all intoxicants included, is said to approach 20¢ of the health dollar. Thus there would appear to be two powerful reasons for effective integration of substance abuse treatment with standard hospitals and health care. One, to prevent inappropriate expensive use of the medical care system, and two, to provide appropriate medical treatment for the many medical conditions that exist in frequent users of alcohol, nicotine, opioids, and so on. If training standards are created and institutionalized, then substance abuse programs will be on a much more firm financial basis because they will be supported by third-party payers. The more treatment that is available and accessible, the more it is likely to be used. When addicts can get to treatment, they use it and at early stages of their substance abuse careers. Treatment can have more of an impact if it is delivered early in a career by reducing "runs" of heroin use, which are usually associated with high degrees of criminality and by reducing mortality from medical conditions (e.g., bacterial endocarditis) and from the violence inherent in the heroin subculture.

The foregoing discussion of outcome data can be summed up by stating that an ethical, trained physician can use methadone in ways that will benefit patients and communities. Methadone can be used for maintenance therapy or in detoxification regimens.

Pharmacology of Methadone

Methadone, first synthesized in Germany in the 1940s, is D,l-4,4-diphenyl-6-dimethyl-amino-3-heptanone (Jaffe and Martin 1975; Kreek 1979). The L isomer accounts for most of its activity. Subjectively, methadone is quite similar to morphine. Both induce euphoria and sedation; 5 to 10 mg of methadone will give analgesia that is quite comparable in intensity and time course to 10 to 15 mg of morphine.

Methadone's effects can be achieved by oral administration. Methadone suppresses the opioid withdrawal syndrome for 12 to 24 hours or longer, much longer suppression than can be achieved with morphine. Day-long suppression of the abstinence syndrome and oral effectiveness define the usefulness of methadone in clinical programs because no other opioid has these two characteristics.

Methadone depresses the respiratory center, has antitussive action, and produces mild hyperglycemia and hypothermia. Methadone inhibits gastrointestinal tone and propulsive activity and will cause biliary tract spasm, but it does not have major effects on the pregnant uterus. Tolerance to miotic effects of methadone develops rapidly. Methadone is well absorbed from the stomach in most individuals, and large concentrations appear in the plasma within minutes after oral administration. The drug enters tissues throughout the body, with only a small amount traversing the blood-brain barrier. Methadone appears to be bound to tissue protein; biotransformation in the liver is probably through N-demethylation and cyclization to form pyrolidines. The half-life of methadone in nontolerant individuals is about 15 hours.

When used as an analgesic in routine practice, delirium, hallucinations, and hemorrhagic urticaria have been reported, although very rarely. There are no reports of such effects in methadone maintenance patients.

Research indicates that with chronic administration, pools of methadone are built up in body tissues and that methadone from these pools provides a fairly steady blood concentration. Like other opioids, methadone crosses the placental barrier, and chronic administration in a pregnant mother will result in a methadone-dependent neonate. Withdrawal from all opioids in neonates, methadone included, seems to be more variable in its expression, more delayed in its onset, and more extended in time in comparison to adult withdrawal.

In the early phases of methadone treatment, several biochemical and physiologic abnormalities have been observed and have been discussed in detail by Kreek (1979). For example, there is a decrease in plasma levels of reproduction-related peptide hormones (e.g., follicle stimulating hormone and luteinizing hormone). All of these abnormalities appear to return to normal after a period of two to 10 months of treatment. Thyroid abnormalities and persistence of protein and immunologic abnormalities, which probably reflect years of use of unsterile needles and solutions, have also been observed. There is no known clinical significance related to these changes. Cicero et al. (1975) found that methadone maintenance patients had decreased ejaculate volume and decreased sperm counts. The time course and clinical significance of these findings are not known.

Overdose of methadone can be treated with naloxone, but it is important to remember that naloxone may have to be repeated because its effects last only two hours whereas the duration of methadone effects is much longer (Kjeldgaard et al. 1971; Waldron et al. 1973). Therefore, methadone overdose needs to be observed closely for 24 to 48 hours, preferably in a hospital.

As noted in the opening paragraphs of this chapter, methadone has been much criticized but no one debates its safety (Kleber et al. 1980). Methadone as used by patients following medical direction has not been associated with serious problems. Common side effects are sedation, if the dose is too high; constipation, which can be treated by increasing fluid intake and using stool softeners and/or reduction in dose; sweating, which can be managed by dose reduction; occasional transient ankle edema; and changes in libido. These latter changes are usually treatable by dose reduction and all the side effects cited above will improve with time alone. Rarely, patients complain of skin problems, but these too improve with time or symptomatic treatment. Daily administration of opioids increases the possibility of synergism with other psychoactive drugs. Patients in many US clinics must take breathalyzer tests before methadone is administered. If blood alcohol concentrations are .05 or above, patients are not given methadone on that day or are given methadone when blood alcohol concentrations are below .05. Users of multiple drugs who are on methadone, of course, are at risk for lethal effects from synergism if they continue polydrug use. The methadone-alcohol interaction can be a complex one. If patients drink heavily on a weekend, for example, they will be more intoxicated than usual because of the additive effects of the drugs. However, the alcohol will lead to hepatic enzyme induction. Once removed, these enzymes will act on methadone so that the patient's usual dose no longer suffices and the patient complains of withdrawal symptoms on Monday.

Studies of the biotransformation of methadone indicate wide interindividual variability in blood levels following identical dosing regimens. This research suggests that poor responders to treatment may not absorb methadone from the gastrointestinal tract normally (Kelley et al. 1978). Liver and renal disease may account for some of the individual variation.

A number of investigators, as reviewed by Gritz et al. (1975), have found that methadone does not appear to interfere with reaction time; methadone-maintained patients also do not appear to have memory deficits as tested by Gritz et al., but chronic administration of methadone was found to differentiate performance of patients from controls on recall: "subtle recall deficits appeared on the more difficult tests." Clinically these effects are not noticeable. In a study of driving records, Maddox et al. (1977) found no evidence to restrict driving privileges of methadone maintenance patients; it is a clinical commonplace that methadone maintenance clinics have patients from most of the occupations necessary to maintain life in modern urban centers.

An extended discussion of the biotransformation of methadone can be found elsewhere (Kreek 1979).

Clinical Aspects of Methadone Maintenance Treatment

The immediate clinical goal of maintenance therapy is to provide a dose of methadone that will suppress opioid abstinence symptoms for the entire 24-hour period between doses without producing euphoria, sedation, or dulling of consciousness (Senay 1983; Wieland and Chambers 1970). This dose relieves the addict of a major source of pressure to use illicit opioids (viz., the dysphoria of opioid abstinence). Staff of a program should be trained to observe the effects of a given dose, and changes should be made in the dose if clinically undesirable effects occur. Many patients will not want to be sedated or euphoric because they want to have their minds clear to work on their problems. Other addicts, however, will seek euphoria or sedation. Their seeking of euphoria should become the subject of clinical interaction. There are sedating and intoxicating doses of any opioid, methadone included, but in a well-run clinic one sees sedation or intoxication infrequently because dose effects are monitored and therapy deals with the issue of frequent intoxication. In the event that a heroin addict is criminally active, the provision of a clinically appropriate dose of methadone, which relieves abstinence dysphoria, relieves the addict of the pressure to get drugs to feel normal. As noted above, studies indicate that rates of crime go down substantially during treatment (McGlothlin 1979).

Another goal of methadone therapy is to engage the addict in a therapeutic relationship both with a counselor and with a program. *Therapeutic* is defined here broadly to include the provision of social, vocational, legal, or other services in addition to psychological help. In many methadone programs in the United States, the counselors have been addicts themselves and have been treated successfully. They provide what might be called affiliative counseling because they personify the transition between addiction and abstinence from drugs. They do not provide counseling in the traditional sense of the word, but they are effective in assisting the addict to achieve abstinence from illicit drugs and in linking the addict with a range of services. Using "professional" psychotherapists (e.g., psychiatrists or psychologists) has been shown to be more effective than drug counselors for patients with mid- or high-level severity of psychiatric symptoms (Woody et al. 1983).

The stereotype of an addict in treatment is one of a manipulative person who has no interest in changing from a life-style centered on intoxiciation. There are addicts who fit the stereotype but to characterize all addicts by this stereotype belies the data and dehumanizes addicts as a group. More often than not, addicts are intensely ambivalent about their habit and life-style and make repeated attempts to change. Therapy depends on building successful links with the healthy pole of the ambivalence. If addicts manipulate, they should be controlled with confrontation and insistence on engagement with the therapeutic process. However, patients who meet DSM-III (American Psychiatric Association 1980) criteria for antisocial personality do not seem to respond particularly well to either psychotherapy or counseling (Woody et al. 1983).

Maintenance therapy, in addition to elimination of abstinence dysphoria, freedom from need to engage in criminal behavior, and provision of a therapeutic relationship, also aims to improve the health status of addicts. On admission to treatment, addicts commonly have a number of health problems. Minor problems such as abscesses, phlebitis, and dental carries, can be and are treated successfully. Major problems such as hepatitis, endocarditis, susceptibility to major infections—such as pneumonia, malaria, tuberculosis, and lately, acquired immune deficiency syndrome (AIDS)—can be identified and referred for therapy. The health status of maintenance patients tends to improve substantially during treatment (Christakis et al. 1973; Finnegan 1979a; Longwell et al. 1979). Addicts usually gain weight and female addicts usually experience a return of normal menstrual cycles (Finnegan 1979a). During runs of heroin use, many female addicts develop menstrual abnormalities; they appear to be more likely to become pregnant during treatment, probably because there is an improvement in nutrition and because, with the provision of legal opioids, there is relative freedom from the stress of a criminal life-style.

Dole and Nyswander (1965, 1968) theorized that methadone would block the reinforcing effects of heroin. Without reinforcement, the conditioned response involved in repeated use of heroin would become weak and disappear. They recommended, therefore, that high doses of methadone, in the order of 80 to 120 mg/day or more, be employed so that addicts could not use enough heroin to achieve euphoria. The issue of dose and outcome efficacy is not resolved. There are studies of both high dose (100 mg/day) versus low dose (30 to 50 mg/day) suggesting that if there are differences in efficacy between high-dose and low-dose regimens, the differences are not large (McGlothlin and Anglin 1981a). Dole and Nyswander also believed that addicts had a metabolic deficit that required exogenous opioids in a fashion similar to the need of diabetics for insulin. There is no evidence to substantiate or to reject the metabolic lesion theory.

The long-range goal of opioid substitution therapy varies. Some programs are based on a philosophy that affirms indefinite maintenance; other programs aim specifically for short periods of maintenance (i.e., a few months to two years) and then require an attempt to become drug-free. Since we have less than two decades of experience with opioid substitution therapy, we have no data that would indicate which of these clinical postures is superior. Certainly the latter is more popular with addicts seeking treatment; the former becomes more acceptable once addicts are in treatment.

Sells and Simpson (1976) worked out a typology of drug treatment programs and divided methadone maintenance programs into those with a high degree of demand for conformity to program guidelines (e.g., a patient must have a certain percentage of urines free from all nonprescribed drugs, cannot miss treatment days) to programs that are more lenient about such matters. A typology of programs is a difficult undertaking because of the variety of positions of such policy matters as program demands for behavioral change, criteria for diagnoses of opioid dependence and therefore of admission to treatment, frequency of required urinalyses, administrative and clinical response to frequent illicit drug use as evidenced by positive urines, program policies concerning patient behavior both in and outside of clinics, and pressure to attempt detoxification. Staffing patterns vary; some programs are heavily staffed with professionals while others have few professionals and a high ratio of ex-addict counselors. The foregoing list is not exhaustive. Changes in just one of these policies can affect every facet of clinic life and have implications for outcome.

Another dimension on which programs differ is the question of "take-home" policy. In some communities with thousands of patients on methadone maintenance, there may be a problem with diversion. Because in the United States many addicts are unemployed and in very serious socioeconomic need, the "street" sale of methadone is not surprising. One of the consequences of diversion is the unsupervised use by persons unaware of the potential of this drug to act synergistically with other intoxicants to produce an overdose. Some communities have therefore created a no-take-home policy; for example, Washington, DC, does not permit any take-home methadone at all.

Many clinicians feel that this is a clinically harmful policy in that it causes the many patients who are doing well an unnecessary hardship in getting to programs on a daily basis. On the other hand, some communities have implemented, on an experimental basis, a policy in which addicts who are doing well on methadone maintenance are permitted, in small numbers (e.g., 20 to 30), to pick up their methadone at a local pharmacy and make trips to the clinic only on a weekly or perhaps monthly basis (Bowden et al. 1976). Most states in the United States, however, permit addicts take-home doses after three to six months of demonstration of favorable progress in treatment. Under current federal regulations, some addicts after two years are permitted to come to the clinic only twice a week and to take home the rest of their daily methadone dose. Why there should be such wide variation in different communities in the scope of the methadone diversion problem is not understood. In addition to the diversion policy, there is an occasional death of the child of an addict because of failure to safeguard take-home doses from children (Aronow et al. 1972; Smialek et al. 1977). Child-proof caps on take-home bottles partially respond to the problem, but ultimately the addict has responsibility for adequate supervision as is the case with any other prescribed drug.

One of the complications of methadone maintenance and detoxification therapy is alcohol abuse (Cohen et al. 1982; Kreek 1981). Estimates of the frequency with which this complication occurs vary widely, but there is no question that it is a significant problem clinically. Referral to Alcoholics Anonymous, use of breathalyzer tests, family therapy, and use of disulfiram can be added to the methadone regimen. Disulfiram can be used concurrently with methadone safely. Alcohol abusers in methadone therapy also tend to abuse other substances more than nonalcohol abusers. Substantial numbers of patients continue to abuse a variety of substances during methadone therapy; diazepam was most common in the past, but has been recently surpassed by cocaine in many programs. This use can be responded to by counseling, urine monitoring (Havassy and Hall 1981; Milby et al. 1980), and, if a reasonable period of time elapses without change, by exclusion from the program.

Patients in most maintenance regimens tend to terminate treatment by dropping out. But they also tend to reenter treatment if re-addicted. Sells' group found that treatment episodes tend to become repeated and that addicts appear to elect methadone maintenance as the number of readmissions grows (Sells 1979; Simpson 1981; Simpson et al. 1982).

Methadone clinics, like mental health clinics, prison half-way houses, and similar kinds of services, are usually not well accepted by surrounding communities. Addiction is a threatening problem, and the stereotype of the addict creates public fear. Community relations are, therefore, extremely important in administering a methadone maintenance clinic. The optimal situation is one in which a community or neighborhood has frequent contact with the leadership of a clinic, and people from the community have jobs in the clinic. If a community has an economic and social stake in a clinic, community relations are usually better. Staff must be trained to discourage congregation of addicts outside clinics to avoid stimulating stereotypic fear. Ideally, methadone clinics should be linked with therapeutic communities, half-way houses, and detoxification centers. Multimodality programming increases the ability to serve and is an important public health model for communities with significant opioid-related problems (Jaffe 1969).

A detailed discussion of staffing and space of a methadone maintenance clinic can be found elsewhere (Lewinson and Mill 1979).

Withdrawal from Methadone Maintenance

Two different kinds of withdrawal regimens are encountered clinically in methadone maintenance clinics. The first is with the successful patient: someone who has a year or two of urine tests negative for all drugs, no alcohol or polydrug problem, stable employment, and good attendance and is functioning well in the family area. Such a patient will ask and/or be asked about detoxification. The preponderance of evidence is that detoxification is difficult for many addicts and that many will lose the gains they have made; but some addicts will be able to withdraw successfully and to maintain a drug-free state (Cushman 1981; Senay et al. 1977; Stimmel et al. 1973). The studies we have on this problem are inadequate in number and in length of the study period. If opioid dependence is a career, then therapeutic intervention must be measured in career terms.

Successful methadone maintenance patients should be advised to attempt detoxification when life stress is as low as possible, and they should be advised to expect a regimen that takes months or possibly years (Senay 1983). In addition, they should be counseled that because of the protracted abstinence syndrome, they will need treatment for at least a year after reaching zero dose. The clinical principles involved in detoxification from maintenance are identical with the principles described later on the use of methadone for detoxification from current dependence on opioids other than methadone.

Addicts should be counseled that failure to achieve zero dose will not affect their status as a patient. The attempt to detoxify carries with it a real risk of losing gains such as job, family function, and avoidance of use of illicit drugs. This risk should not be compounded by program exclusion.

A second category of withdrawal is based on administrative needs. Usually, patients in maintenance will have violated basic program rules. For example, they will have been violent or will have tried to sell drugs in or near clinics. One can almost always assume concurrent use of street heroin or other drugs in these patients. The random urines obtained weekly in maintenance clinics will usually confirm this use. The withdrawal regimen can be shortened, therefore, in comparison to that employed in the first category of patients discussed above. A two- to three-week regimen is humane and will usually meet administrative needs. At times, clinics refuse to detoxify on an outpatient basis patients who have been violent toward staff and insist they go into a facility such as a state psychiatric hospital.

As is the case with detoxification from street drugs, outcomes observed in follow-up studies on successful patients in methadone maintenance do not encourage one to suggest detoxification for patients (Kleber 1981). Cushman observed a 7.6 percent success rate; Dole and Joseph, 18 percent; Millman et al., 27 percent; and Stimmel et al., 8 percent in studies of detoxified methadone maintenance patients (all reported in Cushman 1981). Dole and Joseph studied a stratified sample of 17,000 heroin addicts who received methadone for the first time in 1972 (Cushman 1981). In 1977, 8 percent of the sample, discharged from treatment, were judged to be apparently well. This figure contrasted sharply with those who remained in treatment; 63 percent of them were judged to be apparently well. Studies by Cushman and Stimmel et al. suggest that the methadone maintenance patient with the best chance of achieving and maintaining opioid-free status has made good progress in treatment, is employed steadily, has a social life primarily outside the drug world, and has a long duration of methadone treatment. "Those in treatment for 3 or more years were likely to be abstinent. Those in treatment less than 1 year are much more likely to resume opioid use" (Cushman 1981).

Most clinicians feel, on the basis of the above-mentioned studies as well as clinical experience, that attempts to withdraw successful methadone maintenance patients carry a real risk of relapse, although some patients are successful. The therapeutic detoxification should be slow. Many patients took longer than one year in the studies reviewed by Cushman (1981); alcohol abuse is also a real but not invariable risk.

Use of Methadone for Detoxification in Opioid Dependence Other Than in Methadone Maintenance Patients

Methadone is the opioid of choice for use in detoxification regimens because it is effective orally and because it suppresses the abstinence syndrome for extended periods. The objective of a clinically sound withdrawal regimen is to reduce to a tolerable degree the inevitable opioid withdrawal symptoms. Occasionally, one can have a symptom-free detoxification, but this is unusual. In the last 20 years, many workers in the field have moved in the direction of lengthening the time of detoxification treatment. Some of the impetus for the change from older practices stems from everyday clinical experience. Other factors influencing this change have been the evidence for the existence of a chronic opioid abstinence syndrome (Martin and Jasinski 1969) and clinical research studies indicating that slow withdrawal is indicated (Senay et al. 1977).

Research also indicates, as clinicians in every kind of cultural setting have observed, that expectation or set is an important factor in producing symptoms during withdrawal. Subjects in one study who were being maintained on daily methadone doses without dose changes and who were blind to their study status complained of withdrawal symptoms as much as a second blind group of patients who were being withdrawn in small increments (Senay et al. 1977).

Clinical experience indicates that it is meaningful to discriminate moderate or severe degrees from mild degrees of opioid dependence. If dependence is moderate or severe, the clinical course of detoxification will require many months, if not longer; symptoms will be more severe; adjunctive medication for sleep will be necessary; and there may not be a successful response to clonidine, propoxyphene napsylate, or other weak opioid agonists in the detoxification process. On admission to the withdrawal regimen, the history may help to indicate whether mild degrees or moderate or severe degrees are present. Patients who have a pretreatment history in the two weeks preceding admission of use of heroin of poor quality and a frequency of use of only once or twice a day will quite frequently have mild degrees of dependence; addicts who give a history of using potent heroin more than twice a day, on the average, will tend to have moderate to severe degrees of opioid dependence (Senay 1983).

. Success rates for detoxification using any method (including methadone) are low even when success is defined as the ability to become completely drug-free for one day. When success is defined as the ability to become abstinent and to sustain complete abstinence for any appreciable time, success rates are very low (Kleber 1981). Variations in the length of time taken to detoxify patients may make for marked clinical differences in patient comfort, retention in treatment, and use of illicit opioids. But these differences "wash out" if one examines status at one year after treatment. Detoxification treatment does not appear to result in permanent changes and is not efficacious for the long-term. If one accepts the notion of a career of heroin use defined by repeated "runs," however, detoxification may be viewed as having a great deal to offer because it reduces illicit drug use, lowers rates of commission of crime, and probably contributes to positive health status for patients if one compares their status with untreated active addicts. Certainly addicts seek detoxification frequently, and for some it is the treatment of choice.

There is a growing body of evidence that the population of heroin addicts applying for treatment can be divided into at least two groups. One appears not to have any biologic dependence on opioids; the second distributes itself into subgroups defined by progressively more severe degrees of dependence. Blachly et al. (1975) challenged 32 applicants for a methadone maintenance program with naloxone and found that 34 percent did not manifest opioid withdrawal symptoms. Senay and Shick (1978) found that approximately 25 percent of the sample of 110 applicants to the Illinois Drug Abuse Program showed minimal tolerance to opioids as measured by methadone test dose pupillography. Wang et al. (1974) tested 363 applicants to a methadone maintenance program and found that 59 had minimal response to naloxone challenge. O'Brien et al. (1978) found that 15 percent of 40 applicants to a methadone maintenance program had no response to naloxone challenge.

Such variations in degree of dependence on admission to treatment may explain the disparate experiences with so-called cold turkey detoxification. If a group of addicts coming for detoxification has a high proportion of minimally dependent patients, then cold turkey or nonopioid-assisted detoxification regimens (e.g., acupuncture, propoxyophene napsylate, clonidine, haloperidol or other tranquilizers) may appear to be efficacious. But if the proportion of patients with severe degrees of dependence is high, then cold turkey or nonopioid-assisted detoxification regimens will result in much needless suffering. It is a common clinical experience in every part of the globe that painful withdrawal experiences do not teach addicts anything and do not deter them from re-addiction. Methadone then appears to be the agent of choice if moderate or severe degrees of dependence are present.

Clinically, the best way to determine degree of dependence in a given individual is to observe the effects of administering a known dose of methadone. Then one can build a withdrawal regimen on the basis of the clincal observations made. We do not have adequate studies of the role of adjunctive medication in success or failure of methadone-assisted detoxification regimens. From a clinical point of view, if moderate or severe degrees of dependence are present, sedatives such as phenobarbital, diazepam, or other benzodiazepines for sleep and for other withdrawal discomfort are indicated. These adjunctive medications, because of their abuse potential and potential for street sale, should be dispensed a few at a time and should not be used on a nightly or daily basis. The best regimen is probably two to three nights per week or days per week if insomnia or other withdrawal symptoms are intense.

The setting in which detoxification occurs is unquestionably influential in the expression and intensity of opioid withdrawal. Patients in therapeutic communities who are required to be active and whose minds are focused on a demanding schedule appear to have much less severe withdrawal symptoms than would occur if they were withdrawing in a hospital or in another less demanding environment. It is important to identify the mental set of patients beginning detoxification. Some will deny their perceptions of impending pain ("withdraw me in five days"); others will have phobic responses so strong that they literally cannot think about the coming experience. Relatively brief clinical management of these mental sets can reduce suffering. Probably it is best for most people to withdraw under blind conditions; that is, to set a date by which zero dose will have been reached and then to reduce doses on a schedule that is not known to the patient. Occasionally, patients will want to control their own detoxification, and there is no clinical research or experience to suggest that they should not be given permission to do so (Razani et al. 1975).

Clinicians almost universally have observed that decrements in methadone need to be smaller as the dose approaches zero. Addicts can tolerate reductions of 5 to 10 mg when their methadone dose is in the 40 to 100 mg/day range. But when the 10 to 20 mg/day range is reached, such decrements will not be tolerable, and powerful pressure will be created to use illicit opioids. One research group found that decrements of 3 to 10 percent/week are optimal in terms of patient comfort and ability to refrain from using illicit opioids, with 10 percent decrements early in the course of withdrawal and 3 percent decrements/week at the end of the regimen (Senay et al. 1977). The regimen lasted seven months in this research design. Subjects for this study had been stabilized on methadone and were therefore more uniform in their degree of dependence than addicts coming into treatment for the first time. Therefore, extrapolation from this study to ordinary clinical experience may not be valid.

One report from patients undergoing detoxification signifying that the withdrawal regimen is too fast is that of anergia. If patients experience it, they are impelled powerfully to use illicit narcotics; anergia together with insomnia and bone and muscle aches are the chief symptoms involved in patients' use of illicit opioids during withdrawal. They probably also underlie the use of alcohol and other drugs during the detoxification regimen.

Detoxification from Dependence on Weak Opioid Agonists

If weak opioid agonists (e.g., codeine, propoxyphene) are associated with dependence, methadone, in low doses, may be useful in treating the sometimes difficult withdrawal from these drugs (Raskin 1970). Doses usually are smaller than those necessary to control withdrawal symptoms from moderate or severe degrees of dependence on strong opioid agonists. The withdrawal regimen can also usually be shortened in time.

Clonidine, an alpha adrenergic agonist, will relieve opioid abstinence symptoms and is used widely (Charney et al. 1981a). With the rapid proliferation of detoxification treatment with alpha adrenergic agonists, there have been some serious clinical errors. It is not understood commonly that patients must cease taking methadone or street narcotics altogether before they start the clonidine regimen. Clonidine and methadone are synergistic for sedative effects; therefore, a combination of slow methadone withdrawal supplemented by concurrently administered clonidine is not indicated. Clonidine has an abuse potential because of its sedative properties; street abuse has occasionally been reported in the United States.

Some programs attempt to follow the STEPS (sequential treatment employing pharmacologic supports) procedure described by Goldstein (1976); that is, they try to induct addicts into treatment on methadone and then to detoxify them and maintain them on naltrexone. To date, compliance with the naltrexone regimen has been a problem; a national study found that addicts tended not to take naltrexone as they might have taken methadone over periods of many months or years (National Research Council on Clinical Evaluation of Narcotic Antagonists 1978). Drop-out rates in naltrexone treatment were very large and early in the treatment regimen. It appears to be safe and effective in the doses used. Clonidine or other alpha-adrenergic agonists are logical candidates for inclusion in the STEPS procedure.

Clinically, it is desirable to engage addicts in treatment after they are abstinent because of the protracted abstinence syndrome and because of their need for support. Compliance rates are poor because addicts tend to view the achievement of abstinence as the end point of treatment.

Methadone and Pregnancy

The pregnant opioid-dependent patient presents a dilemma because clinical experience indicates that attempts to detoxify her carry substantial risk of death for her fetus (Finnegan 1979a, 1979b, 1979c). While the human adult rarely dies or has convulsions from opioid withdrawal, the human fetus is much more liable to death and to convulsions. In the United States, several clinical centers have independently arrived at a policy of maintaining a pregnant opioid-dependent woman through her pregnancy and delivery on doses of methadone of less than 25 mg/day. This regimen avoids fetal death from withdrawal and also avoids the death of neonates from withdrawal if doses of methadone in excess of 50 mg/day are used for maintenance through the pregnancy and delivery. When opioid-dependent pregnant women were maintained on 50 to 100 mg/day of methadone, neonatal mortality increased to an unacceptable level. Loss of neonates is unusual with low-dose maintenance regimens. If withdrawal during pregnancy is necessary, it is best to carry it out in the second trimester at a rate not exceeding 5 mg/week.

With low-dose methadone, most neonates need no treatment for the mild withdrawal they experience, but some will require treatment with phenobarbital and/or paregoric. The phenobarbital controls the hyperactivity and the threat of convulsions; the paregoric controls the gastrointestinal manifestations of the neonatal opioid abstinence syndrome. Other drugs occasionally used are diazepam, chlorpromazine, and methadone.

The human fetus and neonate do not have mature enzyme systems to carry out the biotransformation and excretion of opioids, with the result that the onset of withdrawal is frequently delayed in comparison to the adult situation; the neonatal opioid withdrawal syndrome can last many weeks and be more variable in its form. For example, it may manifest itself solely as hyperactivity or as failure to thrive. Common symptoms of opioid withdrawal in neonates are tremor, high-pitched cry, increased muscle tone, hyperactivity, poor sleep, poor feeding, sweating, mottling, excoriation, and yawning. Less common symptoms include convulsions, fever, vomiting, markedly hyperactive Moro reflex, and flapping tremor; gastrointestinal symptoms of watery stools and/or vomiting may predominate. Some clinicians feel that the sudden infant death syndrome is more frequent in opioid-dependent than it is in nonopioid-dependent neonates (Pierson et al. 1972). Close monitoring of dependent neonates is indicated for many weeks, if not months, following birth.

Analgesic needs of the mother can be met with normal doses of usual opioid agonists. It is important to stress that, as in other medical situations, maintenance methadone does not contribute to analgesic needs. In the event that a pregnant opioid-dependent woman is delivering and has a heroin habit, methadone should be used to control withdrawal. In this situation, as in other forms of medical stress, the stress of withdrawal should not be added to the stress of delivery. Stress levels will usually be very high in dependent women and require psychological management (i.e., support, nonjudgmental attitudes, and recognition of her suffering). Additional principles of management of the drug-dependent woman are given by Finnegan (1979a). The mother's drug dependence treatment needs can be determined once she has healed from any sequelae of giving birth. Withdrawal should not be attempted until her psychological and biologic status is stable.

Studies reviewed by Finnegan (1979a) indicate that birth weights of the neonates of methadone maintenance women are elevated when compared to the offspring of heroin-dependent women, although they are still not normal. Finnegan also reviewed the evidence suggesting that if methadone has teratogenic effects or major developmental effects, they are not apparent in the studies carried out to date.

Addiction and Medical-Surgical Illnesses

An opioid-dependent person may sustain injuries requiring hospitalization or may otherwise require medical or surgical treatment. Since opioid withdrawal is stressful under the best of circumstances, it is contraindicated to withdraw an addict who is simultaneously undergoing some medical or surgical stress. The principle is not to sum stresses (Senay 1983). Maintenance regimens with methadone are indicated throughout the period of surgical or medical treatment. Analgesia can be achieved with doses of meperidine, morphine, or other usual opioid analgesics about one-third larger than normal in addition to the methadone required for maintenance purposes. Kreek (1981) pointed out that effective analgesia is poorly brought about by simply increasing the dose of methadone used to treat withdrawal, probably because methadone has minimal peak effects. Pentazocine or other mixed agonist-antagonists (e.g., buprenorphine) are contraindicated for analgesia because these antagonists will selectively displace methadone or other opioids (e.g., heroin) from receptor sites and cause or worsen opioid withdrawal.

In the event that a given medical or surgical patient is on methadone maintenance, the dose given in ordinary maintenance should be continued throughout the medical or surgical crisis. If the opioid addict is a so-called street addict, then, in most cases, smooth control can be achieved with methadone 10 to 30 mg/day. The dose can be divided and will be more effective if it is divided into two or three daily doses; control of withdrawal can be achieved usually with once-a-day administration. Obviously, if anesthesia is necessary, the fact of current dependence on opioids should be communicated to the anesthesiologist.

Once the medical or surgical crisis has passed, a decision can be made about detoxification. If an addict wants to be detoxified, referral to a drug abuse program should be the option of choice. Many patients will not want to be detoxified and will want to return to heroin use in their customary surroundings. They should be permitted to do so. However, if they request detoxification, it should be provided before discharge, even though it is difficult to detoxify most addicts on a medical or surgical ward. The staff on these wards are not equipped by training or experience to treat addiction. More often than not, management problems (e.g., drug use, intoxication in guests, stealing) will occur. If a given patient was on methadone maintenance at admission, he or she should be discharged back to their methadone maintenance program without alteration of the dose.

In the case of multiple simultaneous drug dependence (e.g., a patient physically dependent on barbiturates, heroin, and alcohol), methadone may be used in combination with one or more central nervous system (CNS) depressants for safe withdrawal (Senay 1983). If multiple simultaneous dependence occurs concurrent with medical or surgical illness, then patients should be stabilized on methadone, CNS depressants (e.g., benzodiazepines), and/or barbiturates until the medical or surgical crisis has passed. Withdrawal may then be carried out from the different dependencies either sequentially or concurrently.

Psychological Aspects of Methadone Therapy

A growing number of studies indicate that opioid-dependent patients have high rates of depressive symptoms when entering methadone maintenance therapy. Methadone does not appear to worsen or to improve these disorders (Desmond 1979; Woody

1977; Woody et al. 1983). Patients studied to date appear to improve with respect to depression whether they stay in treatment or drop out early. Although they improve as a group, rates of depressive symptoms are still elevated in comparison to rates in community samples after months have elapsed since entering treatment.

Studies indicate that psychiatric status may be an important factor predicting outcome in opioid-dependent patients. Berzins et al. (1974) suggested that the type of psychopathology, as reflected in Minnesota Multiphasic Personality Inventory profiles, may influence treatment responsiveness. Woody (1977) emphasized the need for further research investigating psychopathology and psychotherapeutic intervention in addicts. Sheppard et al. (1972) found that heroin addicts represented a diverse group in terms of type and degree of psychopathology. McLellan et al. (1982, 1983) studied both alcoholics and drug addicts in six different treatments, including a methadone maintenance clinic, and found that "patients with low psychiatric severity improved in every treatment program. Patients with high psychiatric severity showed virtually no improvement in any treatment. Patients with mid-range psychiatric severity (60% of the sample) showed outcome differences from treatment and especially from patient program matches."

A number of studies indicate that antidepressants may have a role in methadone maintenance populations. Studies of psychopathology in opioid-dependent persons suggest that depression is frequent in addict populations as is the diagnosis of personality disorders and possibly phobias, but these studies have not been carried out on large samples. Generalizability is therefore not established. Addicts in different national settings may differ from each other substantially in kinds and degrees of psychopathology so that cross-cultural studies are needed.

Westermeyer (1979) studied medical and nonmedical treatment methods in the Far East and found that Eastern therapies do not differ greatly from Western therapies in effectiveness, although medical therapies (including methadone detoxification) are becoming more popular.

Future Directions for Methadone Maintenance

The provision of licensing and accreditation standards for narcotic substitution programs should result in the closer liaison of this form of treatment of addiction with the standard health care systems, including the mental health care system, in most countries. In the United States, there already is some movement toward licensing and accreditation, and program regulation has improved to the point where poorly run programs are less and less frequent. It is important to understand that substance abuse treatment in general, narcotics included, is a parallel human service delivery system in most of the countries of the world and does not exist in close liaison with standard care offered by hospitals. This situation in the long-term should be remedied because it means that addicts get second-class care for their many medical and psychiatric problems, and the integration of legal opioid substitution therapy with the standard health care system would greatly enhance the ability of both systems to care for relevant populations. Some data suggest, as noted above, that one in five hospital beds is occupied by a person suffering from some medical or psychiatric problem related to substance abuse. There would seem to be a powerful financial reason for integrating these two treatment systems.

In addition to the probable legitimatization of opioid substitution therapy and its merger with the standard health care systems, it is entirely possible that the technology of legal opioid substitution therapy may be greatly improved in the coming decade. There are a number of adjunctive drugs with which we are gaining important clinical experience, drugs such as clonidine and newer agonist-antagonists such as buprenorphine.

L-Alpha-acetylmethadiol (L-AAM) is a long-acting congener of methadone and has been extensively tried in the United States, although it is not approved for routine use (Jaffe et al. 1972). Treatment results with L-AAM compared to methadone under blind conditions indicate that rates of reduction of drug use, reduction of criminality, and improvement in social and vocational functioning are identical (Ling and Blaine 1979), although retention rates are lower. From a clinical point of view, however, L-AAM seems to be effective with a different subset of addicts.

Under an L-AAM regimen, addicts need only come to the clinic three times a week. They take L-AAM on Monday, Wednesday, and Friday, with the Friday dose being some 10 to 20 percent higher than the Monday and Wednesday doses. Other days of the week can be selected, of course. The provision of long-acting L-AAM therapy appears to offer some fiscal and administrative advantages in that staff time can be reduced and more time made free for the provision of direct clinical services with L-AAM. Less attention need be focused on drug taking and drug prescribing.

One of the unresolved questions in methadone maintenance programming is the precise role played by the various elements. As TOPS demonstrates, programs do provide a wide range of services: legal, vocational, and social (Craddock et al. 1982). Patterns of substance abuse are changing worldwide in the direction of abuse of multiple substances, in rotating fashion, with new intoxicants added constantly to the mix. Opioids, however, continue to be abused. Thus a role for legal opioid substitution therapy seems assured. Despite its controversial status, legal opioid substitution therapy appears to offer a unique service to at least some addicts. It will be needed for the foreseeable future unless current drug abuse levels decrease dramatically.

Chapter 137

Inpatient Treatment of Addiction

Drug addiction is a chronic disease that is associated with progressive medical, psychiatric, and psychosocial deterioration. Severely addicted patients may require hospitalization before they are capable of recovery. This powerful intervention effectively breaks the cycle of addiction and provides the opportunity to conduct a full medical and psychiatric evaluation under controlled conditions. Coexisting disorders can be identified and treated while the patient is abstinent from drugs and involved in rehabilitative treatment. In this chapter, we will outline the inpatient approach to drug addiction and discuss major evaluation and treatment issues.

Indications for Hospitalization

Hospitalization for addiction is indicated when outpatient treatment has consistently failed or is likely to fail (Gold et al. 1985a). Severe addiction represents a life-threatening situation. Death by overdose or due to medical complications associated with drug addiction is common. Psychiatric disturbances may lead to dangerously impaired judgment or suicide. Addicts involved in drug dealing or other antisocial activities may be murdered. Accidental death can occur during intoxication states (Gold et al. 1985b). Given the hazards of drug addiction, hospitalization is a reasonable intervention in cases where absolute control of the patient and the patient's environment is necessary.

Addicts with serious medical complications may be candidates for inpatient treatment. These conditions include overdose, abstinence syndromes, and most diseases related to addiction. Continued drug use in the presence of medical disorders such as seizures, cardiac disease, or serious infections is also an indication for hospitalization. Psychiatric illness associated with suicidal, homocidal, or grossly disorganized states obviously requires hospitalization. Often, patients with anxiety and depression are unable to tolerate outpatient rehabilitation until their psychiatric symptoms are properly evaluated and treated. Intravenous drug users should usually be hospitalized because they respond poorly to outpatient treatment and are particularly vulnerable to medical illness and overdose. Drug dealers may require hospitalization as may other patients with easy access to drugs (Washton et al. 1984a). Inpatient treatment is frequently necessary for addicts who are unwilling to leave work or living environments with extraordinary daily access to drugs. Finally, patients adverse to treatment but externally motivated by legal, family, or job pressure may develop internal motivation during intensive inpatient rehabilitation.

Hospitalization is the safest course when serious medical conditions coexist with active addiction, and either interfere with recovery or are exacerbated by continued drug use. These conditions will be described in the following pages. Often, an effective medical evaluation and treatment approach is impossible without the controlled conditions of inpatient treatment. Similarly, psychiatric disorders are difficult to diagnose and treat in active drug users. The differentiation between preexisting and drug-induced psychiatric symptoms usually requires detoxification and careful observation over a period of several drug-free days. A proper evaluation and treatment is especially crucial when suicidal or homicidal impulses are present. The degree of control afforded by inpatient treatment allows the treatment staff to evaluate co-morbidity and to provide a period of abstinence for patients who are truly unable to cease drug use outside the hospital.

Evaluation

The optimal assessment of drug-addicted patients is conducted on a separate evaluation unit (Gold et al. 1984). The evaluation unit addresses drug intoxication, drug withdrawal, and coexisting psychiatric and medical disorders that would otherwise be disruptive to a treatment unit milieu. A complete medical and psychiatric evaluation is necessary before the evaluation and treatment of addiction can proceed. This complex process involves a thorough, integrated, and structured approach from the moment the patient enters the hospital. The physician must be familiar with the pharmacology of abused drugs and be able to recognize intoxication and withdrawal states (Estroff and Gold 1984; Gold et al. 1985b). Other medical and psychiatric complications of drug addiction should likewise be familiar to the physician and multidisciplinary staff.

Admission Procedures

Certain basic admission procedures and precautions are advisable once the patient enters the locked evaluation unit. The unit serves to protect patients from drug access and impulsive departure during their most vulnerable period of treatment. Visual surveillance is maintained until the completion of a luggage inspection and "strip" body search for hidden drugs. It is naive to assume that all patients will be sufficiently motivated to enter the hospital without bringing their drug(s) of choice along. Vital signs are then measured and communicated to the admitting physician. A urine sample for drug analysis (Table 1) is obtained under direct urethral supervision (Gold et al. 1984; Pottash et al. 1982; Verebey et al. 1986a). The patient is then examined by the admitting physician, with particular attention focused on intoxication and withdrawal signs and conditions to be described further on. Acute overdose syndromes should be rapidly identified and treated medically (Olson et al. 1983). An unstructured psychiatric interview is then conducted and admission orders are written (Table 2). Preliminary DSM-III-R (American Psychiatric Association 1987) diagnoses are made with regard to substance abuse and dependence. Due to the confounding influence of drug withdrawal and intoxication, DSM-III-R diagnoses of psychiatric disorders are usually deferred until the completion of detoxification and a drug-free period of observation. At this point, the patient is oriented to the unit and its rules, and visual surveillance is discontinued unless otherwise indicated.

Unit rules should be promptly stated and conveyed in writing to all patients. The violation of certain rules represents grounds for possible discharge. These include drug use, sexual activity, and physical violence on the unit. Patients are also expected to submit random urines for drug analysis on request and adhere to various medical precautions (e.g., hepatitis precautions, blood testing, and vital sign measurements). All drug unit staff members who are recovering are also expected to submit urine samples for analysis on request. An important point often overlooked by substance

Table 1. Comprehensive Evaluation of Urine for Drugs of Abuse

Specific gravity	Phencyclidine
Opiates	Methaqualone
Methadone	Alcohol
Amphetamine	Propoxyphene
Barbiturates	THC/
Cocaine	marijuana
Benzodiazepines	Glutethimide

Note. This represents the standard urine screen by antibody-based testing for all admitted addicts. Positive results are confirmed by gas chromatography/mass spectrometry (GC/MS). Urine testing for additional substances can be obtained if their use is suspected. Blood samples are analyzed by GS/MS when acute intoxication is suspected. ·

Table 2. Typical Admission Orders for a Heroin and Cocaine User Suspected of Alcohol Dependence

---

Admit to evaluation unit
Withdrawal and seizure precautions
Elopement precautions
Hepatitis precautions
Vital signs qid
Screen all visitors
Laboratory tests:
- Chest film
- CBC, SMA-22, RPR, ESR[1]
- Mantoux test
- Electrocardiogram
- Urinalysis (pregnancy test optional)
- Urine for comprehensive drugs of abuse (see Table 1)
- Comprehensive hepatitis evaluation
- Serum cocaine, serum heroin, serum alcohol, etc. (if acutely intoxicated or under the influence of a drug or drugs at time of mental status)

---

[1]CBC = complete blood count, SMA-22 = simultaneous multiple analyses, RPR = rapid plasma reagin, ESR = erythrocyte sedimentation rate.

abuse units is that all visitors should be screened for drug addiction. Visitors may be asked to submit urine samples or to be searched for drugs before they are allowed to visit. This minimizes access to actively addicted friends or family members who may be likely to bring drugs into the unit or to influence the patient negatively. A status system is useful to define graduated privileges and to restrict patients to the locked unit who are psychiatrically or medically unstable or at risk of elopement.

Withdrawal precautions are necessary for all drug patients during the first several days. Patients are often dependent on several drugs and may minimize or withhold information about drug use. This is particularly important with regard to covert alcohol or sedative-hypnotic dependence because of the perils of these abstinence syndromes. If the initial urine demonstrates the presence of sedative-hypnotics, the index of suspicion for sedative withdrawal should be increased. A pentobarbital test may be performed to assess the degree of barbiturate dependence. Vital signs are monitored at least four times daily, and a tongue depressor is present at the bedside in case of seizures. Observation for seizure and withdrawal symptoms is most effective when the physician and nursing staff are completely familiar with these conditions (Table 3). The most common medical emergencies include seizures, drug overdose, arrythmias, and myocardial infarction. Physician and nursing staff should be familiar with medical emergencies and have the equipment and expertise necessary for cardiopulmonary resuscitation.

Hepatitis precautions are necessary for all patients using or suspected of using needles. This precaution minimizes the transmission of hepatitis to other patients and staff. Precautions are carefully explained to each patient, and a written explanation is supplied. Patients eat on disposable trays with disposable utensils. Linens and towels are bleached, and clothes are washed separately. Patients are instructed that hepatitis transmission can occur via saliva, sputum, urine, feces, blood, and seminal or vaginal fluid. Any contact with other individuals must be accordingly restricted. Hands are washed for 30 seconds with hexachloraphene after contact with any of the listed body fluids. Patients unable or unwilling to adhere to these instructions require

Table 3. Signs and Symptoms Useful in Identifying and Distinguishing Opiate and Sedative-Hypnotic Withdrawal States

	Common to Opiate and Sedative-Hypnotic Withdrawal	Specific to Opiate Withdrawal	Specific to Sedative-Hypnotic Withdrawal
Signs	• hypertension • tachycardia • hyperreflexia • tremor • vomiting • diarrhea • diaphoresis • hyperthermia	• lacrimation • mydriasis • rhinorrhea • fasciculations • yawning • pilomotor erection • decreased light reflex	• seizures • blepharospasm • postural hypertension
Symptoms	• irritability • anxiety • insomnia • nausea • panic	• craving opiates • bone pain • muscle aches • orgasm • hot and cold flashes	• craving sedatives • muscle weakness

confrontation and special supervision. Universal precautions are necessary in patients with suspected acquired immune deficiency syndrome (AIDS), who should receive HTLV-III antibody testing. A comprehensive hepatitis profile of the blood is obtained immediately and analyzed for hepatitis A and B antibodies and antigens. Liver functions are also sequentially analyzed, and signs or symptoms of hepatitis are scrutinized. If infectious hepatitis is found, family members or friends with past exposure to the patient should be advised to consult their physician. The hepatitis precautions can be discontinued only after hepatitis has been actually ruled out or when the patient is no longer infectious.

Medical Evaluation

A full medical history and review of systems must be obtained at the onset of treatment. Family or friend informants are useful sources of information because patients often minimize or omit crucial medical information. This particularly occurs with questions about drugs abused, medical complications of addiction, and abstinence symptoms. Laboratory tests and the physical examination often provide a more objective and accurate evaluation of medical problems. Past medical records should be obtained and reviewed. Drug-related illnesses (outlined in the following paragraphs) should be promptly identified and treated.

The physical examination on admission is first directed toward the possibility of overdose. Most patients enter the hospital intoxicated; some may have ingested all their available drugs. Any patient with signs or symptoms of imminent respiratory or cardiac arrest is obviously treated supportively and transferred to an intensive care unit. Medical procedures for opiate, sedative-hypnotic, and central stimulant overdose have been reviewed elsewhere (Gay 1982; Gold and Estroff 1985; Goldfrank and Bresnitz 1978; Wilkinson 1970). The admitting physician must be familiar with all signs and symptoms of drug overdose, as well as with appropriate emergency therapies.

Withdrawal syndromes and detoxification strategies are discussed in Chapter 134. Several general points, however, are important to emphasize. Sedative-hypnotic and alcohol withdrawal should never be overlooked or untreated because these are potentially fatal conditions. With mixed dependence, sedative-hypnotic withdrawal should be treated appropriately before the other drug dependence can be accurately evaluated. Physical signs of drug withdrawal (Table 3) are much more reliable than subjective symptoms. In addition, there is often significant overlap between withdrawal syndromes. Drug addicts will often attempt to maximize their drug intake during detoxification, and their complaints of withdrawal should be objectively confirmed. Signs of intoxication indicate the need for dose reduction. Medication-seeking behavior may include covert exercise prior to vital sign measures, feigned tremor, and fabricated complaints of cramps, diarrhea, and bone pain. This behavior should be confronted at the onset by the physician and staff. Opiate detoxification with clonidine (Gold et al. 1980) as compared to methadone minimizes drug-seeking behavior.

The physical examination also evaluates routes of drug administration and drug-related diseases. With cocaine abuse, the nasal septum is inspected for signs of necrosis and perforation. Needle marks may be present even when intravenous drug use has been denied. Unusual sites of injection, such as the jugular or femoral veins, should be inspected and auscultated for bruits. The presence of cellulitis, abscess, and inflammation at the injection site raises the possibility of sepsis or bacterial colonization of other organs. Endocarditis, pneumonia, and brain abscesses are evaluated with cardiac, pulmonary, and neurologic examinations. The eyes are carefully examined for exudates, granulomas, and hemorrhages. Abdominal palpation may reveal hepatomegaly from hepatitis or portal hypertension. Generalized lymphadenopathy may be indicative of AIDS. Drug-related disorders must be considered throughout the physical examination and the review of systems.

Laboratory testing includes routine admission studies to identify major medical diseases (Table 2). Additional medical testing should be pursued according to the clinical condition of the patient. The supervised urine sample should be analyzed for specific gravity to ensure that the patient has not diluted it to avoid drug detection. Modern enzyme radioimmunoassay or gas chromatography/mass spectrometry (GC/MS) screening for drugs may be ordered on admission when covert drug use is suspected and greater sensitivity is clinically indicated (Gold et al. 1984; Pottash et al. 1982). Patients who demonstrate altered mood, signs of intoxication, or drastic changes in attitude are best evaluated for covert drug use with blood sample analyzed by GC/MS.

Specific medical complications of drug abuse comprise a wide range of disorders (Table 4). These relate to tissue damage from drugs, their contaminants, and their routes of administration. The means of drug administration account for many of the medical complications of addiction. Intravenous and intraarterial drug administration is associated with the greatest risk of medical disease, followed by intradermal (skin-popping), freebasing, intranasal use, and oral ingestion. Intravenous drug use may involve needles, water, and contaminants that are unsterile. These paraphernalia are frequently shared by addicts, leading to the rapid transmission of infection. Trauma at the site of injection can produce inflammation, granulomas, abscesses, neuropathies, aneurisms, and venous ruptures. Tissue downstream from the injection site (e.g., skin, muscle, and veins) is most commonly involved in the spread of infection, followed by the lungs and endocardium of the right side of the heart. Further metastatic spread of infection from intravenous use can produce sepsis, brain abscesses, meningitis, osteomyelitis, pyelonephritis, and hepatitis. Bacterial infections may involve a mixture of different and unusual organisms (Louria et al. 1967).

Table 4.   Common Medical Complications of Drug Addiction

Infectious
  Hepatitis
  AIDS
  Pneumonia

Neurologic
  Seizures
  Cerebral vascular accidents
  Hematomas (subdural or subarachnoid)
  Peripheral neuropathy
  Meningitis

Cardiopulmonary
  Myocardial infarction
  Arrhythmias
  Cardiopulmonary arrest
  Subacute bacterial endocarditis
  Aspiration
  Pulmonary hypertension

Renal
  Nephrotic syndrome (antigen-antibody complex)
  Pyelonephritis
  Hepatorenal syndrome

Trauma
  Aneurisms and venous ruptures
  Head injuries
  Nasal septum perforation

Other
  Birth defects
  Malnutrition
  Dental problems

Hepatitis occurs commonly in intravenous drug users. Infectious hepatitis should be distinguished from alcohol-induced hepatitis by serial liver enzyme testing and antigen-antibody measurements for hepatitis A and B organisms. Hepatitis B is easily acquired because it can be transmitted in minute amounts of blood (Krugman 1982). Infectious hepatitis is also found in addicts without past needle use who are exposed to intravenous users. Non-A/non-B infectious hepatitis may also be present (Fields et al. 1982), as well as chronic persistent hepatitis.

The identification of intravenous drug use as a risk factor for AIDS is well documented (Marx 1982). Compromised cell-mediated immunity can lead to pneumocystic carinii pneumonia, disseminated herpes simplex, cerebral toxoplasmosis, cytomegalovirus, cryptococcal meningitis, and a variety of disseminated mycobacterial infections. Generalized lymphadenopathy, Kaposi's sarcoma, and diffuse undifferentiated lymphoma may also be found in AIDS patients (Centers for Disease Control 1982). Decreased helper T cell levels (Marx 1982) are postulated to account for the compromised cellular immunity. Because of the high mortality rates in AIDS patients, extreme care must be taken to avoid transmission of the disease.

Neurologic diseases may occur from infection, trauma, or pharmacologic effects of the drug. Subdural or subarachnoid hematomas should be ruled out in cases of head trauma. Cerebral vascular accidents may result from hypertensive crisis after central stimulant use (Shukla 1982) or embolic phenomena (Brust and Richter 1976). Seizures may also result from central stimulant intoxication and from alcohol or sedative-hypnotic withdrawal. At particular risk for seizures are patients with past head injuries, previous withdrawal seizures, or underlying seizure disorder. Tics, myoclonus, and choreoathetoid movements are produced by central stimulants. Volatile solvents may cause brain damage, with ataxia, seizures, and coma (King et al. 1981). Nitrous oxide is associated with peripheral neuropathy (Nevins 1980), and polyradiculoneuropathy has been associated with heroin use (Loizou and Boddie 1978). Neuropsychological testing commonly reveals memory, concentration, and spatial-perceptual impairment in drug addicts, indicative of more subtle brain dysfunction.

Ophthalmologic disorders may result from the intravenous delivery of talc or other contaminants into the retinal circulation (Friberg et al. 1979; Tse and Ober 1980). A visual display of light ("talc flash") is often experienced by addicts during this event. Lodged emboli may form granulomas and progress to macular ischemia (Friberg et al. 1979). Bacterial and fungal infections of the eye have also been reported.

Most pulmonary and cardiac diseases associated with addiction are infectious. These include pneumonia, septic emboli, abscesses, mycotic aneurisms, and endocarditis. Aspiration may occur, particularly during overdose or intoxication states. Pulmonary hypertension from fibrosis can occur with the freebasing of cocaine and its contaminants. Cocaine, especially with intravenous use, may produce cardiac arrhythmias, myocardial infarction, and sudden death (Washton et al. 1984b; Wetli and Wright 1979). Clearly a chest X ray and electrocardiogram are indicated on admission for all drug patients.

Renal disease in addicts may be secondary to antigen-antibody complex deposits in patients with hepatitis or endocarditis (Gutman et al. 1972; Kohler et al. 1974). This possibility should be considered when a nephrotic syndrome is present. Acute or chronic renal failure may also result from amphetamine-induced rhabdomyolysis or polyarteritis nodosa. Hepatitis may also cause renal failure with hepatorenal syndrome.

Endocrine abnormalities have been reported in drug addicts. Opiates appear to inhibit the hypothalamic-pituitary-adrenal (HPA) axis and the production of gonadotropins and testosterone (Gold et al. 1982). Cocaine and opiates produce hyperprolactinemia (Dackis et al. 1984b; Gold et al. 1982). Cocaine-induced hyperprolactinemia has led to the dopamine depletion hypothesis of cocaine addiction (Dackis and Gold 1985b) and recent trials of bromocriptine for cocaine craving and withdrawal in these patients (Dackis and Gold 1985a). Cocaine intoxication may also activate the thyroid axis (Dackis et al. 1985). Marijuana may inhibit testosterone (Kolodny et al. 1974) and sperm motility (Hong et al. 1981), as well as reduce libido. The results of these marijuana studies, however, are mixed and unclear.

Dietary and dental problems are also found with drug addicts. Dental pain is a frequent complaint of drug addicts during detoxification. Dental problems have often been present for months or years, but masked by drug analgesia. The problem may be so advanced that extraction is necessary to avoid acute ulcerative gingivitis (Carter 1978). Vitamin deficiency may be specific to drug use or a reflection of poor dietary patterns. Multivitamin and thiamine replacement during the first two weeks of hospitalization is probably a prudent precaution (Gold and Verebey 1984).

During pregnancy, the effects of drug addiction on the fetus can be tragic. Alcohol produces gross deformity of the newborn (Clarren and Smith 1978). Although opiates are not teratogenic, their use may predispose to attention deficit disorder (Chasnoff et al. 1982). Certain effects of the addict's life-style may lead to poor prenatal care, low birth weight, and diminished fetal prognosis. Congenital malformations may occur with the use of meprobamate, diazepam, and chlordiazepoxide during the first trimester. Phenobarbital use during pregnancy is associated with congenital malformations and altered reproductive function in female offspring. Although the effects of cocaine and other central stimulants on the fetus are not known, increased fetal mortality rates have been reported (Eriksson et al. 1981).

It should be evident that drug addiction is a dangerous, life-threatening disease from a medical standpoint. Medical disorders should be quickly discovered and treated during the first days of hospitalization. The relationship between medical diseases and the addiction is impressed on the patient and family. Although the fear of medical disease or death seldom motivates an addict to cease drug use, it can serve to minimize the initial resistance to treatment. Medical stabilization is always the first priority in the treatment of the addict. Once accomplished, the psychiatric evaluation is conducted.

Psychiatric Evaluation

The psychiatric evaluation of drug addicts is an important part of their overall treatment. Untreated psychiatric illness is associated with morbidity and interferes with recovery from addiction. The complex interface between psychiatric and addictive illness can be reduced to three possible diagnostic situations. First, psychiatric symptoms may be entirely secondary to addiction, as in the case of cocaine-induced hallucinations (Siegel 1978). Secondly, addiction may result entirely from the self-medication of an underlying psychiatric disorder. One example would be a patient with panic anxiety who was dependent on benzodiazepines. The third and most complicated situation involves the coexistence of autonomous psychiatric and addictive illnesses, as with the manic-depressive patient with a 10-year history of intravenous heroin addiction. In these cases, the resolution of one illness will not automatically result from the stabilization of other illness. Even if initial drug use was motivated by psychiatric symptoms, entrenched addictive patterns will not disappear without specific rehabilitative treatment. The only effective approach to these patients involves the skillful coordinaton of psychiatric and drug rehabilitative treatment.

The psychiatric evaluation of drug addicts should clearly define which diagnostic situation exists. Patients with numerous past treatment failures for addiction may have primary psychiatric illness that must be identified and treated. Conversely, addicts with psychiatric symptoms secondary to addiction can often be spared unnecessary pharmacotherapy and psychiatric treatment.

To diagnose psychiatric illness in drug addicts reliably, the clinician must allow some passage of time to eliminate intoxication and withdrawal effects. This time varies according to the drug in question and severity of addiction. Unfortunately, there exists little research regarding this important diagnostic issue. A two-week drug-free period after the completion of detoxification is useful to clarify diagnostic issues. This "wash out" period must sometimes be abandoned when emergency pharmacotherapy is clinically indicated. During the drug-free period, attention is directed toward any diminution of psychiatric symptoms. Substance-induced psychiatric syndromes typically remit gradually, and this pattern justifies further observation.

The psychiatric evaluation is coordinated with the medical evaluation and laboratory testing. Medical conditions capable of mimicking psychiatric illness (e.g., seizure disorders or thyroid disease) should be properly diagnosed and treated. Sudden changes in mental status or motivation may result from clandestine drug use and can be investigated with blood or urine testing for drugs of abuse.

The psychiatric examination of drug addicts is more complicated than that of nonaddicts. The clinician must be familiar with confounding effects of drug intoxication, withdrawal, and protracted withdrawal states. Knowledge of the drug addict mentality, such as a reluctance or inability to describe psychiatric symptoms, will diminish inaccuracies in diagnosis. These patients have experienced feeling states far outside the normal range and may have difficulty discerning more subtle feelings of anxiety, depression, or anger. Intentional distortions may further complicate the evaluation. Patients willing to use unknown street drugs are often surprisingly resistant to taking psychotropics and may minimize psychiatric symptoms. While some addicts are fearful of being psychiatrically diagnosed, others emphasize psychiatric symptoms as a means of minimizing their addiction. Sequential mental status examinations and behavioral observations by the staff must be integrated with patient reports to ensure accuracy of diagnosis.

The past psychiatric history is also difficult to obtain reliably. The diagnosis of psychiatric illness during periods of active addiction is confounded by the many effects of addictive agents. Psychiatric symptoms during significant periods of abstinence, or preceding addiction, are diagnostically useful provided the drug history is accurate. Family reports are usually helpful in identifying past psychiatric symptoms. If major psychiatric illness has been present prior to the onset of addiction, or during significant periods of drug abstinence, then a psychiatric diagnosis is likely. Often a positive psychiatric family history that is confirmatory will be present. The likelihood of past psychiatric illness should alert the clinician to conduct a careful evaluation of present symptoms during the wash-out period.

Evaluation of Specific Psychiatric Disorders

We will now review the diagnostic approach to specific psychiatric conditions in drug addicts. Particular attention will be directed toward aspects of the psychiatric evaluation that differ from the approach in nonaddicted psychiatric patients. Since some drugs of abuse are more likely to generate certain psychiatric symptoms, these agents will be discussed more extensively in sections relating to those symptoms. Similarly, certain addictive drugs are more effective in ameliorating specific symptoms and are abused more commonly by patients with those symptoms. Due to a general lack of research on the psychiatric diagnosis of drug addicts, most of what follows is based on our clinical experience.

Depression

Many addicts feel or appear depressed when they enter the hospital. Depression may result from a number of factors. Drug withdrawal can be associated with depressed mood and vegetative symptoms, such as insomnia, anorexia, anergia, and psychomotor agitation. The full realizaton of the addict's deterioration often leads to feelings of guilt and demoralization in the addict. The habitual use of drugs may disrupt brain centers involved in mood regulation, producing organic affective syndromes. The psychiatric evaluation of depression must distinguish these possibilities from major depression before identifying patients in need of antidepressant medications.

The persistence of major depression (by DSM-III-R criteria) for two weeks after the completion of detoxification is probably an indication to consider an antidepressant trial. The actual diagnosis, however, remains clouded because some addictive agents may cause protracted affective syndromes. Methadone dependence, for example, may induce protracted depressive syndromes that may nonetheless respond to antidepressant treatment (Dackis and Gold 1984). Alcohol dependence is associated with severe but rapidly remitting depressive syndromes. A full understanding of substance-induced affective syndromes awaits further research. Based on our present knowledge and given the high rates of recidivism with depressed addicts (Rounsaville et al. 1982), persistent depression should be treated. The presence of depression during periods of drug abstinence is consistent with affective illness, as is a family history of depression. A history of depression preceding drug abuse is also diagnostic but seldom helpful because drug abuse usually begins long before the usual age of onset for affective illness.

Opiate addicts have been reported by several investigators to have high rates of depression (Dackis and Gold 1984). Prevalence rates of 17 percent were found for major depression in methadone-dependent patients (Rounsaville et al. 1982d), whereas recently detoxified heroin- and methadone-dependent patients had rates of 25 and 60 percent, respectively (Dackis and Gold 1983). Due to the high rates of major depression in detoxified opiate addicts and profound B-endorphin and cortisol disruptions in these patients (Gold and Rea 1983), it has been suggested that opiates may actually induce an organic affective syndrome (Dackis and Gold 1984). Clinicians should maintain a high index of suspicion for major depression in opiate addicts, based on the high prevalence rates. When used in conjunction with a careful diagnostic interview and sequential observations for depression, the dexamethasone suppression test (DST) may be a useful diagnostic adjunct with opiate addicts. This test has sensitivity for depression in opiate addicts when conducted two weeks after detoxification (Dackis et al. 1984a). The recognition and treatment of depression in opiate addicts could significantly improve recovery rates for addiction, as well as reduce the morbidity of depression.

Sedative-hypnotic drugs are widely abused alone or in conjunction with other drugs. The most commonly abused drugs in this class are the widely prescribed benzodiazepines. Iatrogenic sedative dependence may result from the practice of treating depressed individuals with benzodiazepines or other sedative-hypnotics. Conversely, sedative withdrawal may resemble depression when associated with vegetative symptoms and unstable mood. A careful and complete detoxification is necessary before depressive symptoms can be properly evaluated. Unfortunately, sedative detoxification may require several weeks of dose reduction while depressive symptoms persist. When clinically indicated, antidepressant treatment may be necessary before the completion of detoxification. This is particularly prudent when previous depressive episodes or suicidality have been present. In these cases, the diagnosis of major depression, with its implied risk of recurrent future episodes, remains in question. A more accurate evaluation for major depression can be made two weeks after detoxification is completed.

With the current proliferation of cocaine abuse, clinicians are becoming increasingly familiar with central stimulants and their psychiatric complications. Although cocaine and amphetamine abuse differ in some aspects, all central stimulants will be considered to be comparable to cocaine for the purpose of this discussion. Cocaine is a potent euphoriant with profound mood-elevating properties. Freud originally suggested that depressed individuals might self-medicate depression with cocaine (Byck 1974). Conversely, cocaine withdrawal may produce "crashing states" associated with anergia, hypersomnia, psychomotor retardation, depressed mood, and irritability (Dackis and Gold 1985b). The initial evaluation of depressed cocaine abusers should therefore distinguish depressive illness from cocaine-induced affective syndromes, which, although often severe, usually remit within days.

Studies suggest that cocaine is not an effective antidepressant agent. When cocaine was administered to a group of depressed patients, it was found that it worsened depressive symptoms in the majority of cases (Post et al. 1974). Even in nondepressed cocaine abusers, the initial euphoria of cocaine is often followed by much longer periods of dysphoria and irritability. Some cocaine abusers will have major depression, however, regardless of whether self-medication with cocaine is a significant dynamic.

Cocaine is not associated with the protracted withdrawal symptoms seen with opiates and sedative-hypnotics. However, since chronic cocaine abuse may produce protracted periods of depressed or elevated mood, the evaluation of affective disorders in these patients is best conducted after two weeks of abstinence. Cocaine abuse is usually found in conjunction with other substance abuse or dependence. Alcohol dependence is common in cocaine abusers, and alcohol-induced mood effects may confound their evaluation. If other drugs of abuse are found by history or urine testing, the effects of these substances on mood must also be considered. Sedative, marijuana, and opiate use should be suspected. If depressive symptoms persist without significant improvement for two weeks after cocaine abstinence, and other factors cannot be identified, the presence of major depression is likely. These patients generally have other features of major depression, such as a positive family history, previous episodes, or mood disturbance during periods of drug abstinence.

Laboratory testing for major depression in cocaine abusers has not been established as reliable. The DST may be useful in confirming major depression but specificity studies are lacking. In fact, since amphetamine releases plasma cortisol in humans (Besser et al. 1969) and leads to adrenocortical hypertrophy in animals (Kirkby and Petchkovsky 1973), cocaine-induced cortisol hypersecretion may exist in the absence of major depression. The thyrotropin-releasing hormone (TRH) test (Extein et al. 1982) is abnormal in nondepressed cocaine abusers (Dackis et al. 1985). The TRH test does not therefore appear specific for depression in cocaine abusers. On the basis of our current knowledge, the diagnosis of major depression must be made on clinical grounds after at least two weeks of cocaine abstinence.

Patients seldom seek hospitalization for marijuana abuse, but many addicts smoke this drug on a regular basis. Psychiatric patients may also abuse marijuana. It is not uncommon for marijuana to be smuggled into drug units. The staff should be aware of this possibility and cognizant of the psychlogical and physiologic signs of marijuana intoxication that are described below. Due to its prolonged persistence in the urine (Dackis et al. 1982), marijuana abuse is easily recognized in urine samples obtained on admission. Chronic use may be associated with tetrahydrocannabinol (THC) levels for several weeks (Dackis et al. 1982). Marijuana intoxication produces mood effects that might confound the evaluation of depression. Psychomotor retardation, decreased concentration, decreased libido, paranoia, and guilty rumination may be seen during intoxication states. Marijuana intoxication is best demonstrated by plasma levels or clinical signs (e.g., pupillary dilation, conjunctival reddening, and tachycardia). The effects of marijuana on neuroendocrine testing is unknown. In our experience, marijuana-induced mood effects may continue for several days but are seldom sufficiently severe to produce a syndrome comparable to major depression. However, marijuana may trigger depressive disorders in patients with underlying affective illness.

Mania

Drug addicts with manic symptoms on admission require an emergency evaluation with a complete physical examination and laboratory testing of the blood and urine for drugs of abuse. Acute withdrawal from sedative-hypnotics, alcohol, or opiates (Table 3) may mimic mania and should be treated quickly and appropriately. Abstinence syndromes should never be, but often are, confused with mania. Intoxication states, particularly with cocaine, amphetamine, phencyclidine, hallucinogens, anticholinergics, and marijuana, can produce manic symptoms. The physical examination should focus on signs of these intoxication states (Table 5) while the physician awaits the results of blood analysis for these agents. Although intoxication states generally disappear within hours, elevated and irritable mood may continue for several days after the cessation of phencyclidine and central stimulant use. However, there should be a discernible trend of clinical stabilization as the drug is metabolized and eliminated.

When manic symptoms persist beyond three days of drug abstinence and are not attributable to withdrawal states, the diagnosis of acute mania is likely. Past manic or depressive epidodes, particularly during periods of drug abstinence, are confirmatory, as is a positive family history of affective (particularly bipolar) disorder. In some cases, there is an extensive history of manic depression with aborted attempts at lithium therapy. Noncompliance and the persistence of drug addiction have often interfered with the stabilization of bipolar disorder.

The discussion of mania and drug abuse would be incomplete without emphasizing the need to avoid diagnosing addictive illness when it is not present. Manic patients typically possess impaired judgment. They are also keenly aware of violent mood swings and may use addictive drugs as a means of controlling their mood (Estroff et al. 1984). Compulsive drug use may occur only during manic episodes, as does other inappropriate or excessive behavior. When this is the case, as confirmed by family reports, true addictive illness may be absent and rehabilitative treatment unnecessary. Conversely, it is crucial to identify addictive illness that coexists with manic depression. Continued drug addiction may also destabilize mood, rendering lithium less effective. Certain addictive agents, such as central stimulants, may activate

Table 5. Physical Signs Associated with Substance-Induced Psychosis

Stimulants	Hallucinogens	Phencyclidine	Tetrahydrocannabinol	Anticholinergics
tachycardia	tachycardia	tachycardia	tachycardia	tachycardia
hypertension	hypertension	hypertension	tremor	hyperthermia
hyperthermia	hyperthermia	hyperthermia	dry mouth	dry mouth
tremor	diaphoresis	diaphoresis	mydriasis	flushing
diaphoresis	mydriasis	nystagmus	nystagmus	mydriasis
dry mouth	flushing	ataxia	ataxia	urinary
retention		stereotypies		hoarseness
flushing		salivation		dry skin
mydriasis		rigidity		dysphagia
hyperreflexia		myoclonus		
stereotypies		peripheral		
convulsions		neuropathy		
arrhythmias				

mania through their effects of central dopamine circuits (Dackis and Gold 1985b). The patient may also discontinue lithium, fearing drug interactions or interference with drug euphoria. Neither disorder can therefore be treated effectively without stabilization of the other.

Psychotic Disorders

The evaluation of psychotic disorders in drug addicts is similar to that discussed with mania. Drug-induced psychosis should be ruled out by physical examination and with plasma and urine testing. Frequent offenders include central stimulants, phencyclidine, marijuana, and hallucinogens. Psychotic symptoms may be found in alcohol or sedative withdrawal, and detoxification should be completed before a full assessment is made. Generally, drug-induced psychosis should remit over a period of hours or days. A discernible improving trend should also be present. Primary psychotic illness, on the other hand, will usually not improve and may worsen as the patient is observed in a drug-free state. Psychotic symptoms in drug addicts, if not presenting a danger, can be observed for spontaneous remission before instituting neuroleptic maintenance.

With schizophrenic drug addicts, a number of specific drug treatment problems arise. Accurate diagnosis is therefore critical. These patients typically have great difficulty interacting in a therapeutic community setting. Drug rehabilitative groups demand intact social skills and active participation. Schizophrenic patients may decompensate in this setting and require a more supportive and psychiatrically oriented approach to their addictive illness. In many cases, there is an extensive history of schizophrenia with previous hospitalizations and the persistence of psychotic symptoms beyond detoxification. Drug addiction has usually had a destabilizing effect on the psychotic illness and often precedes episodes of relapse and drug noncompliance. The treatment of these patients is problematic.

When schizophrenia is not obviously present by history, the diagnostic evaluation is more complicated. The persistence of psychosis beyond one week of hospitalization generally rules out substance-induced psychosis. However, with phencyclidine abuse, more protracted psychosis may occur. Covert psychotomimetic drug use on the unit should also be ruled out with blood and urine testing. Neurologic disorders may also be associated with psychoses. Temporal lobe epilepsy is more likely to manifest during detoxification and can be evaluated by history or electroencephalography (EEG) testing. A sleep-deprived EEG or 24-hour telemetry EEG provides increased sensitivity and can be performed two weeks after detoxification. Neuropsychological testing after two to four weeks of abstinence is helpful when brain dysfunction is suspected, and structural lesions, such as hematomas or abscesses, can be identified with a computed tomography (CT) scan of the head. Certain viral syndromes may produce psychosis (Henderson and Shelokov 1959) and can be detected with a lumbar puncture for antibody titers. A full neurologic evaluation is especially important when a past history of psychosis is absent.

In cases of schizophrenia or schizoaffective illness, it is important to evaluate the patient's capacity for drug rehabilitative treatment. If insight and judgment are severely impaired, there is usually little benefit from standard therapeutic community treatment. These patients often have histories of intractable relapse to psychotic and addictive illness. Their inability to care for themselves or take responsibility for their recovery indicates the need for a different and more structured treatment approach. Similarly, psychotic patients with grossly impaired interpersonal skills will not benefit satisfactorily from drug groups and will require a modified approach. Some psychotic patients, however, will be appropriate for standard recovery programs, especially if psychotic symptoms can be stabilized.

Anxiety

Anxiety symptoms are particularly common with recently hospitalized drug addicts. All abstinence syndromes involve some degree of anxiety and may even produce panic attacks, which should not be confused with independent anxiety disorders. Conversely, patients with anxiety disorders may become drug-dependent over years of self-medication. These patients particularly abuse sedative-hypnotics, alcohol, and opiates. The evaluation of drug addicts for anxiety should clearly identify those individuals in need of specific pharmacotherapy.

The first step in evaluating a possible anxiety disorder is to rule out organic etiologies. Drug withdrawal represents only one possibility. Drug intoxication with cocaine, marijuana, hallucinogens, and phencyclidine may produce panic symptoms. Evidence for these intoxication states can be evaluated by plasma and urine testing, history, and physical examination. A wash-out period corresponding to the duration of action of the drug in question is essential before diagnosing an anxiety disorder. Medical causes such as hyperthyroidism, mitral valve prolapse, hypoglycemia, and pheochromocytoma should be ruled out. Temporal lobe epilepsy may mimic panic anxiety and is more likely to manifest during drug withdrawal. Complaints of anxiety are frequent among drug-seeking addicts and should be qualified by objective observation and staff reports. Urges for drugs may be experienced as anxiety and will usually dissipate during constructive rehabilitative groups.

Sedative-dependent patients pose complex diagnostic issues with regard to anxiety. Agents such as barbiturates, benzodiazepines, glutethimide, and methaqualone generally require a prolonged detoxification lasting several weeks. Anxiety symptoms experienced during this period may represent an underlying anxiety disorder or result from protracted withdrawal. Physical signs, including hypertension, tremor, diaphoresis, tachycardia, and hyperreflexia, are of limited value, with the latter being most specific for drug withdrawal. Sedatives may be capable of producing protracted anxiety syndromes lasting for several months. These have been described by patients to remit gradually with continued drug abstinence. Temporary treatment with propranolol may be of help in these patients and has also been recommended for the final stages of benzodiazepine withdrawal. Protracted withdrawal states associated with anxiety are also seen after detoxification from methadone. When anxiety improves over several weeks of drug abstinence, protracted withdrawal is the more likely diagnosis, and the diagnosis of generalized anxiety or panic disorder should be avoided.

If primary anxiety disorders coexist with addictive illness, an accurate diagnosis is imperative to assure proper treatment. Patients with anxiety disorders are quite vulnerable to drug addiction during their pursuit of symptom relief. Addictive drugs may be illicitly attained, but are often prescribed by physicians. Sedative-hypnotics, particularly benzodiazepines, have been widely used for generalized anxiety and panic disorders (Rickels et al. 1983; Sheehan 1982) but may lead eventually to physical dependence (Greenblatt and Shader 1978). A reasonably high incidence of anxiety disorders, therefore, is found among drug addicts.

Drug addicts with panic disorders are likely to relapse if their psychiatric illness is not properly diagnosed and treated. These patients typically describe anxiety attacks preceding drug use, with avoidant behavior and phobic patterns. A past history of school phobia may be obtained, and a family history of panic disorder is common. Panic attacks may occur in the hospital and should be distinguished from withdrawal symptoms. The diagnosis of panic disorder is most reliably made after detoxification has been completed. Mitral valve prolapse is often found with echocardiogram studies, and may indicate a beneficial clinical response to beta-adrenergic blockers such as propranolol.

Generalized anxiety disorder may coexist with addictive illness and can be diagnosed after detoxification. This disorder should not be overdiagnosed in recently detoxified patients because anxiety is a hallmark of early recovery. Drug addicts must learn to experience unpleasant feeling states and to cope without artificial means of anxiety regulation. Early recovery also involves the recollection of drug addict behavior, which is anxiety producing. Since the treatment of addiction is often associated with anxiety, excessive or unnecessary pharmacotherapy for anxiety in these patients should be avoided.

Personality Disorders

Characteristic features of personality disorders are commonly found in patients hospitalized for drug addiction. However, to diagnose personality disorders reliably, these features should be typical of long-term functioning and not be molded by demands and priorities of drug addiction. Antisocial behaviors directed toward drug procurement may cease with drug abstinence. Impulsivity during drug intoxication may never occur in a sober state. Persistent lying is necessary to avoid social ostracism or job loss and often ceases with recovery. Therefore, personality disorders should be diagnosed cautiously in individuals during the early stages of their recovery. Caution is especially warranted if drug addiction has persisted for many years or decades. Such individuals may experience profound character transformations with recovery. Although it is well recognized that personality disorders are difficult to diagnose during discrete espisodes of psychiatric illness, there is insufficient appreciation of the extent to which drug addiction can distort an individual's personality.

With these considerations in mind, it is also important to emphasize that individuals with preexisting personality disorders or conduct disorders are at increased risk of drug addiction (Khantzian and Khantzian 1984). The presence of antisocial personality disorder may predispose to drug abuse and negatively affect prognosis. Antisocial and borderline personality disorders include drug abuse as diagnostic criteria. Individuals with avoidant personality disorders may self-medicate social anxiety with drugs or alcohol. Personality disorders may therefore precede or result from drug addiction. This distinction is probably difficult to assess during hospitalization for addiction and is not an essential determination in the treatment of addiction. Unless a compelling historical background exists for a personality disorder, perhaps personality diagnoses should be deferred during the first six months of recovery.

Psychiatric Treatment of the Addict

The treatment of psychiatric illness in drug addicts must be carefully coordinated with drug rehabilitation. Drug addiction should never be viewed as justified by psychiatric illness. The addict will otherwise avoid the responsibility of remaining abstinent and engaging in rehabilitation. Pharmacotherapy for psychiatric illness should not be seen as treatment for addiction. The stabilization of psychiatric illness seldom ends entrenched addiction because addicts use drugs primarily for their euphoria and in response to drug urges. Physicians treating drug addicts must be sufficiently sophisticated regarding addictive illness and its treatment to avoid the undermining of rehabilitative efforts. Even when drug abuse has begun as an attempt at self-medication of an underlying psychiatric disorder, it usually takes on a life of its own, independent of the underlying disorder, and must be treated therefore as a primary, rather than secondary, condition.

In prescribing medications, addictive agents must obviously be avoided once detoxification has been completed. Generally, addictive agents are not effective in the maintenance treatment of psychiatric illness even in patients without addiction. With drug addicts, these agents will usually be abused or will lead to relapse with the drug of choice. Even if indicated and properly selected, the use of psychotropic medications may interfere with drug rehabilitation. The pattern of taking medications daily may bear symbolic resemblance to drug abuse and may undermine the patient's sense of abstinence. Ostracism from self-help groups occasionally results when group members learn of psychotropic use. Therefore, as with many medical decisions, the need for psychotropic medication should clearly outweigh potential disadvantages. During inpatient treatment, the clinician has somewhat more latitude to observe whether untreated psychiatric symptoms will subside.

Drug addicts are often quite resistant to taking prescribed medications, even though indiscriminant use of drugs may have preceded their hospitalization. These patients may fear or deny the existence of psychiatric illness and prefer the sole diagnosis of addiction. Since untreated psychiatric disease leads to morbidity and a greater risk of relapse, this resistance must be confronted and overcome to ensure optimal treatment. Education regarding psychotropic medication is essential. The patient should understand that the medication prescribed is not addictive and does not produce euphoria. Noncompliance or internal conflict will otherwise result. Families should understand the need for medications and the illness for which they are prescribed. A meeting with the essential family members and patient at the end of the psychiatric evaluation is useful to clarify diagnostic and treatment issues. Ironically, even though addicts may have been taking illicit drugs for years without regard to purity or dangerous additives, they will often complain of side effects from prescribed medications as a means of avoiding pharmacotherapy.

The pharmacologic treatment of specific psychiatric disorders in drug addicts does not differ in most respects from that with nonaddicts. Once a psychiatric disorder has been properly diagnosed, its treatment should proceed according to standard psychiatric approaches. The few deviations or modifications of psychiatric treatment in drug addicts will be discussed here according to the disorder treated.

Drug addicts with affective disease generally respond to standard antidepressant medications. Target symptoms are evaluated for improvement while antidepressant blood levels are monitored. The monitoring of blood levels in these patients is useful to ensure compliance, avoid toxicity, and attain therapeutic doses (Gold et al. 1984; Preskorn et al. 1986). Antidepressants with a large degree of anticholinergic activity may be less suitable because of their mild potential for abuse. The two major issues in addicts with affective illness include noncompliance for medications and ascribing the addiction to the self-medication of depressive symptoms. This later resistance can be confronted by focusing on their pursuit of euphoria rather than mere symptom relief. Usually peer groups are most equipped with information about the patient to make this point. Noncompliance may be most effectively addressed in individual therapy and with education. This problem is particularly prevalent among manic patients. To maximize the chances of recovery, each resistance should be confronted and resolved during hospitalization.

Psychotic disorders coexisting with addictive illness often pose the greatest challenge to the physician and treating staff. These patients, especially when schizophrenic, may not relate well in drug rehabilitation units and usually require a specialized psychiatric unit. Compliance with antipsychotic medications and with drug rehabilitation is a perennial problem. Once psychotic symptoms have been stabilized, compliance can be addressed by obtaining periodic, neuroleptic blood levels or by administering depot injections. Family education is essential to emphasize the need for neuroleptic treatment and the dangers of illicit drug use. After these patients have been evaluated and stabilized, efforts should be directed toward providing good outpatient planning with structure and external controls. Half-way house placement with urine screening for drugs of abuse and rehabilitative therapy is the optimal form of treatment.

Addicts with anxiety disorders generally respond to standard pharmacologic treatments. However, they are at great risk for benzodiazepine dependence, and these widely prescribed drugs are counterindicated when addictive illness is present. These patients tend to focus on symptom relief and to minimize their enjoyment of abused drugs. Urges for drugs are denied or confused with anxiety. They may altogether reject drug rehabilitation, insisting that abuse will end once their symptoms have been stabilized. However, the true addict uses drugs to produce a euphoric state in addition to the relief of anxiety and would be unlikely to remain abstinent without rehabilitation.

Patients with panic disorders may have social phobia and experience panic symptoms during rehabilitation groups. Until their anxiety disorder is stabilized, some flexibility with regard to group attendance is justified. Avoidance behavior is not necessarily a resistance to treatment in these cases. Beta-adrenergic blockers may be an effective treatment for the phobia of group meetings. These agents can also be prescribed during detoxification, when anxiety symptoms are intolerable. Patients with addictive illness should always be warned about the future use of addictive agents for anxiety. Even prescribed medications should be carefully scrutinized for addictive potential and avoided until their safety has been assured. The widespread use of alprazolam for panic anxiety, or diazepam for generalized anxiety, raises the possibility that such agents may be inadvertently recommended by physicians unaware of the addiction or unfamiliar with its management. Tricyclic antidepressants and monoamine oxidase inhibitors have proven efficacy in the treatment of panic disorder and should be prescribed in lieu of benzodiazepines.

As previously discussed, personality disorders in drug addicts should be diagnosed cautiously because of the profound effects of addiction on character and behavior. Personality disorders should not be the focus of treatment for addiction. Focusing on a personality disorder during the early stages of recovery may contradict drug rehabilitative treatment by conveying that drug use results from conflict and will cease once conflict has resolved. Specific treatment of personality disorders is indicated when they interfere with drug rehabilitation. Extremely narcissistic patients often have difficulty tolerating peer feedback and forming meaningful therapeutic relationships. Paranoid patients have difficulty with trust and self-disclosure. Antisocial personality disorders limit the patient's capacity for honesty and the adherence to unit rules. These and countless other resistances to treatment must be addressed, but the task of inpatient drug rehabilitation is the attainment of abstinence, not the improvement of personality disorders.

Repeated emphasis has been placed on the coordination of psychiatric and drug rehabilitative care. While the psychiatrist must make the addict available for rehabilitation by treating disruptive psychiatric illness, the psychiatrist must also understand and support the treatment principles for addiction, which will be outlined. This involves an emphasis on self-help groups, the need to make the addict responsible for his or her own treatment, and reliance on other specialized staff to facilitate recovery from addiction.

Treatment of Addiction

The inpatient treatment of addiction is designed to end drug abuse abruptly, to institute rehabilitation, and to prepare the addict for outpatient treatment. This is primarily accomplished by establishing a staff of specialists and recovering addicts on the drug treatment unit and a peer-group community that resembles outpatient self-help groups. Patients are transferred to the locked drug treatment unit after the completion of their evaluation. Patient homogeneity is an important feature of treatment for drug addiction. Patients without addictive illness should not be mixed with drug patients on the treatment unit. A viable peer group is further enhanced if drug patients with similar psychosocial and addictive backgrounds can be grouped. Intravenous heroin and cocaine addicts may comprise one group while sedative-hypnotic addicts and alcoholic patients comprise another. Individual therapy reinforces the group's approach, and family therapy addresses pathologic family dynamics that obstruct recovery. Education is provided to patients and families, with an emphasis on the disease concept of addiction.

A viable, functioning inpatient peer group comprises the most important element of inpatient treatment. Although 12 to 16 appears to be the optimal number of patients in a viable inpatient peer group, larger units may be subdivided into teams. While new patients are often manipulative, irresponsible, and antisocial, dramatic changes in attitude and behavior may be produced by a cohesive group of peers. It is the task of skilled staff to maintain an effective peer group and to avoid the development of cynicism, oppositionalism, and subversion. This is accomplished by placing the responsibility for recovery on each patient, and making the patients accountable for their behavior and attitudes. Drug addicts are expected to self-disclose honestly, to attend all meetings, and to assist each other through caring confrontation. Much of this work occurs in group meetings that are run by professionally trained and recovering staff members.

Individual therapy may be an important adjunct during inpatient treatment. Patients with severe personality disorders may require psychotherapy to facilitate peer-group participation. Therapists should be familiar with the recovery community approach and support its philosophy. The resolution of psychological conflict is not construed as sufficient therapy for addiction or as the major task of inpatient treatment.

Pathologic family patterns are typically present with drug addicts. Families often compensate for the addict's social and occupational dysfunction. As responsibilities are taken over by the family, the addict is freed to pursue addiction further. Family behavior that enables continued addiction must often be identified and changed before the addict is willing to seek recovery seriously. An initial meeting with the patient, family, and family therapist is effective early in treatment. Families may be asked to discuss their experience of the addiction openly. Subsequent family and multiple family meetings serve to improve communication, change pathologic family dynamics, and discuss discharge planning.

Education provides an understanding of addiction and specific directives for recovery. Addicts are taught that they must avoid all addictive agents, including marijuana and alcohol. Actively addicted friends should be likewise avoided. Places and situations that stimulate drug urges are linked to relapse and must be viewed as dangerous. The inability to control drug use is seen as permanent, and even long periods of abstinence will not reverse this vulnerability. Controlled, recreational drug use is not possible. The ability to relapse is therefore ever present, necessitating continued involvement in outpatient self-help groups. Patients are taught to be initially suspicious of their own motives and thoughts and to rely on their peers and the staff for guidance. The desire for drugs does not disappear and may manifest in covert ways.

The typical daily schedule should be busy, with minimal periods of inactivity. This serves to minimize boredom that may lead to drug craving or subversive behavior on the unit. An active schedule also provides a model for outpatient treatment, in which expanses of "free time" should be avoided. Numerous daily drug groups are the most important aspect of inpatient rehabilitation. These may be open-ended groups or devoted toward a particular patient or treatment issue. Generally, small groups are preferable when dealing with particular individuals; educational topics can be handled in larger groups or lectures. Drug groups should encompass the same philosophy of outpatient self-help groups such as Cocaine Anonymous, Narcotics Anonymous, and Alcoholics Anonymous. In this way, the addict becomes comfortable with these highly effective approaches and can smoothly phase into these groups after discharge. Although group treatment is the central modality of inpatient rehabilitation, individual psychotherapy and family therapy may constitute part of the weekly schedule. Exercise and creative therapies may be included in the schedule. During their free time, patients should be encouraged to learn more about each other, develop therapeutic relationships, and discuss treatment issues.

Progress in treatment is based on the development of internal motivation for recovery, honest self-disclosure, and commitment to outpatient treatment. Generally, two weeks is sufficient time for the drug addict to develop internal motivation for recovery. Patients lacking sincere motivation after this period of time are probably not ready for drug abstinence and may sabotage the peer group if they are not discharged or transferred to another facility. A total hospitalization of four to six weeks on the specialized drug unit is usually an adequate period of time for inpatient treatment. Progress in treatment is determined by the full treatment team, and peer feedback represents a useful and usually accurate appraisal of behavior and attitude.

Careful outpatient planning is essential and necessary for the attainment of continued drug abstinence. While inpatient care spans several weeks, relapse remains a lifelong risk. Compliance with outpatient rehabilitation should be discussed and assessed prior to discharge. Patients who lack sufficient motivation for treatment may require longer hospitalization or half-way house placement. Coexisting psychiatric and medical disorders that have been stabilized should be addressed with careful outpatient referrals. Specific discharge recommendations are clearly conveyed to the patient and family prior to discharge. Failure to agree with discharge recommendations represents a negative prognosticator and may suggest the need for protracted inpatient treatment.

Conclusion

In many cases, hospitalization is the only intervention powerful enough to end the active cycle of addiction. With patients sufficiently ill to require hospitalization, inpatient treatment for addiction represents only one phase of total drug rehabilitation. Eventually, the addict must return to the outside world and resume work, family, and social functioning. In nearly all cases, the successful continuation of drug abstinence is dependent on regular participation in outpatient rehabilitation. Hospitalization allows the physician to conduct a comprehensive medical and psychiatric evaluation and to treat coexisting conditions that might otherwise preclude recovery from addiction. Addicts are then exposed to intensive, inpatient rehabilitation in preparation for lifelong participation in self-help groups. The process of recovery that begins in the hospital is often the addict's only chance for survival. The addicts are then given the option to continue the process of recovery that, if successful, will transform their lives.

Chapter 138

Treatment in Residential Therapeutic Communities

Drug-free residential programs for substance abuse appeared a decade later than therapeutic communities (TCs) in psychiatric hospitals pioneered by Jones (1953) and others in the United Kingdom. The name *therapeutic community* evolved in these hospital settings, although the two models arose independently.

The TC for substance abuse emerged in the 1960s as a self-help alternative to existing conventional treatments. Recovering alcoholics and drug addicts were its first participant-developers. While its modern antecedents can be traced to Alcoholics Anonymous and Synanon, the TC prototype is ancient, existing in all forms of communal healing and support.

Contemporary TCs have evolved much beyond their origins into sophisticated human services institutions. Today, the term *therapeutic community* is generic, describing a variety of residential programs serving a wide spectrum of drug and alcohol abusers. About a quarter of these conform to the traditional long-term method. These have made the greatest impact on rehabilitating substance abusers.

The Traditional TC

Traditional TCs are similar in planned duration of stay (15 to 24 months), structure, staffing pattern, perspective, and rehabilitative regime, although they differ in size (30 to 600 beds) and client demographies. Staff are a mixture of TC-trained clinicians and human service professionals. Primary clinical staff are usually former substance abusers who themselves were rehabilitated in TC programs. Ancillary staff consist of professionals in mental health, vocational, educational, family counseling, fiscal, administrative, and legal services.

TCs accommodate a broad spectrum of drug abusers. Although they originally attracted narcotic addicts, a majority of their client populations are nonopioid abusers. Thus this modality has responded to the changing trend in drug use patterns, treating clients with drug problems of varying severity, different life-styles, and various social, economic, and ethnic backgrounds.

Clients in traditional programs are usually male (75 percent) and in their mid-20s (50 percent). TCs are almost all racially mixed, and most are age-integrated, with 25 percent of their clients under 21. A few TCs have separate facilities for adolescents. About half of all admissions are from broken homes or ineffective families, and more than three-quarters have been arrested at some time in their lives.

The TC views drug abuse as a deviant behavior, reflecting impeded personality development or chronic deficits in social, educational, and economic skills. Its antecedents lie in socioeconomic disadvantage, in poor family effectiveness, and in psychological factors.

Thus the principal aim of the therapeutic community is a global change in life-style: abstinence from illicit substances, elimination of antisocial activity, employability, and prosocial attitudes and values. The rehabilitative approach requires multidimensional influence and training, which for most can only occur in a 24-hour residential setting.

The traditional TC can be distinguished from other major drug treatment modalities in three broad ways. First, the TC coordinates a comprehensive rehabilitative offering in a single setting. Vocational counseling, work therapy, recreation, group and individual therapy, education, medical, family, legal, and social services occur within the TC.

Second, the primary "therapist" and teacher in the TC is the community itself, consisting of peers and staff who role model successful personal change. Staff members also serve as rational authorities and guides in the recovery process. Thus the community as a whole provides a crucial 24-hour context for continued learning in which individual change in conduct, attitudes, and emotions are monitored and mutually reinforced in the daily regime.

Third, TCs have an approach to rehabilitation based on an explicit perspective of the drug abuse disorder, the client, and the recovery process. It is this perspective that shapes its organizational structure, staffing, and treatment process.

The TC Perspective

Full accounts of the TC perspective are described elsewhere (De Leon 1981, 1984; De Leon and Ziegenfuss 1986; Deitch 1972; Kaufman and De Leon 1978). Although expressed in a social psychological idiom, this perspective evolved directly from the experience of recovering participants in TCs.

Drug abuse is viewed as a disorder of the whole person, affecting some or all areas of functioning. Cognitive and behavioral problems appear, as do mood disturbances. Thinking may be unrealistic or disorganized; values are confused, nonexistent, or antisocial. Frequently there are deficits in verbal, reading, writing, and marketable skills. Whether couched in existential or psychological terms, moral or even spiritual issues are apparent.

Abuse of any substance is viewed as overdetermined behavior. Physiologic dependency is secondary to the wide range of influences that control the individual's drug use behavior. Thus the problem is the person, not the drug. Addiction is a symptom, not the essence of the disorder. In the TC, chemical detoxification is a condition of entry, not a goal of treatment. Rehabilitation focuses on maintaining a drug-free existence.

Rather than drug-use patterns, individuals are distinguished along dimensions of psychological dysfunction and social deficits. Many clients have never acquired conventional life-styles. Vocational and educational problems are marked; middle-class mainstream values are either missing or unachievable. Usually these clients emerge from a socially disadvantaged sector, where drug abuse is more a social response than a psychological disturbance. Their TC experience is better termed *habilitation*, the development of a socially productive, conventional life-style for the first time in their lives.

Among clients from more advantaged backgrounds, drug abuse is more directly expressive of psychological disorder or existential malaise, and the word *rehabilitation* is more suitable, emphasizing a return to a life-style previously lived, known, and perhaps rejected.

Nevertheless, substance abusers in TCs share important similarities. Either as cause or consequence of their drug abuse, all reveal features of personality disturbance or impeded social function. Thus all residents in the TC follow the same regime. Individual differences are recognized in specific treatment plans that modify the emphasis, not the course, of their experience in the therapeutic community.

In the TC's view of recovery, the aim of rehabilitation is global. The primary psychological goal is to change the negative patterns of behavior, thinking, and feeling that predispose drug use; the main social goal is to develop a responsible drug-free life-style. Stable recovery, however, depends on a successful integration of these social and psychological goals. For example, healthy behavioral alternatives to drug use are reinforced by commitment to the values of abstinence; acquiring vocational or educational skills and social productivity is motivated by the values of achievement and self-reliance. Behavioral change is unstable without insight, and insight is insufficient without felt experience. Thus conduct, emotions, skills, attitudes, and values must be integrated to ensure enduring change.

The rehabilitative regime is shaped by several broad assumptions about recovery.

Motivation. Recovery depends on pressures to change, positive and negative. Some clients seek help, driven by stressful external pressures; others are moved by more intrinsic factors. For all, however, remaining in treatment requires continued motivation to change. Thus elements of the rehabilitation approach are designed to sustain motivation or to detect early signs of premature termination.

Self-help. Although the influence of treatment depends on the person's motivation and readiness, change does not occur in a vacuum. The individual must permit the impact of treatment or learning to occur. Thus rehabilitation unfolds as an interaction between the client and the therapeutic environment.

Social learning. A life-style change occurs in a social context. Negative patterns, attitudes, and roles were not acquired in isolation, nor can they be altered in isolation. Thus recovery depends not only on what has been learned, but how and where learning occurs. This assumption is the basis for the community itself serving as teacher. Learning is active, by doing and participating. A socially responsible role is acquired by acting the role. What is learned is identified with the people involved in the learning process, with peer support and staff as credible role models. Newly learned ways of coping are threatened by isolation and its potential for relapse; a perspective on self, society, and life must be affirmed by a network of others.

Treatment as an episode.   Residency is a relatively brief period in an individual's life, and its influence must compete with the influences of the years before and after treatment. For this reason, unhealthy "outside" influences are minimized until the individual is better prepared to engage these on his or her own; treatment regimen is designed for high impact. Thus life in the TC is necessarily intense, its daily regime demanding, and its therapeutic confrontations unmoderated.

TCs adhere to certain precepts that constitute a view of healthy, proper, social living. Although somewhat philosophical in its focus, this "view of right living" relates to the TC perspective of the client and of recovery.

TCs are explicit in identifying right and wrong behaviors for which there exist appropriate rewards and punishments. Guilt, a moral experience, is a central issue in the recovery process. Particular values are stressed as essential to social learning and personal growth. These include truth and honesty (in word and deed), the work ethic, accountability, self-reliance, responsible concern ("brother's keeper"), and community involvement. On a broader philosophical level, treatment focuses the individual on the personal present (here and now) versus the historical past (then and when). Past behavior and circumstances are explored only to illustrate the current patterns of dysfunctional behavior, negative attitudes, and outlook. Individuals are encouraged and trained to assume personal responsibility for their present reality and destiny.

Who Comes for Treatment

Research has documented that therapeutic admissions reveal a considerable degree of psychosocial dysfunction in addition to their substance abuse.

Social Profiles

Among adult admissions, less than one-third are employed full-time in the year before treatment, more than two thirds have been arrested, and 30 to 40 percent have had prior drug treatment histories (e.g., De Leon 1984; Simpson and Sells 1982). Among adolescents, 70 percent have dropped out of school, more than 70 percent have been arrested at least once, and 40 percent have been legally referred to treatment (compared with 25 percent of adults) (De Leon and Deitch 1985; Holland and Griffen 1984).

Psychological Profiles

Clients may differ in social background and drug-use patterns but psychological profiles obtained with standard instruments appear remarkably uniform, as evident in a number of TC studies (e.g., Biase 1981; Brook and Whitehead 1980; De Leon 1976, 1980, 1984; De Leon et al. 1973; Kennard and Wilson 1979; Zuckerman et al. 1975).

Typically, symptom measures on depression and anxiety are deviantly high, socialization scores are poor, and IQ is in the dull-normal range. On the Tennessee Self-Concept Scales, the self-esteem segment is markedly low, confusion and contradiction concerning self-perception is high, as is the level of the maladjustment segment. The Minnesota Multiphasic Personality Inventory scales are deviant, with prominent peaks reflecting confusion (high F), character disorder (Pd), and disturbed thinking and affect (high Sc). Smaller but still deviant peaks are seen on depression (D) and hypomania (Ma).

The psychological profiles reveal drug abuse as the prominent element in a picture that mirrors features of both psychiatric and criminal populations. For example, the character disorder characteristics and poor self-concept of delinquent and repeated offenders are present, along with the dysphoria and confused thinking of emotionally unstable or psychiatric populations. These profiles vary little across age, sex, race, primary drug, or admission year and are not significantly different from drug abusers in other treatment modalities. Thus the drug abusers who come to the TC do not appear to be sick, as do patients in mental hospitals, nor are they simply hard-core criminal types, but they do reveal a considerable degree of psychological disability.

Psychiatric Diagnoses

The few diagnostic studies of TC admissions confirm the above conclusion. The most frequent Axis I diagnosis is substance abuse dependency, although more than half obtain an additional nondrug diagnosis, usually involving phobic or general anxiety disorder. Less than 15 percent receive a diagnosis of affective disorder, only scattered percentages are diagnosed as psychotic, and about 30 to 40 percent of all admissions obtain an Axis II diagnosis of antisocial personality (Carroll and Sobel 1986; De Leon 1976, 1988; Jainchill et al. 1986).

That the psychological and psychiatric profiles reveal few psychotic features and relatively low variability reflects several factors: exclusionary criteria at admissions, common characteristics among all substance abusers, and self-selection among those who seek admission to residential treatment. Nevertheless, clients do differ, evident in drop-out and success rates, which are discussed later. Rather than fixed background or psychopathologic characteristics, this client diversity points to such factors as motivation for personal change and suitability for the TC treatment.

Contact Referral

Clients contact TCs through three main sources: by self-referral, by referral by agency or individual professionals, and through active recruitment by the program. The outreach team (usually trained graduates of TCs and selected human services staff), working in hospitals, jails, courtrooms, social agencies, and the street, conduct face-to-face interviews to determine receptivity to the TC.

Approximately 30 percent of all referrals enter TCs under some form of legal pressure, parole, probation, or some other court-mandated disposition (CODAP 1979). For some programs, however, legal referrals consist of considerably higher percentages of all admissions. The remainder are voluntary, although large numbers come to treatment under pressure from family, employment difficulties, and the cumulative effects of their history of illegal involvement.

Admission Interview

A full admission evaluation establishes a disposition for the client for referral within the TC treatment system, either outpatient or residential, or referral outside the TC system (e.g., psychiatric, hospital, private counseling). The admissions procedure is a structured interview conducted by trained paraprofessionals. Initial interviews last 60 minutes and may be followed with a second interview, often including significant others. Additionally, records of previous legal, medical, psychiatric, and drug treatment histories are evaluated.

Detoxification

With few exceptions, admissions to residential treatment do not require medically supervised detoxification. Thus traditional TCs do not usually provide this service on the premises. Most primary abusers of opioids, cocaine, alcohol, barbiturates, and amphetamines have undergone self or medical detoxification prior to seeking admission to the TC. A small proportion require detoxification during the admission evaluation, and they are offered the option of a detoxification at a nearby hospital. Barbiturate users are routinely referred for medically supervised detoxification, after which they are assessed for admission. A minor percentage of admissions to TCs have been primarily involved with hallucinogens or phencyclidine (PCP). Among those who appear compromised, a referral is made for psychiatric service, after which the client can return for residential treatment.

Criteria for Residential Treatment

Traditional TCs maintain an "open-door" policy with respect to admission to residential treatment. This understandably results in a wide range of treatment candidates, not all of whom are equally motivated, ready, or suitable for the demands of the residential regime. Relatively few are excluded because the TC policy is to accept individuals who elect residential treatment, regardless of the reasons influencing their choice.

However, there are two major guidelines for excluding clients: suitability and risk. The former refers to the degree to which the client can meet the demands of the TC regime and integrate with others.

This includes participation in groups, fulfilling work assignments, and living with minimal privacy in an open community, usually under dormitory conditions. Risk refers to the extent to which clients present a management burden to the staff or pose a threat to the security and health of the community of others.

Specific exclusionary criteria most often include histories of arson, suicide, and serious psychiatric disorder. Psychiatric exclusion is usually based on documented history of psychiatric hospitalizations or prima facie evidence of psychotic symptoms on interview (e.g., frank delusions, thought disorder, hallucinations, confused orientation or signs of serious affect disorder). An important differential diagnostic issue concerns drug-related mood or mental states. For example, disorientation, dysphoria, and thought or sensory disorders clearly associated with hallucinogens, PCP, and sometimes cocaine may not exclude an otherwise suitable individual from the TC. Where diagnosis remains in question, most TCs will utilize a psychiatric consultation after admission. Appropriate referral, however, is based on the client's suitability or risk rather than on diagnosis alone.

Generally, clients on regular psychotropic regimes will be excluded because use of these usually correlates with chronic or severe psychiatric disorder. Also, the regular administration of medication, particularly in the larger TCs, presents a management and supervisory burden for the relatively few medical personnel in these facilities.

Medication for medical conditions is acceptable in TCs, as are handicapped clients or those who require prosthetics, providing they can meet the participatory demands of the program. A full medical history is obtained during the admission evaluation, which includes questions on current medication regimes (e.g., asthma, diabetes, hypertension), and the necessity for prosthetics. Physical examinations and laboratory workups (blood and urine profiles) are obtained after admission to residency. Although test results occasionally require removal of a client from residency, such cases are relatively rare. Because of concern about communicable disease in a residential setting, some TCs require tests for conditions such as hepatitis prior to entering the facility or at least within the first weeks of admission. Policy considerations concerning testing for acquired immune deficiency syndrome (AIDS) and management of AIDS, or clients diagnosed with AIDS-related complex (ARC) are currently being clarified by most TCs.

The Residential Client

Although there is no typical residential client, the need for long-term treatment in TCs is based on indicators that can be briefly summarized across five main areas:

1. Chronic-acute stress concerning physical, psychological, and social problems associated with drug use. Some indicators are evidence for out-of-control behavior with respect to drug use, criminality, or sexuality; suicidal potential threat through overdose; threat of injury or death through other drug-related means; degree of anxiety or fear concerning violence, jail, illness, or death; and extent of personal losses (e.g., financial, relationships, employment).
2. Severity and chronicity of drug use. This refers to the individual's ability to maintain complete abstinence in a nonresidential treatment setting. Some indicators are previous treatment experiences (number, type, and outcomes), previous self-initiated attempts at abstinence (frequency and longest duration), and current active drug use versus current abstinence.
3. Social and interpersonal function. Some indicators are involvement in the drug life-style (friends, places, activities) and impaired ability to maintain employment or school responsibility or to maintain social relations and responsibilities (e.g., parental, spouse, filial, friendships).
4. Antisocial involvement. Some indicators are active and past criminal history, frequency and duration of incarcerations, and existing legal pressures for treatment.
5. Motivation, readiness, and suitability for therapeutic community life. Some indicators are acceptance of the severity of drug problem; acceptance for the need for treatment ("can't do it alone"); willingness to sever ties with family, friends, and current life-style while in treatment; and willingness to surrender a private life meeting the expectations of a structured community.

The TC Approach

The TC utilizes diverse elements and activities to bring out rehabilitative change. We will now outline TC life in terms of its structure (social organization) and its process in terms of the individual's passage through stages of community life.

TC Structure

TCs are composed of peer groups and staff that constitute the community, or family, in a residential facility. This peer-to-community structure strengthens the individual's identification with a perceived, ordered network of others. More importantly, it arranges relationships of mutual responsibility to others at various levels in the program.

The operation of the community itself is the task of the residents, working together under staff supervision. Work assignments, called job functions, are arranged in a hierarchy, according to seniority, individual progress, and productivity. The new client enters a setting of upward mobility. Job assignments begin with the most menial tasks (e.g., mopping the floor) and lead vertically to levels of coordination and management. Indeed, clients come in as patients and can leave as staff. This social organization reflects the fundamental aspects of the rehabilitative approach, mutual self-help, work as education and therapy, peers as role models, and staff as rational authorities.

Mutual self-help.   The essential dynamic in the TC is mutual self-help. Thus the day-to-day activities of a TC are conducted by the residents themselves. In their jobs, groups, meetings, recreation, and personal and social time, it is residents who continually transmit to each other the main messages and expectations of the community.

The extent of the self-help process in the TC is evident in the broad range of resident job assignments. These include conducting all house services (e.g., cooking, cleaning, kitchen service, minor repair), serving as apprentices, and running all departments, conducting meetings and peer-encounter groups.

The TC is managed as an autocracy, with staff serving as rational authorities. Their psychological relationship with the residents is as role models and parental surrogates, who foster the self-help, developmental process through managerial and clinical means. They monitor and evaluate client status, supervise resident groups, assign and supervise resident job functions, and oversee house operations. Clinically, staff conduct all therapeutic groups, provide individual counseling, organize social and recreational projects, and confer with significant others. They decide matters of resident status, discipline, promotion, transfers, discharges, furloughs, and treatment planning.

Work as education and therapy.   In the TC, work mediates essential educational and therapeutic effects. Work and job changes have clinical relevance for substance abusers in TCs, most of whom have not successfully negotiated the social and occupational world of the larger society.

Vertical job movements carry the obvious rewards of status and privilege. However, lateral job changes are more frequent, providing exposure to all aspects of the community. Typically, residents experience many lateral job changes that enable them to learn new skills and to negotiate the system. This increased involvement also heightens their sense of belonging and strengthens their commitment to the community.

Job changes in the TC are singularly effective therapeutic tools, providing both measures of and incentives for behavioral and attitudinal changes. In the vertical structure of the TC, ascendency marks how well the client has assimilated what the community teaches and expects; hence the job promotion is an explicit measure of the resident's improvement and growth.

Conversely, lateral or downward job movements also create situations that require demonstrations of personal growth. A resident may be removed from one job to a lateral position in another department or dropped back to a lower status position for clinical reasons. These movements are designed to teach new ways of coping with reversals and change that appear to be unfair or arbitrary.

Peers as role models.   Peers as role models and staff as role models and rational authorities are the primary mediators of the recovery process. Indeed, the strength of the community as a context for social learning relates to the number and quality of its role models. All members of the community are expected to be role models—roommates; older and younger residents; junior, senior, and directorial staff. TCs require these multiple role models to maintain the integrity of the community and assure the spread of social learning effects.

Residents who demonstrate the expected behaviors and reflect the values and teachings of the community are viewed as role models. This is illustrated in two main attributes.

Role models "act as if." They behave as the person they should be, rather than as the person they have been. Despite resistances, perceptions, or feelings to the contrary, they engage in the expected behavior and consistently maintain the attitudes and values of the community. These include self-motivation, commitment to work and striving, positive regard for staff as authority, and an optimistic outlook toward the future.

In the TC's view, acting as if is not just an exercise in conformity, but an essential mechanism for more complete psychological change. Feelings, insights, and altered self-perceptions often follow rather than precede behavior change.

Role models display responsible concern. This concept is closely akin to the notion of "I am my brother's keeper." Showing responsible concern involves willingness to confront others whose behavior is not in keeping with the rules of the TC, the spirit of the community, or the knowledge that is consistent with growth and rehabilitation. Role models are obligated to be aware of the appearance, attitude, moods, and performances of their peers, and confront negative signs in these. In particular, role models are aware of their own behavior in the overall community and the process prescribed for personal growth.

Staff as rational authorities.   TC clients often have had difficulties with authorities who have not been trusted or perceived as guides and teachers. Thus they need a successful experience with a rational authority who is credible (recovered), supportive, correcting, and protecting to gain authority over themselves (personal autonomy). Implicit in their role as rational authorities, staff provide the reasons for their decisions and explain the meaning of consequences. They exercise their powers to train and guide, facilitate and correct, rather than punish, control, or exploit.

The TC Process

Rehabilitation in the TC unfolds as a developmental process occurring in a social learning context. Values, conduct, emotions, and cognitive understanding (insight) must be integrated in the evolution of a socially responsible, personally autonomous individual.

The developmental process itself can be understood as a passage through three main stages of incremental learning. The learning that occurs at each stage facilitates change at the next, and each change reflects increased maturity and personal autonomy.

Stage I (Induction: 0 to 60 days).   The main goals of this initial phase of residency are further assessment and orientation to the TC. Assessment of the individual with respect to specific treatment needs or suitability for the TC continues during the first two months of residency because the admission evaluation does not always yield a complete picture of the client.

The goal of orientation in the initial phase of residency is to assimilate the individual into the community through full participation and involvement in all of its activities. Rapid assimilation is crucial at this point, when clients are most ambivalent about the long tenure of residency. Thus the new resident is immediately involved in the daily residential regime, which emphasizes role induction into the community process. For example, seminars focus on: 1) cardinal rules (i.e., no use of drugs, no violence or threat of physical violence); 2) community or house regulations (expected conduct in the community, such as speaking, dressing, punctuality, attendance); 3) program essentials (structure organization, its process stages, its philosophy and perspective); and 4) therapeutic community tools (e.g., encounter and other groups, job functions, the privilege system).

Group process during the initial phase is designed to facilitate peer involvement, acceptance of the regime, and training in using the group itself. The intensity of confrontations is moderate to avoid elevating individual fear.

Success and passage through the induction stage is reflected mainly in retention rather than in overt client change. Although individuals differ greatly in the degree to which they are assimilated into the TC, the fact that they remain 30 to 60 days is sufficient to meet the limited goals of this stage.

Stage II (Primary treatment: 2 to 12 months).   During this stage, the main TC objectives of socialization, personal growth, and psychological awareness are pursued through all of the therapeutic and community resources and activities. These unfold in the daily regime of community life.

Phases

Primary treatment actually consists of three phases in the socialization-developmental process that roughly correlate with time in the program (one to four months, five to eight months, and nine to twelve months). These periods are marked by plateaus of stable behavior that signal further change. Although the daily regime remains the same throughout the phases of primary treatment, client progress is reflected by program status and developmental and psychological changes at the end of each phase.

Four-month Resident

Four-month residents have junior status in the TC system, limited freedom, and lower-level jobs. Developmentally, these residents conform to the TC system. Although they may not completely accept the perspective and regime, they "act as if" they understand and comply with the program, participating fully in daily activities. They follow directions, engage in basic expected behaviors (getting up in the morning, making the bed, keeping the area clean, attending all meetings). They adhere to the cardinal and house rules and accept disciplinary contracts. They display a general knowledge of the TC approach, accept the seriousness of their drug use and other problems, and show some separation from the drug culture, street code, and language.

Psychologically, four-month residents reveal measurable decreases in the dysphoria usually present at admission. Their participation in groups increases, although communication and group skills are not fully acquired. They display limited personal disclosure in groups and in one-on-one sessions.

Eight-month Resident

Eight-month residents "set an example." Their elevated status in the social structure is evident in their privileges and job functions. They have earned greater personal freedom, including the right to leave the facility without escort when going to prescribed places, for brief periods and for specific reasons. They have ascended the job hierarchy and can hold special positions that pay a modest stipend (e.g., $5 to $10 weekly). Their key attitudes reflect acceptance of the program, commitment to continued personal change, and value for the role model attributes of honesty and responsibility.

Developmentally, eight-month residents have moved beyond mere conformity, overcome difficulties with compliance, and consciously control acting-out behavior. Growth is evident in their adaptability to job changes, their acceptance of staff as rational authorities, and their ability to contain their negative thoughts and emotions. This picture reveals some degree of internalization of the TC's perspective on recovery. For the eight-month resident, the precept to "act as if" has become a personal mode of learning, not merely a tactic of compliance.

Psychologically, these residents reveal elevated self-esteem based on the status and progress through the previous eight months. This is most evident in the positive assertions about next steps. Self-awareness is manifest in identification of their characteristic images. More importantly, while they may not indicate special understanding or insight into the origins or "dynamics" of their problems, they accept full responsibility for their behavior, their problems, and their solutions.

For eight-month residents, personal disclosure is less restrained. When confronted, they quickly drop defenses and reveal honest emotional expression. They have acquired group skills and are expected to assist facilitators in the encounter group process.

Twelve-month Resident

Twelve-month residents are established role models in the program. Privileges reflect the increasing degree of personal autonomy. They enjoy more privacy and can obtain bi-weekly furloughs. While they cannot hold jobs outside the facility, their positions within indicate that they effectively run the house. As coordinators, for example, they are responsible for arranging resident movement, trips, and seminars, under staff supervision. Similarly, their stipend status is also elevated; they are eligible to be staff-in-training in executive management offices or special ancillary services. They are expected to assist staff in monitoring the facility overnight and on weekends. For those who have chosen vocational-educational training, at this stage they are highly involved with school and are experiencing its pressures and challenges.

Developmentally, 12-month residents reflect a dual status. As established role models, they provide leadership in the community. But, as they prepare for reentry (the next and final stage of treatment), their focus begins to shift toward future status outside the program. Their maturity is most evident in the degree to which they have internalized therapeutic community values and in their increased autonomy. Their social interactions with staff are more spontaneous and relaxed, and they socialize with a network of positive peers during recreation and furlough.

Psychologically, 12-month residents reveal higher and more stable levels of self-esteem commensurate with their senior status in the community. They display some insight into their drug problems and personalities. They accept responsibility for themselves and for other members in the community.

Twelve-month residents display paradoxical signs of positive change. Although confident and eager to move forward, a certain degree of anxiety and insecurity emerges associated with their uncertainty about the future. Their openness about anticipated problems in the future is considered a positive psychological sign.

After a year, residents are fully trained participants in the group process and often serve as facilitators. A high level of personal disclosure is evident in groups, in peer exchange, and in their increased use of staff counseling.

Stage III (Reentry: 13 to 24 months). Reentry is the stage at which the client must strengthen skills for autonomous decision making and the capacity for self-management with less reliance on rational authorities or a well-formed peer network. There are two phases of the reentry process.

Reentry Phase I (13 to 18 months)

The main goal of this phase, during which clients continue to live in the facility, is preparation for healthy separation from the community.

Emphasis on rational authority decreases under the assumption that the client has acquired a sufficient degree of self-management. This is reflected in more individual decision making about privileges, social plans, and life design. The group process involves fewer leaders at this stage, fewer encounters, and more shared decision making. Particular emphasis is placed on life-skills seminars, which provide didactic training for life outside the community. Attendance is mandated for sessions on budgeting, job seeking, use of alcohol, sexuality, parenting, use of leisure time, and so on.

During this phase, individual plans are a collective task of the client, a key staff member, and peers. These plans are actually blueprints of educational and vocational programs, which include goal attainment schedules, methods of improving interpersonal and family relationships, and social and sexual behavior. Clients may be attending school or holding full-time jobs, either within or outside of the TC at this point. Still, they are expected to participate in house activities when possible and to carry some community responsibilities (e.g., facility coverage at night).

Reentry Phase II (18 to 24 months)

The goal of this phase is to complete a successful separation from residency. Clients are on "live-out" status, involved in full-time jobs or education, maintaining their own households, usually with live-out peers. They may attend such aftercare services as Alcoholics Anonymous or Narcotics Anonymous or take part in family or individual therapy. This phase is viewed as the end of residency, but not of program participation. Contact with the program is frequent at first and only gradually reduced to weekly phone calls and monthly visits with a primary counselor.

Graduation

Completion marks the end of active program involvement. Graduation itself, however, is an annual event conducted in the facility for completees at usually a year beyond their residency.

Thus the TC experience is preparation rather than a cure. Residence in the program facilitates a process of change that must continue throughout life, and what is learned in treatment are the tools to guide the individual on a steady path of continued change. Completion, or graduation, therefore, is not an end but a beginning.

Elements of the TC Process

The typical day in a therapeutic community is highly structured, beginning at 7 AM and ending at 11 PM. It includes a variety of meetings, job functions (work therapy), therapeutic groups, recreation, and individual counseling. The interplay of these activities contribute to the TC process and may be grouped into three main elements: therapeutic-educative, community enhancement, and community and clinical management.

Therapeutic-Educative Element

These activities consist of various group processes and individual counseling. They provide settings for expressing feelings, divert negative acting-out, permit ventilation of feeling, and resolve personal and social issues. They increase communication and interpersonal skills, examine and confront behavior and attitudes, and offer instruction in alternate modes of behavior.

There are four main forms of group activity in the TC: encounters, probes, marathons, and tutorials. These differ somewhat in format, objectives, and method, but all attempt to foster trust, personal disclosure, intimacy, and peer solidarity to facilitate therapeutic change.

The focus of the encounter is behavioral. Its approach is confrontation, and its objective is to modify negative behavior and attitudes directly. Probes and marathons have as their primary objective significant emotional change and psychological insight. Tutorial groups stress learning of skills.

The basic encounter is the cornerstone of group process in the TC. The term *encounter* is generic, describing a variety of forms that utilize confrontational procedures as their main approach. The basic encounter group, composed of 12 to 20 residents, meets at least three times weekly, usually for two hours in the evening, and is followed by an additional 30 minutes for snacks and socializing. The objective of each encounter is modest and limited: to heighten individual awareness of specific attitudes or behavioral patterns that should be modified.

Probes are staff-led group sessions composed of 10 to 15 residents, conducted to obtain in-depth clinical information on clients early in their residency (two to six months). They are scheduled when needed and usually last from four to eight hours. Their main objectives are to increase staff understanding of the individual's background for the purposes of treatment planning and to increase openness, trust, and mutual identification. Unlike the encounter, which stresses confrontation, the probe emphasizes the use of support, understanding, and the empathy of the other group members. Probes go much beyond the here-and-now behavioral incident, which is the material of the encounter, to past events and experiences.

Marathons are extended group sessions, the objective of which is to initiate resolution of life experiences that have impeded the individual's development. During their 18 months of residence, every client participates in at least two marathons.

Marathons are usually composed of large groups of selected residents and meet for 18 to 24 hours. Considerable experience, both personal and professional, is required to assure safe and effective marathons. These groups are conducted by all staff, assisted by senior residents with marathon experience ("shepherds").

The general approach of the marathon is to dissipate defensiveness and resistance toward facilitating an emotional processing ("working through") of a significant life event, and to encourage the individual to continue to address the importance of certain life-altering issues of the past. A wide variety of techniques are employed, including elements from psychodrama, primal therapy, and pure theater, to produce its impact.

Tutorial groups are directed primarily toward training or teaching, as opposed to correcting behavior or facilitating of emotional catharsis and psychological insight. Tutorial groups consist of 10 to 20 residents, are scheduled as needed, and usually address certain themes for purposes of teaching, including: personal growth concepts (e.g., self-reliance, maturity, relationships); job skill training (e.g., managing the department or the reception desk); and clinical skill training (e.g., use of encounter tools).

The four main groups are supplemented by a number of ad hoc groups that convene as needed. These vary in focus, format, and composition. For example, gender-, ethnic-, or age-specific groups may utilize encounter or tutorial formats. Dormitory, room, or departmental encounters may address issues of daily community living.

Counseling. One-to-one counseling balances the needs of the individual with those of the community. While peer exchange is ongoing and constitutes the most consistent counseling in TCs, staff counseling sessions are conducted as needed, usually informally. The staff counseling method in the TC is not traditional, as is evident in its main features: interpersonal sharing, direct support, minimal interpretation, didactic instructions, and confrontation.

Community Enhancement Element

These activities, which facilitate assimilation into the community, include the four main facility-wide meetings: the morning meeting, seminars (held each day), the house meeting (held each day), and the general meeting (called when needed).

Morning meetings convene all residents of the facility and the staff on the premises after breakfast, usually for 30 minutes, to initiate the day's activities with a positive attitude, motivate residents, and strengthen unity. This is accomplished through recitation of the philosophy, songs, readings, and skits. This meeting is particularly important in that most residents of TCs have never adapted to the routine of an ordinary day.

Seminars convene every afternoon, usually for one hour. The seminar collects all the residents together at least once during the working day. Thus staff observation of the entire facility is regularized since the seminar in the afternoon complements the daily morning meeting and the house meeting in the evening. A clinical aim of the seminar, however, is to balance the individual's emotional and cognitive experience. Of the various meetings and group processes in the TC, the seminar is unique in its emphasis on listening, speaking, and conceptual behavior.

House meetings convene nightly, after dinner, usually for one hour. The main aim of these meetings is to transact community business, although they also have a clinical objective. In this forum, social pressure is judiciously employed to facilitate individual change through public acknowledgment of positive or negative behaviors among certain individuals or subgroups.

General meetings convene only when needed, usually to address negative behavior, attitudes, or incidents in the facility. All residents and staff (including those not on duty) are assembled at any time and for indefinite duration. These meetings, conducted by staff, are designed to identify problem people or conditions or to reaffirm motivation and reinforce positive behavior and attitudes. A variety of techniques may be employed (e.g, special sessions to relieve guilt, staff lecturing and testimony, dispensing sanctions for individuals or groups).

Community and Clinical Management Element

These activities maintain the physical and psychological safety of the environment and ensure that resident life is orderly and productive. They protect the community as a whole and strengthen it as a context for social learning. The main activities are privileges, disciplinary sanctions, and surveillance.

Privileges.   In the TC, privileges are explicit rewards that reinforce the value of achievement. Privileges are accorded by overall clinical progress in the program. Displays of inappropriate behavior or negative attitude can result in loss of privileges, which can be regained by demonstrated improvement.

The type of privilege is related to the degree of personal autonomy achieved at different stages of treatment. These may range from phone and letter writing earlier in treatment to overnight furloughs later in treatment. Successful movement through each stage earns privileges that grant wider personal latitude and increased self-responsibility.

Privileges acquire importance because they are earned through investment of time, energy, self-modification, risk of failure, and disappointment. Thus the earning process establishes the value of privileges and gives them potency as social reinforcements.

Although the privileges offered in the TC are quite ordinary, it is their social and psychological relevance to the client that also enhances their importance.

Because privilege is equivalent to status in the vertical social system of the TC, loss of even small privileges is a status setback that is particularly painful for individuals who have struggled to raise their low self-esteem.

Moreover, since substance abusers often cannot distinguish between privilege and entitlement, the privilege system in the TC teaches that productive participation or membership in a family or community is based on an earning process.

Finally, privileges provide explicit feedback in the learning process. They are one of the tangible rewards that are contingent on individual change. This concrete feature of privilege is particularly suitable for individuals with histories of performance failure or incompletion.

Discipline and sanctions.   Therapeutic communities have their own specific rules and regulations that guide the behavior of residents and the management of facilities. The explicit purpose of these is to ensure the safety and health of the community; however, their implicit aim is to train and teach residents through the use of discipline.

In the TC, social and physical safety are prerequisites for psychological trust. Thus sanctions are invoked against any behavior that threatens the safety of the therapeutic environment. For example, breaking one of the TC's cardinal rules—such as no violence or threat of violence—can bring immediate expulsion. Even threats as minor as the theft of a toothbrush or a book must be addressed.

The choice of sanction depends on the severity of the infraction, time in program, and history of infractions. For example, verbal reprimands, loss of privileges, or speaking bans may be selected for less severe infractions; job demotions, loss of residential time, and expulsion may be invoked for more serious infractions.

Although often perceived as punitive, the basic purpose of contracts is to provide a learning experience by compelling residents to attend to their own conduct, to reflect on their own motivation, to feel some consequence of their behavior, and to consider alternate forms of acting under similar situations.

Contracts also have important community functions. The entire facility is made aware of all disciplinary actions. Thus contracts deter violations. They provide vicarious learning experiences for others. As symbols of safety and integrity, they strengthen community cohesiveness.

Surveillance.   Among several forms of surveillance in the TC, the house run is the most comprehensive. Several times a day, staff or senior residents walk through the entire facility from top to bottom, examining its overall condition. This simple procedure has profound clinical implications as well as management goals. House runs provide global "snapshot" impressions of the facility: its cleanliness, routine, safety, and psychological tone. They permit early detection of problems.

The main clinical aims of the house run are to illuminate psychological and social functioning. It provides observable, physical indicators of self-management skills and of the attitudes, emotional status, and awareness of residents and staff.

The sanctions employed for violation of house expectations are consistent with its management and clinical goals and range from reprimands on the spot to bans (restrictions) on roommates, floor mates, or individual residents. Expulsion may be invoked for serious violations of safety, health, and cardinal rules.

Urine testing.   Most TCs utilize unannounced random urine testing, or incident-related urine-testing procedures. Residents who deny the use of drugs or refuse urine testing on request are rejecting a fundamental expectation in the TC, which is to trust staff and peers enough to disclose undesirable behavior. The voluntary admission of drug use initiates a learning experience, which includes exploration of conditions precipitating the infraction. Denial of actual drug use, either before or after urine testing, can block the learning process and may lead to termination or drop-out.

Random urine procedures in the TC usually consist of weekly sampling of urines on an unannounced basis, either routinely or based on suspicions of a "dirty house." The more usual procedure is urine testing on incident or observation. Thus staff's suspicion of drug use in the facility or, more likely, of a client's return from furlough could result in a urine test.

When positive urines are detected, the action taken depends on the drug used, time and status in the program, previous history of drug and other infractions, and locus and condition of use. Actions may involve expulsion, loss of time, radical job demotions, or loss of privileges for specific periods. Review of the "triggers" or reasons for drug use is also an essential part of the action taken.

Effectiveness and New Applications

Success Rates

A substantial literature points to the effectiveness of the TC (TC approach) in rehabilitating drug abusers (see reviews by Bale 1979; Brook and Whitehead 1980; De Leon 1985; De Leon and Rosenthal 1979; Sells 1979). Significant improvements occur on separate outcome variables (drug use, criminality, and employment) and on composite indices for measuring individual success. These studies show maximum to moderately favorable outcomes (based on opioid, nonopioid, and alcohol use; arrest rates; additional treatment; and employment) for more than half of the sample of "completed" clients and drop-outs. With few exceptions, follow-up studies reported a positive relationship between time in the program and posttreatment outcome status (e.g., De Leon 1984; Holland 1983; Simpson and Sells 1982).

In a few studies that investigated psychological outcome, results uniformly showed significant improvement at follow-up. Phoenix House studies, for example, have demonstrated a direct relationship between posttreatment behavioral success and psychological adjustment (De Leon 1984; De Leon and Jainchill 1981).

Retention

High drop-out rates are the rule for all drug treatment modalities. For therapeutic communities, retention is of particular importance because research has established a firm relationship between time spent in treatment and successful outcome. However, most admissions to therapeutic community programs leave residency, many before treatment influences are presumed to be effectively rendered.

Drop-out is highest (30 to 40 percent) the first 30 days of admission, but declines sharply thereafter (De Leon and Schwartz 1984). One-year retention rates range from 10 to 30 percent, although more recent trends suggest gradual increases in annual retention.

While a legitimate concern, retention should not be confused with treatment effectiveness. Therapeutic communities are effective for those who remain long enough for treatment influences to occur. Obviously, however, a critical issue for TCs is maximizing holding power to benefit more clients.

TC Alternatives and Client Diversity

Traditional TCs are highly effective for a certain segment of the drug abuse population. However, those who seek assistance in TC settings represent a broad spectrum of clients, many of whom may not be suitable for long-term residential stay.

The issues of retention and client diversity have encouraged TCs to improve their diagnostic capability and to develop alternatives to long-term residence. Better assessment of individual differences has enhanced the TC's capability for retaining those suitable for residential treatment through more flexible treatment planning and program modification. It has also clarified the need for options other than long-term residential treatment.

For example, the prominence of youth drug abuse has led to adaptations of the traditional TC approach that appear more appropriate for adolescents. These include age-segregated facilities, with considerable emphasis on educational needs and family involvement. Among adults, the spread of drug abuse in the workplace, particularly in cocaine use, has prompted the TC to develop short-term residential and ambulatory models for the employed, more socialized clients.

The participation of families or significant others has been a notable development in TCs for both adolescents and adults. Most traditional TCs do not provide a regular family therapy service because the client in residence is viewed as the primary target of treatment rather than the family unit. Some therapeutic community systems, such as Phoenix House, do offer programs in individual and multiple family therapy as components of their nonresidential and (more recently) short-term residential modalities. Experience has shown, however, that beneficial effects can occur with other forms of significant-other participation. Seminars, support groups, open houses, and other special events focus on how significant others can affect the client's stay in treatment; they teach the TC perspective on recovery and provide a setting for sharing common concerns and strategies for coping with the client's future reentry into the larger community. Thus family participation activities enhance the TC's rehabilitative process for the residential client by establishing an alliance between the significant others and the program.

The TC and Mental Health

The gradual "enculturation" of drug abuse in recent years has resulted in growing numbers of individuals with concurrent substance abuse and psychiatric problems. In mental health settings, for example, young adult chronics (age 18 to 35) constitute a substantial proportion of psychiatric inpatients. For these, drug use produces new symptoms or exacerbates preexisting psychiatric conditions, posing serious management and clinical problems. In psychiatric outpatient populations, undetected drug use presents a formidable diagnostic problem (Nurco 1983). Conversely, increasing numbers of substance abusers seeking admission to drug treatment programs have documented psychiatric histories.

Many TCs have responded to the widening range of client problems. Although the TC self-help approach remains fundamental, modifications in ancillary services, practices, and staffing are evident. For example, psychopharmacologic adjuncts and individual psychotherapy are utilized for selected clients at appropriate stages in treatment. In particular, staff composition has altered to reflect a mix of selected mental health professionals (psychiatrists, psychologists, and social workers) with the traditionally trained TC professionals.

Incorporating these modifications into the TC has been difficult for a variety of reasons. Some of these relate to the TC's drug-free philosophy and self-help perspective, others to staff differences in language, education, role definition, and experience. These difficulties have been minimized through vigorous training and orientation efforts guided by a common perspective of recovery (Carroll and Sobel 1986; De Leon 1985). Indeed, the successful integration of personnel and methods from the traditional TC and mental health approaches portends the evolution of a new treatment model applicable for both substance abuse and psychiatric populations.

Chapter 139

Family Therapy in Substance Abuse Treatment

Substance abuse has a profound effect on the family, and the family is a critical factor in the treatment of the substance abuser. In this chapter, I will focus on the role of the family in substance abuse treatment. Family therapy cannot stand alone in the treatment of serious substance abusers. However, it is a valuable and often necessary adjunct to treatment, particularly when integrated into a comprehensive program. There are three basic phases of the family's involvement in treatment: 1) developing a system for establishing and maintaining a drug-free state, 2) establishing a workable method of family therapy, and 3) dealing with family readjustment after the cessation of substance abuse. These phases will be discussed in detail, with an emphasis on variation in treatment techniques to meet the needs of different types of substance abusers. The variations are based on drugs(s) abused, ethnicity, family type, stage of disease, and gender. Before this material is presented, I will review the efficacy of family treatment of substance abusers to date.

Demonstration of the Efficacy of Family Therapy with Substance Abuse

A major problem in assessing family therapy is that all family therapy is not the same. Thus it is difficult to generalize success or failure from one program or individual to another or to the field in general.

Hersch (1961) advocated group therapy with the parents of adolescent addicts. Granger and Shugart (1966) conducted family therapy with more than 100 male addicts. They concluded that treatment of the addict within his family unit was the treatment of choice.

Several family therapy outcome studies were performed in the 1970s, generally characterized by a lack of methodological sophistication. Silver et al. (1975) have described a methadone program for pregnant addicts and their addicted spouses that included 40 percent of the women in treatment becoming drug-free and the male employment rate increasing from 10 to 55 percent. Both rates are higher than those achieved by traditional methadone programs without family treatment. A problem with this study, as with most evaluations of family approaches to drug abuse, is the lack of follow-up data or control groups.

Ziegler-Driscoll (1977) reported a study conducted at Eagleville that found no difference between treatment groups with family therapy and those without on a four- to six-month follow-up. However, the therapists were new to family therapy and the supervisors new to substance abuse. As the therapists became more experienced, their results improved.

Hendricks (1971) found at one-year follow-up that narcotic addicts who had received five-and-a-half months of multiple family therapy (MFT) were twice as likely to remain in continuous therapy than addicts not responding to MFT. Kaufman and Kaufmann's (1977) work has shown that adolescent addicts with MFT have half the recidivism rate of clients without it.

Stanton (1979) noted that of 68 studies of the efficacy of the family therapy of drug abuse, only 14 quantify their outcome. Only six of these provided comparative data with other forms of treatment or control groups. Four of the six (Hendricks 1971; Scopetta et al. 1979; Stanton and Todd 1982; Wunderlich et al. 1974) showed family treatment to be superior to other modes. Winer et al. (1974) and Ziegler-Driscoll (1977) found no superiority of family treatment. Stanton (1979) concluded that "family treatment shows considerable promise for effectively dealing with problems of drug abuse."

Stanton and Todd (1982) have provided the field with the best documented controlled study of the family therapy of drug abuse to date. Stanton and Todd emphasized concrete behavioral changes, which include a focus on family rules about drug-related behavior and the utilization of weekly urine tests to give tangible indications of progress. They were concerned with interrupting and altering the repetitive family interactional patterns that maintain drug-taking.

In their family treatment groups, they found on one-year follow-up that days free of methadone, illegal opiates, and marijuana all shifted favorably, compared with a nonfamily treatment group. However, there was no significant decrease in alcohol abuse nor increase in work or school productivity. They noted a high mortality rate in nonfamily therapy cases (10 percent) and only 2 percent in those who received family therapy.

However, lack of success in certain aspects of outcome is troubling. Even their best treatment group (paid family) had 31 percent of days on methadone, 19 percent illegal opiates, 12 percent nonopiate illegal drugs, 25 percent marijuana, 44 percent alcohol, and 63 percent of possible work or school days not attended or involved (an important parameter of individuation).

Family therapy evaluation has now reached a high level of sophistication. The National Institute on Drug Abuse (NIDA) has funded several studies utilizing comprehensive evaluation techniques beginning in 1985. These evaluations focus on patient characteristics and heterogeneity, technique variability, deleterious or beneficial aspects of other components, patient and therapist treatment goals, therapist attributes, sample selection and attrition, patient experiences outside of and after treatment, psychiatric diagnosis in all family members, quantification of substance abuse evaluation in relation to treatment, and the analysis and interpretation of data.

Developing a System for Establishing and Maintaining a Drug-Free State

The family treatment of substance abuse begins with developing a system to achieve and maintain abstinence. This system, together with specific family therapeutic techniques and knowledge of family patterns commonly seen in families with a substance-abusing member, provides a workable, therapeutic approach to substance abuse.

Family treatment of substance abuse must begin with an assessment of the extent of substance-dependence as well as the difficulties it presents for the individual and the family. The quantification of substance abuse history can take place with the entire family present; substance abusers often will be honest in this setting, and "confession" is a helpful way to begin communication. Moreover, other family members can often provide more accurate information than the substance abuser (also known as the identified patient or IP). However, some IPs will give an accurate history only when interviewed alone. In taking a drug abuse history, it is important to know what current and past use has been of every type of abusable drug as well as alcohol: quantity, quality, duration, expense, how intake was supported and prevented, physical effects, tolerance, withdrawal, and medical complications. At times, other past and present substance abusers within the family are identified. It is also essential to document the families' patterns of reactivity to drug use and abuse. The specific method necessary to achieve abstinence can only be decided on after the extent and nature of substance abuse is quantified.

Early Establishment of a System for Achieving a Substance-Free State

It is critical first to establish a system for enabling the substance abuser to become drug-free so that family therapy can take place effectively. The specific methods employed to achieve abstinence vary according to the extent of use, abuse, and dependence. Mild to moderate abuse in adolescents can often be controlled if both parents can agree on clear limits and expectations and how to enforce them. Older abusers may also stop if they are made aware of the medical or psychological consequences to themselves or the effects on their family.

If substance abuse is moderately severe or intermittent and without physical dependence, such as intermittent use of hallucinogens or weekend cocaine abuse, then the family is offered a variety of measures, such as regular attendance at Narcotics Anonymous (NA) or Cocaine Anonymous (CA) for the IP and Alanon or Narcanon for family members.

Some mild to moderate substance abusers who are resistant to self-help groups may find that another system (e.g., religion, exercise regime, relaxation techniques, career change) helps them stay off of drugs (Kaufman 1985). If these methods fail, then short-term hospitalization may be necessary to establish a substance-free state and to begin effective treatment even with nondependent patients. In more severe cases of drug abuse and dependence, more aggressive methods are necessary to establish a substance-free state. Heroin addicts can be detoxified on an outpatient basis with clonidine or methadone, the latter only in specialized 21-day programs. However, if substance abuse is so severe that the IP is unable to attend sessions without being under the influence of drugs, if social or vocational functioning is severely impaired, if there is drug-related violence, or if there is physical dependence, then the first priority in treatment is to stop substance use immediately. This involves persuading the family to pull together to achieve at least temporary abstinence. Generally, this is best done in a hospital setting. Thus if the abuse pattern is severe, hospitalization will be set as a requirement very early in therapy.

Establishing a Method for Maintaining a Substance-Free State

The family is urged to adopt some system that will enable the abuser to continue to stay free of abusable substances. This system is part of the therapeutic contract made early in treatment. A lifetime commitment to abstinence is not required. Rather, the "one day at a time" approach of Alcoholics Anonymous (AA) is recommended; the patient is asked to establish a system for abstinence, which is committed to for only one day at a time but which is renewed daily using the basic principles of NA and CA. When the substance abuser has a history of past or present drug dependence, therapy is most successful when total abstinence is advocated.

Many individuals initially have to shop for CA or NA groups in which they feel personally comfortable. Every recovering substance abuser is strongly encouraged to attend small study groups, which work on AA's Twelve Steps, as well as larger open meetings which often have speakers and which anyone can attend. Abstinence can also be achieved in heroin addicts by drug-aided measures such as methadone maintenance or naltrexone blockade. These medications work quite well in conjunction with family therapy, as work with the family enhances compliance and the blocking effects on the primary drug of abuse help calm down the family system so that family and individual therapy can take place. Hospitalization also calms down an overreactive family system. Another advantage of hospitalization is that it provides an intensive 24-hour-a-day orientation to treatment. This total immersion in treatment for a 14- to 30-day period may provide the impetus for the drug abuser to get off and stay off drugs, particularly if there is effective, comprehensive aftercare. Individuals who have been dependent on illicit drugs for more than a few years generally do not do well in short-term programs, although these programs may buy time so that effective individual and family therapy can occur. For drug-dependent patients who fail in outpatient and short-term hospital programs, insistence on long-term residential treatment is the only workable alternative. Most families, however, will not accept this until other methods have failed. To accomplish this end, a therapist must be willing to maintain long-term ties with the family, even through multiple treatment failures. On the other hand, it may be more helpful to terminate treatment if the substance abuser continues to abuse chemicals, as continued family treatment implies that change is occurring when it is not. One way to continue therapist-family ties while not condoning substance abuse is to work with the family without the substance abuser present (this will be described below). In other cases, it is more effective to terminate treatment until all family members are willing and able to adopt a workable program for reinforcing abstinence. Families that believe that therapy is being terminated in their best interest often return a few months or years later, ready and willing to commit to abstinence from drugs of abuse (Kaufman 1985).

Working with Families with Continued Drug Abuse

The family therapist is in a unique position in regard to continued substance abuse and other manifestations of the IP's resistance to treatment, including total nonparticipation. The family therapist still has a workable and highly motivated patient(s): the family. One technique that can be used with an absent or highly resistant patient is the "intervention" (Johnson 1973), which was developed for use with alcoholics but can be readily adapted to work with drug abusers, particularly those who are middle class, involved with their nuclear families, and employed.

In this technique, the family (excluding the abuser) and significant network members (e.g., employer, fellow employees, friends, and neighbors) are coached to confront the substance abuser with concern, but without hostility, about the destructiveness of his or her drug abuse and behavior. They agree in advance about what treatment is necessary and then insist on it. As many family members as possible should be included, as the breakthrough for acceptance of treatment may come from an apparently uninvolved family member such as a grandchild or cousin. The involvement of the employer is crucial and, in some cases, may be sufficient in and of itself to motivate the drug abuser to seek treatment. The employer who clearly makes treatment a precondition of continued employment, who supports time off for treatment, and who guarantees a job on completion of the initial treatment course is a very valuable ally. The employer's model is also a very helpful one for the family who needs to be able to say "we love you and because we love you we will not continue to live with you if you continue to abuse drugs. If you accept the treatment being offered to you and continue to stay off drugs, we will renew our lifetime commitment to you" (Kaufman 1985).

If drug abusers do not meet the above criteria for an intervention or if the intervention has failed, we are left with the problems of dealing with a substance-abusing family. Berenson (1979) offered a workable, three-step therapeutic strategy for dealing with the spouses or other family members of individuals who continue to abuse substances or who are substance dependent. Step one is to calm down the family by explaining problems, solutions, and coping mechanisms. Step two is to create an external supportive network for family members so that the emotional intensity is not all in the relationship with the substance abuser or redirected to the therapist. There are two types of support systems available to these spouses. One type is a self-help group in the Alanon model, Narcanon, or Cocanon, and the other is a significant others (SO) group led by a trained therapist. In the former, the group and sponsor provide emotional support, reinforce detachment, and help calm down the family. An SO group may provide more insight and less support for remaining with a substance-abusing spouse. Step three involves giving the spouse three choices: 1) keep doing exactly what you are doing, 2) detach or emotionally distance yourself from the drug abuser, or 3) separate or physically distance yourself. When the client does not change, it is labeled an overt choice 1. When a client does not choose 2 or 3, the therapist can point out that he or she is in effect choosing not to change. If not changing becomes a choice, then the spouse can be helped to choose to make a change. In choice 2, spouses are helped to avoid overreacting emotionally to drug abuse and related behavior and are taught strategies for emotional detachment. Leaving, choice 3, is often difficult to carry out when the family is emotionally or financially dependent on the substance abuser.

Each of these choices seem impossible to carry out at first. The problem of choosing may be resolved by experiencing the helplessness and powerlessness in pursuing each choice.

As part of the initial contract with a family, it is suggested that the abuser's partner continue individual treatment, NA, CA, or a spouse group even if the abuser drops out. Other family members are also encouraged to continue in family therapy and support groups. It should be reemphasized that whenever we maintain therapy with a family wherein serious drug abuse continues, we have the responsibility of not maintaining the illusion that a family is resolving problems while in fact they are really reinforcing them.

Motivating the Entire Family to Participate

Although I describe above how to deal with a family when the IP is resistant to treatment participation, it should be obvious that treatment works best when the entire family is available for therapy. Once the family therapist has knowledge of the substance-abusing family, a program for dealing with substance abuse, and a workable personal method of family therapy, it becomes remarkably easy to get the entire family to come in for treatment. The person who calls for an initial appointment is generally the one who is best able to get the entire household to come in for therapy. However, in some cases, the therapist may have to contact one or more family members directly. If a reluctant family member claims to no longer be involved with the family, the therapist can truthfully point out that he or she would be valuable because of objectivity. If the member says his or her relationship with the family is too painful, then the therapist can emphasize the potential helpfulness of that person in joining the family therapy. The therapist may emphasize his or her own inability to help the family unless the member attends. Reluctant family members can also be asked to attend to protect their interests, to prevent a skewed view, to ensure that all views are expressed, to preserve fairness, and to attend a therapy session without any obligation to participate (Bauman 1981). Most family members will agree to a single evaluative visit. It then becomes imperative for the therapist to establish a contract with the family that all members feel will relieve their pains as well as that of the IP.

Stanton and Todd (1982) have been successful in getting 70 percent of the families of methadone maintenance patients, a generally unreachable group, into an initial interview. Of those who attended the initial session, 94 percent continued with treatment. Stanton and Todd presented 21 valuable, basic, facilitatory principles. For example, the therapist should deliver a nonblaming message that focuses on helping the patient rather than the family. Family treatment should be presented in such a way that, in opposing it, family members would be stating that they want the IP to remain symptomatic. The program should be structured in a way that does not allow the therapist to back down from enlisting whole families.

The concept of the family as a multigenerational system necessitates that the entire family be involved in treatment. The family members necessary to perform optimum treatment consist of the entire household and any relatives who maintain regular (approximately weekly) contact with the family. Relatively emancipated family members who have less than weekly contact may be very helpful to these families; sessions that include them should be scheduled around their visits home.

The utilization of a multigenerational approach involving grandparents, parents, spouse, and children at the beginning of family therapy as well as certain key points throughout the therapy is advised. However, the key unit with substance abusers younger than about age 24 is the IP with siblings and parents. The critical unit with married substance abusers older than 24 is the IP and spouse. However, the more dependent the IP is on parents, the more critical is work with the parents. The majority of sessions should be held with these family units; the participation of other family members is essential to more thorough understanding and permanent change in the family.

Family therapy limited to any dyad is most difficult. The mother-addicted son dyad is almost impossible to treat; someone else, such as a lover, grandparent, or uncle should be brought in if treatment is to succeed. If there is absolutely no one else available from the natural family network, then surrogate family members in multiple family therapy groups can provide support and leverage to facilitate restructuring maneuvers (Kaufman and Kaufmann 1977).

Treatment for drug addicts and their spouses has been less effective than treatment for alcoholic couples (Kaufman 1985). This led Stanton and Todd (1982) to suggest that family treatment of male narcotic addicts begin with their parents, and that the addict-spouse couple should not be worked with until the addict's parents can "'release" the addict to the spouse. In the experience of Phoenix House, there has been so much difficulty with addicted couples that they insist on separate residential treatment sites for such couples, as a matter of program policy. But, at a therapeutic community at Metropolitan State Hospital in California (The Awakening Family), addicted couples have been successfully treated in the same program by insisting on couples therapy throughout their stay. Another essential aspect of treating couples with children is focusing on their functions as parents, and therapy involving children has the distinct advantage of developing parenting skills.

An Integrated Approach to a Workable System of Family Treatment

Family Diagnosis

Accurate diagnosis is as important a cornerstone of family therapy as it is in individual therapy. In family diagnosis, we look at family interactional and communication patterns and relationships. In assessing a family, it is helpful to construct a map of their basic alliances and roles (Minuchin 1974). We also examine the family rules, boundaries, and adaptability. We look for coalitions, particularly transgenerational ones, shifting alliances, splits, cutoffs, and triangulation. We observe communication patterns, confirmation and disconfirmation, unclear messages, and conflict resolution. We note the family's stage in the family life cycle. We note mind reading (predicting reactions and reacting to them before they happen, or knowing what someone thinks or wants), double binds, and fighting styles. It is helpful to obtain an abbreviated three-generation genogram that focuses on the identified patient (IP), his or her parents and progeny, and the spouse's parents.

The genogram, another contribution of Bowen (1971), has become a basic tool in many family therapy approaches. A genogram is a pictorial chart of the people involved in a three-generational relationship system; it marks marriages, divorces, births, geographical locations, illnesses, and deaths. All significant physical, social, and psychological dysfunctions may be added to it. The genogram is used to examine relationships in the extended family complex (Guerin and Pendagast 1976). Other members of the household and any other significant relatives with whom there is regular or important current contact are also included. In step-families, the initial genogram must include the noncustodial parent(s) and the geographical location and family situation of all children from prior marriages; these may be extremely significant. As therapy progresses, a full but informal family genogram may be gradually developed as other important family members from the past and present are discussed. The genogram provides a cast of significant characters in the family so that a diagnostic map may be constructed. Obviously, the diagnostic frame of reference of the therapist is greatly influenced by the therapeutic system(s) utilized.

An Overview of Family Treatment Techniques

Each of the systems of family therapy presently in use will be briefly summarized in this chapter, with an emphasis on the application of these techniques to substance abusers. They are classified into four schools: structural-strategic, psychodynamic, Bowen's systems theory, and behavioral. Any of these types of family therapy can be applied to substance abusers if their common family patterns are kept in mind and if a method to control substance abuse is implemented.

Structural-strategic therapy. These two types are combined because they were developed by many of the same practitioners, and shifts between the two are frequently made by these therapists, depending on the family's needs. The thrust of structural family therapy is to restructure the system by creating interactional change within the session. The therapist actively becomes a part of the family, yet retains sufficient autonomy to restructure the family (Stanton 1981).

According to strategic therapists, symptoms are maladaptive attempts to deal with difficulties, which develop a homeostatic life of their own and continue to regulate family transactions. The strategic therapist works to substitute new behavior patterns for the destructive repetitive cycles. The techniques used by strategic therapists (Madanes 1981; Stanton 1981) include the following:

1. Using tasks with the therapist responsible for planning a strategy to solve the family's problems.
2. Putting the problem in solvable form.
3. Placing considerable emphasis on change outside the sessions.
4. Learning to take the path of least resistance so that the family's existing behaviors are used positively.
5. Using paradox, including restraining change and exaggerating family roles.
6. Allowing the change to occur in stages. The therapist may create a new problem so that solving it leads to solving the original problem. The family hierarchy may be shifted to a different, abnormal one before reorganizing it into a new functional hierarchy.
7. Using metaphorical directives in which the family members do not know they have received a directive.

Stanton and Todd (1982) successfully utilized an integrated structural-strategic approach with heroin addicts on methadone maintenance treatment.

Psychodynamic therapy.   This approach has rarely been applied to substance abusers because they usually require a more active, limit-setting emphasis on the here and now than is usually associated with psychodynamic techniques. However, if certain basic limitations are kept in mind, psychodynamic principles can be extremely helpful in the family therapy of these patients. As Gurman and Kniskern (1981) noted, most psychodynamic family therapists are pragmatic psychodynamic in that they utilize a broad-based workable system that includes psychodynamic principles and techniques.

The symptoms of the IP are viewed in the context of his or her own historical past as well as that of every family member. Psychodynamic family therapy and strategic therapies have a common ultimate goal: achieving second-order change. The goal is to change the entire family system so that dysfunction does not occur in other family members once the symptoms of the IP have been alleviated.

There are two cornerstones for the implementation of psychodynamic techniques: the therapist's self-knowledge and a detailed family history. Every family member will internalize a therapist's good qualities, such as warmth, trust, trustworthiness, assertion, empathy, and understanding. Likewise, they may incorporate less desirable qualities such as aggression, despair, and emotional distancing. It is absolutely essential that a therapist thoroughly understand his or her own emotional reactions as well as those of the family.

Important elements of psychodynamic family therapy include the following.

Countertransference.   The therapist may have a countertransference problem toward the entire family or any individual member of the family and may get into power struggles or may overreact emotionally to affect, content, or personality. There are several common countertransference reactions to substance abusers and their families. The IP's dependency, relationship suction and repulsion, manipulativeness, denial, impulsivity, and role abandonment may readily provoke countertransference reactions in the therapist. However, family therapists view their emotional reactions to families in a systems framework as well as a countertransference context. Thus they must be aware of how families will replay their problems in therapy by attempting to detour or triangulate their problems onto the therapist. The therapist must be particularly sensitive about becoming an enabler who, like the family, protects or rejects the substance abuser.

The role of interpretation.   Interpretations can be extremely helpful if they are made in a complementary way, without blaming, guilt induction, or dwelling on the hopelessness of longstanding, fixed patterns. Repetitive patterns and their maladaptive aspects to each family member can be pointed out, and tasks can be given to help them change these patterns. Some families need interpretations before they can fulfill tasks. An emphasis on mutual responsibility when making any interpretation is an example of a beneficial fusion of structural and psychodynamic therapy (Kaufman 1985).

Overcoming resistance.   Resistance is defined as behaviors, feelings, patterns, or styles that prevent change (Anderson and Stewart 1983). In substance-abusing families, key resistance behaviors that must be dealt with involve the failure to perform functions that enable the abuser to stay "clean."

Every substance-abusing family has characteristic patterns of resistant behavior in addition to individual resistances. This family style may contribute significantly to resistance; some families may need to deny all conflict and emotion and are almost totally unable to tolerate any displays of anger or sadness; others may overreact to the slightest disagreement. It is important to recognize, emphasize, and interpret the circumstances that arouse resistance patterns (Anderson and Stewart 1983). However, early on, the therapist must avoid labeling the behavior as resistance or directly confronting it because this increases hostility and, in turn, enhances resistance. The reciprocal family interactions that lead to resistant behaviors should be pointed out.

Resistance can be focused on in the treatment contract; each family member agrees to cooperate in overcoming resistance. If a family is willing to perform its assigned tasks, then most resistances are irrelevant or can be overcome. Resistances such as blaming, dwelling on past injustices, and scapegoating can be directly discouraged by the therapist. The therapist may overcome resistance by joining techniques, including minimizing demands on the family to change so that the family moves more slowly, but in the desired direction.

Working through.   This important concept, derived from psychoanalysis, is quite similar to the structural concept of isomorphic transactions. It underscores the need to work repeatedly on many different overt issues, all of which stem from the same dysfunctional core. Thus to have real change, a family must deal with a problem over and over until it has been worked through.

This process is much quicker in family than individual therapy because when an appropriate intervention is made, the entire family system may reinforce the consequent positive change. If the system later pulls the family's behavior back to old maladaptive ways, then it becomes necessary to work the conflicts through in many different transactions until stable change takes place. A specific psychodynamic technique that is often helpful with substance abusers is the family of origin (F of O) technique as developed by Framo (1981). In this technique the F of O of adult substance abusers is worked with to understand how past difficulties are being replayed in the present and to begin to shift these transferential problems.

Bowen's systems family therapy. In Bowen's (1971) approach, the cognitive is emphasized and the use of affect is minimized. Systems theory focuses on triangulation, which implies that whenever there is emotional distance or conflict between two individuals, tensions will be displaced onto a third party, issue, or substance. Drugs are frequently the subject of triangulation.

Behavioral family therapy. This approach is commonly used with substance-abusing adolescents. Its popularity may be attributed to the fact that it can be elaborated in clear, easily learned steps.

Noel and McCrady (1984) developed seven steps in the therapy of alcoholic couples that can readily be applied to married adult drug abusers and their families:

1. Functional analysis. Families are taught to understand the interactions that maintain drug abuse.
2. Stimulus control. Drug use is viewed "as a habit triggered by certain antecedents and maintained by certain consequences." The family is taught to avoid or change these triggers.
3. Rearranging contingencies. The family is taught techniques to provide reinforcement for efforts at achieving a drug-free state by frequent reviewing of positive and negative consequences of drug use and self-contracting for goals and specific rewards for achieving these goals. Covert reinforcement is done by rehearsing in fantasy a scene in which the IP resists a strong urge to use drugs.
4. Cognitive restructuring. IPs are taught to modify self-derogatory, retaliatory, or guilt-related thoughts. IPs question the logic of these "irrational" thoughts and replace them with more "rational" ideations.
5. Planning alternatives to drug use. IPs are taught techniques for refusing drugs through role-playing and covert reinforcement.
6. Problem solving and assertion. The IP and family are helped to decide if a situation calls for an assertive response and then, through role-playing, develop effective assertive techniques. IPs are to perform these techniques twice daily as well as utilize them in a difficult situation that would have previously triggered the urge to use drugs.
7. Maintenance planning. The entire course of therapy is reviewed, and the new armamentarium of skills emphasized. IPs are encouraged to practice these skills regularly as well as reread handout materials that explain and reinforce these skills.

Families can also be taught through behavioral techniques to become aware of their nonverbal communication to make the nonverbal message concordant with the verbal and to learn to express interpersonal warmth nonverbally as well as verbally (Stuart 1980).

Specific Structural Techniques

In this section, I will emphasize those family therapy techniques that I have found most useful in my work with substance abusers. Many of these techniques evolve from the structural family work of Minuchin (1974) and Haley (1977). This approach also borrows from systems and psychoanalytic techniques and integrates these disparate treatment methods into one system. The reader is advised to choose those methods that are compatible with his or her personality, to learn and practice these techniques by rote, and finally to utilize them in a spontaneous manner. These techniques will be described individually, although most techniques are a fusion of several others as they are implemented in clinical practice. These techniques include the contract, joining, actualization, marking boundaries, assigning tasks, reframing, the paradox, balancing and unbalancing, and creating intensity. Lastly, the use of a cotherapist will be discussed.

The Contract

The contract is an agreement to work on mutually agreed on, workable issues. The contract should always promise help with the IP's problem before it is expanded to other issues.

The primary contract is drafted with the family at the end of the first interview. In subsequent sessions, the concept of a contract is always maintained so that family assignments and tasks are agreed on and their implementation contracted by the family. When an individual or agency chooses an initial assessment period of more than one session, then the contract at the end of the first session may include only an agreement by the family to participate in the planned evaluation. However, the likelihood that the family will return after the first session is greatly enhanced by a contract that develops measures for problem resolution. In establishing a contract, the family must choose a system to achieve abstinence and agree to pursue that system after it has been agreed on as part of the initial evaluation.

The family should be provided with the beginnings of a system of shifting overreactivity to substance abuse in the initial contract. They may be coached to disengage from the IP, using strength gained from support groups and the therapist. At times, this disengagement can only be accomplished by powerful restructuring or paradoxical interventions. Later in therapy, contingency contracting principles can be used to facilitate mutual trust, particularly in areas such as adolescent individuation (e.g., a child agrees to be more respectful if curfew is extended).

Joining

In joining, the therapist adjusts himself or herself in a number of different ways to affiliate with the family system. Joining enhances the therapist's leverage to change the system. The therapist alternates between joining that supports the family system and its members and joining that challenges it. Joining with only one part of a family may severely stress or change the rest of the family. The therapist must make contact with all family members so that they will comply with the therapist even when they sense that the therapist is being unfair (Kaufman 1985). The therapist should join by respecting and not challenging the initial defensiveness, which is so common in these families.

Joining begins in the first moment of the session when the therapist makes the family comfortable through social amenities and chatting with each member. There are three types of joining techniques: maintenance, tracking, and mimesis (Minuchin 1974). Joining can also be classified by proximity.

Maintenance. Maintenance requires supporting the family structures and behaving according to the family rules. In its most extreme form, this includes accepting the family scapegoats as the problem when another family member is much more problematic. Maintenance operations include supporting areas of family strength, rewarding, affiliating with a family member, complimenting or supporting a threatened member, and explaining a problem. The therapist uses the family's metaphors, expressions, and language.

Tracking.   In tracking, the therapist follows the content of the family's interactions by listening carefully to what everyone has to say and by providing comments and expressions that help each family member know he or she has been heard and understood.

Mimesis.   Mimesis involves the therapist's adopting the family's style and affect. If a family uses humor, so should the therapist. If a family communicates through touching, then the therapist can also touch. The therapist supports family members or the entire family by means of nonverbal identifications.

Joining classified by proximity.   In joining families from a position of closeness, the therapist must push to find positive aspects in all family members, particularly ones who are disliked (Minuchin and Fishman 1981). A therapist who finds something positive in someone unlikable will find that he or she then begins to like that person. Being able to help difficult patients change positively also helps therapists to like them. Another technique is for therapists to look into their own personality and find similar characteristics. By confirming these positives, the therapist will enhance the individual's self-esteem and help make that person more likable. In general, pointing out several individuals' complementary responsibility for negative behaviors will help the therapist join with the entire system. In joining from a middle position, the therapist gathers important information by observing his or her own ways of interacting with the family without being incorporated into the family system. Here it is often important to shift emphasis by tracking from content to process. In joining from a disengaged position, the therapist may have the role of an expert or director.

Actualization

Patients usually direct their communications to the therapist. They should be trained to talk to each other rather than to the therapist. They should be asked to enact transactional patterns rather than describe them. Manipulating space is a powerful tool for generating actualization. Changing seating may create or strengthen boundaries. Asking two members who have been chronically disengaged or communicating through a third party to sit next to each other can actualize strong conflicts and emotions.

Many families try to look as good as possible when they enter therapy. Actualizations unleash sequences that are beyond their control and permit the therapist to see the family as it really is. Three progressively elaborated types of actualization are utilized (Minuchin and Fishman 1981). The first involves sequences that evolve spontaneously as families are permitted to be themselves in session. In the second, therapist-planned scenarios permit further natural interactions; these may utilize latent issues that are close to the surface and are beginning to evolve in session. The third, the most change-oriented type of actualization, has the family reenacting in session a pattern that is outside of their repetitive, maladaptive system and that demonstrates new ways of problem solving.

Marking Boundaries

Each individual and each subsystem is encouraged to preserve their appropriate boundaries. Each person should be spoken to, not about, and no one should talk, feel, think, answer or act for anyone else. Each family member is encouraged to tell his or her own story and listen to and acknowledge the communications of others. Nonverbal checking and blocking of communications should also be observed and, when appropriate, pointed out and halted. "Mind reading" is very common, and is strongly discouraged because even if the mind reader is correct it almost always starts an argument. No one likes his or her reactions to be anticipated.

Symbolic boundaries are established in the session by the therapist placing his or her body, an arm, or a piece of furniture between members, by rearranging members, or by avoiding eye contact. These boundaries are supported and strengthened by tasks outside of the session. The most important boundary shift in family therapy is weakening the ties between an overinvolved parent and child and strengthening the boundary that protects the parents as a unit and supports them against parents, in-laws, affairs, and the rest of the world external to the nuclear family.

If a role or tie is removed from a family member, this relationship should be replaced by building ties with other family members or people outside of the family. When boundaries are strengthened around a system, that system's functioning invariably improves.

Assigning Tasks

Tasks help gather information, intensify the relationship with the therapist, continue the therapy outside of sessions, and give family members the opportunity to behave differently (Haley 1977). Tasks that work in the framework of family goals, particularly those involving changing the symptoms of the IP, should be chosen. Tasks should involve everyone in the family and bring gains to each member. A task should be successfully completed in session before one is assigned as homework.

When tasks are given they should be specific, clear, and concise. If tasks are performed successfully, they will restructure the family toward optimal functioning. Tasks that fail are used as valuable learning experiences that reveal family dysfunction. Still, the family should not be let off easily, and the reasons for their failing themselves should be explored.

Reframing

In reframing (Minuchin and Fishman (1981), the therapist takes information received from the family and transforms it into a format that will be most helpful to changing the family. Reframing begins at the start of the first session as the therapist receives information from the family, molding it so that the family members feel that their problems are clear and solvable. Reframing is achieved by focusing material as it is received, selecting the elements that will facilitate change, and organizing the information in such a way as to give it new meaning. Perhaps the most common use of reframing is when the symptoms of an IP are broadened to include the entire family system. Another common reframing is describing the positive function of the IP's symptoms for the family.

The Paradox

Paradoxical techniques work best with chronically rigid, repetitive, circular, highly resistant family systems, particularly ones that have had many prior therapeutic failures (Papp 1981).

Paradox is not utilized when family motivation is high, resistance is low, and the family responds readily to direct interventions. Paradox is not used in crisis situations such as violence, suicide, incest, or child abuse; here the therapist needs to provide structure and control. Paradox is often used to slow progress so that a family is chafing at the bit to move faster or to exaggerate a symptom to emphasize the family's need to extrude it. A symptom that is an externalized acting-out of family conflicts (stealing, secret drug taking) can be prescribed to be performed within the family so that the family can deal with it. An individual's behavior is not prescribed without relating it to its function in the family system. The symptom should only be prescribed in a way that changes the functioning of the system. At times, psychodynamic interpretations can be made in a paradoxical way that gives greater impact to reach and change the family.

Balancing and Unbalancing

Balancing techniques, which tend to support a family, are conceptually similar to Minuchin and Fishman's (1981) complementarity. They challenge the family's views of symptoms as part of a linear hierarchy and emphasize the reciprocal involvement of symptom formation, while supporting the family. In using balancing as a technique, mutual responsibility is emphasized, and tasks that involve change in all parties should be given.

Unbalancing involves changing or stressing the existing hierarchy in a family. The therapist unbalances by affiliating with a family member of low power so this person can challenge his or her prescribed family role, or by escalating a crisis, emphasizing differences, blocking typical transactional patterns, developing implicit conflict, and rearranging the hierarchy (Minuchin and Fishman 1981). It should be attempted only after the therapist has achieved a great deal of power through joining.

Creating Intensity

Creating intensity techniques are verbal devices used to ensure that the therapist's message is heard and incorporated by the family. One simple way to be heard is to repeat either the same phrase or different phrases that convey the same concept. Another way of creating intensity is through isomorphic transactions that use many different interventions to attack the same underlying dysfunctional pattern.

The amount of time a family spends on a transaction can be increased or decreased, as can the proximity of members during an interaction. Intensity can also be created by resisting the family's pull to get the therapist to do what they want.

Individual versus Cotherapy

Cotherapy is very helpful in work with these families for a number of reasons. One therapist can join with one segment of the family (e.g., parents) while the other joins with the sibling subsystem. One therapist can join from very close proximity while the other can maintain sufficient distance to remain objective. Cotherapy pairing can also provide the breadth of male-female or professional-ex-addict perspectives.

The relationship between cotherapists may be conflictual, and it is essential that time be set aside both pre- and postsession for therapists to work through these conflicts, or at times to agree to disagree.

Strategic therapists advocate that there should only be one therapist in the room with the family, but that the cotherapist, treatment team or supervisor all remain outside of the room, viewing the session through a one-way mirror. This provides for objectivity for the team and a place for the primary therapist to retreat from the family tension in order to receive consultation. Two therapists or a team is obviously more expensive than one, but the benefits of the former may outweigh its short-term expense.

Variations in Family Treatment Techniques to Meet the Needs of Different Types of Drug Abusers

I will now consider the modification of treatment typologies necessary for optimal treatment of abusers of various types of drugs and their families. In family treatment we must consider the needs of at least one other person and, in most cases, many other persons as we adapt our treatment techniques to each individual family. It is not the drug of abuse that demands modifications in technique, but other variables such as extent and severity of substance abuse, psychopathology, ethnicity, family reactivity, stage of disease, and gender (Kaufman 1985).

Drug Type and Family Treatment

Most of the modifications in family treatment that are based on drug type occur in the first phase of treatment when a system is developed for establishing and maintaining a drug-free state. Family self-help support groups are extremely helpful adjuncts to family therapy. Cocanon is extremely helpful in dealing with the specific problems of the relatives of cocaine abusers. Some relatives of abusers of minor tranquilizers can participate well in Alanon, whereas the relatives of other types of drug abusers may find it difficult to relate to the relatives of alcoholics and would work best in a specialized group. In most areas, groups such as Cocanon and Narcanon do not exist, and it is helpful to utilize groups of significant others that may be organized according to substance of abuse as well as by other factors such as social class and ethnicity.

Substance abuse choice may interact with a variety of factors, such as ethnicity and life-cycle stage. For example, white adolescents abuse mainly alcohol and marijuana and are less involved in the use of heroin and barbiturates than nonwhites (Carlisi 1979). Other studies have found that whites are more likely than blacks to have tried alcohol, marijuana, barbiturates, amphetamines, psychedelics, and inhalants, but are less likely to have tried cocaine or heroin (Kandel et al. 1978). As drug trends have changed, more and more white youths have at least tried cocaine. Mexican Americans are more likely to use phencyclidine (PCP), East Coast Hispanic youths to use inhalants, and so on. Younger substance abusers are more likely to abuse inhalants, hallucinogens, and marijuana; Young adults, heroin; middle-age persons, tranquilizers and alcohol. With younger drug abusers, we focus on the family of origin; with older IPs, we focus on their nuclear family of procreation. When the drug abuse pattern is associated with a high level of criminality or antisocial personality, more intense and prolonged family treatment efforts are necessary, although the prognosis is poorer than with less antisocial patients. When there is drug dependence rather than abuse, family therapy must be more intensive and prolonged.

Ethnicity

Ethnicity exerts a powerful effect on family function, styles, roles, and communication patterns, which supersede the differential effects of various drugs. The effects of ethnicity depend on how many generations of the family have lived in the United States and the homogeneity of the neighborhood in which they live. In describing ethnic characteristics, we must realize that we risk overgeneralizing because of individual variations among ethnic groups (e.g., Northern urban versus Southern rural blacks, Northern versus Southern Italian family of origin).

Italian-American families.   In Italian-American families, the family of origin has the highest priority, often creating difficulties for the spouse, who must cope with a mate's intense and exclusive ties to the family of origin. Therapy with Italian-American families should focus on the renegotiation of their rigid system boundaries, which keep the extended family out of contact with the outside world (Rotunno and McGoldrick 1982). They talk openly and with exaggerated feeling, yet hide their family secrets, which are plentiful. Secrets must be dealt with delicately, as their being made known to the therapist may constitute family betrayal (McGoldrick 1982a).

The therapist must overcome being distrusted as an outsider so that the authority necessary to change the family can be established. Then the therapy can focus on helping the IP differentiate from the family in more adaptive ways than through substance abuse, yet permit them a face-saving way to remain within the family (Rotunno and McGoldrick 1982).

Multiple family groups (Kaufman and Kaufmann 1977) can be very helpful in providing Italian-American families the support that they need to let their children individuate. Given the insularity of the Italian-American extended family, their willingness to open up and change in a group of other families is surprising. The use of an Italian-American cotherapist, their view of the doctor as respected expert, and other Italian-American families in the group who supported the letting go process were also helpful (Kaufman 1985).

Jewish-American families.   There is a very strong family orientation in these families, with marriage and children central (Herz and Rosen 1982). There is also a strong sense of family democracy, with consensual decision making and diffuse generational boundaries (McGoldrick 1982b). They place a high value on verbal explanation and reassurance in child rearing and do not use strong threats (McGoldrick 1982b).

Jewish-American families value credentials and education, and the therapist should not feel threatened by questions about these issues. When credentials are established, they readily consult with the therapist as a wise person, but still retain the right to make the final judgment about which interventions they will or will not use. They prefer complex, sophisticated interventions and consider behavioral types of techniques to be superficial (McGoldrick 1982b). Talking and expressing their feelings is more important to Jewish-American families than actively changing; thus they prefer analytic techniques to strategic ones (Herz and Rosen 1982). However, tasks are essential to shift from intellect to action, and they can be given in the families' own complex terms, utilizing their language and rituals.

The therapist must respect the rules that support enmeshed togetherness at the same time as he or she facilitates some essential boundary making.

White Anglo-Saxon families. White Anglo-Saxon families place a strong emphasis on independence, which extrudes children from the family early and neglects the extended family. They have difficulties in communication and have an inadequate sense of self-worth if they do not meet the expectations of the Calvinistic work ethic (McGill and Pearce 1982).

In these families, the IP's difficulties are perceived as the patient's problem, not the family's (McGill and Pearce 1982). Thus, white Anglo-Saxon families should be encouraged to stay involved, to provide support, and to assume control of the problem. The substance abuser is encouraged to share his or her pain with the family members so they are able to share the responsibility (McGill and Pearce 1982). Since asking for help is so difficult for these families, the therapist should support rather than confront them in the early stage of therapy and should build trust so that their feelings of vulnerability will not be intensified (McGill and Pearce 1982). Once the problem is clearly defined and a treatment contract is made, they will proceed with hard work in therapy, with the belief that this will be sufficient for success in therapy as it is in life.

Irish-American families. Irish-American families tend to view therapy in the same way they view confession; relating sins and gaining forgiveness (McGoldrick 1982a). Yet if the therapist uncovers their sins, they will feel embarrassed. They do not let the therapist know if they are inconvenienced or uncomfortable. Because of their politeness and loyalty, they may comply with the therapist without really changing. They view the therapist like a priest-authority and thus will respond best to a structured, problem-oriented approach or to a specific, clearly spelled out plan such as behavioral therapy (McGoldrick 1982a).

Involving a distant father is often essential to correcting the maternally dominated imbalance that is so common in Irish-American families. Some Irish-American fathers have become so totally removed from the family that it has been impossible to get them to come into therapy. Although the actual therapy may be very uncomfortable for these families, a deep sense of personal responsibility leads them to continue therapeutic work on their own after termination of formal therapy.

Black-American families. The constant impact of racism and discrimination is a continuing and pervasive aspect of black-American family systems and is a crucial factor in their family therapy. Disciplining of children is strict and direct, but the lack of positive support by social structures leads to a high incidence of substance abuse in youth. Talking-oriented therapy is not effective or acceptable in black-American families, particularly those that have become underorganized as a result of social pressures (McGoldrick 1982b). In these families, structural therapy, which strengthens family organization while adding to its flexibility, is the most effective model.

Family Reactivity

Substance-abusing families have been categorized according to four types: functional, enmeshed, disintegrated, and absent, each with different needs for family therapy (Kaufman and Pattison 1981).

Functional families.   Functional families have minimal overt conflict and a limited capacity for insight, as they protect their working homeostasis. Thus the therapist should not be too ambitious to crack the defensive structure of the family, which is likely to be resistant. The initial use of family education is often well received. Explanation of the medical effects of drugs provides a concrete way for the family to face up to the consequences of substance abuse (Kaufman and Pattison 1981). These families can usually be taught appropriate family rules and roles. Cognitive modes of interaction are usually acceptable, as more uncovering and emotional interactions may be resisted.

If abstinence and equilibrium are achieved, the therapist should be content even if the family continues to use a great deal of denial and emotional isolation.

The achievement of a "dry system" is usually feasible. Short-term hospitalization may be required. Drug abusers from functional families are often resistant to long-term residential treatment because they are protected by the family homeostasis.

Enmeshed families.   The therapeutic approach with enmeshed families is much more difficult and prolonged than with functional families. Educational and behavioral methods may provide some initial relief, but are not likely to have much impact on the enmeshed neurotic relationships. Often these families are resistant to ending substance abuse, and the therapist is often faced with working with the family while substance abuse continues.

Although initial hospitalization or detoxification may achieve temporary abstinence, the IP is highly vulnerable to relapse. Therefore, long-term family therapy with substantial restructuring is required to develop an affiliated family system free of substance abuse. An integrated synthesis of several schools of family therapy techniques may be required.

Because of the enmeshment and explosiveness of these families, it is usually necessary to reinforce boundaries, define personal roles, and diminish reactivity. The therapist will have to be active and directive to keep the emotional tensions within workable limits. Disengagement can be assisted by getting family members involved with external support groups.

Disintegrated families.   In disintegrated systems, there is a prior history of reasonable vocational function and family life, but a progressive deterioration of family function, and finally separation from the family. The use of family intervention might seem irrelevant in such a case. However, many of these marriages and families have fallen apart only after severe drug-related behavior. Further, there is often only pseudoindividuation of the substance abuser from marital, family, and kinship ties. These families cannot and will not reconstitute during the early phases of rehabilitation. Early therapeutic sessions are usually characterized by apathy or by intense hostility toward the IP. Thus the early stages of treatment should focus primarily on the substance abuser. However, potential ties to spouse, family, kin, and friends should be explored early in treatment, and some contact should be initiated. When abstinence and personal stability have been achieved over several months, the family can be worked with to reestablish family ties, but reconstitution of the family unit should not be a necessary goal.

Absent families.   In absent family systems, there is a total loss of the family of origin and a lack of other permanent relationships. Nevertheless, there are two types of social network interventions possible. The first is the elaboration of still existing friend and kin contacts. Often these social relationships can be revitalized and provide meaningful social support. Second, in occasional younger patients, there is a positive response to peer-group approaches, such as long-term therapeutic communities, NA, church fellowships and recreational and avocational clubs, which draw them into social relationships and vocational rehabilitation. These patients can develop new skills and the ability to engage in satisfactory marriage and family life.

Life-Cycle Phase of the Family

Often we are dealing with several phases of the family cycle simultaneously because of the high frequency of substance abuse in many generations of the same family. The therapy of 15-year-olds will be quite similar regardless of the substance being abused. The treatment of a 45-year-old corporate executive alcoholic may be quite different from that of a 45-year-old heroin addict because their individual styles and family systems have evolved so differently over a long period of time.

Family therapy in which the IP is an adolescent differs from one in which there is an adult IP in the following ways: less chronicity and severity, peer-group involvement that is susceptible to parental influence, less criminal activity, and fewer involvements in extrafamilial systems. Families with an adolescent IP invariably experience difficulties setting appropriate limits on adolescent individuation. The major therapeutic thrust in these families is to help the parents remain unified when setting limits while permitting flexibility in their negotiating these limits (Fishman, et al. 1982).

For a drug-abusing young adult offspring, separation from the family is often a more desirable goal. To achieve this, the therapist must create intensity, escalate stress, and use other strategic unbalancing techniques. In dealing with older adults, the structural-dynamic techniques that were described in the beginning of this chapter are more often indicated.

The family therapy of a grandparent substance abuser is just beginning to be addressed. Here it may be critical to involve their children and grandchildren to facilitate the IP's entry into treatment. Once a substance-free state is achieved, then the IP grandparent can work toward achieving or reestablishing an executive or consultant position in the hierarchy (Kaufman 1979).

Stages of Family's Reaction to IPs

Every family goes through various phases or cycles in their reactions to substance abuse. After an initial phase of denial, but still early in a substance-using career, families tend to overreact in an enmeshed and chaotic way to drug-related behavior, particularly during periods of intoxication and heavy use. Later on, there is usually more of a tendency to form a new family homeostasis, one that excludes the IP. Unfortunately, some families may stay enmeshed with the IP, and family members may be dragged down to severe depression and substance abuse themselves. Families may also cycle between disengagement and enmeshed reactivity (Steinglass 1980). During highly reactive, enmeshed stages, boundaries must be demarcated to calm down the system. In disengaged families, trust and closeness need to be gradually rebuilt. However, the therapist must realize that repetitive cycling from enmeshed to distant may continue whether the family is in therapy or not and that these cycles must be expected. This is a strong argument for long-term therapy as well as for maintaining a positive alliance after treatment so that the family can return as needed.

Variations According to Gender of the IP

Traditionally, substance abuse treatment in the United States has been male-oriented. In countering this one-sided approach, family therapists must be aware that the families of chemically dependent women demonstrate much greater disturbance than those of male patients seeking treatment. These disturbances include greater incidence of chemical dependency of other family members, mental illness, suicide, violence, and both physical and sexual abuse. Family-related issues also bring far more women than men into treatment, with potential loss of custody of minor children heading the list (Sutker 1981).

In view of the differences in the families of female substance abusers, family intervention strategies with women must differ from those for males. Family therapy may be more essential for female substance abusers because of these symbolic or often actual losses of spouse and children. The therapist should not impose a stereotyped view of femininity on female patients; this could intensify the conflicts that may have precipitated their substance use (Sandmeier 1980). The therapist should be sensitive to the specific problems of women and women substance abusers in our society and address these issues in treatment.

Women substance abusers have special concerns about their children and child care. Family therapy may assist them to see how the parenting role fits into their lives and how to establish parenting skills, perhaps for the very first time. Many women have been victimized in a number of ways in the past, including incest, battering, and rape. Catharsis and understanding of these feelings may be essential before a woman can build new relationships or improve her present ties (Kaufman 1985).

With male patients, special issues such as pride and accepting their own dependency strivings often need to be addressed.

Family Readjustment After the Cessation of Substance Abuse

Once the substance abuse has stopped, the family may enter a honeymoon phase in which major conflicts are denied. The family may maintain a superficial harmony based on relief and suppression of negative feeling. On the other hand, when the drug-dependent person stops using drugs, other family problems may be uncovered, particularly in the parent's marriage or in other siblings. These problems, which were present all along but obscured by the IP's drug use, will be "resolved" by the IP's return to symptomatic behavior if not dealt with in family therapy. In the latter case, the family then reunites around their problem person, according to their old, familiar pathologic style.

Too many treatment programs in the substance abuse field focus their efforts on the 28-day inpatient program, neglecting aftercare. Many of these programs include a one-week intensive family educational and therapeutic experience, but with even less focus on the family in aftercare than the IP. These intensive short-term programs have great impact on the family system, but only temporarily. The pull of the family homeostatic system will draw the IP and/or other family members back to symptomatic behavior. The family must be worked with for months and often years after substance abuse first abates if a drug-free state is to continue. In addition, ongoing family therapy is also necessary for the emotional well-being of the IP and other family members.

Chapter 140

Individual Psychotherapy for Substance Abuse

Many types of individual psychotherapy have been used in the course of substance abuse treatments. This variety of treatment makes it difficult to write a brief yet comprehensive chapter on this topic. The course chosen here is to provide a selection of meaningful guidelines for those who wish to use psychotherapy with substance abuse patients. Throughout this chapter, the term psychotherapy is used to describe a psychological treatment that aims to modify intrapsychic and interpersonal conflicts.

In this chapter, psychotherapy will be contrasted with drug counseling. In this context, drug counseling is defined as the regular management of drug-dependent patients through monitoring of behavior (urinalysis, employment), the enforcement of program rules (no loitering, attendance regulation), and the provision of concrete services such as referral for job counseling, medical services, or legal aid. While it is recognized that drug counseling generally involves group and individual therapy sessions, the nature of these sessions is usually directed to issues of behavior management, crisis intervention, and extrapsychic problems. Drug counseling requires the development of basic interpersonal management skills and a knowledge base regarding behavioral aspects of addiction and the availability of social services.

A Rationale for Using Psychotherapy with Substance Abuse Patients

Various psychiatric disorders are very common among substance abuse patients. In a comprehensive study of opioid addicts in New Haven, Connecticut (Rounsaville et al. 1982), more that 85 percent were found to have a lifetime history of a psychiatric disorder other than opioid dependence, and 70 percent had a current psychiatric illness. Affective disorders, especially depression, were the most common problems, with 74 percent meeting DSM-III (American Psychiatric Association 1980) criteria for having had an affective disorder, either currently or in the past. Almost identical results were found in other similar studies done in Boston (Khantzian and Treece 1985) and Philadelphia (Woody et al. 1983), thus providing replicability of Rounsaville et al.'s findings.

Some have stated that any person with a substance abuse disorder has an additional psychiatric problem (Wurmser 1979). This position has not been supported by the studies mentioned above, where a portion of the patients examined had no psychiatric problem other than substance abuse, at least as defined by the RDC and the DSM-III diagnostic categories. Clinicians have, in fact, stated that some types of drug abuse may begin or be continued as a form of self-medication to treat anxiety, depression, or other psychiatric disorders (Khantzian 1985; Khantzian et al. 1974). This relationship between psychiatric disorders, drug abuse, and self-medication provides one of the main rationales for using psychotherapy with substance abusers. Given this relationship, substance abuse patients with clinically significant psychiatric disorders, in addition to their substance abuse, are individuals who one might consider for psychotherapy.

Studies on Psychotherapy Efficacy with Substance Abusers

Evidence for the efficacy of professional psychotherapy for substance abuse is in an early stage. Only two major outcome studies have been done, and these were both aimed to see if psychotherapy provided benefits that would be greater than and different from those occurring from standard paraprofessional counseling services in methadone maintenance programs. One study found evidence for improved outcome from psychotherapy in the general patient population, but especially with those patients who had clinically significant psychiatric symptoms (Woody et al. 1983). Another study found no benefits beyond those resulting from the standard paraprofessional counseling and the drug treatment milieu created by the program (Rounsaville et al. 1983).

Other reports on outcome of psychotherapy with substance abusers are also available. Table 1 summarizes nine of such studies that used random assignment to treatment and control groups. Seven of the nine studies found evidence that psychotherapy can be helpful with this population. A notable exception to this trend was the well-designed and careful study done by Rounsaville et al. (1983). By way of further review, it is important to consider the settings in which the studies were done. Three of the studies that showed the efficacy of psychotherapy were done in the same clinic (McLellan et al. 1986; Stanton and Todd 1982; Woody et al. 1983). Clearly, it cannot be concluded that data are currently available that support generalization of the trend seen in Table 1 to all programs. It may be the case that psychotherapy works in some situations or with certain types of substance abuse patients, but not with others. Programmatic conditions and the types of patients for whom psychotherapy may be appropriate are just beginning to be explored and defined. It is beyond the scope of this chapter to review these issues in detail; a summary of this topic is available elsewhere (Rounsaville and Kleber 1985).

In this chapter, we will emphasize a "how to do it" approach and thus will draw

Table 1. Psychotherapy Studies with Random Assignment and Controls

Authors	N	Therapy Type	Result
Willett 1973	9	group	better
LaRosa et al. 1974	42	individual	better
Abrams 1979	15	group	better
Connett 1980	19	group	no difference
Stanton and Todd 1982	62	family	better
Resnick et al. 1981	62	individual	better
Rounsaville et al. 1983	72	individual	no difference
Woody et al. 1983	110	individual	better
McLellan et al. 1986b	37	individual	better

heavily on data obtained from those studies that have provided evidence for psychotherapy efficacy with this population. It will consist of three parts: 1) a description of general factors that are important to consider before attempting to do psychotherapy with substance abuse patients; 2) presentation of clinical material from psychotherapy sessions with substance abusers in which supportive expressive psychotherapy will be used as an example of a representative therapy; and 3) a brief discussion of ideas about what types of substance abuse patients might profit from psychotherapy, how they might be identified, and what results one might hope to achieve.

General Factors

Pharmacology, Treatments, and Life-Styles

It is helpful for psychotherapists who treat substance abusers to become familiar with the main effects and adverse effects of the drugs that are abused; with the various treatments, pharmacologic and otherwise, that are commonly used within the substance abuse field; and with the lifestyles, slang words, and cultural habits of substance abuse patients. An excellent source for obtaining much of this information can be found elsewhere (Jaffe 1985). Familiarity with the life-styles of substance abusers can be gained by talking to paraprofessionals or psychotherapists who have treatment experience with substance abusers, or by the first-hand experience gained through treating patients. Hanson et al. (1985) provide excellent descriptive information about the life-styles of opiate addicts.

An experienced therapist knows that substance abuse patients sometimes come to treatment while under the influence of drugs. Obviously, the patient's mental state can vary considerably, depending on whether he or she is intoxicated, withdrawing, or in the more "normal" state that is found between these two extremes. The patient sometimes may be so intoxicated that therapy is impossible, and the session must be rescheduled, postponed, or temporarily discontinued until better control of the drug use is achieved by some other means, such as hospitalization. It is also worth noting that some patients are addicted to multiple drugs such as sedatives and opiates, or alcohol and stimulants. These can be unusually difficult to treat as they are often under the influence of complicated pharmacologic effects in addition to having severe psychiatric problems. For example, such a patient may be withdrawing from one drug and intoxicated with another, while also experiencing a major depressive disorder. Inpatient, abstinence-oriented treatment is often necessary for such patients prior to attempting any type of meaningful psychological intervention. This allows for better control over the substance abuse and thus gives psychotherapy a better chance to be used effectively than would be the case if the patient attended therapy while intoxicated or in a state of withdrawal. In the case of opiate addiction, many find that methadone programs can provide good control over drug use without having to use inpatient facilities.

Types of Patients and Treatments

Few studies are available that carefully define which types of substance abuse patients might benefit from which kind of psychotherapy. Much of the available data on psychotherapy outcome with general psychiatric patients has supported its efficacy, but has provided little reason to suggest that patients with one type of disorder have outcomes similar to those with another, or that one type of psychotherapy is superior to any others (Smith et al. 1980). Both clinical experience and research studies indicate that the part contributed by psychotherapy to overall outcome probably varies considerably among specific disorders. Examples are manic-depressive illness, where lithium accounts for much more of the variance in outcome than psychotherapy (Whybrow et al. 1984) and minor depressive disorder, where psychotherapy most likely plays at least an equal role to pharmacotherapy (Elkin 1986). Knowledge is accumulating rapidly in these areas and new data often quickly change our opinion. The demonstration that tricyclics effectively treat panic disorder (Klein 1981), a condition often previously treated with psychotherapy, and the work demonstrating that family therapy provides significant benefits for schizophrenics often treated only with pharmacotherapy (Fallon et al. 1982) are examples of data that have led to changes in the recommended mix of pharmacotherapy versus psychotherapy for certain disorders. Rounsaville and Kleber (1985) reviewed some of these issues as they apply to substance abusers.

Treatment Settings

Psychotherapy is appropriate for use in both inpatient and outpatient treatment settings. An exception may be the drug-free therapeutic community. Here, the major treatment program is a peer-regulated milieu with an emphasis on self-government, individual responsibility, group meetings, and strict behavioral controls. Psychotherapy does not easily fit into this structure, although it may be used in some programs as an ancillary treatment that is targeted to patients with persistent and overt psychiatric symptoms.

Psychotherapy probably has the best chance to work when it is integrated into an ongoing treatment program that focuses directly on significantly reducing or eliminating drug use as well as reducing any accompanying psychiatric symptoms. In methadone treatment programs, for example, all patients are usually assigned a drug counselor who has a number of specific tasks. These include talking with the patient about current problems, supporting and encouraging the patient's efforts to reduce drug use, monitoring progress, providing liaison or consultation with medical personnel, making job referrals, obtaining legal advice, encouraging limit setting by enforcing program rules, and keeping accurate records. These tasks are both extensive and essential. Some counselors use these techniques much more successfully than others (McLellan et al. 1986). Coordination and integration of psychotherapists into such a program is facilitated by good personal relations between the therapist and staff. Commitment to the overall program by activities such as having the therapist work within the facility, familiarizing the therapist with overall program procedures and policies, and having therapists regularly attend some of the ongoing staff meetings are helpful in this regard.

The psychotherapist may take a very active role in the care of some patients where he or she provides the primary ongoing treatment. At any time in treatment, the psychotherapist may work concomitantly with Alcoholics Anonymous, Narcotics Anonymous, or other self-help groups. These organizations can be invaluable in helping drug-free patients remain abstinent and increase socially desirable behaviors.

Drug treatment programs exhibit tremendous variability in basic aspects of service delivery such as availability of medical services, control of behavioral problems, level of illicit drug use, safety and sanitary conditions, use of psychotropic drugs, level of staff morale, educational level of staff, and types of patients treated (Ball et al. 1986). These programmatic qualities may play a major but as yet undefined role in the feasibility, efficacy, or relative importance that psychotherapy may have in different settings. Data that define these differences and relate them to outcome should be available in the near future. It is likely that some control over drug use and some degree of social stability is necessary if psychotherapy is to have a chance to work.

Psychotherapy, whether conducted in the setting of a clinic or a private office, is most effective when also combined with the structure imposed by regular, observed urine testing. Many clinicians have found that involvement of significant family members in the treatment process is helpful. Therapies usually pay special attention to any factors that exist in the family that would serve to undermine treatment. Excellent descriptions of family therapy with addicts are found in Stanton and Todd (1982), who described techniques used in structural family therapy and presented outcome data from a study conducted by these authors. Some writers have noted that the presence of external pressure, such as threat of job loss or divorce (Herrington et al. 1982), can serve as a valuable motivator for an otherwise resistant patient to become seriously involved in treatment. Such external pressure is sometimes a necessary supplement to therapy. In such cases, the urine tests serve not only to provide structure, but also to document that the patient is in fact succeeding at abstinence. Examples are situations where employers or probation officers need drug-negative urines to justify allowing the patient to work or to stay out of prison.

Therapist Qualities

There is a considerable debate in the literature regarding the effective ingredients of psychotherapy. One major issue is whether changes observed following psychotherapy are the result of the specific techniques of the treatment itself or of the effects of the therapist's personality. Several studies (e.g., Luborsky et al. 1985, 1986) indicate that efficacy is probably determined by a combination of such factors. The personality of the therapist definitely appears to be an important factor and might even play a larger role than the specific interventions of the therapy.

Little evidence is available to indicate the type of therapist who may do best with substance abusers, thus it is difficult to comment with certainty on this issue, perhaps partly because substance abusers are such a heterogeneous group. Some guidelines can be offered, however, from the few available studies that have examined therapist qualities as they relate to outcome.

First, the therapist should be reasonably interested in and comfortable when relating to substance abusers. Therapists who from the beginning of treatment form a positive relationship perceived by the patient as "helping" appear to have a better chance of success than those who form less positive bonds (Luborsky et al. 1985). In contrast, some therapists have strong negative reactions to the manipulative, sociopathic, impulsive, or demanding behavior that is often seen in drug abusers. Others react negatively to the self-induced quality of substance abuse, which sets it apart from many other medical disorders in which the patient has very little to do with the onset or continuation of the illness. Therapists with such predominantly negative reactions will probably not do well with these patients.

Some clinicians feel that therapists probably need to extend themselves a little more with drug abusers than with other types of adult psychiatric patients. The dependency needs of the patients often express themselves in the doctor-patient relationship, and an occasional concrete supportive response is probably useful, especially in the early phases of treatment. This may consist of greeting the patient warmly on entering the office, actively seeking to reestablish contact when an appointment is missed, or seeing the patient occasionally at unscheduled times if the need is present and the time is available.

Examples of How Psychotherapy Can Be Applied to Substance Abusers

Many of the techniques and principles of psychotherapy used with substance abusers are similar to those used in psychotherapy with nonsubstance-abusing patients. The modifications introduced for this special population do not radically change the underlying techniques. We will attempt to illustrate this as it applies to supportive-expressive (SE) therapy. We have chosen to describe this particular form of therapy because we are familiar with it, because many therapists have been trained in an analytic form of therapy such as SE therapy, and because it is used widely. Cognitive-behavioral psychotherapy (Woody et al. 1983) and interpersonal psychotherapy (Rounsaville et al. 1983) are other techniques that have also been used with substance abusers.

SE therapy (Luborsky 1984) derives from psychoanalytic therapy, and thus borrows many concepts from the analytical school. The main concept with which the SE therapist operates is the importance of understanding the patient's wishes and their consequences from the point of view of the patient. These wish-consequence sequences, although largely outside the patient's awareness, can be understood by listening to the flow of what the patient says. After forming a helping relationship with the patient, the therapist can then use the understanding gained to help the patient help himself or herself, both to deal with the drug dependence and to improve general functioning.

Two main classes of techniques, supportiveness and expressiveness, are essential in this form of psychotherapy. The expressive component of the treatment refers to techniques that are aimed at facilitating understanding. The focus is around two main aspects: 1) finding the meanings of the drug dependence, particularly understanding the stresses that precipitate and continue the drug taking, as well as other symptoms, and 2) discerning the core relationship conflicts as they are expressed both inside and outside of treatment, especially in relation to the drug dependence. The expressive component, therefore, is much like what has been called a "focal psychotherapy," in which the therapy focuses around one main problem (Malan 1963; Sifneos 1972). Each patient is to be provided with as much of an expressive component as can be profitably used. This component will be greater for those persons who possess the requisite ego strength and anxiety tolerance along with the capacity for reflection about their interpersonal relationships.

The SE form of psychotherapy used for substance abusers has certain special emphases (Luborsky 1977) as compared with the general type of SE therapy, more completely described in Luborsky (1984). These emphases are the following:

1. Much time and energy on the therapist's part is required to introduce the patients to treatment and to engage them in it.
2. The goals must be formulated early and kept in sight.
3. Much attention must be given by the therapist to developing a positive relationship and supporting the patient. With most drug-dependent patients, a strong supportive component is necessary for the patient to tolerate the expressive aspects.
4. The therapist has to keep abreast of the patient's compliance with the overall drug treatment program, which includes adherence to the rules and avoiding nonprescribed drug taking. This information should come from the patient but may also be provided by family, friends, or other treatment staff (e.g., the drug counselor).

Having this information will allow the therapist to explore the meaning of renewed illicit drug taking or infractions of rules.

5. If the patient is receiving methadone, attention should be given as to when the patient feels therapy is best, before or after the daily dose. Methadone usually is such a central part of the patient's life that interest in therapy might be lost once the daily dose has been taken. This is especially true for patients who are just starting the program and have not yet established a close relationship with the therapist. Thus close attention should be given to setting appointments and looking for the patient at the time he or she is expected to arrive for the daily dose.

Techniques for Beginning Treatment

Orne and Wender (1968) showed the significant advantage of preliminary socialization interviews conducted by a person who knows the form of therapy and scheduled just before the patient is assigned to the psychotherapist. Such an interview explains to the patient how psychotherapy proceeds, what he or she is to do and what the therapist will do, and how the patient is to react to what the therapist will do. This interview is especially important for patients who have no prior experience with psychotherapy, as is the case with many substance abusers. The staff person who refers the patient for psychotherapy is in an ideal position to provide this interview.

Preliminary Socialization

After first meeting the patient, it is important for the therapist to explain the process—what the patient will be doing and what the therapist will be doing. This explanation can be given in small amounts over several sessions and may repeat some of what is in the preliminary socialization interview. Much of the explanation can be accomplished by pointing to examples in the actual conduct of the treatment. From time to time, it should be emphasized that what the patient and therapist do represents an active job of problem solution in the process of making progress toward the goals.

Goal Setting

Goal setting takes place primarily in the early sessions but may extend throughout the treatment as the patient revises the goals. For all these patients, one of the goals will be to control drug use. A more general goal for most patients will be to improve psychological and occupational functioning. For some patients it will be to decrease certain symptoms or to get along better with others. Goals should be set so that they take into account what seems achievable. Setting a time frame within which goals should be attained adds further structure and may serve to stimulate motivation.

Goals are not only important at the beginning and end, but also throughout the process of the treatment. They provide markers of progress, or lack of it. When a goal is achieved during the course of treatment, there will most likely be "internal markers," as observed by Schlesinger (in Luborsky 1977), which signal the change. These are ways of recognizing different phases during the course of the treatment. These phases and subphases allow the patient and therapist to have a recurrent sense of completion and accomplishment. In addition, the setting of reasonable goals is especially helpful for those patients for whom the treatment may appear to be an opportunity for unlimited dependence. Reasonable goal setting acts as a modulation of such regressive developments.

Techniques for Developing a "Helping Relationship"

Usually the patient's experience of a helping relationship will develop as a normal part of the therapist's work. The patient will ordinarily recognize that the therapist is trying to do the job of helping, the patient will then feel helped, and a good therapeutic alliance will form. One main requirement for the development of a therapeutic alliance is that the therapist *feel* an alliance so that it will be conveyed. Sometimes the alliance is expressed through the use by patient and therapist of the word *we*.

One impediment to this therapeutic alliance is that the therapist may dislike the patient. However, after reflection, there is usually a quality of any patient that a therapist can approve of and like; it is useful to make such a search and find that part. Understanding possible psychological determinants of addictive behavior (Khantzian 1985; Khantzian et al. 1974; Wurmser 1979) may be helpful in this regard, as well as being aware of the common countertransference responses (Davidson 1977) of anger, frustration, or overprotectiveness.

The therapist may need to foster the development of a helping relationship by specific techniques, described in detail elsewhere (Luborsky 1977, 1984). They include: 1) conveying a sense of wanting the patient to achieve the stated goals; 2) letting the patient know that the therapist is aware of changes that have taken place; 3) conveying understanding, acceptance, and respect for the patient; 4) using forms of expression that show that the therapist feels a "we" bond with the patient; 5) helping to develop the patient's ability to do what is in his or her best interests; and 6) finding the patient's strengths, including areas of competence and effective defenses, and then supporting them.

As an example of the last point, the following is an excerpt from a session in which the patient tells about trying to get a job and the therapist explores with the patient anything that might interfere with these endeavors.

P: So I got a job in this pizza pie place starting next week.
T: Oh, you do?
P: Yeah.
T: Oh, good! That starts on Monday?
P: Tuesday.
T: You'll be working nights?
P: Uh-huh, yeah.
T: What will you do?
P: Everything. Making hoagies, pizza pies, whatever.
T: Is it near your house?
P: Yeah.
T: So—what do you think? Are you happy about getting it?
P: Yeah! It's something to keep me occupied.
T: Congratulations! That's good. You've been looking around for work.
P: Yeah. It's something to keep me busy.

Another example of bolstering areas of competence is recognizing and supporting the continued reliance of the patient on self-control.

P: It [methadone] wears off in the early part of the morning. I'd start to feel not myself. I'd say, you're going to get it this afternoon. Don't worry about it. You know, it's there.
T: How did you do on the weekend [with take-homes]? Did you wait 'til afternoon to take them?

P: Yeah, every day. I'd take my medicine every day at 3 o'clock in the afternoon. I got up in the morning and didn't think about it.

T: A lot of self-control to do that.

P: That's what I'm basing my thing on: a lot of self-control. And it seems to be working. But like I said, not easy.

T: No, not at all.

P: You know it worked every day.

T: So you really kept to your schedule.

P: Yeah. I kept to it very well. If I can do that, you know—.

Expressive Techniques for Achieving Understanding

For a large part of the time that the therapist is engaged with the patient in a session, attention should be on the task of listening to what the patient is communicating, evaluating it, and then deciding how to communicate understanding. The process from the point of view of the therapist is an alternation of three phases: listening, understanding, and responding.

Listening. In this phase, attention is unreflective; it is just listening and not trying to fit the material to any special conceptual model. The type of listening in the first phase is the best preliminary for the next phase, which is understanding. After such listening, a shift then will occur to a more reflective, evaluative, understanding attitude as hunches and hypotheses develop.

Understanding. In using these techniques with drug-abusing patients, the therapist's mental set is toward finding the main theme of the patient's most important symptoms (usually related to drug-taking and vocational problems) and their interpersonal context. Some patients may be aware of the psychological conditions of their drug-taking when they first come for treatment. However, most are not. Two main ways are available to assist the patient in understanding the meaning of drug-taking as it relates to psychological symptoms: 1) eliciting the circumstances leading to the symptom, which might be the taking of the drug or the temptation to take the drug, and 2) exploring with the patient ways to recognize these circumstances and develop restraints on impulses to use drugs.

The way the therapist gains understanding of the intra- and interpersonal context for the patient's symptoms is mainly by learning of their place in the patient's central relationship pattern, the core conflictual relationship theme (Levine and Luborsky 1981; Luborsky et al. 1985). This theme contains within it the patient's relationship problems. It is prevalent within many different relationships, appearing again and again in the patient's communications about relationships in the present and in the past. It also appears in the treatment relationship with the therapist.

One of the best ways for the therapist to gain experience in identifying the core conflictual relationship theme is to review some sessions in terms of the patient's accounts of interactions with people. Each time the patient describes an interaction with another person, the therapist should attend to two main components: 1) the patient's wishes, needs, or intentions (e.g., "I wish or want something from the person)" and 2) the consequences of having these wishes, needs, or intentions, (e.g., "but I get upset" or "but I will be rejected" or "but I begin to feel down"). Doing this kind of analysis for a series of interactions with people will provide the therapist with an estimate of the most frequent wish and consequence combination (i.e., the core relationship theme).

One of the virtues of formulating the core relationship theme in terms of wish and consequence sequences is that it leads the patient and therapist to think in terms of faulty problem solutions. Drug taking is a prime example. After grasping the wish-consequence theme and thinking of the consequence (e.g., drug taking) in terms of a trial solution, further listening will then allow the patient and therapist to think of alternative solutions. It is usually best for the patient to come up with these trial solutions; if they are not labeled clearly by the patient that way, the therapist should do it. Theoretically, there are always many possible solutions; practically, it may be difficult to tell which type of solution is the one the patient can and will try.

In getting a rounded picture of the main theme, it is valuable to understand how it appears in three spheres: 1) current relationships inside the treatment, 2) current relationships outside the treatment, and 3) past relationships. The therapist should always try to attend to when pattern of relationships with people mirrors the relationship with the therapist. It is not that the therapist will necessarily express this understanding to the patient, although under some conditions this might occur. Understanding of the relationship with the therapist, both its transference and real components, will be a helpful guide at times of crisis, especially if its onset is within one of the sessions, because its understanding might be found in the relationship with the therapist.

It will also help in understanding the patient to keep a sense of the past process of the treatment. The therapist tends to track this process on the basis of three time segments: 1) relationships within the present situation, 2) relationships of the present session and the immediately prior one, and 3) relationships of these two and the longer course of a series of sessions. It is often helpful to refresh one's memory where necessary just before the session by looking over notes on the themes of the last session or the last series of sessions.

Responding

Appropriate and timely responses to the patient's material are another very important part of therapy. Several principles that help guide the therapist's response are described here briefly and in more detail by Luborsky (1977, 1984).

Choice of response.   many of the therapist's responses should be chosen because of their congruence with some aspect of either the context for drug taking and other main symptoms or the core conflictual relationship theme.

The therapist's responses in the following example, taken from a psychotherapy session with a methadone-maintained addict, were selected because they fit with this principle:

> P: You don't get your true recognition because they think "once a junkie, always a junkie." And they always think you're trying to connive and trying to do something, you know. It's not what some person does, like, it's just what goes along with the whole character. They generalize that you are the same as them [other addicts] but, you know, it's hard to generalize everyone in one category. Everybody isn't the same. But they do, you know. They give you the runaround a lot of times. "We'll see about this," "we'll see," "we'll see." I think "Ah, man, the hell with it. Why should I even bother anymore." But then I say to myself, "If I didn't bother—but there's always the chance that I'll get it [a take-home]." There's always that little chance, a hope, you know.
>
> T: Yeah.
>
> P: It makes me strive. But it seems like I'm never getting it, you know. I get upset. I get very—I start to get hostile.

T: Then you need to calm down and then you feel like you want to take some drugs to calm down. So I guess the pattern, if we try to make it more general, is you feel that people don't give you what you deserve. They don't recognize your accomplishments. You meet them halfway and they don't meet you halfway.

P: Right.

T: And then what happens is that you start getting angry about it and it makes you feel anxious you said. And then you end up really craving drugs even more, feeling like you really need something to calm down.

P: Yeah, right. And that turns into doing something.

T: And then you get angry with yourself for having done something. And it goes into a real circular thing.

P: Really. Yeah, really. And it ain't worth it, you know. Cause there's always that hope that I'll get the other take-home. One of these days it's gotta happen. But I feel like what else do I gotta do. You bring in your pay slips to show you're working and so on, keep your urines clean. I've been doing all that. I don't know what else I have to do.

T: So I guess when you start getting angry with one person, you end up angry with a lot of people.

P: Yeah, right.

T: And you feel like, I'm just going to go out and do something. I'm not going to come to therapy. I'm going to take drugs. You end up sort of hurting yourself. . . .

The wish, need, or intention in this case is: I want to be approved and recognized for my efforts and not criticized because they are deficient. The consequences are 1) responses from self: I get upset, I get angry, I take drugs, I keep trying in hopes of getting recognition, and 2) responses from others: I get criticized if I slip, people don't appreciate how hard I'm trying, people who know I'm an addict think very little of me.

The therapist's interpretations attempt to highlight these wish-consequence sequences with the aim of changing the patient's problematic response patterns.

Noting signs of progress in understanding.   Signs of progress may be evident in terms of achieving the goals as well as achieving understanding. Since many of the therapist's responses are guided by attention to the core relationship theme, even after a few sessions the main theme will become clearer to both therapist and patient. The therapist may then say to the patient at an appropriate time, "We begin to see the problem in your relationships, which you are trying to solve. It is . . . ." Such a formulation provides a renewed focus; it also increases the sense of progress.

Having patience.   From time to time the therapist should remember not to be tempted into responding before being certain of what is happening. The best way for the therapist to do this is to consider that it is not natural to understand consistently. Understanding comes periodically and unpredictably, not consistently and gradually. There is no point to responding just to respond or to imply that one is understanding before one really is.

After working together for a while, a parallel process will begin to appear in the patient, who will also be more tolerant of delays in understanding. It is a common observation that at times the patient will get discouraged by not understanding what he or she is expressing and will ask to have it explained. Usually within a short time after such a question, further listening by the patient and therapist will offer some of the answer.

Overcoming countertransference.   It is very easy to be drawn into certain kinds of negative or countertherapeutic responses to the patient. The first type might be called responding without sufficient reflection and understanding. This is usually based on becoming overly involved in the exchange with the patient so that it is hard to get the necessary distancing required for reviewing and understanding.

The second kind might be called the contagion of mood—if the patient is anxious, the therapist becomes anxious; if the patient is happy, the therapist becomes happy.

The third form of countertherapeutic response may be more common than has been realized: the therapist's responding in ways that fit into the patient's negative expectations (Singer and Luborsky 1977). For example, if the patient is communicating a great fear that people dominate him and tell him what to do, the therapist may unwittingly begin to do just that. Of course, the therapist is less vulnerable to these countertherapeutic responses if he or she observes a reasonable balance between listening involvement and reflective uninvolvement. In the latter, one would become aware of the main theme of the patient's fears and expectations and, therefore, have greater protection against fitting into them.

The fourth form is becoming angry or frustrated by the patient, especially when there has been a period of abstinence with subsequent relapse back to drug use. A variant of this response is feeling angry at attempts by the patient to manipulate the therapist. An example might be attempts by the patient to have the therapist undermine efforts of other staff to discipline the patient for behavior that violates the program rules.

A fifth form is becoming overprotective and aligning oneself with the patient in attempts to avoid appropriate discipline. Patients will often attempt to persuade the therapist to write a phoney note for the purpose of obtaining public assistance (e.g., to say that the patient is unable to work, when this is really untrue), to avoid legal consequences of illicit behavior, or to fabricate a story regarding why the patient missed work. It is important to be supportive yet accurate and honest in these situations. A simple explanation of what the therapist can and cannot do and why is usually sufficient.

Testing the "goodness" of a session.   One test of a good session that has worked well in practical applications is the matching-of-messages test. In reviewing a session, the therapist formulates the main message of the patient (which often is the same as the main relationship theme) based on the patient's total communication. Then the therapist reviews the session again to formulate the therapist's main response to the patient. A good session is one in which there is an adequate match between the two messages.

Dealing with Termination

The form of SE psychotherapy we have presented can be carried out as either time-limited or time-unlimited. The form used in the Veterans Administration Penn project was time-limited and the patient was kept adequately informed and aware of this. The choice of time-limited therapy for this project was based on practical as well as scientific considerations. Using this format, the patient often goes through all the phases of a longer treatment in a more condensed time and usually does not experience the ending of treatment as premature. The experience with time-limited psychotherapy is that since the patient and therapist know the time perspective, much of what would be done in a longer treatment gets shaped by the concept of available time. Despite the restricted time, there clearly is a beginning, middle, and end.

Furthermore, it is reassuring to therapists to realize that time-limited treatment is not necessarily less effective than time-unlimited treatment, at least as seen from reviews of available studies (Luborsky et al. 1975). However, it is usual to find a resurgence of initial problems within the weeks or months before termination. If the therapist deals with this by considering it an aspect of the patient's anticipation of the meaning of ending, usually the surge subsides and the patient reattains the gains that were made earlier. Occasionally, symptoms can become severe around termination, and extra efforts, including additional sessions, are necessary to reduce them.

Many patients naturally are interested in knowing whether the therapist wants to be kept up to date on their progress after termination. It is appropriate for the therapist to reveal such an interest. If the patient is engaged in an ongoing treatment program, the therapist may say when this comes up that news of how things are going would be welcome, and the therapist will hear this regularly from the patient's routine follow-ups. Such an exchange at the time of termination can contribute materially to the posttreatment maintenance of the treatment gains.

If at termination new goals are raised or if the old goals are not achievable in the time remaining and the patient wishes to continue treatment, the therapist should help with a referral. In time-limited therapy, the therapist may reevaluate these new goals and extend the treatment until both the therapist and patient feel that the desired progress has been achieved.

What Type of Substance Abusers Might Profit and How Might They Be Identified?

Data to answer this question are extremely limited. Psychotherapy is used extensively in many private and in some publicly funded substance abuse treatment programs, and some writers (Herrington et al. 1982) have stated that it is generally useful. Herrington et al.'s patients, however, were physicians who had been admitted to a comprehensive substance abuse treatment program that started with inpatient treatment and ended with long-term outpatient follow-up. About half of their patients were alcoholic and the rest were addicted to other substances, mainly narcotics or stimulants. Thus although encouraging, their data apply to a subset of the addict population and may not be generalizeable.

The largest study that provides data regarding who might benefit from psychotherapy with substance abusers was that done by Woody et al. (1983). This project compared outcome between methadone-maintained male veteran opiate addicts who received paraprofessional drug counseling with others who received drug counseling plus professional psychotherapy. It thus also deals with a subset of the overall addict population, like Herrington et al.s' (1982) work. Most patients in the therapy and counseling groups improved, but those who received the additional psychotherapy made more gains than those who received drug counseling alone. Overall, the standard program was effective, but psychotherapy generated additional benefits.

Closer examination of the data showed that patients who had few psychiatric symptoms in addition to their opiate dependence made substantial gains with drug counseling alone and that psychotherapy did not add significantly to their benefits. However, patients with moderate or especially high levels of psychiatric symptoms (most commonly anxiety and depression) had significantly better outcomes if they had the additional psychotherapy (Woody et al. 1985). Patients with antisocial personality disorder but no other psychiatric disorder made few gains with either drug counseling or psychotherapy (Woody et al. 1985). Furthermore, not all therapists produced comparable results. Some did much better than others, thus indicating that therapist qualities were important determinants of outcome (Luborsky et al. 1985). Those qualities that seemed most important were the ability of the therapist to form a helping relationship and the degree to which the therapist followed the specifications of the prescribed therapy. These findings suggest that psychotherapy is best reserved for the more psychiatrically symptomatic patients, but that outcome is a complex process that develops as an interaction between diagnosis, sociodemographic factors, and therapist qualities.

The finding that psychotherapy provides additional benefits for those patients having significant additional psychiatric problems also emerges from Rounsaville and Kleber's (1985b) review. The lack of impact that psychotherapy can provide to those with only antisocial personality disorder is also consistent with the experience of others (Shamsie 1981).

It is important to note that although studies generally find significant benefits from psychotherapy, there is little evidence that it "cures" addiction. The available evidence suggests the presence of somewhat fluid relationships between psychiatric symptoms and drug abuse, with one influencing the other. The studies, however, do provide cautiously optimistic data that psychotherapy can provide meaningful benefits beyond those generally attained, but probably only if it is integrated into other aspects of ongoing treatment programs.

Chapter 141

Behavioral Treatment of Drug Abuse

In this chapter we present drug abuse from a behavioral perspective and review the behavior therapy techniques available to assess and treat drug abuse. A behavioral perspective views drug self-administration as a learned response that is maintained primarily by the potent biologic reinforcing effects of drugs, with drug self-administration being the primary target of assessment and intervention.

The chapter will begin by presenting a behavioral model of drug abuse that helps us understand why this is such a pervasive and difficult-to-influence disorder. The principles and application of behavioral therapeutics will then be discussed, including behavioral assessment methods, treatment methods for suppressing undesirable drug-use behavior, and treatment methods for increasing desirable prosocial behaviors. Two types of behavioral interventions will be emphasized as particularly suitable for application with drug abusers: 1) skills training techniques that address adaptive response deficits and 2) contingency management techniques that enhance motivation for behavior change by arranging appropriate environmental consequences for different behavioral options. Other specifically focused behavioral techniques such as relaxation training or counterconditioning might be useful in individual cases where behavior analysis indicates a need. However, the bulk of experience with these techniques suggests that they are not necessary for the broad population of drug abusers.

Drugs as Reinforcers

Perhaps the most striking generality to emerge from behavioral pharmacology and drug-abuse research is that drugs can act as powerful biologic reinforcers in a manner analogous to food and sex. That is, drugs appear to serve as primary reinforcers, with little learning or conditioning required to establish reinforcing effects. Support for this behavioral model comes from the animal laboratory where it has been clearly demonstrated that rats, pigeons, dogs, and monkeys will, without any elaborate training or inducement, perform operant responses to obtain infusions of commonly abused drugs, including opiates, sedatives, and stimulants (Deneau et al. 1969; Johanson and Schuster 1982). Extension of the behavioral model to humans is supported by the striking cross-species similarities that have been noted between animal and human drug self-administration. A review by Griffiths et al. (1980) presented evidence for similarities in the types of drugs that are self-administered by human and nonhuman species, for similarities in patterns of drug intake, and for similarities in the environmental and pharmacologic factors that influence rates and patterns of self-administration. These striking cross-species similarities suggest that the excessive self-administration of certain substances is a biologically normal event, whose etiology and maintenance depend more on the potent reinforcing properties of drugs and less on unique characteristics of the individual than has been previously recognized. Further, drugs can act as reinforcers in animals in the absence of physical dependence (Kelleher and Goldberg 1975), which suggests that the pleasurable or reinforcing properties of drugs exist independently of the need to avoid unpleasant symptoms of withdrawal.

The fact that drugs can act as powerful reinforcers to maintain behavior implies that every human has the potential to become a substance abuser. This clearly does not happen. Rather, large individual differences exist in the amount, type, and pattern of drug use. The factors that determine whether a particular individual will become an abuser are as yet poorly understood. There may be biologic differences in susceptibility to reinforcing drug effects (Goodwin 1985; Schuckit 1985). Other influencing factors may include the availability of abusable substances, the behavior and attitudes of friends and family with regard to substance use, and concurrent involvement in other socially deviant behaviors (Yamaguchi and Kandel 1984). What does seem clear from observation of individuals entering treatment for drug abuse is that the drug reinforcer has by that time become a preeminent influence in their lives, as evidenced by an overriding concern with acquisition and effects of preferred drugs as well as repeated episodes of drug self-administration. In contrast, behavior of nonabusers is controlled to a much greater extent by acquisition of nondrug reinforcers, both material and social. Perhaps the most important difference between abusers and nonabusers is the extent to which the drug reinforcer has attained preeminence in their lives and control over their behavior.

Once drugs have been established as reinforcers, their influence over behavior can be pervasive and powerful. The potency of drug reinforcement is seen not only in the control it exerts over behavior during periods of regular use, but also in the extreme difficulty encountered when abusers try to terminate their drug use. Relapse to drug use is the most common sequela of an abstinence attempt, generally occurring within three months of abstinence initiation. This is a powerful and pervasive relationship that has been observed across a variety of specific substances of abuse (Hunt et al. 1971). Withdrawal symptoms that occur during the early stages of abstinence and that can be relieved by ingesting the drug certainly account for some of the relapse tendencies observed among abusers. However, withdrawal is probably not the only factor operating because relapse frequently occurs long after physiologic signs of withdrawal have abated. Behavioral research suggests that repeatedly reinforced responses are robust and not easily eliminated. Thus, for example, animal studies have shown that drug-reinforced behavior is rapidly responsive to the presence versus absence of reinforcement. Self-administration generally declines when reinforcement is eliminated, but responding is rapidly reestablished when reinforcement again becomes available (Griffiths et al. 1980). This suggests that people trying to remain abstinent must counteract a fundamental behavioral tendency for previously reinforced responding to recur under conditions of drug availability as well as a tendency for the reinforcer to regain rapid control over behavior once reexposure has occurred. This concept is relevant to an analysis of relapse because it suggests that reexposure to the drug reinforcer, especially after a period of deprivation introduced by an abstinence attempt, is very likely to precipitate further relapse.

Once drug-reinforced responding has been established and overlearned in a given individual, it is remarkably difficult to eliminate. Further, although different specific drugs of abuse may have very different biologic effects, experience to date suggests that these differences appear to have little influence on the nature of the behavioral problems of dependence and abuse. Rather, the behavioral processes involved in abuse and dependence and the techniques recommended for treatment are quite similar across a range of drugs that are pharmacologically diverse.

A behavioral model of drug abuse has implications for defining treatment goals, selecting treatment interventions, and evaluating treatment efficacy. From a behavioral perspective, the main goal of drug-abuse treatment is to eliminate behavior maintained by drug reinforcement. Simply reducing drug-reinforced behavior, although possibly an acceptable goal in some individual cases, is not likely to have a lasting impact due to the tendency of drug reinforcement to regain excessive control over behavior. Useful intervention techniques are those designed to suppress the target behavior of drug self-administration and to prevent relapse; techniques for increasing alternative prosocial behaviors may also be useful in some cases. A behavioral approach emphasizes the importance of using objective behavioral end points to characterize the disorder, to provide a target for intervention, and to provide a measure of progress toward treatment goals.

Assessment of Drug Abuse

Behavior therapy seeks to change specific targeted behaviors and utilizes repeated behavioral assessment to evaluate progress toward therapeutic goals. Behavioral assessment tries insofar as possible to sample behaviors in an objective manner, which lends itself to reliable and valid measurement across time, across situations, and across observers to characterize the frequency and patterns of maladaptive behaviors and the circumstances under which they occur. The primary techniques available for behavioral assessment of drug abuse are self-report and urinalysis testing.

Self-Report

Self-report, particularly in face-to-face interviewing, is the most widely used and frequently the most practical method for securing behavioral assessment information, especially historical information relating to drug use. There are no widely accepted standardized interviews for assessment of drug abuse, although the Addiction Severity Index (Kosten et al. 1983b; McLellan et al. 1980) provides some reasonable guidelines for conducting such interviews. Two general principles can be used to guide questioning about drug use. First, because multiple drug use is common among abusers, questions should be asked about use of drugs from all major pharmacologic classes (sedatives, stimulants, tranquilizers, narcotics, and hallucinogens). Alcohol and marijuana use are clearly important assessment topics because concurrent abuse of one or both of these substances may be common among abusers of other drugs. Where any use of pharmaceuticals is suspected, it is quite useful to conduct the interview using the product description section of the *Physicians Desk Reference*. Because patients will often identify drugs by nicknames or appearance, this facilitates accuracy in reporting the types and dosages of drug used. Secondly, questioning should be directed toward specific quantities and patterns of drug ingestion. A detailed review of drug use on each day of the previous week, for example, provides a concrete starting point. For each drug abused, the duration of abuse, typical recent quantities and frequencies, and patterns (e.g., regular versus binge) and circumstances (time, place, relation to other persons and activities) of use should be determined. Detailed drug-use information is useful for assessing the magnitude and chronicity of the drug-abuse problem and the precipitating circumstances of use. The information obtained can be used to design interventions that will counteract or remove the patient from precipitating circumstances.

Self-monitoring or self-recording is a second self-report method commonly used in behavioral assessment. This is essentially a diary-keeping technique in which the individual records each instance of the problem behavior, often along with accompanying circumstances and moods. Self-monitoring can be used to keep track in a quantitative and objective fashion of the patients' drug self-administration, including concurrent use of multiple substances. The circumstances and affect surrounding drug-use occasions can also be recorded. Boudin et al. (1977) provides an example of the use of the self-recording technique in drug abuse treatment. While self-recording can provide a very rich and detailed data set, it is useful only with highly cooperative and motivated subjects, which may exclude its utility with some socially deviant populations of drug abusers.

Behavioral Observation

Direct observation is a hallmark of behavioral assessment methodology. For example, observers might be sent to the home or the schoolroom to assess directly (e.g., with frequency counts) the nature and severity of a child's problem behaviors as well as the circumstances under which the behaviors occur. Direct observation can also take place during analog situations in a clinic setting (e.g., from behind a one-way mirror). Because drug abuse is a clandestine activity, therapists seldom have the opportunity to observe behavior directly. Collateral reports by friends, relatives, or co-workers can sometimes be a useful source of observational information. Observed intoxication or erratic behavior will often be the basis for drug-abuse treatment referral. In such cases, the therapist must confirm a drug-abuse diagnosis because erratic behavior can sometimes have other causes. Collateral report can also be useful during treatment, especially when denial or underreporting of drug use is suspected. However, one would not want to rely completely on collateral report for assessment information. Instead, toxicology testing provides a unique opportunity to obtain indirect objective evidence about the occurrence of recent drug use.

Biologic Testing

Urine is the specimen of choice when toxicology screening for drugs of abuse is performed. Urine is more easily collected than blood. In addition, because urine is a depot site for drug excretion, concentrations will be higher and detection will be possible for longer periods of time than is the case with blood samples. Further, analyses performed on blood may result in failure to detect some substances of abuse (due to short time course) or failure to discern metabolite patterns that are critical in drug identification. Thin-layer chromatography (TLC) is the most widely used analytic technique for urine drug screening. It is a broad spectrum test that can identify a wide variety of drugs during a single analytic procedure. Drugs typically detected include opiates, sedatives and phenothiazines, stimulants (including amphetamines and cocaine), benzodiazepines, antidepressants, and certain hallucinogens such as phencyclidine. Marijuana and its metabolites are not usually detected in standard TLC screens but can be if looked for. TLC testing is relatively inexpensive per drug screened. The assay is widely available through hospital chemistry laboratories or specialized analytic laboratories. TLC testing has a high degree of specificity; drugs within most pharmacologic classes can be individually identified. TLC testing also has a high degree of flexibility; procedures can be developed to improve sensitivity of testing for particular drugs (e.g., marijuana) that are not readily apparent in wide-range screening procedures.

A second urine testing method is the enzyme multiplied immunoassay test (EMIT). This semiquantitative testing method utilizes antigen-antibody reactions to detect the presence of specific drugs in blood or urine. Because antigen-antibody tests are highly specific, separate tests are often needed to detect each drug of interest. Tests for opiates (based on a morphine-specific reagent), methadone, barbiturate sedatives (based on a secobarbital-specific reagent), benzodiazepine tranquilizers (based on an oxazepam-specific reagent), cocaine, amphetamine, methaqualone, phencyclidine, propoxyphene, and cannabinoids are currently available. The opiate, barbiturate, and benzodiazepine tests have cross-reactivity with other compounds from the class but these are detected with less sensitivity than the compound used to develop the test. Because the equipment needed to conduct testing is commercially available, EMIT testing can be set up on-site at treatment clinics to provide virtually immediate feedback about recent drug use. The EMIT is particularly useful when a single drug class is the target of assessment and less useful as well as more expensive with polydrug abusers who may shift their specific drugs of abuse over time.

TLC and EMIT testing generally differ in sensitivity for detection of various drugs. For example, EMIT is generally more sensitive than TLC for cocaine, marijuana, opiates, and barbiturates; TLC is more sensitive for detection of a wide range of benzodiazepines. However, TLC testing is variable across laboratories, depending on specific reagents and extraction procedures employed. Users are advised to obtain current information about detection sensitivities from their laboratory to understand and use urine testing data correctly. Recently, as there has been increased use of toxicologic testing in the general population for prevention or detection of drug abuse (e.g., employee drug testing), there has been increased use of other more expensive but more precise testing procedures such as gas chromatography and mass spectrophotometry. Since information about frequencies, quantities, and circumstances of use is not obtained with urine testing, there may still be considerable reliance on self-report. However, toxicology screening is enormously useful in the treatment of drug abuse, both for initial assessment and for ongoing evaluation of progress during treatment.

Treatment of Drug Abuse

Once drug abuse has been identified and assessed, the primary goals of drug-abuse treatment are to eliminate behavior maintained by drug reinforcement and to prevent reinstatement of drug self-administration behavior after abstinence has been initiated. Although the type of drug being abused will determine the physiologic effects associated with self-administration and withdrawal, it will by and large not influence the type of treatment interventions recommended. The one exception is opiate abuse, where substitution treatment with methadone is a practical, accepted, and effective treatment modality. However, a substitution approach would be neither logical nor practical for many varieties of drug abuse such as alcohol, cocaine, and marijuana. Similarly, the magnitude and chronicity of the drug-abuse problem, while it may influence the prognosis of good treatment outcome, will not by and large influence the long-term abstinence goal of treatment or the methods used to achieve this goal. Thus the four behavioral methods discussed—1) behavioral counseling, 2) relapse prevention skills training, 3) stimulus counterconditioning, and 4) contingency management—can generally be applied across a wide range of specific drug abuse types and treatment situations.

Behavioral Counseling

Behavior therapy techniques have become generally accepted as a useful component of drug-abuse treatment programs, even though these programs may not be formally described as behavioral treatment. Environmental restructuring is often an important treatment element. For example, the therapist may note the circumstances that surround and appear to precipitate drug use and work to eliminate or remove the patient from these circumstances. If arguments with a parent or spouse are associated with episodes of drug use, then an attempt may be to teach the patient new ways to handle interpersonal conflict. If the patient spends time with drug-using friends, then ways to dissolve old social ties and form new ones with nonusers may be a focus of treatment. If contact with dealers is ordinarily frequent, the patient may be advised to move or change his or her telephone number to terminate this contact. A variety of self-control and motivation enhancement strategies may be used to help the patient remain drug-free. For example, patients who enter treatment having experienced negative social, financial, and health effects of chronic drug abuse will be encouraged to reestablish previously rewarding activities and to rehearse verbally the costs of use and the benefits of abstinence. The use of self-reward techniques such as self-praise and material purchases after periods of successful abstinence may be suggested. Finally, the social support of family members may be enlisted to bolster motivation.

An abstinence-oriented multimodal treatment program for cocaine abuse developed by Washton (1985, 1986b) exemplifies the combined use of behavioral and other traditional treatment approaches. Intensive (initially two to three times per week) urine and breath alcohol monitoring is used throughout treatment, serving both as an aid to self-control efforts and a measure of treatment success. Treatment contracting is utilized to bolster motivation for abstinence. At first, treatment availability is made contingent on abstinence. That is, patients are required to demonstrate abstinence from all drugs of abuse, in this case for a 30-day period, to gain entry into the formal treatment program. Patients who fail to achieve initial abstinence may have their probationary period extended; some are required to enter the hospital for inpatient detoxification treatment, an event that most patients wish to avoid. Following successful abstinence initiation, patients enter both professionally led recovery groups and individual psychotherapy. Cognitive-behavioral strategies designed to help patients cope with relapse temptations are taught as part of the treatment program, and environmental restructuring (e.g., changing telephone numbers to avoid contact with dealers) is often advocated. Treatment contracting continues during the second treatment phase. Patients agree to remain in treatment and continue urinalysis testing for at least six more months and also agree that during this time any evidence of drug use, including urine positives, treatment drop-out, or failure to make scheduled appointments, will result in notification of a significant other designated by the patient—usually a family member. After six to nine months of successful treatment, patients graduate into a seniors program where urinalysis testing is reduced to once monthly and therapy begins to focus on collateral problems that may not be directly related to drug use.

The program described above illustrates that behavioral techniques for achieving and maintaining abstinence are compatible with a variety of models concerning the etiology of drug abuse, including both behavioral or learning models and biologic or disease models. Given the difficult goal of promoting long-term abstinence, eclectic treatment programs recognize the importance of using techniques that are effective regardless of the conceptual or theoretical origins of those techniques. The advantage of a multimodal treatment approach is that it provides a rational and flexible system for individualized assessment and treatment delivery in which the behavior problems of the drug abuser are addressed from a variety of perspectives, one or more of which may be effective in promoting change.

Relapse Prevention Skills Training

Once drug use has been interrupted and the patient motivated to avoid future use, the focus of treatment becomes relapse prevention. Among the specific behavior therapies available for treatment of drug abuse, relapse prevention skills training is perhaps the most innovative and promising. In an attempt to understand the relapse process, Marlatt and Gordon (1980, 1985) interviewed recently treated abusers of heroin, cigarettes, and alcohol about the circumstances surrounding their relapse. Reported relapse circumstances were similar across all types of abused substances. Relapse was most frequently associated with negative emotional states and interpersonal conflict and next most frequently with social pressure to use. Initial relapse incidents were often accompanied by feelings of guilt and failure, which appeared to precipitate further relapse, a syndrome labeled the abstinence violation effect by Marlatt and Gordon (1980). This interview study suggested that it is possible to identify a cluster of common potential high-risk relapse circumstances that could be targeted during treatment. Additional research on relapse has shown that the use of either behavioral coping techniques such as delay, avoidance, and substitution, or the use of cognitive coping techniques such as verbal rehearsal, considering consequences and alternatives, and self-praise in the face of a relapse crisis, is associated with continued abstinence; the absence of any coping responses is associated with relapse (Shiffman 1982, 1984).

From this survey research on relapse, coping skills training interventions have been designed with the intent of teaching patients the behavioral and cognitive skills needed to prevent relapse during the long and perilous period following initial cessation. In relapse prevention training, the dangers of relapse are described, and patients are taught specific drug avoidance techniques and adaptive methods of coping with the emotional, interpersonal, and behavioral stimuli that may precipitate relapse. Specifically, patients may be encouraged to avoid circumstances where drugs will be readily available, make public commitments to abstinence, practice drug refusal skills, ask friends and relatives to deny any requests for drugs, and avoid contact with drug suppliers by moving or changing telephone numbers. Cognitive relabeling is an integral part of relapse prevention training designed to counteract the emotional component of the abstinence violation effect. Patients are taught to relabel relapse incidents as "slips" rather than failures, to recognize these as a natural part of the struggle to remain abstinent, and to view slips as the stimulus for increased utilization of coping responses rather than as a stimulus that sets the stage or provides an excuse for total relapse.

Evaluation of coping skills training interventions is still at an early stage. Two innovative aftercare programs designed to prevent relapse in opiate abusers have emphasized these skills training techniques (Catalano and Hawkins 1985; Hawkins et al. 1986; McAuliffe et al. 1985). Evaluation research has shown that drug abusers can learn new relapse prevention skills (e.g., Hawkins et al. 1986). What remains to be demonstrated, however, is generalization of training to the natural environment and beneficial effects on drug relapse outcomes.

Stimulus Counterconditioning

Wikler (1973) proposed that exposure to stimuli previously associated with drug self-administration can precipitate withdrawal-like physiologic responses that are interpreted as drug cravings and that lead to re-addiction. If such conditioned responses could be eliminated, then abusers might find it easier to remain abstinent in the face of exposure to drug-related stimuli. Two approaches, extinction and counterconditioning, have been tried in attempts to eliminate conditioned drug responses.

During classical extinction, responding must occur in the absence of reinforcement. This typically results in an initial increase or "burst" of responding, followed by gradual decline and eventual elimination of responding. In the case of drug abuse, reinforcement can be eliminated by pharmacologic blockade or self-administration of an inert substance. Studies with human opiate abusers (Mello et al. 1981; Meyer et al. 1976) have shown that opiate self-administration does not occur spontaneously during antagonist blockade treatment. Rather, subjects appeared to develop a rapid discrimination between the availability versus nonavailability of opioid drug effects and adjusted their behavior accordingly, only occasionally self-administering the drug to verify the presence of antagonist blockade. When the antagonist was discontinued, drug self-administration returned immediately. This is consistent with extensive animal laboratory and human data (Griffiths et al. 1980) indicating that neither prevention of the response nor temporary elimination of drug reinforcement lead to a lasting suppression of drug self-administration behavior.

It is possible that extinction treatment would be beneficial if abusers were required to perform nonreinforced drug self-administration during antagonist treatment. Studies by O'Brien et al. (1974, 1980) suggested that enforced extinction responding might be a potent intervention. Treatment participants maintained on an opiate antagonist were scheduled to practice repeatedly their usual opioid preparation ("cook-up") and self-injection ritual in the laboratory. In initial trials, patients found the procedure somewhat pleasant; over successive trials, however, the experience became progressively more aversive and ultimately unacceptable, resulting in study drop-out. It is possible that aversive reactions would be eliminated given sufficient practice with nonreinforced responding. However, even if demonstrable extinction could be achieved during treatment, the long-term efficacy of extinction treatment might be questioned on theoretical grounds since formally extinguished responding can be readily reinstated when the active reinforcer again becomes available.

The purpose of counterconditioning is to neutralize or change conditioned responses to internal stimuli (e.g., anxiety, craving) that may lead to drug use. Two specific techniques are available. In the first, relaxation training, patients are taught incompatible relaxation responses to be used in the presence of stressful or drug-related stimuli that normally elicit anxiety of craving. In the second, aversive counterconditioning, a presumptive noxious stimulus (e.g., electric shock, emetic medication, or an unpleasant thought such as the thought of vomiting) is repeatedly paired with either actual or imagined drug-related stimuli such as drug use locations, drug rituals, drug paraphernalia, and drug effects. The intent is to change the nature of the conditioned responses elicited by these drug-related stimuli so they become less likely to trigger drug use.

Although chemical aversion therapies have gained some degree of acceptance in the treatment of alcoholism (Neubuerger et al. 1982), previous reviews of both relaxation training (Hall 1983; Klajner et al. 1984) and aversive counterconditioning (Callner 1975; Stitzer et al. 1983) have concluded that there is little or no evidence demonstrating their utility in the treatment of drug abuse. In the case of relaxation training, it is often difficult to determine whether the technique has been properly learned and almost impossible to determine whether patients consistently practice the technique in appropriate situations. In the case of aversive counterconditioning, ethical concerns over the use of noxious stimuli lead frequently to the use of weak stimuli (e.g., imaginary events) that reduce the potency of treatment and hinder efficacy. Even if counterconditioning were successful, its impact might be expected to diminish over time, especially if the patient is reexposed to the drug reinforcer. Although there may be reason to use these techniques with individual patients where behavioral assessment indicates a need, there is at present no reason to believe that extinction, relaxation, or counterconditioning therapies are useful for the general population of drug abusers.

Contingency Management

Contingency management is a behavior therapy technique that organizes treatment delivery, sets specific objective behavioral goals, and attempts to structure the abuser's environment in a manner that is conducive to behavior change. In essence, a system of incentives and disincentives is set up designed to influence behavior by making abstinence relatively attractive and continued drug use relatively unattractive. By arranging appropriate consequences for different behavioral alternatives, contingency management provides motivation for behavior change. It should be noted that, in the case of drug abuse, contingency management therapy must counteract the reinforcing effects of drugs. This is not easy because the reinforcing effects of drugs are generally more potent, more immediate, and more readily available than are many other potential reinforcers in the abuser's environment.

Contingency management procedures have been applied with drug abusers in several settings that differ widely in the amount of contact they offer with drug-abusing patients and in the access they offer to programmatic reinforcers for use in contingent arrangements. Because contingency management is the most well developed and potentially effective behavioral treatment approach currently available, we will discuss its application in the three most common drug abuse treatment settings: residential therapeutic communities, methadone maintenance clinics, and outpatient drug-free treatment settings.

Application in residential treatment settings

Residential therapeutic communities, although not explicity designed as behavioral interventions, typically incorporate many behavioral elements in their operation. Therapeutic communities provide a highly structured social environment and intensive therapy component designed to produce a major change in the addict's life-style by eliminating drug-related and psychopathic behavior while promoting productive vocational and social involvement. Social reinforcement and punishment are used extensively to shape desired behaviors. Also, graded levels of status and privilege are available within the community and are earned by appropriate therapeutic progress (e.g., appropriate social interactions within the group, expressing commitments to a drug-free life, and making posttreatment plans compatible with this goal).

Although good treatment outcomes have been observed for the self-selected group of voluntary patients who spend several months in residential treatment (e.g., Bale et al. 1980), it seems clear that the most severe limitation to the widespread efficacy of therapeutic community treatment is its low acceptability to patients. For example, four therapeutic communities studied by Bale et al. (1980) designed for six-month enrollment lost half of their patients in less than two months, retained about 20 percent for six months and less than two percent of their patients for 12 months. Retention may be influenced by environmental circumstances. For example, several studies have suggested that criminal justice contingencies can increase the duration of residential treatment participation (Collins and Allison 1983; Copeman and Shaw 1976; Harford et al. 1976). Retention may also be influenced by program structure and the type of treatments employed. For example, Bale et al. (1984) found better retention and treatment outcome associated with programs that were highly structured and provided adequate patient monitoring and behavioral contingencies.

Application in methadone maintenance clinics

The methadone clinic provides unique opportunities to implement contingency management interventions with drug abusers. In methadone treatment, a population of chronic drug abusers living in the community report daily to a specified location to receive medication. This arrangement provides a structured basis for routine, frequent contact with drug abuse patients who have continued exposure to illicit drug availibility. Close monitoring of drug use via urinalysis can be conveniently carried out and is generally a routine part of treatment. Further, the treatment protocol, which includes dispensing of a mildly reinforcing drug (McCaul et al. 1982) in the context of a structured clinic operation, provides numerous opportunities for establishing contingencies that require positive behavior change as a condition of receiving treatment-related privileges and reinforcers. Listed below are examples of the privileges and reinforcers available at the methadone clinic for use in contingency management procedures:

- Continued treatment availability
- Take-home doses
- Clinic attendance frequency (e.g., once versus twice daily)
- Clinic attendance time
- Clinic-controlled dose alteration
- Patient-controlled dose alteration
- Reduced (or increased) counseling requirements
- Reduced (or increased) clinic fee requirements
- Reduced (or increased) urinalysis monitoring requirements
- Access to adjunct clinic services (legal, social, psychological)
- Access to prescribed adjunct medications
- Participation in clinic policy planning
- Provision of methadone for vacations away from the clinic

Not all of these potential reinforcers have been evaluated for their ability to alter behavior when offered in contingent arrangements. Continued treatment availability has been the most widely employed and most extensively evaluated reinforcer for contingency management interventions designed to suppress ongoing drug use during methadone treatment, while contingent take-home privileges have also received some evaluation.

Contingent treatment availability. Aversive control techniques are frequently seen as the treatment approach of choice with antisocial drug abuse patients whose successful treatment may require a high degree of structure and limit setting (McCarthy and Borders 1985). Further, withdrawal of existing reinforcers on evidence of drug use is frequently the most practical approach to contingency management treatment. Patients who are uncooperative with the program and continue supplemental drug use during treatment will typically have their privileges gradually restricted over a period of time. Eventually, patients may be given an ultimatum that requires dramatic immediate improvement (e.g., absence of any drug-positive urine tests after a specified date), with treatment termination being the consequence of failure to meet the requirements. Evaluation studies have shown that contingent treatment availability can be an effective motivator of behavior change.

Liebson et al. (1978), working with a group of methadone maintenance patients who were also chronic alcoholics, showed that continued availability of methadone treatment could be used to motivate concurrent participation in supervised disulfiram therapy. Under one study condition, patients were provided with disulfiram and urged to take it at home; under the contingent treatment condition, patients were required to ingest disulfiram each day at the clinic, with refusal resulting in detoxification and termination of methadone treatment. Study subjects performed much better on measures of abstinence and social functioning during participation in the contingent disulfiram condition than during participation in the control condition. In fact, the group of study subjects ended up spending much more time in the contingent (3,497 days) than in the control (1,634 days) condition because of a provision that control subjects would switch conditions if they showed evidence of heavy drinking. This was an important study because it demonstrated a highly effective and practical treatment approach to a pervasive clinical problem—the treatment of alcoholism among drug abuse patients.

Treatment termination contracting can also influence polydrug supplementation among methadone maintenance patients. In one study (Dolan et al. 1985), any drug use detected during a 30-day period resulted in the start of a gradual (average of 93 days) detoxification, with termination from the treatment program scheduled at the completion of the detoxification. Drug use was eliminated in about half (11 of 21) of the chronic abusers selected for the study and stayed well below baseline levels for these successful subjects during a 60-day postcontract evaluation period. Another study (McCarthy and Borders 1985) showed better outcomes on measures of treatment retention and drug use for patients who were required to have drug-free urines during one out of every four months of their first treatment year or risk treatment termination, as compared with usual care patients who did not have the treatment termination contingency.

Treatment termination contracting can produce dramatic improvement in some patients, but interpretation of the net benefit is difficult because patients forced to leave programs are likely to have worse outcomes when they are off methadone treatment than when they are in treatment (McGlothlin and Anglin 1981).

Take-home reinforcement.   Positive reinforcement procedures utilizing methadone take-home privileges may also be effective for promoting reduced drug supplementation during methadone treatment. In one study (Stitzer et al. 1982), chronic benzodiazepine abusers were offered a choice of reinforcers that included take-homes and money ($30 per week) if they provided benzodiazepine-free urine samples during twice-weekly testing. Reduced benzodiazepine use was noted in eight of 10 subjects during the contingent intervention while half of the subjects remained benzodiazepine-free throughout the three-month intervention. Take-homes were chosen on about half the occasions that reinforcers were earned; money was selected on the remaining occasions. A study by Milby et al. (1978) supports the value of a contingent take-home incentive for reducing supplemental drug use. When patients could earn take-home privileges by delivering drug-free urine samples for seven consecutive weeks, the number of patients delivering such long strings of drug-free urines doubled.

Treatment clinics typically authorize take-home and other privileges for long-standing clients as a reward for being employed, cooperative with clinic rules, and generally drug-free (as measured in urinalysis testing). By delivering these privileges as a reward to patients who are already functioning well, clinics fail to take full advantage of their therapeutic potential. Policies that allow poorly functioning patients to earn take-homes or other privileges for demonstrating concrete evidence of improved performance must be implemented to take advantage of the therapeutic potential of the methadone take-home privilege.

Application in nonresidential drug-free programs

Contingency contracting is the behavioral treatment technique most frequently used in nonresidential drug-free treatment settings. The behavioral objectives of treatment are specified in writing as are the consequences for drug use versus drug abstinence. Since there are few tangible reinforcers and penalties available in a drug-free treatment clinic for dispensing to patients, an increased reliance on therapist ingenuity or patient cooperation may be necessary to incorporate relevant and effective contingencies in contracting procedures. Suitable incentives can sometimes be found within the patient's work and interpersonal environment by involving employers, criminal justice monitors, or family and friends in the treatment process. Care must be taken, however, to ensure adequate documented patient consent prior to involving family and employers in treatment procedures.

Employment reinforcers. Under some circumstances, employers can be involved in treatment to monitor drug-abusing employees and deliver appropriate consequences. For example, partial loss of job privileges such as wages or vacation time might be arranged as a consequence of intoxication detected at the work site. Other positive incentives such as increased vacation time, monetary bonuses, or reductions in health care costs could also be offered based on improvements in work attendance (poor attendance being one of the most frequent signs of drug or alcohol abuse) or good cooperation with treatment. If the employer is unaware of the drug-abuse problem and cannot be directly involved in treatment, it may be possible to use employer notification as an aversive consequence of poor treatment performance. Such a program was developed by Crowley and co-workers for treatment of medical practitioners who were abusing primarily opiates or cocaine (Crowley 1984). At the start of treatment, each patient provided the therapist with a signed letter to their licensing board or employer describing the drug-abuse problem and voluntarily relinquishing the license or job because of continued drug abuse. The patient agreed via a written contract that the letter would be mailed by the therapist if drug use was detected during routine frequent urine monitoring. Thus the license loss contract functioned to change a likely negative consequence of long-term continued drug use to an immediate aversive consequence of relapse to drug use. Outcome evaluation based on 17 patients revealed that the potential loss of a professional license did not totally prevent relapse, but did appear to reduce greatly the frequency and severity of relapse incidents and to result in generally favorable outcomes.

Social reinforcers. Family and friends provide another potential source of reinforcers for use in contingency management. Is some ways, the family is an ideal locus for contingency management because family members usually have frequent close contact with the abuser and control a variety of both material and social reinforcers that could be dispensed in contingent arrangements. For example, the parents or spouses of drug abusers can be taught to reinforce abstinence with attention, praise, and material reinforcers (e.g., cooking favorite meals), while reacting to intoxication with limited social and physical contact, perhaps leaving the house or locking the patient out if this is warranted. With family involvement, of course, a host of communication and interaction issues will generally surface so that more traditional family therapy techniques might usefully be incorporated in treatment.

It is sometimes possible for the therapist to initiate social network changes that promote abstinence rather than drug use. Patients in therapy are routinely encouraged to break off relationships with drug-using friends and to establish closer ties with nondrug-using friends. Relocating in a new city is an extreme but effective strategy for improving drug-use outcomes (Maddox and Desmond 1982). In some recent experimental programs, drug abusers have been introduced to successful ex-addicts or community volunteers who are to serve as models and encourage drug-free activities in the community (Catalano and Hawkins 1985; McAuliffe et al. 1985). Drug-free friends might be formally involved in contingency contracts, although this is not a usual treatment approach. Finally, it may be beneficial to establish drug- and alcohol-free social clubs where social reinforcement can be obtained in a drug-free environment (Hunt and Azrin 1973).

Criminal justice reinforcers.   For patients who are being monitored by the criminal justice system, it may be possible to set up cooperative contingency management systems in which adequate treatment participation results in reduced parole-probation requirements and sentence time while treatment drop-out or poor performance results in intensified parole-probation monitoring and criminal justice sanctions such as incarceration and fines. Polakow and Doctor (1973, 1974) demonstrated that reduced probation time could be used as a reinforcer in a contingency contracting program for probationers with drug-related offenses. However, relapse-contingent incarceration programs have not been very effective, probably due to the long delay between detection of drug use and implementation of the consequence (McCabe et al. 1975; McGlothlin et al. 1977).

Security deposit reinforcers.   Involving family members and employers in contingency contracting may require more active outreach efforts on the part of the therapist than is generally considered desirable or cost-effective. It is sometimes possible, however, to obtain access to reinforcers and punishers directly from the patient. One example previously cited is the license relinquishing letters obtained by Crowley (1984) from his patients at the start of treatment. A more general example of this approach is security deposit contracting, in which the patient deposits with the therapist tangible items such as money, ownership deeds, or some other valued material goods. The deposit can be returned in portions as specified treatment goals are met or at the end of a specified time period. A program described by Boudin et al. (1977) for treatment of community drug abusers exemplifies the security deposit approach. Some patients were persuaded to deposit all earned money into a joint bank account held with the therapist; others gave up a valued possession to the program. In the case of joint bank accounts, a living allowance was paid by the therapist, with the amount contingent on treatment progress; and fines could be levied against the deposit if evidence of drug use or other contract violations were detected.

Community reinforcement model.   Hunt and Azrin (1973) described a community reinforcement program that may serve as the prototype for a comprehensive environmental contingency management program with drug-free patients. The program was implemented with a small group of 20 chronic alcoholics located at a state hospital treatment facility in a small midwestern town. Subjects were randomly assigned to usual aftercare or to a special intervention program that actively restructured the environment to prevent relapse. Jobs were located for unemployed patients and arrangements made with employers to send the worker home and dock pay if the patient were to show up at work intoxicated. Marital and family counseling was given. Couples were taught to define and reestablish mutually satisfying aspects of their relationship. Spouses were taught to reinforce abstinence and to limit social and physical contact in the case of intoxication. Surrogate or foster families were arranged for those who had no biologic families in the area. A nonalcoholic social club where sobriety was required for entry and where socializing could take place in the absence of alcohol was started for study participants. Finally, subjects were encouraged to become more integrated into the social life of the community by subscribing to newspapers, installing a telephone, and buying a radio or television. The six-month evaluation of this project showed greatly improved outcomes for subjects exposed to the community reinforcement program as compared with control subjects. For example, the average percentage of time drinking was 14 percent for community reinforcement versus 79 percent for usual care control subjects. Whether these good outcomes would persist over a longer-term follow-up period is not clear. It is also not clear whether the community reinforcement model could be successfully applied to drug abusers living in an urban environment where it may be more difficult to obtain control over environmental sources of reinforcement. Nevertheless, the community reinforcement approach provides a model that may be usefully applied in whole or in part with drug abusers.

Assessment of Collateral Behaviors

Once drug use has been eliminated and environmental controls for relapse prevention set in place, attention can be turned to collateral behavior problems of individual abusers that may or may not be directly related to their drug-abuse history. Since drug abusers may differ greatly on social competency and achievement, individualized assessment is essential for treatment planning. Only recently has an instrument been developed for use with drug-abuse patients that provides assessment information across the range of collateral behavior problems that may be encountered in this population (McLellan et al. 1980). The Addiction Severity Index uses information obtained during a face-to-face interview to derive a clinical rating problem severity in seven areas of patient functioning: 1) drug use, 2) alcohol use, 3) medical status, 4) legal involvement, 5) employment, 6) family-social relations, and 7) psychiatric status. The global rating scores derived from the employment and family-social test components are useful for identifying individual social competency problem areas. Once general problem areas have been identified, more detailed assessment of individual skills deficits can be conducted using self-report and observational techniques.

The most common form of detailed social competency assessment is informal direct observation of patients' interaction with the therapist or other treatment staff. For example, observation may reveal that a patient is chronically aggressive and argumentative or passive and underassertive. Similarly, the patients' reliability, punctuality, and the ability to follow rules and carry out assigned tasks can be assessed informally by observing his or her compliance with clinic rules or therapist requests. Such informal behavioral observations can be extremely useful, although they fail to provide standardized data that can be used to assess specific treatment needs.

Role-play performance in analog situations is the most useful formal observational assessment technique for assessing behavioral skills associated with social competence. A test developed by Callner and Ross (1978) to assess assertiveness skills in drug abusers will illustrate the technique. Their test, Behavioral Performance Situations, is comprised of 10 brief interpersonal vignettes that require the patient to respond assertively in each of five subject areas: 1) heterosexual interactions, 2) authority interactions, 3) giving and receiving positive feedback, 4) giving and receiving negative feedback, and 5) drug availability situations. To assess assertiveness, patient responses were audiotaped and then coded by trained raters for duration, fluency, and affect of response. By assessing across a range of analog social interaction situations, the nature (e.g., over- versus underassertiveness), extent, and situational generality of deficits can be identified.

A role-play test was also used by Hall et al. (1981a, 1981b) to assess job-interviewing skills in unemployed opiate abusers. Trained raters judged both the adequacy of information provided and the manner in which subjects presented themselves (e.g., posture, eye contact, speech fluency) during a simulated job interview. Another related assessment technique used by Platt and Spivack (1977) asks patients to solve hypothetical interpersonal problem situations presented in a story format. Patients are scored on the number and adequacy of problem-solving steps cited. This story-telling assessment method most likely evaluates the same sorts of skills as does role-playing while using a less personalized and anxiety-provoking procedure. The advantage of the role-play method, however, is that it more directly assesses the subjects ability to perform adaptive behaviors in problematic situations.

Treatment of Collateral Behaviors

In a review of behavior therapy for the treatment of interpersonal dysfunction, Bellack and Morrison (1982) pointed out that social interactions are the hub of human existence, mediating work, leisure, reproduction, and the securing of food and shelter. Thus adequate social skills would appear essential for developing a productive and satisfying life-style. For drug abusers, abstinence from drugs may also require adequate interpersonal skills to plan alternatives to drug-taking activities, to handle interactions with drug-using friends and suppliers, and to decline offers of drugs. Thus social skills may be critical for maintaining a drug-free as well as a satisfying life-style. Since drug-abuse patients exhibit a wide pretreatment range of social skills and social adjustment characteristics, skills levels may need to be individually assessed and skills training tailored to different subpopulations.

There have been several recent attempts to teach social competency skills to drug abusers (Hawkins et al. 1986; Platt et al. 1982). Hawkins et al. attempted to teach relapse prevention skills to abstinent opiate abusers; Platt et al. tried teaching general interpersonal problem-solving skills to methadone maintenance patients. Both programs showed that some skills had been learned, but neither was able to show any impact on measures of drug use. Two focused skills training programs have been developed for drug abusers to remediate employment-related skills deficits. Platt and Metzger (1985) applied their cognitive-behavioral problem-solving approach to unemployed opiate abusers. Hall et al. (1981a, 1981b) adapted a behavioral training approach to improve job-seeking skills among unemployed drug abusers. The Job Seekers' Workshop focuses on job application, job interviewing, and job-finding techniques. Role-playing with videotaped feedback is the primary treatment technique, and information networking is used to aid in job finding. In both of these employment programs, about 50 percent of the unemployed experimental subjects obtained jobs following treatment. The benefits of employment skills training programs may go beyond an economic impact on the patient; interpersonal and problem-solving skills may also generalize to other areas of life function.

An increase in prosocial behaviors is generally accepted as a desirable goal of drug-abuse treatment, but there are few guidelines concerning the particular behaviors that should be the focus of treatment interventions or concerning the timing of interventions for prosocial behavior development. The lack of guidelines is based on a lack of information about the role of prosocial behaviors in initiation and maintenance of drug abstinence. It is well known that patients with higher pretreatment levels of social stability and productivity have a better prognosis for successful resolution of their substance abuse problem during and after treatment (e.g., Gerard and Saenger 1966; McLellan 1983). However, it is not known whether improving prosocial behaviors in poorly functioning patients, if it can be accomplished, would improve the drug-abuse outcome prognosis, or which particular prosocial behaviors might be effective in this regard. In practice, the choice of prosocial target behaviors for therapeutic focus is often determined by program-wide policies (e.g., employment tends to be the top priority in methadone maintenance clinics) or determined by the existing resources and expertise available at the treatment site rather than by careful individualized assessment of specific behavioral deficits. Although there is little concrete information about the most productive timing and sequencing of treatment interventions, there appears to be general agreement in the treatment community that treatment of collateral behaviors should be delayed until after drug use is controlled or eliminated.

Conclusion

This chapter has reviewed the behavior therapy techniques that are available for the treatment of drug abuse and the drug abuser. Behavior therapy provides a valuable approach to assessment that incorporates direct observation and/or collection of objective data whenever possible as part of the assessment battery. A behavioral approach also advocates ongoing assessment of objective end points during treatment as a means of evaluating treatment progress. In the case of drug abuse, urinalysis testing has been widely accepted as the most useful measure of the primary treatment target: drug self-administration. Behavior therapy also offers two unique types of interventions for use in the treatment of drug abuse: skills training for teaching new behaviors including relapse prevention skills, and contingency management for arranging environmental consequences in a manner that discourages drug use and promotes alternative behaviors.

Behavior therapies are seldom used in isolation but have become generally accepted as useful components of multimodal treatment whose goal is long-term abstinence from illicit drug use with or without pharmacologic support (e.g., methadone maintenance). Relapse prevention training and contracting for continued treatment availability in particular are enjoying current popularity as treatment components in multimodal programs. Since there is little evidence to suggest that one type of treatment is superior to another, a multimodal approach may be the most practical one because the problems of the drug abuser will be addressed from a variety of perspectives, one or more of which may be effective in promoting change in a given individual.

Because drug abuse is a chronic relapsing disorder, it may ultimately be necessary to design treatments that continue to monitor and intervene with abusers over a prolonged period of time even after they have achieved apparently stable abstinence. The challenge of a long-term treatment approach would be integrating continued treatment into the life of the abuser to sustain efficacy. Behavior therapies would seem appropriate for this task. Contingency management systems such as those described in Hunt and Azrin's (1973) community reinforcement program are specifically designed to transfer treatment effects to the natural environment by establishing environmental contingencies that promote abstinence. Employers and families may be especially effective change agents if they can be taught to monitor the drug abuser and enforce the limits and consequences that can control behavior. Even when environmental controls have been set in place and the abuser appears to be stably abstinent, it might be useful for the treatment clinic to continue occasional urine monitoring over a prolonged (e.g., several years) posttreatment period. Any detected drug use could set the occasion for instigating renewed interventions that would bolster or correct failing environmental control systems.

Although these techniques hold great promise, there are several potential difficulties with the use of behavioral skills training and contingency management therapy approaches. First, therapists may lack training and expertise in delivery of behavioral techniques. This problem can be addressed by referral to structured training manuals and books describing behavioral therapy techniques. For example, a manual describing the Job Seekers' Workshop has been published (Hall et al. 1985). Similarly, there is at least one good book describing the application of contingency contracting techniques (DeRisi and Butz 1975). However, because drug abusers may be manipulative, deviant, and generally unmotivated for treatment, the talents of skilled and ingenious therapists may be needed to implement effective skills training and contingency management programs with this population. Thus there may be additional expense involved in hiring trained therapists to deliver treatment. If paraprofessional staff are used, there may be resistance to implementation of these techniques either because they are viewed as coercive or because they generally require increased effort on the part of therapists. This suggests that behavior management may be needed for staff as well as patients to ensure both enthusiasm and proficiency in treatment delivery. Treatment implementation may be hindered by insufficient funds for urine testing, especially in publicly supported clinics where reduced urine testing may be viewed as a cost-saving measure. Since adequate urine testing is essential for monitoring the target behavior being treated, this would appear to be a false economy. As far as the ethics of particular treatments are concerned, these must be judged in terms of effects on behavior. In the case of drug abuse, because we are dealing with a behavior problem that is very resistant to treatment and damaging to the patient, all effective treatments deserve consideration.

If drug abusers always eliminated their self-administration behaviors during and after treatment episodes, then the magnitude of the continuing drug-abuse problem would rest only on treatment enrollment variables. The efficacy of all currently available treatments is limited, however, by their imperfect ability to exert control over substance self-administration behaviors. As previously discussed, drugs are potent reinforcers that tend to gain control over large portions of the abusers' behavior; these strongly maintained drug-reinforced behaviors are not easy to eliminate. Further, abusers tend to seek treatment only after the problem has been chronic for many years and generally after associated legal, employment, and/or family problems have developed. Thus although treatment can have demonstrable benefits on drug-use outcomes, especially over the short-term, permanent abstinence from the abused drug along with complete social rehabilitation is achieved in only a minority of patients. Nevertheless, the current state of our knowledge suggests that the efficacy of existing medical (e.g., methadone maintenance) and counseling treatments may be improved by incorporating behavior therapies that offer unique advantages in the areas of assessment, skills training, and behavior management.

References

Section 13
Psychoactive Substance Use Disorders (Not Alcohol)

Abelson HI, Miller JD: A decade of trends in cocaine use in the household population, in Cocaine Use in America: Epidemiologic and Clinical Perspectives. NIDA Research Monograph 61. Edited by Adams EH, Kozel NJ. Rockville, Md, Department of Health and Human Services, 1985

Abrams J: A cognitive behavioral versus nondirective group treatment program for opioid addicted persons: an adjunct to methadone maintenance. Int J Addict 14:503–511, 1979

Adams EH, Durell J: Cocaine: a growing public health problem, in Cocaine: Pharmacology, Effects, and Treatment of Abuse. NIDA Research Monograph 50. Edited by Grabowski J. Rockville, Md, Department of Health and Human Services, 1984, pp 9–14

Adams EH, Kozel NJ (eds): Cocaine use in America: introduction and overview, in Cocaine Use in America: Epidemiologic and Clinical Perspectives. NIDA Research Monograph 61. Edited by Adams EH, Kozel NJ. Rockville, Md, Department of Health and Human Services, 1985

Adams EH, Gfroerer JC, Rouse BA, et al: Trends in prevalence and consequences of cocaine use. Adv Alcohol Subst Abuse 6:49–71, 1987

Akil H, Watson SJ, Young E, et al: Endogenous opioids: biology and function. Annu Rev Neurosci 7:223–255, 1984

American Medical Association: Failure to diagnose barbiturate intoxication The Citation 24:22–23, 1971

American Psychiatric Association: Diagnostic and Statistical Manual of Mental Disorders, 3rd ed. Washington, DC, American Psychiatric Association, 1980

American Psychiatric Association: Diagnostic and Statistical Manual of Mental Disorders, 3rd ed, revised. Washington, DC, American Psychiatric Association, 1987

Anderson CM, Stewart S: Mastering Resistance: A Practical Guide to Family Therapy. New York, Guilford Press, 1983

Anglin MD, McGlothlin WH: Outcome of narcotic addict treatment in California, in Drug Abuse Treatment Evaluation: Strategies, Progress and Projects. NIDA Research Monograph 51. Edited by Tims FM, Ludford JP. Washington, DC, US Government Printing Office, 1984

Anglin MD, Brecht MC, Woodward JA, et al: An empirical study of maturing out: conditioned factors. Int J Addict 21:233–246, 1985

Anker AL, Crowley TJ: Use of contingency in speciality clinics for cocaine abuse, in Problems of Drug Dependence 1981. NIDA Research Monograph 41. Edited by Harris LS. Rockville, Md, Department of Health and Human Services, 1982, pp 452–459

Arndt IO, Cacciola JS, McLellan AT, et al: A re-evaluation of naltrexone toxicity in recovering opiate addicts, in Problems of Drug Dependence 1985. NIDA Research Monograph 67. Edited by Harris LS. Rockville, Md, US Department of Health and Human Services, 1986, p 525

Aronow R, Paul SD, Woolley PV, et al: Childhood poisoning: an unfortunate consequence of methadone availability. JAMA 219:321–324, 1972

Ausubel DP: Drug Addiction: Physiological and Sociological Aspects. New York, Random House, 1958

Ausubel DP: Causes and types of drug addiction: a psychosocial view. Psychiatr Q 35:523–531, 1961

Babor TF, Dolinsky Z, Rounsaville BJ, et al: Unitary versus multidimensional models of alcoholism treatment outcome: an empirical study. J Stud Alcohol 49:167–177, 1988

Baker EFW: LSD psychotherapy. Presented at the Second Conference on the Use of LSD in Psychotherapy. Amityville, NY, 7 May 1985

Bakkar CB: The clinical picture in hallucinogen intoxication. Hospital Medicine November 5:102–114, 1969

Bale RN: Outcome research in therapeutic communities for drug abusers: a critical review—1963–1975. Int J Addictions 14:1053–1074, 1979

Bale RN, Van Stone WW, Kuldau JM, et al: Therapeutic communities vs methadone maintenance. Arch Gen Psychiatry 37:179–193, 1980

Bale RN, Zarcone VP, Van Stone WW, et al: Three therapeutic communities. Arch Gen Psychiatry 41:185–191, 1984

Ball JC, Corty E, Petroski SP, et al: Medical services provided to 2394 patients at methadone programs in three states. Journal of Substance Abuse Treatment 3:203–209, 1986

Balster RH, Woolverton WH: Tolerance and dependence to phencyclidine, in PCP (Phencyclidine): Historical and Current Perspectives. Edited by Domino EF. Ann Arbor, Mich, NPP Books, 1981

Bandura A: Principles of Behavior Modification. New York, Holt, Rinehart, and Winston, 1969

Bandura A: Self-efficacy: toward a unifying theory of behavior change. Psychol Rev 84:191–215, 1977

Banerjee SP, Sharman VK, King-Cheung LS, et al: Cocaine and d-amphetamine induce changes in central B-adrenoceptor sensitivity: effects of acute and chronic drug treatment. Brain Res 175:119–130, 1979

Bant W: Diazepam withdrawal symptoms (letter). Br Med J 4:285, 1975

Barabasz AF, Baer L, Sheehan DV, et al: A three year clinical follow-up of hypnosis and REST for smoking: hypnotizability, absorbption and depression. Int J Clin Exp Hypn 34:169–181, 1986

Basalt RC: Disposition of Toxic Drugs and Chemicals in Man. Davis, Calif, Biomedical Publications, 1982

Bauman MH: Involving resistant family members in therapy, in Questions and Answers in the Practice of Family Therapy. Edited by Gurman A. New York, Guilford Press, 1981, pp 16–19

Beck AT, Ward CH, Mendelson M: An inventory for measuring depression. Arch Gen Psychiatry 4:461–471, 1961

Bell DS: The experimental reproduction of amphetamine psychosis. Arch Gen Psychiatry 127:1170–1175, 1970

Bellack AS, Morrison RL: Interpersonal dysfunction, in International Handbook of Behavior Modification and Therapy. Edited by Bellack AS, Hersen M, Kazdin EA. New York, Plenum, 1982

Benowitz NL: Biochemical measurements of tobacco consumption, in Measurement in the Analysis and Treatment of Smoking. NIDA Research Monograph 48. Edited by Grabowski J, Bell CS. Rockville, Md, Department of Health and Human Services, 1985

Berenson D: The therapist's relationship with couples with an alcoholic member, in

Family Therapy of Drug and Alcohol Abuse. Edited by Kaufman E, Kaufmann P. New York, Gardner Press, 1979, pp 233–242

Berlin RM, Conell LJ: Withdrawal symptoms after long-term treatment with therapeutic doses of flurazepam: a case report. Am J Psychiatry 140:488–490, 1983

Bernhardson G, Gunne LM: Forty six cases of psychosis in cannabis abusers. Int J Addict 7:9–16, 1972

Berzins J, Ross WF, English GE, et al: Subgroups among opiate addicts: a typological investigation. J Abnorm Psychol 83:65–73, 1974

Besser GM, Butler PWP, Landon J, et al: Influence of amphetamines on plasma corticosteroid and growth hormone levels in man. Br Med J 4:528–530, 1969

Best JA, Suedfeld P: Restricted environmental stimulation therapy and self-management in smoking cessation, in Restricted Environmental Stimulation. Edited by Suedfeld P. New York, Wiley Press, 1980

Bewley TH, James IP, LeFevre C, et al: Maintenance treatment of narcotic addicts (not British nor a system, but working now). Int J Addict 7:597–611, 1972

Biase DV: Daytop Miniversity: Advancement in Drug-Free Therapeutic Community Treatment. Evaluation Report No. 1-H81-DA-01911-01A1. Rockville, Md, National Institute on Drug Abuse, 1981

Bickel WK, Johnson RE, Stitzer ML, et al: A clinical trial of buprenorphine, I: comparison with methadone in the detoxification of heroin addicts, II: examination of its opioid blocking properties. NIDA Research Monograph 76, ed. Harris L. Problems of Drug Dependence 1986. DHHS Rockville, MD, 1987, pp 182–195

Billings AG, Moos RH: Social-environmental factors among light and heavy cigarette smokers: a controlled comparison with non-smokers. Addict Behav 8:381–391, 1983

Blachly PH: Progress report on the methadone blockade: treatment of heroin addicts in Portland. Northwest Med 69:172–176, 1970

Blachly PH et al: Titration of the opiate abstinence syndrome with naloxone, in Development in the Field of Drug Abuse. Edited by Senay EC. Cambridge, Mass, Schenkman, 1975

Blane HT: Psychotherapeutic approach, in The Biology of Alcoholism, vol 5. Edited by Kissen B, Begleiter H. New York, Plenum, 1977

Blanken AJ, Adams EH, Durell J. Drug abuse: implications and current trends. Psychol Med 1986

Bloom WA Jr, Sudderth EW: Methadone in New Orleans: patients, problems and police. Int J Addict 5:465–487, 1970

Blum A: Using athletes to push tobacco to children: snuff-dippin' cancer-lipped man. NY State J Med 83:1365–1367, 1983

Blume SB: Psychotherapy in the treatment of alcoholism, in Psychiatric Update: American Psychiatric Association Annual Review, vol 3. Edited by Grinspoon L. Washington, DC, American Psychiatric Press, 1984, pp 338–346

Bobo J, Gilchrist L: Urging the alcoholic client to quit smoking cigarettes. Addict Behav 8:297–305, 1983

Bolter A: Issues for inpatient treatment of chronic PCP abuse. Journal of Psychedelic Drugs 12:287–288, 1980

Borison RL, Hitri A, Klawans HL, et al: A new animal model for schizophrenia: behavioral and receptor binding studies, in Catecholamines: Basic and Clinical Frontiers. Edited by Usdin E. New York, Pergamon Press, 1979

Boudin HM: Contingency contracting as a therapeutic tool in the deceleration of amphetamine use. Behav Ther 3:604–608, 1972

Boudin HM, Valentine VE, Inghram RD, et al: Contingency contracting with drug abusers in the natural environment. Int J Addict 12:1–16, 1977

Bowden CL, Maddox JF, Esquivel M, et al: Methadone dispensing by community pharmacies. Am J Drug Alcohol Abuse 3:243–254, 1976

Bowen M: Family therapy and family group therapy, in Comprehensive Group Psychotherapy. Edited by Kaplan H, Sadock B. Baltimore, Williams and Wilkins, 1971

Bozarth MA, Wise RA: Anatomically distinct opiate receptor fields mediate reward and physical dependence. Science 22:516–517, 1984

Brady JV, Fotin RW, Fischman MW, et al: Behavioral interactions and the effects of marijuana. Alcohol, Drugs and Driving 2:93–103, 1986

Brahen LS, Henderson RK, Copone T, et al: Naltrexone treatment in a jail work-release program. J Clin Psychiatry 45:49, 1984

Brook RC, Whitehead IC: Drug-Free Therapeutic Community. New York, Human Sciences Press, 1980

Brown BS, DuPont RL, Bass UF, et al: Impact of a large-scale narcotics treatment program: a six month experience. Int J Addict 8:49–57, 1973

Brown BS, Watters JK, Iglehart AS: Methadone maintenance dosage levels and program retention. American Journal of Drug and Alcohol Abuse 9:129–139, 1982

Brown D, Fromm E: Hypnosis and Behavioral Medicine. Hillsdale, NJ, Lawrence Erlbaum Associates, 1987

Brown WA, Corrivieau P, Egert MH: Acute psychologic and neuroendocrine effects of dextroamphetamine and methylphenidate. Psychopharmacology 58:189–195, 1978

Brust JCM, Richter RW: Stroke associated with addiction to heroin. J Neurol Neurosurg Psych 39:194–199, 1976

Bry B, McKeon P, Pandina RJ: Extent of drug use as a function of number of risk factors. J Abnorm Psychol 91:273–279, 1982

Burling TA, Ziff DC: Tobacco smoking: a comparison between alcohol and drug abuse in patients. Addict Behav 13:185–190, 1988

Burt Associates, Inc: Drug Treatment in New York City and Washington, D.C.: Followup Studies. Washington, DC, US Government Printing Office, 1977

Bush MN, Rubenstein R, Hoffman I, et al: Spontaneous pneumomediastinum as a consequence of cocaine use. NY State J Med 4:618–619, 1984

Byck R: Cocaine Papers: Sigmund Freud. New York, Stonehill Publishing Co, 1974

Byck R: Cocaine use and research: three histories, in Cocaine: Clinical and Biobehavioral Aspects. Edited by Fisher S, Raskin A, Uhlenhuth EH. New York, Oxford Press, 1986

Cadoret RJ, Troughton E, O'Gorman TW, et al: An adoption study of genetic and environmental factors in drug abuse. Arch Gen Psychiatry 43:1131–1136, 1986

Callner DA: Behavioral treatment approaches to drug abuse: a critical review of the research. Psychol Bull 82:143–164, 1975

Callner DA, Ross SM: The assessment and training of assertive skills with drug addicts: a preliminary study. Int J Addict 13:227–239, 1978

Capone T, Brahen L, Condren R, et al: Retention and outcome in a narcotic antagonist treatment program. J Clin Psychol 42:825–833, 1986

Caracci G, Migoni P, Mukherjee S: Phencyclidine abuse and depression. Psychosomatics 24:932–933, 1983

Carlisi JA: Unique aspects of white ethnic drug use, in Youth Drug Abuse: Problems, Issues, and Treatment. Edited by Breschner G, Friedman A. Lexington, Mass, Lexington Books, 1979

Carroll JFX, Sobel B: Integrating mental health personnel and practices into a therapeutic community, in Therapeutic Communities for Addictions: Readings in Theory, Research, and Practice. Edited by De Leon G, Ziegenfuss J. Springfield, Ill, Charles C Thomas, 1986

Carter EF: Dental implications of narcotic addiction. Aust Dent J 23:308–310, 1978

Carter WE: Cannabis in Costa Rica: A Study of Chronic Marijuana Use. Philadelphia, Institute for the Study of Human Issues, 1980

Catalano RF, Hawkins JD: Project skills: preliminary results from a theoretically based aftercare experiment, in Progress in the Development of Cost-Effective Treatment for Drug Abusers. NIDA Research Monograph 58. Publication ADM 85-1401. Edited by Ashery RS. Washington, DC, US Government Printing Office, 1985

Centers for Disease Control: Epidemiologic aspects of the current outbreak of Kaposi's sarcoma and opportunistic infections. N Engl J Med 306:248–252, 1982

Chait LD, Fischman MW, Schuster CR: "Hangover" effects the morning after marijuana smoking. Drug Alcohol Depend 15:229–238, 1985

Chanda SK, Sharma VK, Banerjee SP: B-adrenoceptor sensitivity following psychotropic drug treatment, in Catecholamines: Basic and Clinical Frontiers. Edited by Usdin E. New York, Pergamon Press, 1979

Charney DS, Menkes DB, Heninger GR: Receptor sensitivity and the mechanism of action of antidepressant treatment. Arch Gen Psychiatry 38:1160–1180, 1981a

Charney DS, Sternberg DE, Kleber HD, et al: The clinical use of clonidine in abrupt withdrawal from methadone. Arch Gen Psychiatry 38:1273–1277, 1981b

Charney DS, Heninger GR, Kleber HD: The combined use of clonidine and naltrexone as a rapid, safe, and effective treatment of abrupt withdrawal from methadone. Am J Psychiatry 143:831–837, 1986

Chasnoff IG, Hatcher R, Burns WJ: Polydrug and methadone-addicted newborns: a continuum of impairment. Pediatrics 7:210–213, 1982

Chasnoff IJ, Burns WJ, Schnoll SH, et al: Cocaine use in pregnancy. N Engl J Med 313:666–669, 1985

Chein I, Gerard DL, Lee RS, et al: The Road to H. New York, Basic Books, 1964

Childress AR, McLellan AT, O'Brien CP: Conditioned responses in a methadone population. Journal of Substance Abuse Treatment 3:173–179, 1986

Chopra GS, Smith JW: Psychotic reactions following cannabis use in East Indians. Arch Gen Psychiatry 30:24–27, 1974

Christakis G, Stimmel B, Rabin J, et al: Nutritional status of heroin users enrolled in methadone maintenance. National Conference on Methadone Treatment Proceedings 1:494–500, 1973

Christian MA: Reproductive toxicity and teratology evaluation of naltrexone. J Clin Psychiatry 45:7, 1984

Cicero TJ, Bell RD, Wiest WG, et al: Function of the male sex organs in heroin and methadone users. N Engl J Med 292:882–887, 1975

Clarren SK, Smith DW: The fetal alcohol syndrome. N Engl J Med 98:1063, 1978

Clayton RR, Voss HL: Youth and Drugs in Manhattan: A Causal Analysis. NIDA Research Monograph 39. Publication ADM 81-1167. Washington, DC, US Government Printing Office, 1981

CODAP: Statistical Series, Trend Report 1976–1979. National Institute on Drug Abuse, DHHS Publication Series E No. 15, 1979

Cohen M et al: The effect of alcoholism in methadone maintained persons on productive activity: a randomized control trial. Alcoholism: Clinical and Experimental Research 6:358–361, 1982

Cohen S: The Substance Abuse Problems. New York, Haworth Press, 1981

Coleman SB: The family trajectory: a circular journey to drug abuse, in Family Factors and Substance Abuse. Edited by Ellis B. Rockville, Md, National Institute on Drug Abuse, 1979

Coleman SB, Stanton MD: The role of death in the addict family. Journal of Marriage and Family Counseling 4:79–91, 1979

Collins JJ, Allison M: Legal coercion and retention in drug abuse treatment. Hosp Community Psychiatry 34:1145–1149, 1983

Colpaert FC, Niemegeers CJ, Janssen PA. Discriminative stimulus properties of cocaine: neuropharmacological characteristics as derived from stimulus generalization experiments. Pharmacol Biochem Behav 10:535–546, 1979

Comptroller General of the United States: Report to the Congress, April 14, 1980. Action Needed to Improve Management and Effectiveness of Drug Abuse Treatment. Publication HRD-80-32. Rockville, Md, US General Accounting Office, 1980

Condiotte MM, Lichtenstein E: Self-efficacy and relapse in smoking cessation programs. J Consult Clin Psychol 49:648–658, 1981

Connell PH: Some observations concerning amphetamine misuse: its diagnosis, management, and treatment with special reference to research needs, in Drugs and Youth. Edited by Wittenborn JR, Brill H, Smith JP, et al. Springfield, Ill, Charles C Thomas, 1970

Connett G: Comparison of progress of patients with professional and paraprofessional counselors in a methadone maintenance program. Int J Addict 15:585–589, 1980

Copemann CD, Shaw PL: Effects of contingent management of addicts expecting commitment to a community based treatment program. Br J Addict 71:187–191, 1976

Covi L, Lipman RS, Pattison JH et al: Length of treatment with anxiolytic sedatives and response to their sudden withdrawal. Acta Psychiatr Scand 49:51–64, 1973

Craddock SG et al: Summary and implications: client characteristics, behaviors and intreatment outcome 1980 TOPS admission cohort. Research Triangle Institute Project 23U-1901, 1982

Craddock VM: Nitrosamines and human cancer: proof of an association? Nature 306:638, 1983

Cregler LL, Mark H: Relation of acute myocardial infarction to cocaine abuse. Am J Cardiol 56:794, 1985

Crowley TJ: Contingency contracting treatment of drug-abusing physicians, nurses, and dentists, in Behavioral Intervention Techniques in Drug Abuse Treatment. NIDA Research Monograph 46. Publication ADM 84-1282. Edited by Grabowski J, Stitzer ML, Henningfield JE. Washington, DC, US Government Printing Office, 1984

Crowley T, Wagner J, Zerbe G, et al: Naltrexone-induced dysphoria in former opioid addicts. Am J Psychiatry 142:1081–1084, 1985

Cumin R, Bonetti EP, Scherschlicht R, et al: Use of the specific benzodiazepine antagonist, Ro 15-1788, in studies of physiological dependence on benzodiazepines. Experientia 38:833–834, 1982

Cushman P Jr: Ten years of methadone maintenance treatment: some clinical observations. Am J Drug Alcohol Abuse 4:543–554, 1977

Cushman P: Detoxification after methadone maintenance, in Substance Abuse: Clinical Problems and Perspectives. Edited by Lowinson JH, Ruiz P. Baltimore, Williams and Wilkins, 1981

Dackis CA, Gold MS: Opiate addiction and depression: cause or effect? Drug Alcohol Depend 11:105–109, 1983

Dackis CA, Gold MS: Depression in opiate addicts, in Substance Abuse and Psychopathology. Edited by Mirin SM. Washington, DC, American Psychiatric Press, 1984, pp 19–40

Dackis CA, Gold MS: Bromocriptine as a treatment of cocaine abuse. Lancet 1:1151–1152, 1985a

Dackis CA, Gold MS: New concepts in cocaine addiction: the dopamine depletion hypothesis. Neurosci Biobehav Rev 9:469–477, 1985b

Dackis CA, Pottash ALC, Annitto W, et al: Persistence of urinary marijuana levels after supervised abstinence. Am J Psychiatry 139:1196–1198, 1982

Dackis CA, Pottash ALC, Gold MS, et al: The dexamethasone suppression test for major depression in opiate addicts. Am J Psychiatry 141:810–811, 1984a

Dackis CA, Gold MS, Estroff TW, et al: Hyperprolactinemia in cocaine abuse. Society for Neuroscience Abstract 10:1099, 1984b

Dackis CA, Estroff TW, Sweeney DR, et al: Specificity of the TRH test for major depression in patients with serious cocaine abuse. Am J Psychiatry 142:1097–1099, 1985

Daghestani AN: Phencyclidine: associated psychosis (letter). J Clin Psychiatry 49:9, 1987

Davidson V: Transference phenomena in the treatment of addictive illness: Love and hate in methadone maintenance. NIDA Research Monograph 12. Rockville, Md, US Department of Health and Human Services, 1977, pp 118–126

Davis JR, Glaros AG: Relapse prevention and smoking cessation. Addict Behav 11:105–114, 1986

Dawley HH, Carroll S, Morrison J: A comparison of hospitalized veteran's attitudes toward smoking and smoking cessation over a four-year period. Addict Behav 5:241–245, 1980

De Angelis GG, Goldstein E: Treatment of adolescent phencyclidine (PCP) abusers. Am J Drug Alcohol Abuse 5:399–414, 1978

Deitch D: Treatment of Drug Abuse in the Therapeutic Community: Historical Influences, Current Considerations and Future Outlooks. National Commission on Marihuana and Drug Abuse, IV, US Govt. Printing Office, Washington DC, 1972, pp 158–175

De Leon G: Psychological and Socio-Demographic Profiles. Final Report of Phoenix House Project Activities. Grant DA-00831-01. Rockville, Md, National Institute on Drug Abuse, 1976

De Leon G: Therapeutic Communities: Training Self-Evaluation. Final Report of Project Activities. Grant 1-H81-DA-01976. Rockville, Md, National Institute on Drug Abuse, 1980

De Leon G: The role of rehabilitation, in Drug Abuse in the Modern World: A Perspective for the Eighties. Edited by Nahas G, Frick HC. New York, Pergamon Press, 1981

De Leon G: The Therapeutic Community: Study of Effectiveness. Treatment Research Monograph Series ADM 84-1286. Rockville, Md, National Institute on Drug Abuse, 1984

De Leon G: The therapeutic community: status and evolution. Int J Addict 20:823–844, 1985

De Leon G: The Therapeutic Community Approach: A Guide to Principles and Practices, in preparation, 1988

De Leon G, Deitch D: Treatment of the adolescent substance abuser in a therapeutic community, in Treatment Services for Adolescent Substance Abusers. Edited by Friedman A, Beschner G. ADM 85-1342. Rockville, Md, 1985

De Leon G, Jainchill N: Male and female drug abusers: social and psychological status two years after treatment in a therapeutic community. Am J Drug Alcohol Abuse 8:465–497, 1981

De Leon G, Rosenthal MS. Therapeutic communities, in Handbook on Drug Abuse. Edited by Dupont R, Goldstein A, O'Donnell J. Rockville, Md, National Institute on Drug Abuse, 1979, pp 39–47

De Leon G, Schwartz S: The therapeutic community: what are the retention rates? Journal of Drug and Alcohol Abuse 10:267–284, 1984

De Leon G, Ziegenfuss J (eds): Therapeutic Communities for Addictions: Readings in Theory, Research and Practice. Springfield, Ill, Charles C Thomas, 1986

De Leon G, Skodol A, Rosenthal MS: The Phoenix therapeutic community for drug addicts: changes in psychopathological signs. Arch Gen Psychiatry 23:131–135, 1973

De Leon G, Jainchill N, Kornreich B, et al: Trends in psychopathology among substance abusers. Presented to the Tenth World Conference of Therapeutic Communities, 1986

Deneau G, Yanagita T, Seevers MH: Self-administration of psychoactive substances in the monkey: a measure of psychological dependence. Psychopharmacology 16:30–48, 1969

DeRisi WJ, Butz G: Writing Behavioral Contracts: A Case Simulation Practice Manual. Champaign, Ill, Research Press, 1975

Derogatis LR: SCL-90-R: Administration Scoring and Procedures Manual I. Baltimore, Clinical Psychometrics Research, 1977

Desmond DP: Effectiveness of psychotherapeutic counselling in methadone maintenance. Drug Alcohol Depend 4:439–447, 1979

Dishotsky NI, Laughman WD, Mogar RE, et al: LSD and genetic damage. Science 172:431–440, 1971

Dobbs WH: Methadone treatment of heroin addicts: early results provide more questions than answers. JAMA 218:1536–1541, 1971

Dolan MP, Black JL, Penk WE, et al: Contracting for treatment termination to reduce illicit drug use among methadone maintenance treatment failures. J Consult Clin Psychol 53:549–551, 1985

Dole VP, Joseph H: Long-term outcome of patients treated with methadone. Ann NY Acad Sci 311:181–187, 1978

Dole VP, Nyswander ME: A medical treatment of diacetylmorphine (heroin) addiction. JAMA 193:646–650, 1965

Dole VP, Nyswander ME: Heroin addiction: a metabolic disease. Arch Intern Med 120:19–24, 1967

Dole VP, Nyswander ME: The use of methadone for narcotic blockade. Br J Addict 63:55–57, 1968

Dupont RL, Green MH: The decline of heroin addiction in the District of Columbia. National Conference on Methadone Treatment Proceedings 2:1474–1483, 1973

Edwards G: The alcohol dependence syndrome: a concept as stimulus to enquiry. Br J Addict 81:171–183, 1986

Edwards G, Gross MM: Alcohol dependence: provisional description of a clinical syndrome. Br Med J 1:1058–1061, 1976

Edwards G, Arif A, Hodgson R: Nomenclature and classification of drug and alcohol related problems. Bull WHO 59:225–242, 1981

Ehrlich P, McGeehan M: Cocaine recovery support groups and the language of recovery. J Psychoactive Drugs 17:11–17, 1985

Elkin I: Results of the NIMH depression collaborative study. Presented at the Annual Meeting of the Society for Psychotherapy Research. Wellesley, Mass, June 1986

Ellingboe J, Mendelson JH, Kuehnle JC: Effects of heroin and naltrexone on plasma prolactin levels in man. Pharmacol Biochem Behav 12:163–165, 1980

Ellinwood EH: Amphetamine psychosis, I: description of the individuals and process. J Nerv Ment Dis 144:273–283, 1967

Ellinwood EH: Assault and homicide associated with amphetamine abuse. Am J Psychiatry 127:1170–1175, 1970

Ellinwood EH: The epidemiology of stimulant abuse, in Drug Use: Epidemiological and Sociological Approaches. Edited by Josephson F, Carroll E. Washington, DC, Hemisphere Press, 1974, pp 303–329

Ellinwood EH, Petrie WM: Dependence on amphetamine, cocaine and other stimulants, in Drug Abuse: Clinical and Basic Aspects. Edited by Pradhan SN. New York, CV Mosby Co, 1977, pp 248–262

Endicott J, Spitzer RL, Fleiss JL, et al: A diagnostic schedule for affective disorders and schizophrenia. Arch Gen Psychiatry 37:837–844, 1978

Eriksson M, Larsson G, Zetterstrom R: Amphetamine addiction and pregnancy. Acta Obstet Gynecol Scand 660:253–259, 1981

Estroff TW, Gold MS: Psychiatric misdiagnosis, in Carman JS (eds): Advances in Psychopharmacology: Predicting and Improving Treatment Response. Edited by Gold MS, Lydiard RB, Carman JS. Boca Raton, Fla, CRC Press, 1984, pp 34–66

Estroff TW, Dackis CA, Sweeney DR, et al: Drug abuse and coexistent bipolar disorder. Presented at the 1984 American Psychiatric Association Meeting. Los Angeles, California, 1984

Ettenburg A, Pettit H, Bloom F, et al: Heroin and cocaine intravenous self-administration in rats: mediation by separate neural systems. Psychopharmacology 78:204, 1982

Extein I, Pottash ALC, Gold MS, et al: Using the protirelin test to distinguish mania from schizophrenia. Arch Gen Psychiatry 39:77–81, 1982

Fagerstrom KO: Measuring degree of physical dependency to tobacco smoking with reference to individualization of treatment. Addict Behav 3:235–241, 1978

Fallon RH, Boyd JL, McGill CW, et al: Family management in the prevention of exacerbations of schizophrenia. N Engl J Med 306:1437–1440, 1982

Farberow NL (ed): The Many Faces of Suicide: Indirect Self-Destructive Behaviors. New York, McGraw-Hill, 1980

Fielding JE: Smoking: health effects and control. N Engl J Med 313:491–498, 1985

Fields HA, Bradley DW, Maynard JE: Non A/Non B hepatitis detection methodology: a review. The Ligand Quarterly 5:28–32, 1982

Fink M, Itil TM: Neurophysiology of phantastica: EEG and behavioral relations in man, in Psychopharmacology: A Review of Progress 1957–1967. Edited by Efrom DH. Washington, DC, US Department of Health, Education and Welfare, 1968

Finnegan LP (ed): Drug Dependence in Pregnancy: Clinical Management of Mother and Child. Publication ADM 79-678. Rockville, Md, US Department of Health, Education and Welfare, 1979a

Finnegan LP: Pathophysiological and behavioural effects of the transplacental transfer of narcotic drugs to the foetuses and neonates of narcotic dependent mothers. Bull Narc 31:1–58, 1979b

Finnegan LP: Women in treatment, in Handbook on Drug Abuse. Edited by Dupont RL, Goldstein A, O'Donnell J. Washington, DC, US Government Printing Office, 1979c

Finnegan LP, Michael H, Leifer B, et al: An evaluation of neonatal abstinence treatment modalities, in Problems on Drug Dependence, 1983. NIDA Research Monograph 49. Publication ADM 84-1316. Edited by Harris LS. Washington, DC, US Government Printing Office, 1984

Fischman MW, Schuster CR, Resnekov I, et al: Cardiovascular and subjective effects of intravenous cocaine administration in humans. Arch Gen Psychiatry 10:535–546, 1976

Fishel R, Hamamoto G, Barbul A, et al: Cocaine colitis: is this a new syndrome? Dis Colon Rectum 28:264–266, 1985

Fishman HC, Stanton MD, Rossman BL: Treating families of adolescent drug abusers, in The Family Therapy of Drug Abuse and Addiction. Edited by Stanton M, Todd T. New York, Guilford Press, 1982

Foxx RM, Brown RA: Nicotine fading and self-monitoring for cigarette abstinence or controlled smoking. J Appl Behav Anal 12:111–125, 1979

Framo JL: Integration of marital therapy with sessions with family of origin, in Handbook of Family Therapy. Edited by Gurman AJ, Kniskern DP. New York, Brunner Mazel, 1981, pp 133–158

Fraser HF, Shaver MR, Maxwell ES, et al: Fatal termination of barbiturate abstinence syndrome in man. J Pharmacol Exp Ther 106:387, 1952

Freud S: Uber Coca. Central BL Ges Therap 2:289–314, 1884

Friberg TR, Gragoudas ES, Regan CDJ: Talc emboli and macular ischemia in intravenous drug abuse. Arch Ophthalmol 97:1089–1091, 1979

Galanter M: Psychotherapy for alcohol and drug abuse: an approach based on learning theory. Journal of Psychiatric Treatment and Evaluation 5:551–556, 1983

Gallant D: PCP: clinical and laboratory diagnostic problems, in PCP (Phencyclidine): Historical and Current Perspectives. Edited by Domino EF. Ann Arbor, Mich, NPP Books, 1981

Gaston EH: Solving the smoking problem on a chronic ward. Journal of Psychiatric Treatment Evaluation 4:397–401, 1982

Gawin FH: Drugs and Eros: reflections on aphrodisiacs. J Psychoactive Drugs 10:227–235, 1978

Gawin FH: Cocaine: psychiatric update. Presented at the 139th Meeting of the American Psychiatric Association. Washington, DC, 15 May 1986a

Gawin FH: Neuroleptic blockade of cocaine induced paranoia but not euphoria. Psychopharmacology 90:142–143, 1986b

Gawin FH, Ellinwood EH: Stimulants: actions, abuse, and treatment. N Engl J Med 318:1173–1183, 1988

Gawin FH, Kleber HD: Cocaine abuse treatment: open pilot trial with desipramine and lithium carbonate. Arch Gen Psychiatry 42:903–910, 1984

Gawin FH, Kleber HD: Cocaine abuse in a treatment population: patterns and diagnostic distractions, in Cocaine Use in America: Epidemiologic and Clinical Perspectives. NIDA Research Monograph 61. Edited by Adams EH, Kozel NJ. Rockville, Md, Department of Health and Human Services, 1985a, pp 182–192

Gawin FH, Kleber HD: Neuroendocrine findings in chronic cocaine abusers. Br J Psychiatry 147:569–573, 1985b

Gawin FH, Kleber HD: Abstinence symptomatology and psychiatric diagnosis in cocaine abusers. Arch Gen Psychiatry 43:107–113, 1986a

Gawin FH, Kleber HD: Pharmacological treatment of cocaine abuse. Psychiatr Clin North Am 9:573–583, 1986b

Gawin FH, Byck R, Kleber HD: Double-blind comparison of desipramine and placebo in chronic cocaine abusers. Presented at the 24th Meeting of the American College of Neuropharmacology. Kaanapali, Hawaii, 13 December 1985a

Gawin F, Riordan C, Kleber HD: Methylphenidate use in non-ADD cocaine abusers: a negative study. Am J Drug Alcohol Abuse 11:193–197, 1985b

Gay GR: Clinical management of acute and toxic cocaine poisoning. Ann Emerg Med 11:562–572, 1982

Gearing FR, Schweitzer MD: An epidemiologic evaluation of long-term methadone maintenance treatment for heroin addiction. Am J Epidemiol 100:101–112, 1974

Gerard DL, Saenger G: Out-Patient Treatment of Alcoholism. Toronto, University of Toronto Press, 1966

Giannini AJ, Malone DA, Giannini MC, et al: Treatment of depression in chronic cocaine and phencyclidine abuse with desipramine. J Clin Pharmacol 26:211–214, 1986

Ginzburg HM, Allison M, Hubbard RL: Depressive symptoms in drug abuse treatment clients: correlates, treatment and changes, in Problems of Drug Dependence, 1983. NIDA Research Monograph 49. Publication ADM 84-1316. Edited by Harris LS. Washington, DC, US Government Printing Office, 1984

Glassman AH, Jackson WK, Walsh BT: Cigarette craving, smoking withdrawal, and clonidine. Science 226:864–866, 1984

Goeders NE, Smith JE: Cortical dopaminergic involvement in cocaine reinforcement. Science 253:195–203, 1982

Gold MS, Estroff TW: The comprehensive evaluation of cocaine and opiate abusers, in Handbook of Psychiatric Diagnostic Procedures, vol 2. Edited by Hall RCW, Beresford TP. Jamaica, NY, Spectrum Publications, 1985, pp 213–230

Gold MS, Rea WS: The role of endorphins in opiate addiction, opiate withdrawal, and recovery. Psychiatr Clin North Am 6:489–520, 1983

Gold MS, Verebey K: The psychopharmacology of cocaine. Psychiatric Annals 14:714–723, 1984

Gold MS, Redmond DE Jr, Kleber HD: Clonidine in opiate withdrawal. Lancet 1:929–930, 1978

Gold MS, Pottash ALC, Extein I, et al: Clonidine in acute opiate withdrawal. N Engl J Med 302:1421–1422, 1980

Gold MS, Dackis CA, Pottash ALC, et al: Naltrexone, opiate addiction and endorphins. Med Res Rev 2:211–246, 1982

Gold MS, Pottash ALC, Annitto WD, et al: Cocaine withdrawal: efficacy of tyrosine. Presented at the 13th Annual Meeting of the Society for Neuroscience. Boston, 7 November 1983

Gold MS, Pottash ALC, Estroff TW, et al: Laboratory evaluation in treatment planning, in The Somatic Therapies. Edited by Karasu TB. Washington, DC, American Psychiatric Association, 1984, pp 31–50

Gold MS, Washton AM, Dackis CA: Cocaine Abuse: Neurochemistry, Phenomenology, and Treatment. NIDA Research Monograph 61. Edited by Kozel MS, Adams EH. Rockville, Md, US Department of Human Services, 1985a, pp 130–150

Gold MS, Estroff TW, Pottash ALC: Substance induced organic mental disorders, in Neuropsychiatry, Psychiatry Update, vol 4. Edited by Yudofsky S. 1985b, pp 223–236

Goldfrank L, Bresnitz E: Toxicologic emergencies: opioids. Hospital Physician 10:26, 1978

Goldfried MR, Davison GC: Clinical Behavior Therapy. New York, Holt, Rinehart, and Winston, 1976

Goldstein A: Heroin addiction: sequential treatment employing pharmacologic supports. Arch Gen Psychiatry 33:353, 1976

Goldstein A: Opioid peptides: function and significance, in Opioids: Past, Present, and Future. Edited by Collier HOJ, Hughes J, Rance MJ, et al. London, Taylor and Frances Ltd, 1984

Goodman LS, Gilman A: The Pharmacological Basis of Therapeutics, 6th ed. New York, Macmillan, 1985

Goodwin DW: Alcoholism and genetics: the sins of the fathers. Arch Gen Psychiatry 42:171–174, 1985

Gorsuch RL, Butler M: Initial drug abuse: a review of predisposing social psychological factors. Psychol Bull 83:120–137, 1976

Grabowski J, O'Brien CP, Greenstein RA: Effects of contigent payment on compliance with a naltrexone regimen. Am J Drug Alcohol Abuse 6:355, 1979

Granger R, Shugart G: The heroin addict's pseudoassertive behavior and family dynamics. Social Caseworks 47:643–649, 1966

Green J, Jaffe JH: Alcohol and opiate dependence. J Stud Alco 38:1274–1293, 1977

Greenblatt DJ, Shader RI: Dependence, tolerance, and addiction to benzodiazepines: clinical and pharmacokinetic considerations. Drug Metab Rev 8:13–28, 1978

Greenstein RA, Evans BD, McLellan AT, et al: Predictors of favorable outcome following naltrexone treatment. Drug Alcohol Depend 12:173–180, 1983

Greenstein RA, Arndt IC, McLellan AT, et al: Naltrexone: a clinical perspective. J Clin Psychiatry 45:25, 1984

Greenwood R, Peachy R: Acute amphetamine poisoning: an account of three cases. Br Med J 30:742–744, 1957

Griffiths RR, Bigelow GE, Henningfield JE: Similarities in animal and human drug-taking behavior, in Advances in Substance Abuse, vol 1. Edited by Mello NK. Greenwich, Conn, JAI Press, 1980

Grinspoon L: Effects of marijuana. Hosp Community Psychiatry 34:307, 1983

Grinspoon L, Bakalar JB: Drug dependence: non-narcotic agents, in Comprehensive Textbook of Psychiatry, 3rd ed. Edited by Kaplan HI, Freedman AM, Sadock BJ. Baltimore: Williams and Wilkins, 1980

Grinspoon L, Bakalar JD: Psychedelics and arylcyclohexylamines, in Psychiatric Update: Annual Review, vol 5. Edited by Frances A, Hales R. Washington, DC, American Psychiatric Press, 1986

Gritz ER, Shiffman SM, Jarvik ME, et al: Physiological and psychological effects of methadone in man. Arch Gen Psychiatry 32:237–242, 1975

Grover D, Yeragani VK, Keshanan MS: Improvement of phencyclidine: associated psychosis with ECT. J Clin Psychiatry 47:477–478, 1986

Grunberg NE: The effects of nicotine and cigarette smoking on food consumption and taste preferences. Addict Behav 7:317–331, 1982

Guerin PJ, Pendagast EF: Evaluation of family system and genogram, in Family Therapy. Edited by Guerin PJ. New York, Gardner Press, 1976, pp 450–464

Gunn RC: Reactions to withdrawal symptoms and success in smoking cessation clinics. Addict Behav 11:49–53, 1986

Gunne LM: The fate of the Swedish methadone maintenance treatment programme. Drug Alcohol Depend 11:99–103, 1983

Gunne LM, Anggard E: Pharmacokinetic studies with amphetamines: relationship to neuropsychiatric disorders. J Pharmacokinet Biopharm 1:481–495, 1973

Gurman AS, Kniskern DP: Handbook of family therapy. New York, Brunner/Mazel, 1981

Gutman RA, Striker GE, Gilliland BC: The immune complex glomerulonephritis of bacterial endocarditis. Medicine 51:1–23, 1972

Haley J: Problem Solving Therapy. San Francisco, Jossey-Bass, 1977

Hall GH: Pharmacology of tobacco smoking in relation to schizophrenia, in Biochemistry of Schizophrenia and Addiction: In Search of a Common Factor. Edited by Hemmings G. Baltimore, University Park Press, 1980

Hall SM: Methadone treatment: a review of the research findings, in Research on the Treatment of Narcotic Addiction: State-of-the-Art. NIDA Research Monograph. Publication ADM 83-1281. Edited by Cooper JR, Altman F, Brown BS, et al. Washington, DC, US Government Printing Office, 1983

Hall SM, Loeb P, Coyne K, et al: Increasing employment in ex-heroin addicts, I: criminal justice sample. Behavior Therapy 12:443–452, 1981a

Hall SM, Loeb P, LeVois M, et al: Increasing employment in ex-heroin addicts, II: methadone maintenance sample. Behavior Therapy 12:453–460, 1981b

Hall SM, Loeb P, LeVois M: Job Seekers' Workshop. Leader's Manual for a Vocational Rehabilitation Strategy. Publication ADM 85-1424. Washington, DC, US Government Printing Office, 1985

Hallgrimsson O: Methadone treatment: the nordic attitude. Journal of Drug Issues 10:463–474, 1980

Hanson B, Beschner G, Walters JM, et al: Life With Heroin: Voices from the Inner City. Lexington, Mass, DC Heath and Company, 1985

Harding T, Knight F: Marijuana-modified mania. Arch Gen Psychiatry 29:635–637, 1973

Harford RJ, Ungerer JC, Kinsella JK: Effects of legal pressure on prognosis for treatment of drug dependence. Am J Psychiatry 133:1399–1404, 1976

Harms E: Some shortcomings of methadone maintenance. Br J Addict 70:77–81, 1975

Hartnoll RL, Mitcheson MC, Battersby A, et al: Evaluation of heroin maintenance in controlled trial. Arch Gen Psychiatry 37:877–884, 1980

Havassy B, Hall S: Efficacy of urine monitoring in methadone maintenance. Am J Psychiatry 138:1497–1500, 1981

Hawkins JD, Catalano RF, Wells EA: Measuring effects of an experimental skills training intervention on drug abusers' skill acquisition. J Consult Clin Pharmacol 54:661–664, 1986

Henderson DA, Shelokov A: Epidemic neuromyasthenia: clinical syndrome? N Engl J Med 260:757–764, 1959

Henderson IWD: Chemical Dependence in Canada: A View From the Hill in Problems of Drug Dependence. Proceedings of the 44th Annual Meeting of the Committee on Problems of Drug Dependence. NIDA Research Monograph 43. Edited by Harris LH. Rockville, Md, US Department of Health and Human Services, 1982

Hendin H: Marijuana use among college students. J Nerv Ment Dis 156:259–270, 1973

Hendin H: Beyond alienation: the end of the psychedelic road. Am J Drug Alcohol Abuse 1:11–23, 1974

Hendin H: The Age of Sensation. New York, WW Norton, 1975

Hendricks WJ: Use of multifamily counseling groups in treatment of male narcotic addicts. Int J Group Psychother 21:34–90, 1971

Henningfield JE: Pharmacologic basis and treatment of cigarette smoking. J Clin Psychiatry 45:24–34, 1984

Herrington RE, Benzer DG, Jacobson GR, et al: Treating substance-use disorders among physicians. JAMA 247:2253–2257, 1982

Hersch R: Group therapy with parents of adolescent drug addicts. Psychiatr Q 35:702–710, 1961

Herz FM, Rosen EJ: Jewish families, in Ethnicity and Family Therapy. Edited by McGoldrick M, Pearce, JK, Giordano J. New York, Guilford Press, 1982

Hesselbrock MN, Meyer RE, Keener JJ: Psychopathology in hospitalized alcoholics. Arch Gen Psychiatry 42:1050–1055, 1985

Hofstetter A, Schutz Y, Jequier E, et al: Increased 24-hours energy expenditure in cigarette smokers. N Engl J Med 314:79–82, 1986

Holland S: Evaluating community based treatment programs: a model for strengthening inferences about effectiveness. International Journal of Therapeutic Community 4:285–306, 1983

Holland S, Griffen A: Adolescent and adult drug treatment clients: patterns and consequences of use. J Psychoactive Drugs 16:79–90, 1984

Hollister L: Report of the National Research Council Committee on Clinical Evaluation of Narcotic Antagonists: clinical evaluation of naltrexone treatment of dependent individuals. Arch Gen Psychiatry 35:335, 1978

Hollister LE: Benzodiazepines 1980: current update. Psychosomatics 21:1–5, 1980

Hollister, LE, Motzenbecker FP, Degan RO: Withdrawal reactions from chlordiazepoxide (Librium). Psychopharmacologia 2:63–68, 1961

Hollister LE, Bennett JL, Kimbell I Jr, et al: Diazepam in newly admitted schizophrenics. Diseases of the Nervous System 24:746–750, 1963

Hollister L, Johnson K, Boukhabza D, et al: Aversive effects of naltrexone in subjects not dependent on opiates. Drug Alcohol Depend 8:37–42, 1982

Holroyd I: Hypnosis treatment for smoking: an evaluative review. Int J Clin Exp Hypn 23:341–357, 1980

Hong CY, Chaput De Saintonge DM, Turner P: Δ^9-tetrahydrocannabinol inhibits human sperm motility. J Pharm Pharmacol 33:746–747, 1981

Huba G, Wingard J, Bentler P: Framework for an interactive theory of drug use, in Theories on Drug Abuse: Selected Contemporary Perspectives. Edited by Lettieri D, Sayers M, Pearson HW. Washington, DC, US Government Printing Office, 1980

Hubbard RL, Allison M, Bray RM, et al: An overview of client characteristics, treatment services, and during treatment outcomes for outpatient prospective study (TOPS), in Research on the Treatment of Narcotic Addiction: State of the Art. NIDA Research Monograph. Publication ADM 83-1281. Edited by Cooper JR, Altman F, Brown BS, et al. Washington, DC, US Government Printing Office, 1983

Hull JG: Self-awareness model of the causes and effects of alcohol consumption. J Abnorm Psychol 90:586–600, 1981

Hunt GM, Azrin NH: A community-reinforcement approach to alcoholism. Behav Res Ther 11:91–104, 1973

Hunt WA, Barnett LW, Branch LG: Relapse rates in addiction programs. J Clin Psychol 27:455–456, 1971

Imerek DE, Woods JH: Kappa receptor mediated opioid dependence in rhesus monkeys. Life Sci 15:987–992, 1986

Imhoff J, Hirsch R, Terenzi RE: Countertransferential and attitudinal considerations in the treatment of drug abuse and addiction. Journal of Substance Abuse Treatment 1:21–30, 1984

Isbell H, Altschul S, Kornetsky CH, et al: Chronic barbiturate intoxications: an experimental study. Archives of Neural Psychiatry 64:1–28, 1950

Istvan J, Matarazzo JD: Tobacco, alcohol and caffeine use: a review of their interrelationships. Psychol Bull 95:301–326, 1984

Itkonen J, Schnoll S, Glassroth J: Pulmonary dysfunction in "freebase" cocaine users. Arch Intern Med 144:219–257, 1984

Jackson G, Richman A: Alcohol use among narcotic addicts. Alcohol Health and Research World 25–28, 1973

Jackson G, Cohen M, Hanbury R, et al: Alcoholism among narcotic addicts and patients on methadone maintenance. J Stud Alcohol 44:499–504, 1983

Jaffe I: Tobacco use as a mental disorder: the rediscovery of a medical problem, in Research on Smoking Behavior. NIDA Research Monograph 23. Edited by Jarvik M, Cullen J, Gritz E, et al. Washington, DC, US Government Printing Office, 1979

Jaffe JH: Experience with the use of methadone in a multi-modality program. Int J Addict 4:481, 1969

Jaffe JH: Drug addiction and drug abuse, in The Pharmacological Basis of Therapeutics, 7th ed. Edited by Gilman AG, Goodman LS, Rall TW, et al. New York, Macmillan, 1985, pp 532–581

Jaffe JH, Martin WR: (1975) Narcotic analgesics and antagonists, in The Pharmacologic Basis of Therapeutics. Edited by Goodman LS, Gilman A. New York, Macmillan, 1975

Jaffe JH, Martin WR: Opioid analgesics and antagonists, in The Pharmacological Basis of Therapeutics, 7th ed. Edited by Gilman AG, Goodman LS, Rall TW, et al. New York, Macmillan, 1985, pp 49–531

Jaffe JH et al: Methadyl acetate vs methadone: a double-blind study in heroin users. JAMA 111:437–442, 1972

Jainchill N, De Leon G, Pinkham L: Psychiatric diagnoses among substance abusers in the therapeutic community treatment. J Psychoactive Drugs 18:209–213, 1986

Jarvik ME, Henningfield JE: Pharmacological treatment of tobacco dependence. Pharmacol Biochem Behav 30:279–294, 1988

Jasinski DR, Pevnick JS, Griffith JD: Human pharmacology and abuse potential of the analgesic buprenorphine. Arch Gen Psychiatry 35:501–516, 1978

Jasinski DR, Johnson RE, Kocher TR: Clonidine in morphine withdrawal: differential effects on signs and symptoms. Arch Gen Psychiatry 42:1063–1066, 1985

Jatlow P, Barash PG, Van Dyke C, et al: Cocaine and succinylcholine sensitivity: a new caution. Anesthesia and Analgesia Current Research 58:235–238, 1979

Jessor R: Predicting time of marijuana use: a developmental study of high school youths, in Predicting Adolescent Drug Abuse: A Review of Issues, Methods, and Correlates. Research Issues II. Edited by Lettieri DJ. Rockville, Md, National Institute on Drug Abuse, 1975

Jessor R, Chase JA, Donovan JE: Psychosocial correlates of marijuana use and problem drinking in a national sample of adolescents. Am J Publ Health 70:604–613, 1980

Jessor R, Donovan J, Costa F: Psychoactive correlates of marijuana use in adolescent and young adulthood: the past as prologue, in Marijuana, Cocaine and Traffic Society. Edited by Moskowitz H. Alcohol, Drugs and Driving, vol 2, no 3–4. Los Angeles, Brain Information Service, Center for Health Sciences, 1986

Johanson CE: Assessment of the dependence potential of cocaine in animals, in Cocaine: Pharmacology, Effects and Treatment of Abuse. NIDA Research Monograph 50. Edited by Grabowski J. Rockville, Md, Department of Health and Human Services, 1984, pp 54–71

Johanson CE, Shuster CR: Animal models of drug self-administration, in Advances in Substance Abuse: Behavioral and Biological Research, vol 2. Edited by Mello NK. Greenwich, Conn, JAI Press, 1982

Johnson V: I'll quit tomorrow. New York, Harper and Row, 1973

Johnston LD, Bachman JG, O'Malley PM: Student Drug Use, Attitudes and Beliefs. Washington, DC, US Government Printing Office, 1982

Johnston LD, O'Malley PM, Backman JG: Illicit Drug Use, Smoking and Drinking by America's High School Students, College Students and Young Adults 1975–1987. Rockville, Md, US Department of Health and Human Services, 1988

Jonas DF, Jonas AD: A bioanthropological overview of addiction. Perspect Biol Med Spring 20:345–354, 1977

Jones M: Therapeutic Community: A New Treatment Method in Psychiatry. New York, Basic Books, 1953

Jones RT: Cannabis and health. Annu Rev Med 34:247–258, 1983

Jonsson LE, Gunne LM, Anggard E: Effects of alpha-methyltyrosine in amphetamine-dependent subjects. Pharmacologia Clinica 2:27–29, 1969

Judson BA, Goldstein A: Naltrexone treatment of heroin addiction: one year follow-up. Drug Alcohol Depend 13:357, 1984

Judson BA, Ortiz S, Crouse L, et al: A follow-up study of heroin addicts five years after first admission to a methadone treatment program. Drug Alcohol Depend 6:295–313, 1980

Judson BA, Carney TM, Goldstein A: Naltrexone treatment of heroin addiction: efficacy and safety in a double-blind dosage comparison. Drug Alcohol Depend 7:325, 1981

Jusko WJ: Smoking and drug response. Pharmacology International 2:10–13, 1981

Kalant H, Kalant OJ: Death in amphetamine users: causes and rates, in Amphetamine Use, Misuse, and Abuse. Edited by Smith DE, Wesson DR, Buxton ME, et al. Boston, GK Hall and Co, 1979

Kandel D: The role of parents and peers in adolescent marijuana use. Science 181:1067–1070, 1973

Kandel D: Stages in adolescent involvement in drug use. Science 190:912–914, 1975

Kandel D (ed): Longitudinal Research on Drug Use: Empirical Findings and Methodological Issues. Washington, DC, Hemisphere, 1978

Kandel D: Developmental stages in adolescent drug involvement, in Theories on Drug Abuse: Selected Contemporary Perspectives. Edited by Lettieri D, Sayers M, Pearson HW. Washington, DC, US Government Printing Office, 1980

Kandel DB, Faust R: Sequence and stages in patterns of adolescent drug use. Arch Gen Psychiatry 32:923–932, 1975

Kandel DB, Kessler RC, Margulies RZ: Antecedents of adolescent initiation into stages of drug use: a developmental analysis. Journal of Youth and Adolescence 7:3–14, 1978

Kaplan HB: Self-Attitudes and Deviant Behavior. Pacific Palisades, Calif, Goodyear Publishing, 1975

Kaplan HB: Antecedents of negative self-attitudes: membership group devaluation and defenselessness. Soc Psychiatry 11:15–25, 1976

Kaplan HB: Self-esteem and self-derogation theory of drug abuse, in Theories on Drug Abuse: Selected Contemporary Perspectives. Edited by Lettieri D, Sayers M, Pearson HW. Washington, DC, US Government Printing Office, 1980

Kaufman E: The application of the basic principles of family therapy to the treatment of drug and alcohol abusers, in Family Therapy of Drug and Alcohol Abuse. Edited by Kaufman E, Kaufmann P. New York, Gardner Press, 1979

Kaufman E: Substance Abuse and Family Therapy. New York, Grune & Stratton, 1985

Kaufman E: A contemporary approach to the family treatment of substance abuse disorders. American Journal of Drug and Alcohol Abuse 12:199–211, 1986

Kaufman E, De Leon G: The therapeutic community: a treatment approach for drug abusers, in Treatment Aspects of Drug Dependence. Edited by Schecter A. Boca Raton, Fla, CRC Press, 1978

Kaufman E, Kaufmann P: Multiple family therapy: a new direction in the treatment of drug abusers. Am J Drug Alcohol Abuse 4:467–468, 1977

Kaufman E, Kaufman PW: Family Therapy of Drug and Alcohol Abuse. New York, Gardner Press, 1979

Kaufman E, Pattison EM: Differential methods of family therapy in the treatment of alcoholism. J Stud Alcohol 42:951–971, 1981

Kelleher RI, Goldberg SR: Control of drug taking behavior by schedules of reinforcement. Pharmacol Rev 27:291–299, 1975

Kelley D, Welch R, McKnelley N, et al: Methadone maintenance: an assessment of potential fluctuations in behavior between doses. Int J Addict 13:1061–1068, 1978

Kennard D, Wilson S: The modification of personality disturbance in a therapeutic community for drug abusers. Br J Med Psychol 52:215–221, 1979

Keup W: Psychotic symptoms due to cannabis abuse. Diseases of the Nervous System 31:119–126, 1970

Khantzian EJ: The ego, the self and opiate addiction: theoretical and treatment considerations. International Review of Psychoanalysis 5:189–198, 1978

Khantzian EJ: An ego/self theory of substance dependence: a contemporary psychoanalytic perspective, in Theories on Drug Abuse: Selected Contemporary Perspectives. Edited by Lettieri D, Sayers M, Pearson HW. Washington, DC, US Government Printing Office, 1980

Khantzian EJ: Cocaine dependence, an extreme case and marked improvement with methylphenidate treatment. Am J Psychiatry 140:784–785, 1983

Khantzian EJ: The self-medication hypothesis of addictive disorders: focus on heroin and cocaine dependence. Am J Psychiatry 142:1259–1264, 1985

Khantzian EJ, Khantzian NJ: Cocaine addiction: is there a psychological predisposition? Psychiatric Annals 14:753–759, 1984

Khantzian EJ, McKenna GJ: Acute toxic and withdrawal reactions associated with drug use and abuse. Ann Intern Med 90:361–373, 1979

Khantzian EJ, Schneider RJ: Treatment implications of a psychodynamic understanding of opioid addicts, in Psychopathology and Addictive Disorders. Edited by Meyer RE. New York, Guilford Press, 1986

Khantzian EJ, Treece C: DSM-III psychiatric diagnosis of narcotic addicts. Arch Gen Psychiatry 42:1067–1071, 1985

Khantzian EJ, Mack JE, Schatzberg AF: Heroin use as an attempt to cope: clinical observations. Am J Psychiatry

Khantzian EJ, Gawin FH, Riordan C, et al: Methylphenidate treatment of cocaine dependence: a preliminary report. Journal of Substance Abuse Treatment 1:107–112, 1984

King MD, Day RE Olive JS, et al: Solvent encephalopathy. Br Med J 283:663–665, 1981

Kirkby RJ, Petchkovsky L: Chronic administration of cocaine: effects on defecation and adrenal hypertrophy in the rat. Neuropharmacology 12:1001, 1973

Kjeldgaard JM, Hahn GN, Heckenlively JR, et al: Methadone-induced pulmonary edema. JAMA 218:882–883, 1971

Klajner F, Hartman LM, Sobell MB: Treatment of substance abuse by relaxation training: a review of its rationale, efficacy and mechanisms. Addict Behav 9:41–55, 1984

Kleber HD: The New Haven methadone maintenance program. Int J Addict 5:449–463, 1970

Kleber HD: Detoxification from narcotics, in Substance Abuse: Clinical Problems and Perspectives. Edited by Lowinson JH, Ruiz P. Baltimore, Williams and Wilkins, 1981

Kleber HD: Concomitant use of methadone with other psychoactive drugs in the treatment of opiate addicts with other DSM-III diagnoses, in Research on the Treatment of Narcotic Addiction: State of the Art. Edited by Cooper JR, Altman F, Brown BS, et al. NIDA Research Monograph. Publication ADM 83-1281. Washington, DC, US Government Printing Office, 1983

Kleber HD, Gawin FH: Cocaine abuse: a review of current and experimental treatments, in Cocaine: Pharmacology, Effects, and Treatment of Abuse. NIDA Research Monograph 50, 1984a

Kleber HD, Gawin FH: The spectrum of cocaine abuse and its treatment. J Clin Psychiatry 45:18–23, 1984b

Kleber HD, Kosten TR: Naltrexone induction: psychologic and pharmacologic strategies. J Clin Psychiatry 45:29, 1984

Kleber HD, Slobetz F, Mezritz M, et al: Medical Evaluation of Long Term Methadone Maintenance Clients. Publication ADM 81-1029. Rockville, Md, US Department of Health and Human Services, 1980

Kleber HD, Weissman MM, Rounsaville BJ, et al: Imipramine as treatment for depression in addicts. Arch Gen Psychiatry 40:649–653, 1983

Kleber HD, Riordan CE, Rounsaville B, et al: Clonidine in outpatient detoxification from methadone maintenance. Arch Gen Psychiatry 42:391–394, 1985a

Kleber HD, Kosten TR, Gaspari J, et al: Nontolerance to the opioid antagonism of naltrexone. Biol Psychiatry 20:66–72, 1985b

Klein DF: Anxiety reconceptualized, in Anxiety: New Research and Changing Concepts. Edited by Klein DF, Rabkin JG. New York, Raven Press, 1981

Knight F: Role of cannabis in psychiatric disturbance. Ann NY Acad Sci 282:64–71, 1976

Knowles R, Lahiri S, Anderson G, et al: Methadone maintenance in St. Louis. Int J Addict 5:407–420, 1970

Knudsen P, Vilmar T: Cannabis and neuroleptic agents in schizophrenia. Acta Psychiatr Scand 69:162–174, 1984

Kohler PF, Cronin RE, Hammond WS: Chronic membranous glomerulonephritis caused by hepatitis B antigen-antibody immune complexes. Ann Intern Med 81:448–451, 1974

Kokkinidis L, Zacharko R: Response sensitization and depression following long-term amphetamine treatment in a self-stimulation paradigm. Psychopharmacology 68:73–76, 1980

Kokkinidis L, Zacharko RM, Predy PA: Post-amphetamine depression of self-stimulation responding from the substantia nigra: reversal by tricyclic antidepressants. Pharmacol Biochem Behav 13:379–383, 1980

Kolodny RC, Masters WH, Kolodner RM, et al: Depression of plasma testosterone levels after chronic intensive marijuana use. N Engl J Med 290:872–874, 1974

Kosten TR, Rounsaville BJ, Kleber HD: Relationship of depression to psychosocial stressors in heroin addicts. J Nerv Ment Dis 171:97–104, 1983a

Kosten TR, Rounsaville BJ, Kleber HD: Concurrent validity of the addiction severity index. J Nerv Ment Dis 171:606–610, 1983b

Kosten TR, Rounsaville BJ, Kleber HD: Parental alcoholism in opioid addicts. J Nerv Ment Dis 173:461–469, 1985

Kosten TR, Gawin FH, Rounsaville BJ, et al: Cocaine abuse among opioid addicts: demographic and diagnostic factors in treatment. American Journal of Drug and Alcohol Abuse 12:1–16, 1986a

Kosten TR, Rounsaville BJ, Kleber HD: A 2.5 year follow-up of depression, life crises, and treatment effects on abstinence among opioid addicts. Arch Gen Psychiatry 43:733–738, 1986b

Kosten TR, Rounsaville BJ, Kleber HD: A 2.5 year follow-up retention and reentry among opioid addicts. Journal of Substance Abuse Treatment 3:181–189, 1986c

Kosten TR, Rounsaville BJ, Kelber HD: A 2.5 year follow-up of cocaine use among treated opioid addicts: have our treatments helped? Arch Gen Psychiatry 44:281–284, 1987a

Kosten TR, Rounsaville BJ, Kleber HD: Multidimensionality in treatment outcome among opioid addicts: 2.5 year follow-up. Compr Psychiatry 28:3–13, 1987b

Kozlowski LT: Psychosocial influences on cigarette smoking, in Behavior Aspects of Smoking, NIDA Research Monograph, no. 26. Krasnegor NA (ed.). USDHEW Pub. Health Service, DHEW Pub. (ADM) 79-882, 1979, pp 97–125

Kramer JC, Fischman VS, Littlefield DC: Amphetamine abuse patterns and effects of high doses taken intravenously. JAMA 201:305–309, 1967

Kreek MJ: Methadone in treatment: physiological and pharmacological issues, in Handbook on Drug Abuse. Edited by Dupont RL, Goldstein A, O'Donnell J. Washington, DC, US Government Printing Office, 1979

Kreek MJ: Health consequences associated with the use of methadone, in Research on the Treatment of Narcotic Addiction: State of the Art. NIDA Research Monograph. Edited by Cooper JR, Altman F, Brown BS, et al. Publication ADM 83-1281. Washington, DC, US Government Printing Office, 1983

Kreek MS: Medical management of methadone-maintained patients, in Substance Abuse: Clinical Problems and Perspectives. Edited by Lowinson JH, Ruiz P. Baltimore, Williams and Wilkins, 1981

Krugman S: The newly licensed hepatitis B vaccine. JAMA 247:2012–2015, 1982

Kuhnert BR, Kuhnert PM: Placental transfer of drugs, alcohol, and components of cigarette smoke and their effects on the human fetus, in Prenatal Drug Exposure: Kinetics and Dynamics. NIDA Research Monograph 60. Edited by Chiang CN, Lee CC. Rockville, Md, US Department of Health and Human Services, 1985

Kumar MSA, Patel V, Millard WI: Effect of chronic administration of delta-9-tetrahydrocannabinol on the endogenous opioid peptide and catecholamine levels in the diencephalon and plasma of the rat. Substance Alcohol Actions Misuse 5:201–210, 1984

Lader M: Dependence on benzodiazepines. J Clin Psychiatry 44:121–127, 1983

Lahmeyer HW, Stock PG: Phencyclidine intoxication, physical restraints, and acute renal failure: case report. J Clin Psychiatry 44:184–185, 1983

Landesman SH, Ginzburg HM, Weiss SH: Special article: the AIDS epidemic. N Engl J Med 312:512–525, 1985

Lando HA, McGovern PG: Nicotine fading as a nonaversive alternative in a broad-spectrum treatment for eliminating smoking. Addict Behav 10:153–161, 1985

Lange R, Jaffe J, Lasovsky D, et al: Unpublished data

Langston JW, Irwin I, Langston EB, et al: Pargyline prevents MPTP-induced parkinsonism in primates. Science 225:1480–1482, 1984

LaRosa JC, Lipsius JH, LaRose JH: Experience with a combination of group therapy and methadone maintenance in the treatment of heroin addiction. Int J Addict 9:605–617, 1974

Lasagna L, von Felsinger JM, Beecher HK: Drug induced mood changes in man, I: observations on healthy subjects, chronically ill patients, and postaddicts. JAMA 157:1066–1020, 1955

LeBellec M, Bismuth CH, Lagier G, et al: Severe withdrawal symptoms after benzodiazepines are discontinued: six clinical cases. Therapie 35:113–118, 1980

Leith NJ, Barrett RJ: Amphetamine and the reward system: evidence for tolerance and post-drug depression. Psychopharmacology 46:19–25, 1976

Leith NJ, Barrett RJ: Self-stimulation and amphetamine: tolerance to d and l isomers and cross tolerance to cocaine and methylphenidate. Psychopharmacology 74:23–28, 1981

Lennard HL et al: The methadone illusion. Science 176:881–884, 1972

Lettieri D (ed): Drugs and Suicide: When Other Coping Strategies Fail. Beverly Hills, Calif, Sage Publications, 1978

Lettieri D: Drug abuse: a review of explanations and models of explanation. Adv Alcohol Subst Abuse 314:9–40, 1985

Lettieri DJ, Sayers M, Pearson HW (eds): Theories on Drug Abuse: Selected Contemporary Perspectives. Washington, DC, US Government Printing Office, 1980

Leventhal H, Cleary P: The smoking problem: a review of the research and theory in behavioral risk modification. Psychol Bull 88:370–405, 1980

Levine FJ, Luborsky L: The core conflictual relationship theme method: a demonstration of reliable clinical inferences by the method of mismatched cases, in Object and Self: A Developmental Approach. Edited by Tuttman S, Kaye C, Zimmerman M. New York, International Universities Press, 1981, pp 501–526

Levy A: Delirium and seizures due to abrupt alprazolam withdrawal: case report. J Clin Psychiatry 45:38–39, 1984

Lewin L: Phantastica. Berlin, Verlang von Georg Stilke, 1924

Lichtenstein E: the smoking problem: a behavioral perspective. J Consult Clin Psychol 50:804–819, 1982

Lichtenstein E, Brown A: Current trends in the modification of cigarette dependence, in International Handbook of Behavior Modification and Therapy, vol 2. Edited by Bellack A, Hersen M, Kazdin AE. New York, Plenum, 1985

Liebson IA, Tommasello A, Bigelow GE: A behavioral treatment of alcoholic methadone patients. Ann Intern Med 89:342–344, 1978

Ling GSF, MacLeod JM, Lee S, et al: Separation of morphine analgesia from physical dependence. Science 226:462–464, 1984

Ling W, Blaine SD: The Use of LAAM in Treatment, in Handbook on Drug Abuse.

Edited by Dupont RL, Goldstein A, O'Donnell J. Washington, DC, US Government Printing Office, 1979

Ling W, Klett CJ, Gillis RD: A cooperative clinical study of methadyl acetate. Arch Gen Psychiatry 35:345–353, 1978

Ling W, Weiss DG, Charuvastra VC, et al: Use of disulfiram for alcoholics in methadone maintenance programs. Arch Gen Psychiatry 40:851–854, 1983

Ling W, Wesson DR: Naltrexone treatment for addicted health-care professionals: a collaborative private practice experience. J Clin Psychiatry 45:46, 1984

Loizou LA, Boddie HG: Polyradiculoneuropathy associated with heroin abuse. J Neurol Neurosurg Psych 41:855–857, 1978

Longwell B, Betz T, Horton H, et al: Weight gain and edema on methadone maintenance therapy. Int J Addict 14:329–335, 1979

Louria DB, Hensle T, Rose F: The major medical complications of heroin addiction. Ann Intern Med 67:1–22, 1967

Lowinson JH, Millman RB: Clinical Aspects of Methadone Maintenance Treatment, in Handbook on Drug Abuse. Edited by Dupont RL, Goldstein A, O'Donnell J. Washington, DC, US Government Printing Office, 1979

Luborsky L: Measuring a pervasive psychic structure in psychotherapy: the core conflictual relationship theme, in Communicative Structures and Psychic Structures. Edited by Freedman N, Grand S. New York, Plenum, 1977, pp 367–395

Luborsky L: Principles of Psychoanalytic Psychotherapy: A Manual for Supportive-Expressive (SE) Treatment. New York, Basic Books, 1984

Luborsky L, Singer B, Luborsky L: Comparative studies of psychotherapy: is it true that "everybody" has won and all must have prizes? Arch Gen Psychiatry 32:995–1008, 1975

Luborsky L, McLellan AT, Woody GE, et al: Therapist success and its determinants. Arch Gen Psychiatry 42:602–611, 1985a

Luborsky L, Mellon J, Alexander K, et al: A verification of Freud's grandest clinical hypothesis: the transference. Clinical Psychology Review 5:231–246, 1985b

Luborsky L, Crits-Christoph P, McLellan T, et al: Do therapists vary in their effectiveness? Findings from four outcome studies. Am J Orthopsychiatry 66:501–512, 1986

Luisada P, Brown B: Clinical management of phencyclidine psychosis. Clinical Toxicology 9:539–545, 1976

Maany I, O'Brien CP, Woody G: Interaction between thioridazine and naltrexone. Am J Psychiatry 144:966, 1987

MacKinnon GL, Parker WA: Benzodiazepine withdrawal syndrome: a literature review and evaluation. Am J Drug Alcohol Abuse 9:19–33, 1982

Madanes C: Elements of strategic family therapy, in Strategic Family Therapy. Edited by Mandanes C. New York, Jossey-Bass, 1981, pp 19–28

Maddox JF, Bowden CL: Critique of success with methadone maintenance. Am J Psychiatry 129:440–446, 1972

Maddox JF, McDonald LK: Status of 100 San Antonio addicts one year after admission to methadone maintenance. Drug Forum 2:239–252, 1973

Maddox JF, Williams TR, Ziegler DA, et al: Driving records before and during methadone maintenance. Am J Drug Alcohol Abuse 4:91–100, 1977

Maddux JF, Desmond DP: Relapse recovery in substance abuse careers, in Relapse and Recovery in Drug Abuse (NIDA Monograph 72). Edited by Tims FM, Leukefeld CG. Rockville, Md, Department of Health and Human Services, 1986, pp 49–71

Maddox JF, Desmond DP: Residence relocation inhibits opioid dependence. Arch Gen Psychiatry 39:1313–1317, 1982

Maher BA: Principles of Psychopathology. New York, McGraw-Hill, 1966

Maier HW: Der Kokainismus. Leipzig, Georg Thieme Verlag, 1926

Malan D: A Study of Brief Psychotherapy. Philadelphia, JB Lippincott Co, 1963

Maletsky BM, Klotter J: Smoking and alcoholism. Am J Psychiatry 131:445–446, 1974

Marcotte DB: Marijuana and mutism. Am J Psychiatry 129:475–477, 1972

Marlatt GA: Relapse prevention: a self-control program for the treatment of addictive behaviors, in Adherence, Compliance and Generalization in Behavioral Medicine. Edited by Stuart RB.

Marlatt GA, Gordon JR: Determinants of relapse: implications for the maintenance of behavior change, in Behavioral Medicine: Changing Health Lifestyles. Edited by Davidson PO, Davidson SM, New York, Brunner/Mazel, 1980, pp 410–452

Marlatt GA, Gordon J (eds): Relapse Prevention. New York, Guilford Press, 1985

Marquardt GM, DiStephano V, Ling LL: Pharmacological effects of (±)-(S)- and (R)MDA, in the Pharmacology of Hallucinations. Edited by Stillman RC, Willette RE. New York, Pergamon Press, 1978

Martin WR, Jasinski DR: Physiological parameters of morphine in man: tolerance, early abstinence, protracted abstinence. J Psychiatr Res 7:9–16, 1969

Martin WR, Jasinski DR, Mansky PA: Naltrexone: an antagonist for the treatment of heroin dependence. Arch Gen Psychiatry 28:784, 1973a

Martin WA, Jasinski DR, Haertzen CA, et al: Methadone—a reevaluation. Arch Gen Psychiatry 28:286–295, 1973b

Marx JL: New disease baffles medical community. Science 217:618–621, 1982

Maslansky R: Methadone maintenance programs in Minneapolis. Int J Addict 5:391–405, 1970

Mathew RJ, Weinman ML, Mirabi M: Physical symptoms of depression. Br J Psychiatry 139:293–296, 1981

May E: Narcotics addiction and control in Great Britain, in Dealing with Drug Abuse. New York, Praeger, 1973

McAuliffe WE, Ch'ien JMN: Recovery training and self help: a relapse-prevention program for treated opiate addicts. Journal of Substance Abuse Treatment 3:9–20, 1986

McAuliffe WE, Gordon RA: A test of Lindesmiths's theory of addiction: the frequency of euphoria among long-term addicts. American Journal of Sociology 79:795–840, 1974

McAuliffe WE, Gordon RA: Reinforcement and the combination of effects: summary of a theory of opiate addiction, in Theories on Drug Abuse: Selected Contemporary Perspectives. Edited by Lettieri D, Sayers M, Pearson IIW. Washington, DC, US Government Printing Office, 1980

McAuliffe WE, Ch'ien JMN, Launer E, et al: The Harvard Group Aftercare Program: preliminary evaluation results and implementation issues, in Progress in the Development of Cost-Effective Treatment for Drug Abusers. NIDA Research Monograph 58. Publication ADM 85-1401. Edited by Ashery RS. Washington, DC, US Government Printing Office, 1985

McCabe OL, Kurland AA, Sullivan D: Paroled narcotic addicts in a verified abstinence program: results of a five-year study. Int J Addict 10:211–228, 1975

McCarthy JJ, Borders OT: Limit setting on drug abuse in methadone maintenance patients. Am J Psychiatry 142:1419–1423, 1985

McCaul ME, Bigelow GE, Stitzer ML, et al: Short-term effects of oral methadone in methadone maintenance subjects. Clin Pharmacol Ther 31:753–761, 1982

McGill D, Pearce JK: British families, in Ethnicity and Family Therapy. Edited by McGoldrick M, Pearce JK, Giordano J. New York, Guilford Press, 1982

McGlothlin W: Drugs and Crime, in Handbook on Drug Abuse. Edited by Dupont RL, Goldstein A, O'Donnell J. Washington, DC, U.S. Government Printing Office, 1979

McGlothlin WH: Distinguishing effects from concomitants of drug use: the case of crime, in Studying Drug Abuse. Edited by Robins LN. New Brunswick, NJ, Rutgers University Press, 1985, pp 153–172

McGlothlin WH, Anglin MD: Shutting off methadone: costs and benefits. Arch Gen Psychiatry 38:885–892, 1981a

McGlothlin WH, Anglin MD: Long-term follow-up of clients of high- and low-dose methadone programs. Arch Gen. Psychiatry 38:1055–1063, 1981b

McGlothlin WH, Anglin MD, Wilson BD: A follow-up of admissions to the California Civil Addict Program. Am J Drug Alcohol Abuse 4:179–199, 1977

McGoldrick M: Irish families, in Ethnicity and Family Therapy. Edited by McGoldrick M, Pearce JK, Giordano J. New York, Guilford Press, 1982a

McGoldrick M: Normal families: an ethnic perspective, in Normal Family Processes. Edited by Walsh F. New York, Guilford Press, 1982b

McLellan AT: Patient characteristics associated with outcome, in Research on the Treatment of Narcotic Addiction: State of the Art. Publication ADM 83-1281. Edited by Cooper JR, Altman F, Brown BS. Rockville, Md, Department of Health and Human Services, Alcohol, 1983

McLellan AT: "Psychiatric severity" as a predictor of outcome from substance abuse treatments, in Psychopathology and Addictive disorders. Edited by Meyer RE. New York, Guilford Press, 1986

McLellan AT, Woody GE, O'Brien CP: Development of psychiatric illness in drug abusers: possible role of drug preference. 301:1310–1304, 1979

McLellan AT, O'Brien CP, Kron R, et al: Matching substance abuse patients to appropriate treatments. Drug Alcohol Depend 5:189–195, 1980a

McLellan AT, Luborsky L, O'Brien CP, et al: An improved diagnostic evaluation instrument for substance abuse patients: the Addiction Severity Index. J Nerv Ment Dis 168:26–33, 1980b

McLellan AT, O'Brien CP, Luborsky L, et al: Are the "addict-related" problems of substance abusers really related? J Nerv Ment Dis 169:232–239, 1981

McLellan AT et al: Is treatment for substance abuse effective? JAMA 247:1423–1428, 1982

McLellan AT, Luborsky L, Woody GE, et al: Predicting response to alcohol and drug abuse treatments. Arch Gen Psychiatry 40:620–625, 1983

McLellan AT, Woody GE, Luborsky L, et al: Does the counselor make a difference in methadone treatment: evidence for differential success rates. Submitted for publication, 1986a

McLellan AT, Childress AR, Ehrman R, et al: Extinguishing conditioned responses during opiate dependence treatment: turning laboratory findings into clinical procedures. Journal of Substance Abuse Treatment 3:33–40, 1986b

McLeod WR, Priest PN: Methadone maintenance in Auckland: the failure of a programme. Br J Addict 68:45–50, 1973

McNicholas LF, Martin WR: New and experimental therapeutic roles for naloxone and related opioid antagonists. Drugs 27:81–93, 1984

Mello NK, Mendelson JH: Buprenorphine suppresses heroin use by heroin addicts. Science 207:657–659, 1980

Mello N, Mendelson JH, Sellers ML, et al: Effect of alcohol and marijuana on tobacco smoking. Clin Pharm 27:202–209, 1980a

Mello NK, Mendelson JH, Kuehnle JC, et al: Operant analysis of human heroin self-administration and the effects of naltrexone. J Pharmacol Exp Ther 216:45–54, 1980b

Mendelson JH, Ellingboe J, Kuehnle JC et al: Heroin and naltrexone effects on pituitary-gonadal hormones in man: interaction of steroid feedback effects, tolerance and supersensitivity. J Pharmacol Exp Ther 214:503–506, 1980

Merz WA, Ballmer U: Symptoms of the barbiturate/benzodiazepine withdrawal syndrome in healthy volunteers: standardized assessment by a newly developed self-rating scale. J Psychoactive Drugs 15:1–2, 1983

Meyer RE, Mirin SM: The Heroin Stimulus: Implication for a Theory of Addiction. New York, Plenum, 1979

Meyer RE, Mirin SM, Altman JL: The clinical usefulness of narcotic antagonists: implications of behavioral research. Am J Drug Alcohol Abuse 2:417–432, 1975

Meyer RE, Mirin SV, Altman JL, et al: A behavioral paradigm for the evaluation of narcotic antagonists. Arch Gen Psychiatry 33:371–377, 1976

Milby JB, Garrett C, English C, et al: Take-home methadone: contingency effects on drug-seeking and productivity of narcotic addicts. Addict Behav 3:215–220, 1978

Milby JB, Clarke C, Toro C, et al: Effectiveness of urine surveillance as an adjunct to outpatient psychotherapy for drug abusers. Int J Addict 15:993–1001, 1980

Milkman H, Frosch WA: On the preferential abuse of heroin and amphetamine. J Nerv Ment Dis 156:242–248, 1973

Millman RB: Considerations on the psychotherapy of the substance of the substance abuser. Journal of Substance Abuse Treatment 3:103–109, 1986

Millman RB, Botvin GJ: Substance use, abuse and dependence, in Developmental Behavioral Pediatrics. Edited by Levine MD, Carey WB, Crocker AS, et al. Philadelphia, WB Saunders, 1983

Millman RB, Sbriglio R: Patterns of use and psychopathology in chronic marijuana users. Psychiatr Clin North Am 9:533, 1986

Minuchin S: Families and Family Therapy. Cambridge, Mass, Harvard University Press, 1974

Minuchin S, Fishman, HC: Family Therapy Techniques. Cambridge, Mass, Harvard University Press, 1981

Mirin SM (ed): Substance Abuse and Psychopathology. Clinical Insights Monograph Series. Washington, DC, American Psychiatric Press, 1984

Mirin SM, Weiss RD, Michael J: Family pedigree of psychopathology in substance abusers, in Psychopathology and Addictive Disorders. Edited by Meyer RE. New York, Guilford Press, 1986

Mohler H, Okada T: Benzodiazepine receptors. Science 198:849–851, 1977

Morgan AH, Hilgard JR: Stanford Hypnotic Clinical Scale (SHCS), in Hypnosis in the Relief of Pain. Edited by Hilgard ER, Hilgard JR. Los Altos, Calif, Kaufmann, 1975

Musto DF: The American Disease. New Haven, Yale University Press, 1973

Nash JD: Taking Charge of Your Smoking. Palo Alto, Calif, Bull Publishing Co, 1981

Nathanson MH: The central action of beta-aminopropyl-benzene (Benzedrine). JAMA 108:528–531, 1937

National Cancer Institute: Quit for Good. Publication 84-2494. Rockville, Md, US Department of Health and Human Services, 1984

National Commission on Marihuana and Drug Abuse: Drug Use in America: Problems in Perspective. Second Report of the National Commission on Marihuana and Drug Abuse. Washington, DC, National Institute on Drug Abuse, March 1973

National Institute on Drug Abuse: Diagnosis and Treatment of Phencyclidine (PCP) Toxicity. Rockville, Md, National Institute on Drug Abuse, 1979

National Institute on Drug Abuse: Treatment Research Report: Effectiveness of Drug Abuse Treatment Programs. Publication ADM 81-1143. Rockville, Md, US Department of Health and Human Services, 1981

National Institute on Drug Abuse: NIDA Capsules: 1985 National Household Survey on Drug Abuse. Rockville, Md, Press Office of the National Institute on Drug Abuse, 1986

National Research Council: Report of the National Research Council Committee on

Clinical Evaluation of Narcotic Antagonists: clinical evaluation of naltrexone in opiate dependent individuals. Arch Gen Psychiatry 35:335–340, 1978

Neubuerger OW, Miller SI, Schmitz RE, et al: Replicable abstinence rates in an alcoholism treatment program. JAMA 248:960–963, 1982

Nevins MA: Neuropathy after nitrous oxide abuse. JAMA 244:2264, 1980

Newman RG: Methadone Treatment in Narcotic Addiction. New York, Academic Press, 1977

Newman RG, Whitehill WB: Double-blind comparison of methadone and placebo maintenance treatments of narcotic addicts in Hong Kong. Lancet 11:485–488, 1979

Noel NE, McCrady BS: Behavioral treatment of an alcohol abuser with the spouse present, in Power to Change: Family Case Studies in the Treatment of Alcoholism. Edited by Kaufman E. New York, Gardner Press, 1984

Nuland W, Field P: Smoking and hypnosis: a systematic clinical approach. Int J Clin Exp Hypn 18:290–306, 1970

Nurco D: Treatment of Drug Abusers in Mental Health Systems. NIDA grant application 1 RO1 DA03271, 1983

Nurco DN, Shaffer JW, Ball JC, et al: Trends in the commission of crime among narcotic addicts over successive trends of addiction and nonaddiction. American Journal of Drug and Alcohol Abuse 10:481–489, 1984

O'Brien CP, Chaddock B, Woody G, et al: Systematic extinction of narcotic drug use using narcotic antagonists. Psychosom Med 36:458, 1974

O'Brien CP, Greenstein R, Mintz J, et al: Clinical experience with naltrexone. Am J Drug Alcohol Abuse 2:365–377, 1975

O'Brien CP, Greenstein R, Ternes J, et al: Clinical pharmacology of narcotic antagonists. Ann NY Acad Sci 311:232–240, 1978

O'Brien CP, Greenstein R, Ternes J, et al: Unreinforced self-injections: effects on rituals and outcome in heroin addicts, in Problems of Drug Dependence, 1979. Proceedings of the 41st Annual Scientific Meeting, The Committee on Problems of Drug Dependence, Inc. NIDA Research Monograph 27. Publication ADM 80-901. Edited by Harris LS. Washington, DC, US Government Printing Office, 1980

O'Brien CP, Terenius L, Wahlstrom A, et al: Endorphin levels in opioid-dependent human subjects: a longitudinal study, in Opioids in Mental Illness: Theories, Clinical Observations and Treatment Possibilities. Edited by Verebey K. Ann NY Acad Sci 398:377–387, 1982

O'Brien CP, Childress AR, McLellan AT, et al: Use of naltrexone to extinguish opioid-conditioned responses. J Clin Psychiatry 45:53, 1984

Ochs HR, Otter H: [Effects of age, sex, and smoking habits on oxazepam kinetics] Verh Dtsch Ges Inn Med 87:1205–1208, 1981

Ockene JK: Changes in cigarette smoking behavior in clinical and community trials, in The Health Consequences of Smoking: Cardiovascular Disease: A Report of the Surgeon General. Edited by Koop CE. Publication PHS 84-50204. Rockville, Md, US Department of Health and Human Services, 1983

Ockene JK, Camic PM: Public health approaches to cigarette smoking cessation. Annals of Behavioral Medicine 7:14–18, 1985

Ockene JK, Nutall R, Benfari RC, et al: A psychosocial model of smoking cessation and maintenance of cessation. Prev Med 10:623–638, 1981

Ockene JK, Bentari RC, Nuttal RL, et al: Relationship of psychosocial factors to smoking behavior change in an intervention program. Preventive Med 11:13–28, 1982

O'Donnel JA, Clayton RR: The stepping stone hypothesis; a reappraisal, in Youth Drug Abuse Problems. Edited by Bechner GM, Friedman AS. Lexington, Mass, Lexington Books, 1979

O'Donnel JA, Voss HL, Clayton RR, et al: Young Men and Drugs: A Nationwide

Survey. NIDA Research Monograph 5. Publication ADM 76-311. Washington, DC, US Government Printing Office, 1976

O'Farrell TJ, Connors, GJ, Upper D: Addictive behaviors among hospitalized psychiatric patients. Addict Behav 8:329–333, 1983

Olsen RW, Loeb-Lundberg F: Convulsant and anticonvulsant drug binding sites related to GABA-regulated chloride ion channels, in GABA and Benzodiazepine Receptors. Edited by Costa E, DiChiari G, Gessa GL. New York, Raven Press, 1981

Olson E, McEnrue J, Greenbaum DM: Recognition general considerations, and techniques in the management of drug intoxication. Heart Lung 12:110–113, 1983

Orne M, Wender P: Anticipatory socialization for psychotherapy: method and rationale. Am J Psychiatry 124:88–89, 1968

Owen RT, Tyrer B: Benzodiazepine dependence: a review of the evidence. Drugs 25:385–398, 1983

Pantuck EJ, Pantuck CB, Anderson KE, et al: Cigarette smoking and chlorpromazine disposition and actions. Pharmacol Ther 31:533–538, 1982

Papp P: Paradoxical strategies and countertransference, in Questions and Answers in the Practice of Family Therapy. Edited by Gurman AS. New York, Brunner Mazel, 1981

Pechacek TF: Modification of smoking behavior, in The Behavioral Aspects of Smoking, NIDA Research Monograph 26. DHEW no. 79-882. Edited by Krashegor NA. Rockville, Md, National Institute of Drug Abuse, 1979

Pederson LL: Compliance with physician advice to quit smoking: a review of the literature. Prev Med 11:71–84, 1982

Peterson RC: Marijuana and health: 1980. NIDA Research Monograph 31. DHEW no. 80-1001. Edited by Peterson RC. Rockville, Md, National Institute of Drug Abuse, 1980

Pevnick JS, Jasinski DR, Haertzen CA: Abrupt withdrawal from therapeutically administered diazepam. Arch Gen Psychiatry 35:995–998, 1978

Perkins ME, Block HI: Survey of a methadone maintenance treatment program. Am J Psychiatry 126:33–40, 1970

Pfohl D, Allen J, Atkinson R, et al: TREXAN (naltrexone hydrochloride): a review of hepatic toxicity at high dosage, in Problems of Drug Dependence 1985. Edited by Harris LS. NIDA Research Monograph Rockville, Md, US Department of Health and Human Services, 1986

Pierson PS et al: Sudden deaths in infants born to methadone-maintained addicts. JAMA 220:1733, 972

Pitts FN Jr: Pharmacological therapies for PCP abuse called fairly effective. Clinical Psychiatry News 12:17, 1984

Platt JJ, Metzger D: The role of employment in the rehabilitation of heroin addicts, in Progress in the Development of Cost-Effective Treatment for Drug Abusers. NIDA Research Monograph 58. Publication ADM 85-1401. Edited by Ashery RS. Washington, DC, US Government Printing Office, 1985

Platt JJ, Spivack G: Measures of Interpersonal Problem-Solving for Adults and Adolescents. Philadelphia, Hahnemann University, 1977

Platt JJ, Morell J, Flaherty E, et al: Controlled Study of Methadone Rehabilitation Process. Final Report, National Institute on Drug Abuse Grant Number R01 DA01929. Philadelphia, Hahnemann Medical College and Hospital, 1982

Pohorecky LA: Interaction of alcohol and stress: a review. Neurosci Biobehav Rev 5:209–229, 1981

Polakow RL, Doctor RM: Treatment of marijuana and barbiturate dependence by contingency contracting. J Behav Ther Exp Psychiatry 4:375–377, 1973

Polakow RL, Doctor RM: A behavioral modification program for adult drug offenders. Journal of Research on Crime and Delinquency 11:63–69, 1974

Pomerleau OF: Underlying mechanisms in substance abuse: examples from research on smoking. Addict Behav 6:187–196, 1981

Pomerleau OF, Pomerleau CS: Neuroregulators and the reinforcement of smoking: Towards a biobehavioral explanation. Neurosci Biobehav Rev 8:503–513, 1984

Post RM, Kotin J, Goodwin FR: The effects of cocaine on depressed patients. Am J Psychiatry 131:511–517, 1974

Post RM, Kopanda RT, Black KE: Progressive effects of cocaine on behavior and central amine metabolism in rhesus monkeys: relationship to kindling and psychosis. Biol Psychiatry 11:403–419, 1976

Pottash ALC, Gold MS, Extein I: The use of the clinical laboratory, in Inpatient Psychiatry Diagnosis and Treatment. Edited by Sederer LI. Baltimore, Williams and Wilkins, 1982

Preskorn SH, Gold MS, Extein I: Therapeutic drug level monitoring in psychiatry, in Diagnostic and Laboratory Testing in Psychiatry. Edited by Gold MS, Pottash ALC. New York, Plenum, 1986, pp 131–154

Prochaska JO, DiClemente CC: Stages and processes of self-change of smoking: toward an integrative model of change. J Consult Clin Psychol 51:390–395, 1983

Prusoff B, Thompson WD, Scholomskos D, et al: Psychosocial stressors and depression among former heroin dependent patients maintained on methadone. J Nerv Ment Dis 165:57–63, 1977

Raskin NN: Methadone for the pentazocine-dependent patient. N Engl J Med 283:1349, 1970

Rauckman EJ, Rosen GM, Cavagnaro J: Norcocaine nitroxide: a potential hepatotoxic metabolite of cocaine. Mol Pharmacol 21:458–462, 1982

Rawson R, Obert J, McCann M, et al: Cocaine treatment outcome: cocaine use following inpatient, outpatient and no treatment, NIDA Research Monograph 67.

Razani J, Chisolm D, Glasser M, et al: Self-regulated methadone detoxification of heroin addicts. Arch Gen Psychiatry 32:909–911, 1975

Redmond DE Jr, Krystal JH: Multiple mechanisms of withdrawal from opioid drugs. Annu Rev Neurosci 7:443–478, 1984

Reith M, Sershen H, Allen DL, et al: A portion of (3H) cocaine binding in brain is associated with serotonergic neurons. Mol Pharmacol 23:600, 1983

Relman A (ed): Marijuana and Health. Washington, DC, Institute of Medicine, National Academy Press, 1982

Resnick R, Resnick E: Psychological issues in the treatment of cocaine abusers. Presented at the Columbia University Symposium on Cocaine Abuse: New Treatment Approaches. New York, 5 January 1985

Resnick RB, Schuyten-Resnick E, Washton AM. Narcotic antagonists in the treatment of opioid dependence: review and commentary. Compr Psychiatry 20:116–125, 1979

Resnick RB, Schuyten-Resnick E, Washton AM: Assessment of narcotic antagonists in the treatment of opioid dependence. Annu Rev Pharmacol Toxicol 20:463–474, 1980

Resnick RB, Washton AM, Stone-Washton N, et al: Psychotherapy and naltrexone in opioid dependence, in Problems of Drug Dependence. NIDA Research Monograph 34. Edited by Harris LS. Rockville, Md, US Department of Health and Human Services, 1981, pp 109–115

Revell AD, Warburton DM, Wesnes K: Smoking as a coping strategy. Addict Behav 10:209–224, 1985

Rickels K. Csanalosi I, Greisman P, et al: A controlled clinical trial of alprazolam for the treatment of anxiety. Am J Psychiatry 140:82–84, 1983

Ricuaurte GA, Schuster CR, Seiden LS: Long-term effects of repeated methylamphet-amine administration on dopamine and serotonin neurons in rat brain: a regional study. Brain Res 193:153, 1980

Rimm DC, Masters JC: Behavior Therapy. New York, Academic Press, 1979

Roberts JR, Quattrochi E, Howland MA: Severe hyperthermia secondary to intrave-nous drug abuse (letter). American Journal of Emergency Medicine 2:373, 1984

Robins LN, Helzer JE, Davis DH: Narcotic use in Southeast Asia and afterwards. Arch Gen Psychiatry 32:955–961, 1975

Rosecan J: The treatment of cocaine abuse with imipramine. L-tyrosine, and L-tryp-tophan. Presented at the VII World Congress of Psychiatry. Vienna, Austria, 14–19 July 1983

Rosen AM, Mukherjee S, Shinbach K: The efficacy of ECT in phencyclidine-induced psychosis. J Clin Psychiatry 45:220–222, 1984

Rosenberg L, Kaufman DW, Helmrich SP, et al: The risk of myocardial infarction after quitting smoking in men under 55 years of age. N Engl J Med 313:1511–1514, 1985

Rotunno M, McGoldrick M: Italian families, in Ethnicity and Family Therapy. Edited by McGoldrick M, Pearce JK, Giordano J. New York, Guilford Press, 1982

Rounsaville BJ, Kleber HD: Untreated opiate addicts. Arch Gen Psychiatry 42:1072–1080, 1985a

Rounsaville BJ, Kleber H: Psychotherapy/counseling for opiate addicts: strategies for use in different treatment settings. Int J Addict 20:869–896, 1985b

Rounsaville BJ, Weissman MM, Rosenberger PH, et al: Detecting depressive disorders in drug abusers. J Affect Disord 1:255–267, 1979

Rounsaville BJ, Rosenberger PH, Wilber CH, et al: A comparison of the SADS/RDC and the DSM-III: diagnosing drug abusers. J Nerv Ment Dis 168:90–97, 1980

Rounsaville BJ, Wilber CH, Rosenberger D, et al: Comparison of opiate addicts' reports of psychiatric history with reports of significant other informants. Am J Drug Alcohol Abuse 8:51–69, 1981

Rounsaville BJ, Tierney T, Crits-Christoph K, et al: Predictors of treatment outcome in opiate addicts: evidence for the multidimensionality of addicts' problems. Compr Psychiatry 23:462–278, 1982a

Rounsaville BJ, Weissman MM, Kleber HD: The significance of alcoholism in treated opiate addicts. J Nerv Ment Dis 170:479–488, 1982b

Rounsaville BJ, Weissman MM, Kleber HD, et al: Heterogeneity of psychiatric diag-nosis in treated opiate addicts. Arch Gen Psychiatry 39:161–166, 1982c

Rounsaville BJ, Weissman MM, Wilber CH, et al: Diagnosis and symptoms of depres-sion in opiate addicts: course and relationship to treatment outcome. Arch Gen Psychiatry 39:151–156, 1982d

Rounsaville BJ, Weissman MM, Wilber CH, et al: Identifying alcoholism in treated opiate addicts. Am J Psychiatry 140:764–766, 1983a

Rounsaville BJ, Weissman MM, Kleber HD: An evaluation of depression in opiate addicts. Research Communications in Mental Health 3:257–289, 1983b

Rounsaville BJ, Glazer W, Wilber CH, et al: Short-term interpersonal psychotherapy in methadone maintained opiate addicts. Arch Gen Psychiatry 40:629–636, 1983c

Rounsaville BJ, Gawin FH, Kleber HD: Interpersonal Psychotherapy (IPT) adapted for ambulatory cocaine abusers. Am J Drug Alcohol Abuse 11:171–191, 1985

Rounsaville BJ, Spitzer RL, Williams JB: Proposed changes in DSM-III substance use disorders: description and rationale. Am J Psychiatry 143:463–468, 1986a

Rounsaville BJ, Kosten TR, Weissman MM, et al: Prognostic significance of psychiatric disorders in treated opiate addicts. Arch Gen Psychiatry 43:739–745, 1986b

Rounsaville BJ, Hesselbrock M, Meyer R: Psychopathology as a predictor of treatment outcome in alcoholics. Arch Gen Psychiatry 44:505–513, 1987

Rowbotham M, Jones RT, Benowitz N, et al: Trazodone-oral cocaine interactions. Arch Gen Psychiatry 41:895–899, 1984

Rubin V, Comitas L: Ganja in Jamaica. The Hague, Mouton, 1975

Rumbaugh C, Bergeron R, Fang H, et al: Cerebral angiographic change in the drug abuse patient. Radiology 101:335–344, 1971

Rumbaugh CL, Fang HCH, Wilson GH, et al: Cerebral CT findings in drug abuse: clinical and experimental observations. J Comput Assist Tomogr 4:330–334, 1980

Ruttenberg AJ, Luke JL: Heroin related deaths: new epidemiological insights. Science 226:14–20, 1984

Salber EJ, Freeman HE, Abelin T: Needed research on smoking: lessons from the Newton study, in Smoking, Health and Behavior. Edited by Borgatta EF, Evans RR. Chicago, Aldine, 1968

Sandmaier M: The Invisible Alcoholics: Women and Alcohol Abuse in America. New York, McGraw-Hill, 1980

Sapira JD, Cherubin CE: Drug Abuse: A Guide for the Clinician. Amsterdam, Excerpta Medica, 1975

Schachter S: Pharmacological and psychological determinants of smoking. Ann Intern Med 88:104–114, 1978

Schneider NG, Jannik ME, Forsythe AB, et al: Nicotine gum in smoking cessation: a placebo-controlled, double-blind trial. Addict Behav 8:253–262, 1983

Schnoll SH: Street PCP scene: issues on synthesis and contamination. Journal of Psychedelic Drugs 12:229–233, 1980

Schnoll S, Daghestani A: Treatment of marijuana abuse: marijuana update. Psychiatric Annals 16:249–254, 1986

Schnoll SH, Karrigan J, Kitchen SB, et al: Characteristics of cocaine abusers presenting for treatment, in Cocaine Use in America: Epidemiologic and Clinical Perspectives. NIDA Research Monograph 61. Edited by Adams EH, Kozel NJ. Rockville, Md, Department of Health and Human Services, 1985, pp 171–181

Schöph J: Withdrawal phenomena after long-term administration of benzodiazepines: a review of recent investigations. Pharmacopsychiatry 16:1–8, 1983

Schuckit MA: The clinical implications of primary diagnostic groups among alcoholics. Arch Gen Psychiatry 42:1043–1049, 1985a

Schuckit MA: Ethanol-induced changes in body sway in men at high alcoholism risk. Arch Gen Psychiatry 42:375–379, 1985b

Schuster CR, Fischman MW: Characteristics of human volunteering for a cocaine research project, in Cocaine Use in America: Epidemiologic and Clinical Perspectives. NIDA Research Monograph 61. Edited by Adams EH, Kozel NJ. Rockville, Md, Department of Health and Human Services, 1985, pp 158–170

Schwartz CJ: The complications of LSD: a review of the literature. J Nerv Ment Dis 146:174–186, 1968

Schwartz RH, Hawks RL: Laboratory detection of marijuana use. JAMA 254:788–792, 1985

Schwartz SR, Goldfinger: The new chronic patient: clinical characteristics of an emerging group. Hosp Community Psychiatry 32:470–474, 1982

Schwarz RM, Burkhart BR, Green SB: Sensation-seeking and anxiety as factors in social drinking. J Stud Alcohol 43:1108–1114, 1982

Scopetta MA, King OE, Szapocznik J, et al: Ecological structural family therapy with Cuban immigrant families. Unpublished 1979

Scott NR, Orzen N, Musillo C, et al: Methadone in the Southwest: a three-year follow-up of Chicano heroin addicts. Am J Orthopsychiatry 43:355–361, 1973

Seiden L: Neurochemical toxic effects of psychomotor stimulants. Presented at the 23rd Annual Meeting of the American College of Neuropsychopharmacology. San Juan, PR, 12 December 1984

Sells SB: Treatment effectiveness, in Handbook on Drug Abuse. Edited by Dupont RL, Goldstein A, O'Donnell J. Washington, DC, US Government Printing Office, 1979, pp 105–118

Sells SB, Simpson DD: The Effectiveness of Drug Abuse Treatment, vol 3. Cambridge, Mass, Balinger, 1976

Selzer ML: The Michigan Alcoholism Screening Test: the quest for a new diagnostic instrument. Am J Psychiatry 127:1653–1658, 1971

Senay EC: Substance Abuse Disorders in Clinical Practice. Littleton, Mass, John Wright, 1983

Senay EC, Schick JFE: Pupillography responses to methadone challenge: aid to diagnosis of opioid dependence. Drug Alcohol Depend 3:133–138, 1978

Senay EC et al: IDAP-five year results. National Conference on Methadone Treatment Proceedings 2:1437–1464, 1973

Senay EC, Dorus W, Goldberg F, et al: Withdrawal from methadone maintenance. Arch Gen Psychiatry 34:361–367, 1977

Seymour RB, Gorton JG, Smith DE: The client with a substance abuse problem, in Practice and Management of Psychiatric Emergency Care. Edited by Gorton JG, Partridge R. St. Louis, CV Mosby Co, 1982

Shafer J: Designer drugs. Science 85:60–67, 1985

Shamsie SJ: Antisocial adolescents: our treatments do not work: where do we go from here? Am J Psychiatry 26:357–364, 1981

Sheehan DV: Current views on the treatment of panic and phobic disorders. Drug Ther 12:74–93, 1982

Sheffet A, Quinones MA, Doyle KM, et al: Assessment of treatment outcomes in a drug abuse rehabilitation network: Newark, New Jersey. Am J Drug Alcohol Abuse 7:141, 1980

Sheppard C, Fracchia J, Ricca E, et al: Indications of psychopathology in male narcotic abusers, their effects, and relation to treatment effectiveness. J Psychol 81:351–360, 1972

Shiffman SM: Relapse following smoking cessation: a situational analysis. J Consult Clin Psychol 50:71–86, 1982

Shiffman S: Coping with temptations to smoke. J Consult Clin Psychol 52:261–267, 1984

Shiffman S, Read L, Maltese J, et al: Preventing relapse in ex-smokers: a self-management approach, in Relapse Prevention. Edited by Marlatt A, Gordon J. New York, Guilford Press, 1985

Shukla D: Intracranial hermorrhage associated with amphetamine use. Neurology 32:917–918, 1982

Sideroff SI, Charuvastra VC, Jarvik ME: Craving in heroin addicts maintained on the opiate antagonist naltrexone. Am J Drug Alcohol Abuse 5:415–423, 1978

Siegel RK: Cocaine hallucinations. Am J Psychiatry 135:309–314, 1978

Siegel RK: Cocaine smoking. J Psychoactive Drugs 14:321–337, 1982

Siegel RK: New patterns of cocaine use: changing doses and routes, in Cocaine Use in America: Epidemiologic and Clinical Perspectives. NIDA Research Monograph 61. Edited by Adams EH, Kozel NJ. Rockville, Md, Department of Health and Human Services, 1985a, pp 204–220

Siegel RK: Treatment of cocaine abuse: historical and contemporary perspectives. J Psychoactive Drugs 17:1–9, 1985b

Sifneos P: Short-term Psychotherapy and Emotional Crisis. Cambridge, Mass, Harvard University Press, 1972

Silver FC, Panepinto WC, Arnon D, et al: A family approach in treating the pregnant addict, in Developments in the Field of Drug Abuse. Edited by Senay E. Cambridge, Mass, Schenkman Pub, 1975

Silverberg R: Drug Themes in Science Fiction. NIDA Research Issues Series No 10. Washington, DC, US Government Printing Office, 1974

Simpson DD: Treatment for drug abuse: follow-up outcomes and length of time spent. Arch Gen Psychiatry 38:875–880, 1981

Simpson DD, Sells SB: Effectiveness of treatment for drug abuse: an overview of the DARP research program. Adv Alcohol Subst Abuse 2:7–29, 1982

Simpson DD, Joe GW, Bracy SA: Six-year follow-up of opioid addicts after admission to treatment. Arch Gen Psychiatry 39:1318–1326, 1982

Singer B, Luborsky L: Countertransference: the status of clinical vs. quantitative research, in The Therapist's Handbook for Effective Psychotherapy: An Empirical Assessment. Edited by Gurman A, Razin A. New York, Pergamon Press, 1977, pp 431–448

Siva Sankar DV: LSD-A Total Study. Westbury, NY, PJD Publications, 1975

Skolnick P, Moncada V, Barber JL: Pentobarbital dual actions to increase brain benzodiazepine receptor affinity. Science 211:1448–1450, 1981

Smialek JE, Monforte JR, Aronon R, et al: Methadone deaths in children: a continuing problem. JAMA 238:2516–2517, 1977

Smith DE: The characteristics of dependence in high-dose methamphetamine abuse. Int J Addict 4:453–459, 1969

Smith DE: Cocaine-alcohol abuse: epidemiological, diagnostic, and treatment considerations. J Psychoactive Drugs 18:117–129, 1986

Smith DE, Wesson DR: A new method for treatment of barbiturate dependence. JAMA 213:294–295, 1970

Smith DE, Wesson DR: A phenobarbital technique for the withdrawal of barbiturate abuse. Arch Gen Psychiatry 24:56–60, 1971

Smith DE, Wesson DR: Barbiturate and other sedative hypnotics, in Treatment Aspects of Drug Dependence. New York, CRC Press, 1978, pp 117–130

Smith DE, Wesson DR: Benzodiazepine dependency syndromes. J Psychoactive Drugs 15:85–95, 1983

Smith D, Wesson D, Seymour R, et al: The diagnosis and treatment of the PCP abuse syndrome, in Phencyclidine (PCP) Abuse: An Appraisal, NIDA Monograph 21. Edited by Peterson R, Stillman R. Rockville, Md, Department of Health and Human Services, 1978

Smith DE, Wesson DR, Damman G: Treatment of the polydrug abuser, in Proceedings of the National Drug Abuse Conference. New York, Marcel Dekker, 1979

Smith DE, Milkman HB, Sunderwirth SG: Addictive disease: concept and controversy, in The Addictions: Multidisciplinary Perspectives and Treatment. Edited by Milkman HB, Shaffer HJ. Lexington, Mass, DC Heath and Co, 1985

Smith M, Glass G, Miller T: The Benefits of Psychotherapy. Baltimore, Johns Hopkins University Press, 1980

Spiegel H: A single-treatment method to stop smoking using ancillary self-hypnosis. Int J Clin Exp Hypn 18:235–250, 1970

Spitzer RL, Williams JBW: Classification of mental disorders and DSM-III, in Comprehensive Textbook of Psychiatry, 3rd ed, vol 1. Edited by Kaplan H, Freedman A, Sadock B. Baltimore, Williams and Wilkins, 1980, 1035–1072

Spotts JV, Shontz FC: Cocaine Users: A Representative Case Approach. New York, Free Press, 1980

Spotts JV, Shontz FC: Ego development, dragon fights, and chronic drug abusers. Int J Addict 17:945–976, 1982

Spyraki C, Fibiger HC, Phillips AC: Cocaine-induced place preference conditioning: lack of effects of neuroleptics and 6 hydroxydopamine lesions. Brain Res 253:195–203, 1982

Squires RF, Braestrup C: Benzodiazepine receptors in rat brain. Nature 266:732–734, 1977

Stanton MD: Family treatment approaches to drug abuse problems: a review. Fam Process 18:251–280, 1979

Stanton MD: An integrated structural/strategic approach to family therapy. Journal of Marital and Family Therapy 7:427–439, 1981

Stanton MD: The Family Therapy of Drug Abuse and Addiction. New York, Guilford Press, 1982

Stanton MD, Todd TC: The Family Therapy of Drug Abuse and Addiction. New York, Guilford Press, 1982

Stefanis C, Boulougouris I, Liakos A: Clinical and psychophysiological effects of cannabis in long-term users, in Pharmacology of Marijuana. Edited by Braude MC, Szara S. New York, Raven Press, 1976

Steffenhagen RA: Drug abuse and related phenomena: an Adlerian approach. Journal of Individual Psychology 30:238–250, 1974

Steinglass P: A life history model of the alcoholic family. Fam Process 19:211–226, 1980

Sterling-Smith R: Pot and pills: toys or therapy? in Drugs and Suicide: When Other Coping Strategies Fail. Edited by Lettieri D. Beverly Hills, Calif, Sage Publications, 1978, pp 279–294

Stimmel BR et al: The prognosis of patients detoxified from methadone maintenance: a follow-up study. National Conference on Methadone Treatment Proceedings 1:270–271, 1973

Stimmel B, Goldberg J, Rotkopf E, et al: Ability to remain abstinent after methadone detoxification: a six year study. JAMA 237:1216–1220, 1977

Stimmel B, Hanbury R, Sturiano V, et al: Alcoholism as a risk factor in methadone maintenance: a randomized controlled trial. Am J Med 73:631–636, 1982

Stimmel B, Cohen M, Sturiano V, et al: Is treatment effective in persons on methadone maintenance? Am J Psychol 140:862–866, 1983

Stimson GV, Oppenheimer E: Heroin Addiction: Treatment and Control in Britain. London, Tavistock Publications Ltd, 1982

Stitzer ML, Griffiths RA, McLellan AT, et al: Diazepam use among methadone maintenance patients: patterns and dosages. Drug Alcohol Depend 8:189–199, 1981

Stitzer ML, Bigelow GE, Liebson IA, et al: Contingent reinforcement for benzodiazepine-free urines: evaluation of a drug abuse treatment intervention. J Appl Behav Anal 15:493–503, 1982

Stitzer ML, Bigelow GE, McCaul ME: Behavioral approaches to drug abuse, in Progress in Behavior Modification, vol 14. Edited by Hersen M. New York, Academic Press, 1983

Stone MH: Drug related schizophrenic syndromes. International Journal of Psychiatry 1985

Strategy Council on Drug Abuse: Federal Strategy for Drug Abuse and Drug Traffic Prevention 1973. Washington, DC, US Government Printing Office, 1973

Stuart RB: Helping Couples Change. New York, Guilford Press, 1980

Suedfeld P, Kristeller JL: Stimulus reduction as a technique in health psychology. Health Psychol 1:337–357, 1982

Sutker PB: Drug dependent women: an overview of the literature, in Treatment Services for Drug Dependent Women, vol 1. Publication (ADM) 81-1177. Edited by Beschner GM, et al. Rockville, Md, National Institute on Drug Abuse, 1981

Swatek R: Marijuana use: persistence and urinary elimination. Journal of Substance Abuse Treatment 1:265–270, 1984

Talbott JA, Teague JW: Marijuana psychosis. JAMA 210:299–302, 1969

Taylor DL, Ho BT, Fagan JD: Increased dopamine receptor binding in rat brain by repeated cocaine injection. Community Psychopharmacology 3:137–142, 1979

Tellegen A, Atkinson G: Openness to absorbing and self altering experiences ("absorption"), a trait related to hypnotic susceptibility. J Abnorm Psychol 83:268–277, 1974

Tennant FS: The clinical syndrome of marijuana dependence. Psychiatric Annals 16:1986

Tennant F, Tarver A: Double-blind comparison of desipramine and placebo in withdrawal from cocaine dependence, in Problems of Drug Dependence. NIDA Research Monograph 55. Edited by Harris LS. Rockville, Md, Department of Health and Human Services, 1986, pp 159–163

Tennant FS, Rawson RA, McCann M: Withdrawal from chronic phencyclidine (PCP) dependence with desipramine Am J Psychiatry 138:845–847, 1981

Tennant F, Rawson R, Cohen A, et al: A clinical experience with naltrexone in suburban opioid addicts. J Clin Psychiatry 45:42–45, 1984

Tennant FS Jr, Rawson RA, Pumphrey E, et al: Clinical experiences with 959 opioid-dependent patients treated with levo-alpha-acetylmethadol (LAAM). Journal of Substance Abuse Treatment 3:195–202, 1986

Tomkins S: Psychological model for smoking behavior. Am J Public Health 56:17–20, 1966

Trueblood B, Judson BA, Goldstein A: Acceptability of methadyl acetate (L-AAM) as compared with methadone in a treatment program for heroin addicts. Drug Alcohol Depend 3:125–132, 1978

Tse DT, Ober RR: Talc retinopathy. Am J Ophthalmol 90:624–640, 1980

Tuason VB, Jones WL: Methadone maintenance treatment: a report on over three years experience. Minn Med 57:899–901, 1974

US Department of Health, Education, and Welfare: Smoking and Health: Report of the Advisory Committee to the Surgeon General of the Public Health Service. Publication PHS 64-1103. Rockville, Md, Centers for Disease Control, 1964

US Department of Health, Education, and Welfare: Smoking and Health: A Report of the Surgeon General. Publication PHS 79-50066. Washington, DC, US Government Printing Office, 1979

US Department of Health and Human Services: The Health Consequences of Smoking: Cardiovascular Disease: A Report of the Surgeon General. Publication PHS 84-50204. Rockville, Md, Office on Smoking and Health, 1983

US Department of Health and Human Services: The Health Consequences of Smoking: Cancer and Chronic Lung Disease in the Workplace: A Report of the Surgeon General. Publication PHS 85-50207. Rockville, Md, Office on Smoking and Health, 1985

US Department of Health and Human Services: The Health Consequences of Smoking: Nicotine Addiction. Publication CDC 88-8406. Rockville, Md, Office on Smoking and Health, 1988

Utena H: Behavioral aberrations in methamphetamine intoxicated animals and chemical correlates in the brain. Prog Brain Res. 21:1902, 1966

Van Dyke C, Ungerer J, Jatlow P, et al: Intranasal cocaine dose relationships of psychological effects and plasma levels. Int J Psychiatry Med 12:1–13, 1982

Verebey K, Jukofsky P, Mule SJ: Evaluation of a new TLC confirmation technique for positive EMIT cannabinoid samples. Research Communications on Substances Abuse 6:1–9, 1985

Verebey K, Martin D, Gold MS: Interpretation of drug abuse testing: strengths and limitations of current methodology, in Psychiatric Medicine. Edited by Hall RCW. Jamaica, Spectrum Publications, 1986a

Verebey K, Gold MS, Mule JS: Laboratory testing in the diagnosis of marijuana intoxication and withdrawal. Psychiatric Annals 16:235, 1986b

Wack J, Rodin L: Smoking and its effects on body weight and the systems of caloric regulation. Am J Clin Nutr 35:366–380, 1982

Waldron VD et al: Methadone overdose treated with naloxone infusion. JAMA 225:53, 1973

Wang RIH, Wiesen RL, Sofian L, et al: Rating the presence and severity of opiate dependence. Clin Pharmacol Ther 16:653–658, 1974

Washton AM: Cocaine abuse treatment. Psychiatry Letters 3:51–56, 1985

Washton A: Nonpharmacologic treatments of cocaine abuse. Psychiatr Clin North Am 9:563–571, 1986a

Washton AM: Treatment of cocaine abuse, in Problems of Drug Dependence, 1985 NIDA Research Monograph 67. Edited by Harris LF. US Government Printing Office, ADM 86-1448, 1986

Washton AM, Resnick RG: Clonidine in opiate withdrawal: review and appraisal of clinical findings. Pharmacotherapy 1:140–146, 1981

Washton AM, Pottash AC, Gold MS: Naltrexone in addicted business executives and physicians. J Clin Psychiatry 45:39–41, 1984

Washton AM, Gold MS, Pottash AC: Successful use of naltrexone in addicted physicians and business executives. Adv Alcohol Subst Abuse 4:89–96, 1984a

Washton AM, Gold MS, Pottash ALC: Survey of 500 callers to a national cocaine helpline. Psychosomatics 25:771–775, 1984b

Washton AM, Gold MS, Pottash ALC: Cocaine abuse: techniques of assessment, diagnosis and treatment. Psychiatric Medicine 1985

Watkins P, Soledad G: My Life with Charles Manson. New York, Bantam Books, 1979

Watson R, Hartmann E, Schildkraut JJ: Amphetamine withdrawal: affective state, sleep patterns and MHPG excretion. Am J Psychiatry 129:263–269, 1972

Way EL: Sites and mechanisms of basic narcotic receptor function based on current research. Ann Emerg Med 15:1021–1025, 1986

Weinstein H, Maayuni S, Glick S, et al: Integrated studies on the biochemical, behavioral and molecular pharmacology of phencyclidine: a progress report, in PCP (Phencyclidine): Historical and Current Perspectives. Edited by Domino EF. Ann Arbor, Mich, NPP Books, 1981

Weiss RD, Goldenheim PD, Mirin SM: Pulmonary dysfunction in cocaine smokers. Am J Psychiatry 138:1110–1112, 1981

Weiss RD, Mirin SM, Michael JL: Psychopathology in chronic cocaine abusers. Presented at the 136th Annual Meeting of the American Psychiatric Association. New York, 4 May 1983.

Weiss RD, Pope HG, Mirin SM: Treatment of chronic cocaine abuse and attention deficit disorder, residual type, with magnesium pemoline. Drug Alcohol Depend 15:69–72, 1985

Weiss RD, Mirin SM, Michael JL, et al: Psychopathology in chronic cocaine abusers. Am J Drug Alcohol Abuse 12:17–29, 1986

Weissman MM, Jarrett RB, Rush AJ: Psychotherapy and its relevance to pharmacotherapy of major depression: a decade later (1976–1986), in Psychopharmacology: The Third Generation of Progress. Edited by Meltzer H. New York, Raven Press, 1987, pp 1059–1069

Weller RA, Halikas JA: Change in effects from marijuana: 5-to-6 year study. J Clin Psychiatry 43:363–365, 1982

Wesson DR, Smith DE: Psychedelics in Treatment Aspects of Drug Dependence. West Palm Beach, Fl, CRC Press 1978

Wesson DR, Smith DE: Low dose benzodiazepine withdrawal syndrome: receptor site mediated. NEWS: California Society for the Treatment of Alcoholism and Other Drug Dependencies 9:1–15, 1982

Westermeyer J: Medical and nonmedical treatment for narcotic addicts: a comparative study from Asia. J Nerv Ment Dis 167:205–211, 1979

Wetli CV, Wright RK: Death caused by recreational cocaine use. JAMA 241:2519–2522, 1979

Whybrow P, Akiskal H, McKinney W: Mood Disorders: Toward a New Psychobiology. New York, Plennum, 1984

Wieland WF, Chambers CD: Two methods of utilizing methadone in the outpatient treatment of narcotic addicts. Int J Addict 5:431–438, 1970

Wikler A: Conditioning factors in opiate addiction and relapse, in Narcotics. Edited by Wilner DI, Kassebaum GG. New York, McGraw-Hill, 1965, pp 85–100

Wikler A: Dynamics of drug dependence: implications of a conditioning theory for research. Arch Gen Psychiatry 28:611–616, 1973

Wikler A: Opioid Dependence: Mechanisms and Treatment. New York, Plenum, 1980

Wilkinson GR: Treatment of drug intoxication: a review of some scientific principles. Clin Toxicol 3:249, 1970

Willett EA: Group therapy in a methadone treatment program: an evaluation of changes in interpersonal behavior. Int J Addict 8:33–39, 1973

Winer LR, Lorio JP, Scrofford I: Effects of treatment on drug abusers and family. Report to SOADAP, 1974

Wise RA: Neural mechanisms of the reinforcing action of cocaine. NIDA Red Monograph Ser. vol. 50: Cocaine: Pharmacology, Effects and Treatment of Abuse. Edited by Grabowski J. 1984

Woody G: Psychiatric aspects of opiate dependence: diagnostic and therapeutic issues, in Psychodynamics of Drug Dependence. NIDA Research Monograph 12. Edited by Blaine J, Julius D. Washington, DC, US Government Printing Office, 1977

Woody GE, O'Brien CP, Greenstein RA: Misuse and abuse of diazepam: an increasingly common medical problem. Int J Addict 10:843–848, 1975

Woody GE, Luborsky L, McLellan AT, et al: Psychotherapy for opiate addicts: does it help? Arch Gen Psychiatry 40:639–645, 1983

Woody GE, McLellan AT, Luborksy L, et al: Severity of psychiatric symptoms as a prediction of benefits from psychotherapy: The Veterans Administration-Penn Study. Am J Psychiatry 141:1172–1177, 1984

Woody GE, McLellan AT, Luborsky L, et al: Sociopathy and psychotherapy outcome. Arch Gen Psychiatry 42:1081–1086, 1985

Woody G, McLellan T, Luborsky L, et al: Sociopathy and psychotherapy outcomes. Arch Gen Psychiatry in press

World Health Organization: Mental Disorders: Glossary and Guide to Their Classification, 9th revision. Geneva, World Health Organization, 1978

Wright TH, Whitaker SB, Welch CB, et al: Hepatic enzyme induction patterns and phenothiazine side effects. Clin Pharmacol Ther 34:533–538, 1983

Wunderlich RA, Lozes J, Lewis J: Recidivism rates of group therapy participants and other adolescents processed by a juvenile court. Psychotherapy: Research and Practice 11:243–245, 1974

Wurmser L: Psychoanalytic considerations of the etiology of compulsive drug use. J Am Psychoanal Assoc. 22:820–843, 1979

Wurmser L: The Hidden Dimension: Psychopathology of Compulsive Drug Use. New York, Jason Aronson, 1979

Yagi B: Studies in general activity, II: the effect of methamphetamine. Annals of Animal Psychology 13:37–47, 1963

Yago KB, Pitts FN Jr, Burgoyne RW, et al: The urban epidemic of phencyclidine (PCP)

use: clinical and laboratory evidence from a public psychiatric hospital emergency service. J Clin Psychiatry 42:193–196, 1981

Yaksh TL, Kohl RL, Rudy TA: Induction of tolerance and withdrawal in rats receiving morphine in the spinal subarachnoid space. Eur J Pharmacol 41:275–284, 1977

Yamaguchi K, Kandel DB: Patterns of drug use from adolescence to young adulthood, III: predictors of progression. Am J Public Health 74:673–681, 1984

Yates AJ, Thain J: Self-efficacy as a predictor of relapse following voluntary cessation of smoking. Addict Behav 10:291–298, 1985

Yesavage JA, Leirer VO, Denari M, et al: Carryover effects of marijuana intoxication on aircraft pilot performance: a preliminary report. Am J Psychiatry 142:1325–1329, 1985

Yokel RA, Wise RA: Increased lever pressing for amphetamine after pimozide in rats: implications for a dopamine theory of reward. Science 221:773–774, 1983

Zangwell BC, McGahan P, Dorozynsky L, et al: How effective is LAAM treatment? Clinical comparison with methadone, in Problems of Drug Dependence, 1985. NIDA Research Monograph 67. Publication ADM 86-1448. Edited by Harris LS. Washington, DC, US Government Printing Office, 1986

Ziegler-Driscoll G: Family research study at Eagleville Hospital and Rehabilitation Center. Fam Process 61:175–189, 1977

Zinberg NE: Alcoholics Anonymous and the treatment and prevention of alcoholism. Alcoholism: Clinical and Experimental Research 1:91–102, 1977

Zuckerman M, Sola S, Masterson J, et al: MMPI patterns in drug abusers before and after treatment in therapeutic communities. J Consult Clin Psychol 43:286–296, 1975

Schizophrenia

Chapter 142

Introduction

The topic of schizophrenia has traditionally stimulated intense debates. Positions tend to be strongly held and often are not based on empirical studies. It is not a surprise that a disorder that is so heterogeneous in its manifestations and that is often so devastating in its consequences mobilizes strong feelings.

The contributors to this section attempt to present a view of the schizophrenias that is based on generally agreed upon current thinking. More controversial issues, including the newest findings, are not presented. The section includes the less controversial findings so as to serve as a "travel guide" to schizophrenia. It cannot be definitive, nor can its recommendations be fixed. New information is continually being generated; therefore, conclusions must change over time. Nevertheless, the authors have a commitment to empirical studies and the use of data as means of drawing and supporting conclusions.

An effort has been made to present the material concerning specific treatment modalities in terms of general principles rather than in terms of every specific possible intervention. There is no doubt that some individuals will attempt to render this document into a set of simple formulae that describe "correct" treatment. However, there can be no correct treatment for an individual who suffers from one variant or another of a heterogeneous disorder. There are, however, treatments that are empirically based and that have been shown to be of value in certain cases. Intelligent and informed empiricism must animate the treatment of schizophrenic patients. There is no textbook in which an individual patient can be looked up to find treatment directions. There is no substitute for clinical judgment and experience. The contributors to this section attempt to transmit current generally supported approaches, and in most cases they provide the evidence on which the belief in the validity of these approaches is based. A scientist may review the data and not find them persuasive and insist that further studies are necessary. Nevertheless, the clinician must treat patients now and cannot merely wait until all questions are resolved at a level of scientific certainty. All medical treatments should be based on empirical studies, and empirical studies obviously can mislead as well as inform. It is the responsibility of clinicians to utilize empirical studies and wed these to their own experience so as to maximize the quality of care given to the individual patient.

This section starts with a highly selective history of both the concept and treatment of the schizophrenic disorders (Chapter 143). It is important to understand the history of the prior thinking about what constitutes this group of illnesses and the previous efforts at its treatment. There is a lesson that can be drawn from the history of the treatment of patients with these illnesses. The illnesses stimulate at times a therapeutic furor in the clinicians responsible for patient care. Obviously, it would be wrong to be indifferent to the suffering, but it is essential that we not add to the suffering in our attempts to relieve it.

In Chapter 144 concepts of illness are discussed in general terms, and the application of these general ideas to the schizophrenic disorders is made clear. Again, it is important that we have some conceptualization of what we are or are not doing before we undertake treatment.

Chapter 145 focuses on the problem of diagnosis. Clearly, in the absence of independent validation any diagnostic effort will be arbitrary. Different diagnostic approaches have different costs and benefits associated with them. The official diagnostic criteria of the American Psychiatric Association are not without fault but do represent an important effort to achieve reliability. The clinician should not refuse to eat bread if cake is not yet available.

In the chapter on psychopharmacologic treatments, the authors attempt to steer a course through the controversies that surround such treatment and to emphasize established approaches. The most recent developments are omitted because they have not yet been adequately validated. In some ways there are more controversies in the area of psychopharmacologic treatment because of the extensive number of studies that have been performed. Where data are available, there will always be contradictions and controversy. Nevertheless, we have more established and verified knowledge in this area than perhaps any other area involving the schizophrenic disorders.

The empirical evidence for the utility of psychoanalytically oriented individual psychotherapy in the treatment of the schizophrenias is not strong. Nevertheless, many mental health professionals including psychiatrists have been and are committed to this particular treatment approach. There are many individual reports of patients deriving benefit from this approach. It seems important, therefore, to include material on the psychoanalytic approach because of the prevalence of its use in clinical practice. It is preceded by a brief chapter reviewing research studies on psychotherapy of schizophrenia.

The interest in group and family therapy approaches has been increasing in recent years. This is true not only in private practice but in many clinic settings. Material has been included in Chapters 149 and 150 that reviews the empirical bases for these approaches and their use in clinical practice.

Finally, Chapter 151 covers the use of rehabilitative techniques in the clinical management of schizophrenic illnesses and in the prevention of deterioration in the course of these illnesses. Clearly, the distinctions between treatment, management, and prevention are at times difficult. The prevention of relapse and the prevention of deterioration are of vital importance whether they are technically included under one or another rubric. The vast majority of these patients will require very long-term care. In the absence of such care, their prognosis deteriorates. Every effort must be made to offer these patients comprehensive care and not to restrict our interventions merely to that particular modality of treatment we as individual practitioners prefer to use.

Chapter 143

Selective History of the Concept and Treatment of Schizophrenia

The activities that best differentiate humans from other species can be subsumed under the concept of mind. Other animals think, but not at the exquisite level of symbolism and logic that is characteristic of our species. It is not surprising that such an extraordinary capacity that evolved so very slowly over time is subject to disorder and derangement. If a mind can function, it can malfunction. There is excellent reason to believe that as long as we have had creatures with minds on the planet, there have been disorders of those very minds.

Many individuals have described the disorders they have observed in others, and in more recent times some have described their own experience of mental disorder. These descriptions and observations have led to an effort to create a nosology of mental disorders that has continued to evolve. No effort thus far has met with universal acceptance, and each generally adapted nosology has had shortcomings and deficiencies.

It will be helpful to review the development of the concept of the schizophrenic disorders and to review selectively the history of treatments applied to the people so diagnosed. Both of these exercises will be of assistance in evaluating our current nosologic and therapeutic efforts and in seeing them with some perspective. The term *démence précoce* was first used by the Belgian psychiatrist Morel (1852–1863) to describe a single patient whose illness had started at the age of 14. Morel used the phrase in the sense of an adjective to describe behaviors and not as a noun to label a disease entity. Earlier, both Pinel (1801) and Haslam (1809) had written clinical descriptions of patients who certainly fulfill the criteria later developed for the schizophrenic disorders.

The entire French school of psychiatry placed a great emphasis on clinical description and avoided the creation of premature categories. German psychiatry by contrast was very much influenced by the discoveries of clinical pathology and attempted thereby to create disease entities. In 1871, Hecker "identified" *hebephrenia* and Kahlbaum in 1874 "identified" *catatonia*. In both cases the terms were nouns referring to disease entities. By 1883, Kraepelin had begun to search for disease entities in psychiatry to parallel those being discovered by the microbiologists. By 1899, Kraepelin classified *dementia praecox*, now translated into Latin from French as one of the two divisions of the illogical psychoses. He differentiated it from the manic-depressive disorders on the basis of the tendency toward deterioration. Kraepelin subsumed hebephrenia and catatonia under his new entity. Although he did modify his opinions and later stated that typical cases can go on to recovery and not end in dementia, he never gave up his quest for disease entities.

Bleuler (1911), who was much influenced by Kant's ideas about mental functioning, did not merely change the name of the illness but rather substituted a syndrome concept. He rejected dementia praecox as a single disease and saw it as a group that included several diseases. He drew a parallel between the group of the schizophrenias and the group of the organic psychoses. He saw the essential clinical feature of this group of disorders to be a splitting or loss of harmony between various groups of mental functions. The fundamental diagnostic features of the schizophrenic disorders were alterations in associations, altered affect, autism, and ambivalence. Meyer (1951) emphasized the interaction between a person and the environment. He therefore implicitly worked with the concepts of stress and tension. In the Kantian tradition Meyer saw mental illnesses as forms of adaptation. This led to diagnostic manuals utilized by the Veterans Administration and formalized by the American Psychiatric Association in 1952 that viewed mental disorders as reactions, in the tradition of Esquirol. This view remained in place until 1968 when the official manual eliminated the concept of schizophrenic reaction and substituted the concept of schizophrenia (American Psychiatric Association 1968). DSM-III and DSM-III-R refer to schizophrenic disorders and thereby avoid the assumptions implicit in the first and second editions.

A study of the history of the treatment of the schizophrenic disorders is particularly informative because it illustrates dangers that are just as prevalent today as they were in the past (Cancro 1978). Madness has frequently evoked both fear and hostility in those who observe it. The fear and hostility have not been restricted to the lay public but can be found in the professionals assigned to the care of mentally ill people.

One of the early devices developed by Rush was a tranquilizing chair. The patient was strapped into this device, and his head was maintained in a fixed position. This control of muscular activity theoretically would reduce the pulse rate and improve the patient's thinking. Rush also developed a device that would increase blood flow to the head by rotating the patient rapidly on a board with the patient's head being at the outermost point of the board. In this way centrifugal forces would drive more blood to the head and improve mentation. In defense of Rush, one can argue that these frightening treatments reflected the primitive state of physiologic knowledge. However, it was stated specifically by Rush and others that terror was an important treatment for madness. Treatments developed by other individuals during this same period were also specifically intended to evoke terror. A stream of water would be applied intensely to the patient's spine, with the hope that the fear of injury would shock the patient back to sanity. Another common method was to chain the patient to the bottom of a well and then add water slowly so as to create a fear of death in the individual.

Another popular treatment was to place the patient into a box with air holes and then immerse the box in water. The technique involved keeping the box under water until the bubbles ceased to rise. The box would then be withdrawn from the water and an attempt made to revive the patient. Needless to add, the efforts of resuscitation were not always successful.

A governor of Bethlehem Hospital stated that the more severely disturbed the patient, the more severe the treatment must be for helping that patient. He suggested throwing patients from extreme heights into bodies of water so as to produce a shock to the nervous system. Shock and terror were the most prevalent forms of treatment for a long period.

Even if we restrict ourselves to the period after World War I when scientific medicine flowered, we shall see that the mentally ill received a different type of scientific medicine. During the 1920s, Cotton claimed an 80 percent recovery rate by removing sources of focal infection. These occult infections often lurked in the tonsils and appendices but primarily in teeth. The diagnosis of schizophrenia was often met with calling in the dentist to remove the patient's teeth. This was done in the absence of any demonstration of infection.

Sinuses and intestines were hosed out with regularity to remove the occult infections that could not otherwise be demonstrated. When the efforts to irrigate out the toxic molecule of schizophrenia were not successful, some patients received an appendicostomy so as to remove the toxic molecule more effectively. Holmes, who developed this aquatic treatment, also reported a 77 percent recovery rate. Carroll reported merely a 67 percent improvement rate through the use of inactivated horse serum introduced into the subarachnoid space. This production of aseptic meningitis was paralleled by surgical removal of testes, thyroid, and any other tissue that someone fantasized might be involved. The therapeutic furor elicited by these patients led to the use of a variety of treatments, many of which were dangerous, destructive, and applied in the absence of a scientific basis for their introduction. The sobering lesson is that good intentions are not sufficient protection for the schizophrenic, and the horror of the illness may evoke inappropriate responses in the physician as well.

The current belief that the group of disorders entitled schizophrenia are multivariate as to their etiology and therefore extremely heterogeneous means that an intervention that is helpful for a given individual who has arrived at the end state called schizophrenia through a particular pathway will be ineffective or even harmful in another individual who has arrived at that etiopathogenically heterogeneous end state through a different pathway. Treatment therefore must be empirical and individualized.

Chapter 144

The Concept of a Disease: Schizophrenia

The approach to the treatment of disease and of illness is partly dictated by knowledge of etiology, pathogenesis, and pathophysiology. In the absence of such knowledge we are forced to resort to the treatment or palliation of symptoms, or to attempt to remove their presumed sources. But the etiology and pathogenesis of most diseases remain unknown. Therefore, we are constrained to resort to empirical observation and to determine the frequency of occurrence of symptoms and signs rather than to their logical ordering according to causal mechanisms.

The physician's ideal is to determine a homogeneous disease entity that can be traced to some common cause(s) and then to remove it (them). This hope has not been fully realized in psychiatry. It was certainly Kraepelin's (1907, reprinted 1971) intent to fulfill it. He attempted to classify characteristic psychiatric diseases, such as dementia praecox and manic-depressive psychosis, on the basis of their unambiguous symptom constellations, their natural histories, regular transitions between phases, and their outcome into disease entities. His contemporary, Bleuler (1911, reprinted 1950), however, believed that schizophrenia was no such entity but represented a syndrome or group of diseases with a variable outcome. Yet he also affirmed the view that the syndrome shared certain common features, consisting of specified disturbances in psychological functions rather than symptoms. The controversy engendered by Kraepelin's belief that dementia praecox and manic-depressive psychosis were disease entities and Bleuler's different concept that schizophrenia was a syndrome remains unresolved up to this day.

The pursuit of the ideal of disease entities is partly based on the fact that we accord special status in medicine to disease, and for good historical reasons. Once Galen's hold on medicine had been loosened, Morgagni began to correlate symptoms with anatomical lesions. Since his time, the same methodology has been pursued. Later the symptoms were progressively correlated with tissue pathology by Bichat and later with cellular pathology by Virchow (1895) and Cohnheim (1882).

In fact, disease thus defined is the subject matter of medicine in the minds of such diverse authorities as Eysenck (1960), Schneider (1950), and Szasz (1961). Only changes in physiologic and psychological functions or processes with an observable and verifiable physical basis qualify as diseases. Such diseases are the proper target of psychiatrists—all else is not. (Indeed the rest of medicine would agree: The only proper concern of physicians is "real" disease, which is based on material changes in the brain and body.)

In psychiatry, the disease criterion was satisfied by Bayle's (1822) discovery that madness could be associated with gross material changes in the brain. (He was, of course, describing paretic neurosyphilis.) Later another form of madness was associated with a vitamin deficiency (pellagra). Indeed, in these two forms of madness, the ideal appears to have been attained, and specific treatment is directed at their specific causes.

But is the ideal really reached, or only approximated? The symptomatic manifestations of paretic neurosyphilis are individual and remarkably varied phenomena that still resist explanation. Therefore, the supposedly close link between the symptom and the anatomical lesion is often illusory.

Furthermore, when the ideal of a homogeneous disease entity is apparently realized, it often turns out that the disease is made up of subforms. Down's syndrome, for example, exists in at least two forms—one that is karyotypically abnormal (trisomy-21) and another that is karyotypically normal. (Incidentally, in the latter the genetic defect is not unitary: Three genes are duplicated [Delabar et al. 1987].)

In the case of bipolar affective illness, the same conclusion applies. The symptomatic manifestations and natural history of this illness are quite characteristic, yet its genetics do not seem to be—three distinct forms have been described (Baron et al. 1987; Egeland et al. 1987; Hodgkinson et al. 1987).

Many well-defined disease entities described by uniform manifestations or pathological lesions—such as essential hypertension, diabetes mellitus, rheumatoid arthritis, or peptic duodenal ulcer—are actually heterogeneous in nature. Cancer may come in 100 different forms. No uniform pathogenesis for all forms of cancer is known. Thus, for instance, oncogenes that are transduced by viruses (Bishop 1987) can either induce growth factors or receptors for these factors or transduce extracellular signals to cell nuclei to promote cell division. Although our knowledge about the sources of this heterogeneity is not complete, it now appears that the anatomical lesion (such as a duodenal ulcer) can come about through a variety of pathways. Furthermore, the symptoms that "typify" the presence of the lesion are often not uniform or may even be absent altogether. Some or all of the "typical" symptoms of duodenal ulcer, e.g., dyspepsia, may be mimicked in nonulcer conditions. A symptom such as aphonia may be associated with the diphtheria toxin or with conversion hysteria.

The heterogeneous nature of a disease can also have significant treatment implications. Type I diabetes mellitus due to insufficient insulin production and secretion requires the replacement of the hormone. Diet and weight loss frequently correct the several different kinds of resistance to insulin that characterize type II diabetes mellitus.

The ideal of categorizing symptoms and signs according to disease entities in medicine has not been easy to attain, except in the case of infections, vitamin deficiency, some metabolic deliria, some forms of dementia, and genetic disorders. Yet even in the case of a genetic-metabolic disorder such as phenylketonuria, we still do not understand how the absence or deficiency of the hepatic enzyme, phenylalanine hydroxylase, "produces" the pleiotropic symptoms and signs of mental deficiency.

Most of the remaining mental illnesses (with the possible exception of manic-depressive disorders) consist of a variety of imprecisely defined conditions and possibly heterogeneous syndromes that cannot as yet be circumscribed into anything approaching a disease entity and that have poorly understood cause(s). No real agreement has been reached among psychiatrists whether to designate schizophrenia as an entity or a syndrome. Sydenham (1676) defined a syndrome as a group of inter-correlated symptoms that were sufficiently distinguishable from other clusters of symptoms. The fact that an official diagnosis of schizoaffective psychosis exists emphasizes the difficulty with which a distinction among symptom clusters can be made in psychiatry.

Disease constructs based on material and measurable deviations or changes help define the symptom clusters, as well as their courses and outcomes. Recently there has been a renewed search for viruses in the brain and their antibody titers in the blood or spinal fluid (DeLisi and Crow 1986). Low monoamine oxidase (type B) levels in blood platelets have been correlated with the paranoid form of schizophrenia (Jeste et al. 1982). Based on the known pharmacologic actions of neuroleptic drugs, a form of schizophrenia is believed to be associated with excessive sensitivity of dopamine receptors (Seeman et al. 1984). In some schizophrenic patients ventricular enlargement, widened cortical sulci, and cerebellar atrophy have been observed by computerized tomography (Weinberger et al. 1979). Spatial disorientation of hippocampal neurons on the left side of the brain has been seen in postmortem specimens of some schizophrenic patients (Scheibel and Kovelman 1981). Position emission tomography scan studies to measure regional rates of glucose metabolism in the brain have shown that in several series of patients the uptake of 18-F-fluorodeoxyglucose was decreased in the frontal lobes (Buchsbaum et al. 1982; Farkas et al. 1984; Wolkin et al. 1985). Depressed patients also showed diminished metabolism in the frontal lobe (Buchsbaum et al. 1984).

These findings were not confirmed using the same techniques by Gur et al. (1987a) or by Sheppard et al. (1983), who employed the oxygen-15 techniques. Gur and her colleagues (1987a) reported that subcortical metabolism was higher than cortical metabolism, despite the fact that in both regions metabolism was lower than that in control subjects. The subcortical-to-cortical gradient was higher, and the metabolism of the left cerebral hemisphere was higher than that of the right. All of these changes, except the last, persisted with medication and clinical improvement (Gur et al. 1987b).

The lack of uniformity in results suggests that schizophrenia is heterogeneous in nature. Many different ways of dividing it into subforms have been proposed. For example, Crow (1980) has suggested that two major subgroups exist:

1. An acute course, with positive symptoms (hallucinations, delusions, excitement, motor manifestations), positive therapeutic responses to neuroleptic medication, and relatively minor disturbances in formal thought processes (overinclusion, idiosyncratic thought, false syllogisms).
2. A chronic course, negative symptoms (anhedonia, apathy, blunted affect, social isolation, or socially deviant behavior, and prominent formal disturbances of thought), a poor response to neuroleptic treatment, and evidence of cerebral atrophy by CT scan.

The idea that schizophrenia is a heterogeneous disorder is also attested to by family aggregation studies: There is considerable variability in different populations in the family aggregation of schizophrenia (Kendler 1982). This variation in the frequency does not seem to be only a function of methodological problems but suggests that the mix of familial and sporadic patients varies in different populations. Family aggregation studies also clarify what the basic psychological defects seem to be in schizophrenia—that is, what the basic liability or predisposition to it is. The common characteristics of families in which aggregation occurs are suspiciousness, poor rapport with other people, social isolation, idiosyncratic use of language, and eccentric behavior: The nonpsychotic members of families share these with their psychotic relatives (Kendler et al. 1985b).

Interestingly enough the root deficit, therefore, seems to be due to disturbances in relating to others and to some of the characteristic negative symptoms. Genetic factors clearly play a role in at least the familial forms of schizophrenia, but the asocial manner of relating to others so far defies understanding in genetic terms.

The evidence is that schizophrenia, like many other diseases, is a heterogeneous disorder. A familial form and a sporadic form exist. Patients with positive symptoms are best treated by neuroleptic agents. Patients with chronic form characterized by negative symptoms, with a relatively poor prognosis, respond to such drugs less well or not at all.

This conclusion may once again be oversimplified. First, the stability of individual subtypes of schizophrenia is only about 50 percent (Kendler et al. 1985a). Second, schizophrenic patients with negative symptoms do not necessarily have a poorer prognosis than those with positive ones (Kay et al. 1986), as Crow suggests.

Nonetheless, recent investigations indicate that at least some forms of schizophrenia qualify as a disease and that some patients, especially those with acute and positive symptoms, respond best to neuroleptic medication. It is also true that pharmacologic treatment improves the formal disturbances in thought, although overinclusive thinking may be a persistent disturbance even in remission.

Pharmacologic treatment seems not to influence the disturbances in social behavior, anhedonia, apathy, or difficulties at work. Logically, it would appear that the social behavior could be encouraged by psychotherapy and social skill training. The apathy, anhedonia, and other forms of amotivational states and some of the formal disturbances in thought have yielded to an "ego-directed" psychotherapeutic approach (Munich 1987).

Yet the matter does not seem to be as simple as stated. Based on the work of

Leff et al. (1985), treatment must still take into account the human environment in which the patient lives. They have shown that schizophrenic patients who have remitted and are being maintained on neuroleptic medication are significantly more liable to relapse into psychosis in families in which there are high levels of "expressed emotion" (a euphemism for hostility and nastiness on the part of family members). Their data indicated that patients who live in supportive homes have a low relapse rate independent of medication.

In conclusion, we have tried to review some general principles in medicine about the current understanding of what constitutes a disease. Recent investigation suggests that schizophrenia is heterogeneous in nature and that at least some forms qualify as a disease. There are even indications of what the shared disturbances are, and that some of the subforms of the disease respond to particular regimens. Nonetheless, we are still very far from fully understanding the riddle of schizophrenia, whose toll in human suffering remains very high.

Chapter 145

Diagnosis of Schizophrenia

DSM-III-R (American Psychiatric Association 1987) contains diagnostic criteria for the schizophrenic disorders (Table 1), including characteristics for five traditionally recognized clinical subtypes. DSM-III-R is an amalgam of ideas from previous diagnostic systems. Diagnostic schemes for schizophrenia have been the subject of a number of reviews (Cancro and Pruyser 1970; Doran et al. 1986; Fenton et al. 1981; Pfohl and Andreasen 1986). The emphasis of this section is the differential diagnosis of schizophrenia-like symptoms.

There are three major changes in the DSM-III-R diagnostic criteria for schizophrenia from those in DSM-III (American Psychiatric Association 1980). First, criterion A has been simplified, and the requirement that symptoms of the active phases be present for one week has been added. Second, the possibility that a child or adolescent may demonstrate a decrease in level of functioning by a failure to exhibit normal psychosocial development has been added. Third, the requirement that onset of the disorder be before age 45 has been eliminated.

Differential Diagnosis

The first diagnostic consideration is whether an organic disorder is causing the psychiatric symptoms (Table 2). Psychiatric symptoms tend to occur early in the course of some organic disorders, often before the development of classical neurologic symp-

Table 1. DSM-III-R Diagnostic Criteria for Schizophrenia

A. Presence of characteristic psychotic symptoms in the active phase: either (1), (2), or (3) for at least one week (unless the symptoms are successfully treated):
  (1) two of the following:
    (a) delusions
    (b) prominent hallucinations (throughout the day for several days or several times a week for several weeks, each hallucinatory experience not being limited to a few brief moments)
    (c) incoherence or marked loosening of associations
    (d) catatonic behavior
    (e) flat or grossly inappropriate affect
  (2) bizarre delusions (i.e., involving a phenomenon that the person's culture would regard as totally implausible, e.g., thought broadcasting, being controlled by a dead person)
  (3) prominent hallucinations [as defined in (1)(b) above] of a voice with content having no apparent relation to depression or elation, or a voice keeping up a running commentary on the person's behavior or thoughts, or two or more voices conversing with each other

B. During the course of the disturbance, functioning in such areas as work, social relations, and self-care is markedly below the highest level achieved before onset of the disturbance (or, when the onset is in childhood or adolescence, failure to achieve expected level of social development).

C. Schizoaffective Disorder and Mood Disorder with Psychotic Features have been ruled out, i.e., if a Major Depressive or Manic Syndrome has ever been present during an active phase of the disturbance, the total duration of all episodes of a mood syndrome has been brief relative to the total duration of the active and residual phases of the disturbance.

D. Continuous signs of the disturbance for at least six months. The six-month period must include an active phase (of at least one week, or less if symptoms have been successfully treated) during which there were psychotic symptoms characteristic of Schizophrenia (symptoms in A), with or without a prodromal or residual phase, as defined below.

Prodromal phase: A clear deterioration in functioning before the active phase of the disturbance that is not due to a disturbance in mood or to a Psychoactive Substance Use Disorder and that involves at least two of the symptoms listed below.

Residual phase: Following the active phase of the disturbance, persistence of at least two of the symptoms noted below, these not being due to a disturbance in mood or to a Psychoactive Substance Use Disorder.

Prodromal or Residual Symptoms:
  (1) marked social isolation or withdrawal
  (2) marked impairment in role functioning as wage-earner, student, or homemaker
  (3) markedly peculiar behavior (e.g., collecting garbage, talking to self in public, hoarding food)
  (4) marked impairment in personal hygiene and grooming
  (5) blunted or inappropriate affect
  (6) digressive, vague, overelaborate, or circumstantial speech, or poverty of speech, or poverty of content of speech
  (7) odd beliefs or magical thinking, influencing behavior and inconsistent with cultural norms, e.g., superstitiousness, belief in clairvoyance, telepathy, "sixth sense," "others can feel my feelings," overvalued ideas, ideas of reference

Table 1. DSM-III-R Diagnostic Criteria for Schizophrenia (continued)

(8) unusual perceptual experiences, e.g., recurrent illusions, sensing the presence of a force or person not actually present

(9) marked lack of initiative, interests, or energy

Examples: Six months of prodromal symptoms with one week of symptoms from A; no prodromal symptoms with six months of symptoms from A; no prodromal symptoms with one week of symptoms from A and six months of residual symptoms.

E. It cannot be established that an organic factor initiated and maintained the disturbance.

F. If there is a history of Autistic Disorder, the additional diagnosis of Schizophrenia is made only if prominent delusions or hallucinations are also present.

toms. The clinician, therefore, should continue to consider an organic explanation for a period of time, even if a complete initial organic workup has been negative.

The differential diagnosis within DSM-III-R for behavior evidently primarily under voluntary control includes malingering and factitious disorder with psychological symptoms. If the patient is a child, autistic disorder is a diagnostic possibility. If, however, a child meets the DSM-III-R criteria for schizophrenia, then that is the diagnosis; there is no specific diagnosis of "childhood schizophrenia" in DSM-III-R. The most commonly considered and problematic differential diagnoses are considered below.

Mood Disorders

It is necessary to recognize a major mood disorder presenting with psychotic symptoms because of differential pharmacologic treatments for mood disorders and schizophrenia. Kraepelin's admonition that these two classes of disorders can have similar clinical presentations is still clinically and theoretically pertinent (Carpenter et al. 1973; Taylor and Abrams 1975). Alternatively stated, no individual sign, symptom, or particular form of thought disorder is specific or pathognomonic for schizophrenia (Pope and Lipinski 1978). Acknowledging the recent trend to assign more importance to the presence of affective symptoms in the differential assessment of major idiopathic psychiatric disorders (Haier 1980; Maj 1984), in its diagnostic criteria for schizophrenia DSM-III-R specifies that a full depressive or manic syndrome, if present, must have developed after psychotic symptoms or be comparatively brief in duration. Because missing the correct diagnosis of a mood disorder can deprive a patient of an effective treatment, some clinicians feel that it is preferable to err on the side of overdiagnosing the presence of a mood disorder. Practically speaking, however, DSM-III-R is a set of guidelines, and it is incumbent on the clinician to utilize clinical experience, as well as assessment of other variables, in making a diagnosis and designing a treatment plan. These other variables include family support, treatment availability, premorbid history, level of functioning, cause of illness, response to treatment, and family history.

Schizoaffective Disorder

The DSM-III-R criteria for schizoaffective disorder require the presence of a major depressive or manic syndrome concurrent with the symptoms of schizophrenia in criterion A (Table 1). The criteria also require that delusions or hallucinations have been present for at least two weeks in the absence of prominent affective symptoms.

Table 2. Organic Diagnoses to Consider in Differentiating Organic Psychoses from Schizophrenia

Drug-induced

Amantadine; amphetamine; belladonna alkaloids; anticholinergic agents; antidepressants; alcohol, short-acting benzodiazepine, or barbiturate withdrawal; cocaine; cimetidine; digitalis; disulfiram; glucocorticoids; L-dopa; lysergic acid diethylamide; mescaline; phenylpropylamine; tetrahydrocannabinol; phencyclidine

Degenerative or metabolic

Alzheimer's disease
B_{12}, thiamine, folate, or niacin deficiency
Cerebral lipoidosis
Electrolyte imbalances—sodium, calcium
Fahr's syndrome
Hallevorden-Spatz disease
Hepatic encephalopathy
Huntington's disease
Metachromatic leukodystrophy and adrenoleukodystrophy
Pellagra
Pick's disease
Porphyria, acute intermittent
Renal failure
Wernicke-Korsakoff's syndrome
Wilson's disease

Seizure disorders (especially interictal changes associated with temporal lobe epilepsy)

Infectious diseases

Acquired immune deficiency syndrome (AIDS)
Creutzfeldt-Jakob disease
Herpes simplex encephalitis
Neurosyphilis

Miscellaneous

Thyroid, parathyroid, and adrenal endocrinopathies
Systemic lupus erythematosus
Normal pressure hydrocephalus
Stroke
Cerebral trauma
Cerebral tumor
Poisoning with carbon monoxide or heavy metals

Many recent studies have suggested that schizoaffective disorder is either indistinguishable from bipolar affective disorder on the basis of treatment response, family history, and outcome (Pope et al. 1980; Rosenthal et al. 1980) or intermediate on the basis of these measures between schizophrenic and affective disorders. However, some researchers suggest that the depressed subtype of schizoaffective disorder may be similar to schizophrenia.

The history of this diagnostic group, as well as previous criteria for it, recently has been reviewed (Brockington and Leff 1979). It is not yet clear whether these patients have atypical mood disorders or atypical schizophrenic disorders that overlap in their clinical presentations. It is possible, however, that these patients represent a distinct diagnostic entity, or that each of these patients has both disorders. The clinician, of course, is responsible for considering other clinical information not covered in the DSM-III-R guidelines.

Brief Reactive Psychosis and Schizophreniform Disorder

The diagnosis of brief reactive psychosis requires psychotic symptoms to have been present for less than one month and for there to be an identifiable and major psychosocial stressor or series of stressors. The criteria for schizophreniform disorder require that schizophrenic symptoms be present for less than the six months required for a diagnosis of schizophrenia. The cut-off point of six months, albeit arbitrary, does differentiate clinically a group of patients with an increased likelihood of poorer outcome (Knesevich et al. 1983). Somewhat akin to patients with schizoaffective disorder, patients with schizophreniform disorder statistically have outcomes that are intermediate between those of patients with schizophrenic or affective disorders (Coryell and Tsuang 1982). Because schizophreniform disorder may be related to the mood disorders (Fogelson et al. 1982; Targum 1983), it probably is warranted in most cases to offer the patient clinical trials of pharmacologic agents used to treat affective disorders. Practically speaking, the diagnosis of schizophreniform disorder encourages the clinician to forestall diagnosing a patient as having schizophrenia until enough time has passed to consider other diagnostic possibilities fully.

Delusional Disorders and Atypical Psychosis

The DSM-III-R diagnosis of delusional disorder delimits a group of patients whose major symptoms are persistent persecutory, jealous, erotomanic, somatic, grandiose, or other type of delusions. These symptoms are present in the absence of other psychotic features seen in schizophrenia and also in the absence of significant affective symptoms. The DSM-III-R separation of delusional disorder is based on research data indicating that this disorder is distinct from either mood or schizophrenic disorders (Kendler 1982; Watt 1985).

The DSM-III-R diagnosis of atypical psychosis is a residual category for a patient who has psychotic symptoms but does not meet the criteria for any other psychotic disorder. These patients particularly must be carefully evaluated for organic disorder.

Personality Disorders

Four preliminary disorders—schizotypal, schizoid, borderline, and paranoid—can have symptoms similar to those of schizophrenia. Schizotypal personality disorder, in particular, prompts the theoretician to consider a "spectrum" of schizophrenic disorders, ranging from more mild symptoms (i.e., schizotypal personality disorder) to severe symptoms (i.e., schizophrenic disorders) (Kety et al. 1971). Children at high risk of developing schizophrenia (because of having a schizophrenic parent) who do have psychological deficits are more likely to develop schizophrenia (Parnas et al. 1982). Within the personality disorders, schizotypal personality disorder is more common in the relatives of schizophrenic probands than in other comparison groups (Kendler et al. 1984), and a weak connection between schizophrenia and paranoid personality disorder may also exist (Kendler and Gruenberg 1982). Although patients with borderline personality disorder may have brief psychotic episodes, there does not appear to be a close connection between this condition and schizophrenia (Pope et al. 1983).

Subtypes of Schizophrenia

DSM-III-R divides schizophrenia into five subtypes based on clinical phenomenology. These are the disorganized (i.e., hebephrenic), paranoid, catatonic, undifferentiated, and residual subtypes. An individual patient often presents with different subtypes over time (Bridge et al. 1978), although some paranoid patients do seem to present consistently with the same phenomenology (in DSM-III-R, paranoid schizophrenia, stable type). Approximately one-third of patients with schizophrenia have the paranoid subtype (Kendler and Tsuang 1981). These patients tend to have a later onset (Fowler et al. 1974) and less frequently have a family history of schizophrenia (Hallgren and Sjogren 1959). Some researchers have suggested that the now-uncommon catatonic subtype may be related to the affective disorders (Abrams and Taylor 1976), and this hypothesis needs to be acknowledged when deciding on treatment modalities for a catatonic patient. Two important diagnostic considerations in a patient with catatonic features are the adverse neurologic effects of neuroleptics and the prodromal symptoms of neuroleptic malignant syndrome. In general, patients with the paranoid and catatonic subtypes have more favorable prognoses than patients with the hebephrenic and undifferentiated subtypes.

Other subtyping schemes or dichotomies have been suggested over the years. In general, these have attempted to differentiate patients with good prognoses from patients with poor prognoses. These dichotomies have included reactive/process, good/poor premorbid personality, exogenous/endogenous, schizophreniform/true, atypical/typical, with/without affective symptoms, latent/psychotic, pseudoneurotic, simple, and oneiroid. One dichotomy that recently has received increased attention divides patients into those with positive (type I) or negative (type II) symptom complexes (Andreasen 1979; Crow et al. 1982; Strauss et al. 1974). This dichotomy has attempted to relate clinical phenomenology to both biologic and prognostic variables. The type I syndrome includes productive psychotic symptoms such as hallucinations and delusions; the type II syndrome includes deficit symptoms such as flat affect and decline of cognitive functioning. An individual patient may have symptoms of both type I and type II. Other features that have been epidemiologically associated with type I include relatively acute onset, a course with exacerbations and remissions, good premorbid functioning, better interepisode adjustment, normal cognitive testing, lack of ventricular enlargement or cortical atrophy on brain CT scan, and positive response to neuroleptic treatment. Patients with the type II syndrome have been shown to have the opposite characteristics in some studies.

Overview of Other Diagnostic Systems

Although DSM-III-R is the most widely accepted set of diagnostic guidelines in the United States, there are other diagnostic systems for schizophrenia in use. In fact, DSM-III-R is a synthesis of previous diagnostic schemes, and its importance can best be appreciated with a knowledge of previous systems.

In 1896, Kraepelin (1907) divided the "illogically insane" into those with manic-depressive illness and those with dementia praecox. In addition to the presence of certain psychotic symptoms, Kraepelin described an onset of symptoms early in life, progression to a "demented" end stage, and a single etiology. In his later writings, Kraepelin acknowledged that the disorder did not always begin in youth and that 12–15 percent of patients did not deteriorate. In 1911, Bleuler (1950) gave the illness of such patients the name "schizophrenias." This term was meant to describe a loss of harmony among mental functions, or a "splitting" of the mind. Although Bleuler proposed four fundamental symptoms, a thought disorder characterized by associational disturbances, particularly looseness, was, perhaps, fundamental in Bleuler's thinking. The other fundamental symptoms were affective disturbances, autism, and ambivalence. Symptoms such as delusions or hallucinations were accessory. Bleuler felt that these patients did not have a uniformly poor outcome. Bleuler's concept of schizophrenias included patients who now would be diagnosed as having bipolar disorder, as well as many more mildly ill patients who may represent contemporary personality disorders.

Perhaps some readers might object to the following simplification, but essentially all subsequent diagnostic schemes merely have rearranged the concepts first explicated by Kraepelin and Bleuler. Schneider (1959) emphasized certain "first rank symptoms" and rejected outcome as a diagnostic criterion. Schneider suggested that these symptoms, such as thought broadcasting, were characteristic of schizophrenia. It has since been shown that there is no symptom unique to schizophrenia (Carpenter and Strauss 1973; Pope and Lipinski 1978). The symptoms of psychosis as described by Schneider, however, have become important aspects of subsequent diagnostic systems, including the Present State Exam (PSE), the Research Diagnostic Criteria (RDC), and the DSM-III-R. Langfeldt (1960) specified somewhat different symptoms and required a deteriorating course for the diagnosis of schizophrenia. More recent systems have tended to word the diagnostic criteria more clearly, to put more emphasis on affective symptoms as exclusion criteria for schizophrenia, and to include information on course.

Twelve prominent diagnostic schemes currently proposed for schizophrenia are the following: Kraepelin's (1907); Bleuler's (1911, reprinted 1950); Schneider's (1959); Langfeldt's (1960); the International Classification of Disease, 9th Edition (ICD-9) (World Health Organization 1978); the St. Louis Criteria (Feighner et al. 1972); the Research Diagnostic Criteria (RDC, Spitzer et al. 1977); the DSM-III-R (American Psychiatric Association 1987); the New Haven Schizophrenia Index (Astrachan et al. 1972); the Flexible System (Carpenter et al. 1973); the Present State Examination (PSE/CATEGO, Wing et al. 1974); and the criteria of Taylor and Abrams (1978). The diagnostic criteria for these systems are contained in a booklet published by the World Psychiatric Association (1983).

All of these schemes include symptoms of psychosis in their criteria. Four (Kraepelin, Langfeldt, St. Louis, DSM-III-R) require a decrease in level of functioning for the diagnosis or a minimum duration of illness (DSM-III-R, RDC, Taylor and Abrams, St. Louis). The St. Louis criteria exclude patients with onset after age 40.

Evaluating Diagnostic Systems

There are five measures by which a diagnostic system should be assessed (Fenton et al. 1981): objectivity of data, reliability, validity, specificity, and comprehensiveness. Each of these qualities is discussed below.

Objectivity of Data

All of the major diagnostic schemes considered in this section are based variously on the presence of certain symptoms, the course of illness (age of onset, duration of symptoms, deterioration in function), and exclusion criteria (mood disorders, organic disorders, and mental retardation). In turn, all of this information is based on what the patient or his family and friends say about past and present symptoms and on what the psychiatrist observes during clinical interviews and mental status examinations. Psychological and neuropsychological testing may sometimes help further to identify and characterize relevant symptoms. The objectivity of these data must be evaluated separately in every instance, but the various diagnostic systems do not differ in their dependence on similar, clinically acquired, but hopefully reliable data.

Reliability

There are two types of reliability, interrater and test-retest. Many studies have merely compared the concordance rates of diagnoses when two or more evaluators diagnosed the same patients. A more recently utilized statistical approach, the kappa statistic, controls for chance agreements among psychiatrists and is reported as a number from 0 to 1, with 1 being perfect agreement (Fleiss et al. 1977). In recent evaluations, kappa has been fairly high for the diagnostic criteria of Schneider, St. Louis, RDC, DSM-III, Flexible System, PSE/CATEGO, and Taylor and Abrams (Brockington et al. 1978; Stephens et al. 1982). The demonstration of good interrater reliability, however, merely shows that clinicians agree on how to apply the criteria as defined and not that the clinicians are necessarily identifying schizophrenia more validly.

Test-retest reliability measures stability of a diagnosis over time. This dimension of diagnostic reliability in schizophrenia has been less well studied than interrater reliability. It has been reported, however, that the more restrictive diagnostic schemes for schizophrenia do have good test-retest reliability over many years of follow-up (Tsuang et al. 1981) and that the DSM-III-R six-month criterion is a useful one to assure stability over time in diagnosing schizophrenia.

Validity

There are four levels of validity: face, descriptive, predictive, and construct. Essentially all of the above schemes for schizophrenia have face and descriptive validity; that is, large numbers of clinicians agree that the criteria describe a fairly specific group of patients. It should be remembered, however, that clinical homogeneity does not guarantee etiological unity. Too, the more stringent validity criteria (predictive and construct) are not met by any diagnostic scheme for schizophrenia. That is, the diagnosis of a particular patient as having schizophrenia by any of the systems can not specifically predict that individual's treatment response, outcome, or heritability. On a statistical basis, however, the diagnostic schemes that include a specific duration of symptoms (St. Louis, RDC, DSM-III-R) are better correlated with poor outcome (Helzer et al. 1981; Kendell et al. 1979; Stephens et al. 1982). Construct validity requires an independent objective measure (e.g., the identification of a specific biological feature) by which to prove a diagnosis. In the absence of such an objective marker or diagnostic test, it should be clearly understood that any diagnostic system for schizophrenia is, essentially, tentative and empirical.

Specificity and Comprehensiveness

An ideal diagnostic system should categorize patients into nonoverlapping groups (specificity), and it should do this for all patients (comprehensiveness). DSM-III-R, in fact, encourages the use of multiple diagnoses, except when not permitted by specific exclusion criteria. This is in accord with diagnostic practice in the rest of medicine; it is possible for a patient to have more than one disorder at a time.

Comprehensiveness varies among systems inasmuch as there is up to a 10-fold difference in the number of patients they each diagnose as having schizophrenia (McGlashan 1984; Stephens et al. 1982). This pattern has led some observers to characterize diagnostic systems as "more" (e.g., DSM-III, Taylor and Abrams, St. Louis) and "less" (e.g., New Haven) restrictive depending on whether they identify, respectively, fewer or more patients. It is not necessarily true, however, that more restrictive definitions of schizophrenia identify "truer" or biologically more homogeneous schizophrenia. More restrictive systems, however, may decrease the range of probable treatment responses and outcomes.

Chapter 146

Psychopharmacologic Treatments

Treatment decisions must, among many other issues, take into consideration the following factors concerning schizophrenic manifestations:

1. Predisposing factors that are mainly genetic or perinatal (e.g., hypoxia) and can influence an individual's vulnerability toward the development of schizophrenia;
2. Precipitating factors that are thought to be found possibly in deviant developmental processes and, probably more importantly, in stressful life events;
3. Sustaining factors that may be genetic but frequently are environmental, e.g., critical and emotionally highly expressive families; and
4. Inhibiting factors that are, in essence, the various therapeutic and protective forces and procedures—both endogenous and exogenous—that constitute substantially the repertoire for any successful therapeutic strategy and management.

From the therapeutic point of view, the most important points are 1) not to misdiagnose and treat neurotic, affective, or personality disorders as schizophrenia and 2) to keep in mind that schizophrenic patients may present at least three different types of psychopathology. There are positive symptoms, like hallucinations and delusions; negative symptoms, like apathy, loss of drive, poverty of speech, or frank dementia; and disturbances of general functioning, including inappropriate behavior and general loss of vocational and social competence. Pharmacotherapy is most effective in suppressing positive symptoms, less effective in reducing the negative symptoms of chronic patients, and least effective against disturbances of general functioning and social interaction except to the extent that these result from drug sensitive symptoms.

Table 1 lists most of the various somatic modalities that are used today or have recently been proposed for the therapeutic management of schizophrenic patients.

Schizophrenia, as a nosological entity, belongs to the class of psychoses. The psychopharmacologic agents that are most specifically effective in all psychotic conditions, except for depressions, are the neuroleptic drugs. (They are also referred to as antipsychotics or major tranquilizers.) There were no effective antipsychotic drugs known until the neuroleptics were discovered in the early 1950s.

For the therapeutic management of the vast majority of schizophrenic patients today, pharmacotherapy offers better effectiveness, easier accessibility, and greater simplicity than most other treatments known. Pharmacotherapy of schizophrenia is certainly a vital option for those physicians who are entrusted with the management of acute or chronic schizophrenic patients in the community, where the uncontrolled pathologic symptoms of these patients may be unacceptable. For hospitalized schizophrenics, pharmacotherapy is usually the most effective means of reducing the patient's stay in the hospital, readying him or her for psychosocial treatments, and preventing future readmissions.

Comparative studies of psychotic patients treated with electroconvulsive treatment (ECT) versus pharmacotherapy at first gave contradictory results (Baker et al. 1958; Tourney 1967). However, the definitive studies of May in 1976, although noting that ECT was associated with fewer days of hospitalization, concluded that pharmacotherapy is generally the treatment of choice (May 1976; May et al. 1976a, 1976b). ECT may still be indicated in special cases, for instance in catatonic patients or if a schizophrenic patient has failed to improve after three months or more of neuroleptic pharmacotherapy. Some clinicians also feel that a combination of ECT and pharmacotherapy gives better and more rapid results than neuroleptic therapy alone, but these claims, so far, have not been substantiated in controlled studies (Taylor and Fleminger 1980).

Megavitamin and "orthomolecular" therapies have received much publicity in recent years, but most systematic and controlled attempts to confirm the claims of those who support this form of treatment have failed to produce positive results. At the present time, neither the theories nor the practice of megavitamin therapy has received any scientific confirmation (Ban and Lehmann 1975).

Propranolol in high doses has been claimed to be effective in the treatment of schizophrenia, but several recent controlled studies have found negative results with this treatment, which is not without hazards (Hanssen et al. 1980).

Hemodialysis, when first proposed as a new treatment modality for schizophrenia, caused considerable, hopeful excitement among psychiatrists, but most attempts to confirm the first promising results since then have failed (Carpenter et al. 1983).

Table 1.   Somatic Treatment Modalities for Schizophrenic Patients

Established	Not Established
1. Pharmacotherapy (antipsychotics)	1. Orthomolecular Treatment
2. Electroconvulsive Treatment (ECT)	2. Propranolol
	3. Lithium
	4. Hemodialysis
	5. Neuropeptides

Lithium has been demonstrated to have some antipsychotic properties. Currently, in many places, therapeutic trials of lithium alone or in combination with antipsychotic drugs have been made in schizophrenic patients, particularly in those who manifest periodic exacerbations or affective symptoms or have proved refractory to other treatments (Small et al. 1975).

Carbamazepine, although not primarily used in schizophrenia, has been found to be helpful in the control of agitation, excitement, and episodic psychotic manifestations.

Reports of favorable results with the administration of endorphins and other neuropeptides have been sporadic and need further confirmation.

When the results of individual psychotherapy, group psychotherapy, and milieu therapy alone were compared with neuroleptic drug treatment in schizophrenic patients, the greatest improvement has consistently occurred with pharmacotherapy (Grinspoon et al. 1968; May 1968). There is also good evidence that psychosocial intervention, especially with an emphasis on education, combined with pharmacotherapy may be more effective than pharmacotherapy alone, particularly during the rehabilitation and maintenance phases of treatment, after the acute symptoms of the psychotic disorder have abated and the problems of social adaptation have moved into the foreground (Liberman et al. 1983).

Family therapy has recently been shown to be successful in reducing the risk of relapses and of rehospitalization of schizophrenic patients and, when used in combination with pharmacotherapy, has made the most substantial new contribution to the therapeutic management of schizophrenic patients in the community (McFarlane 1983).

Choice of an Antipsychotic Drug

In spite of many statements to the contrary in the promotional literature, the therapeutic effectiveness of all nonexperimental neuroleptic drugs available in the United States and Canada today, is identical for all practical purposes. It is true that there are subtle differences in the responses of particular schizophrenic symptoms and syndromes to specific neuroleptics, but we are unable to predict these idiosyncratic responses in advance. Some neuroleptic drugs may be effective in a slightly shorter time—a matter of a few days—than others, but for practical purposes the clinician may consider all neuroleptic drugs as equally effective and differing only in their dosage requirements, the side effects they produce, and their cost.

Nevertheless, as in every other area of therapeutics, there are always individual patients who, for unknown reasons, respond better to one drug than to another. However, these are exceptions. Moreover, certain patients are more susceptible to one type of side effect than to another, and for this reason clinicians should be familiar with several different neuroleptics: one from each of the three types of phenothiazines—1) the aliphatic, 2) the piperazine, and 3) the piperidine derivatives—a butyrophenone, a thioxanthene, a dibenzoxazepine, a dihydroindolone. and a diphenylbutylpiperidine compound.

In general, then, the choice of a neuroleptic for the treatment of schizophrenic patients should mainly be determined not by the drug's novelty—once the diagnosis of schizophrenia has been established—but by the doctor's familiarity with the drug, its side effects, route of administration, and cost (Table 2).

Table 2. Psychopharmacologic Treatments for Schizophrenia

Drugs	Trade Names	Notes	Potency Equivalents	Mode of Administration	Daily Doses
Phenothiazines					
Aliphatic					
Chlorpromazine	Thorazine, Sonazine, Largactil	More sedative and autonomic than extrapyramidal side effects	100 mg	Tablets, liquid Injection	P.O. 25–2000 mg I.M. 12.5–300 mg
Piperidine					
Thioridazine	Mellaril		100 mg	Tablets, concentrate	P.O. 25–600 mg
Mesoridazine	Serentil		50 mg	Tablets, concentrate Injection	P.O. 25–400 mg I.M. 12.5–200 mg
Piperazine					
Perphenazine	Trilafon		10 mg	Tablets, concentrate Injection	P.O. 4–100 mg I.M. 2–30 mg
Trifluoperazine	Stelazine		5 mg	Tablets, liquid Injection	P.O. 2–60 mg I.M. 2–30 mg
Fluphenazine	Permitil, Prolixin, Moditen, Modecate		2 mg	Tablets, elixir Injection Injection depot (every two to four weeks)	P.O. 1–40 mg I.M. 0.5–40 mg I.M. 6.25–100 mg
Thioxanthenes					
Thiothixene	Navane	Reported to be more activating	5 mg	Capsules, concentrate Injection	P.O. 2–90 mg I.M. 2–30 mg
Butyrophenone					
Haloperidol	Haldol	Therapeutic plasma level: 5–20 ng/ml	2 mg	Tablets, solution Injection Injection depot (every two to four weeks)	P.O. 1–100 mg I.M. 0.5–140 mg I.M. 6.25–100 mg
Dibenzoxazepine					
Loxapine	Daxolin, Loxitane, Loxapac	Active metabolite of antidepressant amoxapine	10 mg	Capsules, concentrate Injection	P.O. 10–250 mg I.M. 25–200 mg
Dihydroindoline					
Molindone	Lindone, Moban	Less weight gain reported	10 mg	Tablets, capsules Concentrate	P.O. 10–225 mg
Diphenylbutylpiperidine					
Pimozide	Orap	Frequently sedating	2 mg	Tablets	P.O. 1–25 mg

Dosing Strategy

Four factors determine the dosing strategy in the treatment of schizophrenic patients:

1. Therapeutic goals;
2. Type of drug;
3. State of the schizophrenic illness;
4. Individual differences

The therapeutic goals can be described in terms of the four principal indications for neuroleptic treatment:

1. Symptomatic management and control of pathological excitement;
2. Treatment of acute psychotic disorders;
3. Treatment of chronic schizophrenic conditions;
4. Maintenance treatment of schizophrenic patients in remission.

The first indication, being for symptomatic treatment only, has the limited therapeutic goal of immediate, temporary control of a difficult situation. In this case, dosage requirements are contingent on the particular circumstances and neither a long-term treatment plan nor serious considerations of the side effects and complications that arise from long-continued treatment, play important roles. Megadoses, however, have not been shown to be more helpful than regular doses in this situation.

The second indication calls for a treatment plan with well-defined therapeutic goals. Physicians should follow a predetermined dosage regime and know well in advance what the criteria and measures of improvement will be and for how long they want to treat the acutely ill schizophrenic patient.

The third indication also requires the setting of well-defined therapeutic objectives. Does the physician aim at the complete suppression of symptoms, or only at the elimination or reduction of the most disturbing psychopathology in a chronic schizophrenic? Dosages, length of treatment, and the type of drug administration will be influenced by these considerations.

The fourth indication aims at secondary prevention rather than at the treatment of an illness or the removal of psychopathologic symptoms. This phase of the pharmacotherapeutic management of a schizophrenic patient is the logical consequence of the fact that neither pharmacotherapy nor any other treatment known today can cure schizophrenia and that pharmacotherapy with antipsychotic drugs can only suppress psychotic symptoms.

Modes of Administration

The most assured way of administering neuroleptic drugs is by intramuscular injection. When given in this manner, the drugs are two or three times more bioavailable than when given by mouth.

After parenteral administration, the next most reliable way of giving neuroleptic drugs is in liquid form, orally administered as a concentrate. Patients often succeed in avoiding to swallow their neuroleptic medication by pretending to do so, while they are really "cheeking" it (i.e., hiding the pill in their cheeks or under the tongue) and later getting rid of it. Liquid medication does not lend itself to this practice easily.

Experienced nurses know that they cannot be certain that their patients have taken the medication unless they have them swallow some water after it has been taken and then inspect the mouth. Relatives of patients should be taught the same technique if there is reason to suspect that a nonhospitalized patient is not reliable in taking medication. Crushing pills before offering them to the patients is another way of preventing them from jeopardizing their treatment.

It has been well established in recent years that after the first few days of treatment a single daily administration of a neuroleptic drug is as effective as divided doses of two or more per day. The once-a-day administration reduces the risk of the patient forgetting or otherwise defaulting on his or her medication; it is also more economical in that it saves nursing time and allows use of lower-priced, large-dose tablets.

Long-Acting Neuroleptics

Some physicians like to use injections of one of the long-acting neuroleptic preparations, e.g, fluphenazine enanthate or decanoate or haloperidol decanoate, as the first therapeutic approach to treating new schizophrenic patients, particularly in community-based programs where teams (or the physician) visit mentally ill patients at their homes and often treat them there during the whole acute episode. This practice is not to be recommended as an initial approach, because of problems with side effects that are better monitored initially with short-acting drugs.

Patients receiving the long-acting drugs should be warned of the possible occurrence of extrapyramidal symptoms and should be given instructions to take appropriate antiparkinsonian medication immediately in this event. Some physicians prefer to give such medication prophylactically to every patient on long-acting therapy.

Polypharmacy

A combination that theoretically can induce dangerous complications, although supporting case reports are lacking in the literature, is the simultaneous administration of phenothiazines, tricyclic antidepressants, and antiparkinsonian medication. Any two of these three might be given simultaneously to a patient, but all three of them together may become dangerous for some patients, particularly the elderly, because of the synergistic effect resulting from the anticholinergic action of these agents. However, neuroleptics may be safely combined with tricyclic antidepressants, and such combinations are indicated in schizophrenic patients who become acutely depressed.

There are few established clinical indications for the simultaneous administration of neuroleptics and benzodiazepines, unless the latter are employed for their anticonvulsant properties in patients who are seizure prone. Recently, however, there has been a renewed interest in the combined use of neuroleptics and benzodiazepines as a means of limiting neuroleptic doses, particularly in acute, agitated schizophrenics. Also the use of benzodiazepines for the treatment of anticipatory anxiety in schizophrenics is warranted.

The Acute Schizophrenic

For the systematic treatment of acute schizophrenic conditions a daily dose range of 300–1000 mg per day of chlorpromazine, or its equivalent, is indicated. Smaller doses may sometimes be effective, but the vast majority of acute schizophrenics will require daily amounts of 300 mg or more. A survey of 118 studies with phenothiazines revealed that in all studies where chlorpromazine had been administered in adequate doses, defined in the survey to be 300 mg per day or more, the drug had proved to be superior to placebo (Klein and Davis 1969).

In the early stages of treating a schizophrenic patient it is better to exceed the minimal required dose than to remain below it. Because the acute toxicity of most neuroleptics is remarkably low, there is little risk involved in raising the dose rapidly to achieve maximum control of the most disturbing and distressing symptoms in a few days. However, once this point has been reached, the dose should be lowered gradually so as to optimize the twin goals of safety and clinical efficacy. In certain treatment-resistant patients, daily doses as high as 2,000–3,000 mg of chlorpromazine, or its equivalent, may be required. However, "rapid neuroleptization," i.e., frequent large daily doses of a high-potency neuroleptic, has not proved to have any advantages over a slower, more careful induction of pharmacotherapy and may even yield poorer results.

Dose requirements for neuroleptic drugs often vary widely in different individuals, probably because of differences in the way various individuals metabolize the drugs. Constitutional differences in enzymatic breakdown mechanisms and protein binding are probably responsible for the fact that identical doses of neuroleptic drugs may produce greatly divergent plasma levels in different individuals.

But plasma levels of the drugs are not the answer to the question of what doses an individual patient should receive—at least, not yet and certainly not routinely. In the first place, the determination of plasma levels of neuroleptic drugs is still beset with many technical difficulties and is far from being readily available to most practicing clinicians. Secondly, no strict correlation between plasma levels of neuroleptics and their therapeutic efficacy has been established as yet, although trends in this direction have been demonstrated.

However, for clinical purposes, it currently is more important that a clinical relation exists between the time of response of certain symptoms to treatment and the dose of the neuroleptic drug a patient is receiving; this relation can be used as a guide to a patient's individual drug requirements. It has been observed that symptoms belonging in the category of arousal, e.g., psychomotor excitement, restlessness, irritability, aggressiveness, and insomnia, tend to be the first ones to be controlled by effective doses of neuroleptic drugs, usually in less than one to two weeks of pharmacotherapy. Affective symptoms, e.g., anxiety, depression, and social withdrawal, respond next. Finally, symptoms related to perceptual and cognitive functions such as hallucinations, delusions, and thinking disorder, tend to diminish (usually in that order) or disappear—in many cases, only after 6–8 weeks of treatment (Lehmann 1967). The observation of this "time table" of therapeutic responses to neuroleptic treatment often allows the clinician to determine whether the dose of the drug being prescribed is adequate for a given patient. Clearly, this outline of symptom response should not be considered as constant or fixed. Also in this era of short hospital stays this pattern of symptom remission will often have to be observed after the hospitalization.

Three of the most common errors committed in the neuroleptic treatment of schizophrenia are the use of inadequate doses, overdosage, and too rapid changes of medication. If an impatient physician changes the drug being prescribed every two weeks because of dissatisfaction with its therapeutic results, that physician might never learn what the proper dose and time are for any of the drugs being constantly changed. A good rule of thumb is not to change to another drug or treatment, e.g., electroconvulsive therapy, until the drug that was originally chosen for the acute episode has been given—at gradually increasing doses—for a period of six to eight weeks, without any noticeable improvement.

Dose requirements for the chronic schizophrenic are, in most cases, lower than those for the acute schizophrenic. If the clinical goal is only to render the patient and his environment more comfortable by reducing the intensity of his symptoms, the chronic patient may require from 50–500 mg of chlorpromazine or its equivalent daily. If the goals are more ambitious in the chronic patient, higher doses may be required. One study found that chronic schizophrenics who had been refractory to conventional doses of neuroleptics could still benefit from high doses, i.e., from 1,000–2,000 mg per day of chlorpromazine or its equivalent, given over a six-month period, particularly if the patients were under 40 years of age and had been hospitalized for less than 10 years (Prien and Cole 1968).

There are, however, many chronic schizophrenic patients who are receiving neuroleptic drugs needlessly, because their symptoms do not respond to the medication. They would do as well or better if the drugs were discontinued. The drug treatment of every chronic schizophrenic who has reached a "steady state" of functioning and whose condition has not changed for months should be assessed at regular intervals—at least once a year—to observe his response to the gradual lowering of the drugs. Those patients who within a short time—sometimes within days—manifest an intensification of their symptoms should resume their pharmacotherapy immediately. In those cases where no deterioration appears, the dose should be further decreased gradually until the minimal dose that maintains greatest improvement has been found.

A number of patients improve temporarily when the neuroleptic medication is stopped. They become brighter and their activity level increases. However, after two to four weeks many of these temporarily improved chronic schizophrenics who are off medication relapse and again manifest their old symptoms, sometimes worse than before. These patients obviously need continued pharmacotherapy.

Finally, there are chronic patients who, after discontinuation of their medication, either improve or at least are no worse than they were while receiving neuroleptics. These patients should not be carried indefinitely on drug treatment because there is no obvious clinical advantage to it.

Maintenance Treatment

After the patient has achieved maximum improvement, one should aim at maintaining the same quality of remission with the lowest possible daily doses of antipsychotic drug. Some patients may be successfully protected against recurrences of their illness with as little as 50 mg of chlorpromazine or its equivalent, although these patients are quite rare. Other patients require daily doses of more than 500 mg of chlorpromazine or its equivalent to remain in good remission. This whole area of practice still depends on informed trial and error, although it is guided by a growing body of recent clinical research. It seems that in some patients minimal threshold doses are sufficient to prevent a recurrence of the psychotic breakdown. In general, however, a definite dose-effect relationship prevails in groups of schizophrenics randomly assigned to fixed doses of neuroleptics.

It is probably true that a significant percentage of patients on maintenance treatment do not need to take their medication and would not relapse without it. Unfortunately, there is no adequate way today of telling which patients would remain well even without treatment, although careful assessment of diagnosis and of past history can often help to predict. The clinician has to make a decision whether to embark on a maintenance regimen of possibly indefinite duration or to accept the higher than 70 percent risk that the patient would have another breakdown within a year. Another attack of schizophrenia may ruin the patients' chances in their chosen occupation. (When a young schoolteacher suffered an acute schizophrenic breakdown, the social workers were able to persuade the school board to let her return to her job as soon as she recovered from her attack, that is, after eight weeks. Because she had responded so quickly and completely to treatment, it was felt that it might not be necessary to put her on maintenance therapy. But when she relapsed after three months and recovered again, she lost her job, and a teaching career was closed to her.)

It is well known that noncompliance of patients on maintenance treatment is a common problem. From 25–50 percent of outpatients are estimated to be unreliable drug takers; the percentage is somewhat lower among inpatients. One simple, but very important, response is to reduce the pill taking of a patient on maintenance treatment to once a day, preferably at bedtime. A patient who is expected to take pills regularly more than once or twice a day is very likely to default. If he has no or only minor symptoms, neither he nor his family may consider him to be sick. Families are often opposed to the "doping" of a relative in apparent remission; and to make families take the maintenance treatment seriously is often a real problem that may be more difficult to solve than the one presented by the short-term treatment of the acute schizophrenic breakdown. The use of long-acting depot esters of fluphenazine or haloperidol can be useful in particularly unreliable or drug-reluctant patients. Furthermore, recent experience with low-dose maintenance therapy has been encouraging. The patients frequently accept the lower dose better and decompensations appear to be more gradual in onset, thereby permitting drug dosage adjustment.

How long should maintenance treatment be continued? There are only arbitrary answers to this question. Studies of adequate duration are not available. Clinical experience suggests it is best to continue maintenance treatment after the first schizophrenic attack for at least one to two years, after the second attack for five years, and after three or more relapses indefinitely, possibly for the patient's lifetime. Families should be informed that relapse rates consistently appear to be higher when drugs are discontinued, even when low doses are stopped after one to two years of a stable clinical picture.

Various investigators have demonstrated the important effects of social and other environmental factors on the schizophrenic patient's stability during long-term follow-up. The type of social environment, e.g., whether he lives with members of his family or with strangers, influences the incidence of relapses. Untoward happenings, adverse experiences, and an emotional climate perceived as demanding, harsh, or critical by patients tend to precipitate recurrences of his illness. Some investigators have even shown that the length of daily exposure to such a negative emotional climate—i.e., more or less than 35 hours per week—made a statistically significant difference in the frequency of relapses. The same team also showed that one of the most important protective agents against these unfavorable social factors were neuroleptic drugs taken as maintenance treatment (Vaughn and Leff 1976). These findings lead to the question of whether neuroleptics can be reduced or eliminated if environmental stresses are more successfully managed.

The disadvantages of maintenance treatment, besides the inconvenience and cost associated with any long-term therapy, lie mainly in the uncomfortable side effects that the drugs often elicit and—more importantly—in the risk of developing tardive dyskinesia. As a serious complication this is likely to occur in 15–25 percent of patients on long-term (> six months) neuroleptic therapy. This risk must be carefully discussed with patients and/or their families when long-term neuroleptic therapy is started and again as the need for continued maintenance therapy is regularly reevaluated.

Social Adjustment

How well the schizophrenic patient functioned in his employment and social relations prior to becoming obviously ill is a valuable predictor of the future course of his illness. Several studies, comparing chronic schizophrenic patients before and after the introduction of the neuroleptic drugs, have provided data to indicate that the new chronic patients present much less severe schizophrenic deterioration than the old ones and that the prognosis for schizophrenia has improved over the last 30 years (Lehmann and Cancro 1985). However, the increasing incidence of personality disorders and drug abuse among schizophrenic patients confounds the picture.

It must always be remembered that no drug known today—or possibly ever—can correct manifestations of social maladaptation in chronically psychotic patients, a condition that does on occasion respond to psychosocial treatment methods. Despite the costs of such long-term psychosocial interventions, it is essential that they be studied further. Today 80–90 percent of acutely hospitalized schizophrenic patients receiving pharmacotherapy will leave the hospital within a year. Ten to twenty years later, 60 percent of the patients will be socially recovered in the community, employed about half the time. Thirty percent will live in the community, being handicapped by deficits, and 10 percent will be hospitalized most of the time.

Negative Effects of Pharmacotherapy

Negative effects of antipsychotic drugs may be divided into five categories:

1. Physical symptoms and complications: undesired drug effects such as extrapyramidal signs, dry mouth, constipation, weight gain, sexual dysfunction, etc.; or consequences that seriously impair the patient's health, e.g., cholestatic jaundice or tardive dyskinesia.
2. Subjective dysphoria: subjective feelings of discomfort and/or distress associated with drug use.
3. Behavioral toxicity: noxious modifications of the patient's behavior as a result of the drug's action, e.g., psychomotor retardation, inertia, hypersomnia, restlessness, etc.
4. Compliance problems: irregular or unreliable adherence to the prescribed drug regime by the patient.

5. Reduction of the physicians' therapeutic efficacy: the physician may depend excessively on pharmacotherapy and not develop a sufficiently strong doctor-patient and family relationship (Lehmann 1979).

Physical side effects of most drugs are usually well known to the medical profession and also to many lay people. To patients they sometimes constitute very considerable inconveniences. Because they may also frighten patients and cause them to discontinue their medication prematurely, the common occurrence of typical side effects should be anticipated and explained to the patient by the physician in advance. Although it has been argued that warning against possible side effects may, in fact, induce them by suggestion, the prevalent opinion today is that the reassurance value of the doctor's explanation—even if it is anticipatory—outweighs the potential disadvantage of an iatrogenic production of side effects. It is, of course, to be understood that every good clinician will use some discretion and will not unnecessarily alarm the patient by a complete recital of all possible complications, even if they are extremely uncommon. The almost absurd effects of a "full disclosure" of all possible negative consequences of taking a drug have been well illustrated in some experiments (Epstein and Lasagna 1969).

Most of the antipsychotic drugs have low toxicity. However, they cause a great variety of side effects, which are unpleasant and thus present a serious obstacle to compliance with drug treatment. Some of the physical side effects also interfere with a patient's behavioral performance, e.g., extrapyramidal symptoms, and with his personal and social image, e.g., obesity.

For some of the side effects there are specific counter measures. The most important examples are the use of certain antiparkinsonian drugs (anticholinergics and amantadine). They are fairly specific in reducing acute extrapyramidal side effects, but precisely for this reason they may be overused. Many psychiatrists insist that these antiparkinsonian drugs should only be used when extrapyramidal symptoms have appeared—not prophylactically—and even then they should be stopped after a few weeks to observe whether the symptoms will remain absent even without the continued use of anticholinergic drugs, because these substances by themselves might have toxic effects and might interfere with the therapeutic efficacy of antipsychotic drugs. Other psychiatrists support routine use of antiparkinsonian drugs even with oral neuroleptics. The indications and contraindications for the use of antiparkinsonian drugs are still subject to controversy.

No drug-induced parkinsonism symptoms were known until the advent of the antipsychotic drugs. However, soon after their introduction, it became evident that a variety of extrapyramidal disorders constituted the most important adverse effects of this new class of drugs. Hypokinetic parkinsonism, more recently labeled rigid-akinetic syndrome, occurs usually within a few days or weeks after the start of antipsychotic drug therapy. Akathisia (restlessness) remains frequently unrecognized and is much more common, disabling, and persistent than is usually realized. Dystonia is an acute, brief, dramatic, and often alarming episode of hypertonicity and focal muscle spasm following, sometimes within hours, the start of antipsychotic medication. These episodes tend to occur more frequently following the starting of high-potency neuroleptics in young males, both children and adolescents. They were at first suspected to be of an hysterical nature until their extrapyramidal origin was recognized.

Finally, the most troublesome extrapyramidal complication of antipsychotic pharmacotherapy made its worldwide appearance in the early 1960s—tardive dyskinesia. Unlike hypokinetic parkinsonism, akathisia, and the acute dystonic manifestations, tardive dyskinesia is, in many cases, irreversible.

Hypokinetic Syndrome

The high-potency dopamine-blocking antipsychotics are more likely to produce parkinsonism than the aliphatic and piperidine derivatives of phenothiazine.

This syndrome—hypokinesia, tremor, mask-like faces—responds well to certain antiparkinsonian drugs, e.g., trihexyphenidyl (Artane), benztropine (Cogentin), procyclidine (Kemadrin), or amantadine (Symmetrel). It is still controversial whether these drugs should be prescribed prophylactically, i.e., at the beginning of antipsychotic drug treatment, or only when symptoms appear. If extrapyramidal symptoms have been successfully treated with antiparkinsonian drugs, these drugs can often be given at lower doses or even withdrawn after two or three months without a return of symptoms. It should be noted that these antiparkinsonian drugs have strong anticholinergic properties and, when prescribed in higher doses, not infrequently cause symptoms of toxic psychosis. Furthermore, these drugs have entered the street market because they are capable of inducing euphoria in certain subjects.

Akathisia

The drug-induced restlessness of akathisia can be very distressing to patients. These symptoms must be distinguished from psychotic agitation. They often respond to propranolol or to benzodiazepines. Frequently, all that is needed is a reduction in dosage of antipsychotic medication.

Dystonia

Dystonia is most likely to occur in young male patients within hours of neuroleptic drug administration. The sudden development of a dystonic syndrome with painful spasms of the muscles of the head and neck as well as spasms of the tongue that interfere with speaking and sometimes an oculogyric crisis is extremely alarming to the patient, particularly if the patient is not prepared for its possible occurrence. Fortunately, these symptoms usually respond rapidly to oral or parenteral administration of anticholinergic-antihistaminergic drugs. Because high-potency neuroleptics such as haloperidol or fluphenazine are most likely to produce dystonia (particularly if administered parenterally as long-acting medications), it is generally recommended that antiparkinsonian drugs be given prophylactically with these medications, or that the patients be warned of the possible occurrence of this side effect, be prescribed a supply of an antiparkinsonian drug, and be instructed to take this medication at the first appearance of dystonic symptoms. If dystonic symptoms persist, the patient should obtain emergency medical attention.

Tardive Dyskinesia

This potential complication of antipsychotic pharmacotherapy presents a significant medical problem in the maintenance management of schizophrenic patients. The condition, once developed, is in many cases irreversible, and there is no effective treatment known today. Therefore, the emphasis must be placed on prevention. Tardive dyskinesia is thought to be the result of chronic hypersensitivity of dopaminergic neurons, although this is not certain. It may be observed in 15–25 percent of all patients who have received neuroleptic drugs, particularly large doses, over a period of months or years.

The clinical problems associated with tardive dyskinesia have been discussed in a special task force report of the American Psychiatric Association. The following points should be noted:

- Antipsychotic (neuroleptic) drugs should, as a general principle, be prescribed only for those psychiatric conditions for which there is well established evidence for their specific therapeutic efficacy, e.g., schizophrenia, Tourette's syndrome, etc.
- Every patient on long-term treatment with antipsychotic drugs should be examined at regular intervals for early signs of tardive dyskinesia.
- If tardive dyskinesia symptoms have appeared, discontinuation, or at least reduction, of the dose of antipsychotic medications should be tried.
- If the patient's psychiatric condition does not allow discontinuation of antipsychotic medication, the options for the treating physician are to try some of the many experimental treatments that have been proposed for tardive dyskinesia ranging from reserpine, benzodiazepines, lithium, and L-dopa to ECT, or to continue with antipsychotic medication, which may even have to be increased to mask the dyskinesia symptoms.

In the latter case, the reasons for the decision to continue with antipsychotic medication, in spite of apparent dyskinesia, must be well documented. There is no accepted general standard of practice to be followed when tardive dyskinesia has been diagnosed, as long as it has been documented that good clinical judgment was used.

There is a need to document the decision to institute maintenance therapy with antipsychotic drugs once acute symptoms of psychosis have subsided. The potential for tardive dyskinesia and the risks associated with relapse should be discussed with the patient and family at the beginning of treatment. This discussion may point to actuarial risk factors: a 70–80 percent risk of a psychotic relapse within a year without maintenance pharmacotherapy versus a 20–30 percent risk of relapse within a year and a 15–25 percent risk of tardive dyskinesia within two to five years with pharmacotherapy. The negative consequences of repeated decompensations must be explained. Higher risk groups for tardive dyskinesia include patients over 50 years of age, those with affective disorders, and those with a history of organic brain damage.

Informed consent is recommended in the longer term use of neuroleptics. Certainly in cases likely to require six months or more of neuroleptic treatment, informed consent should be obtained from the family and from the patient if he or she is able to give such consent. It is necessary to give the family and the patient, when possible, an adequate disclosure of what is known about the risks and benefits of maintenance neuroleptic treatment. Even psychotic patients may be competent to choose their preferred risk and if in the clinician's judgment—documented in the record—the patient can make the choice of risk, the clinician must defer to this judgment.

Other Side Effects

Many other side effects of psychotropic drugs cannot always be effectively counteracted, e.g., dry mouth and weight gain occurring with the use of neuroleptics. Sometimes a change in drug will be helpful, e.g., changing to molindone in cases of obesity, or bethanechol and sugarless gum can be used for dryness of the mouth. At other times the patient must be persuaded to accept these side effects in exchange for the overall therapeutic action of the drug that has been prescribed as part of the management of the psychopathology.

Somatic complications are conditions that seriously impair a patient's health (e.g., cholestatic jaundice), are potentially fatal (e.g., agranulocytosis, malignant neuroleptic syndrome, or hepatic necrosis), or produce potentially irreversible damage (e.g., retinitis pigmentosa or tardive dyskinesia). Fortunately, these severe complications are relatively rare.

Certain complications can be neither anticipated nor prevented reliably. For instance, agranulocytosis, which occurs in only one of every 5,000–10,000 patients treated with chlorpromazine, is an idiosyncratic hypersensitivity response and can only be dealt with effectively by constant clinical vigilance (e.g., immediate blood counts in cases of fever and sore throat), which should lead to immediate diagnosis and appropriate treatment of the condition when it occurs.

Many patients reject neuroleptics because they find drug use associated with subjective dysphoria. These dysphoric states range from feeling imprisoned and depressed to a vague discomfiture. These altered states of feeling often lead to a rejection of drug therapy.

Behavioral toxicity may be defined as noxious modifications of the patient's behavior that are the result of a drug's actions and the patient's reaction to them and not necessarily part of the disease itself for which the patient is receiving treatment.

Some authors have reported that long-acting neuroleptics, e.g., fluphenazine esters, may induce depressive mood changes that are sometimes serious enough to lead to suicide (Segal and Kopschitz 1969). These early reports have not been replicated, and the clinician must weigh the important benefits of long-acting drugs versus their problems.

Other dysphoric reactions to neuroleptic drugs are commonly observed—for instance, anhedonia, anxiety, agitation, and anger—and thought by some investigators to signal a poor prognosis. Akinesia or hypomobility characterized by apparent loss of initiative and motivation has been singled out by some authors as a special extrapyramidal side effect (Rifkin et al. 1975).

Noncompliance, or the irregular or unreliable adherence to the prescribed drug regime by the patient, is a common and troublesome problem, particularly with schizophrenic patients in remission. A high proportion of patients, estimated to range from 30 to 50 percent, are unreliable drug takers (Hare and Wilcox 1967). They may refuse to take their prescribed drug because of the unpleasant side effects it produces, or they may discontinue their drug regime for primarily psychological reasons, for instance because they fear that continued taking of a drug may be dangerous, because they refuse to accept the fact that they have to take medicine even though they no longer have symptoms, or because they simply forget to take their medication regularly. There is a definite place for the consideration of long-acting compounds in these patients. Obviously, an improved doctor-patient relationship can also be helpful in improving compliance.

Socially isolated patients with a poor educational background who are hostile in their attitude are at high risk for noncompliance. Physicians can improve the situation if they maintain an interested, positive, respectful attitude, simplify the treatment regime as much as possible, (e.g., by prescribing once-a-day medication or using long-acting depot forms), and keep the patient under close supervision by arranging for regular aftercare visits to the clinic or office (Blackwell 1973).

It is a familiar clinical experience that schizophrenic patients may show some personality deterioration after having suffered repeated psychotic relapses. Even if they again lose their florid symptoms, they may develop personality defects, lose some of their social skills and competencies, and begin to go down on the socioeconomic ladder. This is only one of the reasons why one should take every reasonable precaution against the recurrence of a schizophrenic attack. On the other hand, the clinician has to consider the risk of tardive dyskinesia if the patient is maintained for long periods of time on neuroleptic drugs.

The methodological dangers of neglecting or obscuring an accurate psychiatric diagnosis and evaluation of existing psychopathology by interfering too soon through psychotropic drug action are well known to every experienced and careful clinician and have been pointed out in publications (Cancro 1969; Klein 1975). But even more important, it often happens that a clinician, influenced by the frequently stated—and probably justified—statement that psychotropic drug treatment with neuroleptics is the most important factor in the therapeutic management of acute schizophrenic decompensations (May 1968), forecloses the treatment options too early and generalizes wrongly that no other treatment modalities need be considered then or at any later stages of the illness. Yet psychosocial treatment measures, with or without pharmacotherapy, are essential components of the management of most schizophrenic conditions after the acute symptomatology has abated. Again, the very reliability of certain psychotropic drug effects carries the potential danger that a physician might conclude erroneously that this drug action alone is equivalent to comprehensive and complete psychiatric management. The end result of such faulty psychological attitudes toward psychotropic drug treatment on the part of the physician is a negative therapeutic effect on the patient. As May and others have long argued, proper care of the schizophrenic patient requires the use of a variety of interventions with the exact mix determined by the needs of the individual patient.

Chapter 147

Psychotherapy of Schizophrenia

The value of psychoanalytically oriented individual psychotherapy in the treatment of the schizophrenias has long been a source of controversy. Some, like Freud, doubted the usefulness of intensive psychotherapy in patients who were unable to form a transference relationship. Sullivan, on the other hand, emphasized the "corrective" emotional experience a schizophrenic patient can derive from the doctor-patient relationship (Sullivan 1962). Whether a theoretical basis exists for the use of individual psychotherapy for schizophrenic patients, the empiric evidence is not encouraging.

A series of controlled, prospective studies (Fairweather et al. 1960; Karon and VandenBos 1981; May 1968; Rogers et al. 1967) that compared the effects of individual psychotherapy with other forms of nondrug treatments failed to demonstrate any therapeutic advantages for psychodynamically oriented treatment of schizophrenic patients. Indeed, after reviewing the available evidence, the American Psychiatric Association Commission on Psychotherapies (1984) concluded that the exclusive use of psychotherapy as a treatment modality is much less effective for the management of schizophrenia than for the management of other major mental disorders.

In the early 1950s, psychotherapy alone was the standard treatment of schizophrenia, but by the end of the 1960s there was a sharp shift to pharmacologic treatment. An influential study was conducted with 20 "back ward" schizophrenic patients at Boston State Hospital to see if antipsychotic medication interfered with psychotherapy (Grinspoon et al. 1968). These patients were transferred to the Massachusetts Mental Health Center, which was generally regarded as a more prestigious institution than the state hospital, and were treated by prominent clinicians with a strong theoretical bias in favor of psychoanalytical methods. Half of the patients received phenothiazines. At the end of 20 months of treatment, the authors concluded that psychotherapy alone offered little benefit for chronic schizophrenic patients, but that phenothiazines were one of the most effective treatments available for chronic schizophrenia.

Despite the consistently negative results of controlled, prospective studies, intensive psychotherapy of schizophrenic patients continues to be widely practiced (McGlashan 1983). Proponents of that modality attribute the discouraging research findings to methodological shortcomings in the studies that prevent true observation of clinical realities (Mosher and Keith 1980). These clinicians cite generally positive personal observations, patient testimonials, and retrospective studies as evidence of the efficacy of the psychodynamic treatment approach.

Interpretations of other major studies on the use of analytically oriented therapy indicate that it is not an effective treatment method for schizophrenic patients. In these studies, various types of psychoanalytic treatments were used, usually in conjunction with some type of neuroleptic medication. It is difficult to compare treatments because of the many variables involved. Patients' characteristics and duration of illness varied, and length of treatment, expertise of clinicians, and outcome measures differed from study to study. As Klein (1980) pointed out, a glaring omission in some of the studies was a control group of patients, noting that "it is relatively easy to show the equivalence of two useless interventions."

May (1968) studied first-admission "middle prognosis" schizophrenics who were assigned to an "ego supportive" type of individual psychotherapy in conjunction with milieu therapy. Patients in this group were compared to those receiving milieu therapy alone. No drugs or electroconvulsive therapy was given. Patients received an average of 46 hours of therapy. Assessments done by independent raters failed to discern significant differences in outcome measures between the two groups.

Rogers et al. (1967) compared the effects of client-centered individual psychotherapy with conventional state hospital treatment in a cohort of acute and chronic schizophrenic patients. Patients in both groups received neuroleptic medication. The investigators found no significant differences in outcome between the two groups.

Karon and VandenBos (1972) compared two different forms of psychotherapy used to treat acutely ill, first-admission schizophrenic patients. In addition one group was treated without drugs. The nondrug group received psychoanalytic psychotherapy characterized as "direct analysis." The second group received chlorpromazine plus psychoanalytic psychotherapy described as "ego analytic." A hospital control group also was included. Because of poor design this study provided no useful information (Klein 1980).

Hogarty and Goldberg (1973) used a nontraditional form of individual psychotherapy termed major role therapy with the goal of helping posthospitalization schizophrenics "reassume and maintain their roles in the community." There were four comparison groups with various combinations of therapy, active drug, and placebo. Results of the study suggested not only that psychotherapy was ineffective, but that it was harmful to some patients.

The most recent, and generally regarded as the most rigorous and well designed, of the treatment outcome studies is the Psychotherapy of Schizophrenia Project (Gunderson et al. 1985). This study was undertaken to assess the comparative efficacy in schizophrenic patients of the two most widely used forms of individual psychotherapy, exploratory insight-oriented (EIO) and reality-adaptive supportive (RAS) psychotherapy, over a two-year period. The objective of EIO therapy is self-understanding and the temporal focus is present and past. The objectives of RAS therapy include symptom relief (via drug management and strengthening of existing defenses) and the temporal focus is present and future. Insight-oriented therapy was provided three times a week and supportive therapy once a week. At the start of the study, all patients were hospitalized and received active milieu treatment and individualized pharmacotherapy and appropriate aftercare services in addition to their assigned psychotherapy.

The cohort was selected for the study using narrow DSM-III criteria (American Psychiatric Association 1980) and represented the midrange of schizophrenic patients in terms of prognosis, being neither markedly chronic or acute. All therapists were seasoned clinicians, with an average of 10 years of experience. Treatment assignment was random.

The major findings of the study were that there were minimal outcome differences between the two groups and that each form of treatment had a preferential and specific action on outcome measures. The obvious implication of these results is that since neither form of treatment had a significant advantage over the other, supportive therapy should be, on a cost-benefit basis, the preferred treatment for schizophrenic patients. It is less theoretical, demands less clinical training, and less clinician time.

Although most of the studies mentioned above failed to meet rigorous experimental criteria, clinical experience has demonstrated that certain patients do respond to individual psychotherapy (Cancro 1983). The Psychotherapy of Schizophrenia Project also provides evidence that it may be possible to identify subgroups who might preferentially benefit from a specific therapy. Schizophrenia is currently conceptualized as a group of disorders, making it possible that patients can be subtyped into treatment-relevant subgroups (Carpenter 1986).

At the end of the two-year period, only 51 of the original 164 patients remained in the project study (28 RAS and 23 EIO patients). Gunderson and Frank (1985) found the characteristics of the two groups of patients who completed the study to be different. They observed that "patients who have positive symptoms of schizophrenia . . . but are relatively optimistic about their prospect of recovery, are more likely to be engaged and to remain in supportive treatment. . . . Supportive therapy is a focused treatment which reinforces a patient's expectations of a good response and . . . patients with positive symptoms welcome treatment that is not too emotionally and interpersonally demanding."

Gunderson and Frank (1985) also found that the patients who remained in insight-oriented therapy had more education and had more negative symptoms and more modest expectations regarding the future. They postulate that EIO therapy is more appropriate for patients who have the requisite compulsivity to attend intensive therapy regularly, who are worn down by their illness, and who see the need for long-term treatment to uncover covert causes. In general, insight-oriented therapists "offer hope that a slower, more basic change can be hoped for. This approach makes sense for patients who have some stable but unsatisfactory level of function and who view their illnesses discouragingly."

Data from the Psychotherapy of Schizophrenia Project "suggest that in the areas of recidivism and role performance (i.e., occupational functioning, hospitalization, and to a lesser extent social adaptation), supportive therapy exerts preferential and specific action compared to insight-oriented therapy. In contrast, insight-oriented therapy appears to exert preferential albeit more modest action in the areas of ego functioning and cognition (i.e., adaptive regression and to a lesser extent thought disorganization)." These findings suggest that different forms of treatment produce different benefits (Stanton et al. 1984). Implicit in the finding of differential efficacy is the fact that planned therapeutic interventions can have an impact on the course of some schizophrenic disorders, even if that impact is modest.

To summarize the scientific evidence, intensive insight-oriented psychotherapy has not been shown to have superior beneficial effects when compared to other conventional forms of psychotherapy or standard institutional care. It has not, however, been established that psychoanalytically derived therapies are of no value in the management of schizophrenic patients. Rather, it has been shown that less costly approaches, such as supportive therapies, are equally effective.

When psychodynamic approaches are used, it is generally agreed that traditional techniques should be modified in the direction of more practical, step-by-step, and goal-oriented methods (Schulz 1987). The availability of the clinician for identification and insight represents an important element in effectiveness. Carpenter (1986) has described the clinical relationship as "the cornerstone of treatment" of the schizophrenic patient. By virtue of this relationship the therapist can act to reduce adverse reactions to stressors in the environment, foster awareness of early signs of impending relapse, educate the patient and other household members, provide genetic counseling, monitor dangerousness, and coordinate multiple therapeutic modalities.

Clinicians need to be cognizant of the potential negative effects of psychotherapy on schizophrenic patients. These include the development of increased dependency, destructive acting out when inhibitions are lifted (May and Simpson 1980), and clinical worsening as a result of overly intrusive activity by the therapist, particularly in withdrawn patients.

Drake and Sederer (1986) note that intensive psychotherapy and intensive milieu therapy may be too stimulating for the frightened schizophrenic patient who needs to be reassured and to regain control of his environment. They suggest that excessive uncovering, insight-oriented exploration, and self-disclosure may be harmful for these patients. In the Psychotherapy of Schizophrenia Project, more than half of the patients receiving intensive treatment dropped out within six months, compared to less than one-third of those receiving supportive treatment (Drake and Sederer 1986).

What emerges from the literature on the psychotherapy of schizophrenia is that there is no simple "therapy by rote" (May and Simpson 1980) for all schizophrenic patients. Some therapists appear to be more successful than others in working with schizophrenic patients. Thus, treatment strategies ultimately need to be individualized, depending on the needs of the patient and the "style and creativity" of the therapist (McGlashan 1983). The theoretical stance of the therapist appears to have little correlation with the efficacy of the treatment, but the therapist's attitude and character structure may be of greater importance. Not every therapist is suited to making a long-term commitment to these patients, who have a formidable communication problem and an uncertain future (Cancro 1983; Carpenter 1986).

It is also clear that neuroleptic medication alone is insufficient treatment for schizophrenic patients. These patients need to be monitored to ensure that they take their medication and to avoid irreversible complications of the drugs. Lamb (1986) argues that less emphasis should be placed on attempting to "mainstream" schizophrenic patients and that clinicians should recognize that the majority of patients are incapable of truly independent functioning in the community and will need support and protection for long periods of time. There is a growing consensus that a combined approach to the management of schizophrenia is most appropriate and that perhaps the psychotherapy of schizophrenia should really be conceptualized as "psychosocial help for people with schizophrenia" (Klein 1980).

In schizophrenia, as in every diagnostic category, patients' personality characteristics play a large role in determining their response to psychodynamic psychotherapy.

Chapter 148 describes the application of psychodynamic principles to treatment of schizophrenic patients. It must be understood from the foregoing discussion that psychodynamic psychotherapy may only be a useful part of the treatment plan for a limited subgroup of schizophrenic patients.

Chapter 148

Individual Psychodynamic Psychotherapy of Schizophrenia

The central phenomenon with which all dynamic psychotherapies of schizophrenia contend is the vulnerability of the patient's self. This liability of the patient to experience fragmentation of the self, its results, its avoidances, its fearsome anxieties, and its degree of communicability—as well as the measures that attempt to counteract the fragmentation, the forces that facilitate it, and the fragmented self's desperate attempts at self-repair—are the crucial issues with which such psychotherapies are involved (Pao 1979).

Often this fragmentation of the self and its underlying awesome ego disorganization can be described by the patient. He reports having gone through an inner catastrophe in which he has profoundly changed and in which the world of his reality has changed along with him. Loss of the boundaries of the ego and the self, intense panic and anxiety, inability to modulate, control, or delay or damp down impulses of aggression or sexuality, or affects such as sadness or terror, leave him prey to floods of experience and feeling. Various hallucinatory organizations of sensation and torturing hypochondriasis occupy his mind (Federn 1952). Delusional tormenting symptoms exhibit themselves as painful and partial attempts of the patient to put the self and the world back together, to organize some primitive representation of boundaries amid the chaos of a fractured ego and fragmented self (Freud 1911; reprinted 1958).

Psychiatrists contending with these phenomena in a patient deal mainly with what Sullivan (1962) calls security operations and Sandler (1960) calls the background of safety. They try to help the ego to restore its cohesiveness, to find a position of safety, and to manage its functions, its affects, its experiences, and its perceptions. They try to facilitate the ego's organizing out of that turmoil a viable object and self-organization and to help the patient find some realistically related view of the world and a safe place for the function of a nonfragmented self.

To do this, first of all, these psychiatrists attempt to exist in a regular, reliable, sequential way with the patient in the same shared space (Schwartz 1978). They see that all sequence and much causality have disappeared from the patient's experience of people, of himself, and of his world and from the regulation of that patient's ego function. Thus, regularity of therapeutic meetings, regularity of place to meet, freedom from impingement of ordinary traumatic stimuli, and the ability to have space in which patient and doctor can listen and notice without danger are among the first and foremost conditions that must be sought and provided. The patient must be able to meet with the doctor where he can hear himself think, where he is physically safe from assault, where his general bodily needs are taken care of, where his literal survival is not at stake, and where the bodily safety of him and his therapist can be assured. It is noteworthy that these conditions must be present and assured for the therapist as well as the patient. No one can expect to form an object relation of a significant psychotherapeutic kind in a place where food, shelter, security from physical trauma, and the regular availability of other recognizing, caring persons cannot be achieved. Individual dynamic psychotherapy cannot be done with the patient subject to assault, lying hungry and cold on a subway grate, or meeting irregularly with various and changing therapeutic personnel.

Central to this process of locating the security operations of the self, i.e., the safety of ego functions, are the communicative processes. Schizophrenic patients regularly attempt to put into some representational form the nature of their dilemmas, their strengths and weaknesses, and their inner and outer perceptual experiences for themselves and others to understand. In behavior and talk from birth on, man is a symbol-organizing and experience-representing organism at play and at work, alone, and in relation to others. Schizophrenic patients, no less than anyone else, wish themselves and their doctors to know where they hurt and why, what they perceive and how, and how they experience their own thinking and affects. This communication is complicated by central dynamic problems in all schizophrenic patients (Hill 1955). Two of the rules under which their families have often brought them up are that they are not to exist and they are not to perceive themselves as separate selves.

For such symbol-forming human animals—afflicted with grave troubles and unable to satisfy many of their own needs adequately—to be invited into the presence of a psychiatrist or other mental health personnel who ask about them and notice that they exist, to be asked to help describe what form that existence takes, and to notice what they perceive and put that into words all violate some of the central scruples of their previously learned environment (Lidz 1973). More than any other kind of patient, therefore, schizophrenic patients—to the degree that they are intimately engaged in any treatment—are immediately involved in a conflict related to the central therapeutic processes of individual dynamic psychotherapy, i.e., to notice, to perceive, and to communicate. To be alive for almost all human beings is to represent what they are and what they see. Schizophrenic patients live as if they do not exist and are only subject to the unnamable dangerous forces that surround them (when a therapist approaches them, these dangerous forces are then located in the treating personnel, i.e., in that individual doctor). These "evil forces" of treatment invite them to see and to be. These "evil" treatment forces are experienced as wanting to occupy all available space, possess the patient's soul.

Nevertheless, the therapist's task is to search for a place to be safe and in which to listen, and in that process attempt to evolve a communicative relationship with the patient that will note, for the therapist and for the patient, the patient's security operations. The doctor must notice and ultimately name the places where safety exists, however tenuously, and the forces that disrupt that safety, that security. These disruptive forces are within the patient and within the behavior, feelings, and actions of the therapist. Therefore, learning the patient's communicative language and understanding how to translate that patient's forms of behavior into words are central (Pious 1961). This study of the patient's and the therapist's representing, communicative processes needs to be grounded in an understanding of the developmental learning that is observed in children's play as they form an object relationship with their parents and evolve communicative language (Greenspan 1981). Similar communicative processes are found in the organizational actions of the tenuous therapeutic object relationship, as well as in its evolution and representational forms in the treatment of schizophrenia. Such an appropriate evolution of language processes around the organization of an helpful object and self relationship is crucial to progress in any dynamic, individual psychotherapy (Schwartz 1986).

Special aspects of the fragmentation of the self are the difficult state of the patient's ego boundaries and the vulnerable conditions of the patient's ego organization. Schizophrenic patients not only have suffered a loss of their own sense of self, but struggle with a fragmentation of their own boundary-restoring ego functions. In the presence of others they feel fused with, taken over by, and invaded by the other persons. This is particularly true with any human being that they feel any affection for or to whom they are attracted. Having lost their boundary-forming functions, the capacity to control and delay impulses is impeded, the capacity to distinguish themselves from others is impaired, their ability to sequence is disrupted, their ability to focus attention is impeded, their sense of time is distorted, and ordinary forms of consciousness and directed thought are interfered with. Thus, a therapist who wants to help these patients distinguish between inside and outside, between right now or sometime later, between the feeling of anger and the behavioral response of hitting somebody, and between the feeling of sexual arousal and the impulse to masturbate is always faced with critical, difficult problems. When the therapist asks a patient if he feels angry, the therapist must contend with the fact that the patient often responds angrily and assaultively. It is as if that patient was concretely merged with the behavioral action invitation implicit in the therapist's question. It is as if the therapist, in asking if the patient is feeling angry, had said, "I see you as expressing your anger," and the patient concretely then does just that. The patient's "projective" point of view of what the therapist is doing is part of the loss of ego boundaries, the concretization, and the lack of ability to form distinctions that are attendant upon the debilitated ego and its fragmented self (Searles 1962).

It is for this reason that dynamic therapists of schizophrenic patients are constantly attentive to the intimacy and distance behaviors, i.e., the boundary-forming processes within themselves and their patients. The distance maneuvers are amongst the simplest developmental ways of managing one's own capacity to distinguish between self and other. Even babies turn away from a troubling person, averting their face and their gaze. Thus, not looking at a person, not meeting with a person in too small a space, not communicating with a person, closing one's eyes so that the person goes away, etc., are all human ways to manage the distance (and therefore the boundaries and their character) between two human beings. Schizophrenic patients use all of these mechanisms to disappear from a situation, to modulate, and to move toward a position of separateness in which they can distinguish between themselves and others, in which they can sequence and delay, in which they can distinguish inner from outer worlds, and in which they can modulate their own and other's stimuli. With such a patient the therapist makes every effort to be respectful of these behaviors and adaptive attempts. As long as the behavior is compatible with continued meeting within the shared space, the therapist does not interfere with such distance modulation. These behaviors are the developmental correlates of ego activity, the cornerstones of the patient's ultimate autonomy, separateness, and organized sense of self (Erikson 1964). The therapist does not usually object in general to the patient's silence and uncommunicativeness to the degree that they represent attempts of the patient to resume ownership of, activate, and extend his own ego functions to organize a self. The therapist tries to facilitate this process and to notice when he has unwittingly intruded, taken over, pushed around, and interfered with the patient's activity and initiative and with the patient's capacities to know and distinguish between what is himself and what is the therapist.

Part of this management of distance is the attempt to modulate stimulation. The patient's fragile ego capacity to deal with affects, drives, and stimuli from within and without is disordered. One of the developmentally earliest ways of managing these kinds of stimulation is to move away from them. One moves away from a hot stove; one moves away from a painful object to locate and stop its hurt. One runs away from someone who is tickling you too much. Similarly, in any human relationship, including a therapeutic relationship, one moves away from a therapist when he or she is too friendly or aggressive, too critical or sexual, or too alluringly close. The therapist of a schizophrenic patient helps locate these troublesome stimuli in words and does not interfere with, though he usually names, any survivable, adaptable attempts to move away from them, as long as such movement away is compatible with the overall continuity of the condition for treatment.

In the presence of a disorganized ego and a fragmented self, the schizophrenic patient of course has enormous difficulty in modulating these stimuli that are within. Such patients report they have a seriously lessened ability to delay and damp down painful or unpleasant affects, as well as difficulty in modulating feelings of happiness, sexuality, affection, or anger. Behaviors related to these affects similarly have lost their distinguishing delay-control mechanisms, and thus their established defenses, so that aggressive or sexual acts, as well as feelings, seem to "happen" to that patient (Rapaport 1959). Patients feel as if they get suddenly angry and hit, as if they are sexually beset while doing mundane grocery shopping and ejaculate or must masturbate, or as if they are hungry and must eat. And in that process, while they are extremely critical of themselves as loathsome and despicable in a global way, there is very little focused, useful conscience phenomena. That is, the ability of the patient to delay, modulate, and feel usefully focused on and guilty about an act seems interfered with. Conscience's ability to distinguish the self from other and care about both enough so that some focused, caring sense of the integrity of the other is sustained and established, in a fashion that is not damaging that self or other, is, like other ego functions, interefered with. As this organized representation of value within the self and other is interefered with, behaviors that might damage that self or other seem inadequately checked, inadequately named or labeled, delayed, and held up to prior judgment, that is, to condemnation before action. The conscience in this form seems to function poorly on the patient's behalf. Concomitantly with this absence of delay, loss of focus, and anticipatory condemnation of a particular act, there is a more global organization of the behavioral control function, as in the total immobility of catatonia, and a concomitant dissolution of reality testing and time sequence function (Cameron 1961). Thus, seconds and hours seem equated, and the behavioral destruction of their own body or others' bodies and other persons all seem of less moment, and without some usual reality distinctions. This is accompanied by equally global, unmodulated, totalistic self-condemnation.

For this reason, the therapist is very attentive on behalf of the patient's ego to this missing, interfered with capacity to delay impulses, control behavior, and modulate affect. No behavior is encouraged and no act is examined without part of the therapist's concern being for how that patient's missing delay, control, and the various organizations of conscience phenomena are involved. It really is not all right for the patient to regularly assault the therapist, or himself, or his environment. It really is not beneficial to feel sexual and have intercourse with everything in sight, or simply get rid of sexual feelings through indiscriminate compulsive masturbation. The therapist needs to sustain reality symbolically in image and words, to locate for that patient what that patient holds dear and caring about himself and all other objects with which he is involved. The therapist regularly notices how he, the patient, regards or avoids noting the relation of his behavior to his own experience of his own feelings toward the world around him.

Central to this whole ego function problem and its behavioral delays, organizations of modulation, and defensive structures is the location of affects and naming how they are managed. The way in which ordinary, naturally occurring affects disrupt the security of the patient and the way in which the therapist arouses affects occupy therapeutic focus. The way in which those affects are managed by the patient—how they are soothed, gotten rid of, owned or disavowed, and expressed and represented, as well as what relevant behaviors are allowed and what behaviors are disallowed—is a central concern of the therapist. Where is anger disruptive, for example, how is it managed, what did the therapist do to arouse it, and by what name did the patient call it? These are all questions imbedded in dynamic psychotherapeutic work. What happened to the patient's sense of self as he smiled warmly at the therapist, whether it disappeared and for how long, and what restored it are regular concerns. Similar detailed regularities of therapeutic attention are involved in sexuality, anxiety, and sadness.

Sadness and grief as objects of attention have a special place in this therapeutic regimen. This is in part because it is only as that patient can evolve and then hold symbolically an organization of the other, and be held himself by that organization, that grief emerges and that sadness can occur. When a therapist notices a schizophrenic patient near to tears, this commands his attention very specially because it relates to the very capacities of that patient and his ego to hold himself or another person dear enough and to be organized enough to notice pain and loss (Klein 1975). It is out of such shared experience between the therapist and patient that the schizophrenic patient allows himself to be "held" by another and holds himself reciprocally valuable, seen, and dear (Winnicott 1953).

Out of these regularities experienced in the therapy, a regard for the self and for the ego and its functions on behalf of the self, and a regard for the ego's necessary boundaries and understood fragilities, repeated again and again over time, the patient evolves a sense of trust—of himself, most importantly, and of his doctor—a mutuality with his therapist. In that slow procedure the patient finds himself noticed by himself and his doctor, held in his therapist's and his own merging words and works, and yet separately regarded in the mind's eye of the therapist. The patient then comes to hold that therapist himself valuable, as someone who can see him, who can notice where he, the patient, functions poorly, where he needs help, and where he doesn't. Trust is always partial and mutual, imbedded in this difficult, joint work (Erikson 1950).

As this trust evolves in an individual dynamic psychotherapy, so a new organization of the self emerges and with it the opportunity to examine how the patient has kept himself absent and has avoided being known even to himself. Usually the patient describes his having had a self that was forbidden, a negative self. False and forbidden selfs come close together in this matter (Winnicott 1960, reprinted 1974). Most critically this is played out in the relationship with the therapist; i.e., the question regularly becomes whether the self that the patient is organizing—out of the valued sense of his named perception, out of his felt activities in their idiosyncratic shape, and out of his aggressive, oppositional, separatist strengths—is, in its divergence from the therapist's own self, to be wholly welcomed and viewed as acceptable. It is as this evolving self becomes acceptable to the therapist and patient as different from the patient's old self, as well as the self that the patient feels the therapist wants for him, that the patient finds that he can and must choose what he is and what he is to become (Erikson 1968).

If poor regulation of ego boundaries and the fragmented self are important dynamic state variables within the patients, so dynamic process variables of separation and individuation are amongst the most crucial of factors between the patient and the therapist (Mahler 1975). It is at times involving each of these variables—the ends of the hour, the weekends, the vacations, the cancelled appointments—that the vulnerability of the fragile ego and the fragmented self are most clearly struggled with in the therapy. There is no easy out for either patient or therapist in these matters. Since feeling longing is intolerable and rejection feelings are the rule, and grief is to be avoided, and anger is frighteningly disruptive of the fragile schizophrenic organization of a self, the therapist's ability to aid these schizophrenic patients in including ordinary human qualities, affects, and experiences within themselves as a part of their self and to direct them toward the therapist as a separate other, is amongst the most difficult and important of endeavors.

Early on it is clear that a most troublesome experience for schizophrenic patients in ending an hour or in cases of an absence or missed appointment is the horrible-to-recognize feeling that they, the patients, are powerless to avoid their own responsiveness to that event, a responsiveness that often is based on caring about their relationship with the therapist. They are horrified to notice that they miss the therapist or are angry at him when he goes away or wish that they were with him. And they feel demeaned and contemptuously belittled by such ordinary, to them, loathsome feelings. In the intricacies of such work, while anger, grief, and loneliness are at the work's center, the experience the patient has upon ending the hour or upon losing his therapist for a week—as that patient develops an interest and investment in the therapist-patient relationship—is that the therapist has robbed the patient of himself, has "eaten" bits of him and devoured portions of his personality, and is slowly destroying him by virtue of what, until that moment, had seemed like the patient's and therapist's cooperative investment in the therapy and the therapeutic process as a mutual endeavor. When it is possible for the patient and the therapist repetitively to endure such experiences in ways that help the patient retain a sense of his own dignity and power and his own ego's activity, as well as his own undemeaned sense of autonomy, things may go very well indeed (Will 1961). In the initial stages of such work, the lost, fragmented self and a persecutory world crowd the work, and these experiences threaten the therapy's existence by virtue of the patient's desperate attempts to control such fragmenting and persecutory anxiety through withdrawal and flight, autistic psychotic ritual, or self-destructive activity of a suicidal, aggressive, or sexual kind.

The other regular and major fragmenting change is that involving growth and individuation. No other single category of change is so difficult for patients to manage. For if they grow, they have within them a necessity to acknowledge this accomplishment, this organization of a newly evolved and extant self, and separateness from those past rules of nonexistence and nonbeing. They must separate from their old false self, they must separate from that part of their mother or father that they felt enjoyed them, fused and nonautonomous, and they must separate a bit from their therapists, since the accomplishments are the patients' own. Faced with their own growth, they must acknowledge that to themselves, which then makes them feel open and all too public, a most difficult developmental experience for schizophrenic patients. Add to this the fact that for any growing human being, a time of change is typically a time of ego fragility. In its milder way normal adolescence, that central occasion of human growth and change, mimics in its fluid ego boundaries, its shifting identifications, its unstable alliances, its unsteady impulse control, and its harsh and absent contrasting conscience phenomena the fragility of the ego and self that every schizophrenic experiences as he evolves a small new organization of a self.

Thus, when first a schizophrenic patient reports to his therapist that he has a separate friend, who appears to find something interesting in him and he in that friend, and has had a dream in which they have gone on a trip together, that therapist listens then with special sensitivity to the rather regular accompaniment of that patient's valued growth by painful feelings of dismay and anxiety. The therapist holds in words, in conveyed perspective, as best he can, that patient amidst the new upsurge in symptomatology of a persecutory kind, and helps him manage the grief over the to-be-slowly-abandoned, old parts of the left-behind, isolated, and lonely self. Much of the to-be-expected crises involving work with such patients involve locating clearly the problems of that growth and development in words and their loci in external reality and in inner life, and supporting that achieved and forbidden autonomy, noticing in the midst of the inundation with persecutory symptomatology, the hidden germinal movement in the patient toward an organization of a new accomplishment, toward an organization of a developing talent, and toward the evolution of a newly separate portion of a self and its unique, workable, environmental adaptation (Schwartz 1987).

The processes of negotiating the territory between fusion and separateness, between togetherness and being apart, are the processes of communicative interaction out of which a viable inner world is formed. Early in the work, schizophrenic patients often feel painfully empty of valuable substance. It is as if they were in an empty house in which no one had lived. In the middle of this emptiness the patient wards off feeling, or finds that he feels only loathing toward himself. He finds then residing within him foul images of his self as decayed, rotting, or poisonous. Side-by-side with these images may be the sense of being inhabited by devils, possessed by demonic forms, which are felt as dangerous, unworldly, grand, and powerful objects. Full of loathsome innards these patients are—or feel they are—and tortured by their therapist. And they themselves are poisonous or potentially torturing or lethal toward human contact, in their own view. They must protect then all others, including their treating doctor, from being harmfully contaminated by these inner products, these essences of themselves (Rosenfeld 1965).

During the course of difficult therapeutic time negotiated, work with affects named, boundaries stated, separation managed, sexuality more clearly regarded, and aggression limited, the patient begins to become less chaotically disorganized on each separation, e.g., each weekend. His self appears less loathsome and does not disappear so completely at the end of each hour. He finds himself less occupied with feeling controlled by his doctor and less noticing that his therapist has been gaining his own therapeutic "soul" at the expense of the patient's. At such a time, dynamic therapists keep a special watch. They attend rather regularly to the patient's visual image of that doctor as therapist. Through careful inquiry the therapist learns that it was a better weekend, a time that had more sequence. The nurses and the patient's family appeared less determinedly malicious and persecutory from the patient's point of view, and that patient noticed as well something different. This difference was that the patient kept thinking of the doctor's face, or book, or previous week's comment, or smile at the end of an hour. And though it made him feel more lonely with this image in his mind, it was as if the doctor somehow occupied a space inside him, inside the weekend's memories of that patient. Dynamic therapists then follow these internal visual images, organized as partial unintegrated representations of a small, organized, internalized view of the therapist as the work proceeds. Its progression as an image, its utility as a step to an organized view of the "other" and the self in that process of their evolving, is closely monitored. What makes that image of the therapist appear and when, what makes an organization of the patient's self come and go? Are they separable and discreet? How does anger or sadness or sexuality affect these patients? How do processes of perceived and felt envy and of owned, separate accomplishment modulate these visual images and their vulnerable underlying organizations from the patient's point of view? And with repetitive examination, such organizations of the therapist as other, internalized by the patient, have their concreteness diminished over time; their integration into the ego, into the personality of the patient as a whole, is gradual, progressive, and irregular. By the time of considerable recovery, the patient says such things as "you know, Doc, I used to hear your voice at night. I would sometimes talk to you. And I notice I don't hear that or do that anymore. In fact I don't think very much about you when I am not here; it's as though either you are already a part of me, or I can do more without you as time goes on." In time the patient is usually able to manage this individuating grief and the interactive separation more adaptively.

The process by which an image of the self and other is evolved in the course of treatment is viewed by the dynamic psychotherapist as essentially similar to these processes of growth involved in normal childhood developments. Where the dynamic psychotherapy of schizophrenia works, where it moves forward toward the evolution of a new organization of self and other, a less fragmented ego, and a workable conscience, those normative developmental processes in all of their complexity impose themselves in body and crucial action, in thought and feeling, in memory and perception, and ultimately in words and verbal language upon the therapy and the therapist. Just as there is no way that a child can develop a very full relationship with his mother and father without his body and its behaviors, his feelings and thoughts, his messy impulses, his intelligence and its creativity, and his capacity for destruction all being a part of that interaction, so it is too in the dynamic psychotherapy of schizophrenia. The questions that surround the therapy of such a person are the questions that surround normal developmental growth, with all the added complexities that are introduced by the fact that this is a therapist and his adult patient in all of their complex past historical experience, not a child beginning early on with his mother.

Thus, the question becomes how the therapist manages the transition from body, action, and affect into representation in words. As the child develops an investment in that mother, courts that mother, charms her, leaves her, punishes her, and comes back to expect her delight in his accomplishments so that he can carry that image of his capacity to charm and separate, as well as his mother's responsiveness and delight in regard to his style of individuated affection, so schizophrenic patients, in order to invest in their therapists, do delight them, charm them, abandon them, punish them, and return expecting and finding that therapist excited by that newfound capacity to work, that newfound observation about the world in which the patient lives (Kohut 1977). Those behaviors, bodily and in action, impose themselves upon the therapist within limits—crucial limits—regardless of his wishes. They are accompanied relentlessly by aggressive behaviors, just as in normal developmental processes, children exert their forceful, aggressive, assertive behaviors on their mother and father and spread them out to the rest of the world (Hartmann 1953). Similar phenomena occur in therapy. Just as a child finds ways to tell his mother what he wants to and will eat, how he wants to and will dress, where he likes to play and when, and with whom he will be calmed and where; so all of these processes in their bodily and action terms occur in the course of a dynamic psychotherapy of schizophrenia. It is the patient who decides whether the hour will be useful, how much of it he will take with him, and how much he will discard. It is the patient who asserts what about the therapist he likes and dislikes, how much he will manage his envy, and by what methods, and which of the therapist's words will soothe him. It is the patient who decides how much of himself he will share and how much he will keep separate, whether his affect will be included in the collaboration, whether the hour will be sleepy or interesting, and whether the therapist will succeed or fail.

The therapist's job is to foster the evolution of these behaviors, bodily states, affective arousals, and thoughts, memories, and feelings into organizations of a self and other, into words, into limited named actions, and complex named interactions between himself and the patient. Central to this endeavor is the clear attention to the subject of limits and the nature of each developmental task involved for the patient, including the task of defining the limits of action necessary to that task that define its crucial boundaries (Schwartz 1983). No useful purpose is served if the patient is allowed to destroy the therapist or the therapy. To that end, to the degree that it is possible, the therapist protects himself and protects the therapy as best he can against aggressive assault of whatever kind. The limits of time, agreements about fee and place of meeting, and privacy of the therapist's general personal life are all regularly attended to in the face of aggressive feeling, bodily arousal, and threat. The task of therapy defines the boundary of regularity of time and schedule, that what the therapist is doing is work, for which he receives compensation, and that this work is not coextensive with all of his life. Noting the patient's interest in altering those boundaries, the feelings of anger, the hidden or overt assaults against the schedule, and the judgment and the person of the therapist with respect to what the therapist says and how he says it, what he feels, when he ends the hour, etc., are all central in their naming and their repetitive limit. These define the nature of the task, the boundary of the therapist's self, and the patient's capacity to assert himself effectively. They are all related to this jointly engaged developmental task. Similarly, limits are central to the therapeutic understanding of the patient's bodily involvement in the therapy. No purpose is served by seductive behavior on the therapist's part. The ordinary canons of dynamic therapy move toward the limits of naming in words, not behaviors, as a goal of therapeutic activity between two adult human beings. Sexuality, arousal, and desire all have their place in this process; all are defined by the limits that they are welcomed, noticed, appreciated, and named, and by the limiting lack of behavioral response in the therapist are moved toward their evolution in words of feeling between the patient and therapist.

Out of that constraint in the therapist, out of the limits relative to those tasks of therapy, and out of the high regard for that human being's valued development are formed regularly parts of those processes of delay, boundary formation, modulation, and control that support ordinary ego functions and become defenses. Evolved out of these behaviors, ordinary conscience functions organize with appropriate impulse control and realistic regard for the reparable self and the surviving object.

Given the clear establishment of boundaries and limits, much of the organization of the patient's inner world proceeds with some regularity. This usually involves the patient locating projectively in the therapy and therapist aspects of himself that cannot as yet be integrated, claimed and managed, held and represented, and named. Rather regularly projected in this evolution are all strong feelings, most disclaimed impulses, and real perceptions of the other, partial organizations of the self, previously organized views of parents (feared and loved), and unintegrated ambivalently and split part objects—all are often experienced first in part as belonging to the patient's experience of the therapist. The patient feels, believes, and envisions that they reside in the therapist's attitudes and behaviors, either secretly or openly acknowledged by that therapist. These projected, envisioned images are experienced by the patient as threatening and limiting to the patient's sense of his own self and safety with that therapist.

Much of the therapeutic work involves the management, naming, and negotiation of these projected parts between therapist and patient. In a very real way such projection must be "welcomed" by the therapist, that is, allowed by the therapist, however distorted and unattractive that projection may be, in order to be located, named, defined, and understood (Ogden 1979). That therapist must notice and bear naming what aspect of his faulted, realistically viewed self these distorted projections lean upon. The therapist must find in himself and accept in full view what the patient regards in him—whether the therapist is seen as hateful, pompous, secret, grandiose, a sexual maniac, a saint and savior, or out to control and destroy and absorb that patient under the guise of being therapeutically helpful. In order for the patient to locate within a manageable, communicable object the menace of his own aggression, the idealized, lost, powerful, magically menacing father, and the actual perception of the historically true, real brutality of that father, the actual real callousness of the therapist must often be acknowledged. There is no way in which the persecution by inner "devils" can be named in words outside the self without the patient first finding his therapist to be truly persecuting him in various and not-always-minor ways. Speaking somehow harshly, stopping the hour abruptly and insensitively, and violating sensitive organizations of the patient's understanding all will be used in this projective process.

Crucially difficult in all of this process for schizophrenic patients is that these projective-introjective developmental processes involve a regular threat to their tenuous ego boundaries. Since it is difficult enough for such patients to know what is inside and what is outside, what is them and what is other, the very process of locating these passionate parts of the self, these aroused impulses, and these strange and truthful perceptual observations in another human being threatens their ego's integrity. The very mechanisms used to deal with such unwanted phenomena within themselves, and with their projected locus, need to be named. In that enterprise, blocking, attacks on thought linkage, avoidance, withdrawal, and splitting occur (Bion 1959). The patient feels that the perceptual event, put into words, will destroy either the patient himself or the therapist. Neither, it is felt, will be able to bear the sight of each other and what they see. Confusion and attacks on the therapist's value and the patient's self-esteem all occur with regularity. Negotiating these processes in ways that maintain the therapeutic relationship, that do not violate the therapist or therapeutic boundaries, and that are respectful of the therapist's self and the patient's valued necessities, while limiting the destructive acting out relative to such processes, is one of the most difficult aspects of the psychotherapy of schizophrenia.

No less difficult are the crucial dimensions that the therapist and patient locate and slowly acknowledge that involve the real, irrevocable, historical traumata in the patient's past familial developmental experience (Frosch 1983). Reciprocally, painful places evolve within the therapist for that complexity of his own inner feelings about and experience of each particular patient, as they inform, guide, and torment him while he communicates with himself and comes to know himself and his own personal development a bit more in work with each individual schizophrenic patient (Searles 1975). After the patient and therapist have negotiated these matters, the patient finds a new ability to own his own aggression and to be author of his own life. He begins to tolerate his appreciated capacity to be as relentlessly, cruelly self-assertive as was his much-hated mother (Kernberg 1975). All of this is included in his own ego. It feels located inside his own body and self. He finds his own ego functions strengthened; his self-organization is more steadfast in its value and stability. He reports being aware of a new self in a stronger, but not invulnerable, ordinary personality. The dynamic therapist is enriched as well by having glimpsed himself anew and having come to know more fully another human being.

Chapter 149

Group Therapy in Schizophrenia

Group psychotherapy has been employed for the past 60 years in the treatment of persons with schizophrenic disorders, in both hospital and clinic settings. To its early adherents, group therapy seemed to hold great potential for the treatment of mental patients, since it not only extended the benefits of individual psychotherapy to greater numbers of patients, but also might offer an additional bonus, that of peer support from the group itself. While outcome research has not demonstrated the efficacy of group therapy for schizophrenics in acute psychotic states, recent studies do suggest that interaction-oriented group approaches may be indicated for those who are less disabled by their disorder, while supportive, problem-oriented, "social learning" group approaches may help those with a more severe pattern of illness course.

In this chapter a framework will be presented whereby group therapy interventions can be planned to remediate the specific cognitive and behavioral deficits that are associated with schizophrenic disorders. The principles and methods of interaction-oriented and social-learning-oriented group therapies will then be discussed, and a summary of the relevant outcome research will be presented. Proceeding from an analysis of the implications of the research, the reader will be given a set of procedures for conducting the two forms of group therapy and for determining the suitability of each form of treatment.

Definition of Patient Deficits and Needs

Designing treatment programs to meet the needs of those with schizophrenic disorders is a task that must consider two key factors: the nature and extent of patients' cognitive shortcomings and their sensitivity to social overstimulation. An understanding of these vulnerabilities enables us to plan programs of corrective intervention. An appreciation of the sensitivity to overstimulation enables one both to adjust the intensity of the mode of treatment to the severity of the illness and to deliver therapeutic challenges when patients have sufficiently recovered from the acute episode to respond by achieving higher levels of social and occupational functioning (Heinrichs and Carpenter 1983).

The basic biologic deficit in the schizophrenic syndrome is considered by many to be a breakdown in attention-focusing neural mechanisms (Cutting 1985; Hemsley 1977; Nuechterlein and Dawson 1984; Venables and Wing 1962). Zubin et al. (1983) have suggested that this occurs when individuals with preexisting vulnerabilities are faced with threatening life circumstances. The accompanying psychological stress and hyperarousal of the autonomic nervous system are presumed responsible for cognitive disorganization marked by severe difficulties in processing complex and ambiguous information.

In this acute state, schizophrenics are unable to screen out irrelevant information. They are thus easily distracted by internal and external stimuli and cannot pay attention to key environmental or internal cognitive cues necessary for solving problems in potentially threatening situations. In what appears to be an attempt to reduce this overload, persons in acute psychotic states make fewer efforts to "scan" and explore their memories as well as the outer environment. The nonselective shutdown in the input of corrective information increases the probability of errors in the perception of social cues and the sending of social responses. Thus, patients are unable to understand the meaning of social situations (Wallace 1984) and engage in incoherent speech (with ambiguous referents) and disorganized behavior. Treatment of the acute state consists of the use of antipsychotic medication and removal of the patient from overstimulating environments to calming, structured, and supportive inpatient units (Ciompi 1983; Keith and Matthews 1982). Acutely symptomatic patients are maximally sensitive to social overstimulation. Thus, it is prudent to wait until positive symptoms have remitted before initiating any form of activating psychological or social therapy.

Because patients are still vulnerable to overstimulation even after they have entered the recovery phase, therapeutic interventions must be chosen carefully. The assurance of continued patient progress requires adherence to medication regimens to prevent premature relapse and the gradual acquisition of necessary survival skills (Heinrichs and Carpenter 1983; Wing 1978). For severely chronic patients, convalescence may last several months to a year or longer (Anderson et al. 1980). Breier and Strauss (1984) and Strauss et al. (1985) use the term "moratorium" to describe a phase during the course of chronic psychotic illness when patients are strengthening their resources. At "change points" patients may embark upon new projects, such as performing simple tasks at home, becoming more involved with friends or family members, entering day treatment, or moving away from home. High-functioning, good premorbid patients approach change points more rapidly and negotiate them more successfully, perhaps because they recover their full cognitive powers sooner following the remission of positive symptoms (Wallace 1984). Most forms of outpatient treatment and especially group therapy help patients to meet the challenges of change points and to maintain their equilibrium thereafter. Patients with a history of frequent relapses, poor premorbid functioning, and an intermorbid persistence of residual symptoms may never achieve the goals of independence and social reintegration. (Cole 1976; McGlashan 1986; Zubin et al. 1983).

Chronic psychotic states can be understood as arising from cognitive adaptations to hyperarousal and information overload and from avoidance patterns that become an enduring characteristic of the patient's way of coping with both situations and other people. Residual symptoms consist of a lack of motivation, a reduction in the capacity to feel and express emotion, and a difficulty in perceiving meanings of words in context and communicating intended meanings to others. Thus, depleted, chronic schizophrenics are unaware of the concerns of others and are unable to use praise and attention to generate supportive social interactions (Wallace 1984). Schizophrenics characteristically avoid social interactions with all but members of their immediate family or a single close friend with whom they become overinvolved (Beels 1981). It is these particular deficits in cognitive and social functioning that are the targets of corrective interventions.

Group therapy helps patients with schizophrenic disorders to correct these deficits by 1) enhancing motivation, 2) learning to feel and express emotion, 3) learning to perceive correctly the meanings of words and the actions of others, 4) learning to convey accurately intended meanings to others, 5) learning to devise more realistic interpersonal constructs, 6) learning to generate solutions to problem situations, and 7) learning to use praise and reinforcement to generate supportive social relationships outside the nuclear family.

Wallace (1984) has concluded that cognitive and social impairments in schizophrenia appear to vary directly with the severity of a patient's premorbid status, length of illness, and degree of thought disorder in periods of relative remission. Thus, patients who functioned well before the onset of their first psychotic episode and whose psychotic symptoms are well controlled by medication will experience minimal cognitive interference and resume social and occupational functioning with only minimal impairment. However, patients with a history of poor or marginal adjustment before illness onset tend to have a slower recovery and manifest more severe "residual" symptoms and resultant persistent disability. It follows, then, that one must design quite different programs of hospital treatment and aftercare to meet the needs of these two patient populations. In the remainder of this chapter, the principles of group therapy, the results of outcome research, and a set of techniques for conducting group therapy for persons with schizophrenic disorders will be presented.

Principles of Group Psychotherapy

The recognition and employment of group dynamics to produce change in individuals is a tradition represented by Adler, Sullivan, and Lewin. Adler saw the therapeutic process as the enhancing of self-esteem by integrating the private interests of men and women with "community feeling" (Adler 1967; Ansbacher and Ansbacher 1964). Sullivan believed that persons define themselves on the basis of the "reflected appraisals" of significant others (Sullivan 1940). Lewin (1947) believed that a strong sense of group identity could motivate people to change their ideas and patterns of behavior.

Powles (1964) has written that group psychotherapy takes place when 1) a group of patients is gathered together for a therapeutic goal; 2) an expert leader is present to help group members achieve their goals; and 3) the "group process" is used to help clarify patient problems and mobilize patients for change. Therapy groups typically contain six to 12 patients and one or two therapists.

Functions of Group Therapy for the Schizophrenic Disorders

1. *Reality testing*. In the postacute phase of illness, patients are encouraged to help one another to distinguish between psychotic (or distorted) and consensually validated perceptions or notions of interpersonal and cognitive events and to develop effective strategies for coping with psychosis (Breier and Strauss 1983; Hollon and Evans 1983; Horowitz and Weisberg 1966).
2. *Interaction*. An interaction orientation involves patients in discussions of interpersonal issues particularly as they apply among group members in the here and now (Heinrichs 1984; Horowitz and Weisberg 1966; Kanas 1985; Malm 1982; O'Brien 1975; Pekala et al. 1985; Slavson 1961; Steiner 1979). The leader encourages member disclosure of feelings, intentions, and underlying beliefs as they pertain to themselves, to others, and to the group interactive process.
3. *Insight*. In insight-oriented groups leaders analyze member transference, resistance, and unconscious motivation to help group members to improve self-understanding.
4. *Social skills*. Social skills training teaches members the verbal and nonverbal techniques of good social relations. Leaders guide members through rehearsals of effective approaches to typical and difficult interpersonal situations, while other members are taught to give corrective feedback and encouragement (Brady 1984a; Curran et al. 1982; Liberman et al. 1980).
5. *Problem solving*. Problem-solving techniques teach members effective problem solving applied to the social and pragmatic difficulties of everyday life (Coche and Flick 1975; Finch and Wallace 1974).
6. *Social learning*. Social skills and problem solving also are referred to as guided social learning experiences where leaders systematically employ modeling, rehearsal, and behavioral conditioning to teach members more effective means to achieve their goals.
7. *Education*. Group leaders can employ didactic or educational approaches to provide information and encourage structured discussions of topics presented (Fenn and Dinaburg 1981; Maxmen 1978, 1984; Waxer 1977).
8. *Support*. Leaders may choose to emphasize group support by mobilizing members' caring and nurturance for one another (e.g., Otteson 1979; Parras 1974).

9. *Activities.* Group activities may be organized around the pursuit of a joint task or project (Anthony and Nemec 1984).
10. *Medication management.* Here, patients on psychotropic medications discuss target symptoms and drug side effects; leaders encourage adherence to prescribed regimens and maintain a supportive and didactic approach (Masnik et al. 1971; Olarte and Masnik 1981).
11. *Self-help.* Self-help groups are leaderless; members share experiences with a common problem or condition and give each other encouragement and advice; professionals often serve as consultant "facilitators" during the start-up phase (Cole 1983).

Sources of Change in Group Therapy

Specific factors thought to produce change in small groups include self-disclosure, insight (increased awareness of the intentions of oneself and other group members), member interaction, group acceptance and cohesiveness (emotional support), catharsis, guidance, vicarious learning, altruism, universality, and the instillation of hope (Block et al. 1981). Maxmen (1973) has written that inpatients value the group therapy experience primarily as a source of hope and emotional support, while Yalom (1970) has written that (less disturbed) outpatients place a higher value on interpersonal feedback and catharsis. Problem-solving and social skills groups produce change through the above processes plus the acquisition of specific behavioral skills that are then applied to the setting of the patient's life-world (Curran et al. 1982).

Outcome Research

The past three decades have produced 24 outcome studies with control or contrast groups (individual psychotherapy conditions, all patients maintained on medication) measuring the efficacy of group therapy for persons with schizophrenic disorders. Specific studies employing insight-oriented, interaction-oriented, supportive, and social-learning-oriented group therapy for acute inpatients, postacute inpatients, and schizophrenic outpatients will be reviewed. The results are organized according to the findings.

1. Insight-oriented group therapy is not useful for most acutely ill schizophrenics. *Evidence*: Pattison et al. (1967) concluded that psychoanalytically oriented group therapy was harmful for acute inpatients. Kanas et al. (1980) reported that psychotic patients receiving insight-oriented group therapy did worse than controls. Leszcz et al. (1985) have recently reported that forced disclosure for schizophrenic inpatients may be "noxious and overstimulating." Mosher and Gunderson (1979) and Spitz (1984) in literature reviews concluded that insight-oriented group therapy is deleterious for acutely psychotic schizophrenics.
2. Insight-oriented group therapy is contraindicated for hospitalized chronic schizophrenics. *Evidence*: Fairweather et al. (1960) reported that chronic psychotics who improved with treatment-as-usual deteriorated with 24 sessions of insight-oriented group therapy. In their review, Bednar and Lawlis (1971) concluded that insight-oriented group therapy is not effective for patients with severe withdrawal and thought disorder.

3. Supportive forms of interaction-oriented group therapy may exert a positive effect with chronic inpatients in long-term settings (more than 50 sessions) and in intermediate-term settings (20–30 sessions) that mobilize social support beyond the therapy session. The effect is negative, however, when the patients are pressured to improve. *Evidence*: In a recent literature review, Kanas (1986) has written that chronic schizophrenics hospitalized for many months on long-term inpatient units in the 1950s and 1960s were reported by clinicians in the absence of control or comparison groups to show significant improvement in response to long-term group therapy. Fairweather et al. (1960) reported that "acute psychotics" (with less than one year of previous hospitalization) receiving group therapy plus a structured group living experience were more successful in keeping their jobs on follow-up than a comparison group of hospitalized acute psychotics receiving group therapy alone. Otteson (1979) found that a group of hospitalized chronic schizophrenics in group therapy who were instructed to use the group experience to achieve a "buddy's" discharge spent significantly more time in the community than a comparison group instructed to concern themselves with their own discharge. Schooler and Spohn (1982) have reported that a "total push" program of group, milieu, and individual therapy produced a marked worsening in the clinical condition of a ward of hospitalized chronic schizophrenics.

4. Interaction-oriented group therapy may help some hospitalized patients in the postacute phase to improve their verbal skills and social behavior. *Evidence*: Coons and Peacock (1970) found that patients participating in 30 sessions of interaction group therapy improved in those verbal skills and behaviors that were emphasized in the mode of treatment.

5. Problem-solving and social skills training group therapy helps postpsychotic inpatients, chronic inpatients, and day-hospital patients to improve in specific areas of cognitive and behavioral functioning targeted by the group interventions. *Evidence*: Coche and Flick (1975) reported that patients receiving eight sessions of interpersonal problem-solving group therapy were more socially active and demonstrated more improved problem-solving skills than a comparison group engaged in play reading. Finch and Wallace (1974) and Wallace et al. (1980) reported that in comparison with a control group, withdrawn patients receiving 12 sessions in a month of "receiving, processing, and sending" skills training, demonstrated a significant improvement in problem solving, conversational skills, and social adjustment, which appeared to facilitate a higher rate of discharge into the community in the ensuing three months. Monti et al. (1980) reported that schizophrenic inpatients receiving social skills training showed greater improvement in social skills and social anxiety than a control group receiving sensitivity training. In their comprehensive review of the literature, May and Simpson (1980) recommended "reality-oriented" group therapy for inpatient schizophrenics.

6. Purely interaction-oriented group therapy has produced inconclusive effects with a chronic outpatient population. *Evidence*: Four controlled studies failed to demonstrate a positive effect for reducing delusional and paranoid thinking (Borowski and Tolwinski 1969), reducing hospital readmission rates (Levene et al. 1970), reducing patient contacts with hospital staff (Purvis and Miskimins 1970), or improving patient functional status (Herz et al. 1974). The three controlled studies showing positive results suggest that improvement may occur in realms of behavior targeted by the intervention, such as social effectiveness (O'Brien et al. 1972), promptness and social initiative (Donlon et al. 1973), and awareness and insight (Claghorn et al. 1974). Interaction-oriented group therapy appears to offer a cost savings in terms of staff man-hours compared with individual psychotherapy (Don-

lon et al. 1973), and it is preferred by patients and involved staff to individual treatment interventions (Herz et al. 1974). Parloff and Dies (1977) in a comprehensive review concluded that group therapy does not reduce rehospitalization rate, diminish symptomatology, enhance vocational adjustment, or increase social effectiveness for chronic schizophrenics. May and Simpson (1980) concluded that results for nine outpatient studies of group therapy for persons with schizophrenic disorders were only "weakly positive."

7. Interaction-oriented group therapy may accelerate the recovery of a higher-functioning, less psychotic schizophrenic outpatient population. This effect is maximized when patients continue attending after discharge the same groups they joined when in the hospital. *Evidence*: Malm (1982) found that compared to a control group of the same size receiving their usual inpatient and outpatient treatment, a "semichronic" population (less than two years of previous hospitalization) of 34 schizophrenics receiving 40 weekly sessions of outpatient interaction-oriented group therapy initiated while in the hospital in addition to their usual program of care were found two years later to demonstrate significant improvement in verbal and cognitive skills, observed emotion, affective involvement, and affective communication. Those patients receiving the extra group therapy made more entries and reentries into the social field and learned more new habits, and the less psychotic among them demonstrated a significant reduction in social disability. Keith and Matthews (1984) have cited this study as the most convincing demonstration of the utility of interaction-oriented group therapy for the treatment of schizophrenic disorders.

8. Social learning group approaches may be more effective than interaction-oriented group therapy for outpatient chronic schizophrenics. *Evidence*: Paul and Lentz (1977) compared 1.5 years of outpatient social learning therapy (a token economy teaching social and self-help behaviors) involving milieu treatment plus problem-solving group therapy with traditional outpatient care (including interaction-oriented group therapy) and found the social learning approach to be the most cost-effective and to result in significantly greater community tenure. In reviews, Mosher (1982), Keith and Matthews (1982), and Spitz (1984) have all suggested that outpatient group therapy with this patient population emphasize the teaching of interpersonal, problem-solving, and vocational skills.

9. The effectiveness of outpatient social learning group therapy can be enhanced when chronic schizophrenics are given "homework assignments" or on-the-spot coaching while they are in the process of negotiating problematic situations in the home or in the community. *Evidence*: Brown and Munford (1983) have written that a program of seven weeks of training in life skills that required patients to complete task assignments in the community resulted in a significant improvement in mood, health behavior, social skills, and knowledge of personal finances compared to treatment-as-usual. Stein and Test (1980) and Test (1984) have reported that a program teaching community coping skills via homework and on-the-spot coaching resulted in increased patient employment, more contact with friends, reduced hospital readmission rates, and greater life satisfaction.

Clinical Implications

Integration of the results of outcome studies with our understanding of cognitive functioning in schizophrenia leads us to the following set of clinical guidelines for group therapy:

Proposition 1.   Group therapy may worsen the condition of acutely psychotic patients. Acutely psychotic persons cannot distinguish relevant from irrelevant information, are unable to respond appropriately to ambiguous social situations, and are particularly susceptible to the social overstimulation posed by group situations. Outcome research confirms that group therapy causes clinical deterioration with acutely psychotic patients.

　　Corollary 1.   Postpsychotic schizophrenics may benefit from group therapy. Once positive symptoms have remitted, supportive, reality-testing, and problem-oriented group therapy may be initiated.

Proposition 2.   High-functioning, "active" schizophrenic patients may benefit from interaction-oriented group therapy. Patients with good premorbid functioning and an acute-remitting course of illness often sustain a moderate or full recovery of their cognitive faculties and are thus more able to withstand the stresses of employment, training, and active social interaction. These patients may benefit from interaction-oriented group therapy whose goal is to accelerate social and occupational reintegration through an in-depth understanding of one's involvement with others, particularly as this occurs in the microcosm of the small group setting. Outcome research confirms that interaction-oriented group therapy may be beneficial for a less psychotic cohort of schizophrenics.

　　Corollary 2.   Those high-functioning, "active" patients who appear to be easily threatened or overstimulated by interaction-oriented group therapy should be treated with a less stimulating, more structured, and directive form of group therapy.

Proposition 3.   Poorly functioning chronic schizophrenics may not benefit from interaction-oriented group therapy. These patients may be overstimulated by forced disclosure and interpersonal confrontation. This population suffers from persistent residual manifestations of the disorder resulting in cognitive avoidance. With profound deficits in the capacity to feel and express emotion and in the ability to perceive correctly the meanings of the words and behavior of others in context and to communicate their own intentions, these patients lack the cognitive tools for making sense out of social ambiguity. Thus, they may not benefit from a form of group therapy that presumes that these cognitive functions are intact. The inconclusiveness of outcome findings suggests that severely psychotic schizophrenics should not be assigned to interaction-oriented group therapy.

　　Corollary 3.   Those chronic schizophrenics who demonstrate significant improvement in cognitive and social functioning with time and treatment may be reassigned to interaction-oriented group therapy to facilitate their more complete social and occupational reintegration.

Proposition 4.   Poorly functioning chronic schizophrenics may benefit from group therapy approaches that attempt to "reprogram" cognitive and behavioral deficits directly through the use of social learning principles applied in a structured, supportive, small-group setting. Here, patients are taught new ways to communicate, solve problems, and relate to others through the demonstration and practice of simple techniques embedded through social reinforcement and generalized to real-life situations via community homework assignments and on-the-spot coaching. Here, structure, clarity, simplicity, and encouragement combine to reduce the chance that patients will be overstimulated by the experience. Thus far, outcome findings indicate that intensive programs of problem solving and social skills training produce cognitive and behavioral improvement as long as the training is continued.

Corollary 4. As the members of social-learning-oriented groups demonstrate improvement, they may either "graduate" to interaction-oriented groups or group leaders may begin to introduce cautiously interaction-oriented techniques (O'Brien CP, personal communication, July 10, 1986).

Group Therapy Intervention Assignment

A set of assignment strategies for the group therapy of patients with schizophrenic disorders emerges logically from the preceding discussion.

1. Since insight-oriented group therapy approaches appear to destabilize patients with schizophrenic disorders, they should only be undertaken, if at all, with extreme caution. Therapists must watch carefully for the signs of symptomatic exacerbation and consider treatment reassignment according to the following guidelines.
2. Acutely psychotic patients should be treated with medication and placed in a calm, structured, supportive milieu that minimizes environmental and social stress (e.g., Ciompi 1983; Keith and Matthews 1982; Mosher 1982).
3. Once positive symptoms have remitted sufficiently to permit engagement in normal social conversation, patients may be reassigned to group therapy modalities on the basis of functional status (e.g., Kanas 1985; O'Brien 1975, 1983). Patients with a history of poor premorbid functioning, multiple relapses, and severe impairment between breakdowns are assigned to one form of group therapy, while patients with a history of good premorbid functioning and a relatively high level of occupational and social adjustment between episodes are assigned to the other form of group therapy. Those experiencing a first psychotic break should be assigned on the basis of their level of premorbid functioning. Thus, those doing well before illness onset should be assigned to an interaction-oriented group and observed carefully for signs of persistent, resistant, positive or negative psychotic symptoms, a sign that the patient might better benefit from membership in the social-learning-oriented group. Those with a history of poorer premorbid functioning should be immediately assigned to the social-learning-oriented group.
4. Group therapy for lower-functioning patients should favor a highly structured and supportive approach, conducted according to social learning principles, emphasizing education, reality testing, problem solving, social skills training, and careful adherence to prescribed medication regimens.
5. Group therapy for higher-functioning patients should emphasize group interaction techniques, using the group process to help members enhance their understanding of their own and others' thoughts, feelings, and behavior.
6. Members of the social-learning-oriented group should be strongly encouraged to continue either in the same group after discharge or to attend an outpatient group with a similar orientation that emphasizes the refining of social and community survival skills. As lower-functioning patients demonstrate the capacity to withstand increased social stimulation, their group leaders may either "graduate" them to groups employing interaction-oriented techniques or slowly change the focus of the social learning group to interpersonal issues between group members.
7. Members of the higher-functioning group should be given the option of attending either the same or a similar interaction-oriented group upon discharge.
8. If higher-functioning patients begin to overreact to confrontation or disclosure or deteriorate clinically, their leaders should either refer them to a social-learning-

oriented group, or temporarily adopt a more structured, supportive, skills-oriented approach until these group members demonstrate a greater facility for coping with interpersonal stress.

Group Therapy Procedures

This section provides clinical guidelines concerning patient preparation, group composition, group structure, training and supervision, specific techniques, and examples of how a group leader would respond to typical situations, contrasting the interaction-oriented approach with supportive social-learning-oriented approaches.

Preparation of patients.   Many patients view group therapy as "second class" treatment. To counter such negative expectations, patients may be told that group therapy should provide them with a better understanding of the illness and their prognosis in course of treatment, a chance to learn survival skills and develop better relationships, and an opportunity to learn from others who have lived with the same illness and to become more aware of oneself and others. Patients should be provided with a set of "group rules" emphasizing the importance of attending regularly, coming on time, remaining in the group until the end of the session, not hitting furniture or other patients, and regarding other patients as if they were members of one's own family.

Composition.   Groups should be composed of patients with similarly diagnosed psychotic disorders. It is crucial that patients be assigned according to functional status (see previous section), with good premorbid, high-functioning people in the interaction-oriented group and poor premorbid, low-functioning people in the social learning group. Schizophrenic patients with prominent antisocial traits or a significant history of substance abuse may require assignment to groups composed exclusively of "double diagnoses" or "young adult chronics" (e.g., Bachrach 1982; Pepper et al. 1981). It is useful to maintain a balanced mix of sexes, and social, cultural, and racial backgrounds, and to match each group member with at least one other person with whom these factors are shared to maximize the opportunities for group identification and cohesiveness (e.g., O'Brien 1983).

Structure.   Inpatient groups usually contain four to eight members, last 45 to 60 minutes, and are conducted one or more times a week. Outpatient groups typically contain five to ten members, last 60 to 90 minutes, and are conducted weekly, on alternate weeks, or monthly. Membership in inpatient groups is open, since new members are admitted as their acute symptoms abate and as old members are discharged. In the clinic or private outpatient setting membership may be kept open until a quorum of regular attenders is achieved and the inevitable dropouts have departed. Closing membership enhances group cohesion.

Leadership.   Most inpatient groups are led by cotherapists; this enables the leaders to manage patients more effectively who are out of control and to retain an objective, supportive, and cool-headed approach in potentially confusing or explosive situations. Addition of a cotherapist to the outpatient group provides the possibility of mutual encouragement and support in an otherwise frustrating clinical setting. Cotherapists can assume directive and emotive roles, model effective communication and genuine concern, and demonstrate problem-solving and role-playing exercises.

Clinical training and supervision. The optimal setting for group therapy training involves the pairing of a novice as cotherapist "apprentice" with an experienced group leader. It is essential that group leaders have access to supervision by professionals experienced in working with psychotic patients (Cole 1987; Talbott 1984). Supervisors can assist with inevitable cotherapy conflicts and can help therapists to remain hopeful in the face of persistent patient dependency, passivity, and slow rates of recovery. Use of a video camera and playback facility and a one-way mirror for "live supervision" greatly enhance the process of supervision.

Specific Group Therapy Techniques

1. *Nonspecific factors.* Therapists should strive to foster a sense of caring (Steiner 1979) and unconditional acceptance of the person (Slavson 1961), while being tolerant, open minded, and nonjudgmental (Wolman 1960).
2. *Knowledge of the illness.* Therapists should have a sound scientific understanding of the schizophrenic disorders and an appreciation of the patient's experience with acute and chronic psychosis (Maxmen 1978, 1984; Torrey 1983; Yalom 1983; Terkelsen, unpublished manuscript).
3. *Preventing overstimulation.* In the early postacute phase, care must be taken to prevent overstimulation through forced self-disclosure or escalating confrontation (Strassberg et al. 1975). Poorly functioning patients should not be stressed in this manner while recovering from acute psychosis for six months to a year or more after discharge. As patients demonstrate increased resilience in response to stressful life situations, leaders may prescribe more challenging assignments or allow patients to cope on their own with increasingly complex group interactional events.
4. *Education and reality testing.* In the postacute phase group leaders should give patients an explanation of the scientific basis of schizophrenia, causes of relapse, and principles of relapse prevention and should emphasize the importance of adhering to medication regimens (Fenn and Dinaburg 1981; Maxmen 1978; Waxer 1977). As students learning about their illness and as experts struggling to cope with psychosis, group members share experiences and coping strategies and become more strongly motivated to assume responsibility for their recovery (Cole 1983; Heinrichs 1984). Newly admitted members are encouraged to discuss their psychotic experiences and "older" members are encouraged to provide corrective feedback, reassuring the new arrivals that they will eventually learn how to cope with delusions, hallucinations, and paranoia and get on with the business of struggling to survive.
5. *Focus on current life situations.* Group discussions revolve around current or recent life problems, such as events leading to hospitalization (Maxmen 1984; Russakoff and Oldham 1984; Waxer 1977) and difficulties on the ward, at home, at work, or with other group members (Kanas 1985; Malm 1982; Pekala et al. 1985; Yalom 1983).
6. *Maintaining a positive emphasis.* Leaders should emphasize the positive aspect of patient narratives or performances, noticing accomplishments, highlighting good intentions, and helping members to take satisfaction in success experiences as they proceed toward recovery. Leaders should encourage members to provide one another with mutual support, encouragement, and practical advice.
7. *Focus on group interaction: the high-function group.* In interaction-oriented group therapy (e.g., Kanas 1985; Malm 1982), leaders use approval to encourage members to speak clearly and directly, to express emotion openly, to make "I" statements, and to show interest in one another. Group members are encouraged to share

Table 1. Comparison of Supportive-Social Learning with Interaction-Oriented Group Psychotherapy

Event	Supportive-Social Learning	Interaction-Oriented
1. Opening the session.	Leader opens meeting, states group goals and methods. Asks for members' agendas of problems to be discussed.	Leader opens meeting, waits for members to make first remarks.
2. Closing the session.	Leader closes meeting after summarizing problems addressed and topics discussed.	Leader closes meeting after asking group members to summarize major group events and themes discussed.
3. Member brings up problem related to "outside life."	Leader helps member to define skills amenable to improvement, elicits other members' suggestions, guides member through role rehearsals, suggests "homework" task for continuing practice of specific behaviors.	Leader encourages other members to share similar experiences and to respond with opinions, suggestions, corrective feedback, and emotional support.
4. Member expresses intense feelings of anger, sadness, inferiority, frustration, anxiety.	Leader helps member to identify specific situations that elicit these feelings and specific behaviors that can be modified. Situations are then role-played.	Leader encourages other members to share similar feelings, helps original member to identify automatic thoughts and underlying assumptions.
5. Member discusses conflict with other group member.	Leader helps member to see conflict as a more general difficulty and sets up impersonal role play in which particular behavioral skills are refined.	Leader assists member to approach other member constructively, helping both to work out difficulty with direct and honest expression of feelings and points of view. Elicits feedback and support from other group members.
6. Member expresses hostility toward other member or group leader.	Leader states that group purpose is to improve coping and problem-solving skills. Asks member to rephrase remarks in a positive or constructive way. Reframes hostility as a more general predisposition in social situations. Role play is devised to assist member to come up with alternative interpretations of social events.	Leader elicits feedback from other group members. Helps original member to understand probable origins of hostile feelings in underlying assumptions, events of group formation; helps member to determine positive connotation in place of negative interpretation. Encourages member to "take the position of the other."
7. Member expresses interest in socializing with other group members.	Leader organizes group outing, such as dining out, a picnic, or an excursion to a local place of interest.	Leader asks member to disclose reasons for wishing to establish more intimate relationship, directs member to speak directly to specific objects of affection, promotes expression of positive feelings; discussion of impression management, popularity, and presentation of self.
8. Member discusses delusions, paranoia, or hallucinations.	Leader points out that these experiences are positive symptoms of schizophrenia that usually respond to medication and when one turns one's attention towards more practical concerns such as group problem solving. After asking other members if they wish to share similar experiences, leader refocuses topic to the group task. If member continues to act psychotic, leader suggests that medication dosage be raised and that this be discussed with psychiatrist.	Leader points out that these experiences are positive symptoms of schizophrenia that usually respond to medication and when one turns one's attention towards more practical concerns such as group problem solving. After asking other members if they wish to share similar experiences, leader invites group members to discuss and evaluate strategies they have used to cope with such symptoms. If member continues to act psychotic, leader suggests that medication dosage be raised and that this be discussed with patient's psychiatrist.

Table 1. Comparison of Supportive-Social Learning with Interaction-Oriented Group Psychotherapy (continued)

Event	Supportive-Social Learning	Interaction-Oriented
9. Member announces intention to discontinue medication.	Leader asks for member's reasons for stopping medication, then presents arguments for continuation, acknowledging costs and benefits of antipsychotic medication. Leader praises those members who support efficacy of adhering to maintenance or targeted medication.	Leader probes member to determine reasons for wishing to discontinue, elicits group response, helps member to weigh advantages and disadvantages of adhering to regimen, suggests that member discuss this issue with prescribing doctor.
10. New member joins group.	Leader introduces new member at beginning of session, asks other members to introduce themselves, then proceeds with day's agenda.	Leader introduces new member at beginning of session, asks new and old members to each present thumbnail sketch of self. Toward end of session, new member is either asked to "go-around" or to comment on what has taken place; old members are invited to respond to what new member has said.
11. Group member leaves the room.	Leader continues with activity-in-progress, assuming that absent member is taking "time-out" to reduce level of arousal and will return when feeling calmer.	Leader asks members to comment on reasons for member's exit and then either sends out a group member or goes out him/herself to fetch retreating member. Once having returned, member is asked to discuss what prompted exit and encouraged to discuss such issues in the group meeting before leaving.
12. Group member is absent.	Leader notes absence and plans to phone up absent member to encourage attendance at next meeting. Asks other members if they would be willing to call up absent member.	Leader elicits members' theories explaining the absence and their feelings about people who don't show up; helps present members to identify automatic thoughts and underlying assumptions. Leader then phones up absent member. In next session leader asks this member to discuss reasons for not attending and allows other members to give corrective feedback.
13. Member announces intention to drop out of the group.	Leader discusses the advantages of patient's continued membership in therapy group, emphasizing the importance of learning problem-solving skills and receiving social support during recovery from acute episodes of psychotic disorders. Expresses hope that leave-taking will be temporary and tells leaving member that he or she is free to return at any time. Other members are allowed to encourage member to remain in the group.	Leader asks the member to disclose specific reasons for dropping out and elicits other members to respond, assisting all to discuss openly issues of loyalty, commitment, identity, loss, and so forth.
14. Member recalls psychotic experience as a "bad dream."	Leader remarks that some patients deal with memories of acute psychosis by trying to forget them, whereas others endeavor to learn from them and integrate them into their experience of the world. Members are then asked to discuss the extent to which they have "sealed over" or incorporated psychotic experiences.	Leader asks other group members to recall their psychotic experiences and how they have either tried to forget them or integrate them into their on-going experience of the world. Leader is careful not to express a preference for one recovery style over the other.

experiences, help one another understand problem situations, and give moral support, opinions, and advice. Events occurring in the group process are used as examples to illustrate typical member difficulties or strengths. As patients demonstrate a greater capacity to withstand interpersonal stress, they are encouraged to hold each other accountable for achieving goals in their social and occupational lives. Therapists do not pressure members to disclose confidential information or interpret unconscious motivations, but they do comment on group themes of immediate relevance and ask group members to summarize issues brought up during the course of the session (Horowitz and Weisberg 1966). Therapists may also use cognitive therapy techniques to help patients to become aware of their "automatic thoughts," logical errors, and unrealistic underlying belief systems that help perpetuate negative feeling states and self-defeating patterns of behavior (Hollon and Evans 1983).

8. *Focus on social learning: the low-functioning group.* In social learning group therapy (Brady 1984b; Curran et al. 1982; Liberman et al. 1980), structured group exercises help to improve patients' receiving, processing, and sending skills through problem-solving and role-playing exercises where therapists act as models and coaches. Patients are taught to define problem situations, generate alternative solutions, see events from others' perspectives, appreciate cause and effect, and anticipate the consequences of their actions. Members learn communication skills, assertiveness training, and how to become acquainted and more deeply involved with others. Specific exercises help members to discharge hostile feelings harmlessly (Bowes et al. 1974) and to understand how others think and feel (Pekala et al. 1985; Serok and Zemet 1983; Wilson et al. 1985). "Activities" may be arranged on occasion, such as meeting in a restaurant, going on a picnic, or going to a local place of interest (Wynne 1978). The serving of refreshments and snacks helps to preserve a low-anxiety, homelike atmosphere and reinforces the caring function of the group. Target symptoms and medication side effects can be discussed at the end of the meeting when prescriptions are written out. Group members may be encouraged to drive one another to and from meetings, telephone each other for support and assistance, and dine out together in pairs. Thus, the group can become an arena for the rebuilding of important social ties outside patients' home environments.

Comparison of Group Therapy Techniques: Social Learning Versus Interaction-Oriented

The anecdotes shown in Table 1 illustrate how group leaders practicing interaction-oriented and social-learning-oriented group therapy deal with typical group situations. The 14 representative examples are intended to give the reader a greater appreciation of the difference between the two approaches and of the utility of each for high- and low-functioning patients.

Conclusion

A review of our current knowledge of cognitive and behavioral functioning in schizophrenia combined with outcome research findings suggest that maximal effectiveness may be achieved by treating good premorbid, high-functioning patients with interaction-oriented group therapy and poor premorbid, low-functioning patients with supportive, social-learning-oriented group therapy. The model presented in this chapter most closely resembles that of Keith and Matthews (1984), who have recommended the adoption of problem-oriented group therapy for chronic schizophrenics and interaction-oriented group therapy for a less psychotic, less chronic patient cohort, and that of O'Brien (1983; personal communication, July 10, 1986), who initially takes a supportive, problem-solving approach and introduces interaction-oriented techniques as patients in the group demonstrate the capacity to deal with complex interpersonal stimulations. The treatment model differs from that of Kanas (1985, 1986), who employs interaction-oriented group therapy for both high- and low-functioning patients, and from those of Heinrichs (1984) and Spitz (1984), who have recommended a problem-solving approach for all schizophrenics.

While the subject of this chapter is the use of group psychotherapy for the treatment of persons with schizophrenic disorders, one should understand that the group therapies are only one facet of a complex array of treatment modalities forming a comprehensive plan of care. These interventions include enlightened medication management (Schooler 1984), family psychoeducation and family therapy, supportive-pragmatic individual psychotherapy (Gunderson et al. 1984), and psychosocial rehabilitation (Anthony and Nemec, 1984). In addition, patients and families may benefit from attending community support groups, many of which are chapters of the National Alliance for the Mentally Ill (Hatfield 1984).

The group therapy procedures recommended for the treatment of patients with schizophrenic disorders are based upon an understanding of relevant clinical techniques, an appreciation of patient cognitive and behavioral deficits, and a critical reading of outcome research. These guidelines apply the two methods of group therapy according to illness-specific requirements, the most important of which are the patient's tolerance of stress and cognitive capacities at particular stages of recovery. The passage of time will enable the further refinement of group therapy approaches and techniques for patients with schizophrenic disorders.

Chapter 150

Family Treatment of Schizophrenia

Family therapy was first conducted with schizophrenic patients in the 1950s on a small scale, because the patients who had responded well to hospital-based individual psychotherapy relapsed upon returning to the family home. These years were dominated by the belief among mental health professionals that "functional" psychiatric disorders were caused by intrapsychic, dynamic processes that antedated the onset of illness and continued to reinforce the symptomatic state of the patient. The possibility that family *transactional* processes could contribute to psychotic illness was regarded as deviant from prevailing theories and was of little importance to psychotherapeutic practice (Beels and McFarlane 1982; Wynne LC, personal communication, November 21, 1986). The study of the families of schizophrenics took place primarily as exploratory clinical research, not related to therapeutic change. One aim of this research was to consider how families with schizophrenic members differed on a continuum from other families and how these family characteristics may have helped shape the psychological development of offspring. Reiss and Wyatt (1975) have criticized the family therapists of succeeding decades for their "naive" translation of tentatively posed research hypotheses into confidently proclaimed principles of clinical treatment applicable to all families, with little differentiation in treatment approaches for families of schizophrenics.

This chapter will begin with a historical review of the early family theories of schizophrenia and then present a brief survey of family systems theory and therapy and discuss a family crisis intervention outcome study based in part on these principles. This will be followed by a consideration of the burdens faced by families having to cope with their schizophrenic relatives and with a health care system sometimes unresponsive to their needs. An overview of research efforts defining the family variables that psychoeducational approaches aim to modify will be followed by a detailed description of the methods and findings of four outcome projects employing family management techniques to reduce patients' rate of relapse. The last portion will provide an integrated treatment framework that enables therapists to select interventions based on severity of illness and phase of recovery.

The Early Theories

The early family theorists proposed that etiology, onset, and relapse in schizophrenia, like other psychiatric disorders, were strongly influenced by dysfunctional patterns of interaction within families; psychotic behavior was seen in part as a response to family difficulties in negotiating conflict, acknowledging differences, or enacting appropriate roles. The "double bind" theory of Bateson et al. (1956) proposed that schizophrenic behavior be viewed as an adaptive response to contradictory parental directives on verbal and nonverbal levels. Lidz et al. (1957) pointed to an association of psychotic behavior with the marital dysfunction of the parents, particularly those who were chronically combative or "schizmatic" and dominant-submissive or "skewed" in their relationships. Bowen (1957, 1965) proposed that schizophrenia emerged as a "family projection process," a result of cumulative, multigenerational patterns of undifferentiated, "fused" family relationships. In a classic paper on "pseudomutuality," Wynne et al. (1958) described the ways that families of acute schizophrenics obscured individual differences and erected a kind of "rubber fence" around family boundaries out of a commonly felt fear of developmental change and separation.

These theories, distorted to a degree by polemics against parents by Laing (1967) and others in the antipsychiatry movement, seem to have exerted a considerable effect on the thinking of succeeding generations of family therapists treating psychotic disorders. With the possible exception of Bowen (1957, 1960), the early theorists agreed that schizophrenia was probably caused by multiple factors (genetic and environmental) in complex interaction and intended primarily to call attention to the possible contribution of family factors (e.g., Jackson 1960; Lidz and Fleck 1960; Wynne 1968).

Bowen, Lidz and the "double-bind" theorists investigated these ideas through clinical research studies that were limited by small sample size, lack of control groups, and inconclusive findings. Their efforts were followed during the subsequent 25 years by a host of research studies attempting to isolate the family variables contributing to the expression or onset of schizophrenic disorders. A large body of research on these family factors has provided little substantive evidence that schizophrenia is caused by double binds, abnormal power relations, parental conflict, or symbolic parent-child relations, although these factors have since proven to be important in their association with patient relapse (Goldstein and Doane 1982; Goldstein and Rodnick 1975; Jacob 1975; Liem 1980; Wynne et al. 1979). Recent prospective research indicates that patterns of intrafamilial communication and affect expression do act as contributory factors in the course of the schizophrenic disorders.

Family Therapy

Traditional forms of family systems therapy propose that symptomatic behavior in an individual is but one expression of a basic dysfunction at the next higher level of organization and complexity, that of the family. Families are seen as bounded open systems within an environment, permitting the entry and exit of information, energy, and matter in various stages of organization (Gray et al. 1969; Miller 1965; von Bertalanffy, 1951). Families are governed by "rules" that maintain the organizational patterns of their components and that are expressed as patterned sequences of behavior developing over time to ensure the survival of the family unit (Arensberg 1972; Chapple 1970). These rules act in "error-activated" fashion to maintain "homeostasis" (Jackson 1957) and in "deviation-amplifying" fashion to assure growth and adaptation to new environmental conditions (Maruyama 1968). Systems-oriented family therapy approaches attempt to achieve symptom remission in individuals through the correction or change of either specific dysfunctional sequences of behavior or the "rules" that govern them (Cole 1982).

Two schools of systems-oriented family therapy have claimed success with "psychotic" patients (e.g., Fox, manuscript in preparation). Structural-strategic therapy focuses on modifying sequences of family behavior that appear to represent dysfunctional structural hierarchies and coalitions (Haley 1980; Madanes 1980, 1982). Selvini-Palazzoli's model (Selvini-Palazzoli et al. 1978) attempts to uncover and change through paradoxical prescriptions and rituals the family rules that are said to result in patient psychosis. Therapists contemplating use of these and similar methods may risk overstimulating unstable chronic schizophrenics and thereby precipitating early relapse. The structural-strategic form risks this through pressure exerted by the therapist on the parents, forcing the patient to adhere to "normal" rules of family conduct. A recent statement of the Palazzoli method, which has been criticized for conveying a disrespect for parents (Anderson 1986), uses an "invariant prescription" to free patients from the family's "dirty games": parents are told to announce to their children that they have a "secret," and then are told to leave their psychotic offspring without warning for increasing periods of time (Selvini 1986). To date, neither of these schools has conducted controlled investigations comparing its methods with standard treatments.

Family Crisis Intervention

The one important outcome study applying family systems techniques to the treatment of schizophrenics was that of Langsley et al. in Colorado (Langsley and Kaplan 1968), who used family crisis techniques as an alternative to hospital admission. In this approach, psychosis was viewed as a "personal crisis" resulting from the failure of the patient to master specific tasks presented by environmental or developmental demands and from the failure of the family to protect the patient from the resulting burden of stress presumed responsible for the patient's condition. The goals of the crisis intervention team were: 1) to relieve pressure on the patient; 2) to teach stress management or coping strategies to the patient and family; and 3) to teach them how to resolve intrafamilial conflicts through bargaining and compromise. In six sessions, including one home visit, families were taught how to administer medication, how to identify stressful interpersonal situations, and how to cope more effectively with disturbed patient behavior and with one another. The treatment team sought to establish a positive relationship with the patient and family by providing immediate aid, focusing attention on pragmatic aspects of the present illness, giving advice and positive reinforcement, providing communication training, and setting family tasks with a high probability of success around important unresolved family issues. To discourage patients from retreating into "regressive," nonfunctional roles, patients were prescribed psychotropic medications and encouraged to take part in family task assignments. The treatment directed the family's attention to the family tasks and away from the patient's symptoms in order to "destigmatize" the patient, which was thought to facilitate emergence from "scapegoat" roles enforced by family homeostasis. The patient's psychotic symptoms were viewed as the patient's attempts to communicate and as, in part at least, a response to environmental stress and family conflict that the treatment sought to ameliorate.

This project compared 150 patients receiving the family crisis treatment with 150 controls, who were initially hospitalized and then received their usual pattern of care. Patients in both forms of treatment were expected to utilize the appropriate community treatment programs available to them. Following the final session of family crisis treatment, the treatment team referred the patient and family to the appropriate community agencies and then remained available to all members of the system— patients, family, and agencies—should future crises occur. The control group (which was initially hospitalized and then received all the therapies usually available in the hospital including individual and group psychotherapy, milieu therapy, medication management, and so forth) was treated in the hospital for an average of 26 days. The group receiving family crisis therapy was treated with an average of 4.2 office visits, 1.3 home visits, 5.1 telephone calls, and 1.2 collateral contacts.

The results showed that 29 percent of hospitalized patients were readmitted to the hospital within six months compared to 13 percent of those in family crisis treatment, resulting in a significant decrease in hospital stay. It was calculated that family crisis treatment was one-sixth as expensive as standard hospital treatment (Langsley et al. 1968). These trends continued at one year and at 18-months' follow-up (Langsley et al. 1971).

In a separate interpretation of the data, 50 schizophrenics were compared with nonschizophrenics (character disorders and reactive depressives), half of each group randomized to family crisis intervention and half to hospital treatment. On follow-up, the crisis management techniques of the nonschizophrenics' families had improved, while those of the families of schizophrenics had not improved in the experimental group and had deteriorated in the control group (Langsley et al. 1969). The authors commented that the families of the schizophrenic patients, especially those of chronic patients with multiple hospitalizations, had significant difficulties in accepting the crisis team's interpersonal frame of reference. These families continued to insist that the patient's problems resulted from an illness or disease process located within the patient. This conflict of illness beliefs between the treatment team and the families may have contributed to the team's failure to teach these families how to manage the disruptive behavior of their psychotic relatives.

With the exception of this study and a controlled study by Ro-Trock et al. (1977), involving a small sample size and not yet replicated, no objective evidence has yet emerged demonstrating the efficacy of family systems therapy for the treatment of schizophrenia (Epstein and Vlok 1981; Keith and Matthews 1982, 1984; Massie and Beels 1972; Mosher and Gunderson 1979; Mosher and Keith 1980). There are two principal reasons for the lack of scientifically credible evaluation research on forms of family therapy other than family crisis intervention in the schizophrenic disorders: 1) the one small controlled study has never been replicated, and there have been no others using family therapy in schizophrenia; 2) since systems-oriented therapists appear neither to accept the disease model of mental illness nor to use DSM-III-R or *International Classification of Diseases*, 9th rev., nomenclature, one may legitimately question whether the "symptom bearers" of their "psychotic families" are of the same patient species as those diagnosed as schizophrenic by contemporary criteria. In a recent appraisal of this situation, Gurman (1984) has suggested that family therapy models without a strong research tradition need not be dismissed before well-designed studies are undertaken to assess the strengths and limitations of each.

The Family's Perspective

In designing systems of health care to meet the needs of families and their schizophrenic relatives, it is important to take into account the burdens assumed by family members caring for their mentally ill relatives. Following deinstitutionalization, family members have had to assume the burden of caring for the 70 percent of chronic mental patients who are discharged from the hospital to their homes (Arnhoff 1975; Goldman 1982). Relatives must learn to cope with the incoherent speech and irrational behavior of patients in the acutely psychotic state and with a persistent lack of motivation in periods of remission. Families often sacrifice time and earning power to provide direct care and experience the disruption of important household routines (Grad and Sainsbury 1963, 1968).

The emotional costs to families include anxiety over not knowing the patient's diagnosis or what to expect from the course of illness, guilt from holding themselves responsible for the illness, and anger and frustration over the failure of treatment to bring about a full recovery (Creer and Wing 1975; Doll 1976). Parents have a high incidence of psychiatric disturbance and marital dissatisfaction (Hirsch and Leff 1975). Families of schizophrenics often become isolated from formal and informal sources of social support in the community (Beels et al. 1984). In the absence of support from outside resources, the strain of having to cope with crisis after crisis may exceed the family's knowledge, skills, and resources and lead to the emotional exhaustion of family members (Hatfield 1984b). The worsening of the patient's condition necessitating repeated hospital admissions often leads to the family's gradual estrangement from the patient (Kreisman and Joy 1975).

Family members have complained that psychotherapists have failed to appreciate their plight. Reeling from guilt-inducing reviews of early life events or directives designed to liberate the patient from having to be the "symptom bearer," family members have felt blamed for the patient's disorder (Appleton 1974; Hatfield 1984b). Many therapists, seeking to avoid stigmatizing the patient, did not reveal the patient's diagnosis nor tell the family how the illness would affect the patient's life (Berkowitz 1984; Holden and Lewine 1982; Terkelsen 1983). For many reasons, including the clinical and political advantages of alliances with a growing consumer movement, it is important to recognize the legitimate needs of the families of schizophrenics (Bernheim 1987; Cole 1987).

Some studies indicate that families are eager to learn from professionals and from other families with a schizophrenic member specific information about the nature, course, and treatment of the disease (Hatfield 1979; Holden and Lewine 1982; Platman 1983). This area of family participation has been given considerable prominence in the 1980s by organized groups of families of schizophrenics, e.g., the local and national Alliances for the Mentally Ill. In addition to supporting research, these families wish to be able to use their strengths to help treatment, to set realistic expectations, to learn management techniques that will help the patient to recover more completely through closer adherence to medication and treatment programs, and to find out about available community resources for social, vocational, and occupational rehabilitation and residential services.

The Plight of the Patient

While the nature of the disease process in the schizophrenic disorders is still unknown, one may conceptualize its onset and course through a "biopsychosocial model," the "diathesis-stress" theory (Goldstein and Rodnick 1975; Nuechterlein and Dawson 1984; Wynne 1978; Zubin 1980; Zubin et al. 1983). The basic deficit appears to be expressed by hyperarousal of the autonomic nervous system, with concomitant breakdown in attention-focusing mechanisms, an inability to handle complex information, and a subsequent deterioration in interpersonal functioning (Ciompi 1983; Cutting 1985; Hemsley 1977; Venables and Wing 1962). This breakdown is thought to be "triggered" when a vulnerable individual is subject to a critical level of internal (biological or psychological), ambient (family, social, or job-related), or exogenous (life event) stress (Falloon 1986; McGlashan 1986; Wynne 1969, 1978; Zubin et al. 1983). The theory thus predicts that relapse in schizophrenia can be precipitated by psychostimulating drugs acting directly at brain cell receptor sites (Angrist et al. 1980; Janowsky et al. 1975) or by excessive social pressure encountered in interpersonal situations (Heinrichs and Carpenter 1983). Such overstimulation, whether by internal, ambient, or exogenous causes, may lead to an overload of the patient's information-processing capacity, further arousal, and a resulting impairment in the integration of social stimuli. The tendency of persons with schizophrenic disorders to resort to social withdrawal may be one way to escape from environmental overstimulation.

The long-term course of schizophrenia is often marked by deficit states with "negative symptoms" such as depression, lack of motivation, and social withdrawal. These patients have an inability to comprehend the meaning of words in context, are unable to communicate intended meanings to others (Cutting 1985; Hemsley 1977), and have severe difficulties using attention and praise to generate supportive social relationships (Wallace 1984).

Investigating the Family Variables

The concepts of communication deviance and expressed emotion have emerged over the past several years as the family factors most highly correlated with onset and relapse in schizophrenia. An understanding of these dimensions of family functioning is essential for those who wish to assist families to manage more effectively the problems associated with having to live with a schizophrenic relative.

Communication Deviance

The concept of communication deviance has emerged as the most enduring product of more than 25 years of American research to determine the family variables associated with or contributing to the onset and course of schizophrenic disorder (Doane 1978; Goldstein 1983; Goldstein and Doane 1982; Goldstein and Rodnick 1975; Jacob 1975; Liem 1980; Mishler and Waxler 1968; Riskin and Faunce 1974; Wynne et al. 1979). Wynne and Singer (1963a, 1963b) originally proposed that schizophrenic thought disorder might arise from the inheritance and/or learning of disturbed patterns of parental communication. These patterns were thought to arise from attentional deficits producing a failure to establish shared foci of attention in interactions and a resulting interference in the establishment of shared meanings (Wynne 1968).

To test this hypothesis, Singer and Wynne (1965a, 1965b) transcribed respondents' (parents, siblings, patients) descriptions of each of the 10 Rorschach cards, assigning them to three classes of communication deviance: 1) closure, or inability to make a commitment to an idea or perception; 2) disruptive behavior, speech irrelevant to the task; 3) peculiar language and logic. An index was derived of the total number of deviant communications divided by the total number of transactions (D/T). Their original study recorded the D/T index for 114 patients and each of their parental dyads and one sibling, comparing the profiles of those diagnosed as schizophrenic (N = 44) with "borderlines" (N = 25), neurotics—primarily depressives (N = 25)—and normals (N = 20). The findings showed that the mean level of parental and sibling communication deviance varied directly with the diagnostic severity of the patient's disorder. The protocol thus enabled a properly trained "blind" rater to predict correctly the likelihood of a schizophrenic offspring in the family from a parental Rorschach or Thematic Apperception Test profile. Furthermore, the communication deviance of the parents was consistently and significantly greater than that of the index schizophrenic patient, indicating that the variable was independent of the degree of individual psychopathology.

Using cards from the Thematic Apperception Test, Jones et al. (1977) replicated Wynne and Singer's original work, and in addition discovered that one could more strongly predict the presence of a schizophrenic offspring if both parents scored high in communication deviance. Significantly, a low-scoring parent matched with a higher scorer appeared to exert a "corrective effect," lessening the probability of the occurrence of severe psychopathology in an offspring.

In a five-year follow-up of children selected at risk on the basis of their having at least one parent previously hospitalized with a psychiatric disorder, Doane et al. (1982) have reported that the presence during childhood of a mother with a high degree of communication deviance predicted deviant adolescent behavior and low functioning in multiple settings (e.g., school, home, with peers). Doane and her co-workers speculated that being brought up with a mother with a high degree of communication deviance might interfere with a child's ability to give and receive ambiguous messages and meanings.

Expressed Emotion

In the decade following the work of the early family theorists in America, a team of British investigators began to study the relationship between patient relapse and the attitudes of close relatives toward schizophrenic family members returning home after hospital discharge. The Camberwell Family Interview (Hooley 1985; Koenigsberg and Handley 1986; Kuipers 1979; Leff and Vaughn 1985; Rutter and Brown 1966) recorded the responses by close relatives to open-ended questions about the patient's most recent illness episode and his at-home behavior. The interview was then taped and scored for an index of expressed emotion by 1) counting the number of critical remarks—determined by verbal and vocal characteristics—and 2) determining the level of emotional overinvolvement, of overprotective, intrusive, or self-sacrificing behavior. A home was considered "high" if one relative scored six or more critical comments or was considered to have a high index of emotional overinvolvement.

It was discovered that chronic schizophrenics nine months after hospital discharge to high-expressed-emotion homes relapsed at a rate of about 55 percent, more than three times the rate (15 percent) of those discharged to low-expressed-emotion homes. This finding was originally observed by Brown et al. in 1958 and then confirmed in a prospective study by Brown's team in 1962. In subsequent prospective studies this finding has been replicated twice in England (Brown et al. 1972; Vaughn and Leff 1976), once in California (Vaughn et al. 1984), and once with Mexican Americans (Karno et al. 1987), with a total of 446 patients in all six studies. Vaughn and Leff (1976) found that the relapse rates in high-expressed-emotion homes were significantly lower when 1) the patient spent less time in face-to-face contact with the key high-expressed-emotion relative or 2) the patient was taking neuroleptic medication.

Seeking to confirm the validity of the hypothesis that a family member's expressed emotion could either increase or decrease autonomic arousal, Tarrier et al. (1979) and Sturgeon et al. (1981) measured the skin conductance of patients before and after a high- or low-expressed-emotion relative entered the room. Their findings showed that for both acute psychotics and chronic patients in remission, the patient's skin conductance did not change after a high-expressed-emotion relative entered the room, but dropped, or habituated, upon entry of a low-expressed-emotion relative. It was concluded that low-expressed-emotion family members might exert a "protective effect" upon the autonomic reactivity of their mentally ill relatives, an effect that could account for their lower relapse rates.

Studies by Leff and Vaughn (1980, 1981) and by Leff et al. (1983) have examined the interaction of expressed emotion, neuroleptic medication, and the occurrence of independent stressful life events prior to relapse. Their results indicated that neuroleptic medication could protect a chronic schizophrenic living in a high-expressed-emotion family in the first year following relapse against one form of stress, either the acute stress of threatening life events or the chronic stress of high expressed emotion, but not against both sources of stress. For patients living with high-expressed-emotion relatives, further protection against relapse would seem to require either reducing the patient's contact with a critical or overinvolved parent or helping the parent to adopt low-expressed-emotion attitudes and behaviors.

These efforts have been facilitated by the development by Doane et al. (1981b) of the Affective Style index, which measures the frequency of critical, guilt-inducing, or intrusive remarks made by one or both parents to the patient in a 10-minute "revealed difference" interactive task (Strodtbeck 1954). Affective style is thus the interactive counterpart of expressed emotion. Doane et al. (1985) have shown that negative affective style predicts: 1) nine-month relapse rates of patients receiving antipsychotic medication and supportive, pragmatic individual psychotherapy; and 2) poor patient social functioning three and six months following hospital discharge.

Analysis of data from 54 families in the UCLA Longitudinal Study suggest that "at risk" adolescents, selected for withdrawn, asocial behavior or preexisting family difficulties, growing up with at least one parent high in communication deviance, have a high probability of developing a schizophrenic spectrum disorder (schizophrenia or schizotypal or schizoid personality disorder) at 5 and 15 year follow-up. The power to predict the eventual expression of schizophrenia spectrum disorder is increased further when households high in communication deviance are also high in expressed emotion and negative affective style (Doane et al. 1981a, 1981b, 1985, 1986; Goldstein 1985, 1987; Norton 1982).

Further research has contributed to a greater understanding of the dimensions of expressed emotion—criticism and emotional overinvolvement. 1) Patient relapse appears to be more highly associated with parent's critical attitudes and behavior than with their overinvolvement (Hogarty 1985; Hogarty et al. 1986). 2) Levels of criticism decline as the patient's symptoms and behavior improve (Hogarty et al. 1986). Criticism appears to be a dimension reflecting a) the relatives' success or failure in coping with the patient's disturbed behavior and with stressful life events, in the recent and remote past (Goldstein 1987); and b) the relatives' difficulty defining the patient's problem as a disease for which he or she is not responsible (Vaughn 1986). 3) The relationship between expressed emotion and relapse pertains primarily to male chronic schizophrenics living in their parental homes (as opposed to females), to patients undergoing their first psychotic episode (MacMillan et al. 1986), and to those who have married. 4) Parents with a high degree of emotional overinvolvement have wider social networks than parents who are highly critical (Anderson et al. 1984). 5) Patients from families with a high degree of emotional overinvolvement tend to have been more withdrawn and less socially interactive as teenagers and to have a higher incidence of deficit symptoms following the onset of their schizophrenic disorders, while patients from highly critical families tend to have more positive premorbid adjustments, or more favorable prognoses, and less severe deficit symptoms (Miklowitz et al. 1983). 6) Parents who have a high degree of emotional overinvolvement appear to have the highest levels of communication deviance (Miklowitz et al. 1986).

These findings suggest that both high emotional overinvolvement and high communication deviance could represent either persistent attitudes or traits (Kanter et al. 1987) or the product of living for many years with a mentally disturbed offspring. Doane has speculated that critical or overinvolved attitudes continually expressed by parents in an amorphous or fragmented manner to a genetically vulnerable child might result in confusion and distress and interfere with the child's learning how to transmit and receive messages and to acquire shared meanings in ambiguous or subtle interpersonal situations. After a patient has developed the disorder, this distress and confusion could be exacerbated once the patient experiences the cognitive deficits produced by the disorder itself, which would interfere further with the capacity to perceive, process, and transmit subtle or complex interpersonal cues or messages.

Recent studies have helped to define the clinical and interactional correlates of expressed emotion (Kuipers et al. 1983; Miklowitz et al. 1983; Strachan et al. 1986).

These studies indicate that high-expressed-emotion relatives: 1) talk more and engage in lively, heated discussions; 2) talk with excitability, criticism, intrusiveness, interruptions, and simultaneous speech; 3) exchange fewer glances with the patient and produce fewer changes in facial expression; 4) appear to be less attentive listeners; and 5) are less effective problem solvers. These qualities contrast with low-expressed-emotion relatives who: 1) talk less, with more frequent and longer pauses; 2) are calmer, more affectively neutral, more positive and supportive; 3) make better eye contact with the patient; 4) are better listeners; and 5) are more effective problem solvers.

Expressed emotion also appears to reflect characteristic attitudes and thresholds of tolerance of family members toward the patient and his behavior in crisis situations (Leff and Vaughn 1985; Vaughn 1986; Vaughn and Leff 1981). These attitudes and tolerance thresholds are thought to be strongly influenced by relatives' attributions (Greenley 1986; Hooley et al. 1987) regarding the patient's behavior, beliefs about illness (Tarrier and Barrowclough 1986), and by their characteristic styles of coping.

Vaughn (1986) has suggested that low-expressed-emotion relatives: 1) accept the legitimacy of the particular illness and believe that psychotic experiences are real for the patient; 2) provide reassurance and social support, and respect the patient's need for closeness and distance; 3) are objective and dispassionate, expressing muted dissatisfaction resulting from realistic expectations for a long, slow recovery, with tolerance for poor performance; and 4) are adaptable, self-controlled, and flexible. High-expressed-emotion relatives in comparison: 1) do not believe that the patient suffers from a legitimate illness, and tend to see deficit symptoms as "laziness" that a properly motivated person should voluntarily control; 2) are critical and intolerant and do not respect the patient's needs for reassurance, social support, and closeness and distance; 3) have unrealistic expectations, either pressuring the patient to behave like "normal people," or expecting that the patient will require lifelong care and protection for an incurable condition; and 4) tend to be rigid, inflexible, and emotionally labile in crisis situations.

Psychoeducational Strategies

Psychoeducational strategies were originally developed to reduce patient relapse by teaching high-expressed-emotion family members to adopt more calm and tolerant attitudes and behaviors towards the patient and to pursue a practical approach towards solving the secondary problems posed by chronic mental illness (Anderson et al. 1980, 1986; Barrowclough and Tarrier 1984; Berkowitz 1984; Falloon et al. 1984; Strachan 1986). This model of intervention seeks to meet demonstrated patient and family needs through a combination of educational, behavioral management, self-help, and family therapy techniques. Patients and family members are taught to regard schizophrenia as a disease process for which no one is held responsible, whose origin is extrinsic to the individual and the family system (Hatfield 1984a; Kanter 1984; Lefley 1985). Family members practice communicating with one another in a clear, direct, and unambiguous manner and learn to function as a team to face the difficulties posed by chronic schizophrenic illness. The information introduced includes a full description of the schizophrenic disorders and their biologic and psychosocial treatment, as well as the principles of communication, social skills training, effective problem solving, and behavioral management.

Family Crisis Therapy

Goldstein et al. at UCLA studied the effects of brief family crisis treatment compared to a control receiving no family crisis treatment for a group of acutely psychotic young schizophrenics following their first or second hospital admissions. These patients were medicated with depot fluphenazine at either moderate (1 cc/month) or low (0.25 cc/month) dosage (Goldstein et al. 1978, 1981). The structure of the family intervention resembled that of the Colorado project in that six sessions of crisis management were provided and the therapists helped the patient and family to cope more effectively with stressful situations. However, the intervention differed from that of the Colorado group in two ways: 1) in its timing, being given after the patient had been stabilized on medication in the hospital rather than as an alternative to hospitalization; and 2) in its attribution of the nature of the patient's problem, now accepting the patient's condition as a mental disorder in the patient whose origins were unknown or idiopathic, for which no one was held responsible, rather than the result of interpersonal family difficulties. The goals of the Goldstein project were also more modest: 1) accepting the fact of patient's psychosis; 2) identifying stresses that may have precipitated the acute episode; 3) anticipating stresses that might lead to future episodes of the disorder; and 4) planning steps family members might take to avoid or minimize these episodes in the future.

Ninety-six patients were randomly assigned to either family crisis intervention or treatment as usual and each group was then further randomly assigned to moderate- or low-dosage medication that was continued for six months. The family crisis sessions were given weekly upon hospital discharge. Results showed that while drug treatment alone did not produce a significant reduction in relapse, family therapy did produce a main effect in both drug treatment groups at six weeks and in the group receiving the moderate medication dosage at six-months follow-up. Further analysis of the data showed that the family treatment appeared to be more effective than the control treatment for reducing blunted affect (at six weeks) and social withdrawal (six months). "High achieving" patients (from families achieving three or more goals of treatment) were functioning significantly better at six months, while in the "nonachievers'" (two or less goals) sessions a high degree of family expressed emotion was observed.

Another research group (Glick et al. 1985) has adopted this format successfully for use during a brief inpatient hospitalization. This group reported that the family intervention was accompanied by patient improvement only for those schizophrenics with a history of good prehospital functioning, while those with poor prehospital functioning did not improve at six-months follow-up. Glick et al. augmented the crisis intervention treatment package by training the patient and family in the identification of prodromal signs and symptoms of schizophrenic relapse (Carpenter and Heinrichs 1983; Herz et al. 1982), a procedure that Goldstein (1983) has also endorsed.

Multiple Relatives' Group Intervention

The London group (Berkowitz 1984; Berkowitz et al. 1981, 1984; Leff et al. 1982, 1985) sought to provide a family management approach that reduced the rate of patient relapse by lowering expressed emotion through the relatives' adoption of the disease model of illness and their learning of low-expressed-emotion ways of coping with the patient. This method included three principal components: 1) an educational package of four short lectures delivered in two home visits concerning the relationships of schizophrenia, patient behavior, and relatives' reaction to the behavior; 2) a multiple relatives' group with two therapists and three to four families meeting at the clinic every other week, where low-expressed-emotion relatives would pass on their attitudes and coping strategies to high-expressed-emotion relatives, while the leaders served as facilitators of this process (due to a high dropout rate of low-expressed-emotion relatives, the leaders took a more active role in these groups); and 3) home-based family sessions where the therapist helped the parents oneto set realistic expectations, to seek change in small steps, to act as a united team, and to solve problems more effectively.

Twenty-four patients about to be discharged from the hospital, all on maintenance antipsychotic medication, who were in high contact with high-expressed-emotion relatives, all on maintenance antipsychotic medication, were then randomly assigned either to a routine outpatient course of treatment or to the social intervention package (Leff et al. 1982). Follow-up found that at nine months, six of 12 controls had experienced a clinical relapse (reappearance of symptoms not present at discharge or exacerbation of symptoms stabilized at discharge), whereas only one of 12 of the experimental group had relapsed. At two-year follow-up (Leff et al. 1985), four of 12 in the treatment group had relapsed, compared with nine of 12 in the comparison group. When the rates were adjusted to reflect only those patients complying with medication, 20 percent of those in the experimental group relapsed, compared with 78 percent in the control group, and there were no relapses in the eight families who had converted from high to low expressed emotion.

Within the total sample, patients from families that had converted from high to low expressed emotion or had significantly reduced their face-to-face contacts relapsed at a rate of only 14 percent, compared with a 78 percent rate for patients from families that did not achieve these goals. The treatment team (Berkowitz et al. 1984) suggested that high-expressed-emotion relatives receiving the social intervention had become less pessimistic, had learned more about problem management, had changed their perception of the patient as someone who would always have the condition to someone who could have "well periods," and had come to see the patient more as an individual.

Home-Based Family Management

Falloon (1985) and Falloon et al. (1985) at the University of Southern California conducted a study of the efficacy of home-based behavioral family therapy compared to an individual therapy control group. Both groups were treated with enlightened medication management, maintaining patients on the lowest therapeutic dosages of antipsychotic medication to avoid side effects. The family therapy was given in the patients' homes in 40 sessions over two years, weekly for the first three months, every other week for the next six months, and then monthly starting with the 10th month, at which time the families also were invited to join a monthly multiple family group. Patients assigned to the control group were treated at the same frequency with the same number of sessions, and at 10 months were also given the opportunity to join monthly multiple family groups.

The family therapy provided education about schizophrenia in the first two sessions and then concentrated on the teaching of communication and problem-solving skills. The project focused primarily on teaching a behavioral management package designed to enhance the families' coping skills. The communications training taught family members to express positive and negative feelings, to make positive requests, and to listen carefully to one another. In the problem-solving sessions, the goals were chosen by the family, and the therapists used operant conditioning, with positive reinforcement of desired responses, behavioral rehearsals, modeling, feedback, and contingency contracting. Homework tasks were only assigned if there was a high probability of success. Conflicts were managed by ignoring hostile remarks, taking "time-out," and setting limits. The therapists saw themselves as teachers and advisors and were "on call" around the clock. The individual therapy control included supportive case management, problem solving, and the developing of behavioral strategies.

Thirty-six patients were selected following medication stabilization after hospitalization for a schizophrenic relapse. These patients were all from "at-risk" households, 33 from homes high in expressed emotion and three from single parent households. Nine-months follow-up showed that 56 percent (10/18) of patients in the control group had experienced a clinical relapse compared to 6 percent (1/18) of those receiving family therapy (Falloon et al. 1982). These findings persisted for two years, by which time 83 percent (15/18) of those receiving individual treatment had relapsed, compared with 17 percent (3/18) of the experimental group (Falloon et al. 1985a). The highest relapse rates were for patients receiving individual therapy whose parents had high levels of negative affective style (Doane et al. 1985). Doane et al. (1986) have suggested that parents not receiving family therapy resort to criticism and intrusiveness as they become increasingly frustrated in having to cope with the patient's behavior.

The investigators (Falloon et al. 1985b) also found that patients in the experimental group had less severe exacerbations, less severe deficit symptoms and depression, and more complete remissions and required lower doses of medication and less hospital care. Family members receiving the family therapy reported less disruption of activities, a reduction in physical and mental health problems, and less subjective burden (Falloon and Pederson 1985) and were observed to have enhanced problem-solving abilities, make fewer critical and intrusive remarks, and show increased tolerance for patients' functional limitations.

A cost-benefit analysis showed that the benefits to families and patients in the experimental group were twice as great as those to families in the control group, and the overall cost of the family treatment package was 19 percent less than the individual treatment modality. Falloon calculated that family management was two and a half times more efficient than individual treatment.

Family Management and Social Skills Training

Hogarty et al. in Pittsburgh set out to test the utility of two distinct social interventions for reducing relapse in schizophrenia—patient social skills training and family management. This project followed other efforts (Hogarty et al. 1974a, 1974b, 1979) in which it had been demonstrated that: 1) neuroleptic medication was the most effective preventive treatment against relapse in schizophrenia; 2) pragmatic individual social casework was not effective unless patients were receiving maintenance neuroleptic medication; and 3) the most meaningful predictor for relapse of patients receiving depot neuroleptic medication was a history of "intrafamilial contention" prior to treatment.

The Pittsburgh group developed the hypothesis that patients on maintenance medication could be protected from relapse by: 1) giving patients the skills to manage stress in their own personal lives; and 2) teaching their families to reduce the level of intrafamilial conflict, to adopt realistic expectations based upon an accurate understanding of the illness, and to develop effective coping strategies.

A total of 134 patients from high-expressed-emotion households who had recently been admitted to the hospital in an acute schizophrenic episode were assigned randomly to four treatment conditions, each receiving maintenance medication: 1) family therapy (N = 30); 2) social skills training (N = 30): 3) family therapy plus social skills training (N = 29); and 4) medication management only (N = 45) (Hogarty et al. 1986).

The goals of the family treatment package (Anderson et al. 1980, 1981) were to increase the relatives' understanding of the patient's illness, to decrease the level of family stress, to increase family members' utilization of their social networks, and to lessen the deleterious effects of long-term family problems. The intervention was to be delivered in four phases over a year or more: 1) engagement; 2) a survival skills workshop; 3) supportive family therapy; 4) either termination or long-term family therapy. In the engagement phase, the therapy team sought to establish a therapeutic alliance by focusing on the patient's problems, understanding the family's strengths, and empathizing with their predicament and point of view. A day-long survival skills workshop provided several families with information about the patient's disorder, the patient's experience, and the difficulties that families experience, as well as with concrete advice for coping in the future. Suggestions were included for ensuring patient adherence to medication regimens, revising expectations, setting limits, keeping communications simple, and refraining from overstimulating the patient. Relatives were encouraged to speak informally with other relatives at the workshop and to meet together afterwards in multiple family groups every six weeks.

The survival skills workshop was followed by a course of family therapy held every other week at the clinic for the next year or more. The family therapy proceeded in four phases: engagement, task assignment, problem solving, and structural change leading to enhanced autonomy. The therapists taught patients and family members to recognize "early warning signs" (of relapse); to communicate clearly and to settle conflicts; to establish secure family, generational, and interpersonal boundaries; to control dangerous behavior; to acknowledge the needs of all members; and, toward the end of the treatment, to encourage the patient's greater assumption of role responsibilities. The patient was also encouraged to become involved in programs of psychosocial rehabilitation. After a year of treatment families were given the choice of either renewing or revising the original contract, tapering the frequency of the sessions, or terminating. It was anticipated that some families might wish to enter longer-term family therapy to work on longer-term goals, but very few families chose this option.

A one-year follow-up showed that patient relapse rates were reduced through a main effect both by family treatment (19 percent) and social skills training (20 percent), compared with the relapse rates of patients receiving only medication management (41 percent). Those patients who received both the family and individual skills training did not relapse at all (0 percent). The main effect of family treatment was thought to be due to the lowering of expressed emotion in 39 percent (16/41) of the families so treated. No relapses occurred for *any* families that converted from high to low expressed emotion (always from a reduction in the number of critical remarks). Since several families in the medication management group and the social skills training group had "converted to low" in the absence of family treatment, it appeared that the criticism aspect of the level of expressed emotion was sensitive to the patient's condition (only 6 percent of families in the project were high in emotional overinvolvement). For those families remaining high in expressed emotion, there was a 42 percent relapse rate overall, 33 percent for those who received family treatment and 20 percent for those who had received social skills training. Only the combined treatment was able to sustain remission in families remaining high in expressed emotion, suggesting that all three forms of intervention—medication, personal protection, and environmental protection—were necessary to prevent patient relapse in chronic schizophrenic disorders.

Summary

The results of these four projects strongly suggest that psychoeducational programs of family management training are effective for reducing the rate of patient relapse in cases of chronic schizophrenia. These family treatment approaches meet the stated needs of family members who have requested professionals to give them information and practical advice and to appreciate their special burdens as caretakers. These approaches also serve as a logical response to the research findings on expressed emotion and communication deviance that indicate that reducing environmental stimulation, simplifying communication, and exerting effective coping strategies will result in reduced morbidity in schizophrenic patients. The basic principles of this approach are listed below:

1. While the course of the patient's disorder is seen as idiopathic, the condition is viewed as a disease for which neither the patient nor the family is held responsible.
2. Patients are seen as experts in experiencing the illness, while relatives are seen as experts in experiencing and coping with the patient. Thus, patients and relatives are considered essential members of the health care team, contributing essential information and advice to the overall plan of care.
3. The treatment team is "on-call" 24 hours a day should a crisis arise.
4. Providing information about the disease and course of illness helps patients and families to set realistic expectations and priorities.
5. Patients are protected against excess autonomic arousal at three key levels: 1) at the neurophysiological level through neuroleptic medication, 2) at the social-personal level through the acquisition of social and coping skills, and 3) at the family level through the acquisition of stimulation-reducing techniques and effective coping strategies.
6. Social interventions successful at providing these protections include family crisis treatment, multiple relatives' or multiple family groups, behavioral family management, psychoeducational workshops combined with structural-supportive family therapy, and patient social skills training (described in Chapter 151).

Phase-Oriented Treatment Assignment and Family Therapy Procedures

In this section, a framework is presented to guide therapists in assigning patients and families to specific modes of treatment according to the severity of illness and phase of recovery. It is suggested that two treatment tracks be offered, one for higher-functioning patients and the other for lower-functioning patients (Figure 1). Patients with first psychotic breaks or schizophreniform disorders, with a history of good pre- and intermorbid functioning, receive a course of brief family crisis therapy, followed

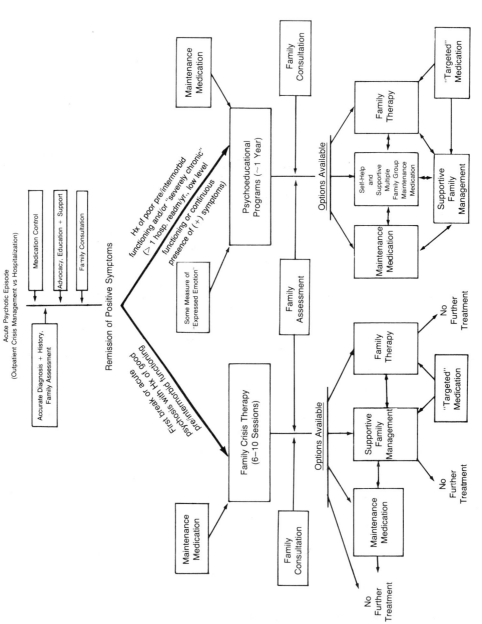

Figure 1. Family intervention strategies for the schizophrenic disorders.

by family consultation and assignment to 1) no further treatment, 2) maintenance medication, 3) supportive family management (plus targeted or maintenance medication), or 4) family therapy. Chronically psychotic patients and all psychotic patients with poor premorbid functioning are enrolled in family psychoeducational treatment for about a year, followed by family consultation and referral to 1) maintenance medication, 2) a multiple family support group, 3) supportive family management (plus targeted medication), or 4) family therapy.

It is useful for the practitioner to think of the family treatment of chronic schizophrenia in three phases (e.g., Wynne 1983): 1) the *acute phase*, when the patient is floridly psychotic and treated for positive symptoms; 2) the *recovery phase*, when the patient's positive symptoms are in relative remission but negative symptoms and sensitivity to social stimulation are important considerations; and 3) the *postrecovery phase*, when the patient may still suffer from negative symptoms but is well enough to tolerate greater environmental change and demands. At each phase, the characteristics of the illness differ and clinical interventions address a different set of priorities.

The Acute Phase: Establishing a Working Alliance

First contact with a patient's family in crisis often follows the onset of an acute psychotic episode. Whether the decompensation is the first or one of many for the patient, it is a time of acute distress for the family. If it is a first psychotic episode, the family will almost certainly be shocked and bewildered; they may not know how to understand what has happened to their relative, how to assess their own responsibility in the illness, or how to cope with the future course of illness (Anderson 1977; Bernheim and Lehman 1985; GAP 1985; Harbin 1979). The therapist should empathize with their feelings and discuss diagnostic and prognostic considerations and treatment options, the most important of which are the need for adequate neuroleptic medication and the selection of the most optimal setting to provide this—whether in the home, a shelter, or a hospital. Because a crisis is often the time of greatest receptivity to help (Hill 1965; Parad and Caplan 1965; Rabkin 1972), the therapist's reliable and empathic assistance will help to establish the mutual trust and credibility necessary for forging an enduring partnership during the course of treatment.

If the patient has been hospitalized, the family therapist should keep family members abreast of developments in the patient's condition and treatment plans, answering their questions and communicating their concerns to the inpatient staff. The therapist can play a key role as a consultant, discussing the diathesis-stress model of schizophrenia, emphasizing the continuing importance of medication, and helping to educate the family about the patient's need for a low stress environment during the lengthy process of recovery. Here, the therapist collaborates with the family, helping them to identify problems and options at all systems' levels and from divergent points of view, to recognize strengths and weaknesses, and to formulate, execute, and revise plans of action (e.g., Epstein and Bishop 1981a; Wynne et al. 1986, 1987).

If the patient is neither violent nor considered a significant risk and is willing to accept treatment, the family and treatment team may decide to manage the acute psychotic episode with outpatient crisis intervention (Flinn and Brown 1977; Hatfield 1984a; Langsley and Kaplan 1968). Here, the most basic principles include being available around the clock; controlling medication with family members acting as nurse surrogates; establishing clear rules for permissible behavior; and maintaining a steady, calm, and nonintrusive presence. It is important to understand that family members who have suffered through the numerous relapses of a severely ill, chronic schizophrenic patient may be reluctant to once again assume the burden of home-care management. Such families are beset with feelings of guilt, anger, frustration, and despair over their relative's unresponsive mental condition. They often experience alienation from a health care system that seems to have promised more help than it has delivered.

Thus, the therapist must convey that the family's needs are as important as the patient's and that the family is not to blame for the illness. Most of this work is done without the patient present, in order to minimize disruptions and to facilitate the candid discussion of stresses associated with the patient's past behavior and most recent activities. To ensure the patient's cooperation and to preserve trust, the patient should later be told in general terms about the meeting and why it was held. It is at this time that families should be made aware of the benefits of joining community support groups for relatives of the mentally ill. Membership in these self-help organizations, many belonging to the National Alliance for the Mentally Ill, can reinforce the education and support provided by the family therapist and health care team, while offering an additional opportunity to share experiences and learn how others have coped with their mentally ill relative (Cole 1983; Hatfield 1987).

The Recovery Phase: Family Crisis Intervention or Psychoeducational Intervention

The main objective of the recovery phase is the development of family skills that will minimize the risk of early patient relapse. As seen in Figure 1, the strategy chosen for establishing these skills depends upon the severity of the patient's illness.

First Psychotic Breaks and High-Functioning Patients

It is important for the consultant team to carefully assess not only the condition of the patient but also that of the family, to discuss the various resources available to them within the mental health treatment system, and to consider whether family crisis therapy is the most appropriate option.

Patients who have experienced a first episode of psychosis with rapid stabilization, or those with good prehospital and premorbid functioning, respond well to the form of family crisis intervention suggested by Mosher, and proven effective by Goldstein et al. (1978, 1981). In Goldstein's original approach, the patient and the family met with a therapist for six weekly problem-focused sessions aimed at identifying and minimizing psychosocial stressors that may have contributed to the patient's breakdown. These weekly sessions may be extended over an eight-week period to provide a realistic time for acute illness to abate. Family crisis treatment begins as soon as the patient has recovered sufficiently to participate and is offered in conjunction with psychotropic medication. Specific education about the causes, expression, treatment, and course of psychotic illness is offered even if a definitive diagnosis may not yet have been made. (For a description of curricula and procedures see the article by McFarlane et al. [1983] and the books by Falloon et al. [1984], Bernheim and Lehmann [1985], and Anderson et al. [1986].)

The therapist then seeks to accomplish some preliminary objectives with the family: 1) helping the family to establish realistic expectations for the patient's optimal recovery (at least six months to a year) so that excessive family demands do not inadvertently contribute to a relapse; 2) discussing each family member's reaction to the patient's psychotic episode to enable them to cope with their fear or shame and to help them see the relationship between stressful events and psychotic decompensation; and 3) explaining the treatment rationale as an effort to identify and manage stressors that may contribute to the risk of future relapse.

These preliminary moves are followed by four further objectives: 1) Identifying a few key stressors apparently affecting the patient. The Smith family may decide, for example, that great stress occurs when John, the patient, and his father argue about John's getting a job, and when John and his mother fight about John's smoking. 2) Developing strategies to prevent stress and cope with it. The family may help John's father approach his son more calmly and with a more realistic request, and John may agree to smoke only in certain areas of the house. 3) Having families implement, evaluate, and refine these strategies. John may have agreed to do some chores around the house until ready for work, while the family helps him plan these activities more effectively. 4) Involving the family in anticipatory planning. Mr. and Mrs. Smith, both teachers, plan ways to avoid increased stress during the summer months when all family members spend more time at home.

Family consultation

Following successful completion of a course of family crisis intervention, patients and families should be given a family consultation to assess their current problems, needs, and options. These options are 1) terminating all treatment; 2) referring the patient to an interaction-oriented psychotherapy group (see Chapter 149) or a self-help group for patients such as Recovery, Inc. (Cole 1983); and 3) placing the patient on maintenance medication or using "targeted" or "low-dose" strategies that teach the patient and family to recognize prodromal signs of impending relapse (Carpenter and Heinrichs 1983; Herz et al. 1982); 4) offering supportive family management, where the therapist remains available on an "as needed" basis to assist the family with stressful situations and to provide practical advice; or 5) conducting family therapy, only if requested, usually for a problem involving spousal or parental marital difficulties or trouble with an acting-out child or adolescent (not the schizophrenic).

Chronic, Severely Ill, and Low-Functioning Schizophrenic Patients: Psychoeducational Methods

Patients with a diagnosis of schizophrenia, who may have had many exacerbations and are unable to hold a job or establish active social lives, require family interventions that teach family members about the illness and how to live with it. This includes specific steps relatives and patients can take to reduce the risk of relapse and minimize their own sense of burden and guilt. A variety of effective interventions have been developed to achieve this objective, including 1) a multifamily workshop followed by individual family sessions; 2) home-based behavioral family therapy sessions; and 3) a multifamily group.

Survival skills workshop and supportive family therapy

In the format developed by Anderson et al. (1980), up to a half-dozen families with a chronic schizophrenic relative are invited to an all-day workshop around the time of the patient's hospital discharge. To maximize relatives' participation, the patients themselves do not attend. In a friendly, informal atmosphere, the workshop staff encourages the families to become collaborators in the recovery process by giving them a wide range of information. The staff presents a state-of-the-art discussion of the causes, course, treatment, and prognosis of schizophrenia in understandable language. Schizophrenia is defined as a disorder with a strong biologic basis producing an increased vulnerability to social stimulation. Psychotrophic medication is emphasized as a crucial component of care. Great care is taken to recognize the courageous efforts the family has made to look after its ill relative. Drawing from the expressed emotion research, the staff explains that intense social interaction with the patient may prove overly stimulating, add to the patient's misery, and may even contribute to the risk of future relapse. Three principles are emphasized: 1) reducing expectations that the patient return rapidly to his premorbid level of functioning; 2) encouraging the family to set limits on bizarre or disruptive behavior by the patient in the calmest possible way; and 3) extending the extrafamilial contacts of the patient and family as far as possible.

Following the workshop, the therapist meets with families individually over the next year or more. Meetings are held every two to three weeks to reinforce the notion that change is slow. The main objectives are the reinforcement of family boundaries and the gradual resumption of responsibility by the patient. The family learns to judge progress by an "internal yardstick," comparing the patient's functioning at present with his functioning six months before, rather than to that of his friends who do not have this illness.

Home-based behavioral family management

An alternative psychoeducational intervention is the home-based behavioral family therapy (which the therapist holds regularly at the family's home) developed by Falloon et al. (1984). In this approach the therapist initially gives the family several discussions about schizophrenia, communication skills, and problem solving. The remainder of the treatment program consists of behavioral exercises in which the therapist teaches family members how to communicate effectively and work together to solve problems. Communication training emphasizes listening skills, recognizing and rewarding positive behavior, expressing positive and negative feelings, and making specific requests for behavior change. Problem-solving training is a systematic process that involves identifying a problem, developing and evaluating possible solutions, and planning, implementing, and revising the one chosen. Family members select key areas in which family stress threatens the stability of the patient, while the therapist helps the family negotiate each step of the problem-solving process. The treatment consists of weekly or twice-monthly family meetings that take place with decreasing frequency over a year or more. The home-based model is labor intensive but ensures a high rate of family participation.

Multiple relatives' or multiple family group treatment

A third method of imparting the psychoeducational message is the multiple relatives' group developed by Berkowitz et al. (1984) and employed by Leff et al. (1982) in their outcome study. Here, information about schizophrenia and its medical management is presented to each family during two home visits. The relatives then meet together with two therapists in a small group of three to four families for the next one to two years. Meeting without the patients allows the relatives to unburden themselves freely of pent-up feelings of anger, frustration, and resentment toward the patients and the illness. In this supportive group environment, family members discuss the problems posed by the illness and can give one another suggestions for coping with their own emotions and for managing difficult patient behavior. The group leaders model low-key tolerant attitudes and offer selective attention to and praise for responses that lower expressed emotion (Berkowitz 1984).

Variants of the third method are the multifamily group approaches developed by Laqueur (1981), Beels (1975), McFarlane (1983), and Cole and Jacobs (manuscript in preparation). In the model proposed by Cole and Jacobs, information about schizophrenia, medication, communication, and problem-solving skills and techniques for managing specific symptoms is presented as a one-year course in twice-monthly meetings to a group of eight to 10 families. In addition to the information provided in the classes, the families receive support and suggestions from each other. During the problem-solving classes, families enact stressful situations in the presence of the other families, who suggest alternative ways to view and solve problems. Including patients in the meetings provides family members with the opportunity to witness psychotic behavior more objectively. Hearing patient-members of other families talk about their voices, strange ideas, and paranoia may help relatives to be more receptive to the notion that schizophrenic symptoms are manifestations of a disease process over which the patient has little control. The presence of patients also permits relatives to learn "by analogy and identification" (Laqueur 1981) and by observing others interact with their parents and relatives, as well as acting, themselves, as cotherapists to other patients and relatives ("cross-parenting") (McFarlane 1983).

During the year or so in which their families are involved in programs of psychoeducational family management, it is important that patients be treated with adequate levels of neuroleptic medication and encouraged to attend programs of psychosocial rehabilitation (e.g., Anderson 1986; Anthony and Nemec 1984) and social skills training (Cole, this volume, Chapter 149; Liberman et al. 1987) once their clinical conditions have stabilized.

Postrecovery Phase

Family consultation

Following completion of a year or so of psychoeducational family management, families are given a family consultation to determine the appropriate plan of care during the postrecovery phase. At this point, some families may wish to practice their newly acquired knowledge and skills on their own and thus elect to leave family treatment.

Family support groups

Others, particularly those involved in multifamily groups, may wish to continue this experience by forming an "alumni group" composed of graduating members of their original multiple family group or by joining a community family support group. In the alumni group, families take major responsibility for the meetings while therapists serve as facilitators of a self-sustaining process of mutual aid. At each monthly or twice-monthly meeting, one family may relate a detailed narrative of its efforts to cope with schizophrenia, after which other group members enumerate the family's strengths, as well as alternative methods the family might use to address specific unsolved problems. In this manner, the alumni group also serves to perpetuate the teachings of the one-year course (Cole 1983).

Supportive family management

Families may also be given the option of supportive family management (e.g., Bernheim 1982) should they elect to call upon the therapist(s) or treatment team for specific problems concerning patient management issues or recurrent patterns of family conflict. Here, the treatment is brief, goal-directed, and conducted according to psychoeducational principles.

Family systems therapy

Rationale. It has been suggested that treatment programs combining social stimulation-reducing psychological interventions with maintenance medication may not only reduce patient arousal, but also dampen motivation and thereby interfere with social recovery (e.g., Buchkramer et al. 1986; Kanter et al. 1987; Schooler 1984). The resolution of lingering residual symptoms and interpersonal difficulties may require the use of lower or intermittent dosages of antipsychotic drugs (Heinrichs and Carpenter 1983). Such an approach requires careful monitoring of the patient and identification of reliable prodromal signs of clinical deterioration (Herz et al. 1982). Both patients and their relatives can be very helpful in this process.

While it is important to maintain a low level of ambient stress during the recovery phase, gradually increasing social pressure on the patient during the postrecovery phase may lead to greater functional improvement. Continued patient progress may require a form of family intervention that encourages relatives to set higher standards of performance for the exercise of behavioral management strategies whose ultimate goal is the launching of the patient to a self-sufficient and independent lifestyle.

Once the patient's condition has stabilized, with no relapse for at least a year, the option of family systems therapy may be selected only if strongly requested by the family and if the therapist or treatment team decide that the patient's further recovery may be facilitated through a more active and concerted effort by the family. Conditions responsive to family therapy include marital problems, persistent patterns of family conflict, continuing overinvolvement with overprotectiveness toward the patient, patient nonparticipation in aftercare programs, or relatives' lingering resentment and despair (Anderson 1986; Haley 1980; Madanes 1982). An alternative use of family systems therapy has been proposed by McFarlane and Beels (1983) for work with "resistant families" who seem unable to learn from psychoeducational approaches.

The family therapy approach to be described is a logical extension of family crisis intervention and psychoeducational strategies. This treatment model proposes the adoption of family methods of therapy but rejects the concept that family dynamics either create or perpetuate sick roles and designate persons to occupy them. Therapists who pursue strategies based on the notion that patient symptoms are derived primarily from family forces may confuse families who have completed psychoeducational programs, and thereby trigger patient overstimulation and early relapse. In contrast, the model proposed here focuses on what families can do to help themselves and the patient cope more effectively with the illness as well as with the demands of everyday life.

Family therapy procedures. A family therapy framework suitable for continuing treatment incorporates behavioral, structural, and structural-strategic methods (Anderson 1986; Cole 1982; Epstein and Bishop 1981a, 1981b; Falloon 1981; Haley 1980; Minuchin 1974). After carefully assessing the family's strengths and specific areas of dysfunction (e.g., Epstein et al. 1978), the therapist secures a working alliance by according top priority to family members' concerns. Therapists model clear, direct, and unambiguous communication by rephrasing family members' comments and model forthrightness by openly revealing the rationale for each action.

The therapy is organized around a logical series of strategic steps for each stage of treatment. These steps are carefully explained to the family and serve as a "cognitive map" for the course of treatment. The therapy involves four problem-solving stages: assessment, contracting, treatment, and closure. Within each stage are four steps: 1) an orientation or explanation of the task to be accomplished; 2) a review of the evidence; 3) a definition of the problem or task; and 4) the execution of a plan of action, evaluation of its effectiveness, and adjustment of the strategy to more closely meet the requirements of the problem. Once the therapist and family have come to a mutual agreement on problems to be worked on, the therapy settles down to the at-home practicing and refinement of problem-solving strategies. The therapist serves as a teacher, guiding the family toward the progressive acquisition of coping and problem-solving skills.

Principles of family therapy. The treatment is facilitated by the following set of principles (by no means exhaustive) for working with families of schizophrenics.

1. Active responsibility. Expect each family member to take an active role in the problem-solving process, either in the carrying out of objectives or serving as monitor or recorder (Epstein and Bishop 1981b).
2. Clear and direct communications. Encourage the use of "I" statements, active listening, and the direct expression of feelings, opinions, and requests. Use simple language and short phrases. Help family members to recognize and clarify verbal and nonverbal messages which are ambiguous.
3. Positive connotation. Emphasize the positive aspects of assumed intentions. Give family members credit for trying as hard as they can (Simon et al. 1985).
4. Positive reinforcement. Teach behavior shaping by giving praise for accomplishments no matter how small, rather than criticism for failure to achieve them. Encourage desired behavior by noticing and praising actions immediately after their commission. Teach relatives to employ principles of operant conditioning to help one another to learn new skills and assume new responsibilities (Falloon 1981).
5. Direct, indirect, and paradoxical directives (Cole 1982; Hoffman 1981; Watzlawick et al. 1974; Weakland et al. 1974). The therapist's aim is to guide the family to make its own suggestions for new solutions to problems. In instances where the family is unable to choose a specific strategy, the therapist may either make a direct suggestion, suggest through analogy (by relating how another family solved the problem or by telling a parable or aphorism), or utilize paradox (e.g., warning the family of probable difficulties each person will encounter once a problem is solved, and advising them against undertaking the anticipated action before each is prepared and ready to cope with the consequences).
6. Conflict management (Falloon et al. 1984). In situations of symmetrical escalation, teach participants to take time out, to take turns being in charge, to acknowledge one another's expertise, and to hold periodic negotiations where contested issues are discussed according to prearranged rules of decorum.
7. Role reallocation (Tharp and Otis 1966). In families that avoid confronting clear inequities in the distribution of roles, deep-seated resentments will interfere with many other aspects of family functioning. In families of the chronically ill, one

family member may often assume a disproportionate share of the caretaking responsibilities (Boszormenyi-Nagy and Spark 1973; Grunebaum 1984). When this situation occurs, the family may benefit from coaching to perceive more clearly the inequity and its untoward consequences, and to consider the advantages and disadvantages of bringing about a more equitable distribution of labor.

8. Enactment. In situations of conflict, problem resolution often involves making changes in the sequences of interaction or the rules that govern them. A more complete picture of characteristic family interactions can be obtained by supplementing reports of how an incident occurred with a live demonstration or enactment of the event at issue (Minuchin 1974). Enactment helps to evoke the emotional "punctuation" (often omitted from retrospective accounts) that may exacerbate difficulties in communication and problem solving.

9. Rehearsal. Once a problem has been defined and a solution has been proposed involving a change in relational patterns, it is helpful to rehearse the solution and critique the rehearsal in the therapy session before practicing it at home.

10. Strengthening behavior control. Studies of formal organizations suggest that stability is improved when the hierarchial structure is clear and effective (Caplow 1968). In families where the children refuse to abide by rules of decorum or to meet reasonable expectations, order can be restored if the senior members (e.g., the parents) can agree on a set of rules and a method of execution. They must be willing to act in unison, suspending persistent marital conflicts until order is firmly restored (Haley 1976).

11. Clarifying expectations and setting limits. Family rules, both explicit and implicit, describe the limits of tolerable behavior, define role expectations, and set deadlines for the achievement of specific goals. In families where chaos abounds, rules and expectations must be made explicit, along with a clear set of rewards and penalties to assure cooperation.

12. Adjusting the degree of affective involvement.

 Underinvolvement. Low individual self-esteem may accompany relationships with family members who ignore one another's needs and feelings. Greater emotional involvement and self-esteem may follow exercises teaching family members to listen actively and empathically to one another (Falloon 1981; Wallace et al. 1980).

 Overinvolvement. Overinvolvement of a relative with the patient can be moderated by: 1) having others share the caretaking duties; 2) encouraging others to spend more time with the caretaker; 3) identifying roles and responsibilities that the patient can begin to assume; and 4) either teaching the patient or coaching the overinvolved relative to teach the patient the requisite skills for more independent functioning.

13. Reducing the intensity of negative affects. Beck et al. (1979), Bedrosian (1983), and Jacobson (1984), among others, have written that cognitive therapy helps to reduce depression, anxiety, and anger through the identification and correction of negative thoughts. One can do cognitive therapy in a family setting by working with one person at a time, while the others are asked to listen in. This helps family members to recognize errors in logical reasoning and negative attributions. Typical patterns include predicting negative outcomes, assigning premature blame, jumping to conclusions, mistaking the part for the whole, and confusing thoughts and feelings with reality (see Burns 1981). (These techniques are usually not effective for persons with acute or chronic thought disorders.)

The course of treatment ends when family members have either solved one or more problems to their satisfaction, or, after repeated attempts, fail to find a solution.

When a solution cannot be found, the therapist explains to the family that: 1) the therapist's attempts to help the family to find a workable solution may not have met their needs; 2) the situation itself may be unresponsive to family therapy; or 3) the family may not have been ready for this form of treatment. This approach to "failure" preserves the therapeutic alliance. Since it does not hold the family responsible for failing to meet unrealizable goals, it maintains morale and helps to ensure continuing involvement with other forms of ongoing patient and family care.

Conclusion

Drawing from the available research on family factors associated with onset and relapse in schizophrenia, and from outcome studies of psychoeducational approaches seeking to reduce expressed emotion and enhance family problem-solving effectiveness, an overview has been presented of the family management approaches found effective for preventing patient relapse. Psychoeducational approaches treat patients and families as partners in the system of care and provide them with information and practical advice for the more effective management of disturbed patient behavior and other stressful life situations encountered at each phase of illness. A treatment assignment strategy has been proposed based upon the severity of the patient's condition and the phase of illness course. When the patient is acutely psychotic, the family therapist serves as crisis manager, educator, and, if the patient is hospitalized, as the family's advocate. When the patient's acute psychotic symptoms have cleared, high-functioning patients undergoing a first psychotic break or a succeeding schizophreniform episode are offered a course of brief family crisis intervention, while the families of low-functioning, chronic patients with a poor premorbid course are advised to enter a year of psychoeducational family management training. Following completion of these primary interventions, a family consultation determines whether they will discontinue family treatment, receive supportive family management, join a family support group, or begin a trial of systems-oriented family therapy if the patients are considered stable enough to withstand the higher level of social stimulation this involves.

Chapter 151

Rehabilitation in Schizophrenic Disorders

The concept of rehabilitation of persons suffering from schizophrenia is a comparatively new one. Inherent in Kraepelin's initial definition of dementia praecox was a steady mental deterioration in which the reacquisition of life skills and reentry into society had no place. Throughout the 1930s and early 1940s, there was relatively little interest in or effort made toward determining how afflicted individuals might be systematically helped to return to the community. After World War II, however, this state of affairs began to change. The 1943 amendments to the United States Vocational Rehabilitation Act extended financial support and vocational rehabilitation services to the psychiatrically disabled. With the advent of effective neuroleptic treatments for schizophrenia in the 1950s and the ensuing deinstitutionalization movement in the 1960s, new hope arose within the mental health professions that even the most chronically impaired and disabled schizophrenic patients might be able to live as relatively independent members of the community. Recent long-term follow-up studies of hospitalized schizophrenics have documented that, given access to continuity of treatment and rehabilitation, upwards of one-half to two-thirds of patients were living in self-sustaining and "normalized" ways in the community (Harding et al. 1987).

In the last 20 years psychiatrists have been forced to confront a disturbing fact: while neuroleptics relieve most symptoms for most schizophrenics, they cannot begin to repair the shattered work, family, and social lives with which most patients are left. This repair requires active rehabilitation efforts (Anthony and Liberman 1986). Rehabilitation mandates a treatment team approach. No one care provider can be expected to remedy vocational deficits, family problems, psychotic symptoms, lack of interpersonal skills, loneliness, and financial difficulties. In this chapter a variety of interventions that are helpful in psychiatric rehabilitation will be discussed. At various times, psychiatrists have assumed primary responsibility for each of these. It is, of course, more typical for other members of the team (e.g., social workers, nurses, psychologists, vocational counselors) to provide most of these services. Nevertheless, we believe that it is imperative that all practitioners, medical and nonmedical, be aware of the rehabilitative needs of the patient and that those treating schizophrenic patients, regardless of discipline, acquire as much expertise in them as possible.

This chapter provides an overview of the currently validated approaches in psychiatric rehabilitation for the interested psychiatrist or psychiatrist-in-training. A more detailed exposition of and practical guide to psychiatric rehabilitation can be found in other recent publications (Liberman 1986, 1987).

For effective and efficient rehabilitation of individuals with schizophrenic disorders, the design and testing of interventions should proceed from a theoretical mapping of the biologic, behavioral, and environmental factors implicated in affecting the course and outcome of the disorders. In the vulnerability-stress-protective model, course and outcome of schizophrenia are in dynamic flux, influenced by environmental, biologic, and personal variables. This model assumes that psychotic symptoms and their accompanying behavioral disabilities emerge or are exacerbated when stressors impinge upon an individual with an underlying and enduring psychobiologic vulnerability to schizophrenic disorder. This vulnerability is manifested by probable genetic predisposition, putative neurotransmitter abnormalities in the central nervous system, and other unknown neurologic factors resulting in cognitive, autonomic, and attentional dysfunctions and poor premorbid social adjustment.

The importance of protective factors that mitigate the impact of stressors superimposed on vulnerability are significant to rehabilitation. Symptom formation and adaptation are bidirectional with the balance potentially determined by the active role of the patient's coping skills and support system in promoting favorable outcomes. The interactional nature of the model clearly targets therapeutic objectives and modalities for interventions. The clinician may prescribe neuroleptic drugs to buffer against the effects of the underlying behavioral factors. From another perspective, environmental modification can be employed to ameliorate the noxious effects of stressors on the vulnerable individual. This accounts for some of the value of hospitalization as asylum, in which the patient is removed temporarily from stressors in family and community settings. Structured, community-based, aftercare environments such as social clubs, day treatment centers, and sheltered workshops can be effective in providing patients with support to compensate for deficits in their community living skills. In addition, treatment such as case management and family therapy may indirectly confer protection against stress and vulnerability by strengthening the patient's social support network.

Neuroleptic drugs are effective in reducing positive symptoms such as delusions and hallucinations, but some patients are refractory to or even worsened by drugs, especially in high doses, and others experience rapid relapse or continuing social and vocational handicaps even with symptomatic improvement and continued medication. The negative or deficit symptoms (Andreasen 1982) of chronic schizophrenia pose a largely unanswered challenge to medical and other treatments. Social withdrawal, apathy, anergy, poor self-care, and anhedonia do not respond well to available treatments. Drugs do not teach life and coping skills either, except indirectly through the removal or reduction of positive symptoms. Most schizophrenic persons need to learn or relearn social and personal skills for survival in the community. The acquisition of living skills, another source of protection from stress and vulnerability, is usually facilitated by the concurrent administration of judicious doses of psychotropic drugs.

The multifactorial and interactional nature of this model of schizophrenic disorder enables the clinician to locate targets suitable for therapeutic goals and interventions. Other chapters of this APA Task Force Report amply describe the value of neuroleptic drugs, other somatic treatments, and psychotherapies for ameliorating psychotic symptoms, delaying relapse, and enhancing adaptation. In this chapter, we will emphasize how behavioral therapies can 1) buffer the noxiousness of stressors through environmental modifications; 2) strengthen the patient's social support network as seen in behavioral family therapy and job clubs; 3) weaken or interrupt psychotic symptoms and bizarre behavior through changing their environmental antecedents and consequences; 4) strengthen patients' assets and competencies, which protect them from future stressors; and 5) interact with pharmacotherapy to yield better outcomes than could be achieved by either modality alone.

Distinctiveness of Behavioral Rehabilitation

Behavioral procedures occupy an increasingly important position among clinical interventions for modifying symptomatic characteristics of schizophrenia and for relearning adaptive skills through well structured learning experiences (Liberman 1976; Wong et al. 1986). The principal distinction between behavioral and other psychosocial approaches to schizophrenia is the firm adherence to specification and measurement by practitioners of behavioral analysis and therapy. In this theoretical framework, psychotic dysfunctions are analyzed in terms of behavioral excesses (e.g., delusional verbalizations), behavioral deficits (e.g., inadequate social skills), and poor behavior-environment fit (e.g., inappropriate affect). Treatment entails alteration of antecedent and consequent stimuli surrounding the problem areas to supplant and suppress psychotic behaviors and to teach and strengthen adaptive skills.

Individuals with schizophrenic disorders may require accentuated prompts, gradual and prolonged shaping of new responses, tangible reinforcement, and other socioenvironmental aids for rehabilitative training; however, their behavior is seen as influenced and determined by the same learning and motivational processes as those that govern the actions of other human beings (Ullmann and Krasner 1969). The modifiability of psychotic behaviors is constrained by the degree of biologic vulnerability and the limitations of environmental resources and consistency (Liberman 1983). While most psychosocial rehabilitation programs currently define their efforts as educational and skill-building, they differ widely in the degree to which they systematically apply behavioral learning principles, and thus in their effectiveness. Positive reinforcement may implicitly occur for appropriate social behavior in a self-help social club or a foster home, but unless it is provided consistently and frequently following that behavior, only higher-functioning and more self-directed persons with schizophrenia are likely to benefit.

Individuals with core psychobiologic dysfunctions that appear to be trait markers in schizophrenia (Nuechterlein and Dawson 1984) have cognitive impairments that require precise and structured training techniques in order for durable social and living skills to be acquired (Liberman et al. 1985). These techniques can be used in hospitals, community mental health centers, vocational settings, home-based family therapy, and clinics or private offices. Behavioral rehabilitation is individualized by specific goal setting and enhanced by active involvement of patients and relatives in the evaluation and treatment enterprise. Techniques are drawn from learning theory (Bandura 1979) and optimized by appropriate psychotropic drug therapy. Behavioral skills are trained most effectively when the learning process is infused by knowledge of psychopathology (Liberman 1982).

Rehabilitation strategies will be presented first for several notable domains of behavioral deviance in schizophrenia. These include social skills deficits, inadequate self-care, bizarre behavior, and lack of vocational skills. Next, innovative and educationally based family interventions that have resulted in marked reductions of symptomatic relapse will be described. Finally, comprehensive treatment programs, both in hospitals and communities that employ behavioral therapies, will be delineated.

Social Skills Training

Social skills training teaches patients specific interpersonal skills and then promotes the maintenance and generalization of these skills through systematic utilization of behavioral learning techniques. In contrast, informal socialization activities can lead to acquisition of skills through incidental learning during spontaneous social interactions. Many schizophrenic patients have learning disabilities that necessitate the use of highly directive behavioral techniques for training social skills. Several training models are available for tailoring to the needs of the individual patient: 1) standard social skills training, 2) a problem-solving model for skills training, and (3) an attention-focusing procedure.

Standard Social Skills Training

Standard training shapes patients' behavior by reinforcing successive approximations of appropriate verbal and nonverbal skills (Liberman et al. 1975). These include assertive responses (Eisler et al. 1978; Hersen et al. 1978), nonverbal behaviors such as eye contact and smiles (Edelstein and Eisler 1976; Kolko et al. 1981), paralinguistic behaviors such as voice volume or speech duration (Eisler et al. 1973; Finch and Wallace 1977), conversational skills such as asking questions and giving compliments (Holmes et al. in press; Urey et al. 1979), community-based instrumental skills (King et al. 1977), and job interview skills (Furman et al. 1979; Kelly et al. 1979). In a typical session the patient role-plays a problematic interpersonal situation with another patient or trainer. The scenes mirror, as much as possible, real and significant life events. After role-playing the scene, the patient receives constructive feedback from the therapist. Positive aspects of the performance are emphasized along with areas that need improvement. Feedback may be accomplished by a videotaped playback of positive segments of the patient's performance. The therapist may also model behaviors that the patient needs to improve. Active coaching, with cueing and prompting, may be offered during the role playing. Following modeling, the patient is asked to repeat the scene and the process begins again. This technique can be used with groups, individuals, or family therapy and can be carried out in hospitals or community-based settings. Standard social skills training procedures have been effective with many chronic psychiatric patients (Christoff and Kelly, in press; McFall 1982; Wallace et al. 1980). Some patients, however, have not shown improvement from standard social skills training (Argyle et al. 1974; Bellack et al. 1976), and the generalizability and durability of treatment gains may be limited (Liberman et al. 1984).

Problem-Solving Social Skills Training

The problem-solving approach to interpersonal skills encompasses three necessary components aimed at enhancing generalization: 1) receiving skills, which include attending to and accurately perceiving cues and contextual elements of interpersonal situations; 2) processing skills, which include generating response alternatives, weighing the consequences of each alternative, and selecting optimal options; and 3) sending skills, using the chosen option for an effective social response that integrates both verbal and nonverbal behaviors.

Interpersonal scenes having both affiliative and instrumental goals are role-played and videotaped as in the standard model. After role playing, the patient is asked specific questions to assess, reinforce, and correct his or her receiving and processing skills. The therapist also assists the patient in considering resources that may be required to employ the skills being learned (e.g., transportation to attend a social club or medication clinic) and in learning ways of obtaining them. With the therapist's coaching, the patient also anticipates obstacles to implementing successfully the learned skills and ways to surmount these obstacles.

Attention-Focusing Procedure

This procedure was designed for chronic schizophrenic patients with severe cognitive, memory, and attentional impairments that preclude them from participating collaboratively in group-based training. The procedure helps focus the patient's attention on relevant training steps while minimizing demands on cognitive abilities (Mosk et al. 1983). This procedure is characterized by multiple, discrete, relatively short training trials that are initiated by the trainer making a statement that serves as a prompt for conversational response by the patient. If the patient makes a correct response he is praised and provided with a small consumable (e.g., food, cigarette). If a correct response is not forthcoming, the trainer implements a prompting sequence. The trainer presents the same statement to the patient and prompts a correct response. The statement is redelivered until he responds correctly several times in succession. After acquisition of the response, the patient is trained in responses to new conversational statements. Typically, patients are taught to make eight to 12 alternative responses in each domain of conversational skills. A study by Massel et al. (1985) found this attention-focusing procedure more effective than standard social skills training with thought-disordered schizophrenic patients.

Personal Grooming Training

Patients need adequate social, vocational, and independent living skills to be maintained successfully in the community. For chronic schizophrenic patients, psychotic symptoms and long hospital stays are typically associated with severe impairments in previous levels of functioning. Even the ability to perform the most basic personal hygiene tasks may be lost due to confusion, apathy, and scarce access to grooming accessories. Psychiatric patients often adopt bizarre styles of make-up, hair, and dress, and their clothes and hair are frequently unkempt. While the debate over the extent to which poor self-care may contribute to their illness has yet to be resolved (Farina et al. 1977; Sussman and Mueser 1983), every service provider working with chronic schizophrenic patients is aware of these deficits in personal grooming.

Deficits in personal hygiene and grooming are among the most stigmatizing features in our culture. Individuals with bizarre dress or who are poorly groomed are frequently ostracized. For schizophrenics, who are likely to already be at a disadvantage due to small networks and deficits in social skills, further ostracism as a result of personal characteristics is especially burdensome. Improvements in hygiene and appearance can be an important first step in the rehabilitative normalization process and can create the potential for the development of social relationships.

Since grooming involves a series of discrete, teachable, and observable components (e.g., tooth brushing, hair combing), it is not surprising that behavioral rehabilitation programs often include training in personal hygiene. One such training approach, successfully developed and implemented at Camarillo State Hospital in California (Wong et al. 1987) begins by training a small group of patients through the use of verbal prompts, modeling, and physical prompts. Grooming goals are specifically defined as clean face, clean hands, hair combed, and clothes neat and appropriate. This specification of objectives is an important element of behavioral training programs. As tangible reinforcers are frequently limited in residential facilities and since social reinforcement is such a critical aspect of personal appearance, the training program emphasizes the use of verbal praise as the primary reinforcer. Training sessions are conducted in front of mirrors, and patients are aided in developing accurate self-assessments and making self-reinforcing verbal statements regarding their improving appearance.

In a pilot study, fifteen 15-minute training sessions led to a 72 percent increase over pretraining levels in the grooming criteria met by four chronic schizophrenics. These improvements were maintained at six-week follow-up. In a wardwide study, grooming training sessions led to a 63 percent posttraining improvement in appearance as measured by staff ratings of 11 factors. This improvement was maintained at six-month follow-up.

Vocational Rehabilitation

While sheltered employment of chronic schizophrenics has a long and utilitarian history extending back to the era of moral treatment in the early nineteenth century, it has been superseded by new methods of vocational rehabilitation to promote movement of schizophrenic patients into gainful jobs in the marketplace. Two promising rehabilitation techniques are transitional employment and the Job Club. Both require identifying the specific work and job-finding skills necessary and the use of reinforcement and behavioral coaching to promote successful work outcomes.

Transitional Employment

Transitional employment opportunities (Beard et al. 1978) are jobs within industrial or commercial establishments that are supervised by rehabilitation professionals. The vocational rehabilitation program contracts with local businesses for the jobs and assumes responsibility for their completion. Each position is assigned to one or more patients. The patients, with staff as backups, are responsible for executing the job at industrial standards and earn the same pay as any other employee would in the same position.

Transitional employment programs were pioneered by Fountain House, a psychosocial rehabilitation club for mental patients with a variety of disorders, in league with a Sears store in New York. In the Fountain House–Sears program, Fountain House assumed responsibility for a custodial position with Sears that was previously filled with a nondisabled employee. Sears agreed to let Fountain House fill the job using as many patients as were required to get the work done. Fountain House assured Sears the job would be completed to industrial standards, even if the staff of Fountain House were required to do the work themselves. The position was split between two patients, with each receiving half of the position's full salary. Each patient worked half a day under the supervision of a Fountain House therapist who counseled the patients directly in their vocational and social situations. The patients remained on the job for three or four months before moving on to their own nonsupervised job, at which time different patients were placed in the position.

Transitional employment offers the patient experience in a competitive position while still having access to therapeutic staff. Patients also have the opportunity to earn a normal wage. By working with a transitional employment program, the "host" business is assured that the position will be filled, the work will be completed, and that they are contributing to their public service image.

Quasi-experimental and randomized controlled trials of transitional employment programs for the chronically mentally ill have been carried out at the Thresholds psychosocial rehabilitation center in Chicago. A very gradual approach to vocational training, using a stepwise progression from volunteer jobs and work adjustment rotations to transitional employment and finally competitive employment, did not appear to yield better nine-month employment rates than those for controls who received no special vocational programming. However, when a more accelerated rehabilitation effort was mounted that launched patients into paid transitional employment within one month of entering the psychosocial center, employment rates almost doubled over those achieved with the more gradual approach (Bond et al. 1984).

Job Club

The Job Club program was developed to instruct and motivate marginally skilled and unemployed individuals in searching for and finding employment (Azrin and Besalel 1980; Azrin and May 1979; Azrin et al. 1975). In its adaptation to unemployed schizophrenic persons, the responsibility for finding a job is shared between the patient and rehabilitation staff. The program assumes that finding a job requires a full-time effort. Patients who are deemed ready for the arduous job search are expected to participate in the program on a full-time basis daily. There are three distinct segments in the Job Club: training in job-seeking skills, the job search itself, and follow-up and job maintenance. While the program has no time limit, successful participants spend an average of 23 days in the program before obtaining employment. For successful participation in the Job Club, schizophrenic patients must be in good remission of their symptoms prior to entry. They must also have held a job within two years of joining the club.

Training in job-seeking skills. During the first week of the program, patients learn basic job-seeking skills (e.g., locating sources of job leads, looking for a job, completing job applications and resumes, appropriate grooming and dressing skills, and interviewing skills). Instruction is based on competency with trainers using programmed materials, didactic instruction, role playing, and in vivo training exercises.

Job search. After completing the job-seeking skills workshop, patients begin a job search. The program provides some of the resources needed to conduct a job search to assist patients in finding jobs. Resources include telephones, desks, fresh leads, secretarial support, and counselors. At the start of each day counselors and patients identify the most advantageous options for the day's job search. They develop outcome expectations for the daily activities, set a time line for accomplishment of each task, and carry out problem solving of potential stumbling blocks that may be encountered during the day. Patients are expected to keep a log of their daily job-seeking activities and account for their time in the program. Monetary token reinforcement systems in conjunction with counselor social support have been used effectively to motivate patients to participate (Jacobs et al. 1984).

Follow-up and job maintenance activities. Job Club graduates are encouraged to attend weekly sessions that teach methods of dealing with problems that threaten job security. Training adheres to a problem-solving model of specifying solutions to an identified issue and role-playing those solutions with feedback before the patient uses the approach in his work setting. Training issues are identified by the participants. Graduates are also free to return to the program if they lose their jobs or wish to upgrade their positions.

Job Clubs have been found to be reasonably effective with psychiatric patients. The Brentwood (Los Angeles, Calif) VA Job Finding Club found that 65 percent of patients entering the program began full-time employment or vocational training following an average of 23 days of participation. At six-month follow-up, almost two-thirds of these individuals were still working. Of patients obtaining employment, approximately 50 percent were diagnosed as schizophrenic. These results stand in contrast with the frequently replicated finding that approximately 20 percent of formerly hospitalized patients are able to secure employment (Anthony et al. 1978). One of the most impressive findings has been that schizophrenia alone does not necessarily preclude the likelihood of finding employment. A study of over 200 Brentwood Job

Finding Club participants indicated that duration of illness and diagnosis did not predict vocational placement. Participation in the Job Club appeared to be the most important determinant, with other predictors of successful outcome being severity of symptoms and age. More recent evaluative findings from the Job Club indicate that schizophrenic persons who are receiving social security pensions, have not worked in two years or longer, and have persisting psychotic symptoms are unlikely to find employment in this program.

Family Interventions

Schizophrenia has an adverse impact, not only on the individual diagnosed with the disorder, but also on his or her family. Family members typically find themselves distressed by the patient's bizarre and asocial behavior; anxious about increased financial burdens for the patient's therapy, medication, and sustenance; uncertain about future plans; and isolated from their own social supports due to time limitations and social embarrassment (Creer and Wing 1974). Even the strongest families can be expected to show signs of strain when a member exhibits schizophrenic symptoms, and increased family stress may be a contributing factor to further symptom exacerbations for the patient (Zubin and Spring 1977).

A variety of family-oriented interventions has been designed to improve the functioning of persons with schizophrenia and their families. One of the most promising recent developments in the treatment of schizophrenia has been the parallel growth of educationally oriented programs in the United States and England for individuals with schizophrenia and their families. Unlike more traditional family therapies, these innovations do not assume that family process has an etiologic influence on the development of schizophrenia. Instead, they are based on the premise that reductions in family stress will have ameliorative and preventive effects on schizophrenic symptoms.

Behavioral family management (Falloon et al. 1984; Liberman et al. 1981), the multiple family social intervention approach (Leff et al. 1982), and psychoeducational family therapy (Anderson et al. 1986) are examples of practical, educationally based treatment for families of schizophrenics. These therapies are offered as an adjunct to appropriate neuroleptic regimens and case management activities and can be delivered in a hospital, clinic, or home. These approaches emphasize providing family members with current scientific thinking on the etiology of schizophrenia, current treatment options (including details on medication and side effects), and useful coping skills. Efforts are concentrated on modifying current family coping *behavior* and problem-solving efforts rather than the underlying family structure. Therapists are directive, providing much support and information and facilitating the development of communication and problem-solving skills.

Research assessment of family education, including controlled studies, indicates that these programs reduce relapse rates (e.g., reemergence or exacerbation of existing symptoms) substantially. For example, in a carefully controlled study of 36 young adult schizophrenics, Falloon et al. (1982) found that, nine months after hospital discharge, only 22 percent of 18 patients who had been randomly assigned to supportive individual aftercare were free of florid schizophrenic symptoms, whereas 56 percent of the 18 patients assigned to the family therapy conditions were in remission (p < 0.01). Two-year follow-ups revealed that 83 percent of the individually treated patients but only 22 percent of the patients assigned to the family therapy experienced exacerbations of psychotic symptoms. In addition, family participants in behavioral family management reported significantly greater reductions in mental and physical problems and patient-imposed burden than were reported by those in the comparison condition (Falloon and Pederson 1985).

Similarly, Leff et al. (1982, 1985) found that schizophrenics from families randomly assigned to receive multiple family social intervention treatment experienced significantly fewer symptoms than those in the traditional treatment condition. Nine percent of patients in the social intervention condition and 50 percent of patients in the control condition relapsed by the nine-month follow-up. This clear superiority of social intervention was still maintained at two years posttreatment, when only 33 percent of the patients in the multiple family social intervention group had relapsed while 83 percent of the control patients had. The family therapy was found to reduce the level of relatives' criticism significantly, a factor that has been associated with heightened likelihood of relapse among individuals with schizophrenia. A report of combined family therapy plus social skills training and low-dose neuroleptic drugs found one-year relapse rates to be zero, compared to 41 percent for patients randomly assigned to drug therapy and customary aftercare (Hogarty et al. 1986).

Inpatient Behavioral Rehabilitation

Despite the advent of neuroleptic medications and the availability of community mental health care centers and community support programs for schizophrenic patients, a residual population of severely impaired, unskilled, and treatment-refractory patients has resisted most efforts at deinstitutionalization. Rehabilitation of this hardcore group of chronic patients requires harnessing all of the behavioral methods described above in a comprehensive, round-the-clock social learning program in patients' living environments.

Utilizing behavioral assessment and therapy, highly trained paraprofessionals and nursing staff have been successful in remediating the bizarre symptoms and social and self-care deficits of most chronic schizophrenic patients. Combining an elegant experimental design with rigorous pursuit of relevant clinical goals, Paul and Lentz (1977) compared the social learning approach with therapeutic community methods and customary custodial care. They found that the results clearly indicated the efficacy of the behavioral approach, even though both the social learning and therapeutic community approaches included the same structured activities and were conducted by the same staff who rotated between the two units.

These investigators randomly assigned 84 long-term, schizophrenic (DSM-II diagnoses) patients to state hospital units utilizing social learning, milieu therapy, or traditional custodial care approaches. The social learning program employed a highly specific token economy with many hours of structured educational activities throughout the day. Patients were positively reinforced with praise and tokens for productive, appropriate behavior (e.g., cleaning rooms, attending classes, grooming) and fined tokens or ignored, or both, for inappropriate activities (e.g., yelling, assaults). They could exchange tokens for backup reinforcers such as consumables (e.g., food, cigarettes) and privileges (e.g., access to grounds). Patients were held accountable for behavior and were provided with training in social skills to equip them for community living.

The milieu program was based on a therapeutic community structure wherein all patients were members of nine- or 10-person "living groups" that were assigned the tasks of identifying problems and promoting change among individual members.

The major vehicle for promoting change was the social and group pressure exerted by living groups on their members. As in the social learning group, patients were scheduled to spend the majority of their time in structured life skills or academic classes. Patients in both programs were scheduled to be in formal treatment 85 percent of their waking time.

A multimodal assessment battery, including reliable time-sampled behavioral observations and nurses' ratings of behavior, revealed impressive and clear-cut results favoring the social learning approach. Improved functioning, enabling long-term community tenure, occurred in 97 percent of the patients in the social learning program. The therapeutic community program was less effective, but its 71 percent release and community maintenance rate was still a favorable outcome when compared to the 45 percent rate for patients released from custodial care and living in the community for 18 months or longer. Differences among the three groups were highly statistically significant. Importantly, the social learning program was clearly the most cost-effective of the three when decreased need for continued hospitalization was included in cost calculations. While the social learning and therapeutic community programs were both slightly more expensive than custodial care on a daily basis ($10.47 versus $10.29 in 1970 dollars), the social learning program resulted in shorter hospital stays, such that average cost over length of stay was $11,794 for social learning patients, $15,252 for therapeutic community patients, and $17,506 for custodial care patients.

The apparently outstanding success in sustaining patients in the community was mirrored by significant clinical and behavioral improvements, which even produced a minority of patients who, by direct observational ratings, could not be distinguished from a normal population. After only 14 weeks of treatment, every resident in the social learning program showed dramatic improvements in overall functioning, regardless of usual prognostic indicators such as duration of hospitalization and pretreatment level of impairment. By the end of the second year of programming, fewer than 25 percent of residents in either experimental condition were on maintenance psychotropic drugs. Two clinically significant conclusions reached by the study were 1) that when older chronic schizophrenics were given active and structured psychosocial therapies, they had little need for maintenance neuroleptic drugs and 2) that it is not how much attention and enthusiasm is offered to patients by staff, but how that attention is given that makes a difference. Patients in the therapeutic community program had more overall staff interaction but improved less than their counterparts in the social learning program.

There are only a few social learning inpatient units for psychiatric patients nationwide, in contrast to the many existing for the developmentally disabled (Boudewyns and Fry 1986). One such program is located at the Clinical Research Unit at Camarillo State Hospital, California, the longest running token economy in a U.S. psychiatric residential facility. The unit's day-to-day programming and token economy are very similar to those used in the Paul and Lentz study. Patients are referred to the Clinical Research Unit when standard hospital programming proves ineffective. On the unit they are provided with training in personal grooming, social skills, room cleanup, and appropriate meal behavior. Special programs also are developed for each patient's unique behavioral problems (e.g., verbal aggression, polydipsia), thus increasing the likelihood of discharge (Liberman et al. 1974b).

Most of the patients' days are structured with specific activities and frequent training sessions as a number of studies indicated that patients exhibit less deviant behavior when they are engaged in formal activities (Liberman et al. 1974b; Rosen et al. 1981). Special attention is paid to helping patients learn to pursue recreational activities. As a series of studies conducted on the Clinical Research Unit indicated, patients' bizarre behavior is reduced when they are engaged in active leisure pursuits (Wong et al. 1987).

Behavioral interventions developed on the Clinical Research Unit have been successful in increasing the social skills of chronic schizophrenics (Massel et al. 1985), controlling the aggressive behavior of treatment-refractory schizophrenics, as well as that of patients with other major psychiatric disorders (Glynn et al. in press), and reducing delusional speech among schizophrenics (Liberman et al. 1973). During its 15 years of operation, 42 percent (38) of the patients referred to the Clinical Research Unit as refractory and requiring more intensive treatment have been discharged into the community, with half of them being successfully maintained in the community postdischarge (length of follow-up ranged from six months to five years) (Banzett et al. 1984). While these percentages are somewhat less than those found by Paul and Lentz, it should be noted that the Clinical Research Unit services clients who are referred for being the most intractable among those in a typical refractory state hospital population.

Behavioral Rehabilitation in Community Mental Health

Responding to the failure of community mental health centers to serve the needs of the chronically mentally ill, Liberman and his associates developed, evaluated, and disseminated behavior therapy modules for skills training in a typical health center. Outpatient, continuing care, and day treatment programs were studied and found to be effective in remediating behavioral deficits of the severely psychiatrically disabled (Liberman and Bryan 1977; Liberman et al. 1976).

As an alternative to and transition from more costly inpatient care, the day treatment center became a focal point for the implementation of behavioral rehabilitation (Liberman et al. 1974a). The services provided in the day hospital were tailored to the needs of individual patients. Upon admission, a functional assessment was conducted identifying each patient's strengths and weaknesses. Treatment goals were determined from this assessment, with input from the patient and relatives. Typically, three to four short-term goals were worked on concurrently. The day hospital engaged patients for six hours a day in an educational program that featured a standard curriculum with scheduled activities and responsibilities. Patients were called "students" to emphasize the educational thrust of the program and to diminish stigma.

A credit incentive system or token economy was implemented in the day treatment center to provide extrinsic motivation for patients' participation in activities. Credits aimed at overcoming the anhedonia and apathy of chronic patients yielded increases in participation of 50 to 100 percent. Upon entry into the program patients were given "credit cards"; credits were earned by participation in therapy or training groups for social and conversational skills, grooming, vocational preparedness, personal finances, shopping on a budget, and anxiety management. Credits were also earned by completing homework assignments in these groups and for developing and achieving personalized goals with a therapist. Other ways to earn credits included prompt arrival at the day hospital, cooking, and dusting furniture.

The backup reinforcers used for credit exchanges included coffee, lunch, outings, time off from the day hospital, private time with a therapist, sitting in a desirable chair, and using the stereo. More important than material awards, however, was the lively interest, praise, and recognition granted by the staff to patients when credits were earned. The credit system, in fact, cued staff members to attend to patients when the latter were demonstrating appropriate social and adaptive behavior (Liberman et al. 1977). A weekly record was maintained on the totals of credits earned and spent by each patient and was reported back to the assembled group of patients and staff together at the community meeting. Patients with the highest number of earned credits were awarded special reinforcers such as free movie passes.

A number of more recent studies indicate that day treatment centers provide behaviorally oriented treatment and rehabilitation and are more effective than other centers with less structured and organized programs. In addition, programs that successfully engage patients in adaptive behavior and endeavor to help patients develop skills are especially influential (Austin et al. 1976; Linn et al. 1980; Milne 1984; Spiegler and Agijian 1977).

Case Management

Whether provided in large institutions or community clinics, behavioral rehabilitation needs to be orchestrated to meet the specific needs of individual patients. Patients' needs change over the lifelong course of schizophrenia (Liberman 1984). Linking patients' needs for treatment and community support with available resources is the process of case management.

Individuals with schizophrenic disorders are frequently resistant to treatment, incapable of securing entitlements for which they are eligible, and unable to mobilize and use community supports. They are, therefore, largely invisible to the public service agencies on whom they theoretically depend for care. Furthermore, an adequate system of community supports is frequently not available even if the patient seeks or accepts treatment. Agencies not specifically designed to work with the mentally ill are especially reluctant to get involved. In addition, the complex and diverse needs of schizophrenics and other chronically mentally ill persons exceed the resources available. Community resistance and stigma have also created barriers to the allocation of funds to develop the needed services. In actuality, community care has become a labyrinth that is functionally inaccessible to many chronically mentally ill patients (National Institute of Mental Health 1977).

Case management can assist chronic mental patients in maximizing their use of existing resources and thereby increase their independence and quality of life. Case management is designed to coordinate the range of services needed by the chronically mentally ill, helping to ensure accountability, continuity of care, accessibility, and efficiency (Intagliata 1982). Case management includes the following functions:

- client identification and outreach;
- individual assessment;
- service planning;
- linkage with required services;
- monitoring of service delivery; and
- client advocacy.

While these functions are often provided by nonmedical personal, supervision and treatment planning should be led by a psychiatrist who is trained and experienced in the care of the chronically mentally ill.

Identification of patients to be served is prerequisite to other case management services. In many cases patients are identified through referrals from mental health professionals and agencies, friends, family, and the patient himself. Unfortunately, many chronically ill persons do not independently seek out assistance, they are not in contact with mental health agencies, and they do not have social support networks. These circumstances necessitate creative attempts at outreach on the part of the case manager (Turner and TenHoor 1978). Case managers are often nurses, social workers, or paraprofessionals who are able to be sustained in their arduous tasks by setting realistic goals and feeling rewarded by small and slow signs of progress.

Assessment of the patient is ideally initiated immediately following referral and should include a detailed assessment of the patient's strengths, deficits, and potential for independent living (Leavitt 1982). The patient's current level of functioning, as well as his or her highest level of functioning prior to hospitalization, needs to be considered. The results of the assessment provide information for making judgments about the patient's requirements for specialized resources that need to be included in the service plan.

The service plan should be a comprehensive written document that can be updated as necessary, based upon the information obtained from the patient assessments. It is imperative that the patient and relatives be involved in the planning (Intagliata 1982; Marlowe 1982). Service plans usually include the following: clearly defined priority areas for needed services; within each of the areas, short- and long-term measurable goals that can be used to evaluate patient progress; specific actions that must be taken to meet the goals; agencies to which the patient is referred; realistic time frames for completing activities; and identification of potential barriers to service utilization and delivery as well as proposed solutions to these problems.

The next step involves linking the patient to the necessary services. This involves not only referring the patient, but doing whatever is necessary to get him or her to the service. This may include providing transportation, establishing interagency agreements, or following up on referrals.

After services have been secured, the case manager needs to monitor the services to assure that the patient receives what is expected and that the services remain appropriate to the patient's needs. The case manager therefore needs to maintain ongoing contact with both the patient and all service providers (Scott and Cassidy 1981). Ideally the case manager should observe the actual services being delivered to the patient. The patient should also be given the opportunity to evaluate the services rendered.

The final responsibility of the case manager is advocacy. Typically, long-term mentally ill persons have not been seen as a priority population, yet they require a multiplicity of services, thus making advocacy a necessity. Advocacy needs to be utilized both for the individual patient's needs and for the medical and social agencies to increase the allocation of resources and give a higher priority for chronically mentally ill individuals and their relatives. At the patient level the case manager needs to assist the patient in receiving all benefits to which he or she is entitled (Willets 1982). At the systems level the advocate applies pressure to service providers for improvements in scope, quality, and accessibility of services (Beatrice 1979). Research is only beginning to identify the elements in case management and other comprehensive rehabilitation programs that are responsible for sustained community tenure and improved quality of life (Franklin et al. 1987; Hoult and Reynolds 1984; Stein and Test 1980; Witheridge and Dincin 1985).

Interactions Between Antipsychotic Drugs and Psychosocial Treatment

The interaction between antipsychotic medication and psychosocial treatment can be mutually facilitative if the combination is offered in judicious ways and keyed to the stage of a patient's disorder (Liberman et al. 1984). Antipsychotic medication, appropriately used, facilitates cognitive functions and therefore enhances the patient's ability to acquire new skills and to utilize other forms of assistance. Psychosocial management and treatment, on the other hand, may enable patients to be treated with lower dosages of neuroleptics and thus reduce the patient's risk of experiencing side effects (Falloon 1985). Studies have shown that antipsychotic medication combined with certain cost-effective and practical behavioral forms of treatment is superior to drugs used alone (Falloon and Liberman 1983; Hogarty et al. 1974; Linn et al. 1980). Further, it has been shown that drugs combined with behaviorally oriented day treatment produce significantly greater improvements in social functioning of chronic mental patients than when drugs were combined with customary psychosocial therapies (Liberman et al. 1976; Linn et al. 1980; Spiegler and Agijian 1977).

The combination of family therapy with drug therapy is one of the more promising treatment strategies. Goldstein et al. (1978) randomly assigned 96 schizophrenic patients to two psychosocial and two neuroleptic dosage treatment conditions (family therapy versus no family therapy and biweekly fluphenazine decanoate 25 mg versus 6.25 mg dosage). The six-week, brief, crisis-oriented family intervention educated patients and their families about the relationship between exacerbations of schizophrenia and stress and also helped to identify strategies for enhancing coping. The six-month relapse rate was 10 percent for patients receiving brief family therapy plus 25 mg of fluphenazine decanoate. Medication dosage levels and family therapy provided important independent benefits.

Obviously, noncompliance with medication regimens greatly reduces the potential benefits patients receive from drug therapy. Chronic schizophrenic outpatients have been found to have high rates of noncompliance, ranging from 40 percent (Van Putten 1974) to 55 percent (Irwin et al. 1971). To improve adherence to maintenance neuroleptic regimens, a comprehensive program for teaching chronic schizophrenic patients how to manage their own medications was developed at the West Los Angeles VA Medical Center, Brentwood Division (Liberman and Evans 1985; Liberman and Foy 1983; Wallace et al. 1985). The medication management module was designed to teach patients four sets of skills: 1) knowledge about medications, 2) safe self-administration, 3) identification of side effects, and 4) negotiating with the physician. In each skill area, patients progress through a sequence of learning activities. The activities include 1) providing a rationale and promoting motivation, 2) videotape modeling of the skills followed by questions and answers, 3) role-playing exercises to practice the skills shown in the video, 4) identifying resources needed to implement the skills and ways to obtain the resources, 5) anticipating barriers to the use of the skills in the natural environment, 6) in vivo exercises, and 7) homework assignments with booster training sessions as needed.

This module was validated using single-subject experimental designs and field tests in typical clinical settings throughout the United States and Canada. Measurements were taken in role-playing exercises designed to simulate real life situations in which patients would need to exhibit the skills that were learned. The results indicated that while patients' performance varied across the four skill areas in the module, they were able to acquire the requisite skills and maintain mastery for at least a three-month follow-up period (Wallace et al. 1985).

Conclusion

Treatment programs for the chronic schizophrenic patient population can be effectively designed and implemented using as a blueprint the view that the course and outcome of schizophrenic disorders are determined by the confluence of an individual's "stress-vulnerability-coping-competence." At any one stage of the disorder, the afflicted individual's impairments and disabilities are minimized by factors (coping and competence as well as neuroleptic drugs) that confer protection from the noxious effects of stress and psychobiological vulnerability. In league with judicious administration of psychotropic drugs and comprehensive community support programs, rehabilitation techniques derived from behavioral learning principles can be clinically effective for both positive and negative symptoms of schizophrenia and for remediating the deficits in self-care, socialization, and work that interfere with community adaptation.

Social skills training methods represent a major strategy for psychiatric rehabilitation. Building skills in patients with schizophrenic and other major mental disorders is based upon the assumption that coping and competence can override stress and vulnerability in reducing relapses and improving psychosocial functioning. For maximum efficiency, skills training needs to incorporate procedures and principles of human learning and information processing. The technology for social skills training has matured, and the empirical validation for its efficacy has grown in the last decade. Its use, however, is still limited to a small number of behaviorally oriented practitioners, of whom very few are psychiatrists. Although many clinics and institutions offer socialization groups for chronically mentally ill patients, few offer structured and systematic social skills training. Fewer still train mental health professionals in these behavioral modalities.

It is important to select the type of training model that will meet the specific needs of the individual patient and his or her stage of disorder. Several models for skills training have been designed and evaluated, each of which has proven to be effective in raising the social competence of chronic schizophrenic patients. The standard model involves role playing by the patient and modeling, prompting, feedback, and reinforcement by the therapist. A problem-solving method of training provides general strategies for dealing with a wide variety of social situations. This model also uses role playing to enhance behavioral performance but highlights the patient's abilities to perceive accurately and to process incoming social messages and meanings. An attention-focusing model, involving discrete training trials that focus the patient's attention on relevant training steps, has been effective with more disabled, thought-disordered schizophrenic patients. It is essential that social skills training be imbedded in a comprehensive program of rehabilitation that features continuity of care, case management, therapeutic relationships, supervised housing, vocational rehabilitation, and judicious prescription of psychotropic drugs.

The controversy over the durability and generalizability of behavioral rehabilitation methods has subsided in recent years with the recognition that training methods must include techniques for assuring transfer of skills to the natural environments of patients. A number of techniques for promoting generalization has been introduced, including 1) issuing "homework assignments" to patients; 2) involving relatives and other community-based caregivers in the rehabilitation program; 3) training patients to use general problem-solving strategies across a broad range of socially challenging situations; 4) building reinforcement contingencies into the patient's natural environments to sustain and strengthen the skills learned in a hospital, clinic, or community center; and 5) fading the frequency and structure of training and adding booster sessions to maintain the skills acquired during more intensive training experiences.

As experience matures in the behavioral rehabilitation of chronic schizophrenics, training activities will be less and less separated from the patient's everyday world and will more and more be fully integrated with it. Training will increasingly occur not solely in settings convenient to the clinician but also in homes, workplaces, schools, stores, and other environments where skills are actually used. Potent reinforcers (i.e., money, edibles, privileges, praise), so crucial in overcoming motivational and cognitive deficits found in schizophrenics, will be more widely accepted as "prostheses" for this population (Liberman et al. 1987).

There is evidence that family tension and stress, experienced as a natural consequence of living with a severe and chronically schizophrenic person in the home, affects the course of schizophrenic illness in negative ways (Imber-Mintz et al. 1987). This relationship between course of illness and emotional climate of the home suggests the need for family intervention and assistance. Newly designed behavioral and educational treatments, which emphasize educating the family about the nature of the illness and useful ways of coping, have been developed and implemented with success. These innovations should hearten the practitioner and guide the implementation of such programs in the general community.

Deficits in personal hygiene represent a major problem and stigma for individuals with schizophrenia; thus, it is encouraging to note the development of successful grooming training programs that are low cost and time-limited. While the long-term effects of such training have yet to be fully established, their immediate benefits have been clearly demonstrated (Wong et al. 1987). In addition, grooming training provides patients with highly visible success experiences that should help motivate them for further training in other areas of community functioning. As cost-effective interventions, grooming skills training can serve as an initial component of a comprehensive psychosocial rehabilitation program.

Chronic schizophrenic patients have been shown to benefit substantially from participation in structured activities; their bizarre behavior is markedly reduced. Unfortunately, this improvement is sustained only as long as patients are involved in the activity. On the positive side, however, providing recreational opportunities to reduce bizarre behavior need not be staff-intensive. Patients benefit when materials are readily available and patients are minimally prompted and monitored for their use. Scheduling many opportunities for structured recreational and educational involvement throughout the day allows patients the optimal situation in which to become less symptomatic and more functional.

The administration of antipsychotic medications is a necessary but not sufficient strategy in the long-term community treatment of schizophrenic patients. Patients benefit most when antipsychotic medications are prescribed in moderate or low doses in combination with other forms of psychological therapy and management. Treatments that utilize behavioral techniques in combination with drug therapy have been especially effective in reducing relapse rates. Further explorations of the nature of drug-psychosocial treatment interactions are essential to the development of community management programs that seek to minimize the morbidity of schizophrenia.

References

Section 14
Schizophrenia

Abrams R, Taylor MA: Catatonia: a prospective clinical study. Arch Gen Psychiatry 33:579–581, 1976

Adler K: Adler's individual psychology, in Psychoanalytic Techniques. Edited by Wolman B. New York, Basic Books, 1967, pp 249–337

American Psychiatric Association: Diagnostic and Statistical Manual of Mental Disorders, 1st ed. Washington, DC, American Psychiatric Association, 1952

American Psychiatric Association: Diagnostic and Statistical Manual of Mental Disorders, 2nd ed. Washington, DC, American Psychiatric Association, 1968

American Psychiatric Association: Diagnostic and Statistical Manual of Mental Disorders, 3rd ed. Washington, DC, American Psychiatric Association, 1980

American Psychiatric Association: The Psychiatric Therapies. Washington, DC, American Psychiatric Association, 1984

American Psychiatric Association: Diagnostic and Statistical Manual of Mental Disorders, 3rd ed, revised. Washington, DC, American Psychiatric Association, 1987

Anderson CM: Family intervention with severely disturbed inpatients. Arch Gen Psychiatry 34:697–702, 1977

Anderson CM: The all-too-short trip from positive to negative connotation. Journal of Marriage and Family Therapy 12:351–354, 1986

Anderson CM, Hogarty GE, Reiss DJ: Family treatment of adult schizophrenic patients: a psychoeducational approach. Schizophr Bull 6:490–505, 1980

Anderson CM, Hogarty G, Reiss DJ: The psychoeducational family treatment of schizophrenia, in New Developments in Interventions with Families of Schizophrenics. Edited by Goldstein MJ. San Francisco, Jossey-Bass, 1981, pp 79–94

Anderson CM, Hogarty G, Bayer T, et al: Expressed emotion and social networks of parents of schizophrenic patients. Br J Psychiatry 144:247–255, 1984

Anderson CM, Reiss DJ, Hogarty GE: Schizophrenia in the Family: A Practitioner's Guide to Psychoeducation and Management. New York, Guilford Press, 1986

Andreasen NC: The clinical assessment of thought, language, and communication disorders, II: diagnostic significance, Arch Gen Psychiatry 36:1325–1330, 1979

Andreason NC: Negative symptoms in schizophrenia. Arch Gen Psychiatry 39:784–788, 1982

Angrist B, Rotrosen J, Gershon S: Responses to apomorphine, amphetamine and neuroleptics in schizophrenic subjects. Psychopharmacology 67:31–38, 1980

Ansbacher HL, Ansbacher RR: The Individual Psychology of Alfred Adler. New York, Harper Torchbooks, 1964, pp 126–162

Anthony WA, Liberman RP: The practice of psychiatric rehabilitation. Schizophr Bull 12:542–559, 1986

Anthony WA, Nemec PB: Psychiatric rehabilitation, in Schizophrenia: Treatment, Management and Rehabilitation. Edited by Bellack AS. New York, Grune & Stratton. 1984, pp 375–413

Anthony WA, Cohen MR, Vitalo R: The measurement of rehabilitation outcome. Schizophr Bull 4:365–383, 1978

Appleton WS: Mistreatment of patients' families by psychiatrists. Am J Psychiatry 131:655–657, 1974

Arensberg CM: Culture as behavior: structure and emergence. Annual Reviews of Anthropology 1:1–26, 1972

Argyle M, Trower P, Bryant B: Explorations in the treatment of personality disorders and neuroses by social skills training. Br J Med Psychol 47:63–72, 1974

Arnhoff FN: Social consequences of policy toward mental illness. Science 188:1277–1281, 1975

Astrachan BM, Harrow M, Adler D, et al: A checklist for the diagnosis of schizophrenia. Br J Psychiatry 121:529–539, 1972

Austin NK, Liberman RP, King LW, et al: A comparative evaluation of two day hospitals. J Nerv Ment Dis 163:253–262, 1976

Azrin NH, Besalel VA: Job Club Counselor's Manual. Baltimore, University Park Press, 1980

Azrin NH, May PRA: The job club method for the job handicapped: a comparative outcome study. Rehabilitation Counseling Bulletin 23:144–155, 1979

Azrin NH, Flores T, Kaplan SJ: Job finding club: A group assisted program for obtaining employment. Behav Res Ther 13:17–27, 1975

Bachrach LL: Young adult chronic patients: an analytical review of the literature. Hosp Community Psychiatry 33:189–197, 1982

Baker A, Game J, Thorpe J: Physical treatment for schizophrenia. Journal of Mental Sciences 104:860–864, 1958

Ban TA, Lehmann HE: Nicotinic acid in the treatment of schizophrenics. Progress report II. Can Psychiatr Assoc J 20: 103–112, 1975

Bandura A: Principles of Behavior Modification. New York, Holt, Rinehart, and Winston, 1979

Banzett LK, Liberman RP, Moore JW, et al: Long-term follow-up of the effects of behavior therapy. Hosp Community Psychiatry 35:277–279, 1984

Baron M, Risch N, Hamburger R, Mandel B, et al: Genetic linkage between X-chromosome markers and bipolar affective illness. Nature (London) 326:289–292, 1987

Barrowclough C, Tarrier N: "Psychosocial" interventions with families and their effects on the course of schizophrenia: a review. Psychol Med 14:629–642, 1984

Bateson G, Jackson DD, Haley J, et al: Towards a theory of schizophrenia. Behav Sci 1:251–264, 1956

Bayle ALJ: Recherches sur l'arachnite chronique. Paris, 1822

Beard JH, Malmud TJ, Rossman E: Pshchiatric rehabilitation and long-term rehospitalization rates: the findings of two research studies. Schizophr Bull 4:622–635, 1978

Beatrice DF: Case management: a policy option for long-term care. Unpublished manuscript, 1979. (Available from the University Health Policy Consortium, Brandeis University, Waltham, Mass)

Beck AT, Rush AJ, Shaw BF, et al: Cognitive Therapy of Depression. New York, Guilford Press, 1979

Bednar RL, Lawlis GF: Empirical research in group psychotherapy, in Handbook of Psychotherapy and Behavior Change: An Empirical Analysis. Edited by Bergin A, Garfield S. New York, Wiley, 1971, pp 812–838

Bedrosian RC: Cognitive therapy in the family system, in Cognitive Therapy with Couples and Groups. Edited by Freeman A. New York, Plenum Press, 1983, pp 95–106

Beels CC: Family and social management of schizophrenia. Schizophr Bull 1:97–118, 1975

Beels CC: Social support and schizophrenia. Schizophr Bull 7:58–72, 1981

Beels CC, McFarlane WR: Family treatment of schizophrenia: background and state of the art. Hosp Community Psychiatry 33:541–550, 1982

Beels CC, Gutwirth L, Berkeley J, et al: Measurement of social support in schizophrenia. Schizophr Bull 10:399–411, 1984

Bellack AS, Hersen M, Turner SM: Generalization effects of social skills training in chronic schizophrenics: an experimental analysis. Behav Res Ther 14:391–398, 1976

Berkowitz R: Therapeutic intervention with schizophrenic patients and their families: a description of a clinical research project. Journal of Family Therapy 6:211–234, 1984

Berkowitz R, Kuipers L, Eberlein-Vries R, et al: Lowering expressed emotion in relatives of schizophrenics, in New Developments in Interventions with Families of Schizophrenics. Edited by Goldstein MJ. New Directions for Mental Health Services no. 12. San Francisco, Jossey-Bass, 1981, pp 27–48

Berkowitz R, Eberlein-Fries R, Kuipers L, et al: Educating relatives about schizophrenia. Schizophr Bull 10:418–429, 1984

Bernheim KF: Supportive family counseling. Schizophr Bull 8:634–641, 1982

Bernheim KF: Family consumerism: coping with the winds of change, in Families of the Mentally Ill: Coping and Adaptation. Edited by Hatfield AB, Lefley HP. New York, Guilford Press, 1987, pp 244–260

Bernheim KF, Lehman AF: Working with Families of the Mentally Ill. New York, Norton, 1985

Bion WR: Attacks on linking. Int J Psychoanal 40:308–315, 1959

Bishop JM: The molecular genetics of cancer. Nature (London) 325:305–311, 1987

Blackwell B: Drug deviation in psychiatric patients, in Future of Pharmacotherapy New Drug Delivery Systems. Edited by Ayd FJ Jr. Baltimore, International Drug Therapy News Letter, 1973

Bleuler E: Dementia Praecox or the Group of Schizophrenias (1911). Translated by Zinkin J. New York, International Universities Press, 1960

Block S, Crouch E, Reibstein J: Therapeutic factors in group psychotherapy: a review. Arch Gen Psychiatry 38:519–526, 1981

Bond GR, Dincin J, Setz PJ, et al: The effectiveness of psychiatric rehabilitation: a summary of research at Thresholds. Psychosocial Rehabilitation Journal 7:6–22, 1984

Borowski T, Tolwinski T: Treatment of paranoid schizophrenics with chlorpromazine and group therapy. Dis Nerv Syst 30:201–202, 1969

Boszormenyi-Nagy I, Spark G: Invisible Loyalties. New York, Harper and Row, 1973

Boudewyns PA, Fry TJ, Nightingale T: Token economy programs in VA medical centers: where are they today? The Behavior Therapist 9:126–127, 1986

Bowen M (with collaboration of Dysinger RH, Brody WM, Basamania B): Treatment of family groups with a schizophrenic member, in Family Therapy in Clinical Practice. Edited by Bowen M. New York, Jason Aronson, 1957, pp 3–15

Bowen M: Family concept of schizophrenia, in The Etiology of Schizophrenia. Edited by Jackson DD. New York, Basic Books, 1960, pp 346–372

Bowen M: Family psychotherapy into schizophrenia in the hospital and private practice, in Intensive Family Therapy. Edited by Boszormenyi-Nagy I, Framo JL. New York, Harper and Row, 1965, pp 213–243

Bowes PF, Banquer M, Bloomfield HH: Utilization of non-verbal exercises in the group therapy of outpatient chronic schizophrenics. Int J Group Psychother 24: 13–24, 1974

Brady JP: Social skills training for psychiatric patients, I: concepts, methods and clinical results. Am J Psychiatry. 141:333–340, 1984a

Brady JP: Social skills training for psychiatric patients, II: clinical outcome studies. Am J Psychiatry 141: 491–498, 1984b

Breier A, Strauss JS: Self-control in psychotic disorders. Arch Gen Psychiatry 40:1141–1145, 1983

Breier A, Strauss JS: The role of social relationships in the recovery from psychiatric disorders. Am J Psychiatry 141:949–955, 1984

Bridge TP, Cannon HE, Wyatt RJ: Burned-out schizophrenia: evidence for age effects on schizophrenic symptomatology. J Gerontol 33:835–839, 1978

Brockington IF, Leff JP: Schizo-affective psychosis: definitions and incidence. Psychol Med 9:91–99, 1979

Brockington IF, Kendell RE, Leff JP: Definition of schizophrenia: concordance and prediction of outcome. Psychol Med 8:387–398, 1978

Brown GW, Carstairs GM, Topping G: Post hospital adjustment of chronic mental patients. Lancet ii: 685–689, 1958

Brown GW, Monck EM, Carstairs GM, et al: Influence of family life on the course of schizophrenic illness. Br J Prev Soc Med 16:55–68, 1962

Brown GW, Birley JLT, Wing JK: Influence of family life on the course of schizophrenic disorders: a replication. Br J Psychol 121:241–258, 1972

Brown MA, Munford AM: Life skills training for chronic schizophrenics. J Nerv Ment Dis 171:466–470, 1983

Buchkramer C, Schulze-Monking H, Lewandowski L, et al: Emotional atmosphere in families of schizophrenic outpatients: relevance of a practice-oriented assessment instrument, in Treatment of Schizophrenia: Family Assessment and Intervention. Edited by Goldstein MJ, Hand I, Hahlweg K. New York, Springer-Verlag, 1986, pp 79–84

Buchsbaum MS, Ingvar DH, Kessler R, et al: Cerebral glucography with positron tomography. Arch Gen Psychiatry 39:251–259, 1982

Buchsbaum MS, DeLisi LE, Holcomb HH, et al: Anteriorposterior gradients in cerebral glucose use in schizophrenia and affective disorder. Arch Gen Psychiatry 41:1159–1166, 1984

Burns D: Feeling Good: The New Mood Therapy. New York, New American Library, 1981

Cameron N: Introjection, reprojection, and hallucination in the interaction between schizophrenic patient and therapist. Int J Psychoanal 42:86–96, 1961

Cancro R: Clinical prediction of outcome in schizophrenia. Comp Psychiatry 10:349–354, 1969

Cancro R: The Healer and Madness. Philadelphia, Strecker Monograph, 1978

Cancro R: Some preliminary thoughts on the psychotherapy of the schizophrenias, in Psychosocial Intervention in Schizophrenia. Edited by Stierlin H, Wynne LC, Wirsching M. Berlin, Springer-Verlag, 1983, pp 143–148

Cancro R, Pruyser PW: A historical review of the development of the concept of schizophrenia. Bull Menninger Clin 34:61–70, 1970

Caplow T: Two Against One: Coalitions in the Triad. New York, Prentice-Hall, 1968

Carpenter WT: Thoughts on the treatment of schizophrenia. Schizophr Bull 12:527–539, 1986

Carpenter WT, Heinrichs DW: Early intervention, time-limited, targeted pharmacotherapy of schizophrenia. Schizophr Bull 9:533–542, 1983

Carpenter WT, Strauss JS: Are there pathognomonic symptoms in schizophrenia? An empiric investigation of Schneider's first rank symptoms. Arch Gen Psychiatry 27:847–852, 1973

Carpenter WT, Strauss JS, Bartko JJ: Flexible system for diagnosis of schizophrenia: report from the WHO international pilot study of schizophrenia. Science 182:1275–1278, 1973

Carpenter WT Jr, Sadler JH, Light PD, et al: The therapeutic efficacy of hemodialysis in schizophrenia. N Engl J Med 308:669–675, 1983

Chapple ED: Culture and Biological Man. New York, Holt, Rinehart and Winston, 1970

Christoff KA, Kelly JA: Social skills training with psychiatric patients, in Handbook of Social Skills Training. Edited by Milan M, L'Abate L. New York, Wiley (in press)

Ciompi L: How to improve the treatment of schizophrenia: a multicausal concept and its therapeutic components, in Psychosocial Intervention in Schizophrenia: An Interactional View. Edited by Stierlin H, Wynne LC, Wirschung M. New York, Springer-Verlag, 1983, pp 53–66

Claghorn JL, Johnstone EE, Cook TH, et al: Group therapy and maintenance treatment of schizophrenics. Arch Gen Psychiatry 31:361–365, 1974

Coche E, Flick A: Problem-solving training groups for hospitalized psychiatric patients. J Psychol 91:19–29, 1975

Cohnheim J: Vorlesungen uber Allgemeine Pathologie, 2nd ed. Berlin, Hirschwald, 1882

Cole SA: Liminality and the sick role. Man Med 2:41–53, 71–73, 1976

Cole SA: Problem-focused family therapy: principles and practical applications, in Psychopathology in Childhood. Edited by Lackenmeyer JR, Gibbs MS. New York, Gardner Press, 1982, pp 342–374

Cole SA: Self-help groups, in Comprehensive Group Psychotherapy, 2nd ed. Edited by Kaplan HI, Saddock BJ. Baltimore, Williams and Wilkins, 1983, pp 144–150

Cole SA (with Cole DS): Professionals who work with families of the chronic mentally ill: current status and suggestions for clinical training, in Families of the Mentally Ill: Coping and Adaptation. Edited by Hatfield A, Lefley H. New York, Guilford Press, 1987, pp 278–306

Cole SA, Jacobs J: Psychoeducation for schizophrenia in a multiple family group setting: clinical guidelines. (manuscript in preparation)

Coons WH, Peacock EP: Interpersonal interaction and personality change in group psychotherapy. Can Psychiatr Assoc J 15:347–355, 1970

Coryell WH, Tsuang MT: DSM-III schizophrenia disorder: comparisons with schizophrenia and affective disorder. Arch Gen Psychiatry 39:66–69, 1982

Creer C, Wing J: Schizophrenia at Home. Surrey, England, National Schizophrenia Fellowship, 1974

Creer C, Wing JK: Living with a schizophrenic patient. Br J Hosp Med July:73–82, 1975

Crow TJ: Molecular pathology of schizophrenia: more than one disease process? Br Med J 180:1–9, 1980

Crow TJ, Cross AJ, Johnstone EC, et al: Two syndromes in schizophrenia and their pathogenesis, in Schizophrenia as a Brain Disease. Edited by Henn FA, Nasrallah HA. New York, Oxford University Press, 1982

Curran JP, Monti PM, Corriveau DP: Treatment of schizophrenia, in International Handbook of Behavior Modification and Therapy. Edited by Bellack AS, Hersen M, Kazdin AE. New York, Plenum Press, 1982, pp 433–466

Cutting J: The Psychology of Schizophrenia. London, Churchill and Livingstone, 1985

Delabar J-M, Goldgaber D, Lamour Y, et al: Amyloid gene duplication in Alzheimer's disease and karyotypically normal Down syndrome. Science 235:1380–1392, 1987

DeLisi LE, Crow TJ: Is schizophrenia a viral or immunologic disorder? Psychiatry Clin North Am 9:115–123, 1986

Doane JA: Family interaction and communication deviance in disturbed and normal families: a review of research. Fam Process 17:357–376, 1978

Doane JA, Goldstein MJ, Rodnick EH: Parental pattern of affective style and the development of schizophrenia spectrum disorders. Fam Process 20:337–349, 1981a

Doane JA, West KL, Goldstein MJ, et al: Parental communication deviance and affective style. Arch Gen Psychiatry 38:679–685, 1981b

Doane JA, Jones JE, Fisher L, et al: Parental communication deviance as a predictor of competence in children at risk for adult psychiatric disorder. Fam Process 21:211–223, 1982

Doane JA, Falloon IRH, Goldstein MJ, et al: Parental affective style and the treatment of schizophrenia: predicting course of illness and social functioning. Arch Gen Psychiatry 42: 34–42, 1985

Doane JA, Goldstein MJ, Miklowitz DJ, et al: The impact of individual and family treatment on the affective climate of families of schizophrenics. Br J Psychiatry 148:279–287, 1986

Doll W: Family coping with the mentally ill: an unanticipated problem of deinstitutionalization. Hosp Community Psychiatry 27:183–185, 1976

Donlon PT, Rada RT, Knight SW: A therapeutic setting for "refractory" chronic schizophrenic patients. Am J Psychiatry 138:1027–1035, 1973

Doran AR, Breier A, Roy A: Differential diagnosis and diagnostic systems in schizophrenia. Psychiatr Clin North Am 9:17–34, 1986

Drake RE, Sederer LI: The adverse effects of intensive treatment of chronic schizophrenia. Compr Psychiatry 27:313–326, 1986

Edelstein BA, Eisler RM: Effects of modeling and modeling with instructions and feedback on the behavioral components of social skills. Behavior Therapy 7:382–389, 1976

Egeland JA, Gerhard DS, Paul DL, et al: Bipolar affective disorders linked to DNA markers on chromosome 11. Nature (London) 325:783–787, 1987

Eisler RM, Hersen M, Miller PM: Effects of modeling on components of assertive behavior. J Behav Ther Exp Psychiatry 4:1–6, 1973

Eisler RM, Blanchard EB, Fitts H, et al: Social skill training with and without modeling in schizophrenic and nonpsychotic hospitalized psychiatric patients. Behav Modif 2:147–172, 1978

Epstein NB, Bishop DS: Problem-centered systems therapy of the family. Journal of Marriage and Family Therapy 7:23–32, 1981a

Epstein NB, Bishop DS: Problem-centered systems therapy of the family, in Handbook of Family Therapy. Edited by Gurman AS, Kniskern DP. New York, Brunner/Mazel, 1981b, pp 444–482

Epstein NB, Vlok LA: Research on the results of psychotherapy: a summary of the evidence. Am J Psychiatry 138:1027–1035, 1981

Epstein NB, Bishop DS, Levin S: The McMaster Model of family functioning. Journal of Marriage and Family Counseling 4:19–31, 1978

Erikson EH: Childhood and Society. New York, Norton, 1950

Erikson EH: Psychological reality and historical actuality, in Insight and Responsibility. New York, Norton, 1964, pp 159–215

Erikson EH: Identity, Youth and Crisis. New York, Norton, 1968

Eysenck HJ: Classification and the problem of diagnosis, in Handbook of Abnormal Psychology. Edited by Eysenck H. London, Pitman Medical, 1960

Fairweather GW, Simon R, Gebhard ME, et al: Relative effectiveness of psychotherapeutic programs: a multi-criterial comparison of four programs for the three different patient groups. Psychol Monogr 74:1–26, 1960

Falloon IRH: Communication and problem-solving skills training with relapsing schizophrenics and their families, in Family Therapy and Major Psychopathology. Edited by Lansky MR. Seminars in Psychiatry. New York, Grune and Stratton, 1981, pp 35–56

Falloon IRH: Family Management of Schizophrenia: A Study of Clinical, Social, Family, and Economic Benefits. Baltimore, Johns Hopkins University Press, 1985

Falloon IRH: Family stress and schizophrenia. Psychiatr Clin North Am, 9:165–182, 1986

Falloon IRH, Liberman RP: Interactions between drug and psychosocial therapy in schizophrenia. Schizophr Bull 9:543–554, 1983

Falloon IRH, Pederson J: Family management in the prevention of morbidity in schizophrenia: the adjustment of the family unit. Br J Psychiatry 147:156–163, 1985

Falloon IRH, Boyd JL, McGill CW, et al.: Family management in the prevention of exacerbations of schizophrenia. N Engl J Med 306:1437–1440, 1982

Falloon IRH, Boyd JL, McGill CW: Family Care of Schizophrenia. New York, Guilford Press, 1984

Falloon IRH, Boyd JL, McGill CW, et al: Family management in the prevention of morbidity in schizophrenia. Arch Gen Psychiatry 42:887–896, 1985

Farina A, Fischer EH, Sherman S, et al: Physical attractiveness and mental illness. J Abnorm Psychol 86:510–517, 1977

Farkas T, Wolf AP, Jaeger J, et al: Regional brain glucose metabolism in chronic schizophrenia. Arch Gen Psychiatry 41:293–300, 1984

Federn S: Ego Psychology and the Psychoses. New York, Basic Books, 1952

Feighner JP, Robins E, Guze SP, et al: Diagnostic criteria for use in psychiatric research. Arch Gen Psychiatry 26:57–63, 1972

Fenn HH, Dinaburg D: Didactic group psychotherapy with chronic schizophrenics. Int J Group Psychother 31:443–452, 1981

Fenton WS, Mosher LR, Matthews SM: Diagnosis of schizophrenia: a critical review of current diagnostic systems. Schizophr Bull 7:452–476, 1981

Finch BE, Wallace CJ: Successful interpersonal skills training with schizophrenic inpatients. J Consult Clin Psychol 45:885–890, 1977

Fleiss JL, Cohen J, Everitt BS: Large sample standard errors of kappa and weighted kappa. Psychol Bull 72:323–327, 1977

Flinn SK, Brown LO: Opening moves in crisis intervention with families of chronic psychotics, in New Directions in Family Therapy. Edited by Buckley TJ, McCarthy JJ, Norman E, et al. Oceanside, NY, Dabor Science Publications, 1977, pp 90–102

Fogelson DL, Cohen BM, Pope HG: A study of DSM-III schizophreniform disorder. Am J Psychiatry 139:1281–1285, 1982

Fowler RC, Tsuang MT, Cadoret RJ, et al: A clinical and family comparison of paranoid and non-paranoid schizophrenia. Br J Psychiatry 124:346–351, 1974

Fox MR: Treating families with a member diagnosed as mentally ill, in When Families Have Trouble. Edited by Fox MR. (manuscript in preparation)

Franklin JL, Solovitz B, Mason M. et al: An evaluation of case management. Am J Public Health 77: 674–678, 1987

Freud S: Psycho-analytic notes on an autobiographical account of a case of paranoia (1911), standard ed. 12. London, Hogarth Press, 1958

Frosch J: The Psychotic Process. New York, International Universities Press, 1983

Furman W, Geller M, Simon SJ, et al: The use of behavioral rehearsal procedure for teaching job-interviewing skills to psychiatric patients. Behavior Therapy 10:157–167, 1979

GAP (Group for the Advancement of Psychiatry—The Committee on the Family): The Family, the Patient and the Psychiatric Hospital. New York, Brunner/Mazel, 1985

Glick ID, Clarkin JF, Spencer JH, et al: A controlled trial of inpatient family intervention. Arch Gen Psychiatry 42:882–886, 1985

Glynn S, Bowen L. Marshall BD, et al: Compliance with less restrictive procedures to control aggression among adult psychiatric inpatients. Hosp Community Psychiatry (in press)

Goldman HH: Mental illness and family burden: a public health perspective. Hosp Community Psychiatry 33:557–560, 1982

Goldstein MJ: Family interaction: patterns of onset and the course of schizophrenia, in Psychosocial Intervention in Schizophrenia. Edited by Stierlin H, Wynne LC, Wirschung M. New York, Springer-Verlag, 1983, pp 5–19

Goldstein MJ: Family factors that antedate the onset of schizophrenia and related disorders: the results of a fifteen year prospective longitudinal study. Acta Psychiatr Scand 71:7–18, 1985

Goldstein MJ: Psychosocial issues. Schizophr Bull 13:157–171, 1987

Goldstein MJ, Doane JA: Family factors in the onset, course and treatment of schizophrenic spectrum disorders: an update on current research. J Nerv Ment Dis 170:692–700, 1982

Goldstein MJ, Kopeikin HS: Short- and-long-term effects of combining drug and family therapy, in New Developments in Interventions with Families of Schizophrenics. Edited by Goldstein MJ. New Directions for Mental Health Services no. 12. San Francisco, Jossey-Bass, 1981, pp 5–26

Goldstein MJ, Rodnick EH: The family's contribution to the etiology of schizophrenia: current status. Schizophr Bull 1:48–63, 1975

Goldstein MJ, Rodnick EH, Evans JR, et al: Drugs and family therapy in the aftercare of acute schizophrenics. Arch Gen Psychiatry 32:1169–1177, 1978

Grad J, Sainsbury P: Mental illness and the family. Lancet i: 544–547, 1963

Grad J, Sainsbury P: The effects that patients have on their families in a community care and control psychiatry service—a two year follow-up. Br J Psychiatry 114:265–278, 1968

Gray W, Duhl FJ, Rizzo ND (eds): General Systems Theory and Psychiatry. Boston, Little Brown, 1969

Greenley JR: Social control and expressed emotion. J Nerv Ment Dis 174:24–30, 1986

Greenspan SI: Psychopathology and Adaptation in Infancy and Early Childhood. New York, International Universities Press, 1981

Grinspoon L, Ewalt JR, Shader R: Psychotherapy and pharmacotherapy in chronic schizophrenia. Am J Psychiatry 124:1945–1952, 1968

Grunebaum H: Comments on Terkelsen's "Schizophrenia and the Family, II: adverse effects of family therapy." Fam Process 23:421–428, 1984

Gunderson JG, Frank AF: Effects of psychotherapy in schizophrenia. Yale J Biol Med 58:373–381, 1985

Gunderson JG, Frank AF, Katz HM, et al: Effects of psychotherapy in schizophrenia, II: comparative outcome of two forms of treatment. Schizophr Bull 10:564–598, 1984

Gur RE, Resnick SM, Alavi A, et al: Regional brain function in schizophrenia, I: a positron emission tomographic study. Arch Gen Psychiatry 44:119–125, 1987a

Gur RE, Resnick SM, Gur RC, et al: Regional brain function in schizophrenia, II: repeated evaluation with positron emission tomography. Arch Gen Psychiatry 44:126–129, 1987b

Gurman A: MFT produces little empirical evidence of effectiveness. Family Therapy News Nov/Dec:8, 17, 1984

Haier JR: The diagnosis of schizophrenia: a review of revent developments. Schizophr Bull 6:417–428, 1980

Haley J: Problem-Solving Therapy. Washington, DC, Jossey-Bass, 1976

Haley J: Leaving Home: The Therapy of Disturbed Young People. New York, McGraw-Hill, 1980

Hallgren B, Sjogren T: A clinical and genetic statistical study of schizophrenia and low grade mental deficiency in a large Swedish rural population. Acta Psychiatrica et Neurologica Scandinavica 34 (Suppl 138):1–65, 1959

Hanssen T, Heyden T, Sunberry I, et al: Propranolol in schizophrenia. Arch Gen Psychiatry 37:685–690, 1980

Harbin HT: A family-oriented psychiatric inpatient unit. Fam Process 18:281–292, 1979

Harding CM, Zubin J, Strauss JS: Chronicity in schizophrenia: fact, partial fact, or artifact. Hosp Community Psychiatry 38:477–486, 1987

Hare EH, Wilcox DRG: Do psychiatric patients take their pills? Br J Psychiatry 113:1435–1439, 1967

Hartmann H: Contribution to the metapsychology of schizophrenia. Psychoanal Stud Child 8:177–198, 1953

Haslam J: Observations on Madness and Melancholy, 2nd ed. London, Hayden, 1809

Hatfield AB: Help-seeking behavior in families of schizophrenics. Am J Community Psychol 7:563–569, 1979

Hatfield AB: Coping with Mental Illness in the Family: A Family Guide. Maryland Department of Health and Mental Hygiene, Mental Hygiene Administration, and the National Alliance for the Mentally Ill, 1984a

Hatfield AB: The family, in The Chronic Mental Patient: Five Years Later. Edited by Talbott JA, New York, Grune & Stratton, 1984b, pp 307–323

Hatfield AB: Families as care givers: a historical perspective, in Families of the Mentally Ill: Coping and Adaptation. Edited by Hatfield AB, Lefley HP. New York, Guilford Press, pp. 3–29, 1987

Hecker D: Die Hebephrenie. Archiv für pathologische Anatomie und Physiologie und klinische Medizin 52:394–429, 1871

Heinrichs DW: Recent developments in the psychosocial treatment of chronic psychotic illness, in The Chronic Mental Patient: Five Years Later. Edited by Talbot JA. New York, Grune and Stratton, 1984, pp 123–136

Heinrichs DW, Carpenter WT: The coordination of family treatment with other treatment modalities, in Family Therapy in Schizophrenia. Edited by McFarlane WR. New York, Guilford Press, 1983, pp 267–287

Helzer JE, Brockington IF, Kendell RE: Predictive validity of DSM-III and Feighner definitions of schizophrenia. Arch Gen Psychiatry 38:791–797, 1981

Hemsley DR: What have cognitive deficits to do with schizophrenic symptoms? Br J Psychiatry 130:167–173, 1977

Hersen M, Bellack AS, Turner SM: Assessment of assertiveness in female psychiatric patients: motor and autonomic measures. J Behav Ther Exp Psychiatry 9:11–16, 1978

Herz MI, Spitzer RL, Gibbon M, et al: Individual vs group aftercare treatment. Am J Psychiatry 131:808–812, 1974

Herz MI, Szymanski NF, Simon JC: Intermittent medication for stable schizophrenic outpatients: an alternative to maintenance medication. Am J Psychiatry 139:918–922, 1982

Hill LP: Psychotherapeutic Intervention in Schizophrenia. Chicago, University of Chicago Press, 1955

Hill R: Generic features of families under stress, in Crisis Intervention. Edited by Parad HJ. New York, Family Service Association, 1965, pp 32–52

Hirsch SR, Leff JP: Abnormalities in parents of schizophrenics. Maudsley Monographs, London, Oxford University Press, pp 94–101, 1975

Hodgkinson S, Sherrington R, Gurling H, et al: Molecular genetic evidence for heterogeneity in manic depression. Nature (London) 325:805–806, 1987

Hoffman L: Foundations of Family Therapy: A Conceptual Framework for Systems Change, New York, Basic Books, 1981

Hogarty GE: Expressed emotion and schizophrenic relapse, in Controversies in Schizophrenia. Edited by Alpert M. New York, Guilford Press, 1985, pp 354–363

Hogarty GE, Goldberg SC, the Collaborative Study Group: Drug and sociotherapy in the aftercare of schizophrenic patients: one-year relapse rates. Arch Gen Psychiatry 28:54–64, 1973

Hogarty GE, Goldberg SC, Schooler NR, et al: Drugs and sociotherapy in the aftercare of schizophrenic patients, II & III. Arch Gen Psychiatry 31:603–618, 1974

Hogarty GE, Goldberg SC, Schooler NR: Drug and sociotherapy and the aftercare of schizophrenic patients. Arch Gen Psychiatry: 31:609–618, 1974a

Hogarty GE, Goldberg SC, Schooler NR, et al: Collaborative Study Group: Drug and sociotherapy and the aftercare of schizophrenic patients, II: two year relapse rates. Arch Gen Psychiatry 31:603–608, 1974b

Hogarty GE, Schooler NR, Ulrich R, et al: Fluphenazine and social therapy in the aftercare of schizophrenic patients. Arch Gen Psychiatry 36:1283–1294, 1979

Hogarty GE, Anderson CM, Reiss DJ, et al (with Environmental/Personal Indicators in the Course of Schizophrenia Research Group): Family psychoeducation, social skills training, and maintenance chemotherapy in the aftercare treatment of schizophrenia. Arch Gen Psychiatry 43:633–642, 1986

Holden DF, Lewine RRJ: How families evaluate mental health professionals, resources and effects of illness. Schizophr Bull 8:626–633, 1982

Hollon SD, Evans MD: Cognitive therapy for depression in a group format, in Cognitive Therapy with Couples and Groups. Edited by Freeman A. New York, Plenum Press, 1983, pp 11–41

Holmes MR, Hansen DJ Sr, Lawrence JS: Conversational skills training with aftercare patients in the community: social validation and generalization. Behavior Therapy 15:84–100, 1984

Hooley JM: Expressed emotion: a review of the critical literature. Clin Psychol Rev 5:119–139, 1985

Hooley JM, Richters JE, Weintraub S, et al: Psychopathology and marital distress: the positive side of positive symptoms. J Abnorm Psychol 96:27–33, 1987

Horowitz MJ, Weisberg PS: Techniques for the group psychotherapy of acute psychosis. Int J Group Psychother 16:42–50, 1966

Hoult J, Reynolds I: Schizophrenia: a comparative trial of community oriented and hospital oriented psychiatric care. Acta Psychiatr Scand 69:359–372, 1984

Imber-Mintz L. Liberman RP, Miklowitz D, et al: Expressed emotion: A call for partnership among relatives, patients and professionals. Schizophr Bull 13:227–235, 1987

Intagliata J: Improving the quality of community care for the chronically mentally disabled: the role of case management. Schizophr Bull 8:655–674, 1982

Irwin DS, Weitzek WD, Morgan DW: Phenothiazine intake and staff attitudes. Am J Psychiatry 127:67–71, 1971

Jackson DD: The question of family homeostasis. Psychoanal Q 31(Suppl):79–90, 1957

Jackson DD (ed): The Etiology of Schizophrenia. New York, Basic Books, 1960

Jacob T: Family interaction in disturbed and normal families: a methodological and substantive view. Psychol Bull 18:35–65, 1975

Jacobs HE, Kardashian S, Kreinbring RK, et al: A skills-oriented model for facilitating employment among psychiatrically disabled persons. Rehabilitation Counseling Bulletin 28:87–96, 1984

Jacobson NS: The modification of cognitive processes in behavioral marital therapy: integrating cognitive and behavioral intervention strategies, in Marital Interaction: Analysis and Modification. Edited by Hahlweg K, Jacobson NS. New York, Guilford Press, 1984, pp 285–308

Janowsky DS, El-Yousel K, Davis JM, et al: Provocation of schizophrenic symptoms by intravenous administration of methylphenidate. Arch Gen Psychiatry 28:185–191, 1975

Jeste DV, Kleinman JE, Potkin SG, et al: Ex uno multi: subtyping the schizophrenic syndrome. Biol Psychiatry 17:199–222, 1982

Jones J, Rodnick E, Goldstein M, et al: Parental transactional style deviance as a possible indicator of risk in schizophrenia. Arch Gen Psychiatry 34:71–74, 1977

Kahlbaum KL: Die Katatonie oder das Spannungsirresein. Berlin, Hirschwald, 1874

Kanas N: Inpatient and outpatient group therapy for schizophrenic patients. Am J Psychother 39:431–439, 1985

Kanas N: Group therapy with schizophrenics: a review of controlled studies. Int J Group Psychother 36:279–296, 1986

Kanas N, Rogers M, Kreth E, et al: The effectiveness of group psychotherapy during the first three weeks of hospitalization: a controlled study. J Nerv Ment Dis 168:487–492, 1980

Kanter JS: Coping Strategies for Relatives of the Mentally Ill, 2nd ed. Washington, DC, The National Alliance for the Mentally Ill, 1984

Kanter J, Lamb HR, Loper C: Expressed emotion in families: a critical review. Hosp Community Psychiatry 38:374–380, 1987

Karno M, Jenkins JH, de la Selva A, et al: Expressed emotion and schizophrenic outcome among Mexican-American families. J Nerv Ment Dis 175:143–151, 1987

Karon BP, VandenBos GR: The consequences of psychotherapy for schizophrenic patients. Psychotherapy: Theory, Research, and Practice 9:111–119, 1972

Karon BP, VandenBos GR: Psychotherapy of Schizophrenia: The Treatment of Choice. New York, Jason Aronson, 1981

Kay SR, Fiszbein A, Lindmeyer JP, et al: Positive and negative syndromes in schizophrenia as a function of chronicity. Acta Psychiatr Scand 74:507–518, 1986

Keith SJ, Matthews SM: Group, family and milieu therapies and psychosocial rehabilitation in the treatment of schizophrenic disorders, in Psychiatry, 1982 Annual Review. Edited by Grinspoon L. Washington, DC, American Psychiatric Press, 1982, pp 166–178

Keith SJ, Matthews SM: Schizophrenia: a review of psychosocial treatment strategies, in Psychotherapy Research: Where Are We and Where Shall We Go? Edited by Williams JBW, Spitzer RL. New York, Guilford Press, 1984, pp 70–88

Kelly JA, Laughlin C, Claiborne M, et al: A group procedure for teaching job interviewing skills to formerly hospitalized psychiatric patients. Behavior Therapy 10:299–310, 1979

Kendell RE, Brockington IF, Leff JP: Prognostic implications of six alternative definitions of schizophrenia. Arch Gen Psychiatry 35:23–31, 1979

Kendler KS: Demography of paranoid psychosis (delusional disorder): a review and comparison with schizophrenia and affective illness. Arch Gen Psychiatry 39:890–902, 1982

Kendler KS, Gruenberg AM: Genetic relationship between paranoid personality disorder and the "schizophrenic spectrum" disorders. Am J Psychiatry 139:1185–1186, 1982

Kendler KS, Tsuang MT: Nosology of paranoid schizophrenia and other paranoid psychoses. Schizophr Bull 7:594–610, 1981

Kendler KS, Masterson C, Ungaro R, et al: A family study of schizophrenia-related personality disorders. Am J Psychiatry 141:424–427, 1984

Kendler KS, Gruenberg AM, Tsuang MD: Subtype stability in schizophrenia. Am J Psychiatry 143:1098–1105, 1985a

Kendler KS, Masterson CC, Davis KL: Psychiatric illness in the first-degree relatives of patients with paranoid psychosis, schizophrenia and medical illness. Br J Psychiatry 147:524–531, 1985b

Kernberg O: Borderline Conditions and Pathological Narcissism. New York, Jason Aronson, 1975

Kety SS, Rosenthal D, Wender PH, et al: Mental illness in the biologic and adoptive families of adopted schizophrenics. Am J Psychiatry 128:302–306, 1971

King LW, Liberman RP, Roberts J, et al: Personal effectiveness: structured therapy for improving social and emotional skills. European Journal of Behavior Analysis and Modification 2:82–91, 1977

Klein DF: Who should not be treated with neuroleptics but often are, in Rational Psychopharmacotherapy and the Right to Treatment. Edited by Ayd FJ Jr. Baltimore, Ayd Medical Communications, 1975

Klein DF: Psychosocial treatment of schizophrenia, or psychosocial help for people with schizophrenia. Schizophr Bull 6:1, 1980

Klein DF, Davis JM: Diagnosis and Drug Treatment of Psychiatric Disorders. Baltimore, Williams and Wilkins, 1969

Klein M: Love, Guilt, and Reparation and Other Works, 1921–1945. New York, Delacorte Press, 1975

Knesevich JW, Zalcman SJ, Clayton PJ: Six-year follow-up of patients with carefully diagnosed good- and poor-prognosis schizophrenia. Am J Psychiatry 140:1507–1510, 1983

Koenigsberg HW, Handley R: Expressed emotion: from predictive index to clinical construct. Am J Psychiatry 143:1361–1373, 1986

Kohut H: The Restoration of the Self. New York, International Universities Press, 1977

Kolko DJ, Dorsett PG, Milan MA: A total-assessment approach to the evaluation of social skills training: the effectiveness of an anger control program for adolescent psychiatric patients. Behavioral Assessment 3:383–402, 1981

Kraepelin E: Compendium der Psychiatrie. Leipzig, Abel, 1883

Kraepelin E: Psychiatrie. Ein Lehrbuch für Studierende und Arzte, 6th ed. Leipzig, Barth, 1899

Kraepelin E: Textbook of psychiatry, 7th ed (abstracted). Translated by Diefendorf. London, Macmillan, 1907

Kraepelin E: Dementia Praecox and Paraphrenia (1907). Translated by Barclay RM, Roberts GM. New York, Robert E. Krieger, 1971

Kreisman DE, Joy VC: The family as reactor to the mental illness of a relative, in Handbook of Evaluation Research, vol 2. Edited by Struening E, Guttentag M. Beverly Hills, Calif, Sage Publications, 1975, pp 483–518

Kuipers L: Expressed emotion: a review. Br J Soc Clin Psychol 18:237–243, 1979

Kuipers L, Sturgeon D, Berkowitz R, et al: Characteristics of expressed emotion: its relationship to speech and looking in schizophrenic patients and their relatives. Br J Clin Psychol 22:257–264, 1983

Laing RD: The politics of experience, in The Politics of Experience and the Bird of Paradise. London, Penguin Books, 1967

Lamb R: Some reflections on treating schizophrenics. Arch Gen Psychiatry 43:1007–1011, 1986

Langfeldt G: Diagnosis and prognosis of schizophrenia. Proc R Soc Med 53:1047–1052, 1960

Langsley DG, Kaplan DM: The Treatment of Families in Crisis. New York, Grune and Stratton, 1968

Langsley DG, Pittman FS, Machotka P, et al: Family crisis therapy—results and implications. Fam Process 7:145–158, 1968

Langsley DG, Pittman FS, Swank GE: Family crises in schizophrenics and other mental patients. J Nerv Ment Dis 149:270–276, 1969

Langsley D, Machotka P, Flomenhaft K: Avoiding mental hospital admission: a follow-up study. Am J Psychiatry 127:1391–1394, 1971

Laqueur HP: Multiple family therapy, in Family Therapy and Major Psychopathology. Edited by Lansky MR. New York, Grune and Stratton, 1981, pp 57–69

Leavitt SS: Case management: a remedy for problems of community care, in Case Management in Mental Health Services. Edited by Sanborn C. New York, Haworth Press, 1982

Leff J, Vaughn C: The interaction of life events and relatives' expressed emotion in schizophrenia and depressive neurosis. Br J Psychiatry 136:146–153, 1980

Leff J, Vaughn C: The role of maintenance therapy and relatives' expressed emotion in relapse of schizophrenia: a two-year follow-up. Br J Psychiatry 139:102–104, 1981

Leff J, Vaughn C: Expressed Emotion in Families: Its Significance for Mental Illness. New York, Guilford Press, 1985

Leff J, Kuipers L, Berkowitz R, et al: A controlled trial of social intervention in the families of schizophrenic patients. Br J Psychiatry 141:121–134, 1982

Leff J, Kuipers L, Berkowitz R, et al: Life events, relatives' expressed emotion and maintenance medication in schizophrenic relapse. Psychol Med 13:799–806, 1983

Leff J, Kuipers L, Berkowitz R, et al: A controlled trial of social intervention in the families of schizophrenic patients: two year follow-up. Br J Psychiatry 146:594–600, 1985

Lefley HP: Families of the mentally ill in cross-cultural perspective. Psychosocial Rehabilitation Journal 8:57–75, 1985

Lehmann HE: Pharmacotherapy of Schizophrenia, in Psychopathology of Schizophrenia. Edited by Hoch P, Zubin J. New York, Grune and Stratton, 1967

Lehmann HE: Negative aspects of psychotherapeutic drug treatment. Prog Neuropsychopharmacol 3:223–229, 1979

Lehmann HE, Cancro R: Schizophrenia: clinical features, in Comprehensive Textbook of Psychiatry, 4th ed. Edited by Kaplan HI, Sadock BJ. Baltimore, Williams and Wilkins, 1985

Leszcz M, Yalom ID, Norden M: The value of inpatient group psychotherapy: patients' perceptions. Int J Group Psychother 35:411–433, 1985

Levene HI, Patterson V, Murphey BG, et al: The aftercare of schizophrenia: an evaluation of group and individual approaches. Psychiatr Q 44:296–304, 1970

Lewin K: Group decision and social change, in Readings in Social Psychology. Edited by Maccoby N, Newcomb TM. New York, Henry Holt, 1947, pp 330–344

Liberman RP: Behavior therapy for schizophrenia, in Treatment of Schizophrenia. Edited by West LJ, Flinn D. New York, Grune and Stratton, 1976

Liberman RP: Sociopolitics of behavioral programs in institutions and community agencies. Analysis and Intervention in Developmental Disabilities 3:131–159, 1983

Liberman RP (ed): Psychiatric Rehabilitation: Special Issue, Schizophr Bull 12:540–723, 1986

Liberman RP: Psychiatric Rehabilitation of Chronic Mental Patients. Washington, DC, American Psychiatric Press, 1987

Liberman RP, Bryan E: Behavior therapy in a community mental health center. Am J Psychiatry 134:401–406, 1977

Liberman RP, Evans C: Behavioral rehabilitation for chronic mental patients. J Clin Psychopharmacol 5:85–145, 1985

Liberman RP, Foy DW: Psychiatric rehabilitation for chronic mental patients. Psychiatric Annals 13:539–545, 1983

Liberman RP, Teigen J, Patterson R, et al: Reducing delusional speech in chronic, paranoid schizophrenics. Journal of Applied Behavior Analysis 6:57–64, 1973

Liberman RP, DeRisi WJ, King LW, et al: Behavioral measurement in a community mental health center, in Evaluating Behavioral Programs in Community, Residential and Educational Settings. Edited by Davidson P, Clark F, Hamerlynck L. Champaign, Ill, Research Press, 1974a

Liberman RP, Wallace CJ, Teigen J, et al: Interventions with psychotics, in Innovative Treatment Methods in Psychopathology. Edited by Calhoun KS, Adams HE, Mitchell EM. New York, Wiley, 1974b

Liberman RP, King LW, DeRisi WJ, et al: Personal Effectiveness: Guiding People to Assert Their Feelings and Improve Their Social Skills. Champaign, Ill, Research Press, 1975

Liberman RP, King LW, DeRisi WJ: Behavior analysis and modification in community mental health, in Handbook of Behavior Therapy and Modification. Edited by Leitenberg H. Englewood Cliffs, NJ, Prentice-Hall, 1976

Liberman RP, Fearn CH, DeRisi WJ, Roberts J, et al: The credit-incentive system: motivating participation of patients in day hospital. British Journal of Social and Clinical Psychology 16:85–94, 1977

Liberman RP, Wallace CJ, Vaughn CE, et al: Social and family factors in the course of schizophrenia: towards an interpersonal problem-solving therapy for schizophrenics and their families, in The Psychotherapy of Schizophrenia. Edited by Strauss JS, Bowers M, Downey TW, et al. New York, Plenum Medical Book Company, 1980, pp 21–54

Liberman RP, Wallace CJ, Falloon IRH, et al: Interpersonal problem-solving therapy for schizophrenics and their families. Compr Psychiatry 22:627–629, 1981

Liberman RP, Nuechterlin KH, Wallace CJ: Social Skills Training and The Nature of Schizophrenia. Kurran JP, Monte PM (eds). New York, Guilford Press, 1982, pp 5–56

Liberman RP, Falloon IRH, Wallace CJ: Drug-psychosocial interactions in the treatment of schizophrenia, in The Chronically Mentally Ill: Research and Services. Edited by Mirabi M. New York, SP Medical and Scientific Books, 1984a

Liberman RP, Lillie F, Falloon IRH, et al: Social Skills training with relapsing schizophrenics. Behav Modif 8:155–179, 1984b

Liberman RP, Massel HK, Mosk M, et al: Social skills training for chronic mental patients. Hosp Community Psychiatry 36:396–403, 1985

Liberman RP, Jacobs HE, Boone SE, et al: Skills training for the community adaptation of schizophrenics, in Psychosocial Treatment of Schizophrenia: Multidimensional Concepts, Psychological, Family and Self-Help Perspectives. Edited by Strauss JS, Boker W, Brenner HD. Toronto, Hans Huber, 1987, pp 94–109

Lidz T: The Origin and Treatment of Schizophrenic Disorders. New York, Basic Books, 1973

Lidz T, Fleck S: Schizophrenia, human interaction and the role of the family, in The Etiology of Schizophrenia. Edited by Jackson DD. New York, Basic Books, 1960, pp 323–345

Lidz T, Cornelison A, Fleck S, Terry D: The intrafamilial environment of schizophrenic patients; II: marital schism and marital skew. Am J Psychiatry 114:241–248, 1957

Liem JH: Family studies of schizophrenia: an update and commentary. Schizophr Bull 6:429–455, 1980

Linn MW, Klett J, Caffey FM: Foster home characteristics and psychiatric patient outcomes. Arch Gen Psychiatry 37:129–132, 1980

MacMillan JF, Gold A, Crowe TJ, et al: Expressed emotion and relapse. Br J Psychiatry 148:133–143, 1986

Madanes C: The prevention of rehospitalization of adolescents and young adults. Fam Process 19:179–191, 1980

Madanes C: Strategic Family Therapy. San Francisco, Jossey-Bass, 1982

Mahler M, Pine F, Bergman A: The Psychological Birth of the Human Infant. New York, Basic Books, 1975

Maj M: Evolution of the American concept of schizoaffective psychosis. Neuropsychobiology 11:7–13, 1984

Malm U: The influence of group therapy on schizophrenia. Acta Psychiatr Scand 65:(Suppl 297), 1982

Marlowe J: The functions of case management, in Proceedings of the 1982 Florida Conference on Deinstitutionalization. Edited by Marlowe H, Weinberg R. Tampa, University of South Florida, 1982

Maruyama M: The second cybernetics: deviation-amplifying mutual causal process, in Modern Systems Research for the Behavioral Scientist. Edited by Buckley W. Chicago, Aldine, 1968, pp 304–313

Masnik R, Bucci L, Isenberg D, et al: "Coffee and . . . ." A way to treat the untreatable. Am J Psychiatry 128:56–59, 1971

Massel HK, Bowen L, Wong SE, et al: The development of a discrete-trials procedure for training social skills to chronic schizophrenics: acquisition and generalization effects. Presented at the meeting of the Association for the Advancement of Behavior Therapy. Houston, Tex, 1985

Massie HN, Beels CC: The outcome of the family treatment of schizophrenia. Schizophr Bull 1:24–36, 1972

Maxmen JS: Group therapy as viewed by hospitalized patients. Arch Gen Psychiatry 28:404–408, 1973

Maxmen JS: An educative model for inpatient group therapy. Int J Group Psychother 28:321–338, 1978

Maxmen JS: Helping patients survive theories: the practice of an educative model. Int J Group Psychother 34:355–368, 1984

May PRA: Treatment of schizophrenia: a comparative study of five treatment methods. New York, Science House, 1968

May PRA: When, what, and why? Psychopharmacotherapy and other treatments in schizophrenia. Compr Psychiatry 17:683–693, 1976

May PRA, Simpson GM: Schizophrenia: overview of treatment methods, in Comprehensive Textbook of Psychiatry, 3rd ed. Edited by Kaplan HI, Freedman AM, Sadock BJ. Baltimore, Williams and Wilkins, 1980a, pp 1192–1216

May PRA, Simpson GM: Schizophrenia: an evaluation of treatment methods, in Comprehensive Textbook of Psychiatry, 3rd ed. Edited by Kaplan HI, Freedman AM, Sadock BJ. Baltimore, Williams and Wilkins, 1980b, 1240–1275

May PRA, Tuma AH, Dixon WJ: Schizophrenia—a follow-up study of results of treatments. Arch Gen Psychiatry 33:474–506, 1976a

May PRA, Tuma AH, Yale C: Schizophrenia: a follow-up study of results of treatment. Hospital stay over two to five years. Arch Gen Psychiatry 33:481–486, 1976b

McFall RM: A review and reformulation of the concept of social skills. Behavioral Assessment 4:1–33, 1982

McFarlane WR: Family Therapy in Schizophrenia. New York, Guilford Press, 1983a

McFarlane WR: Multiple family therapy in schizophrenia, in Family Therapy in Schizophrenia. Edited by McFarlane WR. New York, Guilford Press, 1983b, pp 141–172

McFarlane WR, Beels CC: A decision-tree model for integrating family therapies for schizophrenia, in Family Therapy in Schizophrenia. Edited by McFarlane WR, New York, Guilford Press, 1983, pp 325–335

McFarlane WR, Beels CC, Rosenheck S: New developments in the family treatment of the psychotic disorders, in Psychiatry Update, vol II. Edited by Grinspoon L. Washington, DC, American Psychiatric Press, 1983, pp 242–256

McGlashan TH: Intensive individual psychotherapy of schizophrenia. Arch Gen Psychiatry 40:909–920, 1983

McGlashan TH: Testing four diagnostic systems for schizophrenia. Arch Gen Psychiatry 41:141–144, 1984

McGlashan TH: Schizophrenia: psychosocial treatments and the role of psychosocial factors in its etiology and pathogenesis, in APA Annual Review, vol 5. Edited by Francis AJ, Hales RE. Washington, DC, American Psychiatric Press, 1986, pp 96–111

Meyer A: The life chart and the obligation of specifying positive data in psychopathologic diagnosis, in The Collected Papers of Adolf Meyer, vol 3. Medical Teaching. Edited by Winters EE. Baltimore, Johns Hopkins Press, 1951

Miklowitz DJ, Goldstein MJ, Falloon IRH: Premorbid and symptomatic characteristics of schizophrenics from families with high and low levels of expressed emotion. J Abnorm Psychol 92:359–367, 1983

Miklowitz DJ, Strachan AM, Goldstein MJ, et al: Expressed emotion and communication deviance in the families of schizophrenics. J Abnorm Psychol 95:60–66, 1986

Miller JG: Living systems: basic concepts. Behav Sci 10:193–237, 1965

Milne D: A comparative evaluation of two psychiatric day hospitals. Br J Psychiatry 145:533–537, 1984

Minuchin S: Families and Family Therapy. Cambridge, Mass, Harvard University Press, 1974

Mishler EG, Waxler NE: Interaction in Families: An Experimental Study of Family Processes and Schizophrenia. New York, Wiley, 1968

Monti PM, Curran JP, Corriveau, et al: Effects of social skills training groups and sensitivity training groups with psychiatric patients. J Consult Clin Psychol 48:241–248, 1980

Morel BA: Etudes Cliniques: Traité Théorique et Pratique des Maladies Mentales. Paris, Masson, 1852–1863

Mosher L: A psychosocial approach to the returning schizophrenic. The Schizophrenic Outpatient 1:1–11, 1982

Mosher LR, Gunderson JG: Group, family, milieu and community support systems treatment for schizophrenia, in Disorders of the Schizophrenic Syndrome. Edited by Bellak L. New York, Basic Books, 1979, pp 399–452

Mosher LR, Keith SJ: Psychosocial treatment: individual, group, family and community support approaches, in Schizophrenia, 1980. Washington, DC, National Institute of Mental Health, 1980, pp 127–158

Mosk MD, Wong SE, Massel HK, et al: Graduated and traditional procedures for teaching social skills to chronic low-functioning schizophrenics. Presented at the Annual Meeting of the American Psychological Association. Anaheim, Calif, 1983

Munich RL: Conceptual trends and issues in the psychotherapy of schizophrenia. Am J Psychother 41:23–37, 1987

National Center for Health Statistics: International Classification of Diseases, 9th rev. Washington, DC, US Government Printing Office, 1978

National Institute of Mental Health, Division of Biometry and Epidemiology: Data sheet on state and county mental hospitals. Rockville, Md, National Institute of Mental Health, 1977

Norton JP: Expressed emotion, affective style, voice tone and communication deviance as predictors of offspring schizophrenia spectrum disorders. Doctoral dissertation. University of California, Los Angeles, 1982

Nuechterlein KH, Dawson ME: A heuristic vulnerability/stress model of schizophrenic episodes. Schizophr Bull 10:300–312, 1984a

Nuechterlein KH, Dawson ME: Information processing and attentional functioning in the developmental cause of schizophrenic disorders. Schizophr Bull 10:160–202, 1984b

O'Brien CP: Group therapy for schizophrenia: a practical approach. Schizophr Bull 1:119–130, 1975

O'Brien CP: Group psychotherapy with schizophrenia and affective disorders, in Comprehensive Group Psychotherapy, 2nd ed. Edited by Kaplan HI, Sadock BJ Baltimore, Williams and Wilkins, 1983, pp 242–249

O'Brien CP, Hamm KB, Ray BA, et al: Group vs individual psychotherapy with schizophrenics. Arch Gen Psychiatry 27:474–478, 1972

Ogden T: On projective identification. Int J Psychoanal 60:357–373, 1979

Olarte SW, Masnik R: Enhancing medication compliance in coffee groups. Hosp Community Psychiatry 32:417–419, 1981

Otteson JP: Curative caring: the use of buddy groups with chronic schizophrenics. J Consult Clin Psychol 47:649–651, 1979

Pao P-N: Schizophrenic Disorders. New York, International Universities Press, 1979

Parad HJ, Caplan G: A framework for studying families in crisis, in Crisis Intervention. Edited by Parad HJ. New York, Family Service Association, 1965, pp 53–72

Parloff MB, Dies RR: Group psychotherapy outcome research. Int J Group Psychother 27:281–319, 1977

Parnas J, Schulsinger F, Schulsinger H, et al: Behavioral precursors of schizophrenia spectrum. Arch Gen Psychiatry 39:658–664, 1982

Parras A: The lounge: treatment for chronic schizophrenics. Schizophr Bull 1:93–96, 1974

Pattison EM, Brissenden A, Wohl T: Assessing specific effects of inpatient group psychotherapy. Int J Group Psychother 17:283–297, 1967

Paul GL, Lentz RJ: Psychosocial Treatment of Chronic Mental Patients: Milieu Versus Social Learning Programs. Cambridge, Mass, Harvard University Press, 1977

Paul GL, Lentz RJ: Psychosocial Treatment of Mental Patients. Cambridge, Mass, Harvard University Press, 1979

Pekala RJ, Siegel JM, Farrar DM: The problem-solving support group: structured group therapy with psychiatric inpatients. Int J Group Psychother 35:391–409, 1985

Pepper B, Kirschner MC, Ryglewicz H: The young adult chronic patient: overview of a population. Hosp Community Psychiatry 32:463–469, 1981

Pfohl B, Andreasen NC: Schizophrenia: diagnosis and classification, in Annual Review, vol 5. Edited by Frances AJ, Hales RE. Washington, DC, American Psychiatric Press, 1986, pp 7–24

Pinel P: Traité Médico-Philosophique de l'Aliénation Mentale, ou la Manie. Paris, Richard, Caille et Ravier, 1801

Pious WL: A hypothesis about the nature of schizophrenic behavior, in Psychotherapy of the Psychoses. Edited by Burton A. New York, Basic Books, 1961, pp 43–68

Platman SR: Family caretaking and expressed emotion: an evaluation. Hosp Community Psychiatry 34:921–925, 1983

Pope HG, Lipinski JF: Diagnosis in schizophrenia and manic-depressive illness. Arch Gen Psychiatry 35:811–828, 1978

Pope HG, Lipinski JF, Cohen BM, et al: "Schizoaffective disorder": an invalid diagnosis? A comparison of schizoaffective disorder, schizophrenia, and affective disorder. Am J Psychiatry 137:921–927, 1980

Pope HG, Jonas J, Hudson J, et al: The validity of DSM-III borderline personality disorder. Arch Gen Psychiatry 40:23–30, 1983

Powles WE: Varieties and uses of group psychotherapy. Can Psychiatr Assoc J 9:196–201, 1964

Prien RF, Cole J: High dose chlorpromazine therapy in chronic schizophrenia. Arch Gen Psychiatry 18:482–495, 1968

Psychiatric Rehabilitation Consultants: Social and Independent Living Skills Modules. Trainer's manual, patient's workbook, and training video for "Medication Management," "Recreation for Leisure," "Grooming and Self-Care," and "Symptom Self-Management." Available from Dissemination Coordinator, Camarillo-UCLA Research Center, Box A, Camarillo, CA 93011

Purvis SA, Miskimins RW: Effects of community follow-up on post-hospital adjustment of psychiatric patients. Community Ment Health J 6:374–382, 1970

Rabkin R: Crisis intervention, in The Book of Family Therapy. Edited by Ferber A, Mendelsohn M. New York, Science House, 1972, pp 582–596

Rapaport D: A historical survey of psychoanalytic ego psychology, in Psychological Issues, vol 1, monograph 1. New York, International Universities Press, 1959, pp 5–17

Reiss D, Wyatt RJ: Family and biologic variables in the same etiologic studies of schizophrenia: a proposal. Schizophr Bull 1:64–81, 1975

Rifkin A, Quitkin F, Klein DF: Akinesia. Arch Gen Psychiatry 32:672–674, 1975

Riskin J, Faunce EE: An evaluative review of family interaction research. Fam Process 11:365–455, 1972

Rogers CR, Gendlin EG, Kiesler DJ, et al (eds): The Therapeutic Relationship and Its Impact: Study of Psychotherapy with Schizophrenics. Madison, The University of Wisconsin Press, 1967

Rosen AJ, Sussman S, Mueser KT, et al: Behavioral assessment of psychiatric patients and normal controls across different environmental contexts. Journal of Behavioral Assessment 3:25–36, 1981

Rosenfeld H: Psychotic States: A Psychoanalytic Approach. New York, Basic Books, 1965

Rosenthal NE, Rosenthal LN, Stallone F, et al: The validation of RDC schizoaffective disorder. Arch Gen Psychiatry 37:804–810, 1980

Ro-Trock G, Wellisch D, Schoolar J: A family therapy outcome study in an inpatient setting. Am J Orthopsychiatry 47:514–522, 1977

Russakoff LM, Oldham JM: Group psychotherapy on a short-term treatment unit: an application of object relations theory. Int J Group Psychother 34:339–354, 1984

Rutter M, Brown GW: The reliability and validity of measures of family life and relationships in families containing a psychiatric patient. Soc Psychol 1:38, 1966

Sandler J: The background of safety. Int J Psychoanal 41:352–356, 1960

Scheibel AB, Kovelman JA: Disorientation of the hippocampal pyramidal cell and its processes in the schizophrenic patient. Biol Psychiatry 16:101–102, 1981

Schneider K: Klinische Psychopathologie, 3rd ed. Stuttgart, Thieme Verlag, 1950

Schneider K: Klinische Psychopathologie, 5th ed. Translated by Hamilton MW. New York, Grune and Stratton, 1959

Schooler C, Spohn HE: Social dysfunction and treatment failure in schizophrenia. Schizophr Bull 8:85–98, 1982

Schooler NR: Discussion: alternative drug treatment strategies in schizophrenia, in Drug Maintenance Strategies in Schizophrenia. Edited by Kane JM. Washington, DC, American Psychiatric Press, 1984, pp 84–90

Schulz SC: Progress in the treatment of nonresponders. Presented at the 140th Annual Meeting of the American Psychiatric Association, Chicago, Ill, May 1987

Schwartz DP: Psychotheraphy, in Schizophrenia: Science and Practice. Edited by Shershow JC. Cambridge, Harvard University Press, 1978, pp 197–222

Schwartz DP: The open hospital and the concept of limits, in Psychosocial Intervention in Schizophrenia. Edited by Stierlin H, Wynne LC, Wirsching M. Berlin, Springer-Verlag, 1983, pp 83–92

Schwartz DP: Loving action and the shape of the object, in Towards a Comprehensive

Model for Schizophrenic Disorders. Edited by Feinsilver DB. New York, The Analytic Press, 1986

Schwartz DP: Intrapsychic structure and interaction, in Attachment and the Therapeutic Process. Edited by Akabone Y, Sacksteder JL, Schwartz DP. New York, International Universities Press, 1987

Scott R, Cassidy K: The case management function: a position paper. Unpublished manuscript available from Ms. Cassidy, New Jersey Division of Mental Health and Hospitals, 1981

Searles H: The differentiation between concrete and metaphorical thinking in the recovering schizophrenic patient. J Am Psychoanal Assoc 10:22–49, 1962

Searles H: Countertransference and theoretical model, in Psychotherapy of Schizophrenia. Edited by Gunderson JG, Mosher LR. New York, Jason Aronson, 1975, pp 223–228

Seeman P, Ulpian C, Bergeron C, et al: Bimodal distribution of dopamine receptor densities in brains of schizophrenics. Science 225:728–731, 1984

Segal M, Kopschitz DH: Depressive changes after fluphenazine treatment. Br Med J 4:169, 1969

Selvini MP: Toward a general model of psychotic family games. Journal of Marriage and Family Therapy 12:339–349, 1986

Selvini-Palazzoli M, Ceccin G, Prata G, et al: Paradox and Counterparadox. New York, Jason Aronson, 1978

Serok S, Zimet RM: An experiment of gestalt group therapy with hospitalized schizophrenics. Psychotherapy: Theory, Research and Practice 20:417–424, 1983

Sheppard G, Marchand R, Gruzelier J, et al: O 15 positron emission tomographic scanning predominantly never-treated acute schizophrenic patients. Lancet ii:1448–1452, 1983

Simon FB, Stierlin H, Wynne LC: The Language of Family Therapy: A Systemic Vocabulary and Sourcebook. New York, Family Process Press, 1985, pp 261–263

Singer M, Wynne L: Thought disorder and family relations of schizophrenics, III: methodology using projective techniques. Arch Gen Psychiatry 12: 187–200, 1965a

Singer M, Wynne L: Thought disorder and family relations of schizophrenics, IV: results and implications. Arch Gen Psychiatry 12:201–212, 1965b

Slavson SR: Group psychotherapy and the nature of schizophrenia. Int J Group Psychother 11:3–32, 1961

Small JG, Kellams JJ, Milstein V, et al: A placebo-controlled study of lithium combined with neuroleptics in chronic schizophrenia patients. Am J Psychiatry 132:1315–1317, 1975

Spiegler MD, Agijian H: The Community Training Center: An Educational-Behavioral Social Systems Model for Rehabilitating Psychiatric Patients. New York, Brunner/Mazel, 1977

Spitz HI: Contemporary trends in group psychotherapy: a literature survey. Hosp Community Psychiatry 35:132–142, 1984

Spitzer RL, Endicott J, Robins E: Research Diagnostic Criteria (RDC), 3rd ed. New York, New York State Psychiatric Institute, 1977

Stanton AH, Gunderson JG, Knapp PH, et al: Effects of psychotherapy on schizophrenic patients, I: design and implementation of a controlled study. Schizophr Bull 10:520–563, 1984

Stein LI, Test MA: An alternative to mental hospital treatment, I: conceptual model, treatment program and clinical evaluation. Arch Gen Psychiatry 37:392–397, 1980

Steiner J: Holistic group therapy with schizophrenic patients. Int J Group Psychother 29:195–210, 1979

Stephens JH, Astrup C, Carpenter WT, Jr, et al: A comparison of nine systems to diagnose schizophrenia. Psychiatry Res 6:127–143, 1982

Strachan AM: Family intervention for the rehabilitation of schizophrenia: toward protection and coping. Schizophr Bull 12: 678–698, 1986

Strachan AM, Leff JP, Goldstein MJ, et al: Emotional attitudes and direct communication in the families of schizophrenics: a cross-national replication. Br J Psychiatry 149:279–287, 1986

Strassberg DS, Roback HB, Anchor KM, et al: Self-disclosure in group therapy with schizophrenics. Arch Gen Psychiatry 32:1259–1261, 1975

Strauss JS, Carpenter WT, Bartko JJ: The diagnosis and understanding of schizophrenia, III: speculations on the processes that underlie schizophrenic symptoms and signs. Schizophr Bull 11:61–76, 1974

Strauss JS, Hafez H, Lieberman P, et al: The course of psychiatric disorder. III: longitudinal principles. Am J Psychiatry 142:289–296, 1985

Strodtbeck FL: The family as a three person group. Am Sociol Rev 19:23–29, 1954

Sturgeon D, Kuipers L, Berkowitz R, et al: Psychophysiological responses of schizophrenic patients to high and low expressed emotion relatives. Br J Psychiatry 138:40–45, 1981

Sullivan HS: Conceptions of Modern Psychiatry. New York, Norton Press, 1940, p 22

Sullivan HS: Schizophrenia as a Human Process. New York, Norton, 1962

Sussman S, Mueser KT: Age, socioeconomic status, severity of mental disorder, and chronicity as predictors of physical attractiveness. J Abnorm Psychol 92:255–258, 1983

Sydenham T: Observationes medicae (1676), in The Entire Works of Thomas Sydenham Newly Made English from the Originals. Edited by Swan J. London, Cave, 1742

Szasz TS: The Myth of Mental Illness. London, Secker and Warburg, 1961

Talbott JA: Educational training for treatment and care, in The Chronic Mental Patient: Five Years Later. Edited by Talbott, JA. New York, Grune and Stratton, 1984, pp 91–101

Targum SD: Neuroendocrine dysfunction in schizophreniform disorder: correlation with six month clinical outcome. Am J Psychiatry 140:309–313, 1983

Tarrier N, Barrowclough C: Providing information to relatives about schizophrenia: some comments. Br J Psychiatry 149:458–463, 1986

Tarrier N, Vaughn C, Lader MH, et al: Bodily reactions to people and events in schizophrenia. Arch Gen Psychiatry 36:311–315, 1979

Taylor MA, Abrams R: Acute mania. Arch Gen Psychiatry 32:863–865, 1975

Taylor MA, Abrams R: The prevalence of schizophrenia: a reassessment using modern diagnostic criteria. Am J Psychiatry 135:945–948, 1978

Taylor P, Fleminger II: ECT for schizophrenia. Lancet i:1380, 1980

Terkelsen K: Schizophrenia and the family, II: adverse effects of family therapy. Fam Process 22:191–200, 1983

Terkelsen K: The Humiliation of the patient. Unpublished manuscript

Test MA: Community support programs, in Schizophrenia: Treatment, Management and Rehabilitation. Edited by Bellack AS. New York, Grune and Stratton, 1984, pp 347–373

Tharp RG, Otis GD: Toward a therapeutic intervention in families. Journal of Counseling Psychology 30:426–434, 1966

Torrey EF: Surviving Schizophrenia: A Family Manual. New York, Harper and Row, 1983

Tourney G: A history of therapeutic fashions in psychiatry 1800–1966. Am J Psychiatry 124:784-796, 1967

Tsuang MT, Woolsen RF, Winokur G, et al: Stability of psychiatric diagnosis. Arch Gen Psychiatry 38:535–539, 1981

Turner JC, TenHoor WJ: The NIMH community support program: pilot approach to a needed social reform. Schizophr Bull 4:319–348, 1978

Ullman LP, Krasner L: A Psychological Approach to Abnormal Behavior. Englewood Cliffs, NJ, Prentice-Hall, 1969

Urey JR, Laughlin C, Kelly JA: Teaching heterosocial conversational skills to male psychiatric inpatients. J Behav Ther Exp Psychiatry 10:323–328, 1979

Van Putten T: Why do schizophrenic patients refuse to take their drugs? Arch Gen Psychiatry 31:67–72, 1974

Vaughn CE: Patterns of emotional response in the families of schizophrenic patients, in Treatment of Schizophrenia: Family Assessment and Intervention. Edited by Goldstein MJ, Hand I, Hahlweg K. New York, Springer-Verlag, 1986, pp 97–106

Vaughn CE, Leff JP: The influence of family life and social factors on the course of psychiatric illness: a comparison of schizophrenia and depressed neurotic patients. Br J Psychiatry 129:125–137, 1976

Vaughn CE, Leff JP: Patterns of emotional response in relatives of schizophrenic patients. Schizophr Bull 7:43–44, 1981

Vaughn CE, Snyder KD, Jones S, et al: Family factors in schizophrenic relapse: a California replication of the British research on expressed emotion. Arch Gen Psychiatry 41:1169–1177, 1984

Venables PH, Wing JK: Level of arousal and the subclassification of schizophrenia. Arch Gen Psychiatry 7:114–119, 1962

Virchow R: Hundert Jahre Allgemeiner Pathologie. Berlin, Hirschwald, 1895

von Bertalanffy L: General systems theory: a new approach to the unity of science. Hum Biol 23:339, 1951

Wallace CJ: Community and interpersonal functioning in the course of schizophrenic disorders. Schizophr Bull 19:233–257, 1984

Wallace CJ, Nelson CJ, Liberman RP, et al: A review and critique of social skills training with schizophrenic patients. Schizophr Bull 6:42–63, 1980

Wallace CJ, Boone SE, Donahoe CP, et al: Psychosocial rehabilitation for the chronic mentally disabled: social and independent living skills training, in Behavioral Treatment of Adult Disorders. Edited by Barlow D. New York, Guilford Press, 1985

Watt JAG: The relationship of paranoid states to schizophrenia. Am J Psychiatry 142:1456–1458, 1985

Watzlawick P, Weakland J, Fisch R: Change: Principles of Problem Formation and Problem Resolution. New York, WW Norton, 1974

Waxer PH: Short-term group psychotherapy: some principles and techniques. Int J Group Psychother 27:33–42, 1977

Weakland J, Fisch R, Watzlawick P, et al: Brief therapy: focused problem resolution. Fam Process 13:141–168, 1974

Weinberger DL, Torrey EF, Neophytides AN, et al: Lateral cerebral ventricular enlargement in chronic schizophrenia. Arch Gen Psychiatry 36:735–739, 1979

Will OA: Paranoid development and the concept of self: psychotherapeutic intervention. Psychiatry 24:74–86, 1961

Willets R: Advocacy for case managers, in Proceedings of the 1982 Florida Conference on Deinstitutionalization. Edited by Marlowe H, Weinberg R. Tampa, University of South Florida, 1982

Wilson WH, Diamond RJ, Factor RM: A psychotherapeutic approach to task-oriented groups of severely ill patients. Yale J Biol Med 58:363–372, 1985

Wing JK: Social influence on the course of schizophrenia, in The Nature of Schizophrenia: New Approaches to Research and Treatment. Edited by Wynne LC, Cromwell RL, Matthysse S. New York, John Wiley, 1978, p 606

Wing JK, Cooper JE, Sartorius N: The Description and Classification of Psychiatric

Symptomatology: An Instruction Manual for the PSE and CATEGO System. New York, Cambridge University Press, 1974

Winnicott DW: Transitional objects and transitional phenomena. Int J Psychoanal 34:89–97, 1953

Winnicott DW: Ego distortion in terms of true and false self (1960), in The Maturational Process and the Facilitating Environment. New York, International Universities Press, 1974, pp 140–152

Witheridge TF, Dincin J: The Bridge: an assertive outreach program in an urban setting, in The Training in Community Living Model: A Decade of Experience. New Directions for Mental Health Services, no. 26. Edited by Tein LI, Test MA. San Francisco, Jossey-Bass, 1985

Wolkin A, Jaeger J, Brodie JD, et al: Persistence of cerebral metabolic abnormalities in chronic schizophrenia as determined by positron emission tomography. Am J Psychiatry 142:564–571, 1985

Wolman BB: Group psychotherapy with latent schizophrenics. Int J Group Psychother 10:301–312, 1960

Wong, SE, Massel HK, Mosk MD, et al: Behavioral approaches to the treatment of schizophrenia, in Handbook of Studies on Schizophrenia. Edited by Burrows GD, Norman TR, Rubinstein G. Amsterdam, Elsevier, 1986

Wong SE, Terranova MD, Bowen L, et al: Providing independent recreational activities to reduce stereotypic vocalizations in chronic schizophrenics. Journal of Applied Behavior Analysis 20:77–81, 1987

Wong SE, Flanagan SG, Kuehnel TG, et al: Teaching independent grooming skills to chronic mental patients. Hosp Community Psychiatry. (in press)

World Health Organization: Mental Disorders: Glossary and Guide to their Classification in Accordance with the Ninth Revision of the International Classification of Diseases. Geneva, World Health Organization, 1978

World Psychiatric Association: Diagnostic Criteria for Schizophrenic and Affective Psychoses. World Psychiatric Association, 1983

Wynne AR: Movable group therapy for institutionalized patients. Hosp Community Psychiatry 29:516–519, 1978

Wynne LC: Methodological and conceptual issues in the study of schizophrenics and their families. J Psychiatr Res 6(Suppl 1):185–199, 1968

Wynne LC: Family research on the pathogenesis of schizophrenia: intermediate variables in the study of families at high risk, in Problems of Psychosis. Edited by Doucet R, Laurin C. Excerpta Medica, pp 401–423. Reprinted by U.S. Department of Health, Education and Welfare, National Institutes of Health publication no. 33818, 1969

Wynne LC: From symptoms to vulnerability and beyond: an overview, in The Nature of Schizophrenia: New Approaches to Research and Treatment. Edited by Wynne LC, Cromwell RL, Matthysse S. New York, Wiley, 1978, pp 698–714

Wynne LC: A phase-oriented approach to treatment with schizophrenics and their families, in Family Therapy in Schizophrenia. Edited by McFarlane WR. New York, Guilford Press, 1983, pp 251–265

Wynne LC: Personal communication. November 21, 1986

Wynne LC, Singer M: Thought disorder and family relations of schizophrenics, I: a research study. Arch Gen Psychiatry 9:191–198, 1963a

Wynne LC, Singer M: Thought disorder and family relations of schizophrenics, II: classification of forms of thinking. Arch Gen Psychiatry 9:199–206, 1963b

Wynne LC, Rycoff IM, Day J, et al: I. Pseudomutuality in the family relations of schizophrenics. Psychiatry 21:205–220, 1958

Wynne LC, Toohey ML, Doane J: Family studies, in Disorders of the Schizophrenic Syndrome. Edited by Bellak L. New York, Basic Books, 1979, pp 264–288

Wynne LC, McDaniel SH, Weber TT (eds): Systems Consultation: A New Perspective for Family Therapy. New York, Guilford Press, 1986

Wynne LC, McDaniel SH, Weber TT: Professional politics and the concepts of family therapy, family consultation and systems consultation. Fam Process 26:153–166, 1987

Yalom ID: The Theory and Practice of Group Psychotherapy. New York, Basic Books, 1970

Yalom ID: Inpatient Group Psychotherapy. New York, Basic Books, 1983, pp 275–312

Zubin J: Chronic schizophrenia from the standpoint of vulnerability, in Perspectives in Schizophrenia Research. Edited by Baxter C, Melnechuk T. New York, Raven Press, 1980, pp 269–294

Zubin J, Spring B: Vulnerability: a new view of schizophrenia. J Abnorm Psychol 96:103–126, 1977

Zubin J, Magaziner J, Steinhauer SR: The metamorphosis of schizophrenia: from chronicity to vulnerability. Br J Psychiatry 143:551–571, 1983

Delusional (Paranoid) Disorders

Chapter 152

Delusional (Paranoid) Disorders

Historical Perspective

The delusional (paranoid) disorders can be regarded as a paradigm of those forms of mental illness that can arise in the absence of any detectable cerebral disease or other organic cause known at the present time; for they pose questions about the nature and causation of mental disorders along a wide front.

The progress of psychiatry in recent decades has resolved some of these issues, but less attention has been devoted to the management of paranoid psychoses and disorders than to other forms of illness. In consequence the advances made in refining and validating the diagnosis and classification of this group of disorders, in improving the efficacy of the available methods of treatment, and in gaining an understanding of their causes have not been commensurate with the progress achieved with respect to a number of the major mental disorders.

The paranoid disorders are relatively common forms of illness, particularly when account is taken of the grey area that separates them from the major psychoses and personality disorders. Kendler (1982) reviewing data from a number of countries concludes that the paranoid disorders constitute 1 to 4 percent of all annual admissions to psychiatric hospitals and estimates incidence of first admissions as 1 per 100,000 of the population per year. Among the reasons that render these disorders particularly interesting and significant both from a scientific and clinical point of view is that, in certain respects, they can be regarded, as Kendler and Tsuang (1981) have pointed out, as occupying an intermediate position between the schizophrenic disorders in the strictest sense on the one hand and the affective disorders on the other. Their mean age of onset, prognosis, and the married state of a high proportion of patients brings them closer to affective than schizophrenic disorders. However, with respect to heredity and social class they have more kinship with schizophrenia. The most salient clinical features, the paranoid delusions, have more in common with schizophrenia than affective disorder but they also overlap in their phenomenology with the affective disorders. All the points briefly made here will be more fully explored in the later sections of this chapter.

Toward the end of the nineteenth century (Séglas 1887) discussion about many issues that remain unresolved at the present time was already in progress. How far, it was asked, could paranoid disorder be related to organic disease or psychological factors? What was their relationship to manic and melancholic states? Did all forms of paranoia and related disorders terminate in states of chronic insanity or were there some conditions with a more benign course? At the commencement of the present century the leading schools of psychiatry were inclined to attribute disorders dominated by paranoid symptoms to constitutional and genetic factors. It was already known that alcohol and cocaine could give rise to psychoses that closely resembled the conditions that were seen in the psychiatric clinic. But investigations failed in most cases to bring to light the evidence of organic causation.

Within a short period of time other authorities were already attributing the disorder to the life events and deprivations endured by patients (Gaupp 1910; Kretschmer 1918) while psychoanalytical theory was asserting that the pathology seen in the clinic was an extreme form of the psychopathology of everyday life (Freud 1911, reprinted 1959). The distinction between jealousy that was a universal human propensity and the forms of "morbid jealousy" that commonly present in the psychiatric clinic was viewed as a difference in degree rather than a difference in kind.

That certain paranoid states were understandable as the reactions of individuals with a special kind of sensibility to certain vicissitudes and humiliations was already appreciated 80 or more years ago by some psychiatrists. They had been trained in the classical descriptive and organic tradition but had moved beyond its teaching (Jaspers 1913, reprinted 1963; Kretschmer 1918; Wimmer 1916). The interest and relevance of the new perspective for certain forms of paranoid disorder were soon acknowledged and have continued to influence the clinical practice and scientific work of some groups of psychiatrists, those of Scandinavia and Switzerland in particular (Retterstol 1966, 1970; Staehelin 1946–1947; Strömgren 1958, 1974).

But the precise role and importance of such factors as causal agents in paranoid disorders was unclear and continues to be the subject of debate at the present time. It was possible to conceive that extreme forms of stress and personal conflict might form a jealous, litigious, suspicious, or sexually maladjusted individual who suffers temporary distortion in perception of the world. But no explanation was or is available as to how delusions become entrenched with complete imperviousness to reason and evidence, how certain forms of hallucination erupt, and above all why neither psychoanalysis nor other forms of psychological treatment are able to banish symptoms and restore the ability to perceive the world as it is. Modification of circumstances of life (excepting the rare situational cases) is equally ineffective for promoting recovery.

These issues are related to the nature of the relationship between normal psychological functioning and paranoid disorders. Most psychiatrists would judge lasting paranoid disorders to be closer to such forms of illness as manic-affective and schizophrenic psychoses than to normal mental life.

Minor paranoid traits are a relatively common human attribute but when pronounced may be mistaken for paranoid disorder. It should be possible to discriminate reliably between jealousy, suspicion, and ideas of self-reference that are within the range of normal variation and morbid mental states in which paranoid symptoms are prominent. A brief consideration of the distinction between the paranoid-like thought processes that are manifest in normal mental life and those experienced and observed in paranoid disorders is germane here.

Paranoid forms of thought and behavior derive from the mechanism of projection: a universal mode of thinking in which one tends to attribute one's unacknowledged feelings to others and to believe that happenings in the world are directed toward the self in a meaningful way. It may exert harmful or beneficial effects. Such mechanisms of projection and self-reference have very likely evolved because they promote human survival and adaptation by sharpening perception of the emotions, attitude, and intentions of others.

Certain forms of mistaken self-reference are ingredients of normal psychological experience. The belief that when one enters a room full of people others are paying special attention to one's attire or some feature such as the shape of the nose or a minor blemish has been experienced in mild and transient form by most individuals. Such reactions are likely to occur in exaggerated form among those who live in communities from which they are separated by differences of language, color, culture, or religious belief. However, in the great majority of those exposed to such situations, the reactions are fleeting; insight into their unreality is preserved or restored after a short interval. One characteristic feature of such normal paranoid reactions is their understandability. They develop along paths that can be comprehended in terms of the range of variation in patterns of thought and conduct observed in the normal population.

In the morbid mental states that comprise paranoid symptoms, paranoid syndromes, and paranoid personality disorders, fleeting ideas of this nature are liable to develop into firmly held and lasting convictions. Insight into their illusory nature is undermined, and the influence they exert on the behavior and attitudes of the affected person alienates him or her from others. The responses elicited by such conduct will serve to intensify delusional convictions of persecution and harassment in a vicious circle.

There are some points of similarity between the normal and the pathologic forms of the paranoid mental state. But the loss of insight into the subjective distortion of perception and the fact that the ideas of self-reference are difficult or impossible to explain in the light of the situation, as well as the habitual nature they assume and the irrationally hostile and aggressive action they may cause, set the pathology qualitatively apart from normal mental functioning. Normal functioning is associated with a measure of insight, is rarely acted out in aggressive of dangerous conduct, and is subject to wide individual variation. Sharp and indubitable lines of demarcation do not exist between the normal and morbid variants of paranoid thinking. This does not invalidate the distinction nor the validity of the judgments that attempt to discriminate between them in clinical practice. It is to the pathologic forms of the paranoid mental state and their treatment that this chapter is largely devoted.

Classification of Paranoid Disorders

In DSM-III-R (American Psychiatric Association 1987) paranoid disorders are described under a number of different headings. The main group is to be found under the rubric 297.10 Delusional (Paranoid) Disorders. This condition is defined as follows: "Nonbizarre delusions (i.e., involving mechanisms that occur in real life, such as being followed, poisoned, infected, loved at a distance, having a disease, being deceived by one's spouse or lover) of at least one month's duration." Exclusion criteria are the presence of prominent auditory or visual hallucinations or of obviously "odd or bizarre" behavior. Features of depressive or manic disorder are admissible only if they appear after the delusions or are of brief duration. The disorder does not meet criterion A for schizophrenia and is not due to an organic mental disorder (p. 202). Category 297.0 "paranoid state, simple" in the *International Classification of Diseases*, 9th revision (ICD-9) (World Health Organization 1978) is essentially similar but the term psychosis is retained: "A psychosis, acute or chronic, not classifiable as schizophrenia or affective psychosis, in which delusions, especially of being influenced, persecuted or treated in some special way, are the main symptoms. The delusions are of a fairly fixed elaborate systematised kind."

The subdivisions under the DSM-III-R rubric include "persecutory," "erotomanic," "somatic,". "grandiose," and "jealous" types according to the character of the predominant delusional theme. In Brief Reactive Psychosis (298.80) symptoms appear in impressive association with a stressful life event and the picture would therefore be generally dominated by persecutory or other delusions and hallucinations. This condition has to be of brief duration lasting up to a month with "virtual return to premorbid level of functioning."

A substantial proportion of patients who satisfy the criteria for a diagnosis of schizoaffective disorder (DSM-III-R 295.70) will prove to have paranoid psychoses in that the presence of prominent non-mood-congruent delusions, and hallucinations will be one of the main reasons for allocating them to the schizoaffective group of disorders.

"Induced psychotic disorder" (shared paranoid disorder) (DSM-III-R 297.30) is by definition a paranoid disorder. "Organic delusional syndrome" (DSM-III-R 293.81), in which the psychiatric features with an organic cause are among the exclusion criteria, presents problems of management closely similar to those for cases that fall within the main group of delusional disorders.

ICD-9 retains paranoia (297.1) which has disappeared from DSM-III-R, and paraphrenia (297.2), which was never included. In addition to acute paranoid reaction (298.3), ICD-9 includes psychogenic paranoid psychosis (298.4).

Paranoid symptoms and paranoid syndromes may be present in the setting of a paranoid personality disorder (ICD-9 301.0, DSM-III-R 301.0). The person with paranoid personality disorder exhibits lifelong traits of oversensitiveness, distrust, and suspicion, so that he or she interprets innocent remarks as threatening. It may prove difficult to differentiate between behavior that arises from lifelong paranoid traits and the early stages of a paranoid disorder, which will in some cases have supervened in a paranoid personality.

Finally, there are probably few experienced clinicians who have not made the erroneous diagnosis of paranoid disorder in a manic illness. The signs of elevated mood may be absent or inconspicuous in manic disorders, the picture being dominated by an angry, irritable, hostile mood, overactivity, paranoid or grandiose delusions, and aggressive and litigious conduct.

Theories Regarding the Etiology of Paranoid Disorders and Their Relationship to Other Psychiatric Syndromes

The relationship between paranoid disorders and other forms of psychiatric illness and the theories that have been advanced about their causation require consideration in this chapter. The evidence bearing on these issues needs to be taken into account when making a diagnosis in patients with paranoid symptoms and when making decisions about treatment.

The *International Pilot Study of Schizophrenia* (World Health Organization 1973) showed that many psychiatrists in different parts of the world consider most cases of psychosis dominated by paranoid delusions, whether or not associated with hallucinations, to be variants of schizophrenic illness. In consequence many of the cases classed by the "CATEGO" program (which was employed to arrive at a computerized diagnosis of schizophrenia or other psychoses from data recorded by participants in the International Pilot Study of Schizophrenia) as paranoid psychosis in this inquiry had been diagnosed as schizophrenia. The participants in this study were expressing allegiance to one of the more influential views expressed in the course of the long controversy regarding the affiliations of the paranoid disorders. The failure to resolve this controversy is rooted in the fact that it does not admit of any simple categorical solution in terms of a simple unifying theory.

Three main groups of theories have been advanced since the beginning of this century regarding the character, nosological status, and outcome of paranoid states.

1. The first theory comes from the school of Kraepelin, and implicit in it is the view that mental disorders dominated by paranoid delusions have a close kinship with schizophrenia. In his early writings Kraepelin had described paranoia and paraphrenia as distinct from schizophrenia in their clinical picture and long-term outcome. In particular, observations over a long period showed that the type of deterioration of personality that occurred in schizophrenia did not take place. However, Kraepelin later accepted the testimony adduced by a number of his pupils favoring a close kinship of these paranoid psychoses with schizophrenia.
2. The second theory is highly influential in the Scandinavian countries, where a wide range of paranoid disorders is subsumed under the heading "psychogenic psychosis." These disorders are regarded as arising from an interaction between certain types of predisposition and the onerous life events that impinge upon vulnerable facets of the personality (Faergeman 1963; Retterstol 1966, 1970; Strömgren 1940; Wimmer 1916). The benign outcome of patients with psychogenic psychoses such as paranoia is contrasted with the chronic deterioration of personality in a high proportion of schizophrenic patients. Paranoid symptoms are prominent both in the "schizoaffective" syndrome of Kasanin (1933) and the schizophreniform disorder described by Langfeldt (1939). Each mentions traumatic life events prior to onset, personality factors, and a favorable outcome, and their theories may therefore be classed with the other "reactive" theories in the second group. Langfeldt's concept has been extensively tested in the studies of Retterstol, which will be described in this section. A relatively large body of observations has been published about the treatment and other aspects of schizoaffective disorder, and therefore this will be mainly considered in the chapter devoted to this condition.
3. A third theory is implicit in the French concept of bouffée delirante, which refers to an acute paranoid hallucinatory syndrome that terminates in a matter of days or weeks in a clear remission without lasting deficit. It is considered to be entirely *distinct from schizophrenia*, and antecedent life events are not mentioned as an etiological factor or a consistent feature of the condition. Bouffée delirante is therefore regarded in France as a third psychosis.

The Scandinavian school was powerfully influenced in its early stages by a number of German psychiatrists who considered that at least some paranoid states arose as psychodynamically understandable historical developments culminating in the delusional syndrome. These psychiatrists included Gaupp, who investigated the psychiatric disorder of the mass murderer Wagner (Gaupp 1914, 1920) and Gaupp's pupil Kretschmer (1919). The ideas of Jaspers (1910, 1913, reprinted 1963) were also widely influential. He divided paranoid states into those in which the delusional ideas were primary and the result of a "psychic process" beyond the reach of understanding, in contrast to developmental conditions that were "understandable." He also formulated criteria for the diagnosis of "psychogenic" disorders including psychoses.

These disputes continue to be of importance for contemporary psychiatry. They are relevant for clinical psychiatrists and investigators whether they employ DSM-III in diagnosis and classification or utilize other systems. Because the evidence about the nature, causation, and the lines of demarcation of paranoid states is complex, account has to be taken of all the dimensions selected by these different theories for special emphasis. Each has some relevance for one or more of the syndromes to be described in this chapter.

Delusional (Paranoid) States as a Form of Schizophrenia

Kraepelin described paranoia as "the insidious development of a permanent and unshakeable delusional system arising from internal causes which is accompanied by perfect preservation of clear and orderly thinking, will and acting." Paranoia was distinct in his view from the paranoid forms of dementia praecox, in that it evolved on the basis of an abnormal constitution that had an hereditary basis. He stressed the absence of hallucinations in this condition, but later contributors were less inflexible about the weight to be attached to this feature. He judged paraphrenia, a delusional psychosis with florid hallucinations, to occupy an intermediate position between schizophrenia on the one hand and paranoia on the other. However, a number of pupils of Kraepelin published evidence that appeared to constitute a rebuttal of his views. In fact evidence of schizophrenic deterioration of personality in more than half of 78 patients diagnosed as paraphrenic was found by Kraepelin himself.

Although he was influenced by the findings of his pupils, Kraepelin continued to defend the view that gave independent nosological status to paranoia and paraphrenia. Both conditions are separately treated in the eighth edition of his textbook (Kraepelin 1909–1915). Paranoia was described as incurable and paraphrenia as pursuing a chronic course as far as the persistence of symptoms was concerned but uncomplicated by the deterioration of personality. At a later stage advances in treatment were to uphold the discriminating nature of Kraepelin's clinical insight in relation to this controversy. But some of his views came to be regarded as inflexible and lacking in the historical and dynamic dimension appropriate for study of the origins of some paranoid states.

As far as paranoia was concerned, it was the views of Kraepelin's pupils rather than those of the master himself that were to exert the greater influence in the decades that followed.

The work of Kolle (1931) provided further support for the view that paranoia and kindred delusional states were forms of schizophrenic illness. Kolle investigated 66 patients with this condition. He regarded 62 to exhibit delusions of a primary and incomprehensible character. He also cited genetic observations that purported to demonstrate that paranoia and schizophrenia had a common hereditary basis. Kolle considered that the "true delusion" was incomprehensible and always the symptom of a psychosis. This was usually schizophrenic but occasionally due to organic disorder.

A number of German psychiatrists ranged themselves on the side of Kolle on the basis of phenomenologic evidence about the character of delusions found in paranoia and paraphrenic psychosis. These were judged by Gruhle (1951), famous pupil of Jaspers, as having the character of true delusion, which "does not originate from subliminal wishes or from repressed emotions. It is an organic cerebral symptom which cannot be traced back to any source and with which one cannot empathise." Another distinguished member of the Heidelberg school, Mayer-Gross (1950), was later to express the opinion that most delusional psychoses were variants of schizophrenic illness. He adopted a view regarding the delusions identical with that of Schneider (1952), who considered that there was a sharp categorical distinction between understandable delusional reactions that had no specific diagnostic significance and true delusions or "delusional perception." He was referring to a two-stage phenomenon: the first comprised an ordinary perception and the second comprised the attachment of an abnormal significance to this perception for reasons that defied comprehension.

The findings of Kolle that favored a genetic link with schizophrenia have been confirmed in the case of paraphrenia by the demonstration of an increased morbid risk for schizophrenic illness in the relatives of patients with this disorder. A substantial proportion of paranoid psychoses and disorders are chronic in nature. In more recent years some support for the closeness of these disorders to schizophrenia has come from the response made by "late paraphrenia," among other paranoid disorders, to treatment with neuroleptic drugs.

But there is also evidence that calls in question the view of Kolle and others and argues in favor of a relatively distinct status for the paranoid disorders. As far as genetics is concerned, although morbid risks for relatives of patients with paranoid disorder are higher than those for the relatives of normal subjects, these risks have been found to be substantially lower for first-degree relatives of paranoic and paraphrenia patients (Kay 1959) than the risks for relatives of schizophrenics. A recent enquiry (Kendler et al. 1985) revealed a raised morbid risk for schizophrenia and schizoid/schizotypal personality in first degree relatives of schizophrenics but not in those patients with delusional disorder. The converse held in respect of the morbid risk of paranoid personality. Moreover, a genetic kinship does not establish clinical identity. The same gene may result in markedly divergent clinical consequences. Each clinical syndrome, therefore, has to be judged in its own right. The chronic course experienced by a proportion of Kolle's paranoiac patients and reported also in more recent studies (Kay and Roth 1961) currently represents an out-of-date picture. The prognosis of late paraphrenia and related forms of disorder has been transformed by the advent of neuroleptic compounds. The precise extent to which the prospects for other paranoid syndromes have been favorably altered remains to be determined with the aid of clinical trials in different subgroups. But there is a body of evidence from trials in schizoaffective illness of predominantly paranoid symptomatology that neuroleptic drugs (alone or in combination with antidepressant compounds) promote remission in a substantial proportion of cases.

Paraphrenic and paranoid psychoses of middle life respond to modern treatments in a manner similar to the corresponding psychoses of the aged. Moreover, in a large cohort of Swedish patients first admitted before neuroleptics came into general use and followed up after many years, the observations of Retterstol (1966, 1970) and his colleague (Opjordsmoen 1986) have shown that "paranoid" and "paranoiac" psychoses (regarded as reactive psychoses by Retterstol) have an outcome that is distinctly more favorable than that of DSM-III schizophrenia. It is the far higher proportion of social recovery in the former that is particularly noteworthy, for it rules out the possibility that true schizophrenic deterioration could have been anywhere nearly as common as suggested by Kolle's original findings. This general conclusion remains valid despite the less favorable outcome in these cases reported by some other observers; the subject is dealt with more fully in a later section.

Toward the end of his life, Kolle (1957) was to depart from his earlier views, according to which delusional states were endogenous, determined by genetic and constitutional factors, and closely related to schizophrenia. He acknowledged the existence of a group of "developmental paranoias." These were delusional states that could be partly understood in the light of historical development of the individual, in contrast to "process paranoia" in which delusions were beyond such attempts at empathy and comprehension. The former comprised such conditions as conjugal paranoias, morbid states of jealousy, and the paranoid states of litigious, fanatical, imprisoned, and deaf individuals.

By this time the view that there was a distinct group of "psychogenic" or "reactive" paranoid psychoses with a benign prognosis had received influential support from the work of Gaupp, Kretschmer, and Scandinavian psychiatrists such as Wimmer (1916), Strömgren (1940), and Faergeman (1963). The first of these authors, Wimmer, was familiar with the work of French authors such as Magnan and Janet and was also influenced by Kraepelin and Jaspers in Germany.

Delusional (Paranoid) States as Psychogenic or "Reactive" Disorders

From the second decade of the present century onward a number of attempts have been made to separate paranoia from dementia praecox by observations purported to establish

1. that they were psychologically understandable developments,
2. that they emerged from interaction between a predisposed individual with an Achilles heel in his personality and traumatic life events,
3. that there followed a paranoid delusional psychosis that divorced the patient from his environment, and
4. that despite this rift from reality the personality remained intact in terms of thought, affect, and volition.

The classical description by Gaupp (1914, 1920) of the notorious mass murderer Wagner was a massively documented paradigm of cases of this nature. Ernst Wagner was a highly educated, intelligent schoolmaster, poet, and novelist who on the night of the 3rd–4th of September 1913 killed his wife and four children by cutting their throats while they slept. He then traveled by train and bicycle from Stuttgart to Muhlhausen. On the following night he started four fires in the sleeping village, and when the inhabitants tried to escape from their houses he fired shots from two pistols at all the male inhabitants killing eight of them and severely wounding 12 others. He was then brought down by some of the inhabitants and prevented from completing his entire plan, which was to murder his brother's family, to start other fires in the village, and to set fire to the neighboring castle where he was to commit suicide by shooting himself. The mass murders had been meticulously planned and kept secret over a decade.

Wagner was committed to an asylum where he spent the rest of his life and was observed by Gaupp over a period of almost 25 years. Wagner had already experienced ideas of self-reference in relation to the practice of masturbation from the age of 18. He believed everyone knew his guilty secret. Gaupp considered that Wagner suffered from a paranoid illness that had begun abruptly (against a background of previously circumscribed paranoid personality traits) after he committed a number of acts of indecency with animals while making his way from an inn to his home in a drunken state. Almost immediately he began to observe others commenting, laughing, and making derisive and contemptuous remarks about him. He believed that the whole village of Muhlhausen and people wider afield were aware of his perverted behavior. He developed an intense hatred of his tormentors and planned to murder his enemies in Mühlhausen out of revenge and to kill his family out of compassionate concern for the sufferings they would otherwise endure after his death.

Gaupp considered Wagner's psychotic disorder to be the delusional reaction of a man of paranoid personality to the emotional stress occasioned by indecent acts that caused him guilt and shame. Over a period of 25 years his delusions remained unshakable except for short-lived intervals when they would recede, only to be replaced by a fresh delusional system in which he felt persecuted by Jews, whom he saw all around him, and in particular by the poet Franz Werfel, whom he accused of plagiarizing his works. He welcomed the advent of the Nazi regime and its racial policies with a joyous satisfaction. He died in 1938 at the age of 64. There was at no time any sign of intellectual impairment or personality deterioration. He remained quick witted, powerful in argument, verbally fluent, and coherent to the end when he died of tuberculosis.

Most of Gaupp's psychiatric colleagues, including Eugen Bleuler, thought Wagner suffered from a mild paranoid schizophrenic illness. Gaupp rejected this view although he admitted that two of Wagner's maternal relatives were clearly schizophrenic. In fact one uncle suffered from delusional ideas of self-reference centering around his masturbation that were strongly reminiscent of earlier stages of his nephew's mental development. But the concept of psychogenic psychosis was carried forward by Gaupp's pupil Kretschmer in his work on the sensitive delusion of reference, *Der Sensitive Beziehungswahn* (1918).

Kretschmer's monograph described patients who were sensitive, endowed with a depressive and pessimistic outlook, and had high ambition and low frustration tolerance. The psychosis was initiated by a "key event," which gave rise to a "mental avalanche" after impinging upon vulnerable facets of the individual's morbid personality. The event was usually some error or indiscretion at variance with the individual's moral code, often a minor misdemeanor of a sexual nature. Kretschmer was partly influenced by his familiarity with the case of Wagner, whom he regarded as exemplifying his syndrome. Subsequent investigations were to show that a substantial proportion of Kretschmer's cases developed symptoms of a chronic psychosis. But it is not clear whether the picture in those found to be ill on follow-up was one of schizophrenic personality deterioration with negative symptoms or no more than an encapsulated psychosis that left the personality intact.

Despite the criticisms leveled against it, Kretschmer's work was widely influential in directing attention to the dynamic aspects of certain paranoid states. Kretschmer's work had helped to create the Scandinavian concept of psychogenic psychosis (Strömgren 1940). Retterstol's concept (1966, 1970) was considerably wider than Kretschmer's syndrome and embraced paranoia and paraphrenia as well as schizophreniform psychosis, which are all regarded as "reactive."

More recently the comprehensive long-term studies conducted by Retterstol and his colleagues have adduced a large body of evidence regarding the clinical profile, course, and prognosis of paranoid psychosis. They followed up and compared the outcome of 78 delusional patients with a schizophreniform psychosis, 173 patients with reactive psychosis, and 52 patients with schizophrenia (originally diagnosed by Langfeldt). Five to 19 years after discharge 81 percent of the reactive psychotics had pursued a favorable course compared with 61 percent of those with schizophreniform psychosis and only 23 percent of those with schizophrenia. Fifty-four percent of the reactive psychotics achieved a complete and lasting remission, 36 percent suffered further attacks with good remissions, and 10 percent pursued a chronic course. In contrast only 10 percent of patients with schizophrenia made a complete recovery.

However, a more recent investigation by Opjordsmoen (1986) of a subsample of 125 patients drawn from Retterstol's material after a follow-up period of between 15 and 18 years or 35 and 37 years after the original admission shows that a further proportion of patients had undergone deterioration as assessed with the aid of the Global Assessment Scale. Approximately 58 percent of the patients were unchanged, 30 percent had deteriorated, and 13 percent had improved. The proportion whose status had declined increased with the length of time that had elapsed since discharge from hospital.

Particular interest attaches to the detailed results regarding social outcome and the proportion who remained under psychiatric care. A variety of different criteria were applied in the evaluation of these patients at follow-up.

On the basis of DSM-III criteria for schizophreniform disorder 58.1 percent were at work at the end of the follow-up period and 87.1 percent were residing at home; the corresponding figures for schizophrenia were 18.4 percent and 68.4 percent.

Among those diagnosed with reactive psychosis by ICD-9 criteria, 68 percent were at work and 92 percent were living at home. The findings for paranoid states (ICD-9) and schizoaffective disorder (RDC) were closely similar, while among patients with delusional disorders according to the criteria of Kendler (Kendler and Tsuang 1981) 51.6 percent were at work and 87.1 percent were living at home.

However, from the data provided by Opjoerdsmoen it would seem that a substantial proportion of patients continued to suffer from psychiatric symptoms. More than half of those with reactive psychosis were receiving psychiatric treatment. The proportion under care with schizophreniform disorders was 58 percent and for schizoaffective and reactive psychoses the proportion was 48 percent. The status of schizophrenic patients was far less satisfactory; four-fifths were continuing under psychiatric treatment and only 18.3 percent were employed.

Although the more unfavorable social outcome has been demonstrated in males, it is of interest that a higher proportion of women remain under psychiatric treatment.

Some components of Retterstol's thesis that the paranoid psychoses are relatively distinct from schizophrenia are therefore supported by his own and others' published data. These disorders pursue on the whole a more benign course than schizophrenic disorders. Schizophrenic deterioration of personality leading to a "burnt-out" state is uncommon. Chronicity of some symptoms is more common, but the illness is encapsulated permitting a satisfactory social adjustment in more than two-thirds of the cases. Approximately 90 percent of "reactive" paranoid psychotics and those with non-schizophrenic delusional disorders were living at home.

Retterstol's conclusions were derived from the largest cohort of patients with paranoid psychosis ever studied and therefore have a firm factual basis. But the verdict that emerges from the observations of other workers is more ambiguous. Forty-three of 160 of Faergeman's patients (Faergeman 1945, 1963) originally diagnosed by Wimmer as suffering from "psychogenic" psychosis proved to be suffering from schizophrenia or a closely similar disorder when followed up many years later. The Norwegian study (Noreik 1970) showed 56 percent of patients with "reactive" psychosis to have pursued a course consistent with a diagnosis of schizophrenic illness. Variations in the criteria used in diagnosis and in sampling are the most likely explanation for some of these seemingly contradictory findings. But the most telling statistics come from Retterstol's own data and those of Opjordsmoen. Of the patients with "uncertain" diagnosis (almost a quarter of the total sample) 30 percent were judged to be schizophrenic on follow-up. One-third of the subsample of 125 patients reexamined decades after the initial admission were found to have deteriorated. And at this time almost 50 percent of "reactive" psychosis were under psychiatric care though only a small proportion were in institutions. The outcome of paranoid psychoses, though relatively favorable overall, is indeterminate.

Jaspers' Line of Demarcation Between "Psychogenic" and "Endogenous" Psychoses

The differential diagnostic criteria of Jaspers (1913, English translation 1963) were the first to be set down in specific terms and continue to be influential among contemporary psychiatrists in Europe in particular. He drew a sharp distinction between psychiatric disorders that could be regarded as the result of "a process" (this term referred to a qualitative change in psychic life that emerged spontaneously without any adequate and ascertainable psychological cause) and "development" disorders that arise during the historical unfolding of the individual's patterns of behavior; a developmental disorder can be understood in terms of this history and the personality that evolved in the course of it. In the former there was a break in continuity of psychic life followed by subjective experiences and behavior beyond the range of normal psychological phenomena. In the latter the disorder was merely a variant of normal psychological experience. During a process "true delusions" are often manifest. These cannot be comprehended when set in the context of the patient's life history and situation. In the developmental type of disorder any distortions of reality are closely and comprehensibly related to the prevailing emotional state and the patient's life predicament.

In Jaspers' view, psychotic delusional (paranoid) disorders may be regarded as psychogenic when they satisfy the following criteria:

1. The onset of illness bears a clear time relationship with some stressful life event.
2. The precipitating stress must be adequate; in other words the disorders that follow stress must not be disproportionately severe.
3. There is a meaningful relationship between the content of the precipitating adverse event and that of the mental illness that follows it. It should be possible to construe it as a form of defense, a wish fulfillment, or an escape from onerous circumstances and symptoms.
4. When the primary or precipitating cause is removed, the illness ("abnormal reaction") comes to an end.

Wimmer (1916), the influential Danish psychiatrist who formulated criteria similar to those of Jaspers, added that reactive psychoses *never end in deterioration*.

A small proportion of paranoid disorders would qualify for diagnosis as psychogenic psychosis according to these criteria. They include the paranoid psychoses of prisoners, some of the paranoid reactions of the deaf and of those placed in a situation of isolation, and induced psychoses such as "folie a deux." But the majority of cases of persecutory paranoia, paranoid jealousy, or erotomania and schizoaffective and schizophreniform disorder with predominantly paranoid features seen in clinical practice would fail to qualify for admission to the class of psychogenic disorders. When these paranoid syndromes follow onerous life events they are disproportionate in severity and duration; meaningful connections will usually be few, tenuous, or nonexistent; and elimination of the "primary" event will very rarely eliminate the mental illness that has followed it. This should not be taken to mean that patients' vicissitudes and their personalities may be omitted from consideration in the treatment given to patients.

As far as delusions are concerned, even if one accepts the validity of the broad distinction between "true delusions" and those more comprehensibly related to prevailing emotional state and the patient's predicament, the sharp and unmistakable dividing line applied by Jaspers is open to question. Hallucinations in clear consciousness and delusions of reference and persecution are at times described in cases of "psychogenic" paranoid psychosis as "understandable." But if this is accepted the same verdict has to be passed on delusions of patients indubitably schizophrenic by the criteria of Schneider (1959). Connections between the themes of delusion and premorbid personality may exist. But the fixed and lasting nature of all such ideas and their imperviousness to all evidence that refutes them are beyond "understanding."

In summary, the evidence makes a strong case that there is a developmental and historic dimension in the form of personality factors and threatening events and circumstances in *a proportion* of patients with paranoid disorder. Long-term follow-up investigations established that the pattern of outcome of paranoid disorders is more favorable on the whole than that of schizophrenia. But the term "psychogenic psychosis" overstates the causal importance of key events and the premorbid state. These probably contribute to the development of the disease, but we do not yet understand how they do so and their etiology remains largely obscure.

Theories of Paranoid States as a Distinct but Nonreactive Psychosis

The French Concept of Bouffée Delirante

The special interest of the French concept resides in the fact that a number of the paranoid psychoses and disorders described in ICD-9 and other classifications appear to be subsumed under a single heading "bouffée delirante" (BD). Pichot (1986) has recently traced the origins of the concept to the contributions of Magnan and Legrain in the late nineteenth century and has reviewed his own earlier work in an attempt to bring it into relationship with the related rubrics in ICD-9 and DSM-III in particular.

The psychosis in question is of sudden onset, and the delusions are overpowering in character and protean in form incorporating persecutory, grandiose, mystical, erotic, and other themes. Hallucinations are a secondary and inessential feature. There may be some clouding of consciousness and emotional disorder manifest in anxiety, agitation, impulsiveness, or inertia. Physical signs are absent and there is a rapid return to premorbid functioning in a matter of "a few hours, days or weeks."

Pichot considers that four of the diagnoses presented in DSM-III could be subsumed under the rubric of bouffée delirante. Schizophreniform disorder differs only in that there is no reference either to emotional stability or fragile personality. These disorders would receive a diagnosis of BD in France. Atypical psychosis would also qualify except for the limitation of BD to a duration of two weeks or less. The same statement applies to acute paranoid disorder. Acute paranoid disorder approximates the reactive form of the BD syndrome except that the symptoms do not display the wide variation that is regarded as characteristic of BD whether or not it is reactive. Brief reactive psychosis, which is expected to resolve in two weeks or less, is regarded by Pichot as the exact French equivalent of reactive BD. But the duration of the former disorder has been changed in DSM-III-R to four weeks.

Pichot points out that the French concept of BD places emphasis upon inherent constitutional aspects of etiology (only 15 percent being judged reactive), whereas DSM-III-R as well as the Scandinavian systems place more emphasis upon the reactive character of the disorder. Whether the four syndromes mentioned by Pichot could indeed be brought together could only be decided by investigations of course, outcome, and treatment response. If there were parallel characteristics in all these respects there would be economy in classification, and decision making with respect to prognosis and treatment could be simplified.

However, the jealous, erotomanic, somatic, grandiose, and persecuting types of delusional (paranoid) disorder (DSM-III-R 297.10) and schizoaffective disorders could not be subsumed under the heading of a psychosis such as BD, which is acute, florid, of short duration, and self-terminating in the great majority of cases. The outcome of schizophreniform disorders is also indeterminate.

Further, BD is stated to carry a favorable prognosis with a return to premorbid functioning in "a few hours, days or weeks." It would seem that 40 percent of cases can be expected to prove nonrecurrent, another 40 percent of patients will suffer relapses, and 20 percent of cases have an outcome closely similar to that of schizophrenia. In fact we appear to be not very remote from the findings of Retterstol. There is the same relative indeterminacy; there are no available criteria for predicting in which of the classes of outcome described by Pichot individual patients will be found some years after initial presentation. Yet the etiological basis of BD is conceived quite differently in France than that of psychogenic or reactive psychoses in Scandinavia. Only 15 percent of BD cases were considered reactive and no more than 6 percent of the paranoid cases. This last term is employed in France exclusively in relation to schizophrenia.

The Viennese Concept of Paranoid Psychoses

The Viennese Group of Berner has arrived at a body of theory as distinctive as that of the French and Scandinavian schools. Yet common ground between all can be defined. The Viennese School (Berner et al. 1983) divided the paranoid psychoses on the strength of background features such as apathy, disturbance of mood and affect, disorders of biologic rhythms such as sleep disturbance, and neurologic or phenomenological evidence suggesting a contribution by an organic lesion. Using such background features they defined three relatively distinct syndromes:

1. A schizophrenic axial syndrome associated with thought disorder and affective impoverishment.
2. A cyclothymic axial syndrome, the leading features of which were disturbances of mood and drive, sleep disorder, and derangements of biologic rhythm.
3. The organic axial syndrome derived from biologic evidence of organic brain damage or phenomenological changes in thought and language suggesting organic impairment.

Utilizing research criteria derived from these axial syndromes, they classified their patients into four groups: 1) an endogenomorphic-schizophrenic syndrome, 2) an endogenomorphic-cyclothymic syndrome, 3) an organomorphic syndrome, and 4) a group made up of those patients who could not be assigned on the basis of the criteria employed to any one of the first three groups. The terms employed imply phenomenological rather than etiologic affinities.

Only five patients fell into the first group. This was one of the reasons for the conclusion of the Vienna workers that the "classical" teaching, according to which the majority of paranoid syndromes have a close kinship with schizophrenia, is erroneous. Of the 18 patients classified into the second group, more than two-thirds pursued an episodic course and one-third became chronic suggesting kinship of the cases with affective disorders. Eight of the 12 patients who were classified under the organomorphic syndrome pursued a chronic course. The largest group was the fourth, including 49 patients. More than two-thirds became chronic and less than one-third pursued an episodic course.

Only a small group of patients with stable paranoid symptoms was therefore classified as a nuclear schizophrenic group. The remainder fell into two main classes: episodic cases on the one hand and those with a chronic pattern of outcome on the other. Five-eighths of the patients fell into this latter outcome group.

Although the chronicity rate was high, the findings do not appear markedly discrepant with those of Retterstol, because the proportion of cases in which a schizophrenic burnt-out state with negative symptoms emerged proved to be very small. In the remainder of the cases, one group constituting about one-third of cases had clear affinities with episodic affective disorders. The second and main group exhibited chronic paranoid delusions. The quality of social adaptation of the patients in the different outcome groups would be of interest. Berner et al. (1983) were undecided as to whether there is an adequate case for a third distinct class of psychotic disorders in addition to manic-depressive and schizophrenic psychosis.

The influential view that regarded all forms of paranoid psychosis not due to organic disease as being variants of schizophrenia is not supported in its original form by the findings of the past few decades. The hereditary link with schizophrenia is found in some syndromes, but its strength and importance have probably been overstated. The classification and diagnosis of the paranoid disorders cannot be decided on the basis of genetic evidence alone. Follow-up findings undertaken on a large scale by Scandinavian workers in particular have shown paranoid psychotic and other disorders enjoy a more favorable clinical and social outcome. In about 50 percent of cases symptoms become chronic (though encapsulated), but personality deterioration of schizophrenic type is rare. Stress has to be laid on the indeterminacy of outcome in the individual case. No reliable means are available for predicting at first presentation whether recovery, a chronic course with some paranoid symptoms, or a schizophrenic illness (which evolves in a small proportion of cases) will follow. A developmental and historical dimension can be defined with the aid of appropriate exploration in certain forms of paranoid illness. This comprises a link between premorbid personality and stressful circumstances that impinge on it and the illness that follows. But the term "psychogenic psychosis" overstates the influence of "key events" in the premorbid state and their adequacy as explanations of paranoid delusional states. Knowledge and understanding of the etiology of these conditions remain limited.

The Contributions of Psychoanalysis

Psychoanalytic theories regarding paranoid disorders have been derived from studies of a small number of individual cases and in Freud's writings from the Schreber case in particular. The observations that form the foundation for psychoanalytic theories are made in a situation and during a specific relationship with a patient in which the therapist occupies the role of privileged observer.

Psychoanalytical ideas regarding paranoid disorders can be treated as a set of hypotheses. As will be argued later, the general role in causation claimed for repressed homosexuality is incompatible with existing empirical evidence. The less sweeping propositions contain some insights that can form starting points for the clinical investigation of patients and for more stringent investigations that can test their scientific validity. Freud made contributions to the dynamics of paranoid psychosis at an early stage of his career, but his most important publication (Freud 1911, reprinted 1959) was based upon an autobiographical volume published by Dr. Daniel Paul Schreber, a German lawyer who suffered from two attacks of paranoid-hallucinatory psychosis. A central idea in Dr. Schreber's integrated body of delusional beliefs was that he had a compelling duty to restore the world to a state of blissful happiness that it had lost. To carry out his sacred mission he would first have to be transmuted from man to woman.

Freud concluded that underlying Schreber's delusions and hallucinations a latent homosexual tendency could be detected. Fearing that his hostility toward his father would be punished by castration, he had adopted the defense of a passive feminine attitude toward him. Freud concluded that paranoid delusions as a whole represented attempts to defend the individual from the entry of repressed homosexual tendencies into consciousness. The character of the delusion that resulted was dependent upon the manner in which the patient dealt with the unconscious feelings of love toward a person of the same sex engendered by his latent homosexuality.

Should the patient reject the thought "I love him" because it is conflict-laden, one might expect the proposition to be converted into the opposite "I hate him" as the object of his feelings and to become "he hates and persecutes me." This provides an inner justification for the patient's defensive feelings of hatred and explains how delusional persecutory ideas may come into being.

The individual may repress or deny the object of his love so that his attitudes and his conduct are built around the proposition, "I do not love him, I love her." In individuals with latent homosexuality, the effect of this form of rejection is to lead to an unceasing succession of erotic adventures and conquests without any emotional investment in any of them. This forms the starting point of Don Juanism and other forms of erotic overcompensation. If the individual denies his own love altogether, a new formulation is expressed as "It is not I who love him, it is she." This is regarded by Freud as the source of conjugal and morbid jealousy and related forms of paranoia.

Finally, if love of an object is altogether repressed, libido is directed inwards to his own self and his attitudes then come to be shaped by "I do not love anybody else, I love only myself." This is regarded as the source of the megalomaniacal forms of paranoia when an individual believes himself to have prestige and power without limit and of being of noble or royal descent. He may pursue an unremitting campaign in order to secure the admission of his claims to outstanding distinction or elevated status.

Freud is seeking to provide a comprehensive explanation for a wide range of paranoid disorders in a single sweep from its starting point in repressed and latent homosexuality. The study of a single autobiographical volume by one man, who is now known to have been submitted in childhood by his father to a complex and cruel dogma-laden regime that constrained him physically in a mechanically elaborate contraption for hours at a time, could not of its nature provide a valid basis for a wide-ranging theory regarding paranoid states.

No evidence has been adduced from studies of large numbers of patients with paranoid or delusional states in favor of latent or covert homosexuality as a factor of importance in the causation of these disorders. A proportion of these patients suffer from feelings of sexual inadequacy, and others are partially or wholly impotent. But they do not differ in these respects from many individuals in the population who do not present with paranoid states. A small proportion of patients with morbid jealousy are alcoholic, others have cerebral lesions or physical deformities. Late paranoid and paraphrenic individuals are preponderantly female and are often single or divorced after a brief marriage; some are frigid wives and cold mothers. But these are special facets of lifelong personality disorders to which genetic factors and familial influences probably make an important contribution.

Later psychoanalytic theorists (Fairbairn 1952; Klein 1948) rejected Freud's hypothesis concerning repressed homosexuality and focused instead on the projection of internalized images of negatively charged relationships. This reflected a shift in psychoanalytic thinking from a focus on drives and libidinal instincts as expressed in Freud's writings to an emphasis on the psychology of the ego and object relationships. These ideas provided the basis for less sweeping propositions concerning the causes of paranoia.

Drawing on object relations theory as conceived by Melanie Chaim, Meissner

(1978) has described the psychological processes that underlie the paranoid distortion of reality relationships. The paranoid patient projects negative internalized images, or bad objects formed during early developmental experience, externally and thereby constructs an image of a persecutory external world that is consistent with an internal sense of self within that environment.

Meissner (1982) suggests how an understanding of the paranoid patient's projective system can be used effectively in the psychotherapeutic process. He emphasizes the primary importance of establishing and sustaining the therapeutic alliance with these patients as a prerequisite for any therapeutic progress. This is particularly difficult, since the ability to establish trust is a central defect in the paranoid character. Meissner refers to the necessary therapeutic attitude in this process as one of "respectful unintrusiveness." He describes this as "an attitude of openness and availability without [the therapist] forcing himself on the patient's attention or invading the latter's inner world." Meissner cautions that consistency on the part of the therapist must be maintained. But confrontation as in orthodox psychoanalysis must be avoided in order to establish the therapeutic alliance.

Traditional psychoanalysis, in which a "transference regression" is induced and the patient's resistances are confronted, is contraindicated in the treatment of severe paranoid psychosis. For patients who are less actively psychotic, the concepts and techniques developed by Meissner may find useful application in the psychotherapeutic component of management. However, the efficacy of such treatment will require evaluation before it can be widely recommended. Psychoanalytic psychotherapy remains inadvisable in actively psychotic and disturbed paranoid patients.

General Management of Paranoid Disorders

Examination and Assessment

As the patient's delusional ideas may be among the leading complaints, it may prove relatively easy to elicit them and to explore the entire range of false beliefs. However, in some cases it takes a good deal of skill and effort to encourage patients to communicate. The psychiatrist's attitude should be patient and tolerant. He must allow himself to be side-tracked into talking about irrelevant matters to which he has been deliberately diverted by the patient in his attempts to test whether in the presence of the therapist he is on friendly or hostile terrain.

It is not always easy to decide whether the patient's strange ideas are delusional, and evidence from an independent source may have to be sought to rule out the possibility that they are superstitious or overvalued ideas that are shared by the cultural setting from which he is drawn. A close relative or other observer might also be able to round off the picture by citing ideas that have not been communicated. Suicidal tendencies or actions that place others at risk may thus be brought to attention.

A full psychiatric and physical examination is an indispensable first step toward arriving at a diagnosis of the condition and of any primary psychiatric or physical illness that might be causes of the delusional state. The psychiatric history should be comprehensive, covering biographical and developmental data, family history, sexual, marital, and social adaptation, and previous record of illness. The history of the development of the illness and the results of the mental state examination should be set in the context of this background information. Consumption of alcohol and drugs should be investigated in detail, and whenever possible evidence on this subject should be sought from a close relative or another independent informant. Chronic alcoholic abuse is a frequent cause or a contributory factor to the causation of paranoid disorders. The clinical picture extends beyond the well-known syndromes of alcoholic hallucinosis and related paranoid states. In a recent investigation of 114 patients with alcoholic psychosis (Cutting 1978), 40 percent were given a diagnosis of schizophrenia and a further 18 percent were given one of "possible paranoid psychoses." It is well known that addiction to cocaine or amphetamines may give rise to acute and at times more long-drawn-out paranoid psychoses.

In recent years it has become clear that frequent use of LSD over a period of years may give rise to a chronic psychotic state with paranoid delusions, bizarre and nebulous thought processes revolving around mystic and religious themes, a shallow affect, and an isolated social state (Frosch et al. 1965). A paranoid hallucinatory psychosis may also be generated by the ingestion of cannabis in large doses taken over long periods (Davison 1977). Personality factors invariably contribute to cause such disorders.

Cerebral disease such as a temporal or frontal lobe tumors, Alzheimer's disease, or myxoedema may give rise to a paranoid psychosis in its early states without any obvious organic psychiatric features. Such possibilities should be considered particularly where the psychosis appears to have come out of a clear sky in middle age in the absence of any evidence of personality predisposition for paranoid reaction. All patients should be given a thorough neurologic examination. Focal psychological deficits may be present, particularly in early cases of degenerative diseases of the Alzheimer's type. Cognitive functions should be carefully evaluated in the course of the clinical examination, and a detailed neuropsychological investigation should be arranged in all cases in which the possibility of cerebral disease as a cause remains open.

Management of the Acute Stage

Only a small proportion of patients with paranoid disorders present acutely with abrupt onset of symptoms. The evolution of the disorder tends on the whole to be more gradual than in schizophrenia. However, a proportion do present acutely, often following some traumatic life event and in the setting of either longstanding anxiety or of ideas of self-reference and suspicion that have been kept under control and are subclinical in character.

Admission on a compulsory basis may become imperative in patients who harass and threaten others, make importunate and insistent demands on imaginary lovers, or constitute a danger through their aggressive or violent conduct to wives, relatives, or other members of the community. No matter how intense the delusional hatred and resentment aroused in the patient toward others, including the therapist, by enforced admission, the therapist must strive to maintain a working relationship with the patient through a combination of participant interest in his beliefs, expression of concern about his sufferings, and willingness to provide help and to sustain him by all available means.

Whether or not there is a large psychogenic element in a paranoid disorder, medication, particularly neuroleptics, will often be required to deal with the acute illness, which may be initially floridly psychotic in character. Treatment with drugs plays an important part in the management of this phase, and where a satisfactory relationship has been established with the patient it is generally possible to persuade him or her to take medication orally. Otherwise, intramuscular treatment should be provided. However, if the patient settles into a quiescent state in the environment of a well-run psychiatric ward with experienced nurses, there should not be undue haste in giving medication under compulsion unless the patient presents serious risk to self or others or shows severe agitation and anxiety or his or her condition is deteriorating due to exhaustion. Heroic doses of neuroleptics should be avoided. The equivalent of 200–300 mg of chlorpromazine (100–150 mg intramuscularly) or 10–15 mg of trifluoperazine should suffice to ameliorate and control symptoms in most cases. The regime has of course to be flexibly adjusted according to the needs of the individual case.

The details of psychological treatment on a long-term basis are considered in a separate section at a later stage.

General Principles of Care and Management

To establish a working relationship with a patient who suffers from paranoid delusions demands careful adherence to certain principles and procedures. They are relevant for the management of all those with lasting delusions in a setting of paranoid disorder. One impediment to treatment is that the patient is convinced of the veracity of the delusions and wishes to have his or her tormentors prosecuted and punished. The patient will evince no interest in treatment if it is explicitly aimed at modifying or eliminating the delusional ideas. Arguments and pitched battles, therefore, always have to be avoided. Yet many patients exhibit a measure of insight in seeking help from doctors or being prepared to be referred for a psychiatric consultation rather than lodging complaints with the police. Advantage should be taken of such signs of partial compliance by offering help for the relief of insomnia, physical and psychic concomitants of anxiety, and the feelings of distress and exhaustion to which patients are reduced by the imaginary intimidation and terror of enemies. Such management can often be undertaken on an outpatient basis at least in the initial stages. This can pave the way for initiating appropriate treatment with neuroleptics, which can also be administered to many patients in a day hospital.

Long-Term Management of Paranoid Disorders

The symptoms are usually well encapsulated even in that group of cases in late life, the late paraphrenias in which the phenomenology overlaps with that of schizophrenia of earlier decades. "Negative" symptoms are rare, and the patients' intellectual ability and occupational skills are usually unaffected. As far as deterioration of personality of a schizophrenic character is concerned, it is rare in the paranoiac and paraphrenic psychoses of late life; when decline does set in it is usually secondary to independent cerebral disease or advanced age. In younger patients "deterioration" has been described in a number of long-term follow-up studies. But it is uncertain whether any change beyond chronic entrenchment of the delusional symptoms supervenes. In most cases the disorder leaves the personality intact even after many years. As compared with schizophrenia a relatively high proportion are able, after appropriate treatment, to return to employment and home (Opjordsmoen 1986). Social rehabilitation, therefore, presents fewer problems than in schizophrenias of earlier adult life even in patients whose symptoms are incompletely controlled by medication.

Administration of a neuroleptic drug on a long-term basis has proved of decisive importance in returning patients to the community and keeping them viable there. Patients should therefore be seen regularly in an outpatient department or private setting to provide encouragement and support to ensure that compliance with treatment is sustained. This also provides those patients who have been isolated by illness with a relationship in which they feel themselves secure from threat and persecution and in which their ideas are viewed without ridicule or adverse judgment.

The work done in the course of treatment in hospital or some other form of close supervision will have been provided in the acute stages of the illness and have laid some foundations for such a relationship. Moreover, many patients in whom pharmacologic therapy has succeeded in bringing the paranoid symptoms under complete or considerable control will be powerfully motivated to attend for follow-up sessions by the relief they will have obtained from torments caused by fear, mistrust, a constant sense of threat, and the terrifying sense of incomprehension the rift from reality causes. During the first year patients should be seen at least at monthly intervals. The periods between interviews can then be adjusted according to the progress achieved. It is prudent to continue with follow-up interviews for a period of at least two to four years. But oral or depot medication should be continued for an indefinite time ahead, and attempts at abandoning treatment with neuroleptics should be undertaken gradually and under close supervision.

Psychotherapeutic help should be largely focused on the here and now; on problems encountered by the patient at work, in marriage, and in interpersonal relationships. In a proportion of paranoid patients in the middle and later years in particular, premorbid personality traits will have caused them to sever bonds with family and friends. Some will have lived in a self-isolated state over a period of many years. Successful treatment of the paranoid psychosis may open up the possibility of re-establishing social contacts. And the assistance to the patient enabling him or her to succeed in such efforts will help to fortify the remission from symptoms and the social readjustment achieved. Attempts to transform the style of existence of a lifelong "loner" rarely succeed and are on the whole imprudent. But such patients will benefit from regular visits by a familiar figure from the hospital or clinic, a social worker, or a community nurse.

During active phases of illness, forms of psychotherapy that aim to instill insight are contraindicated. Paranoid patients tend to misconstrue interpretations and questions in the course of such therapies, and they may serve to reinforce the belief that the psychiatrist is colluding with their malevolent oppressors. However, in the case of those in whom paranoid states have been well encapsulated, who have assets of intelligence and personality, and have shown themselves able to acquire a measure of objectivity in relation to their illness, psychotherapy of a systematic kind aimed at resolving current problems and conflicts and defining realistic goals for the future may be justified. This psychotherapy can serve also to help younger patients in particular to resolve problems of fateful importance in their interpersonal relationships and career, ambivalence, confusion, or lack of realism about their assets as individuals, their ambitions, and any difficulties in their sexual and marital life. Excessive consumption of alcohol or drugs also requires exploration, and the planning of a regime that utilizes the patient's assets to ensure freedom from dependence may be essential as a preventive measure. Treatment along such lines has to be continually assessed and carefully monitored.

Pharmacologic Treatment

A large body of evidence has accumulated to establish the efficacy of treatment with neuroleptics in the control of symptoms and in the prevention of relapse in the entire group of schizophrenic and related paranoid hallucinatory disorders. Baldessarini and Davis (1980) have carried out an analysis of nearly 30 studies of patients observed over varying periods after initial improvement and subsequent management with either neuroleptic medication or an inactive placebo. The mean rate of clinical deterioration, relapse, and/or hospitalization was 16.4 percent in those who received active medication compared with 58 percent in those who received placebo. The difference was very highly significant statistically. There was, however, a considerable range of variation in the results recorded in the different studies.

Neuroleptic compounds have also proved the most effective treatment in those paranoid disorders that do not satisfy strict operational criteria for the diagnosis of schizophrenia. However, although these drugs have the widest range of efficacy in some of the conditions to be described in this chapter, other substances such as antidepressants may be indicated. Or a combination of neuroleptics with a tricyclic substance may prove, after systematic clinical observation, to be optimal. Before a decision to administer a neuroleptic is finalized, a careful medical and psychiatric evaluation should be undertaken including information about the drugs already being received by the patient.

It is generally accepted that middle-aged and elderly patients should receive substantially smaller doses of neuroleptic compounds than those under the age of 50–55 years. One-half to one-third of the average dose of 350–400 mg of chlorpromazine employed in ordinary schizophrenia or the equivalent dose of some other neuroleptic compound should suffice for alleviation and control of psychotic symptoms. At the outset divided doses should be administered in paranoid states to reduce the chance of side effects. Thioridazine has in the past been a much favored phenothiazine for the treatment of the paranoid and paraphrenic psychoses of late life because its extrapyramidal side effects are relatively mild. However, it has severe anticholinergic action as well as other autonomic effects, and in high doses it may give rise to confusion, hypotension, and possibly cardiac arrhythmia. It is preferable to use doses of higher potency phenothiazines such as trifluoperazine in doses up to a total of 15–25 mg daily, the dose chosen being adjusted according to clinical response. Substantially smaller doses may suffice for maintenance purposes.

A high proportion of the paranoid psychoses that develop gradually in middle and late life prove chronic, whether the symptoms appear in the setting of lifelong circumscribed abnormalities of personality or out of a clear sky without relevant defects in premorbid personality or vicissitudes in life that may make the disorder partly understandable. Therefore, there has been a temptation to follow in the wake of those who have attempted to optimize the effects of neuroleptic drugs by administering megadoses in cases of ordinary schizophrenia. There is no objective evidence to validate such practices. Quitkin et al. (1975) compared 1200 mg of oral fluphenazine daily (equivalent to a daily dosage of 100,000 mg of chlorpromazine) with 30 mg of fluphenazine in the treatment of patients who were resistant to all treatments. McClelland et al. (1976) compared a weekly dose of 150 mg of depot fluphenazine decanoate with a 12.5-mg dose for a period of six months. In neither case was there a significant advantage in favor of the high-dose regime. Almost the entire literature devoted to this subject has testified to the benefits of low-dose regimes or the lack of further benefit derived from higher doses (Baldessarini 1984, 1986).

Although there are compelling considerations in favor of low-dose regimes in the older patients, they should not be applied inflexibly in clinical practice. A small proportion of patients requires higher doses than those cited, and in others a lower dose will suffice to elicit an optimal effect. Elderly people with paranoid psychoses do not fare well on depot medication with fluphenazine or with other compounds. Side effects tend to be troublesome, and hypotension is common, and is a particular danger in that falls are liable to be complicated by fractures. Depot medication should therefore be reserved for and tried with caution only in those patients in whom there has been failure to secure compliance. This is uncommon in patients who have responded well during preliminary treatment with oral medication in hospital. There is relatively little evidence derived from double-blind controlled studies to testify to the efficacy of phenothiazines, butyrophenones, or thioxanthenes in the treatment of the acute or chronic states of paranoid psychoses of the later years. Some evidence from trials is listed in a later section devoted to late paraphrenia. The success achieved by neuroleptics in treating this disorder, a relatively homogeneous psychotic illness among the paranoid psychoses, is particularly impressive. A few decades ago these patients were doomed to spend their remaining years in the long-stay wards of mental hospitals. But most of these patients are now able to live in their homes or in the community; yet their kinship with schizophrenia in terms of heredity, phenomenology, and life history is well established (Kay and Roth 1961; Roth 1986).

On the basis of such strict evidence as is available and of a large body of clinical observation, neuroleptic drugs can be expected to elicit a favorable response in the short and long term in the most commonly occurring paranoid psychoses of the later years. There are certain exceptions that are discussed under the headings of the individual syndromes. Neuroleptics succeed rather uncommonly in the morbid jealousy psychoses (Mooney 1965), in erotomanic disorders, and in the paranoid states that occur in the setting of severe personality disorder.

Interaction Between Side Effects and the Disease Process

Those receiving maintenance treatment with a neuroleptic in middle or late life are particularly at risk of suffering the consequences of one particular diagnostic error. But the problem arises during treatment of paranoid psychoses at all ages. Baldessarini (1986) has pointed out that there is an interaction between the side effects of the drugs and the disease process that may lead the former to be confused with the deterioration of the psychiatric disorder. Thus, akathisia can be mistaken for agitation and anxiety. The effects of a cholinergic intoxication may give rise to confusional or delirious states and also agitation. Bradykinesia may be misconstrued as apathy, and autism and catatonic features will resemble a relapse into psychosis. Dystonia can elicit an erroneous diagnosis of conversion symptoms or epileptic attacks, and the affective changes due to antipsychotic drugs may be misconstrued as a complication of the clinical picture by a depressive syndrome.

The value of antiparkinsonian and anticholinergic drugs commonly employed in the treatment of the entire range of extrapyramidal complications caused by neuroleptic drugs requires consideration in relation to the stable paranoid states of the later years. Despite their wide use over long periods in cases of schizophrenia in the past, the evidence that these compounds are effective in the relief of drug-induced parkinsonism is ambiguous. In a controlled double-blind crossover trial the effectiveness of amantadine, orphenadrine, and placebo in the relief of parkinsonism induced by depot fluphenazine decanoate was compared in a double-blind crossover trial (Mindham et al. 1972). The standard methods of assessment employed revealed no significant differences among the effects of the three treatments. Even in the trials that reported positive results (Capstick and Pudney 1976), only partial success was achieved in the control of parkinsonian symptoms. Moreover, as far as dyskinesia is concerned, the results of several investigations have offered suggestive evidence that the concurrent administration of a neuroleptic substance and an anticholinergic antiparkinsonian drug may add to the risk of generating tardive dyskinesia (Chouinard et al. 1979; Kiloh et al. 1973).

Antiparkinsonian anticholinergic drugs should not, therefore, be prescribed routinely to middle-aged and elderly people in particular as they are at special risk of developing certain extrapyramidal complications as well as severe anticholinergic effects in the form of an acute toxic delirious state with agitation, hallucinations, restlessness, and exhaustion. Evidence has recently come to light (Westlake and Rastegar 1973) that the "neuroleptic malignant syndrome" manifest as extreme rigidity, catatonia, and hyperthermia with deep coma that has proved a rare complication in treatment with neuroleptic drugs may be particularly likely to occur when neuroleptic substances are given concurrently with antiparkinsonian anticholinergic substances.

Prophylaxis Against Side Effects

The first measure to be taken when extrapyramidal rigidity or other complications arise in the course of long-term treatment with antipsychotic drugs is to reduce the dosage unless this step is contraindicated on clinical grounds. If the first step fails, another neuroleptic compound should be substituted. The addition of an antiparkinsonian drug should be a last-resort measure and used for the shortest period required. The compound chosen should be given for relief of symptoms and never for a period exceeding eight to nine weeks.

Whenever possible neuroleptic compounds should not be continued for longer than two years. At some appropriate time during a remission after 12 to 18 months of treatment, a gradual reduction of treatment should be attempted and a systematic effort made to discover the lowest possible maintenance dose of neuroleptic. If symptoms of relapse should threaten during this scaling-down process rendering a further period of treatment with drugs inescapable, the psychiatrist should seek a conference with patients and relatives for the purpose of setting out in a precise and candid fashion the advantages to be derived from continuing with maintenance treatment as well as the hazards involved. The objective is to arrive at a mutually acceptable decision regarding the continuation of treatment. If this is achieved it should be recorded in the clinical notes and signed by all those who have been party to the decision.

Neuroleptic Malignant Syndrome

Those of advanced age (as well as youthful subjects) are at particular risk of developing the neuroleptic malignant syndrome or hyperthermic syndrome. Contributory factors are very high doses of potent neuroleptics, age, environmental temperature, and use of a combination of drugs. In particular, as already mentioned, concurrent administration of antiparkinsonian preparations with neuroleptics may increase the risk of developing this syndrome, which has a high fatality rate. Neuroleptic drugs must be immediately discontinued. Bromocriptine should be administered in divided oral doses of 10 to 20 mg a day. Management includes attempts to bring the fever under control and the administration of intravenous fluids. The patient should be immediately transferred to an intensive-care unit where the administration of an intravenous muscle relaxant drug by an anesthetist may be indicated if patients do not respond to other measures. Beneficial results have been reported from administration of the dopamine agonist bromocriptine together with the peripheral muscle relaxant dantrolene sodium (Granato et al. 1983).

Patients Refractory to Drug Treatment

A substantial proportion of patients with primary paranoid disorders in middle or late life can be expected to respond to treatment with neuroleptic compounds with improvement or a complete remission from symptoms. The term "primary" refers in this context to conditions not due to some other functional psychosis or organic disorder and not associated with serious and lifelong disorder of personality. When primary disorders such as these fail to respond, the diagnosis and treatment regime have to be reviewed. A number of possibilities require consideration.

Atypical Mania

One common cause of total failure to respond is the presence of a manic state in which persecutory and other delusions are unusually prominent. These may include some noncongruent delusional ideas and at times hallucinations and symptoms that resemble passivity feelings. Elation of mood may be inconspicuous or absent, and aggression, irritability, and litigiousness may be prominent. A review of the clinical findings and of the previous history of illness, family history, and personality and thorough reexamination of the patient to put the fresh hypothesis to the test should make it possible to confirm or rebut the alternative diagnosis. If atypical mania appears to be the explanation for resistance to treatment, lithium carbonate should be given in gradually increasing doses (monitored by blood levels). Should a phenothiazine have been previously used, it is desirable to substitute a butyrophenone in gradual stages.

Overuse of Antiparkinsonian Agents

Continuous or excessive use of antiparkinsonian agents may be responsible for therapeutic failure. There is now a body of evidence indicating that such use may impair therapeutic response (Simpson et al. 1980) and precipitate tardive dyskinesia (Nasrallah 1980). The use of antiparkinsonian drugs should be limited to the early phases of treatment in those groups of patients who then exhibit extrapyramidal side effects and to periods when any of the complications that have been listed are manifest. In paranoid states that have arisen in close association with stressful circumstances or conflicts in the sexual, social, or professional sphere and that prove intractable, extrapyramidal side effects should be dealt with by decreasing the dosage of the drugs employed and antiparkinsonian agents should be avoided. There is no entirely satisfactory solution to the problem of such complications as tardive dyskinesia. The best policy is to work out a strategy for management by trial and error on an individual basis in cases in which it presents.

Undesirability of Escalation of Dosage

Failure to respond to a given neuroleptic in doses adequate by the standards outlined earlier, after a trial period of six to eight weeks, should never be a signal for steep escalation of dosage, particularly in elderly and middle-aged subjects. There is no evidence (as already indicated) that megadoses elicit superior therapeutic effects, and given over a long period they are liable to increase the hazard of producing lasting extrapyramidal effects. Change to another compound is a preferable course of action.

Complication by Depressive Disorder

Failure of neuroleptic treatment may occur in the presence of an independent depressive syndrome, that is, in patients for whom the diagnosis of "schizodepressive" disorder may be appropriate. The possibility that depression is secondary to neuroleptic treatment has to be excluded, and a decrease in dosage may be the first logical step. But such a secondary depression should not present great difficulty in that the clinical picture comprises a limited range of symptoms usually confined to retardation, apathy, inertia, and little or no specific depressive ideation. In the presence of a true depressive syndrome it is justifiable to add tricyclic compounds to the neuroleptics already being used. This strategy succeeds in a proportion of cases of schizodepressive disorder. It should be remembered that neuroleptics and antidepressants may potentiate each other's effects. Further consideration is given to this group of cases in a later section on electroconvulsive treatment.

Laboratory Tests

In the event of failure of neuroleptic treatment in a patient who had been expected to respond, the plasma level of the neuroleptic drug in question should be estimated wherever appropriate facilities are available. It should reveal whether compliance in taking drugs has been satisfactory or whether the explanation for failure might be the rapid metabolization of the drug. Another useful laboratory test is the plasma prolactin, which parallels plasma levels of neuroleptic drugs closely when they have been given in small or moderate doses. Long sustained therapy with neuroleptics causes the plasma prolactin to plateau or to decline. There are also sex and age differences in response that have to be taken into account in interpreting the results elicited (Ohman and Axelsson 1980).

Electroconvulsive Treatment

In a proportion of patients in whom paranoid psychosis first appears in middle or later life, the condition is relatively encapsulated and occurs in the setting of a personality with assets as reflected in achievements in career, interpersonal relationships, marriage, and in at least some of the roles of parent and spouse. It is particularly important to consider electroconvulsive treatment in those patients refractory to other treatments in whom the psychosis has appeared in a steplike manner, in the absence of any life situation that renders it understandable, in patients in whom there is a clear family history of affective disorder in first-degree relatives, or if there is a prominent depressive component in the clinical picture.

A small proportion of paranoid psychoses in late life are atypical affective disorders. The affective coloring and some depressive ideation may come to light after careful phenomenological analysis, but the affective component may be inconsistent, complex, and beyond the reach of empathy. Such patients may suffer from a "mixed" psychosis in the original sense of Kraepelin. The complex affect and ideation of these patients arises from the coexistence and interaction of manic and depressive disorders. They present some of the most difficult problems in psychiatric diagnosis and are often treated as schizophrenics. Be this as it may, psychoses emerging within a short period in relatively intact personalities will often respond to electroconvulsive treatment where previous neuroleptic and other regimes of drug treatment have failed to elicit an adequate or a sufficiently sustained remission.

Such patients may require maintenance treatment with lithium carbonate when the disorder is judged to have been affective in character and with neuroleptic compounds when the condition proves after observation over a period to be an indubitable paranoid disorder. However, patients should not be placed on maintenance therapy with lithium after a solitary attack. The need for long-term treatment should be considered only in the event of relapses that occur within short intervals or when they prove seriously prejudicial to the patient's interests.

Opportunities for Neurobiologic Research Provided by Clinical Observation and Treatment of Delusional States

This chapter covers the management of delusional disorders, but the opportunities afforded for advancing knowledge of the neurobiology of these conditions deserve brief mention. Little attempt has been made to apply or extend new observations that have been recorded in the course of neurobiologic study of schizophrenia to the delusional disorders despite the evidence that there are lines of continuity and areas of overlap between them.

Schizophrenia has been divided hypothetically into two syndromes in recent years. The type 1 syndrome comprises positive symptoms such as delusions and hallucinations. This syndrome responds to neuroleptic treatment. The type 2 syndrome is characterized by negative symptoms such as flattening of emotion, poverty of speech, apathy, some cognitive impairment, and deterioration of behavior (Crow et al. 1982). Type 1 has been attributed by Crow and his colleagues to a disturbed dopaminergic transmission possibly arising from an increase in D2 dopamine receptors (Crow et al. 1981b). The type 2 syndrome is considered to arise from structural changes in the brain and responds poorly to treatment with neuroleptics. The evidence that has been adduced in favor of this subdivision is inconsistent but it has some heuristic value.

Paranoid delusional states very rarely present "negative" symptoms even after many years of chronic illness. Comparison of the postmortem brain in patients with delusional disorder and those with schizophrenia both of positive and negative types might therefore shed further light on the dopaminergic hypothesis, as well as the specifity of the reported increase in D2 dopamine receptors for illnesses of the positive type. Information regarding the efficacy of neuroleptics in the different forms of delusional syndrome is imprecise at the present time and more controlled investigations are needed.

Late paraphrenia has a particularly close genetic relationship to schizophrenia, but cerebral lesions are known to occur in a proportion of cases, although organic psychiatric features are absent. Studies with modern brain imaging techniques such as positron emission tomography have yet to be undertaken in these cases as far as the author's knowledge goes. The results should prove of particular interest. It remains to be determined whether the "hypofrontality" reported in schizophrenia by a number of workers (Andreasen et al. 1986; Buchsbaum et al. 1984) can be replicated in this delusional disorder of late life. The localization of the lesions that are present in a minority of cases should also shed light on the character of the cerebral dysfunction underlying schizophrenia. Finally, lesional disorders that are of relatively late onset offer special opportunities for application of the techniques of molecular genetics which have made such striking advances in human linkage studies.

Application of the techniques brought to light by the new genetics have already succeeded in discovering the genetic locus for Huntington's disease, among other neurologic conditions. The genetic problems of schizophrenia are considerably more complex. But the possibility of discovering markers in close proximity to the gene (or genes) for schizophrenia and transmitted with the schizophrenic gene from parent to child may be within reach, judging from successes achieved in disorders of similar complexity such as diabetes and manic-depressive disorder. Paranoid delusional disorders are sometimes familial (as in Gaupp's case described above), and a substantial proportion of patients are old enough to have had children and grandchildren. Success has recently been achieved (Sherrington et al. 1988) in locating the gene that gives rise to schizophrenia in the rare families in which it seems to be transmitted down generations by a single autosomal gene. Using two restriction fragment length polymorphisms these workers succeeded in mapping the gene to the region 5q11-13 on chromosome 5 with confidence in two families and with less certainty in a number of others. The techniques provided by the new genetics need therefore to be applied to familial delusional disorders. Although these are generally distinct from schizophrenia some of its forms reside in its borderlands.

Clinical Features and Management of Specific Paranoid Conditions

Persecutory Delusional Disorder

In this condition the main delusion is that the individual or those closely related to the individual, or both, are being treated in a critical, hostile, and malevolent manner by others. The condition rarely comes out of a clear sky without predisposing features in the personality that render the individual vulnerable to exaggerated suspiciousness and ideas of reference. Some features of the illness are therefore understandable in the light of the premorbid personality and the situational stresses that precede illness in a proportion of cases. But delusional beliefs that resist all evidence to the contrary and are defended with tortuous and topsy-turvy reasoning and complete lack of insight are not understandable. Such delusional (paranoid) disorders always entail a discontinuity in mental life of the patient even where connections can be traced between the content of the delusions and the premorbid personality. But the vulnerable facets of personality have to be taken into account in the management of the illness and in rehabilitation. These points are illustrated by the following patients:

Case A. A 31-year-old man was admitted after a suicide attempt with an overdose that was potentially lethal. Premonitory symptoms had begun at the age of 13 when other pupils at school teased and ridiculed the patient because of his large ears. He began to look at the three-way mirror to see his face at different angles. After a time his mouth seemed to him to be twisted to the left, the left ear to be bigger than the right, the left nostril higher than the right, and his whole face appeared asymmetrical. His ideas were not set at this time and his parents did not observe behavior to give cause for concern, although they were conscious that he was looking at himself in mirrors for excessive periods of time. At the age of 19 he began to feel that strangers were at times looking at him and laughing. He thought they were ridiculing his protuberant ears. Almost two years later he began to hear them make derogatory remarks. At this stage he retained considerable insight but proceeded to grow his hair long to enable him to conceal his ears. Indubitable psychotic symptoms began at the age of 29 when he was involved in a sexual affair with a married woman and under some threat from her husband. He now began to hear passersby comment "Look at the state of him, he walks like a pouf" (homosexual). There were references to his "baby face" and menacing stares were directed toward him. He heard one man in a public house comment "Is that him?" and his companion replying "Yes that's him; Dave is going to do him in." One day when he went to his car out of a pub the word "Unikor," which he could not understand, had been scraped, he believed, on his frost-covered windscreen. This word might have been a neologistic condensation of "eunuchoid" and "unicorn" but there were no other privately coined words, his speech was clear and coherent, and there was no thought disorder. He began to lipread workmen saying "There is that bastard there" and "that pouf let's go and get him." These comments he construed as referring to his sexual liaison.

Before the onset of the illness he was a shy, sensitive, anxious, self-conscious, and obsessional personality dominated by a powerful mother. An antidepressant with a small dose of a benzodiazepine failed to make any impression. But he made a very good response to treatment with 20 mg of trifluoperazine and psychotherapy of a supportive and explanatory kind. Symptomatic recovery was complete in about five months after the onset of illness. Eighteen months after his initial illness, follow-up showed him to be in good remission and he had returned to work.

Comment. Ideas of reference are a central feature of delusional (paranoid) states of a persecutory type, and they were prominent in this patient. Innocent remarks, facial expressions or gestures, and statements in newspapers or on television are torn out of context and applied to oneself as critical, offensive, or threatening. In the fully developed psychosis these ideas are derived from normal perceptions and are interwoven with each other to form a systematized body of delusional beliefs. In this patient hallucinations were reported, but they were at all times inseparably entwined with the delusions. No themes beyond the scope of the patient's rather simple delusional beliefs had been taken up by hallucinatory voices. He was never observed to be listening to voices and was uncertain in relation to some experiences whether he actually heard people speak or was merely convinced in his mind they were making the offensive remarks he quoted.

The onset of the psychosis constituted a fresh departure in the patient's psychic life associated with loss of insight and potentially fatal self-destructive tendencies. It also responded well to treatment with neuroleptic drugs. These aspects constitute the biologic or "endogenous" or "process" aspects of the disorder. But clear lines of continuity with earlier stages of development are also manifest. Intermittent ideas of reference penetrated by a measure of insight had already been present at the age of 19. His ideas of self-reference can be understood *up to a point* as an extension of the painful feelings of self-consciousness and shame about his physical deformity that he experienced at an early age. But the morbid ideas during the psychotic phase were true delusions carrying total conviction over months. His life had been dominated by a powerful mother who intruded herself into every one of the relationships he established with women. His attitude toward her had been markedly ambivalent since early adolescence, and he had never succeeded in establishing himself in a role independent of her. His symptoms began during a stormy sexual relationship. The condition therefore has some of the features of the paranoid psychosis of sensitive persons described by Kretschmer. Although the short-term outcome was satisfactory it was prudent (having regard to the overall result of follow-up studies of such cases) to maintain caution about the long-term prognosis.

Case B. The second case in this section provides an example of onset after a striking key event. The patient was a shy, reticent, and self-conscious medical student. He had very high levels of aspiration, was regarded as capable and conscientious, and had a number of conspicuous obsessional traits. At the age of about 21 he developed a severe bout of diarrhea followed by constipation. After this he found to his embarrassment that he was often having to expel flatus. He had always been rather anxious, self-conscious, and given to mild ideas of reference in social gatherings, and these symptoms lowered his social confidence and self-esteem. He was investigated for a period of about a year by a gastroenterologist and urologists but all findings were essentially normal.

During this year he began to observe that people stared at him when he entered trains or buses or participated in social events. He concluded that an offensive odor was possibly emanating from him. At this stage he had a measure of insight into the lack of foundation for his ideas of reference. But following a key experience there was a sudden change for the worse. He was walking one day on the university campus when he saw the vice-chancellor of the university, an eminent man for whom he had a high respect, walking toward him. As he approached nearer, the vice-chancellor took a handkerchief from his pocket and blew his nose in a vigorous manner. The patient felt an immediate conviction that a putrifying and intolerable stench emanated from him.

Thereafter whenever he entered a restaurant, a cinema, or the underground it appeared to him that he was invariably greeted with an outburst of nose blowing and people would keep their handkerchiefs to their noses in an attempt to protect themselves from the malodorous newcomer. He described the appearance of handkerchiefs and the epidemic of nose blowing with a vividness and detail that endowed the experience with some of the features of a hallucination. The probability is that he had merely overinterpreted some minimal cues with a consequent distortion of perception. This provides a good example of the kind of quasi-hallucinatory experience closely and entirely tailored to the delusional belief that is found in patients with disorders of the paranoiac type.

Comment. Treatment with neuroleptics was attempted but could not be sustained owing to persistence of the symptoms and severe side effects that were very poorly tolerated probably on account of obsessional and hypochondriacal tendencies. The developmental history was of interest. He was one of two children of elderly parents, and the family had restricted social contacts. Since childhood the patient had been shy, nervous, and in adolescence self-conscious and tense in the company of others. He had never had a girlfriend when he was first seen at 21 years. Dynamic psychotherapy was tried for a period, but the patient did not cooperate. Simple behavioral treatment enabled him to move more freely amongst his peers, and his delusions were gradually penetrated by a measure of insight. He resumed his studies and when followed up three years after presentation was working in a general practice where he was highly regarded. His delusion had become more circumscribed, and he could often override his social aversion. But he was still bothered by the belief in the offensive smell that emanated from him. All attempts at establishing a sexual relationship had proved abortive, but he had recently made a new female acquaintance.

After recovery or significant improvement in such patients psychotherapy combined with behavioral methods is certainly indicated, particularly when the individual in question is gifted, cooperative, and endowed as these patients were with a measure of insight after recovery from the acute attack. Psychotherapy should be focused on current problems, the amelioration of the social anxiety that is often present, and the modification of attitudes toward the self. Every attempt should be made to institute neuroleptic treatment and to maintain it for one or two years as the relapse rate is high and the outcome uncertain even in seemingly favorable cases.

The indications for psychotherapy and appropriate measures have to be decided on an individual basis. Some persecutory delusional states arise from a longstanding suspicion penetrated by varying insight which then evolve abruptly into a complex delusional system present refractory problems. Although the case described appeared sudden in onset it emerged in the setting of an abnormally shy, over-sensitive, acutely self-conscious personality with few friends; in social situations he would often blush, perspire, and believe that his appearance caused him to be the object of special attention. The fixed belief that an unpleasant smell emanated from him was at first penetrated by intermittent insight. It may have been reinforced by the period of more than a year in which he was investigated by two medical departments with the implicit assumption that the offensive odour had an objective basis in organic disease. The apparent aversion of the Head of his University who seemed to hold his handkerchief to his nose when at a distance from him was followed by systematic generalisation of the delusional belief that he was being avoided, ridiculed and humiliated wherever he went.

This patient could be regarded as exhibiting features both of a persecutory and somatic delusional disorder. But he would have also satisfied the criteria for avoidant personality disorder on the strength of the features already cited as also his asocial, asexual and isolated existence and the social disablement he had suffered since adolescence, which would have rendered him exquisitely sensitive to signs of rejection or disapproval.

In the view of the author avoidant personality provides a common setting for the development of delusional disorders. One should add that the line of demarcation of avoidant personality from the Axis I diagnosis of social phobia is indistinct in that the latter disorder also commences in a similar fashion during adolescence.

The delusional disorder changed during the first year of observation. Thereafter the central delusion gradually faded into the background, probably influenced in part by the academic success that boosted his self-confidence, psychotherapy that instilled a measure of insight and the behavioural treatment that gradually enabled him to mix socially with others with greater assurance and physical comfort. However, when contact was lost with him after about 20 months, the belief that there was an unpleasant smell about him continued to surface occasionally on social occasions. He had by then qualified and was succeeding in his profession.

Following detailed exploration in cases of persecutory disorder a range of factors is usually defined as having contributed to illness in varying degrees: heredity, personality setting, life circumstances, physical health, sensory deficits and excessive alcohol consumption. They present in different combinations (Johanson 1964). We do not know the precise importance and weight that should be assigned to the contribution of these different factors. A judgment has to be made on the basis of clinical observation and enquiry in each individual case so as to set objectives and decide on priorities in treatment.

Case C. The following case illustrates the importance of the historical dimension including previous personality, developmental history, and adjustment in a patient with a severe psychotic and relapsing delusional (paranoid) disorder. Although there was evidence that personality factors had probably contributed to breakdown, there were other findings to suggest a specific biologic predisposition. The acute florid symptoms began suddenly with the characteristics of a psychosis or a "process" in the sense of Jaspers. But there was also a prodromal "developmental" phase that paved the way for and was continuous with the explosive onset of psychotic illness. These two types of psychopathology are not mutually exclusive. Relevant data should be gathered and formulations made under each heading in cases of paranoid illness, for they prove complementary in a high proportion of cases, and paying due attention to each aspect will deepen understanding and ensure that treatment is undertaken along all relevant paths.

The disorder had begun two years before the patient was first seen. But the acute psychotic phase commenced abruptly during the first night he spent in his room in a students' hostel attached to a university in which he had embarked upon a course of studies in modern languages. The students were of both sexes but only about one in five were females.

Two years before admission he began to worry that he might be schizophrenic after reading a book on the subject. A few months later after a circumcision for which he had asked after watching a "blue" film and judging his penis to be abnormal, he started to fear that he might be homosexual. He developed a succession of attacks of depression with clear diurnal variation of mood and early morning waking. There were feelings of self-revulsion, and he had described himself as "disgusting" and "so foul that it was best to kill myself off." He was tormented with doubt about his sexual identity.

After the abrupt end of one of his attacks, depression was followed by one of a succession of bouts of elation of mood lasting four to six weeks in which his mind worked with great rapidity and in which he made a deep impression upon his supervisors with the quality of his academic work. He also embarked upon a passionate but unconsummated love affair with an attractive young woman. This terminated rapidly followed by a deep depression in which he made a serious suicide attempt. He had already made a number of attempts during the previous 18 months, but the one preceding admission was potentially lethal. The day before he had consumed a large quantity of alcohol and had taken 30 flupenthixol and 15 phencyclidine tablets leaving a suicide note. He was resuscitated without difficulty.

On examination he was friendly and cooperative but showed marked anxiety and pressured speech with flight of ideas. But the sequence of association could always be followed, and his conversation was witty, brilliant, and entertaining. His mood was cheerful and frivolous, yet his preoccupations were depressive. He thought himself under derisive criticism from his peers. He stated that during his first night in college he had felt himself oppressively surrounded by others who could observe and watch him. Through the walls of his room he heard voices of others calling him "fascist," "communist," "a sh-- bastard," and "fag."

Among delusions he expressed during his six weeks in hospital was the conviction that his thoughts could be read by others and that everyone knew that he had indulged in masturbation. His gaucheness and effeminate gestures made it easy, he believed, to read his thoughts. On numerous occasions he had sensed that he was the reincarnation of a malignant person. He insisted during one long interview that his success in gaining an entry scholarship to University was either hereditary or due to some hypnotic influence to which he had been exposed. He felt unable to explain the nature of this influence.

A few weeks previously he had had some forewarning of what was to come when he had walked out into the street with his girlfriend and he heard a number of young men who passed him commenting in contempt and derision. One of them remarked to the girl, "don't go out with him, he will sodomize you from the back." Another had said, "he's a perverted dangerous queer, you are not safe." On his first night in college the voices were recognizably similar. In the light of this young man's previous uncertainties about his sexual identity and the history that will be briefly outlined, the experience of the night of his first residence in college could be described as "homosexual panic." But there was also indubitable evidence that he had been suffering from a bipolar illness.

The family and personal history were relevant. His father had been alcoholic and unfaithful, and his mother divorced his father when the patient was nine months old. The mother had remarried a 51-year-old Roman Catholic. There was one half-brother 11 years old. The maternal grandmother was a key figure in the family. She disapproved of her daughter's second marriage and changed her will as a result; the patient was deeply devoted to her. He was brought up from the age of four to five years of age by his grandmother, who took over responsibility for the boarding house that was run by the family. At night she would take the patient round on her nocturnal visits rattling her keys and taking meticulous steps to ensure that there were no females hiding in the rooms occupied by mainly male students. The patient began to experience anxiety and a certain terror during some of these visits, but he did not describe them or complain of them to anyone.

There were no neurotic traits in childhood. At school he proved very bright and subsequently gained a scholarship to university. He proved to be exceptionally intelligent and creative with interests in drama, piano, and music. At 19 he went to university to read languages and at first managed to establish some friendships, but he was exceedingly shy and self-conscious with women. At the age of 17 he went through a period in which he believed that he was a homosexual and thereafter was obsessed with his effeminacy in body build and gesture. (There was some objective basis for this belief.) He became quite a good mixer at parties but felt sexually insecure.

He attributed these anxieties to an experience he had when he was about 15 years old. He saw his stepfather and mother in the hall embracing and caressing each other. He was deeply shocked and he thought his disgust was natural: "I was very romantic in spirit." He stated that he was resentful and jealous of his stepfather, and his hostility was intensified by his grandmother's attitude toward her son-in-law.

While in hospital the patient's moods fluctuated markedly during the first two weeks but thereafter stabilized with modest doses of a neuroleptic (thioridazine) in a dose of 125 mg daily. He was discharged after a stay of seven weeks to resume his academic work. He was kept on a maintenance dose of medication. He obtained a very good degree in his final examinations eight months after discharge and proceeded to a post that offered good prospects. He remained well during the period before examinations and declined referral for psychotherapy pleading lack of time. When a follow-up contact was last made with him 18 months after discharge there had been no clear relapses. He was still having difficulties in relating to women and had periodic mild to moderate mood swings but was coping well with his post. He now accepted referral to a psychotherapist who decided to treat him with a combination of dynamic and cognitive methods.

Comment. This highly intelligent and gifted young man broke down first at the age of 19 with symptoms of an affective disorder. After 12 to 15 months this condition presented features of probable bipolar affective disorder, but detailed phenomenological observations about this stage were not available. He made a number of suicide attempts during depressive phases. After 18 months he developed an acute psychotic disorder with hallucinations in clear consciousness and a number of persecutory delusions in which sexual themes were prominent. These extended well beyond explanation in terms of mood disturbance of a depressive or manic kind; some were bizarre and he also experienced thought broadcasting. A diagnosis of acute paranoid psychosis with conspicuous affective coloring was made. The hallucinations were entirely confined to articulation of his persecutory ideas and ambiguously poised feelings about his sexual identity and role.

In adolescence there had been emotional turmoil generated around a "Hamlet" situation with feelings of betrayal by his mother and jealousy and hatred of his stepfather. He experienced severe anxiety and lack of confidence in his relationships with women. The evolution of the acute schizoaffective disorder occurred at first exposure to a sexually threatening environment. Conflicts engendered in the course of development are clearly not a sufficient cause for a delusional or schizoaffective psychosis that continued over many months with a succession of suicidal attempts. However, any view that dismissed the sexual and social conflicts as irrelevant for a clinical formulation and for management of the patient would be doctrinaire.

Account had to be taken of the historical and personality aspects to establish rapport and communicate with this patient. Attempts had to be made to enable him to expand insight into his conflicts to modify his cognition of himself in the light of the new experiences that were buttressing his self-esteem. He also needed support to help him deal with problems in everyday life that he was unable to negotiate in phases of low mood. Such measures can be expected to potentiate the effects of maintenance treatment with drugs in those individuals who have shown themselves liable to develop persecutory delusional disorder under stress. The patient will need to be followed up at regular intervals. The future course may reveal his condition to have been an atypical bipolar affective disorder that requires lithium carbonate as a prophylactic measure.

Late Paraphrenia

Late paraphrenia is a disorder of later life characterized by a well-organized system of paranoid delusions usually with hallucinations existing in the setting of a well-preserved personality and affective response.

The personality of these patients tends to be markedly abnormal before the onset of frank psychotic symptoms. They are often self-isolated and tend to be emotionally cold, suspicious, quarrelsome, and eccentric. Their sexual adaptation in earlier life was poor: a substantial proportion have never married or the marriage was stormy, short-lived, and relatively infertile. The patients make poor mothers, and their attitudes toward their husbands are often tinged with suspicion and hostility (Kay 1963; Kay and Roth 1961).

The management of this condition merits consideration in some detail. Although it does not figure in DSM-III-R, it is widely recognized in different parts of the world and more data have become available from clinical observation and trials about its treatment and course than about any other single form of delusional psychosis. It can also be regarded as a paradigm of the paranoid disorders of the later years. The knowledge gained through research into this condition can therefore shed a certain amount of light on the problem of management posed by delusional disorders in general.

Until phenothiazines were introduced, the outcome of later paraphrenia was almost uniformly unfavorable (Roth 1955). As those affected have a normal life expectancy it was common for such patients to spend many years of their remaining lives in hospital until neuroleptic drugs began to be employed in the treatment of their psychosis (Kay and Roth 1961; Roth 1955).

These patients often possess formidable personalities, being forceful, independent, and determined. Many had been self-isolated and had few social contacts. But prior to illness they had been able, through unusual talents and great energy, to lead successful and at times distinguished lives and to deal effectively with the practical, domestic, and other problems the elderly have to face. Experience with antipsychotic drugs in this group of patients has shown that psychotic symptoms can be brought under control in the majority of cases, and a further proportion achieve a partial remission of satisfactory quality. They are thus enabled to leave hospital, and only rarely is long-term institutional care necessary. A high proportion have proved able to resume independent life in the community.

In an investigation published by Post (1966) 93 patients admitted between 1954 and 1961 were treated and followed up for one to three years. An adequate course of treatment was administered in 71 patients. Forty-three had a complete remission from psychotic symptoms. Six patients were wholly unresponsive to medication. Clinical outcome judged after a three-year follow-up period showed little correlation with the patient's occupational status, but it is of interest that insight into the delusional character of their former beliefs was rarely achieved by the responders. Initial treatment response, compliance by the patient, and some insight into the character of the symptoms endured during illness were all correlated with outcome at follow-up. The pharmacologic treatment employed was 15–25 mg of trifluoperazine (Stelazine) or 150–600 mg of thioridazine (Mellaril). The investigation was uncontrolled, but the outcome in 24 patients of the original sample who had not been given antipsychotic drugs was a striking contrast; the psychosis continued unabated during the follow-up period in each case during the three-year period of observation.

Similar findings were recorded by Herbert and Jacobsen. Of 45 patients admitted to a mental hospital between 1958 and 1961, 21 patients could be discharged from hospital after treatment with antipsychotics. Sixteen patients continued in long-term care and eight patients died. Treatment of such patients with depot medication has proved superior to treatment with oral haloperidol in an inquiry undertaken by Raskind et al. (1979).

It is best to commence with a flexible regime of medication with 10–15 mg of trifluoperazine or 4–6 mg of perphenazine. For maintenance treatment the lowest possible dose that proves adequate on the basis of close observation should be used.

Where insight is lacking and compliance poor, a cautious attempt should be made to institute treatment with depot medication. Flupenthixol (fluphenazine) decanoate in a 20-mg dose monthly (after a trial dose of 10 mg) should suffice in the majority of cases. Unfortunately side effects often prove severe with depot medication; parkinsonism and tardive dyskinesia are common and arterial hypotension is all too liable to be complicated by fractures from falls. A steep fall in blood pressure may give rise to symptoms of cerebral ischemia or actual infarction. Where compliance proves satisfactory or administration of drugs can be supervised by a reliable relative, treatment by means of oral medication is to be preferred.

A coloring of depressive symptoms is relatively common in late paraphrenia. Post (1966) reported affective symptoms in 53 patients, which were severe in 20 cases. Manic symptoms are very rare, although in some cases forceful, assertive behavior, pressure of speech, and overactivity raise a suspicion of concomitant hypomania. If this suspicion is confirmed, a change in pharmacologic treatment may prove necessary.

In most cases associated depressive symptoms subside as the schizophrenic illness recedes. In a minority of patients tricyclic compounds may have to be added, although no therapeutic trials have tested their value in this disorder. In that minority of patients in whom a complete symptomatic profile of an endogenous depressive illness is present in addition to prominent paranoid features, a course of electroconvulsive therapy is indicated when drugs have failed to elicit a response. But it is wise to continue with a maintenance course of neuroleptics when a firm diagnosis of paraphrenia has been reached.

The establishment of good rapport and securing the confidence of the patient are a precondition for effective therapy and can be achieved in many cases with an effort. Under no circumstances should delusions be contested, and the therapists should not allow themselves to be drawn into arguments. His attitude should be detached, empathic, and constructive. Psychotherapy of a simple, explanatory, and supportive kind helps such patients to maintain their hold on reality and to keep hostility and morbid suspicion at bay to some extent.

The correction of sensory deficits as far as possible can be expected to ameliorate the symptoms manifest in patients with late paraphrenic disorder. There is good reason to believe that the isolation from human contact and communication created by such deficits plays some part in the genesis of the disorder. Ideally treatment should be undertaken in middle life or earlier, particularly for those in whom self-referential or paranoid tendencies are noted.

The content of the delusions and hallucinations reflects some of the premorbid personality features and may originate in part from the genetic factors that also contribute to the causation of the psychotic disorder. Themes of being robbed, evicted, and sexually assaulted figure prominently in the psychotic phenomena. In contrast to the abstract, mystical, and symbolic character of the delusions and the language in which they are expressed by young schizophrenics, the corresponding phenomena in late paraphrenic patients are blatantly sexual with fears of erotic approaches by others or frank delusions of sexual interference by occult means. Actual genital hallucinations are commonplace. Such features may be associated with Schneiderian first rank symptoms. Paraphrenic delusions are also distinctive in that persecutory figures are often individuals who are close to the patient such as family members or neighbors.

There is evidence from personality tests including a scale for the assessment of schizoid traits that the 35–40 percent of paraphrenic patients who suffer from deafness (which differs in duration and etiology from the hearing defects of normal subjects) are more intact as individuals and score lower on scales for schizoid traits in particular than paraphrenics without sensory deficits (Cooper et al. 1976). This suggests that rapport may be more easily established with those who are afflicted with sensory deficits. They may prove more ready to make use of whatever means of communication remain open to them so that supportive and explanatory psychotherapy can be more readily and effectively undertaken.

Delusional States of the Morbidly Jealous

The old view that morbid jealousy usually evolved in alcoholic subjects has in recent years been refuted by a large body of evidence that has shown the phenomenon of "conjugal paranoia" as a syndrome in its own right. However, a proportion of cases evolve as a result of transformation from a well-controlled, transient, and circumscribed tendency to jealousy into an overt and delusional form by some other psychiatric disorder that supervenes. In a review of the published literature of morbid jealousy Mooney (1965) found alcoholism to have been present in only 22.5 percent of cases. Langfeldt (1961) and Johanson (1964) came to similar conclusions from a study of their case material.

Jaspers (1910) considered that the paranoiac form of jealousy could develop either as the result of a special form of personality "development" or a consequence of a psychic "process." In the latter cases the systematized delusions make an abrupt appearance and are the expression of a psychiatric disorder that entails a qualitative shift from the norm. Similarly Kolle (1931) regarded "jealousy paranoia" as an endogenous genetically determined psychosis with a close kinship to the schizophrenic group of disorders.

The prominence given to schizophrenia as a causal factor had probably been influenced by the fact that the disorder usually proves exceedingly refractory to treatment. This theory is not supported by the findings in most of the large series of patients investigated, which have brought to light very few schizophrenic cases. In the important study of Vauhkonen (1968) the great majority of the patients were assigned to the following groups: Mild Paranoid Reaction, Mild Paranoid Condition, Paranoid Psychoses, and Paranoia. Only three of 55 patients were judged to be suffering from schizophrenia of paranoid type. It is not clear how far they differed in course and outcome from the other cases. In all the diagnostic groups to which the great majority of the patients were assigned, personality factors and the developmental process that had shaped the personality were judged to have made a substantial contribution to causation. Vauhkonen (1968) also considered that the character of the relationship and the interactions between the partners in the marriage had played a significant role in the genesis of the disorder.

Most of the patients are male and in severe cases the picture assumes a typical form. The wife is accused of committing adultery with strangers picked up in the street, with near relations, and even her own children. The patient suspects her of an insatiable sexual appetite from which only he is excluded. He searches her underclothes for evidence of seminal stains, which may be brought for the inspection of the therapist. When he arrives at home and hears her drawing the curtains in the evening, this is a signal for the sexually aroused men in the neighborhood to assemble in the house for an orgy. On other occasions when she is taken unawares and is seen to be going to the bathroom she does so to put her clothes in order because her lover has just escaped through the window. Shadows around her eyes are certain evidence she has been having sexual intercourse in his absence. Her frigidity to him can only signify that she is obtaining satisfaction elsewhere.

The behavior of patients with morbid jealousy may assume bizarre forms. A private detective may be engaged to secure proof of the spouse's depravity. One of our patients used a special dye to paint unobtrusively the top of a hot water bottle used by the spouse at night to secure evidence that she was masturbating with it to indulge her insatiable sexual appetites.

The spouse is incessantly interrogated in an attempt to prevail on her to confess her extramarital sexual adventures. Under the influence of such coercion some spouses describe imaginary misdemeanors. They may be violently assaulted and in some cases murdered following such confessions. Mowat (1966) in a survey of homicidal patients admitted to Broadmoor, a hospital for the criminally insane in England, found pathologic jealousy among 12 percent of men and 15 percent of women.

A wide range of views has been expressed about the etiology of the syndrome of morbid jealousy or the "Othello" syndrome. As we have already indicated, personality disorder or a lifelong personality problem has emerged as the largest single group in most authoritative studies. A substantial proportion suffer from a paranoiac disorder. This is superimposed and has evolved on the basis of premorbid traits associated with maladaptation. Depressive illness is associated in about 10–15 percent of cases, but it must act in association with personality predisposition as pathologic jealousy is found only in a small fraction of patients with depressive illness. As studies of Johanson (1964) have shown, a range of organic factors may make some contribution to causation. They include alcohol, drug dependence, cerebral lesions such as neoplasm, and the early stages of cerebral degeneration.

Understanding of the etiological basis of morbid jealousy is an essential precondition for appropriate and competent management of disorders and therefore merits further consideration. Some writers (Wendt 1957) have been led by the bizarreness of the delusional symptoms and the intractability of a high proportion of cases to postulate a dichotomy similar to that of Jaspers; a proportion of cases develop in his view on the basis of a "delusional mood" and are in his view always schizophrenic. A number of lines of evidence throw doubt on the possibility that schizophrenia is the underlying causal agent except in a small minority of cases. Although the condition is often chronic, deterioration of personality is virtually never seen. The symptomatology merely remains unchanged unless the patient is separated from his conjugal partner or consort. But any new relationship established is likely to be complicated by a recrudescence of morbid jealousy. Outside the scope of their delusions of unfaithfulness, conduct and even relationships may be relatively normal. In hospitals for the criminally insane, where they are often committed after conviction for murder or violent assault, such patients tend to be conspicuous for their orderly conduct and the absence of overt signs of psychopathology.

Where the jealousy, the accusations, and the attacks upon a spouse cannot be brought under control, a judicial separation is the only means of protecting her from serious injury or murder. In the small proportion of schizophrenic cases with a paranoid state in which the disorder has emerged over a short period out of a relatively clear sky, treatment with neuroleptics combined with counseling of the couple should always be attempted. A favorable response to drugs is elicited in a relatively small proportion of primary delusional cases (Mooney 1965), but in frankly schizophrenic patients the response is considerably better. Depressive illness requires treatment with antidepressants and in resistant cases with electroconvulsive therapy, and alleviation of symptoms or complete recovery may follow. The usual result is that jealousy returns to more normal or more manageable proportions, and when it has come out of an entirely clear sky in the premorbid state the delusional quality attaching to the beliefs and usually the jealous and hostile conduct will be eliminated.

Any concomitant physical disease requires full investigation and appropriate treatment. Feelings of sexual inferiority with an objective basis in impotence or premature ejaculation may benefit from behavioral treatment.

Jealousy is not confined to men, but morbid delusional forms are rare in women and disorders associated with serious violence are even more so. But syndromes in women with jealousy as a central feature have been seen with increasing frequency in psychiatric clinics in recent years.

Particularly in those cases in both sexes in which beliefs in unfaithfulness oscillate between doubt and certainty, joint marital therapy administered by a therapist experienced in this field can make an important contribution in reducing jealousy to manageable proportions and averting a permanent rift in the marriage. Such an approach should not preclude an attempt to institute pharmacologic treatment, which may help to secure an optimal outcome. Neuroleptic or antidepressant drugs may be the treatment of choice according to the character of the clinical profile.

Litigious Delusional States

In these patients there is an enduring tendency to engage in lawsuits in an attempt to seek rectification of or compensation for minimal or imaginary injustices and grievances. Should the verdict go against these patients, as is often the case, some are liable to become enraged and aggressive while others continue to mount lawsuits in unending succession; they constitute the vexatious litigants familiar to judges, lawyers, and psychiatrists in all countries. Some patients harass or attack their imaginary persecutors or the judges who have failed to recognize the justice of their cause. Others pursue an unremitting campaign in an attempt to secure the rectification of social evils or dangers to public health in which they believe with delusional intensity and inflexibility.

One patient pursued a campaign over many years to seek removal of additives to bread, introduced by secret government edict or through covert malevolence by the civil service, and intended to reduce the sexual urges of all members of the community so as to achieve population control. Others seek justice with respect to grievances that may have a small kernel of truth, for example, testing clauses in a will made by a person with whom they were acquainted but who had incurred no debt or obligation to the patient. At the extreme end of the spectrum these syndromes merge with the states of mind of a proportion of subjects who commit violent or murderous acts to achieve some social or political objective. Psychiatry has no role in such cases except with respect to those individuals in whom an indubitable psychiatric diagnosis can be made. Kretschmer regarded the litigious-delusional state as a form of expansive paranoia that was liable to evolve in mainly "sthenic" personalities and that could be regarded as being at the opposite pole from "sensitive" personalities liable to paranoid states dominated by delusional ideas of reference. In other words the querulantly litigious individual was predisposed by personality constituion to assume the role of persecutor and aggressor, whereas his counterpart at the opposite pole saw himself as the victim of persecution.

Somatic Paranoid Disorder

In the first group of these cases patients with somatic forms of delusional disorder are convinced they suffer from some abnormality in their appearance, the shape of the nose or the breasts or ears, to which they consider that others respond with derision, contempt, hostility, and aversion. Surgical treatment is sought to correct imagined deformities of the nose, ears, eyes, breasts, or genitalia. When the results fail to approximate to the patient's image of perfection, which is usually the case, severe emotional disturbance follows and suicide attempts are relatively common.

In the second group the picture is dominated by the fear-laden belief that some serious form of physical ill health such as heart disease, cerebral tumor, leukemia, venereal infection, or advanced carcinoma are present. Death may be believed to be imminent and suicide will be attempted to anticipate it. The condition is more common in men than in women. The patient's state of mind often hovers between doubt and delusion that he or she suffers from a potentially lethal malady. Strong evidence from x-rays or ECGs may for a time diminish the patient's distress. But a state of mind that oscillates between doubt and delusion returns. The favorable reports are declared to be forgeries intended to conceal the agonizing fate awaiting the patient. The inability to eradicate doubt is responsible for some of the duality of anguish suffered in patients. Obsessional traits figure prominently in the premorbid personality, and patients swing unsteadily across the reality line in a delusional state that fluctuates in intensity. But a substantial suicide risk exists. Some patients may suffer initially from a severe anxiety state, and mild hypochondriacal preoccupations have often been present over a long period.

Case D.   In this 37-year-old man, the premorbid personality was shy, self-conscious, reticent, and anxious. He had considerable difficulty in his late teens in establishing a relationship with a girl friend and had feelings of inferiority about his appearance and uncertainty about his ability to function sexually in a masculine role. At the age of 16 he described a distressing but short-lived and isolated experience. When looking in the mirror one day he detected a slight squint in his eye. His eyebrows also seemed excessively prominent. He heard a voice in his head that he could not identify saying, "no, it is quite all right." There were no sequelae to this episode, and his adjustment at work and social relationships remained normal for a number of years. His relatives had not observed any anomalies in his behavior to suggest any form of psychiatric disorder.

At the age of 21 while sitting at a bar of a public house he was informed by one of his friends that the girl with whom he had been going out regularly had become engaged to someone else. He experienced a sudden surge of anxiety. This was followed by a voice in his head saying, "who made me cock-eyed." He experienced an immediate "electrical impulse" from his brain down towards his legs causing him to slide off the high chair on which he was sitting drinking some beer. His knees banged painfully against the wooden panel of the bar. Following this experience he developed the delusional belief over a period of two to three weeks that his eyes were out of alignment, the orbits deformed and misshapen, and his eyebrows protuberant to a severely disfiguring degree. He sought the advice of a plastic surgeon and underwent a succession of four operations in an attempt to eliminate the defects of which he complained. This proved of no avail. Wherever he went contemptuous and derisory attention was paid to him and passers-by commented on his ugliness. In a public house he heard one commenting, "look at that cock-eyed clown." And at a social gathering he heard a man near to him comment, "eyes like piss pools in the snow." He made three determined suicide attempts with overdoses of drugs. Antidepressant drugs and convulsive therapy had no effect. After a period of some months he responded with considerable improvement to thioridazine followed by depot injections of fluphenazine decanoate. He obtained further relief from weekly psychotherapeutic sessions along mainly behavioral lines. But he continued to suffer from a severe social anxiety and at times ideas of reference that bordered on the delusional. He was able to return to work despite continuing symptoms. Contact was lost with the patient after some two years of observation. During this time his symptoms fluctuated a great deal but there was no deterioration in his affective response or personality. It is noteworthy that, in this case, the delusional and quasi-hallucinatory experiences were restricted to specific beliefs about the deformity of his face and the manner in which others reacted to it.

Comment. The somatic delusions in this case were associated with hallucinations on rare occasions. Both of these took the form of unambiguous vocal expression of derisory comments he believed others to be making about him, and in hospital he was never observed to be hallucinating. They can be reconciled with criterion B of DSM-III-R 297.10, which excludes those with prominent auditory or visual hallucinations. He was intermittently very depressed and made three suicide attempts but again failed to respond to antidepressants or electroconvulsive therapy. A case could be made for schizophrenic disorder, but this would not be consistent with the predominance of a single delusional theme, nor would the patient conform to DSM-III or other criteria for this disorder. The psychosis was well encapsulated, and deterioration of personality was not in evidence.

Erotomanic Delusional States

The person affected is usually an unmarried woman who maintains the delusional belief that a person of elevated social status or a famous film star or politician is secretly in love with her. The condition is often described by eponymous attribution to de Clérambault (1921), who first delineated the syndrome. The deluded and infatuated patient regards the imagined lover as a suitor and considers that he will be doomed to an emotionally impoverished and fruitless existence unless he can be united with her. She explains his failure to communicate his love directly by a range of ingenious confabulations; for example in the interests of expediency he may have to be discrete and restrained. His responses may appear to be inexplicably hostile and aggressive; he may lodge complaints with the police or his lawyers may send letters threatening a legal action. She interprets such action as motivated by his need to conduct the affair with cunning and dissimulation. In the course of time the patients may be provoked into public demonstration and harassment of the loved one. The minority of male subjects with this disorder may behave violently towards the imaginary beloved or run into conflict with the law in other ways. The delusional syndrome remains encapsulated over long periods and schizophrenic deterioration of personality does not occur when the delusions are confined to a single theme. Treatment should proceed according the principles outlined in the early general section of this chapter.

Conclusions

Delusional (paranoid) psychoses have assumed increasing importance in recent years. Hare (1974) has drawn attention to the decreasing rate of admission of patients diagnosed as schizophrenia and the concomitant increase in those diagnosed as suffering from paranoid and related forms of paranoid illness. There is independent evidence from Scandinavian studies that reactive psychoses, the term used there to describe most nonschizophrenic paranoid disorders, form a larger proportion of those admitted to hospital than schizophrenic disorders (Retterstol 1966). This group of mental disorders has been treated with neglect in recent decades. The literature contains relatively few records of controlled therapeutic trials of neuroleptics and other physical treatments or of evaluations of the efficacy of psychological methods of treatment. This gap in knowledge needs urgently to be remedied.

Evidence from controlled therapeutic trials has shown that modern biologic methods of treatment are effective in ameliorating or resolving certain forms of paranoid psychoses and disorder, including the paranoid disorders of later life, the main group of persecutory disorders, and certain forms of schizoaffective disorder. This statement does not apply to the morbid jealousy syndromes, litigious paranoia, or the somatic delusional states. Here too further inquiries are needed to define more precisely the groups of cases in which these methods of treatment are effective and to develop reliable indices for the prediction of outcome.

There is a body of evidence to suggest that paranoid disorders as a whole have a better prognosis than schizophrenic illness. Fresh inquiries are needed to establish rates of remission that can be achieved with the aid of optimal courses of treatment combining all available modalities.

There is a solid body of evidence that has established the importance of premorbid personality and its interaction with threatening life events as factors that contribute to causation in a substantial group of paranoid disorders. But the concept of "psychogenic psychosis" implicitly overstates the etiological importance of such factors.

A case has been made for approaching the therapy of paranoid states along a broad front. Historic and developmental dimensions need to be taken into account for understanding patients and for supporting and counseling them and modifying their attitudes with psychological methods of treatment.

On the basis of the larger follow-up studies undertaken, more than half of patients with delusional disorders can be expected to recover. A substantial minority, 30 to 40 percent in different series, suffer from chronic symptoms but these appear to be well encapsulated in the majority and personality is well preserved. A small percentage develop true schizophrenia. Approximately 80 percent or more were found to achieve a social recovery in the largest series studied. But these findings need to be repeated in modern cohorts of cases.

There is a compelling need for controlled therapeutic trials to provide more information regarding the effects of pharmacological and psychological forms of treatment in the different forms of delusional disorder. The trial and error basis that has to be adopted in the treatment of patients in a number of the disorders described in this chapter is unsatisfactory. Fresh investigations drawing upon the recent advances in genetics require also to be mounted to clarify the hereditary basis of the different forms of delusional illness. Finally, research needs to be conducted into a problem that received only brief mention in this chapter. This refers to the body of evidence in the clinical literature (as in the monographs of Retterstol, Johanson, and Gaupp's study of the Wagner family) that excessive alcohol consumption contributes to the aetiology of a substantial proportion of the persecutory delusional states, morbid jealousy syndromes and some of the disorders dominated by auditory hallucinations. The suggestion from the recorded cases is that alcohol exerts its influence by potentiating hereditary, personality and dynamic factors and their interactions. Precise information is also needed about the treatment response and prognosis of patients in whom such syndromes with concomitant alcoholism are manifest.

References

Section 15
Delusional (Paranoid) Disorders

American Psychiatric Association: Diagnostic and Statistical Manual of Mental Disorders, 3rd ed. Washington, DC, American Psychiatric Association, 1980

American Psychiatric Association: Diagnostic and Statistical Manual of Mental Disorders, 3rd ed, revised. Washington, DC, American Psychiatric Association, 1987

Andreasen NC, Nasrallah HA, Dunn V, et al: Structural abnormalities in the frontal system in schizophrenia: a magnetic resonance imaging study. Arch Gen Psychiatry 43:136–144, 1986

Baldessarini RJ: Chemotherapy in Psychiatry. Cambridge, Mass, Harvard University Press, 1984

Baldessarini RJ: Public lecture given at Clarke Institute of Psychiatry, University of Toronto, November 20, 1986

Baldessarini RJ, Davis JM: What is the best maintenance dose of neuroleptics in schizophrenia? Psychiatry Res 3:115–122, 1980

Berner P, Gabriel E, Kathschnig H, et al: Diagnostic Criteria for Schizophrenia and Affective Psychoses. London, World Psychiatric Association, 1983

Brockington IF, Meltzer HY: The nosology of schizoaffective psychosis. Psychiatr Dev 1:317–338, 1983

Buchsbaum MS, Delisi LE, Halcomb HH, et al: Anteroposterior gradients in cerebral glucose use in schizophrenia and affective disorder. Arch Gen Psychiatry 41:1159–1166, 1984

Capstick N, Pudney H: A comparative trial of orphenadrine and tofenacin in the control of depression and extrapyramidal side effects associated with fluphenazine decanoate therapy. J Int Med Res 4:435–440, 1976

Chouinard G, Annable L, Ross-Chouinard A, et al: Factors related to tardive dyskinesia. Am J Psychiatry 136:360–362, 1979

Clérambault, G. de: 1921 Les délires passionels. Erotomanie, revendication, jalousie. Bulletin de la Société clinique de Médicine Mentale 66–71

Cooper AF, Garside RG, Kay DK: A comparison of deaf and non-deaf patients with paranoid and affective psychoses. Br J Psychiatry 129:532–538, 1976

Crow TJ, Cross, AJ, Johnstone EC, et al: Two syndromes in schizophrenia and their pathogenesis, in Schizophrenia as a Brain Disease. Edited by Henn F, Nasrallah HA. New York, Oxford University Press, 1981a, pp 196–234

Crow TJ, Owen F, Cross AJ, et al: Neurotransmitters, enzymes and receptors in post mortem brain in schizophrenia: evidence that an increase in D2 dopamine receptors is associated with the type 1 syndrome, in Transmitter Biochemistry of Human Brain Tissue. Edited by Riederer P, Usdin E. London, Macmillan, 1981b, pp 85–96

Cutting J: A reappraisal of alcoholic psychoses. Psychol Med 8:285–295, 1978

Davison K: Drug induced psychoses and their relationship to schizophrenia, in Schizophrenia Today. Oxford, Pergamon Press, 1977

Faergeman PM: Psychogenic psychoses. A description and follow-up of psychoses following psychological stress. London, Butterworths, 1963

Fairbairn WD: Psychoanalytic Studies of the Personality. London, Tavistock Publications, 1952

Freud S: Psycho-analytic notes upon an autobiographical account of a case of paranoia (Dementia Paranoides) (1911), in Collected Papers, vol III. New York, Basic Books, 1959, pp 387–470

Frosch WA, Robins ES, Stern M: Untoward reactions to LSD resulting in hospitalisation. N Engl J Med 273:1235, 1965

Gaupp R: Uber paranoische Veranlagung und abortive Paranoia. Zentralbl Nervenheilk Psychiatr 33:65–67, 1910

Gaupp R: Zur Psychologie des Massenmordes. Berlin, Hauptlehrer Wagner von Degerloch, 1914

Gaupp R: Der Fall Wagner. Eine Katamnese, zugleich ein Beitrag zur Lehre von Paranoia. Z ges Neurol Psychiatr 60:312–327, 1920

Granato JE, Stern BJ, Ringel A, et al: Neuroleptic malignant syndrome: successful treatment with dantrolene and bromocriptine. Annals of Neurology 14:89–90, 1983

Gruhle HW: Uber den Wahn. Nervenarzt 22:125–126, 1951

Hare EH: The changing content of psychological illness. J Psychosom Res 18:283–289, 1974

Herbert M, Jacobson S: Late Paraphrenia. British Journal of Psychiatry 1, 3:461–469, 1967

Jaspers K: Eifersuchtswahn. Z ges Neurol Psychiatry 1:567–637, 1910

Jaspers K: General Psychopathology (1913), 7th ed. Translated by Hoenig Hamilton. London, Manchester University Press, 1963

Johanson E: Mild paranoia. Description and analysis of fifty-two in-patients from an opern department for mental diseases. Acta Psychiatr Scand Suppl 177, 1964

Kasanin J: The acute schizoaffective psychoses. Am J Psychiatry 13:97–126, 1933

Kay DK: Observations on the natural history and genetics of old age psychoses: Stockholm material 1931–1937 (abridged). Proc R Soc Med 52, 1959

Kay DK: Late paraphrenia and its bearing on the aetiology of schizophrenia. Acta Psychiatr Scand 39:159–302, 1963

Kay DK, Roth M: Environmental and hereditary factors in the schizophrenias of old age ("late paraphrenia") and their bearing on the general problem of causation in schizophrenia. J Ment Sci 107:649–686, 1961

Kendler KS: Demography of paranoid psychosis (delusional disorder): a review and comparison with schizophrenia and affective illness. Arch Gen Psychiatry 39:890–902, 1982

Kendler KS, Gruenberg AM, Tsuang MT: Psychiatric illness in first degree relatives of schizophrenics and surgical control patients. Archives of General Psychiatry 42:770–779, 1985

Kendler KS, Tsuang MT: Nosology of paranoid schizophrenia and other paranoid psychoses. Schizophr Bull 7:597–610, 1981

Kiloh LG, Smith SJ, Williams SE: Anti-parkinson drugs as causal agents in tardive dyskinesias. Med J Aust 2:591–593, 1973

Klein M: Contributions to Psychoanalytic Theory. London, Hogarth Press, 1948

Kolle K: Die primare Verrucktheit. Leipzig, George Thieme, 1931

Kolle K: Der Wahnkranke im Lichte alter und neuer Psychopathologie. Stuttgart, George Thieme, 1957

Kraepelin E: Psychiatrie. Ein Lehrbuch fur Studierende and Arzte, 8th ed. Leipzig, Aufl. J.A. Barth, 1909–1915

Kretschmer E: Der Sensitive Beziehungswahn. Berlin, Julius Springer, 1918

Kretschmer E: Der Sensitive Beziehungswahn. Berlin, Julius Springer, 1918

Langfeldt G: The hypersensitive mind. Acta Psychiatr Scand Suppl 73, 1951

Langfeldt G: The erotic jealousy syndrome. Acta Psychiatr Scand Suppl 151, 1961

Mayer-Gross W: Psychopathology of delusions. Congress International de Psychiatrie I. Tome I, 59–87, 1950

McClelland HA, Farquharson RG, Leyburn P, et al: Very high dose fluphenazine decanoate. Arch Gen Psychiatry 33:1435–1442, 1976

Meissner WW: The Paranoid Process. New York, Jason Aronson, 1978

Meissner WW: Psychotherapy of the paranoid patient, in Technical Factors in the Treatment of the Severely Disturbed Patient. Edited by Giovacchini PL, Boyer LG. New York, Jason Aronson, 1982

Mindham RHS, Gaind R, Anstee BH, et al: Comparison of amantadine, orphenadrine and placebo in the control of phenothiazine-induced parkinsonism. Psychol Med 2:406–413, 1972

Mooney HB: Pathologic jealousy and psychochemotherapy. Br J Psychiatry 111/480:1023–1042, 1965

Mowat RR: Morbid Jealousy and Murder. London, Tavistock, 1966

Nasrallah HA: Neuroleptic plasma levels and tardive dyskinesia: a possible link? Schizophr Bull 6:4, 1980

Opjordsmoen S: Long-term follow-up of paranoid psychoses. Psychopathology 19:44–49, 1986

Pichot P: The Concept of "Bouffée Delirante" with special reference to the Scandinavian concept of reactive psychosis. Psychopathology 19:35–43, 1986

Post F: Persistant Persecutory States of the Elderly. Oxford, Pergamon Press, 1966

Quitkin, F, Rifkin A, Kelin DE: Very high dosage vs. standard dosage fluphenazine in schizophrenia. Arch Gen Psychiatry 32:1276, 1281, 1975

Raskind M, Alvarez C, Herlin RN: Fluphenazine enanthate in the outpatient treatment of late paraphrenia. J Am Geriatr Soc 27:459–463, 1979

Retterstol N: Paranoid and Paranoiac Psychoses. Oslo, Universitetsforlaget, 1966

Retterstol N: Prognosis in Paranoid Psychoses. Springfield, Ill, Charles C Thomas, 1970

Roth M: The natural history of mental disorders arising in old age. J Ment Sci 101:281–301, 1955

Roth M: Diagnosis and prognosis of schizophrenia, in Handbook of Studies on Schizophrenia, part 1, 14:169–182, 1986

Schneider K: Über den Wahn. Stuttgart, 1952

Schneider K: Clinical Psychopathology. Translated by Hamilton MS. New York, Grune and Stratton, 1959

Séglas J: La paranoia. Archives de Neurologie 13:63–76, 393–406, 1887

Sherrington R, Byrnjolfsson J, Petursson H, et al: Localisation of a Susceptibility Locus for Schizophrenia on Chromosome 5. Nature Vol. 336, Issue No. 615, 164–167, 1988

Simpson GM, Varga E, Haher J: Psychotic exacerbations produced by neuroleptics. Dis Nerv Syst 37:367–369, 1976

Simpson GM, et al: Effect of antiparkinsonian medication on plasma levels of chlorpromazine. Arch Gen Psychiatry 37:205, 1980

Staehelin JE: Zur Frage der Emotionspsychosen. Bull Schwiez Akad Med Wiss 2:121–130, 1946–1947

Strömgren E: Episodiske Psykoser. Copenhagen, Munksguard, 1940

Strömgren E: Pathogenese der verschiedenen Formen von psychogenen Psychosen , in Memorial volume to Ernst Kretschmer on his seventieth birthday, Mehrdimensionale Diagnostik und Therapie, pp. 67–7–. Stuttgart: Thieme, 1958

Strömgren E: Psychogenic Psychoses, in Themes and Variations in European Psychiatry. An Anthology. Edited by Hirsch SR, Shepherd M. Bristol, England, John Wright, 1974

Vauhkonen K: On the pathogenesis of morbid jealousy, with special reference to the personality traits of and interaction between jealous patients and their spouses. Acta Psychiatr Scand Suppl 202, 1968

Westlake RJ, Rastegar A: Hyperpyrexia from drug combinations. JAMA 225:1250, 1973

Wimmer A: Psykogene Sindssygdomsformer (in Danish). Copenhagen, Lunds, 1916

World Health Organization: The International Pilot Study of Schizophrenia, vol I. Geneva, World Health Organization, 1973

World Health Organization (ed): International Classification of Diseases, 9th rev. Geneva, World Health Organization, 1978

SECTION 16

Psychotic Disorders
Not Elsewhere Classified

Chapter 153

Introduction

The only two features shared by all of the disorders included in this section of DSM-III-R (American Psychiatric Association 1987) are included in its title, "The Psychotic Disorders Not Elsewhere Classified." Each of the syndromes we will discuss is characterized by the presence of psychosis, and none of the syndromes fits in very well within any of the other sections of the DSM-III-R classification. Before we get on to individual disorders themselves, it may be useful to discuss some of the methodological issues in diagnosis that generate "miscellaneous" categories and the consequent impact this has on treatment planning.

There were two methodological innovations used to develop DSM-III (American Psychiatric Association 1980) that resulted in its promulgation of a very large number of specific disorders, some of which are difficult to collect into homogeneous theme-centered sections. Both of these methods were derived from DSM-III's spiritual predecessor, the Research Diagnostic Criteria (RDC). DSM-III provides explicit diagnostic criteria for each category and attempts to define them in a fairly narrow manner that increases the homogeneity of patients who qualify for the diagnosis. The provision of explicit and narrowly defined categories promotes reliability, increases the accuracy of clinical communication, and furthers the selection of patients for validation research. However, these gains are purchased at a cost—the necessity of including a sufficient number of the narrowly defined categories to ensure coverage of the varied conditions commonly seen in clinical practice that were previously defined in fewer, vaguer, and more heterogeneous categories. Because the RDC included many fewer diagnostic categories than DSM-III, its residual category (undiagnosed psychiatric disorder) was used for the majority of patients seen in clinical practice. DSM-III became a "splitter's" delight (and a "lumper's" nightmare) precisely because it applied the RDC criteria method, but combined it with a necessary ambition to achieve diagnostic comprehensiveness so that the classification system could be used widely in clinical, as well as research, settings.

Whenever, as in DSM-III, the diagnostic pie is cut into smaller slices, it becomes more difficult to determine where to draw the lines between categories. When these lines are drawn explicitly and by criteria, as in DSM-III, it is inevitable that the resulting boundaries will often seem (and be) arbitrary. There is, for instance, very little evidence supporting a six-month duration boundary between schizophrenic and schizophreniform disorders or the two-week limit for brief reactive psychosis (in fact this latter has been changed in DSM-III-R to one month). There has been so much controversy on the border between the schizophrenic and affective disorders that the category created to deal with this difficulty—the schizoaffective disorder—does not even have a set of diagnostic criteria. Thousands of classification decisions had to be made in the creation of DSM-III, and the very explicitness of most of these often highlights their necessary arbitrariness.

Ultimately, of course, all psychiatric diagnostic categories are defined in such a way as to sit at the boundary of several other categories. In fact, patient presentations that straddle these borders are so frequently encountered in clinical practice that the term "atypical" has little meaning, at least in its connotation of low prevalence. The categories included in this section describe patients who are psychotic but who are not classical in their presentation of features that would qualify for a schizophrenic or affective disorder diagnosis. The individual syndromes are defined by criteria that are largely unvalidated, have been modified in DSM-III-R, and undoubtedly will be subject to continued and extensive future modifications. All of the definitions of disorders in DSM-III are tentative, but those that define disorders in this section are probably more tentative than most. None of the DSM-III categories deserves or stands up to reification, and least of all those to be discussed here.

What does this imply about treatment planning? In a few words—humility, flexibility, pluralism, integration, and empiricism. If we do not, with any degree of certainty, know how best to define the disorders covered here, even less do we have prescriptive approaches to each of them. We have learned a great deal about the treatment of psychosis but have a great deal more to learn. It is also not clear how strategies devised and tested in schizophrenic populations (e.g., low or intermittent medication dosing and family therapy to reduce expressed emotion) will transfer to schizophreniform or schizoaffective disorder or how the medication strategies for treating schizophrenic or affective disorders will work alone or in combination for schizoaffective disorder. An empirical, open-minded, wide-ranging, and integrated patient-based approach to treatment planning is desirable (and perhaps necessary) in all psychiatric treatment, but this is particularly the case for conditions such as those addressed here that are less clearly and homogeneously defined and have received less research and clinical attention.

Chapter 154

Treatment of Schizophreniform Disorder

There are many ways to examine the diagnostic category of schizophreniform disorder that have both conceptual and practical implications. We suspect, therefore, that our comments about treatment considerations will have greater utility if we briefly explain our conceptual framework with references to DSM-III and DSM-III-R.

As presented in DSM-III, the diagnosis of schizophreniform disorder symptomatically resembles schizophrenia in all aspects except duration. The illness is described as lasting longer than two weeks but less than six months including the prodromal, active, and residual phases. Although we can theoretically accept the concept of prodrome, the difficulty in dating the onset of prodrome retrospectively and the dearth of data implying the possibility of preventing the onset of psychotic symptomatology if a prodromal period could be identified prospectively suggest that defining the term prodrome is a less than satisfying task. Rather than working with the theoretically defined DSM-III (DSM-III-R) syndrome of schizophreniform disorder, we shall address the issue of a psychotic illness occurring with relatively little warning and not resolving completely within the first two weeks. In terms of the "less than six months" criterion, here again we find room for clinical flexibility. Prognosis or duration of illness is difficult for the treating clinician to predict prospectively with enough certainty to alter the treatment decision. We find, therefore, that in describing the clinical approach to the schizophreniform category, we are potentially examining two "diagnostic" possibilities:

1. A group of people who have relatively recent onset of psychotic symptoms and who will recover completely in six months and form the "true schizophreniform" category.
2. A group of people who have relatively recent onset of psychotic symptoms and who may be waiting out their six months to be rediagnosed schizophrenic and who are the "holding pattern schizophreniform" category.

Because we find the term schizophreniform unwieldy enough without modifiers like "true" and "holding pattern," and because we are unaware of any research data that would allow us to differentiate meaningfully between these two categories on initial presentation either in terms of prognosis or treatment, the remainder of this discussion of treatment of schizophreniform disorder will focus on the *early* treatment phase of a psychotic illness lasting more than two weeks, which through clinical improvement is giving indications that it will resolve within six months. This sense of improvement may be a critical, even if neither completely operational or reliable, concept in schizophreniform disorder. Many alternative treatments, particularly pharmacologic, would be considered if improvement were not being observed. For a full discussion of early treatment options in situations in which improvement is not occurring, we refer the reader to Section 14 on schizophrenia.

The reader should also be aware that much of the research data we refer to has been derived from the treatment of psychosis in clearly mixed populations of both schizophreniform and schizophrenic diagnoses. We acknowledge that there may be some differences in the treatment of these two groups, and where research evidence is available on this point we emphasize it.

We are also committed to the concept that good clinical care emanates from a solid understanding of the available research base and have therefore organized this chapter with an emphasis first on research and second on the clinical implications of research for treatment. There are, of course, many decisions facing the clinician for which we have little empirical research. When this is true in the treatment of schizophreniform disorder, we attempt to differentiate our clinical opinion from research supported data.

Onset of Treatment

Role of Neuroleptics in Acute Psychosis

There is overwhelming evidence supporting the role of neuroleptics in the alleviation of positive symptoms of schizophrenia. Almost no one would question the role of medication during the psychotic state. Eighty to 90 percent of patients who have psychotic symptoms will respond to the use of neuroleptics with a reduction of symptomatology. While there is consensus on this particular point, the particular strategies to be invoked for the treatment of acute symptoms have produced considerable disagreement and clinical opinion unsupported by research data. In an excellent review of this area, Donaldson et al. (1983) emphasized the following points:

1. The treatment of the first appearance of psychotic symptoms may require considerably less medication than previously thought (Cohen et al. 1980). Dosages of less than 300 mg of chlorpromazine equivalents produce a clinical response and increasing the dosage over 500 mg adds little.
2. Rapid neuroleptization, the frequent use of high-potency neuroleptics during the first hours of hospitalization, needs to be reconsidered in light of these findings. The benefit of this procedure may lie in the sedation rather than the antipsychotic benefits of this regimen.
3. The range of blood levels of neuroleptics at which a response has been reported is too variable (40-fold) to be of use in the treatment planning.
4. Family history of response to medication, prior treatment response, and particular side effects should be used in the selection of a particular medication.
5. Research is progressing on "markers" that would predict medication responsiveness, but to date the only strong predictor of a positive drug response is an acute onset of positive symptoms in a good premorbid patient.

Role of Psychosocial Treatment

There is a long tradition of using two major psychosocial interventions, individual and group psychotherapy, with schizophrenic patients on inpatient units. For the purpose of this chapter we will be citing evidence from the four studies that focused on relatively acute patient populations to make the extrapolation to schizophreniform disorder more credible. The evidence to date supports a positive impact of these modalities on patient functioning only when patients are receiving neuroleptic medication. Our data on the limited contributions of inpatient intensive psychotherapy in the absence of medication to early resolution of the psychotic phase of the illness come from the five major studies of individual psychotherapy conducted in inpatient settings.

The study by Karon and VandenBos (1981) has generated many questions regarding its design, and thus the investigators' positive interpretation of the benefits of experienced therapists working with schizophrenic patients is difficult to interpret. The study by Rogers et al. (1967) presents evidence of a minimal positive effect and even that is confounded by the unstated use of medication. The study by Grinspoon et al. (1972) of whether drugs interfered with individual psychotherapy found just the opposite: without drugs, individual psychotherapy was largely ineffective. It should be noted, however, that this study involved far more chronic patients than could conceivably receive a diagnosis of schizophreniform disorder.

The study at the Camarillo State Hospital by May (1968) was an intensive investigation of five standard treatment modalities given to a sample of 228 first-admission, mid-range prognosis schizophrenics between the ages of 16 and 45 in an inpatient setting. Because of the patient population, it is most relevant to schizophreniform disorder. This study attempted to evaluate treatment modalities as they could be provided in a good public treatment program. The five modalities were psychotherapy alone, milieu, electroconvulsive therapy (ECT), neuroleptics alone, and neuroleptics plus psychotherapy. Although the results of this study have been questioned because the therapists were relatively inexperienced and the psychotherapy was not intense, if the study is considered as an evaluation of treatment strategies as they are most likely to be employed in a standard treatment setting, then these criticisms are less germane. The investigation's frequently cited results showed that the two drug conditions (drug alone and drug plus psychotherapy) were associated with significantly higher measures of clinical improvement than were the two nondrug conditions (milieu and psychotherapy alone) with ECT falling in between. The follow-up studies of discharged patients raised an additional point for consideration: does the withholding of neuroleptic medication during the actively psychotic phase of the disorder have long-term consequences? During their follow-up period, no control was attempted over the frequency or the type of treatment received, making definitive conclusions impossible; yet May and Tuma (1970) have reported that the patients who did not receive drugs initially spent twice as many days in the hospital after discharge as those who received drugs, raising the possibility that in a standard inpatient unit initially treating the positive symptoms without drugs may lead to a poorer long-term course of the disorder.

At the conclusion of these four studies the advocates of intensive individual psychotherapy for schizophrenic disorders defended the possibility that the treatment was effective by criticizing the negative studies for not using experienced therapists, not making the therapy intensive or frequent enough, not making the treatment long enough in duration, and not following patients after discharge from the hospital.

Stanton et al. (1984) recently reported on the results of a study conducted at McLean Hospital and Boston University in which intensive individual psychotherapy was provided by experienced therapists three to four hours a week, was begun with acutely psychotic inpatients, and was continued over into the outpatient setting. The comparison group received good clinical management with a well-developed "reality adaptive, supportive psychotherapy." Both groups received medication in accordance with clinical judgment. The results of this well-conducted 10-year study are as follows: First, the patients who were the most severely ill dropped out of the intensive treatment group at a significantly higher rate than that seen in the supportive management group. And second, despite the effects of this differential attrition, which left the supportive group with sicker patients than the intensive therapy group, the magnitude of the differences in outcome between groups was minimal. The supportive psychotherapy was superior in preventing recidivism and improving role performance; the intensive psychotherapy demonstrated a smaller advantage in cognition and ego functioning.

In terms of inpatient group psychotherapy, the results are at least as sobering. It would appear that in a standard inpatient setting for the treatment of patients suffering from psychotic symptomatology, there is little evidence to suggest that specific psychotherapies, individual or group, when used without medication, are beneficial. Indeed, there is some suggestion that without neuroleptics, there may be potential short-term or long-term negative effects of these therapies. Furthermore, the evidence for an additive effect of these therapies when given in combination with drugs is modest. At a time when patients characteristically display dramatic positive symptomatology early in the resolution of psychosis on a standard inpatient unit, pharmacologic therapies are crucial in bringing about a reduction in symptoms. The amount of resources one should devote to intensive psychotherapy in addition to medication at this point in the treatment program must, of course, be an individual clinical decision, but one should certainly not expect major improvement from these therapies alone.

Although some may find this assessment on intensive interpersonal psychotherapies in the floridly psychotic phase of illness disappointing, we feel that the results are not at all surprising. Psychotherapies are better suited for approaching negative symptoms of schizophrenia and schizophreniform illnesses and problems of socialization. During the early hospitalization period, these problems assume far less importance than does the reduction of positive symptomatology. Current societal expectations of rapid response, monetary limitations with third party involvement, and current biologic emphasis also contribute to the deemphasis of individual psychotherapy.

Clinical Implications

Primary concern in approaching the acutely psychotic patient is in providing a safe and rapidly effective treatment. Safe treatment requires the establishment of a diagnosis and a therapeutic plan. We have discussed schizophreniform disorder as if the diagnosis has been established. Clearly this is not how conditions present to the clinician. Initially the differential diagnosis would include many of the other categories of psychotic disorders not elsewhere classified, including brief reactive psychosis and induced psychotic disorder and major disorder categories like schizophrenia and affective disorder with psychotic features. Obviously, in the first two weeks of observation, either as an inpatient or outpatient, physical examination, laboratory work including drug screening, and a thorough family history of physical or psychiatric disorders would be obtained. With the passage of the first two weeks, brief reactive psychosis is ruled out by definition and many acute toxic states will have resolved or been identified in the course of the physical examination or laboratory workup. Perhaps the most difficult differential diagnosis clinically, and one that also may have critical treatment implications, is with respect to affective syndromes with psychotic features in a good premorbid patient. On a cross-sectional approach, or after seeing the patient over only a brief period of time, the clinician is faced with what may be a difficult if not impossible decision on diagnosis. Helpful, of course, is the family history or any prior psychiatric problem. But, for many patients the decision must be made without this kind of help, and usually the strategy will be to treat the psychotic features and carefully observe affect and mood during the recovery from psychosis.

The second element of safe treatment is whether to hospitalize the patient or attempt to treat him or her as an outpatient. The degree of safety (both clinical and "threat to self or others") and degree of comfort in treating a developing psychosis on an outpatient basis will vary depending on a number of issues:

1. Prior experience of the therapist in treating psychosis in an outpatient treatment program.
2. An established relationship with the patient or past history (if any) of the patient.
3. Indications of a robust response to medication (past history or current situation).
4. Availability of support for the patient (family, friends, or clinical resources).

We feel that this particular decision is too individualized for the clinician, patient, and family for any prescription in a treatment manual. Clinical judgment will always be the best guidance.

Once safety has been assured, the next goal is to provide a rapidly effective therapeutic intervention. Although they are not in practice separable, the clinical implications of the role of pharmacology and psychosocial intervention are perhaps best discussed in turn. From the research data described above, we would recommend that neuroleptic medication be initiated early and in dosages approaching 500 mg of chlorpromazine equivalents. For many patients additional neuroleptic medication may seem needed for sedation, but we would like to suggest the possible use of a benzodiazepine derivative drug for the purpose of sedation. Although the data for this choice are not as strong as we would desire, there have been several interesting discussions of this point in *Biological Therapies in Psychiatry* (1986), which suggest that significantly lower doses of neuroleptic are possible with this type of adjunctive support.

The selection of the appropriate neuroleptic is an area for which available research data do not provide much assistance. Despite efforts to identify patient profiles that are associated with response to specific neuroleptics, there are no guidelines available. Side effect profiles, sedation requirements, family or individual history of response, and clinician familiarity with a specific neuroleptic should be the guiding principles. In treating patients who have never received neuroleptics before, high-potency agents with their increased risk of dystonias and other extrapyramidal side effects may be less desirable.

Although we have not been impressed with the results of *intensive* psychotherapies in the early stages of acute psychosis, maintaining a strong clinical management position and alliance with the patient and family during this period is essential. Support for both the patient and family is critical, and this early relationship building on the part of the clinician will pay major dividends later in the recovery process. Information sharing about the disorder and the treatment and providing a responsive and safe environment are critical elements of the early stages of a successful treatment program.

Recovery Period

Once active symptomatology has been brought under control, usually in the hospital setting, the focus and the location of treatment changes. Central in the postpsychotic recovery period are the prevention of relapse and the improvement in skills required for independent living.

Antipsychotic drug treatment is well established as an essential component in the prevention of relapse for psychosis-prone patients in the community (*Biological Therapies in Psychiatry* 1986). In a drug discontinuation study (Davis 1975) remitted patients with schizophrenia had a relapse rate of 68 percent, arguing strongly for the need for some form of medication strategy for the recovery period. However, this study included too few "first episode patients" to draw conclusions specific to the schizophreniform diagnosis.

However, although demonstrably effective, such drug treatment is not without problems. Data from studies that are now 20 years old are in agreement with more recent and perhaps more rigorously designed investigations that show relapse rates after one year of drug treatment to be approximately 30 percent (Davis et al. 1980; Baldessarini and Davis 1980). Estimates of relapse rates after one year even with drug treatment are not markedly reduced even in studies that control for compliance through the use of long-acting injectable medication. Thus drug treatment does not confer the basic benefit of immunity from relapse on all recipients. Further, even among patients who do not relapse, many do not seem to achieve adequate levels of functioning. Simply preventing the gross social disruption of a relapse does not appear sufficient to enable patients to mobilize their own resources to be better after a year or two of drug treatment than they were before. Indeed, in some areas, such as development of symptoms of depression or negative symptoms, drug-treated patients may show increased symptomatology over time (Mandel et al. 1982). Finally, although not necessarily relevant in the first six months of treatment, a recent prospective estimate of cumulative incidence of tardive dyskinesia at the end of seven years of cumulative neuroleptic exposure is 28 percent (Kane 1986).

More recently, attention has turned to alternate reduced drug treatment strategies. Their goal is to provide the advantages of medication while decreasing the risk of tardive dyskinesia and the occurrence of other side effects of neuroleptic drugs such as akinesia. A further goal of the reduced dosage strategies has been the improvement of social functioning.

One such dosage strategy uses a substantially lowered dose administered prophylactically (Kane et al. 1983). Kane's group reported that during a one-year treatment period, patients treated with low-dose neuroleptic drugs (1.25–5 mg every two weeks of prolixin decanoate) were more likely to experience a symptom exacerbation requiring administration of additional medication than were patients receiving standard-dose neuroleptics. However, after a year the patients receiving low-dose neuroleptics had fewer symptoms associated with tardive dyskinesia. In another report from this study Kreisman and Blumenthal (personal communication, 1988) found that patients receiving low dosages who did not relapse during the year were rated significantly more favorably by their families than either patients in the low-dose group who had relapsed or the patients in the standard-dose group who did not. In addition, although the low-dose group required more supplementary medication, the type of symptoms they manifested rarely required hospitalization and was usually treated in the community.

The second variant of reduced dosage has been that of intermittent or targeted medication where patients are kept drug free except during periods of incipient relapse when pharmacologic intervention is vigorously pursued. Although the results of the two projects in which this strategy is being studied (Carpenter et al. 1982; Herz et al. 1982) are not reported on, we look forward to their future development.

At this point in discussing the treatment of schizophreniform disorder, it is important to note that remission of psychotic symptoms is not synonymous with recovery, since the illness may include a "residual phase." While pharmacologic intervention clearly lays the base for control of psychotic symptoms and therefore makes improvement in negative symptoms possible, the persistence or increase in negative symptoms over a sustained period of time with drugs alone has been disappointing. It is here that the understanding of the influence of psychosocial factors in the course of illness and their role in interventions must be considered.

Two particularly thorough studies of individual and group psychotherapy have examined these points. Hogarty et al. (1974, 1979) studied a form of individual sociotherapy and medication. In terms of prevention of relapse they found that after 24 months 80 percent of placebo-treated patients had relapsed compared with 48 percent of drug-treated patients. Over the entire 24-month period, the addition of the individual sociotherapy produced a modest reduction in rate of relapse. Again, medication had the expected impact on positive symptoms. However, for patients who did not relapse in the first six months, the sociotherapy substantially reduced relapse for the final 18 months of the study. At 18 months for those still in the study, a positive effect of therapy on social adjustment appeared, an effect that was stronger at 24 months. It should be noted the frequency of therapy visits was relatively low, but that even at this frequency two points are quite striking: 1) social improvement and protection from relapse late in the study was found for those patients who had not previously relapsed and 2) a toxic association of therapy with increased relapse was found early in the study in newly remitted patients not maintained on neuroleptic medication. It is this latter point that is most relevant for the postdischarge treatment of patients with schizophreniform disorder.

The second study was done by Malm (1982), who evaluated the impact of group therapy in addition to treatment with neuroleptics and social skills training on newly admitted schizophrenic patients. As expected, for all measures of positive symptomatology, there was dramatic improvement over the first 30 days of neuroleptic treatment for all subjects. For all patients who had not completely recovered in the first 30 days, the results of the study indicated that the patients treated with group therapy improved significantly more than those not treated with group therapy in the areas of social functioning including more free time activities, entries and reentries into social fields, and improved personal habits. No difference in relapse rates between the groups was found.

The results of these two examples indicate that if we are to expect improvement from our psychotherapies, they should be continued over an extended period of time and perhaps, more importantly, they should be initiated in the outpatient stabilization period after the control of positive symptomatology has been assured through medication.

Recently there has been a movement to develop treatments that are more environmentally oriented, in part because of the recognition of the importance of environmental factors and in part because perhaps a more thorough and comprehensive treatment strategy could be given. In fact, if one considers the severity and all-pervasiveness of schizophrenia it seems remarkable that circumscribed, time-limited therapies have produced as much improvement as they have. The recent struggle has been to develop mechanisms for the delivery of environmentally oriented treatments that are cost effective and possible to replicate.

There are certainly many therapeutic techniques to deal with the environment in which the person suffering from schizophrenia or schizophreniform illnesses lives: the Training in Community Living program of Stein and Test (1976), the Soteria project of Mosher (1972), and the family management strategies of such groups as Goldstein's (1978), Leff's (1982), or Falloon's (1982). In schizophreniform disorder family therapy is particularly relevant for the following reasons:

1. Over 65 percent of schizophrenic patients discharged from the hospital return to their families (Department of Health and Human Services Steering Committee on the Chronically Mentally Ill 1980). If only patients recovering from early episodes of psychosis are considered, particularly important in the consideration of schizophreniform illness, this figure is much higher.
2. Families are a natural support system (Keith and Matthews 1984). They provide an interested, involved, and available resource that cannot be reproduced readily.
3. Research has indicated that families identify potential relapse better and earlier than do patients, therefore providing an earlier indication for treatment intensification (Herz and Melville 1980).

4. Families provide a natural setting for context-dependent learning, seemingly so essential for full recovery to take place (Keith and Matthews 1984).

In working with families, however, we must also bear in mind that the family's needs must be given equal attention in the following areas:

1. Need for information. Families require information on the range of possibilities in prognosis that the illness has (i.e., our early distinction between "true" and "holding pattern" schizophreniform disorder).
2. Family burden. The illness places tremendous burdens on the family, and a treatment program must recognize this. In general, our experience is that early in the illness, the families are eager to learn the kinds of management skill necessary to help their family member to recover.
3. Family management as a transitional strategy. Mental health programs have frequently looked for new locations to house the mentally ill, from state hospitals to nursing homes. Families should not be expected to become the new "back wards." The goal of family management strategies should be to promote independent living functions. This is especially so for schizophreniform disorder. The family is an available instrument for encouraging positive change. Failure to recognize this essential point will lead to burnout on the part of the family either from being asked to do too much for too long or, in the case of parents, simply from becoming too old to provide the necessary care.
4. Family management as a disguised "finger pointing." Families have become justifiably sensitive to mental health professionals who have in the past accused families of causing schizophrenia. Although relatively few clinicians cling to this belief, the scars of several decades of finger pointing are still present and must be addressed early in any family management program. Families of schizophreniform disorder patients are particularly vulnerable as the illness is new to them and they may experience unnecessary guilt about having "caused" the illness.

Although the specifics of family management strategies may vary, common among them are the following:

1. The enlistment of the family in a positive clinical alliance.
2. The provision of psychoeducational material about schizophrenia.
3. The provision to the family of principles of management skills in the areas of:
   - problem solving
   - communication
   - stress reduction
4. Encouragement to families to expand their social networks, particularly through mutual interest groups.

The family management programs that have been the focus of research study have differed in their location of delivery (home versus clinic), their mode of delivery (individual families versus multiple family groups), timing (acute versus stabilized patients), and even whether to include the patient or not. The results, however, have not differed—they have been uniformly positive. Unlike the more specific psychotherapies (individual and group), which for some psychosis-prone patients prove to be overstimulating and require medication as a sine qua non for treatment, there is some indication that the gains made in family management may allow reduction of medication and therefore interface well with the new lowered dose strategies. When combined with the gains in reduction of negative symptoms and interpersonal relationships, we feel this treatment strategy will merit strong consideration in working with schizophrenic or schizophreniform patients.

Clinical Implications for the Recovery Period

The major goals of this period are stabilization and progress in preparing a patient to reenter a productive role in society. We have discussed our current feelings that a lower dose of neuroleptic medication may be effective and, because of the lowering of the risks associated with prolonged medication, desirable. The establishment of "how low" will be possible only with careful clinical management that will, of course, need to be individualized for each patient. When to initiate the lowering of the dosage is also individualized. While some patients can begin reduction early, most will require a full six months of maintenance medication before it can be attempted. Of particular concern are those patients whose symptom profile remains high or who have a labile clinical course. The lowering of medication levels for these patients will require a full explication of the risk-benefit ratio. In this latter situation, of residual psychotic symptoms or lability, one must be willing to ask whether the patient is indeed responsive to neuroleptic medication at all. Certainly, issues of medication compliance may complicate the clinical picture and if this is a possibility, injectable depot medication should be considered. If psychotic symptoms remain unchanged in the face of guaranteed delivery of neuroleptic medication through depot injection, serious consideration should be given to medication other than neuroleptics, such as lithium. By definition, those with a diagnosis of schizophreniform disorder will be unlikely to be in a category of continuing psychotic symptoms. Those who are should be further treated according to the principles discussed in Section 14 on schizophrenia.

We would like to emphasize again that regardless of what psychosocial intervention one is applying to schizophreniform disorders (individual, group, or other), the inclusion of the family and other major people in the patient's environment (certainly with the patient's consent) in a therapeutic alliance is a critical ingredient for success.

Conclusions

Patients with schizophreniform disorder are few in number relative to those with broader schizophrenic diagnoses and probably are a heterogeneous group as well. Virtually no research specific to this population has been carried out. Schooler and Keith (1983) are coordinating a study of acutely ill patients including both schizophrenic and schizophreniform patients. Among the first 115 patients included in the study, only five received a schizophreniform diagnosis—two with recurrent episodes ("true" schizophreniform) and three in their first episode ("holding pattern" schizophreniform). Thus, one must rely on data generated in studies on the broader populations that we have reviewed above, our inferences from these data, and clinical experience. Our recommendations for treatment, therefore, have emphasized four major points:

1. Intervention with neuroleptic medication early in the course.
2. Education of the patient and family about psychosis and its treatment.
3. The building of the foundation for interpersonal therapies, which may prove to be critical in the recovery phase of the illness.
4. The importance of clinical sensitivity in deciding the degree of treatment and environmental intensity optimal for an individual patient.

Chapter 155

Treatment of Schizoaffective Disorders

Introduction

Historical Issues

The term "schizoaffective disorder" was first used by Kasanin in 1933 to designate a group of patients with an acute onset of psychosis and confusion, normal premorbid history, and an identifiable precipitating event for their illness (Kasanin 1933). All of the patients recovered completely—and unexpectedly, given the severity of their psychotic symptoms when they came to psychiatric care. Since then, after several decades of wide acceptance, the term has fallen into more disfavor than disuse.

The complex nosology of schizoaffective disorder has made it a controversial category. The first two editions of the *Diagnostic and Statistical Manual of Mental Disorders* (DSM-I and DSM-II; American Psychiatric Association 1952, 1968) included schizoaffective illness as a subtype of schizophrenia, in keeping with the then-current thinking in this country that "even a trace of schizophrenia is schizophrenia" (Lewis 1954, quoted in Maj 1984, p. 8). In the late 1960s and early 1970s the exclusion of all severe psychotic symptomatology from affective disorders was questioned (Winokur et al. 1969). Although to accept psychotic symptoms as a part of disorders with predominantly affective symptoms and good response to somatic treatments has not been difficult, the problem of classifying disorders with more mixed symptomatology and chronic course remains. Some are reluctant to accept Kraepelin's dichotomy, much less to add a third psychosis, and see psychiatric illness as a spectrum (Brockington and Leff 1979; Brockington et al. 1980b; Post 1971; Strauss 1983). Others see atypical forms of either affective (Pope et al. 1980; Welner et al. 1974) or schizophrenic illness (Armbruster et al. 1983; Roth and McClelland 1979) in schizoaffective disorder.

Most recent studies address the central question: does schizoaffective disorder exist as a distinct disease? If it is not a separate disorder, is it a form of affective disorder, a form of schizophrenia, two diseases coexisting in one patient, or a label given to a heterogeneous group of disorders including all of the above? Whether the disease exists or not, there are patients who have both affective and schizophrenic symptoms. This chapter intends not to settle metaphysical questions, but simply to discuss the current theories (and their supporting data) for the treatment of schizoaffective disorder.

Background

A variety of diagnostic criteria have been used to select cases of schizoaffective disorder for study. The major criteria are given in Table 1. Kasanin, in creating the term schizoaffective for his nine patients diagnosed originally as suffering from de-

Table 1. Major Definitions of Schizoaffective Disorder

Kasanin: young, good premorbid social adjustment, precipitating social stress, preceding depressive symptoms, sudden onset of dramatic psychosis, clouding of consciousness, complete recovery, probable history of previous episode (Kasanin 1933).

DSM-I, DSM-II: a mixture of schizophrenic symptoms and pronounced elation or depression; excited and depressed types (American Psychiatric Association 1952, 1968).

Welner: 1) full depressive or manic syndrome; 2) at least two of: delusion, hallucination, formal thought disorder, abnormal thought disorder (autistic or dereistic thinking), bizarre or strikingly inappropriate behavior; these of quality and severity enough to make diagnosis of affective disorder "unlikely"; 3) acute onset, episodic course, or confusion; 4) exclusion: organicity (Welner 1974).

ICD-9: a psychosis in which pronounced manic or depressive features are intermingled with pronounced schizophrenic features; tends towards remission and may recur (World Health Organization 1978).

RDC, manic and depressive forms: 1) one or more periods of predominantly depressed or manic mood; 2) enough additional symptoms to meet criteria for manic or depressive episode; 3) one of: delusions of control; thought broadcasting, insertion, or withdrawal; nonaffective hallucinations for several days; auditory hallucinations of commentary or conversation; one week (depressive subtype) or one month (manic) without affective symptoms but with delusions or hallucinations (except those typical of depression); preoccupation with a nondepressive delusion or hallucination; formal thought disorder with either blunted or inappropriate affect, any delusion or hallucination, or grossly disorganized behavior; 4) symptoms have persisted at least one week; 5) affective and schizophrenic symptoms overlap temporally to some degree. Exclusion: psychotic symptoms during substance abuse withdrawal (Spitzer 1978).

DSM-III: "without criteria"; i.e., affective illness with mood-incongruent delusions or hallucinations dominant when affective symptoms are absent; mood-incongruent psychosis and affective syndrome where the course is unknown (American Psychiatric Association 1980).

DSM-III-R: at some time either a major depressive or manic syndrome with symptoms from criterion A for schizophrenia; an episode of two weeks with delusions or hallucinations and no prominent affective symptoms. Exclusions: schizophrenia or organicity (American Psychiatric Association 1987).

---

mentia praecox, reviews the earlier work on mixed clinical presentations of affective and schizophrenic symptoms (Kasanin 1933). While believing that Kraepelin's classification is too rigid and draws attention away from the sources of both illness and recovery in the individual, Kasanin insists on accurate classification of disease and states that the nine patients he treated had a recurrent, but not a deteriorating, illness and therefore not truly a schizophrenia. His description was not used per se to establish formal criteria, but formed the basis from which others have defined and studied the disorder. Through DSM-II, schizoaffective disorder continues as a part of schizophrenia without specific criteria. Those who study schizoaffective disorder using DSM-II generally include patients who meet criteria for both affective and schizophrenic illness in their samples. Welner (1974) includes confusion as a criterion but disregards precipitating factors. He subdivided his patients according to whether they met full affective criteria and by the number of psychotic symptoms. Of those with two or more psychotic symptoms, those who met full affective criteria seemed to have illnesses more closely related to affective disorders by course; the illnesses of those who did not meet full affective criteria appeared closer to schizophrenia (Croughan et al. 1974). He found that acuteness of onset or confusion was not useful for predicting outcome; 71 percent of his patients had a chronic course, and 81 percent deteriorated overall. Those with an episodic course did not deteriorate (Welner et al. 1977). The diagnosis remained, as Welner called it "a persistent enigma" (Welner et al. 1974, p. 628).

The Feighner criteria, published in 1972, did not include schizoaffective disorder but did give a new emphasis to study of family history as one part of the validation of psychiatric diagnoses (Feighner et al. 1972). The current status of schizoaffective disorder depends on the studies based on criteria that followed the Feighner criteria, i.e., the Research Diagnostic Criteria (RDC, Spitzer and Williams 1985), *International Classification of Diseases*, 9th revision (ICD-9) (World Health Organization 1978), and DSM-III (American Psychiatric Association 1980). In general, DSM-III affective disorder with mood-incongruent psychoses is equivalent to RDC schizoaffective disorder, but many DSM-III schizophrenics also satisfy the criteria for RDC schizoaffective disorder. The RDC schizoaffective diagnosis includes as one possible symptom the persistence of psychotic features without affective symptoms during an episode; remission or chronicity are not included in the criteria. Schizoaffective disorder is categorized as a type of schizophrenic psychosis in ICD-9; no minimum duration nor number of affective or psychotic symptoms is specified, only that both types be pronounced. The DSM-III schizoaffective diagnosis is grouped with "other psychoses," removing it from schizophrenic disorders but avoiding classification with affective illness or the status of a third psychosis. The diagnosis is suggested for use when the differential or the history is unclear; by implication, such cases are expected to prove themselves ultimately as either affective or schizophrenic illness when the course is known. Both DSM-III and ICD-9 require a combination of affective and psychotic features, though no more than one psychotic feature is required. The nature of onset, particular symptoms, premorbid history, and outcome are not specified; these items, along with family history and laboratory data, are left to the research which attempts to validate and understand this diagnosis. Undisclosed alcohol and other drug abuse often plays a substantial role in the development of the more bizarre psychotic affective states.

Diagnosis of Schizoaffective Disorder

Characteristics of Schizoaffective Disorder

Epidemiology. Schizoaffective illness begins by age 30 in most studies. Rosenthal et al. (1980), using RDC criteria, found the mean age of onset and first treatment significantly lower in schizoaffectives than bipolar I patients who did not meet RDC schizoaffective criteria ($p < 0.05$). Tsuang et al. (1977) found that the mean age of admission for 52 patients with a DSM-II chart diagnosis of schizoaffective disorder was significantly lower than that for patients with schizophrenia ($p < 0.01$) or affective disorders ($p < 0.001$). Other studies provide descriptive data: by RDC criteria, 40 of 76 patients had onset before age 30 (Brockington et al. 1980b); Clayton found 64 percent under age 30 by DSM-II (Clayton et al. 1968); and Welner, using the Feighner criteria, obtained a mean age at onset of 24.5 years (Welner et al. 1979).

The data on distribution by sex are also consistent. Most find a preponderance of women in groups of schizoaffective patients. The exception is in RDC schizoaffective manics studied by Clayton; slightly more of these were male (Clayton 1982). Other studies generally do not present data for the RDC subtypes; only one study finds an even sex ratio among all RDC schizoaffectives (Brockington et al. 1980b: 36 males, 40 females). Among Clayton's depressed schizoaffectives, as in other studies, the ratio of females to males is 2:1 or more (Angst 1980; Baron et al. 1982; Coryell and Zimmerman, in press; Kemali et al. 1985; Welner et al. 1979).

Other demographic data are rarely presented. Clayton suggests that RDC schizoaffective manics marry less often than the general population (Clayton 1982); Himmelhoch, using RDC criteria, states that the difference is significant (Himmelhoch et al. 1981). In a comparison of nonmanic psychotic patients, Coryell found, after taking age into account, that schizoaffective and depressed patients were about equally likely to marry and significantly more likely to do so than schizophrenics (Coryell and Zimmerman, in press). The overall functioning of schizoaffectives was between that of depressed and schizophrenic patients (Coryell and Zimmerman, in press). Good premorbid functioning and acute onset are generally considered "good prognostic features" here as for schizophrenia, but available data are negligible.

Family history.   Examining the prevalence of various diagnoses in schizoaffective patients' first-degree relatives has been a major tool in the attempt to define schizoaffective disorder. One twin study and several studies of first degree relatives will be reviewed here.

Cohen et al. (1972) reviewed the Veterans Administration charts of 15,909 pairs of twins; from these they found 260 pairs in which one or both members had a major psychiatric diagnosis and zygosity agreed on by his reviewers. Their criteria resembled those of DSM-II and the RDC; these patients had a chronic course with episodes of both significant affective and schizophrenic symptoms. The data for monozygotic twin pairs are as follows: in 14 pairs where at least one had schizoaffective illness, both were schizoaffective in 50 percent of cases; concordance was 38.5 percent in 13 pairs with bipolar illness; and for schizophrenia, concordance was 23.5 percent in 81 pairs. The difference between the schizoaffective and schizophrenic concordance rates was significant at the 0.05 level. Twelve dizygotic schizoaffective pairs and 27 bipolar pairs showed no concordance; dizygotic schizophrenic twins had a concordance of 5.3 percent. There was no instance of different diagnoses within any pair of twins; however, raters were not blind to the diagnosis of the co-twin as the charts were reviewed in pairs.

Angst et al. (1979) examined 150 patients with schizoaffective illness by the criteria of ICD-9 and Welner and sorted incidence of illness by parents, siblings, and children of the probands. If schizoaffective illness were a third psychosis, then schizoaffective illness should be the most frequent diagnosis in all three generations and the incidence should be equal for all three. The age-corrected incidence of affective disorder, schizophrenia, and schizoaffective disorder was not significantly different among parents and siblings; too few children were at risk for those data to be significant. Their conclusion, similar to that of Coryell (in press), is that schizoaffectives include some with affective disorder, some with schizophrenia, some with mixed genetic inheritance, and some patients called schizoaffective who have no other known diagnosis.

The recent trend in genetic studies of schizoaffective illness has been to find heterogeneity. Mendelwicz (1976) found the risk of affective disorders in the families of schizoaffective patients to be more like the risk in the families of patients with affective disorders, but found the risk for schizophrenia to be between the risk for relatives of schizophrenic patients and that for relatives of affectively ill patients. He used Feighner criteria for affective disorder and schizophrenia and devised criteria for schizoaffective disorder. Baron et al. (1982) and Endicott et al. (in press) used RDC criteria and subtypes to suggest that schizoaffective illness is heterogeneous and probably contains a subset of bipolar affective disorder. They found relationships to major depression with psychosis, schizoaffective disorders, and schizophrenic disorders. Coryell et al. (1982), in general agreement with Brockington et al. (1980b) and Walker (1981), found that major depression with mood-incongruent features by DSM-III, i.e., RDC schizoaffective-depressed, cannot, as a whole, be grouped with either schizophrenia or affective illness. Coryell suggests from his review of the literature that schizoaffective illness includes patients with affective disease, patients with schizophrenia, and possibly patients with other, unidentified illnesses (Coryell, in press).

The available studies are inconsistent in which diagnostic criteria they use as well as in what types and subtypes of diagnoses they tabulate. Schizoaffective disorder does seem to be heterogeneous. No study except that of Cohen et al. (1972) finds a significant degree of schizoaffective illness in the families of these patients. It may be that this diagnosis is particularly difficult to make as a lifetime or family history diagnosis, as it requires recall of specific features of psychotic episodes as well as periods of remission in the case of some definitions. Nonetheless, it seems likely that many patients called schizoaffective with predominantly manic affective symptoms are bipolar patients with psychotic features. It cannot be determined at present whether the remaining patients should be reclassified with other diagnoses, whether some have two coexisting genetic disorders, or whether there exists a core of true schizoaffectives unrelated to affective disorder or to schizophrenia.

Course.   Some definitions of schizoaffective disorder imply a particular course of the illness, beginning with Kasanin's description of patients who recovered (Kasanin 1933). Studies of the course of patients so diagnosed, regardless of criteria, usually find a course less favorable than that of affective illness but better than that of schizophrenia.

The percentage of patients with schizoaffective disorder who show complete recovery varies from 5.9 percent (Himmelhoch et al. 1981, using a variant of RDC) to 32 percent (DSM-III affective disorders with mood-incongruent psychotic features; Coryell et al. 1982). Himmelhoch's group required interepisodic formal thought disorder as part of the diagnostic criteria; the duration of follow-up is not specified. They found less response to treatment among the schizoaffective patients than among the affective disorder patients, 49 percent of whom recovered. The mean follow-up time for Coryell et al.'s retrospective chart study of major depression with mood-congruent and mood-incongruent psychotic features was two to three years; recovery rates were 32 percent for the mood-incongruent group, 44 percent for the mood-congruent group, and 69 percent for the affective disorder group without psychotic features. Schizophrenic patients, however, had a recovery rate of only 7 percent. Elsewhere, following these groups for 40 years, they found that patients with mood-incongruent psychoses differ significantly from schizophrenics in all measures of outcome, such as occupational and marital status. The mood-incongruent patients did less well than did the depressed patients with mood-congruent or no psychotic features, however (Coryell and Tsuang 1985). Grossman et al. (1984), after a one-year follow-up, found 10 percent of schizoaffectives versus 36 percent of those with affective disorders to have a good outcome; in general, the schizoaffectives resembled schizophrenics in the number of rehospitalizations and in social functioning, but were more like those with affective disorders in work history and interepisodic psychiatric symptoms. Brockington et al. (1980a, 1980b) found RDC schizoaffective manics to have a course like that of bipolar manics; 21 of 32 were given "final diagnoses" of bipolar affective illness on review of the entire course. The schizoaffective depressed patients, on the other hand, varied. Thirty of 68 were finally called schizophrenic, and 26 of 68 were given various affective diagnoses. A chronic course was observed in 23 percent of the schizoaffective manics and 31 percent of the schizoaffective depressives.

A review of 502 patients diagnosed as schizophrenic by Schneiderian symptoms showed surprisingly slight differences in outcome when various schizoaffective criteria were applied to differentiate them; see Table 2 (Armbruster et al. 1983). Characteristic schizophrenic residual symptoms, the worst outcome in this tabulation, refers to continuing psychotic symptoms or the negative symptoms of affective blunting, avolition, etc.; noncharacteristic symptoms refer to affective or other symptoms. The average time of follow-up in this study was 18.6 years. Remarkably, the patients differentiated by the various definitions of schizoaffective disorder showed similar, and uniformly better, outcomes than the 502 patients in the original sample of schizophrenic patients. Armbruster et al. (1983) were not able to predict outcome by presenting symptoms, although a prevailing catatonic or depressive syndrome initially was more favorable than a paranoid-hallucinatory state.

The available data again use varying diagnostic criteria, varying duration of follow-up, and varying measures of outcome. In general, schizoaffective disorder follows a course between affective and schizophrenic illness. Again, many studies probably contain patients who would not be called schizoaffective by DSM-III criteria, but who should instead be diagnosed as bipolar patients with psychotic features or depressed patients with mood-incongruent psychoses.

Differential Diagnosis

Schizoaffective illness has been referred to by several other names, most of which emphasize its relationship to schizophrenia (see Table 3). The differential diagnosis among DSM-III disorders must also include affective disorder and schizophreniform illness. No adequate differential can be made among these, given our present knowledge, without a longitudinal history. The major difference between schizophrenia and schizoaffective disorders lies not simply in the presence of affective symptoms—since most schizophrenics show affective symptoms at some time—but rather in remissions from either affective or schizophrenic symptoms. A good premorbid adjustment and clear family history of affective disorder may be suggestive of schizoaffective disorder, but cannot prove the diagnosis. The quality of thought disorder

Table 2. Outcome of Schizoaffective Disorder

Criteria	n	No. (%)		
		Recovery	Noncharacteristic residual symptoms	Characteristic residual symptoms
Kasanin	20	8 (40)	11 (55)	1 (5)
RDC	26	11 (42)	12 (46.5)	3 (11)
Angst/ICD	58	18 (31)	34 (58.7)	6 (10.3)
Leonhard cycloid psychosis	53	24 (45)	20 (37.7)	9 (17)
Entire group	502	(22)	(43)	(35)

Note. Derived from Armbruster et al. (1983).

Table 3. Diagnostic Terms Sometimes Considered Equivalent to Schizoaffective Disorder

Psychogenic psychosis	Atypical psychosis
Reactive psychosis	Psychogenic psychosis
Remitting schizophrenia	Cycloid psychosis
Good prognosis schizophrenia	Recovered schizophrenia
Schizophreniform psychosis	

or content of hallucinatory material also does not differentiate patients by outcome or eventual diagnosis.

With increasing recognition that psychotic symptoms may be part of affective symptomatology, it is easy to think that all schizoaffective disorders are simply affective disorders with particularly severe psychotic symptoms. Some psychotic patients, particularly those with prominent affective symptoms, may in fact be atypical affective patients who present with such striking psychotic symptoms that they are diagnosed as schizoaffective. Coryell and Tsuang (1985) suggest that depressed patients with mood-incongruent psychoses, i.e., RDC schizoaffective depressed patients, are a more heterogeneous group than those with mood-congruent psychotic symptoms. Periods of remission are neither a requirement nor an exclusion criterion in the RDC.

Schizophreniform illness as defined in DSM-III includes what would have been called schizoaffective disease in some definitions. Again, a history is necessary: duration is to be less than six months but more than two weeks. The disorder is otherwise defined as equivalent to DSM-III schizophrenia, although the DSM-III discussion differentiates schizophreniform illness also by a relatively acute onset, rapid resolution, and return to premorbid functioning. Symptoms resulting from substance abuse, withdrawal, or other organic or toxic causes might resemble schizoaffective illness acutely, but should be separable by history, physical examination, and laboratory data.

Treatment Outcome

No single treatment has been unequivocally successful in treating schizoaffective disorder. Lithium, tricyclic antidepressants, antipsychotics, electroconvulsive therapy, and various combinations have been tried. It is important to note that some of the uses of the medications as outlined below are not supported by the data in the Product Information Section of the *Physicians Desk Reference*.

Lithium

Angst et al., using ICD-9 criteria, compared bipolar, unipolar, and schizoaffective patients' response to lithium at levels of 0.6–1.6 mEq/liter for 20 months. All had significantly fewer episodes of illness than they had before treatment; for the schizoaffectives the difference was significant at $p < 0.001$ (Angst et al. 1969). Later, in a larger study, they report that schizoaffectives on lithium have significantly fewer episodes, fewer admissions, and longer cycles than those not receiving lithium, but still have a worse outcome than purely affective patients (Angst et al. 1970). Similar results, i.e., significant response but less than the response of affective illness to lithium, have been found by others (Brockington et al. 1980a). In a recent study,

Kemali et al. (1985) found good response to lithium in 38 ICD-9 schizoaffectives; the results remained consistent when other criteria for schizoaffective illness were applied to the patients. Their patients were maintained at levels of 0.6–1.0 mEq/liter for two years.

Some trials of lithium or lithium versus an antipsychotic (usually chlorpromazine) have found that patients who are not overly active, who are acutely psychotic, but who do not have a history of chronic illness may be treated as effectively with lithium as with an antipsychotic. Prien et al. (1972) compared DSM-II diagnosed schizoaffective patients in a collaborative study examining the efficacy of lithium versus chlorpromazine and found chlorpromazine significantly better only for "highly active" patients (p. 188). Braden and co-workers, using RDC criteria on a smaller sample, had similar results (Braden et al. 1982).

Antipsychotics

Fewer data are available on the use of antipsychotics alone in schizoaffective disorder. In a study of RDC schizoaffective depressed patients, Brockington et al. (1980b) found that 61 percent responded to chlorpromazine, haloperidol, or trifluoperazine as the first or second drug given. There are no data to suggest that any particular antipsychotic drug is preferable in schizoaffective disorder. Studies comparing chlorpromazine to lithium, cited above, find chlorpromazine more efficacious only in very active patients. A comparison of lithium (doses to 2,500 mg/day) and chlorpromazine (doses to 400 mg/day) in 14 RDC schizoaffective manics found the effects to be about equal; for schizoaffective depressed patients, chlorpromazine alone did better than amitriptyline (Brockington et al. 1978).

Tricyclic Antidepressants

The brief literature on the use of tricyclic antidepressants in patients with schizoaffective disorder suggests that they are not useful when prescribed alone for most schizoaffective patients. They may have a role, however, for the subset of schizoaffective patients who have predominantly depressed affective symptoms. Brockington et al. (1978) compared amitriptyline (maximum dose 250 mg/day) to chlorpromazine (maximum dose 750 mg/day) to a combination of the two in schizoaffective depressed patients; amitriptyline alone induced recovery in only one patient of 13; chlorpromazine or the combination was more successful. In a later study of depressed patients with psychotic features, Brockington et al. (1980b) found that tricyclics given alone or in combination induced full recovery in 14 of 42 patients; of the initial group of 76 patients, 60 met criteria for RDC schizoaffective depressed type. Most of these patients had predominantly affective symptoms. In those patients whose symptoms are predominantly psychotic, tricyclics may be less useful. Johnson (1981), in a study of schizophrenic patients who had depressive symptoms, found no significant difference in placebo versus nortriptyline in relieving depressive symptoms.

Electroconvulsive Therapy

Electroconvulsive therapy (ECT) has also been used for schizoaffective patients. Brockington et al.'s (1980b) study of RDC schizoaffective depressed patients included four for whom ECT was the first treatment, eight for whom ECT was tried with tricyclics and antipsychotics, and 22 for whom ECT was tried after other treatments failed. Of all patients receiving ECT under any circumstances, 62 percent had full recovery and only 15 percent showed no improvement. These researchers note that ECT tended to be given to the most severely ill patients and conclude that it may be as effective as chlorpromazine for them. Tsuang et al. (1979) studied long-term outcome of 74 schizoaffective patients to examine the differential effect of ECT on mortality. There was significantly lower mortality in the 24 patients who received ECT than in the 50 who did not, though these groups did not differ by age at admission or length of follow-up. Three patients in the non-ECT group committed suicide; none of those who received ECT did so. This difference was not statistically significant, but was considered indicative of the better long-term outcome from ECT. The study group included patients admitted from 1934–1944, so no comparison with other treatments was made.

Recommendations for Treatment

Biologic Treatment

Patients with schizoaffective disorder have different initial presentations. This variety is to be expected, given the apparent heterogeneity included under this label, and the different presentations inevitably affect treatment planning. Some cases resemble bipolar illness in symptoms and course; some resemble psychotic unipolar depression; some resemble schizophrenias. The most difficult patient to treat, of course, is the one who cannot be assigned to one of these subsets at initial presentation.

The patient whose initial presentation and history (if known) suggest a similarity to bipolar disorder with psychotic features should be tried first on lithium at a blood level of 0.8–1.0 mEq/liter. An antipsychotic should be given initially as well. Given the real concerns about long-term effects of antipsychotic medications, such doses should be minimized. Those patients who did not tolerate or do not respond to lithium may be tried on medications recently advocated for control of bipolar affective disease, e.g., carbamazepine. There are studies showing its efficacy in mania, though none for schizoaffective disorder; but patients deserve a trial of medication that has a lesser long-term risk given the risk of tardive dyskinesia. Carbamazepine is given at 200 mg twice a day initially to a maximum of approximately 1400 mg daily in divided doses, or until improvement or toxicity occurs. Anticonvulsant blood levels are a general guide to dosing, and liver function and blood counts should be monitored. Carbamazepine and lithium together may be tried. Drug interactions should be considered as many nonpsychotropic drugs will alter blood levels, sometimes dangerously.

The patient with severe depressive symptoms and enough psychotic features to be diagnosed as schizoaffective may be more difficult to treat. Some would argue that any patient with severe affective symptoms, with or without psychotic symptoms, deserves a trial of ECT, particularly if the episode of illness has lasted less than six months. The data presented above suggest that ECT is very effective, and appropriately administered it is a safe treatment. Many patients (and their families), however, resist ECT and some patients are not seriously ill enough to warrant it. These patients should be treated with a tricyclic antidepressant and an antipsychotic at therapeutic levels. Lithium augmentation of the tricyclic may be tried also, at a lower lithium level than needed for acute treatment with lithium alone. Tricyclic blood levels are available for nortriptyline and imipramine with good evidence for therapeutic ranges (Perry et al. in press). Measurement of haloperidol levels and establishment of a therapeutic range are more recent, but supporting data do exist (Magliozzi et al. 1981). Therapeutic levels of other antipsychotics are not at present well documented.

Patients with a chronic course, or whose symptoms are predominantly psychotic, will need antipsychotic medication. These patients also may be given a trial with the treatments suggested above; severe psychotic symptomatology may mask affective symptoms. Those who do not respond to lithium, carbamazepine, a combination of lithium and carbamazepine, or tricyclics, or any of these with or without antipsychotics, should probably be placed on antipsychotics alone to alleviate the agitation and severe psychotic symptoms that jeopardize their ability to participate in any activities in any setting. Anticholinergics to control extrapyramidal side effects should, of course, be available. The depot antipsychotics now available, haloperidol and fluphenazine, are most useful in patients whose compliance is unsatisfactory. A period of better functioning with the depot medication may provide a chance to show the patient that better overall functioning and social acceptance can be obtained with medication.

Psychosocial Treatments

There is very little data-based research on the psychosocial treatment of schizoaffective disorders. Among the brief psychotherapies, it has been suggested that cognitive therapy is not helpful for schizoaffectives (Rush 1980); other forms may be of benefit. Nevertheless, common sense alone suggests that these patients do often need and deserve long-term supportive and psychosocial therapy in addition to psychopharmacologic management. As do some personality disorder patients, chronically depressed or dysthymic patients, and schizophrenic patients, some patients with schizoaffective disorder may benefit from long-term, nonhospital care such as is provided in long-term residential treatment centers. The published results from the Chestnut Lodge follow-up study, for example, do not include data for schizoaffective patients, but do suggest that one-third of schizophrenic patients may have a functionally adequate outcome; those with affective disorders generally did better (McGlashan 1984). In a study of family management in long-term care of schizophrenia, Falloon et al. (1985) suggest that carefully selected schizophrenic patients do better with family rather than individual management therapies. Patients from higher-expressed-emotion families tended to be assigned to individual management in this study; again, the literature showing benefit from therapies designed to reduce expressed emotion discuss schizophrenic patients primarily (Keith and Mathews 1982). Unfortunately, all such programs are expensive and in many places are not sufficiently available. At the least such patients should have a long-term therapeutic relationship, whether with a psychiatrist, psychologist, nurse-therapist, or social worker, both for on-going supportive therapy and as a means of access to more intensive, physician-directed services during acute episodes.

Acute and Chronic Management

An acutely psychotic, agitated patient should be sedated rapidly for his or her safety and comfort as well as that of hospital staff and other patients. Traditionally such sedation is accomplished with antipsychotic medication, tapering to lower doses as soon as the patient is able to cooperate and show some self-control. Reducing stimulation with seclusion or preventing harm with physical restraints may be necessary initially. When treatment with antipsychotics is initiated, nursing staff should monitor the patient for dystonic reactions so that prompt relief can be provided by the on-call physician. Once initial agitation and psychosis are controlled, treatment can proceed as suggested above.

Chronic management depends on the type of schizoaffective illness the patient shows both by initial presentation and by course. Those with schizoaffective-manic illness should receive lithium (or alternatives as discussed above) if efficacious. A slightly lower level than is needed for acute illness may be effective in prophylaxis against acute episodes; Smulevitch et al. (1974) found significantly fewer episodes and admissions in patients with lithium levels of 0.6–0.8 mEq/liter. Antipsychotics in the lowest possible dose are probably of benefit in patients for whom other treatments alone are insufficient. Consistent, long-term follow-up should be arranged.

Conclusion

Schizoaffective illness remains a disorder difficult to diagnose, treat, or discuss. Some remain convinced that the label hides patients for whom the correct diagnoses— affective disorder or schizophrenia—has not yet been made clear by sufficient history or sufficient diagnostic thought. Most would grant that some patients diagnosed as schizoaffective in earlier decades instead were psychotic manic or depressed patients, diagnosed under systems now replaced. It is not clear, finally, whether the disease really exists or whether it is an undifferentiated early stage of the more identifiable psychiatric disease that will emerge in time. It does remain a useful category for some of the patients we encounter, if only to signify uncertainty as to eventual diagnosis or prognosis.

For this diagnosis to remain useful, it needs to be better understood. Studies of every element are needed using consistent diagnostic categories: family history, symptomatology, course, response to treatment, long-term outcome. Perhaps more studies like those of Armbruster et al. (1983) and Kemali et al. (1985), showing the similarities among patients reclassified by the various current systems, would help distinguish what elements of the criteria are essential. It does seem, from the differences in outcome and treatment response, that manic and depressed schizoaffectives should be separately studied, as Clayton (1982) has suggested.

Very little has been done to validate this disease with laboratory data. Do any of the various neurotransmitters and other substances we can measure differentiate schizoaffective patients from others? Does any biochemical response to medication occur; if so, does that response differentiate these patients from others? Only a few studies address such questions so far (Targum 1980).

Clinically, we have new drugs becoming available, and we need to see whether any of these will help schizoaffective patients, perhaps particularly trying the newer antidepressants with depressed schizoaffective patients now that there are nontricyclic antidepressants available. Finally, as brief psychotherapy becomes both more studied and more economically necessary, we need to study which of these patients will benefit from what form of psychotherapy, and at what point in this illness. Schizoaffective disorder is not only a heterogeneous disorder but also often a fluctuating one, and different treatments may prove most effective at different times within it.

As psychiatry continues to address such questions, eventually the diagnosis of schizoaffective disorder may become less Welner's "persistent enigma" and instead a basis for rational medical and psychotherapeutic help for patients whose disease is, at least partially, understood.

Chapter 156

Treatment of Brief Reactive Psychosis

Brief reactive psychosis is a variously described subtype of functional psychosis distinguished from schizophrenia and from affective psychosis. DSM-III-R (American Psychiatric Association 1987) provides a classification of the so-called functional psychoses and bases differential diagnosis on explicit criteria. The nosology of psychosis has become increasingly important as differential etiologies and therapeutics are explored. To the extent that brief reactive psychosis is a different illness from schizophrenia and from affective disorder, therapeutics must also be distinguished.

The DSM-III-R category of brief reactive psychosis is a rudimentary approximation of the Scandinavian concept of reactive psychosis, "constitutional psychosis," or "psychogenic psychosis." These terms designate a good prognosis psychotic reaction that is distinguished from both schizophrenia and from affective psychosis by its clear relation to a precipitating stressor, its acute onset, its briefness in duration and lack of chronic residual symptoms, and the return of the patient to his previous level of functioning. The types of brief reactive psychoses are described as acute paranoid reactions, reactive confusions with disturbances in attention and orientation, reactive excitations or manias (rare), and reactive depressive psychoses (Faergeman 1963; Strömgren 1974). It is thought that these reactive psychoses occur in individuals who have weaknesses in their personalities making them more vulnerable than others to stress (Wimmer, quoted by Strömgren 1974). It is also considered that the specific features of the psychosis are understandable if one knows the patient's life history and the meaning the stressor has for him (Jaspers 1963). Thus, the European concept is a clinical one, firmly based on evidence that symptomatology is the result of the pathogenic effects of definable stress and is to be understood in each patient according to his makeup.

Differential Diagnosis

The DSM-III Context

DSM-I (American Psychiatric Association 1952) did not list reactive psychoses. DSM-II (American Psychiatric Association 1968) placed the reactive psychoses under "298 other psychoses." Subtypes were "psychotic depressive reaction," "reactive excitation," "reactive confusion," "acute paranoid reaction," and "reactive psychosis unspecified." No criteria for diagnosis were given.

DSM-III (American Psychiatric Association 1980) designated certain essential features: sudden onset, duration less than two weeks, eventual return to the premorbid level of functioning, a recognizable precipitating psychosocial stressor, the invariable presence of emotional turmoil, at least one psychotic symptom, and no period of increasing psychopathology immediately preceding the psychosocial stressor.

The DSM-III definition of brief reactive psychosis was narrow in time frame and deviated from the traditional psychopathologic concept. It limited the illness to two weeks; it required a stressor that would evoke significant symptoms of distress in almost anyone; it required emotional turmoil; it excluded increasing psychopathology immediately prior to the psychosocial stressor. These were major shifts from the Scandinavian descriptive and German phenomenologic approaches.

DSM-III-R diagnostic criteria for brief reactive psychosis are listed in Table 1. There are five main differences between DSM-III-R and DSM-III. One is the extension of maximum allowable duration from two weeks to one month in the revision. Second, whereas DSM-III makes increasing psychopathology immediately prior to the psychosocial stressor an exclusion criterion, the revised version specifically names the presence of prodromal symptoms of schizophrenia as the exclusion criteria. The third difference is that, in the revised version, emotional turmoil is not a necessary feature if there is, instead, overwhelming perplexity or confusion. The fourth and most radical change is that schizotypal personality disorder prior to onset prohibits the diagnosis. Fifth, mood disorders are explicitly excluded by DSM-III-R. Both DSM-III and DSM-III-R eliminate any mention of the subtypes seen in DSM-II and in the literature.

Traditionally, the diagnosis of reactive psychosis has been made very loosely. All epidemiological, genetic, and follow-up studies have been based on nonstringent diagnoses. It remains to be seen whether strict adherence to DSM-III or DSM-III-R criteria will better define brief reactive psychosis as a discreet illness separable from schizophrenia or affective disorder. Clearly, fewer cases will qualify for the diagnosis.

Of special note is the fact that the majority of cases of reactive psychosis in the literature are of the depressive type (Retterstol 1978; Andersen and Laerum 1980). Using DSM-III or DSM-III-R criteria, many of these cases might currently be diagnosed as major depression. DSM-III-R will not allow the diagnosis of brief reactive psychosis

---

Table 1.　DSM-III-R Diagnostic Criteria for Brief Reactive Psychosis

A. Presence of at least one of the following symptoms indicating impaired reality testing (not culturally sanctioned):

   (1) incoherence or marked loosening of associations
   (2) delusions
   (3) hallucinations
   (4) catatonic or disorganized behavior

B. Emotional turmoil, i.e., rapid shifts from one intense affect to another, or overwhelming perplexity or confusion.

C. Appearance of the symptoms in A and B shortly after, and apparently in response to, one or more events that, singly or together, would be markedly stressful to almost anyone in similar circumstances in the person's culture.

D. Absence of the prodromal symptoms of Schizophrenia, and failure to meet the criteria for Schizotypal Personality Disorder before onset of the disturbance.

E. Duration of an episode of the disturbance of from a few hours to one month, with eventual full return to premorbid level of functioning. (When the diagnosis must be made without waiting for the expected recovery, it should be qualified as "provisional.")

F. Not due to a psychotic Mood Disorder (i.e., no full mood syndrome is present), and it cannot be established that an organic factor initiated and maintained the disturbance.

when the criteria for a mood disorder can be met. This will permit very few diagnoses of brief reactive psychosis of the affective type.

Other factors that will eliminate cases formerly diagnosed as reactive psychosis are the stricter requirements for a severe stressor (rather than a severe reaction to a stressor), the duration limitation, and the exclusion of prodromal symptoms or preexisting schizotypal personality disorders.

Making the Diagnosis

Usually the physician's first contact with a patient experiencing a brief reactive psychosis will be in the emergency room. The first priority is to rule out an organic state that presents with psychotic symptoms. This is done by history, physical examination, and laboratory analysis to identify any organic factor that may be etiologically related to the disturbance. If no evidence for an acute or chronic organic brain syndrome is found, the DSM-III decision tree for psychoses directs one to determine whether symptoms are under voluntary control, qualifying for the diagnosis of malingering or factitious disorder. If not, duration of illness is the next consideration. Brief reactive psychosis has a time limit of one month in the revised version. If a functional psychosis in an adolescent or an adult lasts longer than this, it must be diagnosed schizophrenia, major affective disorder, schizoaffective disorder, schizophreniform disorder, paranoid disorder, or atypical psychosis. If duration criteria are met, psychosis must have been precipitated by a stressor to qualify as brief reactive psychosis. Otherwise, it may be one of the above-mentioned disorders or a brief psychosis associated with a personality disorder.

The DSM-III decision tree has its limitations in the acute situation. One cannot know about the eventual duration of the psychosis at the time that the diagnosis must be made and treatment initiated. Therefore, after ruling out an organic cause, factitious disorder, and malingering, the next step, for practical reasons, is to search in the patient's history for evidence of one of the major psychoses. If the patient has had definite schizophrenia or affective psychosis, the current episode, even if brief and even if there is a stressor, is regarded as an exacerbation of one of these chronic illnesses.

If the cross-sectional picture during the acute psychotic episode in question meets the criteria for brief reactive psychosis and also for a major psychosis (except for duration), and the patient has no past history of a major psychosis, uncertainty in the diagnosis will remain until enough time has elapsed to clarify the duration. Admission diagnoses such as schizophreniform disorder, schizoaffective disorder, atypical psychosis, and brief reactive psychosis will frequently require subsequent revision.

If the acute psychotic disorder does not meet the criteria for a major psychosis and also does meet the criteria for brief reactive psychosis (e.g., there may be no stressor or duration may be longer than one month), it may have to be diagnosed as atypical psychosis. This diagnosis is also subject to change as more information becomes available or with the passage of time.

In some cases where severe inability to recall personal information in response to a stressor is the essential feature of the disturbance, one of the dissociative disorders might be a more appropriate diagnosis. Some Axis II personality disorders also permit transitory psychotic symptoms (e.g., borderline).

In uncertain cases, a full appreciation of the underlying psychopathologic concepts and an intuitive grasp of psychopathology will guide the clinician in the initial of individual clinicians, but denotes the formidable powers of pattern recognition by the observing clinician experienced and trained in psychopathology. Jaspers (1963a) viewed this process as central to patient assessment and classification.

Treatment

Diagnosing a patient as having a brief reactive psychosis raises the broadest range of therapeutic considerations. The diagnosis itself has implications of a clinical syndrome where specific vulnerability and etiology are not determined and where the syndromal designation may comprise multiple disease entities. Treatment, therefore, is neither etiologically based (except to the extent that the stressor is viewed as causative) nor physiologically specific to this diagnostic class. Therapeutic considerations necessarily range from providing a secure environment and facilitating the passage of time without complicating the illness process to more restricted goals such as the acute therapeutics of anxiety, depression, and psychosis. Highly individualized treatment planning is necessary to integrate the interpersonal and pharmacologic strategies to provide maximum acute treatment, to minimize complications in the future, and to reduce the patient's vulnerability to subsequent episodes. The following discussion outlines the general principles and techniques available to the clinician in ascertaining the optimal treatment strategy for the individual case.

The Initial Steps

An acute psychosis is a medical emergency best handled in a hospital setting. The patient should be located without restraints in a quiet room to reduce stimulation and lessen behavioral excitation. Attention must first be given to the possibility of life-threatening medical conditions. Restoration of pulmonary or cardiac function and of fluid and electrolyte balance and detoxification or treatment of drug withdrawal states take priority. Serious head trauma or intracerebral hemorrhage or infection must be suspected and ruled out early. Some of the life-threatening medical conditions that can cause delirium and acute psychosis are cerebrovascular accident, hypertensive encephalopathy, hypoglycemia, hypoxia and hypoperfusion states, meningitis and encephalitis, poisoning, Wernicke-Korsakoff syndrome, diabetic ketoacidosis and nonketotic hyperosmolar states, hyperthermia, acute adrenal insufficiency, and thyroid storm (Anderson and Kuehnle 1974; LaBruzza in Tupin et al. 1984). Other serious medical problems to consider are electrolyte and acid-base disturbances, systemic infections, and subdural hematoma. Lastly, drug toxic and drug withdrawal states must be ruled out (LaBruzza in Tupin et al. 1984).

During the time that one is evaluating the patient for the possibility of a medical emergency, the patient is likely to be presenting a behavioral emergency that must be controlled. Reduced stimulation in a quiet room, with only one or two people providing care, or admission to a hospital can calm an agitated patient and reduce danger. Unfortunately, those who are not calmed by these measures are usually the patients with the more serious organic conditions in which great caution must be used with medication. Therefore, if it is absolutely necessary to control violent behavior pharmacologically before the patient's medical status and diagnosis are known, it is usually best to use a small dose of a high-potency neuroleptic that has little anticholinergic or cardiovascular action and little sedation to complicate the clinical picture (Anderson and Kuehnle 1985). If there is reason to believe there is an anticholinergic crisis, physostigmine is the drug of choice (Granacher and Baldessarini 1976). If it is known that the patient is not intoxicated with alcohol or other depressant drug and is not suffering from a neurological insult, a benzodiazepine is safe and effective. In extreme cases, physical restraints may be temporarily necessary.

Admission to the hospital is necessary if there are any signs of delirium or if the patient is homicidal or suicidal. It may also be advisable if there is no social support or if there is no improvement in the psychosis after four to six hours with medication (Anderson and Kuehnle 1985). The hospital may be the optimal setting for establishing the diagnosis, clarifying the nature of the stress precipitant, and assessing environmental support.

The Interpersonal Therapeutic Context

The abruptness of onset, the stressful circumstances, and the bewildering experience of disordered thought and perception make this disorder extremely vexing to patient and close relatives. The clinician can alleviate aspects of the problem by establishing the medical framework with the powerful expectations of sufferer and healer. The exploration of the patient's subjective experience, the ascertainment of the life story, and the detailing of precipitating stress and its interaction with personality and environmental factors is the doctor's initial task. The very process enables the patient to engage in a therapeutic clinical relationship. Many attributes of this relationship may support vulnerable functions, decrease isolation and distortion, clarify the helping process, and enhance identification with a source of stability and perspective.

The dyadic relationship at this initial state is guided by phenomenology rather than the presentiments of therapeutic theory. Developing a broad and deep understanding of the phenomenon is necessary for diagnosis and for the full range of treatment decisions required (Carpenter and Hanlon 1986). An appreciation of the therapeutic potential of pharmacotherapy, modification of environment, psychotherapy, participation of important others in treatment, and the like are gained through the interpersonal phenomenological approach. An early commitment to one treatment approach to the exclusion of others, or basing treatment on a priori etiologic assumptions, is ill advised.

Following the subsidence of psychosis, longer-range therapeutic strategies may be considered. By then the patient's life history is better known, and an informed clinical inference regarding the nature of stress-induced pathogenesis can be derived. Appreciation of lingering problems (e.g., dysphoric affect, weakened sense of self) and likelihood of future episodes provide a basis for formulating psychotherapeutic and pharmacotherapeutic plans.

The fact that this disorder is self-limited by definition does not mean that the impact of stress-related psychosis is brief. Longer-term observation, counseling, and treatment will often prove beneficial. There are a variety of psychotherapeutic approaches to be considered, and currently the clinician does not have empirical evidence clarifying the respective efficacy of these approaches. Nor are these approaches necessarily mutually exclusive. Educational and behavioral approaches to stress reduction and coping may be used together with exploratory psychotherapy aimed at reducing idiosyncratic reaction to specific stressors. In all instances, however, it is important for doctor and patient to realize that rapid improvement in psychosis is the natural history of the disorder. Brief crisis intervention is clearly required, but whether long-term therapeutics are required or are even desirable must be determined in the individual case.

whether long-term therapeutics are required or are even desirable must be determined in the individual case.

Pharmacologic Strategies

Once a medical emergency has been ruled out by thorough investigation in a holding environment, attention may focus on management and treatment of behavior. If behavior is agitated and dangerous, neuroleptics should be given acutely until the patient is calm. The effectiveness of neuroleptics is not confined to a single type of psychosis. Neuroleptics are effective in all psychoses and can be given regardless of the subtype of functional psychosis, whether that be a paranoid, excitational, depressed, or confusional picture. Rapid neuroleptization can be employed to assure that a therapeutic dose is quickly reached, but it is rarely desirable to drive the dosage above standard therapeutic range. It should be well documented why the medication was necessary, that the patient or family, or both, was informed of the need and risks, and that proper approval was obtained. Dosage should usually be reduced as soon as the acute behavioral disturbance subsides. The clinician must be alert to the appearance of acute dystonic or other severe extrapyramidal reactions and treat them accordingly.

Antidepressants and lithium are too slow in their onset of action to be useful in acute management. However, within several days the clinical picture may be less dramatic and predominantly excitational or depressive. Considering the high mortality rate from suicide in brief reactive psychosis and in depressive disease, as well as the destructiveness of manic psychosis, it is prudent to consider lithium or antidepressant pharmacotherapeutics at an early stage. Prolonged prophylaxis with these drugs is not recommended unless the diagnosis has been revised to major affective disorder.

Benzodiazepines may also be used for initial therapy. They are very safe and have antipsychotic efficacy in the acute situation (Cole 1985; Modell 1985). Benzodiazepine therapy should be considered short term with dosage reduction as soon as psychosis wanes. Disinhibition of behavior, including violence and withdrawal seizures, is of concern with higher doses and sustained treatment.

Those patients who were put on medication acutely should be withdrawn from it as soon as they are stabilized so as not to make the error of continuing to treat when the illness has been resolved. There are some who believe that one is less likely to have a reappearance of psychosis if medication is withdrawn gradually, though this has not been established. If the illness recurs when neuroleptics are discontinued, it may be that it is a brief reactive psychosis that has not resolved, or it may be another psychotic disorder such as schizophrenia. In either case, neuroleptics can be reinstituted until the patient has restabilized and stopped later. Neuroleptic medication should rarely be continued for an indefinite period of time, except in schizophrenia, and then only with persistent psychosis or frequent recurrence of disabling symptoms.

Phenomenological Basis for Treatment

Brief reactive psychosis is not a discrete disease with a unitary treatment. All acute psychoses are initially approached in a similar manner on first presentation when it is important to sort out and treat any serious medical condition or behavioral emergency. After the emergency has been dealt with by medical evaluation, isolation, hospitalization, and pharmacologic therapy, it becomes important to understand what coping mechanisms the patient is using and what sort of problem he or she is struggling with, as well as what personality vulnerabilities predisposed to psychosis. If Strömgren's idea is correct that the phenomenological subtype of the psychosis is an indicator of the kind of problem with which the patient is dealing, then it would be useful in paranoid states to search for an injury to the patient's self-esteem and to focus treatment on helping the patient to evaluate himself or herself more realistically. In depressed or excitational states one would look for a conflictual situation that the patient cannot accept and help him or her find ways to resolve it. In confusional or hysterical states, one would look for a stressor that challenged the patient's distorted view of the world and help him or her assess external reality.

It is possible, in contrast to the position of Jaspers, Strömgren, and others, that the form that the psychosis takes does not give a clue to the nature of the stressor or to the patient's personality and defensive style. Psychotic symptoms could be viewed not as a defense, but as phenomena indicating a breakdown of defenses when coping mechanisms are overwhelmed (Hollender and Hirsch 1964).

In either case, patients experiencing brief reactive psychosis are thought to have underlying personality vulnerabilities. Treatment and prophylaxis against future episodes include a long-term effort to define and strengthen specific coping strategies. Developing a comprehensive picture of the circumstances, sequences, and experiences of the acute episode enables the clinician to gain an empathic understanding of the patient's psychodynamics and personality. This, in turn, may help the patient establish a realistic perspective, appreciate factors involved in illness, decrease sense of isolation, and work collaboratively on treatment planning.

Interpersonal Strategies

Skilled interpersonal intervention begins in the emergency setting, especially if there is a threat of violence. Malinek and Halbreich give a very thorough description of how to recognize impending violence and how to intervene when violence threatens or is occurring (Malinek and Halbreich in Tupin et al. 1984). The general principles are: to talk to the patient and others to get as much information as possible about what is bothering the patient; to help the patient clarify that he or she is angry and to explore the consequences of acting on that anger; to remove people who provoke the patient; to have adequate security on hand, evident to the patient; to remove weapons; to physically restrain a violent patient only by using a team of trained people; and to use intramuscular medication if necessary once the patient is restrained.

Strömgren points out that after the acute attack is over ongoing therapy must address itself to strengthening the weaknesses in the personality. "To achieve this it is necessary to make a close analysis of the structure of the images of environment and self. We must find the points at which these different structures are unrealistic, and the patient must be educated to alter them. . . . It will furthermore be a great advantage if it is possible to establish a broader basis for these vulnerable areas of the personality. These patients will often tend to put all their fortune on one card, so to speak, whether it be in themselves or in the environment. This is the reason why it is impossible for them to bear a defeat on this, their only front" (Strömgren 1974).

Integration of Therapeutic Approaches

Treatment of the patient who has recently faced a severe stress, is vulnerable to pathogenic effects of this stress, and has experienced psychosis calls for a range of social, psychological, and biologic therapeutic interventions. We have adumbrated a few techniques in the preceding discussion. There is an available literature providing more detailed discussion of each treatment, especially the literature on crisis management, pharmacology of psychosis, and brief psychotherapy.

The integration of various treatments can be conceptualized within the framework of the biopsychosocial medical model (Engel 1980) and parallels our previous discussion of integrated treatment of schizophrenia (Carpenter 1984; Strauss and Carpenter 1981). The brief reactive psychoses may provide a paradigm for this integrating. Social (stressful event), psychological (patient's psychic reaction), and biologic (vulnerability) are conceptualized in etiology and pathogenesis. Treatment approaches emphasizing social, psychological, and biologic techniques are considered germaine. Additive and synergistic influence among treatments is also expected. Pharmacologic intervention may ameliorate the effect of stress and enable the patient to be more realistically collaborative in the dyadic clinical relationship. Interpersonal therapeutics may enable the patient to avoid some stressors and curb idiosyncratic reaction.

It is deceptive to think of brief reactive psychosis as an acute disorder with a brief and simple treatment. The fact that there is often a personality vulnerability predisposing to repeated episodes means that it is usually necessary to bring to bear a long-term treatment effort composed of the entire constellation of psychosocial treatments available in the modern armamentarium. In this regard it is important to avoid clinical care in a spirit of therapeutic reductionism where commitment to a specific etiologic or therapeutic theory does not allow application of the relevant treatments in an integrative manner.

Treatment Pitfalls and the Role of Follow-up

Psychosocial decline and suicide.   Reactive psychoses as traditionally defined do not have an entirely benign course when conditions other than continued psychosis are examined. Jørgensen (1985) found that on follow-up 21 of 41 patients were not self-supporting on 10-year follow-up. The number of disability pensioners went from 21 to 30 from the beginning to the end of the study. On admission, 28 of the 41 patients belonged to the lowest of five social classes and several underwent a decline during the observation period. Marriage and parenthood were also well below the norms for the culture. Andersen and Laerum (1980) found that of 34 deaths occurring in 110 verified cases of psychogenic-reactive psychoses over a 14-year period, 15 or 30 percent were due to suicide. Faergeman (1963) found that, after 15 years, three of 17 or 18 percent of deaths in patients with verified psychogenic psychoses were suicides. These findings suggest that cases of acute psychosis, in which the psychosis resolves, often have severe sequelae such as psychosocial disability and suicide. The treatment implications of this are that these patients must not be lost to follow-up or be considered to need no more treatment after the acute episode has resolved.

Continued use of neuroleptics.   Neuroleptics should not be continued beyond the resolution of the acute psychotic episodes. Because of their probable long-term undesirable side effects, chronic administration of neuroleptics is appropriate only in cases where it is demonstrated that there is a serious chronic relapsing disease, in which case the probable consequences of nonadministration of neuroleptics are worse than their probable side effects.

Cultural considerations.   Different cultures have differing world views, and they sanction their own special ways of dealing with crises. Thus, there are culture-bound syndromes in different societies that correspond to brief reactive psychoses as they are known in the Western world but that have a different phenomenology. Examples of such psychotic states are "amok," "latah," "imu," and "whitiko psychosis" (Langness 1967). When someone from a very different culture presents in the emergency room with an acute psychosis, it may be impossible for treatment personnel not familiar with that culture to diagnose or treat the illness. It is essential in such cases to confer closely with someone who is familiar with the culture while trying to understand and treat the patient.

Psychotherapy. Faergeman cautions that psychosis can, on occasion, be precipitated by psychotherapy in which the transference can prove destructive for a weak ego. Anxieties can be so intense that evocative, exploratory psychotherapy enhances psychosocial disintegration (Faergeman 1963). The phenomenologically based approach can provide support and reality structuring, reserving formal psychotherapy for carefully selected patients.

Conclusion

Brief reactive psychosis is a clinical syndrome best conceptualized within a broad medical model. Multiple therapeutic considerations are required to address the psychopathology, the vulnerability, and the interaction with stress. Integrative treatment is essential.

Chapter 157

Treatment of Induced Psychotic Disorder

Induced psychotic disorder is a psychiatric condition that has fascinated psychiatrists since its description by Lasègue and Falret in 1877 as folie à deux (Lasègue and Falret 1877). (Earlier accounts have been documented by Greenberg [1956].) It seems to epitomize the worst imaginable form of what may be a ubiquitous concern, a pathological relationship in which one individual adversely affects another, in this case, literally drives the other person crazy. Ingmar Bergman's film, "Cries and Whispers," is a popular dramatization of this theme. In it, a nurse is inexorably drawn into the psychosis of her patient. Induced psychotic disorder is the most recent in a long list of alternative names for the disease entity, each of which emphasizes the concept of sanity, and induced schizophrenia. These and other terms have been collected by Gralnick (1942) and Enoch and Trethowan (1979).

Definition

The original description provided by Lasègue and Falret made eight points:

1. In ordinary circumstances the contagion of insanity does not occur when a healthy person is exposed to an insane individual.
2. The contagion insanity is not possible except under exceptional conditions. a) One individual is an active element; being more intelligent than the other he creates the delusion and gradually imposes it upon the second or passive one; the delusion soon becomes their common cause to be repeated to all in an almost identical fashion. b) To allow this interactual process to take place in two different minds, it is necessary for both individuals to have lived in a very close-knit existence, sharing the same environment for a long period of time. c) The delusion should be kept within the limits of the possible, and based on past events or an apprehension or hope in the future.
3. Folie à deux always occurs in the conditions indicated above. All the observations are analogous, almost identical in character among men and women, children, adults, and old people.
4. This variety of insanity is more frequent among women but it also occurs among men.
5. We might mention heredity as a . . . predisposing cause when two persons from the same family are concerned. . . . However, this etiology cannot account for cases in which the two patients are not blood relatives, for instance when an illness occurs in a husband and wife.
6. A main therapeutic indication is to separate the two patients.
7. In most cases, the second patient is not so deeply affected as the first. It is even possible to consider the second patient as having merely suffered a temporary moral pressure, that is, to be noninsane in the social and legal sense.
8. In some rare cases the moral pressure put by an insane person upon a weak individual may be extended to a third person, or even to a lesser degree to more persons in the environment (Lasègue and Falret 1877).

Contemporary interest in the syndrome originates with Gralnick (1942). In keeping with his emphasis on the transfer of psychosis he renamed it, "psychoses of association" and defined it as the "transfer of delusional ideas and/or abnormal behavior from one person to one or more others who have been in close association with the primarily affected patient." Dewhurst and Todd's (1956) later, widely cited criteria emphasize the similarity of the delusions and evidence of mutual support rather than the transfer: 1) evidence of intimate association, 2) high degree of similarity in general motif and delusional content of the partners' psychoses, and 3) the presence of unequivocal evidence that the partners accept, support, and share each other's delusional ideas.

DSM-III (American Psychiatric Association 1980) emphasized the paranoid nature of the shared delusions and originally classified the condition as a shared paranoid disorder in which there is a persecutory delusional system that develops as a result of a close relationship with a person who already has an established paranoid psychosis. This classification has been criticized for being too restrictive (Lazarus 1985). Although persecutory delusions seemed to be the most common delusion in shared psychotic disorders (70 percent in Gralnick's study), religious, grandiose, and hypochondriacal delusions occur. Also, the primary diagnosis need not always be a paranoid psychosis or paranoid schizophrenia. The newer DSM-III-R (American Psychiatric Association 1987) nomenclature has omitted the criteria of an established paranoid psychosis but omits the Dewhurst and Todd (1956) criteria of a mutually supportive interaction between the partners once the delusion is shared. The DSM-III-R criteria are listed in Table 1.

Clinical Subtypes

Shortly after Lasègue and Falret's definition of folie à deux, four different subgroups were described. These have been summarized by Gralnick (1942) and Grover (1937).

1. Folie imposée (imposed psychosis). The delusions of a psychotic person are transferred to a mentally sound person who offers little resistance to their acceptance. The delusions of the recipient disappear after separation.
2. Folie simultanée (simultaneous psychosis). In this subtype there is a simultaneous but independent appearance of an identical psychosis in two morbidly predisposed individuals.
3. Folie communique (communicated psychosis). The recipient develops psychotic symptoms after a variable period of resistance. After adopting the content of the delusion, the recipient then goes on to develop delusions that are independent of the first subject.
4. Folie induité (induced psychosis). This subtype refers to an already psychotic hospitalized individual who is influenced by another patient. He or she "enriches his [or her] delusions" (Montyel, quoted by Enoch and Trethowan 1979, p. 135).

Although Gralnick (1942) found these subdivisions clinically useful, most investigators have rejected them as confusing. Dewhurst and Todd (1956) reject simultaneous psychoses as a subdivision because of the improbability of two identical delusional systems developing at exactly the same moment. It is likely that one person developed the delusion first, and it is inconceivable given their similarity that one does not influence the other. Induced psychoses seem an unnecessary distinction because it is based on the fact of hospitalization and would otherwise be classified as a communicated psychosis. More controversial is the distinction between imposed and communicated psychosis, which rests on whether or not the delusions disappear on separation.

The only systematic effort to study the frequency of the different types was

Table 1.   DSM-III-R Diagnostic Criteria for Induced Psychotic Disorder
A. A delusion develops (in a second person) in the context of a close relationship with another person, or persons, with an already established delusion (the primary case).
B. The delusion in the second person is similar in content to that in the primary case.
C. Immediately before onset of the induced delusion, the second person did not have a psychotic disorder or the prodromal symptoms of Schizophrenia.

conducted by Gralnick (1942), who in an English language review was able to distinguish 61 cases of imposed psychoses, 24 cases of communicated psychoses, six cases of simultaneous psychoses, and five cases of induced psychoses. This suggests that the distinction between imposed and communicated psychoses is valid and that the stability of the delusional system in the recipient once the subjects are separated is important. Dewhurst and Todd (1956) dismiss stability of the delusion as an artifact of the duration of the psychoses. Another explanation is that it reflects different degrees of pathology in the secondary person(s). We will return to this below.

Another subdivision of shared delusional disorder refers to groups in which more than two persons are involved. There are reports of folie à trois, folie à quatre (Sims et al. 1977), folie à douze (Waltzer 1963), folie à famille (Tseng 1969), and folie à pleusirs (Enoch and Trethowan 1979). The distinction between these group or collective psychoses and mass or epidemic hysteria is not always clearly defined. More problematic are bizarre and unusual cults where the followers act in a deliberate and organized manner on the delusions of their charismatic leaders. These cults will be discussed further in a later section.

Epidemiology

Induced psychotic disorder is usually considered a relatively uncommon syndrome. One investigator reported 29 individuals (1.7 percent) with folie à deux in 1700 consecutive admissions (Spradley 1937). Gralnick (1942) summarized 103 cases, and reports of additional cases have been added every year or so since then. Most hospital clinicians have encountered at least one case (Lehmann 1980), and many cases go unnoticed in admissions statistics because they are classified individually or because only one member of the pair is admitted to the hospital and the diagnosis is not made. The more a hospital is oriented toward careful family evaluation and diagnosis, the more likely a partner in a shared psychotic disorder will be found.

Gralnick (1942) emphasizes the preponderance in induced psychotic disorders of persons who live together in intimate contact for a long time. He reports the following combinations in 103 pairs: two sisters, 40 pairs; husband and wife, 26 pairs; mother and child, 24 pairs; two brothers, 11 pairs; brother and sister, six pairs; father and child, 2 pairs. The greater susceptibility of women to the disease is probably due to the more restricted and submissive roles imposed upon them socially. To this might be added the greater likelihood that they will seek help and be hospitalized.

The Association Between the Subjects

The relationship between the partners in an induced psychotic disorder has been studied from a variety of diagnostic, biologic, and psychodynamic perspectives. Many of these studies are inadequate because of the exclusivity of their approach and a failure to adequately define diagnostic criteria. In the following paragraphs we will consider each of the these perspectives.

Diagnoses of the Partners

The most complete diagnostic study of the partners in induced psychotic disorders is that of Soni and Rochley (1974). They were able to find 109 cases in the English literature with sufficient data to permit a diagnostic evaluation. In nearly all the reported cases the primary partner is schizophrenic (65 cases) or paraphrenic (31 cases). Paraphrenia is used in the European literature to describe a mild late-onset paranoid schizoprenic condition. By DSM-III criteria this condition would likely be divided into a very mixed group of paranoid states, atypical bipolar disease, schizophrenia, and perhaps paranoid-schizotypal personality disorders. Other diagnoses found in the primary partner were affective psychosis (nine cases) and senile arteriopathic psychosis (four cases). More than one-half of the secondary partners in the Soni and Rochley review belonged to a schizophenic-paraphrenic group, but a significant number had either a personality disorder, a dementia, mental retardation, some physical disability such as deafness or a stroke, or a language barrier.

This study, although limited by its dependence on reported literature and lack of diagnostic criteria, does illuminate the controversy surrounding the usefulness of the subtypes of imposed and communicated psychosis. In the communicated psychoses the secondary partner develops a true delusional disease, in which an underlying or latent psychotic condition is shaped by the illness of the primary partner. These patients do not readily abandon their delusions on separation from the primary partner. Those who have an imposed psychosis and do abandon their delusions on separation may have a severe personality disorder or mental retardation and do not have a true delusional disorder. Members of this group are "highly impressionable rather than deluded." (Munro 1982). It is likely then that imposed psychosis and communicated psychosis represent extremes found in induced psychotic disorders and that there are gradations from a partial compliance with the delusions in an impressionable partner to influencing the content of a separate psychosis in a deluded partner. This would account for the varying results regarding the efficacy of separation in the treatment of the disease.

A frequent diagnostic distinction that occurs in the literature is that of one partner being dominant and the other being submissive (Faguet and Faguet 1982). The primary subject or inducer is consistently found to be more dominant as well as intelligent, forceful, autonomous, and imaginative. The secondary or induced partner is submissive and less intelligent, highly suggestible, dependent, more passive, more prone to hysteria, and more likely to be socially deprived and disadvantaged physically. Although Lasègue and Falret in their original communication emphasized the dominance of the primary figure over the recipient they note that the recipient is not entirely a submissive partner since in most of their cases he or she becomes delusional after considerable resistance and then may affect the primary partner sufficiently to modify his or her delusions. It is sometimes difficult to determine which partner is dominant. In one case report reversal of the roles occurred (McNiel 1972).

Both criminal acts (Greenberg 1956) and suicide pacts (Ali Salih 1981) have been described as occurring in induced psychotic disorder. An example of the latter is a husband with a severe depressive illness with pronounced nihilistic and suicidal ideas who convinced his wife to join him in a suicide pact. She survived and, although depressed, was no longer suicidal or nihilistic (Christodoulou 1970).

Genetic Studies

The biologic argument emphasizes the fact that most shared disorders are consanguineous (91 percent by Gralnick's data) and that a similar genetic inheritance forms the basis for the phenomenon. Kallman and Mickey (1946) argued that the genetic similarity was so compelling that "the concept of folie à deux may be useful for the practice of counting in French but not for describing the occurrence of similar schizophrenic symptoms." In those cases of "conjugal psychoses" in which a similar genetic makeup could not be invoked they believed that the effect of assortative mate selection was a likely explanation.

Kallman and Mickey and others who have invoked the genetic argument fail, however, to address the rarity with which consanguineous paranoid patients share each other's delusions under normal conditions. The symptoms may be similar, but their content is not. An intensive study of the Genain quadruplets (Rosenthal 1977) notes that although the presence and onset of hallucinations and perhaps of delusions seem to correlate among the quadruplets, there was no apparent connection in their content. Certainly this is the more common clinical experience. Jaspers (1963b), in his discussion of the phenomenology of schizophrenia, emphasizes that one never finds a community of schizophrenics because the rigidity and the pervading egocentricity of their delusions precludes any communal life. They are normally as uncommunicative and unresponsive to each other as they are to the arguments of family and health professionals. The significant discordance for the presence of schizophrenia in monozygotic twins also supports the contention that something more than genetic similarity is required to explain the "contagion of insanity."

In an important neglected study, Scharfetter (1972) collected 215 reports of 'symbiontic psychoses" (75 inducers and 140 induced) with sufficient information to permit a study of the incidence of schizophrenia, affective disorder, and schizoid personality in the relatives of both partners. Using unspecified criteria he found the incidence of schizophrenia among the relatives of the secondary partners who were not consanguineous with the primary partner to be similar to that among the relatives of secondary partners who did share a blood relationship with the primary partner. The morbid risk in both cohorts was similar to the reported risk value expected for relatives of schizophrenic probands. Scharfetter concluded that these findings support the view that only persons with a genetically determined predisposition to schizophrenia are likely to develop a schizophreniform psychosis under the influence of a schizophrenic partner. Unfortunately he does not distinguish between imposed psychoses and communicated psychoses, although he does make clear that 40 percent of the induced partners were not schizophrenic but showed a schizoid psychopathy. The frequency of this personality disorder in the relatives of the secondary partners is similar to that expected in the relatives of schizophrenics, which suggests that it may be a personality disorder that is related to schizophrenia. This raises the intriguing possibility that those secondary partners with personality disorders may be part of a schizophrenic spectrum although not clearly schizophrenic. This must remain a speculation.

The Environment

Most reports of individuals with shared psychotic disorder note their isolation or seclusiveness from the remainder of society. This sequestration—which may be derived from factors unrelated to illness such as poverty, physical disability, language difficulties, and geographic isolation—may contribute to the vulnerability of the secondary partner because of an increased dependency on the primary partner (Soni and Rockely 1974). Additionally, a process similar to brainwashing may occur. As described by Waltzer (1963) the prisoner is usually removed from any supportive contact with a familiar environment and exposed repetitively to the arguments of his or her warden. This produces a disorganization and regression that is followed by identification with the aggressor and finally a reindoctrination. In most cases, however, the isolation from friends and community in induced psychotic disorders is self-imposed and results from the hostile and rejecting attitude that accompanies the delusions. Whatever the origin of the sequestration of the partners, there is the loss of the possibility of any balancing dialogue or self-correcting impact on the delusional formation.

Psychodynamics

A number of contributions have explored the psychodynamic mechanisms involved in the sharing of the delusional content. Deutsch (1938) first drew attention to the prepsychotic exclusive rapport that exists between the partners as an expression of the unconscious bonds, which later brings both partners to similar delusional ideas. The partners need not live with each other for this to be true. Layman and Cohen (1957) describe two brothers who lived apart for many years. When the old brother telephoned the younger dependent brother for help because of his persecutory delusions and hallucinations, the younger brother came to his aid and promptly adopted his delusions without any prolonged period of transmission or imposition. Layman and Cohen believe that similar underlying needs in the partners allow a delusion to be transmitted because it is "tailor made." It is not communicated, transmitted, or forcibly imposed but *adopted*. This is a shift from the common belief that the delusion is often imposed by a persistent wearing away of the recipient's resistance. Falret and Lasègue did, however, believe that a delusion could only be accepted if it was "sentimental and reasonable."

Early dynamic explanations of induced psychotic disorders sought to use hypnosis, transference, and identification as models to elucidate the illness. More recent contributions have emphasized a conflictual basis for the shared delusional formation. Pulver and Brunt (1961) provide the most detailed analysis. They view the primary partner in the prepsychotic relationship as stressed (angered) by the dependent needs of the secondary partner. Once the primary partner becomes psychotic, the hostility toward the secondary partner is projected outward into the outsider and continues toward the secondary partner in the now persistent demands that the secondary partner accept the primary partner's delusions. The secondary partner, unable to either tolerate the aggressive behavior of the primary partner or to free himself by forming a relationship to another person, resolves this conflict by identifying with the primary partner's delusional aggression. A similar construction utilizing this defense of "identification with the aggressor" could be established for grandiose or religious delusions. An alternative dynamic emphasizes the intense attachment of the secondary partner. He or she seeks to preserve the relationship with the dominant one by adapting his or her delusions because the threat of the loss is greater than the fear of psychosis.

Not surprisingly this phenomenon of induced psychotic disorder has been illuminated by investigators of child behavior. Anthony (1970) found that some children of psychotic mothers seem to adopt their delusions while others did not. He believes this to be related to the child's inability to function autonomously apart from the mother and represented a failure to mature beyond the normal and appropriate developmental stage in which there is a natural "folie à deux" between mother and child (nine to 36 months). Pine (1979) describes this developmental failure in children as a failure in differentiation. They may then develop a folie à deux in childhood.

Family Dynamics

A family dynamic perspective to induced psychotic disorder has been largely neglected in the literature. All families tend to share a common reality and family myths that help the family to maintain a stable cohesiveness or homeostasis in the midst of internal and external threats (Ferreira 1963). These threats may occur as a result of members' unresolved ambivalence, competition, dependency, etc. The shared psychoses of one or more members can be viewed from this background (Wikler 1980).

Case 1. (courtesy of Jeff Halpern, M.D., and Ellen Shapiro, M.S.W.). A 36-year-old woman believed her hospitalization and deteriorating work and social function were the results of a bad hair coloring. She insisted that her hair had turned bright orange, and even though her natural color had grown back her mind remained altered. The mother shared the delusion while the father did not, but the father remained strangely uninvolved. This detachment may have been due to an organic personality disorder, secondary to an undiagnosed cerebellar disease. The patient and mother's delusion coincided with the diagnosis of the father's brain disease five years earlier.

In a diagnostic family interview it became evident that the marriage had never been happy, and following the birth of the daughter the father had moved into another room. The mother and daughter continued to share the same bed into the present. The daughter became the mother's entire life; she hoped that the daughter, unlike herself, would go to college, become a professional, and have a happy marriage. When the daughter became psychotic the mother accepted the daughter's delusion, perhaps as a way to avoid personal grief at the daughter's illness and the failure of her vicarious expectations. The shared delusion may also have represented a psychotic denial of the husband-father's brain ("head") disease.

The daughter was hospitalized and treated with phenothiazines, which decreased somewhat the preemptory occupation with the delusion. The mother's belief in the delusion seemed to rapidly disappear. The parents were successfully encouraged to take a much-talked-of vacation, which they did only to return early to demand the discharge of the daughter because she was "now better." The mother believed her daughter could return to work at an unrealistic level of expectation.

Comment. The investment of both parents in the daughter's delusion became evident in the father's passive acceptance of the mother-daughter induced psychotic disorder. The difficulty in influencing the "family system" was evident in the parents' withdrawing the patient from treatment after an apparently unsuccessful effort to function as a couple without the daughter. The mother and daughter sharing the same bed has been noted (Faguet and Faguet 1982) as not uncommon in shared psychotic disorders.

Collective Psychoses and Cults

There is no consensus in the literature regarding "collective psychosis" as a clinical variant of shared psychotic disorder. Eugen Bleuler (1930, p. 534), for example, did not include members of unusual religious cults within his definition of folie à deux. "But the individual follower of a prophet who represents an undemonstrable view will be declared insane only in the worst cases although most of them cannot be considered responsible or capable of action in matters connected with the induced view" (Enoch and Trethowan 1979, p. 156). They argue that in some instances when large groups of people "become infected, as it were, by irrational ideas leading them into untoward mass behavior the mechanisms may resemble a shared paranoid disorder."

It is important to distinguish epidemic hysteria such as the outbreaks of fainting, globus, convulsions, and abnormal movements involving girls in nunneries, factories, prisons, or schools that have been documented from medieval times to the present. These occur in groups ripe with shared apprehensions, concerns, and conflicts and are triggered by some trivial factor that occurs to one member of the group. The behavior seems more related to a social situation than to individual psychopathology in its spontaneous, unorganized, and contagious nature. Although individual personality features or a latent psychosis may contribute to an individual's membership, the major impression in such hysterical epidemics is one of regressive group phenomenon (Sirois 1974).

In recent years the existence of unusual cults, often religious, have been investigated by psychiatrists. These cults are established by strong charismatic leaders who claim to possess some revealed "vision" and consist of members who are actively recruited into accepting this vision and living in isolation from the remainder of society, which is viewed with distrust and suspicion. Most investigators have avoided psychiatric diagnoses such as shared psychotic disorder or collective psychoses in evaluating the subjects' mystic-like experiences in order to attempt to understand what the member derives from membership in the cult. Galanter (1980) for example, describes a "relief effect" in what seem to be very troubled individuals. Nevertheless, the question occurs of whether beliefs are reflections of the members' atypical spiritual experiences or are pathological manifestations of mental illness (Ross 1983). West and Singer (1980) believe that many indoctrinees can be considered to be victims of traumatic neuroses that in some instances may include delusional thinking. Kriegman and Soloman (1985) believe that the follower is able to stabilize a defective sense of self by forming an idealized self-object relationship to the cult leader.

In 1969 a series of group murders in California were organized by Charles Manson and his followers, the "Family." Manson had had an early history of antisocial behavior with prolonged periods of institutionalization during his adolescence and childhood. In his 30s he gathered a group of young men and women around him who believed his claims of possessing satanic powers such as being able to fortell the future by reading scriptures and interpreting the songs of a rock group. At his behest his followers murdered a number of people in order to prepare for "helter skelter," a worldwide racial conflict with massive devastation. At the trial neither he nor his followers were found to be legally insane, but a psychiatrist described one family member as suffering from "folie à famille, a kind of shared madness within a group situation" (Hockman, quoted by Bugliosi 1974, p. 461). The prosecuting lawyer described Manson as a "sophisticated con man" who used drugs, repetitive preaching, sex, and coercion together with an uncanny ability to detect the needs and fears from those who were drawn to him. Most of the followers were wanderers who had left home in mid-adolescence and were unable to find any prior stability in relationships, school, or career. Manson seemed able to release in them latent tendencies to focus a murderous hatred on a fictitious common enemy so that they became capable of murder (Bugliosi 1974).

Another example is James Jones, the founder of the Peoples Temple in Indianapolis, who fled from his persecutors to California and then to a jungle site in Guyana (Ulman and Abse 1983). When investigated by a congressional committee he had 913 of his followers commit suicide with a specially prepared cyanide cocktail and then shot himself. Jones preached a mixture of politics and hellfire religion and showed marked personality traits of paranoia and explosiveness. Many of his persecutory ideas may have reached a delusional intensity so that Rosen has suggested that the mass suicide was a folie collective (Rosen 1981).

These examples raise questions about the relationship of induced psychotic disorder to group phenomena in which the charisma of the leader and the regressive abrogation of rational thinking by the followers may be amplified by group processes. The reader is referred to articles by Galanter (1980) and West and Singer (1980) for further discussion.

Treatment

The treatment of shared psychotic disorder is complicated by the absence of any systematic treatment outcome studies and the fact that usually only one partner presents for hospitalization. It is only later during a family visit or family evaluation that the induced psychotic disorder becomes evident. The most significant complication is that induced psychotic disorder is not a distinctive psychopathological entity in itself but a description of a relationship and possible influence between individuals who may have very different disease processes.

In those instances where both partners are identified in the emergency room or prior to hospitalization, there is no consensus in the literature on how to proceed. The traditional approach since Falret and Lasègue is separation of the partners. If both members require hospitalization then separate wards or even institutions might be considered. This "classic" approach was first seriously questioned by Layman (1957), who claimed to find only one case report of a successful treatment by separation. More recent reports have emphasized the traumatic impact on the partners that may occur following separation. Rioux (1963) reported two paranoid schizophrenic sisters in which the secondary began to severely deteriorate following separation from the primary. He recommended that treatment be directed toward exploration of the association between the members. Potash and Brunell (1974) also recommend a multiple conjoint psychotherapy.

The advantage of hospitalizing both patients together or hospitalizing one and permitting frequent contact is that it allows an evaluation of the interaction between the two partners as well as a careful diagnostic evaluation of the individual pathologies. The diagnosis of induced psychotic disorder must be determined, and it must be established whether the secondary partner has an "imposed psychosis" (is impressionable) or an autonomous "communicated psychosis" (is delusional). Observing the two together will often clarify this. An automatic quality to the recitation of the delusions or an absence of firm conviction in the secondary partner usually points to an imposed psychosis with an underlying personality disorder. A mutually supportive and interactive elaboration and maintenance of the delusion will suggest that the secondary partner has a primary autonomous disease (communicated psychosis) such as schizophrenia, bipolar disease, etc. If there are doubts regarding the diagnosis, then temporary separation may be necessary to clarify the issue.

In a situation of an imposed psychosis separation or successful treatment of the primary partner relieves the delusions in the secondary subject. Since separation is often undesirable (e.g., a mother and child) or difficult (e.g., two sisters sharing an apartment in a community in which they have lived their entire lives), successful treatment of the primary partner is desirable. This treatment will be the same as that usually recommended for the core disease process of the primary partner. More specific interventions are required when physical disabilities such as mental retardation, deafness, drug dependence, dementia, etc., contribute to the secondary partner's dependency on the primary partner. Foster care may need to be considered for children until the response of the parent to treatment is evaluated. Relapse is always a danger in the secondary partner if the primary partner relapses (Fernando and Frieze 1985).

In cases of communicated psychosis both partners will require specific treatments for the autonomous psychotic process. These may be either neuroleptics, lithium, electroconvulsive therapy, or antidepressants depending on the primary diagnosis.

Once the primary disease has been biologically treated, it is important to treat the relationship between the partners. How this is done will depend on the relationship. In general, therapy needs to be directed toward increasing the autonomy of both the primary and secondary partners by providing alternative supports, activities, and interests so that there is a decrease in the pathologic enmeshment with each other. In some instances a psychotherapeutic approach aimed at insight into issues of aggression, dependency, and separation may prove useful.

The formation of a treatment alliance with the partners often requires considerable tact and skill. They will not, as a rule, accept treatment for their delusional beliefs. Often emphasizing an associated symptom such as insomnia, depression, or anxiety that results from living under the "strain" of the delusion may provide a focus. Attention can then be focused on how the patients are feeling or sleeping without specifically questioning the delusion and provoking an angry withdrawal from treatment.

Case 2.   A 43-year-old housewife-writer was admitted to the hospital in a severely agitated and confused state. Her history revealed a delusional state of 10 years' duration regarding a conspiracy in the literary world that prevented her poems from being published. Her husband and three adolescent children shared these beliefs and confirmed her assertion that strange sounds on the telephone indicated it was tapped. The husband was the only one to state unequivocally that he heard the sounds and to elaborate on the techniques of the "invasion of privacy" that the "establishment" used to control artists. Members of the patient's family were not hospitalized since they functioned well outside the home without any need to mention the conspiracy. If they did, it was usually in generalized terms such as, "the literary establishment has it in for my mother." The patient herself had managed to function remarkably well during her marriage as a housekeeper and mother by keeping the delusion within the family. Her primary diagnosis was paranoid state with a schizophreniform psychosis. A diagnosis of induced psychotic disorder was made in the husband and children. The patient responded quickly to neuroleptic medication. The children and husband agreed after two visits that they had mistakenly gone along with the patient's "over intense imagination" although the treatment team was quite convinced that the husband was just being compliant. He was an impassive college physics teacher who seemed to be an odd caricature of an absent-minded professor. Although attached to his family, he expressed it by distant concerned observation rather than by participation in family activities.

Follow-up over a six-year period revealed the diagnosis in the primary partner to be a chronic paranoid state with periodic affective disruptions. These were easily controlled on an outpatient basis with medication and supportive therapy that encouraged the patient in her commitment to writing despite the failure of the establishment to respond with praise and sympathized with her immense efforts at maintaining the family with the husband's limited income, severe passivity, and interpersonal distance. A decreased need to convince the family of her persistant delusions was sufficient to permit the three children to begin to separate from the family and to enter college without untoward incident, although one of the children showed tendencies toward being isolated and without friends. They had an imposed psychosis. The husband continued to share his wife's delusions regarding the establishment although he accepted his wife's need for treatment to prevent her from getting too "excited" about things. He seemed to have a communicated psychosis.

Comment. A mild supportive intervention that did not question the reality of the delusion and the occasional use of medication had a dramatic effect on this folie à famille. Over time it became clear that much of the wife's passionate and angry involvement with the literary establishment was a displaced reaction against the husband, who supported the involvement because it enabled him to maintain a comfortable emotional distance in the relationship. Conjoint therapy was not recommended in this case because of a tactical decision to enlist the husband as an ally with the therapist in "helping the wife with her overexcitement" in responding to her failures.

Case 3. (courtesy of Thomas Kramer, M.D.). The patient was a single, unemployed 30-year-old woman who was admitted to the hospital with an elaborate delusional system centering around a lawyer whom she believed had bribed the judge in a negligence case in which he had represented the patient 10 years earlier. She believed he currently prevented her from obtaining employment and had hired a "hit man" to rape and kill her. She also felt she had ESP that informed her of danger and experienced "vibes" that made her ears ring and her body ache when the lawyer was unable to sleep. The diagnostic impression was that the patient was suffering from a chronic paranoid schizophrenia.

After admission it was found that the mother also felt "vibes" simultaneously with the patient and shared the same delusional system regarding the lawyer. The patient and the mother had threatened to assault the lawyer one week earlier. Learning of this, the patient's brother contacted the police, who brought the patient to the hospital. It was difficult to date the mother's psychosis, but it seemed to become more severe after her son had moved from the house three years earlier.

The mother was a 65-year-old woman who had never functioned outside of first her parents' home and then her marriage home. She was diagnosed as having Axis I induced psychotic disorder and Axis II dependent personality. The father worked as a newspaper salesman until the age of 75 when he had retired. He had borderline intelligence and poor hearing for which he refused treatment. After the birth of his daughter he had taken to sleeping in another room so that the mother and daughter could be together—a practice that continued to the present.

An intense effort was made to induce the patient to accept treatment with neuroleptics and family counseling. Although she received an adequate dosage of medication for several weeks, she was unable to acknowledge that she had an illness and persisted in believing that her delusions were true. The mother was not hospitalized but encouraged to visit frequently. As a result of the separation the mother improved significantly. She questioned whether the delusions were true and began to acknowledge the daughter's illness.

As a result of the mother's improvement and the daughter's persistent illness, it was suggested that they not see each other for at least a month. The mother responded by anxiously expressing a fear that the daughter could not function without her. However, with support from the social worker she seemed willing to accept the treatment plan. Her daughter protested violently. "My mother will be all alone. She can't do without me. I can't leave her." Despite efforts to keep them separated the patient contacted her mother and demanded that her mother remove her from the hospital. In a family session involving the brother, father, mother, and patient the parents vividly described how the marriage had been characterized by episodes of frightening verbal or physical violence that were stopped by the patient thrusting herself between them. As this was being discussed, the patient became acutely psychotic and accused the laywer of messing up her life. Unsuccessful suggestions were made to the family that it was necessary for the patient to remain at home in order to continue to modulate the difficulties in the marriage and that the daughter's anger at the lawyer in part expressed her anger at the parents for imposing this burden on her. The mother agreed with the daughter to remove her from the hospital while the father maintained an apparently indifferent stance.

Comment. The case demonstrates the immense difficulty in successfully separating the parties. With support and partial separation from the daughter the mother showed a significant improvement despite the daughter's failure to obtain a good response from neuroleptics. The proposal of a one-month separation panicked both the daughter and mother and resulted in an unalterable demand for release. This underscores the need for a family therapy that acknowledges the powerful dynamic factors that keep the individuals pathologically tied to each other. The treatment team strongly believed that the delusional anger at the lawyer served as a siphon for the angry ambivalence among the family members. The patient's belief that the mother could not manage without her represented a projection of her own inadequacy. These dynamics are, of course, not an etiologic explanation for the induced psychotic disorder, but they do illuminate the importance of psychodynamic factors in the maintenance of the shared delusions and the resistence initiated by a proposal of separation.

Conclusion

Although there are no outcome studies in the treatment of shared paranoid disorder, the literature seems to be oddly optimistic regarding the prognosis. The most that could be said at this point is that it is no better than the prognosis for the treatment of the core disease processes in the respective individuals, and perhaps worse because of the complications secondary to the mechanisms sustaining the shared delusions. Until more systematic epidemiologic, phenomenological, diagnostic, treatment, and outcome studies are available on induced psychotic disorder, guidelines for the diagnosis and treatment of this fascinating disorder will have to rest on anecdotal reports and clinical judgment.

Chapter 158

Treatment of Atypical Psychosis

In DSM-III-R (American Psychiatric Association 1987) the "atypical psychosis" label is included parenthetically next to "psychotic disorder not otherwise specified (NOS)," and the two diagnostic labels can be used interchangeably. In this chapter, the atypical psychosis designation is primarily utilized instead of psychotic disorder NOS. Potential confusion can arise from using the atypical psychosis label because over the years the term has carried various meanings. Historically, some important early references to atypical psychosis include those of Kleist (1923), Leonhard (1934), Pauleikhoff (1957), Mitsuda (1962), and Asano (1960). As used by these authors and others, the term atypical psychosis has often implied intermediate conditions between a number of specific diagnostic entities, including schizophrenia, bipolar affective disorder, and organic conditions such as epilepsy (Mitsuda 1962; Monroe 1982; Sawa 1962). There appears to have been an evolving process in which some homogeneous symptom clusters, considered by some in the past to be among the atypical psychoses, have achieved the status of specific diagnostic categories (e.g., schizoaffective disorder, schizophreniform disorder). This has relegated the remaining clinical presentations that seem to defy systematic categorization to the "organization catch-all" of atypical psychosis. The resultant ambiguity of this diagnostic entity is necessarily reflected in the absence of clearly defined therapeutic regimens. Indeed, an ongoing diagnostic evaluation ideally should lead to the determination of a more specific DSM-III-R diagnosis. Following such a determination, the clinician would then be able to select a therapeutic strategy from the constellation of better-defined treatment modalities prescribed for the more specific diagnosis.

DSM Use of Atyptical Psychosis

DSM-I and DSM-II did not utilize the label atypical psychosis, but these earlier diagnostic systems did contain categories under their respective schizophrenic diagnoses for "other and unspecified types" of schizophrenia (American Psychiatric Association 1952, 1968). DSM-III (American Psychiatric Association 1980) included atypical psychosis in its offical nomenclature, under the category of "psychotic disorders not elsewhere classified."

In DSM-III, a diagnosis of atypical psychosis (298.90) carried a meaning similar to that of the DSM-I and DSM-II category of schizophrenia "other and unspecified types," to the extent that it was a residual category for disorders in which there were some psychotic symptoms present, but in which the psychotic symptoms were not of sufficient duration, intensity, or quality to be classified under a more specific DSM diagnosis.

DSM-III-R (American Psychiatric Association 1987) continues to carry atypical psychosis as a diagnostic category under the classification "psychotic disorders not elsewhere classified." In DSM-III-R the preferred designation for atypical psychosis appears to be "psychotic disorder not otherwise specified." Both the DSM-III and DSM-III-R concepts of atypical psychosis are similar, but there are some important differences. For instance, the DSM-III diagnosis of atypical psychosis included some of the monosymptomatic psychotic conditions such as monosymptomatic hypochondriacal psychosis and erotomania. DSM-III-R delegates these disorders to a new categorization under the Delusional (Paranoid) Disorders (297.10) and specifies them as the somatic and erotomanic types, respectively. Additionally, the DSM-III category of atypical psychosis included the late-onset schizophrenias (schizophrenic illness starting after age 45). Now, with the age criterion (less than 45 years of age) removed from the DSM-III-R diagnostic criteria for schizophrenia, the late-onset schizophrenia-like psychoses seem largely absorbed into the DSM-III-R diagnosis of schizophrenia. Furthermore, in contrast to earlier DSM editions, there are specific criteria for schizoaffective disorder (295.70) in DSM-III-R. This might result in some of the patients who would have been diagnosed with schizoaffective disorder according to the DSM-

III nonspecific definition of the disorder failing to meet the more specific criteria in DSM-III-R and now to be diagnosed with atypical psychosis.

There are no specific criteria for the DSM-III-R category of atypical psychosis (298.90). Psychotic symptoms included in the description of atypical psychosis in DSM-III-R include delusions, hallucinations, incoherence, marked loosening of associations, catatonic excitement or stupor, and disorganized violent behavior. Examples of atypical psychoses include psychoses with unusual features, such as persistent auditory hallucinations (e.g., in a patient without decreased social or occupational functioning), transient psychotic episodes associated with other psychiatric diagnoses (e.g., character disorders, anorexia nervosa), as well as psychotic episodes associated with the menstrual cycle or postpartum period (with the requirement that the psychotic disorders not fulfill criteria for other more specific psychotic syndromes). Another clinical presentation that might be classified as atypical psychosis includes a transient psychosis that resembles a brief reactive psychosis (298.80), yet does not appear to be associated with an adequate history of stressor(s).

The atypical psychosis category includes psychotic disorders for which there is simply not enough adequate information to make a more specific diagnosis. According to DSM-III-R the atypical psychosis category is preferred to "diagnosis deferred." The diagnosis of atypical psychosis can be changed as more information becomes available about the patient. Other disorders that might be included are some of the culturally bound transient psychotic syndromes, such as Amok (Malaysia), Latah (Malaysia), and Windigo (some North American Indians) (Lehmann 1985).

In summary, there seem to be a number of different possible meanings for the label atypical psychosis as most currently applied in DSM-III-R. First, its use can imply the presence of a psychotic condition awaiting further investigation to yield a more specific final diagnosis. Resolution of a more specific final diagnosis may be achieved after 1) more information becomes available to the clinician or contradictory information is clarified, or 2) the condition itself, over time, becomes more typical of a specific DSM-III-R diagnosis. At times there might be considerable nosologic debate amongst clinicians about whether or not a possible psychotic disorder belongs to a DSM-III-R category of atypical psychosis or another DSM-III category. For instance, in a possible differentiation of an atypical psychosis from a brief reactive psychosis, differences of opinion might exist among clinicians as to whether or not the stressors the patient complains about or notes as possible precipitants are sufficiently significant to qualify for the diagnosis of brief reactive psychosis.

A second DSM-III-R conceptual issue concerning the application of atypical psychosis involves the use of this category to consolidate a group of heterogeneous and currently poorly defined psychotic disorders that fall out of the described matrices of DSM-III-R diagnoses with specific criteria. Again, it should be noted that atypical psychosis has been used by different authors to connote a multitude of meanings. Many of these authors have not adhered to the prevailing DSM terminology at the time. For instance, some authors have utilized the term atypical psychosis in a manner that might include patients who would meet the DSM-III diagnoses of schizophreniform or schizoaffective psychosis (Perris 1974).

Evaluation

To the extent that atypical psychosis often represents a temporary, conditional diagnosis, attempts must be made during the evaluation to 1) gather all the necessary information possible from all available sources in an attempt to see if the patient's condition can fulfill criteria for another specified diagnosis (e.g., brief reactive psychosis, organic mental disorder), and 2) observe the patient carefully over time to see if the patient's condition will evolve symptoms that meet another more specific diagnosis. Some recommend, if possible, holding off on any treatments in order to observe the patient's symptoms, unmasked, over time (Tsuang and Loyd 1985). This might help to clarify if the patient's "atypical psychosis" is in fact just an atypical presentation of a more common disorder. For instance, Ballenger et al. (1982) have suggested that adolescents with bipolar affective disorder, manic type, can often present with atypical psychotic features.

A careful biopsychosocial evaluation is indicated. Attention needs to be paid to biologic issues (e.g., medical history, physical examination, laboratory tests), psychological factors (e.g., recent life stresses, psychiatric history), and social factors (e.g., family history and cultural background). The significance of certain stressors and psychotic conditions in cross-cultural patients is often best understood if appreciated within the cultural context. A high incidence of psychosis has been suggested in some immigrant groups (Anonymous 1980), which at times can take on an atypical presentation. The labeling of a clinical syndrome as an atypical presentation may reflect cultural relativism. The evaluation of the psychotic patient from another culture can be difficult because of linguistic barriers and differences in the cultural perspective. Consultation with someone (ideally a mental health worker) from the patient's culture, or at least very familiar with that culture, can be quite helpful. Ideally, the consultant would be able to speak the language and evaluate the role of cultural influences on the patient's symptoms.

Additionally, a potential aid in the evaluation of the atypically psychotic patient might be the amobarbital (Amytal) interview. As Perry and Jacobs (1982) point out, the Amytal interview, in general, can be useful in the evaluation of catatonia, stupor, and muteness to help distinguish among different etiologies. Pellegrini and Putman (1984) report on the successful use of the Amytal interview in the evaluation of a patient with atypical psychosis.

Biomedical Evaluation

As noted above, it is necessary to rule out underlying medical conditions that might be causing or exacerbating the patient's psychotic illness (Hall et al. 1980; LaBruzza 1984). Detection of underlying medical pathology can convert an atypical psychosis diagnosis to one of the organic mental disorders in DSM-III-R. Careful mental status, physical, and neurologic examinations with attention to possible signs of organicity are important. Neuropsychological testing can be helpful if the patient is able to cooperate.

The clinician might want to lower his or her threshold for ordering certain laboratory and other diagnostic tests in patients with confusing and atypical psychiatric presentations. In the case of atypical psychosis, a reasonable laboratory test battery might include a complete blood count with differential, chemistry panels (including electrolytes, glucose, renal and hepatic functions, calcium and phosphate levels), thyroid function tests, a serum cortisol level, a screening test for syphilis, B-12 and folate levels, and a urinalysis. Blood levels for any prescribed or over-the-counter medications that the patient is taking that have meaningful therapeutic or toxic levels should be obtained. Bromide intoxication can be suggested by elevations in the serum chloride. Urine for heavy metal screening might be obtained if the patient seems at risk for such environmental intoxication (e.g., manganese madness) (DeLisi 1984). In a young psychotic patient with a movement disorder, Wilson's disease can be ruled out by obtaining serum and urine copper and serum ceruloplasmin levels (Sternberg

1986). Psychotic patients with symptoms consistent with acute intermittent porphyria (AIP), such as episodic abdominal pain, autonomic dysfunction, and neuropathy, should undergo the appropriate urine studies for AIP. However, Tischler et al. (1985) reported that psychiatric symptoms can predominate in patients with AIP, and the "classic" symptoms might be absent. So the clinician might want to still screen urines for porphobilinogen and uroporphyrin in atypically psychotic patients without the classic AIP symptoms. Note that during asymptomatic periods patients typically do not excrete excess amounts of these substances.

Screens for illicit drugs should be ordered. The need to rule out drugs of abuse as a potential component of a patient's psychotic presentation cannot be overemphasized. False-negative results can confuse a patient's diagnosis (Ragen et al. 1986). The clinician needs to become knowledgeable about ways to best detect drug abuse. This can often be accomplished through consultation with the clinician's laboratory.

Exposure to various other substances has been implicated in some atypical psychotic presentations. These can include organic toxins related to occupational or residential exposure or associated with some form of solvent or inhalant abuse. Such suspected organic toxin exposure is typically supported by a thorough history, as laboratory confirmation is often difficult. The clinician's laboratory or local poison center may be of some assistance in locating labs capable of performing analyses for some of these substances. State departments of public health can usually be of assistance in performing analyses related to suspected cases of occupational exposure (e.g., with insecticides, rodenticides, or other organics used by industry). As an example of organic toxin exposure associated with an atypical psychotic presentation, Poe et al. (1987) reported a case of atypical psychosis related to the topical application of N, N-diethyl-m-toluamide (deet), the active ingredient in most topical insect repellents. Deet was reportedly found in this patient's urine more than a week after the last topical application.

Other laboratory tests should be ordered as indicated. A number of disease states have been reported to be associated with atypical psychotic-like illnesses (Gerson and Miclat 1985; Mangotich and Misiaszek 1983). Patients with central nervous system (CNS) human immunodeficiency virus (HIV) infection can present with psychosis. Appropriate testing for this condition might be indicated in patients with symptoms of acquired immunodeficiency syndrome (AIDS) or a history of high-risk behaviors for the disorder. Other medical conditions relevant to a discussion of atypical psychosis include Cushing's and Addison's disease, hyper- or hypothyroidism, hyper- or hypoparathyroidism, multiple sclerosis, seizures, lupus, head trauma, certain vitamin deficiencies, cancer, and CNS infection.

In addition to a chest X ray and electrocardiogram (EKG), an electroencephalogram (EEG) might also be a part of the initial evaluation. Hall et al. (1980) have suggested that a sleep-deprived EEG is probably more sensitive than a routine EEG. Although it has been claimed that the sleep-deprived EEG with nasopharyngeal (NP) leads can increase the diagnostic yield of the EEG (Sternberg 1986), the true value of NP leads has been questioned (Ramani et al, 1985). Grebb et al. (1986) have specifically recommended using both sleep deprivation and NP leads in diagnostic workup of the psychotic patient. However, Lam et al. (1988) reported that an EEG seems most useful when there already is a strong clinical suspicion of an organic mental disorder. Additionally, a negative EEG study does not rule out CNS pathology or a seizure disorder. Monroe (1982) has suggested that some atypical psychoses might be related to seizure phenomena that cannot currently be detected with EEG surface or NP electrodes.

In another aspect of the biomedical evaluation, Weinberger (1984) recommends the use of a computed tomography (CT) scan in patients presenting with confusion, a first episode of psychosis of unknown etiology, or prolonged catatonia. Garber et al. (1988) have suggested the use of magnetic resonance imaging in patients with atypical psychiatric presentations when the CT result has been equivocal.

Psychosocial Assessment

The psychosocial evaluation should include careful attention to the patient's past psychiatric history and treatment. The evaluation should also include exploration of the patient's personality characteristics and recent life stresses. DSM-III-R now allows a diagnosis of Brief Reactive Psychosis (298.80) to be applied not only in a patient with a solitary severe stressor but also in patients with an accumulation of markedly stressful events.

In addition to taking a careful history from a phenomenological point of view (e.g., the presence or absence of specific symptoms such as hallucinations or delusions), listening to the material with a dynamic ear can provide important diagnostic information as well. Attention to the details of the development of the present symptoms in the context of a thorough assessment of the patient's premorbid functioning, both in the interpersonal and vocational spheres, is critical. Is this present psychotic state the culmination of a gradual decline in functioning, or is it of sudden onset in a relatively high-functioning individual? Another area to pay attention to is the content of the symptoms, not just their presence or absence. The nature of the hallucinations or of the delusions may point to the stressors that led to their development. For example, delusions of worthlessness and condemning voices may suggest that the patient has been experiencing guilt as a prelude to the overt atypical psychosis. Grandiose delusions may be a compensatory mechanism for low self-esteem exacerbated by some recent event. It is important to recognize that the stressors that contribute to the development of the psychosis may be symbolic as well as real life events. To neglect the content of the psychotic material may result in missing important diagnostic information as well as material for treatment planning.

Another important task in evaluating an atypical psychotic patient is to pay attention to the patient's present state of ego functioning. Bellak has done extensive work in putting forth an "inventory" of ego functions in his work with psychotic patients (Bellak 1979; Bellak and Siegel 1983), which includes assessment of the psychotic patient's: 1) reality testing, 2) judgment 3) object relations, (degree and kind of relatedness to other people), 4) thought processes, 5) patterns of defenses (e.g., primitive versus higher level defenses). Such an inventory may help in the assessment, diagnosis, and follow-up evaluation of the atypical psychotic patient.

Moving beyond the consideration of the patient as an individual, a thorough psychosocial evaluation should include an assessment of the family. Interviewing family members may yield important observations of the patient's behavior that patient's may not be able to report themselves and may assist in an understanding of possible stressors that the patient may be experiencing. The specific role played by expressed emotion (critical or emotionally overinvolved attitudes of the parents), affective style (parental criticism, guilt induction, intrusiveness, and inadequate support), and communication deviance (unclear parental communication) in families of patients with atypical psychosis is unknown. An association has been made between these pathologic styles of relating and the parents of schizophrenic patients (Doane et al. 1981; Leff et al. 1985), although they do not seem necessarily specific to schizophrenia (Doane et al. 1981; McGlashan 1986). Doane et al. (1981) found a higher frequency of schizophrenic spectrum disorders in families with high affective style and communication deviance compared to that in families with low affective style and communication deviance. However, atypical psychosis does not appear to have been included in the schizophrenic spectrum disorders studied by Doane and colleagues. Finally, an assessment of the family history of psychiatric disturbance may yield information as to biologic contributions to the present psychosis. It should be noted, however, that the genetics and heritability of "atypical psychosis" are far from being fully clarified.

Assessment of Need for Hospitalization

Indications for hospitalization would be similar to those indicated for diagnostic categories involving psychosis. These indications would include suicidal or homicidal risk, or both, poor impulse control, extremely poor judgment or disorganization in which the patient or others are at potential risk, and the need for inpatient observation and evaluation pursuant to a diagnostic resolution.

Treatment

A number of problems exist in evaluating studies and case reports of treatment response in patients with atypical psychosis. First, as previously mentioned, the exact meaning in the literature of what constitutes an atypical psychosis can vary greatly from author to author. Most of these reports of treatment response have not utilized DSM-III or DSM-III-R criteria. Furthermore, most of these studies have not been well controlled and have generally involved small numbers of patients. Therefore, the treatments proposed here should only serve as a general guideline. Importantly, because atypical psychosis is a catch-all diagnosis for what seems to be a heterogeneous group of disorders, no one specific treatment plan can be recommended for this diagnostic category (Tamminga and Carpenter 1982). Any treatment plan for a patient with atypical psychosis needs to be individually tailored for the patient's particular symptom complex and problem list. In general, the major strategy involves the approximation of the "atypically" psychotic picture to other specific DSM-III-R psychotic disorders (e.g., schizophrenia, bipolar disorder), where the various treatments have been more extensively and carefully defined.

A Note on Documentation

A note on documentation of the patient's history, presentation, and treatment response is perhaps in order at this point in the discussion. Although careful documentation of a patient's course of illness and response to treatment is important with all psychiatric disorders, it seems particularly crucial in the patient with a diagnosis of atypical psychosis. Future clinicians will need to rely heavily on this past information to help better piece together the atypical psychotic picture and be able to more effectively decide on appropriate treatment plans.

Treatment of Acute Atypical Psychosis

Hospitalization

The use of the hospital environment in cases of atypical psychosis would be similiar to that for any psychotic condition. If indicated, hospitalization should provide safety (for the patient and others), close observation and supervision, reality testing, and limits on impulses and destructive behavior (e.g., with medications or restraints, or both, if necessary). If a patient refuses hospitalization, conference with the patient and family might be helpful in bringing about an appropriate plan. Involuntary hospitalization for the patient might need to be considered at times, with careful attention to the commitment laws for the clinician's and patient's locality.

Somatic treatments

As mentioned earlier, some recommend delaying the initiation of treatment for the patient with atypical psychosis and observing the patient for as long as possible, in the hope of clarifying the diagnosis (Tsuang and Loyd 1985). In a severely agitated patient, Reid (1983) suggests considering the use of a short-acting barbiturate, which "may be useful without masking important symptoms." In the treatment of atypical psychoses, the use of any somatic treatment (i.e., electronconvulsive shock therapy and pharmacologic agents), as well as the selection and titration of specific agents, must be based upon the individual characteristics of each atypical patient. The clinician can use specific target symptoms as well as a general assessment of patterns of psychopathology to formulate the somatic therapeutic regimen. Treatment of this disorder is approximate and can be complicated by atypical responses to specific somatic treatments.

Recommended guidelines for somatic treatments might include the following For the patient with significant psychotic symptoms, such as hallucinations and delusions, one might consider treatment with antipsychotic medication. The ideal dose of the antipsychotic is probably the lowest dose that controls the patient's symptoms. Although the benzodiazepines have been associated with behavioral disinhibition, this class of drugs has been reported to be useful, both alone and in conjunction with an antipsychotic, in the control of the very agitated psychotic patient (Cohen and Lipinski 1986; Modell et al. 1985; Victor et al. 1984). As many of the atypical psychoses are episodic in nature, attempts should be made to decrease or stop the antipsychotic medication when the symptoms subside or disappear. The severity of recurrence of symptomatology might dictate any necessary reinstatement or increase of the antipsychotic medication. If antipsychotic medications are considered, the clinician must always weigh the potential therapeutic gain versus the possible negative complications and side effects, such as tardive dyskinesia. The successful use of ECT has also been described (Kimura 1980), but its exact role in the treatment of atypical psychosis will require further evaluation.

In patients with significant affective features, treatment would be similar to that for a psychotic affective disorder. In psychotic depressive disorders, treatment with a combination of an antipsychotic plus an antidepressant (Brown et al. 1982), or alternatively ECT, has been described. However, treatment response has been reported using alternate therapeutic regimens. Quitkin et al. (1978) reported on a study supporting the view that tricyclics alone are ineffective for delusional depression. However, Howarth et al. (1985) found that delusional depressives were in fact more likely to respond to tricyclic antidepressants alone than nondelusional depressed patients, but that the delusionally depressed patients might require a longer period of time on the antidepressant (e.g., a few months) before ultimately responding.

It should be noted that some atypical responses to medications in patients with atypical psychotic conditions have been reported. Akiskal et al. (1983) described five patients with atypical paranoid psychosis who responded to treatment with antidepressants alone despite the absence in these patients of a full affective syndrome. Brotman and Jenike (1984) and Jenike (1984) reported on a few cases of patients with monosymptomatic hypochondriacal delusions without clear symptoms or history suggestive of an affective disorder who were reported to be unresponsive to anti-psychotic medications, but who were responsive to treatment with antidepressants alone. The clinician should note that monosymptomatic hypochondriacal psychosis in DSM-III-R is generally classified under the category Delusional (Paranoid) Disorders, somatic type.

The role of specific antipsychotic medication in the treatment of atypical psychosis has not yet been established. No particular antipsychotic medication has been demonstrated to have clear superiority over any other in the treatment of atypical psychosis as currently defined. Anticonvulsants and acetazolamide have been described as useful in some patients with atypical psychosis. However, the use of these medications in atypically psychotic patients is not supported by the data in the Product Information Section of the *Physician's Desk Reference*. The utilization of these medications in cases of atypical psychosis is in part based on a hypothesized relationship between some cases of atypical psychosis and seizure-like phenomena (Monroe 1982), which might be especially relevant in those patients with episodic psychotic conditions associated with confusion, precipitous onset, memory disturbances, and an abnormal EEG. Monroe (1982) has suggested the use of carbamazepine. Frykholm (1985) describes three patients with atypical psychosis who were unresponsive to more conventional pharmacologic agents, such as antipsychotics, lithium, and antidepressants, but who did respond to treatment with clonazepam. Acetazolamide has also been utilized in the treatment of some seizure disorders, and in Japan Inoue et al. (1984) have reported that this medication might have antipsychotic and prophylactic effects in atypical psychosis. Although there is evidence (Monroe 1982) linking some forms of atypical psychosis to electrophysiologic abnormalities, much of the evidence is indirect, and even within this postulated argument it is not clear whether abnormal behavior is linked with ictal or interictal occurrences.

The clinician should note that none of the organic treatments described in this section have been carefully evaluated in controlled clinical trials for patients with atypical psychosis. Therefore, clear recommendations for their use in the atypical psychoses have not been clearly established.

Psychosocial interventions

Profound emphasis must be placed both on 1) the absence of unifying symptom complexes that can be considered pathognomonic of atypical psychosis and 2) the lack of unified treatment approches. Unlike the other diagnoses of DSM-III-R, which have an organizing mainstream of classical presentation and commonly accepted clinical interventions, the diagnostic category of atypical psychosis is characterized by a diversity of presentations that defy any delineation of standard treatment approaches. Thus, in both treatment and symptomatology, the exception is the rule and the wise clinician follows the clues of each individual case.

There has been little reported in the literature on psychosocial interventions (e.g., the various types of psychotherapy, behavioral therapy) in the atypical psychoses. McGlashan (1982) writes that, for the atypical psychoses, "consistent rules-of-thumb" cannot be applied, and that the "choice of strategy depends entirely on the nature of the individual 'atypical' case." Psychosocial interventions during the active phase of an atypical psychosis would seem to be similar to those described for other psychotic disorders, such as exacerbations of bipolar disorders or schizophrenia. A more extensive literature is available concerning the psychosocial treatment of other psychotic conditions. For instance, McGlashan (1986) has outlined some "phase-specific" (e.g., acute phase versus subacute phase) psychosocial treatment guidelines for schizophrenia. Perhaps these strategies as well as others already defined for some psychotic disorders (e.g., schizophrenic, bipolar and delusional disorders) can be used as partial guidelines for the psychosocial treatment of the atypical psychoses. Modalities that might be employed are a supportive, ongoing relationship with a therapist, group therapy, family therapy, and social skills training if indicated (McGlashan 1986). However, the exact application of these psychosocial therapies requires ongoing evaluation of the specific requirements for treatment of the individual with an atypical psychosis.

The clinician should note that the significance of certain stressors in some patients might best be understood if appreciated in the cultural context. For instance, Farmer and Falkowski (1985) describe two cases of atypical psychosis in West African women who failed to respond to conventional treatments but resolved with complete recovery once they had been returned to their country and tribal home. A worker familiar with the patient's culture and language might be better able to work with the patient and provide more effective psychosocial support.

Long-term follow-up

Ongoing psychosocial care for patients with atypical psychosis would seem to be similar to that for patients with other psychotic disorders. The plan for long-term follow-up would depend on the patient's individual needs. In an atypical psychotic patient with another underlying psychiatric disorder, such as a borderline personality disorder or anorexia nervosa, attention should be directed at continuing the psychosocial and possible somatic treatments for these disorders.

There is the overall impression in the literature that patients with atypical psychoses tend to have a better prognosis and function on a higher level than patients with schizophrenia (Kimura 1980). However, as some atypical psychosis may be expected to evolve into more classic schizophrenia or bipolar illness, extensive long-term follow-up may be required. The extent of follow-up will depend upon results derived from diagnostic evaluation, the evolving course of the psychotic process, and treatment response. Follow-up might include periodic contact with a mental health professional for evaluation and support (e.g., with individual, group, or family therapy) and vocational rehabilitation if necessary. If psychotropic medications need to be utilized, the ideal dose is probably the lowest dose that controls the patient's symptoms. As mentioned previously, upon clearing of the patient's symptomatology, attempts should be made to decrease or stop the medication. Recurrence of symptoms would dictate any necessary reinstitution or increase in medications. Some patients may require maintenance treatment with psychotropics. Antidepressant medications would be utilized as they are in the treatment of the major affective disorders. Lithium prophylaxis might be indicated in some recurring atypical psychoses, such as the "cycloid psychoses" (Perris 1978).

Treatment of Some Specific Atypical Psychotic Syndromes

· As previously noted, atypical psychosis is a heterogeneous disorder that includes a number of different types of atypical psychotic syndromes that have been described in the literature. Some specific treatments for these different atypical psychotic syndromes have been proposed. Some of these will be presented here. The clinician should note, however, that the application of these therapies for these specific atypical psychotic disorders has been undergoing investigation and requires significant clarification.

Furthermore, because of the very nature of the atypical psychosis category and these specific subgroups, constraints are placed on the extent of generalizable therapeutic recommendations. Again, it seems that the issue of primary importance in the management of patients with atypical psychoses is not delineating a specific treatment, but rather delineating a specific diagnosis. Thus, the management of all these specific syndromes encompassed in the atypical psychosis category must begin with a rigorous diagnostic evaluation.

Postpartum (puerperal) psychosis not fulfilling criteria for other psychotic condition in DSM-III-R

Postpartum psychosis seems to occur at a rate of about one to two per thousand deliveries (Kendall et al. 1981; Kumar et al. 1983). Although there is a much higher risk of postpartum psychosis in women with a history of bipolar affective illness or a previous history of postpartum psychosis (Kumar et al. 1983), many of these women have no previous psychiatric history (Inwood 1985; Ziporyn 1984). Up to 50 percent of women with a history of postpartum psychosis have been reported to experience a second episode (Inwood 1985). It has been proposed by some that postpartum psychosis should be considered a distinct nosologic entity (Hays and Douglas 1984; Munoz 1985), although a link with bipolar affective illness has been proposed (Brockington et al. 1981). Puerperal psychosis is described as usually beginning within two to three weeks after delivery (Brockington et al. 1982a).

As with any other patient with an atypical psychosis, it is important to rule out other psychiatric or medical conditions that might be responsible for the patient's psychotic condition. No definitive hormonal or physiologic factors have been identified as being etiologically related to postpartum psychosis (Robinson and Stewart 1986), but attempts are being made to do so (Lindstrom et al. 1984; Riley and Wyatt 1985; Robinson and Stewart 1984). No clear psychosocial variables have been associated with the etiology of postpartum psychosis (Robinson and Stewart 1986).

As the patient with postpartum psychosis often has difficulty coping with the care of her infant, close supervision and environmental support of the patient and infant is vital, and an argument could be made that this can be most easily achieved in the hospital. It is important to closely monitor whether the patient is suicidal, homicidal, or specifically infanticidal, with appropriate interventions taken to protect the patient, child, or others, if necessary. Surrogate mother figures might be temporarily needed if the patient is too disorganized to adequately care for the child or is potentially harmful to the infant. Here, the father, grandparents, extended family, friends, and/or trained child care workers have been reported to be helpful in providing the needed support for the child (Inwood 1985). The need for continuing support and supervision for the patient, child, and family after the patient and child have been discharged from the hospital must be carefully assessed.

Psychopharmacologic management of the patient with a postpartum psychosis would be similar to that previously described for the management of patients with atypical psychosis. If the patient presents with psychotic symptoms (e.g., hallucinations, delusions), antipsychotic medications can be utilized in a similar manner as one would use these medications in acute exacerbations of schizophrenia. For the woman who presents with primarily manic-like symptoms, which seems to be the more common presentation for postpartum psychosis (Brockington et al. 1981), lithium can be used in conjunction with an antipsychotic, and treatment can be instituted in a fashion similar to that used for treating an acute manic episode. It has been reported that patients with postpartum psychosis who fail to respond to pharmacologic attempts at management may respond to electroconvulsive shock therapy (ECT). ECT has been reported to sometimes provide a complete remission after about six to eight treatments (Robinson and Stewart 1986). Because of the high risk of recurrence of psychosis with subsequent pregnancies, appropriate counseling of the patient and family might be wise in considering future pregnancies. Prophylactic lithium during subsequent pregnancies is generally contraindicated, however, because of its reported teratogenic potential (Jefferson et al. 1983). Teratogenicity has been reported for psychotropic medications and caution should be exercised in their use during pregnancy until this danger has been more fully elucidated (Goldberg and Di Mascio 1978).

Psychotropic medications can be found in the mother's breast milk. As lithium given to the mother seems to appear in breast milk in appreciable amounts, mothers requiring lithium therapy are probably best advised not to breast feed. The lithium concentration that has been reported in the milk is one-half of the mother's serum lithium level, and reported serum lithium levels in the infant are one-half to one-third of the mother's serum lithium level (Goldberg and Di Mascio 1978). For the other psychotropic medications (e.g., antipsychotics), for which the risk to the infant is not known and the amount found in breast milk is generally low, the potential risk of exposure to the medications, regardless of how small the amount, should be carefully weighed against the potential benefit to the infant and mother of breast feeding. A conservative approach might be to recommend a period of bottle feeding for the infant whose mother is taking psychotropic medication.

Psychosis associated with the menstrual cycle

Transient psychoses associated with the menstrual cycle have been described (Berlin et al. 1982; Dennerstein et al. 1983; Endo et al. 1978). As these disorders have been commonly associated with puberty, they have also been referred to as "periodic psychosis of puberty" (Altschule and Brem 1963; Berlin et al. 1982). The psychotic episodes can begin five to ten days prior to the onset of menstruation. The symptoms generally diminish after the menstrual flow has begun.

Different treatments have been described. These include antipsychotics, lithium, ECT (Endo et al. 1978), danazol (Dennerstein et al. 1983), oral contraceptive (Felthous et al. 1980), medroxyprogesterone acetate (Berlin et al. 1982), clomiphene citrate (Cooksen 1967), phenytoin in a patient with a history of seizure disorder (Kramer 1977), and acetazolamide (Inoue et al. 1984). None of these therapies has been extensively evaluated, and therapy for these patients needs to be individualized and based on a careful psychiatric, medical, gynecologic, and neurologic evaluation. No clear statements of treatment efficacy can be made, except that appropriate conversion to another specific DSM-III-R diagnosis will define more specific treatment strategies. Consultation with gynecologists and psychiatrists knowledgeable and experienced with this disorder might be helpful.

Cycloid psychosis

Cycloid psychosis is described as a periodic psychiatric disorder with polymorphic symptomatology including confusion, acute onset, and possibly delusions, hallucinations, and unusual movements (Brockington et al. 1982b; Perris 1974, 1978). The patient is often described as normal in the intervals between psychotic episodes (Perris 1974). Claims in the literature (Cutting et al. 1978; Vogl and Zaudig 1985) purport an incomplete nosologic overlap between cycloid psychosis and some other disorders that might appear similar, such as bipolar affective illness, schizophrenia, and schizoaffective disorder. Indeed, DSM-III-like criteria for cycloid psychosis have been proposed (Perris 1974, 1978). At this time treatments for cycloid psychosis that have been described are similar to treatments for bipolar and schizoaffective disorders. Lithium has been reported to possibly decrease the overall morbidity of patients with cycloid psychosis (Perris 1978).

Periodic catatonia

Gjessing (1974) has described periodic catatonia as a syndrome with an abrupt appearance of catatonic excitement or stupor separated by relatively symptom-free intervals. Many cases of periodic catatonia might qualify for other DSM-III-R diagnoses (e.g., schizophrenic disorder, catatonic type, or bipolar disorder). However, a few patients may not meet the criteria for another DSM-III-R diagnosis and might qualify for a diagnosis of atypical psychosis. Gjessing (1974) and Petursson (1976) reported that lithium was effective in extending symptom-free intervals, although others have reported little therapeutic benefit from lithium (Sovner 1974). Wald (1978) presented a case report of a woman in whom lithium brought about complete remission of her periodic catatonia. Numerous other agents have been described in the treatment of this condition including antipsychotic medication, thyroxine, alpha-methyldopa, and disulfiram (Gjessing 1973). ECT has been described as helping to end a catatonic state, but ECT does not seem to prevent recurrence of the next psychotic phase (Gjessing 1974).

Substance-induced chronic psychosis

Perhaps another type of atypical psychosis can be the case of the patient with a chronic psychotic condition the onset of which seemed temporarily related to the use of a mind-altering substance and in which there is no evidence of continued drug abuse. These patients would not meet other specific DSM-III-R criteria, including those for psychoactive substance-induced mental disorders, such as an Hallucinogen Delusional Disorder (292.11), Cocaine Delusional Disorder (292.11), or Posthallucinogen Perception Disorder (292.89). Vardy and Kay (1983) found LSD-associated chronic psychotic patients to be fundamentally similar to schizophrenic patients in genealogy, phenomenology, and course of illness. The treatment of a patient with a substance-induced chronic psychotic condition would seem similar to that of a chronic schizophrenic patient. The acute exacerbations of the psychosis would also be handled in a similar manner. The use of appropriate drug screens might help detect those patients who continue to use drugs.

Treatment Summary

Besides the significant limitations placed on treatment recommendations, there is also another major handicap. There is a dearth of research into the nature of these disorders, their natural history, and treatment response. There are virtually no well controlled studies of treatment utilizing sufficiently clear diagnostic definitions and sufficient numbers of patients to provide the basis for a rational therapeutic strategy. Although the blame for this is in large part due to ambiguities surrounding the definition of atypical psychosis, there have also been relatively few attempts to standardize diagnosis and treatment. Indeed, the very nature of this "residual catch-all" category may preclude the development of any standardized treatment regimen.

One might argue that the most valuable contribution to this field of investigation would be carefully conducted multicenter studies applying standardized diagnostic and treatment strategies. Until this is accomplished, treatment recommendations are weakened by the anecdotal and often idiosyncratic nature of the data base.

Prognosis

Few studies on the prognosis and course of atypical psychosis exist. Overall, the sense has been that atypical psychosis has a more benign course than schizophrenia. Kimura et al. (1980) followed the course of 58 patients diagnosed as having atypical psychosis. These authors were aware of some of the semantic confusion surrounding the label atypical psychosis. Kimura et al. (1980) briefly described the criteria they used for a diagnosis for atypical psychosis, which included acute onset of illness, polymorphous clinical picture, disturbed consciousness, well maintained affective rapport, and remittent course. How these patients would be diagnosed utilizing DSM-III-R criteria for psychotic conditions, however, is unclear. Kimura et al. (1980) reported that in these patients with "atypical psychosis," the relative length of hospitalization was shorter than that for the patients with schizophrenia. Although the patients with atypical psychosis seemed to have a more benign course of illness than did the patients with schizophrenia, Kimura et al. (1980) did note that in 19 of the 58 patients with atypical psychosis that were followed, a "defect" state was ultimately recognized.

One possible interpretation of these findings is that within the heterogeneous group of atypical psychoses were patients with a disease process close in many respects to schizophrenia or schizoaffective disorder (e.g., the 19 "defect" state patients). Mixed in with this group, perhaps, were patients with more benign types of pathologic processes. When the prognostic outcome is assessed, the average outcome of these diverse pathologic processes appears to be superior to that associated with schizophrenia or schizoaffective illness, but this may largely reflect an averaging of several pathologic processes. Thus, outcome studies may reflect the past and current diagnostic heterogeneity of atypical psychosis rather than a specific, generalizable, more benign prognosis.

Conclusion and Future Directions for Research

In DSM-III-R, atypical psychosis is a residual category used for patients with a functional psychosis who do not meet criteria for other specific diagnostic entities. Indeed, atypical psychosis ends up being a heterogeneous, "catch-all" category. The DSM-III and DSM-III-R concepts of atypical psychosis, although similar, embody some important differences. For instance, late-onset schizophrenia (schizophrenia occurring after the age of 45), as well as some of the monosymptomatic delusional syndromes, are no longer included in the DSM-III-R category of atypical psychosis as they had been in the DSM-III atypical psychosis category. This might complicate some comparisons of diagnoses of atypical psychosis made with DSM-III criteria and those made utilizing the DSM-III-R description.

The atypical psychoses are undergoing a dynamic evolution, in which pathologic entities are shifted in and out of this diagnostic category, in response to refinements in our system of nomenclature, biologic and psychosocial research, and even specific treatment responses. Indeed, it has even been suggested (Lion 1982) that in the future subgroups of the atypical psychoses may be possibly defined according to their response to specific drugs. For instance, although the concept of a "carbamazepine responsive" subgroup of atypical psychoses is almost a heretical divergence from our traditional strategies of diagnostic nomenclature, it is indicative of the formidable challenges and frustrations of the atypical psychosis diagnostic category.

It is important for the clinician to be aware that there are methodologic problems in reviewing the studies of atypical psychosis and treatment. The studies have been widely scattered in time and location, and different researchers have used different diagnostic systems and different concepts of the diagnostic category of atypical psychosis. Also, the technical aspects of many of these studies vary. Furthermore, many of the investigations of treatment response in atypical psychotic patients have been small case studies. The therapeutic ideas suggested by the preliminary studies and case reports available in the current literature need to be followed up with more careful investigation.

In the future it would seem important to attempt to identify some of the homogeneous disorders amongst the currently heterogeneous atypical psychosis category. The study of these disorders might include investigation of their genetic transmission, relationship to overall psychiatric history, and their associated biologic markers, as well as the study of their long-term prognosis and response to specific treatment. The relationship and overlap with other psychiatric disorders, such as schizophrenia, affective disorders, character disorders, and anxiety disorders need to be more carefully defined.

Additionally, it would appear valuable to achieve some consensus concerning the definition of atypical psychosis on an interntional basis, as much of the work on atypical psychosis has occurred outside of the United States. It might be helpful to investigate operational definitions for some of the different types of atypical psychosis, such as those proposed by Perris (1974) for cycloid psychosis. We would need to attempt investigation of the validity of these new operational definitions and determine if they are truly distinct from other already specified diagnostic categories (Brockington et al. 1982c). Overlap with other diagnostic entities would need to be delineated. It would seem most important to determine whether or not separating out these atypical psychotic disorders from other psychiatric categories is helpful in treatment planning and in establishing prognoses, especially in terms of whether this schema shows clear superiority over deferring the diagnosis.

In the future, the use of biologic markers might help us to pick out which cases of atypical psychosis are actually atypical presentations of other specified psychotic disorders. Unfortunately, at this time no biologic markers have been clearly accepted for routine clinical use in the evaluation of psychiatric disorders and none can yet be incorporated into our diagnostic armamentarium for assessing patients with atypical psychosis (Symthies 1982). However, research into these markers might bring some of these methods into the realm of diagnostic procedures for practicing clinicians. These markers might not only prove to be an aid in diagnostic decision-making in patients with atypical psychosis, but they also might help us in arriving at a prognosis as well as in making treatment plan decisions. Indeed, it is perhaps characteristic of this diagnostic category that if future research is truly successful in providing a consistent and reliable basis for categorization, we might be able to discard the atypical psychosis category and replace it with other specific DSM-III-R diagnoses.

At this time, treatment for patients with atypical psychoses needs to be carefully individualized for each patient's particular constellation of symptoms. The clinician must be alert to cases of atypical psychosis that are actually atypical presentations of other specified diagnostic entities with treatment strategies that have been more extensively evaluated and more specifically defined. Additionally, atypical psychosis can be a manifestation of an underlying medical disorder. Clinicians should also be aware that reports of treatment for atypical psychosis in the literature should be approached cautiously, as definitions of atypical psychosis can vary and the reports are very preliminary. What has been provided in this chapter are some suggestive guidelines based on a meager and often inconsistent literature. Good clinical judgment needs to be the final arbiter for all treatment decisions.

References

Section 16
Psychotic Disorders Not Elsewhere Classified

Akiskal HS, Arana GW, Baldessarini RJ, et al: A clinical report of thymoleptic-response atypical paranoid psychoses. Am J Psychiatry 140:1187–1190, 1983

Ali Salih M: Suicide pact in setting of folie à deux. Br J Psychiatry 139:62–67, 1981

Altschule MD, Brem J: Periodic psychosis of puberty. Am J Psychiatry 119:1176–1178, 1963

American Psychiatric Association: Diagnostic and Statistical Manual of Mental Disorders, 1st ed. Washington DC, American Psychiatric Associaiton, 1952

American Psychiatric Association: Diagnostic and Statistical Manual of Mental Disorders, 2nd ed. Washington, DC, American Psychiatric Association, 1968

American Psychiatric Association: Diagnostic and Statistical Manual of Mental Disorders, 3rd ed. Washington, DC, American Psychiatric Association, 1980

American Psychiatric Association: Diagnostic and Statistical Manual of Mental Disorders, 3rd ed, revised. Washington, DC, American Psychiatric Association, 1987

Andersen J, Laerum H: Psychogenic psychoses. A retrospective study with special reference to clinical course and prognosis. Acta Psychiatr Scand 62:331–342, 1980

Anderson HW, Kuehnle CJ: Strategies for the treatment of acute psychosis. JAMA 229:14, 1974

Angst J: Course of unipolar despressive, bipolar manic-depressive, and schizoaffective disorders. Fortschr Neurol Psychiatr 40:3–30, 1980

Angst J, Dittrich A, Grof P: Course of endogenous affective psychoses and its modification by prophylactic administration of imipramine and lithium. Int Pharmacopsychiatry 2:1–11, 1969

Angst J, Weis P, Grof P, et al: Lithium prophylaxis in recurrent affective disorders. Br J Psychiatry 116:604–614, 1970

Angst J, Felder W, Lohmeyer B: Schizoaffective disorders, I: results of a genetic investigation. J Affective Disord 1:139–153, 1979

Anonymous: Paranoia and immigrants. Br Med J 281:1513–1514, 1980

Anthony EG: The influence of maternal psychosis in children—folie à deux, in Parenthood: Its Psychology and Psychopathology. Edited by Anthony EJ, Benedok T. Boston, Little, Brown, 1970

Armbruster B, Gross G, Huber G: Long-term prognosis and course of schizoaffective, schizophreniform, and cycloid psychoses. Psychiatr Clin North Am 16:156–168, 1983

Asano N: Clinico-genetic study of manic depressive psychoses. Japan Journal of Human Genetics 5:224–253, 1960

Baldessarini RJ, Davis JM: What is the best maintenance dose of neuroleptics in schizophrenia? Psychiatry Res 3:115–122, 1980

Ballenger JC, Reus VI, Post RM: The "atypical" clinical picture of adolescent mania. Am J Psychiatry 139:602–606, 1982

Baron M, Gruen R, Asnis L, et al: Schizoaffective illness, schizophrenia, and affective disorders: morbidity risk and genetic transmission. Acta Psychiatr Scand 65:253–263, 1982

Bellak L: An idiosyncratic overview, in Disorders of the Schizophrenic Syndrome. New York, Basic Books, 1979

Bellak L, Siegel H: Handbook of Intensive Brief and Emergency Psychotherapy. Larchmont, NY, C.P.S., 1983

Berlin FJ, Bergey GK, Money J: Periodic psychosis of puberty: a case report. Am J Psychiatry 139:119–120, 1982

Biological Therapies in Psychiatry. Vol 9, no. 10, October 1986

Bleuler E: Textbook of Psychiatry. New York, Macmillan, 1930

Braden V, Fink EB, Qualls CB, et al: Lithium and chlorpromazine in psychotic inpatients. Psychiatry Res 7:69–81, 1982

Brockington IF, Leff JP: Schizo-affective psychosis: definitions and incidence. Psychol Med 9:91–99, 1979

Brockington IF, Kendell RE, Kellett JM, et al: Trials of lithium, chlorpromazine, and amitriptyline in schizoaffective patients. Br J Psychiatry 133:162–168, 1978

Brockington IF, Wainwright S, Kendell RE: Manic patients with schizophrenic or paranoid symptoms. Psychol Med 10:73–83, 1980a

Brockington IF, Kendell RE, Wainwright S: Depressed patients with schizophrenic or paranoid symptoms. Psychol Med 10:665–675, 1980b

Brockington IF, Cernik KF, Schofield EM, et al: Puerperal psychosis. Phenomena and diagnosis. Arch Gen Psychiatry 38:829–833, 1981

Brockington IF, Winokur G, Dean C: Puerperal psychosis, in Motherhood and Mental Illness. Edited by Brockington IF, Kumar R. New York, Grune and Stratton, 1982a

Brockington IF, Perris C, Kendell RE: The course and outcome of cycloid psychosis. Psychol Med 12:97–105, 1982b

Brockington IF, Perris C, Meltzer HY: Cycloid psychoses: diagnosis and heuristic value. J Nerv Ment Dis 170:651–656, 1982c

Brotman AW, Jenike MA: Monosymptomatic hypochondriasis treated with tricyclic antidepressants. Am J Psychiatry 141:1608–1609, 1984

Bugliosi V: Helter Skelter: The True Story of the Manson Murders. New York, WE Norton, 1974

Carpenter WT Jr: Thoughts on the Treatment of Schizophrenia. Strecker Monograph Series. Philadelphia, The Institute of Pennsylvania Hospital, 1984

Carpenter WT Jr, Hanlon TE: Clinical practice and the phenomenology of schizophrenia, in Handbook of Studies on Schizophrenia. Edited by Burrows GD. Elsevier, Amsterdam, 1986

Carpenter WT, Stephens JH, Rey AC, et al: Early intervention vs. continuous pharmacotherapy of schizophrenia. Psychopharmacol Bull 18:21–23, 1982

Christodoulou GN: Two cases of folie à deux in husband and wife. Acta Psychiatr Scand 46:413–419, 1970

Clayton PJ: Schizoaffective disorders. J Nerv Ment Dis 170:646–650, 1982

Clayton PJ, Rodin L. Winokur G: Family history studies, III: schizoaffective disorder, clinical and genetic factors including a one to two year follow-up. Compr Psychiatry 9:31–49, 1968

Cohen BM, Lipinski JF: Treatment of acute psychosis with non-neuroleptic agents. Psychosomatics 27(Suppl 1):7–16, 1986

Cohen BM, Allen MG, Pollin V, et al: Relationship of schizoaffective psychosis to manic depressive psychosis and schizophrenia. Arch Gen Psychiatry 26:539–545, 1972

Cohen BM, Lipinski, JF, Pope H, et al: Neuroleptic blood levels and therapeutic effect. Psychopharmacology 70:191–194, 1980

Cole JO: Psychopharmacology update: medication and seclusion and restraint. McLean Hosp J 10:37–53, 1985

Cookson BA: Clinical note on the possible use of clomiphene citrate in recurrent psychosis. Can Psychiatr Assoc J 11:271–274, 1967

Coryell W: Schizo-affective and schizophreniform disorders, in Medical Basis of Psychiatry. Edited by G Winokur, P Clayton. Philadelphia, W.B. Saunders (in press)

Coryell W, Tsuang MT: Major depression with mood-congruent or mood-incongruent psychotic features: outcome after 40 years. Am J Psychiatry 142:479–482, 1985

Coryell W, Zimmerman M: Demographic, historical, and symptomatic features of the nonmanic psychoses. J Nerv Ment Dis (in press)

Coryell W, Tsuang MT, McDaniel J: Psychotic features in major depression. J Affective Disord 4:227–236, 1982

Croughan JL, Welner A, Robins E: The group of schizoaffective and related psychoses—critique, record, follow-up, and family studies. Arch Gen Psychiatry 31:632–637, 1974

Cutting JC, Clare AW, Mann AH: Cycloid psychosis: an investigation of the diagnostic concept. Psychol Med 8:637–648, 1978

Davis JM: Overview: maintenance therapy in psychiatry: I. Schizophrenia. Am J Psychiatry 132:1237–1245, 1975

Davis JM, Schaffer CB, Killian GA, et al: Important issues in the drug treatment of schizophrenia. Schizophr Bull 6:70–87, 1980

DeLisi LE: Use of the clinical laboratory, in Biomedical Psychiatric Therapeutics. Edited by Sullivan JL, Sullivan PD. Boston, Butterworth Publishers, 1984

Dennerstein L, Judd F, Davies B: Psychosis and the menstrual cycle. Med J Aust 1:524–526, 1983

Department of Health and Human Services Steering Committee on the Chronically Mentally Ill: Toward a National Plan for the Chronically Mentally Ill. Washington, DC, 1980

Deutsch H: Folie à deux. Psychoanal Q 7:307–318, 1938

Dewhurst K, Todd J: The psychosis of association—folie à deux. J Nerv Ment Dis 124:451–459, 1956

Doane JA, West KL, Goldstein MJ, et al: Parental communication deviance and affective style. Predictors of subsequent schizophrenia spectrum disorders in vulnerable adolescents. Arch Gen Psychiatry 38:679–685, 1981

Donaldson SR, Gelenberg AJ, Baldessarini RJ: The pharmacologic treatment of schizophrenia: a progress report. Schizophr Bull 9:504–527, 1983

Endicott J, Nee J, Coryell W, et al: Major depressive syndrome with psychotic features: evidence of differential familial association. J Affective Disord (in press)

Endo M, Daiguji M, Asano Y, et al: Periodic psychosis recurring in association with menstrual cycle. J Clin Psychiatry 39:456–466, 1978

Engel GL: The clinical application of the biopsychosocial model. Am J Psychiatry 137:535–544, 1980

Enoch MD, Trethowan WH: Uncommon Psychiatric Syndromes, 2nd ed. Bristol, John Wright, 1979, pp 134–159

Faergeman PM: Psychogenic Psychoses. London, Butterworths, 1963

Faguet RA, Faguet KF: Folie à deux, in Extraordinary Disorders of Human Behavior. Edited by Friedmann CTH, Faguet RA. New York, Plenum Press, 1982

Falloon I, Boyd J, McGill CW, et al: Family management in the prevention of exacerbations of schizophrenia: a controlled study. N Engl J Med 306:1437–1440, 1982

Falloon IR, Boyd JL, McGill CW, et al: Family management in the prevention of morbidity in schizophrenia: clinical outcome of a two-year longitudinal study. Arch Gen Psychiatry 42:887–896, 1985

Farmer AE, Falkowski WF: Maggot in the salt, the snake factor and the treatment of atypical psychosis in West African women. Br J Psychiatry 146:446–448, 1985

Feighner JP, Robins E, Guze SB, et al: Diagnostic criteria for use in psychiatric research. Arch Gen Psychiatry 26:57–63, 1972

Felthous AR, Robinson DB, Conroy RW: Prevention of recurrent menstrual psychosis by an oral contraceptive. Am J Psychiatry 137:245–246, 1980

Fernando FP, Frieze M: A relapsing folie à trois. Br J Psychiatry 146:315–316, 1985

Ferreira A: Family myths and homeostasis. Arch Gen Psychiatry 9:457–463, 1963

Frykholm B: Clonazepam-antipsychotic effect in a case of schizophrenia-like psychosis with epilepsy and in three cases of atypical psychosis. Acta Psychiatr Scand 71:539–542, 1985

Galanter M: Psychological induction into the large group: findings from a modern religious sect. Am J Psychiatry 137:1574–1579, 1980

Garber HJ, Weilburg JB, Buonanno FS, et al: Use of magnetic resonance imaging in psychiatry. Am J Psychiatry 145:164–171, 1988

Gerson SN, Miclat R: Cushing disease presenting as atypical psychosis following by sudden death. Can J Psychiatry 30:223–224, 1985

Gjessing LR: Catecholamines and antipsychotic drugs in periodic catatonia, in Catecholamines and Schizophrenia. Edited by Matthysee JW, Kety SS. Oxford, Permagon Press, 1973

Gjessing LR: A review of periodic catatonia. Biol Psychiatry 8:23–45, 1974

Goldberg HL, Di Mascio A: Psychotropic drugs in pregnancy, in Psychopharmacology: A Generation of Progress. Edited by Lipton MA, Di Mascio LA. New York, Raven Press, 1978

Goldstein MJ, Rodnick EH, Evans JR, et al: Drug and family therapy in the aftercare of acute schizophrenics. Arch Gen Psychiatry 35:1169–1177, 1978

Gralnick A: Folie à deux—the psychosis of association. A review of 103 cases and the entire English literature: with case presentations. Part 1. Psychiatr Q 16:230–263, 1942

Grebb JA, Weinberger DR, Morihisa JM: Electroencephalogram and evoked potential studies of schizophrenia, in Handbook of Schizophrenia, vol 1. The Neurology of Schizophrenia. New York, Elsevier Science Publishers, 1986

Greenberg HP: Crime and folie à deux: review and case history. J Ment Sci 102:772–779, 1956

Grinspoon L, Ewalt JR, Shader RI: Schizophrenia: Pharmacotherapy and Psychotherapy. Baltimore, Williams and Wilkins, 1972

Grossman LS, Harrow M, Fudala JL, et al: Longitudinal course of schizoaffective disorders: a prospective follow-up study. J Nerv Ment Dis 172:140–148, 1984

Hall RCW, Garden ER, Stickney SK: Physical illness manifesting as psychiatric disease, II: analysis of a state hospital inpatient population. Arch Gen Psychiatry 37:989–995, 1980

Hays P, Douglas A: A comparison of puerperal psychosis and the schizophrenia variant of manic depression. Acta Psychiatr Scand 69:177–181, 1984

Herz MI, Melville C: Relapse in schizophrenia. Am J Psychiatry 137:801–805, 1980

Herz MI, Szymanski HV, Simon JC: Intermittent medication for stable schizophrenic outpatients: an alternative to maintenance medication. Am J Psychiatry 139:918–922, 1982

Himmelhoch JM, Fuchs CZ, May SJ, et al: When a schizoaffective diagnosis has meaning. J Nerv Ment Dis 169:277–282, 1981

Hirsch SR, Shepherd M (eds): Themes and Variations in European Psychiatry. Charlottesville, University Press of Virginia, 1974

Hogarty GE, Goldberg SC, Schooler NR, et al: Drug and sociotherapy in the aftercare of schizophrenic patients: II, two-year relapse rates. Arch Gen Psychiatry 31:603–608, 1974

Hogarty GE, Schooler NR, Ulrich R, et al: Fluphenazine and social therapy in the after care of schizophrenic patients: relapse analyses of a two-year controlled study of fluphenazine decanoate and fluphenazine hydrochloride. Arch Gen Psychiatry 36:1283–1294, 1979

Hollender MH, Hirsch SJ: Hysterical psychosis. Am J Psychiatry 120:1066–1074, 1964

Howarth BG, Grace MG: Depression, drugs and delusions. Arch Gen Psychiatry 42:1145–1147, 1985

Inoue K, Umezawa Y: Antipsychotic and prophylatic effects of acetazolamide (Diamox) on atypical psychosis. Folia Psychiatr Neurol Jpn 38: 425–436, 1984

Inwood DG: The spectrum of postpartum psychiatric disorders, in Recent Advances in Postpartum Psychiatric Disorders. Edited by Inwood DG. Washington, DC, American Psychiatric Press, 1985

Jaspers K: Allgemeine Psychopathologie (General Psychopathology). Translated by Hoenig J, Hamilton MW. Manchester, England, Manchester University Press, 1963a

Jaspers K: General Psychopathology. Chicago, University of Chicago Press, 1963b

Jefferson JW, Greist JH, Ackerman DC: Lithium Encyclopedia for Clinical Practice. Washington, DC, American Psychiatric Press, 1983

Jenike MS: Successful treatment of dysmorphophobia with tranylcypromine. Am J Psychiatry 141:1462–1463, 1984

Johnson DAW: Studies of depressive symptoms in schizophrenia, I: prevalence of depression and its possible cause. Br J Psychiatry 139:89–100, 1981

Jørgensen P: Long-term course of acute reactive paranoid psychosis. A follow-up study. Acta Psychiatr Scand 71:30–37, 1985

Kallman FJ, Mickey JS: The concept of induced insanity in family units. J Nerv Ment Dis. 104:303–315, 1946

Kane JM: Presented at the 139th Annual Meeting of the American Psychiatric Association. Washington, DC, May 1986

Kane JM, Rifkin A, Woerner M., et al: Low dose neuroleptic treatment of outpatient schizophrenics, I: preliminary results for relapse rates. Arch Gen Psychiatry 40:893–896, 1983

Karon B, VandenBos G: Psychotherapy of Schizophrenia. New York, Jason Aronson, 1981

Kasanin J: The acute schizoaffective psychoses. Am J Psychiatry 10:97–126, 1933

Keith SJ, Mathews SM: Group, family and milieu therapies and psychosocial rehabilitation in the treatment of schizophrenic disorders, in Psychiatry 1982: Annual Review. Edited by Grinspoon L. Washington, DC, American Psychiatric Press, 1982

Keith SJ, Matthews SM: Schizophrenia: a review of psychosocial treatment strategies, in Psychotherapy Research. Edited by Williams JBD, Spitzer RL. New York, Guilford Press, 1984

Kemali D, Maj II, Ariano MG, et al: Prophylaxis of schizoaffective disorder with lithium. Adv Biochem Psychopharmacol 40:153–158, 1985

Kendall RE, Rhme D, Clark JA: The social and obstetric correlates of psychiatric admission in the puerperium. Psychol Med 11:340–350, 1981

Kendler KS, Gruenberg AM: An independent analysis of the Danish adoption study of schizophrenia. Arch Gen Psychiatry 41:555–564, 1984

Kimura S, Fujito T, Wakabayashi T: A contribution to the course and prognosis of the atypical psychosis. Folia Psychiatr Neurol Jpn 34:419–432, 1980

Kleist K: Schizophrenias as system diseases. Klin Wochenschr 1:962–963, 1923

Kramer MS: Menstrual epiletoid psychosis in an adolescent girl. Am J Dis Child 131:316–317, 1977

Kriegman D, Soloman L: Cult groups and the narcissistic personality: the offer to heal defects in the self. Int J Group Psychother 35:239–261, 1985

Kumar R, Isaacs S, Meltzer E: Recurrent post-partum psychosis. A model for prospective clinical investigation. Br J Psychiatry 142:618–620, 1983

LaBruzza AL: Medical illness as a cause for psychosis, in Transient Psychosis. Diagnosis Management and Evaluation. Edited by Tupin JP, Halbreich U, Pena JJ. New York, Brunner/Mazel, 1984

Lam RW, Hurwitz TA, Wada JA: The clinical use of EEG in a general psychiatric setting. Hosptial Commun Psychiatry 39:533–536, 1988

Langness LL: Hysterical psychosis: the cross-cultural evidence. Am J Psychiatry 124:143–152, 1967

Lasèque C, Falret J: La folie à deux (ou foli communiquee). Ann Med Psychol 18:321–355, 1877. English translation and bibliography by Michaud R: Am J Psychiatry 121:Suppl 4, 1964

Layman WA, Cohen L: A modern concept of folie à deux. J Nerv Ment Dis 125:412–419, 1957

Lazarus A: Folie à deux: Psychosis by association or genetic determination? Compr Psychiatry 26:129–133, 1985

Leff J, Kuipers L, Berkowitz R, et al: A controlled trial of social intervention in the families of schizophrenic patients. Br J Psychiatry 141:121–134, 1982

Leff J, Kuipers L, Berkowitz R, et al: A controlled trial of social intervention in the families of schizophrenic patients: two year follow-up: Br J Psychiatry 146:594–600, 1985

Lehmann HE: Unusual psychiatric disorders, atypical psychoses and brief reactive psychoses, in Comprehensive Textbook of Psychiatry, 3rd ed, vol 2. Edited by Kaplan HI, Freedman AM, Saddock BJ. Baltimore, Williams and Wilkins, 1980, pp 1981–2002

Lehmann HE: Unusual psychiatric disorders, atypical psychoses and brief reactive psychoses, in Comprehensive Textbook of Psychiatry, vol IV. Edited by Kaplan HI, Saddock BJ. Baltimore, Williams and Wilkins, 1985

Leonhard K: Atypische endogene Psychosen im Lichte der familien forschung. Z Gesamte Neurol Psychiat 149:520–562, 1934

Lindstrom LH, Nyberg F, Terenius L, et al: CSF and plasma beta-casomorphin-like opioid peptides in postpartum psychosis. Am J Psychiatry 141:1059–1066, 1984

Lion JR: Diagnostic and therapeutic difficulties in atypical illness. J Nerv Ment Dis 170:766–768, 1982

Magliozzi JR, Hollister LE, Arnold KV, et al. Relationship of serum haloperidol levels to clinical response in schizophrenic patients. Am J Psychiatry 133:365–367, 1981

Maj M: Evolution of the American concept of schizoaffective psychosis. Neuropsychobiology 11:7–13, 1984

Malm U: The influence of group therapy on schizophrenia. Acta Psychiatr Scand Suppl 297, 1982

Mandel MR, Severe JB, Schooler NR, et al: Development and prediction of postpsychotic depression in neuroleptic-treated schizophrenics. Arch Gen Psychiatry 39:197–203, 1982

Mangotich M, Misiaszek J: Atypical psychosis in a patient with Usher's Syndrome. Psychosomatics 24:674–675, 1983

May PRA: Treatment of Schizophrenia: A Comparative Study of Five Treatment Methods. New York, Science House, 1968

May PRA, Tuma AH: Methodological problems in psychotherapy research: observations of the Karon-VandenBos study of psychotherapy and drugs in schizophrenia. Br J Psychiatry 117:569–570, 1970

McGlashan TH: DSM-III schizophrenia and individual psychotherapy. J Nerv Ment Dis 170:752–757, 1982

McGlashan TH: Chestnut Lodge follow-up study, II: long-term outcome of schizophrenia and the affective disorders. Arch Gen Psychiatry 41:586–601, 1984

McGlashan TH: Schizophrenia: psychosocial treatments and the role of psychosocial factors in its etiology and pathogenesis, in American Psychiatric Association Annual Review, vol 5. Edited by Frances AJ, Hales RE. Washington, DC, American Psychiatric Press, 1986

McNiel JN, Verwoerdt A, Peat D: Folie à deux in the aged: review and case report of role reversal. J Am Geriatric Soc 20:316–323, 1972

Mendlewicz J: Genetic studies in schizoaffective illness, in Impact of Biology on Modern Psychiatry. Edited by Gershon ES, Belmaker RH, Kety SS, et al. New York, Plenum, 1976

Mitsuda H: The concept of atypical psychoses from the aspect of clinical genetics. Folia Psychiatr Neurol Jpn 16:214–221, 1962

Modell JG, Lenox RH, Weiner S: Inpatient clinical trial of lorazepam for the management of manic agitation. J Clin Psychopharmacol 5:109–113, 1985

Monroe RR: Limbic ictus and atypical psychoses. J Nerv Ment Dis 170:711–716, 1982

Mosher LR: Research design to evaluate psychosocial treatments of schizophrenia, in Psychotherapy of Schizophrenia. Edited by Rubinstein D, Alanen YO. Amsterdam, Excerpta Medica, 1972

Munoz RA: Postpartum psychosis as a discrete entity. J Clin Psychiatry 46:182–184, 1985

Munro A: Paranoia revisited. Br J Psychiatry 141:344–349, 1982

Pauleikoff B: Atypische Psychosen. Bibliotheca Psychiatrica et Neurologica. Supplementa ad, International Monthly Review of Psychiatry and Neurology Fasc. 99:1–141, 1957

Pellegrini AJ, Putman P: the amytal intervention in the diagnosis of late onset psychosis with cultural features presenting as catatonic stupor. J Nerv Ment Dis 172:502–504, 1984

Perris C: A study of cycloid psychosis. Acta Psychiatr Scand Suppl 253, 1974

Perris C: Morbidity suppressive effect of lithium carbonate in cycloid psychosis. Arch Gen Psychiatry 35:328–331, 1978

Perry JC, Jacobs D: Overview: clinical applications of the Amytal interview in psychiatric emergency settings. Am J Psychiatry 139:552–559, 1982

Perry PJ, Pfohl EM, Holstad SG: The relationship between pharmacologic response and tricyclic antidepressant disposition: a critique of the literature using logistic regression analysis. Clin Pharmacokinet (in press)

Petursson H: Lithium treatment of a patient with periodic catatonia. Acta Psychiatr Scand 54:248–253, 1976

Pine F: On the pathology of the separation-individuation process as manifested in later clinical work: an attempt at delineation. Int J Psychoanal 60:225–242, 1979

Poe RO, Snyder JW, Stubbins JF, et al: Psychotic reaction to an insect repellent (letter). Am J Psychiatry 144:1103–1104, 1987

Pope EG, Lipinski JF, Cohen EM, Axelrod DT: "Schizoaffective disorder": an invalid diagnosis? A comparison of schizoaffective disorder, schizophrenia, and affective disorder. Am J Psychiatry 137:921–927, 1980

Post F: Schizo-affective symptomatology in late life. Br J Psychiatry 118:437–445, 1971

Prien RF, Caffey EM Jr, Klett J: A comparison of lithium carbonate and chlorpromazine in the treatment of excited schizo-affectives. Arch Gen Psychiatry 27:182–189, 1972

Pulver SE, Brunt MY: Deflection of hostility in folie à deux. Arch Gen Psychiatry 5:65–73, 1961

Quitkin F, Rifkin A, Klein DF: Imipramine response in deluded depressive patients. Am J Psychiatry 135:806–811, 1978

Ragen FA, Hite SA, Samuels MS, et al: Extended EMIT-DAU phencyclidine screen. J Clin Psychiatry 47:194–195, 1986

Ramani V, Loewenson RB, Torrey F: The limited usefulness of nasopharyngeal EEG recording in psychiatric patients. Am J Psychiatry 142:1099–1100, 1985

Reid WH: Psychotic disorders not elsewhere classified, in Treatment of DSM-III Psychiatric Disorders. Edited by Reid WH. New York, Brunner/Mazel, 1983

Retterstol N: The Scandinavian concept of reactive psychosis, schizophreniform psychosis and schizophrenia. Psychiatr Clin (Basel) 11:180–187, 1978

Riley DM, Wyatt DC: Hypercalcemia in the etiology of puerperal psychosis. Biol Psychiatry 20:479–488, 1985

Rioux B: A review of folie à deux. The psychosis of association. Psychiatr Q 37:405–428, 1963

Robinson GE, Stewart DE: Postpartum psychiatric disorders. Can Med Assoc J 134:31–37, 1986

Rogers CR, Gendlin EG, Kiesler DJ, et al (eds): The Therapeutic Relationship and Its Impact: A Study of Psychotherapy with Schizophrenics. Madison, University of Wisconsin Press, 1967

Rosen BK: Suicide pacts: a review. Psychol Med 11:525–533, 1981

Rosenthal D, Quinn OW: Quadruplet hallucinations. Arch Gen Psychiatry 34:817–827, 1977

Rosenthal NE, Rosenthal LN, Stallone F, et al: Toward the validation of RDC schizoaffective disorder. Arch Gen Psychiatry 37:804–810, 1980

Ross MW: Clinical profiles of Hare Krishna devotees. Am J Psychiatry 140:416–420, 1983

Roth M, McClelland H: Relationship of "nuclear" and "atypical" psychoses: some proposals for a classification. Psychiatr Clin North Am 12:23–54, 1979

Rush AJ: Psychotherapy of the affective psychoses. Am J Psychoanal 40:99–123, 1980

Sawa M: Epileptoid psychosis: a group of atypical endogenous psychoses. Folia Psychiatr Neurol Japan 16:320–329, 1962

Scharfetter C: Studies of heredity in symbiotic psychoses. Int J Ment Health 1:116–123, 1972

Schooler NR, Keith SJ: National Institute of Mental Health Cooperative Agreement Program Protocol for Treatment Strategies in Schizophrenia Study, 1983

Sims A, Salmons P, Humphrey P: Folie à quatre. Br J Psychiatry 130:134–138, 1976

Sirois F. Epidemic hysteria. Acta Psychiatr Scand 252(Suppl):1–44, 1974

Smulevitch AB, Zavidovskaya GI, Igonin AL, et al: Effectiveness of lithium in affective and schizoaffective psychoses. Br J Psychiatry 125:65–72, 1974

Soni SD, Rochley GJ: Socio-clinical substrates of folie à deux. Br J Psychiatry 125:230–235, 1974

Spitzer RL, Williams JBW: Research Diagnostic Criteria (RDC) for a Selected Group of Functional Disorders, 2nd ed. Biometric Research, New York State Psychiatric Institute, 1985

Spradley JB: Discussant in Grover M: Study of cases of folie à deux. Am J Psychiatry 93:1054–1062, 1937

Stanton AH, Gunderson JG, Knapp PH, et al: Effects of psychotherapy in schizophrenia: I, design and implementation of a controlled study. Schizophr Bull 10:520–562, 1984

Stein LI, Test MA: Training in community living: one year evaluation. Am J Psychiatry 133:917–918, 1976

Sternberg DE: Testing for physical illness in psychiatric patients. J Clin Psychiatry 47(Suppl):3–9, 1986

Strauss JS: Schizo-affective disorders: "just another illness" or key to understanding the psychoses. Psychiatr Clin North Am 16:286–296, 1983

Strauss JS, Carpenter WT Jr: Schizophrenia. Edited by Woods SM. New York, Plenum, 1981

Strömgren E: Psychogenic psychoses, in Themes and Variations in European Psychiatry. Edited by Hirsch SR, Shepherd M. Charlottesville, University Press of Virginia, 1974

Symthies JR: Biological markers for the schizophrenic and atypical psychoses. J Nerv Ment Dis 170:732–736, 1982

Tamminga CA, Carpenter WT: The DSM-III diagnosis of schizophrenic-like illness and the clinical pharamacology of psychosis. J Nerv Ment Dis 170:744–751, 1982

Targum SD: Neuroendocrine dysfunction in schizophreniform disorder, correlation with six-month clinical outcome. Am J Psychiatry 140:309–313, 1983

Tischler PV, Woodward B, O'Connor J, et al: High prevalence of intermittent acute porphyria in a psychiatric patient population. Am J Psychiatry 142:1430–1436, 1985

Tseng WS: A paranoid family in Taiwan: a dynamic study of folie à famille. Arch Gen Psychiatry 21:55–63, 1969

Tsuang MT, Loyd DW: Other psychotic disorders, in Psychiatry, Vol 1. Edited by Cavenar JO Jr. Philadelphia, J.B. Lippincott, 1985

Tsuang MT, Dempsey GM, Dvoredsky A, et al: Family history study of schizo-affective disorder. Biol Psychiatry 12:331–338, 1977

Tsuang MT, Dempsey GM, Fleming JA: Can ECT prevent premature death and suicide in schizoaffective patients? J Affective Disord 1:167–171, 1979

Tupin J, Halbreich U, Pena J (eds): Transient Psychosis: Diagnosis Management and Evaluation. New York, Brunner/Mazel, 1984

Ulman RB, Abse DW: The group psychology of mass madness. Jonestown. Political Psychology 4:637–661, 1983

Vardy MM, Kay SR: LSD psychosis or LSD-induced schizophrenia? A multimethod inquiry. Arch Gen Psychiatry 40:877–883, 1983

Victor BS, Link NA, Binder RL, et al: Use of clonazepam in mania and schizoaffective disorders. Am J Psychiatry 141:1111–1112, 1984

Vogl G, Zaudig M: Investigation of operationalized diagnostic criteria in the diagnosis of schizoaffective and cycloid psychoses. Compr Psychiatry 26:1–10, 1985

Wald D, Lerner J: Lithium in the treatment of periodic catatonia: a case report. Am J Psychiatry 135:751–752, 1978

Walker E: Attentional and neuromotor functions of schizophrenics, schizoaffectives, and patients with other affective disorders. Arch Gen Psychiatry 38:1355–1358, 1981

Waltzer H: A psychotic family—folie à douze. J Nerv Ment Dis 137:67–75, 1963

Weinberger DR: Brain disease and psychiatric illness: when should a psychiatrist order a CAT scan? Am J Psychiatry 141:1521–1527, 1984

Welner A, Croughan JL, Robins E: The group of schizoaffective and related psychoses—critique, record, follow-up, and family studies, I: a persistent enigma. Arch Gen Psychiatry 31:628–631, 1974

Welner A, Croughan J, Fishman R, et al: The group of schizoaffective and related psychoses: a follow-up study. Compr Psychiatry 10:413–422, 1977

Welner A, Welner Z, Fishman R: The group of schizoaffective and related psychoses, IV: a family study. Compr Psychiatry 20:21–26, 1979

West LJ, Singer MT: Cults, quacks, and nonprofessional psychotherapies, in Comprehensive Textbook of Psychiatry, 3rd ed, vol 3. Edited by Freedman AM, Kaplan HI, Saddock BJ. Baltimore, Williams and Wilkins, 1980

Wikler L: Folie à famille: a family therapist's perspective. Fam Process 19:257–268, 1980

Winokur G, Clayton PJ, Reich T: Manic Depressive Illness. Saint Louis, C.V. Mosby, 1969

World Health Organization (ed): Glossary and Guide to the Classification of Mental Disorders in accordance with the International Classification of Diseases, 9th rev. Geneva, World Health Organization, 1978

Ziporyn T: "Rip Van Winkle period" ends for puerperal psychiatric problems. JAMA 251:2061–2067, 1984